JOEL WHITBURN'S
TOP POP
Albums
1955-1985

Compiled from Billboard's pop album charts, 1955-1985

Record Research Inc.
P.O. Box 200
Menomonee Falls, Wisconsin 53051

ISBN 0-89820-054-7

Published independently by Record Research Inc.
P.O. Box 200, Menomonee Falls, Wisconsin 53051

CONTENTS

INTRODUCTION

After many years of additional research, I am pleased to welcome music enthusiasts to enjoy my updated and revised pop album book. If patience is a virtue, then you readers certainly can claim this goodness of character, as a thirteen year wait is enough to test anyone's patience. I do hope, however, that you'll find the wait was worthwhile as I have added many new features, symbols and notes to make this the best book I have ever published.

In setting out to prepare for this new edition, I had one primary goal in mind — to obtain an original copy of every charted album for my research library. It seemed to be the only logical way to make every detail in this book accurate and to be able to expound on notes about the artists and the albums themselves. After nearly five years of searching (and an investment of a small fortune) I was able to obtain a copy of every album listed in this book.

After gathering the albums into my newly built library, the research began. One by one, each and every album was carefully scrutinized and listened to, enabling me to accurately list the artist (or artists), album title, label and number, and to add many interesting and trivial bits of information about both artist and album. The entire project took over three years to complete, but I'm sure you'll agree it was well worth the effort. While the book gives us an insight into 30 years of American culture, it is also a definitive account of the entire so-called rock era, and of the dates and popularity of the 14,000 albums that made Billboard's pop album charts during the past three decades.

I hope you'll receive endless enjoyment from this greatly expanded edition. Let me hear from you if you wish to contribute any interesting facts about an artist or album. I can promise you that future editions will be published on a more frequent basis and that each edition will contain even more data about the artists, albums and music that have meant so much to each of our lives.

JOEL WHITBURN

A SYNOPSIS OF THE BILLBOARD ALBUM CHARTS

DATE	POSITIONS	CHART TITLE
1/1/55	15	BEST SELLING POPULAR ALBUMS (mostly biweely charts with the exception of a 7 week gap and several 3 week gaps)
3/24/56	10-15-20-30	BEST SELLING POPULAR ALBUMS (charts published weekly with size varying from a top 10 to a top 30)
6/2/56	15	BEST SELLING POP ALBUMS
9/2/57	25	BEST SELLING POP LP's
5/25/59	50	BEST SELLING MONOPHONIC LP's
5/25/59	30	BEST SELLING STEREOPHONIC LP's (separate Stero and Mono charts published through 8/10/63)
1/4/60	40	MONO ACTION CHARTS (mono albums charted 39 weeks or less)
1/4/60	30	STEREO ACTION CHARTS (stereo albums charted 19 weeks or less — changed to 29 weeks or less on 5/30/60)
1/4/60	25	ESSENTIAL INVENTORY—MONO (mono albums charted 40 weeks or more)
1/4/60	20	ESSENTIAL INVENTORY—STEREO (stereo albums charted 20 weeks or more — changed to 30 weeks or more on 5/30/60)
1/9/61	25	ACTION ALBUMS—MONOPHONIC (mono albums charted 9 weeks or less)
1/9/61	15	ACTION ALBUMS—STEREOPHONIC (stereo albums charted 9 weeks or less)
1/9/61	—	Approximately 200 Albums listed by category (no positions) and shown as essential inventory.
4/3/61	150	TOP LP's — MONAURAL
4/3/61	50	TOP LP's — STEREO
8/17/63	150	TOP LP's (one chart)
4/1/67	175	TOP LP's
5/13/67	200	TOP LP's
11/25/67	200	TOP LP's (3 pages)
2/15/69	200	TOP LP's (2 pages with A-Z artist listing)
2/19/72	200	TOP LP's & TAPE
10/20/84	200	TOP 200 ALBUMS
1/5/85	200	TOP POP ALBUMS

An album appearing on both the Mono and Stereo charts in the same week is tabulated as 1 weekly appearance.

The album's highest position is determined by the chart (Mono or Stereo) on which the album reached its highest position.

The Essential Inventory charts list albums which have already been charted for months on the Mono & Stereo charts, and therefore, it was researched for weeks charted only — its chart positions were not used.

Billboard published a "Most Played by Jockeys" chart from 7/14/56 to 12/8/58 and a "Pop Albums Coming Up Strong" chart from 7/14/56 to 8/26/57. There were 47 albums from the Jockey charts and 39 albums from the Coming Up charts that never hit the "Best Selling Pop Albums" charts. Those albums have been included in this book, however, a weight factor was added the peak position of each album. 10 positions have been added to the peak position of each Jockey album (Ex.: a #1 album is shown with a peak position of 11) and 15 positions have been added to each Coming Up album. 15 positions were added to the Coming Up albums because the "Best Selling Pop Albums" chart was a top 15 and the "Pop Albums Coming Up Strong" chart was like a "Bubbling Under The Top LPs" chart. Although the albums from these charts did not make the Best Selling chart, they were significant, and it did not seem fair to omit them.

Although this book begins with 1955, the album charts actually began as a top 5 in 1945. Those albums charted from 1945-54 will be included in our upcoming pre-1955 pop book.

ALBUMS
BY
ARTIST

This section lists, alphabetically by artist name, every album to hit Billboard's pop album charts from 1955 through March, 1985.

Each artist's charted hits are listed in chronological order. A sequential number is shown in front of each song title to indicate the artist's number of charted hits. All top 10 albums are highlighted in dark type.

All **TOP 10 SINGLES** from Billboard's **HOT 100** are listed below the album they came from. The highest position each single reached is indicated in parenthesis after the title. Singles listed without a highest position are noteworthy non-top 10 hits.

Explanation of Headings & Symbols

DATE CHARTED: Date album debuted on charts

PEAK POS: Album's highest charted position (highlighted in dark type)

WKS CHRT'D: Total weeks charted

LABEL & NUMBER: Original record label and number

( ): Number in parenthesis after #1 and #2 albums indicates total weeks album held that position.

+ : Indicates the highest position and weeks charted data are subject to change since the album was still charted as of the March 30, 1985 cut-off date.

[ ]: Number in brackets following label number indicates amount of records in the album

•: RIAA certified gold album (500,000 units sold)
▲: RIAA certified platinum album (1,000,000 units sold)

The Record Industy Association of America began certifying gold albums in 1958 and platinum albums in 1976. Certain record labels have never requested RIAA certifications for albums which would otherwise have qualified for these awards.

Symbols in brackets after the titles indicate the following:

C — Comedy	M — Mini Album (E.P.)
E — Early Recordings	N — Novelty
EP— 7" Extended Plays	OC— Original Cast
F — Foreign Language	R — Reissue or Re-release
G — Greatest Hits	S — Soundtrack
I — Instrumentals	T — Talk/Spoken Word
K — Compilations	TV— TV Show
L — Live	X — Christmas

DATE CHARTED	PEAK POS	WKS CHRT'D	ARTIST — Album Title	LABEL & NUMBER
			A's Philadelphia-area rock quintet	
7/11/81	146	7	1. A Woman's Got The Power	Arista 9554
			ABBA Swedish: (A)Agnetha (B)Bjorn (B)Benny (A)Anni-Frida	
8/17/74	145	8	1. Waterloo .... "Waterloo"(6)	Atlantic 18101
11/15/75	174	3	2. Abba	Atlantic 18146
9/18/76	48	61	▲ 3. Greatest Hits .... [G]	Atlantic 18189
1/22/77	20	50	● 4. Arrival .... "Dancing Queen"(1)	Atlantic 18207
2/18/78	14	41	▲ 5. The Album .... "Take A Chance On Me"(3)	Atlantic 19164
7/07/79	19	27	● 6. Voulez-Vous	Atlantic 16000
12/22/79	46	14	● 7. Greatest Hits, Vol. 2 .... [G]	Atlantic 16009
12/13/80	17	38	● 8. Super Trouper .... "The Winner Takes It All"(8)	Atlantic 16023
1/09/82	29	17	9. The Visitors	Atlantic 19332
12/18/82	62	18	10. The Singles (The First Ten Years) .... [G]	Atlantic 80036 [2]
			ABC British new wave trio - Martin Fry. lead singer	
9/25/82	24	39	1. the Lexicon of Love .... "The Look Of Love"	Mercury 4059
12/17/83	69	14	2. Beauty Stab	Mercury 814661
			AC/DC Australian heavy-metal quintet led by Angus & Malcolm Young (guitars) and Bon Scott (vocals)-died 2/19/80 (30)	
8/13/77	154	11	● 1. Let There Be Rock	Atco 151
6/24/78	133	17	● 2. Powerage	Atlantic 19180
12/23/78	113	14	● 3. If You Want Blood You've Got It .... [L]	Atlantic 19212
8/25/79	17	83	▲ 4. Highway To Hell	Atlantic 19244
8/23/80	4	92	▲ 5. **Back In Black** .... Brian Johnson replaces Bon Scott as lead singer	Atlantic 16018
4/18/81	3	55	▲ 6. **Dirty Deeds Done Dirt Cheap** .... [R]	Atlantic 16033
7/18/81	146	19	● 7. High Voltage .... [R] above 2 albums recorded in 1976	Atco 142
12/12/81	1(3)-	30	▲ 8. **For Those About To Rock We Salute You** ...	Atlantic 11111
9/10/83	15	23	● 9. Flick Of The Switch	Atlantic 80100
11/17/84	76	14	10. '74 Jailbreak .... [E-M] Australian releases from 1975-76	Atlantic 80178
			ACCEPT German heavy-metal quintet led by vocalist Udo Dirkschneider	
2/04/84	74	26	1. Balls To The Wall	Portrait 39241
3/30/85	112+	2+	2. Metal Heart	Portrait 39974
			ACE British pub-rock quintet - Paul Carrack, lead singer	
3/15/75	11	22	1. Five-A-Side (an Ace album) .... "How Long"(3)	Anchor 2001
12/27/75	153	6	2. Time For Another	Anchor 2013
2/12/77	170	2	3. No Strings	Anchor 2020
			ACE SPECTRUM New York City trio	
8/23/75	138	7	1. Low Rent Rendezvous	Atlantic 18143
			DAVID ACKLES	
8/12/72	167	10	1. American Gothic	Elektra 75032
			BARBARA ACKLIN	
10/05/68	146	5	1. Love Makes A Woman	Brunswick 754137

DATE CHARTED	PEAK POS	WKS CHRT'D	ARTIST — Album Title	LABEL & NUMBER
			ADAM & THE ANTS British - Adam Ant's real name: Stuart Goddard	
2/28/81	44	35	1. Kings Of The Wild Frontier	Epic 37033
12/12/81	94	21	2. Prince Charming	Epic 37615
			ADAM ANT:	
11/06/82	16	36	● 3. Friend Or Foe "Goody Two Shoes"	Epic 38370
12/10/83	65	26	4. Strip	Epic 39108
			BRYAN ADAMS Canadian rock singer/guitarist	
1/30/82	118	13	1. You Want It, You Got It	A&M 4864
2/19/83	8	59	▲ 2. **Cuts Like A Knife** "Straight From The Heart"(10)	A&M 4919
11/24/84	6	20+	▲ 3. **Reckless** "Run To You"(6)	A&M 5013
			ADC BAND Detroit-based sextet	
12/16/78	139	9	1. Long Stroke	Cotillion 5210
			LEO ADDEO & His Orchestra	
1/09/61	143	13	1. Hawaii In Hi-Fi ...... [I]	RCA Camden 510
			CANNONBALL ADDERLEY quintet features Cannonball (alto sax)-died 8/8/75 (46), brother Nat (cornet), and pianists Joe Zawinul (1-8) & George Duke (9,10,12)	
5/05/62	30	21	1. Nancy Wilson/Cannonball Adderley	Capitol 1657
3/30/63	11	25	2. Jazz Workshop Revisited ...... [I-L]	Riverside 444
2/25/67	13	27	3. Mercy, Mercy, Mercy! ...... [I-L]	Capitol 2663
6/10/67	154	12	4. Why Am I Treated So Bad! ...... [I-L]	Capitol 2617
12/09/67	186	2	5. 74 Miles Away - Walk Tall ...... [I-L]	Capitol 2822
3/14/70	136	22	6. Country Preacher ...... [I-L] introduction by Rev. Jesse Jackson	Capitol 404
9/26/70	194	2	7. Experience in E, Tensity, Dialogues ...... [I]	Capitol 484
3/06/71	169	2	8. The Price You Got To Pay To Be Free ...... [L]	Capitol 636 [2]
2/26/72	167	3	9. The Black Messiah ...... [L]	Capitol 846 [2]
7/01/72	74	20	10. Soul Zodiac ...... featuring the Nat Adderley Sextet - narration by Rick Holmes	Capitol 11025 [2]
9/29/73	179	5	11. Inside Straight ...... [I-L]	Fantasy 9435
9/20/75	121	8	12. Phenix ...... [I]	Fantasy 79004 [2]
			ADDRISI BROTHERS Dick & Don Addrisi - Don died of cancer on 11/13/84 (45)	
4/08/72	137	3	1. We've Got To Get It On Again	Columbia 31296
7/02/77	118	14	2. Addrisi Brothers	Buddah 5694
			KING SUNNY ADE & his African Beats Nigerian known for his native 'JuJu Music'	
4/09/83	111	29	1. JuJu Music ...... [F]	Mango 9712
8/20/83	91	10	2. Synchro System ...... [F]	Mango 9737
			AEROSMITH Boston hard-rock quintet featuring Steven Tyler (vocals) & Joe Perry (lead guitar 1-8)	
10/13/73	21	59	● 1. Aerosmith ...... "Dream On"(6)	Columbia 32005
4/06/74	74	86	● 2. Get Your Wings	Columbia 32847
4/26/75	11	128	● 3. Toys In The Attic "Walk This Way"(10)	Columbia 33479
5/29/76	3	53	▲ 4. **Rocks**	Columbia 34165
12/24/77	11	20	▲ 5. Draw The Line	Columbia 34856
11/11/78	13	22	▲ 6. Live! Bootleg ...... [L]	Columbia 35564 [2]
12/01/79	14	19	● 7. Night In The Ruts	Columbia 36050

DATE CHARTED	PEAK POS	WKS CHRT'D	ARTIST — Album Title	LABEL & NUMBER
11/29/80	53	16	● 8. Aerosmith's Greatest Hits .... [G]	Columbia 36865
9/25/82	32	19	9. Rock In A Hard Place	Columbia 38061
			AFRIQUE	
6/16/73	152	8	1. Soul Makossa .... [I]	Mainstream 394
			featuring David T. Walker on guitar	
			AFTER THE FIRE	
			English	
3/12/83	25	20	1. ATF	Epic 38282
			"Der Kommisar"(5)	
			AIR FORCE - see GINGER BAKER	
			AIR SUPPLY	
			Australian group led by Graham Russell & Russell Hitchcock	
5/17/80	22	103	▲ 1. Lost In Love	Arista 4268
			"Lost In Love"(3)/"All Out Of Love"(2)/	
			"Every Woman In The World"(5)	
6/13/81	10	60	▲ 2. **The One That You Love**	Arista 9551
			"The One That You Love"(1)/"Here I Am"(5)/"Sweet Dreams"(5)	
6/19/82	25	38	▲ 3. Now And Forever	Arista 9587
			"Even The Nights Are Better"(5)	
8/20/83	7	43	▲ 4. **Greatest Hits** .... [G]	Arista 8024
			"Making Love Out Of Nothing At All"(2)	
			AIRTO - see DEODATO	
			JAN AKKERMAN	
			Dutch guitarist formerly with Focus	
10/13/73	192	4	1. Profile .... [I]	Sire 7407
3/02/74	195	2	2. Tabernakel .... [I]	Atco 7032
4/08/78	198	2	3. Jan Akkerman .... [I]	Atlantic 19159
			ALABAMA	
			Randy Owen, Jeff Cook, Teddy Gentry (cousins) and Mark Herndon	
7/19/80	71	21	▲ 1. My Home's In Alabama	RCA 3644
3/28/81	16	161	▲ 2. Feels So Right	RCA 3930
3/13/82	14	114	▲ 3. Mountain Music	RCA 4229
3/26/83	10	70	▲ 4. **The Closer You Get...**	RCA 4663
2/11/84	21	61+	▲ 5. Roll On	RCA 4939
2/23/85	28+	7+	6. 40 Hour Week	RCA 5339
			ALARM	
			British rock quartet - Mike Peters, lead singer	
7/30/83	126	37	1. The Alarm .... [M]	I.R.S. 70504
3/10/84	50	22	2. Declaration	I.R.S. 70608
			MORRIS ALBERT	
			Brazilian	
9/06/75	37	31	1. Feelings	RCA 1018
			"Feelings"(6)	
6/12/76	163	7	2. Morris Albert	RCA 1496
			ALCATRAZZ	
			hard rock quintet - Graham Bonnet, lead singer (member of Rainbow and the Michael Schenker Group)	
1/07/84	128	18	1. No Parole From Rock 'N' Roll	Rocshire 22016
6/09/84	133	10	2. Live Sentence .... [L]	Rocshire 22020
			recorded 1/28/84 in Tokyo, Japan	
			RONNIE ALDRICH & His Two Pianos	
10/23/61	20	33	1. Melody And Percussion For Two Pianos..... [I]	London P. 4 44007
10/06/62	36	4	2. Ronnie Aldrich & His Two Pianos .... [I]	London P. 4 44018
5/22/71	169	6	3. Love Story .... [I]	London P. 4 22 [2]
			with the London Festival Orchestra	

DATE CHARTED	PEAK POS	WKS CHRT'D	ARTIST — Album Title	LABEL & NUMBER
			ALIVE 'N KICKIN'	
10/17/70	**129**	3	1. Alive 'N Kickin' .... produced by Tommy James "Tighter, Tighter"(7)	Roulette 42052
			DAVIE ALLAN & THE ARROWS rock instrumental quartet	
10/15/66	**17**	71	1. The Wild Angels .... [S]	Tower 5043
4/22/67	**94**	18	2. The Wild Angels, Vol. II .... [S-I]	Tower 5056
8/19/67	**165**	2	3. Devil's Angels .... [S-I]	Tower 5074
			DAYTON ALLEN comedian on the Steve Allen TV show	
12/19/60	**35**	1	1. Why Not! .... [C]	Grand Award 424
			DEBORAH ALLEN country singer	
12/03/83	**67**	20	1. Cheat The Night .... [M]	RCA 8514
			PETER ALLEN Australian cabaret-style performer	
4/14/79	**171**	3	1. I Could Have Been A Sailor	A&M 4739
11/29/80	**123**	20	2. Bi-Coastal	A&M 4825
3/12/83	**170**	6	3. Not The Boy Next Door	Arista 9613
			STEVE ALLEN founded TV's "The Tonight Show" in 1954	
5/14/55	**7**	9	1. **Music For Tonight** .... [I]	Coral 57004
3/16/63	**70**	11	2. Funny Fone-Calls .... [C] from Steve's TV show	Dot 3472
4/27/63	**41**	22	3. Gravy Waltz And 11 Current Hits! .... [I]	Dot 3515
			WOODY ALLEN screen actor, writer and director	
8/15/64	**63**	11	1. Woody Allen .... [C]	Colpix 518
			ALLMAN BROTHERS BAND America's top Southern rock band featuring brothers Duane & Gregg Allman, and Dickey Betts	
1/24/70	**188**	5	1. The Allman Brothers Band	Atco 308
10/24/70	**38**	22	2. Idlewild South	Atco 342
7/24/71	**13**	47	● 3. At Fillmore East .... [L]	Capricorn 802 [2]
3/18/72	**4**	48	● 4. **Eat A Peach** .... [L] includes Duane's last 3 studio recordings	Capricorn 0102 [2]
3/10/73	**25**	55	● 5. Beginnings .... [R] reissue of albums #1 & 2 above	Atco 805 [2]
8/25/73	**1(5)**	56	● 6. **Brothers And Sisters** .... "Ramblin' Man"(2)	Capricorn 0111
9/13/75	**5**	14	● 7. **Win, Lose Or Draw**	Capricorn 0156
12/13/75	**43**	14	8. The Road Goes On Forever, A Collection Of Their Greatest Recordings .... [G]	Capricorn 0164 [2]
12/04/76	**75**	10	9. Wipe The Windows-Check The Oil-Dollar Gas .... [L] live recordings from 1972-1975	Capricorn 0177 [2]
3/17/79	**9**	24	● 10. **Enlightened Rouges**	Capricorn 0218
8/23/80	**27**	13	11. Reach For The Sky	Arista 9535
8/22/81	**44**	12	12. Brothers Of The Road	Arista 9564
11/21/81	**189**	3	13. The Best Of The Allman Brothers Band . [G]	Polydor 6339
			DUANE ALLMAN died in a cycle accident on 10/29/71 (24)	
12/09/72	**28**	26	● 1. An Anthology .... [K]	Capricorn 0108 [2]
8/31/74	**49**	16	2. An Anthology, Vol. II .... [K] above 2 albums feature Duane's session work	Capricorn 0139 [2]

DATE CHARTED	PEAK POS	WKS CHRT'D	ARTIST — Album Title	LABEL & NUMBER
			DUANE & GREGG ALLMAN	
5/13/72	**129**	8	1. Duane & Gregg Allman .... [E]	Bold 301
			recorded in 1968	
11/03/73	**171**	8	2. Early Allman .... [E]	Dial 6005
			ALLMAN JOYS recorded in 1966	
			GREGG ALLMAN	
11/24/73	**13**	39	● 1. Laid Back	Capricorn 0116
11/16/74	**50**	12	2. The Gregg Allman Tour .... [L]	Capricorn 0141 [2]
			with orchestra, and guest "Cowboy"	
6/11/77	**42**	12	3. Playin' Up A Storm	Capricorn 0181
			LAURINDO ALMEIDA & The Bossa Nova All Stars	
12/08/62	**9**	27	1. Viva Bossa Nova! .... [I]	Capitol 1759
			HERB ALPERT	
			born on 3/31/37 in Los Angeles - co-founder of A&M Records	
			HERB ALPERT & THE TIJUANA BRASS:	
12/29/62	**24**	157	● 1. The Lonely Bull .... [I]	A&M 101
			"The Lonely Bull"(6)	
1/16/65	**6**	163	● 2. South Of The Border .... [I]	A&M 108
5/15/65	**1(8)**	185	● 3. Whipped Cream & Other Delights .... [I]	A&M 110
			"Taste Of Honey"(7)	
10/16/65	**1(6)**	164	● 4. Going Places .... [I]	A&M 112
1/15/66	**17**	56	● 5. Herb Alpert's Tijuana Brass, Volume 2 .... [I]	A&M 103
			Herb's 2nd album, recorded in 1963	
5/14/66	**1(9)**	129	● 6. What Now My Love .... [I]	A&M 4114
12/10/66	**2(6)**	85	● 7. S.R.O. .... [I]	A&M 4119
6/03/67	**1(1)**	53	● 8. Sounds Like .... [I]	A&M 4124
12/23/67	**4**	49	● 9. Herb Alpert's Ninth .... [I]	A&M 4134
5/11/68	**1(2)**	54	● 10. The Beat Of The Brass .... [I]	A&M 4146
			"This Guy's In Love With You"(1)	
7/05/69	**28**	26	● 11. Warm .... [I]	A&M 4190
11/22/69	**30**	20	12. The Brass Are Comin' .... [I]	A&M 4228
3/21/70	**43**	32	● 13. Greatest Hits .... [G-I]	A&M 4245
7/24/71	**111**	10	14. Summertime .... [I]	A&M 4314
6/17/72	**135**	10	15. Solid Brass .... [K-I]	A&M 4341
12/08/73	**196**	4	16. Foursider .... [K-I]	A&M 3521 [2]
			HERB ALPERT & THE T.J.B.:	
6/01/74	**66**	11	17. You Smile-The Song Begins .... [I]	A&M 3620
4/26/75	**88**	10	18. Coney Island .... [I]	A&M 4521
			HERB ALPERT:	
2/11/78	**65**	19	19. Herb Alpert/Hugh Masekela .... [I]	Horizon 728
10/13/79	**6**	39	▲ 20. Rise .... [I]	A&M 4790
			"Rise"(1)	
7/26/80	**28**	12	21. Beyond .... [I]	A&M 3717
8/22/81	**61**	10	22. Magic Man .... [I]	A&M 3728
5/29/82	**100**	26	23. Fandango .... [I]	A&M 3731
9/24/83	**120**	8	24. Blow Your Own Horn .... [I]	A&M 4949
			HERB ALPERT/TIJUANA BRASS:	
8/25/84	**75**	10	25. Bullish .... [I]	A&M 5022
			ALPHAVILLE	
			German synth-pop trio - Marian Gold, lead singer	
12/22/84	**180**	15	1. Forever Young	Atlantic 80186
			AMAZING RHYTHM ACES	
			Memphis-based country/rock sextet - Russell Smith, lead singer	
10/18/75	**120**	8	1. Stacked Deck	ABC 913
6/05/76	**157**	7	2. Too Stuffed To Jump	ABC 940

DATE CHARTED	PEAK POS	WKS CHRT'D	ARTIST — Album Title	LABEL & NUMBER
4/16/77	114	11	3. Toucan Do It Too	ABC 1005
4/15/78	116	9	4. Burning The Ballroom Down	ABC 1063
2/17/79	144	7	5. The Amazing Rhythm Aces	ABC 1123
			re-released on Columbia 36083	
10/04/80	175	3	6. How The Hell Do You Spell Rythum?	Warner 3476

AMBOY DUKES
Detroit rock group led by Ted Nugent

2/10/68	183	4	1. The Amboy Dukes	Mainstream 6104
6/15/68	74	23	2. Journey To The Center Of The Mind	Mainstream 6112
3/21/70	191	2	3. Marriage On The Rocks/Rock Bottom	Polydor 4012
3/06/71	129	5	4. Survival Of The Fittest/Live .... [L]	Polydor 4035
			TED NUGENT & THE AMBOY DUKES	

AMBROSIA
Los Angeles trio: Joe Puerta, Burleigh Drummond & David Pack

5/03/75	22	33	1. Ambrosia	20th Century 434
9/18/76	79	17	2. Somewhere I've Never Travelled	20th Century 510
8/12/78	19	29	3. Life Beyond L.A.	Warner 3135
			"How Much I Feel"(3)	
4/19/80	25	33	4. One Eighty	Warner 3368
			"Biggest Part Of Me"(3)	
5/29/82	115	7	5. Road Island	Warner 3638

DON AMECHE & FRANCES LANGFORD
Don & Frances both began their film careers in 1935

4/07/62	76	12	1. The Bickersons .... [C]	Columbia 1692
11/03/62	109	6	2. The Bickersons Fight Back .... [C]	Columbia 1883
			comedy skits written and created by Philip Rapp	

AMERICA
Dewey Bunnell & Gerry Beckley - with Dan Peek thru album #8

2/19/72	1(5)	40	● 1. **America**	Warner 2576
			"A Horse With No Name"(1)/"I Need You"(9)	
12/02/72	9	32	● 2. **Homecoming**	Warner 2655
			"Ventura Highway"(8)	
11/17/73	28	18	3. Hat Trick	Warner 2728
7/13/74	3	53	● 4. **Holiday**	Warner 2808
			"Tin Man"(4)/"Lonely People"(5)	
4/05/75	4	44	● 5. **Hearts**	Warner 2852
			"Sister Golden Hair"(1)	
11/22/75	3	63	● 6. **History/America's Greatest Hits** .... [G]	Warner 2894
5/01/76	11	22	● 7. Hideaway	Warner 2932
3/12/77	21	14	8. Harbor	Warner 3017
12/17/77	129	7	9. America/Live .... [L]	Warner 3136
			recorded at the Greek Theatre, Los Angeles	
7/07/79	110	6	10. Silent Letter	Capitol 11950
9/06/80	142	6	11. Alibi	Capitol 12098
8/28/82	41	28	12. View From The Ground	Capitol 12209
			"You Can Do Magic"(8)	
7/02/83	81	14	13. Your Move	Capitol 12277
11/10/84	185	3	14. Perspective	Capitol 12370

AMERICAN BREED
Chicago rock quartet - Kevin Murphy was a founding member of Rufus

2/24/68	99	10	1. Bend Me, Shape Me	Acta 38003
			"Bend Me, Shape Me"(5)	

AMERICAN DREAM

2/28/70	194	2	1. The American Dream	Ampex 10101
			Todd Rundgren, producer	

DATE CHARTED	PEAK POS	WKS CHRT'D	ARTIST — Album Title	LABEL & NUMBER
			AMERICAN FLYER Craig Fuller (Pure Prairie League), Eric Kaz (Blues Magoos), Steve Katz (Blood, Sweat & Tears), Doug Yule (Velvet Underground)	
9/04/76	**87**	10	1. American Flyer	United Art. 650
7/02/77	**171**	5	2. Spirit Of A Woman	United Art. 720
			AMES BROTHERS Ed, Gene, Joe & Vic Ames - Vic died on 1/23/78 (51)	
12/02/57	**16**	4	1. There'll Always Be A Christmas .... [X]	RCA 1541
			ED AMES played Mingo on the TV series "Daniel Boone"	
11/05/66	**90**	7	1. More I Cannot Wish You	RCA 3636
3/04/67	**4**	81	● 2. **My Cup Runneth Over** .... "My Cup Runneth Over"(8)	RCA 3774
7/08/67	**77**	38	3. Time, Time	RCA 3834
12/16/67	**24**	25	4. When The Snow Is On The Roses	RCA 3913
2/24/68	**13**	50	● 5. Who Will Answer? And Other Songs Of Our Time	RCA 3961
8/10/68	**135**	14	6. Apologize	RCA 4028
12/21/68	**186**	6	7. The Hits Of Broadway And Hollywood	RCA 4079
3/08/69	**114**	14	8. A Time For Living, A Time For Hope	RCA 4128
7/05/69	**157**	6	9. The Windmills Of Your Mind	RCA 4172
10/18/69	**119**	16	10. The Best Of Ed Ames .... [G]	RCA 4184
1/03/70	**172**	6	11. Love Of The Common People	RCA 4249
7/11/70	**194**	2	12. Sing Away The World	RCA 4381
2/20/71	**199**	1	13. The Songs Of Bacharach And David	RCA 4453
			NANCY AMES	
9/26/64	**133**	4	1. This Is The Girl That Is .... [F]	Liberty 7369
10/29/66	**133**	8	2. Latin Pulse .... [F] both albums are sung in Spanish	Epic 26189
			GENE AMMONS jazz tenor sax player - died in 1974 (49)	
12/22/62	**53**	17	1. Bad! Bossa Nova .... [I]	Prestige 7257
6/06/70	**174**	2	2. The Boss Is Back! .... [I]	Prestige 7739
			GEZA ANDA classical pianist	
6/29/68	**115**	17	1. Mozart: Piano Concertos Nos. 17 & 21 ..... [I] contains the theme from the film "Elvira Madigan"	DG 138783
			ERIC ANDERSEN	
7/15/72	**169**	11	1. Blue River	Columbia 31062
4/19/75	**113**	9	2. Be True To You	Arista 4033
			BILL ANDERSON host of Nashville Network's TV quiz show "Fandango"	
7/06/63	**36**	17	1. Still .... "Still"(8)	Decca 74427
			ERNESTINE ANDERSON vocalist with Eddie Heywood and Lionel Hampton	
10/20/58	**15**	6	1. Hot Cargo!	Mercury 20354
			JOHN ANDERSON country singer	
4/09/83	**58**	12	● 1. Wild & Blue	Warner 23721
10/29/83	**163**	5	2. All The People Are Talkin'	Warner 23912
			JOHN W. ANDERSON - see KASANDRA	

DATE CHARTED	PEAK POS	WKS CHRT'D	ARTIST — Album Title	LABEL & NUMBER
			JON ANDERSON lead singer of Yes - also see Jon & Vangelis	
7/24/76	**47**	13	1. Olias Of Sunhillow	Atlantic 18180
12/06/80	**143**	11	2. Song Of Seven	Atlantic 16021
7/03/82	**176**	5	3. Animation	Atlantic 19355
			LAURIE ANDERSON	
5/29/82	**124**	12	1. Big Science	Warner 3674
3/17/84	**60**	19	2. Mister Heartbreak	Warner 25077
1/26/85	**192**	5	3. United States Live .... [L] recorded at the Brooklyn Academy of Music in February. 1983	Warner 25192 [5]
			LYNN ANDERSON daughter of country singer Liz Anderson	
4/12/69	**197**	2	1. With Love, From Lynn	Chart 1013
5/03/69	**180**	3	2. The Best Of Lynn Anderson .... [G]	Chart 1009
1/09/71	**19**	33	● 3. Rose Garden .... "Rose Garden"(3)	Columbia 30411
7/24/71	**99**	14	4. You're My Man	Columbia 30793
10/30/71	**174**	4	5. The World Of Lynn Anderson .... [R] reissue of Lynn's first two Columbia albums from 1970	Columbia 30902 [2]
12/04/71	**132**	5	6. How Can I Unlove You	Columbia 30925
4/08/72	**114**	9	7. Cry	Columbia 31316
9/09/72	**160**	7	8. Listen To A Country Song	Columbia 31647
11/11/72	**129**	14	9. Lynn Anderson's Greatest Hits .... [G]	Columbia 31641
8/11/73	**179**	3	10. Top Of The World	Columbia 32429
			ANDREWS SISTERS Patty. Maxene & LaVerne - LaVerne died in 1967 (52)	
10/06/73	**126**	9	1. The Best Of Andrews Sisters .... [G]	MCA 4024 [2]
10/13/73	**167**	7	2. Boogie Woogie Bugle Girls .... [K]	Paramount 6075
7/13/74	**137**	3	3. Over Here! .... [OC] Broadway musical featuring Patty & Maxene	Columbia 32961
7/20/74	**198**	1	4. In The Mood .... [K]	Paramount 1023 [2]
			JULIE ANDREWS & CAROL BURNETT	
9/01/62	**85**	9	1. Julie And Carol at Carnegie Hall .... [L] a musical concert performed on 6/11/62	Columbia 2240
			ANGEL East Coast heavy-metal rock quintet featuring Frank DiMino (vocals), Punky Meadows (guitar) and Greg Giuffria (keyboards)	
12/20/75	**156**	6	1. Angel	Casablanca 7021
6/19/76	**155**	10	2. Helluva Band	Casablanca 7028
3/05/77	**76**	12	3. On Earth As It Is In Heaven	Casablanca 7043
2/04/78	**55**	13	4. White Hot	Casablanca 7085
3/03/79	**159**	5	5. Sinful	Casablanca 7127
2/23/80	**149**	4	6. Live Without A Net .... [L]	Casablanca 7203 [2]
			ANGEL CITY Australian hard-rock quintet - Doc Neeson. lead singer	
5/10/80	**152**	7	1. Face To Face	Epic 36344
11/08/80	**133**	6	2. Darkroom	Epic 36543
3/20/82	**174**	5	3. Night Attack	Epic 37702
			ANGELS Peggy Santiglia. lead singer of female trio from New Jersey	
9/28/63	**33**	14	1. My Boyfriend's Back .... "My Boyfriend's Back"(1)	Smash 67039
			ANIMALS British rock quintet led by Eric Burdon	
9/05/64	**7**	27	1. The Animals .... "The House Of The Rising Sun"(1)	MGM 4264
3/20/65	**99**	9	2. The Animals On Tour	MGM 4281

16

DATE CHARTED	PEAK POS	WKS CHRT'D	ARTIST — Album Title	LABEL & NUMBER
9/18/65	**57**	25	3. Animal Tracks	MGM 4305
2/12/66	**6**	113	● 4. **The Best Of The Animals** .... [G]	MGM 4324
8/20/66	**20**	30	5. Animalization	MGM 4384
			"See See Rider"(10)	
12/03/66	**33**	22	6. Animalism	MGM 4414
			ERIC BURDON & THE ANIMALS:	
3/25/67	**121**	13	7. Eric Is Here	MGM 4433
6/10/67	**71**	24	8. The Best Of Eric Burdon And The	
			Animals, Vol. II .... [G]	MGM 4454
9/23/67	**42**	20	9. Winds Of Change	MGM 4484
			"San Franciscan Nights"(9)	
4/06/68	**79**	29	10. The Twain Shall Meet	MGM 4537
8/24/68	**152**	8	11. Every One Of Us	MGM 4553
1/11/69	**123**	10	12. Love Is	MGM 4591 [2]
3/15/69	**153**	6	13. The Greatest Hits Of Eric Burdon And	
			The Animals .... [G]	MGM 4602
			THE ANIMALS:	
8/25/73	**188**	2	14. Best Of The Animals .... [G]	Abkco 4226
8/27/77	**70**	11	15. Before We Were So Rudely Interrupted	United Art. 790
9/10/83	**66**	10	16. Ark	I.R.S. 70037
9/15/84	**193**	4	17. Rip It To Shreds - the Animals greatest	
			hits live! .... [L]	I.R.S. 70043

ANIMOTION
6-member band led by Astrid Plane and Bill Wadhams

DATE CHARTED	PEAK POS	WKS CHRT'D	ARTIST — Album Title	LABEL & NUMBER
2/23/85	**50+**	7+	1. Animotion	Mercury 822580
			"Obsession"	

PAUL ANKA
born in Ottawa, Canada on July 30, 1941

DATE CHARTED	PEAK POS	WKS CHRT'D	ARTIST — Album Title	LABEL & NUMBER
7/04/60	**4**	140	1. **Paul Anka Sings His Big 15** .... [G]	ABC-Para. 323
			"Diana"(1)/"You Are My Destiny"(7)/"Lonely Boy"(1)/ "Put Your Head On My Shoulder"(2)/"It's Time To Cry"(4) "Puppy Love"(2)	
12/05/60	**23**	16	2. Anka At The Copa .... [L]	ABC-Para. 353
9/25/61	**72**	12	3. Paul Anka Sings His Big 15, Vol. 2 .... [G]	ABC-Para. 390
			"My Home Town"(8)/"Dance On Little Girl"(10)	
4/14/62	**61**	12	4. Young, Alive And In Love!	RCA 2502
9/15/62	**137**	2	5. Let's Sit This One Out	RCA 2575
7/06/63	**65**	33	6. Paul Anka's 21 Golden Hits .... [G]	RCA 2691
			newly recorded versions of ABC-Paramount hits	
3/15/69	**101**	11	7. Goodnight My Love	RCA 4142
12/27/69	**194**	2	8. Life Goes On	RCA 4250
1/15/72	**188**	4	9. Paul Anka	Buddah 5093
6/03/72	**192**	4	10. Jubilation	Buddah 5114
8/31/74	**9**	28	● 11. **Anka**	United Art. 314
			"(You're) Having My Baby"(1)/"One Man Woman/One Woman Man"(7)	
12/14/74	**125**	9	12. Paul Anka Gold .... [G]	Sire 3704 [2]
			original ABC-Paramount recordings	
4/05/75	**36**	29	13. Feelings	United Art. 367
			"I Don't Like To Sleep Alone"(8)	
12/13/75	**22**	25	● 14. Times Of Your Life .... [K]	United Art. 569
			9 of 10 cuts from previous 2 United Artists albums "Times Of Your Life"(7)	
10/23/76	**85**	15	15. The Painter	United Art. 653
6/18/77	**195**	3	16. The Music Man	United Art. 746
11/25/78	**179**	7	17. Listen To Your Heart	RCA 2892
5/09/81	**171**	6	18. Both Sides Of Love	RCA 3926
8/13/83	**156**	8	19. Walk A Fine Line	Columbia 38442

ANN-MARGRET - see JOHN GARY/AL HIRT

DATE CHARTED	PEAK POS	WKS CHRT'D	ARTIST — Album Title	LABEL & NUMBER
			ANNETTE born Annette Funicello on 10/22/42 - became a Mousketeer in 1955	
3/21/60	**21**	9	1. Annette Sings Anka	Buena Vista 3302
9/26/60	**38**	3	2. Hawaiiannette	Buena Vista 3303
10/19/63	**39**	13	3. Annette's Beach Party .... [S] half of the songs are from the film "Beach Party"	Buena Vista 3316
			ADAM ANT - see ADAM & THE ANTS	
			RAY ANTHONY trumpet player with the Glenn Miller and Jimmy Dorsey bands	
3/19/55	**10**	4	1. **Golden Horn** .... [I]	Capitol 563
6/23/56	**15**	1	2. Dream Dancing .... [I]	Capitol 723
10/28/57	**11**	21	3. Young Ideas .... [I]	Capitol 866
5/19/58	**12**	10	4. The Dream Girl .... [I]	Capitol 969
7/21/62	**14**	19	5. Worried Mind .... [I]	Capitol 1752
			AORTA rock quartet	
4/12/69	**167**	8	1. Aorta	Columbia 9785
			APOLLO 100 featuring Tom Parker	
2/19/72	**47**	16	1. Joy .... [I] "Joy"(6)	Mega 1010
			APOLLONIA 6 female trio led by Patty (Apollonia) Kotero (co-star of film "Purple Rain") - trio evolved from Vanity 6	
10/27/84	**62**	17	1. Apollonia 6	Warner 25108
			APPALOOSA Boston folk-rock quartet	
8/16/69	**178**	4	1. Appaloosa	Columbia 9819
			CARMINE APPICE - see BECK, BOGERT, APPICE	
			APRIL WINE Canadian rock quintet - Myles Goodwyn, lead singer	
4/14/79	**114**	11	1. First Glance	Capitol 11852
11/10/79	**64**	40	● 2. Harder...Faster	Capitol 12013
1/31/81	**26**	34	▲ 3. The Nature Of The Beast	Capitol 12125
7/10/82	**37**	20	4. Power Play	Capitol 12218
3/17/84	**62**	12	5. Animal Grace	Capitol 12311
			AQUARIAN DREAM	
10/09/76	**154**	6	1. Norman Connors presents Aquarian Dream ..	Buddah 5672
			AQUARIANS Vladimir Vassilieff, piano	
11/01/69	**192**	2	1. Jungle Grass .... [I]	United Art. 73053
			ARBORS group formed at the University of Michigan in Ann Arbor	
2/11/67	**144**	2	1. A Symphony For Susan	Date 3003
			ARCHIES studio group created by Don Kirshner - Ron Dante, lead singer	
11/02/68	**88**	21	1. The Archies	Calendar 101
9/06/69	**66**	36	2. Everthing's Archie .... "Sugar, Sugar"(1)	Calendar 103
1/03/70	**125**	10	3. Jingle Jangle .... "Jingle Jangle"(10)	Kirshner 105
9/12/70	**137**	6	4. Sunshine	Kirshner 107
11/28/70	**114**	12	5. The Archies Greatest Hits .... [G]	Kirshner 109
			AREA CODE 615	
10/18/69	**191**	4	1. Area Code 615 .... [I]	Polydor 4002

18

DATE CHARTED	PEAK POS	WKS CHRT'D	ARTIST — Album Title	LABEL & NUMBER
			ARENA BRASS Robert Mersey, conductor	
1/05/63	**130**	5	1. The Lonely Bull .... [I]	Epic 26039
			ARGENT British rock quartet led by Rod Argent (Zombies)	
7/01/72	**23**	23	1. All Together Now .... "Hold Your Head Up"(5)	Epic 31556
4/07/73	**90**	11	2. In Deep	Epic 32195
5/04/74	**149**	6	3. Nexus	Epic 32573
1/11/75	**151**	4	4. Encore-Live In Concert . ... [L]	Epic 33079 [2]
3/29/75	**171**	3	5. Circus	Epic 33422
			ARMADA ORCHESTRA 37 members of The London Symphony Orchestra	
1/17/76	**196**	2	1. The Armada Orchestra .... [I]	Scepter 5123
			ARMAGEDDON rock quartet led by Keith Relf (Yardbirds)	
6/07/75	**151**	6	1. Armageddon	A&M 4513
			JOAN ARMATRADING born on 12/9/50 in the West Indies	
10/09/76	**67**	27	1. Joan Armatrading	A&M 4588
10/22/77	**52**	21	2. Show Some Emotion	A&M 4663
11/11/78	**125**	12	3. To The Limit	A&M 4732
12/08/79	**136**	18	4. How Cruel .... [M]	A&M 3302
6/07/80	**28**	23	5. Me Myself I	A&M 4809
10/17/81	**88**	32	6. Walk Under Ladders	A&M 4876
4/30/83	**32**	22	7. The Key	A&M 4912
1/21/84	**113**	10	8. Track Record .... [G]	A&M 4987
3/30/85	**115+**	2+	9. Secret Secrets	A&M 5040
			ARMORED SAINT Los Angeles-based rock quintet - John Bush, lead vocals	
12/22/84	**138**	16	1. March Of The Saint	Chrysalis 41476
			LOUIS ARMSTRONG & The All Stars all-time great jazz trumpet player/vocalist - died 7/6/71 (71)	
10/01/55	**10**	1	1. **Satch Plays Fats** .... a tribute to Fats Waller	Columbia 708
12/15/56	**12**	2	2. Ella And Louis .... ELLA FITZGERALD & LOUIS ARMSTRONG backing by the Oscar Peterson Trio, plus Buddy Rich	Verve 4003
5/16/64	**1(6)**	74 ●	3. **Hello, Dolly!** .... "Hello, Dolly"(1)	Kapp 3364
			EDDY ARNOLD Country music's all-time #1 artist - born on 5/15/18 near Henderson, Tennessee	
10/26/63	**131**	5	1. Cattle Call	RCA 2578
10/16/65	**7**	58 ●	2. **My World** .... "Make The World Go Away"(6)	RCA 3466
3/26/66	**26**	28	3. I Want To Go With You	RCA 3507
7/30/66	**46**	22	4. The Last Word In Lonesome	RCA 3622
12/24/66	**36**	30	5. Somebody Like Me	RCA 3715
3/18/67	**57**	24	6. Lonely Again	RCA 3753
5/06/67	**34**	57 ●	7. The Best Of Eddy Arnold .... [G]	RCA 3565
10/07/67	**34**	36	8. Turn The World Around	RCA 3869
2/24/68	**122**	21	9. The Everlovin' World Of Eddy Arnold ...	RCA 3931
6/15/68	**56**	32	10. The Romantic World Of Eddy Arnold	RCA 4009
11/09/68	**70**	13	11. Walkin' In Love Land	RCA 4089
3/08/69	**77**	13	12. Songs Of The Young World	RCA 4110
7/05/69	**167**	5	13. The Glory Of Love	RCA 4179

DATE CHARTED	PEAK POS	WKS CHRT'D	ARTIST — Album Title	LABEL & NUMBER
11/01/69	116	8	14. The Warmth Of Eddy	RCA 4231
5/02/70	191	3	15. Love & Guitars	RCA 4304
5/30/70	146	2	16. The Best Of Eddy Arnold, Volume II .... [G]	RCA 4320
3/13/71	141	4	17. Portrait Of My Woman	RCA 4471

ARPEGGIO

2/10/79	75	16	1. Let The Music Play	Polydor 6180

STEVE ARRINGTON'S Hall Of Fame
former lead singer of Slave

3/12/83	101	17	1. Steve Arrington's Hall Of Fame: I	Atlantic 80049
2/25/84	141	9	2. Positive Power	Atlantic 80127

ARROWS - see DAVIE ALLAN

ART IN AMERICA
family trio: Chris, Dan & Shishonee Flynn

3/26/83	176	3	1. Art In America	Pavillion 38517

ART OF NOISE
techno-pop quartet led by producer Trevor Horn

7/14/84	85	13	1. (Who's Afraid Of?) The Art Of Noise	Island 90179

ASHFORD & SIMPSON
Nickolas Ashford & Valerie Simpson (married)

11/10/73	156	13	1. Gimme Something Real	Warner 2739
7/20/74	195	4	2. I Wanna Be Selfish	Warner 2789
5/08/76	189	4	3. Come As You Are	Warner 2858
2/05/77	180	3	4. So So Satisfied	Warner 2992
10/15/77	52	46	● 5. Send It	Warner 3088
9/09/78	20	28	● 6. Is It Still Good To Ya	Warner 3219
9/01/79	23	23	● 7. Stay Free	Warner 3357
8/23/80	38	12	8. A Musical Affair	Warner 3458
10/17/81	125	6	9. Performance .... [L] 3 of 4 sides recorded live	Warner 3524 [2]
5/29/82	45	20	10. Street Opera	Capitol 12207
9/17/83	84	12	11. High-Rise	Capitol 12282
11/10/84	29	22 +	● 12. Solid	Capitol 12366

ASHTON, GARDNER & DYKE
British: Tony Ashton, Kim Gardner & Roy Dyke

8/07/71	185	6	1. Resurrection Shuffle	Capitol 563

ASIA
British: Steve Howe, Carl Palmer, Geoff Downes & John Wetton

4/03/82	1(9)	61	▲ 1. **Asia** "Heat Of The Moment"(4)	Geffen 2008
8/27/83	6	25	▲ 2. **Alpha** "Don't Cry"(10)	Geffen 4008

ASLEEP AT THE WHEEL
Austin, Texas western swing band

9/20/75	136	8	1. Texas Gold	Capitol 11441
9/18/76	179	3	2. Wheelin' And Dealin'	Capitol 11546
4/16/77	162	4	3. The Wheel	Capitol 11620
9/06/80	191	2	4. Framed	MCA 5131

ASSOCIATION
California soft-rock sextet

8/20/66	5	59	● 1. **And Then...Along Comes The Association** "Along Comes Mary"(7)/"Cherish"(1)	Valiant 5002
1/07/67	34	15	2. Renaissance	Valiant 5004
7/22/67	8	68	● 3. **Insight Out** "Windy"(1)/"Never My Love"(2)	Warner 1696
5/04/68	23	26	4. Birthday "Everything That Touches You"(10)	Warner 1733

DATE CHARTED	PEAK POS	WKS CHRT'D	ARTIST — Album Title	LABEL & NUMBER
12/28/68	4	75	● 5. **Greatest Hits** .... [G]	Warner 1767
5/10/69	99	18	6. Goodbye, Columbus .... [S]	Warner 1786
			soundtrack includes instrumentals by Charles Fox	
10/04/69	32	17	7. The Association	Warner 1800
7/18/70	79	12	8. The Association "Live" .... [L]	Warner 1868 [2]
8/14/71	158	4	9. Stop Your Motor	Warner 1927
5/20/72	194	5	10. Waterbeds In Trinidad!	Columbia 31348

ASTRONAUTS
Boulder, Colorado surf/rock quintet

DATE CHARTED	PEAK POS	WKS CHRT'D	ARTIST — Album Title	LABEL & NUMBER
8/03/63	61	14	1. Surfin' With The Astronauts	RCA 2760
2/08/64	100	9	2. Everything Is A-OK! .... [L]	RCA 2782
3/28/64	123	5	3. Competition Coupe	RCA 2858

ASYLUM CHOIR - see LEON RUSSELL

CHET ATKINS
Nashville's top guitarist - born on 6/20/24 in Luttrell, Tenn.

DATE CHARTED	PEAK POS	WKS CHRT'D	ARTIST — Album Title	LABEL & NUMBER
6/16/58	21	4	1. Chet Atkins At Home .... [I]	RCA 1544
2/22/60	16	12	2. Teensville .... [I]	RCA 2161
2/13/61	7	24	3. **Chet Atkins' Workshop** .... [I]	RCA 2232
7/10/61	119	10	4. The Most Popular Guitar .... [I]	RCA 2346
3/17/62	31	24	5. Down Home .... [I]	RCA 2450
10/13/62	33	9	6. Caribbean Guitar .... [I]	RCA 2549
3/23/63	135	5	7. Our Man In Nashville .... [I]	RCA 2616
9/21/63	93	6	8. Teen Scene .... [I]	RCA 2719
2/29/64	64	8	9. Guitar Country .... [I]	RCA 2783
4/09/66	112	13	10. Chet Atkins Picks On The Beatles .... [I]	RCA 3531
6/18/66	62	23	11. The "Pops" Goes Country .... [I]	RCA 2870
			CHET ATKINS/BOSTON POPS/ARTHUR FIEDLER	
12/17/66	140	4	12. From Nashville With Love .... [I]	RCA 3647
5/06/67	148	9	13. It's A Guitar World .... [I]	RCA 3728
1/20/68	189	2	14. Class Guitar .... [I]	RCA 3885
3/30/68	184	3	15. Solo Flights .... [I]	RCA 3922
10/11/69	160	4	16. Chet Picks On The Pops .... [I]	RCA 3104
			CHET ATKINS/BOSTON POPS/ARTHUR FIEDLER	
12/13/69	150	7	17. Solid Gold '69 .... [I]	RCA 4244
4/25/70	139	5	18. Yestergroovin' .... [I]	RCA 4331
5/29/76	172	5	19. Chester & Lester .... [I]	RCA 1167
			CHET ATKINS & LES PAUL	

ATLANTA
9-man country band

DATE CHARTED	PEAK POS	WKS CHRT'D	ARTIST — Album Title	LABEL & NUMBER
5/26/84	140	7	1. Pictures	MCA 5463

ATLANTA DISCO BAND

DATE CHARTED	PEAK POS	WKS CHRT'D	ARTIST — Album Title	LABEL & NUMBER
1/17/76	172	9	1. Bad Luck .... [I]	Ariola Am. 50004

ATLANTA RHYTHM SECTION
Atlanta studio musicians - Ronnie Hammond, lead singer

DATE CHARTED	PEAK POS	WKS CHRT'D	ARTIST — Album Title	LABEL & NUMBER
9/14/74	74	12	1. Third Annual Pipe Dream	Polydor 6027
9/06/75	113	9	2. Dog Days	Polydor 6041
6/05/76	146	15	3. Red Tape	Polydor 6060
1/15/77	11	39	● 4. A Rock And Roll Alternative	Polydor 6080
			"So In To You"(7)	
4/09/77	154	4	5. Atlanta Rhythm Section .... [R]	MCA 4114 [2]
			reissue of their first two Decca albums from 1972 & 1973	
4/01/78	7	40	▲ 6. **Champagne Jam**	Polydor 6134
			"Imaginary Lover"(7)	
6/23/79	26	21	● 7. Underdog	Polydor 6200
11/10/79	51	12	8. Are You Ready! .... [L]	Polydor 6236 [2]
8/16/80	65	11	9. The Boys From Doraville	Polydor 6285
9/19/81	70	16	10. Quinella	Columbia 37550

DATE CHARTED	PEAK POS	WKS CHRT'D	ARTIST — Album Title	LABEL & NUMBER
			ATLANTIC STARR eight-man, one-woman band from Westchester, New York	
8/26/78	67	13	1. Atlantic Starr	A&M 4711
6/02/79	142	7	2. Straight To The Point	A&M 4764
3/14/81	47	30	3. Radiant	A&M 4833
3/27/82	18	29	4. Brillance	A&M 4883
11/19/83	91	28	5. Yours Forever	A&M 4948
			ATOMIC ROOSTER British rock quartet	
7/03/71	90	15	1. Death Walks Behind You	Elektra 74094
12/11/71	167	9	2. In Hearing Of Atomic Rooster	Elektra 74109
10/07/72	149	8	3. Made In England	Elektra 75039
			AUDIENCE	
6/24/72	175	5	1. Lunch	Elektra 75026
			BRIAN AUGER British jazz-rock keyboardist	
			JULIE DRISCOLL/BRIAN AUGER & THE TRINITY:	
5/10/69	194	2	1. Jools & Brian	Capitol 136
6/14/69	41	16	2. Streetnoise	Atco 701 [2]
			BRIAN AUGER & THE TRINITY:	
8/01/70	184	3	3. Befour	RCA 4372
			BRIAN AUGER'S OBLIVION EXPRESS:	
6/03/72	170	7	4. Second Wind	RCA 4703
8/04/73	64	31	5. Closer To It!	RCA 0140
4/06/74	45	20	6. Straight Ahead	RCA 0454
12/07/74	51	13	7. Live Oblivion, Vol. 1 .... [L]	RCA 0645
10/11/75	115	8	8. Reinforcements	RCA 1210
3/13/76	169	4	9. Live Oblivion, Vol. 2 .... [L]	RCA 1230 [2]
2/19/77	127	5	10. Happiness Heartaches	Warner 2981
			BRIAN AUGER:	
4/23/77	151	3	11. The Best Of Brian Auger .... [G]	RCA 2249
			AURRA Curt Jones & Starleana Young	
6/13/81	103	13	1. Send Your Love	Salsoul 8538
2/27/82	38	15	2. A Little Love	Salsoul 8551
			PATTI AUSTIN	
12/03/77	116	13	1. Havana Candy	CTI 5006
10/03/81	36	44	2. Every Home Should Have One .... "Baby, Come To Me"(1-with James Ingram)	Qwest 3591
3/31/84	87	18	3. Patti Austin	Qwest 23974
			AUTOGRAPH Los Angeles-based rock quintet - Steve Plunkett, lead singer	
1/05/85	29+	14+	1. Sign in Please	RCA 8040
			AUTOMATIC MAN	
10/02/76	120	7	1. Automatic Man	Island 9397
10/08/77	109	8	2. Visitors	Island 9429
			FRANKIE AVALON born Francis Avallone on 9/18/40 in Philadelphia	
12/21/59	9	14	1. **Swingin' On A Rainbow**	Chancellor 5004
10/23/61	59	20	2. A Whole Lotta Frankie .... [G] "Dede Dinah"(7)/"Gingerbread"(9)/"Venus"(1)/ "Bobby Sox To Stockings"(8)/"Just Ask Your Heart"(7)/"Why"(1)	Chancellor 5018
			AVERAGE WHITE BAND Scottish 6-man white-soul band	
9/21/74	1(1)	43	● 1. AWB .... "Pick Up The Pieces"(1)	Atlantic 7308

DATE CHARTED	PEAK POS	WKS CHRT'D	ARTIST — Album Title	LABEL & NUMBER
4/05/75	39	13	2. Put It Where You Want It .... [R] reissue of 1973 album "Show Your Hand"	MCA 475
6/28/75	4	24	● 3. **Cut The Cake** .... "Cut The Cake"(10)	Atlantic 18140
7/17/76	9	32	▲ 4. **Soul Searching**	Atlantic 18179
1/22/77	28	18	● 5. Person To Person .... [L]	Atlantic 1002 [2]
7/23/77	33	21	6. Benny And Us .... AVERAGE WHITE BAND & BEN E. KING	Atlantic 19105
4/01/78	28	17	● 7. Warmer Communications	Atlantic 19162
4/07/79	32	15	8. Feel No Fret	Atlantic 19207
5/31/80	116	12	9. Shine	Arista 9523
9/20/80	182	2	10. Volume VIII .... [G] side two contains their greatest hits	Atlantic 19266

AXE
| 6/26/82 | 81 | 20 | 1. Offering .... | Atco 148 |
| 9/10/83 | 156 | 6 | 2. Nemesis .... | Atco 90099 |

HOYT AXTON
son of songwriter Mae Axton ("Heartbreak Hotel")
| 4/12/75 | 188 | 2 | 1. Southbound .... | A&M 4510 |
| 4/10/76 | 171 | 4 | 2. Fearless .... | A&M 4571 |

ROY AYERS
R&B/jazz vibraphonist

ROY AYERS UBIQUITY:
10/05/74	156	4	1. Change Up The Groove	Polydor 6032
2/21/76	90	18	2. Mystic Voyage	Polydor 6057
8/14/76	51	17	3. Everybody Loves The Sunshine	Polydor 6070
1/15/77	74	12	4. Vibrations	Polydor 6091
7/02/77	72	25	5. Lifeline	Polydor 6108

ROY AYERS:
3/11/78	33	13	6. Let's Do It	Polydor 6126
8/19/78	48	15	7. You Send Me	Polydor 6159
5/26/79	67	15	8. Fever	Polydor 6204
12/15/79	82	18	9. No Stranger To Love	Polydor 6246
11/01/80	157	3	10. Love Fantasy	Polydor 6301
8/15/81	197	2	11. Africa, Center Of The World	Polydor 6327
3/20/82	160	7	12. Feeling Good	Polydor 6348

AZTEC CAMERA
Roddy Frame & backing trio from the British Isles
| 9/10/83 | 129 | 10 | 1. High Land, Hard Rain .... | Sire 23899 |
| 10/13/84 | 175 | 6 | 2. Knife .... | Sire 25183 |

AZTEC TWO-STEP
Rex Fowler & Neal Shulman
| 12/25/76 | 181 | 4 | 1. Two's Company .... | RCA 1497 |

AZTECA
17 member band led by Coke Escovedo
| 1/13/73 | 151 | 9 | 1. Azteca .... | Columbia 31776 |

BABE RUTH
English rock quartet - Jenny Haan, lead singer
8/11/73	178	6	1. First Base	Harvest 11151
2/22/75	75	7	2. Babe Ruth	Harvest 11367
10/25/75	169	6	3. Stealin' Home	Harvest 11451

BABYS
John Waite, lead singer of British foursome
| 3/05/77 | 133 | 13 | 1. The Babys .... | Chrysalis 1129 |
| 10/08/77 | 34 | 26 | 2. Broken Heart .... | Chrysalis 1150 |

DATE CHARTED	PEAK POS	WKS CHRT'D	ARTIST — Album Title	LABEL & NUMBER
1/27/79	22	25	3. Head First	Chrysalis 1195
1/19/80	42	22	4. Union Jacks	Chrysalis 1267
11/15/80	71	15	5. On The Edge	Chrysalis 1305
11/07/81	138	7	6. Anthology .... [G]	Chrysalis 1351

BURT BACHARACH [Chorus & Orchestra]
top composer who often worked with lyricist Hal David

DATE CHARTED	PEAK POS	WKS CHRT'D	ARTIST — Album Title	LABEL & NUMBER
10/28/67	96	65	● 1. Reach Out	A&M 4131
6/28/69	51	87	● 2. Make It Easy On Yourself	A&M 4188
6/19/71	18	24	● 3. Burt Bacharach	A&M 3501
1/05/74	181	6	4. Living Together	A&M 3527
12/14/74	173	5	5. Burt Bacharach's Greatest Hits .... [G]	A&M 3661

BACHELORS
trio from Dublin, Ireland

DATE CHARTED	PEAK POS	WKS CHRT'D	ARTIST — Album Title	LABEL & NUMBER
6/20/64	70	16	1. Presenting: The Bachelors .... "Diane"(10)	London 353
11/07/64	142	3	2. Back Again	London 393
4/03/65	136	4	3. No Arms Can Ever Hold You	London 418
9/04/65	89	6	4. Marie	London 435

BACHMAN-TURNER OVERDRIVE
Canadian quartet led by Randy Bachman (1-8, 11) & C.F. Turner

DATE CHARTED	PEAK POS	WKS CHRT'D	ARTIST — Album Title	LABEL & NUMBER
8/18/73	70	68	● 1. Bachman-Turner Overdrive	Mercury 673
1/19/74	4	75	● 2. **Bachman-Turner Overdrive II** .... "Let It Ride"/"Takin' Care Of Business"	Mercury 696
8/31/74	1(1)	50	● 3. **Not Fragile** .... "You Ain't Seen Nothing Yet"(1)	Mercury 1004
3/08/75	180	3	4. Bachman-Turner-Bachman As Brave Belt . [E] reissue of 1972 LP "Brave Belt II"	Reprise 2210
5/31/75	5	22	● 5. **Four Wheel Drive**	Mercury 1027
1/03/76	23	21	● 6. Head On	Mercury 1067
8/14/76	19	15	● 7. Best Of B.T.O (So Far) .... [G]	Mercury 1101
3/19/77	70	9	8. Freeways	Mercury 3700
3/18/78	130	4	9. Street Action	Mercury 3713
4/07/79	165	4	10. Rock N' Roll Nights .... above 2 albums shown as BTO	Mercury 3748
9/29/84	191	2	11. Bachman Turner Overdrive	Compleat 1010

BACK STREET CRAWLER
British - led by Paul Kossoff (Free)

DATE CHARTED	PEAK POS	WKS CHRT'D	ARTIST — Album Title	LABEL & NUMBER
11/15/75	111	10	1. The Band Plays On	Atco 125
8/14/76	140	5	2. 2nd Street	Atco 138
			CRAWLER:	
9/10/77	85	13	3. Crawler	Epic 34900

BAD COMPANY
British: Paul Rodgers (vocals), Mick Ralphs (guitar), Simon Kirke (drums), Boz Burrell (bass)

DATE CHARTED	PEAK POS	WKS CHRT'D	ARTIST — Album Title	LABEL & NUMBER
7/27/74	1(1)	64	● 1. **Bad Company** .... "Can't Get Enough"(5)	Swan Song 8410
4/19/75	3	33	● 2. **Straight Shooter** .... "Feel Like Makin' Love"(10)	Swan Song 8413
2/14/76	5	28	▲ 3. **Run With The Pack**	Swan Song 8415
3/26/77	15	24	● 4. Burnin' Sky	Swan Song 8500
3/31/79	3	37	▲ 5. **Desolation Angels**	Swan Song 8506
9/04/82	26	18	6. Rough Diamonds	Swan Song 90001

BADFINGER
British quartet originally known as The Iveys - leader Pete Ham committed suicide on 5/1/75 (27)

DATE CHARTED	PEAK POS	WKS CHRT'D	ARTIST — Album Title	LABEL & NUMBER
3/28/70	55	17	1. Magic Christian Music .... "Come And Get It"(7) - also see Soundtrack "Magic Christian"	Apple 3364
11/28/70	28	15	2. No Dice .... "No Matter What"(8)	Apple 3367

DATE CHARTED	PEAK POS	WKS CHRT'D	ARTIST — Album Title	LABEL & NUMBER
12/25/71	**31**	32	3. Straight Up	Apple 3387
			produced by Todd Rundgren & George Harrison "Day After Day"(4)	
12/15/73	**122**	8	4. Ass	Apple 3411
3/09/74	**161**	5	5. Badfinger	Warner 2762
11/09/74	**148**	6	6. With You Were Here	Warner 2827
3/24/79	**125**	8	7. Airwaves	Elektra 175
2/28/81	**155**	6	8. Say No More	Radio 16030

BADGER
British quartet led by Tony Kaye (former keyboardist with Yes)

DATE CHARTED	PEAK POS	WKS CHRT'D	ARTIST — Album Title	LABEL & NUMBER
8/11/73	**167**	8	1. One Live Badger .... [L]	Atco 7022

JOAN BAEZ
folk song stylist born in New York on 1/9/41

DATE CHARTED	PEAK POS	WKS CHRT'D	ARTIST — Album Title	LABEL & NUMBER
11/27/61	**13**	125	● 1. Joan Baez, Vol. 2	Vanguard 2097
3/03/62	**15**	140	● 2. Joan Baez	Vanguard 2077
			Joan's first album, recorded in 1960	
10/27/62	**10**	114	● 3. **Joan Baez In Concert** .... [L]	Vanguard 2122
11/23/63	**45**	18	4. The Best Of Joan Baez .... [E]	Squire 33001
			first recordings from 1959 with Bill Wood & Ted Alevizos	
12/07/63	**7**	36	5. **Joan Baez In Concert, Part 2** .... [L]	Vanguard 2123
11/21/64	**12**	66	6. Joan Baez/5	Vanguard 79160
10/23/65	**10**	27	7. **Farewell, Angelina**	Vanguard 79200
9/02/67	**38**	20	8. Joan	Vanguard 79240
8/10/68	**84**	25	9. Baptism	Vanguard 79275
1/25/69	**30**	20	● 10. Any Day Now	Vanguard 79306 [2]
			Songs of Bob Dylan	
6/07/69	**36**	14	11. David's Album	Vanguard 79308
			dedicated to her imprisoned husband, David Harris	
3/21/70	**80**	14	12. One Day At A Time	Vanguard 79310
11/21/70	**73**	11	13. The First 10 Years .... [K]	Vanguard 6560 [2]
9/18/71	**11**	23	● 14. Blessed Are	Vanguard 6570 [2]
			"The Night They Drove Old Dixie Down"(3)	
1/01/72	**164**	5	15. Carry It On .... [S]	Vanguard 79313
			film features Joan and her husband, David Harris	
5/27/72	**48**	24	16. Come From The Shadows	A&M 4339
12/16/72	**188**	7	17. The Joan Baez Ballad Book .... [K]	Vanguard 41/42 [2]
			selections from first 5 Vanguard LPs	
5/19/73	**138**	9	18. Where Are You Now, My Son?	A&M 4390
			side 2 has actual war sounds recorded in Vietnam	
7/07/73	**163**	8	19. Hits/Greatest & Others .... [G]	Vanguard 79332
5/17/75	**11**	46	● 20. Diamaonds & Rust	A&M 4527
2/07/76	**34**	17	21. From Every Stage .... [L]	A&M 3704 [2]
11/06/76	**62**	17	22. Gulf Winds	A&M 4603
6/25/77	**54**	14	23. Blowin' Away	Portrait 34697
12/17/77	**121**	8	24. The Best Of Joan C. Baez .... [G]	A&M 4668
8/04/79	**113**	7	25. Honest Lullaby	Portrait 35766

PHILIP BAILEY
one of the lead vocalists for Earth, Wind & Fire

DATE CHARTED	PEAK POS	WKS CHRT'D	ARTIST — Album Title	LABEL & NUMBER
9/10/83	**71**	14	1. Continuation	Columbia 38725
11/10/84	**22**	22 +	● 2. Chinese Wall	Columbia 39542
			"Easy Lover"(2-with Phil Collins)	

RAZZY BAILEY
country singer

DATE CHARTED	PEAK POS	WKS CHRT'D	ARTIST — Album Title	LABEL & NUMBER
6/20/81	**183**	2	1. Makin' Friends	RCA 4026
2/27/82	**176**	4	2. Feelin' Right	RCA 4228

DATE CHARTED	PEAK POS	WKS CHRT'D	ARTIST — Album Title	LABEL & NUMBER
			SCOTT BAIO	
			star of new TV series "Charles In Charge"	
9/04/82	181	4	1. Scott Baio	RCA 8025
			BAJA MARIMBA BAND	
			9-man band led by marimbaist Julius Wechter	
4/25/64	88	12	1. Baja Marimba Band .... [I]	A&M 104
4/24/65	127	3	2. Baja Marimba Band Rides Again .... [I]	A&M 109
1/08/66	102	16	3. For Animals Only .... [I]	A&M 113
11/19/66	54	43	4. Watch Out! .... [I]	A&M 4118
5/27/67	77	44	5. Heads Up! .... [I]	A&M 4123
			JULIUS WECHTER & THE BAJA MARIMBA BAND:	
1/20/68	168	9	6. Fowl Play .... [I]	A&M 4136
8/31/68	171	8	7. Do You Know The Way To San Jose? .... [I]	A&M 4150
3/08/69	117	10	8. Those Were The Days .... [I]	A&M 4167
10/18/69	176	3	9. Fresh Air .... [I]	A&M 4200
4/04/70	180	6	10. Greatest Hits .... [G-I]	A&M 4248
			ANITA BAKER	
			former lead singer of Chapter 8	
10/29/83	139	11	1. The Songstress	Beverly G. 10002
			BAKER GURVITZ ARMY	
			British - featuring Ginger Baker (drums) & Adrian Gurvitz (guitar)	
2/15/75	140	7	1. The Baker Guritz Army	Janus 7015
11/15/75	165	5	2. Elysian Encounter	Atco 123
			GEORGE BAKER Selection	
			Dutch group led by Hans Bouwens	
7/04/70	107	6	1. Little Green Bag	Colossus 1002
1/31/76	153	7	2. Paloma Blanca	Warner 2905
			GINGER BAKER'S Air Force	
			British group featuring Steve Winwood and Denny Laine	
5/23/70	33	15	1. Ginger Baker's Air Force .... [L]	Atco 703 [2]
			recorded live at London's Royal Albert Hall	
			BALANCE	
			led by Peppy Castro (Blues Magoos)	
8/29/81	133	12	1. Balance	Portrait 37357
			JOHN BALDRY	
			British	
7/03/71	83	18	1. It Ain't Easy	Warner 1921
5/06/72	180	6	2. Everything Stops For Tea	Warner 2614
			above 2 produced by Rod Stewart & Elton John	
			MARTY BALIN	
			member of Jefferson Starship	
6/06/81	35	23	1. Balin	EMI America 17054
			"Hearts"(8)	
3/12/83	156	6	2. Lucky	EMI America 17088
			KENNY BALL & His Jazzmen	
			English dixieland jazz band	
3/17/62	13	32	1. Midnight In Moscow .... [I]	Kapp 1276
			"Midnight In Moscow"(2)	
			RUSS BALLARD	
			original member of Argent	
8/16/80	187	2	1. Barnet Dogs	Epic 36186
6/09/84	147	13	2. Russ Ballard	EMI America 17108
			BALLIN' JACK	
1/02/71	180	8	1. Ballin' Jack	Columbia 30344

DATE CHARTED	PEAK POS	WKS CHRT'D	ARTIST — Album Title	LABEL & NUMBER
			BALTIMORE & OHIO MARCHING BAND	
1/20/68	177	3	1. Lapland .... [I]	Jubilee 8008
			BANANARAMA	
			female trio from London, England	
4/16/83	63	19	1. Deep Sea Skiving	London 810102
6/02/84	30	36	2. Bananarama	London 820036
			reissued (#820165) October, 1984 with new song "Wild Life" "Cruel Summer"(9)	
			THE BAND	
			Robbie Robertson, Levon Helm, Rick Danko, Richard Manuel & Garth Hudson - also see Bob Dylan	
8/10/68	30	40	1. Music From Big Pink	Capitol 2955
			Big Pink: The Band's communal home in Woodstock	
10/18/69	9	49	● 2. **The Band**	Capitol 132
9/05/70	5	22	● 3. **Stage Fright**	Capitol 425
10/16/71	21	14	4. Cahoots	Capitol 651
9/09/72	6	28	● 5. **Rock Of Ages** .... [L]	Capitol 11045 [2]
11/17/73	28	20	6. Moondog Matinee	Capitol 11214
12/13/75	26	19	7. Northern Lights-Southern Cross	Capitol 11440
9/04/76	51	14	8. The Best Of The Band .... [G]	Capitol 11553
3/26/77	64	10	9. Islands	Capitol 11602
4/29/78	16	20	10. The Last Waltz .... [S-L]	Warner 3146 [3]
			farewell concert at the San Francisco Winterland with guests Bob Dylan, Eric Clapton, Neil Diamond, Ringo Starr & others	
			BAND OF THE BLACK WATCH	
			Scottish military unit	
3/20/76	164	4	1. Scotch On The Rocks .... [I]	Private S. 2007
			MOE BANDY & JOE STAMPLEY	
			country duo	
4/11/81	170	4	1. Hey Joe!/Hey Moe!	Columbia 37003
			BANG	
4/08/72	164	10	1. Bang	Capitol 11015
			BANGLES	
			female rock quartet from Los Angeles	
8/04/84	80	30	1. All Over The Place	Columbia 39220
			BANGOR FLYING CIRCUS	
12/27/69	190	2	1. Bangor Flying Circus	Dunhill 50069
			PETER BANKS	
			former member of Yes, and Flash	
9/08/73	152	8	1. Two Sides Of Peter Banks	Sovereign 11217
			featuring Phil Collins, Steve Hackett & Jan Akkerman	
			TONY BANKS	
			keyboardist with Genesis	
12/15/79	171	5	1. A Curious Feeling	Charisma 2207
			BAR-KAYS	
			Otis Redding's backing band - 4 original members killed with him in plane crash on 12/10/67	
2/27/71	90	12	1. Black Rock	Volt 6011
11/13/76	84	22	2. Too Hot To Stop	Mercury 1099
12/10/77	47	23	● 3. Flying High On Your Love	Mercury 1181
11/11/78	72	15	4. Money Talks	Stax 4106
12/23/78	86	17	5. Light Of Life	Mercury 3732
11/10/79	35	24	● 6. Injoy	Mercury 3781
12/13/80	57	16	7. As One	Mercury 3844
11/14/81	55	29	● 8. Nightcruising	Mercury 4028
11/20/82	51	29	9. Propositions	Mercury 4065
4/21/84	52	22	10. Dangerous	Mercury 818478

DATE CHARTED	PEAK POS	WKS CHRT'D	ARTIST — Album Title	LABEL & NUMBER

FRANK BARBER Orchestra

6/05/82	**94**	16	1. Hooked On Big Bands .... [I] discofied medleys of six big bands	Victory 702

GATO BARBIERI
jazz tenor sax player

5/05/73	**166**	7	1. Last Tango in Paris .... [S-I]	United Art. 045
10/26/74	**160**	3	2. Chapter Three - Viva Emiliano Zapata .... [I] Zapata: revolutionary leader in Mexico (killed in 1919)	Impulse! 9279
10/02/76	**75**	32	3. Caliente! .... [I]	A&M 4597
10/29/77	**66**	20	4. Ruby, Ruby .... [I]	A&M 4655
7/29/78	**96**	7	5. Tropico .... [I]	A&M 4710
8/11/79	**116**	9	6. Euphoria .... [I]	A&M 4774

KEITH BARBOUR

11/01/69	**163**	4	1. Echo Park	Epic 26485

BARCLAY JAMES HARVEST
British art-rock quartet

2/19/77	**174**	3	1. Octoberon	MCA 2234

BOBBY BARE

10/26/63	**119**	3	1. "Detroit City" And Other Hits	RCA 2776
2/01/64	**133**	5	2. 500 Miles Away From Home .... "500 Miles Away From Home"(10)	RCA 2835

BARRABAS
rock sextet led by Jo Tejada

8/23/75	**149**	7	1. Heart Of The City	Atco 118

SYD BARRETT
original lead guitarist of Pink Floyd

8/17/74	**163**	4	1. The Madcap Laughs/Barrett	Harvest 11314 [2]

CLAUDJA BARRY

2/25/78	**131**	10	1. Claudja	Salsoul 5525
6/02/79	**101**	10	2. Boogie Woogie Dancin' Shoes	Chrysalis 1232

LEN BARRY
real name: Leonard Borisoff - lead singer of The Dovells

11/20/65	**90**	13	1. 1-2-3 .... "1-2-3"(2)	Decca 74720

LOU ANN BARTON

4/24/82	**133**	9	1. Old Enough	Asylum 60032

COUNT BASIE
top big-band jazz leader since 1935 - died on 4/26/84 (79)

2/02/63	**5**	42	1. **Sinatra-Basie** .... FRANK SINATRA/COUNT BASIE	Reprise 1008
7/20/63	**19**	27	2. This Time By Basie! Hits of the 50's And 60's .... [I]	Reprise 6070
9/07/63	**123**	5	3. Li'l Ol' Groovemaker...Basie! .... [I]	Verve 8549
10/19/63	**69**	20	4. Ella And Basie! .... ELLA FITZGERALD/COUNT BASIE	Verve 4061
2/22/64	**150**	1	5. More Hits Of The 50's And 60's .... [I]	Verve 8563
8/22/64	**13**	31	6. It Might As Well Be Swing .... FRANK SINATRA/COUNT BASIE	Reprise 1012
3/27/65	**141**	4	7. Our Shining Hour .... SAMMY DAVIS, JR. & COUNT BASIE	Verve 8605
3/26/66	**107**	13	8. Arthur Prysock/Count Basie	Verve 8646
12/10/66	**143**	2	9. Broadway Basie's...Way .... [I]	Command 905
4/06/68	**145**	6	10. The Board Of Directors .... COUNT BASIE & THE MILLS BROTHERS	Dot 25838
6/01/68	**195**	3	11. Manufacturers of Soul .... JACKIE WILSON/COUNT BASIE	Brunswick 754134

DATE CHARTED	PEAK POS	WKS CHRT'D	ARTIST — Album Title	LABEL & NUMBER
			TONI BASIL choreographer/director/dancer	
10/23/82	**22**	30	● 1. Word Of Mouth .... "Mickey"(1)	Chrysalis 1410
			FONTELLA BASS married to jazz trumpeter Lester Bowie	
2/26/66	**93**	8	1. The 'New' Look .... "Rescue Me"(4)	Checker 2997
			SHIRLEY BASSEY Welsh	
4/24/65	**85**	9	1. Shirley Bassey Belts The Best! .... "Goldfinger"(8)	United Art. 6419
10/17/70	**105**	13	2. Shirley Bassey Is Really "Something"	United Art. 6765
6/12/71	**123**	24	3. Something Else	United Art. 6797
3/18/72	**94**	13	4. I Capricorn	United Art. 5565
11/25/72	**171**	8	5. And I Love You So	United Art. 5643
5/26/73	**60**	19	6. Never, Never, Never	United Art. 055
9/22/73	**136**	8	7. Live At Carnegie Hall .... [L] featuring Woody Herman's band	United Art. 111 [2]
9/21/74	**142**	6	8. Nobody Does It Like Me	United Art. 214
11/29/75	**186**	3	9. Good, Bad But Beautiful	United Art. 542
10/09/76	**149**	8	10. Love, Life And Feelings	United Art. 605
			BATDORF & RODNEY John Batdorf & Mark Rodney - also see Silver	
10/28/72	**185**	7	1. Batdorf & Rodney	Asylum 5056
7/12/75	**140**	10	2. Life Is You	Arista 4041
			LES BAXTER & His Orchestra musical arranger for Capitol Records in the fifties	
1/28/56	**6**	1	1. **Tamboo!** .... [I]	Capitol 655
3/16/57	**21**	2	2. Skins! .... [I]	Capitol 774
			BAY CITY ROLLERS Scottish pop/rock quintet	
9/27/75	**20**	35	● 1. Bay City Rollers .... "Saturday Night"(1)	Arista 4049
3/20/76	**31**	16	● 2. Rock N' Roll Love Letter .... "Money Honey"(9)	Arista 4071
9/18/76	**26**	25	● 3. Dedication	Arista 4093
7/23/77	**23**	11	● 4. It's A Game .... "You Made Me Believe In Magic"(10)	Arista 7004
12/03/77	**77**	11	● 5. Greatest Hits .... [G]	Arista 4158
10/14/78	**129**	4	6. Strangers In The Wind	Arista 4194
			BE-BOP DELUXE English techno-rock quartet led by Bill Nelson	
2/07/76	**96**	17	1. Sunburst Finish	Harvest 11478
10/16/76	**88**	8	2. Modern Music	Harvest 11575
8/20/77	**65**	15	3. Live! In The Air Age .... [L]	Harvest 11666 [2]
3/11/78	**95**	9	4. Drastic Plastic	Harvest 11750
			BEACH BOYS California quintet led by Brian Wilson, with brothers Dennis & Carl Wilson, cousin Mike Love and Alan Jardine - Dennis drowned on 12/28/83 (39)	
11/24/62	**32**	37	1. Surfin' Safari	Capitol 1808
5/04/63	**2(2)**	78	● 2. **Surfin' U.S.A.** .... "Surfin' U.S.A."(3)	Capitol 1890
10/12/63	**7**	56	● 3. **Surfer Girl** .... "Surfer Girl"(7)	Capitol 1981
11/09/63	**4**	46	● 4. **Little Deuce Coupe** .... "Be True To Your School"(6)	Capitol 1998

DATE CHARTED	PEAK POS	WKS CHRT'D		ARTIST — Album Title	LABEL & NUMBER
4/11/64	13	38	●	5. Shut Down, Volume 2 .... "Fun, Fun, Fun"(5) Volume 1 - see Miscellaneous section: Cars	Capitol 2027
8/01/64	4	49	●	6. **All Summer Long** .... "I Get Around"(1)	Capitol 2110
11/07/64	1(4)	62	●	7. **Beach Boys Concert** .... [L]	Capitol 2198
3/27/65	4	50	●	8. **The Beach Boys Today!** .... "When I Grow Up"(9)/"Dance, Dance, Dance"(8)	Capitol 2269
7/24/65	2(1)	33	●	9. **Summer Days (And Summer Nights!!)** .... "Help Me Rhonda"(1)/"California Girls"(3)	Capitol 2354
11/27/65	6	24		10. **Beach Boys' Party!** .... "Barbara Ann"(2)	Capitol 2398
5/28/66	10	39		11. **Pet Sounds** .... "Sloop John B"(3)/"Wouldn't It Be Nice"(8)	Capitol 2458
7/23/66	8	78	●	12. **Best Of The Beach Boys** .... [G]	Capitol 2545
8/12/67	50	22	●	13. **Best Of The Beach Boys, Vol. 2** .... [G]	Capitol 2706
9/30/67	41	21		14. Smiley Smile .... "Good Vibrations"(1)	Brother 9001
12/30/67	24	15		15. Wild Honey	Capitol 2859
7/06/68	126	10		16. Friends	Capitol 2895
9/07/68	153	6		17. Best Of The Beach Boys, Vol. 3 .... [G]	Capitol 2945
3/01/69	68	11		18. 20/20	Capitol 133
8/16/69	136	6		19. Close-Up .... [R] reissue of "Surfin' U.S.A."/"All Summer Long" LPs	Capitol 253 [2]
9/26/70	151	4		20. Sunflower	Brother 6382
9/11/71	29	17		21. Surf's Up	Brother 6453
6/03/72	50	20		22. Pet Sounds/Carl And The Passions - So Tough .... [R] reissue of "Pet Sounds" plus new LP "Carl..."	Brother 2083 [2]
1/27/73	36	30		23. Holland	Brother 2118
12/08/73	25	24	●	24. The Beach Boys In Concert .... [L]	Brother 6484 [2]
7/20/74	1(1)	155	●	25. **Endless Summer** .... [K]	Capitol 11307 [2]
8/03/74	50	11		26. Wild Honey & 20/20 .... [R]	Brother 2166 [2]
11/09/74	125	6		27. Friends & Smiley Smile .... [R]	Brother 2167 [2]
5/03/75	8	43	●	28. **Spirit Of America** .... [K]	Capitol 11384 [2]
7/19/75	25	23		29. Good Vibrations-Best Of The Beach Boys .... [G]	Brother 2223
7/17/76	8	27	●	30. **15 Big Ones** .... 15: age of band and number of tracks "Rock And Roll Music"(5)	Brother 2251
12/11/76	75	10		31. Beach Boys '69 (The Beach Boys Live In London) .... [L]	Capitol 11584
4/30/77	53	7		32. Love You	Brother 2258
10/21/78	151	4		33. M.I.U. Album .... MIU: Maharishi International University	Brother 2268
4/07/79	100	13		34. L.A. (Light Album)	Caribou 35752
4/12/80	75	6		35. Keepin' The Summer Alive	Caribou 36283
12/26/81	156	8		36. Ten Years Of Harmony (1970-1980) .... [K]	Caribou 37445 [2]
7/03/82	180	6		37. Sunshine Dream .... [K]	Capitol 12220 [2]

BEACON STREET UNION
Boston quintet

3/09/68	75	16		1. The Eyes Of The Beacon Street Union	MGM 4517
9/14/68	173	10		2. The Clown Died In Marvin Gardens	MGM 4568

BEAST
Denver septet

9/13/69	195	2		1. Beast	Cotillion 9012

30

DATE CHARTED	PEAK POS	WKS CHRT'D	ARTIST — Album Title	LABEL & NUMBER
			BEATLES #1 recording group of all-time from Liverpool, England: John Lennon, Paul McCartney, George Harrison and Ringo Starr	
2/01/64	1(11)	71	● 1. **Meet The Beatles!** .... "I Want To Hold Your Hand"(1)	Capitol 2047
2/08/64	2(9)	49	2. **Introducing...The Beatles** .... 1st U.S. album - released July, 1963 "Please Please Me"(3)/"Twist And Shout"(2)/ "Do You Want To Know A Secret"(2)/"Love Me Do"*(1)/ "P.S. I Love You"*(10) * - only on first pressing	Vee-Jay 1062
2/15/64	68	14	3. The Beatles with Tony Sheridan and Their Guests .... [E] 6 cuts feature Tony & the Beatles/6 others feature the Titans	MGM 4215
4/04/64	104	6	4. Jolly What! The Beatles & Frank Ifield .... [K] 4 cuts by the Beatles/8 cuts by Frank Ifield	Vee-Jay 1085 .
4/25/64	1(5)	55	● 5. **The Beatles' Second Album** .... "She Loves You"(1)	Capitol 2080
6/06/64	20	13	6. The American Tour With Ed Rudy .... [T] interviews with The Beatles	RadioPulsebeat 2
7/18/64	1(14)	51	7. **A Hard Day's Night** .... [S] 8 vocals - 4 instrumentals "Can't Buy Me Love"(1)/"A Hard Day's Night"(1)	United Art. 6366
8/08/64	2(9)	41	● 8. **Something New** .... Capitol 2108 includes 5 tunes from "A Hard Day's Night" album	Capitol 2108
10/10/64	142	2	9. The Beatles vs. The Four Seasons .... [R] "Introducing The Beatles" & "Golden Hits Of The 4 Seasons" LPs	Vee-Jay 30 [2]
10/31/64	63	11	10. Songs, Pictures And Stories Of The Fabulous Beatles .... [R] 2nd reissue of "Introducing The Beatles"	Vee-Jay 1092
12/12/64	7	17	● 11. **The Beatles' Story** .... [T] narrative featuring bits of their hits	Capitol 2222 [2]
1/02/65	1(9)	71	● 12. **Beatles '65** .... "I Feel Fine"(1)/"She's A Woman"(4)	Capitol 2228
4/24/65	43	34	● 13. **The Early Beatles** .... [R] reissue by Capitol of Vee-Jay recordings	Capitol 2309
6/26/65	1(6)	41	● 14. **Beatles VI** .... "Eight Days A Week"(1)	Capitol 2358
8/28/65	1(9)	44	● 15. **Help!** .... [S] 7 vocals - 5 instrumentals "Ticket To Ride"(1)/"Help!"(1)	Capitol 2386
12/25/65	1(6)	59	● 16. **Rubber Soul**	Capitol 2442
7/09/66	1(5)	31	● 17. **"Yesterday"...And Today** .... [G] originally featured the "butcher cover" "Yesterday"(1)/"We Can Work It Out"(1)/"Day Tripper"(5)/ "Nowhere Man"(3)	Capitol 2553
9/03/66	1(6)	77	● 18. **Revolver** .... "Yellow Submarine"(2)	Capitol 2576
6/24/67	1(15)	168	● 19. **Sgt. Pepper's Lonely Hearts Club Band** .... also see Soundtrack of the same name	Capitol 2653
12/23/67	1(8)	87	● 20. **Magical Mystery Tour** .... [S-G] 6 tunes from the film + 5 singles hits "Penny Lane"(1)/"Strawberry Fields Forever"(8)/ "All You Need Is Love"(1)/"Hello Goodbye"(1)	Capitol 2835
12/14/68	1(9)	144	● 21. **The Beatles [White Album]**	Apple 101 [2]
2/08/69	2(2)	24	● 22. **Yellow Submarine** .... [S] side 1: Beatles; side 2: instrumentals by George Martin	Apple 153
10/18/69	1(11)	116	● 23. **Abbey Road** .... "Come Together"(1)/"Something"(1)	Apple 383
3/21/70	2(4)	33	● 24. **Hey Jude** .... [G] "Paperback Writer"(1)/"Lady Madonna"(4)/"Hey Jude"(1)/ "The Ballad Of John And Yoko"(8)	Apple 385
5/16/70	117	7	25. The Beatles featuring Tony Sheridan - In The Beginning (Circa 1960) .... [E]	Polydor 4504
5/30/70	1(4)	55	● 26. **Let It Be** .... [S] film features the Beatles during recording sessions "Get Back"(1)/"Let It Be"(1)/"The Long And Winding Road"(1)	Apple 34001

DATE CHARTED	PEAK POS	WKS CHRT'D	ARTIST — Album Title	LABEL & NUMBER
4/14/73	3	164	● 27. **The Beatles/1962-1966** .... [G]	Apple 3403 [2]
4/14/73	1(1)	169	● 28. **The Beatles/1967-1970** .... [G]	Apple 3404 [2]
6/26/76	2(2)	30	▲ 29. **Rock 'N' Roll Music** .... [K]	Capitol 11537 [2]
			"Got To Get You Into My Life"(7)	
5/21/77	2(2)	17	▲ 30. **The Beatles At The Hollywood Bowl** ... [E-L]	Capitol 11638
			concert recordings of 8/23/64 & 8/30/65	
7/02/77	111	7	31. The Beatles Live! at the Star-Club in	
			Hamburg, Germany; 1962 .... [E-L]	Lingasong 7001 [2]
11/12/77	24	31	● 32. Love Songs .... [K]	Capitol 11711 [2]
4/12/80	21	15	33. Rarities .... [K]	Capitol 12060
4/10/82	19	12	● 34. Reel Music .... [K]	Capitol 12199
			tunes from the Beatles' five films	
11/13/82	50	28	● 35. 20 Greatest Hits .... [G]	Capitol 12245
			The Beatles' 20 #1 singles	

BEAU BRUMMELS
San Francisco rock group

DATE CHARTED	PEAK POS	WKS CHRT'D	ARTIST — Album Title	LABEL & NUMBER
5/08/65	24	21	1. Introducing The Beau Brummels	Autumn 103
			"Just A Little"(8)	
9/30/67	197	2	2. Triangle	Warner 1692
7/05/75	180	3	3. The Beau Brummels	Warner 2842

BECK, BOGERT, APPICE

DATE CHARTED	PEAK POS	WKS CHRT'D	ARTIST — Album Title	LABEL & NUMBER
4/07/73	12	27	1. Jeff Beck, Tim Bogert, Carmine Appice	Epic 32140
			Bogert & Appice formerly with Cactus and Vanilla Fudge	

JEFF BECK
English rock guitarist - formerly with the Yardbirds ('64-'66)

DATE CHARTED	PEAK POS	WKS CHRT'D	ARTIST — Album Title	LABEL & NUMBER
8/24/68	15	33	1. Truth	Epic 26413
7/12/69	15	21	2. Beck-Ola	Epic 26478
			above 2 with Rod Stewart (vocals)	
11/06/71	46	16	3. Rough And Ready	Epic 30973
5/13/72	19	26	4. Jeff Beck Group	Epic 31331
4/12/75	4	25	● 5. **Blow By Blow** .... [I]	Epic 33409
6/26/76	16	25	● 6. **Wired** .... [I]	Epic 33849
4/02/77	23	15	7. Jeff Beck with The Jan Hammer Group	
			Live .... [I-L]	Epic 34433
7/12/80	21	20	8. There And Back .... [I]	Epic 35684

JOE BECK
jazz/funk guitarist - also see Esther Phillips

DATE CHARTED	PEAK POS	WKS CHRT'D	ARTIST — Album Title	LABEL & NUMBER
6/28/75	140	5	1. Beck .... [I]	Kudu 21

BEE GEES
English/Australian trio of brothers: Robin & Maurice (twins), and Barry Gibb

DATE CHARTED	PEAK POS	WKS CHRT'D	ARTIST — Album Title	LABEL & NUMBER
8/26/67	7	52	1. **Bee Gees' 1st**	Atco 223
2/10/68	12	22	2. Horizontal	Atco 233
8/31/68	17	27	3. Idea	Atco 253
			"I've Gotta Get A Message To You"(8)/"I Started A Joke"(6)	
12/07/68	99	12	4. Rare Precious & Beautiful .... [E]	Atco 264
			early Australian recordings (1963-1966)	
2/22/69	20	25	5. Odessa	Atco 702 [2]
7/26/69	9	49	● 6. **Best Of Bee Gees** .... [G]	Atco 292
3/28/70	100	8	7. Rare Precious & Beautiful, Volume 2 .... [E]	Atco 321
			more Australian recordings (1963-1966)	
5/09/70	94	8	8. Cucumber Castle	Atco 327
1/30/71	32	14	9. 2 Years On	Atco 353
			"Lonely Days"(3)	
9/25/71	34	14	10. Trafalgar	Atco 7003
			"How Can You Mend A Broken Heart"(1)	
11/11/72	35	14	11. To Whom It May Concern	Atco 7012
2/03/73	69	13	12. Life In A Tin Can	RSO 870

DATE CHARTED	PEAK POS	WKS CHRT'D	ARTIST — Album Title	LABEL & NUMBER
8/04/73	98	16	13. Best Of Bee Gees, Vol. 2 .... [G] Atco hits (1969-1972)	RSO 875
6/15/74	178	5	14. Mr. Natural	RSO 4800
6/21/75	14	74	● 15. Main Course .... "Jive Talkin"(1)/"Nights On Broadway"(7)	RSO 4807
10/02/76	8	63	▲ 16. **Children Of The World** .... "You Should Be Dancing"(1)/"Love So Right"(3)	RSO 3003
11/13/76	50	33	● 17. Bee Gees Gold, Volume One .... [G] Atco hits (1967-1972)	RSO 3006
6/04/77	8	90	▲ 18. **Here At Last...Bee Gees...Live** .... [L]	RSO 3901 [2]
11/26/77	1(24)	120	▲ 19. **Saturday Night Fever** .... [S] 6 cuts by the Bee Gees/others by various artists - the #1 selling soundtrack album of all-time (25 million) "How Deep Is Your Love"(1)/"Stayin' Alive"(1)/"Night Fever"(1)	RSO 4001 [2]
2/17/79	1(6)	55	▲ 20. **Spirits Having Flown** .... "Too Much Heaven"(1)/"Tragedy"(1)/"Love You Inside Out"(1)	RSO 3041
11/17/79	1(1)	32	▲ 21. **Bee Gees Greatest** .... [G] RSO hits only	RSO 4200 [2]
11/21/81	41	12	22. Living Eyes	RSO 3098
7/16/83	6	27	▲ 23. **Staying Alive** .... [S] side 1: Bee Gees; side 2: various artists	RSO 813269
			HARRY BELAFONTE born in New York City on 3/1/24	
1/28/56	3	7	1. **"Mark Twain" And Other Folk Favorites**	RCA 1022
2/25/56	1(6)	64	● 2. **Belafonte**	RCA 1150
6/16/56	1(31)	99	● 3. **Calypso** .... "Banana Boat"(5)	RCA 1248
3/30/57	2(2)	20	● 4. **An Evening With Belafonte**	RCA 1402
9/16/57	3	16	5. **Belafonte Sings Of The Caribbean**	RCA 1505
10/20/58	16	15	6. Belafonte Sings The Blues	RCA 1972
5/25/59	18	13	7. Love Is A Gentle Thing	RCA 1927
6/15/59	13	21	8. Porgy & Bess .... LENA HORNE/HARRY BELAFONTE	RCA 1507
11/02/59	3	168	● 9. **Belafonte At Carnegie Hall** .... [L]	RCA 6006 [2]
3/21/60	34	1	10. My Lord What A Mornin' .... spirituals	RCA 2022
12/26/60	3	39	● 11. **Belafonte Returns To Carnegie Hall** .... [L] with Odetta-Mariam Makeba-Chad Mitchell Trio	RCA 6007 [2]
8/28/61	3	67	● 12. **Jump Up Calypso**	RCA 2388
5/12/62	8	24	13. **The Midnight Special**	RCA 2449
10/20/62	25	22	14. The Many Moods Of Belafonte	RCA 2574
12/22/62	125	2	15. To Wish You A Merry Christmas .... [X]	RCA 2626
6/22/63	30	26	16. Streets I Have Walked	RCA 2695
4/18/64	17	20	17. Belafonte At The Greek Theatre .... [L]	RCA 6009 [2]
10/17/64	103	7	18. Ballads, Blues And Boasters	RCA 2953
7/10/65	85	11	19. An Evening With Belafonte/Makeba .... HARRY BELAFONTE/MIRIAM MAKEBA	RCA 3420
4/09/66	124	8	20. An Evening With Belafonte/Mouskouri .... HARRY BELAFONTE/NANA MOUSKOURI	RCA 3415
7/16/66	82	10	21. In My Quiet Room	RCA 3571
4/29/67	172	2	22. Calypso In Brass	RCA 3658
7/29/67	199	3	23. Belafonte On Campus	RCA 3779
1/10/70	192	3	24. Homeward Bound	RCA 4255
			ADRIAN BELEW guitarist with Frank Zappa and others	
7/24/82	82	9	1. Lone Rhino	Island 9751
10/01/83	146	7	2. Twang Bar King	Island 90108

DATE CHARTED	PEAK POS	WKS CHRT'D	ARTIST — Album Title	LABEL & NUMBER
			BELL & JAMES LeRoy Bell & Casey James	
2/03/79	31	19	1. Bell & James	A&M 4728
11/03/79	125	4	2. Only Make Believe	A&M 4784
			ARCHIE BELL & THE DRELLS quartet from Houston, Texas	
5/25/68	142	8	1. Tighten Up .... "Tighten Up"(1)	Atlantic 8181
8/16/69	163	3	2. There's Gonna Be A Showdown	Atlantic 8226
1/10/76	95	20	3. Dance Your Troubles Away	TSOP 33844
			MAGGIE BELL lead singer of British group 'Stone The Crows'	
4/20/74	122	13	1. Queen Of The Night	Atlantic 7293
4/05/75	130	8	2. Suicide Sal	Swan Song 8412
			VINCENT BELL	
6/20/70	75	8	1. Airport Love Theme .... [I]	Decca 75212
			WILLIAM BELL	
4/02/77	63	12	1. Coming Back For More .... "Tryin' To Love Two"(10)	Mercury 1146
			BELLAMY BROTHERS David & Howard Bellamy	
5/15/76	69	12	1. Bellamy Brothers .... "Let Your Love Flow"(1)	Warner 2941
			BELLE STARS English female septet	
5/28/83	191	2	1. The Belle Stars	Warner 23866
			BELLS Jacki Ralph & Cliff Edwards, lead singers of Canadian quintet	
5/01/71	90	14	1. Fly, Little White Dove, Fly .... "Stay Awhile"(7)	Polydor 4510
			BELMONTS former trio with Dion	
10/27/62	113	7	1. The Belmonts' Carnival Of Hits .... [G]	Sabina 5001
			PAT BENATAR hard-rock singer from Brooklyn, New York - real name: Patricia Andrzejewski	
10/20/79	12	122	▲ 1. In The Heat Of The Night	Chrysalis 1236
8/23/80	2(5)	93	▲ 2. **Crimes Of Passion** .... "Hit Me With Your Best Shot"(9)	Chrysalis 1275
7/25/81	1(1)	54	▲ 3. **Precious Time**	Chrysalis 1346
11/20/82	4	46	▲ 4. **Get Nervous**	Chrysalis 1396
10/15/83	13	34	▲ 5. Live From Earth .... [L] 2 of the 10 songs are new studio tracks "Love Is A Battlefield"(5)	Chrysalis 41444
11/24/84	14	20+	▲ 6. Tropico .... "We Belong"(5)	Chrysalis 41471
			TONY BENNETT born in Queens, New York, on 8/3/26	
2/23/57	14	9	1. Tony	Columbia 938
7/07/62	5	149	● 2. **I Left My Heart In San Francisco**	Columbia 8669
10/13/62	37	19	3. Tony Bennett At Carnegie Hall .... [L]	Columbia 23 [2]
4/06/63	5	44	4. **I Wanna Be Around**	Columbia 8800
8/24/63	24	30	5. This Is All I Ask	Columbia 8856
2/22/64	20	24	6. The Many Moods Of Tony	Columbia 8941
5/23/64	79	12	7. When Lights Are Low	Columbia 8975
12/19/64	42	19	8. Who Can I Turn To	Columbia 9085

DATE CHARTED	PEAK POS	WKS CHRT'D	ARTIST — Album Title	LABEL & NUMBER
5/22/65	47	22	9. If I Ruled The World - Songs For The Jet Set	Columbia 9143
8/21/65	20	42	● 10. Tony's Greatest Hits, Volume III .... [G]	Columbia 9173
3/12/66	18	29	11. The Movie Song Album	Columbia 9272
10/08/66	68	18	12. A Time For Love	Columbia 9360
5/13/67	178	6	13. Tony Makes It Happen!	Columbia 9453
1/13/68	164	7	14. For Once In My Life	Columbia 9573
5/10/69	174	8	15. Tony Bennett's Greatest Hits, Volume IV .... [G]	Columbia 9814
9/06/69	137	5	16. I've Gotta Be Me	Columbia 9882
2/28/70	144	11	17. Tony Sings The Great Hits Of Today!	Columbia 9980
11/14/70	193	2	18. Tony Bennett's "Something"	Columbia 30280
3/06/71	67	13	19. Love Story	Columbia 30558
11/20/71	195	2	20. Get Happy with the London Philharmonic Orchestra .... [L]	Columbia 30953
2/19/72	182	4	21. Summer Of '42	Columbia 31219
7/01/72	167	14	22. With Love	Columbia 31460
10/21/72	175	7	23. Tony Bennett's All-Time Greatest Hits .... [G] hits from 1951-1972	Columbia 31494 [2]
12/09/72	196	6	24. The Good Things In Life	MGM/Verve 5088
			MARK BENNO also see Leon Russell	
9/23/72	171	8	1. Ambush	A&M 4364
			GEORGE BENSON jazz/pop guitarist, vocalist	
8/23/69	145	3	1. Tell It Like It Is .... [I]	A&M 3020
12/28/74	78	19	2. Bad Benson .... [I]	CTI 6045
4/17/76	1(2)	78	▲ 3. **Breezin'** "This Masquerade"(10)	Warner 2919
6/26/76	51	16	4. Good King Bad .... [I]	CTI 6062
7/24/76	125	8	5. The Other Side Of Abbey Road .... [E] version of Beatles' "Abbey Road" album - recorded 1969	A&M 3028
10/30/76	100	8	6. Benson & Farrell .... [I] GEORGE BENSON & JOE FARRELL (jazz flutist)	CTI 6069
1/29/77	122	8	7. George Benson In Concert-Carnegie Hall .... [I-L] recorded January, 1975 - with guest: Hubert Laws	CTI 6072
2/12/77	9	35	▲ 8. **In Flight**	Warner 2983
2/11/78	5	38	▲ 9. **Weekend In L.A.** .... [L] "On Broadway"(7)	Warner 3139 [2]
3/17/79	7	26	● 10. **Livin' Inside Your Love**	Warner 3277 [2]
8/09/80	3	38	▲ 11. **Give Me The Night** "Give Me The Night"(4)	Warner 3453
11/21/81	14	26	● 12. The George Benson Collection .... [G] "Turn Your Love Around"(5)	Warner 3577 [2]
6/18/83	27	35	● 13. In Your Eyes	Warner 23744
1/26/85	45	11+	14. 20/20	Warner 25178
			BROOK BENTON born Benjamin Peay on 9/19/31 in Camden, South Carolina	
6/05/61	82	20	1. Brook Benton's Golden Hits .... [G] "It's Just A Matter Of Time"(3)/"So Many Ways"(6)/"Kiddio"(7)	Mercury 60607
9/25/61	70	13	2. The Boll Weevil Song And 11 Other Great Hits "The Boll Weevil Song"(2)	Mercury 60641
2/17/62	77	7	3. If You Believe spirituals	Mercury 60619
10/27/62	40	15	4. Singing The Blues - Lie To Me	Mercury 60740

35

DATE CHARTED	PEAK POS	WKS CHRT'D	ARTIST — Album Title	LABEL & NUMBER
4/13/63	82	6	5. Brook Benton's Golden Hits, Volume 2 .... [G] "Hotel Happiness"(3)	Mercury 60774
10/28/67	156	4	6. Laura (What's He Got That I Ain't Got)	Reprise 6268
7/19/69	189	2	7. Do Your Own Thing	Cotillion 9002
2/21/70	27	23	8. Brook Benton Today .... "Rainy Night In Georgia"(4)	Cotillion 9018
8/22/70	199	2	9. Home Style	Cotillion 9028

GERTRUDE BERG
Molly Goldberg of radio & TV shows - died in 1966 (67)

7/17/65	131	12	1. How To Be A Jewish Mother .... [C] announcer: David Ross; writer: Dan Greenburg	Amy 8007

EDGAR BERGEN & CHARLIE McCARTHY - see W.C. FIELDS

POLLY BERGEN

6/10/57	10	5	1. **Bergen Sings Morgan** .... Polly portrayed Helen Morgan in a TV film	Columbia 994
11/04/57	20	1	2. The Party's Over	Columbia 1031

BERLIN
Los Angeles electro-pop trio

2/19/83	30	34	● 1. Pleasure Victim	Geffen 2036
3/31/84	28	30	2. Love Life	Geffen 4025

SHELLEY BERMAN
comedian

4/27/59	2(6)	134	1. **Inside Shelley Berman** .... [C]	Verve 15003
11/30/59	6	73	2. **Outside Shelley Berman** .... [C]	Verve 15007
7/25/60	4	52	3. **The Edge Of Shelley Berman** .... [C]	Verve 15013
11/06/61	25	19	4. A Personal Appearance .... [C]	Verve 15027
9/26/64	94	8	5. The Sex Life Of The Primate (and other Bits of Gossip) .... [C] with Jerry Stiller, Anne Meara and Lovelady Powell	Verve 15043

HERSCHEL BERNARDI
portrayed Tevye in Broadway's "Fiddler On The Roof"

11/12/66	138	5	1. Fiddler On The Roof	Columbia 6610

LEONARD BERNSTEIN
conductor

12/12/60	13	7	1. Bernstein Plays Brubeck Plays Bernstein .... [I] side 1: New York Philharmonic with Dave Brubeck Quartet conducted by Leonard Bernstein; side 2: Dave Brubeck Quartet	Columbia 8257
12/25/71	53	20	2. Mass (from the Liturgy of the Roman Mass) .... created for the opening of the John F. Kennedy Center for the Performing Arts	Columbia 31008 [2]

CHUCK BERRY
legendary rock & roller - born in St. Louis on 10/18/31

8/24/63	29	17	1. Chuck Berry On Stage .... [L] live audience dubbed in	Chess 1480
6/06/64	34	21	2. Chuck Berry's Greatest Hits .... [G] "Maybellene"(5)/"School Day"(3)/"Rock & Roll Music"(8)/ "Sweet Little Sixteen"(2)/"Johnny B. Goode"(8)	Chess 1485
12/12/64	124	7	3. St. Louis To Liverpool .... "No Particular Place To Go"(10)	Chess 1488
5/20/67	191	3	4. Chuck Berry's Golden Decade .... [G]	Chess 1514 [2]
6/10/72	8	47	● 5. **The London Chuck Berry Sessions** .... [L] side 1: studio; side 2: live "My Ding-A-Ling"(1)	Chess 60020
10/21/72	72	17	6. Chuck Berry's Golden Decade .... [R] reissue of album #4 above	Chess 1514 [2]
11/04/72	185	7	7. St. Louie To Frisco To Memphis .... [L] record 1: live at the Fillmore with the Steve Miller Band	Mercury 6501 [2]

DATE CHARTED	PEAK POS	WKS CHRT'D	ARTIST — Album Title	LABEL & NUMBER
2/24/73	110	8	8. Chuck Berry's Golden Decade, Vol. 2 .... [G]	Chess 60023 [2]
9/08/73	175	6	9. Chuck Berry/Bio	Chess 50043
			KAREN BETH	
9/06/69	171	6	1. The Joys Of Life	Decca 75148
			DICKEY BETTS The Allman Brothers' lead guitarist	
8/31/74	19	16	1. Highway Call .... side 1: vocals; side 2: instrumentals	Capricorn 0123
4/30/77	31	12	2. Dickey Betts & Great Southern	Arista 4123
4/29/78	157	5	3. Atlanta's Burning Down	Arista 4168
			B-52's quintet from Athens, Georgia	
8/11/79	59	55	● 1. The B-52's	Warner 3355
9/20/80	18	27	● 2. Wild Planet	Warner 3471
8/08/81	55	11	3. Party Mix! .... [M] 6 cut party remix of "Wild Planet" LP	Warner 3596
2/20/82	35	18	4. Mesopotamia .... [M]	Warner 3641
5/21/83	29	26	5. Whammy!	Warner 23819
			BICKERSONS - **see DON AMECHE & FRANCES LANGFORD**	
			BIDDU ORCHESTRA English studio orchestra	
2/21/76	170	3	1. Biddu Orchestra .... [I]	Epic 33903
			BIG BROTHER & THE HOLDING COMPANY Janis Joplin, lead singer (1,2 & 4)	
9/02/67	60	30	1. Big Brother & The Holding Company	Mainstream 6099
8/31/68	1(8)	66	● 2. **Cheap Thrills**	Columbia 9700
11/28/70	134	6	3. Be A Brother	Columbia 30222
5/15/71	185	4	4. Big Brother & The Holding Company ...... [R] reissue + 2 more cuts of album #1 above	Columbia 30631
9/04/71	157	3	5. How Hard It Is	Columbia 30738
			BIG COUNTRY Scottish four-man rock band	
9/24/83	18	42	● 1. The Crossing	Mercury 812870
5/05/84	65	12	2. Wonderland .... [M]	Mercury 818835
11/24/84	70	17	3. Steeltown	Mercury 822831
			MR. ACKER BILK English clarinetist - with the Leon Young String Chorale	
5/05/62	3	29	● 1. **Stranger On The Shore** .... [I] "Stranger On The Shore"(1)	Atco 129
9/01/62	48	9	2. Above The Stars & Other Romantic Fancies .... [I]	Atco 144
			BILLION DOLLAR BABIES Alice Cooper's backup band	
6/11/77	198	2	1. Battle Axe	Polydor 6100
			BILLY & THE BEATERS Billy Vera	
5/16/81	118	10	1. Billy & The Beaters .... [L]	Alfa 10001
			BILLY SATELLITE rock quartet from Oakland, California, led by Monty Byrom	
9/01/84	139	6	1. Billy Satellite	Capitol 12340
			BIONIC BOOGIE a Gregg Diamond production	
1/28/78	88	16	1. Bionic Boogie	Polydor 6123
			JANE BIRKIN & SERGE GAINSBOURG	
3/07/70	196	2	1. Je T'Aime (Beautiful Love) .... [F]	Fontana 67610

DATE CHARTED	PEAK POS	WKS CHRT'D	ARTIST — Album Title	LABEL & NUMBER
			ELVIN BISHOP guitarist with the Paul Butterfield Blues Band	
7/27/74	100	17	1. Let It Flow	Capricorn 0134
5/10/75	46	17	2. Juke Joint Jump	Capricorn 0151
1/24/76	18	34	3. Struttin' My Stuff .... "Fooled Around And Fell In Love"(3)	Capricorn 0165
11/20/76	70	12	4. Hometown Boy Makes Good!	Capricorn 0176
8/27/77	38	12	5. Live! Raisin' Hell .... [L]	Capricorn 0185 [2]
			STEPHEN BISHOP pop-rock singer/songwriter - also see Soundtrack "Tootsie"	
1/08/77	34	32	1. Careless .... "On And On"	ABC 954
9/16/78	35	19	● 2. Bish	ABC 1082
			JUSSI BJOERLING Swedish tenor - died 9/9/60 (49)	
4/17/61	142	1	1. The Beloved Bjoerling, Volume One .... [E] opera arias 1936-1948	Capitol 7239
			BLACK 'N BLUE Portland, Oregon hard-rock quintet - Jamie St. James, vocals	
9/15/84	116	11	1. Black 'N Blue	Geffen 24041
			BLACKBYRDS pop/soul group founded by Donald Byrd	
6/22/74	96	23	1. The Blackbyrds	Fantasy 9444
12/07/74	30	39	2. Flying Start .... "Walking In Rhythm"(6)	Fantasy 9472
7/05/75	150	6	3. Cornbread, Earl and Me .... [S]	Fantasy 9483
11/22/75	16	40	● 4. City Life	Fantasy 9490
11/27/76	34	24	● 5. Unfinished Business	Fantasy 9518
10/08/77	43	30	● 6. Action	Fantasy 9535
1/06/79	159	7	7. Night Grooves .... [K]	Fantasy 9570
1/17/81	133	11	8. Better Days	Fantasy 9602
			BLACKFOOT Rick "Rattlesnake" Medlocke, lead singer	
5/12/79	42	41	● 1. Strikes	Atco 112
6/21/80	50	20	2. Tomcattin'	Atco 101
7/25/81	48	12	3. Marauder	Atco 107
6/11/83	82	13	4. Siogo	Atco 90080
10/27/84	176	5	5. Vertical Smiles	Atco 90218
			BLACK IVORY New York-based trio	
4/22/72	158	9	1. Don't Turn Around	Today 1005
1/20/73	188	9	2. Baby, Won't You Change Your Mind	Today 1008
			BLACKJACK quartet led by Michael Bolton	
7/21/79	127	7	1. Blackjack	Polydor 6215
			BLACK OAK ARKANSAS Southern rock sextet led by Jim "Dandy" Mangrum	
8/28/71	127	12	● 1. Black Oak Arkansas	Atco 354
2/12/72	103	10	2. Keep The Faith	Atco 381
7/08/72	93	19	3. If An Angel Came To See You, Would You Make Her Feel At Home?	Atco 7008
3/17/73	90	16	● 4. Raunch 'N' Roll/Live .... [L]	Atco 7019
11/24/73	52	22	● 5. High On The Hog	Atco 7035
7/27/74	56	12	6. Street Party	Atco 101
5/31/75	145	8	7. Ain't Life Grand	Atco 111
10/18/75	99	17	8. X-Rated	MCA 2155

DATE CHARTED	PEAK POS	WKS CHRT'D	ARTIST — Album Title	LABEL & NUMBER
2/28/76	194	2	9. Live! Mutha .... [L]	Atco 128
6/12/76	173	7	10. Balls Of Fire	MCA 2199

BLACK PEARL
West Coast group led by Bernie "B.B." Fieldings

5/03/69	130	5	1. Black Pearl	Atlantic 8220
10/17/70	189	2	2. Black Pearl-Live! .... [L]	Prophesy 1001

BLACK SABBATH
British heavy-metal group led by Ozzy Osbourne - replaced by Ronnie James Dio (10-12) and Ian Gillan (13)

8/29/70	23	65	● 1. Black Sabbath	Warner 1871
2/20/71	12	70	● 2. Paranoid	Warner 1887
9/04/71	8	43	● 3. **Master Of Reality**	Warner 2562
10/21/72	13	31	● 4. Black Sabbath, Vol. 4	Warner 2602
1/26/74	11	32	● 5. Sabbath Bloody Sabbath	Warner 2695
8/23/75	28	14	6. Sabotage	Warner 2822
2/28/76	48	10	● 7. We Sold Our Soul For Rock 'N' Roll .... [K]	Warner 2923 [2]
10/30/76	51	12	8. Technical Ecstasy	Warner 2969
10/28/78	69	14	9. Never Say Die!	Warner 3186
6/14/80	28	24	● 10. Heaven And Hell	Warner 3372
11/28/81	29	18	11. Mob Rules	Warner 3605
2/05/83	37	12	12. Live Evil .... [L]	Warner 23742 [2]
10/22/83	39	16	13. Born Again	Warner 23978

BLACK UHURU
reggae quintet led by Michael Rose

7/24/82	146	7	1. Chill Out	Island 9752

BILL BLACK'S Combo
Bill, of "Scotty & Bill" on Elvis Presley's Sun recordings - died on 10/21/65 (39)

11/14/60	23	28	1. Solid And Raunchy .... [I]	Hi 12003
1/20/62	35	19	2. Let's Twist Her .... [I]	Hi 12006
7/11/64	143	4	3. Plays Tunes By Chuck Berry .... [I]	Hi 32017
11/28/64	139	3	4. Bill Black's Combo Goes Big Band .... [I]	Hi 32020
8/19/67	195	2	5. Bill Black's Greatest Hits .... [G-I]	Hi 32012
			"White Silver Sands"(9)	
9/13/69	168	4	6. Solid And Raunchy The 3rd .... [I]	Hi 32052

STANLEY BLACK

2/10/62	30	8	1. Exotic Precussion .... [I]	London P. 4 44004
8/18/62	33	10	2. Spain .... [I]	London P. 4 44016
8/10/63	50	4	3. Film Spectacular .... [I]	London P. 4 44025
6/12/65	148	3	4. Music Of A People .... [I]	London P. 4 44060
			above 2 with the London Festival Orchestra	

RITCHIE BLACKMORE - see RAINBOW

JACK BLANCHARD & MISTY MORGAN
husband and wife

7/04/70	185	5	1. Birds Of A Feather	Wayside 001
			"Tennessee Bird Walk"	

BOBBY BLAND
born in Rosemark, Tennessee on 1/27/30

9/01/62	53	7	1. Here's The Man!!!	Duke 75
7/13/63	11	26	2. Call On Me/Thats The Way Love Is	Duke 77
8/01/64	119	8	3. Ain't Nothing You Can Do	Duke 78
11/03/73	136	19	4. His California Album	Dunhill 50163
8/03/74	172	7	5. Dreamer	Dunhill 50169
10/26/74	43	20	● 6. Together For The First Time...Live .... [L]	Dunhill 50190 [2]
			B.B. KING & BOBBY BLAND	

DATE CHARTED	PEAK POS	WKS CHRT'D	ARTIST — Album Title	LABEL & NUMBER
9/13/75	154	5	7. Get On Down With Bobby Bland	ABC 895
7/17/76	73	14	8. Together Again...Live .... [L]	ABC/Impulse 9317
			BOBBY BLAND & B.B. KING	
5/14/77	185	4	9. Reflections In Blue	ABC 1018
7/01/78	185	3	10. Come Fly With Me	ABC 1075
10/27/79	187	2	11. I Feel Good, I Feel Fine	MCA 3157

BLASTERS
Los Angeles rockabilly group

DATE CHARTED	PEAK POS	WKS CHRT'D	ARTIST — Album Title	LABEL & NUMBER
1/09/82	36	30	1. The Blasters	Slash 3680
10/30/82	117	8	2. Over There-Live At The Venue, London .... [M-L]	Slash 23735
5/14/83	95	8	3. Non Fiction	Slash 23818
3/23/85	111+	3+	4. Hard Line	Slash 25093

ADAM BLESSING - see DAMNATION OF

BLIND FAITH
Eric Clapton, Steve Winwood, Ginger Baker & Rick Grech

DATE CHARTED	PEAK POS	WKS CHRT'D	ARTIST — Album Title	LABEL & NUMBER
8/16/69	1(2)	37	● 1. **Blind Faith**	Atco 304
2/26/77	126	8	2. Blind Faith .... [R]	RSO 3016
			reissue of 1st album	

BLODWYN PIG
British quartet led by Mick Abrahams of Jethro Tull

DATE CHARTED	PEAK POS	WKS CHRT'D	ARTIST — Album Title	LABEL & NUMBER
12/13/69	149	5	1. Ahead Rings Out	A&M 4210
6/27/70	96	5	2. Getting To This	A&M 4243

BLONDIE
New York rock group led by Debbie Harry

DATE CHARTED	PEAK POS	WKS CHRT'D	ARTIST — Album Title	LABEL & NUMBER
2/25/78	72	17	1. Plastic Letters	Chrysalis 1166
9/23/78	6	103	▲ 2. **Parallel Lines**	Chrysalis 1192
			"Heart Of Glass"(1)	
10/20/79	17	51	▲ 3. Eat To The Beat	Chrysalis 1225
12/13/80	7	34	▲ 4. **Autoamerican**	Chrysalis 1290
			"The Tide Is High"(1)/"Rapture"(1)	
10/31/81	30	23	● 5. The Best Of Blondie .... [G]	Chrysalis 1337
			"Call Me"(1)	
6/19/82	33	12	6. The Hunter	Chrysalis 1384

BLOODROCK
rock group from Fort Worth, Texas

DATE CHARTED	PEAK POS	WKS CHRT'D	ARTIST — Album Title	LABEL & NUMBER
4/25/70	160	5	1. Bloodrock	Capitol 435
11/07/70	21	37	2. Bloodrock 2	Capitol 491
4/10/71	27	23	3. Bloodrock 3	Capitol 765
11/06/71	88	7	4. Bloodrock U.S.A.	Capitol 645
6/03/72	67	22	5. Bloodrock Live .... [L]	Capitol 11038 [2]
9/30/72	104	14	6. Bloodrock Passage	Capitol 11109

BLOODSTONE
soul group from Kansas City, Missouri

DATE CHARTED	PEAK POS	WKS CHRT'D	ARTIST — Album Title	LABEL & NUMBER
4/14/73	30	36	1. Natural High	London 620
			"Natural High"(10)	
1/05/74	110	22	2. Unreal	London 634
8/10/74	141	8	3. I Need Time	London 647
2/22/75	147	6	4. Riddle Of The Sphinx	London 645
7/17/82	95	11	5. We Go A Long Way Back	T-Neck 38115

BLOOD, SWEAT & TEARS
New York jazz-rock group formed by Al Kooper, Steve Katz & Bobby Colomby - David Clayton-Thomas, lead singer (1-5; 9-10)

DATE CHARTED	PEAK POS	WKS CHRT'D	ARTIST — Album Title	LABEL & NUMBER
4/13/68	47	55	● 1. Child Is Father To The Man	Columbia 9619
2/01/69	1(7)	109	● 2. **Blood, Sweat & Tears**	Columbia 9720
			"You've Made Me So Very Happy"(2)/"Spinning Wheel"(2)/ "And When I Die"(2)	

DATE CHARTED	PEAK POS	WKS CHRT'D		ARTIST — Album Title	LABEL & NUMBER
7/18/70	1(2)	41	●	3. **Blood, Sweat & Tears 3**	Columbia 30090
7/10/71	10	23	●	4. **B, S & T; 4**	Columbia 30590
3/11/72	19	27	●	5. Blood, Sweat & Tears Greatest Hits .... [G]	Columbia 31170
11/04/72	32	17		6. New Blood	Columbia 31780
8/25/73	72	12		7. No Sweat	Columbia 32180
9/07/74	149	6		8. Mirror Image	Columbia 32929
5/31/75	47	13		9. New City	Columbia 33484
7/31/76	165	3		10. More Than Ever	Columbia 34233

BOBBY BLOOM
died from an accidental shooting on 2/28/74

| 11/28/70 | 126 | 3 | | 1. The Bobby Bloom Album .... | L&R 1035 |
| | | | | "Montego Bay"(8) | |

MIKE BLOOMFIELD
Chicago-born blues guitarist - with Paul Butterfield Blues Band, and Electric Flag - died on 2/15/81 (37)

8/31/68	12	37	●	1. Super Session	Columbia 9701
				MIKE BLOOMFIELD/AL KOOPER/STEVE STILLS	
2/08/69	18	20		2. The Live Adventures Of Mike Bloomfield	
				And Al Kooper .... [L]	Columbia 6 [2]
10/11/69	127	5		3. It's Not Killing Me	Columbia 9883
6/16/73	105	12		4. Triumvirate	Columbia 32172
				MIKE BLOOMFIELD/JOHN PAUL HAMMOND/DR. JOHN	

KURTIS BLOW
real name: Kurt Walker

10/18/80	71	10		1. Kurtis Blow	Mercury 3854
7/18/81	137	5		2. Deuce	Mercury 4020
10/09/82	167	5		3. Tough .... [M]	Mercury 505
10/13/84	83	26+		4. Ego Trip	Mercury 822420

BLOWFLY

| 5/24/80 | 82 | 20 | | 1. Blowfly's Party [X-Rated] .... | Weird World 2034 |

BLUE CHEER
San Francisco heavy-metal band

3/09/68	11	27		1. Vincebus Eruptum	Philips 264
9/28/68	90	16		2. Outsideinside	Philips 278
5/03/69	84	14		3. New! Improved! Blue Cheer	Philips 305
11/07/70	188	5		4. The Original Human Being	Philips 347

BLUE MAGIC
Philadelphia soul quintet

3/16/74	45	34		1. Blue Magic	Atco 7038
				"Sideshow"(8)	
12/28/74	71	13		2. The Magic Of The Blue	Atco 103
10/04/75	50	12		3. Thirteen Blue Magic Lane	Atco 120
9/25/76	170	5		4. Mystic Dragons	Atco 140

BLUE OYSTER CULT
U.S. rock quintet led by Donald "Buck Dharma" Roeser & Eric Bloom

5/20/72	172	8		1. Blue Oyster Cult	Columbia 31063
3/17/73	122	13		2. Tyranny And Mutation	Columbia 32017
4/27/74	53	14		3. Secret Treaties	Columbia 32858
3/15/75	22	13	●	4. On Your Feet Or On Your Knees .... [L]	Columbia 33371 [2]
6/19/76	29	35	▲	5. Agents Of Fortune	Columbia 34164
				"(Don't Fear) The Reaper"	
11/12/77	43	14	●	6. Spectres	Columbia 35019
9/30/78	44	12	●	7. Some Enchanted Evening .... [L]	Columbia 35563
7/07/79	44	17		8. Mirrors	Columbia 36009
7/12/80	34	16		9. Cultosaurus Erectus	Columbia 36550

DATE CHARTED	PEAK POS	WKS CHRT'D	ARTIST — Album Title	LABEL & NUMBER
7/11/81	24	31	● 10. Fire Of Unknown Origin	Columbia 37389
5/15/82	29	19	11. Extraterrestrial Live .... [L]	Columbia 37946 [2]
11/26/83	93	16	12. The Revolution By Night	Columbia 38947

BLUE RIDGE RANGERS
John Fogerty (of CCR) - one man band

DATE CHARTED	PEAK POS	WKS CHRT'D	ARTIST — Album Title	LABEL & NUMBER
5/05/73	47	15	1. The Blue Ridge Rangers	Fantasy 9415

BLUE SWEDE
Swedish sextet

4/06/74	80	17	1. Hooked On A Feeling	EMI 11286
			"Hooked On A Feeling"(1)/"Never My Love"(7)	

BLUES BROTHERS
John Belushi (died on 3/5/82-33) & Dan Aykroyd

12/23/78	1(1)	29	▲ 1. **Briefcase Full Of Blues**	Atlantic 19217
6/28/80	13	19	● 2. The Blues Brothers .... [S]	Atlantic 16017
			with Aretha Franklin, James Brown & Ray Charles	
12/27/80	49	12	3. Made In America .... [L]	Atlantic 16025
1/09/82	143	3	4. Best Of The Blues Brothers .... [G]	Atlantic 19331

BLUES IMAGE
Tampa, Florida quintet led by Mike Pinera

8/16/69	112	9	1. Blues Image	Atco 300
4/25/70	147	13	2. Open	Atco 317
			"Ride Captain Ride"(4)	

BLUES MAGOOS
Bronx, New York rock quintet led by Peppy Castro

12/03/66	21	32	1. Psychedelic Lollipop	Mercury 61096
			"(We Ain't Got) Nothin' Yet"(5)	
4/22/67	74	16	2. Electric Comic Book	Mercury 61104

BLUES PROJECT
New York City blues band - members Al Kooper & Steve Katz formed Blood, Sweat & Tears in 1967

5/21/66	77	21	1. Live At The Cafe Au Go Go .... [L]	Verve Fore. 3000
12/17/66	52	36	2. Projections	Verve Folk. 3008
10/07/67	71	11	3. The Blues Project Live At Town Hall .... [L]	Verve Fore. 3025
8/09/69	199	2	4. Best Of The Blues Project .... [G]	Verve Fore. 3077

BOBBY & THE MIDNITES
rock quintet led by Bob Weir (Grateful Dead)

11/21/81	158	7	1. Bobby & The Midnites	Arista 9568
8/25/84	166	4	2. Where the Beat Meets the Street	Columbia 39276

WILLIE BOBO
latin & jazz percussionist - died 9/15/83 (49)

2/26/66	137	8	1. Spanish Grease .... [I]	Verve 8631

ANGELA BOFILL
performed with Dizzy Gillespie and Cannonball Adderley

2/17/79	47	26	1. Angie	GRP 5000
11/03/79	34	33	2. Angel of the Night	GRP 5501
11/21/81	61	22	3. Something About You	Arista 9576
2/12/83	40	32	4. Too Tough	Arista 9616
11/26/83	81	21	5. Teaser	Arista 8198

TIM BOGERT - see BECK, BOGERT, APPICE

HAMILTON BOHANNON

8/12/78	58	19	1. Summertime Groove	Mercury 3728

RUDI BOHN & his Band
German conductor of polkas

10/16/61	38	9	1. Percussive Oompah .... [I]	London P. 4 44009

DATE CHARTED	PEAK POS	WKS CHRT'D	ARTIST — Album Title	LABEL & NUMBER
			TOMMY BOLIN	
			guitarist with James Gang and Deep Purple - died on 12/4/76 (25)	
12/20/75	**96**	14	1. Teaser	Nemperor 436
10/02/76	**98**	8	2. Private Eyes	Columbia 34329
			MICHAEL BOLTON	
			former lead singer of Blackjack	
5/07/83	**89**	13	1. Michael Bolton	Columbia 38537
			BON JOVI	
			Jon Bon Jovi, lead singer of East Coast quintet	
2/25/84	**43**	37	1. Bon Jovi	Mercury 814982
			ANGELO BOND	
8/02/75	**179**	2	1. Bondage	ABC 889
			JOHNNY BOND	
			died on 6/12/78 (63)	
5/29/65	**142**	3	1. Ten Little Bottles .... [N]	Starday 333
			GARY "U.S." BONDS	
			real name: Gary Anderson	
8/07/61	**6**	28	1. **Dance 'til Quarter To Three**	Legrand 3001
			"New Orleans"(6)/"Quarter To Three"(1)/"School Is Out"(5)	
5/02/81	**27**	20	2. Dedication	EMI America 17051
6/26/82	**52**	17	3. On The Line	EMI America 17068
			above 2 produced by Bruce Springsteen	
			BONEY M	
			German disco quartet	
9/02/78	**134**	10	1. Nightflight To Venus	Sire 6062
			KARLA BONOFF	
			songwriter/singer from Los Angeles	
10/01/77	**52**	40	1. Karla Bonoff	Columbia 34672
9/29/79	**31**	26	2. Restless Nights	Columbia 35799
4/03/82	**49**	35	3. Wild Heart Of The Young	Columbia 37444
			BONZO DOG BAND	
			British satirical band - also see the Rutles	
6/10/72	**199**	2	1. Let's Make Up And Be Friendly	United Art. 5584
			BOOKER T. & PRISCILLA	
			Booker T. Jones & wife Priscilla (sister of Rita Coolidge)	
8/14/71	**106**	6	1. Booker T. & Priscilla	A&M 3504 [2]
7/22/72	**190**	4	2. Home Grown	A&M 4351
			BOOKER T. & THE MG's	
			MG's (Memphis Group): Booker T. Jones, Steve Cropper, Duck Dunn & Al Jackson (died 10/1/75-39)	
11/10/62	**33**	17	1. Green Onions .... [I]	Stax 701
			"Green Onions"(3)	
6/24/67	**35**	29	2. Hip Hug-Her .... [I]	Stax 717
8/26/67	**98**	4	3. Back To Back .... [I-L]	Stax 720
			THE MAR-KEYS/BOOKER T. & THE MG's	
5/18/68	**176**	4	4. Doin' Our Thing .... [I]	Stax 724
10/19/68	**127**	9	5. Soul Limbo .... [I]	Stax 2001
			"Hang 'Em High"(9)	
11/23/68	**167**	11	6. The Best Of Booker T. & The MG's .... [G-I]	Atlantic 8202
2/08/69	**98**	27	7. Uptight .... [S]	Stax 2006
			"Time Is Tight"(6)	
6/14/69	**53**	18	8. The Booker T. Set .... [I]	Stax 2009
5/02/70	**107**	15	9. McLemore Avenue .... [I]	Stax 2027
			version of Beatles' "Abbey Road" album	
11/14/70	**132**	8	10. Booker T. & The M.G.'s Greatest Hits .... [G-I]	Stax 2033
2/13/71	**43**	38	11. Melting Pot .... [I]	Stax 2035

DATE CHARTED	PEAK POS	WKS CHRT'D	ARTIST — Album Title	LABEL & NUMBER
			BOB BOOKER & GEORGE FOSTER - see COMEDY section	
			TAKA BOOM Chaka Khan's sister	
6/09/79	171	4	1. Taka Boom	Ariola 50041
			BOOMTOWN RATS Irish sextet - Bob Geldof, lead singer	
3/03/79	112	13	1. A Tonic For The Troops	Columbia 35750
12/01/79	103	16	2. The Fine Art Of Surfacing	Columbia 36248
2/21/81	116	8	3. Mondo Bongo	Columbia 37062
			DANIEL BOONE English - real name: Peter Lee Stirling	
10/07/72	142	9	1. Beautiful Sunday	Mercury 649
			DEBBY BOONE Pat Boone's daughter	
10/29/77	6	37	▲ 1. **You Light Up My Life** .... "You Light Up My Life"(1)	Warner 3118
8/12/78	147	5	2. Midstream	Warner 3130
			PAT BOONE born Charles Eugene Boone on 6/1/34; son-in-law of Red Foley	
10/27/56	14	4	1. Howdy!	Dot 3030
6/24/57	13	7	2. A Closer Walk with Thee .... [EP] 7" E.P. (4 sacred songs)	Dot 1056
7/08/57	19	3	3. "Pat"	Dot 3050
9/02/57	5	5	4. **Four By Pat** .... [EP] 7" E.P. (4 songs)	Dot 1057
10/07/57	20	2	5. Pat Boone .... Pat's 1st album "Ain't That A Shame"(1)/"At My Front Door"(7)/"I'll Be Home"(4)	Dot 3012
10/21/57	3	36	● 6. **Pat's Great Hits** .... [G] "I Almost Lost My Mind"(1)/"Friendly Persuasion"(5)/ "Don't Forbid Me"(1)/"Why Baby Why"(5)/ "Love Letters In The Sand"(1)/"Remember You're Mine"(6)	Dot 3071
12/23/57	12	13	7. April Love .... [S] "April Love"(1)	Dot 9000
12/23/57	21	4	8. Hymns We Love	Dot 3068
7/28/58	2(1)	32	9. **Star Dust**	Dot 3118
11/24/58	13	2	10. Yes Indeed!	Dot 3121
7/13/59	17	11	11. Tenderly	Dot 3180
5/23/60	26	3	12. Moonglow	Dot 3270
7/17/61	29	30	13. Moody River .... "Moody River"(1)	Dot 3384
1/06/62	39	2	14. White Christmas .... [X]	Dot 3222
9/15/62	66	13	15. Pat Boone's Golden Hits .... [G] "Speedy Gonzales"(6)	Dot 3455
12/29/62	116	1	16. White Christmas .... [X-R]	Dot 3222
			BOOTSY William "Bootsy" Collins with his band "Bootsy's Rubber Band"	
5/01/76	59	27	1. Stretchin' Out In Bootsy's Rubber Band	Warner 2920
2/05/77	16	23	● 2. Ahh...The Name Is Bootsy, Baby!	Warner 2972
2/25/78	16	24	● 3. Bootsy? Player Of The Year	Warner 3093
7/21/79	52	9	4. This Boot Is Made For Fonk-n	Warner 3295
12/06/80	70	9	5. Ultra Wave	Warner 3433
5/29/82	120	8	6. The One Giveth, The Count Taketh Away	Warner 3667
			BOSTON rock quintet from Boston - led by Tom Scholz & Brad Delp	
9/25/76	3	101	▲ 1. **Boston** .... "More Than A Feeling"(5)	Epic 34188
9/02/78	1(2)	35	▲ 2. **Don't Look Back** .... "Don't Look Back"(4)	Epic 35050

44

DATE CHARTED	PEAK POS	WKS CHRT'D	ARTIST — Album Title	LABEL & NUMBER
			BOSTON POPS ORCHESTRA/ARTHUR FIEDLER	
			maestro Fiedler died on 7/10/79 (83)	
2/02/59	9	16	1. Offenbach: Gaite Parisienne;	
			Khachaturian: Gayne Ballet Suite ... [I]	RCA 2267
7/14/62	29	14	2. Pops Roundup .... [I]	RCA 2595
3/09/63	36	6	3. Our Man In Boston .... [I]	RCA 2599
4/06/63	5	23	4. "Jalousie" And Other Favorites In The	
			Latin Flavor .... [I]	RCA 2661
6/22/63	29	14	5. Star Dust .... [I]	RCA 2670
10/19/63	116	4	6. Concert In The Park .... [I]	RCA 2677
9/26/64	18	31	7. "Pops" Goes The Trumpet .... [I]	RCA 2729
			AL HIRT/BOSTON POPS/ARTHUR FIEDLER	
11/21/64	53	14	8. Peter And The Commissar .... [C]	RCA 2773
			ALLAN SHERMAN/BOSTON POPS/ARTHUR FIEDLER	
10/23/65	86	16	9. Nero Goes "Pops" .... [I]	RCA 2821
			PETER NERO/ARTHUR FIEDLER/BOSTON POPS	
5/14/66	145	3	10. The Duke At Tanglewood .... [I-L]	RCA 2857
			DUKE ELLINGTON/BOSTON POPS/ARTHUR FIEDLER	
6/18/66	62	23	11. The "Pops" Goes Country .... [I]	RCA 2870
			CHET ATKINS/BOSTON POPS/ARTHUR FIEDLER	
10/26/68	157	7	12. Up Up And Away .... [I]	RCA 3041
4/05/69	192	2	13. Glenn Miller's Biggest Hits .... [I]	RCA 3064
10/11/69	160	4	14. Chet Picks On The Pops .... [I]	RCA 3104
			CHET ATKINS/BOSTON POPS/ARTHUR FIEDLER	
1/09/71	190	2	15. Fabulous Broadway .... [I]	Polydor 5003
12/04/71	174	5	16. Arthur Fiedler "Superstar" .... [I]	Polydor 5008
2/26/72	196	3	17. The Music Of Paul Simon .... [I]	Polydor 5018
9/08/79	147	6	18. Saturday Night Fiedler .... [I]	Midsong Int. 011
			BOSTON POPS ORCHESTRA/JOHN WILLIAMS	
			John succeeded Arthur Fiedler as the Boston Pops conductor	
12/20/80	181	6	1. Pops In Space .... [I]	Philips 9500 921
			BOSTON SYMPHONY Orchestra	
5/11/63	17	8	1. Ravel: Bolero/Pavan For A Dead	
			Princess/La Valse .... [I]	RCA 2664
			Charles Munch, conductor	
5/18/63	41	4	2. Mahler: Symphony No. 1 .... [I]	RCA 2642
			Erich Leinsdorf, conductor	
3/28/64	82	12	3. Mozart: Requiem Mass	RCA 7030 [2]
			a Requiem Mass conducted by Erich Leinsdorf in memory of President Kennedy - celebrated by Richard Cardinal Cushing on 1/19/64 in Boston, Massachusetts	
			BOW WOW WOW	
			English: Annabella Lwin + 3 of Adam's original Ants	
11/21/81	192	2	1. See Jungle! See Jungle! Go Join Your	
			Gang Yeah! City All Over, Go Ape	
			Crazy	RCA 4147
5/15/82	67	22	2. The Last Of The Mohicans .... [M]	RCA 4314
9/18/82	123	9	3. I Want Candy	RCA 4375
			cuts from first 2 albums above + 2 new songs	
3/26/83	82	13	4. When The Going Gets Tough, The Tough	
			Get Going	RCA 4570
			DAVID BOWIE	
			born David Jones in London, England on 1/8/47	
4/15/72	93	16	1. Hunky Dory	RCA 4623
6/17/72	75	72	● 2. The Rise And Fall Of Ziggy Stardust And	
			The Spiders From Mars	RCA 4702
11/18/72	16	36	3. Space Oddity [R]	RCA 4813
			1st rock album, recorded in 1968	
11/18/72	105	23	4. The Man Who Sold The World .... [R]	RCA 4816
			2nd rock album, recorded in 1970	

DATE CHARTED	PEAK POS	WKS CHRT'D	ARTIST — Album Title	LABEL & NUMBER
3/17/73	144	9	5. Images 1966-1967 .... [E] 1st recordings in London on Pye and Decca labels	London 628/9 [2]
5/12/73	17	22	● 6. Aladdin Sane	RCA 4852
11/10/73	23	21	7. Bowie Pin Ups .... David's versions of his favorite pop hits from '64-'67	RCA 0291
6/15/74	5	25	● 8. **Diamond Dogs**	RCA 0576
10/26/74	8	21	● 9. **David Live** .... [L] recorded at the Tower Theatre, Philadelphia	RCA 0771 [2]
3/22/75	9	50	● 10. **Young Americans** .... "Fame"(1)	RCA 0998
2/07/76	3	32	● 11. **Station To Station** .... "Golden Years"(10)	RCA 1327
6/19/76	10	39	▲ 12. **Changesonebowie** .... [G]	RCA 1732
1/29/77	11	19	13. Low	RCA 2030
11/12/77	35	19	14. "Heroes"	RCA 2522
5/06/78	136	8	15. David Bowie narrates Prokofiev's "Peter and The Wolf" .... DAVID BOWIE/EUGENE ORMANDY & THE PHILADELPHIA ORCHESTRA	RCA 2743
10/21/78	44	13	16. Stage .... [L]	RCA 2913 [2]
6/16/79	20	15	17. Lodger	RCA 3254
10/04/80	12	27	18. Scary Monsters	RCA 3647
12/12/81	68	18	19. Changestwobowie .... [G]	RCA 4202
4/03/82	135	7	20. Christiane F. .... [S] soundtrack features 9 of David's songs	RCA 4239
4/30/83	4	68	▲ 21. **Let's Dance** .... "Let's Dance"(1)/"China Girl"(10)	EMI America 17093
8/27/83	99	9	22. Golden Years .... [G]	RCA 4792
11/12/83	89	15	23. Ziggy Stardust/The Motion Picture .... [S-L] documentary of David's final tour as his character Ziggy	RCA 4862 [2]
4/21/84	147	6	24. Fame and Fashion (David Bowie's All Time Greatest Hits) .... [G]	RCA 4919
10/20/84	11	24	▲ 25. Tonight .... "Blue Jean"(8)	EMI America 17138

BOX OF FROGS
British quartet - 3 members were original Yardbirds

7/07/84	45	20	1. Box Of Frogs	Epic 39327

BOX TOPS
quintet from Memphis area - Alex Chilton, lead singer

11/18/67	87	15	1. The Letter/Neon Rainbow .... "The Letter"(1)	Bell 6011
4/27/68	59	19	2. Cry Like A Baby .... "Cry Like A Baby"(2)	Bell 6017
12/07/68	45	26	3. The Box Tops Super Hits .... [G]	Bell 6025
9/06/69	77	11	4. Dimensions	Bell 6032

TOMMY BOYCE & BOBBY HART
pop songwriting team

9/09/67	200	1	1. Test Patterns	A&M 4126
4/20/68	109	5	2. I Wonder What She's Doing Tonite? .... "I Wonder What She's Doing Tonite"(8)	A&M 4143

CHARLES BOYER
French romantic actor - died 8/26/78 (78)

1/08/66	148	2	1. Where Does Love Go .... spoken versions of love songs	Valiant 5001

TERENCE BOYLAN

11/05/77	181	3	1. Terence Boylan	Asylum 1091

BRAINSTORM

3/26/77	145	16	1. Stormin'	Tabu 2048

DATE CHARTED	PEAK POS	WKS CHRT'D	ARTIST — Album Title	LABEL & NUMBER
			BRAM TCHAIKOVSKY	
			rock quartet led by Bram (real name Peter Bramall)	
6/30/79	**36**	18	1. Strange Man, Changed Man	Polydor 6211
5/17/80	**108**	10	2. Pressure	Polydor 6273
5/23/81	**158**	8	3. Funland	Arista 4292
			BONNIE BRAMLETT	
			former half of Delaney & Bonnie	
2/22/75	**168**	5	1. It's Time	Capricorn 0148
			BRAND X	
			British jazz-fusion group - Phil Collins (Genesis), drummer	
11/13/76	**191**	3	1. Unorthodox Behaviour .... [I]	Passport 98019
5/21/77	**125**	8	2. Moroccan Roll .... [I]	Passport 98022
11/03/79	**165**	6	3. Product .... [I]	Passport 9840
			LAURA BRANIGAN	
			pop vocalist from upstate New York	
9/25/82	**34**	36	● 1. Branigan	Atlantic 19289
			"Gloria"(2)	
4/09/83	**29**	37	2. Branigan 2	Atlantic 80052
			"Solitaire"(7)	
4/28/84	**23**	45	3. Self Control	Atlantic 80147
			"Self Control"(4)	
			BRASS CONSTRUCTION	
			9-man disco ensemble	
2/07/76	**10**	35	▲ 1. **Brass Construction**	United Art. 545
11/20/76	**26**	22	● 2. Brass Construction II	United Art. 677
11/19/77	**66**	14	● 3. Brass Construction III	United Art. 775
11/18/78	**174**	4	4. Brass Construction IV	United Art. 916
12/15/79	**89**	20	5. Brass Construction 5	United Art. 977
9/20/80	**121**	5	6. Brass Construction 6	United Art. 1060
5/22/82	**114**	8	7. Attitudes	Liberty 51121
6/11/83	**176**	6	8. Conversations	Capitol 12268
			BRASS RING featuring Phil Bodner	
6/25/66	**109**	8	1. Love Theme From The Flight Of The Phoenix .... [I]	Dunhill 50008
4/15/67	**157**	3	2. Sunday Night At The Movies .... [I]	Dunhill 50015
6/24/67	**193**	2	3. The Dis-Advantages Of You .... [I]	Dunhill 50017
			BOB BRAUN	
10/27/62	**99**	6	1. Till Death Do Us Part	Decca 74339
			BRAVE BELT - see BACHMAN-TURNER OVERDRIVE	
			BREAD	
			David Gates, leader - James Griffin, Larry Knechtel, Mike Botts	
10/18/69	**127**	9	1. Bread	Elektra 74044
			"It Don't Matter To Me"(10)	
8/08/70	**12**	32	● 2. On The Waters	Elektra 74076
			"Make It With You"(1)	
3/27/71	**21**	25	● 3. Manna	Elektra 74086
			"If"(4)	
2/05/72	**3**	56	● 4. **Baby I'm-A Want You**	Elektra 75015
			"Baby I'm-A Want You"(3)/"Everything I Own"(5)	
11/18/72	**18**	29	● 5. Guitar Man	Elektra 75047
3/31/73	**2(1)**	119	● 6. **The Best Of Bread** .... [G]	Elektra 75056
6/01/74	**32**	18	● 7. The Best Of Bread, Volume Two .... [G]	Elektra 1005
1/15/77	**26**	16	● 8. Lost Without Your Love	Elektra 1094
			"Lost Without Your Love"(9)	
			BREAKWATER	
4/21/79	**173**	5	1. Breakwater	Arista 4208
6/07/80	**141**	5	2. Splashdown	Arista 4264

DATE CHARTED	PEAK POS	WKS CHRT'D	ARTIST — Album Title	LABEL & NUMBER
			BRECKER BROTHERS	
			Mike & Randy Brecker - session instrumentalists (sax & trumpet) - also see Dreams	
6/07/75	**102**	13	1. The Brecker Brothers .... [I]	Arista 4037
2/28/76	**82**	16	2. Back To Back	Arista 4061
5/07/77	**135**	6	3. Don't Stop The Music .... [I]	Arista 4122
6/20/81	**176**	3	4. Straphangin' .... [I]	Arista 9550
			BEVERLY BREMERS	
9/16/72	**124**	8	1. I'll Make You Music	Scepter 5102
			BRENDA & THE TABULATIONS	
			Philadelphian Brenda Payton & male trio	
7/01/67	**191**	4	1. Dry Your Eyes	Dionn 2000
			WALTER BRENNAN	
			Grandpa of TV series "The Real McCoys" - died on 9/21/74 (80)	
6/23/62	**54**	10	1. Old Rivers	Liberty 3233
			"Old Rivers"(5)	
			BREWER & SHIPLEY	
			Mike Brewer & Tom Shipley	
3/06/71	**34**	26	1. Tarkio	Kama Sutra 2024
			"One Toke Over The Line"(10)	
12/25/71	**164**	8	2. Shake Off The Demon	Kama Sutra 2039
1/27/73	**174**	7	3. Rural Space	Kama Sutra 2058
5/11/74	**185**	5	4. ST-11261	Capitol 11261
			album title refers to the label prefix and number	
			BRICK	
			Atlanta-based disco/jazz quintet	
11/13/76	**19**	24	1. Good High	Bang 408
			"Dazz"(3)	
9/10/77	**15**	32	2. Brick	Bang 409
5/19/79	**100**	8	3. Stoneheart	Bang 35969
7/12/80	**179**	5	4. Waiting On You	Bang 36262
9/05/81	**89**	10	5. Summer Heat	Bang 37471
			BRIDES OF FUNKENSTEIN	
			'P-Funk' recording act	
11/04/78	**70**	13	1. Funk Or Walk	Atlantic 19201
2/16/80	**93**	7	2. Never Buy Texas From A Cowboy	Atlantic 19261
			ALICIA BRIDGES	
9/30/78	**33**	32	1. Alicia Bridges	Polydor 6158
			"I Love The Nightlife"(5)	
			DEE DEE BRIDGEWATER	
5/06/78	**170**	7	1. Just Family	Elektra 119
5/26/79	**182**	4	2. Bad For Me	Elektra 188
			MARTIN BRILEY	
			British	
5/07/83	**55**	22	1. One Night With A Stranger	Mercury 810332
2/09/85	**85**	9 +	2. Dangerous Moments	Mercury 822423
			MARTY BRILL & LARRY FOSTER - see COMEDY section	
			JOHNNY BRISTOL	
8/31/74	**82**	17	1. Hang On In There Baby	MGM 4959
			"Hang On In There Baby"(8)	
12/11/76	**154**	11	2. Bristol's Creme	Atlantic 18197
			BRITISH LIONS	
			re-formed Mott The Hoople alumnus	
4/29/78	**83**	15	1. British Lions	RSO 3032

DATE CHARTED	PEAK POS	WKS CHRT'D	ARTIST — Album Title	LABEL & NUMBER
			BENJAMIN BRITTEN	
			conductor - died on 12/4/76 (63)	
9/07/63	68	8	1. Britten: War Requiem	London 4255 [2]
			with The London Symphony Orchestra	
			DAVID BROMBERG	
			New York session guitarist	
3/25/72	194	2	1. David Bromberg	Columbia 31104
2/23/74	167	5	2. Wanted Dead Or Alive	Columbia 32717
7/12/75	173	3	3. Midnight On The Water	Columbia 33397
10/09/76	104	11	4. How Late'll Ya Play 'Til? .... [L]	Fantasy 79007 [2]
			record 1: studio: record 2: live	
11/19/77	132	9	5. Reckless Abandon	Fantasy 9540
6/17/78	130	9	6. Bandit In A Bathing Suit	Fantasy 9555
2/24/79	152	4	7. My Own House	Fantasy 9572
			BRONSKI BEAT	
			British techno-pop trio - vocals: Jimmy Somerville,	
			synthesizers: Steve Bronski & Larry Steinbachek	
1/19/85	36	12+	1. The Age Of Consent	MCA 5538
			HERMAN BROOD	
5/26/79	122	19	1. Herman Brood & His Wild Romance	Ariola 50059
			BROOKLYN BRIDGE	
			Johnny Maestro (Crests), lead singer - also see Isley Brothers	
3/29/69	54	30	1. Brooklyn Bridge	Buddah 5034
			"Worst That Could Happen"(3)	
10/11/69	145	8	2. The Second Brooklyn Bridge	Buddah 5042
			BROOKLYN, BRONX & QUEENS BAND (B.B.&Q. Band)	
8/29/81	109	9	1. The Brooklyn, Bronx & Queens Band	Capitol 12155
			BROOKLYN DREAMS	
			Joe "Bean" Esposito, lead singer	
3/24/79	151	7	1. Sleepless Nights	Casablanca 7135
			MEL BROOKS - see CARL REINER	
			BROTHERHOOD OF MAN	
			British - a Tony Hiller production	
8/08/70	168	8	1. United We Stand	Deram 18046
			BROTHERS FOUR	
			Dick Foley, Bob Flick, John Paine, Mike Kirkland -	
			fraternity brothers at the University of Washington	
4/18/60	11	19	1. The Brothers Four	Columbia 1402
			"Greenfields"(2)	
2/13/61	4	35	2. B.M.O.C. (Best Music On/Off Campus)	Columbia 1578
12/18/61	71	14	3. The Brothers Four Song Book	Columbia 1697
10/06/62	102	4	4. The Brothers Four: In Person .... [L]	Columbia 1828
5/04/63	81	12	5. Cross-Country Concert .... [L]	Columbia 1946
10/12/63	56	20	6. The Big Folk Hits	Columbia 8833
10/31/64	134	4	7. More Big Folk Hits	Columbia 9013
5/01/65	118	5	8. The Honey Wind Blows	Columbia 9105
11/13/65	76	15	9. Try To Remember	Columbia 9179
7/30/66	97	7	10. A Beatles' Songbook (The Brothers Four	
			sing Lennon/McCartney)	Columbia 9302
			BROTHERS JOHNSON	
			funk guitarists George & Louis Johnson	
3/06/76	9	49	▲ 1. **Look Out For #1**	A&M 4567
			"I'll Be Good To You"(3)	
5/21/77	13	31	▲ 2. Right On Time	A&M 4644
			"Strawberry Letter 23"(5)	
8/12/78	7	24	▲ 3. **Blam!!**	A&M 4714

DATE CHARTED	PEAK POS	WKS CHRT'D	ARTIST — Album Title	LABEL & NUMBER
3/08/80	5	30	▲ 4. **Light Up The Night** .... "Stomp!"(7)	A&M 3716
7/18/81	48	13	5. Winners	A&M 3724
1/22/83	138	5	6. Blast! (The Latest And The Greatest)........ [G] side 2: greatest hits	A&M 4927
8/04/84	91	11	7. Out Of Control	A&M 4965

ARTHUR BROWN
British

9/07/68	7	24	1. **The Crazy World Of Arthur Brown** .... "Fire"(2)	Track 8198

CHUCK BROWN & The Soul Searchers

2/17/79	31	14	● 1. Bustin' Loose	Source 3076

DANNY JOE BROWN
lead singer of Molly Hatchet

7/04/81	120	7	1. Danny Joe Brown & The Danny Joe Brown Band	Epic 37385

JAMES BROWN
Black music's all-time #1 artist - born on 5/3/33 near Augusta, Georgia

6/29/63	2(2)	66	1. **Live At The Apollo** .... [L] recorded at the Apollo Theater, New York City, 10/24/62	King 826
9/28/63	73	17	2. Prisoner Of Love	King 851
2/29/64	10	22	3. **Pure Dynamite! Live At The Royal** .... [L] recorded at the Royal Theater, Baltimore, Maryland	King 883
5/09/64	61	18	4. Showtime .... [L]	Smash 67054
4/10/65	124	10	5. Grits & Soul .... [I]	Smash 67057
9/11/65	26	27	6. Papa's Got A Brand New Bag .... "Papa's Got A Brand New Bag"(8)	King 938
11/20/65	42	19	7. James Brown Plays James Brown - Today & Yesterday .... [I]	Smash 67072
1/22/66	36	17	8. I Got You (I Feel Good) .... "I Got You (I Feel Good)"(3)	King 946
4/16/66	101	11	9. James Brown Plays New Breed .... [I]	Smash 67080
9/10/66	90	9	10. It's A Man's Man's Man's World .... "It's A Man's Man's Man's World"(8)	King 985
12/03/66	135	3	11. Handful Of Soul .... [I]	Smash 67084
4/08/67	88	14	12. Raw Soul	King 1016
6/10/67	41	17	13. Live At The Garden .... [L]	King 1018
7/15/67	164	5	14. James Brown Plays The Real Thing .... [I]	Smash 67093
9/16/67	35	17	15. Cold Sweat .... "Cold Sweat"(7)	King 1020
3/23/68	17	14	16. I Can't Stand Myself (When You Touch Me)	King 1030
5/18/68	135	14	17. I Got The Feelin' .... "I Got The Feelin'"(6)	King 1031
8/24/68	150	5	18. James Brown Plays Nothing But Soul .... [I]	King 1034
9/07/68	32	39	19. Live At The Apollo, Volume II .... [L]	King 1022 [2]
4/12/69	53	22	20. Say It Loud-I'm Black And I'm Proud .... "Say It Loud-I'm Black And I'm Proud"(10)	King 1047
5/31/69	99	14	21. Gettin' Down To It	King 1051
8/23/69	40	13	22. James Brown plays & directs The Popcorn .... [I]	King 1055
9/06/69	26	22	23. It's A Mother	King 1063
2/14/70	43	12	24. Ain't It Funky .... [I]	King 1092
5/16/70	125	10	25. Soul On Top .... with the Louie Bellson Orchestra	King 1100
7/04/70	121	6	26. It's A New Day So Let A Man Come In	King 1095
9/12/70	29	31	27. Sex Machine .... [L]	King 1115 [2]
1/30/71	61	15	28. Super Bad .... [L]	King 1127

DATE CHARTED	PEAK POS	WKS CHRT'D	ARTIST — Album Title	LABEL & NUMBER
5/01/71	137	4	29. Sho Is Funky Down Here .... [I]	King 1110
9/04/71	22	18	30. Hot Pants	Polydor 4054
12/25/71	39	21	31. Revolution Of The Mind - Live At The Apollo, Volume III .... [L]	Polydor 3003 [2]
6/17/72	83	16	32. James Brown Soul Classics .... [G]	Polydor 5401
7/08/72	60	21	33. There It Is	Polydor 5028
12/09/72	68	17	34. Get On The Good Foot	Polydor 3004 [2]
3/03/73	31	21	35. Black Caesar .... [S]	Polydor 6014
7/28/73	92	11	36. Slaughter's Big Rip-Off .... [S]	Polydor 6015
1/05/74	34	36	● 37. The Payback	Polydor 3007 [2]
7/27/74	35	19	38. Hell	Polydor 9001 [2]
1/25/75	56	10	39. Reality	Polydor 6039
5/24/75	103	8	40. Sex Machine Today	Polydor 6042
10/04/75	193	2	41. Everybody's Doin' The Hustle & Dead On The Double Bump	Polydor 6054
8/14/76	147	8	42. Get Up Offa That Thing	Polydor 6071
1/15/77	126	10	43. Bodyheat	Polydor 6093
5/06/78	121	22	44. Jam/1980's	Polydor 6140
8/11/79	152	6	45. The Original Disco Man	Polydor 6212
8/16/80	170	5	46. James Brown...Live/Hot On The One .... [L] recorded in Tokyo, Japan	Polydor 6290 [2]
11/22/80	163	3	47. Live And Lowdown At The Apollo, Vol. 1 .... [R] reissue of album #1 above	Solid Smoke 8006

JIM ED BROWN
leader of The Browns - host of Nashville Network's TV talent show "You can be a Star!"

2/06/71	81	9	1. Morning	RCA 4461

JULIE BROWN
2/02/85	168	7	1. Goddess In Progress .... [N-M]	Rhino 610

LES BROWN & His Band of Renown
worked with Bob Hope for over two decades

2/19/55	15	1	1. Concert At The Palladium .... [I-L] recorded at the Hollywood Palladium, September 1953	Coral CX-1 [2]

MAXINE BROWN
11/29/69	195	2	1. We'll Cry Together	Commonwlth 6001

ODELL BROWN & The Organ-Izers
jazz quartet

9/09/67	173	4	1. Mellow Yellow .... [I]	Cadet 788

PETER BROWN
1/14/78	11	44	1. A Fantasy Love Affair .... "Dance With Me"(8)	Drive 104

SHIRLEY BROWN
1/25/75	98	11	1. Woman To Woman	Truth 4206

DUNCAN BROWNE
5/19/79	174	5	1. The Wild Places	Sire 6065

JACKSON BROWNE
born in West Germany on 10/9/48

3/18/72	53	23	● 1. Jackson Browne .... "Doctor My Eyes"(8)	Asylum 5051
11/10/73	43	38	● 2. For Everyman	Asylum 5067
10/12/74	14	29	● 3. Late For The Sky	Asylum 1017
11/20/76	5	35	▲ 4. The Pretender	Asylum 1079
1/07/78	3	65	▲ 5. Running On Empty	Asylum 113
7/19/80	1(1)	38	▲ 6. Hold Out	Asylum 511
8/20/83	8	33	● 7. Lawyers In Love	Asylum 60268

DATE CHARTED	PEAK POS	WKS CHRT'D	ARTIST — Album Title	LABEL & NUMBER
			TOM BROWNE jazz/funk trumpet player	
8/11/79	**147**	6	1. Browne Sugar .... [I]	GRP 5003
7/26/80	**18**	26	● 2. Love Approach .... [I]	GRP 5008
2/21/81	**37**	19	3. Magic	GRP 5503
12/12/81	**97**	14	4. Yours Truly	GRP 5507
12/03/83	**147**	12	5. Rockin' Radio .... [I]	Arista 8107
			BROWNSVILLE STATION Ann Arbor, Michigan trio led by Michael Lutz	
10/07/72	**191**	5	1. A Night On The Town	Big Tree 2010
9/15/73	**98**	19	2. Yeah! .... "Smokin' In The Boy's Room"(3)	Big Tree 2102
6/15/74	**170**	8	3. School Punks	Big Tree 89500
			DAVE BRUBECK Quartet jazz quartet featuring Dave (piano) & Paul Desmond (alto sax)	
2/05/55	**8**	3	1. **Dave Brubeck At Storyville: 1954** .... [I-L]	Columbia 590
3/19/55	**5**	22	2. **Brubeck Time** .... [I]	Columbia 622
11/12/55	**7**	3	3. **Jazz: Red Hot And Cool** .... [I-L]	Columbia 699
7/08/57	**18**	1	4. Jazz Impressions of the U.S.A. .... [I]	Columbia 984
9/30/57	**24**	1	5. Jazz Goes To Junior College .... [I-L]	Columbia 1034
11/28/60	**2(1)**	164	● 6. **Time Out Featuring "Take Five"** .... [I]	Columbia 8192
12/12/60	**13**	7	7. Berstein Plays Brubeck Plays Bernstein .... [I] side 1: New York Philharmonic with Dave Brubeck Quartet conducted by Leonard Bernstein; side 2: Dave Brubeck Quartet	Columbia 8257
12/25/61	**8**	46	8. **Time Further Out** .... [I]	Columbia 8490
6/16/62	**24**	21	9. Countdown - Time In Outer Space .... [I]	Columbia 8575
3/16/63	**14**	15	10. Bossa Nova U.S.A. .... [I]	Columbia 8798
7/27/63	**37**	4	11. The Dave Brubeck Quartet At Carnegie Hall .... [I-L]	Columbia 826 [2]
12/21/63	**137**	3	12. Brandenburg Gate: Revisited .... [I] with Orchestra	Columbia 8763
4/18/64	**81**	9	13. Time Changes .... [I]	Columbia 8927
2/27/65	**142**	4	14. Jazz Impressions Of New York .... [I]	Columbia 9075
10/09/65	**122**	3	15. Angel Eyes .... [I]	Columbia 9148
3/26/66	**133**	5	16. My Favorite Things .... [I]	Columbia 9237
7/30/66	**104**	4	17. Dave Brubeck's Greatest Hits .... [G-I]	Columbia 9284
1/10/76	**167**	5	18. 1975: The Duets .... [I] DAVE BRUBECK & PAUL DESMOND	Horizon 703
			JACK BRUCE Scottish - bass player with Cream - also see West, Bruce & Laing	
10/25/69	**55**	11	1. Songs For A Tailor	Atco 306
12/07/74	**160**	3	2. Out Of The Storm	RSO 4805
5/07/77	**153**	5	3. How's Tricks .... JACK BRUCE BAND	RSO 3021

12/13/80	**182**	2	4. I've Always Wanted To Do This ....
			    JACK BRUCE & FRIENDS
			    friends: Clem Clempson, Billy Cobham, David Sancious
				Epic 36827

1/30/82	**109**	6	5. Truce .... JACK BRUCE/ROBIN TROWER	Chrysalis 1352
			LENNY BRUCE satirical comedian - died 8/3/66 - also see Soundtrack "Lenny"	
3/15/75	**178**	2	1. Lenny Bruce/Carnegie Hall .... [C] the complete show - recorded on 2/4/61	Unit. Art. 9800 [3]
4/05/75	**191**	2	2. The Real Lenny Bruce .... [R-C] recorded 1958-1959	Fant. 79003 [2]

DATE CHARTED	PEAK POS	WKS CHRT'D	ARTIST — Album Title	LABEL & NUMBER
			BILL BRUFORD percussionist with Yes, King Crimson & Genesis	
7/07/79	**123**	5	1. One Of A Kind .... [I]	Polydor 6205
3/29/80	**191**	2	2. Gradually Going Tornado	Polydor 6261
			ANITA BRYANT 2nd runner-up to Miss America in 1958	
9/15/62	**145**	2	1. In A Velvet Mood	Columbia 8685
1/21/67	**146**	4	2. Mine Eyes Have Seen The Glory	Columbia 9373
			RAY BRYANT jazz pianist	
6/25/66	**111**	12	1. Gotta Travel On .... [I]	Cadet 767
5/13/67	**193**	3	2. Slow Freight .... [I]	Cadet 781
			PEABO BRYSON soul ballad singer from South Carolina	
3/11/78	**49**	29	● 1. Reaching For The Sky	Capitol 11729
12/09/78	**35**	26	● 2. Crosswinds	Capitol 11875
12/15/79	**44**	19	3. We're The Best Of Friends .... NATALIE COLE/PEABO BRYSON	Capitol 12019
5/03/80	**79**	16	4. Paradise	Capitol 12063
12/20/80	**52**	19	5. Live & More .... [L] ROBERTA FLACK & PEABO BRYSON	Atlantic 7004 [2]
2/28/81	**82**	11	6. Turn The Hands Of Time	Capitol 12138
11/28/81	**40**	24	7. I Am Love	Capitol 12179
12/04/82	**55**	21	8. Don't Play With Fire	Capitol 12241
8/13/83	**25**	42	● 9. Born To Love .... PEABO BRYSON/ROBERTA FLACK	Capitol 12284
6/16/84	**44**	26	10. Straight From The Heart .... "If Ever You're In My Arms Again"(10)	Elektra 60362
7/14/84	**168**	10	11. The Peabo Bryson Collection .... [G] side 2: duets with Roberta Flack and Natalie Cole	Capitol 12348
			B.T. EXPRESS Brooklyn, New York disco ensemble	
11/23/74	**5**	31	● 1. **Do It ('Til You're Satisfied)** .... "Do It ('Til You're Satisfied)"(2)/"Express"(4)	Roadshow 5117
8/02/75	**19**	19	2. Non-Stop	Roadshow 41001
5/29/76	**43**	12	3. Energy To Burn	Columbia 34178
5/28/77	**111**	5	4. Function at the Junction	Columbia 34702
2/25/78	**67**	11	5. Shout!	Columbia 35078
5/31/80	**164**	4	6. B.T. Express 1980	Columbia 36333
			BUBBLE PUPPY psychedelic rock band from Austin, Texas	
5/17/69	**176**	6	1. A Gathering Of Promises .... "Hot Smoke & Sasafrass"	Int'l. Artists 10
			BUCHANAN & GOODMAN - see DICKIE GOODMAN	
			ROY BUCHANAN rock guitarist	
9/09/72	**107**	12	1. Roy Buchanan	Polydor 5033
3/10/73	**86**	13	2. Second Album .... [I]	Polydor 5046
2/23/74	**152**	10	3. That's What I Am Here For	Polydor 6020
12/28/74	**160**	6	4. In The Beginning	Polydor 6035
5/15/76	**148**	7	5. A Street Called Straight	Atlantic 18170
6/18/77	**105**	8	6. Loading Zone .... [I]	Atlantic 18219
5/20/78	**119**	7	7. You're Not Alone .... [I]	Atlantic 19170
1/24/81	**193**	2	8. My Babe	Waterhouse 12

DATE CHARTED	PEAK POS	WKS CHRT'D	ARTIST — Album Title	LABEL & NUMBER
			LINDSEY BUCKINGHAM member of Fleetwood Mac	
11/07/81	**32**	24	1. Law And Order .... "Trouble"(9)	Asylum 561
9/01/84	**45**	16	2. Go Insane	Elektra 60363
			BUCKINGHAMS Chicago quintet led by Dennis Tufano & Carl Giammarese	
3/25/67	**109**	8	1. Kind Of A Drag .... "Kind Of A Drag"(1)	U.S.A. 107
6/10/67	**58**	23	2. Time & Charges .... "Don't You Care"(6)/"Mercy, Mercy, Mercy"(5)	Columbia 9469
2/10/68	**53**	16	3. Portraits	Columbia 9598
9/21/68	**161**	5	4. In One Ear And Gone Tomorrow	Columbia 9703
5/17/69	**73**	12	5. The Buckinghams' Greatest Hits .... [G]	Columbia 9812
			TIM BUCKLEY died 6/29/75 (28)	
11/04/67	**171**	5	1. Goodbye And Hello	Elektra 7318
4/19/69	**81**	12	2. Happy Sad	Elektra 74045
2/07/70	**192**	2	3. Blue Afternoon	Straight 1060
			BUCKNER & GARCIA Jerry Buckner & Gary Garcia	
3/13/82	**24**	16	● 1. Pac-Man Fever .... [N] album inspired by popular video games "Pac-Man Fever"(9)	Columbia 37941
			BUCKWHEAT	
4/01/72	**179**	6	1. Movin' On	London 609
			BUD & TRAVIS balladeers Bud Dashiel & Travis Edmonson	
11/09/63	**126**	4	1. Bud & Travis...In Concert .... [L] recorded 3/24/60 at Santa Monica's Civic Auditorium	Liberty 11001 [2]
3/28/64	**129**	6	2. Perspective on Bud & Travis	Liberty 7341
			BUFFALO SPRINGFIELD Stephen Stills, Neil Young, Richie Furay, Dewey Martin and Bruce Palmer (replaced Jim Messina)	
3/25/67	**80**	16	1. Buffalo Springfield .... "For What It's Worth"(7)	Atco 200
11/18/67	**44**	14	2. Buffalo Springfield Again	Atco 226
8/17/68	**42**	19	3. Last Time Around	Atco 256
3/01/69	**42**	24	4. Retrospective/The Best Of Buffalo Springfield .... [G]	Atco 283
12/08/73	**104**	13	5. Buffalo Springfield .... [K]	Atco 806 [2]
			JIMMY BUFFETT backed by The Coral Reefer Band	
3/02/74	**176**	13	1. Living and Dying in 3/4 Time	Dunhill 50132
2/08/75	**25**	27	2. A1A .... A1A: beach access road off U.S. 1 in Florida	Dunhill 50183
2/14/76	**65**	14	3. Havana Daydreamin'	ABC 914
2/12/77	**12**	42	▲ 4. Changes In Latitudes, Changes In Attitudes .... "Margaritaville"(8)	ABC 990
4/08/78	**10**	29	▲ 5. **Son Of A Son Of A Sailor**	ABC 1046
11/11/78	**72**	18	● 6. You Had To Be There .... [L]	ABC 1008 [2]
9/15/79	**14**	28	● 7. Volcano	MCA 5102
2/21/81	**30**	18	8. Coconut Telegraph	MCA 5169
1/23/82	**31**	15	9. Somewhere Over China	MCA 5285
10/08/83	**59**	24	10. One Particular Harbour	MCA 5447
9/29/84	**87**	14	11. Riddles In The Sand	MCA 5512

DATE CHARTED	PEAK POS	WKS CHRT'D	ARTIST — Album Title	LABEL & NUMBER
			BUGGLES British - Geoff Downes & Trevor Horne joined "Yes" in 1980	
3/27/82	161	5	1. Adventures In Modern Recording	Carrere 37926
			BULLDOG Gene Cornish & Dino Danelli were members of The Rascals and Fotomaker	
11/18/72	176	11	1. Bulldog	Decca 75370
			VICTOR BUONO character actor - died on 1/1/82 (43)	
9/18/71	66	17	1. Heavy! .... [C]	Dore 325
			ERIC BURDON lead singer of The Animals	
			ERIC BURDON & WAR:	
5/16/70	18	27	1. Eric Burdon Declares "War"	MGM 4663
			"Spill The Wine"(3)	
12/26/70	82	9	2. The Black-Man's Burdon	MGM 4710 [2]
			THE ERIC BURDON BAND:	
12/21/74	51	16	3. Sun Secrets	Capitol 11359
8/09/75	171	5	4. Stop	Capitol 11426
			WAR featuring ERIC BURDON:	
12/25/76	140	5	5. Love Is All Around .... [E] recorded 1969-70	ABC 988
			SOLOMON BURKE soul singer from Philadelphia	
7/31/65	141	3	1. The Best Of Solomon Burke .... [G]	Atlantic 8109
7/05/69	140	4	2. Proud Mary	Bell 6033
			CAROL BURNETT star of TV show 1967-1978 - also see Julie Andrews	
1/29/72	199	2	1. Carol Burnett featuring If I Could Write A Song	Columbia 31048
			T-BONE BURNETT native of Fort Worth, Texas	
10/01/83	188	5	1. Proof Through The Night	Warner 23921
			ROCKY BURNETTE Johnny Burnette's son	
6/21/80	53	14	1. The Son Of Rock And Roll .... "Tired Of Toein' The Line"(8)	EMI America 17033
			BURNING SENSATIONS led by former Motels guitarist Tim McGovern	
7/30/83	175	4	1. Burning Sensations .... [M]	Capitol 15009
			GEORGE BURNS TV and film star born in 1896	
2/09/80	93	10	1. I Wish I Was Eighteen Again	Mercury 5025
			KENNY BURRELL jazz guitarist - also see Jimmy Smith/Kai Winding	
11/30/63	108	4	1. Blue Bash! .... [I] KENNY BURRELL/JIMMY SMITH	Verve 8553
12/17/66	146	2	2. The Tender Gender .... [I]	Cadet 772
8/31/68	191	2	3. Blues-The Common Ground .... [I]	Verve 8746
			JENNY BURTON New Yorker	
3/24/84	181	4	1. In Black And White	Atlantic 80122
			BUS BOYS appeared in the film "48 HRS."	
11/29/80	85	15	1. Minimum Wage Rock & Roll	Arista 4280
8/21/82	139	7	2. American Worker	Arista 9569

DATE CHARTED	PEAK POS	WKS CHRT'D	ARTIST — Album Title	LABEL & NUMBER
			KATE BUSH English	
11/13/82	157	11	1. The Dreaming	EMI America 17084
7/09/83	148	6	2. Kate Bush .... [M]	EMI America 19004
			JOE BUSHKIN [his piano and orchestra]	
5/26/56	14	1	1. Midnight Rhapsody .... [I]	Capitol 711
			JON BUTCHER Axis	
3/26/83	91	13	1. Jon Butcher Axis	Polydor 810059
3/31/84	160	6	2. Stare At The Sun	Polydor 817493
			CARL BUTLER country singer	
4/27/63	104	9	1. Don't Let Me Cross Over	Columbia 2002
			JERRY BUTLER Chicago-bred soul singer born on 12/8/39	
10/03/64	102	11	1. Delicious Together .... BETTY EVERETT & JERRY BUTLER "Let It Be Me"(5)	Vee-Jay 1099
1/20/68	154	7	2. Mr. Dream Merchant	Mercury 61146
3/16/68	178	2	3. Jerry Butler's Golden Hits Live .... [L]	Mercury 61151
7/27/68	195	2	4. The Soul Goes On	Mercury 61171
1/04/69	29	47	5. The Ice Man Cometh .... "Only The Strong Survive"(4)	Mercury 61198
10/04/69	41	23	6. Ice On Ice	Mercury 61234
6/27/70	167	5	7. The Best Of Jerry Butler .... [G]	Mercury 61281
7/11/70	172	4	8. You & Me	Mercury 61269
2/06/71	186	4	9. Jerry Butler Sings Assorted Sounds	Mercury 61320
3/27/71	143	5	10. Gene & Jerry - One & One .... GENE CHANDLER & JERRY BUTLER	Mercury 61330
10/02/71	123	22	11. The Sagittarius Movement	Mercury 61347
6/17/72	92	24	12. The Spice Of Life	Mercury 7502 [2]
2/05/77	199	2	13. The Vintage Years .... [G] featuring 13 hits by Jerry Butler and 13 by The Impressions "He Will Break Your Heart"(7-'60)	Sire 3717 [2]
3/12/77	146	11	14. Suite For The Single Girl	Motown 878
6/18/77	53	12	15. Thelma & Jerry .... THELMA HOUSTON & JERRY BUTLER	Motown 887
1/13/79	160	4	16. Nothing Says I Love You Like I Love You	Phil. Int. 35510
			BILLY BUTTERFIELD - see RAY CONNIFF	
			PAUL BUTTERFIELD Chicago bluesman with guitarists Mike Bloomfield (1-2) & Elvin Bishop (1-4)	
			THE PAUL BUTTERFIELD BLUES BAND:	
12/04/65	123	9	1. The Paul Butterfield Blues Band	Elektra 7294
10/08/66	65	29	2. East-West	Elektra 7315
1/13/68	52	16	3. The Resurrection Of Pigboy Crabshaw .... Pigboy Crabshaw: Elvin Bishop	Elektra 74015
8/24/68	79	17	4. In My Own Dream	Elektra 74025
11/01/69	102	10	5. Keep On Moving	Elektra 74053
1/16/71	72	12	6. The Butterfield Blues Band/Live .... [L]	Elektra 2001 [2]
9/04/71	124	6	7. Sometimes I Just Feel Like Smilin'	Elektra 75013
5/20/72	136	6	8. Golden Butter/The Best Of The Paul Butterfield Blues Band .... [G]	Elektra 2005 [2]
			PAUL BUTTERFIELD'S BETTER DAYS:	
2/03/73	145	13	9. Better Days	Bearsville 2119
11/03/73	156	8	10. It All Comes Back	Bearsville 2170

DATE CHARTED	PEAK POS	WKS CHRT'D	ARTIST — Album Title	LABEL & NUMBER
			BUZZCOCKS British quartet led by Peter Shelley	
2/23/80	**163**	6	1. A Different Kind Of Tension	I.R.S. 009
			CHARLIE BYRD jazz guitarist	
9/15/62	**1(1)**	70	1. **Jazz Samba** .... [I] STAN GETZ/CHARLIE BYRD	Verve 8432
3/23/63	**128**	5	2. Bossa Nova Pelos Passaros .... [I] Pelos Passaros: "By The Birds"	Riverside 9436
6/28/69	**197**	4	3. Aquarius .... [I]	Columbia 9841
9/06/69	**129**	4	4. Let Go .... [I-L]	Columbia 9869
			DONALD BYRD jazz-fusion trumpeter - founder of the Blackbyrds	
7/11/64	**110**	8	1. A New Perspective .... [I] with Herbie Hancock (piano) & Kenny Burrell (guitar)	Blue Note 84124
4/28/73	**36**	34	2. Black Byrd	Blue Note 047
3/30/74	**33**	28	3. Street Lady .... [I]	Blue Note 140
3/29/75	**42**	19	4. Stepping Into Tomorrow .... [I]	Blue Note 368
11/15/75	**49**	29	5. Places And Spaces	Blue Note 549
12/18/76	**167**	4	6. Donald Byrd's Best .... [G]	Blue Note 700
2/12/77	**60**	14	7. Caricatures	Blue Note 633
11/18/78	**191**	4	8. Thank You...For F.U.M.L. (Funking Up My Life)	Elektra 144
10/03/81	**93**	10	9. Love Byrd .... with "125th Street, N.Y.C." and Isaac Hayes	Elektra 531
			BYRDS original Los Angeles-based folk/rock group: Roger McGuinn, Gene Clark, Chris Hillman, Mike Clarke and David Crosby	
6/26/65	**6**	38	1. **Mr. Tambourine Man** .... "Mr. Tambourine Man"(1)	Columbia 9172
1/01/66	**17**	40	2. Turn! Turn! Turn! .... "Turn! Turn! Turn!"(1)	Columbia 9254
8/27/66	**24**	28	3. Fifth Dimension	Columbia 9349
3/18/67	**24**	24	4. Younger Than Yesterday	Columbia 9442
9/02/67	**6**	29	● 5. **The Byrds' Greatest Hits** .... [G]	Columbia 9516
2/03/68	**47**	19	6. The Notorious Byrd Brothers	Columbia 9575
8/31/68	**77**	10	7. Sweetheart Of The Rodeo	Columbia 9670
3/15/69	**153**	7	8. Dr. Byrds & Mr. Hyde	Columbia 9755
9/06/69	**84**	12	9. Preflyte .... [E] recorded in 1964	Together 1001
12/13/69	**36**	17	10. Ballad Of Easy Rider	Columbia 9942
10/17/70	**40**	21	11. The Byrds (Untitled)	Columbia 30127 [2]
7/24/71	**46**	10	12. Byrdmaniax	Columbia 30640
12/25/71	**152**	7	13. Farther Along	Columbia 31050
12/16/72	**114**	13	14. The Best Of The Byrds (Greatest Hits, Volume II) .... [G]	Columbia 31795
3/24/73	**20**	17	15. Byrds .... reunion of original 5 Byrds	Asylum 5058
9/08/73	**183**	3	16. Preflyte .... [R] reissue of album #9 above	Columbia 32183
			DAVID BYRNE leader of the Talking Heads - also see Brian Eno	
12/19/81	**104**	12	1. The Catherine Wheel .... [OC]	Sire 3645
			D.L. BYRON	
2/16/80	**133**	10	1. This Day And Age	Arista 4258

DATE CHARTED	PEAK POS	WKS CHRT'D	ARTIST — Album Title	LABEL & NUMBER
			CACTUS U.S. group formed by Tim Bogert & Carmine Appice (Vanilla Fudge)	
7/25/70	**54**	18	1. Cactus	Atco 340
3/20/71	**88**	13	2. One Way...Or Another	Atco 356
11/27/71	**155**	10	3. Restrictions	Atco 377
10/28/72	**162**	5	4. 'Ot 'N' Sweaty .... [L] side 1 recorded live at the Mar Y Sol Festival in Puerto Rico	Atco 7011
5/12/73	**183**	6	5. Son Of Cactus .... NEW CACTUS BAND - Mike Pinera, leader	Atco 7017
			JOHN CAFFERTY & THE BEAVER BROWN BAND rock sextet from Rhode Island	
10/15/83	**9**	48+▲	1. **Eddie And The Cruisers** .... [S] "On The Dark Side"(7)/"Tender Years"	Scotti Br. 38929
			TANE CAIN wife of Journey's Jonathan Cain	
9/11/82	**121**	10	1. Tane Cain	RCA 4381
			CALDERA progressive latin jazz group	
10/01/77	**159**	4	1. Sky Islands .... [I]	Capitol 11658
			BOBBY CALDWELL formerly with Johnny Winter, Captain Beyond and Armageddon	
11/18/78	**21**	31	1. Bobby Caldwell .... "What You Won't Do For Love"(9)	Clouds 8804
3/29/80	**113**	15	2. Cat In The Hat	Clouds 8810
4/17/82	**133**	13	3. Carry On	Polydor 6347
			J.J. CALE laid-back rock singer/songwriter	
1/22/72	**51**	32	1. Naturally	Shelter 8098
12/30/72	**92**	11	2. Really	Shelter 8912
6/15/74	**128**	11	3. Okie	Shelter 2107
9/25/76	**84**	18	4. Troubadour	Shelter 52002
9/08/79	**136**	9	5. 5	Shelter 3163
2/28/81	**110**	7	6. Shades	MCA 5158
4/03/82	**149**	8	7. Grasshopper	Mercury 4038
			JOHN CALE Welsh - original member of Velvet Underground	
4/11/81	**154**	5	1. Honi Soit (o nee swa)	A&M 4849
			CALL California-based quartet - Michael Been, lead vocals	
3/26/83	**84**	15	1. Modern Romans	Mercury 810307
			MARIA CALLAS operatic soprano	
2/27/65	**87**	8	1. Bizet: Carmen	Angel 3650 [3]
			CAMARATA - see SOUNDTRACK "Parent Trap!"	
			GODFREY CAMBRIDGE comedian - died 11/29/76 (43)	
7/11/64	**42**	13	1. Ready Or Not...Here's Godfrey Cambridge .... [C]	Epic 13101
4/03/65	**142**	9	2. Them Cotton Pickin' Days Is Over .... [C]	Epic 13102
			CAMEL British band led by Peter Bardens	
11/30/74	**149**	13	1. Mirage	Janus 7009
7/19/75	**162**	5	2. The Snow Goose .... [I]	Janus 7016
5/22/76	**123**	13	3. Moonmadness	Janus 7024

DATE CHARTED	PEAK POS	WKS CHRT'D	ARTIST — Album Title	LABEL & NUMBER
11/12/77	136	5	4. Rain Dances	Janus 7035
2/10/79	134	10	5. Breathless	Arista 4206
			CAMEO New York City soul/funk group led by Larry Blackmon	
8/20/77	116	15	1. Cardiac Arrest	Choc. City 2003
2/18/78	58	23	2. We All Know Who We Are	Choc. City 2004
11/04/78	83	15	3. Ugly Ego	Choc. City 2006
7/28/79	46	21	● 4. Secret Omen	Choc. City 2008
5/24/80	25	26	● 5. Cameosis	Choc. City 2011
12/06/80	44	17	● 6. Feel Me	Choc. City 2016
6/20/81	44	13	● 7. Knights Of The Sound Table	Choc. City 2019
4/10/82	23	24	● 8. Alligator Woman	Choc. City 2021
5/07/83	53	12	9. Style	Atlanta A. 811072
3/17/84	27	24	● 10. She's Strange	Atlanta A. 814984
			RAFAEL CAMERON native of Guyana	
8/02/80	67	18	1. Cameron	Salsoul 8535
7/18/81	101	12	2. Cameron's In Love	Salsoul 8542
			GLEN CAMPBELL born in Arkansas on 3/22/36 - also see the Folkswingers	
12/02/67	5	75	● 1. **Gentle On My Mind**	Capitol 2809
12/30/67	15	80	● 2. By The Time I Get To Phoenix	Capitol 2851
4/06/68	26	51	● 3. Hey, Little One	Capitol 2878
6/22/68	24	33	4. A New Place In The Sun	Capitol 2907
10/12/68	11	47	● 5. Bobbie Gentry & Glen Campbell	Capitol 2928
11/16/68	1(5)	46	● 6. **Wichita Lineman** "Wichita Lineman"(3)	Capitol 103
4/12/69	2(1)	42	● 7. **Galveston** "Galveston"(4)	Capitol 210
9/20/69	13	29	● 8. Glen Campbell - "Live" .... [L]	Capitol 0268 [2]
2/07/70	12	28	● 9. Try A Little Kindness	Capitol 389
5/23/70	38	19	10. Oh Happy Day inspirational songs	Capitol 443
6/27/70	90	13	11. Norwood .... [S]	Capitol 475
10/03/70	27	21	12. The Glen Campbell Goodtime Album "It's Only Make Believe"(10)	Capitol 493
4/17/71	39	27	● 13. Glen Campbell's Greatest Hits .... [G]	Capitol 752
8/07/71	87	9	14. The Last Time I Saw Her	Capitol 733
12/11/71	128	8	15. Anne Murray/Glen Campbell	Capitol 869
11/25/72	148	13	16. Glen Travis Campbell	Capitol 11117
6/09/73	154	6	17. I Knew Jesus (Before He Was a Star)	Capitol 11185
11/16/74	166	5	18. Reunion (the songs of Jimmy Webb)	Capitol 11336
8/09/75	17	30	● 19. Rhinestone Cowboy "Rhinestone Cowboy"(1)	Capitol 11430
5/01/76	63	9	20. Bloodline	Capitol 11516
11/27/76	116	6	21. The Best Of Glen Campbell .... [G]	Capitol 11577
3/19/77	22	22	● 22. Southern Nights "Southern Nights"(1)	Capitol 11601
1/07/78	171	5	23. Live At The Royal Festival Hall .... [L] with the Royal Philharmonic Orchestra	Capitol 11707 [2]
12/16/78	164	5	24. Basic	Capitol 11722
2/28/81	178	3	25. It's The World Gone Crazy	Capitol 12124
			CANDYMEN Roy Orbison's former backup band	
11/11/67	195	4	1. The Candymen	ABC 616

DATE CHARTED	PEAK POS	WKS CHRT'D	ARTIST — Album Title	LABEL & NUMBER
			CANNED HEAT Los Angeles group formed by Bob "The Bear" Hite (died 4/6/81-36)	
8/12/67	**76**	23	1. Canned Heat	Liberty 7526
2/24/68	**16**	52	2. Boogie With Canned Heat .... "On The Road Again"	Liberty 7541
12/07/68	**18**	17	3. Living The Blues .... [L] record 2 recorded live "Going Up The Country"	Liberty 27200 [2]
8/09/69	**37**	15	4. Hallelujah	Liberty 7618
12/06/69	**86**	19	5. Canned Heat Cook Book (The Best Of Canned Heat) .... [G]	Liberty 11000
1/17/70	**173**	5	6. Vintage-Canned Heat .... [E]	Janus 3009
9/12/70	**59**	19	7. Future Blues	Liberty 11002
2/27/71	**73**	16	8. Hooker 'N Heat .... CANNED HEAT & JOHN LEE HOOKER	Liberty 35002 [2]
7/17/71	**133**	9	9. Canned Heat Concert (Recorded Live in Europe) .... [L]	United Art. 5509
10/30/71	**182**	2	10. Living The Blues .... [R] reissue of album #3 above	United Art. 9955 [2]
3/04/72	**87**	12	11. Historical Figures And Ancient Heads	United Art. 5557
			CANNIBAL & THE HEADHUNTERS four Mexican-American youths	
5/08/65	**141**	4	1. Land Of 1000 Dances	Rampart 3302
			ACE CANNON alto saxophonist	
5/19/62	**44**	17	1. "Tuff"-Sax .... [I]	Hi 32007
			FREDDY CANNON born Frederick Picariello on 12/4/40 in Lynn, Massachusetts	
9/01/62	**101**	5	1. Freddy Cannon At Palisades Park .... "Palisades Park"(3)	Swan 507
			EDDIE CANO jazz/latin quartet led by Eddie on piano	
9/01/62	**31**	12	1. Eddie Cano At P.J.'s .... [I]	Reprise 6030
			LANA CANTRELL Australian	
11/16/68	**166**	2	1. Lana!	RCA 4026
			JIM CAPALDI English - original member of Traffic	
3/04/72	**82**	11	1. Oh How We Danced	Island 9314
9/07/74	**191**	3	2. Whale Meat Again	Island 9254
2/14/76	**193**	4	3. Short Cut Draw Blood	Island 9336
5/21/83	**91**	12	4. Fierce Heart	Atlantic 80059
			CAPITOLS Detroit trio	
7/23/66	**95**	12	1. Dance The Cool Jerk .... "Cool Jerk"(7)	Atco 190
			CAPTAIN & TENNILLE Daryl Dragon & Toni Tennille (married)	
6/14/75	**2(1)**	104	● 1. **Love Will Keep Us Together** .... "Love Will Keep Us Together"(1)/"The Way I Want To Touch You"(4)	A&M 3405
3/20/76	**9**	61	▲ 2. **Song Of Joy** .... "Lonely Night"(3)/"Shop Around"(4)/"Muskrat Love"(4)	A&M 4570
4/23/77	**18**	15	● 3. Come In From The Rain	A&M 4700
12/10/77	**55**	12	● 4. Captain & Tennille's Greatest Hits .... [G]	A&M 4667
7/22/78	**131**	30	5. Dream .... "You Never Done It Like That"(10)	A&M 4707
11/17/79	**23**	24	● 6. Make Your Move .... "Do That To Me One More Time"(1)	Casablanca 7188

DATE CHARTED	PEAK POS	WKS CHRT'D	ARTIST — Album Title	LABEL & NUMBER
			CAPTAIN BEEFHEART Don Van Vliet - also see Frank Zappa	
2/19/72	**131**	9	1. The Spotlight Kid	Reprise 2050
			CAPTAIN BEEFHEART & THE MAGIC BAND:	
12/23/72	**191**	7	2. Clear Spot	Reprise 2115
4/27/74	**192**	4	3. Unconditionally Guaranteed	Mercury 709
			CAPTAIN BEYOND rock group led by Rod Evans (Deep Purple) & Bobby Caldwell	
8/19/72	**134**	12	1. Captain Beyond	Capricorn 0105
9/01/73	**90**	10	2. Sufficiently Breathless	Capricorn 0115
6/11/77	**181**	2	3. Dawn Explosion	Warner 3047
			CAPTAIN SKY Daryl Cameron	
1/27/79	**157**	12	1. The Adventures Of Captain Sky	AVI 6042
			IRENE CARA star of the film "Fame"	
1/30/82	**76**	17	1. Anyone Can See	Network 60003
12/10/83	**77**	37	2. What A Feelin' .... "Flashdance...What A Feeling"(1)/"Breakdance"(8)	Geffen 4021
			CARAVAN British rock quintet	
8/23/75	**124**	10	1. Cunning Stunts	BTM 5000
			CARAVELLES English duo: Andrea Simpson & Lois Wilkinson	
2/15/64	**127**	4	1. You Don't Have To Be A Baby To Cry ...... "You Don't Have To Be A Baby To Cry"(3)	Smash 67044
			TONY CAREY German - ex-keyboardist with Rainbow - leader of Planet P Project	
4/02/83	**167**	9	1. Toney Carey [I Won't Be Home Tonight]	Rocshire 0001
3/31/84	**60**	24	2. Some Tough City	MCA 5464
			HENSON CARGILL	
3/23/68	**179**	2	1. Skip A Rope	Monument 18094
			GEORGE CARLIN comedian	
2/19/72	**13**	35	● 1. FM & AM .... [C]	Little David 7214
10/14/72	**22**	35	● 2. Class Clown .... [C]	Little David 1004
11/10/73	**35**	21	● 3. Occupation: Foole .... [C]	Little David 1005
12/07/74	**19**	17	● 4. Toledo Window Box .... [C]	Little David 3003
11/08/75	**34**	15	5. An Evening With Wally Londo Featuring Bill Slaszo .... [C]	Little David 1008
5/21/77	**90**	9	6. On The Road .... [C]	Little David 1075
1/06/79	**112**	8	7. Indecent Exposure (some of the best of George Carlin) .... [G-C]	Little David 1076
12/19/81	**145**	13	8. A Place For My Stuff! .... [C]	Atlantic 19326
8/04/84	**136**	11	9. Carlin on Campus .... [C]	Eardrum 1001
			WALTER CARLOS classical music performed on the Moog Synthesizer	
1/18/69	**10**	56	● 1. **Switched-On Bach** .... [I]	Columbia 7194
1/03/70	**199**	2	2. The Well-Tempered Synthesizer .... [I]	Columbia 7286
7/08/72	**146**	9	3. Walter Carlos' Clockwork Orange .... [I] features music from the Soundtrack - also see the Soundtrack	Columbia 31480
7/08/72	**168**	7	4. Sonic Seasonings .... [I]	Columbia 31234 [2]

DATE CHARTED	PEAK POS	WKS CHRT'D	ARTIST — Album Title	LABEL & NUMBER
			CARL CARLTON originally recorded as Little Carl Carlton	
1/18/75	**132**	7	1. Everlasting Love .... "Everlasting Love"(6)	ABC 857
8/08/81	**34**	19	2. Carl Carlton	20th Century 628
10/23/82	**133**	7	3. The Bad C.C.	RCA 4425
			LARRY CARLTON session guitarist - member of The Crusaders 1972-77	
8/26/78	**174**	10	1. Larry Carlton .... [I]	Warner 3221
9/06/80	**138**	8	2. Strikes Twice .... [I]	Warner 3380
1/30/82	**99**	16	3. Sleepwalk .... [I]	Warner 3635
6/18/83	**126**	11	4. Friends .... [I]	Warner 23834
			ERIC CARMEN lead singer of the Raspberries	
11/15/75	**21**	51	● 1. Eric Carmen .... "All By Myself"(2)	Arista 4057
9/10/77	**45**	13	2. Boats Against The Current	Arista 4124
10/28/78	**137**	12	3. Change Of Heart	Arista 4184
6/28/80	**160**	5	4. Tonight You're Mine	Arista 9513
2/09/85	**128**	9+	5. Eric Carmen	Geffen 24042
			JEAN CARN also see Norman Connors	
2/19/77	**122**	10	1. Jean Carn	Phil. Int. 34394
8/15/81	**176**	3	2. Sweet And Wonderful	TSOP 36775
			KIM CARNES singer/songwriter from Los Angeles	
7/05/80	**57**	17	1. Romance Dance .... "More Love"(10)	EMI America 17030
5/02/81	**1(4)**	52	▲ 2. **Mistaken Identity** .... "Bette Davis Eyes"(1)	EMI America 17052
9/25/82	**49**	22	3. Voyeur	EMI America 17078
11/19/83	**97**	16	4. Cafe Racers	EMI America 17106
			CARNIVAL	
12/06/69	**191**	2	1. The Carnival	World Pac. 21894
			CARPENTERS Karen and brother Richard Carpenter - Karen died on 2/4/83 (32)	
9/19/70	**2(1)**	87	● 1. **Close To You** .... "Close To You"(1)/"We've Only Just Begun"(2)	A&M 4271
3/06/71	**150**	16	2. Ticket To Ride .... Carpenters' first album	A&M 4205
6/05/71	**2(2)**	59	● 3. **Carpenters** .... "For All We Know"(3)/"Rainy Days And Mondays"(2)/"Superstar"(2)	A&M 3502
7/08/72	**4**	41	● 4. **A Song For You** .... "Hurting Each Other"(2)/"Goodbye To Love"(7)	A&M 3511
6/02/73	**2(1)**	41	● 5. **Now & Then** .... side 2: medley of '60's hits with D.J. Tony Peluso "Sing"(3)/"Yesterday Once More"(2)	A&M 3519
12/01/73	**1(1)**	49	● 6. **The Singles 1969-1973** .... [G] "Top Of The World"(1)	A&M 3601
6/28/75	**13**	18	● 7. **Horizon** .... "Please Mr. Postman"(1)/"Only Yesterday"(4)	A&M 4530
7/10/76	**33**	16	● 8. A Kind Of Hush	A&M 4581
10/22/77	**49**	18	9. Passage	A&M 4703
12/09/78	**145**	7	● 10. Christmas Portrait .... [X] made top 10 on Billboard's special Xmas charts (1983-84)	A&M 4726
7/04/81	**52**	15	11. Made In America	A&M 3723
11/19/83	**46**	19	12. Voice Of The Heart	A&M 4954
1/05/85	**190**	1	13. An Old-Fashioned Christmas .... [X]	A&M 3270

DATE CHARTED	PEAK POS	WKS CHRT'D	ARTIST — Album Title	LABEL & NUMBER
			VIKKI CARR real name: Florencia Cardona	
7/18/64	**114**	4	1. Discovery!	Liberty 7354
10/21/67	**12**	47	2. It Must Be Him .... "It Must Be Him"(3)	Liberty 7533
3/23/68	**63**	16	3. Vikki!	Liberty 7548
3/29/69	**29**	34	4. For Once In My Life .... [L]	Liberty 7604
5/09/70	**111**	8	5. Nashville by Carr	Liberty 11001
7/10/71	**60**	14	6. Vikki Carr's Love Story	Columbia 30662
1/08/72	**118**	4	7. Superstar	Columbia 31040
6/24/72	**146**	12	8. The First Time Ever (I Saw Your Face)	Columbia 31453
9/09/72	**106**	25	9. En Espanol .... [F]	Columbia 31470
6/23/73	**142**	7	10. Ms. America	Columbia 32251
11/24/73	**172**	7	11. Live At The Greek Theatre .... [L]	Columbia 32656 [2]
9/28/74	**155**	5	12. One Hell Of A Woman	Columbia 32860
			PAUL CARRACK formerly with Ace, and Squeeze	
9/11/82	**78**	14	1. Suburban Voodoo	Epic 38161
			KEITH CARRADINE son of actor John Carradine	
6/26/76	**61**	17	1. I'm Easy	Asylum 1066
			DAVID CARROLL & His Orchestra real name: Nook Schrier	
6/01/59	**21**	6	1. Let's Dance	Mercury 60001
1/11/60	**6**	30	2. **Let's Dance Again**	Mercury 60152
			JIM CARROLL Band New York-based poet/rock singer	
11/15/80	**73**	23	1. Catholic Boy	Atco 132
5/22/82	**156**	7	2. Dry Dreams	Atco 145
			CARS Boston-area quintet led by Ric Ocasek	
7/01/78	**18**	139	▲ 1. The Cars	Elektra 135
6/30/79	**3**	62	▲ 2. **Candy-O**	Elektra 507
9/06/80	**5**	28	▲ 3. **Panorama**	Elektra 514
11/28/81	**9**	41	▲ 4. **Shake It Up** .... "Shake It Up"(4)	Elektra 567
4/07/84	**3**	53 +	▲ 5. **Heartbeat City** .... "You Might Think"(7)/"Drive"(3)	Elektra 60296
			BETTY CARTER - see RAY CHARLES	
			CARLENE CARTER daughter of June Carter Cash - married to Nick Lowe	
10/04/80	**139**	6	1. Musical Shapes	Warner 3465
			CLARENCE CARTER blind since childhood - formerly married to Candi Staton	
12/07/68	**200**	2	1. This Is Clarence Carter .... "Slip Away"(6)	Atlantic 8192
4/05/69	**169**	4	2. The Dynamic Clarence Carter	Atlantic 8199
8/16/69	**138**	3	3. Testifyin'	Atlantic 8238
9/26/70	**44**	12	4. Patches .... "Patches"(4)	Atlantic 8267
5/22/71	**103**	10	5. The Best Of Clarence Carter .... [G] .	Atlantic 8282
2/28/81	**189**	3	6. Let's Burn	Venture 1005
			MEL CARTER born on 4/22/43 in Cincinnati, Ohio	
9/18/65	**62**	12	1. Hold Me, Thrill Me, Kiss Me .... "Hold Me, Thrill Me, Kiss Me"(8)	Imperial 12289
10/01/66	**81**	11	2. Easy Listening	Imperial 12319

DATE CHARTED	PEAK POS	WKS CHRT'D	ARTIST — Album Title	LABEL & NUMBER
			RON CARTER jazz bassist	
3/12/77	**193**	1	1. Pastels .... [I]	Milestone 9073
10/21/78	**178**	3	2. A Song For You .... [I]	Milestone 9086
			VALERIE CARTER	
4/02/77	**182**	5	1. Just A Stone's Throw Away	Columbia 34155
			CASCADES quintet from San Diego	
4/20/63	**111**	10	1. Rhythm Of The Rain .... "Rhythm Of The Rain"(3)	Valiant 405
			JOHNNY CASH born in Dyess, Arkansas on 2/26/32	
12/08/58	**19**	11	1. The Fabulous Johnny Cash	Columbia 1253
3/16/63	**80**	15	2. Blood, Sweat & Tears	Columbia 8730
7/27/63	**26**	68	● 3. Ring Of Fire (The Best Of Johnny Cash) .... [K]	Columbia 8853
7/25/64	**53**	17	● 4. I Walk The Line .... includes 6 newly recorded Sun label hits	Columbia 8990
11/07/64	**47**	13	5. Bitter Tears (Ballads of The American Indian)	Columbia 9048
3/20/65	**49**	13	6. Orange Blossom Special	Columbia 9109
7/09/66	**88**	9	7. Everybody Loves A Nut .... [N]	Columbia 9292
7/22/67	**82**	71	● 8. Johnny Cash's Greatest Hits, Volume 1 .... [G]	Columbia 9478
10/07/67	**194**	3	9. Carryin' On with Johnny Cash & June Carter .... Johnny & June were married in March of 1968	Columbia 9528
6/15/68	**13**	122	● 10. Johnny Cash At Folsom Prison .... [L]	Columbia 9639
2/15/69	**54**	20	11. The Holy Land .... gospel music with narrative	Columbia 9726
7/05/69	**1(4)**	70	● 12. **Johnny Cash At San Quentin** .... [L] "A Boy Named Sue"(2)	Columbia 9827
9/27/69	**95**	13	13. Original Golden Hits, Volume I .... [K]	Sun 100
9/27/69	**98**	8	14. Original Golden Hits, Volume II .... [K]	Sun 101
10/11/69	**168**	2	15. Johnny Cash .... [K] reissue of earlier Columbia recordings	Harmony 11342
11/29/69	**164**	6	16. Get Rhythm [K]	Sun 105
12/27/69	**181**	4	17. Showtime [K]	Sun 106
12/27/69	**197**	2	18. Story Songs Of The Trains And Rivers [K]	Sun 104
2/14/70	**6**	30	● 19. **Hello, I'm Johnny Cash**	Columbia 9943
5/16/70	**186**	3	20. The Singing Story Teller .... [K] all Sun albums were recorded from 1955-1958	Sun 115
6/06/70	**54**	34	● 21. The World Of Johnny Cash .... [K]	Columbia 29 [2]
11/14/70	**44**	18	22. The Johnny Cash Show .... [L] recorded at the Grand Ole Opry	Columbia 30100
12/12/70	**176**	6	23. I Walk The Line .... [S] the film is based on the novel "An Exile"	Columbia 30397
6/26/71	**56**	12	24. Man In Black	Columbia 30550
10/23/71	**94**	8	● 25. The Johnny Cash Collection (His Greatest Hits, Volume II) .... [G]	Columbia 30887
4/29/72	**112**	9	26. A Thing Called Love	Columbia 31332
9/16/72	**176**	7	27. Johnny Cash: America (A 200-Year Salute In Story And Song)	Columbia 31645
2/24/73	**188**	4	28. Any Old Wind That Blows	Columbia 32091
7/17/76	**185**	2	29. One Piece At A Time	Columbia 34193

DATE CHARTED	PEAK POS	WKS CHRT'D	ARTIST — Album Title	LABEL & NUMBER
			ROSANNE CASH	
			Johnny Cash's daughter - married to Rodney Crowell	
3/28/81	**26**	32	● 1. Seven Year Ache	Columbia 36965
7/10/82	**76**	12	2. Somewhere In The Stars	Columbia 37570
			CASHMAN & WEST	
			Terry Cashman & Tommy West	
10/14/72	**168**	8	1. A Song Or Two	Dunhill 50126
8/11/73	**192**	2	2. Moondog Serenade	Dunhill 50141
			CASINOS	
			9-man group from Cincinnati led by Gene Hughes	
5/13/67	**187**	4	1. Then You Can Tell Me Goodbye	Fraternity 1019
			"Then You Can Tell Me Goodbye"(6)	
			DAVID CASSIDY	
			played Keith and was lead singer for TV's "The Partridge Family"	
2/12/72	**15**	23	● 1. Cherish	Bell 6070
			"Cherish"(9)	
11/11/72	**41**	17	2. Rock Me Baby	Bell 1109
			SHAUN CASSIDY	
			Shaun & David are half-brothers	
6/25/77	**3**	57	▲ 1. **Shaun Cassidy**	Warner 3067
			"Da Doo Ron Ron"(1)/"That's Rock 'N' Roll"(3)	
11/26/77	**6**	37	▲ 2. **Born Late**	Warner 3126
			"Hey Deanie"(7)	
8/19/78	**33**	13	▲ 3. Under Wraps	Warner 3222
			JIMMY CASTOR Bunch	
4/22/72	**27**	23	1. It's Just Begun	RCA 4640
			"Troglodyte"(6)	
9/23/72	**192**	4	2. Phase Two	RCA 4783
3/01/75	**74**	17	3. Butt Of Course	Atlantic 18124
9/25/76	**132**	9	4. E-Man Groovin'	Atlantic 18186
			CAT MOTHER & the ALL NIGHT NEWS BOYS	
			New York rock quintet produced by Jimi Hendrix	
7/05/69	**55**	15	1. The Street Giveth...And The Street Taketh Away	Polydor 4001
			Jimi Hendrix, producer	
			CATE BROS.	
			twins Earl & Ernie Cate	
2/07/76	**158**	9	1. Cate Bros.	Asylum 1050
10/30/76	**182**	2	2. In One Eye And Out The Other	Asylum 1080
			CARMEN CAVALLARO	
			pianist imitating Duchin's style	
5/26/56	**1(1)**	99	1. **The Eddy Duchin Story** .... [S-I]	Decca 8289
			biographical film about the popular pianist/orchestra leader	
			C.C.S.	
			British jazz/rock band	
4/03/71	**197**	2	1. Whole Lotta Love	RAK 30559
			CELI BEE & THE BUZZY BUNCH	
			Puerto Rican disco band led by Celinas	
7/23/77	**169**	5	1. Celi Bee & The Buzzy Bunch	APA 77001
			CENTRAL LINE	
			black English quartet	
1/09/82	**145**	9	1. Central Line	Mercury 4033
			CERRONE	
			French disco production by Jean-Marc Cerrone	
2/26/77	**153**	10	1. Love In C Minor	Cotillion 9913
8/06/77	**162**	5	2. Cerrone's Paradise	Cotillion 9917

DATE CHARTED	PEAK POS	WKS CHRT'D	ARTIST — Album Title	LABEL & NUMBER
1/21/78	129	8	3. Cerrone 3 - Supernature	Cotillion 5202
11/18/78	118	13	4. Cerrone IV - The Golden Touch	Cotillion 5208

PETER CETERA
vocalist & guitarist of Chicago

1/23/82	143	10	1. Peter Cetera	Full Moon 3624

FRANK CHACKSFIELD & His Orchestra
English

1/09/61	36	14	1. Ebb Tide	Richmond 30078
11/28/64	120	9	2. The New Ebb Tide	London P. 4 44053

CHAD & JEREMY
English - Chad Stuart & Jeremy Clyde

9/26/64	22	39	1. Yesterday's Gone .... "A Summer Song"(7)	World Art. 2002
3/27/65	69	14	2. Chad & Jeremy Sing For You	World Art. 2005
6/26/65	37	18	3. Before And After	Columbia 9174
11/06/65	77	11	4. I Don't Want To Lose You Baby	Columbia 9198
4/23/66	49	23	5. The Best Of Chad & Jeremy .... [G]	Capitol 2470
8/20/66	144	4	6. More Chad & Jeremy .... above 2 albums feature World Artists' recordings	Capitol 2546
9/24/66	61	14	7. Distant Shores	Columbia 9364
11/11/67	186	5	8. Of Cabbages And Kings	Columbia 9471

CHAIRMEN OF THE BOARD
leader General Johnson formerly led the Showmen

5/02/70	133	10	1. Give Me Just A Little More Time .... "Give Me Just A Little More Time"(3)	Invictus 7300
11/28/70	117	16	2. In Session	Invictus 7304
5/06/72	178	3	3. Bittersweet	Invictus 9801

CHAKACHAS

4/08/72	117	11	1. Jungle Fever .... [F]	Polydor 5504

GEORGE CHAKIRIS
portrayed Bernardo in the film "West Side Story"

9/01/62	28	16	1. George Chakiris	Capitol 1750
2/02/63	45	17	2. Memories Are Made Of These	Capitol 1813

RICHARD CHAMBERLAIN
TV's "Dr. Kildare"

2/02/63	5	36	1. Richard Chamberlain Sings .... "Theme From Dr. Kildare"(10)	MGM 4088

CHAMBERS BROTHERS
four brothers from Mississippi

2/17/68	4	57	● 1. The Time Has Come	Columbia 9522
10/12/68	16	21	2. A New Time-A New Day	Columbia 9671
12/27/69	58	33	3. Love, Peace And Happiness .... [L] record 2: live at Bill Graham's Fillmore East	Columbia 20 [2]
12/05/70	193	2	4. The Chambers Brothers Greatest Hits [E] .... reissue of 1965-1966 recordings	Vault 135 [2]
2/27/71	145	7	5. New Generation	Columbia 30032
12/04/71	166	7	6. The Chambers Brothers' Greatest Hits..... [G]	Columbia 30871

CHAMPAIGN
from Champaign, Illinois

3/21/81	53	20	1. How 'Bout Us	Columbia 37008
4/02/83	64	24	2. Modern Heart	Columbia 38284
11/10/84	184	3	3. Woman in Flames	Columbia 39365

BILL CHAMPLIN
formerly with Sons Of Champlin - current member of Chicago

2/06/82	178	4	1. Runaway	Elektra 563

DATE CHARTED	PEAK POS	WKS CHRT'D	ARTIST — Album Title	LABEL & NUMBER
			GENE CHANDLER	
			born Eugene Dixon in Chicago on 7/6/37	
3/31/62	69	8	1. The Duke Of Earl	Vee-Jay 1040
			"Duke Of Earl"(1)	
1/08/66	124	3	2. Gene Chandler - Live On Stage In '65 .... [L]	Constellation 1425
10/31/70	178	9	3. The Gene Chandler Situation	Mercury 61304
3/27/71	143	5	4. Gene & Jerry - One & One	Mercury 61330
			GENE CHANDLER & JERRY BUTLER	
11/25/78	47	20	5. Get Down	Chi-Sound 578
8/25/79	153	3	6. When You're #1	20th Century 598
6/07/80	87	18	7. Gene Chandler '80	20th Century 605
			CHANGE	
			Italian disco production	
5/10/80	29	25	● 1. The Glow Of Love	RFC 3438
4/18/81	46	22	2. Miracles	Atlantic 19301
5/15/82	66	9	3. Sharing Your Love	Atlantic 19342
4/02/83	161	7	4. This Is Your Time	Atlantic 80053
4/28/84	102	15	5. Change of Heart	Atlantic 80151
			BRUCE CHANNEL	
5/19/62	114	5	1. Hey! Baby (and 11 Other Songs About Your Baby)	Smash 67008
			"Hey! Baby"(1)	
			CHANSON	
10/14/78	41	21	1. Chanson	Ariola 50039
			CHANTAY'S	
			Southern California surf/rock quintet (ages 17-18)	
5/18/63	26	18	1. Pipeline .... [I]	Dot 25516
			"Pipeline"(4)	
			HARRY CHAPIN	
			folk-rock storyteller - died in an auto accident on 7/16/81 (38)	
3/18/72	60	27	1. Heads & Tales	Elektra 75023
10/28/72	160	8	2. Sniper and Other Love Songs	Elektra 75042
12/29/73	61	23	3. Short Stories	Elektra 75065
9/07/74	4	33	● 4. **Verities & Balderdash**	Elektra 1012
			"Cat's In The Cradle"(1)	
10/04/75	53	8	5. Portrait Gallery	Elektra 1041
5/01/76	48	19	● 6. Greatest Stories-Live .... [L]	Elektra 2009 [2]
10/30/76	87	6	7. On The Road To Kingdom Come	Elektra 1082
9/17/77	58	10	8. Dance Band On The Titanic	Elektra 301 [2]
7/01/78	133	8	9. Living Room Suite	Elektra 142
10/27/79	163	3	10. Legends Of The Lost And Found - New Greatest Stories Live .... [L]	Elektra 703 [2]
11/01/80	58	15	11. Sequel	Boardwalk 36872
			CHARLENE	
			Charlene Duncan	
4/10/82	36	20	1. I've Never Been To Me	Motown 6009
			"I've Never Been To Me"(3)	
11/27/82	162	7	2. Used To Be	Motown 6027
			RAY CHARLES	
			born Ray Charles Robinson in Albany, Georgia on 9/23/32	
2/15/60	17	82	1. The Genius Of Ray Charles	Atlantic 1312
7/18/60	13	37	2. Ray Charles In Person .... [L]	Atlantic 8039
			recorded on 5/28/59 at Herndon Stadium, Atlanta, Georgia	
10/10/60	9	50	3. **The Genius Hits The Road**	ABC-Para. 335
			"Georgia On My Mind"(1)	
3/06/61	11	31	4. Dedicated To You	ABC-Para. 355

DATE CHARTED	PEAK POS	WKS CHRT'D	ARTIST — Album Title	LABEL & NUMBER
3/27/61	4	48	5. **Genius + Soul = Jazz** .... featuring top jazz artists including Count Basie's band "One Mint Julep"(8)	Impulse! 2
8/28/61	20	73	6. What'd I Say .... [K] "What'd I Say"(6)	Atlantic 8029
8/28/61	49	17	7. The Genius After Hours .... [K-I]	Atlantic 1369
9/04/61	52	15	8. Ray Charles & Betty Carter	ABC-Para. 385
11/11/61	73	12	9. The Genius Sings The Blues .... [K]	Atlantic 8052
12/18/61	11	52	10. Do The Twist! .... [K]	Atlantic 8054
4/21/62	1(14)	101	● 11. **Modern Sounds In Country And Western Music** .... "I Can Stop Loving You"(1)/"You Don't Know Me"(2)	ABC-Para. 410
8/11/62	14	38	12. The Ray Charles Story .... [K] all of above Atlantic albums recorded 1952-1959	Atlantic 900 [2]
8/18/62	5	47	● 13. **Ray Charles' Greatest Hits** .... [G] "Hit The Road Jack"(1)/"Unchain My Heart"(9)	ABC-Para. 415
11/03/62	2(2)	67	● 14. **Modern Sounds In Country And Western Music (Volume Two)** .... "You Are My Sunshine"(7)/"Take These Chains From My Heart"(8)	ABC-Para. 435
8/31/63	2(2)	36	15. **Ingredients In A Recipe For Soul** .... "Busted"(4)	ABC-Para. 465
3/21/64	9	23	16. **Sweet & Sour Tears**	ABC-Para. 480
8/29/64	36	16	17. Have A Smile With Me	ABC-Para. 495
2/20/65	80	18	18. Ray Charles Live In Concert .... [L]	ABC-Para. 500
9/11/65	116	7	19. Country & Western Meets Rhythm & Blues .	ABC-Para. 520
3/12/66	15	36	20. Crying Time .... "Crying Time"(6)	ABC-Para. 544
9/17/66	52	17	21. Ray's Moods	ABC 550
3/25/67	77	62	● 22. A Man And His Soul .... [G]	ABC 590 [2]
7/08/67	76	34	23. Ray Charles invites you to Listen	ABC/TRC 595
4/13/68	51	24	24. A Portrait Of Ray	ABC/TRC 625
4/05/69	167	11	25. I'm All Yours-Baby!	ABC/TRC 675
7/26/69	172	3	26. Doing His Thing	ABC/TRC 695
7/11/70	155	2	27. My Kind Of Jazz .... [I]	Tangerine 1512
8/22/70	192	4	28. Love Country Style	ABC/TRC 707
5/29/71	52	16	29. Volcanic Action Of My Soul	ABC/TRC 726
11/20/71	152	10	30. A 25th Anniversary in Show Business Salute to Ray Charles .... [G] record 1: Atlantic hits; record 2: ABC hits	ABC 731 [2]
4/29/72	52	22	31. A Message From The People	ABC/TRC 755
11/25/72	186	8	32. Through The Eyes Of Love	ABC/TRC 765
5/19/73	182	5	33. Ray Charles Live .... [R-L] record 1: recorded at The Newport Jazz Festival, 7/5/58 record 2: reissue of album #2 above	Atlantic 503 [2]
6/28/75	175	3	34. Renaissance	Crossover 9005
12/04/76	138	11	35. Porgy & Bess .... RAY CHARLES/CLEO LAINE	RCA 1831 [2]
11/12/77	78	20	36. True To Life	Atlantic 19142
2/23/85	80+	7+	37. Friendship .... duets with 10 superstar country artists	Columbia 39415

RAY CHARLES Singers

DATE CHARTED	PEAK POS	WKS CHRT'D	ARTIST — Album Title	LABEL & NUMBER
4/04/64	11	33	1. Something Special For Young Lovers .... "Love Me With All Your Heart"(3)	Command 866
9/05/64	45	22	2. Al-Di-La and other Extra-Special songs for Young Lovers	Command 870
12/05/64	88	20	3. Songs For Lonesome Lovers	Command 874
8/21/65	125	6	4. Songs For Latin Lovers	Command 886

SONNY CHARLES
leader of the Checkmates, Ltd.

DATE CHARTED	PEAK POS	WKS CHRT'D	ARTIST — Album Title	LABEL & NUMBER
12/25/82	136	7	1. The Sun Still Shines	Highrise 102

DATE CHARTED	PEAK POS	WKS CHRT'D	ARTIST — Album Title	LABEL & NUMBER
			CHARLESTON CITY ALL-STARS conducted by Enoch Light	
7/08/57	16	14	1. The Roaring 20's, Volume 2 .... [I]	Grand Award 340
9/02/57	17	2	2. The Roaring 20's, Volume 3 .... [I]	Grand Award 353
			CHARLIE five-man British group	
6/04/77	111	15	1. No Second Chance	Janus 7032
4/15/78	75	14	2. Lines	Janus 7036
9/01/79	60	10	3. Fight Dirty	Arista 4239
7/23/83	145	9	4. Charlie	Mirage 90098
			CHARO & The Salsoul Orchestra	
11/26/77	100	15	1. Cuchi-Cuchi	Salsoul 5519
			CHASE Bill Chase and 3 other members killed in plane crash on 8/9/74	
5/08/71	22	26	1. Chase	Epic 30472
4/08/72	71	12	2. Ennea	Epic 31097
4/27/74	155	10	3. Pure Music	Epic 32572
			CHEAP TRICK Chicago rock quartet: Rick Nielsen, Bun E. Carlos, Robin Zander, Tom Petersson - replaced by Jon Brant(#7)	
9/24/77	73	12	● 1. In Color	Epic 34884
6/10/78	48	22	● 2. Heaven Tonight	Epic 35312
2/24/79	4	53	▲ 3. **Cheap Trick At Budokan** .... [L] "I Want You To Want Me"(7)	Epic 35795
10/06/79	6	25	▲ 4. **Dream Police**	Epic 35773
7/05/80	39	12	5. Found All The Parts .... [M] 10" mini LP - recorded 1976-1979	Epic 36453
11/15/80	24	15	● 6. All Shook Up	Epic 36498
5/29/82	39	27	7. One On One	Epic 38021
9/10/83	61	11	8. Next Position Please	Epic 38794
			CHUBBY CHECKER born Ernest Evans on 10/3/41 in Philadelphia	
10/31/60	3	86	1. **Twist With Chubby Checker** .... "The Twist"(1)	Parkway 7001
5/29/61	110	16	2. It's Pony Time .... "Pony Time"(1)	Parkway 7003
9/25/61	11	47	3. Let's Twist Again .... "Let's Twist Again"(8)	Parkway 7004
12/04/61	8	38	4. **For Twisters Only**	Parkway 7002
12/11/61	2(6)	67	5. **Your Twist Party** .... [K] features songs from previous 4 albums	Parkway 7007
12/18/61	7	30	6. **Bobby Rydell/Chubby Checker**	Cameo 1013
3/31/62	17	27	7. For Teen Twisters Only .... "The Fly"(7)/"Slow Twistin'"(3)	Parkway 7009
4/28/62	54	11	8. Twistin' Round The World	Parkway 7008
6/09/62	29	20	9. Don't Knock The Twist .... [S] 6 cuts by Chubby, who also stars in the film	Parkway 7011
10/27/62	23	24	10. All The Hits (For Your Dancin' Party) ...... "Limbo Rock"(2)	Parkway 7014
11/17/62	117	4	11. Down To Earth .... CHUBBY CHECKER/DEE DEE SHARP	Cameo 1029
12/15/62	11	24	12. Limbo Party	Parkway 7020
12/29/62	27	23	13. Chubby Checker's Biggest Hits .... [G] "Popeye The Hitchhiker"(10)	Parkway 7022
3/30/63	87	17	14. Let's Limbo Some More	Parkway 7027
8/10/63	90	4	15. Beach Party	Parkway 7030
10/12/63	104	4	16. Chubby Checker In Person .... [L] labeled as "Twist It Up"	Parkway 7026

DATE CHARTED	PEAK POS	WKS CHRT'D	ARTIST — Album Title	LABEL & NUMBER
12/23/72	152	10	17. Chubby Checker's Greatest Hits .... [G]	Abkco 4219 [2]
3/06/82	186	2	18. The Change Has Come	MCA 5291

CHECKMATES, LTD. featuring SONNY CHARLES
quintet from Fort Wayne, Indiana

10/18/69	178	4	1. Love Is All We Have To Give	A&M 4183

CHEECH & CHONG
Richard Marin & Thomas Chong

9/25/71	28	64	● 1. Cheech And Chong .... [C]	Ode 77010
7/01/72	2(1)	111	● 2. Big Bambu .... [C]	Ode 77014
9/08/73	2(1)	69	● 3. Los Cochinos .... [C]	Ode 77019
10/19/74	5	25	● 4. Cheech & Chong's Wedding Album .... [C]	Ode 77025
			"Earache My Eye Featuring Alice Bowie"(9)	
6/26/76	25	13	5. Sleeping Beauty .... [C]	Ode 77040
12/02/78	162	7	6. Up In Smoke .... [C-S]	Warner 3249
7/19/80	173	3	7. Let's Make A New Dope Deal .... [C]	Warner 3391

CHEQUERED PAST
verteran hard-rock quintet - features members of Blondie, the Sex Pistols, & Detective

9/15/84	151	6	1. Chequered Past	EMI America 17123

CHER
real name: Cherilyn LaPierre - also see Sonny & Cher

9/18/65	16	24	1. All I Really Want To Do	Imperial 12292
4/23/66	26	19	2. The Sonny Side Of Cher	Imperial 12301
			"Bang Bang"(9)	
10/01/66	59	16	● 3. Cher	Imperial 12320
11/18/67	47	14	4. With Love - Cher	Imperial 12358
			"You Better Sit Down Kids"(9)	
11/30/68	195	3	5. Cher's Golden Greats .... [G]	Imperial 12406
8/16/69	160	3	6. 3614 Jackson Highway	Atco 298
			address of the Muscle Shoals Sound Studio	
9/25/71	16	45	7. Gypsys, Tramps & Thieves	Kapp 3649
			"Gypsys, Tramps & Thieves"(1)/"The Way of Love"(7)	
1/08/72	92	10	8. Cher Superpak .... [K]	United Art. 88 [2]
7/29/72	43	22	9. Foxy Lady	Kapp 5514
10/07/72	95	9	10. Cher Superpak, Vol. II .... [K]	United Art. 94 [2]
			Superpaks: Imperial recordings	
4/14/73	140	8	11. Bittersweet White Light	MCA 2101
9/22/73	28	25	● 12. Half-Breed	MCA 2104
			"Half-Breed"(1)	
6/01/74	69	14	13. Dark Lady	MCA 2113
			"Dark Lady"(1)	
11/16/74	152	7	14. Greatest Hits .... [G]	MCA 2127
5/10/75	153	7	15. Stars	Warner 2850
2/24/79	25	21	● 16. Take Me Home	Casablanca 7133
			"Take Me Home"(8)	

CHERRELLE
real name: Cheryl Norton

9/08/84	144	8	1. Fragile	Tabu 39144

DON CHERRY
born in Wichita, Texas on 1/11/24

9/22/56	15	7	1. Swingin' For Two	Columbia 893
			with Ray Conniff & His Orchestra	

CHI-LITES
Eugene Record, leader of soul group from Chicago

9/13/69	180	3	1. Give It Away	Brunswick 754152
8/21/71	12	32	2. (For God's Sake) Give More Power To The People	Brunswick 754170
			"Have You Seen Her"(3)	

DATE CHARTED	PEAK POS	WKS CHRT'D	ARTIST — Album Title	LABEL & NUMBER
4/29/72	5	36	3. **A Lonely Man** .... "Oh Girl"(1)	Brunswick 754179
10/21/72	55	24	4. The Chi-Lites Greatest Hits [G]	Brunswick 754184
3/24/73	50	13	5. A Letter To Myself	Brunswick 754188
9/15/73	89	14	6. Chi-Lites	Brunswick 754197
7/13/74	181	5	7. Toby	Brunswick 754200
11/29/80	179	6	8. Heavenly Body	Chi-Sound 619
4/10/82	162	7	9. Me And You	Chi-Sound 635
6/04/83	98	12	10. Bottom's Up	Larc 8103

CHIC
disco group formed by Nile Rodgers & Bernard Edwards

DATE CHARTED	PEAK POS	WKS CHRT'D	ARTIST — Album Title	LABEL & NUMBER
12/17/77	27	40	● 1. Chic .... "Dance, Dance, Dance"(6)	Atlantic 19153
12/02/78	4	48	▲ 2. **C'est Chic** .... "Le Freak"(1)/"I Want Your Love"(7)	Atlantic 19209
8/25/79	5	17	▲ 3. **Risque** .... "Good Times"(1)	Atlantic 16003
12/22/79	88	9	4. Les Plus Grands Succes De Chic - Chic's Greatest Hits .... [G]	Atlantic 16011
7/26/80	30	15	5. Real People	Atlantic 16016
12/19/81	124	9	6. Take It Off	Atlantic 19323
12/04/82	173	6	7. Tongue In Chic	Atlantic 80031

CHICAGO
original band: Terry Kath (1-11, died 1/23/78-31), Robert Lamm, Peter Cetera, James Pankow, Danny Seraphine, Lee Loughnane, Walter Parazaider

DATE CHARTED	PEAK POS	WKS CHRT'D	ARTIST — Album Title	LABEL & NUMBER
5/17/69	17	171	● 1. Chicago Transit Authority .... "Does Anybody Really Know What Time It Is?"(7)/"Beginnings"(7)	Columbia 8 [2]
2/14/70	4	134	● 2. **Chicago II** .... "Make Me Smile"(9)/"25 Or 6 To 4"(4)	Columbia 24 [2]
1/30/71	2(2)	63	● 3. **Chicago III**	Columbia 30110 [2]
11/13/71	3	46	● 4. **Chicago At Carnegie Hall** .... [L] 4 album boxed set	Columbia 30865 [4]
7/29/72	1(9)	51	● 5. **Chicago V** .... "Saturday In The Park"(3)	Columbia 31102
7/14/73	1(5)	73	● 6. **Chicago VI** .... "Feelin' Stronger Every Day"(10)/"Just You 'N' Me"(4)	Columbia 32400
3/30/74	1(1)	69	● 7. **Chicago VII** .... "(I've Been) Searchin' So Long"(9)/"Call On Me"(6)	Columbia 32810 [2]
4/12/75	1(2)	29	● 8. **Chicago VIII** .... "Old Days"(5)	Columbia 33100
11/29/75	1(5)	72	● 9. **Chicago IX - Chicago's Greatest Hits** ...... [G]	Columbia 33900
7/04/76	3	44	▲ 10. **Chicago X** .... "If You Leave Me Now"(1)	Columbia 34200
10/01/77	6	20	▲ 11. **Chicago XI** .... "Baby, What A Big Surprise"(4)	Columbia 34860
10/21/78	12	29	▲ 12. Hot Streets	Columbia 35512
9/01/79	21	10	● 13. Chicago 13	Columbia 36105
8/09/80	71	9	14. Chicago XIV	Columbia 36517
12/12/81	171	5	15. Chicago - Greatest Hits, Volume II .... [G]	Columbia 37682
6/26/82	9	38	▲ 16. **Chicago 16** .... "Hard To Say I'm Sorry"(1)	Full Moon 23689
6/02/84	4	45+	▲ 17. **Chicago 17** .... "Hard Habit To Break"(3)/"You're The Inspiration"(3)	Full Moon 25060

CHIEFTAINS
Irish folk band led by Paddy Moloney

DATE CHARTED	PEAK POS	WKS CHRT'D	ARTIST — Album Title	LABEL & NUMBER
2/28/76	187	4	1. The Chieftains 5 .... [I]	Island 9334

DATE CHARTED	PEAK POS	WKS CHRT'D	ARTIST — Album Title	LABEL & NUMBER
			CHIFFONS New York female quartet led by Judy Craig	
5/18/63	**97**	11	1. He's So Fine .... "He's So Fine"(1)	Laurie 2018
8/20/66	**149**	3	2. Sweet Talkin' Guy .... "Sweet Talkin' Guy"(10)	Laurie 2036
			DESMOND CHILD & ROUGE	
3/24/79	**157**	6	1. Desmond Child and Rouge	Capitol 11908
			CHILLIWACK Canadian	
3/26/77	**142**	13	1. Dreams, Dreams, Dreams	Mushroom 5006
8/12/78	**191**	4	2. Lights From The Valley	Mushroom 5011
10/03/81	**78**	30	3. Wanna Be A Star	Millennium 7759
11/27/82	**112**	10	4. Opus X	Millennium 7766
			CHIPMUNKS David Seville (Alvin, Simon & Theodore's creator) died on 1/16/72 (52)	
11/30/59	**4**	41	1. **Let's All Sing With The Chipmunks** .... [N] "The Chipmunk Song"(1)"Alvin's Harmonica"(3)	Liberty 3132
6/20/60	**31**	5	2. Sing Again With The Chipmunks .... [N]	Liberty 3159
12/22/62	**84**	2	3. Christmas With The Chipmunks .... [N-X]	Liberty 3256
9/05/64	**14**	23	4. The Chipmunks Sing The Beatles Hits ... [N]	Liberty 7388
8/09/80	**34**	26	● 5. Chipmunk Punk .... [N] 'group' resurrected by Seville's son	Excelsior 6008
6/06/81	**56**	35	● 6. Urban Chipmunk .... [N]	RCA 4027
11/21/81	**72**	9	● 7. A Chipmunk Christmas .... [N-X] made top 10 on Billboard's special Xmas charts (1983-84)	RCA 4041
6/05/82	**109**	6	8. Chipmunk Rock .... [N]	RCA 4304
			CHOCOLATE MILK New Orleans soul combo	
10/25/75	**191**	3	1. Action Speaks Louder Than Words	RCA 1188
6/24/78	**171**	5	2. We're All In This Together	RCA 2331
4/14/79	**161**	6	3. Milky Way	RCA 3081
12/12/81	**162**	10	4. Blue Jeans	RCA 3896
			CHRISTIE English trio - Jeff Christie, leader	
12/12/70	**115**	10	1. Yellow River	Epic 30403
			LOU CHRISTIE born Lugee Geno Sacco on 2/19/43 in Glen Willard, Pennsylvania	
8/24/63	**124**	6	1. Lou Christie .... "Two Faces Have I"(6)	Roulette 25208
3/05/66	**103**	14	2. Lightnin' Strikes .... "Lightnin' Strikes"(1)	MGM 4360
			JUNE CHRISTY jazz singer - orchestra conducted by Pete Rugolo	
10/02/54	**8**	11	1. **Something Cool**	Capitol 516
9/29/56	**14**	4	2. The Misty Miss Christy	Capitol 725
7/22/57	**16**	4	3. June - Fair and Warmer!	Capitol 833
			CITY BOY British rock sextet	
8/28/76	**177**	3	1. City Boy	Mercury 1098
2/12/77	**170**	4	2. Dinner At The Ritz	Mercury 1121
9/16/78	**115**	9	3. Book Early	Mercury 3737
			C.J. & CO. Detroit disco/soul band	
7/09/77	**60**	23	1. Devil's Gun	Westbound 6100

DATE CHARTED	PEAK POS	WKS CHRT'D	ARTIST — Album Title	LABEL & NUMBER
			CLANCY BROTHERS & TOMMY MAKEM Irish balladeer quartet	
11/16/63	60	12	1. In Person At Carnegie Hall .... [L]	Columbia 1950
5/02/64	91	6	2. The First Hurrah!	Columbia 2165
			ERIC CLAPTON Britain's premier rock guitarist - formerly with the Yardbirds, John Mayall's Bluesbreakers, Cream, and Blind Faith - also see Derek & The Dominos and Delaney & Bonnie	
7/25/70	13	30	1. Eric Clapton	Atco 329
4/15/72	6	42	● 2. **History Of Eric Clapton** .... [K] recordings with groups listed in above artist notes	Atco 803 [2]
10/14/72	87	17	3. Eric Clapton At His Best .... [K] recordings from 1st Atco album + Derek & The Dominos "Layla" LP	Polydor 3503 [2]
2/17/73	67	11	4. Clapton .... [K] more recordings - same as above note	Polydor 5526
9/22/73	18	14	5. Eric Clapton's Rainbow Concert .... [L] Clapton's comeback concert at London's Rainbow Theatre with Pete Townshend, Steve Winwood, Ron Wood & Jim Capaldi	RSO 877
7/20/74	1(4)	25	● 6. **461 Ocean Boulevard** .... address where recorded in Miami, Florida "I Shot The Sheriff"(1)	RSO 4801
4/12/75	21	14	7. There's One In Every Crowd	RSO 4806
9/06/75	20	13	8. E.C. Was Here .... [L]	RSO 4809
10/16/76	15	21	9. No Reason To Cry	RSO 3004
3/05/77	194	2	10. Eric Clapton .... [R] reissue of album #1 above	RSO 3008
11/26/77	2(5)	74	▲ 11. **Slowhand** .... "Lay Down Sally"(3)	RSO 3030
12/02/78	8	37	▲ 12. **Backless** .... "Promises"(9)	RSO 3039
5/03/80	2(6)	31	● 13. **Just One Night** .... [L] recorded live at the Budokan Theatre, Japan	RSO 4202 [2]
3/21/81	7	21	● 14. **Another Ticket** .... "I Can't Stand It"(10)	RSO 3095
5/22/82	101	14	15. Time Pieces/The Best Of Eric Clapton ...... [G]	RSO 3099
2/19/83	16	19	16. Money And Cigarettes	Duck 23773
			DAVE CLARK FIVE British: Dave Clark, Mike Smith, Lenny Davidson, Rick Huxley, Denny Payton	
4/11/64	3	32	● 1. **Glad All Over** .... "Glad All Over"(6)/"Bits And Pieces"(4)	Epic 26093
6/20/64	5	22	2. **The Dave Clark Five Return!** .... "Can't You See That She's Mine"(4)	Epic 26104
8/29/64	11	28	3. American Tour .... "Because"(3)	Epic 26117
1/02/65	6	21	4. **Coast To Coast**	Epic 26128
4/03/65	24	23	5. Weekend In London	Epic 26139
8/14/65	15	21	6. Having A Wild Weekend .... [S] the Dave Clark Five star in the film "Catch Us If You Can"(4)	Epic 26162
12/11/65	32	16	7. I Like It Like That .... "I Like It Like That"(7)	Epic 26178
2/26/66	9	62	● 8. **The Dave Clark Five's Greatest Hits** .... [G] "Over And Over"(1)	Epic 26185
6/25/66	77	11	9. Try Too Hard	Epic 26198
10/01/66	127	6	10. Satisfied With You	Epic 26212
12/10/66	103	7	11. The Dave Clark Five/More Greatest Hits .... [G]	Epic 26221
3/25/67	119	7	12. 5 By 5	Epic 26236
8/12/67	149	3	13. You Got What It Takes .... "You Got What It Takes"(7)	Epic 26312
			DICK CLARK - **see VARIOUS - Radio/TV Celebrity Compilations**	

DATE CHARTED	PEAK POS	WKS CHRT'D	ARTIST — Album Title	LABEL & NUMBER
			GENE CLARK original member of the Byrds - also see McGuinn, Clark & Hillman	
11/02/74	144	5	1. No Other	Asylum 1016
			PETULA CLARK English - born on 11/15/33 - also see Soundtracks "Finian's Rainbow"/"Goodbye, Mr. Chips"	
2/13/65	21	36	1. Downtown "Downtown"(1)	Warner 1590
5/29/65	42	17	2. I Know A Place "I Know A Place"(3)	Warner 1598
10/23/65	129	9	3. The World's Greatest International Hits!	Warner 1608
4/09/66	68	12	4. My Love "My Love"(1)	Warner 1630
9/03/66	43	16	5. I Couldn't Live Without Your Love "I Couldn't Live Without Your Love"(9)	Warner 1645
2/18/67	49	27	6. Color My World/Who Am I	Warner 1673
9/02/67	27	27	7. These Are My Songs "This Is My Song"(3)/"Don't Sleep In The Subway"(5)	Warner 1698
2/17/68	93	23	8. The Other Man's Grass Is Always Greener	Warner 1719
9/07/68	51	21	9. Petula	Warner 1743
12/28/68	57	17	10. Petula Clark's Greatest Hits, Vol. 1 [G]	Warner 1765
5/17/69	37	11	11. Portrait Of Petula	Warner 1789
12/27/69	176	7	12. Just Pet	Warner 1823
8/08/70	198	2	13. Memphis	Warner 1862
4/10/71	178	3	14. Warm And Tender	Warner 1885
			ROY CLARK co-host of TV's "Hee-Haw"	
7/05/69	50	20	1. Yesterday, When I Was Young	Dot 25953
1/03/70	129	9	2. The Everlovin' Soul Of Roy Clark	Dot 25972
8/29/70	176	6	3. I Never Picked Cotton	Dot 25980
4/03/71	178	8	4. The Best Of Roy Clark [G]	Dot 25986
8/14/71	197	2	5. The Incredible Roy Clark	Dot 25990
7/29/72	112	12	6. Roy Clark Country!	Dot 25997
5/05/73	172	6	7. Roy Clark/Superpicker [I]	Dot 26008
4/13/74	186	3	8. Roy Clark/The Entertainer	Dot 2001
			STANLEY CLARKE jazz-rock bassist - member of Return To Forever	
1/18/75	59	16	1. Stanley Clarke [I]	Nemperor 431
11/01/75	34	19	2. Journey To Love [I]	Nemperor 433
9/25/76	34	22	3. School Days [I]	Nemperor 439
4/29/78	57	19	4. Modern Man [I]	Nemperor 35303
7/21/79	62	14	5. I Wanna Play For You [I-L] 1/2 is live & 1/2 is studio	Nemperor 35680 [2]
6/28/80	95	11	6. Rocks, Pebbles And Sand	Epic 36506
5/09/81	33	23	7. The Clarke/Duke Project STANLEY CLARKE/GEORGE DUKE	Epic 36918
8/21/82	114	8	8. Let Me Know You	Epic 38086
11/26/83	146	10	9. The Clarke/Duke Project II STANLEY CLARKE/GEORGE DUKE	Epic 38934
4/28/84	149	13	10. Time Exposure	Epic 38688
			CLASH leader of Great Britain's new music wave: Joe Strummer, Mick Jones, Paul Simonon, Topper Headon	
2/24/79	128	10	1. Give 'Em Enough Rope	Epic 35543
9/08/79	126	6	2. The Clash	Epic 36060
2/09/80	27	33	3. London Calling	Epic 36328 [2]
11/22/80	74	16	4. Black Market Clash 10" album	Epic 36846

DATE CHARTED	PEAK POS	WKS CHRT'D	ARTIST — Album Title	LABEL & NUMBER
2/07/81	24	20	5. Sandinista!	Epic 37037 [3]
6/12/82	7	61	▲ 6. **Combat Rock**	Epic 37689
			"Rock The Casbah"(8)	

CLASSICS IV
Atlanta, Georgia quartet led by Dennis Yost

3/09/68	140	7	1. Spooky	Imperial 12371
			"Spooky"(3)	
2/01/69	196	3	2. Mamas And Papas/Soul Train	Imperial 12407
			"Stormy"(5)	
4/26/69	45	20	3. Traces	Imperial 12429
			"Traces"(2)	
12/06/69	50	20	4. Dennis Yost & The Classics IV/Golden Greats-Volume I .... [G]	Imperial 16000

CASSIUS CLAY
heavyweight boxing champ Muhammad Ali - also see Soundtrack "The Greatest"

10/12/63	61	20	1. I Am The Greatest! .... [C]	Columbia 2093
			comedy bits and poetry from Clay	

TOM CLAY

8/28/71	92	5	1. What The World Needs Now Is Love	MoWest 103
			"What The World Needs Now Is Love/Abraham, Martin And John"(8)	

RICHARD CLAYDERMAN
French pianist - real name: Phillipe Pages

11/24/84	160	9	1. Amour .... [I]	Columbia 39603

MERRY CLAYTON

11/20/71	180	11	1. Merry Clayton	Ode 77012
9/06/75	146	8	2. Keep Your Eye On The Sparrow	Ode 77030

DAVID CLAYTON-THOMAS
lead singer of Blood, Sweat & Tears

9/27/69	159	8	1. David Clayton-Thomas! .... [E]	Decca 75146
			recordings prior to BS&T days	
4/15/72	184	3	2. David Clayton-Thomas	Columbia 31000

CLEAR LIGHT
Los Angeles rock band

11/25/67	126	13	1. Clear Light	Elektra 74011

CLARENCE CLEMMONS & The Red Bank Rockers
saxophonist with Bruce Springsteen's E Street Band

11/05/83	174	5	1. Rescue	Columbia 38933
			John "J.T." Bowen, lead vocalist	

CLEVELAND ORCHESTRA
Michael Tilson Thomas, conductor

3/29/75	152	4	1. Carl Orff: Carmina Burana	Columbia 33172
			opera composed in 1936	

VAN CLIBURN
classical pianist from Kilgore, Texas

8/04/58	1(7)	125	● 1. **Tchaikovsky: Piano Concerto No. 1** .... [I]	RCA 2252
			Kiril Kondrashin, conductor	
7/13/59	10	60	2. **Rachmaninoff: Piano Concerto No. 3**... [I-L]	RCA 2355
			Carnegie Hall performance of 5/19/58	
1/09/61	134	13	3. Schumann: Piano Concerto in A Minor .... [I]	RCA 2455
			Fritz Reiner conducts the Chicago Symphony Orchestra	
2/03/62	71	29	4. My Favorite Chopin .... [I]	RCA 2576
3/10/62	25	13	5. Brahms: Piano Concerto No. 2 .... [I]	RCA 2581
			Fritz Reiner conducts the Chicago Symphony Orchestra	

DATE CHARTED	PEAK POS	WKS CHRT'D	ARTIST — Album Title	LABEL & NUMBER
			JIMMY CLIFF Jamaican reggae singer/composer - real name: James Chambers	
3/22/75	140	8	1. The Harder They Come .... [S] 6 cuts by Jimmy, who also starred in the film	Mango 9202
11/01/75	195	2	2. Follow My Mind	Reprise 2218
8/14/82	186	2	3. Special	Columbia 38099
			LINDA CLIFFORD former Miss New York State	
5/20/78	22	22	1. If My Friends Could See Me Now	Curtom 5021
4/07/79	26	17	2. Let Me Be Your Woman	RSO 3902 [2]
12/01/79	117	9	3. Here's My Love	RSO 3067
7/19/80	180	4	4. The Right Combination .... LINDA CLIFFORD/CURTIS MAYFIELD	RSO 3084
10/04/80	160	6	5. I'm Yours	RSO 3087
			CLIMAX Sonny Geraci, lead singer (formerly with The Outsiders)	
6/24/72	177	7	1. Climax .... "Precious And Few"(3)	Rocky Road 3506
			CLIMAX BLUES BAND English quartet led by Colin Cooper & Peter Haycock	
11/28/70	197	1	1. The Climax Chicago Blues Band Plays On ...	Sire 97023
2/17/73	150	10	2. Rich Man	Sire 7402
12/01/73	107	30	3. FM/Live .... [L]	Sire 7411 [2]
6/15/74	37	29	4. Sense Of Direction	Sire 7501
9/13/75	69	11	5. Stamp Album	Sire 7507
10/23/76	27	44	6. Gold Plated .... "Couldn't Get It Right"(3)	Sire 7523
4/29/78	71	11	7. Shine On	Sire 6056
6/16/79	170	6	8. Real To Reel	Sire 3334
4/25/81	75	16	9. Flying The Flag	Warner 3493
			PATSY CLINE killed in a plane crash on 3/5/63 (30) with Cowboy Copas and Hawkshaw Hawkins	
3/31/62	73	21	1. Patsy Cline Showcase .... "Crazy"(9)	Decca 4202
8/31/63	74	12	2. The Patsy Cline Story .... [G]	Decca 7176 [2]
			GEORGE CLINTON 'P-Funk' innovator - also see Funkadelic and Parliament	
12/18/82	40	33	1. Computer Games	Capitol 12246
1/07/84	102	18	2. You Shouldn't-Nuf Bit Fish	Capitol 12308
			CLIQUE	
1/17/70	177	3	1. The Clique	White Whale 7126
			ROSEMARY CLOONEY - see HI-LO's	
			BILLY COBHAM jazz/rock drummer - formerly with John McLaughlin	
11/17/73	26	43	1. Spectrum .... [I]	Atlantic 7268
5/04/74	23	21	2. Crosswinds .... [I]	Atlantic 7300
12/21/74	36	13	3. Total Eclipse .... [I]	Atlantic 18121
6/28/75	74	8	4. Shabazz (Recorded Live In Europe) .... [I-L]	Atlantic 18139
11/15/75	79	7	5. A Funky Thide Of Sings .... [I]	Atlantic 18149
4/10/76	128	8	6. Life & Times .... [I]	Atlantic 18166
10/23/76	99	9	7. "Live"-On Tour In Europe .... [L] THE BILLY COBHAM/GEORGE DUKE BAND	Atlantic 18194
6/03/78	172	4	8. Inner Conflicts .... [I]	Atlantic 19174
10/14/78	166	6	9. Simplicity Of Expression-Depth Of Thought	Columbia 35457

DATE CHARTED	PEAK POS	WKS CHRT'D	ARTIST — Album Title	LABEL & NUMBER
			WAYNE COCHRAN flamboyant rock singer, with the C.C. Riders	
3/30/68	167	4	1. Wayne Cochran!	Chess 1519
			BRUCE COCKBURN Canadian	
2/23/80	45	24	1. Dancing In the Dragon's Jaws	Millennium 7747
10/18/80	81	9	2. Humans	Millennium 7752
5/23/81	174	5	3. Bruce Cockburn/Resume	Millennium 7757
8/25/84	74	28+	4. Stealing Fire	Gold Mt. 80012
			JOE COCKER English white blues singer	
5/31/69	35	37	● 1. With A Little Help From My Friends .... with Jimmy Page & Stevie Winwood	A&M 4182
11/22/69	11	53	● 2. Joe Cocker! .... with Leon Russell and The Grease Band	A&M 4224
9/05/70	2(1)	53	● 3. **Mad Dogs & Englishmen** .... [S-L] title refers to Cocker's 1970 concert tour with an entourage of 43 including Leon Russell & Chris Stainton "The Letter"(7)	A&M 6002 [2]
12/02/72	30	21	4. Joe Cocker	A&M 4368
8/24/74	11	36	5. I Can Stand A Little Rain .... "You Are So Beautiful"(5)	A&M 3633
8/30/75	42	10	6. Jamaica Say You Will	A&M 4529
5/15/76	70	10	7. Stingray	A&M 4574
12/10/77	114	8	8. Joe Cocker's Greatest Hits .... [G]	A&M 4670
9/16/78	76	13	9. Luxury You Can Afford	Asylum 145
7/10/82	105	23	10. Sheffield Steel	Island 9750
5/19/84	133	9	11. Civilized Man	Capitol 12335
			DAVID ALLAN COE	
7/09/83	179	5	1. Castles In The Sand	Columbia 38535
			DENNIS COFFEY & The Detroit Guitar Band	
11/13/71	36	25	1. Evolution .... [I] "Scorpio"(6)	Sussex 7004
3/25/72	90	14	2. Goin' For Myself .... [I]	Sussex 7010
1/20/73	189	6	3. Electric Coffey .... [I]	Sussex 7021
1/17/76	147	7	4. Finger Lickin Good .... [I]	Westbound 212
			LEONARD COHEN Canadian poet/singer	
3/02/68	83	14	1. Songs Of Leonard Cohen	Columbia 9533
4/12/69	63	17	2. Songs From A Room	Columbia 9767
5/01/71	145	11	3. Songs Of Love And Hate	Columbia 30103
5/26/73	156	5	4. Leonard Cohen: Live Songs .... [L]	Columbia 31724
			MYRON COHEN comedy story teller	
4/02/66	102	13	1. Everybody Gotta Be Someplace .... [C]	RCA 3534
			COLD BLOOD Bay-area rock group led by Lydia Pense	
12/27/69	23	29	1. Cold Blood	San Francisco 200
1/23/71	60	13	2. Sisyphus	San Francisco 205
4/22/72	133	11	3. First Taste Of Sin	Reprise 2074
4/28/73	97	14	4. Thriller!	Reprise 2130
8/10/74	126	8	5. Lydia	Warner 2806
3/13/76	179	4	6. Lydia Pense & Cold Blood	ABC 917
			COLD CHISEL Australian rock quintet	
6/13/81	171	6	1. East	Elektra 336

DATE CHARTED	PEAK POS	WKS CHRT'D	ARTIST — Album Title	LABEL & NUMBER
			NAT KING COLE	
			formed King Cole Trio in 1939 - died of cancer on 2/15/65 (45)	
4/28/56	16	2	1. Ballads Of The Day	Capitol 680
			"Darling Je Vous Aime Beaucoup"(7)/"A Blossom Fell"(2)	
3/09/57	13	2	2. After Midnight	Capitol 782
			with the King Cole Trio	
4/06/57	1(8)	93	● 3. **Love Is The Thing**	Capitol 824
9/23/57	18	3	4. This Is Nat "King" Cole	Capitol 870
12/16/57	18	6	5. Just One Of Those Things	Capitol 903
5/05/58	18	3	6. St. Louis Blues .... [S]	Capitol 993
			Nat portrayed W.C. Handy in the film about Handy's life	
9/22/58	12	5	7. Cole Espanol .... [F]	Capitol 1031
12/01/58	17	2	8. The Very Thought Of You	Capitol 1084
6/22/59	45	5	9. To Whom It May Concern	Capitol 1190
4/18/60	33	2	10. Tell Me All About Yourself	Capitol 1331
10/24/60	4	11	11. **Wild Is Love**	Capitol 1392
5/15/61	79	17	12. The Touch Of Your Lips	Capitol 1574
5/05/62	27	16	13. Nat King Cole sings/George Shearing plays	Capitol 1675
9/22/62	3	162	● 14. **Ramblin' Rose**	Capitol 1793
			"Ramblin' Rose"(2)	
12/29/62	24	36	15. Dear Lonely Hearts	Capitol 1838
5/25/63	68	6	16. Where Did Everyone Go?	Capitol 1859
7/06/63	14	36	17. Those Lazy-Hazy-Crazy Days Of Summer	Capitol 1932
			"Those Lazy-Hazy-Crazy Days Of Summer"(6)	
8/01/64	18	45	18. I Don't Want To Be Hurt Anymore	Capitol 2118
9/26/64	74	23	19. My Fair Lady	Capitol 2117
2/06/65	4	38	20. **L-O-V-E**	Capitol 2195
3/20/65	30	39	● 21. Unforgettable .... [R]	Capitol 357
			reissue of 1953 10" album	
7/03/65	77	9	22. Songs From "Cat Ballou" And Other Motion Pictures .... [K]	Capitol 2340
			features Nat's film hits	
9/04/65	60	14	23. Looking Back .... [G]	Capitol 2361
			"If I May"(8)/"Send For Me"(6)/"Looking Back"(5)	
2/19/66	74	11	24. Nat King Cole At The Sands .... [L]	Capitol 2434
11/26/66	145	3	25. The Great Songs! .... [E]	Capitol 2558
			recorded in 1957	
9/14/68	187	5	● 26. The Best Of Nat King Cole .... [G]	Capitol 2944
			"Mona Lisa"(1-'50)/"Too Young"(1-'51)	
8/23/69	197	3	27. Close-Up .... [R]	Capitol 252 [2]
			reissue of "Ballads Of The Day"/"Nat King Cole's Top Pops" LPs	
			NATALIE COLE	
			Nat King Cole's daughter	
8/30/75	18	56	● 1. Inseparable	Capitol 11429
			"This Will Be"(6)	
5/29/76	13	30	● 2. Natalie	Capitol 11517
3/05/77	8	28	▲ 3. **Unpredictable**	Capitol 11600
			"I've Got Love On My Mind"(5)	
12/10/77	16	39	▲ 4. Thankful	Capitol 11708
			"Our Love"(10)	
7/15/78	31	16	● 5. Natalie...Live! .... [L]	Capitol 11709 [2]
4/07/79	52	15	● 6. I Love You So	Capitol 11928
12/15/79	44	19	7. We're The Best Of Friends	Capitol 12019
			NATALIE COLE/PEABO BRYSON	
6/14/80	77	22	8. Don't Look Back	Capitol 12079
9/26/81	132	4	9. Happy Love	Capitol 12165
9/17/83	182	3	10. I'm Ready	Epic 38280
			ALBERT COLLINS	
2/12/72	196	2	1. There's Gotta Be A Change	Tumbleweed 103

DATE CHARTED	PEAK POS	WKS CHRT'D	ARTIST — Album Title	LABEL & NUMBER
			JUDY COLLINS folksinger born in Denver, Colorado on 5/1/39	
3/28/64	126	10	1. Judy Collins #3	Elektra 7243
10/02/65	69	13	2. Judy Collins' Fifth Album	Elektra 7300
1/07/67	46	34	● 3. In My Life	Elektra 7320
1/06/68	5	75	● 4. **Wildflowers** .... "Both Sides Now"(8)	Elektra 74012
12/21/68	29	33	● 5. Who Knows Where The Time Goes	Elektra 74033
9/20/69	29	29	6. Recollections .... [K] recorded 1963 thru 1965	Elektra 74055
12/05/70	17	35	● 7. Whales & Nightingales	Elektra 75010
12/04/71	64	13	8. Living	Elektra 75014
5/27/72	37	24	● 9. Colors Of The Day/The Best Of Judy Collins [G]	Elektra 75030
2/10/73	27	20	10. True Stories And Other Dreams	Elektra 75053
4/12/75	17	34	● 11. Judith .... "Send In The Clowns"	Elektra 1032
9/11/76	25	20	12. Bread & Roses	Elektra 1076
8/06/77	42	27	13. So Early In The Spring, The First 15 Years .... [K]	Elektra 6002 [2]
3/17/79	54	16	14. Hard Times For Lovers	Elektra 171
5/03/80	142	6	15. Running For My Life	Elektra 253
3/13/82	190	5	16. Times Of Our Lives	Elektra 60001
			PHIL COLLINS English - drummer and leader of Genesis	
3/14/81	7	76+	● 1. **Face Value**	Atlantic 16029
11/27/82	8	73	▲ 2. **Hello, I Must Be Going!** .... "You Can't Hurry Love"(10)	Atlantic 80035
3/09/85	1(4)+	5+	▲ 3. **No Jacket Required** .... "One More Night"(1)	Atlantic 81240
			WILLIAM COLLINS - see BOOTSY	
			COLOSSEUM British jazz/rock band formed by members of John Mayall's Bluesbreakers	
11/20/71	192	3	1. Colosseum Live	Warner 1942 [2]
			JESSI COLTER Waylon Jenning's wife	
5/03/75	50	27	1. I'm Jessi Colter .... "I'm Not Lisa"(4)	Capitol 11363
2/07/76	109	8	2. Jessi	Capitol 11477
8/07/76	79	8	3. Diamond In The Rough	Capitol 11543
3/21/81	43	19	● 4. Leather and Lace .... WAYLON & JESSI	RCA 3931
			ALICE COLTRANE widow of John Coltrane	
11/13/71	190	2	1. Universal Consciousness .... [I]	Impulse! 9210
10/12/74	79	8	2. Illuminations .... [I] TURIYA ALICE COLTRANE/DEVADIP CARLOS SANTANA	Columbia 32900
			CHI COLTRANE	
9/23/72	148	10	1. Chi Coltrane	Columbia 31275
			JOHN COLTRANE jazz tenor saxophonist - died on 7/17/67 (40)	
11/18/67	194	3	1. Expression .... [I] John's last recording session. February, 1967	Impulse! 9120
11/13/71	186	3	2. Sun Ship .... [I] recorded 8/26/65	Impulse! 9211
			COMMAND ALL-STARS - see ENOCH LIGHT	

DATE CHARTED	PEAK POS	WKS CHRT'D	ARTIST — Album Title	LABEL & NUMBER
			COMMANDER CODY & His Lost Planet Airmen George Frayne is Commander Cody	
11/27/71	82	32	1. Lost In The Ozone .... "Hot Rod Lincoln"(9)	Paramount 6017
9/09/72	94	13	2. Hot Licks, Cold Steel & Truckers Favorites	Paramount 6031
6/16/73	104	9	3. Country Casanova	Paramount 6054
2/16/74	105	14	4. Live From Deep In The Heart Of Texas...... [L]	Paramount 1017
3/01/75	58	10	5. Commander Cody & His Lost Planet Airmen ...	Warner 2847
10/11/75	168	6	6. Tales From The Ozone	Warner 2883
7/31/76	170	3	7. We've Got A Live One Here! .... [L]	Warner 2939 [2]
9/03/77	163	5	8. Rock 'N Roll Again .... COMMANDER CODY BAND	Arista 4125
			COMMODORES Tuskegee, Alabama soul group led by Lionel Richie (1-13)	
8/24/74	138	9	1. Machine Gun	Motown 798
3/22/75	26	33	2. Caught In The Act	Motown 820
11/08/75	29	32	3. Movin' On .... "Sweet Love"(5)	Motown 848
7/10/76	12	39	4. Hot On The Tracks .... "Just To Be Close To You"(7)	Motown 867
4/02/77	3	53	5. **Commodores** .... "Easy"(4)/"Brick House"(5)	Motown 884
11/12/77	3	28	6. **Commodores Live!** .... [L]	Motown 894 [2]
5/27/78	3	33	▲ 7. **Natural High** .... "Three Times A Lady"(1)	Motown 902
11/25/78	23	20	8. Commodores' Greatest Hits .... [G]	Motown 912
8/18/79	3	41	9. **Midnight Magic** .... "Sail On"(4)/"Still"(1)	Motown 926
6/28/80	7	33	▲ 10. **Heroes**	Motown 939
7/11/81	13	40	▲ 11. **In The Pocket** .... "Lady (You Bring Me Up)"(8)/"Oh No"(4)	Motown 955
12/04/82	37	24	● 12. All The Great Hits .... [G]	Motown 6028
6/11/83	141	7	13. Commodores Anthology .... [G]	Motown 6044 [2]
10/01/83	103	11	14. Commodores 13 .... their first album since the departure of Lionel Richie	Motown 6054
2/16/85	24+	8+	15. Nightshift .... "Nightshift"	Motown 6124
			PERRY COMO vocalist with Ted Weems' band from 1936 to 1942	
10/15/55	7	20	1. **So Smooth**	RCA 1085
9/02/57	8	10	2. **We Get Letters**	RCA 1463
12/16/57	8	5	● 3. **Merry Christmas Music** .... [X]	RCA 1243
12/16/57	11	9	4. Dream Along With Me	RCA Camden 403
6/23/58	18	2	5. Saturday Night With Mr. C.	RCA 1004
9/01/58	24	2	6. Como's Golden Records [G] .... "Hot Diggity"(1)/"Round And Round"(1)/"Catch A Falling Star"(1)/ "Magic Moments"(4)	RCA 1007
12/15/58	9	4	7. **Merry Christmas Music** [X-R]	RCA 1243
1/05/59	16	7	8. When You Come To The End Of The Day	RCA 1885
11/02/59	17	3	9. Como Swings	RCA 2010
1/04/60	22	1	● 10. Season's Greetings .... [X]	RCA 2066
12/31/60	27	1	11. Season's Greetings .... [X-R]	RCA 2066
9/25/61	50	13	12. Sing To Me, Mr. C.	RCA 2390
1/06/62	33	3	13. Season's Greetings .... [X-R]	RCA 2066
9/29/62	32	20	14. By Request	RCA 2567
12/08/62	90	6	15. The Best Of Irving Berlin's Songs From "Mr. President" .... with Kaye Ballard & Sandy Stewart	RCA 2630

DATE CHARTED	PEAK POS	WKS CHRT'D	ARTIST — Album Title	LABEL & NUMBER
12/15/62	**74**	3	16. Season's Greetings .... [X-R] made top 10 on Billboard's special Christmas charts (1963)	RCA 2066
9/21/63	**59**	18	17. The Songs I Love	RCA 2708
5/29/65	**47**	17	18. The Scene Changes	RCA 3396
6/11/66	**86**	9	19. Lightly Latin	RCA 3552
10/22/66	**81**	16	20. Perry Como In Italy	RCA 3608
6/21/69	**93**	11	21. Seattle	RCA 4183
1/16/71	**22**	27	22. It's Impossible .... "It's Impossible"(10)	RCA 4473
6/26/71	**101**	9	23. I Think Of You	RCA 4539
5/26/73	**34**	19	● 24. And I Love You So	RCA 0100
8/17/74	**138**	10	25. Perry	RCA 0585
12/20/75	**142**	9	26. Just Out Of Reach	RCA 0863

CON FUNK SHUN
7-man funk/soul band led by Michael Cooper

DATE CHARTED	PEAK POS	WKS CHRT'D	ARTIST — Album Title	LABEL & NUMBER
10/15/77	**51**	28	● 1. Secrets	Mercury 1180
7/01/78	**32**	19	● 2. Loveshine	Mercury 3725
6/02/79	**46**	22	● 3. Candy	Mercury 3754
4/12/80	**30**	20	● 4. Spirit Of Love	Mercury 3806
12/13/80	**51**	19	5. Touch	Mercury 4002
12/12/81	**82**	13	6. Con Funk Shun 7	Mercury 4030
12/04/82	**115**	29	7. To The Max	Mercury 4067
12/03/83	**105**	21	8. Fever	Mercury 814447

CONEY HATCH

DATE CHARTED	PEAK POS	WKS CHRT'D	ARTIST — Album Title	LABEL & NUMBER
9/17/83	**186**	2	1. Outa Hand	Mercury 812869

JOHN CONLEE

DATE CHARTED	PEAK POS	WKS CHRT'D	ARTIST — Album Title	LABEL & NUMBER
6/11/83	**166**	6	1. John Conlee's Greatest Hits .... [G]	MCA 5405

ARTHUR CONLEY
discovered and produced by Otis Redding

DATE CHARTED	PEAK POS	WKS CHRT'D	ARTIST — Album Title	LABEL & NUMBER
5/13/67	**93**	13	1. Sweet Soul Music .... "Sweet Soul Music"(2)	Atco 215
8/19/67	**193**	2	2. Shake, Rattle & Roll	Atco 220
7/06/68	**185**	2	3. Soul Directions	Atco 243

RAY CONNIFF
arranger/conductor for Columbia's leading singers

DATE CHARTED	PEAK POS	WKS CHRT'D	ARTIST — Album Title	LABEL & NUMBER
3/23/57	**11**	7	1. 'S Wonderful! .... [I]	Columbia 925
12/23/57	**10**	34	● 2. 'S Marvelous .... [I]	Columbia 1074
6/23/58	**9**	44	3. 'S Awful Nice .... [I]	Columbia 1137
9/29/58	**9**	48	● 4. Concert In Rhythm .... [I]	Columbia 1163
5/25/59	**10**	11	5. Broadway In Rhythm .... [I]	Columbia 1252
6/29/59	**29**	8	6. Hollywood In Rhythm .... [I]	Columbia 1310
11/23/59	**8**	36	7. Conniff Meets Butterfield .... [I] RAY CONNIFF & BILLY BUTTERFIELD (trumpeter)	Columbia 1346
12/28/59	**14**	2	● 8. Christmas With Conniff .... [X]	Columbia 1390
2/15/60	**8**	54	9. It's The Talk Of The Town	Columbia 1334
3/07/60	**13**	33	10. Concert In Rhythm - Volume II .... [I]	Columbia 1415
8/15/60	**6**	27	11. Young At Heart	Columbia 1489
10/10/60	**4**	58	12. Say It With Music (A Touch Of Latin) ...... [I]	Columbia 1490
12/31/60	**15**	1	13. Christmas With Conniff .... [X-R]	Columbia 1390
2/13/61	**4**	34	● 14. Memories Are Made Of This .... [I]	Columbia 1574
9/11/61	**14**	34	15. Somebody Loves Me	Columbia 1642
12/18/61	**16**	6	16. Christmas With Conniff .... [X-R] made top 10 on Billboard's special Christmas charts (1969)	Columbia 1390
2/17/62	**5**	34	● 17. So Much In Love	Columbia 1720
5/05/62	**6**	25	18. 'S Continental .... [I]	Columbia 1776
10/06/62	**28**	16	19. Rhapsody In Rhythm .... [I]	Columbia 1878

DATE CHARTED	PEAK POS	WKS CHRT'D	ARTIST — Album Title	LABEL & NUMBER
12/08/62	32	4	● 20. We Wish You A Merry Christmas .... [X] made top 10 on Billboard's special Xmas charts ('63/64/72)	Columbia 1892
3/09/63	20	15	21. The Happy Beat .... [I]	Columbia 8749
9/14/63	85	13	22. Just Kiddin' Around .... [I] RAY CONNIFF & BILLY BUTTERFIELD	Columbia 8822
2/15/64	73	17	23. You Make Me Feel So Young .... [I]	Columbia 8918
5/30/64	50	19	24. Speak To Me Of Love	Columbia 8950
10/03/64	23	27	25. Invisible Tears	Columbia 9064
4/03/65	141	5	26. Friendly Persuasion .... [I]	Columbia 9010
6/05/65	34	19	27. Music From Mary Poppins, The Sound Of Music, My Fair Lady, & Other Great Movie Themes	Columbia 9166
9/18/65	54	16	28. Love Affair	Columbia 9152
4/02/66	80	9	29. Happiness Is	Columbia 9261
7/16/66	3	90	● 30. **Somewhere My Love** .... "Somewhere My Love"(9)	Columbia 9319
3/18/67	78	10	31. Ray Conniff's World Of Hits .... [I]	Columbia 9300
5/13/67	180	2	32. En Espanol! .... [F]	Columbia 9408
6/03/67	30	46	33. This Is My Song	Columbia 9476
10/28/67	39	15	34. Hawaiian Album	Columbia 9547
2/17/68	25	41	● 35. It Must Be Him	Columbia 9595
6/01/68	22	39	● 36. Honey	Columbia 9661
10/26/68	70	22	37. Turn Around Look At Me	Columbia 9712
3/08/69	101	14	38. I Love How You Love Me	Columbia 9777
7/12/69	158	5	39. Ray Conniff's Greatest Hits [G]	Columbia 9839
12/20/69	103	21	40. Jean	Columbia 9920
4/25/70	47	28	41. Bridge Over Troubled Water	Columbia 1022
9/26/70	177	5	42. Concert In Stereo/Live At The Sahara/Tahoe .... [L]	Columbia 30122 [2]
12/26/70	120	13	43. We've Only Just Begun	Columbia 30410
3/27/71	98	15	44. Love Story	Columbia 30498
9/11/71	185	5	45. Great Contemporary Instrumental Hits..... [I]	Columbia 30755
2/12/72	138	11	46. I'd Like To Teach The World To Sing	Columbia 31220
6/03/72	114	14	47. Love Theme From "The Godfather"	Columbia 31473
10/07/72	180	10	48. Alone Again (Naturally)	Columbia 31629
2/10/73	165	10	49. I Can See Clearly Now	Columbia 32090
7/07/73	176	5	50. You Are The Sunshine Of My Life	Columbia 32376
10/13/73	194	4	51. Harmony	Columbia 32553

NORMAN CONNORS
jazz drummer featuring vocalists Michael Henderson, Jean Carn, & Phyllis Hyman - also see Aquarian Dream

10/11/75	150	5	1. Saturday Night Special	Buddah 5643
7/24/76	39	24	● 2. You Are My Starship	Buddah 5655
4/09/77	94	16	3. Romantic Journey	Buddah 5682
5/27/78	68	17	4. This Is Your Life	Arista 4177
1/13/79	175	5	5. The Best Of Norman Connors & Friends [G]	Buddah 5716
7/21/79	137	7	6. Invitation	Arista 4216
9/27/80	145	6	7. Take It To The Limit	Arista 9534
12/05/81	197	2	8. Mr. C	Arista 9575

CONTROLLERS

12/17/77	146	6	1. In Control	Juana 200,001

RY COODER
guitar stylist and vocalist

2/12/72	113	8	1. Into The Purple Valley	Reprise 2052
6/08/74	167	6	2. Paradise And Lunch	Reprise 2179
10/23/76	177	5	3. Chicken Skin Music	Reprise 2254

DATE CHARTED	PEAK POS	WKS CHRT'D	ARTIST — Album Title	LABEL & NUMBER
9/10/77	158	5	4. Show Time .... [L]	Warner 3059
8/11/79	62	15	5. Bop Till You Drop	Warner 3358
1/24/81	43	16	6. Borderline	Warner 3489
6/12/82	105	7	7. The Slide Area	Warner 3651

SAM COOKE
born in Chicago, Illinois on 1/22/35 - died in a shooting incident on 12/11/64 (29)

DATE CHARTED	PEAK POS	WKS CHRT'D	ARTIST — Album Title	LABEL & NUMBER
3/10/58	16	2	1. Sam Cooke .... "You Send Me"(1)	Keen 2001
6/30/62	72	8	2. Twistin' The Night Away .... "Twistin' The Night Away"(9)	RCA 2555
10/20/62	22	35	3. The Best Of Sam Cooke .... [G] "Chain Gang"(2)	RCA 2625
3/23/63	94	9	4. Mr. Soul	RCA 2673
9/14/63	62	19	5. Night Beat	RCA 2709
4/04/64	34	19	6. Ain't That Good News .... "Another Saturday Night"(10)	RCA 2899
10/31/64	29	55	7. Sam Cooke At The Copa .... [L]	RCA 2970
2/13/65	44	23	8. Shake .... "Shake"(7)	RCA 3367
7/24/65	128	8	9. The Best Of Sam Cooke, Volume 2 .... [G]	RCA 3373
10/30/65	120	7	10. Try A Little Love	RCA 3435

RITA COOLIDGE
began career as one of the Friends of Delaney & Bonnie

DATE CHARTED	PEAK POS	WKS CHRT'D	ARTIST — Album Title	LABEL & NUMBER
4/03/71	105	10	1. Rita Coolidge	A&M 4291
12/18/71	135	8	2. Nice Feelin'	A&M 3130
11/11/72	46	24	3. The Lady's Not For Sale	A&M 4370
9/22/73	26	24	● 4. Full Moon .... KRIS KRISTOFFERSON & RITA COOLIDGE	A&M 4403
5/25/74	55	15	5. Fall Into Spring	A&M 3627
12/21/74	103	12	6. Breakaway .... KRIS KRISTOFFERSON & RITA COOLIDGE	Monument 33278
12/06/75	85	10	7. It's Only Love	A&M 4531
4/02/77	6	54	▲ 8. **Anytime...Anywhere** .... "(Your Love Has Lifted Me) Higher And Higher"(2)/ "We're All Alone"(7)	A&M 4616
6/17/78	32	22	● 9. Love Me Again	A&M 4699
2/03/79	106	9	10. Natural Act .... KRIS KRISTOFFERSON & RITA COOLIDGE	A&M 4690
9/22/79	95	16	11. Satisfied	A&M 4781
2/14/81	107	8	12. Rita Coolidge/Greatest Hits .... [G]	A&M 4836
9/12/81	160	4	13. Heartbreak Radio	A&M 3727

ALICE COOPER
real name: Vincent Furnier - stage show known as the Theatre Of The Absurd

DATE CHARTED	PEAK POS	WKS CHRT'D	ARTIST — Album Title	LABEL & NUMBER
6/28/69	193	6	1. Pretties For You	Straight 1051
3/20/71	35	38	● 2. Love It To Death	Warner 1883
12/04/71	21	54	● 3. Killer	Warner 2567
7/01/72	2(3)	32	● 4. **School's Out** .... "School's Out"(7)	Warner 2623
3/17/73	1(1)	50	● 5. **Billion Dollar Babies**	Warner 2685
12/08/73	10	21	● 6. **Muscle Of Love**	Warner 2748
8/31/74	8	23	● 7. **Alice Cooper's Greatest Hits** .... [G]	Warner 2803
3/22/75	5	37	● 8. **Welcome To My Nightmare**	Atlantic 18130
7/17/76	27	32	● 9. Alice Cooper Goes To Hell	Warner 2896
5/28/77	42	16	10. Lace And Whiskey .... "You And Me"(9)	Warner 3027
12/17/77	131	6	11. The Alice Cooper Show .... [L]	Warner 3138
12/16/78	60	11	12. From The Inside	Warner 3263

DATE CHARTED	PEAK POS	WKS CHRT'D	ARTIST — Album Title	LABEL & NUMBER
5/24/80	44	17	13. Flush The Fashion	Warner 3436
9/19/81	125	5	14. Special Forces	Warner 3581

PAT COOPER
comedian from Brooklyn, New York

DATE CHARTED	PEAK POS	WKS CHRT'D	ARTIST — Album Title	LABEL & NUMBER
5/28/66	82	42	1. Our Hero...Pat Cooper [C]	United Art. 6446
12/17/66	84	14	2. Spaghetti Sauce & Other Delights [C]	United Art. 6548
3/22/69	193	2	3. More Saucy Stories From...Pat Cooper [C]	United Art. 6690

STEWART COPELAND
drummer of the Police

DATE CHARTED	PEAK POS	WKS CHRT'D	ARTIST — Album Title	LABEL & NUMBER
12/17/83	157	5	1. Rumble Fish [S-I] composed, performed and produced by Copeland	A&M 4983

CHICK COREA
jazz/rock pianist - founded group Return To Forever

DATE CHARTED	PEAK POS	WKS CHRT'D	ARTIST — Album Title	LABEL & NUMBER
3/06/76	42	15	1. The Leprechaun [I]	Polydor 6062
1/15/77	55	12	2. My Spanish Heart [I]	Polydor 9003 [2]
3/11/78	61	14	3. The Mad Hatter [I]	Polydor 6130
8/19/78	86	10	4. Friends [I]	Polydor 6160
3/31/79	100	8	5. An Evening With Herbie Hancock & Chick Corea [I-L]	Columbia 35663 [2]
11/24/79	175	2	6. An Evening With Chick Corea & Herbie Hancock [I-L] above 2 albums recorded during their 1978 concert series	Polydor 6238 [2]
5/10/80	170	3	7. Tap Step [I]	Warner 3425
8/01/81	179	4	8. Three Quartets [I]	Warner 3552

CORNELIUS BROTHERS & SISTER ROSE
Edward, Carter & Rose Cornelius

DATE CHARTED	PEAK POS	WKS CHRT'D	ARTIST — Album Title	LABEL & NUMBER
7/29/72	29	25	1. Cornelius Brothers & Sister Rose "Treat Her Like A Lady"(3)/"Too Late To Turn Back Now"(2)	United Art. 5568

CORPORATION

DATE CHARTED	PEAK POS	WKS CHRT'D	ARTIST — Album Title	LABEL & NUMBER
3/01/69	197	4	1. The Corporation	Capitol 175

DAVE "BABY" CORTEZ
rock and roll organist - real name: David Clowney

DATE CHARTED	PEAK POS	WKS CHRT'D	ARTIST — Album Title	LABEL & NUMBER
9/29/62	107	3	1. Rinky Dink [I] "Rinky Dink"(10)	Chess 1473

LARRY CORYELL
jazz/rock guitarist - also see Eleventh House

DATE CHARTED	PEAK POS	WKS CHRT'D	ARTIST — Album Title	LABEL & NUMBER
5/31/69	196	3	1. Lady Coryell	Vanguard 6509

BILL COSBY
comedian - played Alexander Scott on TV series "I Spy" - star of the new NBC-TV series "The Cosby Show"

DATE CHARTED	PEAK POS	WKS CHRT'D	ARTIST — Album Title	LABEL & NUMBER
6/27/64	21	128	● 1. Bill Cosby Is A Very Funny Fellow, Right! [C]	Warner 1518
11/21/64	32	140	● 2. I Started Out As A Child [C]	Warner 1567
8/28/65	19	152	● 3. Why Is There Air? [C]	Warner 1606
5/28/66	7	106	● 4. **Wonderfulness** [C]	Warner 1634
5/13/67	2(1)	73	● 5. **Revenge** [C]	Warner 1691
9/02/67	18	26	6. Bill Cosby Sings/Silver Throat "Little Ole Man"(4)	Warner 1709
2/24/68	74	11	7. Bill Cosby Sings/Hooray For The Salvation Army Band!	Warner 1728
4/06/68	7	46	● 8. **To Russell, My Brother, Whom I Slept With** [C]	Warner 1734
10/26/68	16	25	● 9. 200 M.P.H. [C]	Warner 1757
2/08/69	37	19	10. It's True! It's True! [C]	Warner 1770
7/12/69	62	16	11. 8:15 12:15 [C] title: times of shows at Harrah's Lake Tahoe	Tetragrm. 5100 [2]

DATE CHARTED	PEAK POS	WKS CHRT'D	ARTIST — Album Title	LABEL & NUMBER
9/06/69	51	25	12. The Best Of Bill Cosby .... [G-C]	Warner 1798
10/18/69	70	24	13. Bill Cosby .... [C]	Uni 73066
3/14/70	80	16	14. More Of The Best Of Bill Cosby .... [G-C]	Warner 1836
9/12/70	165	6	15. "Live" Madison Square Garden Center ..... [C]	Uni 73082
3/06/71	72	8	16. When I Was A Kid .... [C]	Uni 73100
12/11/71	181	7	17. For Adults Only .... [C]	Uni 73112
9/30/72	191	4	18. Inside The Mind of Bill Cosby .... [C]	Uni 73139
6/16/73	187	4	19. Fat Albert .... [C]	MCA 333
6/05/76	100	12	20. Bill Cosby Is Not Himself These Days (Rat Own, Rat Own, Rat Own) .... [N] Bill raps to an instrumental backing	Capitol 11530
12/18/82	64	14	21. Bill Cosby "Himself" .... [C-S] excerpts of his filmed one-man show in Ontario, Canada	Motown 6026

ALEC R. COSTANDINOS & The Syncophonic Orchestra
also see Love & Kisses

3/25/78	92	17	1. Romeo & Juliet .... Shakespeare set to a disco beat	Casablanca 7086

ELVIS COSTELLO & The Attractions
born Declan McManus in Liverpool, England

12/03/77	32	36	● 1. My Aim Is True	Columbia 35037
4/15/78	30	17	2. This Year's Model	Columbia 35331
1/27/79	10	25	● 3. Armed Forces	Columbia 35709
3/22/80	11	15	4. Get Happy!!	Columbia 36347
10/11/80	28	14	5. Taking Liberties .... [K] previously released and unreleased tracks	Columbia 36839
2/14/81	28	15	6. Trust	Columbia 37051
11/14/81	50	13	7. Almost Blue	Columbia 37562
7/24/82	30	24	8. Imperial Bedroom	Columbia 38157
8/13/83	24	24	9. Punch The Clock	Columbia 38897
7/07/84	35	21	10. Goodbye Cruel World	Columbia 39429

JAMES COTTON Band
former sideman with Muddy Waters' band

12/16/67	194	2	1. The James Cotton Blues Band	Verve Fore. 3023
1/18/75	146	9	2. 100% Cotton	Buddah 5620

JOSIE COTTON

8/07/82	147	12	1. Convertible Music	Elektra 60140

COUCHOIS
rock quintet led by Chris, Pat & Mike Couchois - also see Ratchell

4/14/79	170	4	1. Couchois	Warner 3289

JOHN COUGAR
born John Cougar Mellencamp on 10/7/51 in Seymour, Indiana

8/18/79	64	29	1. John Cougar	Riva 7401
10/04/80	37	55	2. Nothin' Matters And What If It Did	Riva 7403
5/08/82	1(9)	93	▲ 3. American Fool .... "Hurts So Good"(2)/"Jack & Diane"(1)	Riva 7501

JOHN COUGAR MELLENCAMP:

11/05/83	9	53	▲ 4. Uh-Huh .... "Crumblin' Down"(9)/"Pink Houses"(8)	Riva 7504

COUNT FIVE
5 teenagers from San Jose, California

12/03/66	122	6	1. Psychotic Reaction .... "Psychotic Reaction"(5)	Double Shot 1001

COUNTRY JOE & THE FISH
Country Joe McDonald - politico-rock leader from San Francisco

6/10/67	39	38	1. Electric Music For The Mind And Body	Vanguard 79244
12/23/67	67	28	2. I-Feel-Like-I'm-Fixin'-To-Die	Vanguard 79266

DATE CHARTED	PEAK POS	WKS CHRT'D	ARTIST — Album Title	LABEL & NUMBER
7/13/68	23	16	3. Together	Vanguard 79277
6/21/69	48	11	4. Here We Are Again	Vanguard 79299
1/03/70	74	9	5. Country Joe & The Fish/Greatest Hits...... [G]	Vanguard 6545
5/02/70	111	9	6. C.J. Fish	Vanguard 6555
8/07/71	185	4	7. War, War, War .... COUNTRY JOE McDONALD	Vanguard 79315
10/30/71	197	2	8. The Life and Times of Country Joe & The Fish from Haight-Ashbury to Woodstock .... [K]	Vanguard 27/28 [2]
			COUNTRY JOE McDONALD:	
2/19/72	179	4	9. Incredible! Live! .... [L]	Vanguard 79316
11/01/75	124	14	10. Paradise With An Ocean View	Fantasy 9495

COUNTS

7/01/72	193	2	1. What's Up Front That-Counts	Westbound 2011

DAVID COURTNEY

2/21/76	194	4	1. David Courtney's First Day	United Art. 553

NOEL COWARD
British actor/writer - died in 1973 (73)

1/28/56	14	1	1. Noel Coward At Las Vegas .... [L]	Columbia 5063

COWSILLS
Barbara (died on 1/31/85 - 56), her daughter and five of her sons

11/04/67	31	17	1. The Cowsills .... "The Rain, The Park & Other Things"(2)	MGM 4498
3/09/68	89	14	2. We Can Fly	MGM 4534
9/07/68	105	12	3. Captain Sad And His Ship Of Fools .... "Indian Lake"(10)	MGM 4554
1/18/69	127	9	4. The Best Of The Cowsills .... [G]	MGM 4597
5/10/69	16	24	5. The Cowsills In Concert .... [L] "Hair"(2)	MGM 4619
5/08/71	200	1	6. On My Side	London 587

CRABBY APPLETON
West Coast rock quintet led by Michael Fennelly

6/27/70	175	6	1. Crabby Appleton	Elektra 74067

CRACK THE SKY

1/24/76	161	6	1. Crack The Sky	Lifesong 6000
10/30/76	142	5	2. Animal Notes	Lifesong 6005
3/11/78	124	8	3. Safety In Numbers	Lifesong 6015

BILLY "CRASH" CRADDOCK
country/rock singer from Greensboro, North Carolina

8/24/74	142	5	1. Rub It In	ABC 817

FLOYD CRAMER
Nashville's top session pianist

8/14/61	70	16	1. On The Rebound .... [I] "On The Rebound"(4)/"San Antonio Rose"(8)	RCA 2359
5/26/62	113	6	2. Floyd Cramer Gets Organ-ized .... [I]	RCA 2488
10/13/62	130	2	3. I Remember Hank Williams .... [I]	RCA 2544
10/23/65	107	13	4. Class Of '65 .... [I]	RCA 3405
9/17/66	123	7	5. Class Of '66 .... [I]	RCA 3650
5/06/67	166	6	6. Here's What's Happening! .... [I]	RCA 3746
4/25/70	183	3	7. The Big Ones, Volume II .... [I]	RCA 4312
5/24/80	170	5	8. Dallas .... [I]	RCA 3613

LES CRANE
TV talk-show host from San Francisco

12/04/71	32	11	1. Desiderata .... Les talks, accompanied by a musical background "Desiderata"(8)	Warner 2570

DATE CHARTED	PEAK POS	WKS CHRT'D	ARTIST — Album Title	LABEL & NUMBER
			HANK CRAWFORD jazz alto saxophonist - formerly with Ray Charles' band	
8/08/64	143	2	1. True Blue .... [I]	Atlantic 1423
4/17/76	159	7	2. I Hear A Symphony .... [I]	Kudu 26
1/29/77	167	3	3. Hank Crawford's Back .... [I]	Kudu 33
			JOHNNY CRAWFORD Mark McCain of TV's "The Rifleman"	
9/01/62	40	10	1. A Young Man's Fancy .... "Cindy's Birthday"(8)	Del-Fi 1223
5/25/63	126	5	2. His Greatest Hits .... [G]	Del-Fi 1229
			RANDY CRAWFORD	
5/31/80	180	7	1. Now We May Begin	Warner 3421
5/23/81	71	19	2. Secret Combination	Warner 3541
6/26/82	148	10	3. Windsong	Warner 23687
11/05/83	164	5	4. Nightline	Warner 23976
			CRAWLER - see BACK STREET CRAWLER	
			CRAZY HORSE Neil Young's back-up group	
3/27/71	84	11	1. Crazy Horse	Reprise 6438
2/05/72	170	6	2. Loose	Reprise 2059
			CRAZY OTTO German pianist - real name: Fritz Schulz-Reichel	
4/16/55	1(2)	21	1. **Crazy Otto** .... [I]	Decca 8113
			PAPA JOHN CREACH rock fiddler - member of Jefferson Airplane	
1/01/72	94	14	1. Papa John Creach	Grunt 1003
			CREAM British: Eric Clapton, Ginger Baker and Jack Bruce	
5/13/67	39	92	● 1. Fresh Cream	Atco 206
12/09/67	4	77	● 2. **Disraeli Gears** .... "Sunshine Of Your Love"(5)	Atco 232
7/13/68	1(4)	46	● 3. **Wheels Of Fire** .... [L] record 1: studio; record 2: Live At The Fillmore "White Room"(6)	Atco 700 [2]
2/15/69	2(2)	26	● 4. **Goodbye**	Atco 7001
7/19/69	3	44	● 5. **Best Of Cream** .... [G]	Atco 291
5/02/70	15	21	6. Live Cream .... [L]	Atco 328
4/01/72	27	16	7. Live Cream - Volume II .... [L]	Atco 7005
10/28/72	135	10	8. Heavy Cream .... [G]	Polydor 3502 [2]
2/19/77	165	6	9. Disraeli Gears .... [R] reissue of album #2 above	RSO 3010
2/19/77	197	4	10. Wheels Of Fire .... [R] reissue of album #3 above	RSO 3802 [2]
			CREATIVE SOURCE	
1/19/74	152	10	1. Creative Source	Sussex 8027
			CREEDENCE CLEARWATER REVIVAL four-man rock group from San Francisco, led by John Fogerty	
7/20/68	52	73	● 1. Creedence Clearwater Revival	Fantasy 8382
2/08/69	7	87	● 2. **Bayou Country** .... "Proud Mary"(2)	Fantasy 8387
9/13/69	1(4)	88	● 3. **Green River** .... "Bad Moon Rising"(2)/"Green River"(2)	Fantasy 8393
12/13/69	3	60	● 4. **Willy and the Poorboys** .... "Down On The Corner"(3)	Fantasy 8397
7/25/70	1(9)	69	● 5. **Cosmo's Factory** .... "Travelin' Band"(2)/"Up Around The Bend"(4)/ "Lookin' Out My Back Door"(2)	Fantasy 8402

DATE CHARTED	PEAK POS	WKS CHRT'D	ARTIST — Album Title	LABEL & NUMBER
12/26/70	5	42	● 6. **Pendulum** .... "Have You Ever Seen The Rain"(8)	Fantasy 8410
4/29/72	12	24	● 7. Mardi Gras .... "Sweet Hitch-Hiker"(6)	Fantasy 9404
12/02/72	15	37	● 8. Creedence Gold .... [G]	Fantasy 9418
7/21/73	61	18	9. More Creedence Gold .... [G]	Fantasy 9430
11/24/73	143	10	10. Live In Europe .... [L] recorded September, 1971	Fantasy CCR-1 [2]
3/06/76	100	14	● 11. Chronicle (The 20 Greatest Hits)............... [G]	Fantasy CCR-2 [2]
12/20/80	62	20	12. The Concert .... [L] originally titled "The Royal Albert Hall Concert", the album was actually recorded at the Oakland Coliseum in 1970	Fantasy 4501
			MARSHALL CRENSHAW	
5/29/82	50	27	1. Marshall Crenshaw	Warner 3673
6/18/83	52	14	2. Field Day	Warner 23873
			CRETONES Los Angeles quartet - Mark Goldenberg, leader	
3/29/80	125	10	1. Thin Red Line	Planet 5
			CREW-CUTS Canadian quartet	
11/27/54	14	1	1. The Crew Cuts On The Campus	Mercury 20140
			BOB CREWE Generation Bob produced many of the Four Seasons' hits	
2/25/67	100	11	1. Music To Watch Girls By .... [I]	DynoVoice 9003
			CRICKETS - see BUDDY HOLLY/BOBBY VEE	
			PETER CRISS drummer of Kiss	
10/14/78	43	20	▲ 1. Peter Criss	Casablanca 7122
			CRITTERS New Jersey quintet	
9/24/66	147	2	1. Younger Girl	Kapp 3485
			JIM CROCE killed in a plane crash on 9/20/73 (30)	
7/01/72	1(5)	93	● 1. **You Don't Mess Around With Jim** .... "You Don't Mess Around With Jim"(8)/"Time In A Bottle"(1)	ABC 756
2/17/73	7	84	● 2. **Life And Times** .... "Bad, Bad Leroy Brown"(1)	ABC 769
12/15/73	2(2)	53	● 3. **I Got A Name** .... "I Got A Name"(10)/"I'll Have To Say I Love You In A Song"(9)	ABC 797
10/05/74	2(2)	46	● 4. **Photographs & Memories/His Greatest Hits** .... [G]	ABC 835
11/01/75	87	18	5. The Faces I've Been .... [E] recordings from 1961-1971	Lifesong 900 [2]
2/26/77	170	3	6. Time In A Bottle/Jim Croce's Greatest Love Songs .... [K]	Lifesong 6007
			STEVE CROPPER - see ALBERT KING	
			BING CROSBY Harry Lillis Crosby - began career with Paul Whiteman in 1926 - died on 10/14/77 (76)	
12/22/56	21	1	1. A Christmas Sing With Bing Around The World .... [X] from the CBS Radio Program - featuring various choirs	Decca 8419
12/02/57	1(1)	7	● 2. **Merry Christmas** .... [X] first charted in 1945 - the #1 Christmas album of all-time "White Christmas"	Decca 8128
3/31/58	13	2	3. Shillelaghs and Shamrocks	Decca 8207
12/15/58	2(1)	4	4. **Merry Christmas** .... [X-R]	Decca 8128
12/28/59	17	2	5. Merry Christmas .... [X-R]	Decca 8128

DATE CHARTED	PEAK POS	WKS CHRT'D	ARTIST — Album Title	LABEL & NUMBER
12/19/60	9	3	6. **Merry Christmas** .... [X-R]	Decca 8128
12/18/61	22	7	7. Merry Christmas .... [X-R]	Decca 8128
12/22/62	46	2	8. Merry Christmas .... [X-R]	Decca 8128
			made top 10 on Billboard's special Christmas charts (1963-73 and 1983)	
12/22/62	50	2	9. I Wish You A Merry Christmas .... [X]	Warner 1484
5/30/64	116	7	10. America, I Hear You Singing	Reprise 2020
			FRANK SINATRA/BING CROSBY/FRED WARING	
3/29/69	162	8	11. Hey Jude/Hey Bing!	Amos 7001
12/10/77	98	9	12. Bing Crosby's Greatest Hits .... [G]	MCA 3031
			recordings from 1939-1947	

DAVID CROSBY
original member of the Byrds

3/20/71	12	18	● 1. If I Could Only Remember My Name	Atlantic 7203
			with West Coast guests Jerry Garcia, Grace Slick, & Joni Mitchell	

DAVID CROSBY/GRAHAM NASH

4/22/72	4	26	● 1. **Graham Nash/David Crosby**	Atlantic 7220
10/11/75	6	31	● 2. **Wind On The Water**	ABC 902
7/24/76	26	15	● 3. Whistling Down The Wire	ABC 956
11/19/77	52	8	4. Crosby/Nash - Live .... [L]	ABC 1042
10/28/78	150	4	5. The Best Of Crosby/Nash .... [G]	ABC 1102

CROSBY, STILLS & NASH
David Crosby/Stephen Stills/Graham Nash/Neil Young (2-4)

6/28/69	6	107	● 1. **Crosby, Stills & Nash**	Atlantic 8229
			CROSBY, STILLS, NASH & YOUNG:	
4/04/70	1(1)	97	● 2. **Deja Vu**	Atlantic 7200
4/24/71	1(1)	42	● 3. **4 Way Street** .... [L]	Atlantic 902 [2]
9/07/74	1(1)	27	● 4. **So Far** .... [G]	Atlantic 18100
			CROSBY, STILLS & NASH:	
7/09/77	2(4)	33	▲ 5. **CSN**	Atlantic 19104
			"Just A Song Before I Go"(7)	
1/10/81	122	5	6. Replay .... [K]	Atlantic 16026
			cuts from C.S.& N. and Stephen Stills albums	
7/17/82	8	41	▲ 7. **Daylight Again**	Atlantic 19360
			"Wasted On The Way"(9)	
7/02/83	43	12	8. Allies .... [L]	Atlantic 80075

CROSS COUNTRY
group evolved from The Tokens

10/13/73	198	2	1. Cross Country	Atco 7024

CHRISTOPHER CROSS
real name: Christopher Geppert

2/16/80	6	116	▲ 1. **Christopher Cross**	Warner 3383
			"Ride Like The Wind"(2)/"Sailing"(1)	
2/19/83	11	31	● 2. Another Page	Warner 23757
			"Think Of Laura"(9)	

CROW
rock/blues quintet - Dave Wagner, lead singer

9/13/69	69	24	1. Crow Music	Amaret 5002
6/06/70	181	4	2. Crow By Crow	Amaret 5006

RODNEY CROWELL
Rosanne Cash's husband

4/26/80	155	10	1. But What Will The Neighbors Think	Warner 3407
10/03/81	105	8	2. Rodney Crowell	Warner 3587

CROWN HEIGHTS AFFAIR
R&B/disco octet led by Phil Thomas

10/04/75	121	17	1. Dreaming A Dream	De-Lite 2017
3/29/80	148	12	2. Sure Shot	De-Lite 9517

DATE CHARTED	PEAK POS	WKS CHRT'D	ARTIST — Album Title	LABEL & NUMBER
			CRUSADERS contemporary jazz group led by Wilton Felder (reeds), Joe Sample (keyboards) & Stix Hooper (drums)	
			JAZZ CRUSADERS:	
1/04/69	184	2	1. Powerhouse .... [I]	Pacific Jz. 20136
10/17/70	90	16	2. Old Socks, New Shoes...New Socks, Old Shoes .... [I]	Chisa 804
			CRUSADERS:	
6/26/71	168	4	3. Pass The Plate .... [I]	Chisa 807
3/04/72	96	29	4. Crusaders 1 .... [I]	Bl. Thumb 6001 [2]
3/10/73	45	29	5. The 2nd Crusade .... [I]	Bl. Thumb 7000 [2]
11/24/73	173	14	6. Unsung Heroes .... [I]	Bl. Thumb 6007
4/13/74	73	20	7. Scratch .... [I-L]	Bl. Thumb 6010
10/26/74	31	23	● 8. Southern Comfort .... [I]	Bl. Thumb 9002 [2]
8/23/75	26	17	9. Chain Reaction .... [I]	Bl. Thumb 6022
5/22/76	38	18	10. Those Southern Knights .... [I]	Bl. Thumb 6024
12/18/76	122	10	11. The Best Of The Crusaders .... [G]	Bl. Thumb 6027 [2]
6/18/77	41	15	12. Free As The Wind .... [I]	Bl. Thumb 6029
7/15/78	34	18	● 13. Images .... [I]	Bl. Thumb 6030
6/09/79	18	39	● 14. Street Life .... [I] with guest vocalist Randy Crawford on "Street Life"	MCA 3094
7/12/80	29	16	15. Rhapsody And Blues .... [I] with guest vocalist Bill Withers on "Soul Shadows"	MCA 5124
10/10/81	59	16	16. Standing Tall .... with guest vocalist Joe Cocker	MCA 5254
7/17/82	144	7	17. Royal Jam .... [L] with B.B. King & The Royal Philharmonic Orchestra	MCA 8017 [2]
4/21/84	79	22	18. Ghetto Blaster	MCA 5429
			CRYAN' SHAMES 6-man band from Chicago	
5/13/67	192	4	1. Sugar & Spice	Columbia 9389
1/13/68	156	5	2. A Scratch In The Sky	Columbia 9586
2/15/69	184	9	3. Synthesis	Columbia 9719
			CRYSTALS Brooklyn female quintet produced by Phil Spector	
3/16/63	131	2	1. He's A Rebel .... "He's A Rebel"(1)	Philles 4001
			JOE CUBA Sextet	
9/17/66	119	3	1. We Must Be Doing Something Right! .... [F]	Tico 1133
1/07/67	131	6	2. Wanted Dead Or Alive (Bang! Bang! Push, Push, Push) .... [F]	Tico 1146
			CUFF LINKS featuring the vocals of Ron Dante (Archies)	
12/06/69	138	11	1. Tracy .... "Tracy"(9)	Decca 75160
			CULTURE CLUB English quartet led by Boy George (real name: George O'Dowd)	
1/08/83	14	88	▲ 1. Kissing To Be Clever .... "Do You Really Want To Hurt Me"(2)/ "Time (Clock Of My Heart)"(2)/"I'll Tumble 4 Ya"(9)	Epic 38398
11/05/83	2(6)	59	▲ 2. **Colour By Numbers** .... "Church Of The Poison Mind"(10)/"Karma Chameleon"(1)/ "Miss Me Blind"(5)	Epic 39107
11/24/84	26	20	▲ 3. Waking Up With The House On Fire	Virgin 39881
			BURTON CUMMINGS lead singer of the Guess Who	
11/06/76	30	20	1. Burton Cummings .... "Stand Tall"(10)	Portrait 34261
7/09/77	51	6	2. My Own Way To Rock	Portrait 34698

DATE CHARTED	PEAK POS	WKS CHRT'D	ARTIST — Album Title	LABEL & NUMBER
			MIKE CURB Congregation	
7/04/70	105	5	1. Come Together	CoBurt 1002
11/21/70	185	2	2. Sweet Gingerbread Man	CoBurt 1003
3/13/71	117	8	3. Burning Bridges and Other Great Motion Picture Themes	MGM 4761
			CURE British duo: Robert Smith and Laurence Tolhurst	
8/13/83	179	8	1. The Walk .... [M]	Sire 23928
2/25/84	181	5	2. Japanese Whispers .... [K] features cuts from mini LP "The Walk" & two 1983 maxi-singles	Sire 25076
6/23/84	180	4	3. The Top	Sire 25086
			TIM CURRY star of "The Rocky Horror Picture Show"	
9/08/79	53	24	1. Fearless	A&M 4773
8/29/81	112	8	2. Simplicity	A&M 4830
			CYMANDE 8-man afro-rock band	
1/13/73	85	17	1. Cymande	Janus 3044
6/30/73	180	4	2. Second Time Round	Janus 3054
			CYMARRON group name taken from the TV series "Cimarron Strip"	
10/02/71	187	3	1. Rings	Entrance 30962
			ANDRE CYMONE Minneapolis native - played bass for Prince	
10/15/83	185	4	1. Survivin' In The 80's	Columbia 38902
			CYRKLE American group managed by the Beatles' manager Brian Epstein	
8/06/66	47	15	1. Red Rubber Ball "Red Rubber Ball"(2)	Columbia 9344
4/01/67	164	2	2. Neon	Columbia 9432
			DALE & GRACE Dale Houston & Grace Broussard	
2/01/64	100	7	1. I'm Leaving It Up To You "I'm Leaving It Up To You"(1)	Montel 100
			DICK DALE & His Del-Tones Southern California surf guitarist	
1/26/63	59	17	1. Surfers' Choice	Deltone 1886
12/14/63	106	11	2. Checkered Flag	Capitol 2002
			KATHY DALTON	
11/16/74	190	3	1. Boogie Bands & One Night Stands	DiscReet 2208
			ROGER DALTREY lead singer of The Who - star of rock opera film "Tommy" - also see Soundtrack "Lisztomania"	
5/26/73	45	20	1. Daltrey	Track 328
8/09/75	28	23	2. Ride A Rock Horse	MCA 2147
7/09/77	46	19	3. One Of The Boys	MCA 2271
8/16/80	22	15	4. McVicar .... [S] Daltrey stars in the film - soundtrack features all members of The Who	Polydor 6284
3/27/82	185	5	5. Best Bits .... [G]	MCA 5301
3/17/84	102	9	6. Parting Should Be Painless	Atlantic 80128
			DAMNATION OF ADAM BLESSING	
3/28/70	181	2	1. The Damnation Of Adam Blessing	United Art. 6738

LIZ DAMON'S Orient Express
Hawaiian

DATE CHARTED	PEAK POS	WKS CHRT'D	ARTIST — Album Title	LABEL & NUMBER
3/06/71	190	2	1. Liz Damon's Orient Express	White Whale 5003

VIC DAMONE
born Vito Farinola on 6/12/28 in Brooklyn, New York

10/13/56	14	8	1. That Towering Feeling!	Columbia 900
3/03/62	64	17	2. Linger Awhile with Vic Damone	Capitol 1646
10/13/62	57	10	3. The Lively Ones	Capitol 1748
7/10/65	86	10	4. You Were Only Fooling	Warner 1602

BILL DANA
comedian a/k/a Jose Jimenez

8/01/60	15	29	1. My Name...Jose Jimenez ...... [C]	Signature 1013
7/17/61	5	51	2. **Jose Jimenez - The Astronaut (The First Man In Space)** ...... [C]	Kapp 1238
12/25/61	109	9	3. More...Jose Jimenez ...... [C]	Kapp 1215
1/13/62	32	22	4. Jose Jimenez In Orbit/Bill Dana On Earth ...... [C]	Kapp 1257
10/13/62	16	20	5. Jose Jimenez Talks To Teenagers Of All Ages ...... [C]	Kapp 1304
2/23/63	30	14	6. Jose Jimenez - Our Secret Weapon ...... [C]	Kapp 1320
12/14/63	128	4	7. Jose Jimenez In Jollywood ...... [C]	Kapp 1332

VIC DANA
born on 8/26/42 in Buffalo, New York

11/16/63	111	9	1. More	Dolton 8026
5/16/64	116	5	2. Shangri-La	Dolton 8028
4/10/65	13	21	3. Red Roses For A Blue Lady "Red Roses For A Blue Lady"(10)	Dolton 8034

RODNEY DANGERFIELD
comedian and star of the film "Caddyshack"

| 8/02/80 | 48 | 19 | 1. No Respect ...... [C] | Casablanca 7229 |
| 11/12/83 | 36 | 20 | 2. Rappin' Rodney ...... [C] | RCA 4869 |

CHARLIE DANIELS Band
Southern rock/boogie band - also see "Volunteer Jam" albums in the Various-Concerts section

7/28/73	164	9	1. Honey In The Rock "Uneasy Rider"(9)	Kama Sutra 2071
12/28/74	38	34	● 2. Fire On The Mountain	Kama Sutra 2603
10/04/75	57	12	3. Nightrider	Kama Sutra 2607
5/15/76	35	18	● 4. Saddle Tramp	Epic 34150
12/04/76	83	10	5. High Lonesome	Epic 34377
11/12/77	105	11	6. Midnight Wind	Epic 34970
5/12/79	5	43	▲ 7. **Million Mile Reflections** "The Devil Went Down To Georgia"(3)	Epic 35751
8/09/80	11	33	▲ 8. **Full Moon**	Epic 36571
4/03/82	26	19	● 9. Windows	Epic 37694
7/23/83	84	12	10. A Decade Of Hits ...... [G]	Epic 38795

RICK DANKO
member (bass) of The Band

| 12/24/77 | 119 | 8 | 1. Rick Danko | Arista 4141 |

BOBBY DARIN
born Walden Robert Cassotto on 5/14/36 in the Bronx, New York - died on 12/20/73 (37)

10/05/59	7	52	1. **That's All** "Mack The Knife"(1)/"Beyond The Sea"(6)	Atco 104
3/07/60	6	38	2. **This Is Darin**	Atco 115
10/17/60	9	38	3. **Darin At The Copa** ...... [L]	Atco 122
5/22/61	18	42	4. The Bobby Darin Story ...... [G] "Splish Splash"(3)/"Queen Of The Hop"(9)/"Dream Lover"(2)	Atco 131

DATE CHARTED	PEAK POS	WKS CHRT'D	ARTIST — Album Title	LABEL & NUMBER
9/11/61	92	10	5. Love Swings	Atco 134
1/27/62	48	31	6. Twist With Bobby Darin	Atco 138
			"You Must Have Been A Beautiful Baby"(5)	
5/12/62	96	11	7. Bobby Darin Sings Ray Charles	Atco 140
10/06/62	45	10	8. Things & Other Things	Atco 146
			"Things"(3)	
11/17/62	100	6	9. Oh! Look At Me Now	Capitol 1791
3/16/63	43	15	10. You're The Reason I'm Living	Capitol 1866
			"You're The Reason I'm Living"(3)	
8/24/63	98	5	11. 18 Yellow Roses	Capitol 1942
			"18 Yellow Roses"(10)	
12/26/64	107	8	12. From Hello Dolly To Goodbye Charlie	Capitol 2194
7/10/65	132	4	13. Venice Blue	Capitol 2322
2/11/67	142	5	14. If I Were A Carpenter	Atlantic 8135
			"If I Were A Carpenter"(8)	

JOHNNY DARRELL

9/06/69	172	3	1. Why You Been Gone So Long	United Art. 6707

JAMES DARREN
born James Ercolani on 10/3/36 in Philadelphia

9/25/61	132	3	1. Gidget Goes Hawaiian (James Darren Sings The Movies)	Colpix 418
5/11/63	48	18	2. Teen-Age Triangle [G]	Colpix 444
			JAMES DARREN/SHELLEY FABARES/PAUL PETERSEN greatest hits of above 3 artists "Goodbye Cruel World"(3)/"Her Royal Majesty"(6)	
6/03/67	187	3	3. James Darren/All	Warner 1688

DARTELLS
6-man band from Oxnard, California

7/06/63	95	5	1. Hot Pastrami!	Dot 25522

SARAH DASH
member of Labelle

1/20/79	182	7	1. Sarah Dash	Kirshner 35477

DAVE & SUGAR
Dave Rowland with female duo

9/17/77	157	4	1. That's The Way Love Should Be	RCA 2477
3/07/81	179	4	2. Dave & Sugar/Greatest Hits [G]	RCA 3915

JOHN DAVIDSON
co-host of TV's "That's Incredible"

10/08/66	19	24	1. The Time Of My Life!	Columbia 9380
4/08/67	125	8	2. My Best To You	Columbia 9448
12/02/67	79	12	3. A Kind Of Hush	Columbia 9534
6/29/68	151	10	4. Goin' Places	Columbia 9654
5/17/69	153	7	5. John Davidson	Columbia 9795
11/22/69	165	5	6. My Cherie Amour	Columbia 9859

DAVE DAVIES
lead guitarist of the Kinks

7/26/80	42	14	1. AFL1-3603	RCA 3603
7/18/81	152	8	2. Glamour	RCA 4036

DANNY DAVIS & THE NASHVILLE BRASS
Danny's real name: George Nowlan

2/15/69	78	24	1. The Nashville Sound [I]	RCA 4059
7/12/69	143	6	2. More Nashville Sounds [I]	RCA 4176
12/27/69	141	20	3. Movin' On [I]	RCA 4232
5/30/70	102	12	4. You Ain't Heard Nothin' Yet [I]	RCA 4334
10/31/70	140	12	5. Down Homers [I]	RCA 4424
4/03/71	161	3	6. Somethin' Else [I]	RCA 4476
9/18/71	184	4	7. Super Country [I]	RCA 4571

DATE CHARTED	PEAK POS	WKS CHRT'D	ARTIST — Album Title	LABEL & NUMBER
11/25/72	193	5	8. Turn On Some Happy! .... [I]	RCA 4803
3/15/80	150	5	9. Danny Davis & Willie Nelson with The Nashville Brass	RCA 3549
			new instrumental backing for earlier recordings by Willie	

MAC DAVIS
born in Lubbock. Texas on 1/21/42

DATE CHARTED	PEAK POS	WKS CHRT'D	ARTIST — Album Title	LABEL & NUMBER
12/25/71	160	17	1. I Believe In Music	Columbia 30926
9/16/72	11	44	● 2. Baby Don't Get Hooked On Me	Columbia 31770
			"Baby Don't Get Hooked On Me"(1)	
4/21/73	120	13	3. Mac Davis	Columbia 32206
5/04/74	13	45	● 4. Stop And Smell The Roses	Columbia 32582
			"Stop And Smell The Roses"(9)	
10/19/74	182	4	5. Song Painter .... [R]	Columbia 9969
			reissue of Mac's first album	
2/08/75	21	14	● 6. All The Love In The World	Columbia 32927
7/05/75	64	10	7. Burnin' Thing	Columbia 33551
4/10/76	156	9	8. Forever Lovers	Columbia 34105
5/24/80	69	15	● 9. It's Hard To Be Humble	Casablanca 7207
10/18/80	67	9	10. Texas In My Rear View Mirror	Casablanca 7239
1/16/82	174	3	11. Midnight Crazy	Casablanca 7257

MILES DAVIS
jazz trumpeteer - began career in 1944 with Billy Eckstine's orchestra

DATE CHARTED	PEAK POS	WKS CHRT'D	ARTIST — Album Title	LABEL & NUMBER
10/02/61	68	19	1. Miles Davis In Person (Friday & Saturday Nights At The Blackhawk, San Francisco) .... [I-L]	Columbia 8494 [2]
3/24/62	116	10	2. Someday My Prince Will Come .... [I]	Columbia 8456
10/06/62	59	7	3. Miles Davis At Carnegie Hall .... [I-L]	Columbia 8612
9/14/63	62	15	4. Seven Steps To Heaven .... [I]	Columbia 8851
4/11/64	93	9	5. Quiet Nights .... [I]	Columbia 8906
9/26/64	116	10	6. Miles Davis In Europe .... [I-L]	Columbia 8983
4/24/65	138	9	7. My Funny Valentine .... [I-L]	Columbia 9106
9/06/69	134	6	8. In A Silent Way .... [I]	Columbia 9875
5/16/70	35	29	● 9. Bitches Brew .... [I]	Columbia 26 [2]
12/12/70	123	12	10. Miles Davis At Fillmore .... [I]	Columbia 30038 [2]
4/24/71	159	8	11. A Tribute To Jack Johnson .... [I-S]	Columbia 30455
			film is a biography of the world heavyweight boxing champ (1908-1915)	
12/25/71	125	13	12. Live-Evil .... [I]	Columbia 30954 [2]
11/18/72	156	11	13. On The Corner .... [I]	Columbia 31906
5/05/73	152	8	14. In Concert .... [I-L]	Columbia 32092 [2]
10/13/73	189	3	15. Basic Miles - The Classic Performances of Miles Davis .... [E-I]	Columbia 32025
			recordings from 1955-1958	
6/08/74	179	5	16. Big Fun .... [I]	Columbia 32866 [2]
1/04/75	141	8	17. Get Up With It .... [I]	Columbia 33236 [2]
			a Duke Ellington tribute album	
3/13/76	168	5	18. Agharta .... [I-L]	Columbia 33967 [2]
5/07/77	190	2	19. Water Babies .... [K-I]	Columbia 34396
			late '60's recordings	
4/11/81	179	2	20. Directions .... [K-I]	Columbia 36472 [2]
			unreleased recordings 1960-1970	
7/25/81	53	18	21. The Man With The Horn .... [I]	Columbia 36790
5/29/82	159	7	22. We Want Miles .... [I-L]	Columbia 38005 [2]
5/21/83	136	7	23. Star People .... [I]	Columbia 38657
6/30/84	169	11	24. Decoy .... [I]	Columbia 38991

DATE CHARTED	PEAK POS	WKS CHRT'D	ARTIST — Album Title	LABEL & NUMBER
			PAUL DAVIS born in Meridian. Mississippi on 4/21/48	
1/11/75	148	6	1. Ride 'Em Cowboy	Bang 401
1/21/78	82	18	2. Singer Of Songs - Teller Of Tales .... "I Go Crazy"(7)	Bang 410
4/26/80	173	4	3. Paul Davis	Bang 36094
12/19/81	52	29	4. Cool Night .... "65 Love Affair"(6)	Arista 9578
			SAMMY DAVIS, JR. Sammy lost his left eye in an auto crash on 11/19/54	
5/14/55	1(6)	27	1. **Starring Sammy Davis, Jr.**	Decca 8118
10/15/55	5	8	2. **Just For Lovers**	Decca 8170
10/20/62	14	22	3. What Kind Of Fool Am I and Other Show-Stoppers	Reprise 6051
3/16/63	96	6	4. Sammy Davis Jr. At The Cocoanut Grove .... [L]	Reprise 6063 [2]
5/25/63	73	15	5. As Long As She Needs Me	Reprise 6082
3/14/64	139	3	6. Sammy Davis Jr. Salutes The Stars Of The London Palladium	Reprise 6095
4/04/64	26	18	7. The Shelter Of Your Arms	Reprise 6114
3/27/65	141	4	8. Our Shining Hour .... SAMMY DAVIS. JR. & COUNT BASIE	Verve 8605
9/04/65	104	4	9. Sammy's Back On Broadway	Reprise 6169
1/11/69	24	25	10. I've Gotta Be Me	Reprise 6324
4/29/72	11	26	11. Sammy Davis Jr. Now .... "The Candy Man"(1)	MGM 4832
10/14/72	128	15	12. Portrait Of Sammy Davis, Jr.	MGM 4852
			SKEETER DAVIS real name: Mary Frances Penick	
4/13/63	61	15	1. The End Of The World .... "The End Of The World"(2)	RCA 2699
			SPENCER DAVIS Group British quartet - Steve Winwood, lead singer	
3/25/67	54	25	1. Gimme Some Lovin' .... "Gimme Some Lovin'"(7)	United Art. 6578
7/15/67	83	9	2. I'm A Man .... "I'm A Man"(10)	United Art. 6589
3/30/68	195	3	3. Spencer Davis' Greatest Hits...................... [G]	United Art. 6641
			TYRONE DAVIS blues singer from Chicago	
3/29/69	146	6	1. Can I Change My Mind .... "Can I Change My Mind"(5)	Dakar 9005
7/11/70	90	11	2. Turn Back The Hands Of Time .... "Turn Back The Hands Of Time"(3)	Dakar 9027
7/01/72	182	6	3. I Had It All The Time	Dakar 76901
8/11/73	174	6	4. Without You In My Life	Dakar 76904
10/02/76	89	9	5. Love And Touch	Columbia 34268
4/07/79	115	12	6. In The Mood With Tyrone Davis	Columbia 35723
1/08/83	137	6	7. Tyrone Davis	Highrise 103
			WILD BILL DAVIS - see JOHNNY HODGES	
			DAWN Tony Orlando. Joyce Vincent Wilson & Telma Hopkins	
12/19/70	35	23	1. Candida .... "Candida"(3)/"Knock Three Times"(1)	Bell 6052
12/18/71	178	2	2. Dawn featuring Tony Orlando	Bell 6069
3/24/73	30	34	● 3. Tuneweaving .... "Tie A Yellow Ribbon Round The Ole Oak Tree"(1)	Bell 1112

DATE CHARTED	PEAK POS	WKS CHRT'D		ARTIST — Album Title	LABEL & NUMBER
10/20/73	43	58	●	4. Dawn's New Ragtime Follies .... "Say. Has Anybody Seen My Sweet Gypsy Rose"(3)/ "Steppin' Out (Gonna Boogie Tonight)"(7)	Bell 1130
				TONY ORLANDO & DAWN:	
12/07/74	16	17		5. Prime Time	Bell 1317
1/11/75	170	4		6. Candida & Knock Three Times .... [R] reissue of album #1 above	Bell 1320
1/18/75	165	5		7. Tony Orlando & Dawn II .... [R] reissue of album #2 above	Bell 1322
4/26/75	20	17		8. He Don't Love You (Like I Love You) .... "He Don't Love You (Like I Love You)"(1)	Elektra 1034
6/28/75	16	32	●	9. Tony Orlando & Dawn/Greatest Hits ...... [G]	Arista 4045
11/01/75	93	6		10. Skybird	Arista 4059
3/20/76	94	6		11. To Be With You	Elektra 1049

DORIS DAY
born Doris Kappelhoff on 4/3/24 - vocalist with Les Brown's band (1943-1946)

DATE CHARTED	PEAK POS	WKS CHRT'D		ARTIST — Album Title	LABEL & NUMBER
2/05/55	15	1		1. Young At Heart .... [S] 10" LP - 6 songs by Doris: 2 by Frank Sinatra	Columbia 6339
6/25/55	1(17)	37		2. **Love Me Or Leave Me** .... [S] Doris portrayed singer Ruth Etting in the film	Columbia 710
2/09/57	11	6		3. Day By Day	Columbia 942
5/30/60	26	7		4. Listen To Day	Columbia DD1
10/02/61	97	8		5. I Have Dreamed	Columbia 8460
3/14/64	102	8		6. Love Him!	Columbia 8931

CORY DAYE
lead singer of Dr. Buzzard's Original Savannah Band

DATE CHARTED	PEAK POS	WKS CHRT'D		ARTIST — Album Title	LABEL & NUMBER
10/13/79	171	5		1. Cory And Me	New York I. 3408

DAZZ BAND
8-man ultrafunk band - formerly known as Kinsman Dazz

DATE CHARTED	PEAK POS	WKS CHRT'D		ARTIST — Album Title	LABEL & NUMBER
6/27/81	154	11		1. Let The Music Play	Motown 957
4/03/82	14	34	●	2. Keep It Live .... "Let It Whip"(5)	Motown 6004
2/12/83	59	16		3. On The One	Motown 6031
12/17/83	73	33		4. Joystick	Motown 6084
10/20/84	83	25 +		5. Jukebox	Motown 6117

DEAD BOYS
American punk-rock quintet

DATE CHARTED	PEAK POS	WKS CHRT'D		ARTIST — Album Title	LABEL & NUMBER
10/22/77	189	4		1. Young, Loud And Snotty	Sire 6038

BILL DEAL & THE RHONDELS
8-man New York City band

DATE CHARTED	PEAK POS	WKS CHRT'D		ARTIST — Album Title	LABEL & NUMBER
4/11/70	185	2		1. The Best Of Bill Deal & The Rhondels ...... [G]	Heritage 35006

JIMMY DEAN
born Seth Ward in Plainview. Texas on 8/10/28

DATE CHARTED	PEAK POS	WKS CHRT'D		ARTIST — Album Title	LABEL & NUMBER
12/04/61	23	28		1. Big Bad John And Other Fabulous Songs And Tales .... "Big Bad John"(1)	Columbia 8535
11/03/62	144	2		2. Portrait Of Jimmy Dean .... "P.T. 109"(8)	Columbia 8694

RONNIE DEAUVILLE

DATE CHARTED	PEAK POS	WKS CHRT'D		ARTIST — Album Title	LABEL & NUMBER
12/09/57	13	2		1. Smoke Dreams	Era 20002

DeBARGE
5-member DeBarge family

DATE CHARTED	PEAK POS	WKS CHRT'D		ARTIST — Album Title	LABEL & NUMBER
9/11/82	24	42	●	1. All This Love	Gordy 6012
10/22/83	36	36	●	2. In A Special Way	Gordy 6061
3/23/85	44 +	3 +		3. Rhythm Of The Night .... "Rhythm Of The Night"	Gordy 6123

DATE CHARTED	PEAK POS	WKS CHRT'D	ARTIST — Album Title	LABEL & NUMBER
			CHRIS DE BURGH British	
4/09/83	**43**	22	1. The Getaway	A&M 4929
6/30/84	**69**	19	2. Man On The Line	A&M 5002
			NICK DE CARO & Orchestra	
4/19/69	**165**	5	1. Happy Heart .... [I]	A&M 4176
			DAVE DEE, DOZY, BEAKY, MICK & TICH English quintet	
8/05/67	**155**	3	1. Greatest Hits .... [G]	Fontana 67567
			JOEY DEE & His Starliters	

12/11/61	**2(6)**	40	1. **Doin' The Twist At The Peppermint**
			    Lounge .... [L]
			    "Peppermint Twist-Part 1"(1)/"Shout"(6)
				Roulette 25166

2/17/62	**18**	23	2. Hey, Let's Twist! .... [S]
			    with Jo-Ann Campbell, Teddy Randazzo & Kay Armen -
			    filmed at New York's Peppermint Lounge
				Roulette 25168

6/30/62	**97**	7	3. Back At The Peppermint Lounge-Twistin' .... [L]	Roulette 25173
			KIKI DEE English	
11/16/74	**28**	18	1. I've Got The Music In Me .... KIKI DEE BAND	Rocket 458
5/14/77	**159**	5	2. Kiki Dee	Rocket 2257
			LENNY DEE organist	
7/09/55	**11**	5	1. Dee-lightful! .... [I]	Decca 8114
6/08/68	**196**	3	2. Gentle On My Mind .... [I]	Decca 74994
3/08/69	**199**	2	3. Turn Around, Look At Me .... [I]	Decca 75073
1/03/70	**189**	3	4. Spinning Wheel .... [I]	Decca 75152
			DEELE Cincinnati soul/funk sextet	
2/04/84	**78**	19	1. Street Beat	Solar 60285
			DEEP PURPLE British heavy-metal band - original lineup: Ritchie Blackmore (guitar), Rod Evans (vocals), Jon Lord (keyboards), Ian Paice (drums), Nicky Simper (bass)	
9/07/68	**24**	23	1. Shades Of Deep Purple .... "Hush"(4)	Tetragram. 102
1/11/69	**54**	14	2. The Book Of Taliesyn	Tetragram. 107
7/12/69	**162**	6	3. Deep Purple	Tetragram. 119

5/16/70	**149**	8	4. Deep Purple/The Royal Philharmonic Ork.
			    "Concerto For Group And
			    Orchestra" .... [L]
			    concert at the Royal Albert Hall - Malcolm Arnold, conductor
			    new members: Roger Glover (replaces Simper), Ian Gillan
			    (replaces Evans)
				Warner 1860

9/12/70	**143**	21	5. Deep Purple In Rock	Warner 1877
8/21/71	**32**	18	6. Fireball	Warner 2564
4/15/72	**7**	118	● 7. **Machine Head** .... "Smoke On The Water"(4)	Warner 2607
10/21/72	**57**	20	8. (Purple Passages) .... [K] highlights from albums 1-3 above	Warner 2644 [2]
1/20/73	**15**	49	● 9. Who Do We Think We Are!	Warner 2678
4/21/73	**6**	52	● 10. **Made In Japan** .... [L]	Warner 2701 [2]

3/02/74	**9**	30	● 11. **Burn** ....
			    new members: David Coverdale (replaces Gillan), Glenn Hughes
			    (replaces Glover)
				Warner 2766

12/07/74	**20**	15	● 12. Stormbringer	Warner 2832

DATE CHARTED	PEAK POS	WKS CHRT'D	ARTIST — Album Title	LABEL & NUMBER
12/06/75	**43**	14	13. Come Taste The Band .... Tommy Bolin replaces Blackmore as lead guitarist (on this album only)	Warner 2895
11/27/76	**148**	6	14. Made In Europe .... [L] European concerts of early 1975	Warner 2995
11/01/80	**148**	4	15. Deepest Purple/The Very Best Of Deep Purple .... [G]	Warner 3486
12/01/84	**17**	19+	● 16. Perfect Strangers .... reunion of Blackmore/Gillan/Glover/Lord/Paice	Mercury 824003

RICK DEES
syndicated television and radio disc jockey

3/05/77	**157**	5	1. The Original Disco Duck .... [N] "Disco Duck (Part 1)"(1)	RSO 3017

DEF LEPPARD
British heavy-metal quintet: Joe Elliott, lead singer

5/03/80	**51**	21	● 1. On Through The Night	Mercury 3828
8/08/81	**38**	28	▲ 2. High 'n' Dry	Mercury 4021
2/05/83	**2(2)**	92	▲ 3. **Pyromania**	Mercury 810308
6/02/84	**72**	17	4. High 'n' Dry .... [R] added remixed version of "Bringin' On The Heartbreak" plus "Me And My Wine" (previously unavailable)	Mercury 818836

DeFRANCO FAMILY featuring Tony DeFranco
5-member family from Canada

10/13/73	**109**	16	1. Heartbeat, It's A Lovebeat .... "Heartbeat - It's A Lovebeat"(3)	20th Century 422
6/29/74	**163**	7	2. Save The Last Dance For Me	20th Century 441

DESMOND DEKKER & THE ACES
Desmond, a Jamaican, was reggae's first successful artist

9/06/69	**153**	3	1. Israelites .... "Israelites"(9)	Uni 73059

DELANEY & BONNIE & FRIENDS
Delaney & Bonnie (Lynn) Bramlett

7/26/69	**175**	3	1. Accept No Substitute - The Original Delaney & Bonnie & Friends	Elektra 74039
4/18/70	**29**	17	2. Delaney & Bonnie & Friends On Tour with Eric Clapton .... [L]	Atco 326
10/10/70	**58**	10	3. To Bonnie From Delaney	Atco 341
4/03/71	**65**	23	4. Motel Shot	Atco 358
4/15/72	**133**	6	5. D&B Together	Columbia 31377

DELEGATION

2/17/79	**84**	16	1. The Promise Of Love	Shadybrook 010

DELFONICS
Philadelphia trio

6/08/68	**100**	6	1. La La Means I Love You .... "La-La-Means I Love You"(4)	Philly Groove 1150
3/08/69	**155**	6	2. Sound Of Sexy Soul	Philly Groove 1151
11/29/69	**111**	19	3. The Delfonics Super Hits .... [G]	Philly Groove 1152
8/15/70	**61**	18	4. The Delfonics .... "Didn't I (Blow Your Mind This Time)"(10)	Philly Groove 1153
6/24/72	**123**	11	5. Tell Me This Is A Dream	Philly Groove 1154

DELLS
Chicago-area R&B quintet formed in 1953

5/25/68	**29**	29	1. There Is .... "Stay In My Corner"(10)	Cadet 804
3/08/69	**146**	10	2. The Dells Musical Menu/Always Together	Cadet 822
6/14/69	**102**	22	3. The Dells Greatest Hits .... [G]	Cadet 824
8/23/69	**54**	24	4. Love Is Blue .... "Oh, What A Night"(10)	Cadet 829
3/14/70	**126**	12	5. Like It Is, Like It Was	Cadet 837

DATE CHARTED	PEAK POS	WKS CHRT'D		ARTIST — Album Title	LABEL & NUMBER
8/28/71	81	16		6. Freedom Means	Cadet 50004
6/24/72	162	5		7. The Dells Sing Dionne Warwicke's	
				Greatest Hits	Cadet 50017
6/23/73	99	9		8. Give Your Baby A Standing Ovation	Cadet 50037
5/04/74	156	6		9. The Dells vs. The Dramatics	Cadet 60027
9/21/74	114	8		10. The Mighty Mighty Dells	Cadet 60030
9/23/78	169	3		11. New Beginnings	ABC 1100
8/30/80	137	12		12. I Touched A Dream	20th Century 618

PACO DE LUCIA - see JOHN McLAUGHLIN

MARTIN DENNY
exotic sounds featuring Martin (piano) & Julius Wechter (vibes)

5/04/59	1(5)	63		1. **Exotica** .... [I]	Liberty 7034
				"Quiet Village"(4)	
8/31/59	8	71		2. **Quiet Village** .... [I]	Liberty 7122
11/23/59	50	1		3. Exotica-Vol. III .... [I]	Liberty 7116
9/29/62	6	27		4. **A Taste Of Honey** .... [I]	Liberty 7237
1/16/65	123	7		5. Hawaii Tattoo .... [I]	Liberty 7394

SANDY DENNY
lead singer of Fairport Convention - died on 4/21/78 (37)

7/20/74	197	2		1. Like An Old Fashioned Waltz	Island 9340

JOHN DENVER
born Henry John Deutchendorf on 12/31/43 in Roswell, New Mexico

10/25/69	148	3		1. Rhymes & Reasons	RCA 4207
5/02/70	197	2		2. Take Me To Tomorrow	RCA 4278
4/17/71	15	80	●	3. Poems, Prayers & Promises	RCA 4499
				"Take Me Home, Country Roads"(2)	
12/04/71	75	16	●	4. Aerie	RCA 4607
9/16/72	4	53	●	5. **Rocky Mountain High**	RCA 4731
				"Rocky Mountain High"(9)	
6/16/73	16	35	●	6. Farewell Andromeda	RCA 0101
12/08/73	1(3)	175	●	7. **John Denver's Greatest Hits** .... [G]	RCA 0374
				"Sunshine On My Shoulders"(1)	
6/29/74	1(1)	96	●	8. **Back Home Again**	RCA 0548
				"Annie's Song"(1)/"Back Home Again"(5)	
3/08/75	2(2)	50	●	9. **An Evening With John Denver** .... [L]	RCA 0764 [2]
				"Thank God I'm A Country Boy"(1)	
10/04/75	1(2)	45	●	10. **Windsong**	RCA 1183
				"I'm Sorry"(1)	
11/08/75	14	16	●	11. Rocky Mountain Christmas .... [X]	RCA 1201
12/20/75	138	6		12. John Denver Gift Pak .... [X]	RCA 1263 [2]
				deluxe Christmas package of previous 2 albums	
9/04/76	7	30	▲	13. **Spirit**	RCA 1694
3/05/77	6	18	▲	14. **John Denver's Greatest Hits,**	
				Volume 2 .... [G]	RCA 2195
12/03/77	45	25	▲	15. I Want To Live	RCA 2521
1/27/79	25	15	●	16. John Denver	RCA 3075
11/10/79	26	12	▲	17. A Christmas Together .... [X]	RCA 3451
				JOHN DENVER & THE MUPPETS	
				made top 10 on Billboard's special Christmas charts (1983)	
3/01/80	39	17		18. Autograph	RCA 3449
7/04/81	32	30	●	19. Some Days Are Diamonds	RCA 4055
3/20/82	39	33	●	20. Seasons Of The Heart	RCA 4256
10/15/83	61	15		21. It's About Time	RCA 4683

DEODATO
Eumir Deodato - Brazilian keyboardist

1/20/73	3	26		1. **Prelude** .... [I]	CTI 6021
				"Also Sprach Zarathustra (2001)"(2)	
8/11/73	19	35		2. Deodato 2 .... [I]	CTI 6029

DATE CHARTED	PEAK POS	WKS CHRT'D	ARTIST — Album Title	LABEL & NUMBER
3/23/74	**114**	9	3. In Concert .... [I] DEODATO/AIRTO (Airto Moreira - Brazilian percussionist)	CTI 6041
5/04/74	**63**	16	4. Whirlwinds .... [I]	MCA 410
11/16/74	**102**	9	5. Artistry .... [I]	MCA 457
9/06/75	**110**	9	6. First Cuckoo .... [I]	MCA 491
10/09/76	**86**	11	7. Very Together .... [I]	MCA 2219
4/29/78	**98**	17	8. Love Island .... [I]	Warner 3132
9/27/80	**186**	3	9. Night Cruiser .... [I]	Warner 3467

DEPECHE MODE
English electro-pop quartet

12/26/81	**192**	9	1. Speak & Spell	Sire 3642
12/04/82	**177**	8	2. A Broken Frame	Sire 23751
7/28/84	**166**	9	3. People Are People	Sire 25124
1/19/85	**172+**	8+	4. Some Great Reward	Sire 25194

DEREK & THE DOMINOS
Eric Clapton, Bobby Whitlock, Jim Gordon, Carl Radle

11/21/70	**16**	65	● 1. Layla .... with Duane Allman "Layla"(10)	Atco 704 [2]
1/27/73	**20**	21	● 2. Derek & The Dominos In Concert .... [L]	RSO 8800 [2]
8/10/74	**107**	10	3. Layla .... [R]	Polydor 3501 [2]
2/19/77	**183**	2	4. Layla .... [R]	RSO 3801 [2]

RICK DERRINGER
member of the McCoys, and Johnny and Edgar Winter's bands

12/01/73	**25**	31	1. All American Boy	Blue Sky 32481
4/26/75	**141**	8	2. Spring Fever	Blue Sky 33423
7/31/76	**156**	9	3. Derringer	Blue Sky 34181
2/19/77	**169**	3	4. Sweet Evil	Blue Sky 34470
7/16/77	**123**	10	5. Derringer Live .... [L]	Blue Sky 34848

TERI DeSARIO

1/19/80	**80**	13	1. Moonlight Madness .... "Yes, I'm Ready"(2-with KC)	Casablanca 7178

JACKIE DeSHANNON
born in Kentucky on 8/21/44

11/01/69	**81**	15	1. Put A Little Love In Your Heart .... "Put A Little Love In Your Heart"(4)	Imperial 12442
7/22/72	**196**	2	2. Jackie	Atlantic 7231

JOHNNY DESMOND - see GLENN MILLER

PAUL DESMOND
alto saxophonist with Dave Brubeck - died 5/30/77 (52)

12/28/63	**129**	3	1. Take Ten .... [I] with Jim Hall (guitar)	RCA 2569
1/10/76	**167**	5	2. 1975: The Duets .... [I] DAVE BRUBECK & PAUL DESMOND	Horizon 703

DETECTIVE
Michael Des Barres, lead singer

5/14/77	**135**	9	1. Detective	Swan Song 8417
1/14/78	**103**	12	2. It Takes One To Know One	Swan Song 8504

DETROIT
7-man Detroit rock group - Mitch Ryder, lead singer

1/29/72	**176**	6	1. Detroit	Paramount 6010

DETROIT EMERALDS
brothers Abe & Ivory Tillmon and James Mitchell

6/19/71	**151**	3	1. Do Me Right	Westbound 2006
2/05/72	**78**	13	2. You Want It, You Got It	Westbound 2013
4/21/73	**181**	4	3. I'm In Love With You	Westbound 2018

DATE CHARTED	PEAK POS	WKS CHRT'D	ARTIST — Album Title	LABEL & NUMBER
			WILLIAM DeVAUGHN	
8/03/74	165	11	1. Be Thankful For What You Got .... "Be Thankful For What You Got"(4)	Roxbury 100
			DEVO Akron, Ohio quintet specializing in robotic rock rhythms	
10/28/78	78	18	1. Q:Are We Not Men? A:We Are Devo!	Warner 3239
6/30/79	73	10	2. Duty Now For The Future	Warner 3337
6/14/80	22	51	● 3. Freedom Of Choice	Warner 3435
4/18/81	50	12	4. DEV-O Live .... [M-L]	Warner 3548
10/10/81	23	25	5. New Traditionalists	Warner 3595
11/20/82	47	20	6. Oh, No! It's Devo	Warner 23741
11/03/84	83	6	7. Shout	Warner 25097
			FRANK DeVOL & the Rainbow Strings	
1/06/62	102	2	1. The Old Sweet Songs Of Christmas ...... [X-I]	Columbia 1543
			BARRY DeVORZON	
11/06/76	42	19	1. Nadia's Theme (The Young And The Restless) .... [I] LP includes 4 cuts by Barry DeVorzon & Perry Botkin, Jr. (others by various artists) "Nadia's Theme"(8) - same version on both albums	A&M 3412
11/06/76	133	12	2. Nadia's Theme (The Young and The Restless) .... [I]	Arista 4104
			DEXYS MIDNIGHT RUNNERS Kevin Rowland, leader of 8-piece Birmingham, England band	
2/12/83	14	24	1. Too-Rye-Ay .... "Come On Eileen"(1)	Mercury 4069
			DENNIS DeYOUNG lead singer of Styx	
10/06/84	29	25	1. Desert Moon .... "Desert Moon"(10)	A&M 5006
			DFX2 San Diego foursome led by twins Douglas & David Farage	
8/20/83	143	8	1. Emotion .... [M]	MCA 36000
			NEIL DIAMOND born in Brooklyn, New York on 1/24/41	
10/29/66	137	4	1. The Feel Of Neil Diamond .... "Cherry, Cherry"(6)	Bang 214
9/16/67	80	19	2. Just For You .... "Girl, You'll Be A Woman Soon"(10)	Bang 217
8/03/68	100	40	3. Neil Diamond's Greatest Hits .... [G]	Bang 219
5/17/69	82	25	4. Brother Love's Travelling Salvation Show .... "Sweet Caroline"(4) - available only on reissues	Uni 73047
12/13/69	30	47	● 5. Touching You Touching Me .... "Holly Holy"(6)	Uni 73071
8/22/70	10	56	● 6. **Neil Diamond/Gold** .... [L] recorded at the Troubadour in Hollywood	Uni 73084
9/12/70	52	25	7. Shilo .... [K]	Bang 221
11/21/70	13	45	● 8. Tap Root Manuscript .... "Cracklin' Rosie"(1)	Uni 73092
2/27/71	100	6	9. Do It! .... [K]	Bang 224
11/13/71	11	25	● 10. Stones .... "I Am...I Said"(4)	Uni 93106
7/15/72	5	41	● 11. **Moods** .... "Song Sung Blue"(1)	Uni 93136
12/09/72	5	78	● 12. **Hot August Night** .... [L] recorded 8/24/72 at the Greek Theatre, Los Angeles	MCA 8000 [2]
1/20/73	36	21	13. Double Gold .... [K]	Bang 227 [2]

DATE CHARTED	PEAK POS	WKS CHRT'D	ARTIST — Album Title	LABEL & NUMBER
9/01/73	**35**	17	● 14. Rainbow .... [K] reissue of cuts from Uni albums	MCA 2103
11/03/73	**2(1)**	34	● 15. **Jonathan Livingston Seagull** .... [S]	Columbia 32550
6/08/74	**29**	42	● 16. Neil Diamond/His 12 Greatest Hits .... [G]	MCA 2106
10/26/74	**3**	27	● 17. **Serenade** .... "Longfellow Serenade"(5)	Columbia 32919
7/04/76	**4**	33	▲ 18. **Beautiful Noise**	Columbia 33965
10/09/76	**102**	5	19. And The Singer Sings His Song .... [K] reissue of selections from Uni & MCA albums	MCA 2227
2/26/77	**8**	21	▲ 20. **Love At The Greek** .... [L] recorded August, 1976 at the Greek Theatre	Columbia 34404 [2]
12/03/77	**6**	24	▲ 21. **I'm Glad You're Here With Me Tonight**	Columbia 34990
12/16/78	**4**	29	▲ 22. **You Don't Bring Me Flowers** .... "You Don't Bring Me Flowers"(1-with Barbra Streisand)	Columbia 35625
1/12/80	**10**	20	▲ 23. **September Morn**	Columbia 36121
11/29/80	**3**	115	▲ 24. **The Jazz Singer** .... [S] "Love On The Rocks"(2)/"Hello Again"(6)/"America"(8) film is a remake of Al Jolson's 1927 classic	Capitol 12120
11/28/81	**17**	27	▲ 25. On The Way To The Sky	Columbia 37628
5/29/82	**48**	42	▲ 26. 12 Greatest Hits, Vol. II .... [G]	Columbia 38068
10/16/82	**9**	34	▲ 27. **Heartlight** .... "Heartlight"(5)	Columbia 38359
6/25/83	**171**	7	28. Classics - The Early Years .... [G] original greatest hits from his Bang label era	Columbia 38792
8/18/84	**35**	25	● 29. Primitive	Columbia 39199
			MANU DIBANGO African	
6/30/73	**79**	13	1. Soul Makossa .... [I]	Atlantic 7267
			DICTATORS Bronx, New York sextet	
7/30/77	**193**	2	1. Manifest Destiny	Asylum 1109
			BO DIDDLEY legendary rock & roller - real name: Elias McDaniel	
11/24/62	**117**	4	1. Bo Diddley	Checker 2984
			DIESEL rock quartet from Holland	
8/08/81	**68**	24	1. Watts In A Tank	Regency 19315
			DIFFORD & TILBROOK Chris Difford & Glenn Tilbrook - vocalists of Squeeze	
7/14/84	**55**	15	1. Difford & Tilbrook	A&M 4985
			DILLARDS country/rock quintet led by Rodney Dillard	
6/10/72	**79**	18	1. Roots And Branches	Anthem 5901
			DILLMAN BAND country/rock quintet led by Steve Solmonson	
4/01/78	**198**	2	1. The Daisy Dillman Band	United Art. 838
5/16/81	**145**	7	2. Lovin' The Night Away	RCA 3909
			AL DI MEOLA guitar virtuoso - member of Return To Forever	
3/27/76	**129**	10	1. Land Of The Midnight Sun .... [I]	Columbia 34074
5/07/77	**58**	12	2. Elegant Gypsy .... [I]	Columbia 34461
4/29/78	**52**	17	3. Casino .... [I]	Columbia 35277
7/12/80	**119**	14	4. Splendido Hotel .... [I]	Columbia 36270 [2]
5/21/81	**97**	13	5. Friday Night In San Francisco .... [I-L] JOHN McLAUGHLIN/AL DI MEOLA/PACO DE LUCIA	Columbia 37152
2/06/82	**55**	13	6. Electric Rendezvous .... [I]	Columbia 37654
12/25/82	**165**	7	7. Tour De Force - "Live" .... [I-L]	Columbia 38373

DATE CHARTED	PEAK POS	WKS CHRT'D	ARTIST — Album Title	LABEL & NUMBER
8/20/83	171	5	8. Passion, Grace & Fire .... [I] JOHN McLAUGHLIN/AL DI MEOLA/PACO DE LUCIA	Columbia 38645
10/29/83	128	6	9. Scenario .... [I]	Columbia 38944
			DINO, DESI & BILLY Jr.'s: Dean Martin & Desi Arnaz - with Billy Hinsche	
9/25/65	51	24	1. I'm A Fool	Reprise 6176
2/12/66	119	6	2. Our Time's Coming	Reprise 6194
			DIO Ronnie James Dio, former lead singer of Black Sabbath & Rainbow	
6/25/83	56	38	● 1. Holy Diver	Warner 23836
7/21/84	23	35	● 2. The Last In Line	Warner 25100
			DION Dion Di Muci - born 7/18/38 in the Bronx, New York	
11/27/61	11	51	1. Runaround Sue .... "Runaround Sue"(1)/"The Wanderer"(2)	Laurie 2009
7/14/62	12	22	2. Lovers Who Wander .... "Lovers Who Wander"(3)/"Little Diane"(8)	Laurie 2012
12/15/62	29	22	3. Dion Sings His Greatest Hits .... [G] 2 cuts: Dion; 10 cuts: Dion & The Belmonts "A Teenager In Love"(5)/"Where Or When"(3)	Laurie 2013
3/23/63	20	21	4. Ruby Baby .... "Ruby Baby"(2)	Columbia 8810
6/22/63	115	6	5. Dion Sings To Sandy (and all his other girls) .... [K] 6 cuts: Dion; 6 cuts: Dion & The Belmonts "Love Came To Me"(10)	Laurie 2017
12/21/68	128	11	6. Dion .... "Abraham, Martin And John"(4)	Laurie 2047
1/01/72	200	2	7. Sanctuary	Warner 1945
12/02/72	197	4	8. Suite For Late Summer	Warner 2642
2/24/73	144	8	9. Reunion-Live at Madison Square Garden 1972 .... [L] DION & THE BELMONTS	Warner 2664
3/24/73	194	5	10. Dion's Greatest Hits .... [G] Dion(4) and Dion & The Belmonts(6) original Laurie hits	Columbia 31942
			DIRE STRAITS English quintet led by Mark Knopfler	
1/06/79	2(1)	41	▲ 1. **Dire Straits** .... "Sultans Of Swing"(4)	Warner 3266
6/30/79	11	19	● 2. Communique	Warner 3330
11/15/80	19	31	● 3. Making Movies	Warner 3480
10/16/82	19	32	4. Love Over Gold	Warner 23728
3/12/83	53	15	5. Twisting By The Pool .... [M]	Warner 29800
4/21/84	46	18	6. Dire Straits Live - Alchemy .... [L]	Warner 25085 [2]
			SENATOR EVERETT McKINLEY DIRKSEN Senator from Illinois ('50-'69) - died on 9/7/69 (73)	
1/07/67	16	16	1. Gallant Men .... [T]	Capitol 2643
8/05/67	148	3	2. Man Is Not Alone .... [T] narration with musical background, conducted by John Cacavas	Capitol 2754
			DIRT BAND - see NITTY GRITTY DIRT BAND	
			DISCO TEX & THE SEX-O-LETTES featuring Sir Monti Rock III	
5/03/75	36	22	1. Disco Tex & His Sex-O-Lettes .... "Get Dancin'"(10)	Chelsea 505
			DIXIE CUPS female trio from New Orleans	
8/29/64	112	5	1. Chapel Of Love .... "Chapel Of Love"(1)	Red Bird 100

DATE CHARTED	PEAK POS	WKS CHRT'D	ARTIST — Album Title	LABEL & NUMBER
			DIXIE DREGS instrumental rock quintet led by Steve Morse	
5/27/78	182	4	1. What If .... [I]	Capricorn 0203
5/19/79	111	13	2. Night Of The Living Dregs .... [I-L] side 2 recorded live at the Montreux Jazz Festival	Capricorn 0216
5/10/80	81	17	3. Dregs of the Earth .... [I]	Arista 9528
			DREGS:	
4/18/81	67	14	4. Unsung Heroes .... [I]	Arista 9548
3/27/82	56	15	5. Industry Standard .... [I]	Arista 9588
			DR. BUZZARD'S ORIGINAL "SAVANNAH" BAND '30s-style group - evolved into Kid Creole	
8/21/76	22	49	● 1. Dr. Buzzard's Original Savannah Band	RCA 1504
2/11/78	36	9	2. Dr. Buzzard's Original Savannah Band Meets King Penett	RCA 2402
			DR. DEMENTO - see **VARIOUS - Radio/TV Celebrity Compilations**	
			DR. HOOK 7-man band led by Ray (eye patch) Sawyer & Dennis Locorriere	
			DR. HOOK & THE MEDICINE SHOW:	
4/29/72	45	23	1. Dr. Hook & The Medicine Show .... "Sylvia's Mother"(5)	Columbia 30898
12/02/72	41	31	2. Sloppy Seconds .... "The Cover Of Rolling Stone"(6)	Columbia 31622
10/27/73	141	6	3. Belly Up!	Columbia 32270
			DR. HOOK:	
7/05/75	141	16	4. Bankrupt .... "Only Sixteen"(6)	Capitol 11397
5/15/76	62	31	5. A Little Bit More	Capitol 11522
11/18/78	66	34	● 6. Pleasure & Pain .... "Sharing The Night Together"(6)/ "When You're In Love With A Beautiful Woman"(6)	Capitol 11859
11/24/79	71	32	7. Sometimes You Win... .... "Sexy Eyes"(5)	Capitol 12018
12/06/80	175	8	8. Rising	Casablanca 7251
12/20/80	142	12	9. Dr. Hook/Greatest Hits .... [G]	Capitol 12122
4/03/82	118	7	10. Players In The Dark	Casablanca 7264
			DR. JOHN real name: Malcolm Rebennack	
10/09/71	184	5	1. Dr. John, The Night Tripper (The Sun, Moon & Herbs) .... with Eric Clapton and Mick Jagger	Atco 362
5/13/72	112	11	2. Dr. John's Gumbo	Atco 7006
3/24/73	24	33	3. In The Right Place .... "Right Place Wrong Time"(9)	Atco 7018
6/16/73	105	12	4. Triumvirate .... MIKE BLOOMFIELD/JOHN PAUL HAMMOND/DR. JOHN	Columbia 32172
5/04/74	105	8	5. Desitively Bonnaroo	Atco 7043
			DOKKEN Los Angeles rock quartet led by Don Dokken	
10/15/83	136	13	1. Breaking The Chains	Elektra 60290
10/13/84	71	26 +	2. Tooth And Nail	Elektra 60376
			THOMAS DOLBY British	
2/05/83	20	31	1. Blinded By Science .... [M] "She Blinded Me With Science"(5)	Harvest 15007
3/19/83	13	28	2. The Golden Age Of Wireless	Capitol 12271
3/17/84	35	18	3. The Flat Earth	Capitol 12309

DATE CHARTED	PEAK POS	WKS CHRT'D	ARTIST — Album Title	LABEL & NUMBER
			JOE DOLCE	
			born of Italian-American parents in Painesville, Ohio	
6/27/81	**181**	4	1. Shaddap You Face	MCA 5211
			featuring Lyn Van Hecke	
			PLACIDO DOMINGO	
			Spanish operatic tenor	
11/07/81	**18**	27	● 1. Perhaps Love	CBS 37243
			with John Denver on the title cut	
3/13/82	**164**	6	2. Domingo-Con Amore	RCA 4265
4/09/83	**117**	11	3. My Life For A Song	CBS 37799
			FATS DOMINO	
			born Antoine Domino on 2/26/28 in New Orleans	
11/10/56	**18**	6	1. Fats Domino - Rock And Rollin'	Imperial 9009
			"I'm In Love Again"(3)	
2/23/57	**19**	2	2. This Is Fats Domino!	Imperial 9028
			"Blueberry Hill"(2)/"Blue Monday"(5)	
3/23/57	**17**	4	3. Rock And Rollin' With Fats Domino	Imperial 9004
			Fats' first album "Ain't That A Shame"(10)	
7/21/62	**113**	6	4. Million Sellers By Fats .... [G]	Imperial 9195
			greatest hits from 1960-1962 "Walking To New Orleans"(6)	
10/05/63	**130**	4	5. Here Comes...Fats Domino	ABC-Para. 455
10/19/68	**189**	2	6. Fats Is Back	Reprise 6304
			DON & THE GOODTIMES	
			Pacific Northwest quintet led by Li'l Don Gallucci	
8/05/67	**109**	4	1. So Good	Epic 26311
			BO DONALDSON & THE HEYWOODS	
			Cincinnati, Ohio septet	
7/06/74	**97**	16	1. Bo Donaldson & The Heywoods	ABC 824
			"Billy, Don't Be A Hero"(1)	
			LOU DONALDSON	
			jazz alto saxophonist	
6/15/63	**141**	2	1. The Natural Soul .... [I]	Blue Note 84108
10/07/67	**141**	11	2. Alligator Bogaloo .... [I]	Blue Note 84263
10/26/68	**182**	6	3. Midnight Creeper .... [I]	Blue Note 84280
			above 2 with George Benson (guitar) & Lonnie Smith (organ)	
4/05/69	**153**	7	4. Say It Loud! .... [I]	Blue Note 84299
10/04/69	**158**	6	5. Hot Dog .... [I]	Blue Note 84318
7/11/70	**190**	2	6. Everything I Play Is Funky .... [I]	Blue Note 84337
9/22/73	**176**	4	7. Sassy Soul Strut .... [I]	Blue Note 109
9/28/74	**185**	3	8. Sweet Lou .... [I]	Blue Note 259
			DONOVAN	
			born Donovan Leitch in Glasgow, Scotland on 2/10/46	
7/17/65	**30**	23	1. Catch The Wind	Hickory 123
12/18/65	**85**	13	2. Fairytale	Hickory 127
9/24/66	**11**	29	3. Sunshine Superman	Epic 26217
			"Sunshine Superman"(1)	
10/01/66	**96**	7	4. The Real Donovan .... [K]	Hickory 135
2/18/67	**14**	21	5. Mellow Yellow	Epic 26239
			"Mellow Yellow"(2)	
12/30/67	**60**	15	6. Wear Your Love Like Heaven	Epic 26349
1/06/68	**185**	3	7. For Little Ones	Epic 26350
1/13/68	**19**	22	● 8. A Gift From A Flower To A Garden	Epic 171 [2]
			deluxe box set of previous 2 albums	
4/06/68	**177**	4	9. Like It Is, Was And Evermore Shall Be .... [K]	Hickory 143
7/27/68	**18**	31	10. Donovan In Concert .... [L]	Epic 26386

DATE CHARTED	PEAK POS	WKS CHRT'D	ARTIST — Album Title	LABEL & NUMBER
10/19/68	20	20	11. The Hurdy Gurdy Man .... "Hurdy Gurdy Man"(5)	Epic 26420
2/22/69	4	56	● 12. **Donovan's Greatest Hits** .... [G]	Epic 26439
9/13/69	23	24	13. Barabajagal .... with The Jeff Beck Group on 2 cuts "Atlantis"(7)	Epic 26481
11/08/69	144	7	14. The Best Of Donovan .... [K]	Hickory 149
7/18/70	16	19	15. Open Road	Epic 30125
11/14/70	128	8	16. Donovan P. Leitch .... [K] compilation of Hickory recordings	Janus 3022 [2]
3/31/73	25	20	17. Cosmic Wheels	Epic 32156
2/02/74	174	5	18. Essence To Essence	Epic 32800
12/14/74	135	6	19. 7-Tease	Epic 33245
6/05/76	174	3	20. Slow Down World	Epic 33945

DOOBIE BROTHERS
California group - lead singers: Tom Johnston ('71-'78), Patrick Simmons ('71-'81) and Michael McDonald ('76-'81)
also see Patrick Simmons

DATE CHARTED	PEAK POS	WKS CHRT'D	ARTIST — Album Title	LABEL & NUMBER
8/26/72	21	119	● 1. Toulouse Street	Warner 2634
3/31/73	7	102	● 2. **The Captain And Me** .... "Long Train Runnin'"(8)	Warner 2694
3/16/74	4	62	● 3. **What Were Once Vices Are Now Habits** .... "Black Water"(1)	Warner 2750
5/17/75	4	25	● 4. **Stampede**	Warner 2835
4/03/76	8	44	▲ 5. **Takin' It To The Streets**	Warner 2899
11/20/76	5	93	▲ 6. **Best Of The Doobies** .... [G]	Warner 2978
9/10/77	10	21	● 7. **Livin' On The Fault Line**	Warner 3045
12/23/78	1(5)	87	▲ 8. **Minute By Minute** .... "What A Fool Believes"(1)	Warner 3193
10/11/80	3	28	▲ 9. **One Step Closer**	Warner 3452
11/21/81	39	15	● 10. Best Of The Doobies, Volume II .... [G]	Warner 3612
7/23/83	79	9	11. The Doobie Brothers Farewell Tour .... [L]	Warner 23772 [2]

DOORS
Jim Morrison (vocals - died 7/3/71-27), Robby Krieger (guitar), Ray Manzarek (keyboards), John Densmore (drums)

DATE CHARTED	PEAK POS	WKS CHRT'D	ARTIST — Album Title	LABEL & NUMBER
3/25/67	2(2)	121	● 1. **The Doors** .... "Light My Fire"(1)	Elektra 74007
11/04/67	3	63	● 2. **Strange Days**	Elektra 74014
8/10/68	1(4)	41	● 3. **Waiting For The Sun** .... "Hello, I Love You"(1)	Elektra 74024
8/09/69	6	28	● 4. **The Soft Parade** .... "Touch Me"(3)	Elektra 75005
3/07/70	4	27	● 5. **Morrison Hotel/Hard Rock Cafe**	Elektra 75007
8/08/70	8	20	● 6. **Absolutely Live** .... [L]	Elektra 9002 [2]
12/19/70	25	21	● 7. 13 .... [G]	Elektra 74079
5/08/71	9	34	● 8. **L.A. Woman**	Elektra 75011
11/06/71	31	15	9. Other Voices	Elektra 75017
2/12/72	55	11	● 10. Weird Scenes Inside The Gold Mine .... [K]	Elektra 6001 [2]
8/05/72	68	15	11. Full Circle	Elektra 75038
9/29/73	158	8	12. The Best Of The Doors .... [G]	Elektra 5035
12/16/78	54	13	13. An American Prayer - Jim Morrison .... Morrison recites his poems, supported musically by the Doors	Elektra 502
11/01/80	17	80	▲ 14. The Doors Greatest Hits .... [G]	Elektra 515
11/05/83	23	20	15. Alive, She Cried .... [E-L] recorded 1968-1970	Elektra 60269

DATE CHARTED	PEAK POS	WKS CHRT'D	ARTIST — Album Title	LABEL & NUMBER
			ANTAL DORATI conductor	
3/16/59	3	54	● 1. **Tchaikovsky: 1812 Festival Overture/Capriccio Italien** .... [I] with the Minneapolis Symphony Orchestra	Mercury 50054
2/27/61	20	16	2. Beethoven: Wellington's Victory/Leonore Overture No. 3/Prometheus Overture .... [I] with the London Symphony Orchestra	Mercury 9000
			CHARLIE DORE British female vocalist	
4/26/80	145	7	1. Where To Now	Island 9559
			JIMMY DORSEY Orchestra & Chorus alto sax & clarinet soloist and bandleader beginning in 1935 - died on 6/12/57 (53)	
10/07/57	19	4	1. The Fabulous Jimmy Dorsey .... 8 of 12 cuts were recorded after Jimmy's death "So Rare"(2)	Fraternity 1008
			LEE DORSEY former professional boxer from New Orleans	
11/12/66	129	5	1. The New Lee Dorsey .... "Working In The Coal Mine"(8)	Amy 8011
			TOMMY DORSEY Orchestra trombone soloist and bandleader beginning in 1934 - died on 11/26/56 (51)	
5/25/59	38	2	1. Tea For Two Cha Chas .... [I] band led by Warren Covington	Decca 8842
			TOMMY & JIMMY DORSEY	
5/19/58	15	6	1. The Fabulous Dorseys In Hi-Fi .... [I] Tommy Dorsey & his orchestra featuring Jimmy Dorsey	Columbia 1190
			DOUBLE EXPOSURE	
8/21/76	129	11	1. Ten Percent	Salsoul 5503
			DOUCETTE Jerry Doucette - Canadian	
3/25/78	159	8	1. Mama Let Him Play	Mushroom 5009
			CARL DOUGLAS Jamaican	
12/14/74	37	17	1. Kung Fu Fighting And Other Great Love Songs .... "Kung Fu Fighting"(1)	20th Century 464
			CAROL DOUGLAS	
3/29/75	177	3	1. The Carol Douglas Album	Midland Int. 0931
11/06/76	188	6	2. Midnight Love Affair	Midland Int. 1798
7/16/77	139	10	3. Full Bloom	Midland Int. 2222
			MIKE DOUGLAS TV talk show host - vocalist with Kay Kyser's band ('45-'49)	
1/29/66	46	15	1. The Men In My Little Girl's Life .... "The Men In My Little Girl's Life"(6)	Epic 26186
			RONNIE DOVE born on 9/7/40 in Baltimore, Maryland	
7/24/65	119	41	1. One Kiss For Old Times' Sake	Diamond 5003
4/02/66	35	21	2. The Best Of Ronnie Dove .... [G]	Diamond 5005
10/22/66	122	5	3. Ronnie Dove Sings The Hits For You	Diamond 5006
3/04/67	121	12	4. Cry	Diamond 5007
			DOVELLS Len Barry, lead singer of Philadelphia quartet	
7/13/63	119	7	1. You Can't Sit Down .... "You Can't Sit Down"(3)	Parkway 7025

DATE CHARTED	PEAK POS	WKS CHRT'D	ARTIST — Album Title	LABEL & NUMBER

LAMONT DOZIER
1/3 of songwriting team Holland-Dozier-Holland

1/26/74	**136**	13	1. Out Here On My Own	ABC 804
1/25/75	**186**	2	2. Black Bach	ABC 839

CARMEN DRAGON
Carmen conducts the Capitol Symphony Orchestra - died on 3/28/84 (69) - father of Daryl Dragon (of Captain & Tennille) - also see Leonard Pennario

4/14/62	**36**	8	1. Nightfall .... [I]	Capitol 8575
			classical melodies	

PETE DRAKE & His Talking Steel Guitar
Grand Ole Opry steel guitarist

5/02/64	**85**	14	1. Forever	Smash 67053

DRAMATICS
Detroit quintet - Ron Banks, lead singer

1/22/72	**20**	24	1. Whatcha See Is Whatcha Get	Volt 6018
			"Whatcha See Is Whatcha Get"(9)/"In The Rain"(5)	
10/13/73	**86**	18	2. A Dramatic Experience	Volt 6019
5/04/74	**156**	6	3. The Dells vs. The Dramatics	Cadet 60027
3/22/75	**31**	18	4. The Dramatic Jackpot	ABC 867
11/15/75	**93**	12	5. Drama V	ABC 916
10/30/76	**103**	25	6. Joy Ride	ABC 955
8/13/77	**60**	19	7. Shake It Well	ABC 1010
5/13/78	**44**	15	● 8. Do What You Wanna Do	ABC 1072
3/08/80	**61**	12	9. 10 1/2	MCA 3196

DREAMBOY
Detroit quintet - Jeff Stanton, lead singer/songwriter

1/14/84	**168**	11	1. Dreamboy .... [M]	Qwest 23988

DREAM SYNDICATE
rock quartet - Steve Wynn, lead singer

8/04/84	**171**	4	1. Medicine Show	A&M 4990

DREAMS
jazz/rock group formed by Mike & Randy Brecker

11/28/70	**146**	6	1. Dreams	Columbia 30225

DREGS - see DIXIE DREGS

DRIFTERS
trend setting R&B vocal group formed in 1953

6/08/63	**110**	9	1. Up On The Roof - The Best Of The Drifters .... [G]	Atlantic 8073
			"There Goes My Baby"(2)/"Save The Last Dance For Me"(1)/ "Up On The Roof"(5)	
8/15/64	**40**	22	2. Under The Boardwalk	Atlantic 8099
			"On Broadway"(9)/"Under The Boardwalk"(4)	
2/06/65	**103**	6	3. The Good Life With The Drifters	Atlantic 8103
3/16/68	**122**	8	4. The Drifters' Golden Hits .... [G]	Atlantic 8153
			greatest hits from 1959-1964	

JULIE DRISCOLL - see BRIAN AUGER

"D" TRAIN
James Williams, lead singer

6/26/82	**128**	9	1. "D" Train	Prelude 14105

EDDY DUCHIN - see CARMEN CAVALLARO

LES DUDEK
session guitarist

4/23/77	**107**	12	1. Say No More	Columbia 34397
5/06/78	**100**	11	2. Ghost Town Parade	Columbia 35088

DATE CHARTED	PEAK POS	WKS CHRT'D	ARTIST — Album Title	LABEL & NUMBER
			DUKE JUPITER rock quartet from Rochester, NY	
6/02/84	**122**	12	1. White Knuckle Ride	Morocco 6097
			GEORGE DUKE jazz keyboard virtuoso	
2/01/75	**141**	6	1. Feel	MPS/BASF 25355
5/31/75	**111**	10	2. The Aura Will Prevail	MPS/BASF 25613
1/24/76	**169**	6	3. I Love The Blues, She Heard My Cry	MPS/BASF 25671
10/23/76	**99**	9	4. "Live"-On Tour In Europe .... [L] THE BILLY COBHAM/GEORGE DUKE BAND	Atlantic 18194
12/04/76	**190**	2	5. Liberated Fantasies .... [I]	MPS/BASF 22835
5/14/77	**192**	3	6. From Me To You	Epic 34469
10/29/77	**25**	24	● 7. Reach For It	Epic 34883
6/03/78	**39**	14	8. Don't Let Go	Epic 35366
3/17/79	**56**	11	9. Follow The Rainbow	Epic 35701
11/24/79	**125**	11	10. Master Of The Game	Epic 36263
5/31/80	**119**	9	11. A Brazilian Love Affair	Epic 36483
5/09/81	**33**	23	12. The Clarke/Duke Project .... STANLEY CLARKE/GEORGE DUKE	Epic 36918
3/06/82	**48**	12	13. Dream On	Epic 37532
4/30/83	**147**	7	14. Guardian Of The Light	Epic 38513
11/26/83	**146**	10	15. The Clarke/Duke Project II .... STANLEY CLARKE/GEORGE DUKE	Epic 38934
			PATTY DUKE star of TV's "Patty Duke Show"	
9/18/65	**90**	12	1. Don't Just Stand There .... "Don't Just Stand There"(8)	United Art. 3452
			DUKES OF DIXIELAND Dixieland jazz combo	
9/09/57	**6**	25	1. **Marching Along With The Dukes Of Dixieland, Vol. 3** .... [I]	Audio Fidel. 1851
12/11/61	**10**	21	2. **The Best Of The Dukes Of Dixieland** .... [G-I]	Audio Fidel. 1956
			ROBBIE DUPREE	
6/14/80	**51**	24	1. Robbie Dupree .... "Steal Away"(6)	Elektra 273
6/13/81	**169**	5	2. Street Corner Heroes	Elektra 344
			DUPREES Jersey City quintet - Joey Vann, lead singer - died 2/28/84 (40)	
12/15/62	**101**	5	1. You Belong To Me .... "You Belong To Me"(7)	Coed 905
			DURAN DURAN British: Simon Le Bon (vocals), Andy Taylor (guitar), John Taylor (bass), Roger Taylor (drums), Nick Rhodes (keyboards)	
6/05/82	**6**	129	▲ 1. **Rio** .... "Hungry Like The Wolf"(3)	Harvest 12211
10/02/82	**98**	15	2. Carnival .... [M] new mixes of previously released material	Harvest 15006
2/19/83	**10**	87	▲ 3. **Duran Duran** .... [R] their first album, released in 1981 "Is There Something I Should Know"(4)	Capitol 12158
12/10/83	**8**	64	▲ 4. **Seven And The Ragged Tiger** .... "Union Of The Snake"(3)/"New Moon On Monday"(10)/ "The Reflex"(1)	Capitol 12310
12/01/84	**4**	19+	▲ 5. **Arena** .... [L] "The Wild Boys"(2)	Capitol 12374
			JIMMY DURANTE Jimmy died on 1/28/80 (86)	
9/21/63	**30**	19	1. September Song .... serious singing by the great comedian	Warner 1506

DATE CHARTED	PEAK POS	WKS CHRT'D	ARTIST — Album Title	LABEL & NUMBER
			IAN DURY & The Blockheads Britain's 'poet of punk' - crippled by polio during childhood	
5/06/78	168	5	1. New Boots And Panties!!!	Stiff 0002
7/21/79	126	6	2. Do It Yourself	Stiff 36104
2/07/81	159	4	3. Laughter	Stiff 36998
			DYKE & THE BLAZERS Dyke is Arlester Christian	
11/04/67	186	4	1. The Funky Broadway	Original Snd. 8876
			BOB DYLAN born Robert Allen Zimmerman on 5/24/41 in Duluth, Minnesota - Bob was the spokesman of the folk-protest movement	
9/07/63	22	32	● 1. The Freewheelin' Bob Dylan	Columbia 8786
3/07/64	20	21	2. The Times They Are A-Changin'	Columbia 8905
9/19/64	43	41	3. Another Side Of Bob Dylan	Columbia 8993
5/01/65	6	43	● 4. **Bringing It All Back Home**	Columbia 9128
10/02/65	3	47	● 5. **Highway 61 Revisited** "Like A Rolling Stone"(2)	Columbia 9189
7/23/66	9	34	● 6. **Blonde On Blonde** "Rainy Day Women #12 & 35"(2)	Columbia 841 [2]
5/06/67	10	94	● 7. **Bob Dylan's Greatest Hits** [G] "Positively 4th Street"(7)	Columbia 9463
1/27/68	2(4)	52	● 8. **John Wesley Harding**	Columbia 9604
5/03/69	3	46	● 9. **Nashville Skyline** "Lay Lady Lay"(7)	Columbia 9825
7/04/70	4	22	● 10. **Self Portrait**	Columbia 30050 [2]
11/14/70	7	23	● 11. **New Morning**	Columbia 30290
12/11/71	14	36	● 12. Bob Dylan's Greatest Hits, Vol. II [G]	Columbia 31120 [2]
8/04/73	16	30	13. Pat Garrett & Billy The Kid [S] Dylan appeared as Alias in the film - (3 vocals by Dylan)	Columbia 32460
12/22/73	17	15	● 14. Dylan [K] outtake recordings from 1969-70	Columbia 32747
2/09/74	1(4)	21	● 15. **Planet Waves** with The Band	Asylum 1003
7/13/74	3	19	● 16. **Before The Flood** [L] the Bob Dylan/Band concert tour	Asylum 201 [2]
2/08/75	1(2)	24	● 17. **Blood On The Tracks**	Columbia 33235
7/26/75	7	14	18. **The Basement Tapes** [E] recorded at Big Pink in Woodstock with The Band in 1967	Columbia 33682 [2]
1/24/76	1(5)	35	▲ 19. **Desire**	Columbia 33893
10/02/76	17	12	● 20. Hard Rain [L] recorded during his tour, the "Rolling Thunder Revue"	Columbia 34349
7/08/78	11	23	● 21. Street-Legal	Columbia 35453
5/12/79	13	25	22. Bob Dylan At Budokan [L] recorded in Japan on 3/1/78	Columbia 36067 [2]
9/08/79	3	26	▲ 23. **Slow Train Coming**	Columbia 36120
7/12/80	24	11	24. Saved	Columbia 36553
9/05/81	33	9	25. Shot Of Love	Columbia 37496
11/19/83	20	24	● 26. Infidels	Columbia 38819
1/05/85	115	9	27. Real Live [L]	Columbia 39944
			DYNAMIC SUPERIORS	
8/09/75	130	10	1. Pure Pleasure	Motown 841
			DYNASTY	
8/02/80	43	21	1. Adventures In The Land Of Music	Solar 3576
10/10/81	119	4	2. The Second Adventure	Solar 20

DATE CHARTED	PEAK POS	WKS CHRT'D	ARTIST — Album Title	LABEL & NUMBER
			RONNIE DYSON 19 year old singer from Brooklyn	
9/05/70	**55**	18	1. (If You Let Me Make Love To You Then) Why Can't I Touch You? .... "(If You Let Me Make Love To You Then) Why Can't I Touch You?"(8)	Columbia 30223
4/07/73	**142**	7	2. One Man Band	Columbia 32211
			EAGLES Don Henley, Glenn Frey, Randy Meisner (1-6), Bernie Leadon (1-5), Don Felder (3-9), Joe Walsh (6-9), Timothy B. Schmit (7-9)	
6/24/72	**22**	49	● 1. Eagles .... "Witchy Woman"(9)	Asylum 5054
5/05/73	**41**	70	● 2. Desperado	Asylum 5068
4/20/74	**17**	87	● 3. On The Border .... "Best Of My Love"(1)	Asylum 1004
6/28/75	**1(5)**	56	● 4. **One Of These Nights** .... "One Of These Nights"(1)/"Lyin' Eyes"(2)/"Take It To The Limit"(4)	Asylum 1039
3/06/76	**1(5)**	133	▲ 5. **Eagles/Their Greatest Hits 1971-1975**... [G]	Asylum 1052
12/25/76	**1(8)**	107	▲ 6. **Hotel California** .... "New Kid In Town"(1)/"Hotel California"(1)	Asylum 1084
10/20/79	**1(9)**	57	▲ 7. **The Long Run** .... "Heartache Tonight"(1)/"The Long Run"(8)/"I Can't Tell You Why"(8)	Asylum 508
11/29/80	**6**	26	▲ 8. **Eagles Live** .... [L]	Asylum 705 [2]
11/13/82	**52**	15	● 9. Eagles Greatest Hits, Volume 2 .... [G]	Asylum 60205
			CHARLES EARLAND jazz organist	
7/11/70	**108**	19	1. Black Talk! .... [I]	Prestige 7758
11/21/70	**131**	10	2. Black Drops .... [I]	Prestige 7815
5/15/71	**176**	7	3. Living Black! .... [I-L]	Prestige 10009
4/03/76	**155**	11	4. Odyssey	Mercury 1049
			EARTH OPERA Boston quartet led by David Grisman & Peter Rowan	
3/22/69	**181**	4	1. The Great American Eagle Tragedy	Elektra 74038
			EARTHQUAKE San Francisco quintet - John Doukas, lead singer	
9/04/76	**151**	4	1. 8.5	Beserkley 0047
			EARTH, WIND & FIRE Chicago group, led by vocalists Maurice White and Philip Bailey	
5/15/71	**172**	13	1. Earth, Wind & Fire	Warner 1905
1/15/72	**89**	13	2. The Need Of Love	Warner 1958
11/25/72	**87**	25	3. Last Days And Time	Columbia 31702
6/09/73	**27**	71	● 4. Head To The Sky	Columbia 32194
3/30/74	**15**	37	● 5. Open Our Eyes	Columbia 32712
9/07/74	**97**	10	6. Another Time .... [R]	Warner 2798 [2]
3/15/75	**1(3)**	55	● 7. **That's The Way Of The World** .... [S] group portrayed a rock band in the film "Shining Star"(1)	Columbia 33280
12/06/75	**1(3)**	54	● 8. **Gratitude** .... [L] contains some studio cuts "Sing A Song"(5)	Columbia 33694 [2]
10/16/76	**2(2)**	30	● 9. **Spirit**	Columbia 34241
12/03/77	**3**	47	▲ 10. **All 'N All**	Columbia 34905
12/02/78	**6**	60	▲ 11. **The Best Of Earth, Wind & Fire, Vol. I** .... [G] "Got To Get You Into My Life"(9)/"September"(8)	ARC 35647
6/16/79	**3**	38	▲ 12. **I Am** .... "Boogie Wonderland"(6)/"After The Love Has Gone"(2)	ARC 35730
11/22/80	**10**	21	● 13. **Faces**	ARC 36795 [2]

DATE CHARTED	PEAK POS	WKS CHRT'D	ARTIST — Album Title	LABEL & NUMBER
11/14/81	5	25	▲ 14. **Raise!** .... "Let's Groove"(3)	ARC 37548
3/12/83	12	21	● 15. Powerlight	Columbia 38367
12/03/83	40	16	16. Electric Universe	Columbia 38980
			ELLIOT EASTON lead guitarist of the Cars	
3/09/85	99+	5+	1. Change No Change	Elektra 60393
			SHEENA EASTON born Sheena Orr on 4/27/59 in Glasgow, Scotland	
3/14/81	24	38	● 1. Sheena Easton .... "Morning Train (Nine To Five)"(1)	EMI America 17049
11/28/81	47	53	● 2. You Could Have Been With Me	EMI America 17061
10/16/82	85	12	3. Madness, Money And Music	EMI America 17080
9/17/83	33	38	4. Best Kept Secret .... "Telefone (Long Distance Love Affair)"(9)	EMI America 17101
10/20/84	15	25+	▲ 5. A Private Heaven .... "Strut"(7)/"Sugar Walls"(9)	EMI America 17132
			EASYBEATS Australian quintet - members George Young & Harry Vanda formed "Flash & The Pan"	
6/10/67	180	5	1. Friday On My Mind	United Art. 6588
			EBN/OZN New York duo: Ebn (instruments)/Ozn (vocals)	
3/31/84	185	4	1. Feeling Cavalier	Elektra 60319
			EBONEE WEBB	
9/12/81	157	7	1. Ebonee Webb	Capitol 12148
			ECHO & THE BUNNYMEN British quartet - Ian McCulloch, lead singer	
7/25/81	184	2	1. Heaven Up Here	Sire 3569
3/26/83	137	9	2. Porcupine	Sire 23770
2/11/84	188	3	3. Echo & The Bunnymen .... [M-L]	Sire 23987
6/09/84	87	11	4. Ocean Rain	Sire 25084
			BILLY ECKSTINE leader of big band from 1944-47	
11/17/62	92	6	1. Don't Worry 'Bout Me	Mercury 60736
			DUANE EDDY born in Corning, New York on 4/26/38 - Duane, with his "twangy" guitar, is rock and roll's #1 instrumentalist	
1/19/59	5	82	1. **Have 'Twangy' Guitar-Will Travel** .... [I] "Rebel-'Rouser"(6)	Jamie 3000
8/03/59	24	17	2. Especially For You... . ... [I]	Jamie 3006
1/25/60	18	13	3. The "Twangs" The "Thang" .... [I]	Jamie 3009
12/26/60	11	21	4. $1,000,000.00 Worth Of Twang .... [I-G] "Forty Miles Of Bad Road"(9)/"Because They're Young"(4)	Jamie 3014
7/17/61	93	15	5. Girls! Girls! Girls! .... [I]	Jamie 3019
5/26/62	82	13	6. Twistin' 'N' Twangin' .... [I]	RCA 2525
10/27/62	72	6	7. Twangy Guitar-Silky Strings .... [I]	RCA 2576
1/19/63	47	17	8. Dance With The Guitar Man	RCA 2648
10/05/63	93	8	9. "Twangin'" Up A Storm!	RCA 2700
5/16/64	144	2	10. Lonely Guitar .... vocal background on above 3 albums by the Anita Kerr Singers	RCA 2798
			EDEN'S CHILDREN Boston-based rock trio led by 'Sham' Schamack	
3/09/68	196	2	1. Eden's Children	ABC 624

DATE CHARTED	PEAK POS	WKS CHRT'D	ARTIST — Album Title	LABEL & NUMBER
			GRAEME EDGE Band featuring Adrian Gurvitz	
			British group led by the Moody Blues' drummer (Edge)	
10/11/75	107	9	1. Kick Off Your Muddy Boots	Threshold 15
7/09/77	164	4	2. Paradise Ballroom	London 686
			DAVE EDMUNDS	
			Welsh - leader of Rockpile	
8/04/79	54	15	1. Repeat When Necessary	Swan Song 8507
5/16/81	48	14	2. Twangin...	Swan Song 16034
1/09/82	163	5	3. The Best Of Dave Edmunds .... [G]	Swan Song 8510
5/01/82	46	14	4. D.E. 7th	Columbia 37930
5/21/83	51	20	5. Information	Columbia 38651
10/13/84	140	4	6. Riff Raff	Columbia 39273
			EDWARD BEAR	
			Canadian trio led by Larry Evoy	
2/10/73	63	16	1. Edward Bear	Capitol 11157
			"Last Song"(3)	
7/07/73	183	6	2. Close Your Eyes	Capitol 11192
			DENNIS EDWARDS	
			member of the Temptations	
3/03/84	48	27	1. Don't Look Any Further	Gordy 6057
			JONATHAN EDWARDS	
11/20/71	42	20	1. Jonathan Edwards	Capricorn 862
			"Sunshine"(4)	
11/18/72	167	9	2. Honky-Tonk Stardust Cowboy	Atco 7015
			VINCENT EDWARDS	
			star of TV series "Ben Casey"	
7/07/62	5	21	1. **Vincent Edwards Sings**	Decca 4311
12/29/62	125	6	2. Sometimes I'm Happy...Sometimes I'm Blue	Decca 4336
			WALTER EGAN	
5/14/77	137	6	1. Fundamental Roll	Columbia 34679
4/15/78	44	31	2. Not Shy	Columbia 35077
			above 2 albums feature Stevie Nicks & Lindsey Buckingham "Magnet And Steel"(8)	
5/28/83	187	2	3. Wild Exhibitions	Backstreet 5400
			EGG CREAM featuring ANDY ADAMS	
5/28/77	197	4	1. Egg Cream	Pyramid 9008
			EGYPTIAN LOVER	
2/09/85	146	9+	1. On The Nile	Egyptian Em. 0663
			8TH DAY	
			Detroit session musicians	
8/07/71	131	16	1. 8th Day	Invictus 7306
			EL CHICANO	
			Mexican-American band led by Bobby Espinosa	
6/13/70	51	17	1. Viva Tirado .... [I]	Kapp 3632
4/17/71	178	9	2. Revolucion	Kapp 3640
5/06/72	173	13	3. Celebration	Kapp 3663
8/04/73	162	16	4. El Chicano	MCA 312
4/06/74	194	3	5. Cinco	MCA 401
			EL COCO	
10/15/77	82	23	1. Cocomotion	AVI 6012
			DONNIE ELBERT	
1/01/72	153	9	1. Where Did Our Love Go	All Platinum 3007

DATE CHARTED	PEAK POS	WKS CHRT'D	ARTIST — Album Title	LABEL & NUMBER
			ELECTRIC FLAG	
			Chicago blues band formed by Mike Bloomfield & Buddy Miles	
4/20/68	31	35	1. A Long Time Comin'	Columbia 9597
1/18/69	76	12	2. The Electric Flag	Columbia 9714
			ELECTRIC INDIAN	
10/04/69	104	9	1. Keem-O-Sabe .... [I]	United Art. 6728
			ELECTRIC LIGHT ORCHESTRA	
			British symphonic rock band led by Jeff Lynne	
6/03/72	196	2	1. No Answer	United Art. 5573
4/21/73	62	22	2. Electric Light Orchestra II	United Art. 040
12/29/73	52	24	3. On The Third Day	United Art. 188
10/19/74	16	32	● 4. Eldorado	United Art. 339
			"Can't Get It Out Of My Head"(9)	
10/25/75	8	48	● 5. **Face The Music**	United Art. 546
			"Evil Woman"(10)	
7/04/76	32	43	● 6. Ole ELO .... [K]	United Art. 630
10/30/76	5	69	▲ 7. **A New World Record**	United Art. 679
			"Telephone Line"(7)	
11/26/77	4	58	▲ 8. **Out Of The Blue**	Jet 823 [2]
6/23/79	5	35	▲ 9. **Discovery**	Jet 35769
			"Shine A Little Love"(8)/"Don't Bring Me Down"(4)	
12/08/79	30	15	▲ 10. ELO's Greatest Hits .... [G]	Jet 36310
7/12/80	4	36	▲ 11. **Xanadu** .... [S]	MCA 6100
			side 1: Olivia Newton-John: side 2: ELO	
			"Xanadu"(8 - with Olivia Newton John)	
8/22/81	16	20	● 12. Time	Jet 37371
			"Hold On Tight"(10)	
7/16/83	36	16	13. Secret Messages	Jet 38490
			ELECTRIC PRUNES	
			Seattle rock quartet led by James Lowe	
4/15/67	113	12	1. The Electric Prunes	Reprise 6248
9/02/67	172	4	2. Underground	Reprise 6262
1/06/68	135	13	3. Mass In F Minor .... [F]	Reprise 6275
			electric rock mass, sung in Latin	
			ELECTRONIC CONCEPT ORCHESTRA	
10/18/69	175	2	1. Electric Love .... [I]	Limelight 86072
			featuring Eddie Higgins on the Moog Synthesizer	
			ELEPHANTS MEMORY	
			rock/jazz group from New York	
5/10/69	200	2	1. Elephants Memory	Buddah 5033
			ELEVENTH HOUSE with LARRY CORYELL	
			jazz/rock quartet	
4/13/74	163	11	1. Introducing The Eleventh House with Larry Coryell .... [I]	Vanguard 79342
8/09/75	163	4	2. Level One .... [I]	Arista 4052
			LARRY ELGART & his Manhattan Swing Orchestra	
6/19/82	24	41	▲ 1. Hooked On Swing .... [I]	RCA 4343
2/12/83	89	14	2. Hooked On Swing 2 .... [I]	RCA 4589
			LES ELGART & His Orchestra	
11/03/56	13	7	1. The Elgart Touch .... [I]	Columbia 875
8/19/57	14	7	2. For Dancers Also .... [I]	Columbia 1008
			LES & LARRY ELGART	
			Les & Larry (brothers) each led his own band in the forties	
10/10/64	128	5	1. Command Performance! Les & Larry Elgart Play The Great Dance Hits .... [I]	Columbia 2221

DATE CHARTED	PEAK POS	WKS CHRT'D	ARTIST — Album Title	LABEL & NUMBER
			YVONNE ELLIMAN	
			Hawaiian - portrayed Mary Magdalene in "Jesus Christ Superstar"	
3/12/77	**68**	16	1. Love Me	RSO 3018
3/11/78	**40**	17	2. Night Flight	RSO 3031
			"If I Can't Have You"(1)	
11/10/79	**174**	6	3. Yvonne	RSO 3038
			DUKE ELLINGTON	
			jazz music's leading bandleader, composer and arranger - died on 5/24/74 (75)	
6/24/57	**14**	1	1. Ellington At Newport .... [I-L]	Columbia 934
			recorded at the Newport Jazz Festival on 7/7/56	
10/03/64	**133**	7	2. Ellington '65: Hits of the 60's/This	
			Time By Ellington .... [I]	Reprise 6122
5/14/66	**145**	3	3. The Duke At Tanglewood .... [I-L]	RCA 2857
			DUKE ELLINGTON/BOSTON POPS/ARTHUR FIEDLER	
2/24/68	**78**	13	4. Francis A. & Edward K.	Reprise 1024
			FRANK SINATRA & DUKE ELLINGTON	
			CASS ELLIOT - see MAMA CASS	
			JOE ELY	
			native of Lubbock, Texas	
4/11/81	**135**	11	1. Musta Notta Gotta Lotta	SouthCoast 5183
10/24/81	**159**	3	2. Live Shots .... [L]	SouthCoast 5262
			KEITH EMERSON	
			member of Emerson, Lake & Palmer - also see Nice	
5/02/81	**183**	3	1. Nighthawks .... [S-I]	Backstreet 5196
			soundtrack produced, composed and performed by Emerson	
			EMERSON, LAKE & PALMER	
			English: Keith Emerson (keyboards), Greg Lake (guitar, vocals), & Carl Palmer (drums)	
2/06/71	**18**	42	● 1. Emerson, Lake & Palmer	Cotillion 9040
7/03/71	**9**	26	● 2. **Tarkus**	Cotillion 9900
1/22/72	**10**	23	● 3. **Pictures At An Exhibition** .... [L]	Cotillion 66666
			based on Mussorgsky's classical composition	
7/29/72	**5**	37	● 4. **Trilogy**	Cotillion 9903
12/15/73	**11**	47	● 5. Brain Salad Surgery	Manticore 66669
9/07/74	**4**	24	● 6. **Welcome back, my friends, to the show**	
			that never ends, Ladies and	
			Gentlemen- .... [L]	Manticore 200 [3]
4/09/77	**12**	26	● 7. Works, Volume 1	Atlantic 7000 [2]
12/10/77	**37**	14	● 8. Works, Volume 2	Atlantic 19147
			above 2 albums feature mostly solo material	
12/09/78	**55**	9	● 9. Love Beach	Atlantic 19211
12/01/79	**73**	10	10. Emerson, Lake & Palmer In Concert .... [L]	Atlantic 19255
			from the 1978 U.S.A.-Canadian tour	
11/29/80	**108**	7	11. The Best Of Emerson, Lake & Palmer ..... [G]	Atlantic 19283
			EMOTIONS	
			sisters Wanda, Sheila, & Jeanette Hutchinson from Chicago	
8/28/76	**45**	27	● 1. Flowers	Columbia 34163
6/25/77	**7**	33	▲ 2. Rejoice	Columbia 34762
			"Best Of My Love"(1)	
12/03/77	**88**	15	3. Sunshine .... [E]	Stax 4100
			reissue of Volt label recordings	
8/26/78	**40**	12	● 4. Sunbeam	Columbia 35385
12/08/79	**96**	10	5. Come Into Our World	ARC 36149
9/26/81	**168**	4	6. New Affair	ARC 37456

DATE CHARTED	PEAK POS	WKS CHRT'D	ARTIST — Album Title	LABEL & NUMBER
			ENCHANTMENT	
			Detroit soul quintet	
3/05/77	104	19	1. Enchantment	United Art. 682
1/21/78	46	21	2. Once Upon A Dream	Roadshow 811
3/17/79	145	8	3. Journey To The Land Of...Enchantment	Roadshow 3269
			ENGLAND DAN & JOHN FORD COLEY	
			Texas duo - Dan Seals is Jim Seals (Seals & Crofts) brother	
8/21/76	17	31	● 1. Nights Are Forever	Big Tree 89517
			"I'd Really Love To See You Tonight"(2)/ "Nights Are Forever Without You"(10)	
4/23/77	80	15	2. Dowdy Ferry Road	Big Tree 76000
4/08/78	61	14	3. Some Things Don't Come Easy	Big Tree 76006
			"We'll Never Have To Say Goodbye Again"(9)	
4/14/79	106	12	4. Dr. Heckle And Mr. Jive	Big Tree 76015
			"Love Is The Answer"(10)	
1/05/80	194	2	5. Best Of England Dan & John Ford Coley .... [G]	Big Tree 76018
			ENGLISH BEAT	
			English ska sextet led by Ranking Roger & Dave Wakeling of General Public	
8/09/80	142	14	1. I Just Can't Stop It	Sire 6091
6/27/81	126	6	2. Wha'ppen?	Sire 3567
11/13/82	39	44	3. Special Beat Service	I.R.S. 70032
12/17/83	87	22	4. What Is Beat? .... [K]	I.R.S. 70040
			ETHEL ENNIS	
3/21/64	147	2	1. This Is Ethel Ennis	RCA 2786
			BRIAN ENO	
			British - founding member of Roxy Music	
8/24/74	151	6	1. Here Come The Warm Jets	Island 9268
5/27/78	171	5	2. Before And After Science	Island 9478
3/21/81	44	13	3. My Life In The Bush Of Ghosts .... [I]	Sire 6093
			BRIAN ENO-DAVID BYRNE	
			JOHN ENTWISTLE	
			British - bass guitarist of The Who	
10/23/71	126	9	1. Smash Your Head Against The Wall	Decca 79183
11/18/72	138	13	2. Whistle Rymes	Track 79190
7/07/73	174	7	3. Rigor Mortis Sets In	Track 321
3/01/75	192	1	4. Mad Dog	Track 2129
			JOHN ENTWISTLE'S OX	
10/10/81	71	9	5. Too Late The Hero	Atco 142
			PRESTON EPPS	
8/15/60	35	1	1. Bongo Bongo Bongo .... [I]	Original Snd. 5002
			ERUPTION	
			Jamaican band featuring Precious Wilson	
4/01/78	133	13	1. Eruption	Ariola 50033
			COKE ESCOVEDO	
			formerly with Santana and Azteca	
3/13/76	195	2	1. Coke	Mercury 1041
5/29/76	190	3	2. Comin' At Ya!	Mercury 1085
2/12/77	195	1	3. Disco Fantasy	Mercury 1132
			ESSEX	
			formed quintet at the U.S. Marine Corps. Camp LeJune	
8/03/63	119	5	1. Easier Said Than Done	Roulette 25234
			"Easier Said Than Done"(1)	

DATE CHARTED	PEAK POS	WKS CHRT'D	ARTIST — Album Title	LABEL & NUMBER
			DAVID ESSEX British - leading actor in London's "Godspell" musical	
1/05/74	32	21	1. Rock On .... "Rock On"(5)	Columbia 32560
			ROY ETZEL trumpet virtuoso from Germany	
12/18/65	140	5	1. The Silence (Il Silenzio) .... [I]	MGM 4330
			EUROGLIDERS Australian pop/rock sextet - Grace Knight, lead singer	
12/22/84	140	11	1. This Island	Columbia 39588
			EURYTHMICS British: Annie Lennox & David Stewart (formerly The Tourists)	
5/28/83	15	59	● 1. Sweet Dreams (Are Made Of This) .... "Sweet Dreams (Are Made Of This)"(1)	RCA 4681
2/04/84	7	37	▲ 2. **Touch** .... "Here Comes The Rain Again"(4)	RCA 4917
7/07/84	115	11	3. Touch Dance .... vocal & instrumental dance remixes of 4 cuts from "Touch" LP	RCA 5086
1/05/85	93	14	4. 1984 (for the love of big brother) .... [S]	RCA 5349
			BETTY EVERETT - see JERRY BUTLER	
			EVERLY BROTHERS born in Brownie, Kentucky - Don on 2/1/37; Phil on 1/19/39	
2/10/58	16	3	1. The Everly Brothers .... "Bye Bye Love"(2)/"Wake Up Little Susie"(1)	Cadence 3003
5/23/60	9	10	2. **It's Everly Time!** .... "So Sad (To Watch Good Love Go Bad)"(7)	Warner 1381
8/22/60	23	8	3. The Fabulous Style Of The Everly Brothers .... [K] "(Til) I Kissed You"(4)/"Let It Be Me"(7)/ "When Will I Be Loved"(8)	Cadence 3040
12/05/60	9	24	4. **A Date With The Everly Brothers** .... "Cathy's Clown"(1)	Warner 1395
8/25/62	35	17	5. The Golden Hits Of The Every Brothers....[G] "Ebony Eyes"(8)/"Walk Right Back"(7)/"Crying In The Rain"(6)/ "That's Old Fashioned"(9)	Warner 1471
8/25/62	35	17	6. The Golden Hits Of The Everly Brothers .... [G]	Warner 1471
9/25/65	141	3	7. Beat & Soul	Warner 1605
7/18/70	180	8	8. The Everly Brothers' Original Greatest Hits .... [G] original Cadence label hits "All I Have To Do Is Dream"(1)/"Bird Dog"(1)/"Problems"(2)	Barnaby 350 [2]
3/10/84	162	5	9. The Everly Brothers Reunion Concert .... [L]	Passport 11001 [2]
10/13/84	38	17	10. EB 84	Mercury 822431
			EVERY MOTHERS' SON New York quintet	
6/10/67	117	11	1. Every Mothers' Son .... "Come On Down To My Boat"(6)	MGM 4471
			EXILE 6-man group from Lexington, Kentucky	
8/19/78	14	26	● 1. Mixed Emotions .... "Kiss You All Over"(1)	Warner 3205
			EXOTIC GUITARS featuring the lead guitar work of Al Casey	
8/03/68	155	5	1. The Exotic Guitars .... [I]	Ranwood 8002
1/04/69	167	11	2. Those Were The Days .... [I]	Ranwood 8040
5/31/69	162	6	3. Indian Love Call .... [I]	Ranwood 8051

DATE CHARTED	PEAK POS	WKS CHRT'D	ARTIST — Album Title	LABEL & NUMBER
			EYE TO EYE duo: Deborah Berg & Julian Marshall (of Marshall Hain)	
6/19/82	99	15	1. Eye To Eye	Warner 3570
			SHELLEY FABARES Nanette Fabray's niece - also see James Darren	
7/21/62	106	11	1. Shelley! "Johnny Angel"(1)	Colpix 426
10/27/62	121	5	2. The Things We Did Last Summer	Colpix 431
			FABIAN Fabian Forte - born in Philadelphia on 2/6/43	
5/18/59	5	21	1. **Hold That Tiger!** "Turn Me Loose"(9)	Chancellor 5003
12/28/59	3	19	2. **Fabulous Fabian**	Chancellor 5005
			BENT FABRIC & His Piano Bent Fabricius-Bierre - from Denmark	
10/27/62	13	39	1. Alley Cat [I] "Alley Cat"(7)	Atco 148
			FABULOUS POODLES English rock quartet	
2/10/79	61	17	1. Mirror Stars	Epic 35666
12/01/79	185	3	2. Think Pink	Epic 36256
			FABULOUS RHINESTONES	
7/29/72	193	6	1. The Fabulous Rhinestones	Just Sunshine 1
9/22/73	193	3	2. Freewheelin'	Just Sunshine 9
			FABULOUS THUNDERBIRDS Texas quartet	
3/28/81	176	7	1. Butt Rockin'	Chrysalis 1319
			FACE TO FACE Boston rock quintet - lead singer Laurie Sargent was featured in the film "Streets Of Fire"	
6/16/84	126	16	1. Face To Face	Epic 38857
			FACES Rod Stewart (joined by Ron Wood of the Jeff Beck Group) replaced Steve Marriott as leader of the revamped British group Small Faces	
4/18/70	119	12	1. First Step group shown as Small Faces	Warner 1851
3/13/71	29	19	2. Long Player	Warner 1892
12/18/71	6	24	● 3. **A Nod Is As Good As A Wink...To A Blind Horse**	Warner 2574
4/21/73	21	16	4. Ooh La La	Warner 2665
1/05/74	63	11	5. Rod Stewart/Faces Live - Coast To Coast Overture and Beginners [L]	Mercury 697
			FACTS OF LIFE	
4/09/77	146	7	1. Sometimes	Kayvette 802
			DONALD FAGEN member of Steely Dan	
10/30/82	11	27	● 1. The Nightfly	Warner 23696
			FAIRPORT CONVENTION English folk/rock group	
12/04/71	200	1	1. Angel Delight	A&M 4319
3/25/72	195	3	2. "Babbacombe" Lee based on the story of condemned prisoner John Lee	A&M 4333
8/16/75	143	8	3. Rising For The Moon	Island 9313

DATE CHARTED	PEAK POS	WKS CHRT'D	ARTIST — Album Title	LABEL & NUMBER
			FAITH, HOPE & CHARITY	
8/30/75	100	14	1. Faith, Hope & Charity	RCA 1100
			PERCY FAITH	
			Canadian conductor-arranger - died on 2/9/76 (67)	
7/28/56	18	2	1. Passport To Romance .... [I]	Columbia 880
5/06/57	8	2	2. **My Fair Lady** .... [I]	Columbia 895
5/25/59	17	14	3. Porgy And Bess .... [I]	Columbia 8105
1/11/60	7	17	● 4. **Bouquet** .... [I]	Columbia 8124
11/28/60	7	8	5. **Jealousy** .... [I]	Columbia 8292
1/09/61	6	19	6. **Camelot** .... [I]	Columbia 8370
10/09/61	38	7	7. Mucho Gusto! More Music Of Mexico .... [I]	Columbia 8439
4/14/62	26	6	8. Bouquet Of Love .... [I]	Columbia 8481
9/29/62	105	5	9. The Music Of Brazil! .... [I]	Columbia 8622
6/22/63	12	36	● 10. Themes for Young Lovers .... [I]	Columbia 8823
10/19/63	80	15	11. Shangri-La! .... [I]	Columbia 8824
2/15/64	103	12	12. Great Folk Themes .... [I]	Columbia 8908
5/30/64	110	7	13. More Themes for Young Lovers .... [I]	Columbia 8967
12/04/65	101	5	14. Broadway Bouquet .... [I]	Columbia 9156
5/27/67	152	5	15. The Academy Award Winner and Other Great Movie Themes .... [I]	Columbia 9450
9/16/67	111	17	16. Today's Themes For Young Lovers	Columbia 9504
3/23/68	121	22	17. For Those In Love	Columbia 9610
9/21/68	95	11	18. Angel Of The Morning (Hit Themes For Young Lovers)	Columbia 9706
2/15/69	88	14	19. Those Were The Days	Columbia 9762
5/31/69	194	4	20. Windmills Of Your Mind .... [I]	Columbia 9835
9/27/69	134	11	21. Love Theme From "Romeo & Juliet"	Columbia 9906
2/14/70	88	14	22. Leaving On A Jet Plane	Columbia 9983
6/13/70	196	2	23. Held Over! Today's Great Movie Themes .... [I]	Columbia 1019
10/17/70	179	4	24. The Beatles Album .... [I]	Columbia 30097
1/23/71	200	2	25. A Time For Love .... [K]	Columbia 30330 [2]
2/27/71	198	2	26. I Think I Love You	Columbia 30502
7/31/71	184	5	27. Black Magic Woman .... [I]	Columbia 30800
12/18/71	186	6	28. Jesus Christ, Superstar .... [I]	Columbia 31042
4/01/72	176	6	29. Joy .... [I]	Columbia 31301
9/23/72	197	4	30. Day By Day	Columbia 31627
			MARIANNE FAITHFULL	
			English	
6/05/65	12	31	1. Marianne Faithfull	London 423
12/25/65	81	16	2. Go Away From My World	London 452
11/19/66	147	2	3. Faithfull Forever...	London 482
4/05/69	171	10	4. Marianne Faithfull's Greatest Hits .... [G]	London 547
2/02/80	82	15	5. Broken English	Island 9570
10/17/81	104	9	6. Dangerous Acquaintances	Island 9648
3/26/83	107	7	7. A Child's Adventure	Island 90066
			FALCO	
			Austrian	
5/07/83	64	13	1. Einzelhaft	A&M 4951
			contains original version of "Der Kommissar"	
			AGNETHA FALTSKOG	
			member of Abba	
9/17/83	102	11	1. Wrap Your Arms Around Me	Polydor 813242
			FAME - see KIDS FROM "FAME"	

DATE CHARTED	PEAK POS	WKS CHRT'D	ARTIST — Album Title	LABEL & NUMBER
			GEORGIE FAME English	
5/01/65	**137**	3	1. Yeh Yeh	Imperial 12282
5/11/68	**185**	4	2. The Ballad Of Bonnie And Clyde .... "The Ballad Of Bonnie And Clyde"(7)	Epic 26368
			FAMILY British quintet - Roger Chapman, lead singer	
2/05/72	**177**	7	1. Fearless	United Art. 5562
10/28/72	**183**	5	2. Bandstand	United Art. 5644
			FANNY female rock quartet	
10/23/71	**150**	7	1. Charity Ball	Reprise 6456
4/01/72	**135**	6	2. Fanny Hill	Reprise 2058
			FANTASTIC FOUR	
6/21/75	**99**	16	1. Alvin Stone (The Birth And Death Of A Gangster)	Westbound 201
			FANTASY rock quintet (aged 16-21)	
8/15/70	**194**	3	1. Fantasy	Liberty 7643
			DONNA FARGO Donna was stricken with multiple sclerosis in 1979	
7/15/72	**47**	43	● 1. The Happiest Girl In The Whole U.S.A. .... "Funny Face"(5)	Dot 26000
3/17/73	**104**	11	2. My Second Album	Dot 26006
			FARQUAHR brothers Barnswallow, Hummingbird, Condor & Flamingo Farquahr	
12/05/70	**195**	3	1. Farquahr	Elektra 74083
			EILEEN FARRELL operatic soprano	
2/13/61	**15**	17	1. I've Got A Right To Sing The Blues	Columbia 1465
			JOE FARRELL - see GEORGE BENSON	
			FASTWAY British rock trio led by Fast Eddie Clarke (Motorhead)	
5/28/83	**31**	32	1. Fastway	Columbia 38662
7/21/84	**59**	14	2. All Fired Up	Columbia 39373
			FATBACK disco/funk band	
2/28/76	**158**	8	1. Raising Hell	Event 6905
8/28/76	**182**	5	2. Night Fever	Spring 6711
8/12/78	**73**	12	3. Fired Up 'N' Kickin'	Spring 6718
9/29/79	**89**	12	4. Fatback XII	Spring 6723
4/19/80	**44**	27	● 5. Hot Box	Spring 6726
11/01/80	**91**	7	6. 14 Karat	Spring 6729
6/20/81	**102**	8	7. Tasty Jam	Spring 6731
1/09/82	**148**	4	8. Gigolo	Spring 6734
			FAT BOYS rap trio	
1/05/85	**48**	14+	● 1. Fat Boys	Sutra 1015
			FAT MATTRESS English rock quartet	
11/15/69	**134**	10	1. Fat Mattress	Atco 309
			FAZE-O Chicago R&B/disco quintet	
3/04/78	**98**	17	1. Riding High	She 740
11/11/78	**145**	3	2. Good Thang	She 741

DATE CHARTED	PEAK POS	WKS CHRT'D	ARTIST — Album Title	LABEL & NUMBER
			FCC [Funky Communication Committee]	
9/08/79	**192**	2	1. Baby I Want You	Free Flight 3405
			BUZZ FEITEN - see **LARSEN/FEITEN BAND**	
			DON FELDER	
			lead guitarist of The Eagles	
12/03/83	**178**	8	1. Airborne	Elektra 60295
			WILTON FELDER	
			member of the Crusaders	
12/09/78	**173**	14	1. We All Have A Star	ABC 1109
11/08/80	**142**	13	2. Inherit The Wind	MCA 5144
3/09/85	**91+**	5+	3. Secrets .... [I]	MCA 5510
			featuring 2 vocal tracks by Bobby Womack	
			JOSE FELICIANO	
			Puerto Rican - born blind on 9/8/45	
7/20/68	**2(3)**	59	● 1. **Feliciano!**	RCA 3957
			"Light My Fire"(3)	
12/07/68	**24**	19	2. Souled	RCA 4045
7/05/69	**16**	36	● 3. Feliciano/10 To 23	RCA 4185
			featuring a recording by Jose at age 10	
12/20/69	**29**	14	● 4. Alive Alive-O! .... [L]	RCA 6021 [2]
			in concert at the London Palladium	
5/30/70	**57**	20	5. Fireworks	RCA 4370
4/17/71	**92**	10	6. Encore! Jose Feliciano's Finest Performances .... [G]	RCA LSP-1005
11/13/71	**173**	9	7. That The Spirit Needs	RCA 4573
5/19/73	**156**	8	8. Compartments	RCA 0141
12/21/74	**136**	7	9. And The Feeling's Good	RCA 0407
9/06/75	**165**	4	10. Just Wanna Rock 'N' Roll	RCA APL-1005
			FELONY	
			Los Angeles rock quintet - Jeffrey Spry, lead singer	
3/26/83	**185**	5	1. The Fanatic	Rock 'n' R. 38453
			FREDDY FENDER	
			Mexican-American - real name: Baldemar Huerta	
4/19/75	**20**	43	● 1. Before The Next Teardrop Falls	ABC/Dot 2020
			"Before The Next Teardrop Falls"(1)/ "Wasted Days And Wasted Nights"(8)	
10/18/75	**41**	18	2. Are You Ready For Freddy	ABC/Dot 2044
2/28/76	**59**	11	3. Rock 'n' Country	ABC/Dot 2050
11/06/76	**170**	3	4. If You're Ever In Texas	ABC/Dot 2061
5/21/77	**155**	7	5. The Best Of Freddy Fender .... [G]	ABC/Dot 2079
			JAY FERGUSON	
			lead singer of Spirit and Jo Jo Gunne	
3/25/78	**72**	12	1. Thunder Island	Asylum 1115
			"Thunder Island"(9)	
4/14/79	**86**	16	2. Real Life Ain't This Way	Asylum 158
4/17/82	**178**	5	3. White Noise	Capitol 12196
			MAYNARD FERGUSON	
			Canadian - played trumpet for Stan Kenton's Band (1950-53)	
7/28/73	**128**	8	1. M.F. Horn/3 .... [I]	Columbia 32403
4/17/76	**131**	14	2. Primal Scream .... [I]	Columbia 33953
4/02/77	**22**	26	● 3. Conquistador .... [I]	Columbia 34457
11/26/77	**124**	8	4. New Vintage .... [I]	Columbia 34971
10/07/78	**113**	9	5. Carnival .... [I]	Columbia 35480
9/01/79	**188**	3	6. Hot .... [I]	Columbia 36124
9/27/80	**188**	2	7. It's My Time .... [I]	Columbia 36766
5/22/82	**185**	4	8. Hollywood .... [I]	Columbia 37713

DATE CHARTED	PEAK POS	WKS CHRT'D	ARTIST — Album Title	LABEL & NUMBER
			FERRANTE & TEICHER piano duo: Arthur Ferrante & Louis Teicher	
11/18/61	10	47	1. West Side Story & Other Motion Picture & Broadway Hits .... [I] "Tonight"(8)	United Art. 6166
12/18/61	23	16	2. Love Themes .... [I]	United Art. 8514
2/10/62	30	27	3. Golden Piano Hits .... [I] "Exodus"(2)	United Art. 8505
3/17/62	11	38	4. Tonight .... [I]	United Art. 6171
6/16/62	61	11	5. Golden Themes From Motion Pictures ...... [I]	United Art. 6210
9/29/62	43	7	6. Pianos In Paradise .... [I]	United Art. 6230
12/15/62	60	11	7. Snowbound .... [I]	United Art. 6233
6/29/63	23	13	8. Love Themes From Cleopatra .... [I]	United Art. 6290
12/14/63	63	17	9. Concert For Lovers .... [I]	United Art. 6315
3/21/64	128	7	10. 50 Fabulous Piano Favorites .... [I]	United Art. 6343
7/18/64	128	5	11. The Enchanted World of Ferrante & Teicher .... [I]	United Art. 6375
11/14/64	145	9	12. My Fair Lady .... [I]	United Art. 6361
11/28/64	35	20	13. The People's Choice .... [I]	United Art. 6385
4/24/65	130	6	14. Springtime .... [I]	United Art. 6406
6/12/65	120	4	15. By Popular Demand .... [I]	United Art. 6416
9/11/65	49	13	16. Only The Best .... [I]	United Art. 6434
1/01/66	134	5	17. The Ferrante And Teicher Concert .... [I-L]	United Art. 6444
6/25/66	119	5	18. For Lovers Of All Ages .... [I]	United Art. 6483
9/24/66	57	21	19. You Asked For It! .... [I]	United Art. 6526
2/18/67	133	5	20. A Man And A Woman & Other Motion Picture Themes .... [I]	United Art. 6572
12/02/67	177	2	21. Our Golden Favorites .... [I]	United Art. 6556
12/21/68	198	4	22. A Bouquet Of Hits .... [I]	United Art. 6659
10/11/69	93	27	● 23. 10th Anniversary - Golden Piano Hits .... [G-I] "Theme From The Apartment"(10-'60)	United Art. 70 [2]
11/22/69	61	26	24. Midnight Cowboy .... [I] "Midnight Cowboy"(10)	United Art. 6725
5/30/70	97	10	25. Getting Together .... [I]	United Art. 5501
12/05/70	188	2	26. Love Is A Soft Touch .... [I]	United Art. 6771
3/06/71	134	9	27. The Best Of Ferrante & Teicher .... [K-I] recordings from 1967-1970	United Art. 73 [2]
5/08/71	172	4	28. The Music Lovers .... [I]	United Art. 6792
10/09/71	172	5	29. It's Too Late .... [I]	United Art. 5531
1/01/72	186	3	30. Fiddler On The Roof .... [I]	United Art. 5552
			BRYAN FERRY British - lead singer of Roxy Music	
10/16/76	160	5	1. Let's Stick Together	Atlantic 18187
4/23/77	126	5	2. In Your Mind	Atlantic 18216
11/04/78	159	5	3. The Bride Stripped Bare	Atlantic 19205
			FESTIVAL	
2/09/80	50	18	1. Evita .... a Boris Midney production of the Broadway show	RSO 3061
			FEVER TREE Texas rock quintet - Dennis Keller, lead singer	
5/18/68	156	21	1. Fever Tree	Uni 73024
12/28/68	83	13	2. Another Time, Another Place	Uni 73040
2/07/70	97	6	3. Creation	Uni 73067
			ARTHUR FIEDLER - see BOSTON POPS	

DATE CHARTED	PEAK POS	WKS CHRT'D	ARTIST — Album Title	LABEL & NUMBER
			SALLY FIELD TV and movie actress	
12/23/67	172	4	1. The Flying Nun	Colgems 106
			RICHARD "DIMPLES" FIELDS	
7/25/81	33	17	1. Dimples	Boardwalk 33232
3/06/82	63	20	2. Mr. Look So Good!	Boardwalk 33249
			W.C. FIELDS classic comedian of American film - died on 12/25/46 (67)	
1/04/69	30	29	1. The Original Voice Tracks From His Greatest Movies .... [C]	Decca 79164
10/18/69	197	2	2. W. C. Fields On Radio .... [C] with Edgar Bergen & Charlie McCarthy	Columbia 9890
			5TH DIMENSION Marilyn McCoo, Billy Davis Jr., Lamonte McLemore, Florence LaRue, & Ron Townson	
6/17/67	8	83	● 1. **Up, Up And Away** .... "Up-Up And Away"(7)	Soul City 92000
1/13/68	105	31	2. The Magic Garden	Soul City 92001
8/24/68	21	21	3. Stoned Soul Picnic .... "Stoned Soul Picnic"(3)	Soul City 92002
5/31/69	2(2)	72	● 4. **The Age Of Aquarius** .... "Aquarius/Let The Sunshine In"(1)/"Wedding Bell Blues"(1)	Soul City 92005
5/09/70	20	50	● 5. Portrait .... "One Less Bell To Answer"(2)	Bell 6045
5/16/70	5	55	● 6. **The 5th Dimension/Greatest Hits** .... [G]	Soul City 33900
8/15/70	63	8	7. The July 5th Album .... [K]	Soul City 33901
3/13/71	17	23	● 8. Love's Lines, Angles And Rhymes	Bell 6060
10/23/71	32	18	● 9. The 5th Dimension/Live!! .... [L]	Bell 9000 [2]
11/06/71	112	7	10. Reflections .... [K]	Bell 6065
4/01/72	58	32	11. Individually & Collectively .... "(Last Night) I Didn't Get To Sleep At All"(8)/ "If I Could Reach You"(10)	Bell 6073
9/30/72	14	24	● 12. Greatest Hits On Earth .... [G] greatest hits from both Soul City and Bell labels	Bell 1106
3/24/73	108	11	13. Living Together, Growing Together	Bell 1116
8/23/75	136	8	14. Earthbound	ABC 897
			50 GUITARS OF TOMMY GARRETT A Tommy "Snuff" Garrett production — guitar solos by Tommy Tedesco	
12/18/61	36	6	1. 50 Guitars Go South Of The Border .... [I]	Liberty 14005
12/14/63	94	8	2. Maria Elena .... [I]	Liberty 14030
6/13/64	142	2	3. 50 Guitars Go Italiano .... [I]	Liberty 14028
11/26/66	99	4	4. 50 Guitars In Love .... [I]	Liberty 14037
7/08/67	168	3	5. More 50 Guitars In Love .... [I]	Liberty 14039
5/03/69	147	9	6. The Best Of The 50 Guitars Of Tommy Garrett .... [G-I]	Liberty 14045
			TIM FINN co-founder and vocalist of The Split Enz	
9/17/83	161	5	1. Escapade	A&M 4972
			ALBERT FINNEY English actor	
9/03/77	199	1	1. Albert Finney's Album	Motown 889
			FIONA Fiona Flanagan - hard-rock singer from New York	
3/30/85	154+	2+	1. Fiona	Atlantic 81242
			FIREBALLET	
9/06/75	151	8	1. Night On Bald Mountain	Passport 98010

DATE CHARTED	PEAK POS	WKS CHRT'D	ARTIST — Album Title	LABEL & NUMBER
			FIREBALLS - see JIMMY GILMER	
			FIREFALL	
			Denver quintet - Rick Roberts, lead singer	
5/08/76	**28**	67	● 1. Firefall	Atlantic 18174
			"You Are The Woman"(9)	
8/20/77	**27**	28	● 2. Luna Sea	Atlantic 19101
10/28/78	**27**	24	▲ 3. Elan	Atlantic 19183
4/12/80	**68**	15	4. Undertow	Atlantic 16006
1/10/81	**102**	13	5. Clouds Across The Sun	Atlantic 16024
12/26/81	**186**	4	6. The Best Of Firefall .... [G]	Atlantic 19316
3/12/83	**199**	3	7. Break Of Dawn	Atlantic 80017
			FIRESIGN THEATRE	
			satirical comedy foursome	
10/18/69	**195**	2	1. How Can You Be In Two Places At Once When You're Not Anywhere At All .... [C]	Columbia 9884
9/19/70	**106**	10	2. Don't Crush That Dwarf, Hand Me The Pliers .... [C]	Columbia 30102
9/25/71	**50**	14	3. I Think We're All Bozos On This Bus .... [C]	Columbia 30737
2/26/72	**75**	11	4. Dear Friends .... [K-C]	Columbia 31099 [2]
11/25/72	**115**	8	5. Not Insane Or Anything You Want To ...... [C]	Columbia 31585
3/02/74	**172**	5	6. The Tale Of The Giant Rat Of Sumatra ....[C]	Columbia 32730
11/02/74	**147**	6	7. Everything You Know Is Wrong .... [C]	Columbia 33141
6/11/77	**184**	2	8. Just Folks...A Firesign Chat .... [C]	Butterfly 001
			FIRM	
			British: Jimmy Page (Led Zeppelin/guitar), Paul Rodgers (Bad Company/vocals), Chris Slade (Manfred Mann/drums), Tony Franklin (keyboards)	
3/02/85	**18+**	6+	1. The Firm	Atlantic 81239
			FIRST CHOICE	
			Philadelphia trio	
10/27/73	**184**	4	1. Armed And Extremely Dangerous	Philly Groove 1400
10/26/74	**143**	7	2. The Player	Philly Groove 1502
10/01/77	**103**	8	3. Delusions	Gold Mind 7501
3/31/79	**135**	12	4. Hold Your Horses	Gold Mind 9502
			FIRST EDITION - see KENNY ROGERS	
			EDDIE FISHER	
			born in Philadelphia on 8/10/28	
4/30/55	**8**	9	1. **I Love You**	RCA 1097
3/30/63	**128**	3	2. Eddie Fisher At The Winter Garden .... [L]	Ramrod 1 [2]
7/24/65	**52**	10	3. Eddie Fisher Today!	Dot 25631
11/26/66	**72**	10	4. Games That Lovers Play	RCA 3726
7/01/67	**193**	3	5. People Like You	RCA 3820
			ELLA FITZGERALD	
			1st lady of Jazz - born in Newport News, Virginia on 4/25/18	
9/17/55	**7**	9	1. **Songs from Pete Kelly's Blues**	Decca 8166
			PEGGY LEE & ELLA FITZGERALD	
7/28/56	**15**	1	2. Ella Fitzgerald sings the Cole Porter Song Book	Verve 4001 [2]
12/15/56	**12**	2	3. Ella And Louis	Verve 4003
			ELLA FITZGERALD & LOUIS ARMSTRONG backing by the Oscar Peterson Trio, plus Buddy Rich	
3/16/57	**11**	4	4. Ella Fitzgerald sings the Rodgers and Hart Song Book	Verve 4002 [2]
			albums 2 & 4 above arranged and conducted by Buddy Bregman	
9/12/60	**11**	51	5. Mack The Knife - Ella In Berlin .... [L]	Verve 4041
11/11/61	**35**	34	6. Ella In Hollywood .... [L]	Verve 4052

DATE CHARTED	PEAK POS	WKS CHRT'D	ARTIST — Album Title	LABEL & NUMBER
10/19/63	69	20	7. Ella And Basie! .... ELLA FITZGERALD/COUNT BAISE	Verve 4061
3/28/64	111	5	8. Ella Fitzgerald sings the George and Ira Gershwin Song Books .... recorded 1958-59 - arranged & conducted by Nelson Riddle	Verve V-29-5 [5]
8/22/64	146	2	9. Hello, Dolly!	Verve 4064
8/19/67	172	2	10. Brighten The Corner .... sacred songs	Capitol 2685
10/18/69	196	2	11. Ella	Reprise 6354

FIVE AMERICANS
Dallas quintet

DATE CHARTED	PEAK POS	WKS CHRT'D	ARTIST — Album Title	LABEL & NUMBER
4/30/66	136	5	1. I See The Light	HBR 9503
7/08/67	121	10	2. Western Union .... "Western Union"(5)	Abnak 2067

FIVE MAN ELECTRICAL BAND
Canadian - Les Emmerson, lead singer

DATE CHARTED	PEAK POS	WKS CHRT'D	ARTIST — Album Title	LABEL & NUMBER
7/31/71	148	9	1. Good-Byes & Butterflies .... "Signs"(3)	Lionel 1100
2/12/72	199	2	2. Coming Of Age	Lionel 1101

FIVE SPECIAL
R&B/funk quintet from Detroit

DATE CHARTED	PEAK POS	WKS CHRT'D	ARTIST — Album Title	LABEL & NUMBER
8/11/79	118	11	1. Five Special	Elektra 206

FIVE STAIRSTEPS
Chicago family group

DATE CHARTED	PEAK POS	WKS CHRT'D	ARTIST — Album Title	LABEL & NUMBER
3/25/67	139	4	1. The Five Stairsteps	Windy C 6000
			5 STAIRSTEPS & CUBIE:	
1/27/68	195	3	2. Our Family Portrait	Buddah 5008
4/26/69	198	2	3. Love's Happening	Curtom 8002
			STAIRSTEPS:	
6/13/70	83	12	4. Stairsteps .... "O-o-h Child"(8)	Buddah 5061
12/12/70	199	2	5. Step by Step by Step .... [K] 9 of 11 cuts are from album #1 above	Buddah 5068

FIXX
London-based techno-pop group - Cy Curnin, lead singer

DATE CHARTED	PEAK POS	WKS CHRT'D	ARTIST — Album Title	LABEL & NUMBER
11/13/82	106	51	1. Shuttered Room	MCA 5345
5/28/83	8	54	▲ 2. **Reach The Beach** .... "One Thing Leads To Another"(4)	MCA 39001
9/08/84	19	29	● 3. Phantoms	MCA 5507

ROBERTA FLACK
born on 2/10/39 in Asheville, North Carolina

DATE CHARTED	PEAK POS	WKS CHRT'D	ARTIST — Album Title	LABEL & NUMBER
1/31/70	1(5)	54	● 1. **First Take** .... "The First Time Ever I Saw Your Face"(1)	Atlantic 8230
8/29/70	33	82	● 2. Chapter Two	Atlantic 1569
12/11/71	18	48	● 3. Quiet Fire	Atlantic 1594
5/13/72	3	39	● 4. **Roberta Flack & Donny Hathaway** .... "Where Is The Love"(5)	Atlantic 7216
9/01/73	3	53	● 5. **Killing Me Softly** .... "Killing Me Softly With His Song"(1)	Atlantic 7271
3/29/75	24	26	6. Feel Like Makin' Love .... "Feel Like Makin' Love"(1)	Atlantic 18131
1/07/78	8	32	● 7. **Blue Lights In The Basement** .... "The Closer I Get To You"(2)	Atlantic 19149
9/30/78	74	10	8. Roberta Flack	Atlantic 19186
3/29/80	25	24	● 9. Roberta Flack Featuring Donny Hathaway ...	Atlantic 16013
12/20/80	52	19	10. Live & More .... [L] ROBERTA FLACK & PEABO BRYSON	Atlantic 7004 [2]

DATE CHARTED	PEAK POS	WKS CHRT'D	ARTIST — Album Title	LABEL & NUMBER
6/27/81	161	11	11. Bustin' Loose .... [S]	MCA 5141
6/19/82	59	21	12. I'm The One	Atlantic 19354
8/13/83	25	42	● 13. Born To Love	Capitol 12284
			PEABO BRYSON/ROBERTA FLACK	

FANNIE FLAGG
comedienne

9/23/67	183	3	1. Rally 'Round The Flagg .... [C]	RCA 3856

FLAME

5/14/77	147	5	1. Queen Of The Neighborhood	RCA 2160

FLAMING EMBER
Detroit rock quartet

8/29/70	188	3	1. Westbound #9	Hot Wax 702

FLAMIN' GROOVIES
San Francisco rock quintet

8/21/76	142	7	1. Shake Some Action	Sire 7521
			produced by Dave Edmunds	

FLASH
English quartet led by Peter Banks (guitar) & Colin Carter (vocals)

5/20/72	33	29	1. Flash	Capitol 11040
12/09/72	121	13	2. Flash In The Can	Capitol 11115
9/01/73	135	8	3. Out Of Our Hands	Capitol 11218

FLASH & THE PAN
Australian duo: George Young & Harry Vanda - formerly with the Easybeats

5/26/79	80	16	1. Flash And The Pan	Epic 36018
5/31/80	159	6	2. Lights In The Night	Epic 36432

LESTER FLATT & EARL SCRUGGS
masters of bluegrass music - Lester died on 5/11/79 (64) - als~ see Earl Scruggs

4/13/63	115	4	1. Hard Travelin' featuring The Ballad Of Jed Clampett	Columbia 8751
9/28/63	134	6	2. Flatt And Scruggs At Carnegie Hall! .... [L]	Columbia 8845
3/30/68	194	4	3. Changin' Times featuring Foggy Mountain Breakdown	Columbia 9596
6/08/68	161	4	4. Original Theme From Bonnie & Clyde ..... [E]	Mercury 61162
			their first recordings from 1948-1950	
7/06/68	187	5	5. The Story Of Bonnie & Clyde	Columbia 9649

FLEETWOOD MAC
English/American band: Mick Fleetwood, Christine McVie, John McVie, Stevie Nicks & Lindsey Buckingham

8/17/68	198	3	1. Fleetwood Mac	Epic 26402
2/08/69	184	6	2. English Rose	Epic 26446
12/13/69	109	22	3. Then Play On	Reprise 6368
			Peter Green was a member on above albums	
10/31/70	69	14	4. Kiln House	Reprise 6408
			Christine McVie joins group - original member Jeremy Spencer quits after this LP	
7/03/71	190	6	5. Fleetwood Mac In Chicago .... [E]	Blue Horiz. 3801 [2]
			recorded Jan. 1969 - featuring various American blues singers	
10/16/71	143	7	6. Black Magic Woman .... [R]	Epic 30632 [2]
			reissue of albums 1 & 2 above	
10/30/71	91	12	7. Future Games	Reprise 6465
			Bob Welch joins group (stays thru "Heroes" LP)	
4/22/72	70	27	● 8. Bare Trees	Reprise 2080
4/28/73	49	13	9. Penguin	Reprise 2138
11/17/73	67	26	● 10. Mystery To Me	Reprise 2158
10/05/74	34	26	11. Heroes Are Hard To Find	Reprise 2196

DATE CHARTED	PEAK POS	WKS CHRT'D	ARTIST — Album Title	LABEL & NUMBER
3/01/75	138	9	12. Vintage Years .... [E-K] recordings from 1967-1969	Sire 3706 [2]
8/02/75	1(1)	148	● 13. **Fleetwood Mac** .... Americans Stevie Nicks & Lindsey Buckingham join group	Reprise 2225
12/06/75	118	16	14. Fleetwood Mac In Chicago .... [R]	Sire 3715 [2]
2/26/77	1(31)	134	▲ 15. **Rumours** .... "Go Your Own Way"(10)/"Dreams"(1)/"Don't Stop"(3)/ "You Make Loving Fun"(9)	Warner 3010
11/03/79	4	37	▲ 16. **Tusk** .... "Tusk"(8)/"Sara"(7)	Warner 3350 [2]
12/27/80	14	18	● 17. Fleetwood Mac Live .... [L]	Warner 3500 [2]
7/17/82	1(5)	45	▲ 18. **Mirage** .... "Hold Me"(4)	Warner 23607

MICK FLEETWOOD
founder/drummer of Fleetwood Mac

7/18/81	43	14	1. The Visitor .... recorded in Ghana, West Africa	RCA 4080

FLEETWOODS
Gary Troxel, Barbara Ellis and Gretchen Christopher - met while attending high school in Olympia, Washington

12/29/62	71	6	1. The Fleetwoods' Greatest Hits .... [G] "Come Softly To Me"(1)/"Mr. Blue"(1)/"Tragedy"(10)	Dolton 8018

FLESHTONES
Peter Zaremba, lead vocalist of New York-based quartet

3/06/82	174	5	1. Roman Gods	I.R.S. 70018

FLOATERS
four-man soul group from Detroit

6/25/77	10	25	▲ 1. **Floaters** .... "Float On"(2)	ABC 1030
4/22/78	131	8	2. Magic	ABC 1047

FLOCK
7-man rock group from Chicago

9/20/69	48	20	1. The Flock	Columbia 9911
10/17/70	96	9	2. Dinosaur Swamps	Columbia 30007

FLOCK OF SEAGULLS
British techno-rock quartet - Mike Score, lead singer

5/22/82	10	50	● 1. **A Flock Of Seagulls** .... "I Ran (So Far Away)"(9)	Jive 66000
5/28/83	16	23	2. Listen	Jive 8013
8/25/84	66	10	3. The Story Of A Young Heart	Jive 8250

FLYING BURRITO BROTHERS
group formed by ex-Byrds Gram Parsons & Chris Hillman

5/03/69	164	7	1. The Gilded Palace Of Sin	A&M 4175
6/12/71	176	9	2. The Flying Burrito Bros.	A&M 4295
6/03/72	171	7	3. Last Of The Red Hot Burritos .... [L]	A&M 4343
7/13/74	158	5	4. Close Up The Honky Tonks .... [K] recordings from 1968-1972	A&M 3631 [2]
10/25/75	138	3	5. Flying Again	Columbia 33817
5/22/76	185	4	6. Sleepless Nights .... [E] 9 tracks recorded in 1970; 3 tracks recorded in 1973 for Gram Parsons' album "Grievous Angel"	A&M 4578

FLYING LIZARDS
British electronic production by David Cunningham

2/23/80	99	8	1. The Flying Lizards	Virgin 13137

FLYING MACHINE
English quartet

12/27/69	179	7	1. The Flying Machine .... "Smile A Little Smile For Me"(5)	Janus 3007

DATE CHARTED	PEAK POS	WKS CHRT'D	ARTIST — Album Title	LABEL & NUMBER
			FOCUS Dutch rock quartet led by guitar virtuoso Jan Akkerman	
1/20/73	8	38	● 1. **Moving Waves** .... [I] "Hocus Pocus"(9)	Sire 7401
4/14/73	35	22	● 2. Focus 3 .... [I]	Sire 3901 [2]
6/30/73	104	9	3. In And Out Of Focus .... their first album - recorded in 1970	Sire 7404
11/17/73	132	10	4. Live At The Rainbow .... [I-L]	Sire 7408
8/03/74	66	19	5. Hamburger Concerto .... [I]	Atco 100
3/01/75	120	9	6. Dutch Masters - A Selection Of Their Finest Recordings 1969-1973 .... [K-I]	Sire 7505
9/27/75	152	6	7. Mother Focus .... [I]	Atco 117
6/04/77	163	7	8. Ship Of Memories .... [K]	Sire 7531
			DAN FOGELBERG born in Peoria, Illinois on 8/13/51	
12/07/74	17	27	● 1. Souvenirs .... Joe Walsh producer and guitarist	Full Moon 33137
10/04/75	23	19	● 2. Captured Angel	Full Moon 33499
6/04/77	13	39	▲ 3. Nether Lands	Full Moon 34185
9/16/78	8	35	▲ 4. **Twin Sons Of Different Mothers** .... DAN FOGELBERG & TIM WEISBERG	Full Moon 35339
12/08/79	3	39	▲ 5. **Phoenix** .... "Longer"(2)	Full Moon 35634
9/12/81	6	62	▲ 6. **The Innocent Age** .... "Same Old Lang Syne"(9)/"Hard To Say"(7)/ "Leader Of The Band"(9)	Full Moon 37393 [2]
11/13/82	15	35	▲ 7. Dan Fogelberg/Greatest Hits .... [G]	Full Moon 38308
2/18/84	15	27	● 8. Windows And Walls	Full Moon 39004
			JOHN FOGERTY leader of Creedence Clearwater Revival - also see Blue Ridge Rangers	
10/04/75	78	7	1. John Fogerty	Asylum 1046
1/26/85	1(1)	11+	▲ 2. **Centerfield** .... "The Old Man Down The Road"(10)	Warner 25203
			TOM FOGERTY John Fogerty's brother - guitarist with CCR	
6/03/72	180	6	1. Tom Fogerty	Fantasy 9407
			FOGHAT British quartet led by Lonesome Dave Peverett - formerly with Savoy Brown	
7/15/72	127	21	1. Foghat	Bearsville 2077
3/31/73	67	19	● 2. Foghat .... picture of a rock and a roll on the cover	Bearsville 2136
2/02/74	34	30	● 3. Energized	Bearsville 6950
11/09/74	40	19	● 4. Rock And Roll Outlaws	Bearsville 6956
10/11/75	23	52	● 5. Fool For The City	Bearsville 6959
11/20/76	36	21	● 6. Night Shift	Bearsville 6962
9/10/77	11	29	▲ 7. Foghat Live .... [L]	Bearsville 6971
5/20/78	25	23	● 8. Stone Blue	Bearsville 6977
10/13/79	35	21	9. Boogie Motel	Bearsville 6990
6/21/80	106	10	10. Tight Shoes	Bearsville 6999
7/25/81	92	9	11. Girls To Chat & Boys To Bounce	Bearsville 3578
11/13/82	162	5	12. In The Mood For Something Rude	Bearsville 23747
6/25/83	192	2	13. Zig-Zag Walk	Bearsville 23888
			ELLEN FOLEY female vocalist on Meat Loaf's "Bat Out of Hell" album	
9/29/79	137	6	1. Nightout	Cleve. I. 36052
4/04/81	152	4	2. Spirit Of St. Louis .... produced by Mick Jones of the Clash	Cleve. I. 36984

DATE CHARTED	PEAK POS	WKS CHRT'D	ARTIST — Album Title	LABEL & NUMBER
			FOLKSWINGERS instrumental quartet led by Glen Campbell	
9/28/63	**132**	4	1. 12 String Guitar! .... [I]	World Pac. 1812
			JANE FONDA - see AEROBICS section	
			FRANK FONTAINE "Crazy Guggenheim" on the Jackie Gleason TV show	
2/09/63	**1(5)**	53	● 1. **Songs I Sing On The Jackie Gleason Show**	ABC-Para. 442
8/24/63	**44**	25	2. Sings Like Crazy	ABC-Para. 460
3/07/64	**92**	12	3. How Sweet It Is	ABC-Para. 470
			WAYNE FONTANA - see MINDBENDERS	
			FOOLS Boston-based quintet - Mike Girard, lead singer	
4/05/80	**151**	8	1. Sold Out	EMI America 17024
3/28/81	**158**	4	2. Heavy Mental	EMI America 17046
			FOOLS GOLD	
4/24/76	**113**	13	1. Fools Gold	Morning Sky 5500
			STEVE FORBERT	
2/10/79	**82**	15	1. Alive On Arrival	Nemperor 35538
11/10/79	**20**	26	2. Jackrabbit Slim	Nemperor 36191
10/11/80	**70**	9	3. Little Stevie Orbit	Nemperor 36595
7/24/82	**159**	6	4. Steve Forbert	Nemperor 37434
			FORCE M.D.'S Staten Island-based soul/rap quintet	
12/15/84	**185**	4	1. Love Letters	Tommy Boy 1003
			LITA FORD member of the Runaways at age 15	
8/04/84	**66**	16	1. Dancin' On The Edge	Mercury 818864
			TENNESSEE ERNIE FORD host of his own TV show from 1956-1961	
4/28/56	**12**	3	1. This Lusty Land!	Capitol 700
1/05/57	**2(3)**	277	● 2. **Hymns**	Capitol 756
5/06/57	**5**	69	● 3. **Spirituals**	Capitol 818
6/09/58	**5**	77	● 4. **Nearer The Cross**	Capitol 1005
12/22/58	**4**	3	● 5. **The Star Carol** .... [X]	Capitol 1071
12/28/59	**7**	2	6. **The Star Carol** .... [X-R]	Capitol 1071
5/02/60	**23**	14	7. Sing A Hymn With Me .... includes a hymn book	Capitol 1332
12/31/60	**28**	1	8. The Star Carol .... [X-R]	Capitol 1071
12/25/61	**110**	3	9. The Star Carol .... [X-R]	Capitol 1071
1/27/62	**67**	19	10. Hymns At Home .... recorded at Ernie's home town church in Bristol, Tennessee	Capitol 1604
5/26/62	**110**	12	11. Here Comes The Mississippi Showboat	Capitol 1684
11/10/62	**43**	2	12. I Love To Tell The Story	Capitol 1751
12/22/62	**48**	2	13. The Star Carol .... [X-R]	Capitol 1071
1/05/63	**71**	12	14. Book Of Favorite Hymns .... [K]	Capitol 1794
4/25/70	**192**	2	15. America The Beautiful	Capitol 412
			FOREIGNER English-American rock group led by Mick Jones (guitar) and Lou Gramm (vocals)	
3/26/77	**4**	113	▲ 1. **Foreigner** .... "Feels Like The First Time"(4)/"Cold As Ice"(6)	Atlantic 18215
7/08/78	**3**	88	▲ 2. **Double Vision** .... "Hot Blooded"(3)/"Double Vision"(2)	Atlantic 19999
9/29/79	**5**	41	▲ 3. **Head Games**	Atlantic 29999

DATE CHARTED	PEAK POS	WKS CHRT'D			ARTIST — Album Title	LABEL & NUMBER
7/25/81	1(10)	81	▲	4. **4**		Atlantic 16999
				"Urgent"(4)/"Waiting For A Girl Like You"(2)		
12/25/82	10	25	●	5. **Foreigner Records** .... [G]		Atlantic 80999
1/05/85	4	14+	▲	6. **Agent Provocateur**		Atlantic 81999
				"I Want To Know What Love Is"(1)		
				FOREVER MORE		
3/07/70	180	3		1. Yours Forever More		RCA 4272
				FORTUNES		
				British		
7/10/71	134	10		1. Here Comes That Rainy Day Feeling Again ..		Capitol 809
				FOTOMAKER		
				members include Dino Danelli & Gene Cornish (Rascals) and Wally Bryson (Raspberries)		
3/25/78	88	13		1. Fotomaker		Atlantic 19165
				FOUNDATIONS		
				English - Clem Curtis, leader		
3/08/69	92	11		1. Build Me Up Buttercup .... [L]		Uni 73043
				side 1: live; side 2: studio		
				"Build Me Up Buttercup"(3)		
				PETE FOUNTAIN		
				New Orlean's clarinetist formerly on Lawrence Welk's TV show		
2/22/60	8	87		1. **Pete Fountain's New Orleans** .... [I]		Coral 57282
5/09/60	31	4		2. Pete Fountain Day .... [I-L]		Coral 57313
9/11/61	43	4		3. Pete Fountain's French Quarter .... [I]		Coral 57359
				Pete's nightclub on Bourbon St. in New Orleans		
2/03/62	41	2		4. Bourbon Street .... [I]		Coral 57389
				PETE FOUNTAIN/AL HIRT		
7/28/62	30	6		5. Music From Dixie .... [I]		Coral 57401
9/07/63	91	9		6. South Rampart Street Parade .... [I]		Coral 57440
6/13/64	53	14		7. New Orleans At Midnight .... [I]		Coral 57429
8/22/64	48	44		8. Licorice Stick .... [I]		Coral 57460
1/02/65	121	7		9. Pete's Place .... [I-L]		Coral 57453
				recorded at Pete's French Quarter Inn, New Orleans		
5/08/65	64	14		10. Mr. Stick Man .... [I]		Coral 57473
4/23/66	100	8		11. A Taste Of Honey		Coral 57486
6/15/68	187	2		12. For The First Time		Decca 74955
				BRENDA LEE & PETE FOUNTAIN		
3/22/69	186	6		13. Those Were The Days .... [I]		Coral 57505
				FOUR FRESHMEN		
				formed in Indianapolis at Butler University		
2/25/56	6	35		1. **Four Freshmen and 5 Trombones**		Capitol 683
10/13/56	11	8		2. Freshmen Favorites .... [G]		Capitol 743
3/02/57	9	7		3. **4 Freshmen and 5 Trumpets**		Capitol 763
11/18/57	25	1		4. Four Freshmen and Five Saxes		Capitol 844
9/29/58	17	1		5. The Four Freshmen In Person .... [L]		Capitol 1008
11/03/58	11	6		6. Voices In Love		Capitol 1074
1/11/60	40	1		7. The Four Freshmen and Five Guitars		Capitol 1255
				FOUR JACKS AND A JILL		
				South African quintet - Jill: Glenys Lynne		
6/22/68	155	6		1. Master Jack		RCA 4019
				FOUR LADS		
				Canadian - background vocalists on Johnnie Ray's hit "Cry"		
10/06/56	14	2		1. On The Sunny Side		Columbia 912
				FOUR PREPS		
				Bruce, Glen, Ed & Marv formed group at Hollywood High School		
8/21/61	8	26		1. **The Four Preps On Campus** .... [L]		Capitol 1566
3/24/62	40	17		2. Campus Encore .... [L]		Capitol 1647

FOUR SEASONS

formed in Newark, New Jersey in 1956 as The Four Lovers - original lineup (1-12): Frankie Valli (lead singer), Bob Gaudio (keyboards), Nick Massi (bass), Tommy DeVito (guitar)

DATE CHARTED	PEAK POS	WKS CHRT'D	ARTIST — Album Title	LABEL & NUMBER
10/27/62	6	27	1. **Sherry & 11 others** .... "Sherry"(1)/"Big Girls Don't Cry"(1)	Vee-Jay 1053
3/02/63	8	19	2. **Big Girls Don't Cry and Twelve others** .... "Walk Like A Man"(1)	Vee-Jay 1056
7/13/63	47	12	3. Ain't That A Shame and 11 others .... "Candy Girl"(3)	Vee-Jay 1059
9/07/63	15	56	4. Golden Hits of the 4 Seasons .... [G]	Vee-Jay 1065
2/29/64	84	9	5. Born To Wander	Philips 129
3/28/64	6	25	6. **Dawn (Go Away) and 11 other great songs** . "Dawn (Go Away)"(3)	Philips 124
6/06/64	100	5	7. Stay & Other Great Hits .... [K] originally titled "Folk-Nanny"	Vee-Jay 1082
8/08/64	7	26	8. **Rag Doll** .... "Ronnie"(6)/"Rag Doll"(1)/"Save It For Me"(10)	Philips 146
9/05/64	105	5	9. More Golden Hits By The Four Seasons ... [K]	Vee-Jay 1088
10/10/64	142	2	10. The Beatles vs. The Four Seasons .... [R] "Introducing The Beatles" & "Golden Hits Of The 4 Seasons" LPs	Vee-Jay 30 [2]
4/10/65	77	13	11. The 4 Seasons Entertain You	Philips 164
12/11/65	10	88	● 12. **The 4 Seasons' Gold Vault of Hits** .... [G] "Let's Hang On!"(3)	Philips 196
12/18/65	106	10	13. Big Hits by Burt Bacharach...Hal David...Bob Dylan...	Philips 193
1/29/66	50	15	14. Working My Way Back To You .... "Working My Way Back To You"(9)	Philips 201
12/03/66	22	53	● 15. 2nd Vault Of Golden Hits .... [G] 9 of 12 cuts are Vee-Jay hits "I've Got You Under My Skin"(9)	Philips 221
12/17/66	107	9	16. Lookin' Back .... [K] recordings from their first 3 Vee-Jay albums	Philips 222
6/24/67	37	25	17. New Gold Hits .... "Tell It To The Rain"(10)/"C'mon Marianne"(9)	Philips 243
12/28/68	37	21	● 18. Edizione D'Oro (The 4 Seasons Gold Edition-29 Gold Hits) .... [G]	Philips 6501 [2]
2/15/69	85	11	19. The Genuine Imitation Life Gazette	Philips 290
6/13/70	190	2	20. Half & Half .... 5 songs by Frankie Valli, 5 songs by The 4 Seasons	Philips 341
11/29/75	38	31	21. Who Loves You .... "Who Loves You"(3)/"December, 1963 (Oh, What A Night)"(1)	Warner 2900
12/13/75	51	17	22. The Four Seasons Story .... [G] all their top hits 1962-1968	Private S. 7000 [2]
5/14/77	168	5	23. Helicon	Warner 3016

FOUR TOPS

from Detroit: Levi Stubbs, Duke Fakir, Lawrence Payton & Obie Benson

DATE CHARTED	PEAK POS	WKS CHRT'D	ARTIST — Album Title	LABEL & NUMBER
2/27/65	63	27	1. Four Tops	Motown 622
11/13/65	20	35	2. Four Tops Second Album .... "I Can't Help Myself"(1)/"It's The Same Old Song"(5)	Motown 634
8/27/66	32	22	3. 4 Tops On Top	Motown 647
12/17/66	17	43	4. Four Tops Live! .... [L]	Motown 654
4/08/67	79	15	5. 4 Tops On Broadway	Motown 657
8/12/67	11	59	6. Four Tops Reach Out .... "Reach Out I'll Be There"(1)/ "Standing In The Shadows Of Love"(6)/"Bernadette"(4)	Motown 660
9/30/67	4	73	7. **The Four Tops Greatest Hits** .... [G]	Motown 662
9/28/68	93	16	8. Yesterday's Dreams	Motown 669
7/05/69	74	10	9. Four Tops Now!	Motown 675
12/13/69	163	6	10. Soul Spin	Motown 695
4/11/70	21	42	11. Still Waters Run Deep	Motown 704
10/17/70	109	12	12. Changing Times	Motown 721

DATE CHARTED	PEAK POS	WKS CHRT'D	ARTIST — Album Title	LABEL & NUMBER
10/17/70	113	16	13. The Magnificent 7 .... SUPREMES & FOUR TOPS	Motown 717
6/26/71	154	6	14. The Return Of The Magnificent Seven .... SUPREMES & FOUR TOPS	Motown 736
9/25/71	106	10	15. Four Tops Greatest Hits, Vol. 2 .... [G]	Motown 740
1/08/72	160	6	16. Dynamite .... SUPREMES & FOUR TOPS	Motown 745
5/27/72	50	28	17. Nature Planned It	Motown 748
11/11/72	33	31	18. Keeper Of The Castle .... "Keeper Of The Castle"(10)/ "Ain't No Woman (Like The One I've Got)"(4)	Dunhill 50129
5/12/73	103	9	19. The Best Of The 4 Tops .... [G]	Motown 764 [2]
9/22/73	66	14	20. Main Street People	Dunhill 50144
4/27/74	118	11	21. Meeting Of The Minds	Dunhill 50166
10/26/74	92	9	22. Live & In Concert .... [L]	Dunhill 50188
6/14/75	148	5	23. Night Lights Harmony	ABC 862
11/13/76	124	8	24. Catfish	ABC 968
9/12/81	37	21	25. Tonight!	Casablanca 7258

KIM FOWLEY
pop music producer in the early 60's

4/19/69	198	3	1. Outrageous	Imperial 12423

VIRGIL FOX
organ virtuoso - died on 10/25/80 (68)

5/29/71	183	2	1. Bach Live At Fillmore East .... [I-L] Johann Sebastian Bach compositions	Decca 75263

REDD FOXX
real name: John Elroy Sanford - "King of the Party Records"

6/03/72	198	3	1. Sanford & Foxx .... [C-E] most of these comedy bits were recorded in the 50's	Dooto 853
7/29/72	155	8	2. Sanford and Son .... [C-TV] actual comedy excerpts from the TV series	RCA 4739
1/03/76	87	13	3. You Gotta Wash Your Ass .... [C] recorded live at the Apollo Theater in Harlem, 1975	Atlantic 18157

FOXY
Miami Latino dance band

7/22/78	12	27	1. Get Off .... "Get Off"(9)	Dash 30005
4/14/79	29	16	2. Hot Numbers.	Dash 30010

PETER FRAMPTON
English - guitarist/vocalist with The Herd and Humble Pie

10/07/72	177	6	1. Wind Of Change	A&M 4348
6/09/73	110	22	2. Frampton's Camel .... title refers to Frampton's four-member band	A&M 4389
3/30/74	125	9	3. Somethin's Happening	A&M 3619
3/29/75	32	64	● 4. Frampton	A&M 4512
1/31/76	1(10)	97	▲ 5. **Frampton Comes Alive!** .... [L] "Show Me The Way"(6)/"Do You Feel Like We Do"(10)	A&M 3703 [2]
6/25/77	2(4)	32	▲ 6. **I'm In You** .... "I'm In You"(2)	A&M 4704
6/23/79	19	16	● 7. Where I Should Be	A&M 3710
6/13/81	43	13	8. Breaking All The Rules	A&M 3722
8/28/82	174	8	9. The Art Of Control	A&M 4905

SERGIO FRANCHI
Italian tenor

11/24/62	17	18	1. Sergio Franchi	RCA 2640
2/09/63	66	21	2. Our Man From Italy	RCA 2657
7/06/63	103	5	3. Broadway...I Love You	RCA 2674

DATE CHARTED	PEAK POS	WKS CHRT'D	ARTIST — Album Title	LABEL & NUMBER
1/25/64	97	7	4. The Dream Duet .... ANNA MOFFO/SERGIO FRANCHI	RCA 2675
3/27/65	114	4	5. Live At The Cocoanut Grove .... [L] with the Freddy Martin Orchestra	RCA 3310

CONNIE FRANCIS
born Constance Franconero on 12/12/38 in Newark, New Jersey

2/08/60	4	81	1. **Italian Favorites** .... [F] "Mama"(8)	MGM 3791
2/22/60	17	100	2. Connie's Greatest Hits .... [G] "Who's Sorry Now"(4)/"My Happiness"(2)/ "Lipstick On Your Collar"(5)/"Frankie"(9)	MGM 3793
12/12/60	9	20	3. **More Italian Favorites** .... [F]	MGM 3871
5/08/61	65	19	4. Connie Francis At The Copa .... [L]	MGM 3913
5/29/61	69	10	5. Jewish Favorites .... [F]	MGM 3869
7/03/61	39	17	6. More Greatest Hits .... [G] "Among My Souvenirs"(7)/"Everybody's Somebody's Fool"(1)/ "My Heart Has A Mind Of Its Own"(1)/"Many Tears Ago"(7)/ "Where The Boys Are"(4)	MGM 3942
10/30/61	11	34	7. Never On Sunday and other title songs from motion pictures	MGM 3965
4/14/62	47	17	8. Do The Twist	MGM 4022
8/25/62	111	9	9. Connie Francis sings .... [G] "Breakin' In A Brand New Broken Heart"(7)/"Together"(6)/ "When The Boy In Your Arms"(10)/"Second Hand Love"(7) "Don't Break The Heart That Loves You"(1)	MGM 4049
10/13/62	22	14	10. Country Music Connie Style	MGM 4079
2/16/63	103	5	11. Modern Italian Hits .... [F]	MGM 4102
3/30/63	66	11	12. Follow The Boys .... [S] only side 1 features songs from the soundtrack	MGM 4123
6/15/63	108	5	13. Award Winning Motion Picture Hits	MGM 4048
10/05/63	94	17	14. Greatest American Waltzes	MGM 4145
10/19/63	70	13	15. Mala Femmena & Connie's Big Hits From Italy .... [K-F]	MGM 4161
11/02/63	68	23	● 16. The Very Best Of Connie Francis .... [G] "Vacation"(9)	MGM 4167
2/01/64	126	2	17. In The Summer Of His Years .... a tribute to President John F. Kennedy	MGM 4210
8/01/64	122	9	18. Looking For Love .... [S]	MGM 4229
12/05/64	149	2	19. A New Kind Of Connie...	MGM 4253
5/01/65	78	15	20. Connie Francis sings For Mama	MGM 4294
1/29/66	61	9	21. When The Boys Meet The Girls .... [S] Connie sings 5 of the 12 songs film is a remake of "Girl Crazy"	MGM 4334

FRANKE & THE KNOCKOUTS
East Coast quintet led by Frankie Previte

3/28/81	31	27	1. Franke & The Knockouts .... "Sweetheart"(10)	Millennium 7755
4/10/82	48	18	2. Below The Belt	Millennium 7763

FRANKIE GOES TO HOLLYWOOD
British rock quintet - vocals by Holly Johnson & Paul Rutherford

11/24/84	33	20+	● 1. Welcome To The Pleasuredome .... "Relax"(10)/"Two Tribes"	Island 90232 [2]

ARETHA FRANKLIN
"Lady Soul" was born on 3/25/42 in Memphis, Tennessee

11/17/62	69	12	1. The Tender, The Moving, The Swinging Aretha Franklin	Columbia 8676
12/19/64	84	13	2. Runnin' Out Of Fools	Columbia 9081
7/10/65	101	8	3. Yeah!!! .... [L]	Columbia 9151
8/06/66	132	4	4. Soul Sister	Columbia 9321
4/08/67	2(3)	79	● 5. **I Never Loved A Man The Way I Love You** . "I Never Loved A Man (The Way I Love You)"(9)/"Respect"(1)	Atlantic 8139

DATE CHARTED	PEAK POS	WKS CHRT'D	ARTIST — Album Title	LABEL & NUMBER
6/10/67	94	14	6. Aretha Franklin's Greatest Hits .... [K] featuring her Columbia recordings from 1961-66	Columbia 9473
8/26/67	5	41	7. **Aretha Arrives** .... "Baby I Love You"(4)	Atlantic 8150
10/21/67	173	8	8. Take A Look .... [K] more early Columbia recordings	Columbia 9554
2/24/68	2(2)	52	● 9. **Aretha: Lady Soul** .... "A Natural Woman"(8)/"Chain of Fools"(2)/ "(Sweet Sweet Baby) Since You've Been Gone"(5)	Atlantic 8176
7/13/68	3	35	● 10. **Aretha Now** .... "Think"(7)/"I Say A Little Prayer"(10)	Atlantic 8186
11/23/68	13	20	11. Aretha In Paris .... [L] record at the Olympia Theatre in Paris, France, on 5/7/68	Atlantic 8207
2/15/69	15	32	12. Aretha Franklin: Soul '69	Atlantic 8212
7/19/69	18	33	13. Aretha's Gold .... [G] "The House That Jack Built"(6)	Atlantic 8227
2/14/70	17	30	14. This Girl's In Love With You	Atlantic 8248
9/12/70	25	22	15. Spirit In The Dark	Atlantic 8265
6/05/71	7	34	● 16. **Aretha Live At Fillmore West** .... [L]	Atlantic 7205
9/25/71	19	34	17. Aretha's Greatest Hits .... [G] "Bridge Over Troubled Water"(6)/"Spanish Harlem"(2)	Atlantic 8295
2/19/72	11	31	● 18. Young, Gifted & Black .... "Rock Steady"(9)/"Day Dreaming"(5)	Atlantic 7213
6/17/72	7	23	● 19. **Amazing Grace** .... [L] with James Cleveland & The Southern California Comm. Choir	Atlantic 906 [2]
6/24/72	160	9	20. In The Beginning/The World Of Aretha Franklin 1960-1967 .... [K]	Columbia 31355 [2]
7/14/73	30	20	21. Hey Now Hey (The Other Side Of The Sky) ...	Atlantic 7265
3/16/74	14	25	22. Let Me In Your Life .... "Until You Come Back To Me (That's What I'm Gonna Do)"(3)	Atlantic 7292
12/21/74	57	13	23. With Everything I Feel In Me	Atlantic 18116
11/15/75	83	11	24. You	Atlantic 18151
6/19/76	18	24	● 25. Sparkle .... [S]	Atlantic 18176
12/25/76	135	8	26. Ten Years Of Gold .... [G]	Atlantic 18204
6/18/77	49	19	27. Sweet Passion	Atlantic 19102
5/13/78	63	11	28. Almighty Fire	Atlantic 19161
10/13/79	146	6	29. La Diva	Atlantic 19248
10/25/80	47	30	30. Aretha	Arista 9538
8/29/81	36	17	31. Love All The Hurt Away	Arista 9552
8/14/82	23	30	● 32. Jump To It	Arista 9602
7/30/83	36	18	33. Get It Right	Arista 8019

ERMA FRANKLIN
Aretha's sister

DATE CHARTED	PEAK POS	WKS CHRT'D	ARTIST — Album Title	LABEL & NUMBER
10/18/69	199	2	1. Soul Sister	Brunswick 754147

RODNEY FRANKLIN
jazz pianist

DATE CHARTED	PEAK POS	WKS CHRT'D	ARTIST — Album Title	LABEL & NUMBER
4/19/80	104	13	1. You'll Never Know .... [I]	Columbia 36122
1/22/83	190	3	2. Learning To Love	Columbia 38198
2/25/84	187	3	3. Marathon	Columbia 38953

MICHAEL FRANKS
jazz/pop singer from Los Angeles

DATE CHARTED	PEAK POS	WKS CHRT'D	ARTIST — Album Title	LABEL & NUMBER
7/31/76	131	13	1. The Art Of Tea	Reprise 2230
2/19/77	119	9	2. Sleeping Gypsy	Warner 3004
4/08/78	90	10	3. Burchfield Nines	Warner 3167
3/17/79	68	16	4. Tiger In The Rain	Warner 3294
5/10/80	83	21	5. One Bad Habit	Warner 3427
1/30/82	45	14	6. Objects Of Desire	Warner 3648
10/29/83	141	11	7. Passionfruit	Warner 23962

DATE CHARTED	PEAK POS	WKS CHRT'D	ARTIST — Album Title	LABEL & NUMBER
			LINDA FRATIANNE - see AEROBICS section	
			STAN FREBERG	
			master-satirist	
7/03/61	34	24	1. Stan Freberg Presents The United States Of America .... [C] with Jesse White and Paul Frees - musical score by Billy May	Capitol 1573
			JOHN FRED & His Playboy Band	
			John Fred Gourrier from Baton Rouge, Louisiana	
2/03/68	154	10	1. Agnes English .... "Judy In Disguise (With Glasses)"(1)	Paula 2197
			FREDDIE & THE DREAMERS	
			Freddie Garrity, leader of quintet from Manchester, England	
4/17/65	19	19	1. Freddie & The Dreamers	Mercury 61017
5/08/65	86	10	2. I'm Telling You Now .... "I'm Telling You Now"(1) although label shows Freddie & The Dreamers as the artist, they are featured on only 2 songs - 5 unknown English groups do the other 10 songs	Tower 5003
6/19/65	85	12	3. Do The Freddie	Mercury 61026
			FREE	
			British quartet - Paul Rodgers (vocals) & Simon Kirke (drums) retired group in 1973 to form Bad Company	
9/13/69	197	2	1. Tons Of Sobs	A&M 4198
9/05/70	17	27	2. Fire And Water .... "All Right Now"(4)	A&M 4268
2/27/71	190	2	3. Highway	A&M 4287
9/11/71	89	8	4. Free Live! .... [L]	A&M 4306
5/27/72	69	16	5. Free At Last	A&M 4349
2/03/73	47	16	6. Heartbreaker	Island 9217
5/24/75	120	7	7. Best Of Free .... [G]	A&M 3663
			FREE MOVEMENT	
1/29/72	167	8	1. I've Found Someone Of My Own .... "I've Found Someone Of My Own"(5)	Columbia 31136
			ALAN FREED - **see VARIOUS - Radio/TV Celebrity Compilations**	
			ACE FREHLEY	
			Kiss' lead guitarist	
10/14/78	26	23	▲ 1. Ace Frehley	Casablanca 7121
			GLENN FREY	
			Eagles' guitarist	
6/26/82	32	38	● 1. No Fun Aloud	Asylum 60129
7/14/84	37	23+	2. The Allnighter	MCA 5501
			FRIDA	
			member of Abba	
11/13/82	41	28	1. Something's Going On	Atlantic 80018
			DEAN FRIEDMAN	
			New Jersey vocalist	
6/04/77	192	6	1. Dean Friedman	Lifesong 6008
			KINKY FRIEDMAN	
			Jewish country singer/satirist	
2/01/75	132	6	1. Kinky Friedman	ABC 829
			FRIENDS OF DISTINCTION	
			Los Angeles-based pop/soul quartet	
5/03/69	35	25	1. Grazin' .... "Grazing In The Grass"(3)	RCA 4149
10/25/69	173	6	2. Highly Distinct	RCA 4212

DATE CHARTED	PEAK POS	WKS CHRT'D	ARTIST — Album Title	LABEL & NUMBER
3/28/70	68	21	3. Real Friends .... "Love Or Let Me Be Lonely"(6)	RCA 4313
10/31/70	179	3	4. Whatever	RCA 4408
8/07/71	166	7	5. Friends & People	RCA 4492

FRIJID PINK
Michigan rock quartet

1/24/70	11	30	1. Frijid Pink .... "House Of The Rising Sun"(7)	Parrot 71033
10/31/70	149	12	2. Defrosted	Parrot 71041

ROBERT FRIPP
British rock avant gardist - founder of King Crimson

5/26/79	79	14	1. Exposure	EG 6201
4/26/80	110	6	2. God Save The Queen/Under Heavy Manners .... [I] features Fripp's "Frippertronics" electronic music	Polydor 6266
4/04/81	90	7	3. The League Of Gentlemen .... [I] title also refers to the name of Fripp's eclectic band	Polydor 6317
			ANDY SUMMERS/ROBERT FRIPP:	
11/06/82	60	11	4. I Advance Masked .... [I]	A&M 4913
10/20/84	155	5	5. Bewitched .... [I]	A&M 5011

FROST
Detroit rock quartet - Dick Wagner, lead singer

6/21/69	168	10	1. Frost Music	Vanguard 6520
11/29/69	148	8	2. Rock And Roll Music .... [L] 4 of 7 cuts are live	Vanguard 6541
10/17/70	197	2	3. Through The Eyes Of Love	Vanguard 6556

DAVID FRYE
comedian/impressionist

12/27/69	19	18	1. I Am The President .... [C]	Elektra 75006
3/27/71	123	6	2. Radio Free Nixon .... [C]	Elektra 74085
12/11/71	60	13	3. Richard Nixon Superstar .... [C]	Buddah 5097
8/11/73	45	15	4. Richard Nixon: A Fantasy .... [C]	Buddah 1600

FUGS
New York City "underground" group - Ed Sanders, leader

7/02/66	95	26	1. The Fugs	ESP 1028
10/29/66	142	4	2. The Fugs First Album	ESP 1018
10/19/68	167	10	3. It Crawled Into My Hand, Honest	Reprise 6305

BOBBY FULLER Four
El Paso, Texas rock band - Bobby died on 7/18/66 (22)

4/02/66	144	2	1. The Bobby Fuller Four .... "I Fought The Law"(9).	Mustang 901

FUN BOY THREE
British trio - formerly with the Specials

7/30/83	104	7	1. Waiting	Chrysalis 41417

FUNKADELIC
part of George Clinton's "P.Funk" battalion

3/21/70	126	17	1. Funkadelic	Westbound 2000
10/31/70	92	11	2. Free Your Mind...And Your Ass Will Follow	Westbound 2001
8/14/71	108	16	3. Maggot Brain	Westbound 2007
6/17/72	123	15	4. America Eats Its Young	Westbound 2020 [2]
7/21/73	112	13	5. Cosmic Slop	Westbound 2022
9/07/74	163	5	6. Standing On The Verge Of Getting It On	Westbound 1001
7/19/75	102	16	7. Let's Take It To The Stage	Westbound 215
10/09/76	103	10	8. Tales Of Kidd Funkadelic	Westbound 227
11/27/76	96	12	9. Hardcore Jollies	Warner 2973

DATE CHARTED	PEAK POS	WKS CHRT'D	ARTIST — Album Title	LABEL & NUMBER
10/07/78	16	22	▲ 10. One Nation Under A Groove	Warner 3209
10/13/79	18	17	● 11. Uncle Jam Wants You	Warner 3371
8/29/81	105	4	12. The Electric Spanking Of War Babies	Warner 3482

FUNKADELIC
includes 3 members of original Funkadelic clan, however, they are not associated with George Clinton

4/11/81	151	4	1. Connections & Disconnections	LAX 37087

FUNKY COMMUNICATION COMMITTEE - see FCC

RICHIE FURAY Band
member of Buffalo Springfield, Poco and Souther, Hillman, Furay Band

8/07/76	130	8	1. I've Got A Reason	Asylum 1067

FUSE ONE
supergroup of contemporary jazz artists

2/13/82	139	8	1. Silk [I]	CTI 9006

FUZZ
Washington, D.C. female soul trio

10/02/71	196	3	1. The Fuzz	Calla 2001

PETER GABRIEL
English - leader of Genesis from 1966-1975

3/12/77	38	17	1. Peter Gabriel	Atco 147
7/22/78	45	10	2. Peter Gabriel	Atlantic 19181
6/21/80	22	29	3. Peter Gabriel	Mercury 3848
10/02/82	28	31	4. Peter Gabriel (Security)	Geffen 2011
6/25/83	44	16	5. Peter Gabriel/Plays Live [L]	Geffen 4012 [2]

ERIC GALE
jazz/soul session guitarist

4/09/77	148	12	1. Ginseng Woman [I]	Columbia 34421
7/21/79	154	5	2. Part Of You [I]	Columbia 35715

RORY GALLAGHER
Irish blues-rock guitarist/vocalist - also see Taste

8/26/72	101	15	1. Rory Gallagher/Live! [L]	Polydor 5513
4/21/73	147	7	2. Blueprint	Polydor 5522
12/01/73	186	7	3. Tattoo	Polydor 5539
9/14/74	110	11	4. Irish Tour '74 [L]	Polydor 9501 [2]
2/22/75	156	5	5. Sinner...And Saint	Polydor 6510
11/29/75	121	13	6. Against The Grain	Chrysalis 1098
10/30/76	163	11	7. Calling Card	Chrysalis 1124
11/04/78	116	15	8. Photo-Finish	Chrysalis 1170
10/06/79	140	4	9. Top Priority	Chrysalis 1235

GALLERY
Jim Gold, leader of Detroit sextet

8/05/72	75	15	1. Nice To Be With You	Sussex 7017
			"Nice To Be With You"(4)	

JAMES GALWAY
classical flutist - also see Cleo Laine

3/03/79	153	5	1. Annie's Song and Other Galway Favorites [I]	RCA 3061
			with the National Phil. Orch., Charles Gerhardt, conductor	

GAMMA
formed by Ronnie Montrose after break-up of Montrose

9/22/79	131	17	1. Gamma 1	Elektra 219
9/13/80	65	19	2. Gamma 2	Elektra 288
3/20/82	72	12	3. Gamma 3	Elektra 60034

DATE CHARTED	PEAK POS	WKS CHRT'D	ARTIST — Album Title	LABEL & NUMBER
			GANG OF FOUR British - Jon King, lead singer	
6/06/81	**190**	2	1. Solid Gold	Warner 3565
2/13/82	**195**	2	2. Another Day/Another Dollar .... [M]	Warner 3646
6/26/82	**175**	3	3. Songs Of The Free	Warner 23683
10/08/83	**168**	4	4. Hard	Warner 23936
			GAP BAND brothers Charles, Ronnie, and Robert Wilson from Tulsa	
5/19/79	**77**	18	1. The Gap Band	Mercury 3758
12/22/79	**42**	28	● 2. The Gap Band II	Mercury 3804
12/27/80	**16**	37	▲ 3. The Gap Band III	Mercury 4003
6/12/82	**14**	52	▲ 4. Gap Band IV	Total Exp. 3001
9/10/83	**28**	43	● 5. Gap Band V - Jammin'	Total Exp. 3004
1/19/85	**58**	12+	6. Gap Band VI	Total Exp. 5705
3/09/85	**108+**	5+	7. Gap Gold/Best of the Gap Band .... [G]	Total Exp. 824343
			JERRY GARCIA founder/lead guitarist of the Grateful Dead	
1/29/72	**35**	14	1. Garcia	Warner 2582
6/22/74	**49**	15	2. Garcia	Round 102
2/14/76	**42**	14	3. Reflections	Round 565
4/15/78	**114**	5	4. Cats Under The Stars	Arista 4160
11/20/82	**100**	8	5. Run For The Roses	Arista 9603
			DAVE GARDNER comedian "Brother" Dave Gardner	
6/20/60	**5**	69	1. **Rejoice, Dear Hearts!** .... [C]	RCA 2083
8/29/60	**5**	56	2. **Kick Thy Own Self** .... [C]	RCA 2239
9/18/61	**15**	30	3. Ain't That Weird? .... [C]	RCA 2335
9/01/62	**49**	13	4. Did You Ever? .... [C]	RCA 2498
3/09/63	**52**	10	5. All Seriousness Aside .... [C]	RCA 2628
5/04/63	**28**	13	6. It Don't Make No Difference .... [C]	Capitol 1867
			ART GARFUNKEL born on 10/13/42 in New York City - also see Simon & Garfunkel	
9/29/73	**5**	25	● 1. **Angel Clare** .... "All I Know"(9)	Columbia 31474
10/25/75	**7**	28	● 2. **Breakaway** .... "My Little Town"(9-Simon & Garfunkel)	Columbia 33700
2/04/78	**19**	16	● 3. **Watermark**	Columbia 34975
4/07/79	**67**	14	4. Fate For Breakfast	Columbia 35780
9/12/81	**113**	8	5. Scissors Cut	Columbia 37392
			JUDY GARLAND star of MGM film musicals from 1935-1954 - died on 1/22/69 (46)	
10/29/55	**5**	6	1. **Miss Show Business**	Capitol 676
11/10/56	**17**	5	2. Judy	Capitol 734
6/17/57	**17**	3	3. Alone	Capitol 835
7/31/61	**1(13)**	97	● 4. **Judy At Carnegie Hall** .... [L]	Capitol 1569 [2]
8/25/62	**33**	14	5. The Garland Touch	Capitol 1710
5/11/63	**45**	6	6. I Could Go On Singing .... [S] Judy's first singing/acting role since 1954's "A Star Is Born"	Capitol 1861
1/04/64	**136**	2	7. The Best Of Judy Garland .... [G]	Decca 7172 [2]
9/04/65	**41**	14	8. "Live" At The London Palladium .... [L] JUDY GARLAND & LIZA MINNELLI	Capitol 2295 [2]
9/16/67	**174**	3	9. Judy Garland At Home At The Palace - Opening Night .... [L]	ABC 620

DATE CHARTED	PEAK POS	WKS CHRT'D	ARTIST — Album Title	LABEL & NUMBER
8/16/69	161	3	10. Judy Garland's Greatest Hits .... [G] condensation of album #7 above	Decca 75150
6/09/73	164	8	11. "Live" At The London Palladium .... [R-L] JUDY GARLAND & LIZA MINNELLI condensation of album #8 above	Capitol 11191

ERROLL GARNER
jazz pianist - died 1/2/77 (53)

11/25/57	16	2	1. Other Voices .... [I] featuring the juke-box hit "Misty"	Columbia 1014
3/10/58	12	7	2. Concert By The Sea .... [I-L] recorded in 1956 in Carmel, California	Columbia 883
6/26/61	35	31	3. Dreamstreet .... [I]	ABC-Para. 365
7/06/63	94	6	4. One World Concert .... [I-L] recorded at Seattle World's Fair	Reprise 6080

GALE GARNETT

9/26/64	43	22	1. My Kind Of Folk Songs .... "We'll Sing In The Sunshine"(4)	RCA 2833

LEIF GARRETT
born on 11/8/61 in Hollywood, California

12/17/77	37	24	● 1. Leif Garrett	Atlantic 19152
11/25/78	34	19	● 2. Feel The Need .... "I Was Made For Dancin'"(10)	Scotti Br. 7100
12/15/79	129	22	3. Same Goes For You	Scotti Br. 16008
12/12/81	185	7	4. My Movie Of You	Scotti Br. 37625

TOMMY GARRETT - see 50 GUITARS

JOHN GARY
born in Watertown, New York on 11/29/32

11/09/63	20	63	1. Catch A Rising Star	RCA 2745
2/22/64	16	46	2. Encore	RCA 2804
8/15/64	42	28	3. So Tenderly	RCA 2922
11/14/64	141	4	4. David Merrick presents Hits From His Broadway Hits .... JOHN GARY/ANN-MARGRET Merrick: Broadway's leading producer	RCA 2947
1/23/65	17	33	5. A Little Bit Of Heaven	RCA 2994
7/24/65	11	29	6. The Nearness Of You	RCA 3349
10/30/65	21	25	7. Your All-Time Favorite Songs	RCA 3411
3/12/66	51	20	8. Choice	RCA 3501
7/09/66	65	12	9. Your All-Time Country Favorites	RCA 3570
10/08/66	73	17	10. A Heart Filled With Song	RCA 3666
2/11/67	117	14	11. Especially For You	RCA 3695
5/13/67	90	11	12. Spanish Moonlight	RCA 3785
10/07/67	76	19	13. The John Gary Carnegie Hall Concert ..... [L]	RCA 1139
4/19/69	192	3	14. Love Of A Gentle Woman	RCA 4134

GARY'S GANG
Gary Turnier (drums) & Eric Matthew (guitar & lead vocal)

3/31/79	42	10	1. Keep On Dancin'	Columbia 35793

LUIS GASCA
jazz trumpet player

5/27/72	195	3	1. Luis Gasca .... [I] with Joe Henderson (sax), Carlos Santana (guitar) & Stanley Clarke (bass)	Blue Thumb 37

DAVID GATES
lead singer of Bread

10/27/73	107	10	1. First	Elektra 75066
2/15/75	102	9	2. Never Let Her Go	Elektra 1028
8/12/78	165	4	3. Goodbye Girl	Elektra 148

DATE CHARTED	PEAK POS	WKS CHRT'D	ARTIST — Album Title	LABEL & NUMBER
			LARRY GATLIN & the GATLIN BROTHERS BAND	
			although albums 1-3 are shown only as Larry Gatlin, he is backed on them by his brothers Steve and Rudy	
4/01/78	175	5	1. Love Is Just A Game	Monument 7616
7/22/78	140	8	2. Oh! Brother	Monument 7626
12/23/78	171	9	● 3. Larry Gatlin's Greatest Hits .... [G]	Monument 7628
11/17/79	102	16	● 4. Straight Ahead	Columbia 36250
11/01/80	118	4	5. Help Yourself	Columbia 36582
10/17/81	184	2	6. Not Guilty...	Columbia 37464
			MARVIN GAYE	
			born in Washington, D.C. on 4/2/39 - shot to death by his father on 4/1/84 (44)	
5/16/64	42	16	1. Together .... MARVIN GAYE & MARY WELLS	Motown 613
5/30/64	72	14	2. Marvin Gaye/Greatest Hits .... [G] "Pride And Joy"(10)	Tamla 252
2/27/65	128	10	3. How Sweet It Is To Be Loved By You .... "How Sweet It Is To Be Loved By You"(6)	Tamla 258
7/16/66	118	10	4. Moods Of Marvin Gaye .... "I'll Be Doggone"(8)/"Ain't That Peculiar"(8)	Tamla 266
9/30/67	178	5	5. Marvin Gaye/Greatest Hits, Vol. 2 .... [G]	Tamla 278
10/07/67	69	14	6. United .... MARVIN GAYE & TAMMI TERRELL "Your Precious Love"(5)/ "If I Could Build My Whole World Around You"(10)	Tamla 277
9/21/68	60	21	7. You're All I Need .... MARVIN GAYE & TAMMI TERRELL "Ain't Nothing Like The Real Thing"(8)/ "You're All I Need To Get By"(7)	Tamla 284
11/02/68	63	27	8. In The Groove .... "I Heard It Through The Grapevine"(1)	Tamla 285
6/14/69	33	18	9. M.P.G. .... "Too Busy Thinking About My Baby"(4)/ "That's The Way Love Is"(7)	Tamla 292
6/14/69	183	7	10. Marvin Gaye And His Girls .... [K] with Tammi Terrell, Mary Wells, & Kim Weston	Tamla 293
10/18/69	184	2	11. Easy .... MARVIN GAYE & TAMMI TERRELL	Tamla 294
11/01/69	189	3	12. That's The Way Love Is	Tamla 299
6/13/70	171	3	13. Marvin Gaye & Tammi Terrell Greatest Hits .... [G]	Tamla 302
11/07/70	117	6	14. Marvin Gaye Super Hits .... [G]	Tamla 300
6/12/71	6	53	15. **What's Going On** .... "What's Going On"(2)/"Mercy Mercy Me"(4)/ "Inner City Blues"(9)	Tamla 310
12/30/72	14	21	16. Trouble Man .... [S] Marvin sings on 3 of the 13 cuts (others are instrumentals) "Trouble Man"(7)	Tamla 322
9/15/73	2(1)	61	17. **Let's Get It On** .... "Let's Get It On"(1)	Tamla 329
11/17/73	26	47	18. Diana & Marvin .... DIANA ROSS & MARVIN GAYE	Motown 803
4/20/74	61	29	19. Marvin Gaye Anthology .... [G]	Motown 791 [3]
7/13/74	8	28	20. **Marvin Gaye Live!** .... [L]	Tamla 333
4/03/76	4	28	21. **I Want You**	Tamla 342
10/02/76	44	8	22. Marvin Gaye's Greatest Hits .... [G]	Tamla 348
4/02/77	3	26	23. **Marvin Gaye Live At The London Palladium** .... [L] "Got To Give It Up"(1)	Tamla 352 [2]
1/06/79	26	21	24. Here, My Dear	Tamla 364 [2]
2/07/81	32	17	25. In Our Lifetime	Tamla 374

DATE CHARTED	PEAK POS	WKS CHRT'D	ARTIST — Album Title	LABEL & NUMBER
11/20/82	7	41	▲ 26. **Midnight Love** .... "Sexual Healing"(3)	Columbia 38197
10/22/83	80	16	27. Every Great Motown Hit Of Marvin Gaye .... [G]	Motown 6058
			CRYSTAL GAYLE younger sister of Loretta Lynn	
9/03/77	12	35	▲ 1. We Must Believe In Magic .... "Don't It Make My Brown Eyes Blue"(2)	United Art. 771
7/15/78	52	39	▲ 2. When I Dream	United Art. 858
8/11/79	128	8	3. We Should Be Together	United Art. 969
9/29/79	36	28	● 4. Miss The Mississippi	Columbia 36203
11/17/79	62	22	● 5. Classic Crystal .... [G]	United Art. 982
5/03/80	149	6	6. Favorites .... [K]	United Art. 1034
9/27/80	79	11	7. These Days	Columbia 36512
9/19/81	99	16	8. Hollywood, Tennessee	Columbia 37438
12/04/82	120	12	9. True Love	Elektra 60200
9/10/83	169	8	10. Crystal Gayle's Greatest Hits .... [G]	Columbia 38803
11/12/83	171	6	11. Cage The Songbird	Warner 23958
			GAYLORD & HOLIDAY Ronnie Gaylord & Burt Holiday - formerly known as the Gaylords	
2/21/76	180	8	1. Second Generation	Prodigal 10009
			GLORIA GAYNOR Newark, New Jersey disco queen	
2/01/75	25	15	1. Never Can Say Goodbye .... "Never Can Say Goodbye"(9)	MGM 4982
10/11/75	64	21	2. Experience Gloria Gaynor	MGM 4997
8/14/76	107	14	3. I've Got You	Polydor 6063
3/19/77	183	4	4. Glorious	Polydor 6095
1/06/79	4	34	▲ 5. **Love Tracks** .... "I Will Survive"(1)	Polydor 6184
10/20/79	58	11	6. I Have A Right	Polydor 6231
5/24/80	178	4	7. Stories	Polydor 6274
			J. GEILS BAND Boston sextet led by Peter Wolf (vocals). Seth Justman (keyboards) & Jerome Geils (guitar)	
1/30/71	195	2	1. The J. Geils Band	Atlantic 8275
11/06/71	64	17	2. The Morning After	Atlantic 8297
10/21/72	54	26	● 3. "Live" - Full House .... [L]	Atlantic 7241
4/28/73	10	44	● 4. **Bloodshot**	Atlantic 7260
12/01/73	51	18	5. Ladies Invited	Atlantic 7286
10/19/74	26	22	6. Nightmares...and other tales from the vinyl jungle	Atlantic 18107
9/27/75	36	9	7. Hotline	Atlantic 18147
5/22/76	40	11	8. Live - Blow Your Face Out .... [L]	Atlantic 507 [2]
7/09/77	51	17	9. Monkey Island	Atlantic 19103
12/16/78	49	22	● 10. Sanctuary	EMI America 17006
7/21/79	129	5	11. Best of the J. Geils Band .... [G]	Atlantic 19234
2/09/80	18	42	● 12. Love Stinks	EMI America 17016
11/14/81	1(4)	70	▲ 13. **Freeze-Frame** .... "Centerfold"(1)/"Freeze-Frame"(4)	EMI America 17062
12/04/82	23	19	● 14. Showtime! .... [L] Peter Wolf's last album with group	EMI America 17087
11/24/84	80	10	15. You're Gettin' Even While I'm Gettin' Odd	EMI America 17137
			GENERAL PUBLIC fronted by English Beat vocalists Dave Wakeling & Ranking Roger	
10/27/84	26	24 +	1. ...All The Rage	I.R.S. 70046

DATE CHARTED	PEAK POS	WKS CHRT'D	ARTIST — Album Title	LABEL & NUMBER
			GENESIS English group formed in 1966 featuring Peter Gabriel (vocalist/founder - left group in '75), Phil Collins (vocalist/drummer), Mike Rutherford (bass), Tony Banks (keyboards) & Steve Hackett (guitar)	
12/15/73	70	29	1. Selling England By The Pound	Charisma 6060
5/18/74	105	14	2. Genesis Live .... [L] recorded in Manchester, England, February 1973	Charisma 1666
10/12/74	170	4	3. From Genesis To Revelation .... [E] their first album, released in 1969	London 643
12/14/74	41	16	4. The Lamb Lies Down On Broadway	Atco 401 [2]
3/20/76	31	19	5. A Trick Of The Tail	Atco 129
1/22/77	26	21	6. Wind & Wuthering	Atco 144
12/03/77	47	16	7. Seconds Out .... [L]	Atlantic 9002 [2]
4/15/78	14	33	● 8. And Then There Were Three... .... from here on, group consists of Banks, Collins & Rutherford	Atlantic 19173
4/26/80	11	31	● 9. Duke	Atlantic 16014
10/17/81	7	57	▲ 10. **Abacab**	Atlantic 19313
6/26/82	10	25	● 11. **Three Sides Live** .... [L] side four: studio cuts from '79-'81	Atlantic 2000 [2]
10/29/83	9	48	▲ 12. **Genesis** .... "That's All"(6)	Atlantic 80116
			GENTLE GIANT British progressive-rock band led by brothers Ray & Derek Shulman	
10/21/72	197	5	1. Three Friends	Columbia 31649
3/31/73	170	9	2. Octopus	Columbia 32022
10/12/74	78	13	3. The Power And The Glory	Capitol 11337
8/16/75	48	11	4. Free Hand	Capitol 11428
5/29/76	137	5	5. Interview	Capitol 11532
2/19/77	89	6	6. The Official "Live" Gentle Giant - Playing The Fool .... [L]	Capitol 11592 [2]
10/15/77	81	7	7. The Missing Piece	Capitol 11696
			BOBBIE GENTRY born in Chickasaw County, Mississippi on 7/27/44	
9/16/67	1(2)	30	● 1. **Ode To Billie Joe** .... "Ode To Billie Joe"(1)	Capitol 2830
3/23/68	132	12	2. The Delta Sweete	Capitol 2842
10/12/68	11	47	● 3. Bobbie Gentry & Glen Campbell	Capitol 2928
8/09/69	164	4	4. Touch 'em With Love	Capitol 155
12/27/69	180	2	5. Bobbie Gentry's Greatest! .... [G]	Capitol 381
5/09/70	96	17	6. Fancy	Capitol 428
			GENTRYS Memphis-based 7-man band - Larry Raspberry, leader	
12/18/65	99	10	1. Keep On Dancing .... "Keep On Dancing"(4)	MGM 4336
			LOWELL GEORGE founder of Little Feat - died on 6/29/79 (34)	
4/14/79	71	9	1. Thanks I'll Eat It Here	Warner 3194
			GERRY & THE PACEMAKERS quartet from Liverpool, England - led by Gerry Marsden	
7/11/64	29	12	1. Don't Let The Sun Catch You Crying .... "Don't Let The Sun Catch You Crying"(4)/ "How Do You Do It?"(9)	Laurie 2024
11/21/64	129	9	2. Gerry & The Pacemakers Second Album	Laurie 2027
2/27/65	13	20	3. Ferry Cross The Mersey .... [S] 9 of 12 songs by Gerry & The Pacemakers (they star in the film which was set in Liverpool) "Ferry Cross The Mersey"(6)	United Art. 6387
2/27/65	120	7	4. I'll Be There!	Laurie 2030
5/15/65	44	22	5. Gerry & The Pacemakers Greatest Hits.... [G]	Laurie 2031

DATE CHARTED	PEAK POS	WKS CHRT'D	ARTIST — Album Title	LABEL & NUMBER
			STAN GETZ jazz tenor saxophonist	
9/15/62	1(1)	70	1. Jazz Samba .... [I] STAN GETZ/CHARLIE BYRD (guitar)	Verve 8432
12/22/62	13	23	2. Big Band Bossa Nova .... [I] with the Gary McFarland Orchestra	Verve 8494
5/18/63	88	11	3. Jazz Samba Encore! .... [I-F] with Luiz Bonfa (guitar) & Maria Toledo (vocals)	Verve 8523
4/11/64	122	6	4. Reflections .... [I]	Verve 8554
6/06/64	2(2)	96	● 5. Getz/Gilberto .... STAN GETZ/JOAO GILBERTO (Brazilian singer/guitarist) "The Girl From Ipanema"(5-vocal by Joao's wife Astrud)	Verve 8545
12/19/64	24	46	6. Getz Au Go Go .... [L] The New Stan Getz Quartet featuring Astrud Gilberto (vocals)	Verve 8600
9/02/67	195	2	7. Sweet Rain .... [I]	Verve 8693
3/01/75	191	1	8. Captain Marvel .... [I] above 2 feature pianist Chick Corea	Columbia 32706
			ANDY GIBB Bee Gees' younger brother	
7/02/77	19	68	▲ 1. Flowing Rivers .... "I Just Want To Be Your Everything"(1)/ "(Love Is) Thicker Than Water"(1)	RSO 3019
6/17/78	7	43	▲ 2. Shadow Dancing .... "Shadow Dancing"(1)/"An Everlasting Love"(5)/ "(Our Love) Don't Throw It All Away"(9)	RSO 3034
3/01/80	21	15	● 3. After Dark .... "Desire"(4)	RSO 3069
12/06/80	46	18	4. Andy Gibb's Greatest Hits .... [G]	RSO 3091
			BARRY GIBB eldest brother of the Bee Gees	
10/20/84	72	8	1. Now Voyager	MCA 5506
			TERRI GIBBS Terri, blind since birth, is from Augusta, Georgia	
2/14/81	53	25	1. Somebody's Knockin'	MCA 5173
			GIBSON BROTHERS Alex, Patrick & Chris	
7/28/79	185	2	1. Cuba	Island 9579
			DON GIBSON born on 3/3/28 in Shelby, North Carolina	
11/02/63	134	3	1. I Wrote A Song... .... featuring new versions of Don's biggest hits	RCA 2702
			ASTRUD GILBERTO Brazilian - wife of composer-guitarist Joao Gilberto - also see Stan Getz	
5/15/65	41	18	1. The Astrud Gilberto Album .... with Antonio Carlos Jobim (guitar)	Verve 8608
10/09/65	68	18	2. The Shadow Of Your Smile	Verve 8629
			JOAO GILBERTO - see STAN GETZ	
			NICK GILDER Canadian - member of Sweeny Todd	
9/23/78	33	20	1. City Nights .... "Hot Child In The City"(1)	Chrysalis 1202
7/07/79	127	8	2. Frequency	Chrysalis 1219
			JOHNNY GILL - see STACY LATTISAW	
			GILLAN Ian Gillan - Deep Purple's lead singer - portrayed Jesus in the rock opera "Jesus Christ Superstar"	
12/06/80	183	3	1. Glory Road	RSO/Virgin 1001

DATE CHARTED	PEAK POS	WKS CHRT'D	ARTIST — Album Title	LABEL & NUMBER
			MICKEY GILLEY	
			owner of "Gilleys" club in Pasadena, Texas	
8/30/80	**177**	3	1. That's All That Matters To Me	Epic 36492
8/22/81	**170**	6	2. You Don't Know Me	Epic 37416
			JIMMY GILMER & THE FIREBALLS	
			Amarillo, Texas native	
11/16/63	**26**	14	1. Sugar Shack	Dot 25545
			"Sugar Shack"(1)	
			DAVID GILMOUR	
			guitarist/vocalist with Pink Floyd	
7/01/78	**29**	18	1. David Gilmour	Columbia 35388
3/17/84	**32**	28	2. About Face	Columbia 39296
			JIM GILSTRAP	
8/30/75	**179**	7	1. Swing Your Daddy	Roxbury 102
			NIKKI GIOVANNI & The New York Community Choir	
8/21/71	**165**	13	1. Truth Is On Its Way [T]	Right-On 5001
			Nikki recites her poems to the music of famous spirituals	
			GIRLSCHOOL	
			heavy-metal female quartet from England	
5/22/82	**182**	5	1. Hit And Run	Stiff 18
			GIUFFRIA	
			California-based rock quintet led by Gregg Giuffria (keyboardist with Angel) and David Glen Eisley (vocals)	
12/08/84	**26**	18+	1. Giuffria	MCA 5524
			GLASS HARP	
			Ohio rock trio led by Phil Keaggy (now a religious artist)	
11/27/71	**192**	3	1. Synergy	Decca 75306
			GLASS MOON	
			U.S. rock trio	
5/10/80	**148**	9	1. Glass Moon	Radio 2003
			PHILIP GLASS	
			composer with his Ensemble	
4/10/82	**121**	6	1. Glassworks [I]	CBS 37265
			synthesized classical-flavored instrumentals	
			TOM GLAZER & The Do-Re-Mi Children's Chorus	
7/27/63	**114**	8	1. On Top Of Spaghetti [N]	Kapp 3331
			JACKIE GLEASON	
			although famous as a TV comedian, Jackie's albums feature dreamy mood music by studio orchestras featuring the trumpets of Bobby Hackett & Pee Wee Erwin	
3/05/55	**5**	14	1. **Music To Remember Her** [I]	Capitol 570
6/25/55	**1(2)**	24	2. **Lonesome Echo** [I]	Capitol 627
11/12/55	**2(2)**	18	3. **Romantic Jazz** [I]	Capitol 568
1/28/56	**7**	8	4. **Music For Lovers Only/Music To Make You Misty** [R-I]	Capitol 475 [2]
			reissue of albums from 1953 & 1954	
2/25/56	**8**	7	5. **Music To Change Her Mind** [I]	Capitol 632
6/09/56	**10**	10	6. **Night Winds** [I]	Capitol 717
12/08/56	**16**	3	7. Merry Christmas [X-I]	Capitol 758
8/26/57	**13**	2	● 8. Music For The Love Hours [I]	Capitol 816
9/09/57	**16**	10	9. Velvet Brass [I]	Capitol 859
12/09/57	**14**	4	10. Jackie Gleason presents "Oooo!" [I]	Capitol 905
8/10/63	**82**	5	11. Movie Themes - For Lovers Only [I]	Capitol 1877
12/07/63	**115**	8	12. Today's Romantic Hits/for lovers only [I]	Capitol 1978

DATE CHARTED	PEAK POS	WKS CHRT'D	ARTIST — Album Title	LABEL & NUMBER
6/06/64	82	10	13. Today's Romantic Hits/for lovers only, Vol. 2 .... [I]	Capitol 2056
2/05/66	141	4	14. Silk 'N' Brass .... [I]	Capitol 2409
11/26/66	71	11	15. How Sweet It Is for lovers .... [I]	Capitol 2582
6/24/67	200	2	16. A Taste Of Brass for lovers only .... [I]	Capitol 2684
8/23/69	192	2	17. Close-Up .... [R-I] reissue of "Music For Lovers Only" ('53) & "Music, Martinis & Memories" ('54)	Capitol 255 [2]

GARY GLITTER
British - real name: Paul Gadd

| 10/28/72 | 186 | 8 | 1. Glitter .... "Rock And Roll Part 2"(7) | Bell 1108 |

ROGER GLOVER
bass player of Deep Purple

| 1/24/76 | 142 | 8 | 1. The Butterfly Ball and the Grasshopper's Feast .... with guests: David Coverdale & Glenn Hughes (Deep Purple), and Ronnie Dio (Rainbow) | UK 56000 |
| 6/16/84 | 101 | 12 | 2. Mask .... | 21 Records 9009 |

GO-GO'S
Belinda Carlisle, lead singer of Los Angeles female quintet

8/01/81	1(6)	72	▲ 1. **Beauty And The Beat** .... "We Got The Beat"(2)	I.R.S. 70021
8/14/82	8	28	● 2. **Vacation** .... "Vacation"(8)	I.R.S. 70031
4/07/84	18	32	3. Talk Show	I.R.S. 70041

GO WEST
British duo: Peter Cox & Richard Drummie

| 3/23/85 | 101+ | 3+ | 1. Go West .... | Chrysalis 41495 |

GOANNA
Australian group - Shane Howard, lead singer

| 6/25/83 | 179 | 5 | 1. Spirit Of Place .... | Atco 90081 |

GODZ
Flint, Michigan rock quartet

| 4/08/78 | 191 | 5 | 1. The Godz .... | Millennium 8003 |
| 2/17/79 | 189 | 2 | 2. Nothing Is Sacred .... | Casablanca 7134 |

LOUISE GOFFIN
Carole King's daughter

| 8/04/79 | 87 | 13 | 1. Kid Blue .... | Asylum 203 |

ANDREW GOLD
son of composer Ernest Gold ("Exodus") & singer Marni Nixon

1/10/76	190	2	1. Andrew Gold	Asylum 1047
5/07/77	95	16	2. What's Wrong With This Picture? .... "Lonely Boy"(7)	Asylum 1086
2/25/78	81	14	3. All This And Heaven Too	Asylum 116

MARTY GOLD & His Orchestra

| 4/13/63 | 10 | 18 | 1. **Soundpower!** .... [I] | RCA 2620 |

GOLDDIGGERS
female singing/dancing troupe from Dean Martin's TV show

| 8/02/69 | 142 | 7 | 1. The Golddiggers .... | Metromedia 1009 |

GOLDEN EARRING
Dutch rock quartet

5/04/74	12	29	● 1. Moontan	Track 396
4/12/75	108	8	2. Switch	Track 2139
2/28/76	156	4	3. To The Hilt	MCA 2183
5/28/77	182	2	4. Mad Love	MCA 2254

DATE CHARTED	PEAK POS	WKS CHRT'D	ARTIST — Album Title	LABEL & NUMBER
12/11/82	**24**	30	5. Cut .... "Twilight Zone"(10)	21 Records 9004
3/17/84	**107**	9	6. N.E.W.S.	21 Records 9008
11/24/84	**158**	6	7. Something Heavy Going Down - Live From The Twilight Zone .... [L]	21 Records 823717
			GOLDEN GATE STRINGS producer: Stu Phillips: conductor: Sid Feller	
5/27/67	**200**	2	1. The Monkees Song Book .... [I]	Epic 26248
			BOBBY GOLDSBORO born on 1/18/41 in Marianna, Florida	
5/06/67	**165**	3	1. Solid Goldsboro - Bobby Goldsboro's Greatest Hits .... [G] "See The Funny Little Clown"(9)	United Art. 6561
4/20/68	**5**	48	● 2. **Honey** .... "Honey"(1)	United Art. 6642
9/21/68	**116**	13	3. Word Pictures featuring Autumn Of My Life	United Art. 6657
6/07/69	**60**	13	4. Today	United Art. 6704
1/17/70	**139**	11	5. Muddy Mississippi Line	United Art. 6735
7/04/70	**103**	10	6. Bobby Goldsboro's Greatest Hits .... [G]	United Art. 5502
1/23/71	**120**	13	7. We Gotta Start Lovin'	United Art. 6777
8/28/71	**142**	5	8. Come Back Home	United Art. 5516
9/29/73	**150**	11	9. Summer (The First Time)	United Art. 124
11/16/74	**174**	3	10. Bobby Goldsboro's 10th Anniversary Album .... [G]	United Art. 311 [2]
			IAN GOMM English - member of Brinsley Schwarz	
9/22/79	**104**	12	1. Gomm With The Wind	Stiff 36103
			GONZALEZ English disco band	
1/20/79	**67**	14	1. Shipwrecked	Capitol 11855
			BENNY GOODMAN "King of Swing" - clarinetist/big band leader since the 1930's	
3/19/55	**7**	15	1. B.G. In Hi-Fi .... [I]	Capitol 565
3/24/56	**4**	10	2. The Benny Goodman Story .... [S-I] Benny is portrayed by Steve Allen in the film, although Benny and his musicians play the music	Decca 8252/3 [2]
11/10/62	**80**	6	3. Benny Goodman In Moscow .... [L-I] recorded during his tour of Russia, July, 1962	RCA 6008 [2]
3/07/64	**90**	10	4. Together Again! .... [I] reunion of his quartet: Gene Krupa, Lionel Hampton & Teddy Wilson	RCA 2698
4/03/71	**189**	7	5. Benny Goodman Today .... [L-I] recorded live in Stockholm	Lond.Phase 4 21 [2]
			DICKIE GOODMAN	
12/06/75	**144**	8	1. Mr. Jaws and other Fables .... [G-N] "Mr. Jaws"(4) side 2: Buchanan & Goodman's top hits including "The Flying Saucer"(3-'56)	Cash 6000
			JERRY GOODMAN & JAN HAMMER jazz/rock duo - formerly with John McLaughlin	
2/08/75	**150**	3	1. Like Children	Nemperor 430
			STEVE GOODMAN Chicago-born folk singer/writer - died on 9/20/84 (36)	
8/23/75	**144**	6	1. Jessie's Jig & Other Favorites	Asylum 1037
5/15/76	**175**	4	2. Words We Can Dance To	Asylum 1060

DATE CHARTED	PEAK POS	WKS CHRT'D	ARTIST — Album Title	LABEL & NUMBER
			GOOSE CREEK SYMPHONY	
			country rock septet	
6/03/72	**167**	8	1. Words Of Earnest	Capitol 11044
			ROBERT GORDON	
			rockabilly singer from Washington, D.C.	
10/01/77	**142**	8	1. Robert Gordon with Link Wray	Private S. 2030
3/18/78	**124**	7	2. Fresh Fish Special	Private S. 7008
			with Link Wray (guitar)	
3/24/79	**106**	12	3. Rock Billy Boogie	RCA 3294
2/02/80	**150**	9	4. Bad Boy	RCA 3523
4/18/81	**117**	15	5. Are You Gonna Be The One	RCA 3773
			LESLEY GORE	
			born on 5/2/46 in New York City	
7/13/63	**24**	15	1. I'll Cry If I Want To	Mercury 60805
			"It's My Party"(1)/"Judy's Turn To Cry"(5)	
1/25/64	**125**	8	2. Lesley Gore Sings Of Mixed-Up Hearts	Mercury 60849
			"She's A Fool"(5)/"You Don't Own Me"(2)	
7/18/64	**127**	6	3. Boys, Boys, Boys	Mercury 60901
12/12/64	**146**	2	4. Girl Talk	Mercury 60943
7/17/65	**95**	24	5. The Golden Hits Of Lesley Gore .... [G]	Mercury 61024
12/04/65	**120**	4	6. My Town, My Guy & Me	Mercury 61042
5/13/67	**169**	5	7. California Nights	Mercury 61120
			EYDIE GORME	
			married to Steve Lawrence since December, 1957	
5/06/57	**14**	10	1. Eydie Gorme	ABC-Para. 150
10/28/57	**19**	4	2. Eydie Swings The Blues	ABC-Para. 192
3/31/58	**19**	4	3. Eydie Gorme Vamps The Roaring 20's	ABC-Para. 218
11/03/58	**20**	1	4. Eydie In Love...	ABC-Para. 246
4/06/63	**22**	22	5. Blame It On The Bossa Nova	Columbia 8812
			"Blame It On The Bossa Nova"(7)	
2/15/64	**143**	3	6. Gorme Country Style	Columbia 8920
9/12/64	**54**	22	7. Amor .... [F]	Columbia 9003
8/28/65	**53**	11	8. More Amor .... [F]	Columbia 9176
			above 2 albums feature the Trio Los Panchos (Spanish)	
6/04/66	**22**	37	9. Don't Go To Strangers	Columbia 9276
2/18/67	**85**	18	10. Softly, As I Leave You	Columbia 9394
5/20/67	**136**	6	11. Together On Broadway	Columbia 9436
			STEVE LAWRENCE & EYDIE GORME	
12/02/67	**148**	9	12. Eydie Gorme's Greatest Hits .... [G]	Columbia 9564
3/08/69	**141**	6	13. What It Was, Was Love	RCA 4115
			STEVE LAWRENCE & EDDIE GORME	
5/10/69	**188**	3	14. Real True Lovin'	RCA 4107
			STEVE LAWRENCE & EYDIE GORME	
3/07/70	**105**	12	15. Tonight I'll Say A Prayer	RCA 4303
			BARRY GOUDREAU	
			lead guitarist of Boston - also see Orion The Hunter	
9/20/80	**88**	8	1. Barry Goudreau	Portrait 36542
			MORTON GOULD & His Orchestra	
11/09/59	**5**	52	1. Tchaikovsky: 1812 Overture/	
			Ravel: Bolero .... [I]	RCA 2345
7/18/60	**3**	41	2. Grofe: Grand Canyon Suite/	
			Beethoven: Wellington's Victory...... [I]	RCA 2433
			ROBERT GOULET	
			played Sir Lancelot in Broadway's "Camelot"	
3/17/62	**43**	65	1. Always You	Columbia 8476
9/01/62	**27**	55	2. Two Of Us	Columbia 8626
1/05/63	**9**	48	3. Sincerely Yours...	Columbia 8731

DATE CHARTED	PEAK POS	WKS CHRT'D	ARTIST — Album Title	LABEL & NUMBER
4/27/63	11	29	4. The Wonderful World Of Love	Columbia 8793
10/19/63	16	23	5. Robert Goulet In Person [L] recorded live at the Chicago Opera House	Columbia 8888
5/02/64	31	22	6. Manhattan Tower/The Man Who Loves Manhattan composed & conducted by Gordon Jenkins	Columbia 2450
10/17/64	72	16	7. Without You	Columbia 9000
12/26/64	5	29	● 8. **My Love Forgive Me**	Columbia 9096
6/05/65	69	16	9. Begin To Love	Columbia 9142
8/14/65	31	19	10. Summer Sounds	Columbia 9180
12/11/65	33	22	11. Robert Goulet On Broadway	Columbia 9218
4/30/66	73	12	12. I Remember You	Columbia 9282
3/11/67	145	3	13. Robert Goulet On Broadway, Volume 2	Columbia 9386
9/14/68	162	15	14. Woman, Woman	Columbia 9695
4/12/69	135	13	15. Both Sides Now	Columbia 9763
9/06/69	174	3	16. Souvenir d'Italie	Columbia 9874
11/14/70	198	2	17. I Wish You Love [K]	Columbia 30011 [2]

GQ
Bronx, New York soul trio

4/07/79	13	35	▲ 1. Disco Nights	Arista 4225
4/05/80	46	20	2. Two	Arista 9511
11/14/81	140	8	3. Face To Face	Arista 9547

GRAHAM CENTRAL STATION
soul/dance band led by Larry Graham

2/09/74	48	26	1. Graham Central Station	Warner 2763
10/05/74	51	18	2. Release Yourself	Warner 2814
8/02/75	22	24	● 3. Ain't No 'Bout-A-Doubt It	Warner 2876
6/26/76	46	16	4. Mirror	Warner 2937
4/23/77	67	10	5. Now Do U Wanta Dance	Warner 3041
			LARRY GRAHAM & GRAND CENTRAL STATION:	
7/01/78	105	11	6. My Radio Sure Sounds Good To Me	Warner 3175
7/14/79	136	4	7. Star Walk	Warner 3322

LARRY GRAHAM
former bass player with Sly & The Family Stone

6/21/80	26	24	● 1. One In A Million You "One In A Million You"(9)	Warner 3447
8/08/81	46	13	2. Just Be My Lady	Warner 3554
6/26/82	142	9	3. Sooner Or Later	Warner 3668
7/30/83	173	4	4. Victory	Warner 23878

GRAND FUNK RAILROAD
Flint, Michigan hard-rock band: Mark Farner, Don Brewer & Mel Schacher - also see Terry Knight & The Pack

10/11/69	27	55	● 1. On Time	Capitol 307
1/31/70	11	67	● 2. Grand Funk	Capitol 406
7/11/70	6	63	● 3. **Closer To Home**	Capitol 471
12/05/70	5	62	● 4. **Live Album** [L]	Capitol 633 [2]
5/01/71	6	40	● 5. **Survival**	Capitol 764
12/04/71	5	30	● 6. **E Pluribus Funk**	Capitol 853
5/13/72	17	27	● 7. Mark, Don & Mel 1969-71 [K]	Capitol 11042 [2]
10/14/72	7	27	● 8. **Phoenix**	Capitol 11099
			GRAND FUNK:	
8/18/73	2(2)	35	● 9. **We're An American Band** "We're An American Band"(1)	Capitol 11207
3/30/74	5	29	● 10. **Shinin' On** "The Loco-Motion"(1)	Capitol 11278

DATE CHARTED	PEAK POS	WKS CHRT'D	ARTIST — Album Title	LABEL & NUMBER
12/21/74	10	24	● 11. **All The Girls In The World Beware!!!** .... "Some Kind Of Wonderful"(3)/"Bad Time"(4)	Capitol 11356
			GRAND FUNK RAILROAD:	
9/13/75	21	10	12. Caught In The Act .... [L]	Capitol 11445 [2]
1/31/76	47	11	13. Born To Die	Capitol 11482
8/28/76	52	8	14. Good Singin' Good Playin'	MCA 2216
11/20/76	126	5	15. Grand Funk Hits .... [G]	Capitol 11579
10/17/81	149	5	16. Grand Funk Lives	Full Moon 3625

GRANDMASTER FLASH & THE FURIOUS FIVE
New York disco DJ & his rap group

10/16/82	53	24	1. The Message	SugarHill 268

EARL GRANT
organist/pianist/vocalist - died on 6/10/70 (39)

8/21/61	7	45	● 1. **Ebb Tide** .... [I]	Decca 74165
4/07/62	17	32	2. Beyond The Reef .... [I]	Decca 74231
12/01/62	92	10	3. Earl Grant At Basin Street East .... [L]	Decca 74299
1/04/64	139	5	4. Fly Me To The Moon .... [I]	Decca 74454
7/11/64	149	2	5. Just For A Thrill .... [I]	Decca 74506
5/15/65	143	4	6. Trade Winds .... [I]	Decca 74623
3/23/68	192	2	7. Gently Swingin' .... [I]	Decca 74937

EDDY GRANT
native of Guyana - former leader of The Equals

4/23/83	10	30	● 1. **Killer On The Rampage** .... "Electric Avenue"(2)	Portrait 38554
6/23/84	64	17	2. Going For Broke	Portrait 39261

GOGI GRANT -
see SOUNDTRACK "Helen Morgan Story"

STEPHANE GRAPPELLI/DAVID GRISMAN
Stephane: jazz violinist: David: jazz/bluegrass mandolinist

6/06/81	108	10	1. Live .... [I-L]	Warner 3550

GRASS ROOTS
Los Angeles-based group - original members: Warren Entner, Rob Grill, Creed Bratton & Rick Coonce

8/19/67	75	15	1. Let's Live For Today .... "Let's Live For Today"(8)	Dunhill 50020
11/23/68	25	43	● 2. Golden Grass .... [G] "Midnight Confessions"(5)	Dunhill 50047
3/29/69	73	16	3. Lovin' Things	Dunhill 50052
12/06/69	36	21	4. Leaving It All Behind	Dunhill 50067
10/24/70	152	27	5. More Golden Grass .... [G]	Dunhill 50087
10/02/71	58	20	● 6. Their 16 Greatest Hits .... [G] "Sooner Or Later"(9)	Dunhill 50107
6/24/72	86	14	7. Move Along	Dunhill 50112

GRATEFUL DEAD
San Francisco rock band led by Jerry Garcia

5/06/67	73	28	● 1. The Grateful Dead	Warner 1689
8/31/68	87	17	2. Anthem Of The Sun	Warner 1749
6/21/69	73	11	3. Aoxomoxoa	Warner 1790
1/03/70	64	15	4. Live/Dead .... [L]	Warner 1830 [2]
6/27/70	27	26	● 5. Workingman's Dead	Warner 1869
10/31/70	127	10	6. Vintage Dead .... [E-L] recorded at San Francisco's Avalon Ballroom in 1966	Sunflower 5001
12/12/70	30	19	● 7. American Beauty	Warner 1893
6/26/71	154	7	8. Historic Dead .... [E-L] more early recordings from 1966	Sunflower 5004
10/16/71	25	12	9. Grateful Dead .... [L]	Warner 1935 [2]
12/02/72	24	24	● 10. Europe '72 .... [L]	Warner 2668 [3]

DATE CHARTED	PEAK POS	WKS CHRT'D	ARTIST — Album Title	LABEL & NUMBER
7/28/73	60	11	11. History Of The Grateful Dead, Vol. 1 (Bear's Choice) .... [L] recorded at Fillmore East, February, 1970	Warner 2721
10/27/73	18	19	12. Wake Of The Flood	Grateful Dead 01
3/09/74	75	10	● 13. The Best Of/Skeleton's From The Closet .... [G]	Warner 2764
7/13/74	16	20	14. Grateful Dead From The Mars Hotel	Grateful Dead 102
9/06/75	12	13	15. Blues For Allah	Grateful Dead 494
7/04/76	56	9	16. Steal Your Face .... [L] recorded at Winterland, San Francisco, October, 1974	Gratfl. Dead 620 [2]
8/20/77	28	16	17. Terrapin Station	Arista 7001
11/12/77	121	8	18. What A Long Strange Trip It's Been: The Best Of The Grateful Dead .... [G]	Warner 3091 [2]
12/09/78	41	19	19. Shakedown Street	Arista 4198
5/17/80	23	21	20. Go To Heaven	Arista 9508
4/18/81	43	16	21. Reckoning .... [L]	Arista 8604 [2]
9/19/81	29	11	22. Dead Set .... [L] above 2 albums recorded live in New York City and San Francisco in 1980	Arista 8606 [2]

DOBIE GRAY
born Leonard Ainsworth, Jr. on 7/26/42 in Brookshire, Texas

DATE CHARTED	PEAK POS	WKS CHRT'D	ARTIST — Album Title	LABEL & NUMBER
3/10/73	64	21	1. Drift Away .... "Drift Away"(5)	Decca 75397
11/10/73	188	3	2. Loving Arms	MCA 371
2/17/79	174	4	3. Midnight Diamond	Infinity 9001

GLEN GRAY & The Casa Loma Orchestra
swing band organized in 1929 - Glen died on 8/23/63 (57)

DATE CHARTED	PEAK POS	WKS CHRT'D	ARTIST — Album Title	LABEL & NUMBER
2/23/57	18	9	1. Casa Loma In Hi-Fi! .... [I]	Capitol 747
6/29/59	28	2	2. Sounds Of The Great Bands! .... [I]	Capitol 1022
2/02/63	63	13	3. Themes Of The Great Bands .... [I]	Capitol 1812
10/19/63	69	15	4. Today's Best .... [I]	Capitol 1938

CHARLES RANDOLPH GREAN Sounde
former artist & repertoire director at RCA & Dot Records

DATE CHARTED	PEAK POS	WKS CHRT'D	ARTIST — Album Title	LABEL & NUMBER
7/26/69	23	15	1. Quentin's Theme .... [I] title cut is from TV's "Dark Shadows"	Ranwood 8055

GREASE BAND
Joe Cocker's backup band

DATE CHARTED	PEAK POS	WKS CHRT'D	ARTIST — Album Title	LABEL & NUMBER
4/17/71	190	3	1. Grease Band	Shelter 8904

GREAT SOCIETY -see GRACE SLICK

GREAT WHITE

DATE CHARTED	PEAK POS	WKS CHRT'D	ARTIST — Album Title	LABEL & NUMBER
3/24/84	144	12	1. Great White	EMI America 17111

R.B. GREAVES
full name: Ronald Bertram Aloysius Greaves, III

DATE CHARTED	PEAK POS	WKS CHRT'D	ARTIST — Album Title	LABEL & NUMBER
1/03/70	85	14	1. R.B. Greaves .... "Take A Letter Maria"(2)	Atco 311

RICK GRECH
bass player with Family, Traffic, Blind Faith & Ginger Baker's Air Force

DATE CHARTED	PEAK POS	WKS CHRT'D	ARTIST — Album Title	LABEL & NUMBER
9/29/73	195	3	1. The Last Five Years .... [K] compiled from his work with groups in above artist notes	RSO 876

GEORGE GREELEY
guest pianist with the Warner Bros. Orchestra - also see Soundtrack "Parrish"

DATE CHARTED	PEAK POS	WKS CHRT'D	ARTIST — Album Title	LABEL & NUMBER
5/22/61	29	16	1. The Best Of The Popular Piano Concertos .... [I-K]	Warner 1410

AL GREEN
born in Forrest City, Arkansas on 4/13/46

DATE CHARTED	PEAK POS	WKS CHRT'D	ARTIST — Album Title	LABEL & NUMBER
8/28/71	58	43	1. Al Green Gets Next To You	Hi 32062
2/12/72	8	56	● 2. **Let's Stay Together** .... "Let's Stay Together"(1)	Hi 32070
9/16/72	162	9	3. Al Green .... [E] recordings from 1967-1968	Bell 6076
10/21/72	4	67	● 4. **I'm Still In Love With You** .... "Look What You Done For Me"(4)/ "I'm Still In Love With You"(3)	Hi 32074
1/06/73	19	28	5. Green Is Blues .... [E] Al's first album on the Hi label	Hi 32055
5/19/73	10	41	● 6. **Call Me** .... "You Ought To Be With Me"(3)/"Call Me (Come Back Home)"(10)/ "Here I Am (Come And Take Me)"(10)	Hi 32077
12/29/73	24	30	● 7. Livin' For You	Hi 32082
11/23/74	15	33	● 8. **Al Green Explores Your Mind** .... "Sha-La-La (Make Me Happy)"(7)	Hi 32087
3/22/75	17	21	9. Al Green/Greatest Hits .... [G]	Hi 32089
9/13/75	28	23	10. Al Green Is Love	Hi 32092
3/20/76	59	16	11. Full Of Fire	Hi 32097
11/27/76	93	14	12. Have A Good Time	Hi 32103
7/02/77	134	9	13. Al Green's Greatest Hits. Volume II .... [G]	Hi 32105
12/24/77	103	12	14. The Belle Album	Hi 6004

GRANT GREEN
jazz guitarist

DATE CHARTED	PEAK POS	WKS CHRT'D	ARTIST — Album Title	LABEL & NUMBER
10/16/71	151	9	1. Visions .... [I]	Blue Note 84373

JACK GREEN
Scottish - former lead guitarist of T. Rex and Pretty Things

DATE CHARTED	PEAK POS	WKS CHRT'D	ARTIST — Album Title	LABEL & NUMBER
10/18/80	121	8	1. Humanesque	RCA 3639

PETER GREEN
English - blues guitarist who co-founded Fleetwood Mac in 1967

DATE CHARTED	PEAK POS	WKS CHRT'D	ARTIST — Album Title	LABEL & NUMBER
10/25/80	186	5	1. Little Dreamer	Sail 0112

NORMAN GREENBAUM

DATE CHARTED	PEAK POS	WKS CHRT'D	ARTIST — Album Title	LABEL & NUMBER
2/28/70	23	25	1. Spirit In The Sky .... "Spirit In The Sky"(3)	Reprise 6365

JACK GREENE
ex-drummer for Ernest Tubb's band

DATE CHARTED	PEAK POS	WKS CHRT'D	ARTIST — Album Title	LABEL & NUMBER
2/25/67	66	21	1. There Goes My Everything	Decca 74845
7/22/67	151	12	2. All The Time	Decca 74904

LORNE GREENE
Ben Cartwright of TV's "Bonanza"

DATE CHARTED	PEAK POS	WKS CHRT'D	ARTIST — Album Title	LABEL & NUMBER
11/28/64	35	19	1. Welcome To The Ponderosa .... "Ringo"(1)	RCA 2843

LEE GREENWOOD
country singer - also see Barbara Mandrell

DATE CHARTED	PEAK POS	WKS CHRT'D	ARTIST — Album Title	LABEL & NUMBER
5/28/83	73	21	● 1. Somebody's Gonna Love You	MCA 5403
6/09/84	150	20	● 2. You've Got A Good Love Comin'	MCA 5488

JOANIE GREGGAINS - see AEROBICS section

DICK GREGORY
comedian - civil rights activist

DATE CHARTED	PEAK POS	WKS CHRT'D	ARTIST — Album Title	LABEL & NUMBER
6/05/61	23	27	1. In Living Black & White .... [C]	Colpix 417
8/16/69	182	8	2. The Light Side: The Dark Side .... [C]	Poppy 60001 [2]

GREY & HANKS
Zane Grey & Len Ron Hanks

DATE CHARTED	PEAK POS	WKS CHRT'D	ARTIST — Album Title	LABEL & NUMBER
2/03/79	97	11	1. You Fooled Me	RCA 3069
2/23/80	195	3	2. Prime Time	RCA 3477

DATE CHARTED	PEAK POS	WKS CHRT'D	ARTIST — Album Title	LABEL & NUMBER
			GRIM REAPER British heavy-metal foursome - Steve Gimmett, lead singer	
8/25/84	**73**	27	1. See you in Hell	RCA 8038
			GRIN Nils Lofgren, lead guitar, keyboards & vocals	
8/07/71	**192**	3	1. Grin	Spindizzy 30321
2/05/72	**180**	6	2. 1 + 1	Spindizzy 31038
3/10/73	**186**	7	3. All Out	Spindizzy 31701
			GRINDER SWITCH southern rock quintet	
11/19/77	**144**	8	1. Redwing	Atco 152
			DAVID GRISMAN jazz/bluegrass mandolin player - formed Earth Opera in 1967 - also see Stephane Grappelli	
9/13/80	**152**	8	1. David Grisman - Quintet '80 .... [I]	Warner 3469
10/24/81	**174**	3	2. Mondo Mando .... [I]	Warner 3618
			LARRY GROCE	
3/27/76	**187**	2	1. Junkfood Junkie .... [L] "Junk Food Junkie"(9)	Warner 2933
			HENRY GROSS original lead guitarist of Sha-Na-Na	
2/08/75	**26**	23	1. Plug Me Into Something	A&M 4502
2/14/76	**64**	28	2. Release .... "Shannon"(6)	Lifesong 6002
3/12/77	**176**	7	3. Show Me To The Stage	Lifesong 6010
			DAVE GRUSIN jazz pianist - composer/producer of music for the soundtracks "On Golden Pond" and "Tootsie"	
3/21/81	**74**	18	1. Mountain Dance .... [I]	GRP 5010
7/18/81	**140**	7	2. Dave Grusin and the GRP All-Stars/Live In Japan .... [I-L] with Sadao Watanabe, Dave Valentin & Tom Browne	GRP 5506
8/07/82	**88**	9	3. Out Of The Shadows .... [I]	GRP 5510
4/16/83	**181**	6	4. Dave Grusin and the NY/LA Dream Band .... [I-L] with Lee Ritenour, Steve Gadd & Eric Gale	GRP 1001
			VINCE GUARALDI Trio jazz trio led by Vince on piano - died on 2/6/76 (43)	
2/02/63	**24**	28	1. Jazz Impressions of Black Orpheus .... [I] "Cast Your Fate To The Wind"	Fantasy 3337
			DAVE GUARD & The Whiskeyhill Singers Dave was a member of the Kingston Trio from 1957-1961	
6/30/62	**92**	11	1. Dave Guard & The Whiskeyhill Singers	Capitol 1728
			GUESS WHO Canadian group featuring Burton Cummings (lead singer) and Randy Bachman (lead guitar - left group after "American Woman")	
4/26/69	**45**	19	1. Wheatfield Soul .... "These Eyes"(6)	RCA 4141
10/04/69	**91**	17	2. Canned Wheat Packed by The Guess Who .... "Laughing"(10)	RCA 4157
2/14/70	**9**	55	● 3. **American Woman** .... "No Time"(5)/"American Woman"(1)	RCA 4266
10/17/70	**14**	25	● 4. Share The Land .... "Share The Land"(10)	RCA 4359
4/17/71	**12**	45	● 5. The Best of The Guess Who .... [G]	RCA 1004
8/21/71	**52**	16	6. So Long, Bannatyne	RCA 4574
3/18/72	**79**	10	7. Rockin'	RCA 4602
8/19/72	**39**	21	8. Live At The Paramount (Seattle) .... [L]	RCA 4779

DATE CHARTED	PEAK POS	WKS CHRT'D	ARTIST — Album Title	LABEL & NUMBER
1/20/73	112	10	9. Artificial Paradise	RCA 4830
7/14/73	155	8	10. #10	RCA 0130
1/12/74	186	4	11. The Best of The Guess Who, Volume II..... [G]	RCA 0269
5/11/74	60	26	12. Road Food	RCA 0405
			"Clap For The Wolfman"(6)	
2/01/75	48	9	13. Flavours	RCA 0636
7/26/75	87	7	14. Power In The Music	RCA 0995
4/30/77	173	4	15. The Greatest of The Guess Who .... [G]	RCA 2253

GREG GUIDRY

4/17/82	147	7	1. Over The Line	Badland 37735

ADRIAN GURVITZ
see BAKER GURVITZ ARMY/GRAEME EDGE BAND

ARLO GUTHRIE
Woody Guthrie's son

11/18/67	17	99	● 1. Alice's Restaurant	Reprise 6267
			side one is the 18 minute tale of "Alice's Restaurant Massacree"	
10/26/68	107	12	2. Arlo .... [L]	Reprise 6299
10/18/69	63	17	3. Alice's Restaurant .... [S]	United Art. 5195
			Arlo stars in the film and sings on only 2 cuts	
10/25/69	54	19	4. Running Down The Road	Reprise 6346
11/07/70	33	17	5. Washington County	Reprise 6411
6/10/72	52	38	6. Hobo's Lullabye	Reprise 2060
			"The City Of New Orleans"	
4/28/73	87	14	7. Last Of The Brooklyn Cowboys	Reprise 2142
6/08/74	165	10	8. Arlo Guthrie	Reprise 2183
5/17/75	181	4	9. Together In Concert .... [L]	Reprise 2214 [2]
			PETE SEEGER & ARLO GUTHRIE	
10/02/76	133	6	10. Amigo	Reprise 2239
6/27/81	184	3	11. Power Of Love	Warner 3558

WOODY GUTHRIE
legendary American folk singer/songwriter - died on 10/3/67 (55)

4/29/72	183	2	1. A Tribute To Woody Guthrie - Part One .... [L]	Columbia 31171
4/29/72	189	2	2. A Tribute To Woody Guthrie - Part Two .... [L]	Warner 2586
			above 2 albums are highlights from concerts at Carnegie Hall (1968), and the Hollywood Bowl (1970) - guests include Bob Dylan, Pete Seeger, Judy Collins & Arlo Guthrie	

GYPSY
James "Owl" Walsh, leader of 5-man rock band

10/10/70	44	20	1. Gypsy	Metromed. 1031 [2]
8/07/71	173	8	2. In The Garden	Metromedia 1044

STEVE HACKETT
former guitarist of Genesis (1969-1977)

4/17/76	191	4	1. Voyage Of The Acolyte	Chrysalis 1112
4/29/78	103	14	2. Please Don't Touch	Chrysalis 1176
7/07/79	138	4	3. Spectral Mornings	Chrysalis 1223
8/30/80	144	6	4. Defector	Charisma 3103
10/24/81	169	3	5. Cured	Epic 37632

SAMMY HAGAR
lead singer of Montrose (1973-1975)

2/26/77	167	9	1. Sammy Hagar	Capitol 11599
1/21/78	100	11	2. Musical Chairs	Capitol 11706
8/19/78	89	9	3. All Night Long .... [L]	Capitol 11812

DATE CHARTED	PEAK POS	WKS CHRT'D		ARTIST — Album Title	LABEL & NUMBER
9/08/79	**71**	13		4. Street Machine	Capitol 11983
6/21/80	**85**	12		5. Danger Zone	Capitol 12069
1/30/82	**28**	32	●	6. Standing Hampton	Geffen 2006
12/25/82	**17**	34	●	7. Three Lock Box	Geffen 2021
1/08/83	**171**	9		8. Rematch .... [K]	Capitol 12238
8/11/84	**32**	35+	●	9. VOA	Geffen 24043
				HAGAR, SCHON, AARONSON, SHRIEVE Sammy Hagar, Neal Schon (Journey), Kenny Aaronson, Michael Shrieve (Santana)	
3/31/84	**42**	18		1. Through The Fire .... [L]	Geffen 4023
				NINA HAGEN East German	
6/05/82	**184**	3		1. Nunsexmonkrock	Columbia 38008
1/28/84	**151**	8		2. Fearless	Columbia 39214
				MERLE HAGGARD born in Bakersfield, California on 4/6/37	
5/13/67	**165**	10		1. I'm A Lonesome Fugitive	Capitol 2702
10/21/67	**174**	4		2. Branded Man	Capitol 2789
3/15/69	**189**	7		3. Pride In What I AM	Capitol 168
6/14/69	**67**	18		4. Same Train, A Different Time .... featuring the songs of Jimmie Rodgers	Capitol 223 [2]
8/23/69	**140**	6		5. Close-Up .... [R] reissue of "Strangers" and "Swinging Doors" albums	Capitol 259 [2]
10/18/69	**99**	11		6. A Portrait Of Merle Haggard	Capitol 319
1/24/70	**46**	52	●	7. Okie From Muskogee .... [L] recorded live in Muskogee, Oklahoma	Capitol 384
7/25/70	**68**	33	●	8. The Fightin' Side Of Me .... [L] recorded live in Philadelphia	Capitol 451
12/19/70	**58**	9		9. A Tribute To The Best Damn Fiddle Player In The World (or, My Salute To Bob Wills) .... with members of Bob Wills original Texas Playboy's band	Capitol 638
4/17/71	**66**	15		10. Hag	Capitol 735
9/18/71	**108**	10		11. Someday We'll Look Back	Capitol 835
4/08/72	**166**	8		12. Let Me Tell You About A Song	Capitol 882
10/07/72	**137**	9	●	13. The Best Of The Best Of Merle Haggard .... [G]	Capitol 11082
8/25/73	**126**	11		14. I Love Dixie Blues...so I recorded "Live" in New Orleans .... [L]	Capitol 11200
3/23/74	**190**	3		15. If We Make It Through December	Capitol 11276
6/28/75	**129**	9		16. Keep Movin' On	Capitol 11365
11/19/77	**133**	5		17. My Farewell To Elvis .... Merle sings 9 of Elvis Presley's hits	MCA 2314
11/07/81	**161**	28	●	18. Big City	Epic 37593
9/25/82	**123**	12		19. A Taste Of Yesterday's Wine .... MERLE HAGGARD & GEORGE JONES	Epic 38203
2/12/83	**37**	53	▲	20. Poncho & Lefty .... MERLE HAGGARD/WILLIE NELSON	Epic 37958
				HAIRCUT ONE HUNDRED British sextet led by Nick Heyward	
4/24/82	**31**	37		1. Pelican West	Arista 6600
				BILL HALEY & His Comets Bill, a rock and roll pioneer, died on 2/9/81 (55)	
1/28/56	**12**	5		1. Rock Around The Clock .... [G] "Shake, Rattle And Roll"(7-'54)/"Rock Around The Clock"(1)/ "Burn That Candle"(9)	Decca 8225
10/13/56	**18**	5		2. Rock 'n Roll Stage Show	Decca 8345

DATE CHARTED	PEAK POS	WKS CHRT'D	ARTIST — Album Title	LABEL & NUMBER
			DARYL HALL half of Hall & Oates duo	
3/29/80	58	12	1. Sacred Songs	RCA 3573
			DARYL HALL & JOHN OATES Daryl: born on 10/11/49 in Pottstown, Pennsylvania; John: born on 4/7/49 in New York City	
2/23/74	33	38	● 1. Abandoned Luncheonette .... "She's Gone"(7)	Atlantic 7269
10/26/74	86	10	2. War Babies .... produced by Todd Rundgren	Atlantic 18109
9/13/75	17	76	● 3. Daryl Hall & John Oates .... "Sara Smile"(4)	RCA 1144
8/28/76	13	57	● 4. Bigger Than Both Of Us .... "Rich Girl"(1)	RCA 1467
3/26/77	92	6	5. No Goodbyes .... [K]	Atlantic 18213
9/17/77	30	17	● 6. Beauty On A Back Street	RCA 2300
5/27/78	42	10	7. Livetime .... [L]	RCA 2802
9/09/78	27	22	● 8. Along The Red Ledge	RCA 2804
10/27/79	33	24	9. X-Static	RCA 3494
8/16/80	17	100	▲ 10. Voices .... "Kiss On My List"(1)/"You Make My Dreams"(5)	RCA 3646
9/26/81	5	61	▲ 11. **Private Eyes** .... "Private Eyes"(1)/"I Can't Go For That"(1)/ "Did It In A Minute"(9)	RCA 4028
10/30/82	3	68	▲ 12. **H2O** .... "Maneater"(1)/"One On One"(7)/"Family Man"(6)	RCA 4383
11/19/83	7	44	▲ 13. **Rock 'N Soul, Part 1** .... [G] "Say It Isn't So"(2)/"Adult Education"(8)	RCA 4858
10/27/84	5	24+	▲ 14. **Big Bam Boom** .... "Out Of Touch"(1)/"Method Of Modern Love"(5)	RCA 5309
			JIMMY HALL former member of Wet Willie	
11/22/80	183	2	1. Touch You	Epic 36516
			JOHN HALL Band former leader of Orleans	
12/05/81	158	13	1. All Of The Above	EMI America 17058
3/05/83	147	5	2. Searchparty	EMI America 17082
			TOM T. HALL country music storyteller	
10/09/71	137	6	1. In Search Of A Song	Mercury 61350
6/09/73	181	4	2. The Rhymer And Other Five And Dimers	Mercury 668
1/26/74	149	11	3. For The People In The Last Hard Town	Mercury 687
4/19/75	180	2	4. Songs Of Fox Hollow	Mercury 500
			HAMILTON, JOE FRANK & REYNOLDS Dan Hamilton, Joe Frank Carollo & Tom Reynolds	
6/19/71	59	15	1. Hamilton, Joe Frank & Reynolds .... "Don't Pull Your Love"(4)	Dunhill 50103
2/19/72	191	4	2. Hallway Symphony	Dunhill 50113
12/13/75	82	14	3. Fallin' In Love .... "Fallin' In Love"(1)	Playboy 407
			CHICO HAMILTON jazz drummer	
12/19/64	145	4	1. Man From Two Worlds .... [I] with Charles Lloyd (sax), Gabor Szabo (guitar) & Albert Stinson (bass)	Impulse! 59
			GEORGE HAMILTON IV	
10/05/63	77	8	1. Abilene	RCA 2778

DATE CHARTED	PEAK POS	WKS CHRT'D	ARTIST — Album Title	LABEL & NUMBER
			MARVIN HAMLISCH pianist/composer/conductor for numerous soundtracks	
8/31/74	170	5	1. The Entertainer .... [I] includes adaptations of 5 Scott Joplin tunes "The Entertainer"(3) - also see Soundtrack 'The Sting'	MCA 2115
			JAN HAMMER - see JEFF BECK/JERRY GOODMAN/NEAL SCHON	
			ALBERT HAMMOND English	
12/09/72	77	15	1. It Never Rains In Southern California .... "It Never Rains In Southern California"(5)	Mums 31905
9/01/73	193	4	2. The Free Electric Band	Mums 32267
			JOHN PAUL HAMMOND - see MIKE BLOOMFIELD	
			JOHNNY HAMMOND jazz organist	
9/11/71	125	14	1. Breakout .... [I]	Kudu 01
5/20/72	174	6	2. Wild Horses/Rock Steady .... [I]	Kudu 04
			HERBIE HANCOCK jazz keyboardist - formerly with Miles Davis (1963-1968)	
5/13/67	197	2	1. Blow-Up .... [S-I] includes one vocal track by the Yardbirds	MGM 4447
6/02/73	176	6	2. Sextant .... [I]	Columbia 32212
1/12/74	13	47	● 3. Head Hunters .... [I]	Columbia 32731
10/05/74	13	23	4. Thrust .... [I]	Columbia 32965
10/12/74	158	3	5. Treasure Chest .... [E-I] tracks from 3 albums, recorded 1969-1970	Warner 2807 [2]
10/18/75	21	24	6. Man-Child .... [I]	Columbia 33812
9/11/76	49	17	7. Secrets .... [I]	Columbia 34280
5/07/77	79	7	8. V.S.O.P .... [I-L] recorded at the Newport Jazz Festival	Columbia 34688 [2]
7/08/78	58	13	9. Sunlight .... Herbie's vocals are electronically synthesized	Columbia 34907
3/17/79	38	22	10. Feets Don't Fail Me Now	Columbia 35764
3/31/79	100	8	11. An Evening With Herbie Hancock & Chick Corea .... [I-L]	Columbia 35663 [2]
11/24/79	175	2	12. An Evening With Chick Corea & Herbie Hancock .... [I-L] above 2 albums recorded during their 1978 concert series	Polydor 6238 [2]
4/19/80	94	18	13. Monster	Columbia 36415
11/29/80	117	6	14. Mr. Hands .... [I]	Columbia 36578
10/03/81	140	6	15. Magic Windows	Columbia 37387
5/29/82	151	6	16. Lite Me Up	Columbia 37928
9/03/83	43	65	● 17. Future Shock .... [I] "Rockit"	Columbia 38814
9/01/84	71	14	18. Sound-System .... [I]	Columbia 39478
			JOHN HANDY jazz saxophonist	
6/05/76	43	21	1. Hard Work .... [I]	ABC/Impulse 9314
4/16/77	200	2	2. Carnival .... [I]	ABC/Impulse 9324
			BO HANSSON Scandinavian organist	
5/05/73	154	8	1. Lord Of The Rings .... [I] inspired by the J.R.R. Tolkien classic tale	Charisma 1059
			HAPPENINGS Paterson, New Jersey quartet	
10/15/66	61	12	1. The Happenings .... "See You In September"(3)	B.T. Puppy 1001
7/22/67	134	6	2. Back To Back .... HAPPENINGS (side 2)/TOKENS (side 1) "I Got Rhythm"(3)	B.T. Puppy 1002

DATE CHARTED	PEAK POS	WKS CHRT'D	ARTIST — Album Title	LABEL & NUMBER
8/10/68	156	4	3. The Happenings Golden Hits! .... [G]	B.T. Puppy 1004
9/06/69	181	2	4. Piece Of Mind	Jubilee 8028
			PEARL HARBOUR - see PEARL HARBOR	
			PAUL HARDCASTLE British keyboardist	
3/23/85	71+	3+	1. Rain Forest .... [I]	Profile 1206
			HARDEN TRIO Bobby Harden and sisters Arleen & Robbie	
6/25/66	146	5	1. Tippy Toeing	Columbia 9306
			TIM HARDIN folk-blues singer/songwriter - died on 12/29/80 (39)	
4/26/69	129	8	1. Suite For Susan Moore And Damion- We Are-One, One, All In One	Columbia 9787
7/31/71	189	1	2. Bird On A Wire	Columbia 30551
			HARDY BOYS singing group for the animated TV show	
11/15/69	199	2	1. Here Come The Hardy Boys	RCA 4217
			HAGOOD HARDY Canadian vibraphonist	
1/03/76	112	14	1. The Homecoming .... [I]	Capitol 11468
			HARMONICATS Jerry Murad, Al Fiore & Don Les	
3/27/61	17	4	1. Cherry Pink And Apple Blossom White ..... [I]	Columbia 8356
			JOE HARNELL his piano & orchestra	
1/26/63	3	36	1. Fly Me To The Moon and the Bossa Nova Pops .... [I]	Kapp 3318
			HARPERS BIZARRE Santa Cruz, California quintet	
5/06/67	108	7	1. Feelin' Groovy	Warner 1693
12/09/67	76	13	2. Anything Goes	Warner 1716
			EDDIE HARRIS jazz tenor saxophonist	
5/29/61	2(1)	37	1. **Exodus To Jazz** .... [I]	Vee-Jay 3016
4/13/68	36	41	2. The Electrifying Eddie Harris .... [I]	Atlantic 1495
8/03/68	120	16	3. Plug Me In .... [I]	Atlantic 1506
2/22/69	199	2	4. Silver Cycles .... [I]	Atlantic 1517
8/16/69	122	9	5. High Voltage .... [I-L]	Atlantic 1529
12/13/69	29	38	6. Swiss Movement .... [I-L] LES McCANN & EDDIE HARRIS recorded live at The Montreux Jazz Festival, Switzerland	Atlantic 1537
4/18/70	191	3	7. The Best Of Eddie Harris .... [I-G]	Atlantic 1545
5/29/71	41	27	8. Second Movement .... [I] EDDIE HARRIS & LES McCANN	Atlantic 1583
11/27/71	164	10	9. Eddie Harris Live At Newport .... [I-L]	Atlantic 1595
7/22/72	185	7	10. Instant Death .... [I]	Atlantic 1611
2/16/74	150	11	11. E.H. in the U.K. .... [I] with Jeff Beck, Stevie Winwood & Albert Lee	Atlantic 1647
10/12/74	100	11	12. Is It In .... [I]	Atlantic 1659
4/19/75	125	9	13. I Need Some Money .... [I]	Atlantic 1669
9/27/75	133	6	14. Bad Luck Is All I Have .... [I]	Atlantic 1675
			EMMYLOU HARRIS contemporary country vocalist supported by all-star backing musicians & artists - also see Gram Parsons	
3/15/75	45	15	1. Pieces Of The Sky	Reprise 2213
1/24/76	25	23	● 2. Elite Hotel	Reprise 2236

DATE CHARTED	PEAK POS	WKS CHRT'D		ARTIST — Album Title	LABEL & NUMBER
1/22/77	21	21	●	3. Luxury Liner	Warner 3115
2/04/78	29	18		4. Quarter Moon In A Ten Cent Town	Warner 3141
12/02/78	81	17	●	5. Profile/Best Of Emmylou Harris .... [G]	Warner 3258
5/05/79	43	22	●	6. Blue Kentucky Girl	Warner 3318
5/24/80	26	34	●	7. Roses In The Snow	Warner 3422
11/29/80	102	9		8. Light Of The Stable .... [X]	Warner 3484
2/21/81	22	24	●	9. Evangeline	Warner 3508
12/12/81	46	20		10. Cimarron	Warner 3603
11/13/82	65	17		11. Last Date .... [L]	Warner 23740
11/19/83	116	13		12. White Shoes	Warner 23961
10/06/84	176	6		13. Profile II - The Best Of Emmylou Harris .... [G]	Warner 25161

MAJOR HARRIS
member of the Delfonics (1971-1973)

DATE CHARTED	PEAK POS	WKS CHRT'D		ARTIST — Album Title	LABEL & NUMBER
3/29/75	28	22		1. My Way .... "Love Won't Let Me Wait"(5)	Atlantic 18119
2/28/76	153	6		2. Jealousy	Atlantic 18160

RICHARD HARRIS
British actor

5/18/68	4	42		1. A Tramp Shining .... "MacArthur Park"(2)	Dunhill 50032
11/16/68	27	15		2. The Yard Went On Forever...	Dunhill 50042
12/18/71	71	14		3. My Boy	Dunhill 50116
12/16/72	181	6		4. Slides	Dunhill 50133
9/08/73	25	27		5. Jonathan Livingston Seagull .... [T] narration from the book - music composed by Terry James	Dunhill 50160
12/28/74	29	15		6. The Prophet by Kahlil Gibran .... [T] Harris recites Gibran's classic work	Atlantic 18120

ROLF HARRIS
Australian

| 8/03/63 | 29 | 9 | | 1. Tie Me Kangaroo Down, Sport & Sun Arise .... [N] "Tie Me Kangaroo Down, Sport"(3) | Epic 26053 |

SAM HARRIS
winner of TV's "Star Search" male vocalist category in 1984

| 9/29/84 | 35 | 28+ | ● | 1. Sam Harris .... | Motown 6103 |

DON HARRISON Band
members Stu Cook & Doug Clifford were with Creedence Clearwater Revival

| 5/01/76 | 159 | 6 | | 1. The Don Harrison Band .... | Atlantic 18171 |

GEORGE HARRISON
Beatles' lead guitarist - born on 2/25/43 in Liverpool, England

1/11/69	49	16		1. Wonderwall Music .... [S-I] Indian influenced instrumentals for the unreleased film "Wonderwall"	Apple 3350
7/05/69	191	2		2. Electronic Sound .... [I] sounds made by a Moog synthesizer	Zapple 3358
12/19/70	1(7)	38	●	3. All Things Must Pass .... "My Sweet Lord"(1)/What Is Life"(10)	Apple 639 [3]
1/08/72	2(6)	41	●	4. The Concert For Bangla Desh .... [L] Madison Square Garden benefit concert on 8/1/71 - with guests Bob Dylan, Eric Clapton & Ringo Starr	Apple 3385 [3]
6/16/73	1(5)	26	●	5. Living In The Material World .... "Give Me Love (Give Me Peace On Earth)"(1)	Apple 3410
12/28/74	4	17	●	6. Dark Horse	Apple 3418
10/11/75	8	11	●	7. Extra Texture (Read All About It)	Apple 3420
11/27/76	31	15	●	8. The Best of George Harrison .... [G] side 1: hits while with The Beatles; side 2: solo hits	Capitol 11578
12/11/76	11	21	●	9. Thirty-Three & 1/3 .... 33 1/3: record playing speed and George's age	Dark Horse 3005

DATE CHARTED	PEAK POS	WKS CHRT'D	ARTIST — Album Title	LABEL & NUMBER
3/17/79	14	18	● 10. George Harrison	Dark Horse 3255
6/20/81	11	13	11. Somewhere In England "All Those Years Ago"(2)	Dark Horse 3492
11/27/82	108	7	12. Gone Troppo	Dark Horse 23734
			NOEL HARRISON actor/singer - Rex Harrison's son	
12/09/67	135	9	1. Collage	Reprise 6263
			WES HARRISON sound effects comedian	
11/02/63	83	5	1. You Won't Believe Your Ears [C]	Philips 103
			WILBERT HARRISON born on 1/6/29 in Charlotte, North Carolina	
1/24/70	190	2	1. Let's Work Together	Sue 8801
			DEBBIE HARRY lead singer of Blondie	
8/29/81	25	12	● 1. KooKoo	Chrysalis 1347
			COREY HART Canadian rock singer/songwriter	
7/14/84	31	36	1. First Offense "Sunglasses At Night"(7)	EMI America 17117
			FREDDIE HART country singer from Lochapoka, Alabama	
10/09/71	37	20	● 1. Easy Loving	Capitol 838
3/18/72	89	11	2. My Hang-Up Is You	Capitol 11014
7/01/72	93	16	3. Bless Your Heart	Capitol 11073
9/22/73	188	6	4. Trip To Heaven	Capitol 11197
			MICKEY HART former Grateful Dead drummer	
10/21/72	190	4	1. Rolling Thunder with Jerry Garcia, Bob Weir, Grace Slick & Stephen Stills	Warner 2635
			JOHN HARTFORD wrote "Gentle On My Mind" for Glen Campbell	
6/14/69	137	9	1. John Hartford	RCA 4156
11/27/71	193	4	2. Aereo-Plain	Warner 1916
			KEEF HARTLEY Band English blues band	
11/28/70	191	3	1. The Time Is Near	Deram 18047
			DAN HARTMAN member of the Edgar Winter Group (1972-76)	
12/16/78	80	19	1. Instant Replay	Blue Sky 35641
3/15/80	189	2	2. Relight My Fire	Blue Sky 36302
11/03/84	55	23+	3. I Can Dream About You "I Can Dream About You"(6)	MCA 5525
			Sensational ALEX HARVEY Band English rock quintet - Alex died on 2/5/82 (46)	
3/01/75	197	1	1. The Impossible Dream	Vertigo 2000
11/01/75	100	4	2. "Live" [L]	Atlantic 18148
			ANNIE HASLAM lead singer of Renaissance	
12/24/77	167	13	1. Annie In Wonderland	Sire 6046
			DONNY HATHAWAY died on 1/13/79 (33) - also see Soundtrack "Come Back Charleston Blue"	
5/15/71	89	21	1. Donny Hathaway	Atco 360
5/29/71	73	25	2. Everything Is Everything Donny's first album	Atco 332

DATE CHARTED	PEAK POS	WKS CHRT'D	ARTIST — Album Title	LABEL & NUMBER
3/04/72	18	38	● 3. Donny Hathaway Live .... [L]	Atco 386
5/13/72	3	39	● 4. **Roberta Flack & Donny Hathaway**	Atlantic 7216
			"Where Is The Love"(5)	
7/21/73	69	13	5. Extension Of A Man	Atco 7029
3/29/80	25	24	● 6. Roberta Flack Featuring Donny Hathaway ...	Atlantic 16013

RICHIE HAVENS
black folksinger/guitarist

2/24/68	184	7	1. Something Else Again	Verve Fore. 3034
7/06/68	182	2	2. Mixed Bag	Verve Folk. 3006
			Richie's first album for Verve (1967)	
11/30/68	192	3	3. Electric Havens .... [E]	Douglas 780
			Richie's second album for Douglas (1966)	
1/11/69	80	11	4. Richard P. Havens, 1983	Verve Fore. 3047 [2]
1/10/70	155	14	5. Stonehenge	Stormy F. 6001
11/07/70	190	2	6. Mixed Bag .... [R]	MGM 4698
1/09/71	29	34	7. Alarm Clock	Stormy F. 6005
			"Here Comes The Sun"	
11/13/71	126	11	8. The Great Blind Degree	Stormy F. 6010
9/23/72	55	18	9. Richie Havens On Stage .... [L]	Stormy F. 6012 [2]
6/09/73	182	4	10. Portfolio	Stormy F. 6013
10/12/74	186	3	11. Mixed Bag II	Stormy F. 6201
10/02/76	157	4	12. The End Of The Beginning	A&M 4598

EDWIN HAWKINS Singers
formerly the Northern California State Youth Choir -
also see Isley Brothers

5/03/69	15	23	1. Let Us Go Into The House Of The Lord	Pavilion 10001
			"Oh Happy Day"(4)	
10/02/71	180	8	2. Children (Get Together)	Buddah 5086
5/27/72	171	4	3. I'd Like To Teach The World To Sing	Buddah 5101

HAWKWIND
British space-rock band - Dave Brock, leader

11/24/73	179	8	1. Space Ritual/Alive In Liverpool And London .... [L]	United Art. 120 [2]
10/05/74	110	12	2. Hall Of The Mountain Grill	United Art. 328
6/14/75	150	5	3. Warrior On The Edge Of Time	Atco 115

ISAAC HAYES
born on 8/6/38 in Covington, Tennessee

7/12/69	8	81	● 1. **Hot Buttered Soul**	Enterprise 1001
4/18/70	8	75	2. **The Isaac Hayes Movement**	Enterprise 1010
12/05/70	11	56	3. To Be Continued	Enterprise 1014
8/21/71	1(1)	60	4. **Shaft** .... [S-I]	Enterprise 5002 [2]
			3 of 15 tracks feature vocals	
			"Theme From Shaft"(1)	
12/11/71	10	34	5. **Black Moses**	Enterprise 5003 [2]
2/26/72	102	12	6. In The Beginning .... [R-E]	Atlantic 1599
			reissue of his first album "Presenting Isaac Hayes" (1967)	
5/19/73	14	26	● 7. Live At The Sahara Tahoe .... [L]	Enterprise 5005 [2]
10/27/73	16	27	● 8. Joy	Enterprise 5007
6/15/74	146	8	9. Tough Guys .... [S-I]	Enterprise 7504
			music from the soundtrack of "Three Tough Guys"	
8/03/74	156	9	10. Truck Turner .... [S-I]	Enterprise 7507 [2]
6/21/75	18	19	● 11. Chocolate Chip	HBS 874
8/23/75	165	4	12. The Best Of Isaac Hayes .... [G]	Enterprise 7510
1/17/76	85	17	13. Disco Connection	HBS 923
2/21/76	45	12	14. Groove-A-Thon	HBS 925
7/24/76	124	7	15. Juicy Fruit (Disco Freak)	HBS 953
2/19/77	49	13	16. A Man And A Woman .... [L]	HBS 996 [2]
			ISAAC HAYES & DIONNE WARWICK	
12/17/77	78	12	17. New Horizon	Polydor 6120

DATE CHARTED	PEAK POS	WKS CHRT'D	ARTIST — Album Title	LABEL & NUMBER
11/18/78	**75**	18	18. For The Sake Of Love	Polydor 6164
9/29/79	**39**	30	● 19. Don't Let Go	Polydor 6224
10/20/79	**80**	19	20. Royal Rappin's	Polydor 6229
			MILLIE JACKSON & ISAAC HAYES	
5/17/80	**59**	15	21. And Once Again	Polydor 6269
			JUSTIN HAYWARD	
			joined the Moody Blues in 1967	
3/12/77	**37**	16	1. Songwriter	Deram 18073
8/09/80	**166**	5	2. Night Flight	Deram 4801
			JUSTIN HAYWARD/JOHN LODGE	
			guitarists of the Moody Blues	
3/29/75	**16**	23	1. Blue Jays	Threshold 14
			album title also refers to the name of their duo	
			LEON HAYWOOD	
			pianist with Big Jay McNeely and Sam Cooke	
8/16/75	**140**	13	1. Come And Get Yourself Some	20th Century 476
5/17/80	**92**	10	2. Naturally	20th Century 613
			ROBERT HAZARD	
			Philadelphia rocker	
3/26/83	**102**	11	1. Robert Hazard .... [M]	RCA 8500
			LEE HAZLEWOOD - see NANCY SINATRA	
			HEADBOYS	
			Scottish rock quartet	
11/10/79	**113**	15	1. The Headboys	RSO 3068
			HEAD EAST	
			St. Louis rock quintet - John Schlitt, lead singer	
8/30/75	**126**	17	● 1. Flat As A Pancake	A&M 4537
5/22/76	**161**	6	2. Get Yourself Up	A&M 4579
4/02/77	**136**	7	3. Gettin' Lucky	A&M 4624
3/11/78	**78**	14	4. Head East	A&M 4680
2/03/79	**65**	14	5. Head East Live! .... [L]	A&M 6007 [2]
11/17/79	**96**	16	6. A Different Kind Of Crazy	A&M 4795
11/08/80	**137**	6	7. U.S. 1	A&M 4826
			HEADHUNTERS	
			Herbie Hancock's super-funk backup band	
4/19/75	**126**	10	1. Survival Of The Fittest .... [I]	Arista 4038
			HEADPINS	
			Canadian rock quartet - Darby Mills, lead singer	
1/21/84	**114**	9	1. Line Of Fire	Solid Gold 9031
			ROY HEAD	
			from San Marcos, Texas	
12/04/65	**122**	8	1. Treat Me Right	Scepter 532
			"Treat Her Right"(2)	
			HEART	
			Seattle-based group led by Ann Wilson (vocals) & sister Nancy (guitar)	
4/10/76	**7**	100	▲ 1. **Dreamboat Annie**	Mushroom 5005
			"Magic Man"(9)	
5/28/77	**9**	41	▲ 2. **Little Queen**	Portrait 34799
4/22/78	**17**	25	▲ 3. Magazine	Mushroom 5008
			recorded in 1976 but not released until 1978 because of a legal fight	
10/07/78	**17**	36	▲ 4. Dog & Butterfly	Portrait 35555
3/08/80	**5**	22	● 5. **Bebe Le Strange**	Epic 36371
12/06/80	**13**	25	● 6. Greatest Hits/Live .... [G-L]	Epic 36888 [2]
			6 of 18 tracks are live "Tell It Like It Is"(8)	

DATE CHARTED	PEAK POS	WKS CHRT'D	ARTIST — Album Title	LABEL & NUMBER
6/12/82	25	14	7. Private Audition	Epic 38049
9/17/83	39	21	8. Passionworks	Epic 38800

HEARTSFIELD
6-man Chicago band

8/16/75	159	7	1. Foolish Pleasures	Mercury 1034

TED HEATH & His Music
English - Ted died on 11/18/69 (69)

10/09/61	28	10	1. Big Band Percussion .... [I]	London P. 4 44002
9/15/62	36	2	2. Big Band Bash .... [I]	London P. 4 44017

JOEY HEATHERTON
movie/TV actress

10/21/72	154	13	1. The Joey Heatherton Album	MGM 4858

HEATWAVE
multinational London-based disco band

8/06/77	11	45	▲	1. Too Hot To Handle	Epic 34761
				"Boogie Nights"(2)	
4/22/78	10	26	▲	2. Central Heating	Epic 35260
				"The Groove Line"(7)	
5/12/79	38	14	●	3. Hot Property	Epic 35970
12/13/80	71	10		4. Candles	Epic 36873
7/10/82	156	6		5. Current	Epic 38065

HEAVEN 17
Glen Gregory, lead singer of British electro-pop trio

2/12/83	68	28	1. Heaven 17	Arista 6606
6/04/83	72	13	2. The Luxury Gap	Arista 8020

BOBBY HEBB
one of the first black artists to perform at the Grand Ole Opry

9/10/66	103	12	1. Sunny	Philips 212
			"Sunny"(2)	

NEAL HEFTI & his Orchestra

2/05/55	8	1	1. Music Of Rudolf Friml .... [I]	"X" 3021
			10" album	
3/12/66	41	21	2. Batman Theme .... [I]	RCA 3573

RAY HEINDORF/MATTY MATLOCK
Ray Heindorf conducting the Warner Bros. Orchestra/
Matty Matlock & his Jazz Band - also see Jack Webb

9/03/55	9	5	1. Pete Kelly's Blues .... [I]	Columbia 690

HEINTJE
14-year-old Dutch boy

12/05/70	108	11	1. Mama	MGM 4739

HELIX
heavy-metal quintet from Ontario, Canada - Brian Vollmer, leader

10/22/83	186	4	1. No Rest For The Wicked	Capitol 12281
8/18/84	69	16	2. Walkin' The Razor's Edge	Capitol 12362

HELLO PEOPLE
mime-rock quartet produced by Todd Rundgren

11/30/74	145	13	1. The Handsome Devils	Dunhill 50184

LEVON HELM & THE RCO ALL-STARS
drummer & vocalist of the Band

11/19/77	142	10	1. Levon Helm & The RCO All-Stars	ABC 1017
			with Paul Butterfield, Steve Cropper, Duck Dunn, Mac Rebennack & Booker T. Jones	

JOE HENDERSON

10/13/62	93	5	1. Snap Your Fingers	Todd 2701
			"Snap Your Fingers"(8)	

DATE CHARTED	PEAK POS	WKS CHRT'D	ARTIST — Album Title	LABEL & NUMBER
			MICHAEL HENDERSON vocalist with Norman Connors - former bass player with Miles Davis	
12/04/76	173	7	1. Solid	Buddah 5662
8/27/77	49	13	2. Goin' Places	Buddah 5693
7/08/78	38	28	● 3. In The Night-Time	Buddah 5712
8/04/79	64	12	4. Do It All	Buddah 5719
8/30/80	35	18	5. Wide Receiver	Buddah 6001
9/19/81	86	11	6. Slingshot	Buddah 6002
6/04/83	169	5	7. Fickle	Buddah 6004
			SKITCH HENDERSON Skitch conducts "The Tonight Show" Orchestra	
10/09/65	103	8	1. Skitch...Tonight! [I]	Columbia 9167
			JIMI HENDRIX psychedelic-blues guitarist - Jimi Hendrix Experience: with Noel Redding (bass) & Mitch Mitchell (drums 1,3-5) - Jimi died on 9/18/70 (27)	
8/26/67	5	106	● 1. **Are You Experienced?** "Purple Haze"/"Hey Joe"	Reprise 6261
12/30/67	75	12	2. Get That Feeling [E] Jimi plays guitar, backing vocalist Curtis Knight (1964)	Capitol 2856
2/10/68	3	53	● 3. **Axis: Bold As Love**	Reprise 6281
10/19/68	1(2)	37	● 4. **Electric Ladyland**	Reprise 6307 [2]
8/02/69	6	35	● 5. **Smash Hits** [G]	Reprise 2025
5/02/70	5	61	● 6. **Band Of Gypsys** [L] with Buddy Miles (drums) & Billy Cox (bass) - recorded New Year's Eve 1969 at New York's Fillmore East	Capitol 472
9/19/70	16	20	● 7. Monterey International Pop Festival [S-L] OTIS REDDING/THE JIMI HENDRIX EXPERIENCE recorded June, 1967 & featured in film "Monterey Pop"	Reprise 2029
3/06/71	3	39	● 8. **The Cry Of Love** Jimi's last self-authorized album	Reprise 2034
3/20/71	127	4	9. Two Great Experiences Together! [E-I] with Lonnie Youngblood (sax)	Maple 6004
10/09/71	15	21	● 10. Rainbow Bridge [S] recordings from 1968-1970	Reprise 2040
3/04/72	12	19	● 11. Hendrix In The West [K-L]	Reprise 2049
9/02/72	82	11	12. Rare Hendrix [E] recorded 6/10/66 with Lonnie Youngblood	Trip 9500
12/09/72	48	18	13. War Heroes [K]	Reprise 2103
7/14/73	89	18	14. sound track recordings from the film Jimi Hendrix [S-L] featuring interviews from the documentary soundtrack	Reprise 6481 [2]
3/22/75	5	20	● 15. **Crash Landing** [K]	Reprise 2204
11/29/75	43	11	16. Midnight Lightning [K]	Reprise 2229
8/12/78	114	15	17. The Essential Jimi Hendrix [K]	Reprise 2245 [2]
8/18/79	156	7	18. The Essential Jimi Hendrix, Volume Two [K]	Reprise 2293
4/26/80	127	7	19. Nine To The Universe [K] jam sessions while working on his last album (1969)	Reprise 2299
9/25/82	79	8	20. The Jimi Hendrix Concerts [K-L]	Reprise 22306 [2]
11/17/84	148	5	21. Kiss The Sky [K] recordings from 1967-69	Reprise 25119
			NONA HENDRYX former member of Labelle	
4/23/83	83	19	1. Nona	RCA 4565
5/05/84	167	7	2. The Art of Defense	RCA 4999

DATE CHARTED	PEAK POS	WKS CHRT'D	ARTIST — Album Title	LABEL & NUMBER
			DON HENLEY drummer/vocalist with the Eagles	
9/04/82	**24**	35	● 1. I Can't Stand Still .... "Dirty Laundry"(3)	Asylum 60048
12/15/84	**13+**	17+	● 2. Building The Perfect Beast .... "The Boys Of Summer"(5)	Geffen 24026
			CAROL HENSEL - see AEROBICS section	
			KEN HENSLEY keyboardist with Uriah Heep	
4/07/73	**173**	7	1. Proud Words On A Dusty Shelf	Mercury 661
			WOODY HERMAN progressive jazz bandleader since 1936	
2/19/55	**11**	1	1. The 3 Herds .... [K-I] recordings from 1945-1954	Columbia 592
8/17/63	**136**	4	2. Encore: Woody Herman - 1963 .... [I-L]	Philips 092
3/21/64	**148**	2	3. Woody Herman: 1964 .... [I]	Philips 118
			HERMAN'S HERMITS Manchester, England quintet led by Peter Noone	
2/20/65	**2(4)**	40	● 1. **Introducing Herman's Hermits** .... "Mrs. Brown You've Got A Lovely Daughter"(1)	MGM 4282
6/19/65	**2(6)**	39	● 2. **Herman's Hermits On Tour** .... "Can't You Hear My Heartbeat"(2)/"Silhouettes"(5)/ "I'm Henry VIII, I Am"(1)	MGM 4295
11/20/65	**5**	105	● 3. **The Best Of Herman's Hermits** .... [G] "Wonderful World"(4)/"Just A Little Bit Better"(7)	MGM 4315
3/26/66	**14**	26	4. Hold On! .... [S] "A Must To Avoid"(8)/"Leaning On The Lamp Post"(9)	MGM 4342
8/20/66	**48**	21	5. Both Sides Of Herman's Hermits	MGM 4386
12/03/66	**20**	32	● 6. The Best Of Herman's Hermits, Volume 2 .... [G] "Listen People"(3)/"Dandy"(5)	MGM 4416
3/18/67	**13**	35	● 7. There's A Kind Of Hush All Over The World .... "There's A Kind Of Hush"(4)	MGM 4438
10/07/67	**75**	9	8. Blaze	MGM 4478
1/13/68	**102**	8	9. The Best Of Herman's Hermits, Volume III .... [G]	MGM 4505
9/28/68	**182**	3	10. Mrs. Brown, You've Got A Lovely Daughter .... [S] group stars in the film and in #4 above	MGM 4548
			PATRICK HERNANDEZ Belgian disco artist	
7/28/79	**61**	15	1. Born To Be Alive	Columbia 36100
			HESITATIONS Cleveland 7-man soul group	
2/24/68	**193**	3	1. The new Born Free	Kapp 3548
			NICK HEYWARD British - lead singer of Haircut One Hundred	
1/14/84	**178**	4	1. North of a Miracle	Arista 8106
			EDDIE HEYWOOD jazz pianist/composer	
5/25/59	**16**	4	1. Canadian Sunset .... [I] title song not the same version as with Hugo Winterhalter in 1956	RCA 1529
			HEYWOODS - see BO DONALDSON	

DATE CHARTED	PEAK POS	WKS CHRT'D	ARTIST — Album Title	LABEL & NUMBER
			HI-LO'S	
4/13/57	13	3	1. Suddenly It's The Hi-Lo's	Columbia 952
7/22/57	14	7	2. Ring Around Rosie	Columbia 1006
			ROSEMARY CLOONEY & THE HI-LO'S	
10/14/57	19	4	3. Now Hear This	Columbia 1023
			AL HIBBLER	
			born blind - vocalist with Duke Ellington 1943-1951	
8/04/56	20	2	1. Starring Al Hibbler	Decca 8328
			DAN HICKS & HIS HOT LICKS	
			California jazzy jug-band group	
10/02/71	195	8	1. Where's The Money? ... [L]	Blue Thumb 29
5/20/72	170	5	2. Striking It Rich!	Blue Thumb 36
6/09/73	67	18	3. Last Train To Hicksville...the home of happy feet	Blue Thumb 51
3/25/78	165	3	4. It Happened One Bite	Warner 3158
			shown only as Dan Hicks	
			BERTIE HIGGINS	
2/27/82	38	25	1. Just Another Day In Paradise	Kat Family 37901
			"Key Largo"(8)	
			HIGH INERGY	
			Pasadena, Calif. soul quartet - Barbara Mitchell, lead singer	
11/05/77	28	25	1. Turnin' On	Gordy 978
7/22/78	42	13	2. Steppin' Out	Gordy 982
5/26/79	147	5	3. Shoulda Gone Dancin'	Gordy 987
			HIGHWAYMEN	
			folk quintet formed at Wesleyan University, Connecticut	
10/09/61	42	22	1. The Highwaymen	United Art. 6125
			"Michael"(1)	
3/24/62	99	14	2. Standing Room Only!	United Art. 6168
9/07/63	79	9	3. Hootenanny with The Highwaymen ... [L]	United Art. 6294
			DAN HILL	
			Canadian	
12/06/75	104	17	1. Dan Hill	20th Century 500
12/10/77	21	24	● 2. Longer Fuse	20th Century 547
			"Sometimes When We Touch"(3)	
1/21/78	79	14	3. Hold On	20th Century 526
9/23/78	118	6	4. Frozen In The Night	20th Century 558
			Z.Z. HILL	
			R&B vocalist from Naples, Texas - died on 4/27/84 (48)	
1/22/72	194	2	1. The Brand New Z.Z. Hill	Mankind 201
			side 1 is a mini opera "Blues At The Opera"	
2/05/83	165	5	2. The Rhythm & The Blues	Malaco 7411
1/07/84	170	9	3. I'm A Blues Man	Malaco 7415
			STEVE HILLAGE	
			British	
1/15/77	130	9	1. L	Atlantic 18205
			produced by Todd Rundgren & featuring his group Utopia	
			CHRIS HILLMAN	
			member of the Byrds, & the Flying Burrito Bros. - also see McGuinn, Clark & Hillman	
6/19/76	152	6	1. Slippin' Away	Asylum 1062
9/17/77	188	3	2. Clear Sailin'	Asylum 1104
			HILLSIDE SINGERS	
1/08/72	71	16	1. I'd Like To Teach The World To Sing	Metromedia 1051

DATE CHARTED	PEAK POS	WKS CHRT'D	ARTIST — Album Title	LABEL & NUMBER
			HIROSHIMA Los Angeles jazz/pop band of Japanese ancestry	
12/22/79	51	27	1. Hiroshima	Arista 4252
11/15/80	72	18	2. Odori	Arista 9541
8/20/83	142	9	3. Third Generation .... [I]	Epic 38708
			AL HIRT New Orleans "Trumpet King"	
5/15/61	21	32	1. The Greatest Horn In The World .... [I]	RCA 2366
10/09/61	61	11	2. Al (He's the King) Hirt and His Band......... [I]	RCA 2354
2/03/62	41	2	3. Bourbon Street .... [I] PETE FOUNTAIN/AL HIRT	Coral 57389
2/10/62	24	25	4. Horn A-Plenty .... [I]	RCA 2446
1/19/63	96	7	5. Trumpet and Strings .... [I]	RCA 2584
3/23/63	44	3	6. Our Man In New Orleans .... [I]	RCA 2607
9/21/63	3	104	● 7. **Honey In The Horn** .... Anita Kerr Singers do background vocals on some tracks "Java"(4)	RCA 2733
2/29/64	83	9	8. Beauty and the Beard .... AL HIRT/ANN-MARGRET	RCA 2690
5/23/64	8	53	● 9. **Cotton Candy** .... [I]	RCA 2917
8/22/64	9	48	● 10. **Sugar Lips**	RCA 2965
9/26/64	18	31	11. "Pops" Goes The Trumpet .... [I] AL HIRT/BOSTON POPS/ARTHUR FIEDLER	RCA 2729
1/30/65	13	43	● 12. The Best Of Al Hirt .... [G-I]	RCA 3309
3/13/65	28	26	13. That Honey Horn Sound	RCA 3337
7/24/65	47	22	14. Live At Carnegie Hall .... [I-L]	RCA 3416
2/12/66	39	18	15. They're Playing Our Song .... [I]	RCA 3492
7/30/66	125	6	16. The Happy Trumpet .... [I]	RCA 3579
3/18/67	127	5	17. Music To Watch Girls By .... [I]	RCA 3773
2/10/68	116	13	18. Al Hirt Plays Bert Kaempfert .... [I]	RCA 3917
			DON HO & The Aliis Hawaiian	
3/05/66	117	5	1. Don Ho-Again! .... [L]	Reprise 6186
12/17/66	15	50	2. Tiny Bubbles	Reprise 6232
5/27/67	115	5	3. East Coast/West Coast .... [L]	Reprise 6244
3/22/69	199	3	4. Suck 'Em Up .... [L]	Reprise 6331
8/23/69	162	6	5. Don Ho-Greatest Hits! .... [G]	Reprise 6357
10/18/69	88	2	6. The Don Ho TV Show .... summer replacement show for "The Kraft Music Hall"	Reprise 6367
			JOHNNY HODGES/WILD BILL DAVIS jazz duo: Hodges (alto sax) & Davis (organ)	
2/20/65	148	2	1. Blue Rabbit .... [I]	Verve 8599
			ROGER HODGSON founding member/lead singer of Supertramp	
10/27/84	46	22	1. In The Eye Of The Storm	A&M 5004
			BILLIE HOLIDAY all-time great jazz singer "Lady Day" - died on 7/17/59 (44) - also see Diana Ross "Lady Sings The Blues"	
12/23/72	85	21	1. The Billie Holiday Story .... [K] recordings from 1944-1950	Decca 161 [2]
1/13/73	108	16	2. Strange Fruit .... [K] recordings from 1939 and 1944	Atlantic 1614
2/24/73	135	9	3. The Original Recordings .... [K] recordings from 1935-1958	Columbia 32060
			AMY HOLLAND daughter of country singer Esmeraldy & opera singer Harry Boersma	
8/30/80	146	14	1. Amy Holland	Capitol 12071

DATE CHARTED	PEAK POS	WKS CHRT'D	ARTIST — Album Title	LABEL & NUMBER
			JENNIFER HOLLIDAY Tony award winner for Best Actress in Broadway's "Dreamgirls"	
10/22/83	31	22	1. Feel My Soul	Geffen 4014
			HOLLIES Manchester, England quintet formed by Allan Clarke (vocals) & Graham Nash (guitar 1-5)	
2/12/66	145	3	1. Hear! Here!	Imperial 12299
10/22/66	75	11	2. Bus Stop .... "Bus Stop"(5)	Imperial 12330
2/25/67	91	8	3. Stop! Stop! Stop! .... "Stop Stop Stop"(7)	Imperial 12339
6/03/67	11	40	4. The Hollies' Greatest Hits .... [G]	Imperial 12350
8/05/67	43	14	5. Evolution .... "Carrie-Anne"(9)	Epic 26315
4/04/70	32	14	6. He Ain't Heavy, He's My Brother .... "He Ain't Heavy, He's My Brother"(7)	Epic 26538
2/13/71	183	2	7. Moving Finger	Epic 30255
7/15/72	21	21	8. Distant Light .... "Long Cool Woman (In A Black Dress)"(2)	Epic 30958
1/27/73	84	12	9. Romany	Epic 31992
10/20/73	157	7	10. The Hollies' Greatest Hits .... [G] includes both Imperial and Epic hits	Epic 32061
5/11/74	28	23	11. Hollies .... "The Air That I Breathe"(6)	Epic 32574
3/29/75	123	10	12. Another Night	Epic 33387
7/09/83	90	9	13. What Goes Around... .... reunion of Graham Nash with group	Atlantic 80076
			LOLEATTA HOLLOWAY	
12/02/78	187	2	1. Queen Of The Night	Gold Mind 9501
			HOLLY & THE ITALIANS Holly Vincent, leader of Los Angeles rock group	
7/11/81	177	3	1. The Right To Be Italian	Virgin 37359
			BUDDY HOLLY Lubbock, Texas rock 'n roll legend - died on 2/3/59 (22) - also see "Buddy Holly Story" soundtrack	
4/27/59	11	181	● 1. The Buddy Holly Story .... [G] includes 4 songs with the Crickets "That'll Be The Day"(1)/"Peggy Sue"(3)/"Oh, Boy!"(10)	Coral 57279
3/16/63	40	17	2. Reminiscing .... [K] instrumental backing by the Fireballs dubbed in (1962)	Coral 57426
8/05/78	55	12	● 3. Buddy Holly/The Crickets 20 Golden Greats .... [G]	MCA 3040
			HOLLYRIDGE STRINGS Stu Phillips - arranger/conductor	
6/20/64	15	25	1. The Beatles Song Book .... [I]	Capitol 2116
10/10/64	82	12	2. The Beach Boys Song Book .... [I]	Capitol 2156
2/13/65	144	3	3. Hits Made Famous By Elvis Presley .... [I]	Capitol 2221
4/24/65	136	3	4. The Nat King Cole Song Book .... [I]	Capitol 2310
6/04/66	142	3	5. The New Beatles Song Book .... [I]	Capitol 2429
			HOLLYWOOD BOWL SYMPHONY ORCHESTRA - see LEONARD PENNARIO	
			HOLLYWOOD STUDIO ORCHESTRA	
3/27/61	23	17	1. Exodus .... [I] this is not the original soundtrack album	United Art. 6123
			EDDIE HOLMAN Norfolk, Virginia soul singer	
2/14/70	75	13	1. I Love You .... "Hey There Lonely Girl"(2)	ABC 701

DATE CHARTED	PEAK POS	WKS CHRT'D	ARTIST — Album Title	LABEL & NUMBER
			CECIL HOLMES Soulful Sounds	
			Tony Camillo - producer/arranger	
4/28/73	141	10	1. The Black Motion Picture Experience .... [I]	Buddah 5129
			themes from black soundtracks	
			CLINT HOLMES	
5/26/73	122	12	1. Playground In My Mind	Epic 32269
			"Playground In My Mind"(2)	
			JAKE HOLMES	
11/14/70	135	6	1. So Close, So Very Far To Go	Polydor 4034
			LEROY HOLMES & His Orchestra	
9/09/67	42	29	1. For A Few Dollars More and other Motion Picture Themes .... [I]	United Art. 6608
6/01/68	138	8	2. The Good, The Bad And The Ugly and other Motion Picture Themes .... [I]	United Art. 6633
			RICHARD "GROOVE" HOLMES	
			jazz organist	
5/14/66	89	26	1. Soul Message .... [I]	Prestige 7435
10/29/66	143	3	2. Living Soul .... [I-L]	Prestige 7468
			recorded at Count Basie's club in Harlem	
12/24/66	134	6	3. Misty	Prestige 7485
			RUPERT HOLMES	
			pop songwriter/arranger	
11/10/79	33	31	● 1. Partners In Crime	Infinity 9020
			"Escape (The Pina Colada Song)"(1)/"Him"(6)	
			HOMBRES	
			Memphis, Tennessee foursome	
12/09/67	180	4	1. Let It Out (Let It All Hang Out)	Verve Fore. 3036
			HONDELLS	
			Southern California quartet led by Ritchie Burns	
11/28/64	119	4	1. Go Little Honda	Mercury 60940
			"Little Honda"(9)	
			HONEYCOMBS	
			English quintet - Dennis D'ell, lead singer	
1/02/65	147	2	1. Here Are The Honeycombs	Interphon 88001
			"Have I The Right?"(5)	
			HONEY CONE	
			West Coast black female background vocal trio	
6/19/71	137	8	1. Sweet Replies	Hot Wax 706
			"Want Ads"(1)	
12/11/71	72	20	2. Soulful Tapestry	Hot Wax 707
9/23/72	189	4	3. Love, Peace & Soul	Hot Wax 713
			HONEYDRIPPERS	
			Robert Plant, Jimmy Page, Jeff Beck, Nile Rodgers	
10/20/84	4	25 +	▲ 1. **Volume One** .... [M]	Es Paranza 90220
			"Sea Of Love"(3)	
			HONEYMOON SUITE	
			Canadian rock quintet - Johnny Dee, lead singer	
8/25/84	60	17	1. Honeymoon Suite	Warner 25098
			JOHN LEE HOOKER	
			blues singer/guitarist from Clarksdale, Mississippi	
2/27/71	73	16	1. Hooker 'N Heat	Liberty 35002 [2]
			CANNED HEAT & JOHN LEE HOOKER	
3/27/71	126	13	2. Endless Boogie	ABC 720 [2]
3/18/72	130	6	3. Never Get Out Of These Blues Alive	ABC 736
			STIX HOOPER	
			The Crusader's drummer	
11/10/79	166	5	1. The World Within .... [I]	MCA 3180

DATE CHARTED	PEAK POS	WKS CHRT'D	ARTIST — Album Title	LABEL & NUMBER
			BOB HOPE	
7/04/76	175	4	1. America Is 200 Years Old...And There's Still Hope! .... [C] comedy sketches featuring Jim Backus, Phyllis Diller & Dudley Moore	Capitol 11538
			MARY HOPKIN British	
3/29/69	28	20	1. Post Card .... produced by Paul McCartney "Those Were The Days"(2)	Apple 3351
			NICKY HOPKINS British session pianist for the Rolling Stones and others	
2/12/72	33	11	1. Jamming With Edward! .... [I] jam session with Ry Cooder, Mick Jagger, Bill Wyman & Charlie Watts	Rolling S. 39100
5/05/73	108	10	2. The Tin Man Was A Dreamer	Columbia 32074
			JIMMY "BO" HORNE	
7/01/78	122	10	1. Dance Across The Floor	Sunshine S. 7801
			LENA HORNE legendary singer/actress/Broadway star	
9/16/57	24	2	1. Lena Horne at the Waldorf Astoria .... [L]	RCA 1028
11/17/58	20	1	2. Give The Lady What She Wants	RCA 1879
6/15/59	13	21	3. Porgy & Bess .... LENA HORNE/HARRY BELAFONTE	RCA 1507
4/14/62	102	8	4. Lena On The Blue Side	RCA 2465
2/09/63	102	5	5. Lena...Lovely And Alive	RCA 2587
5/16/70	162	10	6. Lena & Gabor .... LENA HORNE & GABOR SZABO (jazz guitarist)	Skye 15
9/26/81	112	9	7. Lena Horne: The Lady And Her Music .... [OC-L] Lena won a Tony in this Broadway musical	Qwest 3597 [2]
			VLADIMIR HOROWITZ classical pianist - born in the U.S.S.R.	
11/10/62	14	22	1. Vladimir Horowitz (Chopin, Schumann, Rachmaninoff, Liszt) .... [I]	Columbia 6371
6/22/63	129	8	2. The Sound Of Horowitz .... [I]	Columbia 6411
7/24/65	22	32	3. Horowitz at Carnegie Hall - An Historic Return .... [I-L]	Columbia 728 [2]
11/16/68	185	4	4. Horowitz On Television .... [I-L] a Carnegie Hall performance on 2/1/68	Columbia 7106
4/29/78	102	14	5. Golden Jubilee Concert - Rachmaninoff Concerto No. 3 .... [I-L] a Carnegie Hall concert with Eugene Ormandy & The New York Philharmonic	RCA 2633
			HORSLIPS Dublin, Ireland rock quintet	
2/25/78	98	9	1. Aliens	DJM 16
3/10/79	155	9	2. The Man Who Built America	DJM 20
			JOHNNY HORTON killed in an auto crash on 11/5/60 (33)	
2/27/61	8	34	● 1. **Johnny Horton's Greatest Hits** .... [G] "The Battle Of New Orleans"(1)/"Sink The Bismarck"(3)/ "North To Alaska"(4)	Columbia 8396
4/28/62	104	10	2. Honky-Tonk Man .... [K]	Columbia 8779
			HOT female soul/pop trio	
5/28/77	125	15	1. Hot .... "Angel In Your Arms"(6)	Big Tree 89522

DATE CHARTED	PEAK POS	WKS CHRT'D	ARTIST — Album Title	LABEL & NUMBER
			HOT BUTTER Stan Free plays the Moog synthesizer	
10/21/72	137	7	1. Popcorn .... [I] "Popcorn"(9)	Musicor 3242
			HOT CHOCOLATE Errol Brown, lead singer of British interracial rock/soul group	
3/01/75	55	17	1. Cicero Park .... "Emma"(8)	Big Tree 89503
11/22/75	41	21	2. Hot Chocolate .... "You Sexy Thing"(3)	Big Tree 89512
9/18/76	172	6	3. Man To Man	Big Tree 89519
1/06/79	31	16	4. Every 1's A Winner .... "Every 1's A Winner"(6)	Infinity 9002
7/28/79	112	6	5. Going Through The Motions	Infinity 9010
			HOT TUNA formed by Jefferson Airplane members Jorma Kaukonen & Jack Casady	
7/18/70	30	19	1. Hot Tuna .... [L]	RCA 4353
6/26/71	43	13	2. First Pull Up Then Pull Down .... [L]	RCA 4550
3/18/72	68	23	3. Burgers	Grunt 1004
2/09/74	148	7	4. The Phosphorescent Rat	Grunt 0348
5/10/75	75	11	5. America's Choice	Grunt 0820
11/29/75	97	9	6. Yellow Fever	Grunt 1238
11/20/76	116	10	7. Hoppkorv	Grunt 1920
4/15/78	92	10	8. Double Dose .... [L]	Grunt 2545 [2]
			DAVID HOUSTON country singer from Shreveport, Louisiana	
8/06/66	57	20	1. Almost Persuaded	Epic 26213
9/13/69	143	5	2. David .... an album of spiritual songs	Epic 26482
4/18/70	194	2	3. Baby, Baby	Epic 26539
9/26/70	170	3	4. Wonders Of The Wine	Epic 30108
			THELMA HOUSTON	
12/25/76	11	37	1. Any Way You Like It .... "Don't Leave Me This Way"(1)	Tamla 345
6/18/77	53	12	2. Thelma & Jerry .... THELMA HOUSTON & JERRY BUTLER	Motown 887
11/12/77	64	11	3. The Devil In Me	Tamla 358
5/30/81	144	6	4. Never Gonna Be Another One	RCA 3842
			WHITNEY HOUSTON daughter of Cissy Houston (Sweet Inspirations)	
3/30/85	136+	2+	1. Whitney Houston	Arista 8212
			GEORGE HOWARD saxophone player from Philadelphia	
9/01/84	178	4	1. Steppin' Out .... [I]	TBA 201
			STEVE HOWE former lead guitarist of Yes	
12/20/75	63	11	1. Beginnings	Atlantic 18154
2/16/80	164	4	2. The Steve Howe Album .... [I]	Atlantic 19243
			HOWLIN' WOLF real name: Chester Arthur Burnett - died on 1/10/76 (65)	
8/21/71	79	15	1. The London Howlin' Wolf Sessions .... with Eric Clapton, Steve Winwood, Bill Wyman, Charlie Watts	Chess 60008
			FREDDIE HUBBARD jazz trumpeter	
3/10/73	165	7	1. Sky Dive .... [I]	CTI 6018
1/19/74	186	5	2. Keep Your Soul Together .... [I]	CTI 6036
9/14/74	153	7	3. High Energy .... [I]	Columbia 33048

DATE CHARTED	PEAK POS	WKS CHRT'D	ARTIST — Album Title	LABEL & NUMBER
1/11/75	127	7	4. The Baddest Hubbard .... [K-I]	CTI 6047
5/17/75	167	4	5. Polar AC .... [I]	CTI 6056
7/19/75	149	6	6. Liquid Love .... [I]	Columbia 33556
9/04/76	85	9	7. Windjammer .... [I]	Columbia 34166
10/29/77	149	6	8. Bundle Of Joy .... [I]	Columbia 34902
7/15/78	131	5	9. Super Blue .... [I]	Columbia 35386

HUDSON & LANDRY
Bob Hudson & Ron Landry - Los Angeles disc jockeys (KGBS)

DATE CHARTED	PEAK POS	WKS CHRT'D	ARTIST — Album Title	LABEL & NUMBER
4/10/71	30	26	1. Hanging In There .... [C]	Dore 324
11/27/71	33	23	2. Losing Their Heads .... [C]	Dore 326
1/06/73	147	9	3. Right-Off! .... [C]	Dore 329

HUDSON BROTHERS
Bill, Brett & Mark Hudson from Portland, Oregon

11/30/74	179	4	1. Totally Out Of Control	Rocket 460
12/07/74	176	4	2. Hollywood Situation	Casablanca 7004
12/13/75	165	6	3. Ba-Fa	Rocket 2169

DAVID HUDSON

8/23/80	184	2	1. To You Honey, Honey With Love	Alston 4412

HUES CORPORATION
Los Angeles black disco/soul trio

6/29/74	20	18	1. Freedom For The Stallion	RCA 0323
			"Rock The Boat"(1)	
7/05/75	147	5	2. Love Corporation	RCA 0938

HUGO & LUIGI Chorus
producers Hugo Peretti & Luigi Creatore

4/27/63	14	13	1. The Cascading Voices of the Hugo & Luigi Chorus	RCA 2641
10/26/63	125	2	2. Let's Fall In Love	RCA 2717

HUMAN BEINZ
Cleveland bar band

3/09/68	65	10	1. Nobody But Me	Capitol 2906
			"Nobody But Me"(8)	

HUMAN LEAGUE
British 6-member electronic pop band, led by Philip Oakey

2/27/82	3	38	● 1. **Dare**	A&M 4892
			"Don't You Want Me"(1)	
9/18/82	135	7	2. Love And Dancing .... [I]	A&M 3209
			THE LEAGUE UNLIMITED ORCHESTRA instrumental versions of songs from album #1 above	
6/18/83	22	29	3. Fascination! .... [M]	A&M 12501
			"(Keep Feeling) Fascination"(8)	
6/16/84	62	13	4. Hysteria	A&M 4923

HUMBLE PIE
English quartet led by Steve Marriott (vocals) & Peter Frampton (guitar 1,2 & 4)

5/08/71	118	23	1. Rock On	A&M 4301
11/06/71	21	32	● 2. Performance-Rockin' The Fillmore .... [L]	A&M 3506 [2]
4/01/72	6	34	● 3. **Smokin'**	A&M 4342
9/30/72	37	20	4. Lost And Found .... [E-R]	A&M 3513 [2]
			reissue of their first two albums "Town And Country" & "As Safe As Yesterday Is"	
3/24/73	13	21	5. Eat It	A&M 3701 [2]
			side 4 recorded live in Glasgow, Scotland	
3/09/74	52	14	6. Thunderbox	A&M 3611
4/26/75	100	8	7. Street Rats	A&M 4514
4/12/80	60	14	8. On To Victory	Atco 122
5/09/81	154	6	9. Go For The Throat	Atco 131

DATE CHARTED	PEAK POS	WKS CHRT'D	ARTIST — Album Title	LABEL & NUMBER
			ENGELBERT HUMPERDINCK real name: Arnold Dorsey - born in India and raised in England	
6/17/67	7	118	● 1. **Release Me** .... "Release Me"(4)	Parrot 71012
12/23/67	10	60	● 2. **The Last Waltz**	Parrot 71015
8/24/68	12	78	● 3. A Man Without Love	Parrot 71022
3/22/69	12	33	● 4. Engelbert	Parrot 71026
1/03/70	5	41	● 5. **Engelbert Humperdinck**	Parrot 71030
7/11/70	19	40	● 6. We Made It Happen	Parrot 71038
2/20/71	22	24	● 7. Sweetheart	Parrot 71043
9/11/71	25	15	● 8. Another Time, Another Place	Parrot 71048
1/01/72	48	13	9. Live At The Riviera, Las Vegas .... [L]	Parrot 71051
8/19/72	72	14	10. In Time	Parrot 71056
8/11/73	113	10	11. King Of Hearts	Parrot 71061
12/21/74	103	14	12. His Greatest Hits .... [G]	Parrot 71067
11/27/76	17	28	▲ 13. After The Lovin' .... "After The Lovin'"(8)	Epic 34381
7/16/77	167	5	14. Miracles by Engelbert Humperdinck	Epic 34730
12/24/77	156	4	● 15. Christmas Tyme .... [X]	Epic 35031
5/19/79	164	4	16. This Moment In Time	Epic 35791
			BOBBI HUMPHREY jazz flautist	
3/30/74	84	21	1. Blacks and Blues .... [I]	Blue Note 142
12/07/74	30	18	2. Satin Doll	Blue Note 344
11/29/75	133	5	3. Fancy Dancer .... [I]	Blue Note 550
7/01/78	89	14	4. Freestyle	Epic 35338
			PAUL HUMPHREY & The Cool Aid Chemists West Coast session drummer	
6/12/71	170	6	1. Paul Humphrey & The Cool Aid Chemists .... [I]	Lizard 20106
			IAN HUNTER English - leader of Mott The Hoople	
5/17/75	50	14	1. Ian Hunter	Columbia 33480
5/22/76	177	7	2. All-American Alien Boy	Columbia 34142
4/28/79	35	24	3. You're Never Alone With A Schizophrenic	Chrysalis 1214
4/26/80	69	17	4. Ian Hunter Live/Welcome To The Club ..... [L]	Chrysalis 1269 [2]
8/29/81	62	11	5. Short Back N' Sides	Chrysalis 1326
8/06/83	125	8	6. All Of The Good Ones Are Taken	Columbia 38628
			JOHN HUNTER rock singer/keyboardist from Chicago	
2/09/85	148	9	1. Famous At Night	Private I 39626
			CHET HUNTLEY & DAVID BRINKLEY formerly co-anchors of TV's NBC Nightly News	
3/14/64	115	7	1. A Time To Keep: 1963 .... [T] a recall of the voices and events of 1963	RCA 1088
			WILLIE HUTCH composer/arranger/guitarist	
6/02/73	114	16	1. The Mack .... [S]	Motown 766
10/13/73	183	6	2. Fully Exposed	Motown 784
5/25/74	179	4	3. Foxy Brown .... [S]	Motown 811
11/15/75	150	6	4. Ode To My Lady	Motown 838
4/03/76	163	6	5. Concert In Blues	Motown 854
			LeROY HUTSON replaced Curtis Mayfield in the Impressions (1972)	
3/06/76	170	8	1. Feel The Spirit	Curtom 5010

DATE CHARTED	PEAK POS	WKS CHRT'D	ARTIST — Album Title	LABEL & NUMBER
			BRIAN HYLAND	
			born in Queens, New York on 11/12/43	
4/19/69	160	5	1. Tragedy/A Million To One	Dot 25926
1/30/71	171	4	2. Brian Hyland	Uni 73097
			produced by Del Shannon "Gypsy Woman"(3)	
			DICK HYMAN	
			arranger/conductor/pianist/organist	
11/25/57	21	2	1. 60 Great All Time Songs, Vol. 3 .... [I]	MGM 3537
			groups of medleys played by Dick on the piano	
11/09/63	117	7	2. Electrodynamics .... [I]	Command 856
4/04/64	132	5	3. Fabulous .... [I]	Command 862
			above 2: Dick Hyman at the Lowrey Organ	
4/27/68	179	2	4. Mirrors - Reflections Of Today .... [I]	Command 924
4/19/69	30	30	5. Moog - The Electric Eclectics of Dick	
			Hyman .... [I]	Command 938
9/27/69	110	11	6. The Age Of Electronicus .... [I]	Command 946
			above 2: synthesized songs on the Moog	
			PHYLLIS HYMAN	
			former singer with Norman Connors' band	
4/30/77	107	14	1. Phyllis Hyman	Buddah 5681
2/03/79	70	17	2. Somewhere In My Lifetime	Arista 4202
12/08/79	50	21	3. You Know How To Love Me	Arista 9509
8/01/81	57	13	4. Can't We Fall In Love Again	Arista 9544
6/18/83	112	12	5. Goddess Of Love	Arista 8021
			IAN & SYLVIA	
			Canadian folk/country duo: Ian Tyson & wife Sylvia Fricker	
9/28/63	115	6	1. Four Strong Winds	Vanguard 79133
9/05/64	70	12	2. Northern Journey	Vanguard 79154
6/19/65	77	18	3. Early Morning Rain	Vanguard 79175
5/28/66	142	6	4. Play One More	Vanguard 79215
4/01/67	130	7	5. So Much For Dreaming	Vanguard 79241
7/08/67	148	10	6. Lovin' Sound	MGM 4388
			JANIS IAN	
			real name: Janis Fink - born in New York City on 5/7/51	
6/17/67	29	28	1. Janis Ian	Verve Folk. 3017
			"Society's Child"	
12/30/67	179	5	2. For All The Seasons Of Your Mind	Verve Fore. 3024
6/01/74	83	20	3. Stars	Columbia 32857
3/22/75	1(1)	64	● 4. **Between The Lines**	Columbia 33394
			"At Seventeen"(3)	
1/24/76	12	19	5. Aftertones	Columbia 33919
1/29/77	45	12	6. Miracle Row	Columbia 34440
9/16/78	120	11	7. Janis Ian	Columbia 35325
7/04/81	156	3	8. Restless Eyes	Columbia 37360
			ICEHOUSE	
			Australian - led by singer/guitarist Iva Davies	
7/25/81	82	15	1. Icehouse	Chrysalis 1350
10/09/82	129	6	2. Primitive Man	Chrysalis 1390
			ICICLE WORKS	
			Liverpool rock trio - Ian McNabb, leader	
4/21/84	40	18	1. Icicle Works	Arista 8202
			ICON	
			Phoenix-based rock quintet - Stephen Clifford, lead singer	
6/09/84	190	2	1. icon	Capitol 12336

DATE CHARTED	PEAK POS	WKS CHRT'D	ARTIST — Album Title	LABEL & NUMBER
			IDES OF MARCH Chicago group led by Jim Peterik (Survivor)	
6/27/70	55	12	1. Vehicle .... "Vehicle"(2)	Warner 1863
			BILLY IDOL English - born William Broad - former leader of British punk group Generation X	
10/24/81	71	68	1. Don't Stop .... [M]	Chrysalis 4000
7/31/82	45	104	● 2. Billy Idol	Chrysalis 41377
12/03/83	6	71+	▲ 3. **Rebel Yell** .... "Eyes Without A Face"(4)	Chrysalis 41450
			IF British jazz-rock combo	
10/31/70	187	2	1. If	Capitol 539
9/25/71	171	3	2. If 3	Capitol 820
10/28/72	195	4	3. Waterfall	Metromedia 1057
			FRANK IFIELD - see BEATLES	
			IGGY & THE STOOGES - see IGGY POP	
			JULIO IGLESIAS Spanish vocalist	
4/02/83	32	89	▲ 1. Julio .... [F]	Columbia 38640
8/25/84	159	9	2. In Concert .... [L-F] recorded in London, Paris, Melbourne & Tokyo in 1983	Columbia 39570 [2]
9/01/84	5	32+	▲ 3. **1100 Bel Air Place** .... "To All The Girls I've Loved Before"(5-with Willie Nelson)	Columbia 39157
9/01/84	179	6	4. Hey! .... [F] originally released in 1980 (not in U.S.A.)	Columbia 39567
9/01/84	181	6	5. From A Child To A Woman .... [F] originally released in 1981 (not in U.S.A.)	Columbia 39569
9/15/84	191	4	6. Moments .... [F] originally released in 1982 (not in U.S.A.)	Columbia 39568
			ILLINOIS SPEED PRESS Chicago rock quintet led by Paul Cotton (Poco)	
5/24/69	144	4	1. The Illinois Speed Press	Columbia 9792
			ILLUSION rock quintet led by John Vinci	
5/10/69	69	27	1. The Illusion	Steed 37003
			ILLUSION jazz-rock sextet formed by members of Renaissance	
7/02/77	163	7	1. Out Of The Mist	Island 9489
			IMPRESSIONS Chicago-based soul group led by Curtis Mayfield (1-13)	
8/31/63	43	33	1. The Impressions .... "It's All Right"(4)	ABC-Para. 450
3/28/64	52	22	2. The Never Ending Impressions	ABC-Para. 468
8/08/64	8	34	3. **Keep On Pushing** .... "Keep On Pushing"(10)/"Amen"(7)	ABC-Para. 493
3/06/65	23	19	4. People Get Ready	ABC-Para. 505
3/20/65	83	15	5. The Impressions Greatest Hits .... [G]	ABC-Para. 515
9/18/65	104	9	6. One By One	ABC-Para. 523
3/05/66	79	10	7. Ridin' High	ABC-Para. 545
7/15/67	184	11	8. The Fabulous Impressions	ABC 606
3/02/68	35	27	9. We're A Winner	ABC 635
9/21/68	172	15	10. The Best Of The Impressions .... [G]	ABC 654
12/07/68	107	13	11. This Is My Country	Curtom 8001
5/24/69	104	17	12. The Young Mods' Forgotten Story	Curtom 8003
3/20/71	180	6	13. 16 Greatest Hits .... [G]	ABC 727
4/29/72	192	2	14. Times Have Changed	Curtom 8012

DATE CHARTED	PEAK POS	WKS CHRT'D	ARTIST — Album Title	LABEL & NUMBER
3/03/73	180	6	15. Curtis Mayfield/His Early Years With The Impressions .... [G]	ABC 780 [2]
7/06/74	176	3	16. Finally Got Myself Together	Curtom 8019
8/09/75	115	5	17. First Impressions	Curtom 5003
3/13/76	195	3	18. Loving Power	Curtom 5009
2/05/77	199	2	19. The Vintage Years .... [G] 13 hits by The Impressions and 13 by Jerry Butler (solo)	Sire 3717 [2]
			INCREDIBLE BONGO BAND	
8/18/73	197	2	1. Bongo Rock .... [I]	Pride 0028
			INCREDIBLE STRING BAND eclectic Scottish folk group led by Mike Heron & Robin Williamson	
7/20/68	161	9	1. The Hangman's Beautiful Daughter	Elektra 74021
3/22/69	174	3	2. Wee Tam	Elektra 74036
3/22/69	180	3	3. The Big Huge	Elektra 74037
12/06/69	166	3	4. Changing Horses	Elektra 74057
7/25/70	196	2	5. I Looked Up	Elektra 74061
1/23/71	183	3	6. 'U'	Elektra 2002 [2]
2/19/72	189	3	7. Liquid Acrobat As Regards The Air	Elektra 74112
			INDEPENDENTS Chicago-based soul trio	
5/19/73	127	9	1. The First Time We Met	Wand 694
			JAMES INGRAM Akron, Ohio native - vocalist on Quincy Jones' album "The Dude"	
11/12/83	46	42	● 1. It's Your Night	Qwest 23970
			LUTHER INGRAM	
1/15/72	175	11	1. I've Been Here All The Time	Koko 2201
9/30/72	39	21	2. If Loving You Is Wrong I Don't Want To Be Right .... "(If Loving You Is Wrong) I Don't Want To Be Right"(3)	Koko 2202
			INMATES British rock quartet led by Peter Gunn	
12/01/79	49	17	1. First Offence	Polydor 6241
			INSTANT FUNK 9-man funk ensemble led by James Carmichael	
2/17/79	12	22	● 1. Instant Funk	Salsoul 8513
12/08/79	129	13	2. Witch Doctor	Salsoul 8529
10/18/80	130	6	3. The Funk Is On	Salsoul 8536
4/10/82	147	7	4. Looks So Fine	Salsoul 8545
			INTERNATIONAL ALL STARS directed by Harry Frekin	
12/04/61	47	2	1. Percussion Around The World .... [I]	London P. 4 44010
			INTRUDERS Philadelphia quartet led by "Little Sonny" Brown	
7/27/68	112	9	1. Cowboys To Girls .... "Cowboys To Girls"(6)	Gamble 5004
1/25/69	144	6	2. The Intruders Greatest Hits .... [G]	Gamble 5005
5/19/73	133	18	3. Save The Children	Gamble 31991
			INVISIBLE MAN'S BAND formed by 4 of the Burke Brothers from the 5 Stairsteps	
5/31/80	90	14	1. The Invisible Man's Band	Mango 9537
			INXS Australian quintet - Michael Hutchence, lead singer	
3/19/83	46	31	1. Shabooh Shoobah	Atco 90072
10/01/83	148	6	2. Dekadance .... [M] 4 extended tracks from album #1 above	Atco 90115

DATE CHARTED	PEAK POS	WKS CHRT'D	ARTIST — Album Title	LABEL & NUMBER
5/26/84	**52**	28	3. The Swing	Atco 90160
8/18/84	**164**	3	4. Inxs .... [E]	Atco 90184
			originally released in 1980 (not in the U.S.A.)	

DONNIE IRIS
leader of The Jaggerz

DATE CHARTED	PEAK POS	WKS CHRT'D	ARTIST — Album Title	LABEL & NUMBER
12/13/80	**57**	23	1. Back On The Streets	MCA 3272
9/26/81	**84**	31	2. King Cool	MCA 5237
11/27/82	**180**	4	3. The High And The Mighty	MCA 5358
7/02/83	**127**	12	4. Fortune 410	MCA 5427
3/16/85	**158+**	4+	5. No Muss...No Fuss	HME 39949

IRISH ROVERS
Irish-born folk quintet - group formed in Canada

DATE CHARTED	PEAK POS	WKS CHRT'D	ARTIST — Album Title	LABEL & NUMBER
4/06/68	**24**	43	1. The Unicorn	Decca 74951
			"The Unicorn"(7)	
11/09/68	**119**	8	2. All Hung Up	Decca 75037
5/10/69	**182**	5	3. Tales To Warm Your Mind	Decca 75081
			ROVERS:	
4/25/81	**157**	8	4. Wasn't That A Party	Cleve. I. 37107

IRON BUTTERFLY
San Diego heavy-metal rock band led by Doug Ingle

DATE CHARTED	PEAK POS	WKS CHRT'D	ARTIST — Album Title	LABEL & NUMBER
3/09/68	**78**	49	1. Heavy	Atco 227
7/20/68	**4**	140	● 2. **In-A-Gadda-Da-Vida**	Atco 250
			side 2 is a 17 minute version of the album title	
2/15/69	**3**	44	● 3. **Ball**	Atco 280
5/23/70	**20**	23	4. Iron Butterfly Live .... [L]	Atco 318
			side 2 is a 19 minute version of "In-A-Gadda-Da-Vida"	
8/29/70	**16**	23	5. Metamorphosis	Atco 339
			with guitarists Mike Pinera & Larry Reinhardt	
12/25/71	**137**	6	6. The Best Of Iron Butterfly/Evolution .... [G]	Atco 369
2/15/75	**138**	6	7. Scorching Beauty	MCA 465

IRONHORSE
Randy Bachman (BTO), leader

DATE CHARTED	PEAK POS	WKS CHRT'D	ARTIST — Album Title	LABEL & NUMBER
4/07/79	**153**	10	1. Ironhorse	Scotti Br. 7103

IRON MAIDEN
heavy-metal quintet from London - Paul Di'anno, lead singer

DATE CHARTED	PEAK POS	WKS CHRT'D	ARTIST — Album Title	LABEL & NUMBER
6/06/81	**78**	23	1. Killers	Harvest 12141
10/31/81	**89**	30	2. Maiden Japan .... [L-M]	Harvest 15000
4/10/82	**33**	65	● 3. The Number Of The Beast	Harvest 12202
			featuring new lead singer Bruce Dickinson	
6/11/83	**14**	45	● 4. Piece Of Mind	Capitol 12274
9/29/84	**21**	28+	● 5. Powerslave	Capitol 12321

ISLEY BROTHERS
family group from Cincinnati led by Ronald, Rudolph & O'Kelly

DATE CHARTED	PEAK POS	WKS CHRT'D	ARTIST — Album Title	LABEL & NUMBER
9/29/62	**61**	13	1. Twist & Shout	Wand 653
6/18/66	**140**	5	2. This Old Heart Of Mine	Tamla 269
5/03/69	**22**	18	3. It's Our Thing	T-Neck 3001
			"It's Your Thing"(20)	
10/18/69	**169**	4	4. Live At Yankee Stadium .... [L]	T-Neck 3004 [2]
			side A: Isley Brothers; side B: Edwin Hawkins Singers; side C: Brooklyn Bridge; side D: Various Artists	
10/18/69	**180**	3	5. The Brothers: Isley	T-Neck 3002
9/25/71	**71**	25	6. Givin' It Back	T-Neck 3008
7/01/72	**29**	33	7. Brother, Brother, Brother	T-Neck 3009
3/17/73	**139**	13	8. The Isleys Live .... [L]	T-Neck 3010 [2]
9/08/73	**8**	37	● 9. 3 + 3	T-Neck 32453
			"That Lady"(6)	
12/22/73	**195**	3	10. Isleys' Greatest Hits .... [G]	T-Neck 3011
9/07/74	**14**	28	● 11. Live It Up	T-Neck 33070

DATE CHARTED	PEAK POS	WKS CHRT'D	ARTIST — Album Title	LABEL & NUMBER
6/14/75	1(1)	40	● 12. **The Heat Is On** .... "Fight The Power"(4)	T-Neck 33536
5/29/76	9	26	● 13. **Harvest For The World**	T-Neck 33809
4/16/77	6	34	▲ 14. **Go For Your Guns**	T-Neck 34432
8/27/77	58	11	15. Forever Gold .... [G]	T-Neck 34452
4/22/78	4	21	▲ 16. **Showdown**	T-Neck 34930
6/16/79	14	20	● 17. Winner Takes All	T-Neck 36077 [2]
4/19/80	8	22	▲ 18. **Go All The Way**	T-Neck 36305
3/21/81	28	17	● 19. Grand Slam	T-Neck 37080
10/31/81	45	13	20. Inside You	T-Neck 37533
8/21/82	87	12	21. The Real Deal	T-Neck 38047
6/04/83	19	23	● 22. **Between The Sheets**	T-Neck 38674

ISLEY, JASPER, ISLEY
Ernie Isley, Chris Jasper, Marvin Isley - youngest members of the Isley Brothers

DATE CHARTED	PEAK POS	WKS CHRT'D	ARTIST — Album Title	LABEL & NUMBER
2/09/85	135	9 +	1. Broadway's Closer To Sunset Blvd.	CBS Assoc. 39873

IT'S A BEAUTIFUL DAY
San Francisco group led by David LaFlamme (1-4)

DATE CHARTED	PEAK POS	WKS CHRT'D	ARTIST — Album Title	LABEL & NUMBER
6/14/69	47	70	● 1. It's A Beautiful Day .... "White Bird"	Columbia 9768
7/04/70	28	21	2. Marrying Maiden	Columbia 1058
12/11/71	130	16	3. Choice Quality Stuff/Anytime	Columbia 30734
11/11/72	144	9	4. It's A Beautiful Day At Carnegie Hall .... [L]	Columbia 31338
4/07/73	114	10	5. It's A Beautiful Day...Today	Columbia 32181

BURL IVES
folk singer/actor

DATE CHARTED	PEAK POS	WKS CHRT'D	ARTIST — Album Title	LABEL & NUMBER
2/17/62	35	34	1. The Versatile Burl Ives! .... "A Little Bitty Tear"(9)	Decca 4152
6/02/62	24	36	2. It's Just My Funny Way Of Laughin' .... "Funny Way Of Laughin'"(10)	Decca 4279
12/05/64	65	15	3. Pearly Shells	Decca 74578

TERRY JACKS
Canadian - Terry and wife Susan were the Poppy Family

DATE CHARTED	PEAK POS	WKS CHRT'D	ARTIST — Album Title	LABEL & NUMBER
3/16/74	81	9	1. Seasons In The Sun .... "Seasons In The Sun"(1)	Bell 1307

JANET JACKSON
sister of the Jacksons (last of 9 children)

DATE CHARTED	PEAK POS	WKS CHRT'D	ARTIST — Album Title	LABEL & NUMBER
11/20/82	63	25	1. Janet Jackson	A&M 4907
10/27/84	147	6	2. Dream Street	A&M 4962

JERMAINE JACKSON
member of the Jackson 5 (1970-1975)

DATE CHARTED	PEAK POS	WKS CHRT'D	ARTIST — Album Title	LABEL & NUMBER
8/12/72	27	36	1. Jermaine .... "Daddy's Home"(9)	Motown 752
6/16/73	152	6	2. Come Into My Life	Motown 775
9/25/76	164	11	3. My Name Is Jermaine	Motown 842
8/27/77	174	3	4. Feel The Fire	Motown 888
4/12/80	6	29	● 5. **Let's Get Serious** .... "Let's Get Serious"(9)	Motown 928
12/06/80	44	23	6. Jermaine	Motown 948
9/26/81	86	10	7. I Like Your Style	Motown 952
8/21/82	46	16	8. Let Me Tickle Your Fancy	Motown 6017
5/19/84	19	47 +	● 9. Jermaine Jackson	Arista 8203

DATE CHARTED	PEAK POS	WKS CHRT'D	ARTIST — Album Title	LABEL & NUMBER
			JOE JACKSON English	
4/07/79	**20**	39	● 1. Look Sharp!	A&M 4743
10/27/79	**22**	25	2. I'm The Man	A&M 4794
11/08/80	**41**	16	3. Beat Crazy	A&M 4837
8/01/81	**42**	13	4. Joe Jackson's Jumpin' Jive .... featuring jazz classics of the 1940s	A&M 4871
7/17/82	**4**	57	● 5. **Night And Day** .... "Steppin' Out"(6)	A&M 4906
9/24/83	**64**	13	6. Mike's Murder .... [S]	A&M 4931
4/07/84	**20**	29	7. Body and Soul	A&M 5000
			LaTOYA JACKSON sister of the Jacksons (5th of 9 children)	
10/18/80	**116**	13	1. LaToya Jackson	Polydor 6291
9/12/81	**175**	3	2. My Special Love	Polydor 6328
6/09/84	**149**	6	3. Heart Don't Lie	Private I 39361
			MAHALIA JACKSON gospel singer - died on 1/27/72 (60)	
1/06/62	**130**	2	1. Sweet Little Jesus Boy .... [X]	Columbia 702
			MICHAEL JACKSON member of the Jacksons - born in Gary, Indiana on 8/29/58	
2/19/72	**14**	23	1. Got To Be There .... "Got To Be There"(4)/"Rockin' Robin"(2)	Motown 747
8/26/72	**5**	32	2. **Ben** .... "Ben"(1)	Motown 755
5/05/73	**92**	12	3. Music & Me	Motown 767
2/15/75	**101**	9	4. Forever, Michael	Motown 825
9/27/75	**156**	5	5. The Best Of Michael Jackson .... [G]	Motown 851
9/01/79	**3**	169	▲ 6. Off The Wall .... "Don't Stop 'Til You Get Enough"(1)/"Rock With You"(1)/ "Off The Wall"(10)/"She's Out Of My Life"(10)	Epic 35745
4/25/81	**144**	10	7. One Day In Your Life .... [E-K] recordings from 1973-75 - 4 of 10 tracks with the Jackson 5	Motown 956
12/25/82	**1(37)**	120+	▲ 8. **Thriller** .... the best selling album in history "The Girl Is Mine"(2)/"Billie Jean"(1)/"Beat It"(1)/ "Wanna Be Startin' Somethin'"(5)/"Human Nature"(7)/ "P.Y.T. (Pretty Young Thing)"(10)/"Thriller"(4)	Epic 38112
6/02/84	**46**	15	9. Farewell My Summer Love 1984 .... [E] recordings from 1973	Motown 6101
6/23/84	**168**	7	10. Michael Jackson & The Jackson 5 - 14 Greatest Hits .... [G] picture disc - 9 cuts by Jackson 5; 5 cuts by Michael Jackso	Motown 6099
			MILLIE JACKSON raunchy soul singer from Georgia	
9/16/72	**166**	11	1. Millie Jackson	Spring 5703
9/29/73	**175**	6	2. It Hurts So Good	Spring 5706
11/02/74	**21**	21	● 3. Caught Up	Spring 6703
7/26/75	**112**	16	4. Still Caught Up	Spring 6708
2/19/77	**175**	6	5. Lovingly Yours	Spring 6712
10/22/77	**34**	23	● 6. Feelin' Bitchy	Spring 6715
7/22/78	**55**	14	● 7. Get It Out'cha System	Spring 6719
4/21/79	**144**	6	8. A Moment's Pleasure	Spring 6722
10/20/79	**80**	19	9. Royal Rappin's .... MILLIE JACKSON & ISAAC HAYES	Polydor 6229
12/22/79	**94**	18	10. Live & Uncensored .... [L]	Spring 6725 [2]
6/21/80	**100**	10	11. For Men Only	Spring 6727
2/07/81	**137**	4	12. I Had To Say It	Spring 6730
3/13/82	**113**	13	13. Live And Outrageous (Rated XXX) .... [L]	Spring 6735

DATE CHARTED	PEAK POS	WKS CHRT'D	ARTIST — Album Title	LABEL & NUMBER
			REBBIE JACKSON eldest sister of the Jacksons	
10/27/84	**63**	18	1. Centipede	Columbia 39238
			WALTER JACKSON died on 6/20/83 (45)	
6/24/67	**194**	5	1. Speak Her Name	Okeh 12120
10/09/76	**113**	18	2. Feeling Good	Chi-Sound 656
4/30/77	**141**	5	3. I Want To Come Back As A Song	Chi-Sound 733
			WILLIS JACKSON jazz tenor saxophonist	
7/23/66	**137**	4	1. Together Again! .... [I] WILLIS JACKSON with JACK McDUFF (organ)	Prestige 7364
8/30/75	**182**	3	2. The Way We Were	Atlantic 18145
			JACKSONS brothers Jackie, Tito, Jermaine (1-13 & 19), Marlon, Michael & Randy (14-19)	
			JACKSON 5:	
1/17/70	**5**	32	1. **Diana Ross Presents The Jackson 5** .... "I Want You Back"(1)	Motown 700
6/06/70	**4**	50	2. **ABC** .... "ABC"(1)/"The Love You Save"(1)	Motown 709
9/26/70	**4**	50	3. **Third Album** .... "I'll Be There"(1)/"Mama's Pearl"(2)	Motown 718
5/01/71	**11**	41	4. Maybe Tomorrow .... "Never Can Say Goodbye"(2)	Motown 735
10/09/71	**16**	26	5. Goin' Back To Indiana .... [TV] TV special with guests Bill Cosby & Tom Smothers	Motown 742
1/01/72	**12**	41	6. Jackson 5 Greatest Hits .... [G] "Sugar Daddy"(10)	Motown 741
6/03/72	**7**	33	7. **Lookin' Through The Windows**	Motown 750
4/14/73	**44**	16	8. Skywriter	Motown 761
10/06/73	**100**	29	9. Get It Together .... "Dancing Machine"(2)	Motown 783
10/05/74	**16**	21	10. Dancing Machine	Motown 780
6/14/75	**36**	15	11. Moving Violation	Motown 829
7/17/76	**84**	9	12. Jackson Five Anthology .... [G] also includes Michael's & Jermaine's solo hits	Motown 868 [3]
			JACKSONS:	
12/04/76	**36**	27	● 13. The Jacksons .... "Enjoy Yourself"(6)	Epic 34229
10/29/77	**63**	11	14. Goin' Places	Epic 34835
12/16/78	**11**	41	▲ 15. Destiny .... "Shake Your Body (Down To The Ground)"(7)	Epic 35552
10/18/80	**10**	29	▲ 16. **Triumph**	Epic 36424
11/28/81	**30**	19	17. Jacksons Live .... [L]	Epic 37545 [2]
6/23/84	**168**	7	18. Michael Jackson & The Jackson 5 - 14	
			Greatest Hits .... [G] picture disc - 9 cuts by Jackson 5; 5 cuts by Michael Jackson	Motown 6099
7/21/84	**4**	30	▲ 19. **Victory** .... "State Of Shock"(3)	Epic 38946
			LOU JACOBI also see Comedy section	
11/12/66	**134**	3	1. Al Tijuana and his Jewish Brass .... [N-I] a Herb Alpert spoof	Capitol 2596
			DEBBIE JACOBS	
9/01/79	**153**	8	1. Undercover Lover	MCA 3156
2/09/80	**178**	7	2. High On Your Love	MCA 3202
			JADE WARRIOR British progressive rock trio led by Glyn Havard	
5/06/72	**194**	2	1. Released	Vertigo 1009

DATE CHARTED	PEAK POS	WKS CHRT'D	ARTIST — Album Title	LABEL & NUMBER
			CHRIS JAGGER Mick Jagger's brother	
11/03/73	186	4	1. Chris Jagger	Asylum 5069
			MICK JAGGER lead singer of the Rolling Stones	
3/16/85	14+	4+	1. She's The Boss	Columbia 39940
			JAGGERZ Donnie Iris, leader of Pittsburgh sextet	
4/11/70	62	11	1. We Went To Different Schools Together .... "The Rapper"(2)	Kama Sutra 2017
			JAM British new wave trio: Paul Weller, Bruce Foxton & Rick Buckler	
2/16/80	137	8	1. Setting Sons	Polydor 6249
2/07/81	72	11	2. Sound Affects	Polydor 6315
12/19/81	176	7	3. The Jam .... [M] 5 British hit singles	Polydor 503
3/27/82	82	16	4. The Gift	Polydor 6349
11/27/82	135	14	5. The Bitterest Pill (I ever had to swallow) .... [M] 4 more British hit singles	Polydor 506
1/15/83	131	9	6. Dig The New Breed .... [L] live recordings from 1977-1982	Polydor 6365
4/09/83	171	4	7. Beat Surrender .... [M] their last studio recording - 5 tracks (1982)	Polydor 810751
			AHMAD JAMAL jazz pianist	
9/22/58	3	107	1. **But Not For Me/Ahmad Jamal at the Pershing** .... [I-L]	Argo 628
11/17/58	11	18	2. Ahmad Jamal, volume IV .... [I-L]	Argo 636
2/01/60	32	7	3. Jamal At The Penthouse .... [I]	Argo 646
12/30/67	168	8	4. Cry Young .... vocal chorus by the Howard Roberts Chorale	Cadet 792
3/15/80	173	5	5. Genetic Walk .... [I-K]	20th Century 600
			JAMES GANG Cleveland hard-rock band led by Joe Walsh (1-4, 7-8)	
11/01/69	83	24	1. Yer' Album	BluesWay 6034
7/25/70	20	66	● 2. James Gang Rides Again	ABC 711
4/17/71	27	30	● 3. Thirds	ABC 721
9/11/71	24	16	● 4. James Gang Live In Concert .... [L]	ABC 733
3/18/72	58	19	5. Straight Shooter	ABC 741
10/07/72	72	15	6. Passin' Thru	ABC 760
2/10/73	79	16	7. The Best Of The James Gang featuring Joe Walsh .... [G]	ABC 774
12/08/73	181	5	8. 16 Greatest Hits .... [G]	ABC 801 [2]
1/05/74	122	18	9. Bang	Atco 7037
9/14/74	97	10	10. Miami	Atco 102
5/31/75	109	9	11. Newborn	Atco 112
			BOB JAMES jazz keyboardist/composer/arranger	
11/02/74	85	14	1. One .... [I]	CTI 6043
4/12/75	75	14	2. Two .... [I]	CTI 6057
7/04/76	49	27	3. Three .... [I]	CTI 6063
4/09/77	38	17	4. BJ4 .... [I]	CTI 7074
11/26/77	47	31	5. Heads .... [I]	Tappan Zee 34896
12/16/78	37	29	● 6. Touchdown .... [I]	Tappan Zee 35594
8/25/79	42	14	7. Lucky Seven .... [I]	Tappan Zee 36056
11/03/79	23	33	● 8. One On One .... [I] BOB JAMES & EARL KLUGH	Tappan Zee 36241

DATE CHARTED	PEAK POS	WKS CHRT'D	ARTIST — Album Title	LABEL & NUMBER
7/12/80	47	18	9. "H" .... [I]	Tappan Zee 36422
2/21/81	66	16	10. All Around The Town .... [I-L]	Tapn. Zee 36786[2]
9/12/81	56	14	11. Sign Of The Times	Tappan Zee 37495
7/17/82	72	17	12. Hands Down .... [I]	Tappan Zee 38067
11/06/82	44	29	13. Two Of A Kind .... [I] EARL KLUGH & BOB JAMES	Capitol 12244
6/04/83	77	11	14. The Genie (Themes & Variations From The TV Series "Taxi") .... [I]	Columbia 38678
10/08/83	106	13	15. Foxie .... [I]	Tappan Zee 38801
10/27/84	136	10	16. 12 .... [I]	Tappan Zee 39580

ETTA JAMES
top R&B singer discovered by Johnny Otis in 1955

8/21/61	68	12	1. At Last!	Argo 4003
8/24/63	117	4	2. Etta James Top Ten .... [G]	Argo 4025
2/01/64	96	10	3. Etta James Rocks The House .... [L]	Argo 4032
3/09/68	82	13	4. Tell Mama	Cadet 802
9/15/73	154	9	5. Etta James	Chess 50042

HARRY JAMES
star trumpet player and bandleader - died on 7/5/83 (67)

11/12/55	10	1	1. **Harry James in Hi-Fi** .... featuring vocals by Helen Forrest	Capitol 654

JIMMY JAMES & The Vagabonds
English

11/29/75	139	16	1. You Don't Stand A Chance If You Can't Dance	Pye 12111

RICK JAMES
Buffalo, New York "punk-funk" rocker

6/24/78	13	36	● 1. Come Get It!	Gordy 981
2/10/79	16	27	2. Bustin' Out Of L' Seven	Gordy 984
11/03/79	34	20	3. Fire It Up	Gordy 990
3/22/80	122	8	4. In 'n' Out .... shown as Rick James presents the Stone City Band	Gordy 991
8/23/80	83	10	5. Garden Of Love	Gordy 995
5/02/81	3	74	▲ 6. **Street Songs**	Gordy 1002
6/05/82	13	23	● 7. Throwin' Down	Gordy 6005
8/27/83	16	29	● 8. Cold Blooded	Gordy 6043
8/25/84	41	19	9. Reflections .... [G] includes 3 new recordings	Gordy 6095

SONNY JAMES
real name: Jimmy Loden - Sonny had 16 consecutive #1 country singles from 1967-1971

12/24/66	141	4	1. The Best of Sonny James .... [G] "Young Love"(1-'57)	Capitol 2615
4/12/69	161	3	2. Only The Lonely	Capitol 193
8/23/69	184	3	3. Close-Up .... [R] reissue of "True Love's A Blessing" & "I'll Never Find Another You" albums	Capitol 258 [2]
10/18/69	83	13	4. The Astrodome Presents In Person Sonny James .... [L]	Capitol 320
4/11/70	177	4	5. It's Just A Matter Of Time	Capitol 432
9/19/70	197	2	6. My Love/Don't Keep Me Hangin' On	Capitol 478
11/28/70	187	4	7. #1 .... featuring BMI's "million performance" country songs	Capitol 629
4/24/71	150	5	8. Empty Arms	Capitol 734
9/11/71	197	2	9. The Sensational Sonny James	Capitol 804
9/23/72	190	5	10. When The Snow Is On The Roses	Columbia 31646

DATE CHARTED	PEAK POS	WKS CHRT'D	ARTIST — Album Title	LABEL & NUMBER
			TOMMY JAMES lead singer of The Shondells - born in Dayton, Ohio on 4/29/47	
9/11/71	131	8	1. Christian Of The World .... "Draggin' The Line"(4)	Roulette 3001
3/22/80	134	7	2. Three Times In Love	Millennium 7748
			TOMMY JAMES & THE SHONDELLS Tommy formed the group in 1960 in Niles, Michigan	
7/30/66	46	15	1. Hanky Panky .... "Hanky Panky"(1)	Roulette 25336
4/29/67	74	18	2. I Think We're Alone Now .... "I Think We're Alone Now"(4)/"Mirage"(10)	Roulette 25353
2/24/68	174	5	3. Something Special! The Best Of Tommy James & The Shondells .... [G]	Roulette 25355
7/27/68	193	2	4. Mony Mony .... "Mony Mony"(3)	Roulette 42012
2/01/69	8	35	5. **Crimson & Clover** .... "Crimson & Clover"(1)/"Crystal Blue Persuasion"(2)	Roulette 42023
10/25/69	141	6	6. Cellophane Symphony .... "Sweet Cherry Wine"(7)	Roulette 42030
12/13/69	21	41	7. The Best Of Tommy James & The Shondells .... [G]	Roulette 42040
4/11/70	91	9	8. Travelin'	Roulette 42044
			JAN & DEAN Jan Berry & Dean Torrence - Jan was partially paralyzed in a car accident, April, 1966	
6/22/63	71	10	1. Jan & Dean take Linda Surfin'	Liberty 7294
8/10/63	32	21	2. Surf City And Other Swingin' Cities .... "Surf City"(1)	Liberty 7314
1/18/64	22	14	3. Drag City .... "Drag City"(10)	Liberty 7339
5/23/64	80	21	4. Dead Man's Curve/The New Girl In School ... "Dead Man's Curve"(8)	Liberty 7361
10/10/64	40	20	5. The Little Old Lady From Pasadena .... "The Little Old Lady (From Pasadena)"(3)	Liberty 7377
10/17/64	66	19	6. Ride The Wild Surf .... [S]	Liberty 7368
2/27/65	33	16	7. Command Performance/Live In Person .... [L]	Liberty 7403
10/02/65	107	6	8. Jan & Dean Golden Hits, Volume 2 .... [G]	Liberty 7417
1/15/66	145	3	9. Folk 'n Roll	Liberty 7431
5/14/66	127	5	10. Filet Of Soul .... [L]	Liberty 7441
			CHAS JANKEL member of Ian Dury & The Blockheads	
3/06/82	126	14	1. Questionnaire	A&M 4885
			HORST JANKOWSKI German pianist/arranger	
5/22/65	18	31	1. The Genius Of Jankowski! .... [I] "A Walk In The Black Forest"	Mercury 60993
12/04/65	65	13	2. More Genius Of Jankowski .... [I]	Mercury 61054
12/03/66	107	2	3. So What's New? .... [I]	Mercury 61093
			JEAN-MICHEL JARRE French electronic keyboard/synthesizer soloist	
10/15/77	78	19	1. Oxygene .... [I]	Polydor 6112
2/03/79	126	8	2. Equinoxe .... [I]	Polydor 6175
7/11/81	98	12	3. Magnetic Fields .... [I]	Polydor 6325
			AL JARREAU Grammy winning jazz vocalist from Milwaukee	
8/28/76	132	11	1. Glow	Reprise 2248
6/25/77	49	15	2. Look To The Rainbow/Live In Europe........ [L]	Warner 3052 [2]
10/14/78	78	28	3. All Fly Home	Warner 3229
6/21/80	27	35	● 4. This Time	Warner 3434

182

DATE CHARTED	PEAK POS	WKS CHRT'D	ARTIST — Album Title	LABEL & NUMBER
8/22/81	9	103	▲ 5. **Breakin' Away**	Warner 3576
4/16/83	13	43	● 6. Jarreau	Warner 23801
11/24/84	49	20+	7. High Crime	Warner 25106

KEITH JARRETT
jazz pianist/composer

DATE CHARTED	PEAK POS	WKS CHRT'D	ARTIST — Album Title	LABEL & NUMBER
8/02/75	160	5	1. El Juicio (The Judgement) .... [I]	Atlantic 1673
3/13/76	195	1	2. In The Light .... [I]	ECM 1033 [2]
7/10/76	179	3	3. Arbour Zena .... [I]	ECM 1070
7/17/76	184	2	4. Mysteries .... [I]	ABC/Impulse 9315
2/12/77	174	4	5. Shades .... [I]	ABC/Impulse 9322
8/06/77	141	12	6. Staircase/Hourglass/Sundial/Sand .... [I]	ECM 1090 [2]
10/01/77	117	6	7. Byablue .... [I]	ABC/Impulse 9331
9/02/78	174	2	8. My Song .... [I]	ECM 1115
			with Jan Garbarek, Palle Danielsson & Jon Christensen	

JASON & THE SCORCHERS
Jason Ringenberg, lead singer

DATE CHARTED	PEAK POS	WKS CHRT'D	ARTIST — Album Title	LABEL & NUMBER
3/10/84	116	14+	1. Fervor .... [M]	EMI America 19008
3/30/85	128+	2+	2. Lost & Found	EMI America 17153

JAY & THE AMERICANS
Jay Black, lead singer of Brooklyn group

DATE CHARTED	PEAK POS	WKS CHRT'D	ARTIST — Album Title	LABEL & NUMBER
12/12/64	131	4	1. Come A Little Bit Closer .... "Come A Little Bit Closer"(3)	United Art. 6407
6/12/65	113	17	2. Blockbusters .... "Cara, Mia"(4)	United Art. 6417
11/20/65	21	20	3. Jay & The Americans Greatest Hits! .... [G]	United Art. 6453
3/19/66	141	4	4. Sunday And Me	United Art. 6474
3/15/69	51	21	5. Sands Of Time .... "This Magic Moment"(6)	United Art. 6671
2/28/70	105	11	6. Wax Museum	United Art. 6719

JAY & THE TECHNIQUES
Jay Proctor, lead singer of Allentown, Pennsylvania group

DATE CHARTED	PEAK POS	WKS CHRT'D	ARTIST — Album Title	LABEL & NUMBER
10/28/67	129	13	1. Apples, Peaches, Pumpkin Pie .... "Apples, Peaches, Pumpkin Pie"(6)	Smash 67095

JERRY JAYE
country/rock singer from Manilla, Arkansas

DATE CHARTED	PEAK POS	WKS CHRT'D	ARTIST — Album Title	LABEL & NUMBER
7/29/67	195	2	1. My Girl Josephine	Hi 32038

JAZZ CRUSADERS - see CRUSADERS

J.B.'s
James Brown's super-funk backup band - also see Fred Wesley

DATE CHARTED	PEAK POS	WKS CHRT'D	ARTIST — Album Title	LABEL & NUMBER
7/28/73	77	13	1. Doing It To Death	People 5603
6/29/74	197	3	2. Damn Right I Am Somebody .... FRED WESLEY & the J.B.'s	People 6602

JEFFERSON AIRPLANE
formed in San Francisco by Marty Balin & Paul Kantner - featuring lead singer Grace Slick - evolved into Jefferson Starship - also see Paul Kantner

DATE CHARTED	PEAK POS	WKS CHRT'D	ARTIST — Album Title	LABEL & NUMBER
9/17/66	128	11	1. Jefferson Airplane Takes Off	RCA 3584
3/25/67	3	56	● 2. **Surrealistic Pillow** .... "Somebody To Love"(5)/"White Rabbit"(8)	RCA 3766
12/23/67	17	23	3. After Bathing At Baxter's	RCA 1511
9/07/68	6	25	● 4. **Crown Of Creation**	RCA 4058
3/01/69	17	20	5. Bless It's Pointed Little Head .... [L]	RCA 4133
11/22/69	13	44	● 6. Volunteers	RCA 4238
12/12/70	12	40	● 7. The Worst Of Jefferson Airplane .... [G]	RCA 4459
9/18/71	11	21	● 8. Bark	Grunt 1001
8/19/72	20	21	● 9. Long John Silver	Grunt 1007
4/14/73	52	16	10. Thirty Seconds Over Winterland .... [L]	Grunt 0147

DATE CHARTED	PEAK POS	WKS CHRT'D	ARTIST — Album Title	LABEL & NUMBER
5/04/74	110	8	11. Early Flight .... [K] _includes previously unreleased material (1965-1970)_	Grunt 0437
			JEFFERSON STARSHIP:	
10/26/74	11	37	● 12. Dragon Fly	Grunt 0717
7/19/75	1(4)	87	● 13. **Red Octopus** .... _"Miracles"(3)_	Grunt 0999
7/10/76	3	38	▲ 14. **Spitfire**	Grunt 1557
1/29/77	37	15	● 15. Flight Log (1966-1976) .... [K] _anthology of Airplane, Starship, Hot Tuna, Slick and Kantner solo releases_	Grunt 1255 [2]
3/18/78	5	34	▲ 16. **Earth** .... _"Count On Me"(8)_	Grunt 2515
2/17/79	20	14	● 17. Gold .... [G]	Grunt 3247
12/01/79	10	28	● 18. **Freedom At Point Zero**	Grunt 3452
4/18/81	26	33	● 19. Modern Times	Grunt 3848
10/30/82	26	31	20. Winds Of Change	Grunt 4372
6/16/84	28	23	● 21. Nuclear Furniture	Grunt 4921

GARLAND JEFFREYS
New York City R&B/rock/reggae singer

3/26/77	140	10	1. Ghost Writer	A&M 4629
4/15/78	99	10	2. One-Eyed Jack	A&M 4681
9/22/79	151	5	3. American Boy & Girl	A&M 4778
3/21/81	59	18	4. Escape Artist	Epic 36983
10/31/81	163	4	5. Rock & Roll Adult	Epic 37436
2/26/83	176	4	6. Guts For Love	Epic 38190

GORDON JENKINS & His Orchestra
composer/conductor - died on 5/1/84 (73)

11/24/56	13	4	1. Gordon Jenkins complete Manhattan Tower .. _a musical narrative originally composed by Jenkins in 1945_	Capitol 766

WAYLON JENNINGS
outlaw country singer - bass player with Buddy Holly 1958-59

10/04/69	169	4	1. Country-Folk .... _WAYLON JENNINGS & THE KIMBERLYS_	RCA 4180
5/16/70	192	2	2. Waylon	RCA 4260
8/11/73	185	5	3. Honky Tonk Heroes	RCA 0240
10/05/74	105	17	4. The Ramblin' Man	RCA 0734
7/05/75	49	21	● 5. Dreaming My Dreams	RCA 1062
4/17/76	189	4	6. Mackintosh & T.J. .... [S] _includes performances by Willie Nelson and The Waylors_	RCA 1520
7/17/76	34	35	● 7. Are You Ready For The Country	RCA 1816
12/18/76	46	17	● 8. Waylon Live .... [L] _recorded live in Dallas & Austin, Texas (1974)_	RCA 1108
5/21/77	15	33	▲ 9. Ol' Waylon	RCA 2317
2/04/78	12	29	▲ 10. Waylon & Willie .... _WAYLON JENNINGS & WILLIE NELSON_	RCA 2686
10/21/78	48	24	● 11. I've Always Been Crazy	RCA 2979
5/05/79	28	115	▲ 12. Greatest Hits .... [G]	RCA 3378
11/10/79	49	28	● 13. What Goes Around Comes Around	RCA 3493
6/07/80	36	43	● 14. Music Man	RCA 3602
3/21/81	43	19	● 15. Leather and Lace .... _WAYLON & JESSI (wife Jessi Colter)_	RCA 3931
3/06/82	39	23	16. Black On Black	RCA 4247
10/30/82	57	22	● 17. WWII .... _WAYLON & WILLIE_	RCA 4455
4/23/83	60	16	18. Take It To The Limit .... _WILLIE NELSON with WAYLON JENNINGS_	Columbia 38562
4/30/83	109	11	19. It's Only Rock & Roll	RCA 4673

DATE CHARTED	PEAK POS	WKS CHRT'D	ARTIST — Album Title	LABEL & NUMBER
			HENRY JEROME & His Orchestra bandleader of the '40s & '50s	
10/09/61	42	2	1. Brazen Brass Goes Hollywood .... [I]	Decca 4085
			JETHRO TULL English progressive rock group led by Ian Anderson	
3/01/69	62	17	1. This Was	Reprise 6336
10/11/69	20	40	● 2. Stand Up	Reprise 6360
5/09/70	11	41	● 3. Benefit	Reprise 6400
5/15/71	7	76	● 4. **Aqualung**	Reprise 2035
5/20/72	1(2)	46	● 5. **Thick As A Brick**	Reprise 2072
11/11/72	3	31	● 6. **Living In The Past** .... [K] primarily features unreleased material (1968-1971) - side 3 recorded live in Carnegie Hall	Chrysalis 2106 [2]
7/21/73	1(1)	32	● 7. **A Passion Play**	Chrysalis 1040
10/26/74	2(3)	31	● 8. **War Child**	Chrysalis 1067
9/27/75	7	14	● 9. **Minstrel In The Gallery**	Chrysalis 1082
1/24/76	13	23	▲ 10. **M.U. - The Best Of Jethro Tull** .... [G]	Chrysalis 1078
5/29/76	14	21	11. Too Old To Rock 'N' Roll: Too Young To Die!	Chrysalis 1111
3/05/77	8	22	● 12. **Songs From The Wood**	Chrysalis 1132
12/03/77	94	6	13. Repeat-The Best Of Jethro Tull, Vol. II .... [G]	Chrysalis 1135
4/29/78	19	17	● 14. Heavy Horses	Chrysalis 1175
10/21/78	21	15	● 15. Jethro Tull Live - Bursting Out .... [L]	Chrysalis 1201 [2]
10/06/79	22	17	● 16. Stormwatch	Chrysalis 1238
9/13/80	30	12	17. "A"	Chrysalis 1301
5/01/82	19	17	18. The Broadsword And The Beast	Chrysalis 1380
10/27/84	76	12	19. Under Wraps	Chrysalis 41461
			JOAN JETT & THE BLACKHEARTS Joan was former leader of Los Angeles girl band The Runaways	
3/14/81	51	21	1. Bad Reputation	Boardwalk 37065
12/19/81	2(3)	59	▲ 2. **I Love Rock-n-Roll** .... "I Love Rock 'N Roll"(1)/"Crimson And Clover"(7)	Boardwalk 33243
7/16/83	20	20	● 3. **Album**	Blackheart 5437
10/27/84	67	21	4. Glorious Results Of A Misspent Youth	MCA 5476
			JIGSAW Australian quartet	
12/13/75	55	19	1. Sky High .... "Sky High"(3)	Chelsea 509
			JOSE JIMENEZ - see BILL DANA	
			JO JO GUNNE Los Angeles quartet formed by Jay Ferguson (Spirit)	
2/26/72	57	22	1. Jo Jo Gunne	Asylum 5053
3/17/73	75	17	2. Bite Down Hard	Asylum 5065
12/22/73	169	7	3. Jumpin' The Gunne	Asylum 5071
12/28/74	198	1	4. So...Where's The Show?	Asylum 1022
			DAMITA JO Damita Jo DeBlanc - former lead singer of Steve Gibson's Red Caps	
3/27/65	121	4	1. This Is Damita Jo	Epic 26131
5/06/67	169	2	2. If You Go Away	Epic 26244
			ANTONIO CARLOS JOBIM Brazilian guitarist/pianist/vocalist - also see Astrud Gilberto	
9/11/65	57	14	1. The Wonderful World Of Antonio Carlos Jobim	Warner 1611
4/15/67	19	28	2. Francis Albert Sinatra & Antonio Carlos Jobim	Reprise 1021

DATE CHARTED	PEAK POS	WKS CHRT'D	ARTIST — Album Title	LABEL & NUMBER
1/13/68	**114**	11	3. Wave .... [I]	A&M 3002
1/09/71	**196**	2	4. Stone Flower .... [I]	CTI 6002

JoBOXERS
Dig Wayne, leader of British quintet

10/15/83	**70**	15	1. Like Gangbusters	RCA 4847

JOE & EDDIE
Joe Gilbert & Eddie Brown - black folk duo

1/18/64	**119**	7	1. There's A Meetin' Here Tonite .... [L]	Crescendo 86
2/15/64	**140**	4	2. Coast To Coast	Crescendo 96

BILLY JOEL
born in Long Island, New York on 5/9/49

1/05/74	**27**	40	● 1. Piano Man	Columbia 32544
11/02/74	**35**	18	● 2. Streetlife Serenade	Columbia 33146
6/05/76	**122**	12	● 3. Turnstiles	Columbia 33848
10/08/77	**2(6)**	137	▲ 4. **The Stranger** .... "Just The Way You Are"(3)	Columbia 34987
10/28/78	**1(8)**	76	▲ 5. **52nd Street** .... "My Life"(3)	Columbia 35609
3/22/80	**1(6)**	73	▲ 6. **Glass Houses** .... "You May Be Right"(7)/"It's Still Rock And Roll To Me"(1)	Columbia 36384
10/03/81	**8**	27	▲ 7. **Songs In The Attic** .... [L] 1980 concert tour recordings of pre-"Stranger" songs	Columbia 37461
10/16/82	**7**	35	▲ 8. **The Nylon Curtain**	Columbia 38200
8/20/83	**4**	86+	▲ 9. **An Innocent Man** .... "Tell Her About It"(1)/"Uptown Girl"(3)/"An Innocent Man"(10)	Columbia 38837
1/14/84	**158**	8	10. Cold Spring Harbor .... [R-E] remix/reissue of Joel's first album (1971)	Columbia 38984

DAVID JOHANSEN
lead singer of punk rock group: the New York Dolls

9/29/79	**177**	4	1. In Style	Blue Sky 36082
7/11/81	**160**	3	2. Here Comes The Night	Blue Sky 36589
7/03/82	**148**	15	3. Live It Up .... [L]	Blue Sky 38004

ELTON JOHN
born Reginald Kenneth Dwight on 3/25/47 in Pinner, England

10/03/70	**4**	51	● 1. **Elton John** .... "Your Song"(8)	Uni 73090
1/23/71	**5**	37	● 2. **Tumbleweed Connection**	Uni 73096
3/27/71	**36**	19	● 3. **"Friends"** .... [S]	Paramount 6004
5/29/71	**11**	22	4. 11-17-70 .... [L] title is date of a live New York radio concert broadcast	Uni 93105
11/27/71	**8**	51	● 5. **Madman Across The Water**	Uni 93120
6/17/72	**1(5)**	61	● 6. **Honky Chateau** .... "Rocket Man"(6)/"Honky Cat"(8)	Uni 93135
2/10/73	**1(2)**	89	● 7. **Don't Shoot Me I'm Only The Piano Player** .... "Crocodile Rock"(1)/"Daniel"(2)	MCA 2100
10/20/73	**1(8)**	91	● 8. **Goodbye Yellow Brick Road** .... "Goodbye Yellow Brick Road"(2)/"Bennie And The Jets"(1)	MCA 10003 [2]
7/06/74	**1(4)**	54	● 9. **Caribou** .... "Don't Let The Sun Go Down On Me"(2)/"The Bitch Is Back"(4)	MCA 2116
11/23/74	**1(10)**	104	● 10. **Elton John - Greatest Hits** .... [G]	MCA 2128
2/01/75	**6**	18	11. **Empty Sky** .... [E-R] Elton's first album originally released in 1969	MCA 2130
6/07/75	**1(7)**	43	● 12. **Captain Fantastic And The Brown Dirt Cowboy** .... "Someone Saved My Life Tonight"(4)	MCA 2142
11/08/75	**1(3)**	26	● 13. **Rock Of The Westies** .... "Island Girl"(1)	MCA 2163
5/22/76	**4**	20	● 14. **Here And There** .... [L] side 1: live in London; side 2: live in New York (both 1974)	MCA 2197

DATE CHARTED	PEAK POS	WKS CHRT'D	ARTIST — Album Title	LABEL & NUMBER
11/13/76	3	22	▲ 15. **Blue Moves** .... "Sorry Seems To Be The Hardest Word"(6)	MCA/Rck.11004[2]
10/22/77	21	20	▲ 16. Elton John's Greatest Hits, Volume II .... [G] "Lucy In The Sky With Diamonds"(1)/ "Philadelphia Freedom"(1)/"Don't Go Breaking My Heart"(1)	MCA 3027
11/11/78	15	18	▲ 17. A Single Man	MCA 3065
6/30/79	51	18	18. The Thom Bell Sessions .... [M] 3 songs recorded in 1977 "Mama Can't Buy You Love"(9)	MCA 13921
10/27/79	35	10	19. Victim Of Love	MCA 5104
5/31/80	13	21	● 20. 21 At 33 .... "Little Jeannie"(3)	MCA 5121
6/06/81	21	19	21. The Fox	Geffen 2002
5/08/82	17	33	● 22. Jump Up!	Geffen 2013
6/11/83	25	54	● 23. Too Low For Zero .... "I Guess That's Why They Call It The Blues"(4)	Geffen 4006
7/21/84	20	34	● 24. Breaking Hearts .... "Sad Songs (Say So Much)"(5)	Geffen 24031
			ROBERT JOHN real name: Robert Pedrick, Jr.	
8/25/79	68	14	1. Robert John .... "Sad Eyes"(1)	EMI America 17007
			JOHNNY & THE DISTRACTIONS Johnny Koonce, leader of Portland rock quintet	
2/20/82	152	9	1. Let It Rock	A&M 4884
			JOHNNY & THE HURRICANES Toledo, Ohio rock instrumental quintet, led by Johnny Paris	
4/18/60	34	3	1. Stormsville .... [I]	Warwick 2010
			SAMMY JOHNS	
3/29/75	148	12	1. Sammy Johns .... "Chevy Van"(5)	GRC 5003
			HOWARD JOHNSON former lead singer of Niteflyte	
9/11/82	122	9	1. Keepin' Love New	A&M 4895
			JESSE JOHNSON'S REVUE former guitarist/vocalist with The Time	
3/16/85	45+	4+	1. Jesse Johnson's Revue	A&M 5024
			MICHAEL JOHNSON	
7/15/78	81	17	1. The Michael Johnson Album	EMI America 17002
9/15/79	157	12	2. Dialogue	EMI America 17010
			ROBERT JOHNSON Memphis session guitarist	
1/13/79	174	8	1. Close Personal Friend	Infinity 9000
			TOM JOHNSTON lead singer of the Doobie Brothers (1971-78)	
10/20/79	100	13	1. Everthing You've Heard Is True	Warner 3304
5/16/81	158	7	2. Still Feels Good	Warner 3527
			FRANCE JOLI 16-year-old French Canadian singer	
9/08/79	26	17	1. France Joli	Prelude 12170
6/28/80	175	3	2. Tonight	Prelude 12179
			PETE JOLLY Trio and Friends jazz pianist	
6/08/63	139	2	1. Little Bird .... [I]	Ava 22

DATE CHARTED	PEAK POS	WKS CHRT'D	ARTIST — Album Title	LABEL & NUMBER
			AL JOLSON one of America's all-time great entertainers - died 10/23/50 (64)	
9/22/62	**40**	42	1. The Best Of Jolson .... [G] Al's recordings for the soundtracks "The Jolson Story" & "Jolson Sings Again"	Decca 169 [2]
			JON & VANGELIS Jon Anderson (British) of Yes & Greek keyboardist Vangelis	
5/31/80	**125**	15	1. Short Stories	Polydor 6272
8/08/81	**64**	34	2. The Friends Of Mr. Cairo	Polydor 6326
8/13/83	**148**	7	3. Private Collection	Polydor 813174
			JONES GIRLS sisters Shirley, Brenda & Valorie	
6/09/79	**50**	16	1. The Jones Girls	Phil. Int. 35757
10/18/80	**96**	24	2. At Peace With Woman	Phil. Int. 36767
12/05/81	**155**	15	3. Get As Much Love As You Can	Phil. Int. 37627
			DAVID JONES English - member of The Monkees	
5/27/67	**185**	6	1. David Jones .... recorded prior to Davy's Monkee career	Colpix 493
			GEORGE JONES the reigning monarch of Country male vocalists	
3/20/65	**141**	4	1. George Jones & Gene Pitney	Musicor 3044
6/26/65	**149**	2	2. The Race Is On	United Art. 3422
8/02/69	**185**	5	3. I'll Share My World With You	Musicor 3177
11/13/71	**169**	6	4. We Go Together .... TAMMY WYNETTE & GEORGE JONES	Epic 30802
6/13/81	**132**	14	▲ 5. I Am What I Am	Epic 36586
11/28/81	**115**	21	6. Still The Same Ole Me	Epic 37106
9/25/82	**123**	12	7. A Taste Of Yesterday's Wine .... MERLE HAGGARD & GEORGE JONES	Epic 38203
			GRACE JONES Jamaican-born rock/disco singer	
10/22/77	**109**	20	1. Portfolio	Island 9470
8/05/78	**97**	8	2. Fame	Island 9525
9/01/79	**156**	7	3. Muse	Island 9538
6/21/80	**132**	10	4. Warm Leatherette	Island 9592
5/23/81	**32**	20	5. Nightclubbing	Island 9624
12/11/82	**86**	20	6. Living My Life	Island 90018
			HOWARD JONES British synth wizard	
3/24/84	**59**	31	1. Human's Lib	Elektra 60346
			JACK JONES son of actor Allan Jones & actress Irene Hervey	
6/29/63	**98**	25	1. Call Me Irresponsible	Kapp 3328
12/28/63	**18**	53	2. Wives And Lovers	Kapp 3352
6/20/64	**43**	19	3. Bewitched	Kapp 3365
8/29/64	**62**	23	4. Where Love Has Gone	Kapp 3396
1/09/65	**11**	25	5. Dear Heart	Kapp 3415
5/08/65	**29**	22	6. My Kind Of Town	Kapp 3433
9/18/65	**86**	13	7. There's Love & There's Love & There's Love	Kapp 3435
3/26/66	**147**	2	8. For The "In" Crowd	Kapp 3465
7/16/66	**9**	64	9. **The Impossible Dream**	Kapp 3486
11/26/66	**75**	12	10. Jack Jones Sings	Kapp 3500
3/25/67	**23**	25	11. Lady	Kapp 3511
10/14/67	**148**	7	12. Our Song	Kapp 3531
12/16/67	**146**	7	13. Without Her	RCA 3911

DATE CHARTED	PEAK POS	WKS CHRT'D	ARTIST — Album Title	LABEL & NUMBER
2/24/68	**167**	6	14. What The World Needs Now Is Love! .... [K]	Kapp 3551
4/27/68	**198**	3	15. If You Ever Leave Me	RCA 3969
9/21/68	**195**	3	16. Where Is Love?	RCA 4048
8/16/69	**183**	4	17. A Time For Us	RCA 4209
			JONAH JONES jazz trumpet player	
3/10/58	**7**	17	1. **Muted Jazz** .... [I]	Capitol 839
4/28/58	**7**	19	2. **Swingin' On Broadway** .... [I]	Capitol 963
9/08/58	**14**	5	3. Jumpin' With Jonah .... [I]	Capitol 1039
			QUINCY JONES jazz musician - arranger/producer/writer - president of Qwest Records - produced Michael Jackson's "Thriller" album	
12/29/62	**112**	8	1. Big Band Bossa Nova .... [I]	Mercury 60751
11/22/69	**56**	39	2. Walking In Space .... [I]	A&M 3023
9/05/70	**63**	16	3. Gula Matari .... [I]	A&M 3030
10/16/71	**56**	33	4. Smackwater Jack .... [I]	A&M 3037
3/04/72	**173**	9	5. Ndeda .... [I-K]	Mercury 623 [2]
6/02/73	**94**	24	6. You've Got It Bad Girl	A&M 3041
5/25/74	**6**	43	● 7. **Body Heat**	A&M 3617
8/23/75	**16**	30	8. Mellow Madness .... this album introduces the Brothers Johnson	A&M 4526
10/02/76	**43**	15	9. I Heard That!! .... [K]	A&M 3705 [2]
2/19/77	**21**	14	● 10. Roots .... [TV]	A&M 4626
6/24/78	**15**	20	▲ 11. Sounds...And Stuff Like That!!	A&M 4685
4/04/81	**10**	80	▲ 12. **The Dude** .... featuring James Ingram's vocals on "Just Once" & "One Hundred Ways"	A&M 3721
7/17/82	**122**	17	13. The Best .... [G]	A&M 3200
			RICKIE LEE JONES pop jazz-styled vocalist - born on 11/8/54 in Chicago, Illinois	
4/07/79	**3**	36	▲ 1. **Rickie Lee Jones** .... "Chuck E.'s In Love"(4)	Warner 3296
8/08/81	**5**	29	● 2. **Pirates**	Warner 3432
7/02/83	**39**	16	3. Girl At Her Volcano .... [M] 10" album - 2 of the 7 tracks are live performances	Warner 23805
10/13/84	**44**	21	4. The Magazine	Warner 25117
			SPIKE JONES "King of Corn" bandleader - died on 5/1/64 (52)	
11/23/63	**113**	4	1. Washington Square .... [I]	Liberty 3338
			TOM JONES Welsh - born Thomas Jones Woodward on 6/7/42	
7/03/65	**54**	42	1. It's Not Unusual .... "It's Not Unusual"(10)	Parrot 71004
9/18/65	**114**	5	2. What's New Pussycat? .... "What's New Pussycat?"(3)	Parrot 71006
3/04/67	**65**	45	● 3. Green, Green Grass Of Home	Parrot 71009
6/15/68	**14**	82	● 4. The Tom Jones Fever Zone	Parrot 71019
2/01/69	**5**	54	● 5. **Help Yourself**	Parrot 71025
3/15/69	**13**	58	● 6. Tom Jones Live! .... [L] originally recorded & released in 1967	Parrot 71014
6/14/69	**4**	43	● 7. **This Is Tom Jones**	Parrot 71028
11/15/69	**3**	51	● 8. **Tom Jones Live In Las Vegas** .... [L]	Parrot 71031
5/09/70	**6**	26	● 9. Tom .... "Without Love (There Is Nothing)"(5)	Parrot 71037
11/14/70	**23**	40	● 10. I (Who Have Nothing)	Parrot 71039
5/22/71	**17**	20	● 11. She's A Lady .... "She's A Lady"(2)	Parrot 71046
11/06/71	**43**	14	● 12. Tom Jones Live At Caesars Palace .... [L]	Parrot 71049 [2]
6/17/72	**64**	20	13. Close Up	Parrot 71055

DATE CHARTED	PEAK POS	WKS CHRT'D	ARTIST — Album Title	LABEL & NUMBER
6/16/73	93	10	14. The Body And Soul of Tom Jones	Parrot 71060
1/05/74	185	4	15. Tom Jones' Greatest Hits .... [G]	Parrot 71062
			"I'll Never Fall In Love Again"(6-'69)	
3/05/77	76	16	16. Say You'll Stay Until Tomorrow	Epic 34468
3/05/77	191	3	17. Tom Jones Greatest Hits .... [G]	London 50002
5/23/81	179	3	18. Darlin'	Mercury 4010

JONZUN CREW
Michael Jonzun, leader of electronic instrumentation group

5/14/83	66	20	1. Lost In Space	Tommy Boy 1001

JANIS JOPLIN
"Pearl", lead singer of Big Brother & The Holding Company, died on 10/4/70 (27)

10/11/69	5	28	● 1. **I Got Dem Ol' Kozmic Blues Again Mama!**	Columbia 9913
1/30/71	1(9)	42	● 2. **Pearl**	Columbia 30322
			"Me And Bobby McGee"(1)	
5/13/72	4	27	● 3. **Joplin In Concert** .... [L]	Columbia 31160 [2]
			side 1: with Big Brother & The Holding Co.	
			side 2: with Full Tilt Boogie Band	
7/14/73	37	22	● 4. Janis Joplin's Greatest Hits .... [G]	Columbia 32168
5/17/75	54	9	5. Janis .... [S]	Columbia 33345 [2]
			soundtrack includes her early recordings from 1963-1965	
2/13/82	104	11	6. Farewell Song .... [K]	Columbia 37569
			recordings from 1967-1970	

SCOTT JOPLIN -
see **MARVIN HAMLISCH/JOSHUA RIFKIN/NEW ENGLAND RAGTIME/SOUNDTRACK "The Sting"/Original Cast "Treemonisha"**

JERRY JORDAN
country/religious humorist

5/31/75	79	12	1. Phone Call From God .... [C]	MCA 473

LONNIE JORDAN
keyboardist of War

2/25/78	158	5	1. Different Moods Of Me	MCA 2329

MARGIE JOSEPH

2/06/71	67	14	1. Margie Joseph Makes A New Impression	Volt 6012
8/17/74	165	3	2. Sweet Surrender	Atlantic 7277

JOURNEY
San Francisco rock group led by Steve Perry (vocals) & Neal Schon (guitar)

5/03/75	138	9	1. Journey	Columbia 33388
2/14/76	100	15	2. Look Into The Future	Columbia 33904
2/19/77	85	10	3. Next	Columbia 34311
2/11/78	21	123	▲ 4. Infinity	Columbia 34912
4/14/79	20	96	▲ 5. Evolution	Columbia 35797
1/05/80	152	8	6. In The Beginning .... [K]	Columbia 36324 [2]
			recordings from their first 3 albums above	
3/22/80	8	57	▲ 7. **Departure**	Columbia 36339
2/21/81	9	69	▲ 8. **Captured** .... [L]	Columbia 37016 [2]
8/08/81	1(1)	146	▲ 9. **Escape**	Columbia 37408
			"Who's Crying Now"(4)/"Don't Stop Believin'"(9)/ "Open Arms"(2)	
2/19/83	2(9)	85	▲ 10. **Frontiers**	Columbia 38504
			"Separate Ways (Worlds Apart)"(8)	

JOY OF COOKING
Berkeley, California rock quintet led by Terry Garthwaite

3/06/71	100	17	1. Joy Of Cooking	Capitol 661
10/09/71	136	7	2. Closer To The Ground	Capitol 828
6/10/72	174	6	3. Castles	Capitol 11050

DATE CHARTED	PEAK POS	WKS CHRT'D	ARTIST — Album Title	LABEL & NUMBER
			JUDAS PRIEST British heavy-metal band - Rob Halford. lead singer	
4/08/78	173	3	1. Stained Glass	Columbia 35296
3/31/79	128	7	2. Hell Bent For Leather	Columbia 35706
10/06/79	70	11	3. Unleashed In The East (Live In Japan) .... [L]	Columbia 36179
5/31/80	34	18	● 4. British Steel	Columbia 36443
4/04/81	39	25	5. Point Of Entry	Columbia 37052
7/24/82	17	53	▲ 6. Screaming For Vengeance	Columbia 38160
2/04/84	18	37	● 7. Defenders Of The Faith	Columbia 39219
			JUDDS country duo: Naomi & daughter Wynonna Judd	
12/01/84	71	19+	1. Why Not Me	RCA 5319
12/08/84	153	15	2. The Judds .... [M] their first album	RCA 8515
			JULUKA South African sextet led by Johnny Clegg & Sipho Mchunu	
8/13/83	186	5	1. Scatterlings	Warner 23898
			JUNIOR British - Junior Giscombe	
5/08/82	71	16	1. "Ji"	Mercury 4043
7/23/83	177	6	2. Inside Lookin' Out	Mercury 812325
			BILL JUSTIS Sun Records' musical director in the '50s - died on 7/15/82 (55)	
11/24/62	94	8	1. Bill Justis plays 12 big instrumental hits (Alley Cat/Green Onions) .... [I]	Smash 67021
2/23/63	89	6	2. Bill Justis plays 12 more big instrumental hits (Telstar/The Lonely Bull) .... [I]	Smash 67030
			PATRICK JUVET Swiss-born disco artist	
7/01/78	125	14	1. Got A Feeling	Casablanca 7101
			BERT KAEMPFERT & His Orchestra German - produced 1st Beatles' recording - died on 6/21/80 (56)	
12/31/60	1(5)	40	● 1. **Wonderland By Night** .... [I] "Wonderland By Night"(1)	Decca 74101
11/18/61	92	6	2. Dancing In Wonderland .... [I]	Decca 74161
4/21/62	82	13	3. Afrikaan Beat and other favorites .... [I]	Decca 74273
9/22/62	14	17	4. That Happy Feeling .... [I]	Decca 74305
7/06/63	87	12	5. Living It Up! .... [I]	Decca 74374
11/30/63	79	6	6. Lights Out, Sweet Dreams .... [I]	Decca 74265
1/23/65	5	55	● 7. **Blue Midnight** .... [I]	Decca 74569
7/10/65	42	22	8. Three O'Clock In The Morning .... [I]	Decca 74670
9/04/65	27	23	9. The Magic Music Of Far Away Places .... [I]	Decca 74616
3/12/66	46	28	10. Bye Bye Blues .... [I]	Decca 74693
7/09/66	39	21	11. Strangers In The Night .... [I]	Decca 74795
10/08/66	30	40	● 12. Bert Kaempfert's Greatest Hits .... [G-I]	Decca 74810
5/13/67	122	7	13. Hold Me .... [I]	Decca 74860
10/07/67	136	7	14. The World We Knew .... [I]	Decca 74925
11/02/68	186	2	15. My Way Of Life .... [I]	Decca 75059
3/29/69	194	5	16. Warm and Wonderful .... [I]	Decca 75089
11/01/69	153	10	17. Traces Of Love .... [I]	Decca 75140
3/28/70	87	7	18. The Kaempfert Touch .... [I]	Decca 75175

DATE CHARTED	PEAK POS	WKS CHRT'D	ARTIST — Album Title	LABEL & NUMBER
2/13/71	140	6	19. Orange Colored Sky .... [I]	Decca 75256
9/25/71	188	2	20. Bert Kaempfert Now! .... [I]	Decca 75305

KAJAGOOGOO
English quintet led by Limahl

6/11/83	38	20	1. White Feathers .... "Too Shy"(5)	EMI America 17094

KALEIDOSCOPE
rock/folk band led by David Lindley

6/14/69	139	8	1. Kaleidoscope	Epic 26467

GUNTER KALLMANN Chorus
German chorus

5/01/65	97	10	1. Serenade For Elisabeth...........................[F]	4 Corners 4209
12/24/66	126	8	2. With Me A Rainbow	4 Corners 4235

KALYAN
14-man soul/calypso band from Trinidad

4/16/77	173	4	1. Kalyan	MCA 2245

KANO
Italian disco band

1/09/82	189	4	1. New York Cake	Mirage 19327

KANSAS
progressive rock group from Topeka led by Steve Walsh (1-8) & Kerry Livgren

6/15/74	174	10	1. Kansas	Kirshner 32817
3/22/75	57	15	● 2. Song For America	Kirshner 33385
12/27/75	70	20	● 3. Masque	Kirshner 33806
11/06/76	5	42	▲ 4. **Leftoverture** .... "Carry On Wayward Son"	Kirshner 34224
10/15/77	4	51	▲ 5. **Point Of Know Return** .... "Dust In The Wind"(6)	Kirshner 34929
11/18/78	32	19	▲ 6. Two For The Show .... [L]	Kirshner 35660 [2]
6/09/79	10	24	● 7. **Monolith**	Kirshner 36008
10/04/80	26	21	● 8. Audio-Visions	Kirshner 36588
6/12/82	16	20	9. Vinyl Confessions	Kirshner 38002
8/13/83	41	21	10. Drastic Measures	CBS Assoc. 38733
9/08/84	154	5	11. The Best of Kansas .... [G]	CBS Assoc. 39283

PAUL KANTNER
original member of Jefferson Airplane & Starship

12/19/70	20	23	● 1. Blows Against The Empire .... PAUL KANTNER/JEFFERSON STARSHIP with Grace Slick, Jerry Garcia, David Crosby & Graham Nash	RCA 4448
12/25/71	89	9	2. Sunfighter .... PAUL KANTNER/GRACE SLICK with Jerry Garcia, David Crosby & Graham Nash	Grunt 1002
6/23/73	120	12	3. Baron von Tollbooth & The Chrome Nun ...... PAUL KANTNER, GRACE SLICK & DAVID FREIBERG	Grunt 0148

KaSANDRA
John W. Anderson is KaSandra

11/23/68	142	8	1. John W. Anderson Presents KaSandra	Capitol 2957

KASHIF

4/09/83	54	33	1. Kashif	Arista 9620
7/21/84	51	21	2. Send Me Your Love	Arista 8205

JORMA KAUKONEN & Vital Parts
former lead guitarist of Jefferson Airplane and Hot Tuna

2/14/81	163	6	1. Barbeque King	RCA 3725

JOHN KAY
Steppenwolf leader

4/29/72	113	11	1. Forgotten Songs & Unsung Heroes	Dunhill 50120
7/14/73	200	2	2. My Sportin' Life	Dunhill 50147

DATE CHARTED	PEAK POS	WKS CHRT'D	ARTIST — Album Title	LABEL & NUMBER
			KAYAK rock quintet from Holland - Max Werner, lead singer	
1/17/76	**199**	2	1. Royal Bed Bouncer	Janus 7023
3/04/78	**117**	9	2. Starlight Dancer	Janus 7034
3/03/79	**145**	7	3. Phantom Of The Night	Janus 7039
			SAMMY KAYE & His Orchestra leader of dance band since 1932	
8/04/56	**20**	1	1. My Fair Lady (For Dancing) .... [I]	Columbia 885
11/17/56	**19**	1	2. What Makes Sammy Swing and Sway .... [I]	Columbia 891
5/30/64	**97**	9	3. Come Dance To The Hits .... [I]	Decca 74502
			KAY-GEES 7-man disco/funk band	
3/01/75	**199**	1	1. Keep On Bumpin' & Masterplan	Gang 101
			KC & THE SUNSHINE BAND Florida disco band led by KC (Harry Wayne Casey)	
8/02/75	**4**	47	1. **KC And The Sunshine Band**	TK 603
			"Get Down Tonight"(1)/"That's The Way (I Like It)"(1)	
10/04/75	**131**	8	2. The Sound Of Sunshine .... [I]	TK 604
			shown only as The Sunshine Band	
10/23/76	**13**	77	3. Part 3	TK 605
			"(Shake, Shake, Shake) Shake Your Booty"(1)/ "I'm Your Boogie Man"(1)/"Keep It Comin' Love"(2)	
8/19/78	**36**	13	4. Who Do Ya (Love)	TK 607
7/07/79	**50**	37	5. Do You Wanna Go Party	TK 611
			"Please Don't Go"(1)	
3/22/80	**132**	11	6. Greatest Hits .... [G]	TK 612
2/04/84	**93**	18	7. KC Ten	Meca 8301
			shown only as KC	
			KEEL heavy-metal quintet led by Ron Keel (vocals/guitar)	
3/09/85	**113+**	5+	1. The Right to Rock	Gold Mt. 5041
			KEITH James Barry Keefer from Philadelphia	
3/25/67	**124**	5	1. 98.6/Ain't Gonna Lie	Mercury 61102
			"98.6"(7)	
			MANNY KELLEM [His Orchestra & Voices] record producer from Philadelphia	
4/13/68	**197**	2	1. Love Is Blue	Epic 26367
			EDDIE KENDRICKS lead singer of the Temptations thru 1971	
5/22/71	**80**	32	1. All By Myself	Tamla 309
6/03/72	**131**	14	2. People...Hold On	Tamla 315
6/16/73	**18**	40	3. Eddie Kendricks	Tamla 327
			"Keep On Truckin'"(1)	
3/16/74	**30**	17	4. Boogie Down!	Tamla 330
			"Boogie Down"(2)	
12/07/74	**108**	14	5. For You	Tamla 335
7/12/75	**63**	25	6. The Hit Man	Tamla 338
1/31/76	**38**	19	7. He's A Friend	Tamla 343
10/09/76	**144**	7	8. Goin' Up In Smoke	Tamla 346
4/22/78	**180**	3	9. Vintage '78	Arista 4170
			JOHN FITZGERALD KENNEDY tributes to President Kennedy who was assassinated on 11/22/63 (46) - also see Leonard Bernstein/Boston Symphony Orch.	
12/28/63	**5**	15	1. **That Was The Week That Was** .... [T]	Decca 9116
			the BBC telecast tribute to Kennedy on 11/23/63	
12/28/63	**8**	14	2. **The Presidential Years 1960-1963** .... [T]	20th Century 3127
			narrated by David Teig	

DATE CHARTED	PEAK POS	WKS CHRT'D	ARTIST — Album Title	LABEL & NUMBER
1/11/64	**42**	8	3. JFK The Man, The President .... [T] narrated by Barry Gray	Documentaries Un.
1/18/64	**18**	9	● 4. A Memorial Album .... [T] narrated by Ed Brown - a broadcast by WMCA, New York on 11/22/63	Premier 2099
1/18/64	**109**	5	5. Actual Speeches of Franklin D. Roosevelt and John F. Kennedy .... [T] side 1: Kennedy's complete Inaugural Address (1/20/61); side 2: Roosevelt speeches	Somerset 16100
1/25/64	**101**	4	6. John F. Kennedy - A Memorial Album ...... [T]	Diplomat 10000
1/25/64	**119**	4	7. The Presidential Years (1960-1963) .... [T]	Pickwick 169
2/08/64	**29**	10	8. Four Days That Shocked The World .... [T] Nov. 22-25, 1963 (complete story narrated by Reid Collins)	Colpix 2500
12/26/64	**49**	11	9. The Kennedy Wit .... [T] narrated by David Brinkley; introduction by Adlai E. Stevenson	RCA 101
12/11/65	**93**	8	10. John Fitzgerald Kennedy...As We Remember Him .... [T] narrated by Charles Kuralt - includes a 240 page book	Legacy 1017 [2]

JOYCE KENNEDY
member of Mother's Finest

9/08/84	**79**	13	1. Lookin' For Trouble	A&M 4996

ROBERT FRANCIS KENNEDY
assassinated during Presidential campaign on 6/5/68 (42)

1/11/69	**187**	4	1. A Memorial .... [T] record 1: highlights of speeches 1964-1968; record 2: excerpts from the High Requiem Mass at St. Patrick's Cathedral - 6/9/68	Columbia 792 [2]

KENNY G
Kenny Gorelick - saxophonist

3/24/84	**62**	21	1. G Force	Arista 8192

STAN KENTON
progressive jazz big band leader - died on 8/25/79 (67)

9/08/56	**13**	2	1. Kenton in Hi-Fi .... [I]	Capitol 724
9/15/56	**17**	4	2. Cuban Fire! .... [I]	Capitol 731
10/23/61	**16**	28	3. Kenton's West Side Story .... [I]	Capitol 1609
7/01/72	**146**	14	4. Stan Kenton Today .... [I-L] recorded live in London, England	Ln. Ph. 4 44179 [2]

ANITA KERR SINGERS
backup singers for many popular artists - also see San Sebastian
 Singers

3/22/69	**162**	6	1. The Anita Kerr Singers Reflect on the hits of Burt Bacharach & Hal David	Dot 25906
9/20/69	**172**	3	2. Velvet Voices And Bold Brass	Dot 25951

NIK KERSHAW
English

5/05/84	**70**	20	1. Human Racing	MCA 39020

DICK KESNER & his Stradivarius Violin

1/12/59	**22**	2	1. Lawrence Welk Presents Dick Kesner .... [I]	Brunswick 54044

KGB
Ray Kennedy, Rick Grech, Mike Bloomfield, Carmine Appice,
 Barry Goldberg

3/06/76	**124**	6	1. KGB	MCA 2166

CHAKA KHAN
lead singer of Rufus - real name: Yvette Marie Stevens

11/04/78	**12**	21	● 1. Chaka	Warner 3245
6/21/80	**43**	16	2. Naughty	Warner 3385
5/09/81	**17**	18	● 3. What Cha' Gonna Do For Me	Warner 3526

DATE CHARTED	PEAK POS	WKS CHRT'D		ARTIST — Album Title	LABEL & NUMBER
12/18/82	**52**	18		4. Chaka Khan	Warner 23729
10/20/84	**14**	25+ ▲		5. I Feel For You	Warner 25162
				"I Feel For You"(3)	

STEVE KHAN
jazz guitarist

2/04/78	**157**	5		1. Tightrope .... [I]	Tappan Zee 34857

KICK AXE
George Criston, lead singer of Canadian heavy metal quintet

6/30/84	**126**	15		1. Vices	Pasha 39297

KID CREOLE & THE COCONUTS
group evolved from Dr. Buzzard's Original Savannah Band

7/18/81	**180**	2		1. Fresh Fruit In Foreign Places	Sire 3534
7/03/82	**145**	12		2. Wise Guy	Sire 3681

KIDS FROM "FAME"
cast members of the TV series "Fame"

4/03/82	**146**	8		1. The Kids From "Fame"	RCA 4249
1/15/83	**181**	4		2. Songs	RCA 4525
3/26/83	**98**	11		3. The Kids From "Fame" Live! .... [L]	RCA 4674
				recorded at the Royal Albert Hall in London	

GREG KIHN Band
group formed in Berkeley, California

9/16/78	**145**	12		1. Next Of Kihn	Beserkley 0056
8/11/79	**114**	7		2. With The Naked Eye	Beserkley 10063
4/26/80	**167**	5		3. Glass House Rock	Beserkley 10068
4/11/81	**32**	32		4. Rockihnroll	Beserkley 10069
4/10/82	**33**	17		5. Kihntinued	Beserkley 60101
3/12/83	**15**	24		6. Kihnspiracy	Beserkley 60224
				"Jeopardy"(2)	
6/16/84	**121**	9		7. Kihntagious	Beserkley 60354
				GREG KIHN:	
3/23/85	**56+**	3+		8. Citizen Kihn	EMI America 17152

ANDY KIM
Canadian - real name: Andrew Joachim

8/02/69	**82**	14		1. Baby I Love You	Steed 37004
				"Baby, I Love You"(9)	
9/14/74	**21**	17		2. Andy Kim	Capitol 11318
				"Rock Me Gently"(1)	
12/21/74	**190**	6		3. Andy Kim's Greatest Hits .... [G]	Dunhill 50193

WARREN KIME & his Brass Impact orchestra
Chicago orchestra leader/arranger

4/15/67	**89**	12		1. Brass Impact .... [I]	Command 910
11/11/67	**177**	7		2. Explosive Brass Impact .... [I]	Command 919

KINGBEES
Jamie James, lead singer of 3-man Los Angeles band

5/31/80	**160**	12		1. The Kingbees	RSO 3075

KING BISCUIT BOY with CROWBAR
Canadian blues-rock band - King Biscuit Boy: Richard Newell

12/26/70	**194**	2		1. Official Music	Paramount 5030

KING CRIMSON
English progressive rock group led by Robert Fripp

12/13/69	**28**	25	●	1. In The Court Of The Crimson King - An Observation By King Crimson	Atlantic 8245
9/12/70	**31**	13		2. In The Wake Of Poseidon	Atlantic 8266
				Greg Lake, lead singer on above 2 albums	
3/20/71	**113**	10		3. Lizard	Atlantic 8278
				Gordon Haskell, lead singer	

DATE CHARTED	PEAK POS	WKS CHRT'D	ARTIST — Album Title	LABEL & NUMBER
2/05/72	**76**	12	4. Islands .... Boz Burrell, lead singer	Atlantic 7212
5/05/73	**61**	14	5. Larks' Tongues In Aspic	Atlantic 7263
5/04/74	**64**	11	6. Starless And Bible Black	Atlantic 7298
11/23/74	**66**	11	7. Red	Atlantic 18110
5/24/75	**125**	5	8. USA .... John Wetton (Asia), lead singer on above 4 albums	Atlantic 18136
10/31/81	**45**	17	9. Discipline	Warner 3629
7/03/82	**52**	14	10. Beat	Warner 23692
4/07/84	**58**	17	11. Three of a Perfect Pair .... Adrian Belew, lead singer on above 3 albums	Warner 25071

KING CURTIS
R&B saxophonist Curtis Ousley - died on 8/14/71 (37)

6/13/64	**103**	12	1. Soul Serenade .... [I]	Capitol 2095
6/03/67	**185**	12	2. The Great Memphis Hits .... [I]	Atco 211
12/09/67	**168**	9	3. King Size Soul .... [I]	Atco 231
8/17/68	**198**	2	4. Sweet Soul .... [I]	Atco 247
12/21/68	**190**	4	5. The Best of King Curtis .... [G-I]	Atco 266
7/19/69	**160**	3	6. Instant Groove .... [I] guitar solos by Duane Allman	Atco 293
8/29/70	**198**	2	7. Get Ready .... [I]	Atco 338
8/21/71	**54**	15	8. Live At Fillmore West .... [I-L] with Billy Preston on organ	Atco 359
3/25/72	**189**	3	9. Everybody's Talkin' .... [I]	Atco 385

KING FAMILY
featuring songs by the entire cast of the TV show

7/10/65	**34**	16	1. The King Family Show!	Warner 1601
10/02/65	**142**	3	2. The King Family Album	Warner 1613

KINGFISH
rock group led by Bob Weir (Grateful Dead)

3/27/76	**50**	9	1. Kingfish	Round 564
5/21/77	**103**	10	2. Live 'N' Kickin' .... [L]	Jet 732

KING FLOYD

5/29/71	**130**	5	1. King Floyd .... "Groove Me"(6)	Cotillion 9047

KING HARVEST

1/27/73	**136**	10	1. Dancing In The Moonlight	Perception 36

KING RICHARD'S FLUEGEL KNIGHTS
King Richard: Dick Behrke

1/27/68	**198**	2	1. Something Super! .... [I]	MTA 5005

ALBERT KING
blues guitarist

11/16/68	**150**	10	1. Live Wire/Blues Power .... [I-L]	Stax 2003
3/01/69	**194**	5	2. King Of The Blues Guitar	Atlantic 8213
5/17/69	**133**	4	3. Years Gone By	Stax 2010
7/12/69	**179**	5	4. Jammed Together .... [I] ALBERT KING/STEVE CROPPER/POP STAPLES	Stax 2020
7/03/71	**188**	6	5. Lovejoy	Stax 2040
10/07/72	**140**	8	6. I'll Play The Blues For You	Stax 3009
3/20/76	**166**	6	7. Truckload Of Lovin'	Utopia 1387
3/12/77	**182**	3	8. Albert Live .... [L]	Utopia 2205 [2]

B.B. KING
Riley B. ("Blues Boy") King - "King of The Blues" -
also see Crusaders

10/12/68	**192**	3	1. Lucille .... Lucille: B.B.'s Gibson guitar	BluesWay 6016
6/14/69	**56**	34	2. Live & Well .... [L] side 1: live; side 2: studio	BluesWay 6031

DATE CHARTED	PEAK POS	WKS CHRT'D	ARTIST — Album Title	LABEL & NUMBER
12/27/69	**38**	30	3. Completely Well .... "The Thrill Is Gone"	BluesWay 6037
4/11/70	**193**	2	4. The Incredible Soul of B.B. King .... [E]	Kent 539
10/17/70	**26**	28	5. Indianola Mississippi Seeds	ABC 713
2/20/71	**25**	33	6. Live In Cook County Jail .... [L]	ABC 723
9/25/71	**78**	8	7. Live At The Regal .... [E-L] recorded in Chicago on 11/21/64	ABC 724
10/16/71	**57**	17	8. B.B. King In London	ABC 730
2/26/72	**53**	17	9. L.A. Midnight	ABC 743
9/09/72	**65**	20	10. Guess Who	ABC 759
2/24/73	**101**	11	11. The Best Of B.B. King .... [G]	ABC 767
9/08/73	**71**	25	12. To Know You Is To Love You	ABC 794
8/17/74	**153**	6	13. Friends	ABC 825
10/26/74	**43**	20	● 14. Together For The First Time...Live .... [L] B.B. KING & BOBBY BLAND	Dunhill 50190 [2]
11/08/75	**140**	5	15. Lucille Talks Back	ABC 898
7/17/76	**73**	14	16. Together Again...Live .... [L] BOBBY BLAND & B.B. KING	ABC/Impulse 9317
2/12/77	**154**	7	17. King Size	ABC 977
5/20/78	**124**	24	18. Midnight Believer	ABC 1061
8/25/79	**112**	12	19. Take It Home	MCA 3151
4/26/80	**162**	4	20. "Now Appearing" at Ole Miss .... [L]	MCA 8016 [2]
2/28/81	**131**	10	21. There Must Be A Better World Somewhere ...	MCA 5162
5/15/82	**179**	5	22. Love Me Tender	MCA 5307
7/02/83	**172**	4	23. Blues 'N' Jazz .... recorded on his 57th birthday (9/16/82)	MCA 5413

BEN E. KING
real name: Benjamin Nelson - lead singer of the Drifters ('59-'60)

DATE CHARTED	PEAK POS	WKS CHRT'D	ARTIST — Album Title	LABEL & NUMBER
8/07/61	**57**	7	1. Spanish Harlem .... "Spanish Harlem"(10)	Atco 133
5/03/75	**39**	14	2. Supernatural .... "Supernatural Thing"(5)	Atlantic 18132
7/23/77	**33**	21	3. Benny And Us .... AVERAGE WHITE BAND & BEN E. KING	Atlantic 19105

CAROLE KING
Carole Klein - one of pop music's most prolific songwriters

DATE CHARTED	PEAK POS	WKS CHRT'D	ARTIST — Album Title	LABEL & NUMBER
4/10/71	**1(15)**	302	● 1. **Tapestry** .... "It's Too Late"(1)	Ode 77009
5/01/71	**84**	27	2. Writer: Carole King .... originally released before "Tapestry"	Ode 77006
12/11/71	**1(3)**	44	● 3. **Music** .... "Sweet Seasons"(9)	Ode 77013
11/04/72	**2(5)**	31	● 4. **Rhymes & Reasons**	Ode 77016
6/23/73	**6**	37	● 5. **Fantasy**	Ode 77018
9/28/74	**1(1)**	29	● 6. **Wrap Around Joy** .... "Jazzman"(2)/"Nightingale"(9)	Ode 77024
3/08/75	**20**	15	7. Really Rosie .... [TV] from the original animated TV soundtrack	Ode 77027
2/07/76	**3**	21	● 8. **Thoroughbred**	Ode 77034
8/06/77	**17**	14	● 9. **Simple Things**	Capitol 11667
4/01/78	**47**	13	● 10. **Her Greatest Hits** .... [G]	Ode 34967
6/17/78	**104**	8	11. Welcome Home	Avatar 11785
6/23/79	**104**	9	12. Touch The Sky	Capitol 11953
6/07/80	**44**	17	13. Pearls-Songs of Goffin and King .... Gerry Goffin: Carole's songwriting partner of the '60s	Capitol 12073
4/03/82	**119**	11	14. One To One	Atlantic 19344

DATE CHARTED	PEAK POS	WKS CHRT'D	ARTIST — Album Title	LABEL & NUMBER
			CLAUDE KING country singer from Shreveport, Louisiana	
8/11/62	**80**	7	1. Meet Claude King .... "Wolverton Mountain"(6)	Columbia 8610
			EVELYN "CHAMPAGNE" KING born in the Bronx, New York on 6/29/60	
5/27/78	**14**	45	● 1. Smooth Talk .... "Shame"(9)	RCA 2466
4/14/79	**35**	17	● 2. Music Box	RCA 3033
10/11/80	**124**	7	3. Call On Me	RCA 3543
7/25/81	**28**	18	4. I'm In Love	RCA 3962
9/11/82	**27**	32	● 5. Get Loose	RCA 4337
12/24/83	**91**	20	6. Face To Face	RCA 4725
			FREDDIE KING blues guitarist/singer - died on 12/27/76 (42)	
7/21/73	**158**	8	1. Woman Across The River	Shelter 8919
			MORGANA KING	
8/22/64	**118**	15	1. With A Taste Of Honey	Mainstream 6015
10/27/73	**184**	5	2. New Beginnings...	Paramount 6067
			REV. DR. MARTIN LUTHER KING, JR. America's civil rights leader - assassinated on 4/4/68 (39)	
10/26/63	**141**	9	1. The Great March To Freedom .... [T] King's speech at Detroit's Freedom Rally (6/23/63)	Gordy 906
11/02/63	**102**	5	2. The March On Washington .... [T] side 1: History of Negro Contributions; side 2: recorded in Washington, D.C. on 8/28/63	Mr. Maestro 1000
11/09/63	**119**	5	3. Freedom March On Washington .... [T] highlights of the 8/28/63 gathering	20th Century 3110
5/04/68	**69**	8	4. I Have A Dream .... [T] speeches from the March on Washington (8/28/63)	Creed 3201
5/18/68	**173**	4	5. The American Dream .... [T] recorded during a Freedom Rally at the Los Angeles Coliseum	Dooto 841
6/08/68	**150**	3	6. In Search Of Freedom .... [T] King's speeches from 1964-1968	Mercury 61170
6/08/68	**154**	3	7. In The Struggle For Freedom And Human Dignity .... [T] King's speech on 12/17/64 in New York City	Unart 21033
			KINGS Canadian quartet - David Diamond, lead singer	
8/16/80	**74**	26	1. The Kings Are Here	Elektra 274
9/26/81	**170**	4	2. Amazon Beach	Elektra 543
			KINGSMEN Portland quintet led by Lynn Easton	
1/18/64	**20**	131	1. The Kingsmen In Person .... [L] "Louie, Louie"(2)	Wand 657
9/26/64	**15**	37	2. The Kingsmen, Volume II .... [L]	Wand 659
2/20/65	**22**	18	3. The Kingsmen, Volume 3 .... [L] "The Jolly Green Giant"(4)	Wand 662
10/30/65	**68**	17	4. The Kingsmen On Campus .... [L]	Wand 670
8/20/66	**87**	8	5. 15 Great Hits .... [K] 7 cuts from first 3 albums; 8 new recordings	Wand 674
			KINGSTON TRIO Bob Shane, Nick Reynolds & Dave Guard (replaced by John Stewart)	
11/03/58	**1(1)**	195	● 1. The Kingston Trio .... "Tom Dooley"(1)	Capitol 996
2/16/59	**2(10)**	178	● 2. From The Hungry i .... [L]	Capitol 1107
6/22/59	**1(15)**	118	● 3. The Kingston Trio At Large	Capitol 1199
11/09/59	**1(8)**	126	● 4. Here We Go Again!	Capitol 1258
4/25/60	**1(12)**	73	● 5. Sold Out	Capitol 1352

DATE CHARTED	PEAK POS	WKS CHRT'D	ARTIST — Album Title	LABEL & NUMBER
8/15/60	1(10)	60	● 6. **String Along**	Capitol 1407
9/05/60	15	13	7. Stereo Concert .... [L]	Capitol 1183
			concert in Liberty Hall, El Paso, Texas	
12/05/60	11	4	8. The Last Month Of The Year .... [X]	Capitol 1446
2/27/61	2(1)	39	9. **Make Way!**	Capitol 1474
7/03/61	3	41	10. **Goin' Places**	Capitol 1564
10/09/61	3	46	11. **Close-Up**	Capitol 1642
			John Stewart replaces Dave Guard here-on	
3/10/62	3	51	12. **College Concert** .... [L]	Capitol 1658
			concert on the campus of UCLA	
6/09/62	7	105	● 13. **The Best Of The Kingston Trio** .... [G]	Capitol 1705
8/18/62	7	37	14. **Something Special**	Capitol 1747
			with orchestral and chorus background	
12/15/62	16	36	15. New Frontier	Capitol 1809
3/30/63	4	29	16. **The Kingston Trio #16**	Capitol 1871
			"Reverend Mr. Black"(8)	
8/17/63	7	25	17. **Sunny Side!**	Capitol 1935
1/11/64	69	14	18. Sing A Song with The Kingston Trio .... [I]	Capitol 2005
2/01/64	18	21	19. Time To Think	Capitol 2011
5/30/64	22	20	20. Back In Town .... [L]	Capitol 2081
			recorded at San Francisco's "Hungry i"	
1/16/65	53	13	21. The Kingston Trio (Nick-Bob-John)	Decca 74613
6/19/65	126	10	22. Stay Awhile	Decca 74656
7/12/69	163	6	23. Once Upon A Time .... [L]	Tetragrm. 5101[2]
			recorded at the Sahara-Tahoe Hotel in Las Vegas (1966)	

KINKS

English group led by brothers Ray & Dave Davies

DATE CHARTED	PEAK POS	WKS CHRT'D	ARTIST — Album Title	LABEL & NUMBER
12/12/64	29	26	1. You Really Got Me	Reprise 6143
			"You Really Got Me"(7)	
4/03/65	13	29	2. Kinks-Size	Reprise 6158
			"All Day And All Of The Night"(7)/	
			"Tired Of Waiting For You"(6)	
8/28/65	60	9	3. Kinda Kinks	Reprise 6173
12/25/65	47	17	4. Kinks Kinkdom	Reprise 6184
4/30/66	95	12	5. The Kink Kontroversy	Reprise 6197
8/27/66	9	64	● 6. **The Kinks Greatest Hits!** .... [G]	Reprise 6217
2/11/67	135	3	7. Face To Face	Reprise 6228
9/09/67	162	4	8. The Live Kinks .... [L]	Reprise 6260
3/02/68	153	2	9. Something Else By The Kinks	Reprise 6279
11/22/69	105	20	10. Arthur (or the decline and fall of The British Empire)	Reprise 6366
			rock opera written for a British TV show	
12/26/70	35	12	11. Lola Versus Powerman and The Moneygoround, Part One	Reprise 6423
			"Lola"(9)	
12/18/71	100	14	12. Muswell Hillbillies	RCA 4644
4/15/72	94	13	13. The Kink Kronikles .... [K]	Reprise 6454 [2]
9/23/72	70	14	14. Everybody's In Show-Biz .... [L]	RCA 6065 [2]
			record 1: studio recordings; record 2: live recordings	
2/24/73	145	5	15. The Great Lost Kinks Album .... [K]	Reprise 2127
			recordings which were never released in the U.S.	
12/15/73	177	6	16. Preservation Act 1	RCA 5002
6/15/74	114	11	17. Preservation Act 2	RCA 5040 [2]
5/17/75	51	13	18. Soap Opera	RCA 5081
12/06/75	45	14	19. Schoolboys In Disgrace	RCA 5102
6/26/76	144	5	20. The Kink's Greatest-Celluloid Heroes .... [K]	RCA 1743
2/26/77	21	16	21. Sleepwalker	Arista 4106
6/03/78	40	21	22. Misfits	Arista 4167
7/28/79	11	18	● 23. Low Budget	Arista 4240
6/28/80	14	33	● 24. One For The Road .... [L]	Arista 8401 [2]

DATE CHARTED	PEAK POS	WKS CHRT'D	ARTIST — Album Title	LABEL & NUMBER
9/20/80	177	4	25. Second Time Around .... [K]	RCA 3520
9/12/81	15	36	● 26. Give The People What They Want	Arista 9567
6/11/83	12	25	27. State of Confusion	Arista 8018
			"Come Dancing"(6)	
12/15/84	57	17+	28. Word Of Mouth	Arista 8264

KISS
Gene Simmons, Paul Stanley, Ace Frehley & Peter Criss

DATE CHARTED	PEAK POS	WKS CHRT'D	ARTIST — Album Title	LABEL & NUMBER
4/20/74	87	23	● 1. Kiss	Casablanca 9001
11/16/74	100	15	● 2. Hotter Than Hell	Casablanca 7006
4/19/75	32	29	● 3. Dressed To Kill	Casablanca 7016
10/11/75	9	110	● 4. **Alive!** .... [L]	Casablanca 7020 [2]
4/03/76	11	78	▲ 5. Destroyer	Casablanca 7025
			"Beth"(7)	
8/21/76	36	17	6. The Originals .... [R]	Casablanca 7032 [3]
			reissue of their first 3 albums	
11/20/76	11	45	▲ 7. Rock And Roll Over	Casablanca 7037
7/09/77	4	26	▲ 8. **Love Gun**	Casablanca 7057
11/26/77	7	33	▲ 9. **Alive II** .... [L]	Casablanca 7076 [2]
5/20/78	22	24	▲ 10. Double Platinum .... [G]	Casablanca 7100 [2]
			during October, 1978, each member of Kiss issued a solo album - see each name for chart details	
6/23/79	9	25	▲ 11. **Dynasty**	Casablanca 7152
6/21/80	35	14	● 12. Kiss Unmasked	Casablanca 7225
12/05/81	75	11	13. Music From The Elder	Casablanca 7261
			Eric Carr replaces Peter Criss	
11/20/82	45	19	14. Creatures Of The Night	Casablanca 7270
			Vinnie Vincent replaces Ace Frehley	
10/15/83	24	30	● 15. Lick It Up	Mercury 814297
			group shown unmasked for the first time	
10/06/84	19	27+	▲ 16. Animalize	Mercury 822495

KIX
Maryland quintet led by vocalist Steve Whiteman

DATE CHARTED	PEAK POS	WKS CHRT'D	ARTIST — Album Title	LABEL & NUMBER
5/28/83	177	8	1. Cool Kids	Atlantic 80056

KLAATU
Canadian rock quartet

DATE CHARTED	PEAK POS	WKS CHRT'D	ARTIST — Album Title	LABEL & NUMBER
4/02/77	32	11	1. Klaatu	Capitol 11542
10/15/77	83	7	2. Hope	Capitol 11633

KLEEER
formerly the Jam Band for Monte Rock's 'Disco Tex' show

DATE CHARTED	PEAK POS	WKS CHRT'D	ARTIST — Album Title	LABEL & NUMBER
4/26/80	140	10	1. Winners	Atlantic 19262
3/07/81	81	16	2. License To Dream	Atlantic 19288
2/20/82	139	8	3. Taste The Music	Atlantic 19334

ROBERT KLEIN

DATE CHARTED	PEAK POS	WKS CHRT'D	ARTIST — Album Title	LABEL & NUMBER
4/28/73	191	3	1. Child Of The 50's .... [C]	Brut 6001

JOHN KLEMMER
jazz tenor saxophonist

DATE CHARTED	PEAK POS	WKS CHRT'D	ARTIST — Album Title	LABEL & NUMBER
9/13/69	176	5	1. Blowin' Gold .... [I]	Cadet Concept 321
12/27/75	90	40	2. Touch .... [I]	ABC 922
9/18/76	66	16	3. Barefoot Ballet .... [I]	ABC 950
6/18/77	51	17	4. LifeStyle (Living & Loving) .... [I]	ABC 1007
6/17/78	83	10	5. Arabesque .... [I]	ABC 1068
11/18/78	178	3	6. Cry .... [I]	ABC 1106
6/02/79	192	9	7. Brazilia .... [I]	ABC 1116
11/24/79	187	2	8. The Best Of John Klemmer, Volume One/Mosaic .... [K-I]	MCA 8014 [2]

DATE CHARTED	PEAK POS	WKS CHRT'D	ARTIST — Album Title	LABEL & NUMBER
8/09/80	146	11	9. Magnificent Madness	Elektra 284
6/13/81	99	9	10. Hush .... [I]	Elektra 527
			KLIQUE Howard Huntsberry, and Isaac & Debbie Suthers (brother & sister)	
10/08/83	70	14	1. Try It Out	MCA 39008
			KLOWNS	
12/12/70	184	2	1. The Klowns	RCA 4438
			EARL KLUGH jazz acoustic guitarist	
7/10/76	124	6	1. Earl Klugh .... [I]	Blue Note 596
12/11/76	188	2	2. Living Inside Your Love .... [I]	Blue Note 667
7/09/77	84	8	3. Finger Paintings .... [I]	Blue Note 737
7/01/78	139	9	4. Magic In Your Eyes .... [I]	United Art. 877
5/19/79	49	21	5. Heart String .... [I]	United Art. 942
11/03/79	23	33	● 6. One On One .... [I] BOB JAMES & EARL KLUGH	Tappan Zee 36241
4/19/80	42	19	7. Dream Come True .... [I]	United Art. 1026
9/27/80	134	4	8. How To Beat The High Cost Of Living .... [S-I] HUBERT LAWS & EARL KLUGH	Columbia 36741
12/06/80	98	23	9. Late Night Guitar .... [I]	Liberty 1079
11/14/81	53	27	10. Crazy For You .... [I]	Liberty 51113
11/06/82	44	29	11. Two Of A Kind .... [I] EARL KLUGH & BOB JAMES	Capitol 12244
5/07/83	38	24	12. Low Ride .... [I]	Capitol 12253
3/31/84	69	23	13. Wishful Thinking .... [I]	Capitol 12323
10/27/84	107	17	14. Nightsongs .... [I]	Capitol 12372
			KLYMAXX female sextet from Los Angeles	
2/02/85	81+	10+	1. Meeting In The Ladies Room	Constell. 5529
			KNACK Los Angeles rock quartet led by Doug Fieger (vocals) & Berton Averre (guitar)	
6/30/79	1(5)	40	▲ 1. **Get The Knack** .... "My Sharona"(1)	Capitol 11948
3/01/80	15	14	● 2. But The Little Girls Understand	Capitol 12045
11/07/81	93	6	3. Round Trip	Capitol 12168
			KNICKERBOCKERS New Jersey rock quartet - Buddy Randell, leader	
2/12/66	134	5	1. Lies	Challenge 622
			CURTIS KNIGHT - see JIMI HENDRIX	
			GLADYS KNIGHT & THE PIPS The Pips: Gladys' brother Merald, and cousins William Guest and Edward Patten	
10/14/67	60	24	1. Everybody Needs Love "I Heard It Through The Grapevine"(2)	Soul 706
6/08/68	158	13	2. Feelin' Bluesy	Soul 707
1/11/69	136	16	3. Silk N' Soul	Soul 711
10/25/69	81	10	4. Nitty Gritty	Soul 713
4/04/70	55	16	5. Gladys Knight & The Pips Greatest Hits .... [G]	Soul 723
5/15/71	35	26	6. If I Were Your Woman "If I Were Your Woman"(9)	Soul 731
1/08/72	60	24	7. Standing Ovation	Soul 736
3/10/73	9	30	8. **Neither One Of Us** "Neither One Of Us (Wants To Be The First To Say Goodbye)"(2)	Soul 737
7/14/73	70	21	9. All I Need Is Time	Soul 739

DATE CHARTED	PEAK POS	WKS CHRT'D	ARTIST — Album Title	LABEL & NUMBER
10/27/73	9	61	● 10. **Imagination** .... "Midnight Train To Georgia"(1)/ "I've Got To Use My Imagination"(4)/ "Best Thing That Ever Happened To Me"(3)	Buddah 5141
2/16/74	77	23	11. Anthology .... [G]	Motown 792 [2]
3/16/74	139	11	12. Knight Time .... [K]	Soul 741
3/23/74	35	34	● 13. Claudine .... [S] "On And On"(5)	Buddah 5602
11/16/74	17	41	● 14. I Feel A Song	Buddah 5612
4/26/75	164	4	15. A Little Knight Music .... [K]	Soul 744
10/18/75	24	16	● 16. 2nd Anniversary .... title refers to their signing with Buddah Records	Buddah 5639
2/07/76	36	15	17. The Best Of Gladys Knight & The Pips..... [G]	Buddah 5653
11/27/76	94	12	18. Pipe Dreams .... [S]	Buddah 5676
4/23/77	51	21	19. Still Together	Buddah 5689
9/16/78	145	6	20. The One And Only...	Buddah 5701
5/31/80	48	18	21. About Love	Columbia 36387
9/05/81	109	8	22. Touch	Columbia 37086
5/21/83	34	33	● 23. Visions	Columbia 38205
3/23/85	135+	3+	24. Life	Columbia 39423
			JEAN KNIGHT	
8/21/71	60	11	1. Mr. Big Stuff .... "Mr. Big Stuff"(2)	Stax 2045
			JERRY KNIGHT a founding member (with Ray Parker) of Raydio	
5/24/80	165	7	1. Jerry Knight	A&M 4788
4/11/81	146	6	2. Perfect Fit	A&M 4843
			ROBERT KNIGHT	
12/16/67	196	2	1. Everlasting Love	Rising Sons 17000
			TERRY KNIGHT & THE PACK Terry founded, managed & produced Grand Funk Railroad	
11/26/66	127	13	1. Terry Knight And The Pack	Lucky Eleven 8000
11/04/72	192	3	2. Mark, Don & Terry 1966-67 .... [K] Mark Farner, Don Brewer (both of Grand Funk) & Terry Knight	Abkco 4217 [2]
			FRED KNOBLOCK	
10/04/80	179	5	1. Why Not Me	Scotti Br. 7109
			KOKOMO English jazz/rock nine-member band	
6/07/75	159	9	1. Kokomo	Columbia 33442
4/17/76	194	2	2. Rise And Shine!	Columbia 34031
			KONGAS disco production by Cerrone	
3/18/78	120	8	1. Africansim	Polydor 6138
			KOOL & THE GANG Jersey City group led by Robert "Kool" Bell (bass) & James Taylor (lead vocals 13-18)	
2/27/71	122	19	1. Live At The Sex Machine .... [I-L]	De-Lite 2008
9/25/71	157	8	2. The Best Of Kool And The Gang .... [G]	De-Lite 2009
1/01/72	171	7	3. Live At P.J.'S .... [I-L]	De-Lite 2010
3/17/73	142	7	4. Good Times	De-Lite 2012
10/13/73	33	60	● 5. Wild And Peaceful .... "Jungle Boogie"(4)/"Hollywood Swinging"(6)	De-Lite 2013
1/12/74	187	4	6. Kool Jazz .... [K-I]	De-Lite 4001
10/05/74	63	34	● 7. Light Of Worlds	De-Lite 2014
3/08/75	81	23	8. Kool & The Gang Greatest Hits! .... [G]	De-Lite 2015

DATE CHARTED	PEAK POS	WKS CHRT'D	ARTIST — Album Title	LABEL & NUMBER
8/30/75	**48**	14	9. Spirit Of The Boogie	De-Lite 2016
3/20/76	**68**	20	10. Love & Understanding	De-Lite 2018
			3 of 8 cuts recorded live in London, England	
11/20/76	**110**	18	11. Open Sesame	De-Lite 2023
1/28/78	**142**	7	12. The Force	De-Lite 9501
9/22/79	**13**	45	▲ 13. Ladies' Night	De-Lite 9513
			"Ladies Night" (8)/"Too Hot" (5)	
10/18/80	**10**	44	▲ 14. **Celebrate!**	De-Lite 9518
			"Celebration"(1)	
10/17/81	**12**	67	▲ 15. Something Special	De-Lite 8502
			"Get Down On It"(10)	
10/09/82	**29**	24	● 16. As One	De-Lite 8505
12/10/83	**29**	37	● 17. In The Heart	De-Lite 8508
			"Joanna"(2)	
12/15/84	**28**	17+	● 18. Emergency	De-Lite 822943
			"Misled"(10)	

AL KOOPER
top session keyboardist/guitarist - founded Blood, Sweat & Tears

DATE CHARTED	PEAK POS	WKS CHRT'D	ARTIST — Album Title	LABEL & NUMBER
8/31/68	**12**	37	● 1. Super Session	Columbia 9701
			MIKE BLOOMFIELD/AL KOOPER/STEVE STILLS	
2/08/69	**18**	20	2. The Live Adventures Of Mike Bloomfield And Al Kooper .... [L]	Columbia 6 [2]
2/08/69	**54**	13	3. I Stand Alone	Columbia 9718
10/11/69	**125**	6	4. You Never Know Who Your Friends Are	Columbia 9855
1/24/70	**182**	5	5. Kooper Session	Columbia 9951
			Al Kooper introduces Shuggie Otis	
9/19/70	**105**	6	6. Easy Does It	Columbia 30031 [2]
7/03/71	**198**	3	7. New York City (You're A Woman)	Columbia 30506
5/06/72	**200**	2	8. A Possible Projection Of The Future/ Childhood's End	Columbia 31159
1/08/77	**182**	5	9. Act Like Nothing's Wrong	United Art. 702

KORGIS
British trio

DATE CHARTED	PEAK POS	WKS CHRT'D	ARTIST — Album Title	LABEL & NUMBER
11/08/80	**113**	12	1. Dumb Waiters	Asylum 290

PAUL KOSSOFF
British guitarist - member of Free and Back Street Crawler - died on 3/19/76 (25)

DATE CHARTED	PEAK POS	WKS CHRT'D	ARTIST — Album Title	LABEL & NUMBER
9/06/75	**191**	2	1. Back Street Crawler .... [I]	Island 9264
			recorded 1973 - Paul formed new band (named after LP title) in 1975	

ANDRE KOSTELANETZ & His Orchestra
Russian immigrant - conductor on radio and records - died on 1/13/80 (78) - also see Beverly Sills

DATE CHARTED	PEAK POS	WKS CHRT'D	ARTIST — Album Title	LABEL & NUMBER
10/01/55	**4**	10	1. **Meet Andre Kostelanetz** .... [K-I]	Columbia KZ 1
5/23/64	**68**	7	2. New York Wonderland .... [I]	Columbia 2138
6/07/69	**200**	2	3. Traces .... [I]	Columbia 9823
11/01/69	**194**	2	4. Sounds Of Love .... [K-I]	Columbia 10 [2]
4/10/71	**183**	2	5. Love Story .... [I]	Columbia 30501

LEO KOTTKE
acoustic guitarist

DATE CHARTED	PEAK POS	WKS CHRT'D	ARTIST — Album Title	LABEL & NUMBER
6/19/71	**168**	7	1. Mudlark	Capitol 682
2/12/72	**127**	9	2. Greenhouse	Capitol 11000
4/07/73	**108**	11	3. My Feet Are Smiling .... [I-L]	Capitol 11164
2/02/74	**69**	18	4. Ice Water	Capitol 11262
11/09/74	**45**	12	5. Dreams and all that stuff .... [I]	Capitol 11335
10/25/75	**114**	7	6. Chewing Pine	Capitol 11446
11/27/76	**153**	4	7. Leo Kottke 1971-1976 - Did You Hear Me? .... [K-I]	Capitol 11576

DATE CHARTED	PEAK POS	WKS CHRT'D	ARTIST — Album Title	LABEL & NUMBER
1/29/77	**107**	9	8. Leo Kottke .... [I]	Chrysalis 1106
9/02/78	**143**	12	9. Burnt Lips	Chrysalis 1191

KRAFTWERK
German duo specializing in synthesized robotic rock

DATE CHARTED	PEAK POS	WKS CHRT'D	ARTIST — Album Title	LABEL & NUMBER
2/08/75	**5**	22	1. **Autobahn** .... [I]	Vertigo 2003
			side 1 is a 22 1/2 minute recording of "Autobahn"	
9/20/75	**160**	5	2. Ralf And Florian .... [I]	Vertigo 2006
12/13/75	**140**	8	3. Radio-Activity	Capitol 11457
4/16/77	**119**	10	4. Trans-Europe Express	Capitol 11603
5/13/78	**130**	9	5. The Man-Machine .... [I]	Capitol 11728
6/06/81	**72**	42	6. Computer-World .... [I]	Warner 3549

BILLY J. KRAMER with the Dakotas
English - managed by Brian Epstein; produced by George Martin

DATE CHARTED	PEAK POS	WKS CHRT'D	ARTIST — Album Title	LABEL & NUMBER
6/20/64	**48**	15	1. Little Children	Imperial 12267
			"Little Children"(7)/"Bad To Me"(9)	

KRIS KRISTOFFERSON
songwriter/vocalist/actor - also see Barbra Streisand "A Star Is Born"

DATE CHARTED	PEAK POS	WKS CHRT'D	ARTIST — Album Title	LABEL & NUMBER
7/31/71	**21**	28	● 1. The Silver Tongued Devil And I	Monument 30679
9/11/71	**43**	22	● 2. Me And Bobby McGee	Monument 30817
3/18/72	**41**	16	3. Border Lord	Monument 31302
11/25/72	**31**	54	● 4. Jesus Was A Capricorn	Monument 31909
			"Why Me"	
9/22/73	**26**	33	● 5. Full Moon	A&M 4403
			KRIS KRISTOFFERSON & RITA COOLIDGE	
5/25/74	**78**	14	6. Spooky Lady's Sideshow	Monument 32914
12/21/74	**103**	12	7. Breakaway	Monument 33278
			KRIS KRISTOFFERSON & RITA COOLIDGE	
12/06/75	**105**	11	8. Who's To Bless...And Who's To Blame	Monument 33379
8/21/76	**180**	2	9. Surreal Thing	Monument 34254
5/07/77	**45**	18	● 10. Songs Of Kristofferson .... [K]	Monument 34687
4/01/78	**86**	7	11. Easter Island	Monument 35310
2/03/79	**106**	9	12. Natural Act	A&M 4690
			KRIS KRISTOFFERSON & RITA COOLIDGE	
11/10/84	**152**	5	13. Music from SongWriter .... [S]	Columbia 39531
			WILLIE NELSON & KRIS KRISTOFFERSON (co-stars of the film)	

KROKUS
Zurich, Switzerland heavy metal quintet - Marc Storace, lead singer

DATE CHARTED	PEAK POS	WKS CHRT'D	ARTIST — Album Title	LABEL & NUMBER
4/04/81	**103**	12	1. Hardware	Ariola 1508
4/10/82	**53**	20	2. One Vice At A Time	Arista 9591
4/16/83	**25**	41	● 3. Headhunter	Arista 9623
9/08/84	**31**	27	● 4. The Blitz	Arista 8243

BOB KUBAN & the In-Men
8-man St. Louis band - Walter Scott, lead singer

DATE CHARTED	PEAK POS	WKS CHRT'D	ARTIST — Album Title	LABEL & NUMBER
4/23/66	**129**	5	1. Look Out For The Cheater	Musicland 3500

KWICK

DATE CHARTED	PEAK POS	WKS CHRT'D	ARTIST — Album Title	LABEL & NUMBER
6/07/80	**197**	2	1. Kwick	EMI America 17025

L.A. BOPPERS
R&B-Bop quartet led by Vance Tenort

DATE CHARTED	PEAK POS	WKS CHRT'D	ARTIST — Album Title	LABEL & NUMBER
3/15/80	**85**	11	1. L.A. Boppers	Mercury 3816

L.A. EXPRESS
jazz quintet minus Tom Scott - also see Tom Scott

DATE CHARTED	PEAK POS	WKS CHRT'D	ARTIST — Album Title	LABEL & NUMBER
3/06/76	**167**	8	1. L.A. Express .... [I]	Caribou 33940

DATE CHARTED	PEAK POS	WKS CHRT'D	ARTIST — Album Title	LABEL & NUMBER
			LaBELLE Patti LaBelle, Sarah Dash & Nona Hendryx - formerly the Blue-Belles - also see Laura Nyro	
12/21/74	7	28	● 1. **Nightbirds** .... "Lady Marmalade"(1)	Epic 33075
9/20/75	44	13	2. Phoenix	Epic 33579
9/25/76	94	10	3. Chameleon	Epic 34189
			PATTI LaBELLE	
9/24/77	62	16	1. Patti LaBelle	Epic 34847
6/24/78	129	7	2. Tasty	Epic 35335
3/31/79	145	16	3. It's Alright With Me	Epic 35772
4/12/80	114	13	4. Released	Epic 36381
10/03/81	156	4	5. The Spirit's In It	Phil. Int. 37380
1/07/84	40	35	● 6. I'm In Love Again	Phil. Int. 38539
			CHERYL LADD Kris Monroe of TV's "Charlie's Angels"	
8/12/78	129	11	1. Cheryl Ladd	Capitol 11808
4/28/79	179	3	2. Dance Forever	Capitol 11927
			DAVID LAFLAMME leader of It's A Beautiful Day	
12/25/76	159	6	1. White Bird	Amherst 1007
			LAID BACK Danish duo: Tim Stahl and John Guldberg	
3/31/84	67	15	1. Keep Smiling	Sire 25058
			CLEO LAINE English - married to bandleader Johnny Dankworth	
4/06/74	157	8	1. Cleo Laine Live!!! at Carnegie Hall .... [L]	RCA 5015
7/20/74	199	1	2. Day By Day	Buddah 5607
12/28/74	168	5	3. A Beautiful Thing	RCA 5059
2/07/76	158	10	4. Born On A Friday	RCA 5113
12/04/76	138	11	5. Porgy & Bess .... RAY CHARLES/CLEO LAINE	RCA 1831 [2]
7/26/80	150	6	6. Sometimes When We Touch .... CLEO LAINE & JAMES GALWAY	RCA 3628
			FRANKIE LAINE born Frank LoVecchio in Chicago on 3/30/13	
4/20/57	13	12	1. Rockin'	Columbia 975
10/23/61	71	37	2. Hell Bent For Leather! .... "Rawhide"	Columbia 8415
5/13/67	16	29	3. I'll Take Care Of Your Cares	ABC 604
10/14/67	162	2	4. I Wanted Someone To Love	ABC 608
3/23/68	127	9	5. To Each His Own	ABC 628
4/19/69	55	11	6. You Gave Me A Mountain	ABC 682
			LAKE German progressive rock sextet	
8/20/77	92	15	1. Lake	Columbia 34763
			GREG LAKE member of King Crimson and Emerson, Lake & Palmer	
10/31/81	62	17	1. Greg Lake	Chrysalis 1357
			LAKESIDE 9-man funk aggregation from Dayton, Ohio	
1/06/79	74	19	1. Shot Of Love	Solar 2937
11/03/79	141	18	2. Rough Riders	Solar 3490
11/29/80	16	35	● 3. Fantastic Voyage	Solar 3720
12/12/81	109	10	4. Keep On Moving Straight Ahead	Solar 3974
1/09/82	58	23	5. Your Wish Is My Command	Solar 26

DATE CHARTED	PEAK POS	WKS CHRT'D	ARTIST — Album Title	LABEL & NUMBER
5/28/83	42	18	6. Untouchables	Solar 60204
7/28/84	68	15	7. Outrageous	Solar 60355

MAJOR LANCE
born on 4/4/41 in Chicago, Illinois

10/05/63	113	3	1. The Monkey Time "The Monkey Time"(8)	Okeh 12105
3/28/64	100	9	2. Um, Um, Um, Um, Um, Um/The Best Of Major Lance .... [G] "Um, Um, Um, Um, Um, Um"(5)	Okeh 12106
9/04/65	109	6	3. Major's Greatest Hits .... [G]	Okeh 12110

ROBIN LANE & THE CHARTBUSTERS
Robin is the daughter of Dean Martin's pianist Ken Lane

4/25/81	172	4	1. Imitaiton Life	Warner 3537

RONNIE LANE - see PETE TOWNSHEND

LESTER LANIN & His Orchestra
leader of society-styled dance bands - albums 1-5 contain
medleys of 25-50 songs with a party atmosphere background

6/24/57	7	10	1. Dance To The Music Of Lester Lanin ...... [I]	Epic 3340
11/11/57	18	2	2. Lester Lanin And His Orchestra .... [I]	Epic 3242
2/03/58	17	2	3. Lester Lanin At The Tiffany Ball .... [I]	Epic 3410
6/09/58	19	3	4. Lester Lanin Goes To College .... [I]	Epic 3474
11/17/58	12	4	5. Have Band, Will Travel .... [I]	Epic 3520
1/20/62	37	20	6. Twistin' in High Society! .... [I]	Epic 3825

MARIO LANZA
operatic tenor/movie actor - died on 10/7/59 (38)

4/28/56	9	6	1. Serenade .... [S]	RCA 1996
3/17/58	7	8	2. Seven Hills Of Rome .... [S] side 1: soundtrack; side 2: various Lanza recordings	RCA 2211
11/02/59	5	46	3. For The First Time .... [S] Mario sings and stars in the above 3 films	RCA 2338
12/14/59	4	4	4. Lanza Sings Christmas Carols .... [X]	RCA 2333
5/16/60	4	53	5. Mario Lanza Sings Caruso Favorites ...... [F] recorded in Rome, June, 1959	RCA 2393
12/18/61	67	5	6. Lanza Sings Christmas Carols .... [X-R]	RCA 2333
10/06/62	64	41	7. I'll Walk With God .... [E]	RCA 2607
8/08/64	87	15	8. The Best Of Mario Lanza .... [G]	RCA 2748

BILLY LARKIN & THE DELEGATES
soul/funk quartet led by Billy on organ

4/02/66	148	2	1. Hole In The Wall .... [I]	World Pac. 1837

LARKS
Don Julian, Charles Morrison & Ted Walters

1/23/65	143	4	1. The Jerk "The Jerk"(7)	Money 1102

NEIL LARSEN

9/01/79	139	7	1. High Gear .... [I]	Horizon 738

LARSEN/FEITEN BAND
Neil Larsen (keyboards) & Buzz Feiten (guitar)

9/13/80	142	10	1. Larsen-Feiten Band	Warner 3468

NICOLETTE LARSON
former backup harmony singer with Neil Young

11/18/78	15	37	● 1. Nicolette "Lotta Love"(8)	Warner 3243
11/03/79	47	21	2. In The Nick Of Time	Warner 3370
1/24/81	62	12	3. Radioland	Warner 3502
8/14/82	75	10	4. All Dressed Up & No Place To Go	Warner 3678

DATE CHARTED	PEAK POS	WKS CHRT'D	ARTIST — Album Title	LABEL & NUMBER
			D.C. LaRUE	
6/26/76	139	13	1. Ca-the-drals	Pyramid 9003
1/08/77	115	11	2. The Tea Dance	Pyramid 9006
			DENISE LaSALLE	
2/05/72	120	9	1. Trapped By A Thing Called Love	Westbound 2012
			LAST POETS	
			Black protest poetry set to music	
6/20/70	29	30	1. The Last Poets	Douglas 3
3/06/71	106	6	2. Right On! [S]	Juggernaut 8802
4/03/71	104	15	3. This Is Madness	Douglas 30583
			JAMES LAST	
			German producer/arranger	
2/19/72	160	5	1. Music From Across The Way	Polydor 5505
8/16/75	172	3	2. Well Kept Secret [I]	Polydor 6040
6/28/80	148	8	3. Seduction [I]	Polydor 6283
			YUSEF LATEEF	
			jazz tenor saxophonist/flutist	
8/16/69	183	5	1. Yusef Lateef's Detroit [I]	Atlantic 1525
			LATIMORE	
			Benny Latimore	
3/26/77	181	5	1. It Ain't Where You Been...	Glades 7509
			STACY LATTISAW	
			born on 11/25/66 in Washington, D.C.	
7/05/80	44	28	1. Let Me Be Your Angel	Cotillion 5219
7/25/81	46	15	2. With You	Cotillion 16049
8/28/82	55	16	3. Sneakin' Out	Cotillion 90002
8/27/83	160	8	4. Sixteen	Cotillion 90106
3/31/84	139	8	5. Perfect Combination	Cotillion 90136
			STACY LATTISAW & JOHNNY GILL	
			CYNDI LAUPER	
			pop-rock singer/songwriter from Brooklyn, New York	
12/24/83	4	68 + ▲	1. She's So Unusual	Portrait 38930
			"Girls Just Want To Have Fun"(2)/"Time After Time"(1)/ "She Bop"(3)/"All Through The Night"(5)	
			STEVE LAWRENCE	
			a charter member of Steve Allen's "Tonight" show	
6/02/58	19	2	1. Here's Steve Lawrence	Coral 57204
8/14/61	76	10	2. Portrait Of My Love	United Art. 6150
			"Portrait Of My Love"(9)	
2/09/63	27	29	3. Winners!	Columbia 8753
			"Go Away Little Girl"(1)	
2/15/64	135	5	4. Academy Award Losers	Columbia 8921
9/12/64	73	9	5. Everybody Knows	Columbia 9027
12/11/65	133	2	6. The Steve Lawrence Show	Columbia 9219
			STEVE LAWRENCE & EYDIE GORME:	
5/20/67	136	6	7. Together On Broadway	Columbia 9436
3/08/69	141	6	8. What It Was, Was Love	RCA 4115
5/10/69	188	3	9. Real True Lovin'	RCA 4107
			VICKI LAWRENCE	
			star of TV's "Mama's Family"	
4/28/73	51	14	1. The Night The Lights Went Out In Georgia	Bell 1120
			"The Night The Lights Went Out In Georgia"(1)	
			DEBRA LAWS	
			sister of Eloise, Hubert & Ronnie Laws	
4/11/81	70	27	1. Very Special	Elektra 300

DATE CHARTED	PEAK POS	WKS CHRT'D	ARTIST — Album Title	LABEL & NUMBER
			ELOISE LAWS	
2/04/78	156	5	1. Eloise	ABC 1022
2/14/81	175	7	2. Eloise Laws	Liberty 1063
			HUBERT LAWS	
			jazz flutist	
2/24/73	148	9	1. Morning Star .... [I]	CTI 6022
			"Amazing Grace"	
6/30/73	175	6	2. Carnegie Hall .... [I-L]	CTI 6025
6/21/75	42	18	3. The Chicago Theme .... [I]	CTI 6058
11/06/76	139	6	4. Romeo & Juliet .... [I]	Columbia 34330
4/08/78	71	18	5. Say It With Silence .... [I]	Columbia 35022
4/28/79	93	8	6. Land Of Passion	Columbia 35708
9/27/80	134	4	7. How To Beat The High Cost Of Living .... [S-I]	Columbia 36741
			HUBERT LAWS & EARL KLUGH	
11/08/80	133	13	8. Family .... [I]	Columbia 36396
			RONNIE LAWS	
			jazz saxophonist	
9/27/75	73	29	1. Pressure Sensitive .... [I]	Blue Note 452
6/12/76	46	21	2. Fever .... [I]	Blue Note 628
5/07/77	37	28	● 3. Friends And Strangers .... [I]	Blue Note 730
11/04/78	51	22	4. Flame	United Art. 881
2/16/80	24	19	5. Every Generation	United Art. 1001
10/10/81	51	19	6. Solid Ground	Liberty 51087
8/13/83	98	11	7. Mr. Nice Guy	Capitol 12261
			LEAGUE UNLIMITED ORCHESTRA - see HUMAN LEAGUE	
			LE PAMPLEMOUSSE	
1/21/78	116	11	1. Le Spank	AVI 6032
			LE ROUX	
			6-man Louisiana rock band - Jeff Pollard, lead singer	
7/08/78	135	15	1. Louisiana's Le Roux	Capitol 11734
6/09/79	162	4	2. Keep The Fire Burnin'	Capitol 11926
			above 2 shown as Louisiana's LeRoux	
8/23/80	145	6	3. Up	Capitol 12092
2/06/82	64	21	4. Last Safe Place	RCA 4195
			BERNIE LEADON/MICHAEL GEORGIADES Band	
			Bernie was a member of the Eagles from 1972-1976	
8/20/77	91	6	1. Natural Progressions	Asylum 1107
			LEAVES	
			Los Angeles rock quintet - John Beck, lead singer	
7/30/66	127	5	1. Hey Joe	Mira 3005
			LeBLANC & CARR	
			Lenny LeBlanc & Pete Carr	
3/18/78	145	7	1. Midnight Light	Big Tree 89521
			LED ZEPPELIN	
			British: Robert Plant (vocals), Jimmy Page (guitar), John Paul Jones (bass/keyboards) & John Bonham (drums) - Bonham died on 9/25/80 (33)	
2/15/69	10	95	● 1. **Led Zeppelin**	Atlantic 8216
11/08/69	1(7)	98	● 2. **Led Zeppelin II**	Atlantic 8236
			"Whole Lotta Love"(4)	
10/24/70	1(4)	42	● 3. **Led Zeppelin III**	Atlantic 7201
			"Immigrant Song"	
11/27/71	2(4)	234	● 4. **Led Zeppelin IV (untitled)**	Atlantic 7208
			"Stairway To Heaven"	
4/14/73	1(2)	99	● 5. **Houses Of The Holy**	Atlantic 7255

DATE CHARTED	PEAK POS	WKS CHRT'D	ARTIST — Album Title	LABEL & NUMBER
3/15/75	1(6)	41	● 6. **Physical Graffiti**	Swan Song 200 [2]
4/24/76	1(2)	30	▲ 7. **Presence**	Swan Song 8416
11/06/76	2(3)	48	▲ 8. **The Soundtrack From The Film "The Song Remains The Same"** .... [S-L] soundtrack recorded live at Madison Square Garden	Swan Song 201 [2]
9/08/79	1(7)	41	▲ 9. **In Through The Out Door**	Swan Song 16002
12/18/82	6	16	▲ 10. **Coda** .... [K] previously unreleased recordings from 1969-1978	Swan Song 90051

ALVIN LEE
British - former lead guitarist/vocalist of Ten Years After

1/12/74	138	8	1. On The Road To Freedom .... ALVIN LEE & MYLON LeFEVRE with guests Steve Winwood. Jim Capaldi, George Harrison & Ron Wood	Columbia 32729
1/04/75	65	12	2. In Flight .... [L]	Columbia 33187 [2]
9/06/75	131	5	3. Pump Iron!	Columbia 33796
6/03/78	115	11	4. Rocket Fuel	RSO 3033
5/26/79	158	5	5. Ride On .... above 2 with new group Ten Years Later	RSO 3049
12/20/80	198	4	6. Free Fall	Atlantic 19287

BRENDA LEE
born Brenda Mae Tarpley on 12/11/44 in Atlanta, Georgia

8/22/60	5	57	1. **Brenda Lee** .... "Sweet Nothin's"(4)/"I'm Sorry"(1)/ "That's All You Gotta Do"(6)	Decca 74039
11/21/60	4	41	2. **This Is.....Brenda** .... "I Want To Be Wanted"(1)	Decca 74082
5/08/61	24	33	3. Emotions .... "Emotions"(7)	Decca 74104
8/28/61	17	39	4. All The Way .... "Dum Dum"(4)	Decca 74176
3/24/62	29	23	5. Sincerely	Decca 74216
11/03/62	20	22	6. Brenda, That's All .... "You Can Depend On Me"(6)/"Fool #1"(3)	Decca 74326
3/09/63	25	31	7. All Alone Am I .... "All Alone Am I"(3)	Decca 74370
12/21/63	39	13	8. Let Me Sing .... "Break It To Me Gently"(4)/"Losing You"(6)	Decca 74439
6/13/64	90	11	9. By Request	Decca 74509
9/25/65	36	14	10. Too Many Rivers	Decca 74684
4/09/66	94	13	11. Bye Bye Blues	Decca 74755
6/25/66	70	14	12. 10 Golden Years .... [G] featuring one hit for each year from 1956-1965	Decca 74757
12/24/66	94	12	13. Coming On Strong	Decca 74825
6/15/68	187	2	14. For The First Time .... BRENDA LEE & PETE FOUNTAIN	Decca 74955
5/24/69	98	9	15. Johnny One Time	Decca 75111

DICKEY LEE
born Dick Lipscomb on 9/21/41 in Memphis

11/10/62	50	12	1. The Tale Of Patches .... "Patches"(6)	Smash 67020

JACKIE LEE
member of the Hollywood Flames - also recorded as Earl Cosby for Bob & Earl

2/05/66	85	9	1. The Duck	Mirwood 7000

JOHNNY LEE
performed with Mickey Gilley at his club in Pasadena, Texas

11/15/80	132	21	● 1. Lookin' For Love .... "Lookin' For Love"(5)	Asylum 309
10/24/81	147	8	2. Bet Your Heart On Me	Full Moon 541

DATE CHARTED	PEAK POS	WKS CHRT'D	ARTIST — Album Title	LABEL & NUMBER
			LAURA LEE	
1/29/72	**117**	11	1. Women's Love Rights	Hot Wax 708
			LEAPY LEE English	
1/18/69	**71**	12	1. Little Arrows	Decca 75076
			PEGGY LEE born Norma Jean Egstrom on 5/26/20 in Jamestown, North Dakota - vocalist with Benny Goodman from 1941-1943	
9/17/55	**7**	9	1. **Songs from Pete Kelly's Blues** .... PEGGY LEE & ELLA FITZGERALD	Decca 8166
9/23/57	**20**	1	2. The Man I Love .... orchestra conducted by Frank Sinatra	Capitol 864
7/14/58	**15**	2	3. Jump For Joy	Capitol 979
12/08/58	**16**	1	4. Things Are Swingin'	Capitol 1049
4/11/60	**11**	58	5. Latin ala Lee!	Capitol 1290
9/11/61	**77**	22	6. Basin Street East .... [L]	Capitol 1520
8/25/62	**85**	6	7. Bewitching-Lee! .... [G] "Fever"(8-'58)	Capitol 1743
11/17/62	**40**	21	8. Sugar 'N' Spice	Capitol 1772
3/09/63	**18**	26	9. I'm A Woman	Capitol 1857
7/27/63	**42**	9	10. Mink Jazz	Capitol 1850
9/26/64	**97**	6	11. In The Name Of Love	Capitol 2096
5/22/65	**145**	4	12. Pass Me By	Capitol 2320
7/30/66	**130**	3	13. Big Spender	Capitol 2475
12/13/69	**55**	18	14. Is That All There Is?	Capitol 386
6/06/70	**142**	9	15. Bridge Over Troubled Water	Capitol 463
12/19/70	**194**	2	16. Make It With You	Capitol 622
			MYRON LeFEVRE - see ALVIN LEE	
			RAYMOND LEFEVRE & His Orchestra French	
3/30/68	**117**	16	1. Soul Coaxing (Ame Caline) ....[I]	4 Corners 4244
			LEFT BANKE New York quintet - Steve Martin, lead singer	
3/25/67	**67**	11	1. Walk Away Renee/Pretty Ballerina .... "Walk Away Renee"(5)	Smash 67088
			MICHEL LEGRAND & His Orchestra French pianist-composer-conductor & arranger - also see Soundtracks "Summer Of '42"/"Thomas Crown Affair"	
5/28/55	**5**	17	1. **Holiday In Rome** .... [I]	Columbia 647
9/17/55	**13**	1	2. Vienna Holiday .... [I]	Columbia 706
6/30/56	**9**	4	3. **Castles In Spain** .... [I]	Columbia 888
3/11/72	**127**	10	4. "Brian's Song" themes & variations .... [I]	Bell 6071
7/01/72	**173**	12	5. Sarah Vaughan/Michel Legrand	Mainstream 361
			TOM LEHRER satirist (in song) who performed on the TV show "That Was The Week That Was"	
11/06/65	**18**	51	1. That Was The Year That Was .... [C]	Reprise 6179
3/26/66	**133**	8	2. An Evening wasted With Tom Lehrer .... [C] recorded March, 1959 in Cambridge, Massachusetts	Reprise 6199
			ERICH LEINSDORF - see BOSTON SYMPHONY ORCHESTRA	
			LEMON PIPERS Cincinnati quintet - Ivan Browne, lead singer	
2/17/68	**90**	18	1. Green Tambourine .... "Green Tambourine"(1)	Buddah 5009

DATE CHARTED	PEAK POS	WKS CHRT'D	ARTIST — Album Title	LABEL & NUMBER
			LENNON SISTERS Dianne, Peggy, Kathy & Janet	
12/25/61	**95**	4	1. Christmas With The Lennon Sisters .... [X]	Dot 25343
5/27/67	**77**	18	2. Somethin' Stupid	Dot 25797
			JOHN LENNON The Beatles' guitarist/lyricist - born on 10/9/40 in Liverpool, England - murdered on 12/8/80 (40) in New York City	
2/08/69	**124**	8	1. Unfinished Music No. 1: Two Virgins	Apple 5001
6/28/69	**174**	8	2. Unfinished Music No. 2: Life With The Lions	Zapple 3357
12/13/69	**178**	3	3. Wedding Album .... above 3 albums feature experimental music and avant-garde sounds by John & Yoko	Apple 3361
1/10/70	**10**	32	● 4. **The Plastic Ono Band - Live Peace In Toronto 1969** .... [L] 9/13/69 concert featuring Eric Clapton on guitar	Apple 3362
12/26/70	**6**	33	● 5. **John Lennon/Plastic Ono Band** .... Plastic Ono Band: John's backing musicians - also see Yoko Ono/Plastic Ono Band	Apple 3372
9/18/71	**1(1)**	45	● 6. **Imagine** .... "Imagine"(3)	Apple 3379
7/01/72	**48**	17	7. Some Time In New York City .... record 1: studio recordings backed by Elephants Memory record 2: "Live Jam" featuring concert recordings with the Mothers of Invention	Apple 3392 [2]
11/24/73	**9**	31	● 8. **Mind Games**	Apple 3414
10/12/74	**1(1)**	35	● 9. **Walls And Bridges** .... "Whatever Gets You Thru The Night"(1)/"#9 Dream"(9)	Apple 3416
3/08/75	**6**	15	10. Rock 'N' Roll	Apple 3419
11/08/75	**12**	32	11. Shaved Fish .... [G] "Instant Karma"(3-70)	Apple 3421
12/06/80	**1(8)**	74	▲ 12. **Double Fantasy** .... 7 songs by John, and 7 by Yoko "(Just Like) Starting Over"(1)/"Woman"(2)/"Watching The Wheels"(10)	Geffen 2001
12/04/82	**33**	16	13. The John Lennon Collection .... [G]	Geffen 2023
1/14/84	**94**	12	14. Heart Play -unfinished dialogue- .... [T] excerpts from a Playboy interview done shortly before John's death	Polydor 817238
2/11/84	**11**	19	● 15. Milk And Honey .... 6 songs by John and 6 by Yoko - recorded in 1980 "Nobody Told Me"(5)	Polydor 817160
			JULIAN LENNON John Lennon's son from his marriage to Cynthia Twist	
11/10/84	**17**	22 +	▲ 1. Valotte .... "Valotte"(9)/"Too Late For Goodbyes"(5) title refers to the French studio where album was recorded	Atlantic 80184
			KETTY LESTER	
6/09/62	**53**	11	1. Love Letters .... "Love Letters"(5)	Era 108
			LET'S ACTIVE North Carolina pop/rock trio	
2/18/84	**154**	11	1. Afoot .... [M]	I.R.S. 70505
11/10/84	**138**	16	2. Cypress	I.R.S. 70648
			LETTERMEN original trio: Tony Butala, Jim Pike and Bob Engemann - Gary Pike (Jim's brother) replaced Bob Engemann in 1968	
2/24/62	**6**	55	1. **A Song For Young Love** .... "The Way You Look Tonight"/"When I Fall In Love"(7)	Capitol 1669
6/09/62	**30**	24	2. Once Upon A Time	Capitol 1711
10/13/62	**59**	19	3. Jim, Tony And Bob	Capitol 1761
4/13/63	**65**	10	4. College Standards	Capitol 1829
8/31/63	**76**	10	5. The Lettermen in Concert .... [L]	Capitol 1936

DATE CHARTED	PEAK POS	WKS CHRT'D	ARTIST — Album Title	LABEL & NUMBER
2/08/64	**31**	32	6. A Lettermen Kind Of Love	Capitol 2013
6/20/64	**94**	10	7. The Lettermen Look At Love	Capitol 2083
11/14/64	**41**	20	8. She Cried	Capitol 2142
3/13/65	**27**	23	9. Portrait Of My Love	Capitol 2270
8/21/65	**13**	24	10. The Hit Sounds Of The Lettermen	Capitol 2359
10/30/65	**73**	13	11. You'll Never Walk Alone	Capitol 2213
2/19/66	**57**	17	12. More Hit Sounds Of The Lettermen!	Capitol 2428
6/25/66	**52**	15	13. A New Song For Young Love	Capitol 2496
10/08/66	**17**	27	● 14. The Best Of The Lettermen [G]	Capitol 2554
2/04/67	**58**	17	15. Warm	Capitol 2633
7/08/67	**31**	26	16. Spring!	Capitol 2711
11/25/67	**10**	48	● 17. **The Lettermen!!!...and "Live!"** [L]	Capitol 2758
			"Goin' Out Of My Head/Can't Take My Eyes Off You"(7)	
4/13/68	**13**	44	● 18. Goin' Out Of My Head	Capitol 2865
9/14/68	**82**	14	19. Special Request [K]	Capitol 2934
12/14/68	**43**	21	20. Put Your Head On My Shoulder	Capitol 147
2/22/69	**128**	10	21. The Best Of The Lettermen, Vol. 2 [G]	Capitol 138
4/05/69	**74**	18	22. I Have Dreamed	Capitol 202
8/23/69	**90**	8	23. Close-Up [R]	Capitol 251 [2]
			reissue of albums #6 & #7 above	
9/06/69	**17**	30	● 24. Hurt So Bad	Capitol 269
2/07/70	**42**	23	25. Traces/Memories	Capitol 390
9/05/70	**134**	11	26. Reflections	Capitol 496
2/06/71	**119**	10	27. Everything's Good About You	Capitol 634
6/26/71	**192**	6	28. Feelings	Capitol 781
10/09/71	**88**	13	29. Love Book	Capitol 836
3/18/72	**136**	6	30. Lettermen 1	Capitol 11010
6/23/73	**193**	7	31. "Alive" Again...Naturally [L]	Capitol 11183
2/23/74	**186**	4	32. All-Time Greatest Hits [G]	Capitol 11249

BARBARA LEWIS
born on 2/9/44 in Detroit, Michigan

DATE CHARTED	PEAK POS	WKS CHRT'D	ARTIST — Album Title	LABEL & NUMBER
9/25/65	**118**	7	1. Baby, I'm Yours [G]	Atlantic 8110
			"Hello Stranger"(3-'63)	

GARY LEWIS & The Playboys
Gary is the eldest son of comedian Jerry Lewis

DATE CHARTED	PEAK POS	WKS CHRT'D	ARTIST — Album Title	LABEL & NUMBER
3/27/65	**26**	25	1. This Diamond Ring	Liberty 7408
			"This Diamond Ring"(1)	
9/18/65	**18**	20	2. A Session With Gary Lewis And The Playboys	Liberty 7419
			"Count Me In"(2)/"Save Your Heart For Me"(2)	
12/04/65	**44**	16	3. Everybody Loves A Clown	Liberty 7428
			"Everybody Loves A Clown"(4)	
3/12/66	**71**	17	4. She's Just My Style	Liberty 7435
			"She's Just My Style"(3)	
5/28/66	**47**	24	5. Hits Again!	Liberty 7452
			"Sure Gonna Miss Her"(9)/"Green Grass"(8)	
10/22/66	**10**	46	● 6. **Golden Greats** [G]	Liberty 7468
2/11/67	**79**	16	7. (You Don't Have To) Paint Me A Picture	Liberty 7487
7/08/67	**185**	4	8. New Directions	Liberty 7519
8/17/68	**150**	9	9. Gary Lewis Now!	Liberty 7568

HUEY LEWIS & THE NEWS
San Francisco 6-man rock band - Huey was born Hugh Cregg III in New York

DATE CHARTED	PEAK POS	WKS CHRT'D	ARTIST — Album Title	LABEL & NUMBER
2/27/82	**13**	59	1. Picture This	Chrysalis 1340
			"Do You Believe In Love"(7)	
10/08/83	**1(1)**	79+ ▲	2. **Sports**	Chrysalis 41412
			"Heart And Soul"(8)/"I Want A New Drug"(6)/	
			"The Heart Of Rock & Roll"(6)/"If This Is It"(6)	

DATE CHARTED	PEAK POS	WKS CHRT'D	ARTIST — Album Title	LABEL & NUMBER
			JERRY LEWIS popular comedian/actor	
12/22/56	**3**	19	1. **Jerry Lewis Just Sings** .... "Rock-A-Bye Your Baby With A Dixie Melody"(10)	Decca 8410
			JERRY LEE LEWIS one of the Fifties leading rockers - born on 9/29/35 in Ferriday, Louisiana	
3/28/64	**116**	8	1. The Golden Hits Of Jerry Lee Lewis .... 1963 recordings of Jerry's biggest Sun hits	Smash 67040
12/05/64	**71**	17	2. The Greatest Live Show On Earth .... [L] recorded on 7/1/64 in Birmingham, Alabama	Smash 67056
6/05/65	**121**	5	3. The Return Of Rock	Smash 67063
5/14/66	**145**	3	4. Memphis Beat	Smash 67079
6/29/68	**160**	12	5. Another Place Another Time	Smash 67104
2/08/69	**149**	7	6. She Still Comes Around (To Love What's Left Of Me)	Smash 67112
5/10/69	**127**	10	7. Jerry Lee Lewis Sings The Country Music Hall Of Fame Hits, Vol. 1	Smash 67117
5/10/69	**124**	10	8. Jerry Lee Lewis Sings The Country Music Hall Of Fame Hits, Vol. 2	Smash 67118
9/27/69	**119**	4	9. Original Golden Hits - Volume 1 .... [G] "Whole Lot Of Shakin' Going On"(3)/"Great Balls Of Fire"(2)/ "Breathless"(7)	Sun 102
9/27/69	**122**	5	10. Original Golden Hits - Volume 2 .... [G]	Sun 103
2/28/70	**186**	2	11. She Even Woke Me Up To Say Goodbye	Smash 67128
5/09/70	**114**	14	12. The Best Of Jerry Lee Lewis .... [G] Jerry's country hits from 1968-1970	Smash 67131
10/10/70	**149**	6	13. Live At The International, Las Vegas .... [L]	Mercury 61278
1/30/71	**190**	6	14. There Must Be More To Love Than This	Mercury 61323
7/24/71	**152**	3	15. Touching Home	Mercury 61343
11/27/71	**115**	12	16. Would You Take Another Chance On Me?	Mercury 61346
4/22/72	**105**	12	17. The "Killer" Rocks On	Mercury 637
3/17/73	**37**	19	18. The Session .... recorded in London with Peter Frampton, Rory Gallagher, Albert & Alvin Lee and others	Mercury 803 [2]
4/28/79	**186**	3	19. Jerry Lee Lewis	Elektra 184
			RAMSEY LEWIS keyboardist born on 5/27/35 in Chicago, Illinois	
12/22/62	**129**	2	1. Sound Of Christmas .... [X-I] made top 10 on Billboard's special Christmas charts (1964-67 and 1969)	Argo 687
7/04/64	**125**	7	2. Bach To The Blues .... [I]	Argo 732
10/17/64	**103**	13	3. The Ramsey Lewis Trio At The Bohemian Caverns .... [I-L]	Argo 741
8/14/65	**2(1)**	47	4. **The In Crowd** .... [I-L] "The 'In' Crowd"(5)	Argo 757
11/06/65	**54**	19	5. Choice! The Best Of The Ramsey Lewis Trio .... [G-I]	Cadet 755
2/19/66	**15**	27	6. Hang On Ramsey! .... [I-L] above albums by The Ramsey Lewis Trio (Elder Young & Red Holt)	Cadet 761
9/10/66	**16**	34	7. Wade In The Water .... [I]	Cadet 774
3/25/67	**95**	16	8. Goin' Latin .... [I]	Cadet 790
7/22/67	**124**	5	9. The Movie Album .... [I]	Cadet 782
10/28/67	**59**	16	10. Dancing In The Street .... [I-L]	Cadet 794
3/09/68	**52**	31	11. Up Pops Ramsey Lewis .... [I]	Cadet 799
7/20/68	**55**	20	12. Maiden Voyage .... [I]	Cadet 811
3/29/69	**191**	14	13. Mother Nature's Son .... [I] all tunes composed by John Lennon & Paul McCartney	Cadet 821
9/06/69	**139**	14	14. Another Voyage .... [I]	Cadet 827

DATE CHARTED	PEAK POS	WKS CHRT'D	ARTIST — Album Title	LABEL & NUMBER
3/14/70	**172**	12	15. The Best Of Ramsey Lewis .... [G-I]	Cadet 839
3/21/70	**157**	8	16. Ramsey Lewis, The Piano Player .... [I]	Cadet 836
10/24/70	**177**	7	17. Them Changes ....[I-L]	Cadet 844
6/19/71	**163**	9	18. Back To The Roots .... [I]	Cadet 6001
6/24/72	**79**	21	19. Upendo Ni Pamoja .... [I]	Columbia 31096
3/03/73	**117**	10	20. Funky Serenity .... [I]	Columbia 32030
10/13/73	**198**	3	21. Ramsey Lewis' Newly Recorded All-Time Non-Stop Golden Hits .... [I]	Columbia 32490
12/28/74	**12**	30	● 22. Sun Goddess .... with Earth, Wind & Fire on 2 of 6 cuts	Columbia 33194
10/04/75	**46**	22	23. Don't It Feel Good	Columbia 33800
5/22/76	**77**	11	24. Salongo .... [I]	Columbia 34173
5/28/77	**79**	10	25. Love Notes .... [I]	Columbia 34696
12/24/77	**111**	9	26. Tequila Mockingbird .... [I]	Columbia 35018
10/28/78	**149**	5	27. Legacy .... [I]	Columbia 35483
8/23/80	**173**	8	28. Routes .... [I]	Columbia 36423
6/20/81	**152**	5	29. Three Piece Suite .... [I]	Columbia 37153
9/08/84	**144**	9	30. The Two Of Us .... RAMSEY LEWIS & NANCY WILSON	Columbia 39326

WEBSTER LEWIS
keyboardist

3/15/80	**114**	9	1. 8 For The 80's	Epic 36197

LORI LIEBERMAN

8/18/73	**192**	6	1. Becoming	Capitol 11203

ENOCH LIGHT & His Orchestra
innovator/producer of stereo percussion albums - Enoch's studio musicians variously billed as Terry Snyder & The All-Stars: The Command All-Stars; Enoch Light & The Light Brigade - died on 7/31/78 (71) - also see Charleston City All-Stars/Los Admiradores/Tony Mottola

6/15/59	**38**	4	1. I Want To Be Happy Cha Cha's .... [I]	Grand Award 388
1/25/60	**1(13)**	124	● 2. **Persuasive Percussion** .... [I]	Command 800
1/25/60	**2(5)**	97	3. **Provocative Percussion** .... [I]	Command 806
8/22/60	**3**	53	4. **Persuasive Percussion, Volume 2** .... [I]	Command 808
9/19/60	**4**	46	5. **Provocative Percussion, Volume 2** .... [I]	Command 810
4/24/61	**3**	20	6. **Persuasive Percussion, Volume 3** .... [I]	Command 817
10/09/61	**1(7)**	57	7. **Stereo 35/MM** .... [I] 35/MM: magnetic film used in recording process	Command 826
2/17/62	**8**	27	8. **Stereo 35/MM, Volume Two** .... [I]	Command 831
2/24/62	**34**	8	9. Persuasive Percussion, Volume 4 .... [I]	Command 830
4/21/62	**27**	12	10. Great Themes From Hit Films .... [I]	Command 835
11/03/62	**44**	4	11. Enoch Light And His Orchestra At Carnegie Hall Play Irving Berlin .... [I]	Command 840
12/15/62	**8**	33	12. **Big Band Bossa Nova** .... [I]	Command 844
11/02/63	**133**	3	13. 1963-The Year's Most Popular Themes ..... [I]	Command 854
4/04/64	**121**	7	14. Rome 35/MM .... [I]	Command 863
5/30/64	**78**	9	15. Dimension "3" .... [I]	Command 867
6/13/64	**129**	4	16. Command Performances .... [K-I]	Command 868
10/03/64	**143**	4	17. Great Themes From Hit Films .... [I]	Command 871
11/07/64	**84**	15	18. Discotheque Dance...Dance...Dance .... [I]	Command 873
9/11/65	**105**	10	19. Magnificent Movie Themes .... [I]	Command 887
5/21/66	**144**	6	20. Persuasive Percussion 1966 .... [I]	Command 895
4/15/67	**173**	2	21. Film On Film - Great Movie Themes............ [I]	Project 3 5005
4/22/67	**163**	4	22. Spanish Strings .... [I]	Project 3 5000
4/26/69	**192**	7	23. Enoch Light & The Brass Menagerie .... [I]	Project 3 5036
3/21/70	**191**	4	24. Spaced Out .... [I]	Project 3 5043
7/24/71	**176**	5	25. Big Band Hits Of The 30's & 40's! .... [I]	Project 3 5056

DATE CHARTED	PEAK POS	WKS CHRT'D	ARTIST — Album Title	LABEL & NUMBER
			GORDON LIGHTFOOT born on 11/17/38 in Orillia, Ontario, Canada	
11/15/69	143	6	1. Sunday Concert .... [L] recorded in Massey Hall, Toronto, Canada	United Art. 6714
5/30/70	12	37	● 2. Sit Down Young Stranger .... "If You Could Read My Mind"(5)	Reprise 6392
5/29/71	38	20	3. Summer Side Of Life	Reprise 2037
6/26/71	178	5	4. Classic Lightfoot (The Best Of Lightfoot/Volume 2) .... [K]	United Art. 5510
3/25/72	42	17	5. Don Quixote	Reprise 2056
11/18/72	95	12	6. Old Dan's Records	Reprise 2116
2/02/74	1(2)	42	● 7. **Sundown** .... "Sundown"(1)/"Carefree Highway"(10)	Reprise 2177
7/27/74	155	9	8. The Very Best Of Gordon Lightfoot .... [K]	United Art. 243
3/01/75	10	20	9. **Cold On The Shoulder**	Reprise 2206
11/22/75	34	24	● 10. Gord's Gold .... [G] record 1 features re-recordings of his Sixties songs	Reprise 2237 [2]
6/26/76	12	41	▲ 11. Summertime Dream .... "Wreck Of The Edmund Fitzgerald"(2)	Reprise 2246
2/04/78	22	20	● 12. Endless Wire	Warner 3149
4/05/80	60	11	13. Dream Street Rose	Warner 3426
2/20/82	87	12	14. Shadows	Warner 3633
8/13/83	175	5	15. Salute	Warner 23901
			LIGHTHOUSE Canadian rock band - Bob McBride, lead singer	
5/09/70	133	3	1. Peacing It All Together	RCA 4325
7/24/71	80	21	2. One Fine Morning	Evolution 3007
1/29/72	157	7	3. Thoughts Of Movin' On	Evolution 3010
7/29/72	178	7	4. Lighthouse Live! .... [L] recorded at Carnegie Hall on 2/6/72	Evolution 3014 [2]
1/13/73	190	9	5. Sunny Days	Evolution 3016
			LIMELITERS Glen Yarbrough (tenor), Lou Gottlieb (bass) & Alex Hassilev (baritone)	
2/27/61	5	74	1. **Tonight: In Person** .... [L] recorded at the Ash Grove, Hollywood, California	RCA 2272
9/04/61	40	18	2. The Limeliters	Elektra 7180
10/02/61	8	36	3. **The Slightly Fabulous Limeliters** .... [L]	RCA 2393
2/03/62	14	31	4. Sing Out!	RCA 2445
6/09/62	25	29	5. Through Children's Eyes .... [L] featuring 70 children from Berkeley, California	RCA 2512
9/29/62	21	12	6. Folk Matinee	RCA 2547
2/02/63	37	25	7. Our Men In San Francisco .... [L]	RCA 2609
5/25/63	83	6	8. Makin' A Joyful Noise	RCA 2588
9/28/63	73	8	9. Fourteen 14K Folk Songs	RCA 2671
5/09/64	118	5	10. More Of Everything! .... Glen Yarbrough replaced by Ernie Sheldon	RCA 2844
			BOB LIND	
4/16/66	148	2	1. Don't Be Concerned .... "Elusive Butterfly"(5)	World Pac. 1841
			DAVID LINDLEY former guitarist/violinist for Jackson Browne	
5/16/81	83	18	1. El Rayo-X	Asylum 524
			MARK LINDSAY lead singer of Paul Revere & The Raiders	
3/07/70	36	19	1. Arizona .... "Arizona"(10)	Columbia 9986
9/05/70	82	10	2. Silverbird	Columbia 30111
10/09/71	180	2	3. You've Got A Friend	Columbia 30735

DATE CHARTED	PEAK POS	WKS CHRT'D	ARTIST — Album Title	LABEL & NUMBER
			ART LINKLETTER radio and TV personality	
12/31/66	143	3	1. For Children Of The World, Art Linkletter narrates "The Bible...In The Beginning" .... [S-T] Art adds narration to music, dialogue and sound effects from the soundtrack	20th Century 3187
			LINX British duo: David Grant & Sketch (Peter Martin)	
6/20/81	175	4	1. Intuition	Chrysalis 1332
			LIPPS, INC. a Steve Greenberg production with vocals by Cynthia Johnson	
4/19/80	5	26	● 1. **Mouth To Mouth** .... "Funkytown"(1)	Casablanca 7197
10/11/80	63	9	2. Pucker Up	Casablanca 7242
			LITTER Detroit hard-rock quintet - Mark Gallagher, lead singer	
8/16/69	175	5	1. Emerge	Probe 4504
			LITTLE ANTHONY & THE IMPERIALS Anthony Gourdine, lead singer of Brooklyn doo-wop quartet	
1/16/65	135	4	1. I'm On The Outside (Looking In) .... includes a new version of "Tears On My Pillow"	DCP 6801
2/20/65	74	13	2. Goin' Out Of My Head .... "Goin' Out Of My Head"(6)/"Hurt So Bad"(10)	DCP 6808
3/05/66	97	23	3. The Best Of Little Anthony & The Imperials .... [G]	DCP 6809
10/04/69	172	5	4. Out Of Sight, Out Of Mind	United Art. 6720
			LITTLE EVA Eva Boyd - discovered while baby sitting at Carole King & Gerry Goffin's home	
11/03/62	97	6	1. Llllloco-Motion .... "The Loco-Motion"(1)	Dimension 6000
			LITTLE FEAT Los Angeles seminal rock sextet led by Lowell George (vocals) & Paul Barrere (lead guitar)	
9/07/74	36	16	1. Feats Don't Fail Me Now	Warner 2784
11/15/75	36	15	2. The Last Record Album	Warner 2884
5/14/77	34	18	3. Time Loves A Hero	Warner 3015
3/11/78	18	25	● 4. Waiting For Columbus .... [L]	Warner 3140 [2]
12/08/79	29	21	5. Down On The Farm	Warner 3345
8/22/81	39	13	6. Hoy-Hoy! .... [K]	Warner 3538 [2]
			LITTLE MILTON Milton Campbell, Jr. from Leland, Mississippi	
6/05/65	101	14	1. We're Gonna Make It	Checker 2995
6/14/69	159	7	2. Grits Ain't Groceries	Checker 3011
3/28/70	197	2	3. If Walls Could Talk	Checker 3012
			LITTLE RICHARD Richard Penniman - born on 12/25/35 in Macon, Georgia	
8/05/57	13	5	1. Here's Little Richard .... [G] "Long Tall Sally"(6)/"Jenny, Jenny"(10)/"Tutti-Frutti"/ "Rip It Up"/"Ready Teddy"	Specialty 2100
8/19/67	184	3	2. Little Richard's Greatest Hits .... [L]	Okeh 14121
11/13/71	193	4	3. King Of Rock And Roll	Reprise 6462
			LITTLE RIVER BAND Australian - Glenn Shorrock, lead singer	
10/02/76	80	24	1. Little River Band	Harvest 11512
6/25/77	49	48	● 2. Diamantina Cocktail	Harvest 11645
6/17/78	16	61	▲ 3. Sleeper Catcher .... "Reminiscing"(3)/"Lady"(10)	Harvest 11783

DATE CHARTED	PEAK POS	WKS CHRT'D	ARTIST — Album Title	LABEL & NUMBER
8/04/79	**10**	33	▲ 4. **First Under The Wire** .... "Lonesome Loser"(6)/"Cool Change"(10)	Capitol 11954
4/19/80	**44**	10	5. Backstage Pass .... [L]	Capitol 12061 [2]
9/19/81	**21**	50	● 6. Time Exposure .... "The Night Owls"(6)/"Take It Easy On Me"(10)	Capitol 12163
12/04/82	**33**	30	● 7. Little River Band/Greatest Hits .... [G]	Capitol 12247
6/18/83	**61**	21	8. The Net .... John Farnham replaces Glenn Shorrock as lead singer	Capitol 12273
			LRB:	
2/09/85	**75**	9+	9. Playing To Win	Capitol 12365
			LITTLE STEVEN & the DISCIPLES OF SOUL Miami Steve Van Zandt of Bruce Springsteen's E Street Band	
12/04/82	**118**	18	1. Men Without Women	EMI America 17086
6/09/84	**55**	17	2. Voice Of America	EMI America 17120
			RICH LITTLE comedian/impressionist	
2/13/82	**29**	13	1. The First Family Rides Again .... [C] with Melanie Chartoff, Michael Richards, Shelley Hack, Jenilee Harrison, Earle Doud (producer), & Vaughn Meader	Boardwalk 33248
			LIVING STRINGS European orchestra	
2/27/61	**26**	6	1. Living Strings Play All The Music From Camelot .... [I]	RCA Camden 657
2/27/61	**42**	7	2. Living Strings Play Music Of The Sea........ [I]	RCA Camden 639
			CHARLES LLOYD Quartet jazz tenor saxophonist	
7/15/67	**188**	4	1. Forest Flower .... [I-L] recorded at the Monterey Jazz Festival on 9/18/66	Atlantic 1473
8/19/67	**171**	7	2. Love-In .... [I-L] recorded at the Fillmore in San Francisco	Atlantic 1481
			LOBO Kent LaVoie from Florida	
6/05/71	**178**	10	1. Introducing Lobo .... "Me And You And A Dog Named Boo"(5)	Big Tree 2003
10/14/72	**37**	31	2. Of A Simple Man .... "I'd Love You To Want Me"(2)/ "Don't Expect Me To Be Your Friend"(8)	Big Tree 2013
5/05/73	**163**	5	3. Introducing Lobo .... [R] reissue of album #1 above	Big Tree 2100
6/30/73	**128**	14	4. Calumet	Big Tree 2101
8/10/74	**183**	4	5. Just A Singer	Big Tree 89501
4/05/75	**151**	7	6. A Cowboy Afraid Of Horses	Big Tree 89505
			JOHN LODGE Moody Blues' guitarist - also see Justin Hayward	
4/23/77	**121**	9	1. Natural Avenue	London 683
			NILS LOFGREN leader of Grin (1969-1974)	
3/22/75	**141**	9	1. Nils Lofgren	A&M 4509
4/17/76	**32**	16	2. Cry Tough	A&M 4573
3/19/77	**36**	12	3. I Came To Dance	A&M 4628
10/29/77	**44**	10	4. Night After Night .... [L]	A&M 3707 [2]
7/21/79	**54**	14	5. Nils	A&M 4756
9/26/81	**99**	11	6. Night Fades Away	Backstreet 5251
			LOGGINS & MESSINA Kenny Loggins & Jim Messina	
3/18/72	**70**	113	● 1. Sittin' In	Columbia 31044
11/11/72	**16**	61	● 2. Loggins And Messina .... "Your Mama Don't Dance"(4)	Columbia 31748
11/10/73	**10**	49	● 3. **Full Sail**	Columbia 32540

DATE CHARTED	PEAK POS	WKS CHRT'D	ARTIST — Album Title	LABEL & NUMBER
5/11/74	5	37	● 4. **On Stage** .... [L]	Columbia 32848 [2]
11/09/74	8	29	● 5. **Mother Lode**	Columbia 33175
9/13/75	21	13	6. So Fine	Columbia 33810
			featuring popular Fifties tunes	
1/31/76	16	17	● 7. Native Sons	Columbia 33578
12/11/76	61	12	▲ 8. The Best Of Friends .... [G]	Columbia 34388
11/12/77	83	8	9. Finale .... [L]	Columbia 34167 [2]

DAVE LOGGINS

11/02/74	54	16	1. Apprentice (In A Musical Workshop)	Epic 32833
			"Please Come To Boston"(5)	

KENNY LOGGINS
born on 1/7/48 in Everett, Washington -
also see Soundtrack "Caddyshack"

5/07/77	27	33	▲ 1. Celebrate Me Home	Columbia 34655
7/22/78	7	31	▲ 2. **Nightwatch**	Columbia 35387
			"Whenever I Call You 'Friend'"(5)	
10/20/79	16	43	● 3. Keep The Fire	Columbia 36172
10/04/80	11	31	● 4. Kenny Loggins Alive .... [L]	Columbia 36738 [2]
			"I'm Alright"(live version)	
9/25/82	13	44	● 5. High Adventure	Columbia 38127

JACKIE LOMAX
singer/songwriter from Liverpool, England

6/21/69	145	9	1. Is This What You Want?	Apple 3354
			produced by George Harrison - with Eric Clapton, Paul McCartney & Ringo Starr	

GUY LOMBARDO & His Royal Canadians
Canadian - #1 dance band of the 30s & 40s - died 11/5/77 (75)

1/19/57	18	2	1. Your Guy Lombardo Medley .... [I]	Capitol 739
			medley of 40 tunes	
7/28/58	12	4	2. Berlin By Lombardo .... [I]	Capitol 1019
			medley of 40 Irving Berlin songs	

LONDON FESTIVAL ORCHESTRA - see RONNIE ALDRICH/STANLEY BLACK

LONDON SYMPHONY ORCHESTRA
performed on many of the top Soundtrack scores - also see
Benjamin Britten/Antal Dorati/Rock Operas: "Tommy"

4/14/79	185	2	1. Classic Rock - Volume One .... [I]	RSO 3043
3/05/83	145	3	2. Hooked On Rock Classics .... [I]	RCA 4608

JULIE LONDON
Dixie McCall of TV's "Emergency" - former wife of Jack Webb

1/28/56	2(2)	18	1. **Julie Is Her Name**	Liberty 3006
			"Cry Me A River"(9)	
8/11/56	16	8	2. Lonely Girl	Liberty 3012
12/15/56	18	6	3. Calendar Girl	Liberty 9002
7/22/57	15	4	4. About The Blues	Liberty 3043
6/01/63	127	3	5. The End Of The World	Liberty 7300
11/23/63	136	4	6. The Wonderful World Of Julie London	Liberty 7324

LORETTA LONG - see CHILDRENS section

CLAUDINE LONGET
French - formerly married to Andy Williams

4/15/67	11	54	● 1. Claudine	A&M 4121
10/07/67	33	29	2. The Look Of Love	A&M 4129
4/13/68	29	21	3. Love Is Blue	A&M 4142
2/01/69	155	7	4. Colours	A&M 4163

LOOKING GLASS
New Jersey quartet

7/01/72	113	18	1. Looking Glass	Epic 31320
			"Brandy (You're A Fine Girl)"(1)	

DATE CHARTED	PEAK POS	WKS CHRT'D	ARTIST — Album Title	LABEL & NUMBER
			TRINI LOPEZ born on 5/15/37 in Dallas, Texas	
7/20/63	2(6)	102	● 1. **Trini Lopez At PJ'S** .... [L] "If I Had A Hammer"(3)	Reprise 6093
12/07/63	11	19	2. More Trini Lopez At PJ'S .... [L]	Reprise 6103
4/11/64	32	33	3. On The Move .... [L]	Reprise 6112
8/22/64	18	24	4. The Latin Album .... [F]	Reprise 6125
10/24/64	30	22	5. Live At Basin St. East .... [L]	Reprise 6134
1/30/65	18	23	6. The Folk Album	Reprise 6147
6/12/65	32	19	7. The Love Album	Reprise 6165
8/28/65	46	12	8. The Rhythm & Blues Album	Reprise 6171
12/18/65	101	10	9. The Sing-Along World Of Trini Lopez	Reprise 6183
5/07/66	54	16	10. Trini	Reprise 6196
8/27/66	110	8	11. The Second Latin Album .... [F]	Reprise 6215
11/26/66	47	11	12. Greatest Hits! .... [G]	Reprise 6226
3/04/67	114	6	13. Trini Lopez In London	Reprise 6238
9/02/67	162	7	14. Trini Lopez - Now!	Reprise 6255
			JEFF LORBER Fusion jazz fusion keyboardist	
9/08/79	119	14	1. Water Sign .... [I]	Arista 4234
5/31/80	123	12	2. Wizard Island .... [I]	Arista 9516
4/18/81	77	15	3. Galaxian .... guest vocals by Donnie Gerrard	Arista 9545
3/27/82	73	13	4. It's A Fact	Arista 9583
5/05/84	106	7	5. In The Heat Of The Night	Arista 8025
3/09/85	96+	5+	6. Step By Step .... above 3 shown only as Jeff Lorber	Arista 8269
			LORD SUTCH & Heavy Friends	
2/21/70	84	13	1. Lord Sutch and Heavy Friends .... Friends: Jimmy Page, Jeff Beck, John Bonham, Nicky Hopkins & Noel Redding	Cotillion 9015
			LOS ADMIRADORES percussion group produced by Enoch Light	
8/29/60	2(1)	50	1. **Bongos Bongos Bongos** .... [I]	Command 809
10/24/60	3	34	2. **Bongos/Flutes/Guitars** .... [I]	Command 812
			LOS BRAVOS rock quintet from Spain - Mike Kogel (Kennedy), lead singer	
11/12/66	93	7	1. Black Is Black .... "Black Is Black"(4)	Press 83003
			LOS INDIOS TABAJARAS Brazilian brothers: Natalicio & Antenor Moreyra Lima	
11/16/63	7	31	1. Maria Elena .... [I] "Maria Elena"(6)	RCA 2822
5/16/64	85	10	2. Always In My Heart .... [I]	RCA 2912
			LOS LOBOS Los Angeles-based Chicano quintet	
12/15/84	47	17+	1. How Will The Wolf Survive?	Slash 25177
			LOUDNESS Japanese heavy-metal quartet - Minoru Nihara, lead singer	
3/02/85	76	6+	1. Thunder In The East	Atco 90246
			LOUISIANA'S LE ROUX - see LE ROUX	
			LOVE Los Angeles rock group led by Arthur Lee	
5/14/66	57	18	1. Love .... "My Little Red Book"	Elektra 74001
2/11/67	80	11	2. Da Capo .... "7 And 7 Is"	Elektra 74005

DATE CHARTED	PEAK POS	WKS CHRT'D	ARTIST — Album Title	LABEL & NUMBER
1/06/68	**154**	10	3. Forever Changes	Elektra 74013
9/06/69	**102**	12	4. Four Sail	Elektra 74049
12/27/69	**176**	5	5. Out Here	Blue Thmb.9000[2]
9/05/70	**142**	7	6. Revisited .... [G]	Elektra 74058
12/26/70	**184**	3	7. False Start	Blue Thumb 8822

LOVE & KISSES
disco production by Alec Costandinos

7/30/77	**135**	14	1. Love And Kisses	Casablanca 7063
5/13/78	**85**	17	2. How Much, How Much I Love You	Casablanca 7091

LOVE CHILDS AFRO CUBAN BLUES BAND
disco production by Michael Zager

7/12/75	**168**	5	1. Out Among 'Em .... [I]	Roulette 3016

LOVE UNLIMITED
Barry White's vocal back-up trio

4/29/72	**151**	12	1. Love Unlimited	Uni 73131
9/08/73	**3**	44	● 2. **Under The Influence Of...**	20th Century 414
10/12/74	**85**	27	3. In Heat	20th Century 443
2/26/77	**192**	3	4. He's All I've Got	Un. Gold 101

LOVE UNLIMITED ORCHESTRA
studio orchestra conducted by Barry White

2/09/74	**8**	25	● 1. **Rhapsody In White** .... [I] "Love's Theme"(1) - first appeared in Love Unlimited album (#414 above)	20th Century 433
7/06/74	**96**	10	2. Together Brothers .... [I-S] includes 2 vocals by Barry White & Love Unlimited	20th Centry.ST-101
11/09/74	**28**	27	● 3. White Gold .... [I]	20th Century 458
1/10/76	**92**	15	4. Music Maestro Please .... [I]	20th Century 480
10/30/76	**123**	8	5. My Sweet Summer Suite .... [I]	20th Century 517

LOVERBOY
Canadian quintet led by Mike Reno (vocals) & Paul Dean (guitar)

1/31/81	**13**	105	▲ 1. Loverboy .... "Turn Me Loose"	Columbia 36762
11/14/81	**7**	122	▲ 2. **Get Lucky** .... "Working For The Weekend"	Columbia 37638
7/02/83	**7**	39	▲ 3. **Keep It Up** .... "Hot Girls In Love"	Columbia 38703

LENE LOVICH
new wave singer, born in Detroit; moved to England at age 13

8/04/79	**137**	10	1. Stateless	Stiff 36102
3/08/80	**94**	8	2. Flex	Stiff 36308
1/15/83	**188**	4	3. No-Man's-Land	Stiff 38399

LOVIN' SPOONFUL
John Sebastian, lead singer and co-founder with Zal Yanovsky, Steve Boone & Joe Butler

12/04/65	**32**	35	1. Do You Believe In Magic .... "Do You Believe In Magic"(9)/ "Did You Ever Have To Make Up Your Mind"(2)	Kama Sutra 8050
4/02/66	**10**	31	2. **Daydream** .... "You Didn't Have To Be So Nice"(10)/"Daydream"(2)	Kama Sutra 8051
9/24/66	**126**	9	3. What's Up, Tiger Lily? .... [S] The Lovin' Spoonful star in this Woody Allen film	Kama Sutra 8053
12/17/66	**14**	26	4. Hums Of The Lovin' Spoonful .... "Summer In The City"(1)/"Rain On The Roof"(10)/ "Nashville Cats"(8)	Kama Sutra 8054
3/18/67	**3**	52	● 5. **The Best Of The Lovin' Spoonful** .... [G]	Kama Sutra 8056
4/15/67	**160**	5	6. You're A Big Boy Now .... [S]	Kama Sutra 8058
1/20/68	**118**	7	7. Everything Playing	Kama Sutra 8061

DATE CHARTED	PEAK POS	WKS CHRT'D	ARTIST — Album Title	LABEL & NUMBER
3/30/68	**156**	5	8. The Best Of The Lovin' Spoonful, Volume 2 .... [G]	Kama Sutra 8064
4/24/76	**183**	3	9. The Best...Lovin' Spoonful .... [G]	Kama Sutr. 2608[2]

NICK LOWE
English - member of Brinsley Schwarz ('70-'75)

DATE CHARTED	PEAK POS	WKS CHRT'D	ARTIST — Album Title	LABEL & NUMBER
4/29/78	**127**	10	1. Pure Pop For Now People	Columbia 35329
7/14/79	**31**	22	2. Labour Of Lust .... "Cruel To Be Kind"	Columbia 36087
2/20/82	**50**	14	3. Nick The Knife	Columbia 37932
4/02/83	**129**	7	4. The Abominable Showman	Columbia 38589
6/23/84	**113**	12	5. Nick Lowe and his Cowboy Outfit	Columbia 39371

L.T.D.
Jeffrey Osborne, lead singer of 10 man R&B/funk band

DATE CHARTED	PEAK POS	WKS CHRT'D	ARTIST — Album Title	LABEL & NUMBER
8/21/76	**52**	30	1. Love To The World	A&M 4589
8/13/77	**21**	34	● 2. Something To Love .... "(Every Time I Turn Around) Back In Love Again"(4)	A&M 4646
6/17/78	**18**	26	▲ 3. Togetherness	A&M 4705
7/21/79	**29**	24	● 4. Devotion	A&M 4771
9/06/80	**28**	28	5. Shine On	A&M 4819
11/28/81	**83**	12	6. Love Magic	A&M 4881

NORMAN LUBOFF Choir

DATE CHARTED	PEAK POS	WKS CHRT'D	ARTIST — Album Title	LABEL & NUMBER
10/15/55	**15**	2	1. Songs Of The West	Columbia 657
7/14/56	**19**	2	2. Songs Of The South	Columbia 860
5/27/57	**19**	4	3. Calypso Holiday	Columbia 1000
1/13/58	**22**	1	4. Songs Of Christmas .... [X]	Columbia 926

CARRIE LUCAS

DATE CHARTED	PEAK POS	WKS CHRT'D	ARTIST — Album Title	LABEL & NUMBER
4/23/77	**183**	5	1. Simply Carrie	Soul Train 2220
5/19/79	**119**	10	2. Carrie Lucas In Danceland	Solar 3219
1/31/81	**185**	3	3. Portrait Of Carrie	Solar 3579
9/11/82	**180**	3	4. Still In Love	Solar 60008

LULU
British - real name Marie Lawrie - formerly married to Maurice Gibb (Bee Gees)

DATE CHARTED	PEAK POS	WKS CHRT'D	ARTIST — Album Title	LABEL & NUMBER
11/11/67	**24**	20	1. To Sir With Love .... "To Sir With Love"(1) - also see Soundtrack of same title	Epic 26339
2/21/70	**88**	14	2. New Routes	Atco 310
9/26/81	**126**	10	3. Lulu	Alfa 11006

ARTHUR LYMAN
percussionist (vibes/marimba) from Hawaii

DATE CHARTED	PEAK POS	WKS CHRT'D	ARTIST — Album Title	LABEL & NUMBER
5/12/58	**6**	62	1. **Taboo** .... [I]	HiFi 806
7/24/61	**10**	30	2. **Yellow Bird** .... [I] "Yellow Bird"(4)	HiFi 1004
3/30/63	**36**	6	3. I Wish You Love .... [I]	HiFi 1009

FRANKIE LYMON - see TEENAGERS

CHERYL LYNN
discovered on TV's "Gong Show"

DATE CHARTED	PEAK POS	WKS CHRT'D	ARTIST — Album Title	LABEL & NUMBER
11/18/78	**23**	30	● 1. Cheryl Lynn	Columbia 35486
1/19/80	**167**	4	2. In Love	Columbia 36145
7/11/81	**104**	13	3. In The Night	Columbia 37034
7/17/82	**133**	20	4. Instant Love	Columbia 38057
4/28/84	**161**	5	5. Preppie	Columbia 38961

LORETTA LYNN
born Loretta Webb on 4/14/35 in Butcher's Hollow, Kentucky

DATE CHARTED	PEAK POS	WKS CHRT'D	ARTIST — Album Title	LABEL & NUMBER
3/04/67	**140**	9	1. You Ain't Woman Enough	Decca 74783
4/08/67	**80**	20	● 2. Don't Come Home A Drinkin'	Decca 74842
4/05/69	**168**	5	3. Your Squaw Is On The Warpath	Decca 75084

DATE CHARTED	PEAK POS	WKS CHRT'D	ARTIST — Album Title	LABEL & NUMBER
8/09/69	148	4	4. Woman Of The World/To Make A Man	Decca 75113
2/28/70	146	11	5. Wings Upon Your Horns	Decca 75163
2/13/71	81	17	● 6. Coal Miner's Daughter	Decca 75253
			also see Soundtrack "Coal Miner's Daughter"	
3/13/71	78	14	7. We Only Make Believe	Decca 75251
			LORETTA LYNN & CONWAY TWITTY	
6/26/71	110	7	8. I Wanna Be Free	Decca 75282
3/04/72	106	13	● 9. Lead Me On	Decca 75326
			CONWAY TWITTY & LORETTA LYNN	
4/08/72	109	9	10. One's On The Way	Decca 75334
8/25/73	153	9	11. Louisiana Woman-Mississippi Man	MCA 335
			CONWAY TWITTY-LORETTA LYNN	
9/22/73	183	2	12. Love Is The Foundation	MCA 355
4/19/75	182	2	13. Back To The Country	MCA 471

GLORIA LYNNE
jazz singer from New York City

DATE CHARTED	PEAK POS	WKS CHRT'D	ARTIST — Album Title	LABEL & NUMBER
9/18/61	51	13	1. I'm Glad There Is You	Everest 5126
			with the Earl May Trio	
10/16/61	101	7	2. He Needs Me	Everest 5128
10/30/61	57	18	3. This Little Boy Of Mine	Everest 5131
4/07/62	58	22	4. Gloria Lynne at Basin Street East .... [L]	Everest 5137
2/09/63	39	27	5. Gloria Lynne at the Las Vegas Thunderbird .... [L]	Everest 5208
9/21/63	27	22	6. Gloria, Marty & Strings	Everest 5220
			arranged and conducted by Marty Paich	
6/06/64	43	19	7. I Wish You Love	Everest 5226
6/05/65	82	10	8. Soul Serenade	Fontana 27541

LYNYRD SKYNYRD
Jacksonville, Florida, Southern rock band - plane crash on 10/20/77 killed leader Ronnie Van Zant (28) and members Steve & Cassie Gaines - also see Rossington Collins Band

DATE CHARTED	PEAK POS	WKS CHRT'D	ARTIST — Album Title	LABEL & NUMBER
9/22/73	27	79	● 1. Lynyrd Skynyrd (pronounced leh-nerd skin-nerd)	MCA/Sounds 363
			"Free Bird"	
5/04/74	12	45	● 2. Second Helping	MCA/Sounds 413
			"Sweet Home Alabama"(8)	
4/12/75	9	20	● 3. Nuthin' Fancy	MCA 2137
2/21/76	20	16	● 4. Gimme Back My Bullets	MCA 2170
10/02/76	9	43	▲ 5. One More From The Road .... [L]	MCA 6001 [2]
11/05/77	5	34	▲ 6. Street Survivors	MCA 3029
			album released 3 days before the plane crash	
9/23/78	15	18	▲ 7. Skynyrd's First And...Last .... [E]	MCA 3047
			recordings from 1970-1972	
12/15/79	12	65	▲ 8. Gold & Platinum .... [G]	MCA 11008 [2]
11/20/82	171	7	9. Best Of The Rest .... [K]	MCA 5370

JOHNNY LYTLE
jazz vibraphonist

DATE CHARTED	PEAK POS	WKS CHRT'D	ARTIST — Album Title	LABEL & NUMBER
2/26/66	141	2	1. The Village Caller! .... [I]	Riverside 480

M
M is Robin Scott

DATE CHARTED	PEAK POS	WKS CHRT'D	ARTIST — Album Title	LABEL & NUMBER
12/22/79	79	8	1. New York-London-Paris-Munich	Sire 6084
			"Pop Muzik"(1)	

MOMS MABLEY
comedienne - real name: Loretta Mary Aiken - died 5/23/75 (78)

DATE CHARTED	PEAK POS	WKS CHRT'D	ARTIST — Album Title	LABEL & NUMBER
5/01/61	16	57	1. Moms Mabley At The "UN" .... [C]	Chess 1452
7/10/61	121	5	2. Moms Mabley Onstage .... [C]	Chess 1447
10/30/61	39	27	3. Moms Mabley at The Playboy Club .... [C]	Chess 1460
3/31/62	28	24	4. Moms Mabley At Geneva Conference .... [C]	Chess 1463

DATE CHARTED	PEAK POS	WKS CHRT'D	ARTIST — Album Title	LABEL & NUMBER
9/01/62	27	21	5. Moms Mabley Breaks It Up .... [C]	Chess 1472
1/12/63	19	18	6. Young Men, Si' - Old Men, No .... [C]	Chess 1477
6/29/63	41	16	7. I Got Somethin' To Tell You! .... [C]	Chess 1479
1/04/64	134	5	8. The Funny Sides Of Moms Mabley .... [C]	Chess 1482
2/29/64	48	24	9. Out On A Limb .... [C]	Mercury 60889
7/18/64	118	10	10. Moms Wows .... [E-C]	Chess 1486
			recorded 1961 at the Playboy Club, Chicago	
9/19/64	128	4	11. Moms The Word .... [C]	Mercury 60907
11/13/65	133	3	12. Now Hear This .... [C]	Mercury 61012
9/06/69	173	3	13. The Youngest Teenager .... [C]	Mercury 61229

JEANETTE MacDONALD & NELSON EDDY
top movie duo of the '30s - Jeanette died on 1/14/65 (63); Nelson died on 3/6/67 (65)

5/25/59	40	3	● 1. Favorites In Hi-Fi	RCA 1738

RALPH MacDONALD
session percussionist

9/25/76	114	16	1. Sound Of A Drum .... [I]	Marlin 2202
3/04/78	57	17	2. The Path .... [I]	Marlin 2210
7/14/79	110	10	3. Counterpoint	Marlin 2229
10/13/84	108	10	4. Universal Rhythm	Polydor 823323

MARY MacGREGOR
pop singer from St. Paul, Minnesota

1/15/77	17	19	1. Torn Between Two Lovers	Ariola Am. 50015
			"Torn Between Two Lovers"(1)	

MACHO
disco production by Mauro Malavasi

10/07/78	101	14	1. I'm A Man	Prelude 12160

LONNIE MACK
full name: Lonnie McIntosh

11/30/63	103	9	1. The Wham Of That Memphis Man!	Fraternity 1014
			"Memphis"(5)	

MAD LADS

8/09/69	180	2	1. The Mad, Mad, Mad, Mad, Mad Lads	Volt 6005

MADNESS
septet from London, England

3/08/80	128	9	1. One Step Beyond...	Sire 6085
11/22/80	146	4	2. Absolutely	Sire 6094
4/30/83	41	29	3. Madness	Geffen 4003
			"Our House"(7)	
3/17/84	109	8	4. Keep Moving	Geffen 4022

MADONNA
Madonna Ciccone from Detroit

9/03/83	8	84+ ▲	1. **Madonna**	Sire 23867
			"Borderline"(10)/"Lucky Star"(4)	
12/01/84	1(3)	19+ ▲	2. Like A Virgin	Sire 25157
			"Like A Virgin"(1)/"Material Girl"(2)	

MAD RIVER

8/09/69	192	2	1. Paradise Bar And Grill	Capitol 185

MADURA

10/30/71	186	2	1. Madura	Columbia 30794 [2]

CLEDUS MAGGARD & The Citizen's Band
Cledus' real name: Jay Huguely

3/13/76	135	8	1. The White Knight .... [N]	Mercury 1072
			novelty "C.B." songs	

MAGIC ORGAN
Jerry Smith on organ

5/06/72	135	7	1. Street Fair .... [I]	Ranwood 8092

DATE CHARTED	PEAK POS	WKS CHRT'D	ARTIST — Album Title	LABEL & NUMBER
			MAGNIFICENT MEN 7-man white R&B group from Pennsylvania	
4/08/67	**171**	2	1. The Magnificent Men	Capitol 2678
7/29/67	**89**	9	2. The Magnificent Men "Live!" .... [L]	Capitol 2775
			TAJ MAHAL blues guitarist/vocalist - real name: Henry Fredericks	
2/22/69	**160**	14	1. The Natch'l Blues	Columbia 9698
10/11/69	**85**	9	2. Giant Step/De Ole Folks At Home	Columbia 18 [2]
6/12/71	**84**	13	3. The Real Thing .... [L]	Columbia 30619 [2]
1/15/72	**181**	6	4. Happy Just To Be Like I Am	Columbia 30767
11/04/72	**177**	4	5. Recycling The Blues & Other Related Stuff .... with The Pointer Sisters on 2 cuts	Columbia 31605
12/01/73	**190**	5	6. Oooh So Good 'N Blues	Columbia 32600
10/12/74	**165**	6	7. Mo' Roots	Columbia 33051
10/18/75	**155**	7	8. Music Keeps Me Together	Columbia 33801
1/29/77	**134**	8	9. Music Fuh Ya' (Musica Para Tu)	Warner 2994
			GEORGE MAHARIS Buz Murdock of TV's "Route 66"	
6/02/62	**10**	30	1. George Maharis Sings!	Epic 26001
9/08/62	**32**	24	2. Portrait In Music	Epic 26021
3/30/63	**129**	10	3. Just Turn Me Loose!	Epic 26037
9/14/63	**77**	7	4. Where Can You Go For A Broken Heart?	Epic 26064
			MAHAVISHNU ORCHESTRA - see JOHN McLAUGHLIN	
			MAHOGANY RUSH heavy metal rock trio formed in Montreal, Canada - Frank Marino (guitar, vocals), Paul Harwood (bass), Jim Ayoub (drums)	
8/24/74	**74**	15	1. Child Of The Novelty	20th Century 451
3/01/75	**159**	4	2. Maxoom	20th Century 463
6/21/75	**84**	13	3. Strange Universe	20th Century 482
6/05/76	**175**	3	4. Mahogany Rush IV	Columbia 34190
			FRANK MARINO & MAHOGANY RUSH:	
5/28/77	**184**	2	5. World Anthem	Columbia 34677
3/11/78	**129**	11	6. Frank Marino & Mahogany Rush Live ...... [L]	Columbia 35257
5/12/79	**129**	10	7. Tales Of The Unexpected .... [L] side 1: studio cuts; side 2: recorded live	Columbia 35753
3/08/80	**88**	9	8. What's Next .... brother Vince Marino (rhythm guitar) joins band	Columbia 36204
8/14/82	**185**	4	9. Juggernaut .... shown only as Frank Marino	Columbia 38023
			MAIN INGREDIENT New York soul trio - original lead singer, Don McPherson, died on 7/4/71 (29) - replaced by Cuba Gooding	
8/22/70	**200**	1	1. The Main Ingredient L.T.D.	RCA 4253
3/13/71	**146**	9	2. Tasteful Soul	RCA 4412
10/02/71	**176**	5	3. Black Seeds	RCA 4483
6/24/72	**79**	27	4. Bitter Sweet .... "Everybody Plays The Fool"(3)	RCA 4677
5/05/73	**132**	13	5. Afrodisiac .... with guest Stevie Wonder	RCA 4834
3/09/74	**52**	31	6. Euphrates River .... "Just Don't Want To Be Lonely"(10)	RCA 0335
5/10/75	**90**	12	7. Rolling Down A Mountainside	RCA 0644
12/13/75	**158**	8	8. Shame On The World	RCA 1003
3/05/77	**177**	3	9. Music Maximus	RCA 1558
			MIRIAM MAKEBA native of South Africa - married to Hugh Masekela	
11/16/63	**86**	10	1. The World Of Miriam Makeba	RCA 2750
5/30/64	**122**	4	2. The Voice Of Africa	RCA 2845

DATE CHARTED	PEAK POS	WKS CHRT'D	ARTIST — Album Title	LABEL & NUMBER
7/10/65	85	11	3. An Evening With Belafonte/Makeba .... HARRY BELAFONTE/MIRIAM MAKEBA	RCA 3420
11/18/67	182	4	4. Miriam Makeba In Concert! .... [L]	Reprise 6253
12/09/67	74	22	5. Pata Pata	Reprise 6274

TOMMY MAKEM - see CLANCY BROTHERS

MALO
latin-rock band formed by Jorge Santana (brother of Carlos)

2/12/72	14	31	1. Malo .... "Suavecito"	Warner 2584
11/11/72	62	14	2. Dos	Warner 2652
4/28/73	101	11	3. Evolution	Warner 2702
3/23/74	188	3	4. Ascencion	Warner 2769

MAMA CASS
Cass Elliot of The Mamas & The Papas - died on 7/29/74 (30)

10/19/68	87	10	1. Dream A Little Dream	Dunhill 50040
7/05/69	91	14	2. Bubble Gum, Lemonade &....Something For Mama	Dunhill 50055
12/06/69	169	6	3. Make Your Own Kind Of Music .... [R] reissue of "Bubble Gum" LP plus song "Make Your Own Kind Of Music"	Dunhill 50071
3/13/71	49	7	4. Dave Mason & Cass Elliot	Blue Thumb 25
3/13/71	194	1	5. Mama's Big Ones .... [G] includes 2 cuts with The Mamas & The Papas	Dunhill 50093

MAMA'S BOYS
British rock trio: brothers Pat, John, & Tommy McManus

8/11/84	172	8	1. Mama's Boys	Jive 8214

MAMAS & THE PAPAS
Cass Elliot, Michelle Phillips, John Phillips & Denny Doherty

3/12/66	1(1)	105	• 1. **If You Can Believe Your Eyes And Ears** ...... "California Dreamin'"(4)/"Monday, Monday"(1)	Dunhill 50006
10/01/66	4	76	• 2. **The Mamas & The Papas** .... "I Saw Her Again"(5)/"Words Of Love"(5)	Dunhill 50010
3/18/67	2(7)	55	• 3. **The Mamas & The Papas Deliver** .... "Dedicated To The One I Love"(2)/"Creeque Alley"(5)	Dunhill 50014
11/11/67	5	65	• 4. **Farewell To The First Golden Era** .... [G]	Dunhill 50025
5/25/68	15	34	5. The Papas & The Mamas	Dunhill 50031
9/28/68	53	13	6. Golden Era, Vol. 2 .... [G]	Dunhill 50038
9/27/69	61	26	7. 16 Of Their Greatest Hits .... [G]	Dunhill 50064
11/06/71	84	8	8. People Like Us	Dunhill 50106
3/03/73	186	4	9. 20 Golden Hits .... [G]	Dunhill 50145 [2]

MANASSAS - see STEPHEN STILLS

MELISSA MANCHESTER
singer/songwriter/pianist - born 2/15/51 in the Bronx, New York

6/23/73	156	13	1. Home To Myself	Bell 1123
5/04/74	159	5	2. Bright Eyes	Bell 1303
3/01/75	12	41	• 3. Melissa .... "Midnight Blue"(6)	Arista 4031
2/21/76	24	17	4. Better Days & Happy Endings	Arista 4067
11/20/76	60	13	5. Help Is On The Way	Arista 4095
7/23/77	60	11	6. Singin'...	Arista 4136
12/09/78	33	27	7. Don't Cry Out Loud .... "Don't Cry Out Loud"(10)	Arista 4186
11/03/79	63	21	8. Melissa Manchester	Arista 9506
9/13/80	68	11	9. For The Working Girl	Arista 9533
5/15/82	19	39	10. Hey Ricky .... "You Should Hear How She Talks About You"(5)	Arista 9574
2/26/83	43	21	11. Greatest Hits .... [G]	Arista 9611
12/03/83	135	9	12. Emergency	Arista 8094

DATE CHARTED	PEAK POS	WKS CHRT'D	ARTIST — Album Title	LABEL & NUMBER
			MANCHILD 7-man Chicago soul band	
10/15/77	154	6	1. Power And Love	Chi-Sound 765
			HENRY MANCINI top movie-TV composer/arranger/conductor	
2/09/59	1(10)	117	● 1. **The Music From Peter Gunn** .... [TV-I]	RCA 1956
6/22/59	7	35	2. **More Music From Peter Gunn** .... [TV-I]	RCA 2040
3/28/60	2(1)	70	3. **Music From Mr. Lucky** .... [TV-I]	RCA 2198
5/08/61	28	26	4. Mr. Lucky Goes Latin .... [I]	RCA 2360
10/09/61	1(12)	96	● 5. **Breakfast At Tiffany's** .... [S-I] "Moon River"	RCA 2362
3/03/62	28	14	6. Combo! .... [I] recorded June, 1960	RCA 2258
6/02/62	37	12	7. Experiment In Terror .... [S-I]	RCA 2442
7/21/62	4	50	8. **Hatari!** .... [S-I] "Baby Elephant Walk"	RCA 2559
2/16/63	12	40	9. Our Man In Hollywood .... "Days Of Wine And Roses"	RCA 2604
6/29/63	5	22	10. **Uniquely Mancini** .... [I]	RCA 2692
12/28/63	6	42	11. **Charade** .... [S-I]	RCA 2755
4/11/64	8	88	● 12. **The Pink Panther** .... [S-I]	RCA 2795
8/01/64	15	19	13. The Concert Sound of Henry Mancini .... [I] medleys of 30 tunes - with a 70-piece orchestra	RCA 2897
8/08/64	42	35	● 14. **The Best Of Mancini** .... [G]	RCA 2693
1/30/65	11	25	15. Dear Heart and Other Songs About Love	RCA 2990
6/26/65	46	17	16. The Latin Sound of Henry Mancini .... [I]	RCA 3356
10/02/65	63	22	17. The Great Race .... [S-I]	RCA 3402
3/12/66	74	13	18. The Academy Award Songs .... features the Oscar winning songs from 1934-1964	RCA 6013 [2]
9/10/66	142	4	19. Arabesque .... [S-I]	RCA 3623
9/10/66	148	2	20. What Did You Do In The War, Daddy?.... [S-I]	RCA 3648
12/17/66	121	19	21. Music of Hawaii .... [I]	RCA 3713
3/18/67	65	13	22. Mancini '67 .... [I]	RCA 3694
10/28/67	183	3	23. Two For The Road .... [S-I]	RCA 3802
12/09/67	126	12	24. Encore! More Of The Concert Sound Of Henry Mancini .... [I] medleys of 21 songs - featuring medley of 6 Beatles' tunes	RCA 3887
5/03/69	5	42	● 25. **A Warm Shade Of Ivory** .... [I] "Love Theme From Romeo & Juliet"(1)	RCA 4140
11/01/69	91	16	26. Six Hours Past Sunset .... [I]	RCA 4239
4/25/70	111	17	27. Theme From "Z" and Other Film Music .... [I]	RCA 4350
9/26/70	196	2	28. This Is Henry Mancini .... [G]	RCA 6029 [2]
12/19/70	91	17	29. Mancini Country .... [I]	RCA 4307
1/23/71	26	22	30. Mancini plays the Theme From Love Story ..	RCA 4466
7/31/71	85	11	31. Mancini Concert .... [I] medleys of 23 tunes	RCA 4542
1/29/72	109	15	32. Big Screen - Little Screen	RCA 4630
4/29/72	74	19	33. Brass On Ivory .... [I] HENRY MANCINI & DOC SEVERINSEN	RCA 4629
9/23/72	195	5	34. The Mancini Generation .... [I]	RCA 4689
6/09/73	185	3	35. Brass, Ivory & Strings .... [I] HENRY MANCINI & DOC SEVERINSEN	RCA 0098
2/14/76	159	6	36. Symphonic Soul .... [I]	RCA 1025
9/18/76	161	4	37. A Legendary Performer .... [G]	RCA 1843
6/11/77	126	8	38. Mancini's Angels .... [I]	RCA 2290

DATE CHARTED	PEAK POS	WKS CHRT'D	ARTIST — Album Title	LABEL & NUMBER
			HARVEY MANDEL progressive rock guitarist - formerly with Canned Heat	
5/10/69	187	3	1. Righteous .... [I]	Philips 306
9/20/69	169	4	2. Cristo Redentor .... [I]	Philips 281
7/22/72	198	3	3. The Snake .... [I]	Janus 3037
			MANDRE disco-funk artist Andre Lewis	
9/17/77	64	13	1. Mandre	Motown 886
			BARBARA MANDRELL born on 12/25/48 in Houston, Texas	
2/24/79	170	4	● 1. The Best of Barbara Mandrell .... [G]	ABC 1119
5/26/79	132	9	2. Moods	ABC 1088
10/13/79	166	5	3. Just For The Record	MCA 3165
9/27/80	175	6	4. Love Is Fair	MCA 5136
9/05/81	86	24	● 5. Barbara Mandrell Live .... [L]	MCA 5243
5/29/82	153	6	6. ...in Black & White	MCA 5295
9/03/83	140	4	7. Spun Gold	MCA 5377
9/08/84	89	13	8. Meant For Each Other .... BARBARA MANDRELL/LEE GREENWOOD	MCA 5477
			MANDRILL 7-man Latin jazz/rock band	
4/24/71	48	22	1. Mandrill	Polydor 4050
4/29/72	56	24	2. Mandrill Is	Polydor 5025
2/17/73	28	30	3. Composite Truth	Polydor 5043
10/13/73	82	15	4. Just Outside Of Town	Polydor 5059
4/26/75	92	14	5. Solid	United Art. 408
7/26/75	194	2	6. The Best Of Mandrill .... [G]	Polydor 6047
2/07/76	143	8	7. Beast From The East	United Art. 577
11/12/77	124	10	8. We Are One	Arista 4144
1/13/79	154	5	9. New Worlds	Arista 4195
			MANFRED MANN British band led by keyboardist Manfred Mann	
11/21/64	35	18	1. the Manfred Mann album .... "Do Wah Diddy Diddy"(1)	Ascot 16015
3/06/65	141	4	2. the five faces of Manfred Mann	Ascot 16018
6/01/68	176	5	3. The Mighty Quinn .... "Mighty Quinn (Quinn The Eskimo)"(10)	Mercury 61168
			MANFRED MANN'S EARTH BAND:	
2/26/72	138	6	4. Manfred Mann's Earth Band	Polydor 5015
6/23/73	196	2	5. Get Your Rocks Off	Polydor 5050
3/02/74	96	15	6. Solar Fire	Polydor 6019
11/30/74	157	3	7. The Good Earth	Warner 2826
9/13/75	120	10	8. Nightingales & Bombers	Warner 2877
9/25/76	10	37	● 9. **The Roaring Silence** .... "Blinded By The Light"(1) Chris Thompson replaces Mick Rogers as lead singer	Warner 2965
3/11/78	83	6	10. Watch	Warner 3157
5/12/79	144	13	11. Angel Station	Warner 3302
1/24/81	87	16	12. Chance	Warner 3498
1/28/84	40	21	13. Somewhere In Afrika	Arista 8194
			CHUCK MANGIONE pop-jazz flugelhornist/composer	
7/03/71	116	11	1. Friends & Love...a Chuck Mangione Concert .... [I-L] "Hill Where The Lord Hides"	Mercury 800 [2]
11/20/71	194	4	2. Together: A New Chuck Mangione Concert .... [I-L] above 2 with the Rochester Philharmonic Orchestra	Mercury 7501 [2]

DATE CHARTED	PEAK POS	WKS CHRT'D	ARTIST — Album Title	LABEL & NUMBER
7/15/72	**180**	6	3. The Chuck Mangione Quartet .... [I]	Mercury 631
12/08/73	**157**	12	4. Land Of Make Believe .... [L] with the Hamilton Philharmonic Orchestra	Mercury 684
4/26/75	**47**	19	● 5. Chase The Clouds Away .... [I]	A&M 4518
11/29/75	**68**	15	6. Bellavia .... [I] Bellavia: Chuck Mangione's mother's maiden name	A&M 4557
12/06/75	**102**	10	7. Encore/The Chuck Mangione Concerts [K-L] excerpts from albums 1,2 & 4 above	Mercury 1050
11/20/76	**86**	24	8. Main Squeeze .... [I]	A&M 4612
10/29/77	**2(2)**	88	▲ 9. **Feels So Good** .... [I] "Feels So Good"(4)	A&M 4658
9/16/78	**105**	6	10. The Best Of Chuck Mangione .... [K-L] same as album #7 above - only full length recordings	Mercury 8601 [2]
9/23/78	**14**	44	● 11. Children Of Sanchez .... [S-I]	A&M 6700 [2]
6/30/79	**27**	23	12. An Evening Of Magic - Chuck Mangione Live At The Hollywood Bowl .... [I-L]	A&M 6701 [2]
2/23/80	**8**	23	● 13. **Fun And Games** .... [I]	A&M 3715
5/16/81	**55**	15	14. Tarantella .... [I-L] benefit concert for Italy's earthquake victims - with guests Dizzy Gillespie, Chick Corea and brother Gap Mangione	A&M 6513 [2]
7/17/82	**83**	10	15. Love Notes .... [I]	Columbia 38101
6/25/83	**154**	7	16. Journey To A Rainbow .... [I]	Columbia 38686
9/15/84	**148**	8	17. Disguise	Columbia 39479

MANHATTAN TRANSFER
versatile vocal harmony quartet

5/03/75	**33**	38	1. The Manhattan Transfer	Atlantic 18133
9/18/76	**48**	9	2. Coming Out	Atlantic 18183
2/18/78	**66**	10	3. Pastiche	Atlantic 19163
12/08/79	**55**	37	4. Extensions	Atlantic 19258
6/13/81	**22**	27	5. Mecca For Moderns	Atlantic 16036
			"Boy From New York City"(7)	
12/12/81	**103**	11	6. The Best Of The Manhattan Transfer .... [G]	Atlantic 19319
10/08/83	**52**	27	7. Bodies And Souls	Atlantic 80104
1/05/85	**127**	11	8. Bop Doo-Wopp .... [L] 6 of 10 cuts are live	Atlantic 81233

MANHATTANS
soul ballad quartet formed in 1962

8/11/73	**150**	8	1. There's No Me Without You	Columbia 32444
3/01/75	**160**	4	2. That's How Much I Love You	Columbia 33064
5/01/76	**16**	27	● 3. The Manhattans .... "Kiss And Say Goodbye"(1)	Columbia 33820
2/26/77	**68**	20	● 4. It Feels So Good	Columbia 34450
3/04/78	**78**	12	5. There's No Good In Goodbye	Columbia 35252
4/14/79	**141**	7	6. Love Talk	Columbia 35693
4/19/80	**24**	26	● 7. After Midnight .... "Shining Star"(5)	Columbia 36411
12/13/80	**87**	10	8. Manhattans Greatest Hits .... [G]	Columbia 36861
8/08/81	**86**	10	9. Black Tie	Columbia 37156
8/06/83	**104**	8	10. Forever By Your Side	Columbia 38600

BARRY MANILOW
pop singer/songwriter born on 6/17/46 in Brooklyn, New York

11/23/74	**9**	58	● 1. **Barry Manilow II** .... "Mandy"(1)	Arista 4016
8/02/75	**28**	51	● 2. Barry Manilow I .... above 2 albums previously released on the Bell label "Could It Be Magic"(6)	Arista 4007
11/08/75	**5**	87	● 3. **Tryin' To Get The Feeling** .... "I Write The Songs"(1)/"Tryin' To Get The Feeling Again"(10)	Arista 4060

DATE CHARTED	PEAK POS	WKS CHRT'D	ARTIST — Album Title	LABEL & NUMBER
8/21/76	6	60	▲ 4. **This One's For You** .... "Weekend In New England"(10)/"Looks Like We Made It"(1)	Arista 4090
5/28/77	1(1)	67	▲ 5. **Barry Manilow/Live** .... [L]	Arista 8500 [2]
2/25/78	3	58	▲ 6. **Even Now** .... "Can't Smile Without You"(3)/"Copacabana (At The Copa)"(8)/ "Somewhere In The Night"(9)	Arista 4164
12/02/78	7	75	▲ 7. **Greatest Hits** .... [G]	Arista 8601 [2]
10/20/79	9	25	▲ 8. **One Voice** .... "Ships"(9)	Arista 9505
12/13/80	15	20	▲ 9. **Barry** .... "I Made It Through The Rain"(10)	Arista 9537
10/17/81	14	25	● 10. If I Should Love Again	Arista 9573
9/25/82	69	9	11. Oh, Julie! .... [M]	Arista 2500
12/18/82	32	27	● 12. Here Comes The Night	Arista 9610
12/03/83	30	19	● 13. Barry Manilow/Greatest Hits, Vol. II ....[G]	Arista 8102
12/15/84	28	17+	● 14. 2:00 AM Paradise Cafe .... with jazz greats, Sarah Vaughan, Gerry Mulligan & Mel Torme	Arista 8254

HERBIE MANN
jazz flautist - born on 4/16/30 in Brooklyn, New York

DATE CHARTED	PEAK POS	WKS CHRT'D	ARTIST — Album Title	LABEL & NUMBER
7/28/62	30	41	1. Herbie Mann at the Village Gate .... [I-L]	Atlantic 1380
11/24/62	100	4	2. Right Now .... [I]	Atlantic 1384
3/02/63	86	7	3. Do The Bossa Nova With Herbie Mann ..... [I] recorded in Rio De Janeiro, Brazil	Atlantic 1397
12/21/63	104	8	4. Herbie Mann Live At Newport .... [I-L]	Atlantic 1413
11/27/65	143	3	5. Standing Ovation At Newport .... [I-L]	Atlantic 1445
10/08/66	139	6	6. Our Mann Flute .... [I]	Atlantic 1464
2/03/68	151	12	7. Glory Of Love .... [I]	A&M 3003
5/24/69	22	44	8. Memphis Underground .... [I] with Roy Ayers (vibes) & Larry Coryell (guitar)	Atlantic 1522
11/22/69	139	10	9. Live At The Whisky A Go Go .... [I-L]	Atlantic 1536
3/07/70	184	3	10. Stone Flute .... [I]	Embryo 520
3/28/70	189	2	11. The Best Of Herbie Mann .... [G-I]	Atlantic 1544
4/17/71	137	3	12. Memphis Two-Step .... [I]	Embryo 531
10/30/71	119	23	13. Push Push .... [I] featuring guitar solos by Duane Allman	Embryo 532
2/03/73	172	8	14. The Evolution Of Mann .... [K-I]	Atlantic 300 [2]
6/16/73	163	6	15. Hold On, I'm Comin' .... [I-L]	Atlantic 1632
9/22/73	146	8	16. Turtle Bay .... [I]	Atlantic 1642
3/30/74	109	10	17. London Underground .... [I] recorded in London with guests Albert Lee, Mick Taylor, Ian McDonald & Stephane Grappelli	Atlantic 1648
8/17/74	141	11	18. Reggae ....[I] also recorded in London with Mick Taylor & Albert Lee (guitars)	Atlantic 1655
4/19/75	27	18	19. Discotheque .... [I]	Atlantic 1670
9/27/75	75	7	20. Waterbed	Atlantic 1676
5/08/76	178	2	21. Surprises .... featuring vocalist Cissy Houston	Atlantic 1682
2/12/77	132	7	22. Bird In A Silver Cage .... [I]	Atlantic 18209
10/01/77	122	7	23. Herbie Mann & Fire Island	Atlantic 19112
5/27/78	165	5	24. Brazil-Once Again .... [I]	Atlantic 19169
2/24/79	77	13	25. Super Mann	Atlantic 19221

JOHNNY MANN Singers
Johnny was musical director for the Joey Bishop talk show

DATE CHARTED	PEAK POS	WKS CHRT'D	ARTIST — Album Title	LABEL & NUMBER
10/12/63	90	4	1. Golden Folk Song Hits, Volume Two	Liberty 7296
10/03/64	77	15	2. Invisible Tears	Liberty 7387
7/15/67	51	23	3. We Can Fly! Up-Up And Away	Liberty 7523

MANFRED MANN - see MANFRED

DATE CHARTED	PEAK POS	WKS CHRT'D	ARTIST — Album Title	LABEL & NUMBER
			CHARLIE MANNA comedian from New York	
7/24/61	**27**	14	1. Manna Overboard!! .... [C]	Decca 4159
			MANNHEIM STEAMROLLER classical-rock group from Omaha, Nebraska - best known for their Fresh Aire album series	
12/22/84	**110**	6	1. Mannheim Steamroller Christmas .... [X-I] made top 10 on Billboard's special Christmas charts (1984)	American G. 1984
			MANTOVANI & His Orchestra Annunzio Paolo Mantovani, born in Venice, Italy - died on 3/29/80 (74)	
2/19/55	**13**	1	1. The Music Of Rudolf Friml .... [I]	London 1150
3/19/55	**14**	1	2. Waltz Time .... [I] "Charmaine"(10-'51)	London 1094
7/09/55	**8**	7	● 3. **Song Hits From Theatreland** .... [I]	London 1219
5/26/56	**12**	7	4. Waltzes Of Irving Berlin .... [I]	London 1452
5/27/57	**1(1)**	231	● 5. **Film Encores** .... [I]	London 1700
12/09/57	**4**	6	● 6. **Christmas Carols** .... [X-I]	London 913
3/24/58	**22**	1	7. Mantovani Plays Tangos .... [I] above 2 albums released in 1953	London 768
5/19/58	**5**	105	● 8. **Gems Forever...** .... [I]	London 3032
11/24/58	**7**	68	● 9. **Strauss Waltzes** .... [I] first released in 1953	London 685
12/22/58	**3**	3	10. **Christmas Carols** .... [X-R]	London 913
2/16/59	**13**	34	11. Continental Encores .... [I]	London 3095
6/01/59	**6**	11	12. **Mantovani Stereo Showcase** .... [K-I]	London SS1
6/08/59	**14**	17	13. Film Encores, Vol. 2 .... [I]	London 3117
12/21/59	**16**	3	14. Christmas Carols .... [X-R]	London 913
1/04/60	**8**	18	15. **All-American Showcase** .... [K-I] 1 side each: Sigmund Romberg/Victor Herbert/Irving Berlin/ Rudolf Friml	London 3122 [2]
3/28/60	**11**	30	16. The American Scene .... [I] side 1 features the music of Stephen Foster	London 3136
7/25/60	**21**	53	17. Songs To Remember .... [I]	London 3149
12/05/60	**2(5)**	71	● 18. **Mantovani plays music from Exodus and other great themes** .... [I]	London 3231
12/19/60	**8**	3	19. **Christmas Carols** .... [X-R]	London 913
2/20/61	**22**	1	20. Operetta Memories .... [I]	London 3181
5/29/61	**8**	50	21. **Italia Mia** .... [I]	London 3239
8/14/61	**29**	10	22. Themes From Broadway .... [I]	London 3250
12/18/61	**36**	6	23. Christmas Carols .... [X-R]	London 913
1/13/62	**83**	8	24. Songs Of Praise .... [I]	London 245
6/09/62	**8**	26	25. **American Waltzes** .... [I]	London 248
10/27/62	**24**	15	26. Moon River and other great film themes .... [I]	London 249
1/05/63	**136**	4	27. Stop The World-I Want To Get Off/ Oliver! .... [I]	London 270
6/01/63	**10**	18	28. **Latin Rendezvous** .... [I]	London 295
6/08/63	**41**	12	29. Classical Encores .... [I]	London 269
11/09/63	**51**	22	30. Mantovani/Manhattan .... [I]	London 328
3/14/64	**134**	3	31. Kismet .... with opera stars Robert Merrill & Regina Resnik and chorus	London 44043
4/18/64	**135**	6	32. Folk Songs Around The World .... [I]	London 360
11/07/64	**37**	43	33. The Incomparable Mantovani .... [I]	London 392
3/20/65	**26**	31	34. The Mantovani Sound - Big Hits From Broadway And Hollywood .... [I]	London 419
10/23/65	**41**	21	35. Mantovani Ole .... [I]	London 422
3/05/66	**23**	26	36. Mantovani Magic .... [I]	London 448
10/08/66	**27**	35	37. Mr. Music...Mantovani .... [I]	London 474

DATE CHARTED	PEAK POS	WKS CHRT'D	ARTIST — Album Title	LABEL & NUMBER
3/11/67	53	33	● 38. Mantovani's Golden Hits .... [G-I]	London 483
9/23/67	49	22	39. Mantovani/Hollywood .... [I]	London 516
3/02/68	64	25	40. The Mantovani Touch .... [I]	London 526
6/15/68	148	7	41. Mantovani/Tango .... [I] includes new versions of 4 tunes from album #7 above	London 532
11/09/68	143	7	42. Mantovani...Memories .... [I]	London 542
4/05/69	73	17	43. The Mantovani Scene .... [I]	London 548
11/01/69	92	17	44. The World Of Mantovani .... [I]	London 565
4/04/70	77	24	45. Mantovani Today .... [I]	London 572
11/07/70	167	3	46. Mantovani in Concert .... [I-L] from the Royal Festival Hall, London	London 578
3/27/71	105	15	47. From Monty, With Love .... [K-I]	London 585 [2]
10/30/71	150	9	48. To Lovers Everywhere U.S.A. .... [I]	London 598
5/27/72	156	12	49. Annunzio Paolo Mantovani .... [I] album celebrates his 25th Anniversary with London Records	London 610

PHIL MANZANERA
guitarist of Roxy Music

| 2/10/79 | 176 | 3 | 1. K-Scope .... | Polydor 6178 |

RAY MANZAREK
The Doors' keyboardist

| 2/08/75 | 150 | 6 | 1. The Whole Thing Started With Rock & Roll Now It's Out Of Control .... | Mercury 1014 |

LITTLE PEGGY MARCH
Philadelphian - born on 3/7/48

| 8/17/63 | 139 | 3 | 1. I Will Follow Him ....
"I Will Follow Him"(1) | RCA 2732 |

BENNY MARDONES
Savage, Maryland native

| 6/07/80 | 65 | 22 | 1. Never Run Never Hide ....
"Into The Night" | Polydor 6263 |

MARIACHI BRASS featuring Chet Baker

| 2/26/66 | 120 | 4 | 1. A Taste Of Tequila .... [I] | World Pac. 21839 |

TEENA MARIE
white soul singer from California - real name: Mary Brocker

5/05/79	94	20	1. Wild and Peaceful .... backed by Rick James & The Stone City Band	Gordy 986
3/15/80	45	23	2. Lady T	Gordy 992
9/13/80	38	29	3. Irons In The Fire	Gordy 997
6/13/81	23	25	● 4. It Must Be Magic	Gordy 1004
11/26/83	119	24	5. Robbery	Epic 38882
12/15/84	31+	17+	6. Starchild .... "Lovergirl"(4)	Epic 39528

MARILLION
English quintet led by Fish

| 6/25/83 | 175 | 7 | 1. Script For A Jester's Tear .... | Capitol 12269 |

FRANK MARINO - see MAHOGANY RUSH

MARK-ALMOND
British sessionmen Jon Mark & Johnny Almond

6/05/71	154	15	1. Mark-Almond	Blue Thumb 27
1/15/72	87	16	2. Mark-Almond II	Blue Thumb 32
10/21/72	103	14	3. Rising	Columbia 31917
5/26/73	177	7	4. The Best of Mark-Almond .... [G]	Blue Thumb 50
8/25/73	73	14	5. Mark-Almond 73 .... [L] side 1: live; side 2: studio	Columbia 32486
7/31/76	112	14	6. To The Heart	ABC 945

DATE CHARTED	PEAK POS	WKS CHRT'D	ARTIST — Album Title	LABEL & NUMBER
			MARKETTS West Coast instrumental surf group	
2/08/64	**37**	14	1. Out Of Limits! .... [I] "Out Of Limits"(3)	Warner 1537
3/12/66	**82**	12	2. The Batman Theme .... [I]	Warner 1642
			MAR-KEYS - see BOOKER T. & THE MG's	
			PIGMEAT MARKHAM vaudeville comedian - died on 12/13/81	
7/20/68	**109**	9	1. Here Come The Judge .... [C] comedy sketches, except for the title song	Chess 1523
			BOB MARLEY & THE WAILERS Bob & his Jamaican band are the masters of reggae - Bob died on 5/11/81 (36)	
5/10/75	**92**	28	1. Natty Dread	Island 9281
10/11/75	**151**	6	2. Burnin'	Island 9256
11/08/75	**171**	5	3. Catch A Fire	Island 9241
5/15/76	**8**	22	4. **Rastaman Vibration**	Island 9383
			"Roots, Rock, Reggae"	
10/23/76	**90**	9	5. Live! .... [L]	Island 9376
6/11/77	**20**	24	6. Exodus	Island 9498
4/22/78	**50**	17	7. Kaya	Island 9517
12/16/78	**102**	16	8. Babylon By Bus .... [L]	Island 11 [2]
11/17/79	**70**	14	9. Survival	Island 9542
8/09/80	**45**	23	10. Uprisins	Island 9596
10/31/81	**117**	6	11. Chances Are .... [E] recorded 1968-1972	Cotillion 5228
7/02/83	**55**	15	12. Confrontation	Island 90085
8/18/84	**54**	34+	13. Legend .... [K] recordings from 1972-1981	Island 90169
			MARMALADE British quintet - Dean Ford, lead singer	
6/20/70	**71**	13	1. Reflections Of My Life .... "Reflections Of My Life"(10)	London 575
			NEVILLE MARRINER conductor of English chamber orchestra, Academy Of St. Martin-In-The-Fields, formed by Marriner in 1959	
11/24/84	**60+**	21+	1. Amadeus .... [S]	Fantasy 1791 [2]
			BRANFORD MARSALIS jazz saxophonist - older brother of Wynton Marsalis	
5/19/84	**164**	7	1. Scenes In The City .... [I]	Columbia 38951
			WYNTON MARSALIS jazz/classical trumpeter - son of jazz pianist Ellis Marsalis	
3/06/82	**165**	5	1. Wynton Marsalis .... [I]	Columbia 37574
7/09/83	**102**	29	2. Think Of One... .... [I]	Columbia 38641
10/13/84	**90**	26+	3. Hot House Flowers .... [I]	Columbia 39530
			MARSHALL TUCKER BAND South Carolina Southern rock band - Doug Gray, lead singer; Toy Caldwell, lead guitarist	
7/07/73	**29**	40	● 1. The Marshall Tucker Band	Capricorn 0112
3/09/74	**37**	28	● 2. A New Life	Capricorn 0124
12/21/74	**54**	14	● 3. Where We All Belong .... [L] record 1: studio; record 2: live	Capricorn 0145 [2]
9/13/75	**15**	34	● 4. Searchin' For A Rainbow	Capricorn 0161
6/26/76	**32**	20	5. Long Hard Ride	Capricorn 0170
2/26/77	**23**	36	▲ 6. Carolina Dreams	Capricorn 0180
5/13/78	**22**	16	● 7. Together Forever	Capricorn 0205
10/21/78	**67**	32	● 8. Greatest Hits .... [G]	Capricorn 0214

DATE CHARTED	PEAK POS	WKS CHRT'D		ARTIST — Album Title	LABEL & NUMBER
5/05/79	30	22		9. Running Like The Wind	Warner 3317
3/22/80	32	15		10. Tenth	Warner 3410
5/23/81	53	12		11. Dedicated	Warner 3525
				in memory of bassist Tommy Caldwell - died in an auto accident on 4/28/80 (30)	
6/12/82	95	7		12. Tuckerized	Warner 3684

MARTHA & THE MUFFINS
Canadian - Martha Johnson, lead singer

DATE CHARTED	PEAK POS	WKS CHRT'D		ARTIST — Album Title	LABEL & NUMBER
9/13/80	186	3		1. Metro Music	Virgin 13145
5/21/83	184	4		2. Danseparc	RCA 4664
7/28/84	163	4		3. Mystery Walk	Current 3
				shown as M+M	

MARTHA & THE VANDELLAS
Detroit trio led by Martha Reeves

DATE CHARTED	PEAK POS	WKS CHRT'D		ARTIST — Album Title	LABEL & NUMBER
11/23/63	125	5		1. Heat Wave	Gordy 907
				"Heat Wave"(4)	
5/29/65	139	3		2. Dance Party	Gordy 915
				"Dancing In The Street"(2)/"Nowhere To Run"(8)	
6/11/66	50	15		3. Greatest Hits .... [G]	Gordy 917
				"Quicksand"(8)	
1/21/67	116	8		4. Watchout!	Gordy 920
				"I'm Ready For Love"(9)/"Jimmy Mack"(10)	
10/07/67	140	5		5. Martha & The Vandellas Live! .... [L]	Gordy 925
				MARTHA REEVES & THE VANDELLAS:	
6/01/68	167	8		6. Ridin' High	Gordy 926
4/01/72	146	7		7. Black Magic	Gordy 958

BOBBI MARTIN

DATE CHARTED	PEAK POS	WKS CHRT'D		ARTIST — Album Title	LABEL & NUMBER
3/06/65	127	5		1. Don't Forget I Still Love You	Coral 57472
5/30/70	176	5		2. For The Love Of Him	United Art. 6700

DEAN MARTIN
born Dino Crocetti in Steubenville, Ohio on 6/7/17

DATE CHARTED	PEAK POS	WKS CHRT'D		ARTIST — Album Title	LABEL & NUMBER
5/12/62	73	16		1. Dino - Italian love songs	Capitol 1659
1/26/63	99	5		2. Dino Latino	Reprise 6054
3/30/63	109	4		3. Country Style	Reprise 6061
8/15/64	2(4)	49	●	4. **Everybody Loves Somebody**	Reprise 6130
				"Everybody Loves Somebody"(1)	
8/29/64	15	31	●	5. Dream With Dean	Reprise 6123
11/14/64	9	30	●	6. **The Door Is Still Open To My Heart**	Reprise 6140
				"The Door Is Still Open To My Heart"(6)	
2/13/65	13	29	●	7. Dean Martin Hits Again	Reprise 6146
8/28/65	13	39	●	8. (Remember Me) I'm The One Who Loves You	Reprise 6170
11/20/65	11	34	●	9. Houston	Reprise 6181
				"I Will"(10)	
3/12/66	40	27	●	10. Somewhere There's A Someone	Reprise 6201
7/02/66	108	3		11. The Silencers .... [S]	Reprise 6211
				Dean's first film as secret agent Matt Helm	
8/27/66	50	25		12. The Hit Sound Of Dean Martin	Reprise 6213
12/03/66	34	31		13. The Dean Martin TV Show	Reprise 6233
12/17/66	95	13		14. The Best Of Dean Martin .... [G]	Capitol 2601
				"That's Amore"(2-'53)/"Memories Are Made Of This"(1-'56)/ "Return To Me"(4-'58)	
5/13/67	46	25		15. Happiness Is Dean Martin	Reprise 6242
9/02/67	20	48	●	16. Welcome To My World	Reprise 6250
6/01/68	26	38	●	17. Dean Martin's Greatest Hits! Vol. 1 .... [G]	Reprise 6301
9/07/68	83	21	●	18. Dean Martin's Greatest Hits! Vol. 2 .... [G]	Reprise 6320
1/04/69	14	25	●	19. Gentle On My Mind	Reprise 6330
2/22/69	145	7		20. The Best Of Dean Martin, Vol. 2 .... [G]	Capitol 140
10/04/69	90	17		21. I Take A Lot Of Pride In What I Am	Reprise 6338
9/12/70	97	12		22. My Woman, My Woman, My Wife	Reprise 6403

DATE CHARTED	PEAK POS	WKS CHRT'D	ARTIST — Album Title	LABEL & NUMBER
2/27/71	113	15	23. For The Good Times	Reprise 6428
2/05/72	117	4	24. Dino	Reprise 2053

ERIC MARTIN Band

9/24/83	191	2	1. Sucker For A Pretty Face	Elektra 60238

GEORGE MARTIN & His Orchestra
English - the Beatles' producer from 1962-1970

9/05/64	111	10	1. Off The Beatle Track .... [I] instrumental versions of the Beatles' hits	United Art. 3377

MOON MARTIN

9/08/79	80	11	1. Escape From Domination	Capitol 11933
11/15/80	138	15	2. Street Fever	Capitol 12099

RAY MARTIN & His Orchestra
British conductor

8/14/61	43	6	1. Dynamica .... [I]	RCA 2287

STEVE MARTIN
popular television and film comedian

10/08/77	10	68	▲ 1. **Let's Get Small** .... [C]	Warner 3090
11/04/78	2(6)	26	▲ 2. **A Wild And Crazy Guy** .... [C]	Warner 3238
10/06/79	25	22	● 3. Comedy Is Not Pretty! .... [C]	Warner 3392
11/14/81	135	4	4. The Steve Martin Brothers .... [C-I] side 1: comedy; side 2: banjo music by Steve	Warner 3477

AL MARTINO
born Alfred Cini in Philadelphia on 10/7/27

12/01/62	109	6	1. The Exciting Voice Of Al Martino	Capitol 1774
6/15/63	7	60	2. **I Love You Because** .... "I Love You Because"(3)	Capitol 1914
10/12/63	9	44	3. **Painted, Tainted Rose**	Capitol 1975
2/08/64	13	28	4. Living A Lie	Capitol 2040
4/18/64	57	15	5. The Italian Voice Of Al Martino .... Al's second Capitol album	Capitol 1907
6/27/64	31	25	6. I Love You More And More Every Day/ Tears And Roses .... "I Love You More And More Every Day"(9)	Capitol 2107
2/06/65	41	15	7. We Could	Capitol 2200
6/19/65	42	12	8. Somebody Else Is Taking My Place	Capitol 2312
9/11/65	19	47	9. My Cherie	Capitol 2362
2/19/66	8	73	● 10. **Spanish Eyes**	Capitol 2435
6/18/66	116	6	11. Think I'll Go Somewhere And Cry Myself To Sleep	Capitol 2528
10/29/66	57	13	12. This Is Love	Capitol 2592
3/25/67	99	12	13. This Love For You	Capitol 2654
6/24/67	23	21	14. Daddy's Little Girl	Capitol 2733
10/14/67	63	21	15. Mary In The Morning	Capitol 2780
3/30/68	129	4	16. This Is Al Martino	Capitol 2843
4/20/68	56	17	17. Love Is Blue	Capitol 2908
8/31/68	108	16	18. The Best Of Al Martino .... [G]	Capitol 2946
7/19/69	189	4	19. Sausalito	Capitol 180
12/20/69	196	2	20. Jean	Capitol 379
4/11/70	184	5	21. Can't Help Falling In Love	Capitol 405
11/28/70	172	6	22. My Heart Sings	Capitol 497
6/03/72	138	10	23. Love Theme From "The Godfather" .... portrayed singer Johnny Fontane in the film	Capitol 11071
2/08/75	129	8	24. To The Door Of The Sun	Capitol 11366

DATE CHARTED	PEAK POS	WKS CHRT'D	ARTIST — Album Title	LABEL & NUMBER
			MARVELETTES	
			Detroit trio led by Gladys Horton	
3/19/66	84	16	1. Greatest Hits .... [G]	Tamla 253
			"Please Mr. Postman"(1)/"Playboy"(7)/ "Don't Mess With Bill"(7)	
4/08/67	129	8	2. The Marvelettes	Tamla 274
			GROUCHO MARX	
			America's great comedian - died on 8/19/77 (86)	
10/11/69	155	3	1. The Marx Bros. (The Original Voice Tracks From Their Greatest Movies) .... [C]	Decca 79168
			narration by Gary Owens	
11/25/72	160	15	2. An Evening With Groucho .... [C]	A&M 3515 [2]
			transcription of his one-man concert tour	
			MARY JANE GIRLS	
			female "funk & roll" quartet formed and produced by Rick James	
5/14/83	56	41	1. Mary Jane Girls	Gordy 6040
3/16/85	66+	4+	2. Only Four You	Gordy 6092
			CAROLYNE MAS	
9/22/79	172	3	1. Carolyne Mas	Mercury 3783
			HUGH MASEKELA	
			native of South Africa - married to Miriam Makeba	
8/05/67	151	10	1. Hugh Masekela's Latest	Uni 73010
1/06/68	90	10	2. Hugh Masekela Is Alive And Well At The Whisky .... [L]	Uni 73015
6/08/68	17	22	3. The Promise Of A Future	Uni 73028
			"Grazing In The Grass"(1)	
3/29/69	195	2	4. Masekela	Uni 73041
9/28/74	149	4	5. I Am Not Afraid	Blue Thumb 6015
8/09/75	132	9	6. The Boy's Doin' It	Casablanca 7017
2/11/78	65	19	7. Herb Alpert/Hugh Masekela .... [I]	Horizon 728
			MASKED MARAUDERS	
			Canadian group masquerading as Bob Dylan, Mick Jagger, John Lennon and Paul McCartney	
1/03/70	114	12	1. The Masked Marauders	Deity 6378
			MASON PROFFIT	
			Chicago country-rock band led by brothers Terry & John Talbot (now inspirational artists)	
4/17/71	177	8	1. Movin' Toward Happiness	Happy Tiger 1019
11/06/71	186	14	2. Last Night I Had The Strangest Dream	Ampex 10138
5/19/73	198	5	3. Bareback Rider	Warner 2704
			BARBARA MASON	
			born on 8/9/47 in Philadelphia	
10/02/65	129	8	1. Yes, I'm Ready	Arctic 1000
			"Yes, I'm Ready"(5)	
2/03/73	95	12	2. Give Me Your Love	Buddah 5117
2/22/75	187	2	3. Love's The Thing	Buddah 5628
			DAVE MASON	
			English - original member of Traffic	
7/04/70	22	25	● 1. Alone Together	Blue Thumb 19
			with guests Leon Russell, Jim Capaldi, Rita Coolidge and Delaney & Bonnie	
3/13/71	49	7	2. Dave Mason & Cass Elliot	Blue Thumb 25
2/26/72	51	14	3. Headkeeper .... [L]	Blue Thumb 34
			side 1: studio: side 2: live	
4/21/73	116	11	4. Dave Mason is Alive! .... [L]	Blue Thumb 54
11/10/73	50	28	5. It's Like You Never Left	Columbia 31721
			with guests Graham Nash and Stevie Wonder	
6/29/74	183	9	6. The Best Of Dave Mason .... [G]	Blue Thumb 6013

DATE CHARTED	PEAK POS	WKS CHRT'D	ARTIST — Album Title	LABEL & NUMBER
11/02/74	25	25	● 7. Dave Mason	Columbia 33096
3/22/75	133	3	8. Dave Mason At His Best .... [K]	Blue Thumb 880
			same as album #6 except for one song	
10/18/75	27	17	9. Split Coconut	Columbia 33698
			with guests The Manhattan Transfer, David Crosby and Graham Nash	
11/27/76	78	17	10. Certified Live .... [L]	Columbia 34174 [2]
4/30/77	37	49	● 11. Let It Flow	Columbia 34680
			"We Just Disagree"	
7/01/78	41	19	● 12. Mariposa de Oro	Columbia 35285
10/28/78	179	4	13. Very Best Of Dave Mason .... [K]	Blue Thumb 6032
6/14/80	74	10	14. Old Crest On A New Wave	Columbia 36144

HARVEY MASON
session drummer

4/28/79	149	8	1. Groovin' You	Arista 4227
5/30/81	186	3	2. M.V.P.	Arista 4283

JACKIE MASON

7/14/62	77	7	1. I'm The Greatest Comedian In The World Only Nobody Knows It Yet .... [C]	Verve 15033

NICK MASON'S Fictitious Sports
Nick is Pink Floyd's drummer

7/04/81	170	3	1. Nick Mason's Fictitious Sports	Columbia 37307

MASS PRODUCTION
10-member R&B/funk band from Norfolk, Virginia

1/08/77	142	10	1. Welcome To Our World	Cotillion 9910
8/27/77	83	9	2. Believe	Cotillion 9918
7/21/79	43	17	3. In The Purest Form	Cotillion 5211
3/29/80	133	9	4. Massterpiece	Cotillion 5218
5/16/81	166	6	5. Turn Up The Music	Cotillion 5226

MUIR MATHIESON
conducting The London Sinfonia orchestra

5/29/61	50	21	1. Gone With The Wind .... [I]	Warner 1322
			newly recorded version of the Max Steiner original score	

MIREILLE MATHIEU
French singer

10/04/69	118	8	1. Mireille Mathieu .... [F]	Capitol 306

JOHNNY MATHIS
born in San Francisco on 9/30/35

9/09/57	4	26	1. **Wonderful Wonderful**	Columbia 1028
			the title song is not included on the album	
12/23/57	2(4)	114	● 2. **Warm**	Columbia 1078
4/07/58	10	12	3. **Good Night, Dear Lord**	Columbia 1119
4/14/58	1(3)	490	● 4. **Johnny's Greatest Hits** .... [G]	Columbia 1133
			"Wonderful! Wonderful!"/"It's Not For Me To Say"(5)/ "Chances Are"(1)/"The Twelfth Of Never"(9)	
9/08/58	6	16	● 5. **Swing Softly**	Columbia 1165
12/15/58	3	4	● 6. **Merry Christmas** .... [X]	Columbia 1195
2/09/59	4	97	● 7. **Open Fire, Two Guitars**	Columbia 1270
7/27/59	2(2)	93	● 8. **More Johnny's Greatest Hits** .... [G]	Columbia 1344
			"A Certain Smile"/"Small World"	
9/21/59	1(5)	295	● 9. **Heavenly**	Columbia 1351
			"Misty"	
12/21/59	10	3	10. **Merry Christmas** .... [X-R]	Columbia 1195
1/18/60	2(1)	75	● 11. **Faithfully**	Columbia 8219
			"Maria"	
8/29/60	4	65	12. **Johnny's Mood**	Columbia 8326
10/03/60	6	27	13. **The Rhythms And Ballads Of Broadway**	Columbia 803 [2]
12/26/60	10	2	14. **Merry Christmas** .... [X-R]	Columbia 8021

DATE CHARTED	PEAK POS	WKS CHRT'D	ARTIST — Album Title	LABEL & NUMBER
5/15/61	38	23	15. I'll Buy You A Star	Columbia 8423
8/28/61	2(7)	63	16. **Portrait Of Johnny** .... [G]	Columbia 8444
12/18/61	31	7	17. Merry Christmas .... [X-R]	Columbia 8021
2/24/62	14	39	18. Live It Up!	Columbia 8511
10/27/62	12	37	19. Rapture	Columbia 8715
12/08/62	12	4	20. Merry Christmas .... [X-R] made top 10 on Billboard's special Christmas charts (1963-68 and 1973)	Columbia 8021
4/20/63	6	45	21. **Johnny's Newest Hits** .... [G] "Gina"(6)/"What Will Mary Say"(9)	Columbia 8816
8/24/63	20	27	22. Johnny	Columbia 8844
12/28/63	23	27	23. Romantically	Columbia 8898
2/15/64	13	28	24. Tender Is The Night	Mercury 60890
5/09/64	35	16	25. I'll Search My Heart and Other Great Hits .... [K]	Columbia 8943
7/25/64	75	10	26. The Wonderful World Of Make Believe	Mercury 60913
8/01/64	88	10	27. The Great Years .... [G]	Columbia 834 [2]
10/17/64	40	20	28. This Is Love	Mercury 60942
3/20/65	52	11	29. Love Is Everything	Mercury 60991
10/16/65	71	26	30. The Sweetheart Tree	Mercury 61041
4/02/66	9	45	31. **The Shadow Of Your Smile**	Mercury 61073
10/08/66	50	18	32. So Nice	Mercury 61091
4/01/67	103	11	33. Johnny Mathis Sings	Mercury 61107
12/23/67	60	20	34. Up, Up And Away	Columbia 9526
4/13/68	26	40	35. Love Is Blue	Columbia 9637
12/14/68	60	21	36. Those Were The Days	Columbia 9705
8/16/69	163	4	37. The Impossible Dream	Columbia 9872
9/13/69	192	2	38. People	Columbia 9871
9/20/69	52	24	39. Love Theme From "Romeo And Juliet"	Columbia 9909
4/04/70	38	26	40. Raindrops Keep Fallin' On My Head	Columbia 1005
10/10/70	61	9	41. Close To You	Columbia 30210
1/23/71	169	7	42. Johnny Mathis sings the music of Bacharach & Kaempfert	Columbia 30350 [2]
3/13/71	47	18	43. Love Story	Columbia 30499
9/04/71	80	10	44. You've Got A Friend	Columbia 30740
2/05/72	128	7	45. Johnny Mathis In Person .... [L] recorded at Caesar's Palace in Las Vegas	Columbia 30979 [2]
6/10/72	71	15	46. The First Time Ever (I Saw Your Face)	Columbia 31342
6/24/72	141	15	● 47. Johnny Mathis' All-Time Greatest Hits .... [G]	Columbia 31345 [2]
10/21/72	83	18	48. Song Sung Blue	Columbia 31626
2/17/73	83	14	49. Me And Mrs. Jones	Columbia 32114
6/30/73	120	7	50. Killing Me Softly With Her Song	Columbia 32258
11/17/73	115	22	51. I'm Coming Home	Columbia 32435
12/28/74	139	7	52. The Heart Of A Woman	Columbia 33251
4/19/75	99	13	53. When Will I See You Again	Columbia 33420
11/08/75	97	21	● 54. Feelings	Columbia 33887
6/26/76	79	15	55. I Only Have Eyes For You	Columbia 34117
3/19/77	139	5	56. Mathis Is...	Columbia 34441
4/01/78	9	24	▲ 57. **You Light Up My Life** "Too Much, Too Little, Too Late"(1-with Deniece Williams)	Columbia 35259
7/29/78	19	16	● 58. That's What Friends Are For JOHNNY MATHIS & DENIECE WILLIAMS	Columbia 35435
2/24/79	122	7	59. The Best Days Of My Life	Columbia 35649
8/09/80	164	5	60. Different Kinda Different	Columbia 36505
12/27/80	140	7	61. The Best Of Johnny Mathis 1975-1980 . [G]	Columbia 36871

DATE CHARTED	PEAK POS	WKS CHRT'D	ARTIST — Album Title	LABEL & NUMBER
7/25/81	173	4	62. The First 25 Years - The Silver Anniversary Album .... [G]	Columbia 37440 [2]
5/08/82	147	9	63. Friends In Love	Columbia 37748
3/10/84	157	19	64. A Special Part Of Me	Columbia 38718

MATTY MATLOCK - see RAY HEINDORF/JACK WEBB

MATTHEWS' SOUTHERN COMFORT
English sextet - Ian Matthews, lead singer (album #1 only)

4/17/71	72	15	1. Later That Same Year .... "Woodstock"	Decca 75264
			SOUTHERN COMFORT:	
8/14/71	196	2	2. Frog City	Capitol 800

DAVID MATTHEWS
jazz arranger/songwriter

9/03/77	169	7	1. Dune .... [I] with Hiram Bullock, Eric Gale, David Sanborn and Grover Washington, Jr.	CTI 5005

IAN MATTHEWS
English - founder of Fairport Convention and Matthews' Southern Comfort

2/12/72	196	3	1. Tigers Will Survive	Vertigo 1010
9/22/73	181	7	2. Valley Hi	Elektra 75061
11/11/78	80	24	3. Stealin' Home .... "Shake It"	Mushroom 5012

PAUL MAURIAT & His Orchestra
French conductor/arranger

12/16/67	1(5)	50	● 1. **Blooming Hits** .... [I] "Love Is Blue"(1)	Philips 248
3/30/68	122	22	2. More Mauriat .... [I]	Philips 226
6/08/68	71	18	3. Mauriat Magic .... [I]	Philips 270
10/12/68	142	7	4. Prevailing Airs .... [I]	Philips 280
3/01/69	77	18	5. Doing My Thing .... [I]	Philips 292
5/03/69	157	8	6. The Soul Of Paul Mauriat .... [I]	Philips 299
11/01/69	183	3	7. L.O.V.E. .... [I]	Philips 320
9/19/70	184	3	8. Gone Is Love .... [I]	Philips 345
5/29/71	180	3	9. El Condor Pasa .... [I]	Philips 352

MAX DEMIAN BAND
rock quintet - named after musician in the novel "Demian"

3/03/79	159	5	1. Take It To The Max	RCA 3273

ROBERT MAXWELL His Harp & Orchestra

4/18/64	17	24	1. Shangri-La .... [I]	Decca 74421

BILLY MAY & His Orchestra
arranger/conductor/sideman for many of the big bands

3/05/55	7	5	1. **Sorta-May** .... [I]	Capitol 562

BRIAN MAY & FRIENDS
lead guitarist of Queen, with friends Eddie Van Halen, Alan Gratzer (REO Speedwagon), Phil Chen and Fred Mandel

11/19/83	125	9	1. Star Fleet Project .... [M]	Capitol 15014

JOHN MAYALL
British bluesman John Mayall & his Bluesbreakers band spawned many of Britain's leading rock musicians

2/17/68	136	14	1. John Mayall's Blues Breakers Crusade .... with Mick Taylor, John McVie, Keef Hartley	London 529
6/15/68	128	5	2. The Blues Alone .... all instruments (except drums) played by Mayall	London 534
9/14/68	59	19	3. Bare Wires .... with the Bluesbreakers	London 537
2/22/69	68	17	4. Blues From Laurel Canyon .... John's first album after disbanding the Bluesbreakers	London 545

DATE CHARTED	PEAK POS	WKS CHRT'D	ARTIST — Album Title	LABEL & NUMBER
9/13/69	79	12	5. Looking Back .... [K] featuring Bluesbreakers greats Eric Clapton & Mick Fleetwood (1964-67)	London 562
9/20/69	32	55	● 6. The Turning Point .... [L] featuring Jon Mark & Johnny Almond	Polydor 4004
2/28/70	93	11	7. The Diary Of A Band .... [E-L] recordings taped by Mayall in clubs during 1967	London 570
3/14/70	33	19	8. Empty Rooms	Polydor 4010
10/24/70	22	22	9. USA Union .... featuring Harvey Mandel and other American artists	Polydor 4022
4/17/71	52	15	10. Back To The Roots .... reunion of Bluesbreaker's alumni including Eric Clapton & Mick Taylor	Polydor 3002 [2]
5/01/71	146	8	11. John Mayall-Live In Europe .... [E-L] volume 2 of album #7 above	London 589
11/13/71	164	7	12. Thru The Years .... [K]	London 600 [2]
11/13/71	179	5	13. Memories .... with Jerry McGee (guitar) & Larry Taylor (bass)	Polydor 5012
6/17/72	64	18	14. Jazz Blues Fusion .... [L]	Polydor 5027
10/28/72	116	11	15. Moving On .... [L]	Polydor 5036
2/10/73	158	7	16. Down The Line .... [K-L] record 1: studio cuts 1965-68; record 2: 1964 live concert (Mayall's first British LP)	London 618 [2]
10/06/73	157	7	17. Ten Years Are Gone .... last 3 Polydor albums feature Blue Mitchell (trumpet) & Freddy Robinson (guitar)	Polydor 3005 [2]
3/15/75	140	4	18. New Year, New Band, New Company .... featuring female vocalist Dee McKinnie	Blue Thumb 6019

CURTIS MAYFIELD
lead singer of The Impressions from 1961-1970

DATE CHARTED	PEAK POS	WKS CHRT'D	ARTIST — Album Title	LABEL & NUMBER
10/03/70	19	49	● 1. Curtis	Curtom 8005
5/29/71	21	38	2. Curtis/Live! .... [L]	Curtom 8008 [2]
11/06/71	40	19	3. Roots	Curtom 8009
8/26/72	1(4)	46	● 4. **Superfly** .... [S] "Freddie's Dead"(4)/"Superfly"(8)	Curtom 8014
3/03/73	180	6	5. Curtis Mayfield/His Early Years With The Impressions .... [G]	ABC 780 [2]
6/09/73	16	26	● 6. Back To The World	Curtom 8015
11/17/73	135	10	7. Curtis In Chicago .... [L] with Chicago soul guests Jerry Butler, The Impressions and Gene Chandler	Curtom 8018
5/25/74	39	22	8. Sweet Exorcist	Curtom 8601
11/16/74	76	7	9. Got To Find A Way	Curtom 8604
6/07/75	120	11	10. There's no place like America Today	Curtom 5001
7/04/76	171	8	11. Give, Get, Take And Have	Curtom 5007
3/26/77	173	3	12. Never Say You Can't Survive	Curtom 5013
8/11/79	42	16	13. Heartbeat	RSO 3053
7/19/80	180	4	14. The Right Combination .... LINDA CLIFFORD/CURTIS MAYFIELD	RSO 3084
7/26/80	128	10	15. Something To Believe In	RSO 3077

LYLE MAYS - see PAT METHENY

MAZE Featuring Frankie Beverly
8-member R&B group formed in San Francisco

DATE CHARTED	PEAK POS	WKS CHRT'D	ARTIST — Album Title	LABEL & NUMBER
2/26/77	52	45	● 1. Maze featuring Frankie Beverly	Capitol 11607
2/04/78	27	22	● 2. Golden Time Of Day	Capitol 11710
4/07/79	33	22	● 3. Inspiration	Capitol 11912
8/02/80	31	23	● 4. Joy And Pain	Capitol 12087
7/04/81	34	27	● 5. Live In New Orleans .... [L] side 4 contains new studio recordings	Capitol 12156 [2]
5/28/83	25	26	6. We Are One	Capitol 12262
3/30/85	75+	2+	7. Can't Stop The Love	Capitol 12377

DATE CHARTED	PEAK POS	WKS CHRT'D	ARTIST — Album Title	LABEL & NUMBER
			LETTA MBULU	
3/19/77	192	3	1. There's Music In The Air	A&M 4609
			produced by Herb Alpert	
			MC5	
			Detroit hard rock quintet - Rob Tyner, lead singer	
3/08/69	30	23	1. Kick Out The Jams .... [L]	Elektra 74042
2/21/70	137	7	2. Back In The USA	Atlantic 8247
			produced by rock critic Jon Landau	
			C.W. McCALL	
			real name: Bill Fries - an advertising agent from Omaha	
4/12/75	143	9	1. Wolf Creek Pass	MGM 4989
11/29/75	12	19	● 2. Black Bear Road	MGM 5008
			"Convoy"(1)	
5/08/76	143	4	3. Wilderness	Polydor 6069
			DAVID McCALLUM	
			Illya Kuryakin of TV's "The Man From U.N.C.L.E."	
2/26/66	27	24	1. Music - A Part Of Me .... [I]	Capitol 2432
6/11/66	79	12	2. Music: A Bit More Of Me .... [I]	Capitol 2498
			on above albums. David conducts a studio orchestra	
			LES McCANN	
			jazz keyboardist	
3/29/69	169	10	1. Much Les .... [I]	Atlantic 1516
12/13/69	29	38	2. Swiss Movement .... [I-L]	Atlantic 1537
			LES McCANN & EDDIE HARRIS	
			recorded live at the Montreux Jazz Festival, Switzerland	
5/29/71	41	27	3. Second Movement .... [I]	Atlantic 1583
			EDDIE HARRIS & LES McCANN	
4/08/72	141	6	4. Invitation To Openness .... [I]	Atlantic 1603
10/07/72	181	6	5. Talk To The People	Atlantic 1619
1/18/75	166	4	6. Another Beginning	Atlantic 1666
11/22/75	161	4	7. Hustle To Survive	Atlantic 1679
			PETER McCANN	
			staffwriter with ABC Music	
7/30/77	82	12	1. Peter McCann	20th Century 544
			"Do You Wanna Make Love"(5)	
			PAUL McCARTNEY	
			The Beatles' bass guitarist/songwriter - born on 6/18/42	
			in Liverpool, England	
5/09/70	1(3)	47	● 1. McCartney	Apple 3363
			recorded at home by Paul as a one-man band	
			"Maybe I'm Amazed"	
			PAUL & LINDA McCARTNEY:	
6/05/71	2(2)	37	● 2. RAM	Apple 3375
			"Uncle Albert/Admiral Halsey"(1)	
			WINGS:	
12/25/71	10	18	● 3. Wild Life	Apple 3386
5/12/73	1(3)	31	● 4. Red Rose Speedway	Apple 3409
			"My Love"(1)	
12/22/73	1(4)	116	● 5. Band On The Run	Apple 3415
			"Helen Wheels"(10)/"Jet"(7)/"Band On The Run"(1)	
6/14/75	1(1)	77	● 6. Venus And Mars	Capitol 11419
			"Listen To What The Man Said"(1)	
4/10/76	1(7)	51	▲ 7. Wings At The Speed Of Sound	Capitol 11525
			"Silly Love Songs"(1)/"Let 'Em In"(3)	
12/25/76	1(1)	86	▲ 8. Wings Over America .... [L]	Capitol 11593 [3]
			30 tracks from their 1976 U.S. tour	
			"Maybe I'm Amazed"(10)	
4/15/78	2(6)	28	▲ 9. London Town	Capitol 11777
			"With A Little Luck"(1)	
12/09/78	29	18	▲ 10. Wings Greatest .... [G]	Capitol 11905
			"Another Day"(5-'71)/"Hi. Hi. Hi"(10-'73)/	
			"Live And Let Die"(2-'73)/"Junior's Farm"(3-'75)	

DATE CHARTED	PEAK POS	WKS CHRT'D	ARTIST — Album Title	LABEL & NUMBER
6/30/79	8	24	▲ 11. **Back To The Egg**	Columbia 36057
			PAUL McCARTNEY:	
6/14/80	3	19	● 12. **McCartney II**	Columbia 36511
			recorded solely by Paul at his home "Coming Up"(1)	
1/31/81	158	3	13. The McCartney Interview .... [T]	Columbia 36987
5/15/82	1(3)	29	▲ 14. **Tug Of War**	Columbia 37462
			"Ebony And Ivory"(1-with Stevie Wonder)/"Take It Away"(10)	
11/19/83	15	24	▲ 15. **Pipes Of Peace**	Columbia 39149
			"Say Say Say"(1-with Michael Jackson)	
11/10/84	21	18	● 16. Give my regards to Broad Street .... [S]	Columbia 39613
			13 of 16 cuts are re-recordings of Beatles/McCartney hits "No More Lonely Nights"(6)	
			### ALTON McCLAIN & DESTINY	
3/31/79	88	16	1. Alton McClain & Destiny	Polydor 6163
			### DELBERT McCLINTON	
			played harmonica on Bruce Channel's hit "Hey Baby" - leader of the Ron-Dels	
6/30/79	146	6	1. Keeper Of The Flame	Capricorn 0223
11/22/80	34	28	2. The Jealous Kind	Capitol 12115
			"Giving It Up For Your Love"(8)	
12/05/81	181	9	3. Plain' From The Heart	Capitol 12188
			### MARILYN McCOO & BILLY DAVIS, JR.	
			Marilyn & husband Billy were members of the 5th Dimension	
9/18/76	30	38	● 1. I Hope We Get To Love In Time	ABC 952
			"You Don't Have To Be A Star (To Be In My Show)"(1)	
8/20/77	57	8	2. The Two Of Us	ABC 1026
10/07/78	146	6	3. Marilyn & Billy	Columbia 35603
			### GAYLE McCORMICK	
			former lead singer of the group Smith	
10/16/71	198	3	1. Gayle McCormick	Dunhill 50109
			### CHARLIE McCOY	
			Nashville's #1 session harmonica player	
5/06/72	98	25	1. The Real McCoy .... [I]	Monument 31359
11/25/72	120	13	2. Charlie McCoy .... [I]	Monument 31910
7/21/73	155	6	3. Good Time Charlie .... [I]	Monument 32215
			### VAN McCOY	
			session keyboardist/composer/producer - died on 7/6/79 (35)	
4/26/75	12	23	1. Disco Baby	Avco 69006
			"The Hustle"(1)	
8/16/75	181	4	2. From Disco To Love .... [E]	Buddah 5648
			originally released in 1972	
10/18/75	80	7	3. The Disco Kid	Avco 69009
5/08/76	106	17	4. The Real McCoy	H&L 69012
1/08/77	193	2	5. The Hustle And Best Of Van McCoy .... [G]	H&L 69016
			### McCOYS	
			Rick Derringer, lead singer/guitarist	
11/20/65	44	19	1. Hang On Sloopy	Bang 212
			"Hang On Sloopy"(1)/"Fever"(7)	
			### GEORGE McCRAE	
8/03/74	38	15	1. Rock Your Baby	TK 501
			"Rock Your Baby"(1)	
7/05/75	152	5	2. George McCrae	TK 602
			albums produced by KC with background music by The Sunshine Band	
			### GWEN McCRAE	
			formerly married to George McCrae	
6/28/75	121	10	1. Rockin' Chair	Cat 2605
			"Rockin' Chair"(9)	

DATE CHARTED	PEAK POS	WKS CHRT'D	ARTIST — Album Title	LABEL & NUMBER
			McCRARYS	
			Linda, Charity, Alfred & Sam McCrary	
9/09/78	**138**	9	1. Loving Is Living	Portrait 34764
			COUNTRY JOE McDONALD - see COUNTRY JOE	
			KATHI McDONALD	
			backing vocalist for Joe Cocker, Leon Russell and others	
4/06/74	**156**	11	1. Insane Asylum	Capitol 11224
			MICHAEL McDONALD	
			former lead singer of The Doobie Brothers	
8/28/82	**6**	32	● 1. If That's What It Takes	Warner 23703
			"I Keep Forgettin'"(4)	
			BROTHER JACK McDUFF	
			jazz organist	
6/15/63	**101**	4	1. Screamin' .... [I]	Prestige 7259
11/09/63	**81**	14	2. Live! .... [I-L]	Prestige 7274
			with George Benson (guitar)	
7/23/66	**137**	4	3. Together Again! .... [I]	Prestige 7364
			WILLIS JACKSON with JACK McDUFF	
12/13/69	**192**	6	4. Down Home Style .... [I]	Blue Note 84322
			McFADDEN & WHITEHEAD	
			songwriting duo Gene McFadden & John Whitehead	
6/02/79	**23**	17	● 1. McFadden & Whitehead	Phil. Int. 35800
			"Ain't No Stoppin' Us Now"	
10/04/80	**153**	6	2. I Heard It In A Love Song	TSOP 36773
			GARY McFARLAND	
			jazz arranger/composer/conductor	
4/19/69	**189**	3	1. America The Beautiful .... [I]	Skye 8
			a jazz lament for America	
			MAUREEN McGOVERN	
			born on 7/27/49 in Youngstown, Ohio	
7/28/73	**77**	16	1. The Morning After	20th Century 419
			"The Morning After"(1)	
9/08/79	**162**	10	2. Maureen McGovern	Warner 3327
			BOB McGRATH - see CHILDRENS section	
			JIMMY McGRIFF	
			jazz organist	
12/01/62	**22**	27	1. I've Got A Woman .... [I]	Sue 1012
11/21/64	**146**	2	2. Topkapi .... [I]	Sue 1033
5/29/65	**130**	6	3. Blues For Mister Jimmy .... [I]	Sue 1039
12/28/68	**161**	19	4. The Worm .... [I]	Solid State 18045
			McGUFFEY LANE	
			sextet from Columbus, Ohio	
1/23/82	**193**	6	1. Aqua Dream	Atco 144
			McGUINN, CLARK & HILLMAN	
			Roger McGuinn, Gene Clark & Chris Hillman of the Byrds	
2/24/79	**39**	19	1. McGuinn, Clark & Hillman	Capitol 11910
2/16/80	**136**	7	2. City	Capitol 12043
			ROGER McGUINN	
			founder and leader of the Byrds	
7/14/73	**137**	9	1. Roger McGuinn	Columbia 31946
9/28/74	**92**	6	2. Peace On You	Columbia 32956
7/05/75	**165**	5	3. Roger McGuinn & Band	Columbia 33541
			McGUINNESS FLINT	
			British - Tom McGuinness/Hughie Flint (formerly with Manfred Mann) - vocals by Benny Gallagher & Graham Lyle	
1/30/71	**155**	8	1. McGuinness Flint	Capitol 625
9/11/71	**198**	2	2. Happy Birthday, Ruthy Baby	Capitol 794

DATE CHARTED	PEAK POS	WKS CHRT'D	ARTIST — Album Title	LABEL & NUMBER
			McGUIRE SISTERS Phyllis, Dorothy & Christine from Middletown, Ohio	
3/05/55	11	5	1. By Request... .... [M] 10" album of 8 songs "Sincerely"(1)	Coral 56123
			BARRY McGUIRE member of the New Christy Minstrels	
9/25/65	37	21	1. Eve Of Destruction .... "Eve Of Destruction"(1)	Dunhill 50003
			McKENDREE SPRING folk/pop quintet led by Fran McKendree	
11/28/70	192	2	1. Second Thoughts	Decca 75230
5/20/72	163	7	2. McKendree Spring 3	Decca 75332
5/03/75	118	8	3. Get Me To The Country	Pye 12108
3/27/76	193	3	4. Too Young To Feel This Old	Pye 12124
			BOB & DOUG McKENZIE Rick Moranis & Dave Thomas of 'SCTV'	
1/09/82	8	21	● 1. **Great White North** .... [C] "Take Off"	Mercury 4034
			SCOTT McKENZIE	
12/09/67	127	7	1. The Voice of Scott McKenzie .... "San Francisco (Be Sure To Wear Flowers In Your Hair)"(4)	Ode 44002
			RAY McKINLEY - see GLENN MILLER	
			ROD McKUEN poet/singer/composer - also see San Sebastian Strings and Glenn Yarbrough	
1/27/68	178	6	1. Listen To The Warm	RCA 3863
11/16/68	175	5	2. Lonesome Cities	Warner 1758
3/01/69	149	10	3. Greatest Hits Of Rod McKuen .... [K]	Warner 1772
8/16/69	175	4	4. The Best Of Rod McKuen .... [K]	RCA 4127
10/11/69	96	16	5. Rod McKuen At Carnegie Hall .... [L]	Warner 1794 [2]
3/14/70	126	13	6. New Ballads	Warner 1837
9/19/70	148	8	7. Rod McKuen's Greatest Hits-2 .... [K]	Warner 2560
3/20/71	182	4	8. Pastorale .... with The Westminster Symphony Orchestra	Warner 1894 [2]
11/06/71	177	3	9. Rod McKuen Grand Tour .... [L]	Warner 1947 [2]
			IAN McLAGAN English - charter member (keyboards) of "Small Faces" & "Faces"	
1/19/80	125	9	1. Troublemaker	Mercury 3786
			MALCOM McLAREN & The World's Famous Supreme Team	
2/18/84	173	6	1. D'ya Like Scratchin' .... [M]	Island 90124
2/02/85	190	6	2. Fans .... shown only as Malcom McLaren	Island 90242
			JOHN McLAUGHLIN English-jazz fusion guitar virtuoso	
1/29/72	89	26	1. The Inner Mounting Flame .... [I] MAHAVISHNU ORCHESTRA With JOHN McLAUGHLIN	Columbia 31067
7/01/72	194	4	2. My Goal's Beyond .... [I]	Douglas 30766
10/21/72	152	6	3. Extrapolation .... [E-I] John's first album, recorded in 1969	Polydor 5510
2/10/73	15	37	4. Birds Of Fire .... [I] MAHAVISHNU ORCHESTRA	Columbia 31996
7/07/73	14	24	● 5. Love Devotion Surrender .... [I] CARLOS SANTANA/MAHAVISHNU JOHN McLAUGHLIN	Columbia 32034
12/22/73	41	14	6. Between Nothingness & Eternity .... [I-L]	Columbia 32766
6/01/74	43	14	7. Apocalypse .... [I] with the London Symphony Orchestra conducted by Michael Tilson Thomas	Columbia 32957

DATE CHARTED	PEAK POS	WKS CHRT'D	ARTIST — Album Title	LABEL & NUMBER
3/22/75	68	11	8. Visions Of The Emerald Beyond .... [I]	Columbia 33411
2/21/76	118	7	9. Inner Worlds	Columbia 33908
			MAHAVISHNU ORCHESTRA (above 4)	
6/12/76	194	2	10. Shakti with John McLaughlin .... [I]	Columbia 34162
4/02/77	168	4	11. A Handful Of Beauty .... [I]	Columbia 34372
			SHAKTI with JOHN McLAUGHLIN (above 2)	
5/27/78	105	14	12. Electric Guitarist .... [I]	Columbia 35326
			reunited with Carlos Santana, Tony Williams, Jack Bruce, Chick Corea, Stanley Clarke, Jerry Goodman & Billy Cobham	
4/28/79	147	5	13. Electric Dreams .... [I]	Columbia 35785
			JOHN McLAUGHLIN with THE ONE TRUTH BAND	
5/21/81	97	13	14. Friday Night In San Francisco .... [I-L]	Columbia 37152
			JOHN McLAUGHLIN/AL DI MEOLA/PACO DE LUCIA	
12/12/81	172	4	15. Belo Horizonte .... [I]	Warner 3619
8/20/83	171	5	16. Passion, Grace & Fire .... [I]	Columbia 38645
			JOHN McLAUGHLIN/AL DI MEOLA/PACO DE LUCIA	
			DON McLEAN	
			born on 10/2/45 in New Rochelle, New York	
11/13/71	1(7)	48	● 1. **American Pie**	United Art. 5535
			"American Pie"(1)/"Vincent"	
2/12/72	111	10	2. Tapestry	United Art. 5522
			Don's first album release	
12/23/72	23	19	3. Don McLean	United Art. 5651
11/23/74	120	8	4. Homeless Brother	United Art. 315
2/14/81	28	21	5. Chain Lightning	Millennium 7756
			"Crying"(5)	
11/28/81	156	11	6. Believers	Millennium 7762
			KRISTY & JIMMY McNICHOL	
			Kristy (Jimmy's sister) played Buddy Lawrence on TV's "Family"	
8/19/78	116	4	1. Kristy & Jimmy McNichol	RCA 2875
			CARMEN McRAE	
			jazz singer	
1/14/67	150	2	1. Alfie	Mainstream 56084
			CHRISTINE McVIE	
			English - vocalist with Fleetwood Mac since 1970	
8/14/76	104	10	1. The Legendary Christine Perfect Album	Sire 7522
			recorded in 1969 under her maiden name, after her departure from Chicken Shack	
2/18/84	26	23	2. Christine McVie	Warner 25059
			"Got A Hold On Me"(10)	
			VAUGHN MEADER	
			President John F. Kennedy immitator - produced by Bob Booker & Earle Doud	
12/08/62	1(12)	49	● 1. **The First Family** .... [C]	Cadence 3060
5/25/63	4	17	2. **The First Family, volume two** .... [C]	Cadence 3065
			above albums feature Naomi Brossart as Jackie Kennedy	
			MEAT LOAF	
			real name: Marvin Lee Aday - played Eddie in the film "The Rocky Horror Picture Show"	
10/29/77	14	82	▲ 1. Bat Out Of Hell	Cleve. I. 34974
			"Two Out Of Three Ain't Bad"	
9/19/81	45	11	2. Dead Ringer	Cleve. I. 36007
			MECO	
			discofied instrumentals by producer Meco Monardo	
8/06/77	13	28	▲ 1. Star Wars And Other Galactic Funk .... [I]	Millennium 8001
			"Star Wars Theme/Cantina Band"(1)	
1/14/78	62	13	2. Encounters Of Every Kind .... [I]	Millennium 8004
9/23/78	68	12	3. The Wizard Of Oz .... [I]	Millennium 8009
8/02/80	140	8	4. Meco Plays Music From The Empire Strikes Back .... [M-I]	RSO 3086
			10" album	

DATE CHARTED	PEAK POS	WKS CHRT'D	ARTIST — Album Title	LABEL & NUMBER
12/13/80	**61**	6	5. Christmas In The Stars/Star Wars Christmas Album .... [X]	RSO 3093
4/03/82	**68**	9	6. Pop Goes The Movies .... [I] *medleys of 28 movie themes*	Arista 9598
			BILL MEDLEY *one of the Righteous Brothers*	
10/12/68	**188**	4	1. Bill Medley 100%	MGM 4583
4/05/69	**152**	4	2. Soft And Soulful	MGM 4603
			ZUBIN MEHTA *conducting the Los Angeles Philharmonic Orchestra -* *also see Soundtrack "Manhattan"*	
6/10/72	**175**	10	1. Gustav Holst: The Planets .... [I]	London 6734
3/04/78	**130**	8	2. Star Wars and Close Encounters Of The Third Kind .... [I]	London 1001
			RANDY MEISNER *member of Poco and the Eagles*	
11/01/80	**50**	33	1. One More Song	Epic 36748
8/21/82	**94**	11	2. Randy Meisner	Epic 38121
			MEL & TIM *cousins Mel Harden & Tim McPherson*	
1/06/73	**175**	7	1. Starting All Over Again	Stax 3007
			GEORGE MELACHRINO & His Orchestra	
1/08/55	**10**	1	1. **Christmas in High Fidelity** .... [X-I]	RCA 1045
5/25/59	**30**	1	2. Under Western Skies .... [I]	RCA 1676
			MELANIE *born Melanie Safka on 2/3/47 in Queens, New York*	
11/15/69	**196**	2	1. Melanie	Buddah 5041
5/09/70	**17**	37	● 2. Candles In The Rain *"Lay Down (Candles In The Rain)"(6)*	Buddah 5060
9/26/70	**33**	19	3. Leftover Wine .... [L]	Buddah 5066
2/27/71	**80**	10	4. The Good Book	Buddah 95000
11/13/71	**15**	27	● 5. Gather Me .... *"Brand New Key"(1)*	Neighbor. 47001
12/04/71	**115**	12	6. Garden In The City	Buddah 5095
4/01/72	**103**	9	7. Four Sides Of Melanie .... [K]	Buddah 95005 [2]
11/11/72	**70**	20	8. Stoneground Words	Neighbor. 47005
5/12/73	**109**	11	9. Melanie At Carnegie Hall .... [L]	Neighbor. 49001 [2]
5/11/74	**192**	4	10. Madrugada	Neighbor. 48001
			HAROLD MELVIN & THE BLUE NOTES *Philadelphia soul quintet - Teddy Pendergrass, lead singer (1-5)*	
9/02/72	**53**	31	1. Harold Melvin & The Blue Notes .... *"If You Don't Know Me By Now"(3)*	Phil. Int. 31648
11/10/73	**57**	20	2. Black & Blue .... *"The Love I Lost"(7)*	Phil. Int. 32407
3/01/75	**26**	32	● 3. To Be True	Phil. Int. 33148
12/13/75	**9**	24	● 4. **Wake Up Everybody**	Phil. Int. 33808
7/04/76	**51**	14	5. All Their Greatest Hits! .... [G]	Phil. Int. 34232
2/05/77	**56**	10	6. Reaching For The World	ABC 969
3/22/80	**95**	20	7. The Blue Album .... *featuring Sharon Paige on 2 Songs*	Source 3197
			MEMPHIS HORNS	
6/10/78	**163**	9	1. The Memphis Horns Band II .... *guest vocalists: Michael McDonald. Anita Pointer &* *James Gilstrap*	RCA 2643

DATE CHARTED	PEAK POS	WKS CHRT'D	ARTIST — Album Title	LABEL & NUMBER
			MEN AT WORK Australian quintet, led by Colin Hay	
7/03/82	1(15)	90	▲ 1. **Business As Usual** .... "Who Can It Be Now?"(1)/"Down Under"(1)	Columbia 37978
5/07/83	3	49	▲ 2. **Cargo** .... "Overkill"(3)/"It's A Mistake"(6)	Columbia 38660
			MEN WITHOUT HATS trio from Montreal, Canada	
8/06/83	13	26	● 1. Rhythm Of Youth .... "The Safety Dance"(3)	Backstreet 39002
10/06/84	127	4	2. Folk Of The '80s (Part III)	MCA 5487
			SERGIO MENDES & BRASIL '66 Latin stylists led by pianist Sergio Mendes	
9/10/66	7	126	● 1. **Sergio Mendes & Brasil '66**	A&M 4116
4/29/67	24	46	● 2. Equinox	A&M 4122
3/09/68	5	51	● 3. **Look Around** .... "The Look Of Love"(4)	A&M 4137
6/08/68	197	4	4. Sergio Mendes' Favorite Things .... [E-I]	Atlantic 8177
12/07/68	3	30	● 5. **Fool On The Hill** .... "The Fool On The Hill"(6)	A&M 4160
8/16/69	33	17	6. Crystal Illusions	A&M 4197
12/13/69	71	16	7. Ye-Me-Le	A&M 4236
7/04/70	101	20	8. Greatest Hits .... [G]	A&M 4252
1/09/71	130	9	9. Stillness	A&M 4284
			SERGIO MENDES & BRASIL '77:	
10/16/71	166	6	10. Pais Tropical	A&M 4315
7/15/72	164	5	11. Primal Roots	A&M 4353
6/02/73	116	15	12. Love Music	Bell 1119
5/18/74	176	5	13. Vintage 74	Bell 1305
2/15/75	105	10	14. Sergio Mendes	Elektra 1027
3/27/76	180	2	15. Homecooking	Elektra 1055
8/20/77	81	12	16. Sergio Mendes And The New Brasil '77	Elektra 1102
5/07/83	27	27	17. Sergio Mendes .... "Never Gonna Let You Go"(4)	A&M 4937
5/19/84	70	22	18. Confetti	A&M 4984
			MENUDO Puerto Rican teen quintet - superstar group of Latin America	
3/10/84	108	12	1. Reaching Out .... 9 of 10 songs are English versions of their Spanish hits	RCA 4993
			YEHUDI MENUHIN - see RAVI SHANKAR	
			MERCY	
6/21/69	38	15	1. The Mercy & Love (Can Make You Happy) ..... "Love (Can Make You Happy)"(2)	Sundi 803
			ROBERT MERRILL - see MANTOVANI	
			MERRY-GO-ROUND Emitt Rhodes, lead singer of Los Angeles-area pop quartet	
11/18/67	190	2	1. The Merry-Go-Round	A&M 4132
			MERRYWEATHER Neil Merryweather	
10/04/69	199	2	1. Word Of Mouth .... with guests Steve Miller, Dave Mason, & Barry Goldberg	Capitol 278 [2]
			JIM MESSINA also see Loggins & Messina	
10/20/79	58	14	1. Oasis	Columbia 36140
6/20/81	95	11	2. Messina	Warner 3559

DATE CHARTED	PEAK POS	WKS CHRT'D	ARTIST — Album Title	LABEL & NUMBER
			METALLICA heavy-metal San Francisco-based quartet - vocals: James Hetfield	
9/29/84	**100**	28+	1. Ride The Lightning .... reissued on Elektra 60396 in Nov. '84	Megaforce 769
			METERS New Orleans' funk band led by Art Neville (Aaron's brother)	
6/21/69	**108**	15	1. The Meters .... [I]	Josie 4010
1/24/70	**198**	2	2. Look-Ka Py Py	Josie 4011
7/18/70	**200**	2	3. Struttin'	Josie 4012
9/06/75	**179**	3	4. Fire On The Bayou .... also see Neville Brothers "Fiyo On The Bayou"	Reprise 2228
			PAT METHENY jazz guitarist	
8/26/78	**123**	12	1. Pat Metheny Group .... [I]	ECM 1114
5/05/79	**44**	22	2. New Chautauqua .... [I]	ECM 1131
11/24/79	**53**	24	3. American Garage .... [I]	ECM 1155
11/01/80	**89**	14	4. 80/81 .... [I] with Charlie Haden, Jack DeJohnette, Dewey Redman, Mike Brecker	ECM 1180 [2]
6/20/81	**50**	21	5. As Falls Wichita, So Falls Wichita Falls .... PAT METHENY & LYLE MAYS (keyboards)	ECM 1190
5/22/82	**50**	28	6. Offramp .... [I]	ECM 1216
6/25/83	**62**	17	7. Travels .... [I-L]	ECM 23791 [2]
5/12/84	**116**	9	8. Rejoicing .... [I] with Charlie Haden & Billy Higgins	ECM 25006
10/13/84	**91**	26+	9. First Circle .... [I]	ECM 25008
3/09/85	**54+**	5+	10. The Falcon And The Snowman .... [S-I] "This Is Not America"(with David Bowie)	EMI America 17150
			MFSB MFSB = Mother Father Sister Brother - studio musicians	
4/21/73	**131**	10	1. MFSB .... [I]	Phil. Int. 32046
1/19/74	**4**	35	● 2. **Love Is The Message** .... [I] "TSOP (The Sound Of Philadelphia)"(1)	Phil. Int. 32707
6/14/75	**44**	13	3. Universal Love .... [I]	Phil. Int. 33158
12/06/75	**39**	12	4. Philadelphia Freedom .... [I]	Phil. Int. 33845
7/10/76	**106**	9	5. Summertime	Phil. Int. 34238
			LEE MICHAELS rock organist/vocalist from Los Angeles	
8/30/69	**53**	26	1. Lee Michaels	A&M 4199
8/01/70	**51**	19	2. Barrel	A&M 4249
6/05/71	**16**	36	3. "5th" .... "Do You Know What I Mean"(6)	A&M 4302
3/25/72	**78**	13	4. Space & First Takes	A&M 4336
4/07/73	**135**	8	5. Lee Michaels Live .... [L]	A&M 3518 [2]
6/02/73	**172**	5	6. Nice Day For Something	Columbia 32275
			BETTE MIDLER born on 12/1/45 in Paterson, New Jersey	
12/09/72	**9**	76	● 1. **The Divine Miss M** .... "Boogie Woogie Bugle Boy"(8)	Atlantic 7238
12/08/73	**6**	27	● 2. **Bette Midler** .... accompanied by Barry Manilow (piano) on above 2 LPs	Atlantic 7270
1/31/76	**27**	15	3. Songs For The New Depression	Atlantic 18155
5/28/77	**49**	11	4. Live At Last .... [L]	Atlantic 9000 [2]
12/17/77	**51**	14	5. Broken Blossom	Atlantic 19151
9/22/79	**65**	17	6. Thighs And Whispers	Atlantic 16004
12/22/79	**12**	45	▲ 7. The Rose .... [S-L] "The Rose"(3)	Atlantic 16010

DATE CHARTED	PEAK POS	WKS CHRT'D		ARTIST — Album Title	LABEL & NUMBER
11/29/80	34	14		8. Divine Madness .... [S-L]	Atlantic 16022
				film captures a live concert at Pasadena Civic Auditorium	
8/27/83	60	13		9. No Frills	Atlantic 80070

MIDNIGHT OIL
Australian quintet led by Peter Garrett

| 2/04/84 | 178 | 5 | | 1. 10,9,8,7,6,5,4,3,2,1 .... | Columbia 38996 |

MIDNIGHT STAR
8-man, 1-woman R&B/funk group formed at Kentucky State University

| 7/30/83 | 27 | 89+ | ▲ | 1. No Parking On The Dance Floor .... | Solar 60241 |
| 12/08/84 | 32 | 18+ | ● | 2. Planetary Invasion .... | Solar 60384 |

MIDNIGHT STRING QUARTET
Snuff Garrett, producer

11/19/66	17	59		1. Rhapsodies For Young Lovers .... [I]	Viva 6001
4/08/67	76	12		2. Spanish Rhapsodies For Young Lovers ..... [I]	Viva 36004
7/29/67	67	15		3. Rhapsodies For Young Lovers, Volume Two .... [I]	Viva 36008
3/30/68	129	17		4. Love Rhapsodies .... [I]	Viva 36013
8/17/68	194	3		5. The Look Of Love And Other Rhapsodies For Young Lovers .... [I]	Viva 36015

MIGHTY CLOUDS OF JOY
soul/gospel quintet

| 10/26/74 | 165 | 5 | | 1. It's Time .... | Dunhill 50177 |
| 1/24/76 | 168 | 6 | | 2. Kickin' .... | ABC 899 |

BUDDY MILES
rock/R&B drummer - member of Electric Flag and Jimi Hendrix's Band Of Gypsys

6/07/69	145	4		1. Electric Church	Mercury 61222
				BUDDY MILES EXPRESS produced by Jimi Hendrix	
7/04/70	35	74		2. Them Changes	Mercury 61280
11/14/70	53	26		3. We Got To Live Together	Mercury 61313
4/10/71	60	24		4. A Message To The People	Mercury 608
10/02/71	50	24		5. Buddy Miles Live .... [L]	Mercury 7500 [2]
7/08/72	8	33	●	6. **Carlos Santana & Buddy Miles! Live!** .... [L]	Columbia 31308
3/10/73	123	9		7. Chapter VII	Columbia 32048
1/19/74	194	3		8. Booger Bear	Columbia 32694
				BUDDY MILES EXPRESS	
8/23/75	68	11		9. More Miles Per Gallon	Casablanca 7019

JOHN MILES
English

| 5/22/76 | 171 | 4 | | 1. Rebel .... | London 669 |
| 3/19/77 | 93 | 15 | | 2. Stranger In The City .... | London 682 |

FRANKIE MILLER
Scottish

6/18/77	124	12		1. Full House	Chrysalis 1128
5/13/78	177	10		2. Double Trouble	Chrysalis 1174
6/26/82	135	9		3. Standing On The Edge	Capitol 12206

GLENN MILLER & His Orchestra
#1 dance band of all-time - Glenn disappeared on a plane flight from England to France on 12/15/44 (40)

9/16/57	16	6		1. Marvelous Miller Moods .... [E]	RCA 1494
				Glenn Miller Army Air Force Band with Johnny Desmond (vocals) - from radio broadcasts during 1943-44	
12/09/57	17	4		2. The New Glenn Miller Orchestra In Hi Fi	RCA 1522
				directed by Ray McKinley (leader of the band after Glenn's death)	

DATE CHARTED	PEAK POS	WKS CHRT'D	ARTIST — Album Title	LABEL & NUMBER
2/24/58	19	3	3. The Glenn Miller Carnegie Hall Concert .... [E-L] recorded on 10/06/39	RCA 1506
1/25/75	115	9	4. A Legendary Performer .... [E] previously unreleased performances from 1939-1942	RCA 0693 [2]
			JODY MILLER born in Phoenix, Arizona on 11/29/41	
6/26/65	124	6	1. Queen Of The House	Capitol 2349
8/28/71	117	8	2. He's So Fine	Epic 30659
			MITCH MILLER & The Gang producer/conductor/arranger for the male sing-along chorus	
7/14/58	1(8)	204	● 1. **Sing Along With Mitch**	Columbia 1160
11/10/58	4	171	● 2. **More Sing Along With Mitch**	Columbia 1243
12/08/58	1(2)	5	● 3. **Christmas Sing-Along With Mitch** .... [X]	Columbia 1205
3/23/59	4	131	● 4. **Still More! Sing Along With Mitch**	Columbia 1283
6/01/59	11	89	● 5. Folk Songs Sing Along With Mitch	Columbia 1316
8/31/59	7	100	● 6. **Party Sing Along With Mitch**	Columbia 1331
12/14/59	8	4	● 7. **Christmas Sing-Along With Mitch** .... [X-R]	Columbia 1205
12/28/59	10	92	8. **Fireside Sing Along With Mitch**	Columbia 1389
4/04/60	8	90	● 9. **Saturday Night Sing Along With Mitch**	Columbia 1414
6/27/60	5	107	● 10. **Sentimental Sing Along With Mitch**	Columbia 1457
10/10/60	40	16	11. March Along With Mitch .... [I]	Columbia 1475
10/31/60	5	78	● 12. **Memories Sing Along With Mitch**	Columbia 8342
12/19/60	6	3	● 13. **Christmas Sing-Along With Mitch** .... [X-R]	Columbia 8027
3/13/61	5	73	● 14. **Happy Times! Sing Along With Mitch**	Columbia 8368
3/13/61	9	27	15. Mitch's Greatest Hits .... [G] "The Yellow Rose Of Texas"(1-'55)/ "Song For A Summer Night"(8-'56)	Columbia 8344
5/29/61	3	45	16. **TV Sing Along With Mitch**	Columbia 8428
9/18/61	6	44	17. **Your Request Sing Along With Mitch**	Columbia 8471
11/06/61	1(1)	18	● 18. **Holiday Sing Along With Mitch** .... [X]	Columbia 8501
12/04/61	9	8	● 19. **Christmas Sing-Along With Mitch** .... [X-R]	Columbia 8027
3/10/62	21	23	20. Rhythm Sing Along With Mitch	Columbia 8527
6/09/62	27	15	21. Family Sing Along With Mitch	Columbia 8573
12/08/62	33	4	● 22. Holiday Sing Along With Mitch .... [X-R] made top 10 on Billboard's special Christmas charts (1963)	Columbia 8501
12/22/62	37	2	● 23. Christmas Sing-Along With Mitch .... [X-R]	Columbia 8027
			MRS. MILLER Mrs. Elva Miller	
5/07/66	15	17	1. Mrs. Miller's Greatest Hits .... featuring the novel operatic voice of housewife Mrs. Miller	Capitol 2494
			NED MILLER	
3/30/63	50	13	1. From A Jack To A King .... "From A Jack To A King"(6)	Fabor 1001
			ROGER MILLER born in Fort Worth, Texas on 1/2/36	
6/27/64	37	46	● 1. Roger And Out .... [N] "Dang Me"(7)/"Chug-A-Lug"(9)	Smash 67049
2/06/65	4	47	● 2. **The Return Of Roger Miller** .... "King Of The Road"(4)	Smash 67061
7/24/65	13	24	3. The 3rd Time Around .... "Engine Engine #9"(7)	Smash 67068
11/13/65	6	57	● 4. **Golden Hits** .... [G] "England Swings"(8)	Smash 67073
11/19/66	108	13	5. Words And Music	Smash 67075
7/01/67	118	8	6. Walkin' In The Sunshine	Smash 67092
8/24/68	173	8	7. A Tender Look At Love	Smash 67103

DATE CHARTED	PEAK POS	WKS CHRT'D		ARTIST — Album Title	LABEL & NUMBER
8/30/69	163	7		8. Roger Miller	Smash 67123
2/14/70	200	2		9. Roger Miller 1970	Smash 67129

STEVE MILLER Band
rock band formed in 1966 in San Francisco

DATE CHARTED	PEAK POS	WKS CHRT'D		ARTIST — Album Title	LABEL & NUMBER
6/15/68	134	18		1. Children Of The Future	Capitol 2920
11/02/68	24	17		2. Sailor	Capitol 2984
				Boz Scaggs was a band member on above albums	
6/28/69	22	26		3. Brave New World	Capitol 184
11/29/69	38	14		4. Your Saving Grace	Capitol 331
7/25/70	23	26		5. Number 5	Capitol 436
10/09/71	82	9		6. Rock Love	Capitol 748
4/01/72	109	10		7. Recall The Beginning...A Journey From Eden	Capitol 11022
11/18/72	56	39	●	8. Anthology [K]	Capitol 11114 [2]
10/20/73	2(1)	38	●	9. **The Joker**	Capitol 11235
				"The Joker"(1)	
5/29/76	3	97	▲	10. **Fly Like An Eagle**	Capitol 11497
				"Rock'n Me"(1)/"Fly Like An Eagle"(2)	
5/21/77	2(2)	68	▲	11. **Book Of Dreams**	Capitol 11630
				"Jet Airliner"(8)	
12/09/78	18	18	▲	12. Greatest Hits 1974-78 [G]	Capitol 11872
11/14/81	26	17	●	13. Circle Of Love	Capitol 12121
6/26/82	3	33	▲	14. **Abracadabra**	Capitol 12216
				"Abracadabra"(1)	
4/30/83	125	7		15. Steve Miller Band - Live! [L]	Capitol 12263
11/10/84	101	10		16. Italian X Rays	Capitol 12339

MILLS BROTHERS
Harry, Herbert & Donald - formed vocal group in 1930 - Harry died on 6/28/82 (68)

DATE CHARTED	PEAK POS	WKS CHRT'D		ARTIST — Album Title	LABEL & NUMBER
3/16/68	21	26		1. Fortuosity	Dot 25809
				"Cab Driver"	
4/06/68	145	6		2. The Board Of Directors	Dot 25838
				COUNT BASIE & THE MILLS BROTHERS	
8/10/68	190	3		3. My Shy Violet	Dot 25872
5/17/69	184	5		4. Dream	Dot 25927

FRANK MILLS
pianist/composer/producer/arranger

DATE CHARTED	PEAK POS	WKS CHRT'D		ARTIST — Album Title	LABEL & NUMBER
3/17/79	21	16	●	1. Music Box Dancer [I]	Polydor 6192
				"Music Box Dancer"(3)	
11/24/79	149	9		2. Sunday Morning Suite [I]	Polydor 6225

STEPHANIE MILLS
starred in the Broadway show "The Wiz"

DATE CHARTED	PEAK POS	WKS CHRT'D		ARTIST — Album Title	LABEL & NUMBER
5/19/79	22	34	●	1. Whatcha Gonna Do...With My Lovin'?	20th Century 583
5/03/80	16	44	●	2. Sweet Sensation	20th Century 603
				"Never Knew Love Like This Before"(6)	
5/16/81	30	23	●	3. Stephanie	20th Century 700
8/07/82	48	19		4. Tantalizingly Hot	Casablanca 7265
9/17/83	104	19		5. Merciless	Casablanca 811364
10/13/84	73	15		6. I've Got The Cure	Casablanca 822421

RONNIE MILSAP
born blind in Robbinsville, North Carolina on 1/16/46

DATE CHARTED	PEAK POS	WKS CHRT'D		ARTIST — Album Title	LABEL & NUMBER
2/15/75	138	7		1. A Legend In My Time	RCA 0846
11/29/75	191	2		2. Night Things	RCA 1223
9/10/77	97	15	●	3. It Was Almost Like A Song	RCA 2439
6/24/78	109	12	●	4. Only One Love In My Life	RCA 2780
6/16/79	98	15		5. Images	RCA 3346
4/05/80	137	13		6. Milsap Magic	RCA 3563
10/25/80	36	41	▲	7. Greatest Hits [G]	RCA 3772

DATE CHARTED	PEAK POS	WKS CHRT'D	ARTIST — Album Title	LABEL & NUMBER
4/18/81	89	29	8. Out Where The Bright Lights Are Glowing ... featuring the hits of Jim Reeves	RCA 3932
9/05/81	31	31	● 9. There's No Gettin' Over Me .... "(There's) No Gettin' Over Me"(5)	RCA 4060
7/03/82	66	14	10. Inside Ronnie Milsap	RCA 4311
4/30/83	36	19	11. Keyed Up	RCA 4670
6/02/84	180	3	12. One More Try For Love	RCA 5016

GARNET MIMMS & The Enchanters
Enchanters: soul trio from Philadelphia

11/23/63	91	5	1. Cry Baby And 11 Other Hits .... "Cry Baby"(4)	United Art. 3305

MINDBENDERS
Manchester, England group

5/01/65	58	9	1. The Game Of Love .... WAYNE FONTANA & THE MINDBENDERS "Game Of Love"(1)	Fontana 27542
7/16/66	92	9	2. A Groovy Kind Of Love .... "A Groovy Kind Of Love"(2)	Fontana 27554

MINISTRY
Chicago duo: Alain Jourgensen and Stephen George

6/25/83	96	14	1. With Sympathy	Arista 6608

MINK DeVILLE
U.S. rock band led by Willy DeVille

8/13/77	186	2	1. Mink DeVille	Capitol 11631
6/10/78	126	5	2. Return To Magenta	Capitol 11780
9/13/80	163	3	3. Le Chat Bleu	Capitol 11955
10/24/81	161	5	4. Coup De Grace	Atlantic 19311

LIZA MINNELLI
daughter of Judy Garland and director Vincente Minnelli

11/21/64	115	8	1. Liza! Liza!	Capitol 2174
9/04/65	41	14	2. "Live" At The London Palladium .... [L] JUDY GARLAND & LIZA MINNELLI	Capitol 2295 [2]
11/28/70	158	3	3. New Feelin'	A&M 4272
9/30/72	19	23	4. Liza With A "Z" .... [TV-L]	Columbia 31762
3/24/73	38	20	5. Liza Minnelli The Singer	Columbia 32149
6/09/73	164	8	6. "Live" At The London Palladium .... [L-R] JUDY GARLAND & LIZA MINNELLI condensation of album #2 above	Capitol 11191
5/18/74	150	4	7. Live At The Winter Garden .... [L]	Columbia 32854

MINOR DETAIL
Irish duo: brothers John & Willie Hughes

10/01/83	187	2	1. Minor Detail	Polydor 815004

MIRABAI

8/30/75	128	6	1. Mirabai	Atlantic 18144

MIRACLES
led by singer/songwriter/producer Smokey Robinson, The Miracles were Motown's first successful recording group

6/08/63	118	8	1. The Fabulous Miracles .... "You've Really Got A Hold On Me"(8)	Tamla 238
10/05/63	139	5	2. The Miracles On Stage .... [L]	Tamla 241
1/04/64	113	4	3. doin' Mickey's Monkey .... "Mickey's Monkey"(8)	Tamla 245
4/17/65	21	25	4. Greatest Hits From The Beginning .... [G] "Shop Around"(2-'61)	Tamla 254 [2]

SMOKEY ROBINSON & THE MIRACLES:

11/27/65	8	40	5. Going To A Go-Go	Tamla 267
12/17/66	41	27	6. Away We A Go-Go	Tamla 271
9/30/67	28	23	7. Make It Happen .... "The Tears Of A Clown"(1-'70)	Tamla 276

DATE CHARTED	PEAK POS	WKS CHRT'D	ARTIST — Album Title	LABEL & NUMBER
2/24/68	7	44	8. **Greatest Hits, Vol. 2** .... [G] "I Second That Emotion"(4)	Tamla 280
10/05/68	42	23	9. Special Occasion	Tamla 290
2/15/69	71	14	10. Live! .... [L]	Tamla 289
8/09/69	25	19	11. Time Out for Smokey Robinson & The Miracles .... "Baby, Baby Don't Cry"(8)	Tamla 295
12/06/69	78	12	12. Four In Blue	Tamla 297
5/30/70	97	11	13. What Love Has...Joined Together	Tamla 301
10/24/70	56	11	14. A Pocket Full Of Miracles	Tamla 306
12/26/70	143	12	15. The Tears Of A Clown .... [R] reissue (new title) of album #7 above	Tamla 276
9/25/71	92	10	16. One Dozen Roses	Tamla 312
8/19/72	46	22	17. Flying High Together	Tamla 318
1/06/73	75	16	18. 1957-1972 .... [L] Smokey's last performance with the group	Tamla 320 [2]
			MIRACLES:	
6/02/73	174	4	19. Renaissance	Tamla 325
2/16/74	97	17	20. Smokey Robinson & The Miracles' Anthology .... [G]	Motown 793 [3]
9/14/74	41	21	21. Do It Baby	Tamla 334
2/08/75	96	9	22. Don't Cha Love It	Tamla 336
10/25/75	33	30	23. City Of Angels .... "Love Machine"(1)	Tamla 339
10/16/76	178	3	24. The Power Of Music	Tamla 344
3/19/77	117	5	25. Love Crazy	Columbia 34460

JUDI SHEPPARD MISSETT - see AEROBICS section

MISSING PERSONS
Dale Bozzio, lead singer (former Playboy bunny from Boston)

5/15/82	46	47	1. Missing Persons .... [M]	Capitol 15001
10/30/82	17	40	● 2. Spring Session M .... title is an anagram of artist's name	Capitol 12228
3/31/84	43	16	3. Rhyme & Reason	Capitol 12315

MISSOURI

6/23/79	174	4	1. Welcome Two Missouri	Polydor 6206

MR. MISTER
Los Angeles rock quartet led by Richard Page (Pages)

4/14/84	170	7	1. I Wear The Face	RCA 4864

MISTRESS

9/15/79	100	14	1. Mistress	RSO 3059

CHAD MITCHELL Trio
Chad Mitchell, Mike Kobluk & Joe Frazier - formed while sophomores at Gonzaga University in Spokane, Washington

3/24/62	39	21	1. Mighty Day On Campus .... [L]	Kapp 3262
9/01/62	81	9	2. The Chad Mitchell Trio At The Bitter End .... [L] Jim McGuinn (Byrds) played guitar on above 2 albums	Kapp 3281
4/13/63	87	30	3. Blowin' In The Wind	Kapp 3313
9/28/63	63	28	4. The Best Of Chad Mitchell Trio .... [G]	Kapp 3334
11/09/63	39	22	5. Singin' Our Mind	Mercury 60838
3/07/64	29	30	6. Reflecting	Mercury 60891
11/14/64	128	11	7. The Slightly Irreverent Mitchell Trio	Mercury 60944
5/01/65	130	3	8. Typical American Boys	Mercury 60992

JONI MITCHELL
born Roberta Joan Anderson on 11/7/43 in Alberta, Canada

5/18/68	189	9	1. Joni Mitchell	Reprise 6293
6/14/69	31	36	2. Clouds	Reprise 6341

DATE CHARTED	PEAK POS	WKS CHRT'D		ARTIST — Album Title	LABEL & NUMBER
4/11/70	**27**	33	●	3. Ladies Of The Canyon .... "Big Yellow Taxi"	Reprise 6376
7/03/71	**15**	28	●	4. Blue	Reprise 2038
12/02/72	**11**	28	●	5. For The Roses	Asylum 5057
2/09/74	**2(4)**	64	●	6. **Court And Spark** .... "Help Me"(7)	Asylum 1001
12/14/74	**2(1)**	22	●	7. **Miles Of Aisles** .... [L] with Tom Scott & The L.A. Express	Asylum 202
12/06/75	**4**	17	●	8. **The Hissing Of Summer Lawns**	Asylum 1051
12/11/76	**13**	18	●	9. Hejira	Asylum 1087
1/07/78	**25**	13	●	10. Don Juan's Reckless Daughter	Asylum 701 [2]
7/07/79	**17**	18		11. Mingus .... Joni performs music composed by Charles Mingus who died on 1/5/79 (56)	Asylum 505
10/04/80	**38**	16		12. Shadows And Light .... [L] with guests Pat Metheny, Michael Brecker & Jaco Pastorius	Asylum 704 [2]
11/20/82	**25**	21		13. Wild Things Run Fast	Geffen 2019

RUBIN MITCHELL
jazz/pop pianist

4/15/67	**164**	2		1. Presenting Rubin Mitchell .... [I]	Capitol 2658

WILLIE MITCHELL
soul trumpeter/arranger/conductor of combo

3/16/68	**172**	5		1. Willie Mitchell Live .... [I-L] recorded at the Manhattan Club in Memphis	Hi 32042
5/11/68	**151**	7		2. Soul Serenade .... [I]	Hi 32039
11/07/70	**188**	2		3. Robbin's Nest .... [I]	Hi 32058

MOBY GRAPE
rock group from San Francisco

7/01/67	**24**	27		1. Moby Grape .... 10 of 13 cuts released simultaneously on 45s	Columbia 9498
5/04/68	**20**	28		2. Wow .... includes bonus LP titled "Grape Jam" (jam sessions with Al Kooper & Mike Bloomfield)	Columbia 9613 [2]
3/01/69	**113**	10		3. Moby Grape '69	Columbia 9696
9/20/69	**157**	6		4. Truly Fine Citizen	Columbia 9912
9/18/71	**177**	5		5. 20 Granite Creek	Reprise 6460

MOCEDADES
sextet from Bilbao, Spain featuring the Amezaga sisters

3/16/74	**152**	7		1. Eres Tu "Touch The Wind" .... "Eres Tu"(9)	Tara 53000

MODERN ENGLISH
British fivesome - Robbie Grey, lead singer

3/19/83	**70**	28		1. After The Snow	Sire 23821
3/24/84	**93**	12		2. Ricochet Days	Sire 25066

DOMENICO MODUGNO
native of Sicily

9/15/58	**8**	6		1. **Nel Blu Dipinto Di Blu (Volare) and other Italian favorites** .... [F] "Nel Blu Dipinto Di Blu"(1)	Decca 8808

ANNA MOFFO - see SERGIO FRANCHI

MOLLY HATCHET
Southern hard rock sextet from Jacksonville, Florida - Danny Joe Brown, lead singer (1,2 & 5,6)

11/11/78	**64**	42	▲	1. Molly Hatchet	Epic 35347
9/29/79	**19**	48	▲	2. Flirtin' With Disaster	Epic 36110
9/20/80	**25**	21	●	3. Beatin' The Odds	Epic 36572
12/05/81	**36**	14		4. Take No Prisoners .... Jimmy Farrar, lead singer on above 2 albums	Epic 37480

DATE CHARTED	PEAK POS	WKS CHRT'D	ARTIST — Album Title	LABEL & NUMBER
3/26/83	**59**	20	5. No Guts...No Glory	Epic 38429
11/24/84	**117**	13	6. The Deed Is Done	Epic 39621

MOM & DADS
four piece polka/dance band from Spokane, Washington

11/13/71	**85**	23	1. The Rangers Waltz .... [I]	GNP Cres. 2061
5/06/72	**165**	6	2. In The Blue Canadian Rockies	GNP Cres. 2063

MOMENTS
also see Ray, Goodman & Brown

3/27/71	**184**	7	1. Moments Greatest Hits .... [G]	Stang 1004
			"Love On A Two-Way Street"(3)	
5/15/71	**147**	8	2. The Moments Live at the New York State	
			Womans Prison .... [L]	Stang 1006
7/12/75	**132**	8	3. Look At Me	Stang 1026

EDDIE MONEY
real name: Edward Mahoney

1/07/78	**37**	49	▲ 1. Eddie Money	Columbia 34909
			"Baby Hold On"	
1/27/79	**17**	26	● 2. Life For The Taking	Columbia 35598
8/09/80	**35**	17	3. Playing For Keeps	Columbia 36514
7/10/82	**20**	44	● 4. No Control	Columbia 37960
11/05/83	**67**	19	5. Where's The Party?	Columbia 38862

THELONIOUS MONK
jazz pianist - died on 2/17/82 (61)

11/30/63	**127**	3	1. Criss-Cross .... [I]	Columbia 8838

T.S. MONK
Thelonious Monk Jr. - son of the legendary jazz artist

1/31/81	**64**	22	1. House Of Music	Mirage 19291
1/09/82	**176**	8	2. More Of The Good Life	Mirage 19324

MONKEES
Davy Jones, Michael Nesmith, Micky Dolenz & Peter Tork

10/08/66	**1(13)**	78	● 1. **The Monkees**	Colgems 101
			"Last Train To Clarksville"(1)	
2/04/67	**1(18)**	70	● 2. **More Of The Monkees**	Colgems 102
			"I'm A Believer"(1)	
6/10/67	**1(1)**	51	● 3. **Headquarters**	Colgems 103
11/25/67	**1(5)**	47	● 4. **Pisces, Aquarius, Capricorn & Jones Ltd** ...	Colgems 104
			"Pleasant Valley Sunday"(3)	
5/11/68	**3**	39	● 5. **The Birds, The Bees & The Monkees**	Colgems 109
			"Daydream Believer"(1)/"Valleri"(3)	
12/21/68	**45**	15	6. Head .... [S]	Colgems 5008
			The Monkees starred in the film	
3/01/69	**32**	15	7. Instant Replay	Colgems 113
6/28/69	**93**	12	8. The Monkees Greatest Hits .... [G]	Colgems 115
			"A Little Bit Me, A Little Bit You"(2)	
11/01/69	**100**	14	9. The Monkees Present	Colgems 117
			Peter Tork no longer a member	
8/07/76	**58**	16	10. The Monkees Greatest Hits .... [G]	Arista 4089
			some of the tracks are different than album #8 above	

MATT MONRO
English - died of liver cancer on 2/7/85 (54)

10/02/61	**87**	14	1. My Kind Of Girl	Warwick 2045
3/13/65	**126**	3	2. Walk Away	Liberty 7402
5/13/67	**86**	22	3. Invitation To The Movies/Born Free	Capitol 2730

MARILYN MONROE
Hollywood sex queen - died on 8/5/62 (36)

10/20/62	**111**	10	1. Marilyn	20th Fox 5000
			Marilyn sings selections from 3 of her films	

DATE CHARTED	PEAK POS	WKS CHRT'D	ARTIST — Album Title	LABEL & NUMBER
			MONROES five-man rock band from San Diego	
6/19/82	109	9	1. The Monroes .... [M]	Alfa 15015
			MONTANA ORCHESTRA Vincent Montana, Jr., conductor - also see Salsoul Orchestra	
12/19/81	195	4	1. Merry Christmas/Happy New Year's .... [X] side 1: Christmas medley; side 2: New Year's eve party medley	MJS 3302
			LOU MONTE	
12/22/62	9	25	1. Pepino The Italian Mouse & Other Italian Fun Songs .... [N] "Pepino The Italian Mouse"(5)	Reprise 6058
			HUGO MONTENEGRO & His Orchestra conductor-arranger-composer - died on 2/6/81 (55) - also see Soundtrack "Hurry Sundown"	
1/29/66	52	20	1. Original Music from The Man From U.N.C.L.E. .... [I]	RCA 3475
2/17/68	9	39	● 2. Music From "A Fistful Of Dollars" & "For A Few Dollars More" & "The Good, The Bad And The Ugly" .... [I] "The Good, The Bad And The Ugly"(2)	RCA 3927
9/21/68	166	5	3. Hang 'Em High	RCA 4022
8/30/69	182	4	4. Moog Power	RCA 4170
			CHRIS MONTEZ protege of Ritchie Valens	
7/02/66	33	24	1. The More I See You/Call Me	A&M 4115
1/14/67	106	11	2. Time After Time	A&M 4120
			WES MONTGOMERY jazz guitarist - died on 6/15/68 (43)	
12/11/65	116	13	1. Bumpin' .... [I]	Verve 8625
9/03/66	51	32	2. Tequila .... [I]	Verve 8653
3/25/67	65	32	3. California Dreaming .... [I]	Verve 8672
5/20/67	129	23	4. Jimmy & Wes The Dynamic Duo .... [I] JIMMY SMITH & WES MONTGOMERY	Verve 8678
10/07/67	13	67	● 5. A Day In The Life .... [I] "Windy"	A&M 3001
12/09/67	56	38	6. The Best Of Wes Montgomery .... [K-I]	Verve 8714
5/04/68	38	30	7. Down Here On The Ground .... [I]	A&M 3006
9/07/68	187	8	8. The Best Of Wes Montgomery, Vol. 2 ...... [K-I]	Verve 8757
11/16/68	94	16	9. Road Song .... [I] album recorded one month before his death	A&M 3012
4/04/70	175	9	10. Greatest Hits .... [G-I]	A&M 4247
			MONTROSE heavy-metal rock band led by Ronnie Montrose (guitar) and Sammy Hagar (vocals 1&2) - also see Gamma	
5/11/74	133	12	● 1. Montrose	Warner 2740
11/16/74	65	14	2. Paper Money	Warner 2823
10/18/75	79	7	3. Warner Bros. presents Montrose!	Warner 2892
9/25/76	118	7	4. Jump On It	Warner 2963
2/11/78	98	10	5. Open Fire .... shown as Ronnie Montrose - produced by Edgar Winter	Warner 3134
			MONTY PYTHON British comedy troupe: Eric Idle, John Cleese, Terry Jones, Graham Chapman, Michael Palin, Terry Gilliam	
5/24/75	48	13	1. Matching Tie & Handkerchief .... [C]	Arista 4039
8/02/75	83	15	2. Monty Python's Flying Circus .... [C]	Pye 12116
8/23/75	87	11	3. The Album Of The Soundtrack Of The Trailer Of The Film Of "Monty Python And The Holy Grail" .... [S-C]	Arista 4050

DATE CHARTED	PEAK POS	WKS CHRT'D	ARTIST — Album Title	LABEL & NUMBER
6/05/76	186	3	4. Monty Python Live! At City Center .... [C]	Arista 4073
11/10/79	155	2	5. Life Of Brian .... [S-C]	Warner 3396
11/15/80	164	9	6. Monty Python's Contractual Obligation Album .... [C]	Arista 9536

MOODY BLUES
English classical-rock group: Justin Hayward, John Lodge, Graeme Edge, Mike Pinder & Ray Thomas

DATE CHARTED	PEAK POS	WKS CHRT'D	ARTIST — Album Title	LABEL & NUMBER
5/04/68	3	102	● 1. **Days Of Future Passed** .... with The London Festival Orchestra "Nights In White Satin" (2-'72)	Deram 18012
9/14/68	23	29	● 2. In Search Of The Lost Chord	Deram 18017
5/31/69	20	136	● 3. On The Threshold Of A Dream	Deram 18025
1/10/70	14	44	● 4. To Our Children's Children's Children	Threshold 1
9/12/70	3	74	● 5. **A Question Of Balance**	Threshold 3
8/14/71	2(3)	43	● 6. **Every Good Boy Deserves Favour**	Threshold 5
11/18/72	1(5)	44	● 7. **Seventh Sojourn**	Threshold 7
11/23/74	11	25	● 8. This Is The Moody Blues .... [G]	Threshold 12/13 [2]
6/04/77	26	15	9. Caught Live +5 .... [L] first 3 sides recorded live at the Royal Albert Hall in '69; side 4: previously unreleased studio recordings	London 690/1 [2]
7/01/78	13	30	▲ 10. Octave	London 708
6/13/81	1(3)	39	▲ 11. **Long Distance Voyager** .... Patrick Moraz replaces Mike Pinder on keyboards	Threshold 2901
9/10/83	26	22	12. The Present	Threshold 2902
3/23/85	146+	3+	13. Voices in the Sky/The Best Of The Moody Blues .... [G] their top hits from 1967-83	Threshold 820155

MOOG MACHINE
Kenny Ascher plays the Moog Synthesizer

DATE CHARTED	PEAK POS	WKS CHRT'D	ARTIST — Album Title	LABEL & NUMBER
9/27/69	170	8	1. Switched-On Rock .... [I]	Columbia 9921

KEITH MOON
The 'Who's drummer - died on 9/7/78 (32)

DATE CHARTED	PEAK POS	WKS CHRT'D	ARTIST — Album Title	LABEL & NUMBER
4/05/75	155	3	1. Two Sides Of The Moon .... with guests Ringo Starr, Joe Walsh, Harry Nilsson & Rick Nelson	Track 2136

MOONGLOWS
classic fifties R&B group led by Harvey Fuqua

DATE CHARTED	PEAK POS	WKS CHRT'D	ARTIST — Album Title	LABEL & NUMBER
8/05/72	193	4	1. The Return Of The Moonglows	RCA 4722

BOB MOORE & His Orchestra

DATE CHARTED	PEAK POS	WKS CHRT'D	ARTIST — Album Title	LABEL & NUMBER
11/11/61	33	18	1. Mexico and Other Great Hits! .... [I] "Mexico"(7)	Monument 4005

DOROTHY MOORE
lead singer of The Poppies

DATE CHARTED	PEAK POS	WKS CHRT'D	ARTIST — Album Title	LABEL & NUMBER
5/29/76	29	23	1. Misty Blue .... "Misty Blue"(3)	Malaco 6351
8/06/77	120	13	2. Dorothy Moore	Malaco 6353

GARY MOORE
former guitarist of Thin Lizzy

DATE CHARTED	PEAK POS	WKS CHRT'D	ARTIST — Album Title	LABEL & NUMBER
4/23/83	149	13	1. Corridors Of Power	Mirage 90077
6/09/84	172	5	2. Victims Of The Future	Mirage 90154

MELBA MOORE
award winning performer as Lutiebelle in the musical "Purlie"

DATE CHARTED	PEAK POS	WKS CHRT'D	ARTIST — Album Title	LABEL & NUMBER
2/20/71	157	5	1. Look What You're Doing To The Man	Mercury 61321
7/05/75	176	4	2. Peach Melba	Buddah 5629
5/08/76	145	5	3. This Is It	Buddah 5657
12/25/76	177	7	4. Melba	Buddah 5677
11/18/78	114	18	5. Melba	Epic 35507

DATE CHARTED	PEAK POS	WKS CHRT'D	ARTIST — Album Title	LABEL & NUMBER
11/13/82	**152**	19	6. The Other Side Of The Rainbow	Capitol 12243
12/24/83	**147**	14	7. Never Say Never	Capitol 12305
			TIM MOORE	
10/12/74	**119**	9	1. Tim Moore	Asylum 1019
8/02/75	**181**	3	2. Behind The Eyes	Asylum 1042
			PATRICK MORAZ former keyboardist with Yes - currently with the Moody Blues	
6/05/76	**132**	5	1. i	Atlantic 18175
			JANE MORGAN	
12/09/57	**13**	3	1. Fascination with the violins of The Troubadors "Fascination"(7)	Kapp 1066
11/26/66	**134**	4	2. Fresh Flavor	Epic 26211
			LEE MORGAN jazz trumpeter - shot and killed on 2/19/72 (33)	
10/10/64	**25**	30	1. The Sidewinder .... [I]	Blue Note 84157
11/26/66	**143**	3	2. Search For The New Land .... [I]	Blue Note 84169
3/01/69	**190**	3	3. Caramba! .... [I]	Blue Note 84289
			MORMON TABERNACLE CHOIR Richard P. Condie directs the 375-voice choir	
10/19/59	**1(1)**	80	● 1. **The Lord's Prayer** "Battle Hymn Of The Republic"	Columbia 6068
12/28/59	**5**	2	2. **The Spirit Of Christmas** .... [X]	Columbia 6100
10/30/61	**47**	1	3. Songs Of The North & South 1861-1865	Columbia 6259
12/25/61	**118**	3	4. The Spirit Of Christmas .... [X-R]	Columbia 6100
1/05/63	**49**	8	5. The Lord's Prayer, Volume II .... albums 1 & 5 feature The Philadelphia Orchestra, Eugene Ormandy, conductor	Columbia 6367
			GIORGIO MORODER electronic composer/conductor for numerous soundtracks	
10/29/77	**130**	7	1. From Here To Eternity .... shown only as Giorgio	Casablanca 7065
			GARY MORRIS country singer/songwriter from Ft. Worth, Texas	
10/15/83	**174**	8	1. Why Lady Why	Warner 23738
			VAN MORRISON Irish blue-eyed soul singer/songwriter - leader of Them	
10/07/67	**182**	7	1. Blowin' Your Mind! "Brown Eyed Girl"(10)	Bang 218
3/14/70	**29**	22	● 2. Moondance	Warner 1835
12/26/70	**32**	17	3. His Band And The Street Choir "Domino"(9)	Warner 1884
10/30/71	**27**	24	● 4. Tupelo Honey	Warner 1950
8/05/72	**15**	28	5. Saint Dominic's Preview	Warner 2633
8/04/73	**27**	19	6. Hard Nose The Highway	Warner 2712
1/26/74	**181**	4	7. T.B. Sheets .... [E] previously unreleased takes from same sessions as album #1	Bang 400
3/16/74	**53**	17	8. It's Too Late To Stop Now .... [L] featuring The Caledonia Soul Orchestra	Warner 2760 [2]
11/09/74	**53**	10	9. Veedon Fleece	Warner 2805
5/07/77	**43**	11	10. A Period Of Transition featuring Dr. John (Mac Rebennack) on keyboards	Warner 2987
10/14/78	**28**	23	11. Wavelength	Warner 3212
9/08/79	**43**	13	12. Into The Music	Warner 3390
9/20/80	**73**	10	13. Common One	Warner 3462
3/06/82	**44**	11	14. Beautiful Vision	Warner 3652

DATE CHARTED	PEAK POS	WKS CHRT'D	ARTIST — Album Title	LABEL & NUMBER
4/09/83	116	8	15. Inarticulate Speech Of The Heart	Warner 23802
3/09/85	61+	5+	16. A Sense Of Wonder	Mercury 822895

STEVE MORSE BAND
lead guitarist of the Dregs

9/01/84	101	12	1. The Introduction .... [I]	Musician 60369

JOHNNY & JONIE MOSBY
husband and wife Country duo

10/11/69	197	1	1. Hold Me	Capitol 286

MOTELS
Martha Davis, lead singer of quintet from Los Angeles

12/01/79	175	2	1. Motels	Capitol 11996
7/12/80	45	20	2. Careful	Capitol 12070
4/24/82	16	41	● 3. All Four One	Capitol 12177
			"Only The Lonely"(9)	
10/15/83	22	24	● 4. Little Robbers	Capitol 12288
			"Suddenly Last Summer"(9)	

MOTHER EARTH
Tracy Nelson, lead singer of Nashville sextet

2/22/69	144	8	1. Living With The Animals	Mercury 61194
8/23/69	95	9	2. Make A Joyful Noise	Mercury 61226
5/15/71	199	2	3. Bring Me Home	Reprise 6431

MOTHER'S FINEST
R&B/rock group led by Joyce Kennedy & Glenn Murdock

9/11/76	148	8	1. Mother's Finest	Epic 34179
9/17/77	134	8	2. Another Mother Further	Epic 34699
9/30/78	123	21	3. Mother Factor	Epic 35546
5/23/81	168	8	4. Iron Age	Atlantic 19302

MOTHERLODE
Canadian pop quartet led by "Smitty" Smith

10/04/69	93	12	1. When I Die	Buddah 5046

MOTHERS OF INVENTION - see FRANK ZAPPA

MOTLEY CRUE
Los Angeles-based rock band; Vince Neil, lead singer

10/15/83	17	78+	▲ 1. Shout At The Devil	Elektra 60289
12/17/83	77	49	● 2. Too Fast For Love	Elektra 60174
			their first album	

MOTORHEAD
British heavy-metal trio - Fast Eddie Clarke, lead guitarist

5/22/82	174	6	1. Iron Fist	Mercury 4042
7/23/83	153	7	2. Another Perfect Day	Mercury 811365

MOTORS
British duo: Andy McMaster & Nick Garvey

4/12/80	174	8	1. Tenement Steps	Virgin 13139

MOTT THE HOOPLE
British rock group led by Ian Hunter (vocals 1-6) &
Mick Ralphs (guitar 1-3)

7/04/70	185	2	1. Mott The Hoople	Atlantic 8258
11/11/72	89	19	2. All The Young Dudes	Columbia 31750
			produced by David Bowie	
8/25/73	35	29	3. Mott	Columbia 32425
4/27/74	28	23	4. The Hoople	Columbia 32871
6/15/74	112	11	5. Rock And Roll Queen .... [E-K]	Atlantic 7297
11/30/74	23	13	6. Mott The Hoople Live .... [L]	Columbia 33282
11/01/75	160	5	7. Drive On	Columbia 33705
			shown only as Mott	

DATE CHARTED	PEAK POS	WKS CHRT'D	ARTIST — Album Title	LABEL & NUMBER
			TONY MOTTOLA Latin-style guitarist - produced by Enoch Light	
4/07/62	**26**	26	1. Roman Guitar .... [I]	Command 816
7/21/62	**41**	6	2. Roman Guitar, Volume Two .... [I]	Command 836
12/11/65	**85**	13	3. Love Songs - Mexico/S.A. .... [I]	Command 889
12/02/67	**198**	3	4. A Latin Love-In .... [I]	Project 3 5010
5/16/70	**189**	3	5. Tony Mottola's Guitar Factory .... [I]	Project 3 5044
			MOUNTAIN New York power-rock group led by Leslie West & Felix Pappalardi (shot to death on 4/17/83-44) - also see West, Bruce & Laing	
9/06/69	**72**	14	1. Leslie West - Mountain .... solo album by West (West formed the group Mountain named after this album title)	Windfall 4500
3/14/70	**17**	39	● 2. Mountain Climbing! .... "Mississippi Queen"	Windfall 4501
2/06/71	**16**	29	● 3. Nantucket Sleighride	Windfall 5500
12/18/71	**35**	16	4. Flowers Of Evil	Windfall 5501
5/13/72	**63**	18	5. Mountain Live (the road goes ever on) .... [L]	Windfall 5502
2/24/73	**72**	16	6. The Best Of Mountain .... [G]	Columbia 32079
3/09/74	**142**	8	7. Twin Peaks .... [L] recorded live at Osaka, Japan on 8/30/73	Columbia 32818 [2]
8/10/74	**102**	9	8. Avalanche	Columbia 33088
			NANA MOUSKOURI - see HARRY BELAFONTE	
			MOUTH & MacNEAL Dutch duo: Willem Duyn & Maggie MacNeal	
7/01/72	**77**	16	1. How Do You Do? .... "How Do You Do?"(8)	Philips 700
			ALPHONSE MOUZON	
12/04/82	**146**	11	1. Distant Lover	Highrise 100
			MOVE British group which evolved into the Electric Light Orchestra	
3/03/73	**172**	8	1. Split Ends .... [K] includes singles releases plus bulk of the 1971 album "Message from the Country"	United Art. 5666
			MOVING PICTURES Alex Smith, lead singer of Australian 6-man group	
12/04/82	**101**	16	1. Days Of Innocence	Network 60202
			MTUME progressive funk band led by James Mtume	
10/18/80	**119**	4	1. In Search Of The Rainbow Seekers	Epic 36017
5/28/83	**26**	22	2. Juicy Fruit	Epic 38588
9/15/84	**77**	19	3. You, Me And He	Epic 39473
			IDRIS MUHAMMAD session drummer	
6/18/77	**127**	19	1. Turn This Mutha Out	Kudu 34
			MARIA MULDAUR Maria and former husband Geoff Muldaur were members of Jim Kweskin's Jug Band	
9/22/73	**3**	56	● 1. Maria Muldaur .... "Midnight At The Oasis"(6)	Reprise 2148
11/09/74	**23**	26	2. Waitress In The Donut Shop	Reprise 2194
3/13/76	**53**	12	3. Sweet Harmony	Reprise 2235
4/08/78	**143**	5	4. Southern Winds	Warner 3162
			MARTIN MULL master of double entendre pop songs	
3/26/77	**184**	2	1. I'm Everyone I've Ever Loved .... [C]	ABC 997
6/17/78	**157**	3	2. Sex & Violins .... [C]	ABC 1064

DATE CHARTED	PEAK POS	WKS CHRT'D	ARTIST — Album Title	LABEL & NUMBER
			GERRY MULLIGAN'S Jazz Combo jazz baritone saxophonist	
5/25/59	39	10	1. I Want To Live! .... [S-I] with Shelly Manne (drums) & Art Farmer (trumpet)	United Art. 5006
			CHARLES MUNCH - see BOSTON SYMPHONY ORCHESTRA	
			MUNGO JERRY British skiffle quartet - Ray Dorset, lead singer	
9/12/70	64	11	1. Mungo Jerry .... "In The Summertime"(3)	Janus 7000
			MUNICH MACHINE a Giorgio Moroder/Pete Bellotte electronic disco production	
7/01/78	190	3	1. A Whiter Shade Of Pale .... featuring vocals by Chris Bennett	Casablanca 7090
			MUPPETS - see CHILDRENS section	
			MICHAEL MURPHEY progressive country singer/songwriter from Austin, Texas	
9/23/72	160	9	1. Geronimo's Cadillac	A&M 4358
6/16/73	196	2	2. Cosmic Cowboy Souvenir	A&M 4388
2/22/75	18	38	● 3. Blue Sky-Night Thunder .... "Wildfire"(3)	Epic 33290
12/06/75	44	13	4. Swans Against The Sun .... with guests Charlie Daniels, John Denver & Willie Nelson	Epic 33851
11/20/76	130	5	5. Flowing Free Forever	Epic 34220
4/01/78	99	6	6. Lonewolf	Epic 35013
9/04/82	69	16	7. Michael Martin Murphey	Liberty 51120
10/29/83	187	3	8. The Heart Never Lies	Liberty 51150
			EDDIE MURPHY television and film comedian/actor	
8/14/82	52	53	● 1. Eddie Murphy .... [C]	Columbia 38180
11/19/83	35	36+	● 2. Eddie Murphy: Comedian .... [C]	Columbia 39005
			WALTER MURPHY keyboardist, composer and arranger of disco music	
9/04/76	15	29	● 1. A Fifth Of Beethoven .... "A Fifth Of Beethoven"(1)	Private S. 2015
7/16/77	175	3	2. Rhapsody In Blue	Private S. 2028
			MURRAY THE "K" - see VARIOUS - Radio/TV Celebrity Compilations	
			ANNE MURRAY born in Springhill, Nova Scotia, Canada on 6/20/46	
10/03/70	41	31	● 1. Snowbird .... "Snowbird"(8)	Capitol 579
4/03/71	121	9	2. Anne Murray	Capitol 667
10/09/71	179	4	3. Talk It Over In The Morning	Capitol 821
12/11/71	128	8	4. Anne Murray/Glen Campbell	Capitol 869
5/20/72	143	8	5. Annie	Capitol 11024
4/28/73	39	24	6. Danny's Song .... "Danny's Song"(7)	Capitol 11172
3/09/74	24	33	7. Love Song .... "You Won't See Me"(8)	Capitol 11266
8/31/74	32	16	8. Country .... [K]	Capitol 11324
12/14/74	70	13	9. Highly Prized Possession	Capitol 11354
12/06/75	142	11	10. Together	Capitol 11433
10/02/76	96	6	11. Keeping In Touch	Capitol 11559
3/04/78	12	52	▲ 12. Let's Keep It That Way .... "You Needed Me"(1)	Capitol 11743
2/17/79	23	29	● 13. New Kind Of Feeling	Capitol 11849
11/03/79	24	23	● 14. I'll Always Love You	Capitol 12012

DATE CHARTED	PEAK POS	WKS CHRT'D	ARTIST — Album Title	LABEL & NUMBER
2/09/80	73	9	15. A Country Collection .... [K]	Capitol 12039
5/03/80	88	15	16. Somebody's Waiting	Capitol 12064
10/04/80	16	64	▲ 17. Anne Murray's Greatest Hits .... [G]	Capitol 12110
5/02/81	55	15	● 18. Where Do You Go When You Dream	Capitol 12144
11/28/81	54	8	● 19. Christmas Wishes .... [X]	Capitol 16232
			made top 10 on Billboard's special Xmas charts (1983-84)	
8/28/82	90	12	20. The Hottest Night Of The Year	Capitol 12225
10/15/83	72	24	● 21. A Little Good News	Capitol 12301
10/27/84	92	24+	22. Heart Over Mind	Capitol 12363

MUSCLE SHOALS HORNS
studio backing band from Muscle Shoals, Alabama

7/04/76	154	8	1. Born To Get Down	Bang 403

MUSIC EXPLOSION
Jamie Lyons, lead singer of pop/rock quintet from Ohio

8/26/67	178	2	1. Little Bit O' Soul	Laurie 2040
			"Little Bit O' Soul"(2)	

MUSIC MACHINE
Los Angeles rock quintet - Sean Bonniwell, lead singer

1/21/67	76	16	1. (Turn On) The Music Machine	Original Snd. 5015
			"Talk Talk"	

MUSICAL YOUTH
5 English boys, ages 11 to 16

1/08/83	23	22	1. The Youth Of Today	MCA 5389
			"Pass The Dutchie"(10)	
12/17/83	144	12	2. Different Style!	MCA 5454

MUSIQUE
a Patrick Adams disco production

9/30/78	62	17	1. Keep On Jumpin'	Prelude 12158

ALICIA MYERS

12/08/84	186	5	1. I Appreciate	MCA 5485

GARY MYRICK

8/06/83	186	3	1. Language .... [M]	Epic 38637

MYSTIC MOODS ORCHESTRA
lush orchestrations featuring sound effects of rain, surf, etc.

4/30/66	63	14	1. One Stormy Night .... [I]	Philips 205
10/08/66	110	10	2. Nighttide .... [I]	Philips 213
3/25/67	157	4	3. More Than Music .... [I]	Philips 231
11/25/67	164	3	4. Mexican Trip .... [I]	Philips 250
2/24/68	182	4	5. The Mystic Moods Of Love .... [I]	Philips 260
11/09/68	194	3	6. Emotions .... [I]	Philips 277
5/03/69	155	9	7. Extensions .... [I]	Philips 301
11/22/69	165	8	8. Love Token .... [I]	Philips 321
5/23/70	165	15	9. Stormy Weekend .... [I]	Philips 342
11/28/70	174	9	10. English Muffins .... [I]	Philips 349
4/29/72	184	3	11. Love The One You're With .... [I]	Warner 2577
5/05/73	190	4	12. Awakening .... [I]	Warner 2690

JIM NABORS
Gomer Pyle on TV's "Andy Griffith Show" & "Gomer Pyle-U.S.M.C."

10/15/66	24	56	● 1. Jim Nabors Sings Love Me With All Your Heart	Columbia 9358
5/20/67	50	40	2. Jim Nabors By Request	Columbia 9465
9/16/67	147	6	3. The Things I Love	Columbia 9503
			adaptations of classical music	
7/13/68	153	26	4. Kiss Me Goodbye	Columbia 9620

DATE CHARTED	PEAK POS	WKS CHRT'D		ARTIST — Album Title	LABEL & NUMBER
11/16/68	173	12	●	5. The Lord's Prayer And Other Sacred Songs	Columbia 9716
6/14/69	145	19		6. Galveston	Columbia 9817
6/27/70	34	23		7. The Jim Nabors Hour titled after his TV variety show (1969-1971)	Columbia 1020
9/05/70	124	26		8. Everything Is Beautiful	Columbia 30129
3/27/71	75	13		9. For The Good Times/The Jim Nabors Hour [L]	Columbia 30449
7/24/71	122	9		10. Help Me Make It Through The Night	Columbia 30810
10/23/71	166	4		11. How Great Thou Art	Columbia 30671
6/17/72	157	8		12. The Way Of Love	Columbia 31336

NAKED EYES
English duo: Pete Byrne (vocals) & Rob Fisher (keyboards)

DATE CHARTED	PEAK POS	WKS CHRT'D		ARTIST — Album Title	LABEL & NUMBER
4/16/83	32	42		1. Naked Eyes "Always Something There To Remind Me"(8)	EMI America 17089
9/08/84	83	10		2. Fuel For The Fire	EMI America 17116

GRAHAM NASH
English - co-founder of the Hollies - also see Crosby/Nash, and Crosby, Stills & Nash

DATE CHARTED	PEAK POS	WKS CHRT'D		ARTIST — Album Title	LABEL & NUMBER
6/19/71	15	24	●	1. Songs For Beginners	Atlantic 7204
1/26/74	34	14		2. Wild Tales	Atlantic 7288
3/08/80	117	5		3. Earth & Sky	Capitol 12014

JOHNNY NASH
reggae/R&B singer from Houston, Texas

DATE CHARTED	PEAK POS	WKS CHRT'D		ARTIST — Album Title	LABEL & NUMBER
11/23/68	109	12		1. Hold Me Tight "Hold Me Tight"(5)	JAD 1207
10/07/72	23	31		2. I Can See Clearly Now "I Can See Clearly Now"(1)	Epic 31607
7/14/73	169	6		3. My Merry-Go-Round	Epic 32158

NASHVILLE BRASS - see DANNY DAVIS

NATIONAL LAMPOON
comedy troupe spawned from the magazine of the same name - also see soundtrack "Animal House"

DATE CHARTED	PEAK POS	WKS CHRT'D		ARTIST — Album Title	LABEL & NUMBER
9/02/72	132	12		1. Radio Dinner [C] featuring Christopher Guest and Melissa Manchester	Banana 38
6/23/73	107	13		2. Lemmings [C] satirical rock revue recorded at New York's Village Gate	Banana 6006
3/16/74	118	8		3. Missing White House Tapes [C] above 2 albums feature John Belushi & Chevy Chase	Banana 6008

NATURAL FOUR
soul foursome from San Francisco

DATE CHARTED	PEAK POS	WKS CHRT'D		ARTIST — Album Title	LABEL & NUMBER
7/05/75	182	3		1. Heaven Right Here On Earth	Curtom 5004

NATURE'S DIVINE
10-member soul group from Detroit

DATE CHARTED	PEAK POS	WKS CHRT'D		ARTIST — Album Title	LABEL & NUMBER
11/10/79	91	8		1. In The Beginning	Infinity 9013

NAZARETH
hard-rock group from Scotland - Dan McCafferty, lead singer

DATE CHARTED	PEAK POS	WKS CHRT'D		ARTIST — Album Title	LABEL & NUMBER
8/18/73	157	13		1. Razamanaz	A&M 4396
3/09/74	150	8		2. Loud 'N' Proud	A&M 3609
7/13/74	157	9		3. Rampant	A&M 3641
4/26/75	17	40	●	4. Hair Of The Dog "Love Hurts"(8)	A&M 4511
5/08/76	24	14		5. Close Enough For Rock 'N' Roll	A&M 4562
12/04/76	75	9		6. Play 'N' The Game	A&M 4610
7/02/77	120	6		7. Hot Tracks [G]	A&M 4643
11/19/77	82	16		8. Expect No Mercy	A&M 4666
2/03/79	88	14		9. No Mean City	A&M 4741

DATE CHARTED	PEAK POS	WKS CHRT'D	ARTIST — Album Title	LABEL & NUMBER
2/16/80	**41**	19	10. Malice In Wonderland	A&M 4799
2/14/81	**70**	13	11. The Fool Circle	A&M 4844
10/10/81	**83**	9	12. 'Snaz .... [L]	A&M 6703 [2]
7/10/82	**122**	10	13. 2XS	A&M 4901

NAZZ
Philadelphia rock quartet featuring Todd Rundgren (guitar) & Stewkey (vocals)

DATE CHARTED	PEAK POS	WKS CHRT'D	ARTIST — Album Title	LABEL & NUMBER
10/19/68	**118**	26	1. Nazz .... "Hello It's Me"	SGC 5001
5/10/69	**80**	15	2. Nazz Nazz	SGC 5002

SAM NEELY
singer/songwriter from Corpus Christi, Texas

DATE CHARTED	PEAK POS	WKS CHRT'D	ARTIST — Album Title	LABEL & NUMBER
9/16/72	**147**	11	1. Loving You Just Crossed My Mind	Capitol 11097
2/10/73	**175**	6	2. Sam Neely-2	Capitol 11143

NEKTAR
English art-rock quartet based in Germany

DATE CHARTED	PEAK POS	WKS CHRT'D	ARTIST — Album Title	LABEL & NUMBER
7/20/74	**19**	28	1. Remember The Future	Passport 98002
2/15/75	**32**	20	2. Down To Earth	Passport 98005
4/03/76	**89**	14	3. Recycled	Passport 98011
9/18/76	**141**	4	4. A Tab In The Ocean .... [I]	Passport 98017
11/05/77	**172**	3	5. Magic Is A Child	Polydor 6115

RICKY NELSON
born Eric Hilliard Nelson on 5/8/40 in Teaneck, New Jersey

DATE CHARTED	PEAK POS	WKS CHRT'D	ARTIST — Album Title	LABEL & NUMBER
11/11/57	**1(2)**	33	1. **Ricky** .... "Be-Bop Baby"(3)	Imperial 9048
7/28/58	**7**	9	2. **Ricky Nelson** .... Poor Little Fool"(1)	Imperial 9050
2/02/59	**14**	19	3. Ricky Sings Again .... "Believe What You Say"(4)/"Lonesome Town"(7)/ "Never Be Anyone Else But You"(6)/"It's Late"(9)	Imperial 9061
9/28/59	**22**	26	4. Songs By Ricky .... "Just A Little Too Much"(9)/"Sweeter Than You"(9)	Imperial 9082
8/29/60	**18**	11	5. More Songs By Ricky	Imperial 9122
5/29/61	**8**	49	6. **Rick Is 21** .... "Travelin' Man"(1)/"Hello Mary Lou"(9)	Imperial 9152
4/14/62	**27**	20	7. Album Seven By Rick	Imperial 9167
3/02/63	**112**	4	8. Best Sellers By Rick Nelson ...... [G] "Stood Up"(2-'58)	Imperial 9218
5/04/63	**137**	5	9. It's Up To You .... [K] It's Up To You"(6)	Imperial 9223
6/08/63	**20**	19	10. For Your Sweet Love	Decca 74419
1/04/64	**14**	22	11. Rick Nelson sings "For You" .... "For You"(6)	Decca 74479
2/21/70	**54**	19	12. Rick Nelson In Concert .... [L] recorded at The Troubadour Club in Los Angeles	Decca 75162
11/07/70	**196**	2	13. Rick Sings Nelson	Decca 75236
12/09/72	**32**	18	14. Garden Party .... "Garden Party"(6)	Decca 75391
2/23/74	**190**	4	15. Windfall .... above 4 albums feature the Stone Canyon Band	MCA 383
2/21/81	**153**	6	16. Playing To Win	Capitol 12109

SANDY NELSON
drummer - born on 12/1/38 in Santa Monica, California

DATE CHARTED	PEAK POS	WKS CHRT'D	ARTIST — Album Title	LABEL & NUMBER
1/20/62	**6**	48	1. **Let There Be Drums** .... [I] "Let There Be Drums"(7)	Imperial 9159
4/14/62	**29**	24	2. Drums Are My Beat! .... [I]	Imperial 9168
7/14/62	**55**	11	3. Drummin' Up A Storm .... [I]	Imperial 9189
11/03/62	**141**	3	4. Compelling Percussion .... [I]	Imperial 9204
12/01/62	**106**	3	5. Golden Hits .... [I]	Imperial 9202

DATE CHARTED	PEAK POS	WKS CHRT'D	ARTIST — Album Title	LABEL & NUMBER
11/21/64	**122**	11	6. Live! In Las Vegas .... [I-L]	Imperial 12272
3/06/65	**135**	5	7. Teen Beat '65 .... [I]	Imperial 12278
7/10/65	**120**	8	8. Drum Discotheque .... [I]	Imperial 12283
10/02/65	**118**	11	9. Drums A Go-Go .... [I]	Imperial 12287
1/08/66	**126**	7	10. Boss Beat .... [I]	Imperial 12298
4/23/66	**148**	2	11. "In" Beat .... [I]	Imperial 12305

TRACY NELSON
lead singer of Mother Earth

10/19/74	**145**	5	1. Tracy Nelson	Atlantic 7310

WILLIE NELSON
prolific country singer/songwriter from Austin, Texas - born on 4/30/33

7/26/75	**28**	43	● 1. Red Headed Stranger .... "Blue Eyes Crying In The Rain"	Columbia 33482
11/08/75	**196**	3	2. What Can You Do To Me Now .... [E]	RCA 1234
3/20/76	**48**	15	● 3. The Sound In Your Mind	Columbia 34092
5/08/76	**149**	7	4. Willie Nelson Live .... [R-L] originally released in 1966 as "Country Music Concert"	RCA 1487
6/05/76	**187**	3	5. Phases And Stages .... [E] recorded in 1964 - produced by Jerry Wexler	Atlantic 7291
10/16/76	**60**	7	6. The Troublemaker .... gospel songs - title song refers to Christ	Columbia 34112
5/21/77	**78**	15	7. Before His Time .... [E] re-mix by Waylon Jennings of earlier recordings	RCA 2210
7/09/77	**91**	12	8. To Lefty From Willie .... a tribute to Lefty Frizzell who died in 1975	Columbia 34695
2/04/78	**12**	29	▲ 9. Waylon & Willie .... WAYLON JENNINGS & WILLIE NELSON	RCA 2686
5/13/78	**30**	117	▲ 10. Stardust .... an album of pop standards from 1926-1955 (produced by Booker T. Jones)	Columbia 35305
12/02/78	**32**	55	▲ 11. Willie and Family Live .... [L] recorded at Harrah's, Lake Tahoe, Nevada	Columbia 35642 [2]
3/03/79	**154**	5	12. Sweet Memories .... [E]	RCA 3243
6/30/79	**25**	18	● 13. One For The Road .... WILLIE NELSON & LEON RUSSELL	Columbia 36064 [2]
11/17/79	**42**	25	● 14. Willie Nelson sings Kristofferson .... songs written by Kris Kristofferson	Columbia 36188
12/01/79	**73**	8	● 15. Pretty Paper .... [X] made top 10 on Billboard's special Christmas charts (1983)	Columbia 36189
1/12/80	**52**	25	● 16. The Electric Horseman .... [S] side 1: songs performed by Willie; side 2: instrumental score by Dave Grusin	Columbia 36327
3/15/80	**150**	5	17. Danny Davis & Willie Nelson with The Nashville Brass .... [E] new instrumental backing for earlier recordings by Willie	RCA 3549
6/14/80	**70**	25	● 18. San Antonio Rose .... WILLIE NELSON & RAY PRICE Willie played bass with Ray's backing band in the early '60s	Columbia 36476
9/06/80	**11**	36	▲ 19. Honeysuckle Rose .... [S-L] "On The Road Again"	Columbia 36752 [2]
3/21/81	**31**	23	▲ 20. Somewhere Over The Rainbow	Columbia 36883
8/01/81	**148**	7	21. The Minstrel Man .... [E]	RCA 4045
9/19/81	**27**	93	▲ 22. Willie Nelson's Greatest Hits (& Some That Will Be) .... [G]	Columbia 37542 [2]
3/20/82	**2(4)**	99	▲ 23. **Always On My Mind** .... "Always On My Mind"(5)	Columbia 37951
10/30/82	**57**	22	● 24. WWII .... WAYLON & WILLIE	RCA 4455
2/12/83	**37**	53	▲ 25. Poncho & Lefty .... MERLE HAGGARD/WILLIE NELSON	Epic 37958
3/19/83	**39**	20	26. Tougher Than Leather	Columbia 38248

DATE CHARTED	PEAK POS	WKS CHRT'D	ARTIST — Album Title	LABEL & NUMBER
4/23/83	**60**	16	27. Take It To The Limit .... WILLIE NELSON with WAYLON JENNINGS	Columbia 38562
11/26/83	**54**	34	● 28. Without A Song	Columbia 39110
12/03/83	**182**	5	29. My Own Way .... [E]	RCA 4819
6/16/84	**116**	7	30. Angel Eyes .... featuring the guitar of Jackie King	Columbia 39363
8/04/84	**69**	26	● 31. City Of New Orleans	Columbia 39145
11/10/84	**152**	5	32. Music from SongWriter .... [S] WILLIE NELSON & KRIS KRISTOFFERSON (co-stars of the film)	Columbia 39531
3/30/85	**164**+	2+	33. Me & Paul .... title song refers to Willie and his drummer Paul English	Columbia 40008
			NENA German - real name: Gabriele Kerner	
3/24/84	**27**	14	1. 99 Luftballons .... "99 Luftballons"(2)	Epic 39294
			PETER NERO pop/jazz/classical pianist from Brooklyn	
7/10/61	**34**	22	1. Piano Forte .... [I]	RCA 2334
9/18/61	**32**	62	2. New Piano In Town .... [I]	RCA 2383
3/17/62	**22**	24	3. Young And Warm And Wonderful .... [I]	RCA 2484
7/07/62	**16**	38	4. For The Nero-Minded .... [I]	RCA 2536
2/02/63	**40**	9	5. The Colorful Peter Nero .... [I]	RCA 2618
3/30/63	**5**	28	6. **Hail The Conquering Nero**	RCA 2638
9/07/63	**31**	23	7. Peter Nero In Person .... [I-L]	RCA 2710
2/29/64	**133**	4	8. Sunday In New York .... [S-I]	RCA 2827
6/06/64	**38**	26	9. Reflections .... [I]	RCA 2853
10/10/64	**42**	21	10. Songs You Won't Forget .... [I]	RCA 2935
2/20/65	**123**	4	11. The Best Of Peter Nero .... [G-I]	RCA 2978
5/29/65	**147**	3	12. Career Girls .... [I]	RCA 3313
10/23/65	**86**	16	13. Nero Goes "Pops" .... [I] PETER NERO/ARTHUR FIEDLER/BOSTON POPS	RCA 2821
2/19/66	**114**	6	14. The Screen Scene .... [I]	RCA 3496
7/16/66	**141**	3	15. Peter Nero-Up Close .... [I]	RCA 3550
5/13/67	**193**	2	16. Peter Nero plays Born Free and others .... [I]	RCA Camden 2139
4/20/68	**180**	4	17. Peter Nero plays Love Is Blue and ten other great songs .... [I]	RCA 3936
5/10/69	**193**	3	18. I've Gotta Be Me .... [I]	Columbia 9800
11/27/71	**23**	27	● 19. Summer of '42 .... [I]	Columbia 31105
7/08/72	**172**	9	20. The First Time Ever (I Saw Your Face) .... [I]	Columbia 31335
			MICHAEL NESMITH & The First National Band Michael was a member of The Monkees	
10/17/70	**143**	3	1. Magnetic South	RCA 4371
1/02/71	**159**	4	2. Loose Salute	RCA 4415
8/04/79	**151**	9	3. Infinite Rider On The Big Dogma .... shown only as Michael Nesmith	Pacific Arts 130
			NEVILLE BROTHERS Aaron, Art, Charles & Cyril Neville - also see the Meters	
8/29/81	**166**	3	1. Fiyo On The Bayou	A&M 4866
			NEWBEATS Larry Henley (lead singer) with Dean & Marc Mathis	
10/03/64	**56**	19	1. Bread & Butter .... "Bread And Butter"(2)	Hickory 120
1/22/66	**131**	4	2. Run Baby Run	Hickory 128

NEW BIRTH
12 member soul-funk band founded by Harvey Fuqua

10/30/71	189	2	1. Ain't No Big Thing, But It's Growing	RCA 4526
3/10/73	31	29	2. Birth Day	RCA 4797
11/17/73	50	31	● 3. It's Been A Long Time	RCA 0285
8/17/74	56	15	4. Comin' From All Ends	RCA 0494
5/24/75	57	17	5. Blind Baby	Buddah 5636
7/19/75	175	2	6. The Best Of The New Birth .... [G]	RCA 1021
8/28/76	168	4	7. Love Potion	Warner 2953
12/10/77	164	6	8. Behold The Mighty Army	Warner 3071

NEW CACTUS BAND - see CACTUS

NEW CHRISTY MINSTRELS
folk/balladeer troupe named after the Christy Minstrels, formed in 1842 by Edwin P. Christy

10/20/62	19	92	1. The New Christy Minstrels	Columbia 8672
2/23/63	30	20	2. The New Christy Minstrels In Person .... [L]	Columbia 8741
5/25/63	20	22	3. Tall Tales! Legends & Nonsense	Columbia 8817
8/24/63	15	77	● 4. Ramblin' featuring Green, Green	Columbia 8855
4/18/64	9	34	5. **Today** .... [S] featuring songs from the film "Advance To The Rear"	Columbia 8959
8/29/64	48	23	6. Land Of Giants .... above albums under the direction of founder Randy Sparks	Columbia 8987
2/13/65	62	11	7. Cowboys And Indians	Columbia 9103
6/26/65	22	22	8. Chim Chim Cher-ee	Columbia 9169
10/16/65	125	9	9. The Wandering Minstrels	Columbia 9184
6/18/66	76	16	10. Greatest Hits .... [G]	Columbia 9279
11/28/70	195	2	11. You Need Someone To Love	Gregar 102

NEW COLONY SIX
soft-rock group from Chicago

9/02/67	172	7	1. Colonization	Sentar 3001
7/20/68	157	6	2. Revelations	Mercury 61165
11/01/69	179	4	3. Attacking A Straw Man	Mercury 61228

NEW EDITION
5 teenage boys from the Roxbury district of Boston - Ralph Tresvant, lead singer

9/03/83	90	33	1. Candy Girl	Streetwise 3301
10/13/84	6	26+ ▲	2. **New Edition** .... "Cool It Now"(4)/"Mr. Telephone Man"	MCA 5515

NEW ENGLAND
East Coast melodic rock quartet

5/19/79	50	17	1. New England	Infinity 9007
7/18/81	176	4	2. Walking Wild .... produced by Todd Rundgren	Elektra 346

NEW ENGLAND CONSERVATORY RAGTIME ENSEMBLE
Gunther Schuller, conductor

5/19/73	65	36	1. Scott Joplin: The Red Back Book .... [I] Red Back Book: collection of famous Joplin rags	Angel 36060

NEW RIDERS OF THE PURPLE SAGE
San Francisco country-rock band formed by Jerry Garcia as an offshoot of the Grateful Dead

9/11/71	39	15	1. New Riders Of The Purple Sage	Columbia 30888
5/06/72	33	18	2. Powerglide	Columbia 31284
12/09/72	85	13	3. Gypsy Cowboy	Columbia 31930
10/20/73	55	18	● 4. The Adventures of Panama Red	Columbia 32450
4/27/74	68	12	5. Home, Home on the Road .... [L]	Columbia 32870
11/02/74	68	9	6. Brujo	Columbia 33145

DATE CHARTED	PEAK POS	WKS CHRT'D	ARTIST — Album Title	LABEL & NUMBER
11/08/75	144	4	7. Oh, What A Mighty Time	Columbia 33688
6/12/76	145	8	8. New Riders	MCA 2196
			NEW SEEKERS	
			group formed by Keith Potger after disbandment of The Seekers	
4/03/71	136	6	1. Beautiful People	Elektra 74088
			"Look What They've Done To My Song Ma"	
12/25/71	37	14	2. We'd Like To Teach The World To Sing	Elektra 74115
			"I'd Like To Teach The World To Sing (In Perfect Harmony)"(7)	
7/15/72	166	10	3. Circles	Elektra 75034
5/19/73	190	4	4. Pinball Wizards	MGM/Verve 5098
			NEW VAUDEVILLE BAND	
			English - Geoff Stevens, vocals	
12/10/66	5	31	● 1. **Winchester Cathedral**	Fontana 27560
			"Winchester Cathedral"(1)	
			NEW WORLD THEATRE ORCHESTRA	
			also shown as the Cinema Sound Stage Orchestra	
10/21/57	8	4	1. **Around The World In 80 Days** .... [I]	Stereo-Fid. 2800
			NEW YORK CITY	
			R&B quartet - first tenor John Brown was a member of the Five Satins	
6/16/73	122	10	1. I'm Doin' Fine Now	Chelsea 0198
			NEW YORK DOLLS	
			glitter-rock band led by David Johansen & Sylvain Sylvain	
9/01/73	116	12	1. New York Dolls	Mercury 675
			produced by Todd Rundgren	
6/01/74	167	5	2. in Too Much Too Soon	Mercury 1001
			NEW YORK PHILHARMONIC - see LEONARD BERNSTEIN	
			MICKEY NEWBURY	
11/13/71	58	15	1. 'Frisco Mabel Joy	Elektra 74107
3/10/73	173	5	2. Heaven Help The Child	Elektra 75055
4/05/75	172	3	3. Lovers	Elektra 1030
			NEWCLEUS	
			New York rap group	
9/08/84	74	28	1. Jam On Revenge	Sunnyview 4901
			BOB NEWHART	
			Bob's situation comedy series debuted on 9/16/72	
5/16/60	1(14)	108	● 1. **The Button-Down Mind Of Bob Newhart** . [C]	Warner 1379
11/14/60	1(1)	70	● 2. **The Button-Down Mind Strikes Back!** ... [C]	Warner 1393
10/30/61	10	30	3. **Behind The Button-Down Mind Of Bob Newhart** .... [C]	Warner 1417
9/08/62	28	26	4. The Button-Down Mind On TV .... [C]	Warner 1467
			Bob hosted a comedy variety show from 1961-62	
2/29/64	113	11	5. Bob Newhart Faces Bob Newhart (faces Bob Newhart) .... [C]	Warner 1517
4/24/65	126	5	6. The Windmills Are Weakening .... [C]	Warner 1588
			RANDY NEWMAN	
			nephew of composers Alfred, Emil and Lionel Newman - also see soundtrack "Ragtime"	
10/02/71	191	3	1. Randy Newman/Live .... [L]	Reprise 6459
6/17/72	163	18	2. Sail Away	Reprise 2064
10/05/74	36	23	3. Good Old Boys	Reprise 2193
			background vocals by the Eagles' Glen Frey & Don Henley	
10/22/77	9	29	● 4. **Little Criminals**	Warner 3079
			guest appearances by members of the Eagles "Short People"(2)	

DATE CHARTED	PEAK POS	WKS CHRT'D	ARTIST — Album Title	LABEL & NUMBER
9/01/79	41	11	5. Born Again .... vocal harmonies by Stephen Bishop	Warner 3346
2/12/83	64	13	6. Trouble In Paradise .... guests include Bob Seger, Linda Ronstadt, Paul Simon & Christine McVie	Warner 23755

JUICE NEWTON
country-pop singer born in Virginia Beach, Virginia

DATE CHARTED	PEAK POS	WKS CHRT'D	ARTIST — Album Title	LABEL & NUMBER
3/07/81	22	86	▲ 1. Juice .... "Angel Of The Morning"(4)/"Queen Of Hearts"(2)/ "The Sweetest Thing (I've Ever Known)"(7)	Capitol 12136
5/29/82	20	46	● 2. Quiet Lies .... "Love's Been A Little Bit Hard On Me"(7)	Capitol 12210
9/10/83	52	15	3. Dirty Looks	Capitol 12294
7/14/84	128	10	4. Can't Wait All Night	RCA 4995
7/21/84	178	5	5. Greatest Hits .... [G]	Capitol 12353

WAYNE NEWTON
Las Vegas's #1 entertainer - born on 4/3/42 in Roanoke, Virginia

DATE CHARTED	PEAK POS	WKS CHRT'D	ARTIST — Album Title	LABEL & NUMBER
10/12/63	55	9	1. Danke Schoen	Capitol 1973
5/01/65	17	20	2. Red Roses For A Blue Lady	Capitol 2335
10/23/65	114	6	3. Summer Wind	Capitol 2389
6/04/66	80	21	4. Wayne Newton - Now!	Capitol 2445
2/04/67	131	13	5. It's Only The Good Times	Capitol 2635
10/07/67	194	4	6. The Best Of Wayne Newton .... [G]	Capitol 2797
6/01/68	186	5	7. One More Time	MGM 4549
8/31/68	196	3	8. Walking On New Grass	MGM 4523
6/17/72	34	21	9. Daddy Don't You Walk So Fast .... "Daddy Don't You Walk So Fast"(4)	Chelsea 1001
11/18/72	164	11	10. Can't You Hear The Song?	Chelsea 1003

OLIVIA NEWTON-JOHN
born on 9/26/48 in Cambridge, England - raised in Melbourne, Australia

DATE CHARTED	PEAK POS	WKS CHRT'D	ARTIST — Album Title	LABEL & NUMBER
11/27/71	158	4	1. If Not For You	Uni 73117
12/29/73	54	20	● 2. Let Me Be There .... includes 6 tracks from album #1 above "Let Me Be There"(6)	MCA 389
6/08/74	1(1)	61	● 3. If You Love Me, Let Me Know .... "If You Love Me (Let Me Know)"(5)/"I Honestly Love You"(1)	MCA 411
2/22/75	1(1)	31	● 4. Have You Never Been Mellow .... "Have You Never Been Mellow"(1)/"Please Mr. Please"(3)	MCA 2133
10/11/75	12	22	● 5. Clearly Love	MCA 2148
3/20/76	13	24	● 6. Come On Over	MCA 2186
11/06/76	30	28	● 7. Don't Stop Believin'	MCA 2223
7/09/77	34	16	8. Making A Good Thing Better	MCA 2280
11/12/77	13	19	▲ 9. Olivia Newton-John's Greatest Hits .... [G]	MCA 3028
5/20/78	1(12)	77	▲ 10. Grease .... [S] 5 songs by Olivia/others by various artists "You're The One That I Want"(1)/ "Hopelessly Devoted To You"(3)/"Summer Nights"(5)	RSO 4002 [2]
12/09/78	7	39	▲ 11. Totally Hot .... "A Little More Love"(3)	MCA 3067
7/12/80	4	36	▲ 12. Xanadu .... [S] side 1: Olivia; side 2: ELO "Magic"(1)/"Xanadu"(8)	MCA 6100
10/31/81	6	57	▲ 13. Physical .... "Physical"(1)/"Make A Move On Me"(5)	MCA 5229
10/09/82	16	86	▲ 14. Olivia's Greatest Hits, Vol. 2 .... [G] "Heart Attack"(3)	MCA 5347
12/03/83	26	17	▲ 15. Two Of A Kind .... [S] 4 songs by Olivia/others by various artists "Twist Of Fate"(5)	MCA 6127

DATE CHARTED	PEAK POS	WKS CHRT'D	ARTIST — Album Title	LABEL & NUMBER
			NICE British classical/rock trio led by keyboardist Keith Emerson	
8/29/70	**197**	5	1. Five Bridges .... [I-L] with the Sinfonia of London Orchestra	Mercury 61295
2/26/72	**152**	8	2. Keith Emerson with The Nice .... [R] reissue of "Five Bridges" and "Elegy" albums	Mercury 6500 [2]
			MIKE NICHOLS & ELAINE MAY improvisational comedy team	
6/01/59	**39**	7	1. Improvisations To Music .... [C] with Marty Rubenstein at the piano	Mercury 20376
2/06/61	**10**	32	2. **An evening with Mike Nichols and Elaine May** .... [OC-C] opened on Broadway on 10/8/60	Mercury 2200
2/24/62	**17**	29	3. Mike Nichols & Elaine May Examine Doctors .... [C]	Mercury 20680
			STEVIE NICKS lead singer of Fleetwood Mac	
8/15/81	**1(1)**	141	▲ 1. **Bella Donna** .... "Stop Draggin' My Heart Around"(3)/"Leather And Lace"(6)	Modern 139
7/02/83	**5**	52	▲ 2. **The Wild Heart** .... "Stand Back"(5)	Modern 90048
			NIGHT Stevie Lange & Chris Thompson (Manfred Mann), lead singers	
8/11/79	**113**	10	1. Night .... second pressings of LP include Thompson's "If You Remember Me" "Hot Summer Nights"	Planet 3
			NIGHTHAWKS Washington, D.C. rock/blues quartet led by Mark Wenner	
7/26/80	**166**	4	1. The Nighthawks	Mercury 3833
			MAXINE NIGHTINGALE English	
5/29/76	**65**	9	1. Right Back Where We Started From .... "Right Back Where We Started From"(2)	United Art. 626
7/21/79	**45**	18	2. Lead Me On .... "Lead Me On"(5)	Windsong 3404
1/08/83	**176**	4	3. It's A Beautiful Thing	Highrise 101
			NIGHT RANGER rock quintet from California	
12/25/82	**38**	69	1. Dawn Patrol	Boardwalk 33259
11/19/83	**15**	69	▲ 2. Midnight Madness .... "Sister Christian"(5)	MCA 5456
			WILLIE NILE rock singer/songwriter from Buffalo, New York	
4/12/80	**145**	6	1. Willie Nile	Arista 4260
5/02/81	**158**	8	2. Golden Down	Arista 4284
			NILSSON Harry Nilsson - born on 6/15/41 in Brooklyn, New York	
8/23/69	**120**	15	1. Harry	RCA 4197
3/06/71	**25**	32	2. The Point! .... [TV] songs & narration from his animated TV special	RCA 1003
7/17/71	**149**	3	3. Aerial Pandemonium Ballet .... [K] selections from "Pandemonium Shadow Show" & "Aerial Ballet" LPs "Everybody's Talkin'"(6-'69)	RCA 4543
12/04/71	**3**	46	● 4. **Nilsson Schmilsson** .... "Without You"(1)/"Coconut"(8)	RCA 4515
7/22/72	**12**	31	● 5. Son Of Schmilsson	RCA 4717
6/23/73	**46**	17	6. A Little Touch Of Schmilsson In The Night .... with orchestra conducted by Gordon Jenkins	RCA 0097

DATE CHARTED	PEAK POS	WKS CHRT'D	ARTIST — Album Title	LABEL & NUMBER
5/04/74	160	9	7. Son Of Dracula .... [S] the film stars are Nilsson and Ringo Starr	Rapple 0220
9/07/74	60	12	8. Pussy Cats .... produced by John Lennon	RCA 0570
4/05/75	141	7	9. Duit On Mon Dei	RCA 0817
2/07/76	111	7	10. Sandman	RCA 1031
7/10/76	158	6	11. ...That's The Way It Is	RCA 1119
8/06/77	108	10	12. Knnillssonn	RCA 2276
6/17/78	140	5	13. Greatest Hits .... [G]	RCA 2798

LEONARD NIMOY
portrays Mr. Spock on "Star Trek"

DATE CHARTED	PEAK POS	WKS CHRT'D	ARTIST — Album Title	LABEL & NUMBER
6/10/67	83	25	1. Mr. Spock's Music From Outer Space .... Leonard sings 3 songs & narrates 3 others - others are instrumentals by Charles Green	Dot 25794
2/24/68	97	13	2. Two Sides Of Leonard Nimoy .... side 1: performs as Mr. Spock: side 2: performs as Leonard Nimoy	Dot 25835

999
Nick Cash, lead singer of British new wave quintet

DATE CHARTED	PEAK POS	WKS CHRT'D	ARTIST — Album Title	LABEL & NUMBER
2/23/80	177	3	1. The Biggest Prize In Sport	Polydor 6256
6/27/81	192	2	2. Concrete	Polydor 6323

1910 FRUITGUM CO.
bubblegum group assembled by producers Jerry Kasenetz & Jeff Katz

DATE CHARTED	PEAK POS	WKS CHRT'D	ARTIST — Album Title	LABEL & NUMBER
4/20/68	162	8	1. Simon Says .... "Simon Says"(4)	Buddah 5010
10/05/68	163	12	2. 1,2,3 Red Light .... "1,2,3 Red Light"(5)	Buddah 5022
4/05/69	147	8	3. Indian Giver .... "Indian Giver"(5)	Buddah 5036

NITE-LITERS
funk 'n' roll band produced by Harvey Fuqua

DATE CHARTED	PEAK POS	WKS CHRT'D	ARTIST — Album Title	LABEL & NUMBER
7/24/71	167	13	1. Morning, Noon & The Nite-Liters .... [I]	RCA 4493
5/20/72	198	2	2. Instrumental Directions .... [I]	RCA 4580

NITTY GRITTY DIRT BAND
country-rock-folk group led by Jeff Hanna & John McEuen

DATE CHARTED	PEAK POS	WKS CHRT'D	ARTIST — Album Title	LABEL & NUMBER
4/08/67	151	8	1. The Nitty Gritty Dirt Band	Liberty 7501
12/05/70	66	32	2. Uncle Charlie & His Dog Teddy .... "Mr. Bojangles"(9)	Liberty 7642
2/05/72	162	10	3. All The Good Times	United Art. 5553
12/30/72	68	32	● 4. Will The Circle Be Unbroken .... with Mother Maybelle Carter, Earl Scruggs, Doc Watson, Roy Acuff & Merle Travis	United Art. 9801 [3]
7/13/74	28	21	5. Stars & Stripes Forever .... [L]	United Art. 184 [2]
10/04/75	66	9	6. Dream	United Art. 469
12/18/76	77	13	7. Dirt, Silver & Gold .... [K]	United Art. 670 [3]
			DIRT BAND:	
7/08/78	163	6	8. The Dirt Band	United Art. 854
1/26/80	76	14	9. An American Dream	United Art. 974
7/19/80	62	16	10. Make A Little Magic	United Art. 1042
9/05/81	102	9	11. Jealousy	Liberty 1106

NITZINGER
rock trio: John Nitzinger, Linda Waring & Curly Benton

DATE CHARTED	PEAK POS	WKS CHRT'D	ARTIST — Album Title	LABEL & NUMBER
9/02/72	170	8	1. Nitzinger	Capitol 11091

DON NIX

DATE CHARTED	PEAK POS	WKS CHRT'D	ARTIST — Album Title	LABEL & NUMBER
9/11/71	197	3	1. Living By The Days	Elektra 74101

CLIFF NOBLES & Co.

DATE CHARTED	PEAK POS	WKS CHRT'D	ARTIST — Album Title	LABEL & NUMBER
9/21/68	159	3	1. The Horse .... "The Horse"(2)	Phil-L.A. S. 4001

DATE CHARTED	PEAK POS	WKS CHRT'D	ARTIST — Album Title	LABEL & NUMBER
			KENNY NOLAN	
3/26/77	**78**	16	1. Kenny Nolan .... "I Like Dreamin'"(3)	20th Century 532
			NORMA JEAN Norma Jean Wright - former member of Chic	
8/26/78	**134**	11	1. Norma Jean	Bearsville 6983
			FREDDIE NORTH	
1/01/72	**179**	5	1. Friend .... "She's All I Got"	Mankind 204
			ALDO NOVA rock singer/songwriter from Montreal, Canada	
2/20/82	**8**	37	● 1. **Aldo Nova** .... "Fantasy"	Portrait 37498
10/15/83	**56**	20	2. Subject: Aldo Nova	Portrait 38721
			NOVO COMBO New York-based rock quartet led by Michael Shrieve (Santana)	
10/10/81	**167**	6	1. Novo Combo	Polydor 6331
			NRBQ NRBQ: New Rhythm & Blues Quintet	
7/19/69	**162**	4	1. NRBQ	Columbia 9858
			TED NUGENT heavy-metal rock guitarist from Detroit - also see Amboy Dukes	
11/22/75	**28**	62	● 1. Ted Nugent	Epic 33692
10/02/76	**24**	32	▲ 2. Free-For-All .... featuring vocals by Meat Loaf	Epic 34121
6/25/77	**17**	39	▲ 3. Cat Scratch Fever	Epic 34700
2/11/78	**13**	22	▲ 4. Double Live Gonzo! .... [L]	Epic 35069 [2]
11/11/78	**24**	20	▲ 5. Weekend Warriors	Epic 35551
6/02/79	**18**	18	● 6. State Of Shock	Epic 36000
5/31/80	**13**	18	● 7. Scream Dream	Epic 36404
3/21/81	**51**	10	8. Intensities In 10 Cities .... [L]	Epic 37084
11/28/81	**140**	8	9. Great Gonzos! The Best Of Ted Nugent.... [G]	Epic 37667
7/17/82	**51**	14	10. Nugent	Atlantic 19365
2/18/84	**56**	15	11. Penetrator	Atlantic 80125
			GARY NUMAN British synthesized techno-rock artist	
9/15/79	**124**	10	1. Replicas .... with Tubeway Army	Atco 117
2/02/80	**16**	30	2. The Pleasure Principle .... "Cars"(9)	Atco 120
10/04/80	**64**	10	3. Telekon	Atco 103
10/24/81	**167**	4	4. Dance	Atco 143
			BOBBY NUNN	
10/23/82	**148**	8	1. Second To Nunn	Motown 6022
			LAURA NYRO white soul-gospel singer/songwriter	
8/10/68	**181**	7	1. Eli And The Thirteenth Confession	Columbia 9626
11/01/69	**32**	17	2. New York Tendaberry	Columbia 9737
12/26/70	**51**	14	3. Christmas And The Beads Of Sweat	Columbia 30259
12/25/71	**46**	17	4. Gonna Take A Miracle .... backing vocals by LaBelle	Columbia 30987
2/03/73	**97**	11	5. The First Songs .... [R] reissue of her first album "More Than A New Discovery"	Columbia 31410
3/13/76	**60**	14	6. Smile	Columbia 33912

DATE CHARTED	PEAK POS	WKS CHRT'D	ARTIST — Album Title	LABEL & NUMBER
7/02/77	137	5	7. Season of Lights...Laura Nyro in Concert .... [L]	Columbia 34786
3/10/84	182	3	8. Mother's Spiritual	Columbia 39215

OAK RIDGE BOYS
formed in Oak Ridge, Tennessee in 1957 as a gospel quartet

2/18/78	120	9	● 1. Y'all Come Back Saloon	ABC/Dot 2093
6/17/78	164	11	● 2. Room Service	ABC 1065
3/29/80	154	6	● 3. Together	MCA 3220
11/22/80	99	21	▲ 4. Greatest Hits .... [G]	MCA 5150
6/13/81	14	48	▲ 5. Fancy Free	MCA 5209
			"Elvira"(5)	
2/20/82	20	21	● 6. Bobbie Sue	MCA 5294
12/04/82	73	7	● 7. Christmas .... [X]	MCA 5365
2/26/83	51	23	● 8. American Made	MCA 5390
11/19/83	121	14	● 9. Deliver	MCA 5455
9/08/84	71	24	● 10. Greatest Hits 2 .... [G]	MCA 5496

JOHN O'BANION
from Kokomo, Indiana

5/16/81	164	4	1. John O'Banion	Elektra 342

O'BRYAN
O'Bryan Burnette II

4/10/82	80	12	1. Doin' Alright	Capitol 12192
3/12/83	87	27	2. You And I	Capitol 12256
5/26/84	64	21	3. Be My Lover	Capitol 12332

RIC OCASEK
lead singer of the Cars

1/29/83	28	16	1. Beatitude	Geffen 2022

OCEAN
Canadian quintet

5/29/71	60	13	1. Put Your Hand In The Hand	Kama Sutra 2033
			"Put Your Hand In The Hand"(2)	

BILLY OCEAN
born in Trinidad - raised in London

7/25/81	152	3	1. Nights (Feel Like Getting Down)	Epic 37406
8/25/84	9	33 +	▲ 2. **Suddenly**	Jive 8213
			"Caribbean Queen (No More Love On The Run)"(1)/"Loverboy"(2)	

PHIL OCHS
folk-protest singer/songwriter - committed suicide on 4/9/76 (35)

7/09/66	149	2	1. Phil Ochs In Concert .... [L]	Elektra 7310
12/09/67	168	5	2. Pleasures Of The Harbor	A&M 4133
6/14/69	167	7	3. Rehearsals For Retirement	A&M 4181
3/14/70	194	2	4. Phil Ochs Greatest Hits	A&M 4253
			album contains all new recordings	

CARROLL O'CONNOR
Archie Bunker of TV's "All In The Family"

6/17/72	118	13	1. Remembering You	A&M 4340
			Carroll sings and narrates songs of the '30's	

ALAN O'DAY
wrote Helen Reddy's #1 hit "Angie Baby"

9/03/77	109	9	1. Appetizers	Pacific 4300
			"Undercover Angel"(1)	

ODETTA
folksinger Odetta Holmes

9/28/63	75	8	1. Odetta sings Folk Songs	RCA 2643

DATE CHARTED	PEAK POS	WKS CHRT'D	ARTIST — Album Title	LABEL & NUMBER
			ODYSSEY	
			lead vocals by sisters Lillian & Louise Lopez	
10/08/77	**36**	38	1. Odyssey	RCA 2204
11/11/78	**123**	5	2. Hollywood Party Tonight	RCA 3031
6/14/80	**181**	4	3. Hang Together	RCA 3526
7/18/81	**175**	5	4. I Got The Melody	RCA 3910
			OFF BROADWAY usa	
			Oak Park, Illinois rock quintet - Cliff Johnson, lead singer	
2/16/80	**101**	11	1. On	Atlantic 19263
			OHIO EXPRESS	
			bubblegum group assembled by producers Jerry Kasenetz & Jeff Katz	
7/06/68	**126**	11	1. Ohio Express	Buddah 5018
			"Yummy Yummy Yummy"(4)	
2/08/69	**191**	2	2. Chewy, Chewy	Buddah 5026
			OHIO PLAYERS	
			R&B/funk group originally formed in Dayton, Ohio in 1959 as the Ohio Untouchables	
3/04/72	**177**	7	1. Pain	Westbound 2015
2/24/73	**63**	22	2. Pleasure	Westbound 2017
9/29/73	**70**	19	3. Ecstasy	Westbound 2021
4/27/74	**11**	48	● 4. Skin Tight	Mercury 705
11/02/74	**102**	8	5. Climax .... [K]	Westbound 1003
11/23/74	**1(1)**	29	● 6. **Fire**	Mercury 1013
			"Fire"(1)	
2/22/75	**92**	7	7. Ohio Players Greatest Hits .... [G]	Westbound 1005
8/23/75	**2(1)**	36	● 8. **Honey**	Mercury 1038
			"Love Rollercoaster"(1)	
12/20/75	**61**	14	9. Rattlesnake .... [K]	Westbound 211
6/12/76	**12**	20	● 10. Contradiction	Mercury 1088
11/13/76	**31**	17	● 11. Ohio Players Gold .... [G]	Mercury 1122
4/09/77	**41**	27	12. Angel	Mercury 3701
12/24/77	**68**	10	13. Mr. Mean	Mercury 3707
9/09/78	**69**	9	14. Jass-Ay-Lay-Dee	Mercury 3730
4/14/79	**80**	14	15. Everybody Up	Arista 4226
4/11/81	**165**	3	16. Tenderness	Boardwalk 37090
			OINGO BOINGO	
			8-man new wave rock group from Los Angeles	
10/25/80	**163**	5	1. Oingo Boingo .... [M]	I.R.S. 70400
			10" 4-song E.P.	
8/15/81	**172**	5	2. Only A Lad	A&M 4863
9/04/82	**148**	9	3. Nothing To Fear	A&M 4930
9/10/83	**144**	7	4. Good For Your Soul	A&M 4959
			O'JAYS	
			soul group formed in Canton, Ohio in 1958: Eddie Levert, Walt Williams, William Powell (died 5/26/77) - replaced by Sam Strain	
9/09/72	**10**	44	● 1. **Back Stabbers**	Phil. Int. 31712
			"Back Stabbers"(3)/"Love Train"(1)	
4/28/73	**156**	8	2. The O'Jays In Philadelphia .... [E]	Phil. Int. 32120
			recordings from 1969 (Neptune label)	
11/10/73	**11**	48	● 3. Ship Ahoy	Phil. Int. 32408
			"Put Your Hands Together"(10)/"For The Love Of Money"(9)	
6/29/74	**17**	24	● 4. The O'Jays Live In London .... [L]	Phil. Int. 32953
4/26/75	**11**	24	● 5. Survival	Phil. Int. 33150
11/29/75	**7**	34	● 6. **Family Reunion**	Phil. Int. 33807
			"I Love Music"(5)	
10/02/76	**20**	22	● 7. Message In The Music	Phil. Int. 34245
6/04/77	**27**	16	● 8. Travelin' At The Speed Of Thought	Phil. Int. 34684
1/07/78	**132**	6	9. The O'Jays: Collectors' Items .... [G]	Phil. Int. 35024 [2]

DATE CHARTED	PEAK POS	WKS CHRT'D	ARTIST — Album Title	LABEL & NUMBER
4/29/78	6	28	▲ 10. **So Full Of Love** .... "Use Ta Be My Girl"(4)	Phil. Int. 35355
9/15/79	16	30	▲ 11. Identify Yourself	Phil. Int. 36027
8/30/80	36	12	12. The Year 2000	TSOP 36416
5/15/82	49	13	13. My Favorite Person	Phil. Int. 37999
8/13/83	142	5	14. When Will I See You Again	Epic 38518

O'KAYSIONS
white soul group from North Carolina - Donny Weaver, lead singer

11/09/68	153	4	1. Girl Watcher .... "Girl Watcher"(5)	ABC 664

DANNY O'KEEFE

9/02/72	87	16	1. O'Keefe .... "Good Time Charlie's Got The Blues"(9)	Signpost 8404
8/11/73	172	9	2. Breezy Stories	Atlantic 7264

OLD & IN THE WAY
bluegrass band: Jerry Garcia, David Grisman, Peter Rowan, John Kahn & Vassar Clements

3/29/75	99	8	1. Old & In The Way .... [L]	Round 103

MIKE OLDFIELD
English electronic prodigy

11/10/73	3	45	● 1. **Tubular Bells** .... [I] "Tubular Bells"(7) - one 49 minute recording (excerpts used in film "The Exorcist")	Virgin 105
9/21/74	87	10	2. Hergest Ridge .... [I]	Virgin 109
12/20/75	146	7	3. Ommadawn .... [I]	Virgin 33913
7/04/81	174	3	4. QE2 .... [I]	Epic 37358
5/08/82	164	5	5. Five Miles Out	Epic 37983

OLIVER
William Oliver Swofford - from North Carolina

8/02/69	19	38	1. Good Morning Starshine .... "Good Morning Starshine"(3)/"Jean"(2)	Crewe 1333
5/16/70	71	13	2. Oliver Again	Crewe 1344

DAVID OLIVER

5/27/78	128	8	1. David Oliver	Mercury 1183

JANE OLIVOR
lyrical stylist from New York

10/22/77	86	8	1. Chasing Rainbows	Columbia 34917
7/08/78	108	12	2. Stay The Night	Columbia 35437
2/23/80	58	12	3. The Best Side Of Goodbye	Columbia 36355
5/29/82	144	6	4. In Concert .... [L] recorded at Berkley School Of Music, Boston	Columbia 37938

NIGEL OLSSON
drummer for Elton John's band

3/24/79	140	5	1. Nigel	Bang 35792

101 STRINGS
European orchestra under the direction of D.L. Miller

5/25/59	9	58	1. **The Soul of Spain** .... [I] this album was #1 for 46 of the 47 weeks that Billboard published a special "Best Selling Low Price LP's" chart (2/19/60-1/8/61)	Somerset 6600
1/09/61	21	19	2. The Soul of Spain, Volume II .... [I]	Somerset 9900
1/09/61	46	15	3. 101 Strings Play The Blues .... [I] a tribute to W.C. Handy	Somerset 5800
1/09/61	104	13	4. Concerto Under The Stars .... [I] featuring Harry Heineman at the piano	Somerset 6700

100 PROOF Aged In Soul

12/12/70	151	7	1. Somebody's Been Sleeping In My Bed .... "Somebody's Been Sleeping"(8)	Hot Wax 704

DATE CHARTED	PEAK POS	WKS CHRT'D	ARTIST — Album Title	LABEL & NUMBER
			ONE WAY Detroit-based soul band - Al Hudson, lead singer	
11/17/79	**181**	5	1. One Way featuring Al Hudson	MCA 3178
8/02/80	**128**	12	2. One Way Featuring Al Hudson	MCA 5127
3/07/81	**157**	8	3. Love Is...One Way	MCA 5163
9/26/81	**79**	19	4. Fancy Dancer	MCA 5247
4/03/82	**51**	23	5. Who's Foolin' Who	MCA 5279
8/20/83	**164**	6	6. Shine On Me	MCA 5428
5/26/84	**58**	20	7. Lady	MCA 5470
			YOKO ONO born in Japan on 2/18/33 - married John Lennon on 3/20/69 - also see John Lennon	
2/06/71	**182**	3	1. Yoko Ono/Plastic Ono Band .... front cover identical to "John Lennon/Plastic Ono Band"	Apple 3373
11/13/71	**199**	2	2. Fly	Apple 3380 [2]
2/24/73	**193**	4	3. Approximately Infinite Universe	Apple 3399 [2]
6/27/81	**49**	9	4. Season Of Glass .... recorded shortly after John's death	Geffen 2004
12/25/82	**98**	13	5. It's Alright (I See Rainbows)	Polydor 6364
			ROY ORBISON born in Wink, Texas on 4/23/36	
4/07/62	**21**	31	1. Crying .... "Running Scared"(1)/"Crying"(2)	Monument 4007
9/01/62	**14**	140	● 2. Roy Orbison's Greatest Hits .... [G] "Only The Lonely"(2)/"Blue Angel"(9)/"Dream Baby"(4)	Monument 4009
8/17/63	**35**	23	3. In Dreams .... "In Dreams"(7)/"Blue Bayou"	Monument 18003
8/22/64	**19**	30	4. More Of Roy Orbison's Greatest Hits .... [G] "It's Over"(9)/"Mean Woman Blues"(5)	Monument 18024
10/17/64	**101**	11	5. Early Orbison .... [K] selections from "Lonely & Blue" and "Crying" albums	Monument 18023
9/04/65	**55**	17	6. There Is Only One Roy Orbison	MGM 4308
11/06/65	**136**	11	7. Orbisongs .... [K] "Oh, Pretty Woman"(1)	Monument 18035
3/05/66	**128**	3	8. The Orbison Way	MGM 4322
8/13/66	**94**	9	9. The Very Best Of Roy Orbison .... [G]	Monument 18045
			ORCHESTRAL MANOEUVRES IN THE DARK English synthesizer duo: Paul Humphreys & Andy McCluskey	
2/06/82	**144**	12	1. Architecture & Morality	Epic 37721
4/23/83	**162**	6	2. Dazzle Ships	Epic 38543
11/24/84	**182**	6	3. Junk Culture	A&M 5027
			ORIGINALS Detroit soul quartet	
1/17/70	**174**	4	1. Baby, I'm For Real	Soul 716
7/11/70	**198**	2	2. Portrait Of The Originals .... "The Bells"	Soul 724
			ORION THE HUNTER rock quartet led by former Boston guitarist Barry Goudreau	
5/19/84	**57**	14	1. Orion The Hunter	Portrait 39239
			TONY ORLANDO - see DAWN	
			ORLEANS rock group founded by John Hall	
3/29/75	**33**	32	1. Let There Be Music .... "Dance With Me"(6)	Asylum 1029
8/28/76	**30**	16	2. Waking And Dreaming .... "Still The One"(5)	Asylum 1070
5/05/79	**76**	13	3. Forever .... "Love Takes Time"	Infinity 9006

DATE CHARTED	PEAK POS	WKS CHRT'D	ARTIST — Album Title	LABEL & NUMBER
			ORLONS Philadelphia quartet - Shirley Brickley, lead singer	
9/01/62	**80**	10	1. The Wah-Watusi .... "The Wah Watusi"(2)	Cameo 1020
7/06/63	**123**	5	2. South Street .... "South Street"(3)	Cameo 1041
			EUGENE ORMANDY - **see PHILADELPHIA ORCHESTRA**	
			ORPHEUS New York soft-rock quartet	
3/09/68	**119**	14	1. Orpheus	MGM 4524
9/28/68	**159**	12	2. Ascending	MGM 4569
10/11/69	**198**	1	3. Joyful	MGM 4599
			ROBERT ELLIS ORRALL	
4/16/83	**146**	9	1. Special Pain .... [M]	RCA 8502
			OSBORNE BROTHERS progressive bluegrass duo: Bobby & Sonny Osborne	
7/04/70	**193**	1	1. Ru-beeeee	Decca 75204
			JEFFREY OSBORNE former lead singer of L.T.D.	
6/19/82	**49**	43	1. Jeffrey Osborne	A&M 4896
8/06/83	**25**	88+	● 2. Stay With Me Tonight	A&M 4940
10/20/84	**39**	25+	● 3. Don't Stop	A&M 5017
			OZZY OSBOURNE British - former lead singer of Black Sabbath	
4/18/81	**21**	104	▲ 1. Blizzard Of Ozz	Jet 36812
11/21/81	**16**	73	▲ 2. Diary Of A Madman	Jet 37492
5/08/82	**120**	18	3. Mr. Crowley .... [M-L] live EP picture disk	Jet 37640
12/11/82	**14**	20	● 4. Speak Of The Devil .... [L] recorded at The Ritz, New York	Jet 38350 [2]
12/10/83	**19**	29	● 5. Bark At The Moon	CBS Assoc. 38987
			OSIBISA African/West Indian band led by Teddy Osei	
7/03/71	**55**	19	1. Osibisa	Decca 75285
2/12/72	**66**	17	2. Wcyaya	Decca 75327
10/28/72	**125**	8	3. Heads	Decca 75368
7/21/73	**159**	7	4. Super Fly T.N.T. .... [S]	Buddah 5136
9/28/74	**175**	4	5. Osibirock	Warner 2802
4/24/76	**200**	2	6. Welcome Home	Island 9355
			LEE OSKAR harmonica player with War	
4/03/76	**29**	24	1. Lee Oskar	United Art. 594
9/16/78	**86**	12	2. Before The Rain	Elektra 150
8/01/81	**162**	6	3. My Road Our Road	Elektra 526
			DONNY OSMOND born on 12/9/57 in Ogden, Utah	
7/10/71	**13**	37	● 1. The Donny Osmond Album .... "Sweet And Innocent"(7)	MGM 4782
11/06/71	**12**	33	● 2. To You With Love, Donny .... "Go Away Little Girl"(1)	MGM 4797
5/27/72	**6**	36	● 3. **Portrait Of Donny** .... "Hey Girl"(9)/"Puppy Love"(3)	MGM 4820
7/22/72	**11**	30	● 4. Too Young	MGM 4854
12/16/72	**29**	20	● 5. My Best To You .... [G]	MGM 4872
3/24/73	**26**	29	6. Alone Together .... "The Twelfth Of Never"(8)	MGM 4886

DATE CHARTED	PEAK POS	WKS CHRT'D	ARTIST — Album Title	LABEL & NUMBER
12/08/73	**58**	13	7. A Time For Us	MGM 4930
12/07/74	**57**	17	8. Donny	MGM 4978
8/21/76	**145**	8	9. Disco Train	Polydor 6067
9/03/77	**169**	5	10. Donald Clark Osmond	Polydor 6109

DONNY & MARIE OSMOND
co-hosts of a musical/variety TV show, 1976-1978

DATE CHARTED	PEAK POS	WKS CHRT'D	ARTIST — Album Title	LABEL & NUMBER
9/07/74	**35**	30	● 1. I'm Leaving It All Up To You "I'm Leaving It (All) Up To You"(4)/ "Morning Side Of The Mountain"(8)	MGM 4968
6/28/75	**133**	6	2. Make The World Go Away	MGM 4996
4/03/76	**60**	38	● 3. Donny & Marie - Featuring Songs From Their Television Show	Polydor 6068
11/27/76	**85**	14	● 4. Donny & Marie - New Season	Polydor 6083
1/07/78	**99**	12	5. Winning Combination	Polydor 6127
11/11/78	**98**	8	● 6. Goin' Coconuts ... [S] 4 of 12 songs are from the film	Polydor 6169

LITTLE JIMMY OSMOND
born on 4/16/63 in Canoga Park, California

DATE CHARTED	PEAK POS	WKS CHRT'D	ARTIST — Album Title	LABEL & NUMBER
12/02/72	**105**	14	1. Killer Joe	MGM 4855

MARIE OSMOND
born on 10/13/59 in Odgen, Utah

DATE CHARTED	PEAK POS	WKS CHRT'D	ARTIST — Album Title	LABEL & NUMBER
9/22/73	**59**	23	1. Paper Roses "Paper Roses"(5)	MGM 4910
7/20/74	**164**	9	2. In My Little Corner Of The World	MGM 4944
3/08/75	**152**	6	3. Who's Sorry Now above 3 albums produced & arranged by Sonny James	MGM 4979
4/30/77	**152**	6	4. This Is The Way That I Feel	Polydor 6099

OSMONDS
Alan, Wayne, Merrill, Jay & Donny - albums 9,11 & 12 also feature Marie and Jimmy

DATE CHARTED	PEAK POS	WKS CHRT'D	ARTIST — Album Title	LABEL & NUMBER
1/30/71	**14**	43	● 1. Osmonds "One Bad Apple"(1)	MGM 4724
6/26/71	**22**	34	● 2. Homemade	MGM 4770
1/29/72	**10**	35	● 3. **Phase-III** "Yo-Yo"(3)/"Down By The Lazy River"(4)	MGM 4796
6/17/72	**13**	29	● 4. The Osmonds "Live" ... [L]	MGM 4826 [2]
10/14/72	**14**	22	● 5. Crazy Horses	MGM 4851
7/07/73	**58**	20	6. The Plan	MGM 4902
11/02/74	**47**	14	7. Love Me For A Reason "Love Me For A Reason"(10)	MGM 4939
8/30/75	**160**	5	8. The Proud One	MGM 4993
12/20/75	**148**	8	9. Around The World - Live In Concert ... [L]	MGM 5012 [2]
10/23/76	**145**	6	10. Brainstorm	Polydor 6077
12/18/76	**127**	5	11. The Osmond Christmas Album ... [X]	Polydor 8001 [2]
1/14/78	**192**	3	12. The Osmonds Greatest Hits ... [G]	Polydor 9005 [2]

GILBERT O'SULLIVAN
Irish

DATE CHARTED	PEAK POS	WKS CHRT'D	ARTIST — Album Title	LABEL & NUMBER
8/12/72	**9**	29	1. **Gilbert O'Sullivan-Himself** "Alone Again (Naturally)"(1)	MAM 4
1/06/73	**48**	19	2. Back To Front "Clair"(2)	MAM 5
10/13/73	**101**	10	3. I'm A Writer, Not A Fighter "Get Down"(7)	MAM 7

SHUGGIE OTIS
blues-rock guitarist - son of R&B pioneer Johnny Otis

DATE CHARTED	PEAK POS	WKS CHRT'D	ARTIST — Album Title	LABEL & NUMBER
1/24/70	**182**	5	1. Kooper Session Al Kooper introduces Shuggie Otis	Columbia 9951
3/07/70	**199**	2	2. Here Comes Shuggie Otis	Epic 26511
3/22/75	**181**	3	3. Inspiration Information	Epic 33059

DATE CHARTED	PEAK POS	WKS CHRT'D	ARTIST — Album Title	LABEL & NUMBER
			OUTLAWS Southern rock band from Tampa, Florida	
8/09/75	13	16	● 1. Outlaws	Arista 4042
4/10/76	36	12	2. Lady In Waiting	Arista 4070
5/28/77	51	27	3. Hurry Sundown	Arista 4135
3/25/78	29	21	● 4. Bring It Back Alive .... [L]	Arista 8300 [2]
11/25/78	60	18	5. Playin' To Win	Arista 4205
11/03/79	55	18	6. In The Eye Of The Storm	Arista 9507
12/13/80	25	26	● 7. Ghost Riders	Arista 9542
5/01/82	77	9	8. Los Hombres Malo	Arista 9584
11/27/82	136	9	9. Greatest Hits Of The Outlaws/High Tides Forever .... [G]	Arista 9614
			OUTSIDERS Cleveland rock quintet - Sonny Geraci, lead singer	
5/28/66	37	16	1. Time Won't Let Me .... "Time Won't Let Me"(5)	Capitol 2501
9/17/66	90	10	2. The Outsiders Album #2	Capitol 2568
8/26/67	103	10	3. Happening 'Live!' .... [L]	Capitol 2745
			BUCK OWENS & His Buckaroos country singer from Bakersfield, California - co-host of "Hee-Haw" since 1969	
7/18/64	46	31	● 1. The Best Of Buck Owens .... [G]	Capitol 2105
9/05/64	88	18	2. Together Again/My Heart Skips A Beat	Capitol 2135
12/12/64	135	5	3. I Don't Care	Capitol 2186
4/03/65	43	22	4. I've Got A Tiger By The Tail	Capitol 2283
3/12/66	106	10	5. Roll out the red carpet for Buck Owens and his Buckaroos	Capitol 2443
9/24/66	114	10	6. Carnegie Hall Concert .... [L]	Capitol 2556
9/30/67	177	7	7. Your Tender Loving Care	Capitol 2760
2/15/69	199	2	8. I've Got You On My Mind Again	Capitol 131
7/05/69	113	5	9. Buck Owens In London .... [L]	Capitol 232
8/16/69	185	5	10. Close-Up .... [R] reissue of "Together Again" & "No One But You" albums	Capitol 257 [2]
11/08/69	122	10	11. Tall Dark Stranger	Capitol 212
2/07/70	141	6	12. Big In Vegas .... [L] with son Buddy Alan, Susan Raye, and The Hagars	Capitol 413
4/25/70	198	2	13. Your Mother's Prayer	Capitol 439
5/16/70	154	6	14. We're Gonna Get Together .... BUCK OWENS & SUSAN RAYE	Capitol 448
9/19/70	196	2	15. The Kansas City Song	Capitol 476
11/28/70	190	2	16. I Wouldn't Live In New York City	Capitol 628
			OXO West Coast quartet led by former Foxy member, Ish Angel	
4/30/83	117	7	1. Oxo	Geffen 4001
			OZARK MOUNTAIN DAREDEVILS country-rock group from Springfield, Missouri	
2/16/74	26	25	● 1. The Ozark Mountain Daredevils ...	A&M 4411
12/14/74	19	31	2. It'll Shine When It Shines .... "Jackie Blue"(3)	A&M 3654
11/08/75	57	15	3. The Car Over The Lake Album	A&M 4549
10/02/76	74	10	4. Men From Earth	A&M 4601
11/19/77	132	10	5. Don't Look Down	A&M 4662
9/30/78	176	3	6. It's Alive .... [L]	A&M 6006 [2]
5/24/80	170	4	7. Ozark Mountain Daredevils	Columbia 36375
			OZONE 	
9/04/82	152	6	1. Li'l Suzy	Motown 6011

DATE CHARTED	PEAK POS	WKS CHRT'D	ARTIST — Album Title	LABEL & NUMBER

PABLO CRUISE
San Francisco quartet led by Dave Jenkins (Stoneground)

DATE CHARTED	PEAK POS	WKS CHRT'D	ARTIST — Album Title	LABEL & NUMBER
8/16/75	**174**	4	1. Pablo Cruise	A&M 4528
4/17/76	**139**	13	2. Lifeline	A&M 4575
3/05/77	**19**	46	▲ 3. A Place In The Sun .... "Whatcha Gonna Do?"(6)	A&M 4625
6/17/78	**6**	43	▲ 4. **Worlds Away** .... "Love Will Find A Way"(6)	A&M 4697
11/17/79	**39**	17	5. Part Of The Game	A&M 3712
7/18/81	**34**	18	6. Reflector	A&M 3726

PACIFIC GAS & ELECTRIC
West Coast blues-rock quintet - Charlie Allen, lead singer

DATE CHARTED	PEAK POS	WKS CHRT'D	ARTIST — Album Title	LABEL & NUMBER
2/01/69	**159**	12	1. Get It On...	Power 701
9/13/69	**91**	8	2. Pacific Gas And Electric	Columbia 9900
7/04/70	**101**	11	3. Are You Ready	Columbia 1017
8/28/71	**182**	8	4. PG&E	Columbia 30362

GENE PAGE

DATE CHARTED	PEAK POS	WKS CHRT'D	ARTIST — Album Title	LABEL & NUMBER
2/01/75	**156**	4	1. Hot City .... [I] conducted by Gene Page - produced by Barry White	Atlantic 18111

JIMMY PAGE
lead guitarist of Led Zeppelin/The Firm

DATE CHARTED	PEAK POS	WKS CHRT'D	ARTIST — Album Title	LABEL & NUMBER
4/03/82	**50**	10	1. Death Wish II .... [S] Jimmy plays guitar, and produced and composed the music for the film	Swan Song 8511

PATTI PAGE
born Clara Ann Fowler in Claremore, Oklahoma on 11/8/27

DATE CHARTED	PEAK POS	WKS CHRT'D	ARTIST — Album Title	LABEL & NUMBER
11/24/56	**18**	2	1. Manhattan Tower .... a version of Gordon Jenkin's musical narrative	Mercury 20226
9/01/62	**115**	5	2. Golden Hits Of The Boys .... Patti's versions of male vocalist hits	Mercury 20712
9/21/63	**83**	6	3. Say Wonderful Things	Columbia 8849
5/22/65	**27**	26	4. Hush, Hush, Sweet Charlotte .... "Hush, Hush, Sweet Charlotte"(8)	Columbia 9153
7/27/68	**168**	6	5. Gentle On My Mind	Columbia 9666

PALM BEACH BAND BOYS

DATE CHARTED	PEAK POS	WKS CHRT'D	ARTIST — Album Title	LABEL & NUMBER
1/28/67	**149**	1	1. Winchester Cathedral .... featuring vocals by Roger Rigney	RCA 3734

ROBERT PALMER
British blue-eyed soul singer

DATE CHARTED	PEAK POS	WKS CHRT'D	ARTIST — Album Title	LABEL & NUMBER
6/14/75	**107**	15	1. Sneakin' Sally Through The Alley	Island 9294
11/22/75	**136**	8	2. Pressure Drop	Island 9372
10/23/76	**68**	16	3. Some People Can Do What They Like	Island 9420
4/01/78	**45**	25	4. Double Fun	Island 9476
7/21/79	**19**	24	5. Secrets .... "Bad Case Of Loving You"	Island 9544
10/11/80	**59**	17	6. Clues	Island 9595
5/15/82	**148**	5	7. Maybe It's Live .... [L] 6 of 10 tracks are live	Island 9665
4/30/83	**112**	19	8. Pride	Island 90065

PAPER LACE
English quintet - Phil Wright, lead singer

DATE CHARTED	PEAK POS	WKS CHRT'D	ARTIST — Album Title	LABEL & NUMBER
9/07/74	**124**	8	1. Paper Lace .... "The Night Chicago Died"(1)	Mercury 1008

NORRIE PARAMOR [His Strings & Orchestra]
British conductor

DATE CHARTED	PEAK POS	WKS CHRT'D	ARTIST — Album Title	LABEL & NUMBER
9/08/56	**18**	3	1. In London, In Love... .... [I]	Capitol Int. 10025

DATE CHARTED	PEAK POS	WKS CHRT'D		ARTIST — Album Title	LABEL & NUMBER
				PARIS British rock trio led by Bob Welch (Fleetwood Mac)	
2/07/76	**103**	9		1. Paris	Capitol 11464
9/11/76	**152**	6		2. Big Towne, 2061	Capitol 11560
				GRAHAM PARKER & The Rumour British pub-rocker with backing band The Rumour (led by guitarist Brinsley Schwarz)	
1/29/77	**169**	7		1. Heat Treatment	Mercury 1117
11/05/77	**125**	5		2. Stick To Me	Mercury 3706
7/01/78	**149**	3		3. The Parkerilla .... [L] sides 1,2 & 3: live: side 4: 12" single studio recording	Mercury 100 [2]
4/14/79	**40**	24		4. Squeezing Out Sparks	Arista 4223
5/31/80	**40**	15		5. The Up Escalator .... Bruce Springsteen sings on one track	Arista 9517
				GRAHAM PARKER:	
4/10/82	**51**	16		6. Another Grey Area	Arista 9589
8/20/83	**59**	14		7. The Real Macaw	Arista 8023
				RAY PARKER JR. originally a session guitarist for Marvin Gaye and Stevie Wonder	
				RAYDIO:	
2/11/78	**27**	23	●	1. Raydio .... "Jack And Jill"(8)	Arista 4163
4/14/79	**45**	30	●	2. Rock On .... "You Can't Change That"(9)	Arista 4212
				RAY PARKER JR. & RAYDIO:	
4/12/80	**33**	21	●	3. Two Places At The Same Time	Arista 9515
4/18/81	**13**	26	●	4. A Woman Needs Love .... "A Woman Needs Love (Just Like You Do)"(4)	Arista 9543
				RAY PARKER JR.:	
4/24/82	**11**	27	●	5. The Other Woman .... "The Other Woman"(4)	Arista 9590
12/18/82	**51**	22		6. Greatest Hits .... [G] includes tracks from all previous 5 albums	Arista 9612
11/26/83	**45**	23		7. Woman Out Of Control	Arista 8087
12/15/84	**60**	15		8. Chartbusters .... [G] "Ghostbusters"(1)	Arista 8266
				MICHAEL PARKS portrayed Jim Bronson on TV's "Then Came Bronson"	
11/08/69	**35**	46		1. Closing The Gap	MGM 4646
5/23/70	**24**	21		2. Long Lonesome Highway	MGM 4662
10/10/70	**71**	8		3. Blue	MGM 4717
3/13/71	**195**	1		4. Lost And Found	Verve 5079
				PARLIAMENT part of George Clinton's "P-Funk" battalion - featuring Bootsy Collins, Bernie Worrell, Fred Wesley, Maceo Parker - also see George Clinton/Funkadelic	
5/03/75	**91**	18		1. Chocolate City	Casablanca 7014
2/21/76	**13**	37	▲	2. Mothership Connection	Casablanca 7022
10/16/76	**20**	22	●	3. The Clones Of Dr. Funkenstein	Casablanca 7034
5/21/77	**29**	19	●	4. Parliament Live/P. Funk Earth Tour .... [L]	Casablanca 7053 [2]
12/24/77	**13**	34	▲	5. Funkentelechy Vs. The Placebo Syndrome ...	Casablanca 7084
12/16/78	**23**	18	●	6. Motor-Booty Affair	Casablanca 7125
12/22/79	**44**	19	●	7. Gloryhallastoopid (Or Pin The Tale On The Funky)	Casablanca 7195
1/10/81	**61**	7		8. Trombipulation	Casablanca 7249
				JOHN PARR	
12/15/84	**48**	17 +		1. John Parr	Atlantic 80180

DATE CHARTED	PEAK POS	WKS CHRT'D		ARTIST — Album Title	LABEL & NUMBER

ALAN PARSONS Project
English session musicians headed by producer/engineer Parsons, and his partner Eric Woolfson

DATE CHARTED	PEAK POS	WKS CHRT'D		ARTIST — Album Title	LABEL & NUMBER
5/15/76	**38**	46		1. Tales Of Mystery And Imagination - Edgar Allan Poe .... *musical interpretation of Poe's most notable works*	20th Century 508
7/16/77	**9**	54	▲	2. **I Robot**	Arista 7002
7/01/78	**26**	25	●	3. Pyramid	Arista 4180
9/15/79	**13**	27	●	4. Eve	Arista 9504
11/15/80	**13**	58	▲	5. The Turn Of A Friendly Card	Arista 9518
6/19/82	**7**	41	▲	6. **Eye In The Sky** .... "Eye In The Sky"(3)	Arista 9599
11/19/83	**53**	29		7. The Best Of The Alan Parsons Project ...... [G]	Arista 8193
3/17/84	**15**	26	●	8. Ammonia Avenue	Arista 8204
3/09/85	**46+**	5+		9. Vulture Culture	Arista 8263

GRAM PARSONS
country-rock singer - died on 9/19/73 (26) - also see Flying Burrito Brothers

DATE CHARTED	PEAK POS	WKS CHRT'D		ARTIST — Album Title	LABEL & NUMBER
2/16/74	**195**	3		1. Grievous Angel .... *with Emmylou Harris*	Reprise 2171

DOLLY PARTON
born on 1/19/46 in Sevierville, Tennessee - also see Soundtrack "Best Little Whorehouse In Texas"

DATE CHARTED	PEAK POS	WKS CHRT'D		ARTIST — Album Title	LABEL & NUMBER
3/22/69	**184**	4		1. Just The Two Of Us .... PORTER WAGONER & DOLLY PARTON	RCA 4039
8/16/69	**162**	5		2. Always, Always .... PORTER WAGONER & DOLLY PARTON	RCA 4186
11/22/69	**194**	2		3. My Blue Ridge Mountain Boy	RCA 4188
4/04/70	**137**	7		4. Porter Wayne And Dolly Rebecca ...... PORTER WAGONER & DOLLY PARTON	RCA 4305
8/15/70	**154**	2		5. A Real Live Dolly .... [L] *recorded at her alma mater, Sevier County High School, Tennessee (with Porter Wagoner on 4 songs)*	RCA 4387
10/10/70	**191**	2		6. Once More .... PORTER WAGONER & DOLLY PARTON	RCA 4388
3/13/71	**142**	3		7. Two Of A Kind .... PORTER WAGONER & DOLLY PARTON	RCA 4490
6/12/71	**198**	1		8. Joshua	RCA 4507
4/02/77	**71**	21		9. New Harvest...First Gathering	RCA 2188
10/29/77	**20**	47	▲	10. Here You Come Again .... "Here You Come Again"(3)	RCA 2544
8/12/78	**27**	34	●	11. Heartbreaker	RCA 2797
6/23/79	**40**	17	●	12. Great Balls Of Fire	RCA 3361
5/03/80	**71**	13		13. Dolly Dolly Dolly	RCA 3546
12/06/80	**11**	34	●	14. 9 to 5 and Odd Jobs .... "9 to 5"(1)	RCA 3852
4/24/82	**106**	12		15. Heartbreak Express	RCA 4289
10/16/82	**77**	23	●	16. Greatest Hits .... [G]	RCA 4422
6/04/83	**127**	11		17. Burlap & Satin	RCA 4691
2/18/84	**73**	14		18. The Great Pretender .... *featuring Dolly's versions of 50's & 60's hits*	RCA 4940
7/21/84	**135**	7		19. Rhinestone .... [S]	RCA 5032
12/08/84	**31**	8	▲	20. Once Upon A Christmas .... [X] KENNY ROGERS & DOLLY PARTON *made top 10 on Billboard's special Christmas charts (1984)*	RCA 15307

PARTRIDGE FAMILY
David Cassidy, lead singer; with stepmother Shirley Jones

DATE CHARTED	PEAK POS	WKS CHRT'D		ARTIST — Album Title	LABEL & NUMBER
10/31/70	**4**	68	●	1. **The Partridge Family Album** ...... "I Think I Love You"(1)	Bell 6050
4/03/71	**3**	53	●	2. **Up To Date** .... "Doesn't Somebody Want To Be Wanted"(6)/ "I'll Meet You Halfway"(9)	Bell 6059

DATE CHARTED	PEAK POS	WKS CHRT'D	ARTIST — Album Title	LABEL & NUMBER
8/28/71	9	35	● 3. **The Partridge Family Sound Magazine**	Bell 6064
3/25/72	18	17	● 4. The Partridge Family Shopping Bag	Bell 6072
9/09/72	21	23	● 5. The Partridge Family at home with their Greatest Hits .... [G]	Bell 1107
12/16/72	41	16	6. The Partridge Family Notebook	Bell 1111
7/07/73	167	5	7. Crossword Puzzle	Bell 1122

PASSPORT
German jazz fusion group led by Klaus Doldinger (sax/keyboards)

3/15/75	137	7	1. Cross-Collateral .... [I]	Atco 107
4/23/77	191	3	2. Iguacu .... [I]	Atco 149
6/03/78	140	7	3. Sky Blue .... [I]	Atlantic 19177
4/05/80	163	4	4. Oceanliner .... [I]	Atlantic 19265
8/29/81	175	3	5. Blue Tattoo .... [I]	Atlantic 19304

JACO PASTORIUS
bassist of jazz-rock group Weather Report

8/15/81	161	3	1. Word Of Mouth .... [I]	Warner 3535

ROBBIE PATTON
English

8/15/81	162	6	1. Distant Shores	Liberty 1107
			co-produced by Fleetwood Mac's Christine McVie	

PAUL & PAULA
Ray Hildebrand & Jill Jackson

2/23/63	9	25	1. **Paul & Paula Sing For Young Lovers**	Philips 078
			"Hey Paula"(1)/"Young Lovers"(6)	
8/10/63	99	5	2. We Go Together	Philips 089

BILLY PAUL
born Paul Williams on 12/1/34 in Philadelphia

8/22/70	183	5	1. Ebony Woman	Neptune 201
10/16/71	197	2	2. Going East	Phil. Int. 30580
11/25/72	17	27	● 3. 360 Degrees Of Billy Paul	Phil. Int. 31793
			"Me And Mrs. Jones"(1)	
4/28/73	186	3	4. Ebony Woman .... [R]	Phil. Int. 32118
11/17/73	110	26	5. War Of The Gods	Phil. Int. 32409
7/06/74	187	4	6. Live In Europe .... [L]	Phil. Int. 32952
3/15/75	140	9	7. Got My Head On Straight	Phil. Int. 33157
12/27/75	139	20	8. When Love Is New	Phil. Int. 33843
1/22/77	88	18	9. Let 'Em In	Phil. Int. 34389
1/28/78	152	4	10. Only The Strong Survive	Phil. Int. 34923

HENRY PAUL Band
Southern rock band led by former Outlaws member, Henry Paul

6/02/79	107	12	1. Grey Ghost	Atlantic 19232
8/02/80	120	9	2. Feel The Heat	Atlantic 19273
12/26/81	158	8	3. Anytime	Atlantic 19325

LES PAUL & MARY FORD
husband & wife (separated May, 1963) - Mary died on 9/30/77 (53) - also see Chet Atkins

5/14/55	15	3	1. Les and Mary	Capitol 577
			10 songs feature Mary's vocals; 6 are instrumentals by Les	

PAT PAULSEN
regular comedian on TV's "Smothers Brothers Comedy Hour"

10/19/68	71	10	1. Pat Paulsen For President .... [C]	Mercury 61179
			with commentary by Ralph Story	

PAUPERS
rock/folk quartet from Toronto, Canada

11/11/67	178	2	1. Magic People	Verve Fore. 3026

DATE CHARTED	PEAK POS	WKS CHRT'D	ARTIST — Album Title	LABEL & NUMBER
			LUCIANO PAVAROTTI Italian operatic tenor	
11/24/79	**77**	21	● 1. O Sole Mio - Favorite Neapolitan Songs .... [F]	London 26560
6/07/80	**94**	18	2. Pavarotti's Greatest Hits .... [F-G]	London 2003-4 [2]
4/24/82	**141**	7	3. Luciano .... [F-K]	London 2013
11/06/82	**158**	3	4. Yes, Giorgio .... [S]	London 9001
9/08/84	**103**	14	5. Mamma .... popular Italian songs arranged & conducted by Henry Mancini	London 411959
			PAVLOV'S DOG New York rock septet - David Surkamp, lead singer	
4/05/75	**181**	6	1. Pampered Menial	ABC 866
			RITA PAVONE pop singer from Italy	
6/20/64	**60**	14	1. Rita Pavone	RCA 2900
			TOM PAXTON topical folk singer/songwriter	
8/16/69	**155**	4	1. The Things I Notice Now	Elektra 74043
6/06/70	**184**	4	2. Tom Paxton 6	Elektra 74066
8/14/71	**120**	3	3. How Come The Sun	Reprise 6443
8/26/72	**191**	4	4. Peace Will Come	Reprise 2096
			JOHNNY PAYCHECK country singer - real name: Don Lytle	
2/18/78	**72**	14	● 1. Take This Job And Shove It	Epic 35045
			FREDA PAYNE sang with Duke Ellington in the late '60s	
8/22/70	**60**	13	1. Band Of Gold .... "Band Of Gold"(3)	Invictus 7301
6/12/71	**76**	18	2. Contact	Invictus 7307
4/15/72	**152**	8	3. The Best Of Freda Payne .... [G]	Invictus 9804
			PEACHES & HERB Peaches: Francine Barker (1-3); Linda Greene (4-7) & Herb Fame	
3/25/67	**30**	25	1. Let's Fall In Love .... "Close Your Eyes"(8)	Date 4004
9/02/67	**135**	12	2. For Your Love	Date 4005
9/21/68	**187**	3	3. Peaches & Herb's Greatest Hits .... [G]	Date 4012
11/25/78	**2(6)**	46	▲ 4. 2 Hot! .... "Shake Your Groove Thing"(5)/"Reunited"(1)	Polydor 6172
11/10/79	**31**	30	● 5. Twice The Fire	Polydor 6239
10/11/80	**120**	6	6. Worth The Wait	Polydor 6298
9/12/81	**168**	3	7. Sayin' Something!	Polydor 6332
			PEANUT BUTTER CONSPIRACY California psychedelic rock quintet - Sandi Robison, lead singer	
5/20/67	**196**	3	1. The Peanut Butter Conspiracy Is Spreading	Columbia 2654
			PEARL HARBOR & THE EXPLOSIONS San Francisco "punkabilly" rock group led by German-born Pearl E. Gates	
1/26/80	**107**	11	1. Pearl Harbor And The Explosions	Warner 3404
2/21/81	**170**	3	2. Don't Follow Me, I'm Lost Too .... PEARL HARBOUR	Warner 3515
			PEARLS BEFORE SWINE New York underground folk quartet led by Tom Rapp	
9/27/69	**200**	2	1. These Things Too	Reprise 6364

DATE CHARTED	PEAK POS	WKS CHRT'D	ARTIST — Album Title	LABEL & NUMBER
			DUKE PEARSON	
			jazz pianist	
4/05/69	193	2	1. The Phantom	Blue Note 84293
			featuring Bobby Hutcherson (vibes) & Jerry Dodgion (flute)	
			ANN PEEBLES	
4/22/72	188	3	1. Straight From The Heart	Hi 32065
3/09/74	155	7	2. I Can't Stand The Rain	Hi 32079
			DAVID PEEL & THE LOWER EAST SIDE	
			New York 'hippie' rock group	
5/24/69	186	3	1. Have A Marijuana	Elektra 74032
5/27/72	191	3	2. The Pope Smokes Dope	Apple 3391
			produced by John Lennon & Yoko Ono	
			TEDDY PENDERGRASS	
			lead singer of Harold Melvin & The Blue Notes (1970-1976) - paralyzed from the shoulders down in an auto crash on 3/18/82	
3/19/77	17	35	▲ 1. Teddy Pendergrass	Phil. Int. 34390
7/01/78	11	35	▲ 2. Life Is A Song Worth Singing	Phil. Int. 35095
6/23/79	5	31	▲ 3. **Teddy**	Phil. Int. 36003
12/22/79	33	15	● 4. Teddy Live! Coast To Coast .... [L]	Phil. Int. 36294 [2]
			side 4: interviews and new studio recordings	
8/23/80	14	34	▲8 5. TP	Phil. Int. 36745
10/03/81	19	27	● 6. It's Time For Love	Phil. Int. 37491
8/21/82	59	15	7. This One's For You	Phil. Int. 38118
1/07/84	123	9	8. Heaven Only Knows	Phil. Int. 38646
6/16/84	38	35	● 9. Love Language	Asylum 60317
			LEONARD PENNARIO	
			classical pianist	
6/15/59	29	1	1. Concertos under the Stars .... [I]	Capitol 8326
			with The Hollywood Bowl Symphony Orchestra, conducted by Carmen Dragon	
			PENTANGLE	
			traditional English folk quintet featuring Bert Jansch & John Renbourn (acoustic guitars) & Jacqui McShee (vocals)	
12/21/68	192	3	1. The Pentangle	Reprise 6315
1/31/70	200	2	2. Basket Of Light	Reprise 6372
3/13/71	193	1	3. Cruel Sister	Reprise 6430
12/04/71	183	3	4. Reflection	Reprise 6463
10/28/72	184	4	5. Solomon's Seal	Reprise 2100
			PEOPLE	
			San Jose, California pop-rock sextet	
7/27/68	128	8	1. I Love You	Capitol 2924
			PEOPLE'S CHOICE	
			soul/disco group led by Frankie Brunson	
9/06/75	56	15	1. Boogie Down U.S.A.	TSOP 33154
			"Do It Any Way You Wanna"	
6/26/76	174	3	2. We Got The Rhythm	TSOP 34124
			PEPPERMINT RAINBOW	
8/02/69	106	9	1. Will You Be Staying After Sunday	Decca 75129
			ITZHAK PERLMAN - see ANDRE PREVIN	
			JOE PERRY Project	
			original lead guitarist of Aerosmith	
4/12/80	47	13	1. Let The Music Do The Talking	Columbia 36388
7/04/81	100	10	2. I've Got The Rock 'N' Rolls Again	Columbia 37364
			STEVE PERRY	
			lead singer of Journey	
4/28/84	12	50+	▲ 1. Street Talk	Columbia 39334
			"Oh Sherrie"(3)	

DATE CHARTED	PEAK POS	WKS CHRT'D		ARTIST — Album Title	LABEL & NUMBER
				PERSUADERS	
3/11/72	141	7		1. Thin Line Between Love And Hate	Win Or Lose 387
4/07/73	178	4		2. The Persuaders	Atco 7021
				PERSUASIONS soul acappella quintet from Brooklyn	
9/18/71	189	3		1. We Came To Play	Capitol 791
2/12/72	88	12		2. Street Corner Symphony	Capitol 872
11/18/72	195	3		3. Spread The Word	Capitol 11101
6/09/73	178	3		4. We Still Ain't Got No Band	MCA 326
				PETER & GORDON British: Peter Asher & Gordon Waller	
7/04/64	21	14		1. A World Without Love .... "A World Without Love"(1)	Capitol 2115
1/02/65	95	11		2. I Don't Want To See You Again	Capitol 2220
5/22/65	51	15		3. I Go To Pieces .... "I Go To Pieces"(9)	Capitol 2324
8/14/65	49	13		4. True Love Ways	Capitol 2368
4/16/66	60	14		5. Woman	Capitol 2477
7/30/66	72	12		6. The Best Of Peter And Gordon ...... [G]	Capitol 2549
2/04/67	80	13		7. Lady Godiva .... "Lady Godiva"(6)	Capitol 2664
				PETER, PAUL & MARY folk trio formed at Greenwich Village, New York: Peter Yarrow, Paul Stookey & Mary Travers	
4/28/62	1(7)	185	●	1. **Peter, Paul & Mary** .... "If I Had A Hammer"(10)	Warner 1449
1/19/63	2(9)	99	●	2. **(Moving)** .... "Puff The Magic Dragon"(2)	Warner 1473
10/26/63	1(5)	80	●	3. **In The Wind** .... "Blowin' In The Wind"(2)/ "Don't Think Twice, It's All Right"(9)	Warner 1507
8/15/64	4	54	●	4. **Peter, Paul and Mary In Concert** ...... [L]	Warner 1555 [2]
4/10/65	8	38	●	5. **A Song Will Rise**	Warner 1589
10/30/65	11	39	●	6. See What Tomorrow Brings	Warner 1615
8/27/66	22	53		7. Peter, Paul and Mary Album	Warner 1648
9/02/67	15	82	●	8. Album 1700 .... "I Dig Rock And Roll Music"(9)/"Leaving On A Jet Plane"(1)	Warner 1700
9/14/68	14	22		9. Late Again	Warner 1751
6/14/69	12	25		10. Peter, Paul and Mommy	Warner 1785
6/20/70	15	40	●	11. 10 Years Together/The Best Of Peter, Paul and Mary .... [G]	Warner 2552
10/21/78	106	7		12. Reunion	Warner 3231
				BERNADETTE PETERS film comedienne	
5/03/80	114	14		1. Bernadette Peters	MCA 3230
10/03/81	151	9		2. Now Playing	MCA 5244
				PAUL PETERSEN - see JAMES DARREN	
				OSCAR PETERSON Trio jazz trio: Oscar (piano), Ray Brown (bass), Ed Thigpen (drums)	
2/09/63	145	2		1. Bursting Out With The All Star Big Band! .... [I]	Verve 8476
6/08/63	127	2		2. Affinity .... [I]	Verve 8516
10/31/64	81	12		3. Oscar Peterson Trio + One .... [I] with Clark Terry (trumpet)	Mercury 60975
				TOM PETTY & The HEARTBREAKERS rock quintet formed in Los Angeles	
9/24/77	55	42		1. Tom Petty & The Heartbreakers	Shelter 52006
6/10/78	23	24	●	2. You're Gonna Get It!	Shelter 52029

DATE CHARTED	PEAK POS	WKS CHRT'D	ARTIST — Album Title	LABEL & NUMBER
11/10/79	2(7)	66	▲ 3. **Damn The Torpedoes** .... "Don't Do Me Like That"(10)	Backstreet 5105
5/23/81	5	31	▲ 4. **Hard Promises**	Backstreet 5160
11/20/82	9	32	● 5. **Long After Dark**	Backstreet 5360

P.F.M.
P.F.M.: Premiata Forneria Marconi - progressive rock quintet from Italy

DATE CHARTED	PEAK POS	WKS CHRT'D	ARTIST — Album Title	LABEL & NUMBER
10/20/73	180	6	1. Photos Of Ghosts	Manticore 66668
12/28/74	151	8	2. P.F.M. 'Cook' .... [I-L]	Manticore 502

PHILADELPHIA ORCHESTRA
Eugene Ormandy, conductor (died 3/12/85-85) - also see Mormon Tabernacle Choir

DATE CHARTED	PEAK POS	WKS CHRT'D	ARTIST — Album Title	LABEL & NUMBER
5/19/62	17	13	1. The Magnificent Sound Of The Philadelphia Orchestra .... [K-I] compiled from 16 of their albums	Columbia 1 [2]
12/22/62	109	2	● 2. The Glorious Sound Of Christmas .... [X] with The Temple University Concert Choir	Columbia 6369
5/06/78	136	8	3. David Bowie narrates Prokofiev's "Peter and The Wolf" .... side 1: above title; side 2: Britten: Young Person's Guide to the Orchestra - both sides feature The Philadelphia Orch.	RCA 2743

ANTHONY PHILLIPS
former guitarist of Genesis

DATE CHARTED	PEAK POS	WKS CHRT'D	ARTIST — Album Title	LABEL & NUMBER
3/26/77	191	3	1. The Geese & The Ghost .... with Mike Rutherford & Phil Collins (both of Genesis)	Passport 98020

ESTHER PHILLIPS
real name: Esther Mae Jones - Esther had 5 top ten singles on the R&B charts in 1950 (with Johnny Otis) - died on 8/7/84 (48)

DATE CHARTED	PEAK POS	WKS CHRT'D	ARTIST — Album Title	LABEL & NUMBER
1/05/63	46	14	1. Release Me! .... country songs (with the Anita Kerr Singers) "Release Me"(8)	Lenox 227
1/02/71	115	15	2. Burnin' .... [L] recorded at Freddie Jett's Pied Piper Club, L.A.	Atlantic 1565
3/18/72	137	15	3. From A Whisper To A Scream	Kudu 05
12/30/72	177	8	4. Alone Again, Naturally	Kudu 09
8/02/75	32	17	5. What A Diff'rence A Day Makes .... with jazz guitarist Joe Beck	Kudu 23
1/31/76	170	4	6. Confessin' The Blues .... side 2: live recording at same club as in album #2 above	Atlantic 1680
1/08/77	150	4	7. Capricorn Princess	Kudu 31

JOHN PHILLIPS
co-founder of The Mamas & The Papas

DATE CHARTED	PEAK POS	WKS CHRT'D	ARTIST — Album Title	LABEL & NUMBER
5/02/70	181	9	1. John Phillips (John The Wolfking of L.A.)	Dunhill 50077

SHAWN PHILLIPS

DATE CHARTED	PEAK POS	WKS CHRT'D	ARTIST — Album Title	LABEL & NUMBER
12/02/72	57	20	1. Faces .... includes 3 recordings from 1969	A&M 4363
12/15/73	72	13	2. Bright White	A&M 4402
11/30/74	50	12	3. Furthermore...	A&M 3662
9/13/75	101	9	4. Do You Wonder	A&M 4539

JIM PHOTOGLO

DATE CHARTED	PEAK POS	WKS CHRT'D	ARTIST — Album Title	LABEL & NUMBER
5/24/80	194	3	1. Photoglo	20th Century 604
6/06/81	119	11	2. Fool In Love With You	20th Century 621

BOBBY (BORIS) PICKETT & The Crypt-Kickers

DATE CHARTED	PEAK POS	WKS CHRT'D	ARTIST — Album Title	LABEL & NUMBER
11/03/62	19	13	1. The Original Monster Mash .... [N] "Monster Mash"(1)	Garpax 57001
9/29/73	173	4	2. The Original Monster Mash .... [N-R] reissue of Garpax album, less 4 songs "Monster Mash"(10)	Parrot 71063

DATE CHARTED	PEAK POS	WKS CHRT'D	ARTIST — Album Title	LABEL & NUMBER
			WILSON PICKETT	
			born on 3/18/41 in Prattville, Alabama	
10/30/65	**107**	6	1. In The Midnight Hour	Atlantic 8114
8/27/66	**21**	29	2. The Exciting Wilson Pickett	Atlantic 8129
			"Land Of 1000 Dances"(6)	
1/21/67	**42**	31	3. The Wicked Pickett	Atlantic 8138
8/12/67	**54**	11	4. The Sound Of Wilson Pickett	Atlantic 8145
			"Funky Broadway"(8)	
11/11/67	**35**	54	5. The Best Of Wilson Pickett .... [G]	Atlantic 8151
2/24/68	**70**	15	6. I'm In Love	Atlantic 8175
7/13/68	**91**	13	7. The Midnight Mover	Atlantic 8183
3/01/69	**97**	14	8. Hey Jude	Atlantic 8215
4/04/70	**197**	3	9. Right On	Atlantic 8250
10/03/70	**64**	19	10. Wilson Pickett In Philadelphia	Atlantic 8270
5/22/71	**73**	13	11. The Best Of Wilson Pickett, Vol. II .... [G]	Atlantic 8290
12/25/71	**132**	14	12. Don't Knock My Love	Atlantic 8300
2/10/73	**178**	8	13. Wilson Pickett's Greatest Hits .... [G]	Atlantic 501 [2]
4/28/73	**187**	3	14. Mr. Magic Man	RCA 4858
			PIECES OF A DREAM	
			jazz trio - produced by Grover Washington, Jr.	
10/31/81	**170**	6	1. Pieces Of A Dream	Elektra 350
8/28/82	**114**	15	2. We Are One	Elektra 60142
2/25/84	**90**	15	3. Imagine This	Elektra 60270
			PILOT	
			Scottish trio	
5/31/75	**82**	14	1. Pilot	EMI 11368
			"Magic"(5)	
			MICHAEL PINDER	
			former keyboardist of the Moody Blues	
5/01/76	**133**	8	1. The Promise	Threshold 18
			PINK FLOYD	
			English progressive rock band: David Gilmour (guitar), Roger Waters (bass), Nick Mason (drums), Rick Wright (keyboards)	
12/02/67	**131**	11	1. Pink Floyd	Tower 5093
			a condensation of their first British album, "The Piper At The Gates Of Dawn"	
1/03/70	**74**	27	● 2. Ummagumma .... [L]	Harvest 388 [2]
			record 1: live; record 2: studio - half a side by each member of the group - David Gilmour replaced Syd Barrett as lead guitarist	
11/07/70	**55**	13	3. Atom Heart Mother	Harvest 382
			with the John Aldiss Choir on side 1	
7/31/71	**152**	7	4. Relics .... [K]	Harvest 759
			recordings from 1967-69	
11/06/71	**70**	73	● 5. Meddle	Harvest 832
6/24/72	**46**	25	6. Obscured By Clouds .... [S]	Harvest 11078
			music from the film "The Valley"	
3/17/73	**1(1)**	566+	● 7. **The Dark Side Of The Moon**	Harvest 11163
			although the LP has sold over 10 million copies, it is not certified platinum because RIAA rules an album cannot be considered for platinum if released prior to 1/1/76	
9/01/73	**153**	7	8. More .... [S-E]	Harvest 11198
			soundtrack originally released in 1969	
12/22/73	**36**	17	9. A Nice Pair .... [R]	Harvest 11257 [2]
			reissue of their first 2 British albums "The Piper At The Gates Of Dawn" & "A Saucerful Of Secrets"	
9/27/75	**1(2)**	39	● 10. **Wish You Were Here**	Columbia 33453
2/19/77	**3**	28	▲ 11. **Animals**	Columbia 34474
12/15/79	**1(15)**	115	▲ 12. **The Wall**	Columbia 36183 [2]
			"Another Brick In The Wall (Part II)"(1)	
12/12/81	**31**	16	● 13. A Collection Of Great Dance Songs............ [G]	Columbia 37680
			recordings from albums #5,7,10,11 & 12 above	

DATE CHARTED	PEAK POS	WKS CHRT'D	ARTIST — Album Title	LABEL & NUMBER
4/09/83	6	23	▲ 14. **The Final Cut** .... group now a trio (minus Rick Wright)	Columbia 38243
6/18/83	68	9	15. Works .... [K] Harvest label recordings (1968-73)	Capitol 12276

PIPKINS
British studio group - Tony Burrows, lead singer

DATE CHARTED	PEAK POS	WKS CHRT'D	ARTIST — Album Title	LABEL & NUMBER
8/08/70	132	4	1. Gimme Dat Ding! .... [N] "Gimme Dat Ding"(9)	Capitol 483

GENE PITNEY
born on 2/17/41 in Hartford, Connecticut

DATE CHARTED	PEAK POS	WKS CHRT'D	ARTIST — Album Title	LABEL & NUMBER
12/01/62	48	15	1. Only Love Can Break A Heart .... "(The Man Who Shot) Liberty Valance"(4)/ "Only Love Can Break A Heart"(2)	Musicor 3003
5/18/63	85	7	2. Gene Pitney Sings Just For You	Musicor 3004
8/03/63	41	31	3. World-Wide Winners .... [G]	Musicor 3005
11/23/63	105	6	4. Blue Gene	Musicor 3006
4/04/64	87	9	5. Gene Pitney's Big Sixteen .... [G]	Musicor 3008
11/14/64	42	17	6. It Hurts To Be In Love .... "It Hurts To Be In Love"(7)/"I'm Gonna Be Strong"(9)	Musicor 3019
3/20/65	141	4	7. George Jones & Gene Pitney	Musicor 3044
7/17/65	112	9	8. I Must Be Seeing Things	Musicor 3056
9/18/65	43	24	9. Looking Through The Eyes Of Love	Musicor 3069
3/19/66	123	8	10. Big Sixteen, Vol. 3 .... [G]	Musicor 3085
12/17/66	61	51	11. Greatest Hits Of All Times .... [G]	Musicor 3102
9/14/68	193	3	12. She's A Heartbreaker	Musicor 3164

PLANET P PROJECT
session musicians assembled by German producer Peter Hauke - Tony Carey, lead singer

DATE CHARTED	PEAK POS	WKS CHRT'D	ARTIST — Album Title	LABEL & NUMBER
3/26/83	42	23	1. Planet P	Geffen 4000
12/01/84	121	14	2. Pink World	MCA 8019 [2]

ROBERT PLANT
lead singer of Led Zeppelin/The Honeydrippers

DATE CHARTED	PEAK POS	WKS CHRT'D	ARTIST — Album Title	LABEL & NUMBER
7/17/82	5	53	● 1. **Pictures At Eleven**	Swan Song 8512
7/30/83	8	40	▲ 2. **The Principle Of Moments** .... "Big Log"/"In The Mood"	Atlantic 90101

PLASMATICS
New York rock quintet - Wendy O. Williams, lead singer (former porn star)

DATE CHARTED	PEAK POS	WKS CHRT'D	ARTIST — Album Title	LABEL & NUMBER
2/21/81	134	10	1. New Hope For The Wretched	Stiff 9
6/06/81	142	9	2. Beyond The Valley Of 1984	Stiff 11
12/05/81	177	3	3. Metal Priestess .... [M]	Stiff 666

PLASTIC COW
Mike Melvoin performs on the Moog Synthesizer

DATE CHARTED	PEAK POS	WKS CHRT'D	ARTIST — Album Title	LABEL & NUMBER
11/08/69	184	2	1. The Plastic Cow Goes Mooooooog .... [I]	Dot 25961

PLASTIC ONO BAND - see JOHN LENNON

PLATTERS
Los Angeles R&B quintet: Tony Williams, lead singer (1-5); David Lynch, Paul Robi, Herb Reed & Zola Taylor

DATE CHARTED	PEAK POS	WKS CHRT'D	ARTIST — Album Title	LABEL & NUMBER
7/14/56	7	27	1. The Platters .... "My Prayer"(1)	Mercury 20146
1/19/57	12	8	2. The Platters, Volume Two	Mercury 20216
3/30/59	15	8	3. Remember When? .... "Smoke Gets In Your Eyes"(1)	Mercury 20410
3/14/60	6	174	● 4. **Encore Of Golden Hits** .... [G] "Only You (And You Alone)"(5)/"The Great Pretender"(1)/ "(You've Got) The Magic Touch"(4)/"Twilight Time"(1)	Mercury 20472

DATE CHARTED	PEAK POS	WKS CHRT'D	ARTIST — Album Title	LABEL & NUMBER
11/14/60	20	18	• 5. More Encore Of Golden Hits .... [G] "Harbor Lights"(8)	Mercury 20591
7/09/66	100	6	6. I Love You 1,000 Times .... includes new versions of 4 of their top ten hits - with new lead singer, Sonny Turner	Musicor 3091

PLAYER
pop/rock group formed in Los Angeles - Peter Beckett, lead singer

DATE CHARTED	PEAK POS	WKS CHRT'D	ARTIST — Album Title	LABEL & NUMBER
11/05/77	26	34	• 1. Player .... "Baby Come Back"(1)/"This Time I'm In It For Love"(10)	RSO 3026
9/09/78	37	23	• 2. Danger Zone	RSO 3036
2/06/82	152	7	3. Spies Of Life	RCA 4186

PLEASURE
R&B group from Portland, Oregon

DATE CHARTED	PEAK POS	WKS CHRT'D	ARTIST — Album Title	LABEL & NUMBER
8/28/76	162	5	1. Accept No Substitutes	Fantasy 9506
4/23/77	113	11	2. Joyous	Fantasy 9526
5/13/78	119	13	3. Get To The Feeling	Fantasy 9550
8/11/79	67	29	4. Future Now	Fantasy 9578
7/12/80	97	14	5. Special Things	Fantasy 9600
5/15/82	164	6	6. Give It Up	RCA 4209

PLIMSOULS
Peter Case, lead singer of Los Angeles rock quartet

DATE CHARTED	PEAK POS	WKS CHRT'D	ARTIST — Album Title	LABEL & NUMBER
4/04/81	153	4	1. The Plimsouls	Planet 13
7/23/83	186	4	2. Everywhere At Once	Geffen 4002

POCKETS
R&B group from Baltimore, Maryland

DATE CHARTED	PEAK POS	WKS CHRT'D	ARTIST — Album Title	LABEL & NUMBER
10/22/77	57	24	1. Come Go With Us	Columbia 34879
10/28/78	85	6	2. Take It On Up	Columbia 35384

POCO
Los Angeles country-rock band formed by Rusty Young and Buffalo Springfield members Richie Furay & Jim Messina

DATE CHARTED	PEAK POS	WKS CHRT'D	ARTIST — Album Title	LABEL & NUMBER
6/28/69	63	21	1. Pickin' Up The Pieces	Epic 26460
6/06/70	58	19	2. Poco .... Timothy B. Schmit joins group	Epic 26522
2/06/71	26	21	3. Deliverin' .... [L]	Epic 30209
9/25/71	52	11	4. From The Inside .... Paul Cotton replaces Jim Messina	Epic 30753
11/25/72	69	20	5. A Good Feelin' To Know	Epic 31601
9/15/73	38	23	6. Crazy Eyes .... Richie Furay's last album as a member	Epic 32354
5/11/74	68	13	7. Seven	Epic 32895
11/30/74	76	11	8. Cantamos	Epic 33192
7/19/75	43	18	9. Head Over Heels	ABC 890
8/02/75	90	8	10. The Very Best Of Poco .... [G]	Epic 33537 [2]
4/03/76	169	4	11. Live .... [L] recorded November, 1974	Epic 33336
5/29/76	89	15	12. Rose Of Cimarron	ABC 946
5/14/77	57	18	13. Indian Summer .... Tim Schmit's last album before joining the Eagles	ABC 989
11/25/78	14	52	• 14. Legend .... "Crazy Love"/"Heart Of The Night"	ABC 1099
7/26/80	46	16	15. Under The Gun	MCA 5132
7/25/81	76	10	16. Blue And Gray	MCA 5227
2/20/82	131	8	17. Cowboys & Englishmen	MCA 5288
12/04/82	195	3	18. Ghost Town	Atlantic 80008
5/19/84	167	6	19. Inamorata	Atlantic 80148

POINT BLANK
6-man rock band from Texas

DATE CHARTED	PEAK POS	WKS CHRT'D	ARTIST — Album Title	LABEL & NUMBER
9/11/76	175	3	1. Point Blank	Arista 4087
8/18/79	175	9	2. Airplay	MCA 3160

DATE CHARTED	PEAK POS	WKS CHRT'D	ARTIST — Album Title	LABEL & NUMBER
5/31/80	110	13	3. The Hard Way	MCA 5114
4/25/81	80	24	4. American Exce$$	MCA 5189
4/17/82	119	17	5. On A Roll	MCA 5312

POINTER SISTERS
Ruth, Anita, June & Bonnie Pointer - from Oakland, California

6/23/73	13	37	● 1. The Pointer Sisters .... "Yes We Can Can"	Blue Thumb 48
3/09/74	82	10	● 2. That's A Plenty	Blue Thumb 6009
9/14/74	96	15	3. Live At The Opera House .... [L]	Blue Thmb. 8002[2]
6/14/75	22	22	4. Steppin	Blue Thumb 6021
12/04/76	164	6	5. The Best Of The Pointer Sisters .... [G]	Blue Thmb. 6026[2]
12/24/77	176	3	6. Having A Party .... Bonnie's last album with her sisters	Blue Thumb 6023
12/02/78	13	32	● 7. Energy .... "Fire"(2)	Planet 1
9/22/79	72	8	8. Priority	Planet 9003
8/30/80	34	24	9. Special Things .... "He's So Shy"(3)	Planet 9
7/11/81	12	22	● 10. Black & White .... "Slow Hand"(2)	Planet 18
7/17/82	59	28	11. So Excited!	Planet 4355
11/13/82	178	3	12. Pointer Sisters' Greatest Hits .... [G]	Planet 60203
11/26/83	8	72+	▲ 13. **Break Out** .... "Automatic"(5)/"Jump (For My Love)"(3)/ "I'm So Excited"(9-originally released on album #11 above)/ "Neutron Dance"(6)	Planet 4705

BONNIE POINTER
one of the Pointer Sisters

12/16/78	96	15	1. Bonnie Pointer .... "Heaven Must Have Sent You"	Motown 911
12/22/79	63	14	2. Bonnie Pointer .... Motown 911: red cover; Motown 929: purple cover	Motown 929

NOEL POINTER
jazz-fusion violin prodigy from Brooklyn

6/18/77	144	8	1. Phantazia .... [I]	Blue Note 736
3/18/78	95	13	2. Hold-On	United Art. 848
9/01/79	138	7	3. Feel It .... [I]	United Art. 973
8/16/80	167	4	4. Calling	United Art. 1050

POLICE
English/U.S. trio: Sting (Gordon Sumner - lead singer), Andy Summers (guitar), Stewart Copeland (drums - from U.S.)

3/03/79	23	63	▲ 1. Outlandos d'Amour .... "Roxanne"	A&M 4753
11/03/79	25	100	● 2. Reggatta de Blanc	A&M 4792
10/25/80	5	153	▲ 3. Zenyatta Mondatta .... "De Do Do Do, De Da Da Da"(10)/ "Don't Stand So Close To Me"(10)	A&M 4831
10/24/81	2(6)	109	▲ 4. **Ghost In The Machine** .... "Every Little Thing She Does Is Magic"(3)/ "Spirits In The Material World"	A&M 3730
7/02/83	1(17)	75	▲ 5. **Synchronicity** .... "Every Breath You Take"(1)/"King Of Pain"(3)/ "Wrapped Around Your Finger"(8)	A&M 3735

MICHEL POLNAREFF

2/21/76	117	13	1. Michel Polnareff	Atlantic 18153

JEAN-LUC PONTY
French jazz-rock violinist - member of Mahavishnu Orchestra

7/26/75	158	5	1. Upon The Wings Of Music .... [I] with Patrice Rushen (keyboards) & Ray Parker, Jr. (guitar)	Atlantic 18138
4/10/76	123	13	2. Aurora .... [I]	Atlantic 18165
12/04/76	67	23	3. Imaginary Voyage .... [I]	Atlantic 18195

DATE CHARTED	PEAK POS	WKS CHRT'D		ARTIST — Album Title	LABEL & NUMBER
9/12/70	**28**	59	●	3. For The Good Times	Columbia 30106
6/12/71	**49**	24		4. I Won't Mention It Again	Columbia 30510
12/04/71	**146**	5		5. Welcome To My World .... [K]	Columbia 30878 [2]
7/29/72	**145**	12		6. The Lonesomest Lonesome	Columbia 31546
9/09/72	**165**	10	●	7. Ray Price's All-Time Greatest Hits .... [G]	Columbia 31364 [2]
4/21/73	**161**	7		8. She's Got To Be A Saint	Columbia 32033
6/14/80	**70**	25	●	9. San Antonio Rose	Columbia 36476
				WILLIE NELSON & RAY PRICE	
				Willie played bass with Ray's backing band in the early '60s	

CHARLEY PRIDE
country singer born on 3/18/38 in Sledge, Mississippi - Charley's had 29 #1 hits on the Country charts (1969-83)

DATE CHARTED	PEAK POS	WKS CHRT'D		ARTIST — Album Title	LABEL & NUMBER
3/30/68	**199**	2	●	1. The Country Way	RCA 3895
2/15/69	**78**	27	●	2. Charley Pride-In Person .... [L]	RCA 4094
				recorded at Panther Hall, Fort Worth, Texas	
6/28/69	**44**	39	●	3. The Sensational Charley Pride	RCA 4153
11/01/69	**24**	65	●	4. The Best Of Charley Pride .... [G]	RCA 4223
2/28/70	**22**	27	●	5. Just Plain Charley	RCA 4290
7/18/70	**30**	38	●	6. Charley Pride's 10th Album	RCA 4367
2/06/71	**42**	26	●	7. From Me To You	RCA 4468
4/17/71	**76**	15	●	8. Did You Think To Pray	RCA 4513
7/24/71	**50**	19		9. I'm Just Me	RCA 4560
12/04/71	**38**	26	●	10. Charley Pride Sings Heart Songs	RCA 4617
				"Kiss An Angel Good Mornin'"	
3/18/72	**50**	15	●	11. The Best Of Charley Pride, Volume 2 .... [G]	RCA 4682
8/19/72	**115**	15		12. A Sunshine Day with Charley Pride	RCA 4742
1/06/73	**189**	8		13. The Imcomparable Charley Pride .... [K]	RCA Camden 2584
2/17/73	**149**	8		14. Songs of Love by Charley Pride	RCA 4837
7/28/73	**166**	6		15. Sweet Country	RCA 0217
1/22/77	**188**	2		16. The Best of Charley Pride, Vol. III .... [G]	RCA 2023
11/21/81	**185**	7		17. Greatest Hits .... [G]	RCA 4151
				hits from 1976-1981	

LOUIS PRIMA
jazz trumpeter - band/combo leader since mid-30s - died on 8/24/78 (67)

DATE CHARTED	PEAK POS	WKS CHRT'D		ARTIST — Album Title	LABEL & NUMBER
1/16/61	**9**	11		1. **Wonderland By Night** .... [I]	Dot 25352

LOUIS PRIMA & KEELY SMITH
husband & wife (divorced in '62) - back-up band: Sam Butera & The Witnesses

DATE CHARTED	PEAK POS	WKS CHRT'D		ARTIST — Album Title	LABEL & NUMBER
6/09/58	**37**	2		1. Hey Boy! Hey Girl! .... [S]	Capitol 1160
				Louis & Keely portray Las Vegas entertainers in the film	
6/23/58	**12**	4		2. Las Vegas Prima Style .... [L]	Capitol 1010
11/02/59	**43**	4		3. Louis and Keely!	Dot 3210

PRINCE
born Prince Rogers Nelson on 6/7/60 in Minneapolis

DATE CHARTED	PEAK POS	WKS CHRT'D		ARTIST — Album Title	LABEL & NUMBER
10/28/78	**163**	5		1. Prince-For You	Warner 3150
11/17/79	**22**	28	▲	2. Prince	Warner 3366
				"I Wanna Be Your Lover"	
11/08/80	**45**	52	●	3. Dirty Mind	Warner 3478
11/07/81	**21**	63	▲	4. Controversy	Warner 3601
11/20/82	**9**	125+	▲	5. **Prince **1999****	Warner 23720 [2]
				"Little Red Corvette"(6)/"Delirious"(8)	
7/14/84	**1(24)**	39+	▲	6. **Purple Rain** .... [S]	Warner 25110
				"When Doves Cry"(1)/"Let's Go Crazy"(1)/"Purple Rain"(2)/ "I Would Die 4 U"(8)/"Take Me With U" film is a semi-autobiographical story about Prince's career	

JOHN PRINE
country-folk singer/songwriter

DATE CHARTED	PEAK POS	WKS CHRT'D		ARTIST — Album Title	LABEL & NUMBER
2/26/72	**154**	3		1. John Prine	Atlantic 8296
10/28/72	**148**	10		2. Diamonds In The Rough	Atlantic 7240

DATE CHARTED	PEAK POS	WKS CHRT'D	ARTIST — Album Title	LABEL & NUMBER
11/24/73	135	11	3. Sweet Revenge	Atlantic 7274
4/26/75	66	10	4. Common Sense	Atlantic 18127
1/15/77	196	2	5. Prime Prine-The Best Of John Prine .... [G]	Atlantic 18202
7/08/78	116	13	6. Bruised Orange	Asylum 139
9/08/79	152	7	7. Pink Cadillac	Asylum 222
8/30/80	144	7	8. Storm Windows	Asylum 286

PRISM
Canadian rock group

10/01/77	137	10	1. Prism	Ariola 50020
7/29/78	158	8	2. See Forever Eyes	Ariola 50034
2/06/82	53	20	3. Small Change	Capitol 12184

PROCOL HARUM
British rock group led by Gary Brooker (vocals/piano) & Robin Trower (guitar 1-5)

9/23/67	47	16	1. Procol Harum .... "A Whiter Shade Of Pale"(5)	Deram 18008
10/12/68	24	20	2. Shine On Brightly	A&M 4151
5/10/69	32	20	3. A Salty Dog	A&M 4179
7/11/70	34	15	4. Home	A&M 4261
5/08/71	32	20	5. Broken Barricades	A&M 4294
5/13/72	5	28	● 6. **Procol Harum Live In Concert with the Edmonton Symphony Orchestra** .... [L] "Conquistador"	A&M 4335
3/31/73	21	22	7. Grand Hotel	Chrysalis 1037
10/20/73	131	10	8. The Best Of Procol Harum .... [G]	A&M 4401
4/20/74	86	9	9. Exotic Birds and Fruit	Chrysalis 1058
8/23/75	52	8	10. Procol's Ninth	Chrysalis 1080
3/26/77	147	6	11. Something Magic	Chrysalis 1130

PRODUCERS
pop/rock quartet from Atlanta, Georgia

6/06/81	163	2	1. The Producers	Portrait 37097

DOROTHY PROVINE
portrayed songstress Pinky Pinkham in the TV series "The Roaring Twenties"

5/15/61	39	66	1. The Roaring 20's .... medleys of 30 songs from the 20's	Warner 1394

JEANNE PRUETT
country singer/songwriter

7/07/73	122	9	1. Satin Sheets	MCA 338

RICHARD PRYOR
ribald comedian

6/15/74	29	53	1. That Nigger's Crazy .... [C]	Partee 2404
8/23/75	12	25	● 2. Is It Something I Said? .... [C]	Reprise 2227
10/09/76	22	19	● 3. Bicentennial Nigger .... [C]	Warner 2960
5/28/77	58	9	4. Are You Serious??? .... [E-C]	Laff 196
6/04/77	114	5	5. L.A. Jail .... [E-C]	Tiger Lily 14023
6/25/77	68	12	● 6. Richard Pryor's Greatest Hits .... [C-K]	Warner 3057
12/16/78	32	20	● 7. Wanted .... [C]	Warner 3364 [2]
9/08/79	176	4	8. Outrageous .... [E-C]	Laff 206
4/17/82	21	17	9. Richard Pryor Live On The Sunset Strip .... [C-S] filmed live at the Hollywood Palladium	Warner 3660
11/12/83	71	13	10. Richard Pryor: Here And Now .... [C-S] filmed live at the Saenger Theater in New Orleans	Warner 23981

DATE CHARTED	PEAK POS	WKS CHRT'D	ARTIST — Album Title	LABEL & NUMBER
			ARTHUR PRYSOCK	
			blues-ballad vocalist with Buddy Johnson's band from 1944-1952	
7/13/63	138	7	1. Coast To Coast	Old Town 2005
12/28/63	97	7	2. A Portrait Of Arthur Prysock	Old Town 2006
8/15/64	131	8	3. Everlasting Songs For Everlasting Lovers	Old Town 2007
7/17/65	116	7	4. A Double Header with Arthur Prysock	Old Town 2009
3/26/66	107	13	5. Arthur Prysock/Count Basie	Verve 8646
1/29/77	153	4	6. All My Life	Old Town 12-004
			PSYCHEDELIC FURS	
			English - brothers Richard (vocals) & Tim Butler (bass) & John Ashton (guitar)	
11/22/80	140	7	1. The Psychedelic Furs	Columbia 36791
6/27/81	89	14	2. Talk Talk Talk	Columbia 37339
11/13/82	61	32	3. Forever Now	Columbia 38261
			produced by Todd Rundgren	
5/26/84	43	27	4. Mirror Moves	Columbia 39278
			PUBLIC IMAGE LTD.	
			Johnny Lydon, lead singer - a.k.a. Johnny Rotten (Sex Pistols)	
5/10/80	171	3	1. Second Edition	Island 3288 [2]
5/30/81	114	4	2. The Flowers Of Romance	Warner 3536
			GARY PUCKETT	
			leader of The Union Gap	
10/16/71	196	2	1. The Gary Puckett Album	Columbia 30862
			GARY PUCKETT & THE UNION GAP	
			formed in San Diego - named after the town of Union Gap, Wash.	
2/17/68	22	45	1. Woman, Woman	Columbia 9612
			"Woman, Woman"(4)	
5/18/68	21	39	● 2. Young Girl	Columbia 9664
			"Young Girl"(2)	
11/02/68	20	20	3. Incredible	Columbia 9715
			"Lady Willpower"(2)/"Over You"(7)	
12/06/69	50	14	4. The New Gary Puckett And The Union Gap Album	Columbia 9935
			"This Girl Is A Woman Now"(9)	
7/11/70	50	33	● 5. Gary Puckett & The Union Gap's Greatest Hits ..... [G]	Columbia 1042
			PURE LOVE & PLEASURE	
4/25/70	195	2	1. A Record Of Pure Love & Pleasure	Dunhill 50076
			PURE PRAIRIE LEAGUE	
			country-rock group formed in Cincinnati	
2/08/75	34	24	● 1. Bustin' Out	RCA 4769
			"Amie"	
6/07/75	24	14	2. Two Lane Highway	RCA 0933
2/07/76	33	16	3. If The Shoe Fits	RCA 1247
11/20/76	99	14	4. Dance	RCA 1924
9/10/77	68	11	5. Live!! Takin' The Stage ..... [L]	RCA 2404 [2]
5/13/78	79	11	6. Just Fly	RCA 2590
6/23/79	124	6	7. Can't Hold Back	RCA 3335
5/17/80	37	24	8. Firin' Up	Casablanca 7212
			"Let Me Love You Tonight"(10)	
5/02/81	72	15	9. Something In The Night	Casablanca 7255
			country singer Vince Gill, lead singer on above 3 albums	
			FLORA PURIM	
			born in Rio de Janeiro - married to Brazilian jazz artist Airto Moreira	
2/15/75	172	5	1. Stories To Tell	Milestone 9058
3/13/76	59	15	2. Open Your Eyes You Can Fly	Milestone 9065

DATE CHARTED	PEAK POS	WKS CHRT'D	ARTIST — Album Title	LABEL & NUMBER
10/16/76	146	5	3. 500 Miles High .... [L] recorded at the Montreux Jazz Festival (7/6/74)	Milestone 9070
3/26/77	163	4	4. Nothing Will Be As It Was...Tomorrow	Warner 2985
8/13/77	194	3	5. Encounter	Milestone 9077
6/03/78	174	4	6. Everyday, Everynight .... accompaniment on all albums by a host of famous jazz musicians	Warner 3168
			BILL PURSELL pianist from Tulare, California	
4/06/63	28	14	1. Our Winter Love .... [I] arrangements by Bill Justis; orchestra directed by Grady Martin "Our Winter Love"(9)	Columbia 1992
			PYRAMIDS West Coast surf band	
3/14/64	119	6	1. The Original Penetration! and other favorites	Best 16501
			PYTHON LEE JACKSON English studio band led by David Bentley	
10/07/72	182	6	1. In A Broken Dream .... [E] recorded in 1968 - Rod Stewart sings lead on 3 tracks	GNP Cres. 2066
			Q	
6/18/77	140	2	1. Dancin' Man	Epic 34691
			QUARTERFLASH rock group from Portland area originally known as Seafood Mama	
10/31/81	8	52	▲ 1. **Quarterflash** .... "Harden My Heart"(3)	Geffen 2003
7/09/83	34	21	2. Take Another Picture	Geffen 4011
			BILL QUATEMAN 1. Night After Night	
2/12/77	129	8	1. Night After Night	RCA 2027
			SUZI QUATRO portrayed Leather Tuscadero on TV's "Happy Days"	
3/30/74	142	13	1. Suzi Quatro	Bell 1302
10/05/74	126	10	2. Quatro	Bell 1313
5/10/75	146	6	3. Your Mama Won't Like Me	Arista 4035
3/24/79	37	20	4. If You Knew Suzi... .... "Stumblin' In"(4-with Chris Norman)	RSO 3044
10/06/79	117	14	5. Suzi...And Other Four Letter Words	RSO 3064
11/01/80	165	5	6. Rock Hard	Dreamland 5006
			QUAZAR 9-member funk group	
11/11/78	121	5	1. Quazar	Arista 4187
			QUEEN British: Freddie Mercury (vocals), Brian May (guitar), John Deacon (bass), Roger Taylor (drums)	
11/03/73	83	22	● 1. Queen	Elektra 75064
5/11/74	49	13	2. Queen II	Elektra 75082
12/14/74	12	32	● 3. Sheer Heart Attack .... "Killer Queen"	Elektra 1026
12/27/75	4	56	● 4. **A Night At The Opera** .... "Bohemian Rhapsody"(9)	Elektra 1053
1/15/77	5	19	● 5. **A Day At The Races** .... "Somebody To Love"	Elektra 101
11/26/77	3	37	▲ 6. **News Of The World** .... "We Are The Champions"(4)/"We Will Rock You"	Elektra 112
12/09/78	6	18	▲ 7. **Jazz**	Elektra 166
7/07/79	16	14	● 8. Queen Live Killers .... [L]	Elektra 702 [2]

DATE CHARTED	PEAK POS	WKS CHRT'D	ARTIST — Album Title	LABEL & NUMBER
7/19/80	1(5)	43	▲ 9. **The Game** .... "Crazy Little Thing Called Love"(1)/ "Another One Bites The Dust"(1)	Elektra 513
12/27/80	23	15	10. Flash Gordon .... [S]	Elektra 518
11/14/81	14	26	▲ 11. Greatest Hits .... [G]	Elektra 564
5/29/82	22	21	● 12. Hot Space	Elektra 60128
3/17/84	23	20	● 13. The Works	Capitol 12322

QUEENSRYCHE
Geoff Tate, lead singer of heavy-metal quintet from Seattle

9/17/83	81	22	1. Queensryche .... [M]	EMI America 19006
10/13/84	61	23	2. The Warning	EMI America 17134

? (QUESTION MARK) & THE MYSTERIANS
Mexican-born quintet - formed group in Detroit

11/19/66	66	15	1. 96 Tears .... "96 Tears"(1)	Cameo 2004

QUICKSILVER MESSENGER SERVICE
San Francisco acid-rock group featuring John Cipollina (guitar) & David Freiberg (bass - left after album #5 to join Jefferson Starship)

6/22/68	63	25	1. Quicksilver Messenger Service	Capitol 2904
3/29/69	27	30	2. Happy Trails .... [L] includes several studio tracks	Capitol 120
1/24/70	25	24	3. Shady Grove	Capitol 391
8/22/70	27	24	4. Just For Love	Capitol 498
1/23/71	26	20	5. What About Me .... Nicky Hopkins (piano) featured on above 3 albums	Capitol 630
12/04/71	114	9	6. Quicksilver	Capitol 819
5/06/72	134	10	7. Comin' Thru	Capitol 11002
5/19/73	108	10	8. Anthology .... [K]	Capitol 11165 [2]
11/15/75	89	12	9. Solid Silver	Capitol 11462

QUIET RIOT
heavy-metal rock quartet from L.A. - Kevin DuBrow, lead singer

4/23/83	1(1)	81	▲ 1. **Metal Health** .... "Cum On Feel The Noize"(5)	Pasha 38443
8/04/84	15	28	▲ 2. Condition Critical	Pasha 39516

CARMEL QUINN
Miss Quinn sings favorites from her native country, Ireland

4/02/55	4	9	1. **Arthur Godfrey presents Carmel Quinn**	Columbia 629

EDDIE RABBITT
born Edward Thomas on 11/27/44 in Brooklyn, New York

6/24/78	143	7	1. Variations	Elektra 127
6/09/79	91	20	2. Loveline	Elektra 181
11/24/79	151	12	● 3. The Best of Eddie Rabbitt .... [G]	Elektra 235
7/12/80	19	54	▲ 4. Horizon .... "Drivin' My Life Away"(5)/"I Love A Rainy Night"(1)	Elektra 276
8/22/81	23	34	● 5. Step By Step .... "Step By Step"(5)	Elektra 532
11/06/82	31	25	6. Radio Romance .... "You And I"(7-with Crystal Gayle)	Elektra 60160
10/01/83	131	11	7. Greatest Hits, Volume II .... [G]	Warner 23925

TREVOR RABIN
British rocker

12/09/78	192	4	1. Trevor Rabin	Chrysalis 1196

RACING CARS
British rock quintet

4/02/77	198	3	1. Downtown Tonight	Chrysalis 1099

DATE CHARTED	PEAK POS	WKS CHRT'D	ARTIST — Album Title	LABEL & NUMBER
			GILDA RADNER	
			portrayed Rosanne Rosanna-Dana on NBC's "Saturday Night Live"	
12/01/79	69	12	1. Live From New York .... [C]	Warner 3320
			RAES	
			Canadian disco group	
3/24/79	161	5	1. Dancing Up A Storm	A&M 4754
			GERRY RAFFERTY	
			Scottish - co-leader of Stealers Wheel	
5/06/78	1(1)	49	▲ 1. **City to City**	United Art. 840
			"Baker Street"(2)	
6/16/79	29	21	● 2. Night Owl	United Art. 958
6/14/80	61	9	3. Snakes And Ladders	United Art. 1039
			RAIDERS - see PAUL REVERE	
			RAIL	
			hard-rock quartet led by vocalist Terry Young	
8/25/84	143	10	1. Rail .... [M]	EMI America 19010
			RAINBOW	
			hard-rock band led by British guitarist Ritchie Blackmore & bassist Roger Glover (5-9), both former members of Deep Purple	
9/06/75	30	15	1. Ritchie Blackmore's R-A-I-N-B-O-W	Oyster 6049
6/05/76	40	17	2. Rainbow Rising	Oyster 1601
7/16/77	65	9	3. On Stage .... [L]	Oyster 1801 [2]
			Tony Carey (keyboards) on above 2 albums	
5/06/78	89	11	4. Long Live Rock 'n' Roll	Polydor 6143
			Ronnie James Dio (vocals) on above albums	
8/25/79	66	15	5. Down To Earth	Polydor 6221
			Cozy Powell (drums) on above 4 albums	
3/07/81	50	16	6. Difficult To Cure	Polydor 6316
11/14/81	147	4	7. Jealous Lover .... [M]	Polydor 502
			2 of 4 songs from album #6	
5/08/82	30	23	8. Straight Between The Eyes	Mercury 4041
10/01/83	34	21	9. Bent Out Of Shape	Mercury 815305
			BONNIE RAITT	
			singer/guitarist - daughter of Broadway's John Raitt	
10/21/72	138	15	1. Give It Up	Warner 2643
10/27/73	87	20	2. Takin My Time	Warner 2729
11/02/74	80	8	3. Streetlights	Warner 2818
10/11/75	43	12	4. Home Plate	Warner 2864
4/23/77	25	22	● 5. Sweet Forgiveness	Warner 2990
10/13/79	30	21	6. The Glow	Warner 3369
3/06/82	38	18	7. Green Light	Warner 3630
			RAM JAM	
			East Coast rock quartet led by Bill Bartlett (Lemon Pipers)	
9/10/77	34	12	1. Ram Jam	Epic 34885
			"Black Betty"	
			RAMATAM	
			rock quintet featuring Mike Pinera (guitar/vocals)	
9/02/72	182	7	1. Ramatam	Atlantic 7236
			EDDIE RAMBEAU	
			singer/songwriter from Hazleton, Pennsylvania	
7/24/65	148	2	1. Concrete And Clay	DynoVoice 9001
			SID RAMIN & Orchestra	
5/25/63	34	6	1. New Thresholds in Sound .... [I]	RCA 2658
			RAMONES	
			punk rock quartet from New York City	
6/05/76	111	18	1. Ramones	Sire 7520
2/12/77	148	10	2. Leave Home	Sire 7528

DATE CHARTED	PEAK POS	WKS CHRT'D	ARTIST — Album Title	LABEL & NUMBER
11/26/77	49	25	3. Rocket To Russia	Sire 6042
10/21/78	103	11	4. Road To Ruin	Sire 6063
2/23/80	44	14	5. End Of The Century .... produced by Phil Spector	Sire 6077
8/08/81	58	11	6. Pleasant Dreams	Sire 3571
3/26/83	83	9	7. Subterranean Jungle	Sire 23800
11/03/84	171	6	8. Too Tough To Die	Sire 25187

JEAN-PIERRE RAMPAL/CLAUDE BOLLING
Rampal: flute; Bolling: pianist/composer

1/31/76	173	4	● 1. Suite for Flute and Jazz Piano .... [I] Rampal's first non-classical recording	Columbia 33233

BOOTS RANDOLPH
premier Nashville session saxophonist

6/15/63	79	49	● 1. Boots Randolph's Yakety Sax .... [I]	Monument 18002
11/13/65	118	5	2. Boots Randolph plays More Yakety Sax! .... [I]	Monument 18037
1/14/67	36	47	● 3. Boots with Strings .... [I]	Monument 18066
2/03/68	189	5	4. Boots Randolph with the Knightsbridge Strings & Voices .... [I]	Monument 18082
3/23/68	76	12	5. Sunday Sax .... [I] gospel songs	Monument 18092
8/31/68	60	24	6. The Sound Of Boots .... [I]	Monument 18099
5/10/69	82	17	7. ...with love/The Seductive Sax of Boots Randolph .... [I]	Monument 18111
1/10/70	113	18	8. Yakety Revisited .... [I]	Monument 18128
10/10/70	157	9	9. Hit Boots 1970 .... [I]	Monument 18144
1/09/71	168	3	10. Boots With Brass .... [I]	Monument 18147
6/12/71	141	11	11. Homer Louis Randolph, III .... [I]	Monument 30678
11/27/71	144	8	12. The World Of Boots Randolph .... [K-I]	Monmnt. 30963[2]
12/02/72	192	3	13. Boots Randolph Plays The Great Hits Of Today .... [I]	Monument 31908

RANK & FILE
country-rock quartet led by brothers Chip & Tony Kinman

5/07/83	165	5	1. Sundown	Slash 23833

BILLY RANKIN
native of Glasgow, Scotland - formerly with Nazareth

3/24/84	119	11	1. Growin' Up Too Fast	A&M 4977

KENNY RANKIN
singer/songwriter/acoustic guitarist

9/09/72	184	8	1. Like A Seed	Little David 1003
11/16/74	63	25	2. Silver Morning	Little David 3000
12/13/75	81	15	3. Inside	Little David 1009
3/12/77	99	23	4. The Kenny Rankin Album	Little David 1013
6/28/80	171	6	5. After The Roses	Atlantic 19271

RARE BIRD
Steve Gould, lead singer of British rock group

3/07/70	117	13	1. Rare Bird	Probe 4514
8/18/73	194	2	2. Epic Forest	Polydor 5530

RARE EARTH
Detroit rock group

12/06/69	12	77	1. Get Ready .... "Get Ready"(4) side 2 is a 21-1/2 minute version of the title song	Rare Earth 507
7/11/70	15	49	2. Ecology .... "(I Know) I'm Losing You"(7)	Rare Earth 514
7/17/71	28	25	3. One World .... "I Just Want To Celebrate"(7)	Rare Earth 520

DATE CHARTED	PEAK POS	WKS CHRT'D	ARTIST — Album Title	LABEL & NUMBER
1/01/72	29	21	4. Rare Earth In Concert .... [L]	Rare Earth 534 [2]
11/25/72	90	20	5. Willie Remembers..	Rare Earth 543
6/16/73	65	23	6. Ma	Rare Earth 546
7/12/75	59	11	7. Back To Earth	Rare Earth 548
10/01/77	187	6	8. Rare Earth	Prodigal 10019
6/03/78	156	6	9. Band Together	Prodigal 10025

RASCALS
Felix Cavaliere, Dino Danelli, Eddie Brigati, Gene Cornish

YOUNG RASCALS:

DATE CHARTED	PEAK POS	WKS CHRT'D	ARTIST — Album Title	LABEL & NUMBER
5/07/66	15	84	● 1. The Young Rascals .... "Good Lovin'"(1)	Atlantic 8123
1/21/67	14	74	● 2. Collections	Atlantic 8134
8/12/67	5	59	● 3. Groovin' .... "Groovin'"(1)/"A Girl Like You"(10)/"How Can I Be Sure"(4)	Atlantic 8148

RASCALS:

3/02/68	9	30	4. Once Upon A Dream	Atlantic 8169
7/13/68	1(1)	58	● 5. Time Peace/The Rascals' Greatest Hits .... [G] "A Beautiful Morning"(3)	Atlantic 8190
3/29/69	17	16	● 6. Freedom Suite .... record 2 entitled "Music Music" is all instrumental "People Got To Be Free"(1)	Atlantic 901 [2]
1/10/70	45	16	7. See	Atlantic 8246
3/20/71	198	1	8. Search And Nearness .... last album with Brigati and Cornish	Atlantic 8276
6/05/71	122	12	9. Peaceful World	Columbia 30462 [2]
5/13/72	180	3	10. The Island Of Real	Columbia 31103

RASPBERRIES
Cleveland, Ohio pop/rock quartet - Eric Carmen, lead singer

5/20/72	51	30	1. Raspberries .... "Go All The Way"(5)	Capitol 11036
12/09/72	36	16	2. Fresh	Capitol 11123
10/06/73	128	7	3. Side 3	Capitol 11220
10/19/74	143	6	4. Starting Over	Capitol 11329
6/12/76	138	4	5. Raspberries' Best Featuring Eric Carmen .... [G]	Capitol 11524

RATCHELL
rock quartet featuring Chris & Pat Couchois

4/15/72	176	3	1. Ratchell	Decca 75330

RATT
hard-rock quintet from Los Angeles - Stephen Pearcy, lead singer

3/24/84	7	55+	▲ 1. Out Of The Cellar	Atlantic 80143
6/30/84	133	19	2. Ratt .... [M] first released in 1983	Time Coast 2203

GENYA RAVAN
born Goldie Zelkowitz in Poland - lead singer of Ten Wheel Drive

9/02/78	147	6	1. Urban Desire	20th Century 562
9/29/79	106	6	2. ...And I Mean It!	20th Century 595

RAVEN
Southern California metal trio

3/23/85	120+	3+	1. Stay Hard	Atlantic 81241

LOU RAWLS
born on 12/1/35 in Chicago, Illinois

4/06/63	130	3	1. Black And Blue	Capitol 1824
5/07/66	4	74	● 2. Lou Rawls Live! .... [L]	Capitol 2459
9/10/66	7	51	● 3. Lou Rawls Soulin'	Capitol 2566
1/21/67	20	31	4. Lou Rawls Carryin' On!	Capitol 2632

DATE CHARTED	PEAK POS	WKS CHRT'D	ARTIST — Album Title	LABEL & NUMBER
5/06/67	**18**	22	5. Too Much!	Capitol 2713
8/26/67	**29**	20	6. That's Lou	Capitol 2756
3/09/68	**103**	22	7. Feelin' Good	Capitol 2864
7/20/68	**165**	6	8. You're Good For Me	Capitol 2927
8/31/68	**103**	16	9. The Best Of Lou Rawls [G]	Capitol 2948
6/14/69	**71**	23	10. The way it was - The way it is	Capitol 215
8/23/69	**191**	3	11. Close-Up [R]	Capitol 261 [2]
			reissue of "Black And Blue" & "Tobacco Road" albums	
12/20/69	**200**	2	12. Your Good Thing	Capitol 325
4/18/70	**172**	3	13. You've Made Me So Very Happy	Capitol 427
9/04/71	**68**	24	14. Natural Man	MGM 4771
2/26/72	**186**	4	15. Silk & Soul	MGM 4809 [2]
6/05/76	**7**	35	▲ 16. **All Things In Time**	Phil. Int. 33957
			"You'll Never Find Another Love Like Mine"(2)	
4/16/77	**41**	29	● 17. Unmistakably Lou	Phil. Int. 34488
12/10/77	**41**	34	● 18. When You Hear Lou, You've Heard It All	Phil. Int. 35036
11/11/78	**108**	8	19. Lou Rawls Live [L]	Phil. Int. 35517[2]
6/02/79	**49**	15	20. Let Me Be Good To You	Phil. Int. 36006
1/12/80	**81**	18	21. Sit Down And Talk To Me	Phil. Int. 36304
1/10/81	**110**	6	22. Shades Of Blue	Phil. Int. 36774
5/14/83	**163**	4	23. When The Night Comes	Epic 38553

RAY, GOODMAN & BROWN
Harry Ray, Al Goodman & William Brown - formerly known as The Moments

1/26/80	**17**	23	● 1. Ray, Goodman & Brown	Polydor 6240
			"Special Lady"(5)	
10/04/80	**84**	12	2. Ray, Goodman & Brown II	Polydor 6299
1/09/82	**151**	7	3. Stay	Polydor 6341

DON RAY
German disco producer/arranger/composer

9/23/78	**113**	11	1. The Garden Of Love	Polydor 6150

JOHNNIE RAY
born in Roseburg, Oregon on 1/10/27

3/02/57	**19**	2	1. The Big Beat	Columbia 961

RAYDIO - see RAY PARKER JR.

SUSAN RAYE
a regular on TV's "Hee Haw" show

5/16/70	**154**	6	1. We're Gonna Get Together	Capitol 448
			BUCK OWENS & SUSAN RAYE	
9/26/70	**190**	2	2. One Night Stand	Capitol 543

CHRIS REA
English

8/12/78	**49**	12	● 1. Whatever Happened To Benny Santini?	United Art. 879
			"Fool (If You Think It's Over)"	

REAL LIFE
Australian quartet

1/07/84	**58**	24	1. Heartland	Curb 5459
			"Send Me An Angel"	

REBELS - see ROCKIN' REBELS

RECORDS
British rock quartet

8/25/79	**41**	14	1. The Records	Virgin 13130
			includes special edition 4 track EP record	

REDBONE
American Indian rock group led by brothers Pat & Lolly Vegas

11/07/70	**99**	17	1. Potlatch	Epic 30109
2/05/72	**75**	9	2. Message From A Drum	Epic 30815

DATE CHARTED	PEAK POS	WKS CHRT'D	ARTIST — Album Title	LABEL & NUMBER
3/16/74	66	16	3. Wovoka .... "Come And Get Your Love"(5)	Epic 32462
10/26/74	174	3	4. Beaded Dreams Through Turquoise Eyes	Epic 33053

LEON REDBONE
mysterious performer of '20s and '30s blues and ragtime

DATE CHARTED	PEAK POS	WKS CHRT'D	ARTIST — Album Title	LABEL & NUMBER
7/31/76	87	15	1. On The Track	Warner 2888
1/22/77	38	13	2. Double Time	Warner 2971
9/16/78	163	4	3. Champagne Charlie	Warner 3165
4/11/81	152	11	4. From Branch To Branch	Emerald City 136

OTIS REDDING
soulful blues singer - born 9/9/41 in Dawson, Georgia; killed in a plane crash on 12/10/67 (26)

DATE CHARTED	PEAK POS	WKS CHRT'D	ARTIST — Album Title	LABEL & NUMBER
5/02/64	103	8	1. Pain In My Heart	Atco 161
4/10/65	147	3	2. The Great Otis Redding Sings Soul Ballads	Volt 411
10/16/65	75	34	3. Otis Blue/Otis Redding Sings Soul	Volt 412
4/30/66	54	29	4. The Soul Album	Volt 413
11/26/66	73	15	5. Complete & Unbelievable....The Otis Redding Dictionary Of Soul	Volt 415
4/22/67	36	31	6. King & Queen .... OTIS REDDING/CARLA THOMAS	Stax 716
8/19/67	32	41	7. Otis Redding Live In Europe .... [L]	Volt 416
12/02/67	9	50	8. **History Of Otis Redding** .... [G]	Volt 418
3/23/68	4	42	9. **The Dock Of The Bay** .... "(Sittin' On) The Dock Of The Bay"(1)	Volt 419
7/20/68	58	21	10. The Immortal Otis Redding	Atco 252
11/30/68	82	17	11. Otis Redding In Person At The Whisky A Go Go .... [L] recorded April, 1966	Atco 265
7/19/69	46	14	12. Love Man .... [K]	Atco 289
8/29/70	200	2	13. Tell The Truth .... [K] albums 9,10,12 & 13 consist of Otis' last recordings from '67	Atco 333
9/19/70	16	20	● 14. Monterey International Pop Festival .... [S-L] OTIS REDDING/THE JIMI HENDRIX EXPERIENCE recorded June, 1967 & featured in film "Monterey Pop"	Reprise 2029
9/16/72	76	15	15. The Best Of Otis Redding .... [G]	Atco 801 [2]

REDDINGS
Dexter & Otis Redding III (sons of Otis Redding) and cousin Mark Locket

DATE CHARTED	PEAK POS	WKS CHRT'D	ARTIST — Album Title	LABEL & NUMBER
12/20/80	174	12	1. The Awakening	Believe 36875
8/01/81	106	5	2. Class	Believe 37175
5/29/82	153	12	3. Steamin' Hot	Believe 37974

HELEN REDDY
born on 10/4/42 in Melbourne, Australia - also see Soundtrack "Pete's Dragon"

DATE CHARTED	PEAK POS	WKS CHRT'D	ARTIST — Album Title	LABEL & NUMBER
6/05/71	100	37	● 1. I Don't Know How To Love Him	Capitol 762
12/04/71	167	7	2. Helen Reddy	Capitol 857
12/09/72	14	62	● 3. I Am Woman .... "I Am Woman"(1)	Capitol 11068
8/11/73	8	43	● 4. **Long Hard Climb** .... "Delta Dawn"(1)/"Leave Me Alone (Ruby Red Dress)"(3)	Capitol 11213
4/20/74	11	35	● 5. Love Song For Jeffrey .... "You And Me Against The World"(9)	Capitol 11284
11/02/74	8	28	● 6. **Free And Easy** .... "Angie Baby"(1)	Capitol 11348
7/12/75	11	34	● 7. No Way To Treat A Lady .... "Ain't No Way To Treat A Lady"(8)	Capitol 11418
12/06/75	5	51	● 8. **Helen Reddy's Greatest Hits** .... [G]	Capitol 11467

DATE CHARTED	PEAK POS	WKS CHRT'D	ARTIST — Album Title	LABEL & NUMBER
8/14/76	16	13	● 9. Music, Music	Capitol 11547
5/21/77	75	19	10. Ear Candy	Capitol 11640

REDEYE
rock quartet led by Dave Hodgkins & Douglas "Red" Mark

| 12/12/70 | 113 | 12 | 1. Redeye .... "Games" | Pentagram 10003 |

RED RIDER
Canadian quintet - Tom Cochrane, leader (cousin of Eddie Cochran)

4/26/80	146	5	1. Don't Fight It	Capitol 12028
9/12/81	65	24	2. As Far As Siam	Capitol 12145
2/05/83	66	16	3. Neruda	Capitol 12226
6/23/84	137	8	4. Breaking Curfew	Capitol 12317

RED ROCKERS
New Orleans foursome - John Griffith, lead singer

| 5/14/83 | 71 | 16 | 1. Good As Gold .... | Columbia 38629 |

JERRY REED
Elvis Presley recorded 2 of Reed's songs: "U.S. Male" & "Guitar Man"

5/16/70	194	2	1. Cookin'	RCA 4293
3/06/71	102	11	2. Georgia Sunshine .... "Amos Moses"(8)	RCA 4391
5/01/71	45	20	3. When You're Hot, You're Hot .... "When You're Hot, You're Hot"(9)	RCA 4506
9/18/71	153	5	4. Ko-Ko Joe	RCA 4596
4/01/72	196	2	5. Smell The Flowers	RCA 4660
7/15/72	116	12	6. The Best Of Jerry Reed .... [G]	RCA 4729
8/11/73	183	4	7. Lord, Mr. Ford	RCA 0238

JIMMY REED
blues singer, guitarist, harmonica player - died on 8/29/76 (50)

| 10/16/61 | 46 | 31 | 1. Jimmy Reed at Carnegie Hall .... [G] record 1: studio re-creation of his Carnegie Hall program; record 2: The Best of Jimmy Reed | Vee-Jay 1035 [2] |
| 10/20/62 | 103 | 6 | 2. Just Jimmy Reed .... side 2 is an unrehearsed recording session | Vee-Jay 1050 |

LOU REED
lead singer of New York seminal rock band, the Velvet Underground

6/24/72	189	2	1. Lou Reed .... with Steve Howe (guitar) & Rick Wakeman (piano)	RCA 4701
12/16/72	29	31	2. Transformer .... produced by David Bowie "Walk On The Wild Side"	RCA 4807
10/20/73	98	11	3. Berlin	RCA 0207
3/02/74	45	27	● 4. Rock N Roll Animal .... [L] recorded at New York's Academy of Music	RCA 0472
10/05/74	10	14	5. **Sally Can't Dance**	RCA 0611
4/05/75	62	10	6. Lou Reed Live .... [L] from same live sessions as album #4	RCA 0959
2/07/76	41	14	7. Coney Island Baby	RCA 0915
11/13/76	64	8	8. Rock And Roll Heart	Arista 4100
4/16/77	156	6	9. Walk On The Wild Side-The best of Lou Reed .... [G]	RCA 2001
4/08/78	89	9	10. Street Hassle	Arista 4169
6/02/79	130	4	11. The Bells	Arista 4229
5/10/80	158	5	12. Growing Up In Public	Arista 9522
12/20/80	178	4	13. Rock And Roll Diary 1967-1980 .... [K] record 1: all cuts but one are with the Velvet Underground	Arista 8603 [2]
2/27/82	169	4	14. The Blue Mask	RCA 4221

DATE CHARTED	PEAK POS	WKS CHRT'D	ARTIST — Album Title	LABEL & NUMBER
4/09/83	159	7	15. Legendary Hearts	RCA 4568
6/16/84	56	32	16. New Sensations	RCA 4998

DELLA REESE
born Dellareese Taliaferro on 7/6/32 in Detroit, Michigan

3/07/60	35	2	1. Della	RCA 2157
10/23/61	113	6	2. Special Delivery	RCA 2391
4/07/62	94	6	3. The Classic Della	RCA 2419
			"Don't You Know"(2-'59)	
10/22/66	149	2	4. Della Reese Live .... [L]	ABC 569
			with Bill Doggett (organ) & Shelly Manne (drums)	

JIM REEVES
Country Music Hall Of Famer - born on 8/20/24 in Galloway, Texas - killed in a plane crash on 7/31/64 (39)

5/23/60	18	26	1. He'll Have To Go	RCA 2223
			"He'll Have To Go"(2)	
6/16/62	97	11	2. A Touch Of Velvet	RCA 2487
6/13/64	30	30	3. Moonlight and Roses	RCA 2854
8/08/64	9	43	● 4. **The Best Of Jim Reeves** .... [G]	RCA 2890
3/06/65	45	13	5. The Jim Reeves Way	RCA 2968
2/12/66	100	6	6. The Best Of Jim Reeves, Vol. II .... [G]	RCA 3482
6/04/66	21	29	● 7. Distant Drums .... [K]	RCA 3542
7/15/67	185	5	8. Blue Side Of Lonesome .... [K]	RCA 3793

MARTHA REEVES - see MARTHA & THE VANDELLAS

RE-FLEX
British techno-rock quartet

12/24/83	53	28	1. The Politics Of Dancing	Capitol 12314

TERRY REID
English rock singer/guitarist

12/21/68	153	8	1. bang, bang you're Terry Reid	Epic 26427
10/18/69	147	5	2. Terry Reid	Epic 26477
4/07/73	172	8	3. River	Atlantic 7259

CARL REINER & MEL BROOKS
TV and film comedy producers

11/24/73	150	12	1. 2000 and Thirteen .... [C]	Warner 2741
			revival of the 1961 "2000 Year Old Man" act	

R.E.M.
Athens, Georgia rock quartet

5/14/83	36	30	1. Murmur	I.R.S. 70604
5/05/84	27	49 +	2. Reckoning	I.R.S. 70044

RENAISSANCE
a Snuff Garrett production

1/09/71	198	2	1. Bacharach Baroque .... [I]	Ranwood 8084
			baroque treatments of Burt Bacharach songs	

RENAISSANCE
British classical-rock group - Annie Haslam, lead singer

9/22/73	171	4	1. Ashes Are Burning	Sovereign 11216
8/03/74	94	21	2. Turn Of The Cards	Sire 7502
8/30/75	48	13	3. Scheherazade and other stories	Sire 7510
			side 2: contemporary version of Rimsky-Korsakov's "Scheherazade"	
6/05/76	55	20	4. Live At Carnegie Hall .... [L]	Sire 3902 [2]
			with the New York Philharmonic, conducted by Tony Cox	
2/05/77	46	16	5. Novella	Sire 7526
3/25/78	58	14	6. A Song For All Seasons	Sire 6049
6/16/79	125	9	7. Azure d'or	Sire 6068
12/12/81	196	4	8. Camera Camera	I.R.S. 70019

DATE CHARTED	PEAK POS	WKS CHRT'D	ARTIST — Album Title	LABEL & NUMBER
			DIANE RENAY Philadelphian Renee Diane Kushner	
4/04/64	**54**	11	1. Navy Blue .... "Navy Blue"(6)	20th Century 3133
			RENE & ANGELA Rene Moore and Angela Winbush	
8/22/81	**100**	8	1. Wall To Wall	Capitol 12161
			RENE & RENE Rene Ornelas & Rene Herrera	
1/11/69	**129**	9	1. Lo Mucho Que Te Quiero	White Whale 7119
			REO SPEEDWAGON Champaign, Illinois rock quintet led by Kevin Cronin (vocals-#4 on) & Gary Richrath (guitar)	
1/12/74	**171**	8	● 1. Ridin' The Storm Out	Epic 32378
11/16/74	**98**	14	2. Lost In A Dream	Epic 32948
8/02/75	**74**	10	3. This Time We Mean It .... Mike Murphy, lead singer on above albums	Epic 33338
6/19/76	**159**	5	4. R.E.O.	Epic 34143
3/19/77	**72**	50	▲ 5. REO Speedwagon Live/You Get What You Play For .... [L]	Epic 34494 [2]
4/22/78	**29**	48	▲ 6. You can Tune a piano, but you can't Tuna fish	Epic 35082
8/11/79	**33**	23	● 7. Nine Lives	Epic 35988
4/19/80	**55**	34	● 8. A Decade Of Rock And Roll 1970 To 1980 .... [K]	Epic 36444 [2]
12/13/80	**1(15)**	101	▲ 9. **Hi Infidelity** .... "Keep On Loving You"(1)/"Take It On The Run"(5)	Epic 36844
7/10/82	**7**	24	▲ 10. **Good Trouble** .... "Keep The Fire Burnin'"(7)	Epic 38100
11/24/84	**7**	20+	▲ 11. **Wheels are turnin'** .... "Can't Fight This Feeling"(1)	Epic 39593
			RETURN TO FOREVER jazz/rock band: Chick Corea (keyboards), Stanley Clarke (bass), Lenny White (drums), Al Di Meola (guitar)	
12/08/73	**124**	12	1. Hymn Of The Seventh Galaxy .... [I]	Polydor 5536
9/28/74	**32**	23	2. Where Have I Known You Before .... [I]	Polydor 6509
3/15/75	**39**	13	3. No Mystery .... [I]	Polydor 6512
4/03/76	**35**	15	4. Romantic Warrior .... [I]	Columbia 34076
4/02/77	**38**	17	5. Musicmagic .... [I]	Columbia 34682
3/03/79	**155**	4	6. Return To Forever Live .... [L] recorded May, 1977	Columbia 35281
			REVERBERI Italian	
2/21/76	**169**	7	1. Reverberi & Schumann, Chopin, Liszt ..... [I] contemporary stylings of above named classical composers	Pausa 7003
			PAUL REVERE & THE RAIDERS Portland, Oregon pop/rock quintet led by Paul Revere (organ) & Mark Lindsay (vocals)	
7/03/65	**71**	45	1. Here They Come!	Columbia 9107
2/05/66	**5**	43	● 2. **Just Like Us!**	Columbia 9251
6/11/66	**9**	43	● 3. **Midnight Ride** .... "Kicks"(4)	Columbia 9308
12/31/66	**9**	33	● 4. The Spirit Of '67 .... "Hungry"(6)/"Good Thing"(4)	Columbia 9395
5/13/67	**15**	47	● 5. Greatest Hits .... [G]	Columbia 9462
9/02/67	**25**	21	6. Revolution! .... "Him or Me-What's It Gonna Be?"(5) Freddy Weller joins group as lead guitarist	Columbia 9521
3/02/68	**61**	23	7. Goin' To Memphis	Columbia 9605
9/14/68	**122**	14	8. Something Happening	Columbia 9665

DATE CHARTED	PEAK POS	WKS CHRT'D	ARTIST — Album Title	LABEL & NUMBER
4/05/69	**51**	19	9. Hard 'N' Heavy (With Marshmallow)	Columbia 9753
8/23/69	**48**	12	10. Alias Pink Puzz	Columbia 9905
11/08/69	**166**	4	11. Two All-Time Great Selling LP's .... [R] reissue of albums #4 & #6 above	Columbia 12 [2]
			RAIDERS:	
4/11/70	**154**	9	12. Collage	Columbia 9964
6/19/71	**19**	20	13. Indian Reservation .... "Indian Reservation"(1)	Columbia 30768
7/08/72	**143**	8	14. All-Time Greatest Hits .... [G]	Columbia 31464 [2]

DEBBIE REYNOLDS
movie actress - also see Aerobics section

DATE CHARTED	PEAK POS	WKS CHRT'D	ARTIST — Album Title	LABEL & NUMBER
4/30/66	**23**	25	1. The Singing Nun .... [S] film is a fictionalized story about Soeur Sourire	MGM 7

ROBERT RHEIMS

DATE CHARTED	PEAK POS	WKS CHRT'D	ARTIST — Album Title	LABEL & NUMBER
1/05/59	**25**	1	1. Merry Christmas in Carols .... [X-I]	Rheims 6006
1/04/60	**39**	1	2. We Wish You A Merry Christmas .... [X]	Rheims 6008

RHINOCEROS
Los Angeles-based rock group - John Finley, lead singer

DATE CHARTED	PEAK POS	WKS CHRT'D	ARTIST — Album Title	LABEL & NUMBER
12/28/68	**115**	22	1. Rhinoceros .... "Apricot Brandy"	Elektra 74030
9/27/69	**105**	9	2. Satin Chickens	Elektra 74056
7/11/70	**178**	6	3. Better Times Are Coming	Elektra 74075

EMITT RHODES
lead singer of Merry-Go-Round

DATE CHARTED	PEAK POS	WKS CHRT'D	ARTIST — Album Title	LABEL & NUMBER
12/12/70	**29**	20	1. Emitt Rhodes .... "Fresh As A Daisy"	Dunhill 50089
4/17/71	**194**	1	2. The American Dream .... [E] recorded 1967-68	A&M 4254
11/27/71	**182**	4	3. Mirror .... Emitt plays all instruments on albums 1 & 3	Dunhill 50111

RHYTHM HERITAGE
a disco production by Steve Barri & Michael Omartian

DATE CHARTED	PEAK POS	WKS CHRT'D	ARTIST — Album Title	LABEL & NUMBER
3/06/76	**40**	17	1. Disco-Fied .... [I] "Theme From S.W.A.T."(1)	ABC 934
2/19/77	**138**	6	2. Last Night On Earth	ABC 987

BUDDY RICH
all-time great drummer - with Tommy Dorsey 1939-46

DATE CHARTED	PEAK POS	WKS CHRT'D	ARTIST — Album Title	LABEL & NUMBER
12/31/66	**91**	27	1. Swingin' New Big Band .... [I-L]	Pacific Jz. 20113
7/15/67	**97**	21	2. Big Swing Face .... [I-L]	Pacific Jz. 20117
11/30/68	**186**	6	3. Mercy, Mercy .... [I-L]	World Pac. 20133
9/13/69	**186**	3	4. Buddy & Soul .... [I-L]	World Pac. 20158
5/20/72	**180**	5	5. Rich In London .... [I-L]	RCA 4666

CHARLIE RICH
originally signed by Sam Phillips' Sun label as a rockabilly artist

DATE CHARTED	PEAK POS	WKS CHRT'D	ARTIST — Album Title	LABEL & NUMBER
5/19/73	**8**	105	● 1. **Behind Closed Doors** .... "The Most Beautiful Girl"(1)	Epic 32247
2/23/74	**36**	27	● 2. There Won't Be Anymore .... [E]	RCA 0433
3/23/74	**24**	31	● 3. Very Special Love Songs	Epic 32531
4/27/74	**89**	19	4. The Best Of Charlie Rich .... new recordings of early non-Epic hits	Epic 31933
10/19/74	**177**	4	5. Charlie Rich Sings the Songs of Hank Williams & Others .... [E-R] previously released as "Charlie Rich Sings Country & Western"	Hi 32084
10/26/74	**84**	15	6. She Called Me Baby .... [E]	RCA 0686
12/07/74	**25**	17	7. The Silver Fox	Epic 33250
6/21/75	**54**	20	8. Every Time You Touch Me (I Get High)	Epic 33455
6/21/75	**162**	4	9. Greatest Hits .... [E-K] includes 4 original Sun recordings "Lonely Weekends"('60)	RCA 0857

DATE CHARTED	PEAK POS	WKS CHRT'D	ARTIST — Album Title	LABEL & NUMBER
4/03/76	168	6	10. Silver Linings .... *gospel songs*	Epic 33545
7/04/76	148	6	11. Greatest Hits .... [G]	Epic 34240
10/29/77	180	3	12. Rollin' With The Flow	Epic 34891
			CLIFF RICHARD born Harry Webb in India on 10/14/40 - Britain's most popular solo vocalist	
4/18/64	115	7	1. It's All In The Game	Epic 26089
8/07/76	76	15	2. I'm Nearly Famous .... "Devil Woman"(6)	Rocket 2210
12/08/79	93	15	3. We Don't Talk Anymore .... "We Don't Talk Anymore"(7)	EMI America 17018
10/11/80	80	34	4. I'm No Hero .... "Dreaming"(10)	EMI America 17039
10/17/81	132	4	5. Wired For Sound	EMI America 17059
			LIONEL RICHIE singer/songwriter/producer - Commodores' lead singer ('74-'81)	
10/23/82	3	129+ ▲	1. **Lionel Richie** .... "Truly"(1)/"You Are"(4)/"My Love"(5)	Motown 6007
11/12/83	1(3)	74+ ▲	2. **Can't Slow Down** .... "All Night Long (All Night)"(1)/"Running With The Night"(7)/ "Hello"(1)/"Stuck On You"(3)/"Penny Lover"(8)	Motown 6059
			SVIATOSLAV RICHTER classical pianist from Russia	
12/12/60	5	26	1. **Brahms: Piano Concerto No. 2** .... [I] with the Chicago Symphony Orchestra; Erich Leinsdorf, conducting	RCA 2466
			DON RICKLES "Mr. Warmth" - master of insulting comedy	
6/15/68	54	29	1. Hello Dummy! .... [C]	Warner 1745
4/12/69	180	4	2. Don Rickles Speaks! .... [C]	Warner 1779
			NELSON RIDDLE & His Orchestra leading pop-jazz arranger/conductor since 1940	
5/27/57	20	1	1. Hey...Let Yourself Go! .... [I]	Capitol 814
2/17/58	20	1	2. C'mon...Get Happy! .... [I]	Capitol 893
10/20/62	48	9	3. Route 66 Theme and Other Great TV Themes .... [I]	Capitol 1771
			JOSHUA RIFKIN classical/jazz/ragtime pianist	
12/11/65	83	17	1. The Baroque Beatles Book .... [I] classical variations of Beatles' tunes - Rifkin conducts the Baroque Ensemble Of The Merseyside Kammermusikgesellschaft	Elektra 7306
6/22/74	75	15	2. Piano Rags By Scott Joplin, Volumes I & II .... [I]	Nonesuch 73026 [2]
12/14/74	126	5	3. Piano Rags By Scott Joplin, Volume III .... [I] music on above albums written by Joplin between 1899 & 1914	Nonesuch 71305
			RIGHTEOUS BROTHERS Southern California blue-eyed soul duo: Bill Medley & Bobby Hatfield	
1/02/65	11	21	1. Right Now! .... [E]	Moonglow 1001
1/16/65	14	20	2. Some Blue-Eyed Soul .... [E]	Moonglow 1002
1/23/65	4	67	3. **You've Lost That Lovin' Feelin'** .... "You've Lost That Lovin' Feelin'"(1)	Philles 4007
5/29/65	9	41	4. **Just Once In My Life...** .... "Just Once In My Life"(9)/"Unchained Melody"(4)	Philles 4008
6/19/65	39	20	5. This Is New! .... [E]	Moonglow 1003
12/25/65	16	26	6. Back To Back .... "Ebb Tide"(5)	Philles 4009
4/30/66	7	32	● 7. **Soul & Inspiration** .... "(You're My) Soul And Inspiration"(1)	Verve 5001

DATE CHARTED	PEAK POS	WKS CHRT'D	ARTIST — Album Title	LABEL & NUMBER
5/21/66	**130**	11	8. The Best Of The Righteous Brothers .... [E-K] all 4 Moonglow albums recorded from 1962-63	Moonglow 1004
9/03/66	**32**	20	9. Go Ahead And Cry	Verve 5004
4/08/67	**155**	15	10. Sayin' Somethin'	Verve 5010
9/16/67	**21**	50	● 11. Greatest Hits .... [G] Philles and Moonglow label hits	Verve 5020
10/28/67	**198**	2	12. Souled Out.	Verve 5031
12/14/68	**187**	2	13. One For The Road .... [L]	Verve 5058
4/05/69	**126**	5	14. Greatest Hits, Vol. 2 .... [G] Verve, Philles and Moonglow label hits	Verve 5071
8/31/74	**27**	18	15. Give It To The People .... "Rock And Roll Heaven"(3)	Haven 9201

JEANNIE C. RILEY
born on 10/19/45 in Anson, Texas

10/12/68	**12**	27	● 1. Harper Valley P.T.A. .... all songs about characters mentioned in the title song "Harper Valley P.T.A."(1)	Plantation 1
3/15/69	**187**	5	2. Yearbooks and Yesterdays	Plantation 2
9/13/69	**142**	7	3. Things Go Better With Love	Plantation 3

RINGS
rock quartet from Boston

2/21/81	**164**	6	1. The Rings	MCA 5165

MIGUEL RIOS
native of Granada, Spain

8/22/70	**140**	4	1. A Song Of Joy .... orchestra directed by Waldo de Los Rios	A&M 4267

WALDO DE LOS RIOS
died on 3/28/77

6/05/71	**53**	16	1. Sinfonias .... [I] contemporary stylings of classical symphonies	United Art. 6802

RIOT
New York heavy-metal rock quintet - Guy Speranza, lead singer

9/12/81	**99**	11	1. Fire Down Under	Elektra 546
1/14/84	**175**	6	2. Born In America	Quality 1008

RIP CHORDS
Southern California quartet

2/22/64	**56**	17	1. Hey Little Cobra and other Hot Rod Hits ...... "Hey Little Cobra"(4)	Columbia 8951

MINNIE RIPERTON
lead singer of Rotary Connection - Minnie died on 7/12/79 (30)

8/17/74	**4**	47	● 1. Perfect Angel .... "Lovin' You"(1)	Epic 32561
11/16/74	**160**	4	2. Come To My Garden .... [E] recorded in 1969	Janus 7011
5/31/75	**18**	23	3. Adventures In Paradise	Epic 33454
3/19/77	**71**	10	'4. Stay In Love	Epic 34191
5/19/79	**29**	27	5. Minnie	Capitol 11936
9/06/80	**35**	15	6. Love Lives Forever .... recordings from 1978 with new accompaniment	Capitol 12097

CYRIL RITCHARD
British actor

1/09/61	**19**	3	1. Alice In Wonderland: The Mad Tea Party/The Lobster Quandrille .... [T] Cyril reads (and sings) selections from the classic story	Riverside 1406

RITCHIE FAMILY
female disco trio produced by Jacques Morali

10/04/75	**53**	12	1. Brazil	20th Century 498
7/24/76	**30**	25	2. Arabian Nights	Marlin 2201
2/12/77	**100**	10	3. Life Is Music	Marlin 2203

DATE CHARTED	PEAK POS	WKS CHRT'D	ARTIST — Album Title	LABEL & NUMBER
7/30/77	**164**	12	4. African Queens	Marlin 2206
9/02/78	**148**	6	5. American Generation	Marlin 2215

LEE RITENOUR
jazz-fusion guitar virtuoso

6/04/77	**178**	5	1. Captain Fingers .... [I]	Epic 34426
6/24/78	**121**	7	2. The Captain's Journey .... [I]	Elektra 136
6/16/79	**136**	6	3. Feel The Night .... [I]	Elektra 192
5/09/81	**26**	23	4. "Rit" "Is It You"	Elektra 331
4/17/82	**163**	6	5. Rio .... [I]	Musician 60024
12/04/82	**99**	14	6. Rit/2	Elektra 60186
6/23/84	**145**	8	7. Banded Together	Elektra 60358

JOAN RIVERS
popular comedienne

4/23/83	**22**	21	1. What Becomes A Semi-Legend Most? ...... [C]	Geffen 4007

JOHNNY RIVERS
born John Ramistella on 11/7/42 in New York City

6/20/64	**12**	45	1. Johnny Rivers At The Whisky a Go Go .... [L] "Memphis"(2)	Imperial 12264
10/17/64	**38**	23	2. Here We a Go Go Again! .... [L]	Imperial 12274
2/20/65	**42**	14	3. Johnny Rivers In Action! .... "Mountain Of Love"(9)	Imperial 12280
6/26/65	**21**	19	4. Meanwhile Back At The Whisky a Go Go.. [L] "Seventh Son"(7)	Imperial 12284
9/25/65	**91**	18	5. Johnny Rivers Rocks The Folk	Imperial 12293
4/16/66	**52**	21	6. "...and I know you wanna dance" .... [L] "Secret Agent Man"(3)	Imperial 12307
9/24/66	**29**	36	● 7. Johnny Rivers' Golden Hits .... [G]	Imperial 12324
12/17/66	**33**	46	8. Changes .... "Poor Side Of Town"(1)	Imperial 12334
6/24/67	**14**	21	9. Rewind .... "Baby I Need Your Lovin'"(3)/"The Tracks Of My Tears"(10)	Imperial 12341
6/29/68	**5**	41	● 10. **Realization** .... "Summer Rain"	Imperial 12372
6/14/69	**26**	25	● 11. A Touch Of Gold .... [G]	Imperial 12427
8/08/70	**100**	9	12. Slim Slo Slider	Imperial 16001
9/11/71	**148**	4	13. Home Grown	United Art. 5532
11/04/72	**78**	20	14. L.A. Reggae .... "Rockin' Pneumonia-Boogie Woogie Flu"(6)	United Art. 5650
9/20/75	**147**	6	15. New Lovers and Old Friends	Epic 33681
1/14/78	**142**	8	16. Outside Help .... "Swayin' To The Music (Slow Dancin')"(10)	Big Tree 76004

RIVIERAS
rock sextet from Indiana - Bill Dobslaw, lead singer

6/13/64	**115**	5	1. Let's Have A Party .... "California Sun"(5)	U.S.A. 102

ROAD

1/31/70	**199**	2	1. The Road	Kama Sutra 2012

MARTY ROBBINS
born in Glendale, Arizona on 9/26/25, and died on 12/8/82 (57) - Marty's had hits on the Country charts every year since 1956

12/28/59	**6**	57	● 1. **Gunfighter Ballads and Trail Songs** .... "El Paso"(1)	Columbia 1349
1/09/61	**21**	2	2. More Gunfighter Ballads and Trail Songs	Columbia 1481
11/03/62	**35**	22	3. Devil Woman	Columbia 1918
12/14/68	**160**	7	4. I Walk Alone	Columbia 9725
7/19/69	**194**	4	5. It's A Sin	Columbia 9811
5/23/70	**117**	16	6. My Woman, My Woman, My Wife	Columbia 9978

DATE CHARTED	PEAK POS	WKS CHRT'D	ARTIST — Album Title	LABEL & NUMBER
5/08/71	143	10	7. Marty Robbins' Greatest Hits, Vol. III .... [G]	Columbia 30571
9/18/71	175	6	8. Today	Columbia 30816
1/22/83	170	9	9. Biggest Hits .... [G]	Columbia 38309
			except for "El Paso" all hits are from 1966-1981	

ROCKIE ROBBINS
6/07/80	71	16	1. You And Me	A&M 4805
9/12/81	147	6	2. I Believe In Love	A&M 4869

ROBBS
Milwaukee rock quartet - Dee Robb, leader
1/13/68	200	1	1. The Robbs	Mercury 61130

ROBERTINO
Robertino Loreti - 15-year-old from Italy
12/01/62	96	6	1. The Young Italian Singing Sensation .... [F]	Kapp 3293

FREDDY ROBINSON
guitarst for Little Walter's Band and for Howling Wolf
9/19/70	133	7	1. The Coming Atlantis .... [I]	Pacific Jz. 20162

SMOKEY ROBINSON
black music's all-time great singer/songwriter/producer - currently vice-president of Motown Records - also see Miracles
7/14/73	70	19	1. Smokey	Tamla 328
4/13/74	99	17	2. Pure Smokey	Tamla 331
4/19/75	36	42	3. A Quiet Storm	Tamla 337
3/06/76	57	15	4. Smokey's Family Robinson	Tamla 341
2/19/77	47	14	5. Deep In My Soul	Tamla 350
4/15/78	75	19	6. Love Breeze	Tamla 359
1/20/79	165	6	7. Smokin' .... [L]	Tamla 363 [2]
6/30/79	17	47	8. Where There's Smoke.. "Cruisin'"(4)	Tamla 366
3/15/80	14	21	9. Warm Thoughts	Tamla 367
3/14/81	● 10	28	10. Being With You "Being With You"(2)	Tamla 375
2/20/82	33	17	11. Yes It's You Lady	Tamla 6001
1/29/83	50	17	12. Touch The Sky	Tamla 6030
9/03/83	124	7	13. Blame It On Love & All The Great Hits .... [G]	Tamla 6064
6/30/84	141	11	14. Essar	Tamla 6098

TOM ROBINSON BAND
British rock band led by political/gay rights activist, Robinson
7/15/78	144	8	1. Power In The Darkness	Harvest 11778 [2]
5/12/79	163	7	2. TRB Two .... produced by Todd Rundgren	Harvest 11930

VICKI SUE ROBINSON
performed on Broadway in "Hair" & "Jesus Christ Superstar"
4/10/76	49	39	1. Never Gonna Let You Go .... "Turn The Beat Around"(10)	RCA 1256
10/23/76	45	16	2. Vicki Sue Robinson	RCA 1829
2/11/78	110	9	3. Half And Half	RCA 2294

WANDA ROBINSON
10/16/71	186	13	1. Black Ivory .... [T] Wanda recites her poems to a musical background	Perception 18

ROCHES
sisters Maggie, Suzzy & Terre Roche
6/16/79	58	11	1. The Roches	Warner 3298
11/22/80	130	7	2. Nurds	Warner 3475
11/13/82	183	3	3. Keep On Doing .... Robert Fripp produced albums 1 & 3	Warner 23735

DATE CHARTED	PEAK POS	WKS CHRT'D	ARTIST — Album Title	LABEL & NUMBER
			ROCKETS rock band from Detroit led by David Gilbert (vocals) & Jim McCarty (guitar)	
4/14/79	**56**	26	1. Rockets	RSO 3047
2/02/80	**53**	15	2. No Ballads	RSO 3071
8/08/81	**165**	5	3. Back Talk	Elektra 351
			ROCKIN' REBELS originally known as the Hot-Toddys and then as the Rebels	
3/23/63	**53**	19	1. Wild Weekend .... [I] "Wild Weekend"(8)/"Rockin' Crickets"('59)	Swan 509
			ROCKPILE British: Dave Edmunds, Nick Lowe, Billy Bremner, Terry Williams	
11/15/80	**27**	19	1. Seconds Of Pleasure .... includes a 7" EP of Edmunds & Lowe singing 4 Everly Brother's tunes	Columbia 36886
			ROCKWELL Motown chairman Berry Gordy's son, Kennedy Gordy	
2/11/84	**15**	30	● 1. Somebody's Watching Me .... "Somebody's Watching Me"(2)	Motown 6052
2/23/85	**120**	7+	2. Captured	Motown 6122
			JIMMIE RODGERS born on 9/18/33 in Camus, Washington	
12/16/57	**15**	3	1. Jimmie Rodgers .... "Honeycomb"(1)/"Kisses Sweeter Than Wine"(3)	Roulette 25020
7/30/66	**145**	4	2. It's Over	Dot 25717
1/06/68	**162**	4	3. Child Of Clay	A&M 4130
8/30/69	**183**	4	4. Windmills Of Your Mind	A&M 4187
			PAUL RODGERS British - lead singer of Free/Bad Company/The Firm	
11/26/83	**135**	10	1. Cut Loose	Atlantic 80121
			JOHNNY RODRIGUEZ Chicano country singer	
4/07/73	**156**	14	1. introducing Johnny Rodriguez	Mercury 61378
10/27/73	**174**	4	2. All I Ever Meant To Do Was Sing	Mercury 686
			TOMMY ROE born on 5/9/42 in Atlanta, Georgia	
11/10/62	**110**	3	1. Sheila .... "Sheila"(1)	ABC-Para. 432
11/05/66	**94**	13	2. Sweet Pea .... [K] "Everybody"(3-'63)/"Sweet Pea"(8)/"Hooray For Hazel"(6)	ABC-Para. 575
4/22/67	**159**	3	3. It's Now Winters Day	ABC 594
4/12/69	**25**	18	4. Dizzy .... "Dizzy"(1)	ABC 683
12/27/69	**21**	29	5. 12 In A Roe/A Collection of Tommy Roe's Greatest Hits .... [G] "Jam Up Jelly Tight"(8)	ABC 700
10/31/70	**134**	6	6. We Can Make Music	ABC 714
			ROGER Roger Troutman - leader of Zapp	
10/03/81	**26**	25	● 1. The Many Facets Of Roger	Warner 3594
6/02/84	**64**	14	2. The Saga Continues...	Warner 23975
			D.J. ROGERS	
9/18/76	**175**	5	1. On The Road Again	RCA 1697
			ERIC ROGERS & his Orchestra	
12/04/61	**37**	8	1. The Percussive Twenties .... [I]	London P. 4 44006
11/12/66	**114**	3	2. Vaudeville! .... [L] re-creation of a vaudeville show, complete with a Master of Ceremonies	London P. 4 44083

DATE CHARTED	PEAK POS	WKS CHRT'D		ARTIST — Album Title	LABEL & NUMBER
				KENNY ROGERS born on 8/21/41 in Houston, Texas	
5/07/77	**30**	25	●	1. Kenny Rogers .... "Lucille"(5)	United Art. 689
8/20/77	**39**	21	●	2. Daytime Friends	United Art. 754
2/04/78	**33**	103	▲	3. Ten Years Of Gold .... [G] side 1: new versions of his First Edition hits	United Art. 835
7/29/78	**53**	12	●	4. Love Or Something Like It	United Art. 903
12/16/78	**12**	112	▲	5. The Gambler .... "She Believes In Me"(5)	United Art. 934
4/14/79	**82**	23	●	6. Classics .... KENNY ROGERS & DOTTIE WEST	United Art. 946
9/29/79	**5**	53	▲	7. **Kenny** .... "You Decorated My Life"(7)/"Coward Of The County"(3)	United Art. 979
1/05/80	**186**	3		8. Every Time Two Fools Collide .... KENNY ROGERS & DOTTIE WEST	United Art. 864
4/12/80	**12**	34	▲	9. Gideon .... "Don't Fall In Love With A Dreamer"(4-with Kim Carnes)	United Art. 1035
10/18/80	**1(2)**	181	▲	10. **Kenny Rogers' Greatest Hits** .... [G] "Lady"(1)	Liberty 1072
7/11/81	**6**	60	▲	11. **Share Your Love** .... album produced by Lionel Richie "I Don't Need You"(3)	Liberty 1108
11/21/81	**34**	9	▲	12. Christmas .... [X]	Liberty 51115
7/24/82	**34**	24	●	13. Love Will Turn You Around	Liberty 51124
12/25/82	**149**	4	▲	14. Christmas .... [X-R] made top 10 on Billboard's special Xmas charts (1983-84)	Liberty 51115
3/12/83	**18**	27	●	15. We've Got Tonight .... "We've Got Tonight"(6-with Sheena Easton)	Liberty 51143
9/24/83	**6**	38	▲	16. **Eyes That See In The Dark** .... RCA 4697 album produced by Barry Gibb "Islands In The Stream"(1-with Dolly Parton)	RCA 4697
11/12/83	**22**	30	▲	17. Twenty Greatest Hits .... [G]	Liberty 51152
5/05/84	**85**	11		18. Duets .... [K] with Dottie West (8 of 10 cuts), Kim Carnes & Sheena Easton	Liberty 51154
9/22/84	**31**	29+	▲	19. What About Me?	RCA 5043
12/08/84	**31**	8	▲	20. Once Upon A Christmas .... [X] KENNY ROGERS & DOLLY PARTON made top 10 on Billboard's special Christmas charts (1984)	RCA 15307
				KENNY ROGERS & THE FIRST EDITION Kenny and 3 other members were with the New Christy Minstrels	
				THE FIRST EDITION:	
1/13/68	**118**	15		1. The First Edition .... "Just Dropped In (To See What Condition My Condition Was In)"(5)	Reprise 6276
3/22/69	**164**	4		2. The First Edition 69	Reprise 6328
				KENNY ROGERS & THE FIRST EDITION:	
10/11/69	**48**	18		3. Ruby, Don't Take Your Love To Town .... "Ruby, Don't Take Your Love To Town"(6)	Reprise 6352
4/18/70	**26**	24		4. Something's Burning	Reprise 6385
10/31/70	**61**	16		5. Tell It All Brother	Reprise 6412
2/20/71	**57**	16	●	6. Greatest Hits .... [G]	Reprise 6437
9/25/71	**155**	3		7. Transition	Reprise 2039
2/05/72	**118**	14		8. The Ballad Of Calico .... inspired by the 1889 mining town of Calico, California	Reprise 6476 [2]
				ROLLING STONES English: Mick Jagger (vocals), Keith Richards (guitar), Bill Wyman (bass), Charlie Watts (drums), Brian Jones (guitar - died 7/3/69-27), replaced by Mick Taylor, who was replaced in 1975 by Ron Wood	
6/27/64	**11**	35		1. England's Newest Hit Makers/The Rolling Stones .... "Not Fade Away"/"Tell Me"	London 375
11/14/64	**3**	38		2. **12 x 5** .... "Time Is On My Side"(6)/"It's All Over Now"	London 402

DATE CHARTED	PEAK POS	WKS CHRT'D	ARTIST — Album Title	LABEL & NUMBER
3/20/65	5	53	3. **The Rolling Stones, Now!** .... "Heart Of Stone"	London 420
8/07/65	1(3)	65	● 4. **Out Of Our Heads** .... "The Last Time"(9)/"(I Can't Get No) Satisfaction"(1)	London 429
12/11/65	4	33	● 5. **December's Children (and everybody's)** ...... "Get Off Of My Cloud"(1)/"As Tears Go By"(6)	London 451
4/16/66	3	99	● 6. **Big Hits (High Tide And Green Grass)** ... [G] "19th Nervous Breakdown"(2)	London 1
7/09/66	2(2)	50	● 7. **Aftermath** .... "Paint It, Black"(1)	London 476
12/17/66	6	48	● 8. **got Live if you want it!** .... [L] recorded at the Royal Albert Hall, London	London 493
2/18/67	2(4)	47	● 9. **Between The Buttons** .... "Ruby Tuesday"(1)/"Let's Spend The Night Together"	London 499
7/22/67	3	35	● 10. **Flowers** .... [G] "Mothers Little Helper"(8)/ "Have You Seen Your Mother, Baby, Standing In The Shadow?"(9)	London 509
12/23/67	2(6)	30	● 11. **Their Satanic Majesties Request**	London 2
12/14/68	5	32	● 12. **Beggars Banquet**	London 539
9/13/69	2(2)	32	● 13. **Through The Past, Darkly (Big Hits Vol. 2)** .... [G] "Jumpin' Jack Flash"(3)/"Honky Tonk Women"(1)	London 3
12/06/69	3	44	● 14. **Let It Bleed** .... Brian Jones' last appearance/Mick Taylor's first with band	London 4
10/17/70	6	23	● 15. **'Get Yer Ya-Ya's Out!'** .... [L] recorded at New York's Madison Square Garden, November, 1969	London 5
5/15/71	1(4)	62	● 16. **Sticky Fingers** .... "Brown Sugar"(1)	Rolling S. 59100
1/08/72	4	233	● 17. **Hot Rocks 1964-1971** .... [G]	London 606/7 [2]
6/10/72	1(4)	43	● 18. **Exile On Main St.** .... "Tumbling Dice"(7)	Rolling S. 2900 [2]
12/30/72	9	29	● 19. **More Hot Rocks (big hits & fazed cookies)** .... [G]	London 626/7 [2]
9/29/73	1(4)	37	● 20. **Goats Head Soup** .... "Angie"(1)	Rolling S. 59101
11/02/74	1(1)	20	● 21. **It's Only Rock 'N Roll**	Rolling S. 79101
6/21/75	6	17	● 22. **Made In The Shade** .... [G]	Rolling S. 79102
6/21/75	8	13	23. **Metamorphosis** .... [K]	Abkco 1
5/08/76	1(4)	24	▲ 24. **Black And Blue** .... Ron Wood's first appearance with band "Fool To Cry"(10)	Rolling S. 79104
10/08/77	5	17	● 25. **Love You Live** .... [L]	Rolling S. 9001 [2]
6/24/78	1(2)	82	▲ 26. **Some Girls** .... "Miss You"(1)/"Beast Of Burden"(8)	Rolling S. 39108
7/19/80	1(7)	51	▲ 27. **Emotional Rescue** .... "Emotional Rescue"(3)	Rolling S. 16015
4/04/81	15	12	● 28. Sucking In The Seventies .... [G]	Rolling S. 16028
9/12/81	1(9)	58	▲ 29. **Tattoo You** .... "Start Me Up"(2)	Rolling S. 16052
6/26/82	5	23	● 30. **"Still Life" (American Concert 1981)** .... [L]	Rolling S. 39113
11/26/83	4	23	▲ 31. **Undercover** .... "Undercover Of The Night"(9)	Rolling S. 90120
7/28/84	86	11	32. Rewind (1971-1984) .... [G]	Rolling S. 90176
			ROMAN HOLLIDAY 7-man jive/rock band from London, England	
9/03/83	142	11	1. Roman Holliday .... [M] 4 of the 5 cuts are also included in the album below	Jive 8086
10/22/83	116	6	2. Cookin' On The Roof	Jive 8101
			ROMANTICS rock quartet from Detroit	
2/02/80	61	15	1. The Romantics	Nemperor 36273
12/06/80	176	7	2. National Breakout	Nemperor 36881

DATE CHARTED	PEAK POS	WKS CHRT'D		ARTIST — Album Title	LABEL & NUMBER
11/14/81	**182**	2		3. Strictly Personal	Nemperor 37435
10/22/83	**14**	36	●	4. In Heat	Nemperor 38880
				"Talking In Your Sleep"(3)	

ROMEO VOID
San Francisco new-wave quintet - Debora Iyall, lead singer

3/06/82	**147**	6		1. Never Say Never .... [M]	415 Records 0007
				produced by the Cars' Ric Ocasek	
9/04/82	**119**	13		2. Benefactor	Columbia 38182
8/25/84	**68**	19		3. Instincts	Columbia 39155

RONETTES
New York trio: Veronica Bennett (Ronnie Spector) and sister Estelle Bennett, with cousin Nedra Talley

12/26/64	**96**	8		1. ...presenting the fabulous Ronettes featuring Veronica	Philles 4006
				"Be My Baby"(2)	

RONNY & THE DAYTONAS
Ronny is Bucky Wilkin

12/05/64	**122**	6		1. G.T.O.	Mala 4001
				"G.T.O."(4)	

MICK RONSON
English - guitarist with David Bowie and Mott The Hoople

4/06/74	**156**	5		1. Slaughter On 10th Avenue	RCA 0353
2/08/75	**103**	9		2. Play Don't Worry	RCA 0681

LINDA RONSTADT
born on 7/15/46 in Tucson, Arizona

12/02/67	**100**	15		1. Evergreen, Vol. 2	Capitol 2763
				THE STONE PONEYS (with Bob Kimmel & Ken Edwards) "Different Drum"	
10/24/70	**103**	10		2. Silk Purse	Capitol 407
				"Long Long Time"	
2/12/72	**163**	10		3. Linda Ronstadt	Capitol 635
				backing by all 4 of the original Eagles	
10/20/73	**45**	56	●	4. Don't Cry Now	Asylum 5064
2/02/74	**92**	15		5. Different Drum .... [K]	Capitol 11269
				5 of 10 songs are with The Stone Poneys	
12/07/74	**1(1)**	51	●	6. **Heart Like A Wheel**	Capitol 11358
				"You're No Good"(1)/"When Will I Be Loved"(2)	
6/14/75	**172**	4		7. The Stone Poneys Featuring Linda Ronstadt .... [E-R]	Capitol 11383
				reissue of Linda's first album (released January, 1967)	
10/04/75	**4**	28	●	8. **Prisoner In Disguise**	Asylum 1045
				"Heat Wave"(5)	
8/28/76	**3**	36	▲	9. **Hasten Down The Wind**	Asylum 1072
				"That'll Be The Day"	
12/18/76	**6**	80	▲	10. **Greatest Hits** .... [G]	Asylum 1092
				includes her hits on Capitol	
5/21/77	**46**	9	●	11. A Retrospective .... [K]	Capitol 11629 [2]
9/24/77	**1(5)**	47	▲	12. **Simple Dreams**	Asylum 104
				"Blue Bayou"(3)/"It's So Easy"(5)	
10/07/78	**1(1)**	32	▲	13. **Living In The USA**	Asylum 155
				"Ooh Baby Baby"(7)	
3/15/80	**3**	36	▲	14. **Mad Love**	Asylum 510
				"How Do I Make You"(10)/"Hurt So Bad"(8)	
11/08/80	**26**	21	●	15. Greatest Hits, Volume Two .... [G]	Asylum 516
10/16/82	**31**	28	●	16. Get Closer	Asylum 60185
10/01/83	**3**	80+	▲	17. **What's New**	Asylum 60260
12/08/84	**13**	18+	▲	18. Lush Life	Asylum 60387
				above 2 arranged and conducted by Nelson Riddle	

ROOFTOP SINGERS
Erik Darling, leader (founder of the Tarriers and a member of the Weavers)

2/16/63	**15**	20	1. Walk Right In! .... "Walk Right In"(1)	Vanguard 9123

EDMUNDO ROS & His Orchestra
native of Caracas, Venezuela

5/25/59	**28**	2	1. Hollywood Cha Cha Cha .... [I]	London 152
12/04/61	**41**	4	2. Bongos From The South .... [I]	London P. 4 44003
9/22/62	**31**	6	3. Dance Again .... [I]	London P. 4 44015

ROSE GARDEN
West Virginia quintet - Diana Di Rose, lead singer

3/16/68	**176**	2	1. The Rose Garden .... "Next Plane To London"	Atco 225

ROSE ROYCE
former backing band for the Temptations and Undisputed Truth - Gwen Dickey, lead singer (1-4)

10/09/76	**14**	40	● 1. Car Wash .... [S] "Car Wash"(1)/"I Wanna Get Next To You"(10)	MCA 6000 [2]
8/27/77	**9**	33	▲ 2. **Rose Royce II/In Full Bloom**	Whitfield 3074
9/09/78	**28**	24	● 3. Rose Royce III/Strikes Again!	Whitfield 3227
9/08/79	**74**	8	4. Rose Royce IV/Rainbow Connection	Whitfield 3387
1/24/81	**160**	7	5. Golden Touch	Whitfield 3512

ROSE TATTOO
Australian heavy-metal rock quintet - Angry Anderson, leader

11/29/80	**197**	3	1. Rock 'N' Roll Outlaw	Mirage 19280

BIFF ROSE
singer/songwriter/pianist

2/08/69	**75**	14	1. The Thorn In Mrs. Rose's Side	Tetragramm. 103
7/12/69	**181**	7	2. Children Of Light	Tetragramm. 116

DAVID ROSE & His Orchestra
born in London, England - orchestra leader/composer/arranger for films and TV - also see Andre Previn

6/30/62	**3**	50	● 1. **The Stripper and other fun Songs for the family** .... [I] "The Stripper"(1)	MGM 4062

JIMMY ROSELLI
Italian singer

6/26/65	**96**	11	1. Life & Love Italian Style .... [F]	United Art. 6429
9/11/65	**145**	2	2. The Great Ones!	United Art. 6438
11/18/67	**191**	3	3. There Must Be A Way	United Art. 6611
6/21/69	**184**	3	4. Core Spezzato .... [F]	United Art. 6698

DIANA ROSS
born on 3/26/44 in Detroit - also see Supremes

7/11/70	**19**	28	1. Diana Ross .... "Ain't No Mountain High Enough"(1)	Motown 711
11/21/70	**42**	16	2. Everything Is Everything	Motown 724
4/24/71	**46**	15	3. Diana! .... [TV] with guests: Jackson 5, Bill Cosby & Danny Thomas	Motown 719
8/07/71	**56**	17	4. Surrender	Motown 723
11/25/72	**1(2)**	54	5. **Lady Sings The Blues** .... [S] Diana portrayed Billie Holiday in the film	Motown 758 [2]
7/14/73	**5**	28	6. **Touch Me In The Morning** .... "Touch Me In The Morning"(1)	Motown 772
11/17/73	**26**	47	7. Diana & Marvin .... DIANA ROSS & MARVIN GAYE	Motown 803
12/29/73	**52**	17	8. Last Time I Saw Him	Motown 812
6/15/74	**64**	17	9. Diana Ross Live At Caesars Palace .... [L]	Motown 801

DATE CHARTED	PEAK POS	WKS CHRT'D	ARTIST — Album Title	LABEL & NUMBER
11/08/75	19	26	10. Mahogany .... [S-I] Diana sings only the title song - instrumentals conducted by Lee Holdridge "Theme From Mahogany (Do You Know Where You're Going To)"(1)	Motown 858
3/06/76	5	32	11. **Diana Ross** .... "Love Hangover"(1) - also includes "Theme From Mahogany"	Motown 861
8/07/76	13	23	12. Diana Ross' Greatest Hits .... [G]	Motown 869
2/12/77	29	14	13. An Evening With Diana Ross .... [L] recorded at the Ahmanson Theatre, Los Angeles	Motown 877 [2]
10/08/77	18	19	14. Baby It's Me	Motown 890
10/21/78	49	17	15. Ross	Motown 907
6/16/79	14	37	● 16. The Boss	Motown 923
6/14/80	2(2)	52	▲ 17. **Diana** .... "Upside Down"(1)/"I'm Coming Out"(5)	Motown 936
3/14/81	32	14	18. To Love Again .... [K] "It's My Turn"(9)	Motown 951
10/24/81	37	32	● 19. All The Great Hits .... [G] includes medleys with the Supremes "Endless Love"(1-with Lionel Richie)	Motown 960 [2]
11/07/81	15	33	▲ 20. Why Do Fools Fall In Love .... "Why Do Fools Fall In Love"(7)/"Mirror, Mirror"(8)	RCA 4153
10/23/82	27	24	● 21. Silk Electric .... "Muscles"(10)	RCA 4384
6/11/83	63	12	22. Diana Ross Anthology .... [G]	Motown 6049 [2]
7/16/83	32	17	23. Ross	RCA 4677
9/29/84	26	28+	● 24. Swept Away .... "Missing You"	RCA 5009
			ROSSINGTON COLLINS BAND band formed by 4 surviving members of Lynyrd Skynyrd, including Gary Rossington & Allen Collins	
7/12/80	13	29	● 1. Anytime, Anyplace, Anywhere	MCA 5130
10/10/81	24	16	2. This Is The Way	MCA 5207
			ROTARY CONNECTION Canadian rock/R&B sextet - Minnie Riperton, lead singer	
3/16/68	37	31	1. Rotary Connection	Cadet Concept 312
10/19/68	176	5	2. Aladdin	Cadet Concept 317
			DAVID LEE ROTH lead singer of Van Halen	
2/23/85	15	7+	1. Crazy From The Heat .... ⌐ [M] "California Girls"(3)	Warner 25222
			ROUGH DIAMOND English rock quintet - David Byron (Uriah Heep), lead singer	
5/07/77	103	8	1. Rough Diamond	Island 9490
			DEMIS ROUSSOS Greek singer	
6/17/78	184	6	1. Demis Roussos	Mercury 3724
			ROUTERS rock instrumental quintet	
3/02/63	104	4	1. Let's Go! with The Routers .... [I]	Warner 1490
			ROVERS - see IRISH ROVERS	
			JOHN ROWLES native of New Zealand	
3/20/71	197	1	1. Cheryl Moana Marie	Kapp 3637
			ROXY MUSIC English art-rock band led by Bryan Ferry (vocals/keyboards)	
7/28/73	193	2	1. For Your Pleasure	Warner 2696
5/18/74	186	4	2. Stranded	Atco 7045
1/25/75	37	15	3. Country Life	Atco 106

DATE CHARTED	PEAK POS	WKS CHRT'D	ARTIST — Album Title	LABEL & NUMBER
11/29/75	50	20	4. Siren .... "Love Is The Drug"	Atco 127
8/07/76	81	7	5. Viva! Roxy Music .... [L]	Atco 139
3/31/79	23	16	6. Manifesto	Atco 114
6/28/80	35	19	7. Flesh + Blood	Atco 102
6/19/82	53	27	8. Avalon	Warner 23686
4/09/83	67	22	9. Musique/The High Road .... [M-L] recorded at the Apollo Theatre, Glasgow, Scotland	Warner 23808
1/21/84	183	6	10. The Atlantic Years 1973-1980 .... [K]	Atco 90122

ROYAL GUARDSMEN
Florida sextet led by Barry Winslow and Chris Nunley

2/11/67	44	22	1. Snoopy vs. The Red Baron .... "Snoopy Vs. The Red Baron"(2)/"Baby Let's Wait"	Laurie 2038
12/23/67	46	11	2. Snoopy And His Friends .... [N-X] side 1: 3 Snoopy songs, including "Snoopy's Christmas" made top 10 on Billboard's special Christmas charts (1967)	Laurie 2042
8/31/68	189	2	3. Snoopy For President .... albums 1 & 3 each feature only one Snoopy song	Laurie 2046

ROYAL PHILHARMONIC ORCHESTRA
British - Louis Clark, conductor (arranger for ELO) - also see Glen Campbell/Crusaders/Deep Purple

11/14/81	4	68	▲ 1. **Hooked On Classics** .... [I] "Hooked On Classics"(10)	RCA 4194
8/28/82	33	41	● 2. Hooked On Classics II (Can't Stop the Classics) .... [I]	RCA 4373
4/23/83	89	14	3. Hooked On Classics III (Journey Through the Classics) .... [I]	RCA 4588

ROYAL SCOTS DRAGOON GUARDS
The Pipes and Drums and Military Band of Scotland's armoured Regiment

6/24/72	34	15	1. Amazing Grace .... [I]	RCA 4744

BILLY JOE ROYAL
native of Atlanta, Georgia

9/18/65	96	7	1. Down In The Boondocks .... "Down In The Boondocks"(9)	Columbia 9203
1/03/70	100	9	2. Cherry Hill Park	Columbia 9974

RUBBER BAND
arranged and conducted by Michael Lloyd

8/02/69	135	6	1. Cream Songbook .... [I]	GRT 10000
9/06/69	116	8	2. Hendrix Songbook .... [I]	GRT 10007

RUBICON
Jerry Martini, leader (member of Sly & The Family Stone '66-'76)

3/25/78	147	7	1. Rubicon	20th Century 552

ARTHUR RUBINSTEIN
classical pianist, born in Lodz, Poland - died on 12/20/82 (95)

1/09/61	117	15	1. Rachmaninoff: Piano Concerto No. 2/ Liszt: Piano Concerto No. 1 .... [I]	RCA 2068
2/13/61	30	12	2. Heart of the Piano Concerto .... [I] favorite movements from 6 piano concertos	RCA 2495

RUBY & THE ROMANTICS
Akron, Ohio quintet featuring Ruby Nash

5/11/63	120	6	1. Our Day Will Come .... "Our Day Will Come"(1)	Kapp 3323

ED RUDY - see BEATLES

RUFFIN BROTHERS
Jimmy & David Ruffin

11/07/70	178	3	1. I Am My Brother's Keeper	Soul 728

DATE CHARTED	PEAK POS	WKS CHRT'D	ARTIST — Album Title	LABEL & NUMBER
			DAVID RUFFIN	
			lead singer of the Temptations from 1964-1968	
6/21/69	31	17	1. My Whole World Ended	Motown 685
			"My Whole World Ended (The Moment You Left Me)"(9)	
12/13/69	148	7	2. Feelin' Good	Motown 696
3/17/73	160	7	3. David Ruffin	Motown 762
11/15/75	31	27	4. Who I Am	Motown 849
			"Walk Away From Love"(9)	
6/12/76	51	12	5. Everything's Coming Up Love	Motown 866
			JIMMY RUFFIN	
5/13/67	133	11	1. Top Ten	Soul 704
			"What Becomes Of The Brokenhearted"(7)/	
			"I've Passed This Way Before"	
4/19/69	196	2	2. Ruff'N Ready	Soul 708
5/31/80	152	6	3. Sunrise	RSO 3078
			"Hold On To My Love"(10)	
			RUFUS	
			soul group formed in Chicago - Chaka Khan, lead singer (all albums except #7 & 9)	
8/04/73	175	6	1. Rufus	ABC 783
6/29/74	4	30	● 2. **Rags To Rufus**	ABC 809
			"Tell Me Something Good"(3)	
1/04/75	7	24	● 3. **Rufusized**	ABC 837
			"Once You Get Started"(10)	
12/06/75	7	32	● 4. **Rufus featuring Chaka Khan**	ABC 909
			"Sweet Thing"(5)	
2/05/77	12	25	▲ 5. Ask Rufus	ABC 975
2/11/78	14	26	● 6. Street Player	ABC 1049
2/10/79	81	9	7. Numbers	ABC 1098
11/17/79	14	26	● 8. Masterjam	MCA 5103
3/28/81	73	11	9. Party 'Til You're Broke	MCA 5159
10/31/81	98	14	10. Camouflage	MCA 5270
9/03/83	50	33	11. Live-Stompin' At The Savoy .... [L]	Warner 23679 [2]
			recorded at the Savoy Theatre, New York (February, 1982) side 4: newly-recorded studio cuts	
			RUMOUR	
			English pub-rock quintet led by Brinsley Schwarz - also see Graham Parker	
8/13/77	124	10	1. Max	Mercury 1174
8/04/79	160	3	2. Frogs Sprouts Clogs And Krauts	Arista 4235
			RUN-D.M.C.	
			rap duo: Joseph Simmons (Run) & Dayrll McDaniels (D.M.C.)	
6/23/84	53	42+	● 1. Run-D.M.C.	Profile 1202
2/23/85	52	7+	2. King Of Rock	Profile 1205
			RUNAWAYS	
			Los Angeles female hard-rock band - lead singers: Cherie Currie & Joan Jett	
8/21/76	194	2	1. The Runaways	Mercury 1090
2/05/77	172	4	2. Queens Of Noise	Mercury 1126
			TODD RUNDGREN	
			virtuoso musician, songwriter, producer, engineer - also see Nazz and Utopia	
1/09/71	185	6	1. Runt	Ampex 10105
			"We Gotta Get You A Woman"	
3/25/72	29	48	● 2. Something/Anything?	Bearsville 2066 [2]
			"Hello It's Me"(5)/"I Saw The Light"	
3/31/73	86	15	3. A Wizard/A True Star	Bearsville 2133
3/16/74	54	17	4. Todd	Bearsville 6952 [2]
6/14/75	86	7	5. Initiation	Bearsville 6957
5/15/76	54	15	6. Faithful	Bearsville 6963

DATE CHARTED	PEAK POS	WKS CHRT'D	ARTIST — Album Title	LABEL & NUMBER
5/06/78	**36**	26	7. Hermit Of Mink Hollow .... "Can We Still Be Friends"	Bearsville 6981
12/02/78	**75**	16	8. Back To The Bars .... [L]	Bearsville 6986 [2]
2/21/81	**48**	13	9. Healing	Bearsville 3522
1/22/83	**66**	13	10. The Ever Popular Tortured Artist Effect	Bearsville 23732

RUNNER
English rock quartet - Steve Gould, lead singer

6/23/79	**167**	4	1. Runner	Island 9536

RUSH
Candian power-rock trio: Geddy Lee (vocals/bass), Alex Lifeson (guitar), Neil Peart (drums)

9/21/74	**105**	13	1. Rush	Mercury 1011
3/15/75	**113**	8	2. Fly By Night	Mercury 1023
10/18/75	**148**	6	3. Caress Of Steel	Mercury 1046
4/10/76	**61**	34	▲ 4. 2112	Mercury 1079
10/02/76	**40**	23	▲ 5. All The World's A Stage .... [L]	Mercury 7508 [2]
9/24/77	**33**	17	● 6. A Farewell To Kings	Mercury 1184
4/15/78	**121**	6	7. Archives .... [R] reissue of albums 1,2 & 3	Mercury 9200 [3]
11/18/78	**47**	21	● 8. Hemispheres	Mercury 3743
2/02/80	**4**	36	▲ 9. **Permanent Waves**	Mercury 4001
3/07/81	**3**	68	▲ 10. **Moving Pictures** .... "Limelight"/"Tom Sawyer"	Mercury 4013
11/14/81	**10**	21	● 11. **Exit...Stage Left** .... [L]	Mercury 7001 [2]
10/02/82	**10**	33	▲ 12. **Signals** .... "New World Man"	Mercury 4063
5/05/84	**10**	27	▲ 13. **Grace Under Pressure**	Mercury 818476

MERRILEE RUSH & The Turnabouts
Seattle, Washington native

10/19/68	**196**	4	1. Angel Of The Morning .... "Angel Of The Morning"(7)	Bell 6020

TOM RUSH
eclectic singer from Portsmouth, New Hampshire

6/11/66	**122**	7	1. Take A Little Walk With Me	Elektra 7308
4/20/68	**68**	14	2. The Circle Game	Elektra 74018
3/14/70	**76**	16	3. Tom Rush	Columbia 9972
12/26/70	**110**	9	4. Wrong End Of The Rainbow	Columbia 30402
3/27/71	**198**	1	5. Classic Rush .... [K]	Elektra 74062
4/29/72	**128**	10	6. Merrimack County	Columbia 31306
10/19/74	**124**	9	7. Ladies Love Outlaws	Columbia 33054
2/07/76	**184**	3	8. The Best Of Tom Rush .... [K]	Columbia 33907

PATRICE RUSHEN
singer, composer, keyboardist from Los Angeles

4/16/77	**164**	4	1. Shout It Out	Prestige 10101
2/17/79	**98**	6	2. Patrice	Elektra 160
11/24/79	**39**	22	3. Pizzazz	Elektra 243
11/29/80	**71**	18	4. Posh	Elektra 302
5/01/82	**14**	28	5. Straight From The Heart .... "Forget Me Nots"	Elektra 60015
6/16/84	**40**	25	6. Now	Elektra 60360

BOBBY RUSSELL
songwriter of "Honey" and "Little Green Apples"

10/16/71	**183**	3	1. Saturday Morning Confusion	United Art. 5548

BRENDA RUSSELL
Canadian

9/22/79	**65**	20	1. Brenda Russell	Horizon 739
4/11/81	**107**	8	2. Love Life	A&M 4811

DATE CHARTED	PEAK POS	WKS CHRT'D	ARTIST — Album Title	LABEL & NUMBER
			LEON RUSSELL top multi-instrumentalist sessionman - also see Joe Cocker	
4/11/70	**60**	19	1. Leon Russell	Shelter 1001
5/29/71	**17**	29	● 2. Leon Russell & The Shelter People	Shelter 8903
12/04/71	**70**	20	3. Asylum Choir II [E] LEON RUSSELL & MARC BENNO recorded April, 1969	Shelter 8910
7/15/72	**2(4)**	35	● 4. **Carney** "Tight Rope"	Shelter 8911
7/07/73	**9**	26	● 5. **Leon Live** [L] recorded at the Long Beach Arena, Long Beach, California	Shelter 8917 [3]
9/22/73	**28**	15	6. Hank Wilson's Back, Vol. I an album of Country & Western songs	Shelter 8923
6/22/74	**34**	16	7. Stop All That Jazz	Shelter 2108
5/03/75	**30**	40	● 8. Will O' The Wisp "Lady Blue"	Shelter 2138
5/01/76	**34**	28	9. Wedding Album LEON & MARY RUSSELL (wife Mary McCreary)	Paradise 2943
10/23/76	**40**	16	● 10. Best Of Leon [G]	Shelter 52004
6/25/77	**142**	5	11. Make Love To The Music LEON & MARY RUSSELL	Paradise 3066
8/12/78	**115**	10	12. Americana	Paradise 3172
6/30/79	**25**	18	● 13. One For The Road WILLIE NELSON & LEON RUSSELL	Columbia 36064 [2]
4/04/81	**187**	2	14. The Live Album [L] Leon Russell & New Grass Revival (bluegrass band)	Paradise 3532
			RUSTIX	
11/15/69	**200**	2	1. Bedlam	Rare Earth 508
			MIKE RUTHERFORD bassist of Genesis	
4/05/80	**163**	11	1. Smallcreep's Day	Passport 9843
10/09/82	**145**	6	2. Acting Very Strange	Atlantic 80015
			RUTLES parody of the Beatles. starring Neil Innes (Bonzo Dog Band) & Eric Idle (Monty Python)	
3/25/78	**63**	9	1. The Rutles	Warner 3151
			BOBBY RYDELL born Robert Ridarelli on 4/26/42 in Philadelphia	
2/27/61	**12**	34	1. Bobby's Biggest Hits [G] "We Got Love"(6)/"Wild One"(2)/"Swingin' School"(5)/ "Volare"(4)	Cameo 1009
10/23/61	**56**	9	2. Rydell At The Copa [L]	Cameo 1011
12/18/61	**7**	30	3. **Bobby Rydell/Chubby Checker** "Jingle Bell Rock"	Cameo 1013
9/01/62	**88**	11	4. All The Hits	Cameo 1019
12/22/62	**61**	12	5. Bobby Rydell/Biggest Hits, Volume 2 [G] "The Cha-Cha-Cha"(10)	Cameo 1028
1/18/64	**67**	9	6. the Top Hits of 1963	Cameo 1070
3/07/64	**98**	4	7. Forget Him "Forget Him"(4)	Cameo 1080
			MITCH RYDER & The Detroit Wheels white soul singer from Detroit - real name William Levise. Jr. - also see Detroit	
3/05/66	**78**	7	1. Take A Ride "Jenny Take A Ride"(10)	New Voice 2000
8/06/66	**23**	34	2. Breakout...!!! "Devil With A Blue Dress On & Good Golly Miss Molly"(4)	New Voice 2002
4/08/67	**34**	16	3. Sock It To Me! "Sock It To Me-Baby!"(6)	New Voice 2003

DATE CHARTED	PEAK POS	WKS CHRT'D	ARTIST — Album Title	LABEL & NUMBER
10/14/67	**37**	26	4. All Mitch Ryder Hits! .... [G]	New Voice 2004
			MITCH RYDER:	
7/09/83	**120**	9	5. Never Kick A Sleeping Dog	Riva 7503
			produced by John Cougar	

SUE SAAD & THE NEXT

3/01/80	**131**	12	1. Sue Saad And The Next	Planet 4

SAD CAFE
Manchester, England pop-rock group - Paul Young, lead singer

1/27/79	**94**	14	1. Misplaced Ideals .... [K]	A&M 4737
			recordings from first two British releases	
9/15/79	**146**	5	2. Facades	A&M 4779
8/15/81	**160**	6	3. Sad Cafe	Swan Song 16048

SADE
Falosade Adu - Nigerian-born vocalist (pronounced Shaw-Day)

2/23/85	**20+**	7+	1. Diamond Life	Portrait 39581

SSgt BARRY SADLER
Staff Sergeant of the U.S. Army Special Forces

2/26/66	**1(5)**	32	● 1. **Ballads of the Green Berets**	RCA 3547
			"The Ballad Of The Green Berets"(1)	
7/09/66	**130**	3	2. The "A" Team	RCA 3605

SAGA
Canadian rock quintet - Michael Sadler, lead singer

10/23/82	**29**	36	● 1. Worlds Apart	Portrait 38246
10/22/83	**92**	9	2. Heads Or Tales	Portrait 38999

CAROLE BAYER SAGER
pop songwriter - married Burt Bacharach in 1982

5/16/81	**60**	22	1. Sometimes Late At Night	Boardwalk 37069

MORT SAHL
topical satirist

10/24/60	**22**	4	1. Mort Sahl At The Hungry i .... [C]	Verve 15012
6/30/73	**149**	7	2. Sing A Song of Watergate... .... [C]	GNP Cres. 2070

DOUG SAHM & Band
also see Sir Douglas Quintet

2/17/73	**125**	10	1. Doug Sahm And Band	Atlantic 7254
			with guests Bob Dylan, Dr. John and David Bromberg	

SAILCAT
country-rock duo: Court Pickett & John Wyker

8/12/72	**38**	14	1. Motorcycle Mama	Elektra 75029

BUFFY SAINTE-MARIE
folk singer - born of Cree Indian parents

5/21/66	**97**	10	1. Little Wheel Spin And Spin	Vanguard 79211
7/08/67	**126**	6	2. Fire & Fleet & Candlelight	Vanguard 79250
8/03/68	**171**	7	3. I'm Gonna Be A Country Girl Again	Vanguard 79280
			recorded with top Nashville musicians	
10/24/70	**142**	7	4. The Best Of Buffy Sainte-Marie .... [G]	Vanguard 3/4 [2]
4/10/71	**182**	6	5. She Used To Wanna Be A Ballerina	Vanguard 79311
			backing musicians: Ry Cooder and Neil Young & Crazy Horse	
5/06/72	**134**	8	6. Moonshot	Vanguard 79312

SAINT TROPEZ
French disco production

11/26/77	**131**	10	1. Je T'aime .... [F]	Butterfly 002
5/05/79	**65**	11	2. Belle de Jour	Butterfly 3100

DATE CHARTED	PEAK POS	WKS CHRT'D	ARTIST — Album Title	LABEL & NUMBER
			KYU SAKAMOTO from Kawasaki, Japan	
6/15/63	14	17	1. Sukiyaki and other Japanese hits .... [F] "Sukiyaki"(1)	Capitol 10349
			SOUPY SALES slapstick comedian	
4/24/65	102	7	1. Spy With A Pie .... [N] songs and sketches from his children's TV series	ABC-Para. 503
5/15/65	80	7	2. Soupy Sales Sez do The Mouse and other teen hits .... [N]	ABC-Para. 517
			SALSOUL ORCHESTRA disco orchestra conducted by Vincent Montana, Jr.	
11/29/75	14	45	1. The Salsoul Orchestra .... [I]	Salsoul 5501
10/23/76	61	14	2. Nice 'N' Naasty	Salsoul 5502
12/11/76	48	13	3. Christmas Jollies .... [X]	Salsoul 5507
6/25/77	61	20	4. Magic Journey	Salsoul 5515
11/26/77	100	15	5. Cuchi-Cuchi .... CHARO & THE SALSOUL ORCHESTRA	Salsoul 5519
3/25/78	117	8	6. Up The Yellow Brick Road	Salsoul 8500
9/09/78	97	13	7. Greatest Disco Hits/Music For Non-Stop Dancing .... [G]	Salsoul 8508
12/19/81	170	5	8. Christmas Jollies II .... [X]	Salsoul 8547
			SAM & DAVE Sam Moore & Dave Prater	
8/06/66	45	15	1. Hold On, I'm Comin'	Stax 708
1/21/67	118	13	2. Double Dynamite	Stax 712
11/18/67	62	13	3. Soul Men .... "Soul Man"(2)	Stax 725
2/15/69	87	17	4. The Best Of Sam & Dave .... [G] "I Thank You"(9)	Atlantic 8218
			SAM THE SHAM & The Pharaohs Sam is Domingo Samudio from Dallas, Texas	
6/12/65	26	18	1. Wooly Bully .... "Wooly Bully"(2)	MGM 4297
9/24/66	82	7	2. Li'l Red Riding Hood .... "Lil' Red Riding Hood"(2)	MGM 4407
3/11/67	98	17	3. the best of Sam the Sham and the pharaohs .... [G]	MGM 4422
			JOE SAMPLE keyboardist for the Crusaders	
2/25/78	62	25	1. Rainbow Seeker .... [I]	ABC 1050
2/10/79	56	26	2. Carmel .... [I]	ABC 1126
1/31/81	65	20	3. Voices In The Rain .... [I]	MCA 5172
4/16/83	125	14	4. The Hunter .... [I]	MCA 5397
			SAN FRANCISCO SYMPHONY ORCHESTRA Seiji Ozawa, conductor	
4/07/73	105	15	1. William Russo: Three Pieces for Blues Band and Orchestra/Leonard Bernstein: Symphonic Dances from West Side Story .... [I] Russo side: with the Siegel-Schwall Band	DG 2530 309
			SAN SEBASTIAN STRINGS music composed by Anita Kerr (with sound effects) and featuring narration of the words of Rod McKuen	
3/25/67	52	143	● 1. The Sea .... [I-T]	Warner 1670
9/23/67	115	13	2. The Earth .... [I-T]	Warner 1705
2/17/68	68	25	3. The Sky .... [I-T]	Warner 1720
1/18/69	20	20	4. Home To The Sea .... [I-T]	Warner 1764

DATE CHARTED	PEAK POS	WKS CHRT'D	ARTIST — Album Title	LABEL & NUMBER
11/22/69	84	17	5. For Lovers .... [I-T]	Warner 1795
1/17/70	162	5	6. The Complete Sea .... [R]	Warner 1827 [3]
			reissue of albums 1 and 4, plus album 7 (forthcoming)	
9/26/70	171	5	7. The Soft Sea .... [I-T]	Warner 1839

DAVID SANBORN
top session saxophonist

DATE CHARTED	PEAK POS	WKS CHRT'D	ARTIST — Album Title	LABEL & NUMBER
8/28/76	125	8	1. Sanborn .... [I]	Warner 2957
6/03/78	151	6	2. Heart To Heart .... [I]	Warner 3189
3/08/80	63	19	3. Hideaway .... [I]	Warner 3379
4/18/81	45	22	4. Voyeur .... [I]	Warner 3546
7/10/82	70	23	5. As We Speak .... [I]	Warner 23650
11/26/83	81	33	6. Backstreet .... [I]	Warner 23906
2/09/85	64	9+	7. Straight To The Heart .... [I-L]	Warner 25150
			featuring live studio cuts of his well known compositions	

SANDALS
Southern California instrumental rock quintet

DATE CHARTED	PEAK POS	WKS CHRT'D	ARTIST — Album Title	LABEL & NUMBER
2/04/67	110	13	1. The Endless Summer .... [S-I]	World Pac. 1832
			film is a surfing documentary by Bruce Brown	

PHAROAH SANDERS
avant-garde jazz saxophonist

DATE CHARTED	PEAK POS	WKS CHRT'D	ARTIST — Album Title	LABEL & NUMBER
8/16/69	188	4	1. Karma .... [I]	Impulse! 9181
7/31/71	175	3	2. Thembi .... [I]	Impulse! 9206
5/20/78	163	5	3. Love Will Find A Way	Arista 4161

TONY SANDLER & RALPH YOUNG
MOR vocal duo - Tony (Belgian-born) & Ralph (New York-born)

DATE CHARTED	PEAK POS	WKS CHRT'D	ARTIST — Album Title	LABEL & NUMBER
12/17/66	85	19	1. Side By Side	Capitol 2598
4/15/67	166	3	2. On The Move	Capitol 2686
7/05/69	188	4	3. Pretty Things Come In Twos	Capitol 241
7/11/70	199	2	4. Honey Come Back	Capitol 449

SANDPIPERS
Los Angeles-based trio - met in the Mitchell Boys Choir

DATE CHARTED	PEAK POS	WKS CHRT'D	ARTIST — Album Title	LABEL & NUMBER
10/29/66	13	37	● 1. Guantanamera	A&M 4117
			"Guantanamera"(9)	
5/27/67	53	28	2. The Sandpipers	A&M 4125
1/13/68	135	5	3. Misty Roses	A&M 4135
9/07/68	180	5	4. Softly	A&M 4147
5/10/69	194	3	5. The Wonder Of You	A&M 4180
4/18/70	160	10	6. Greatest Hits .... [G]	A&M 4246
8/15/70	96	11	7. Come Saturday Morning	A&M 4262

TOMMY SANDS
singer/actor - married to Nancy Sinatra ('60-'65)

DATE CHARTED	PEAK POS	WKS CHRT'D	ARTIST — Album Title	LABEL & NUMBER
5/06/57	4	18	1. **Steady Date with Tommy Sands**	Capitol 848
2/24/58	17	4	2. Sing Boy Sing .... [S]	Capitol 929
			Tommy portrays fictional singer Virgil Walker in the film	

SANFORD/TOWNSEND Band
Ed Sanford/John Townsend

DATE CHARTED	PEAK POS	WKS CHRT'D	ARTIST — Album Title	LABEL & NUMBER
8/13/77	57	15	1. The Sanford/Townsend Band	Warner 2966
			"Smoke From A Distant Fire"(9)	
2/11/78	92	8	2. Duo-Glide	Warner 3081

SAMANTHA SANG
Australian

DATE CHARTED	PEAK POS	WKS CHRT'D	ARTIST — Album Title	LABEL & NUMBER
3/11/78	29	14	● 1. Emotion	Private S. 7009
			"Emotion"(3)	

DATE CHARTED	PEAK POS	WKS CHRT'D	ARTIST — Album Title	LABEL & NUMBER
			SANTA ESMERALDA Spanish-flavored disco band featuring Leroy Gomez	
11/12/77	**25**	23	● 1. Don't Let Me Be Misunderstood	Casablanca 7080
2/25/78	**41**	14	2. The House Of The Rising Sun	Casablanca 7088
9/02/78	**141**	6	3. Beauty	Casablanca 7109
			MONGO SANTAMARIA Cuban-born band leader and bongo player	
5/04/63	**42**	10	1. Watermelon Man! .... [I] "Watermelon Man"(10)	Battle 96120
3/27/65	**112**	10	2. El Pussy Cat .... [I]	Columbia 9098
8/28/65	**79**	15	3. La Bamba .... [I]	Columbia 9175
6/04/66	**135**	5	4. Hey! Let's Party .... [I]	Columbia 9273
8/10/68	**171**	18	5. Soul Bag .... [I]	Columbia 9653
3/01/69	**62**	24	6. Stone Soul .... [I]	Columbia 9780
11/29/69	**193**	2	7. Workin' On A Groovy Thing .... [I]	Columbia 9937
4/11/70	**171**	3	8. Feelin' Alright .... [I]	Atlantic 8252
10/03/70	**195**	2	9. Mongo '70 .... [I]	Atlantic 1567
			SANTANA Latin-rock band formed in San Francisco, led by guitarist/ vocalist Carlos Santana	
9/13/69	**4**	108	● 1. **Santana** .... "Evil Ways"(9)	Columbia 9781
10/10/70	**1(6)**	88	● 2. **Abraxas** .... "Black Magic Woman"(4)/"Oye Como Va" ⌐	Columbia 30130
10/16/71	**1(5)**	39	● 3. **Santana III** .... "Everybody's Everything"	Columbia 30595
11/04/72	**8**	32	● 4. **Caravanserai**	Columbia 31610
12/01/73	**25**	21	● 5. Welcome	Columbia 32445
7/27/74	**17**	21	● 6. Santana's Greatest Hits .... [G]	Columbia 33050
11/02/74	**20**	19	7. Borboletta	Columbia 33135
4/10/76	**10**	26	● 8. **Amigos**	Columbia 33576
1/22/77	**27**	19	● 9. Festival	Columbia 34423
11/05/77	**10**	24	● 10. **Moonflower** .... [L] set also features some new studio recordings	Columbia 34914 [2]
11/04/78	**27**	33	● 11. Inner Secrets	Columbia 35600
10/20/79	**25**	22	12. Marathon	Columbia 36154
4/18/81	**9**	32	● 13. **Zebop!** .... "Winning"	Columbia 37158
9/04/82	**22**	23	14. Shango .... "Hold On"	Columbia 38122
3/23/85	**55+**	3+	15. Beyond Appearances	Columbia 39527
			CARLOS SANTANA Mexican-born rock and jazz-fusion guitarist (Santana leader)	
7/08/72	**8**	33	● 1. **Carlos Santana & Buddy Miles! Live!** ..... [L] recorded in Hawaii's Diamond Head volcano crater	Columbia 31308
7/07/73	**14**	24	● 2. Love Devotion Surrender .... [I] CARLOS SANTANA/MAHAVISHNU JOHN McLAUGHLIN	Columbia 32034
10/12/74	**79**	8	3. Illuminations .... [I] TURIYA ALICE COLTRANE/DEVADIP CARLOS SANTANA	Columbia 32900
3/31/79	**87**	9	4. Oneness/Silver Dreams-Golden Reality .... [I] 1/2 of side 1 recorded live in Osaka, Japan	Columbia 35686
9/06/80	**65**	10	5. The Swing Of Delight .... [I] with guests: Herbie Hancock, Wayne Shorter & Ron Carter	Columbia 36590 [2]
4/23/83	**31**	17	6. Havana Moon .... with guests: Willie Nelson, Booker T. Jones and The Fabulous Thunderbirds	Columbia 38642

DATE CHARTED	PEAK POS	WKS CHRT'D	ARTIST — Album Title	LABEL & NUMBER
			SANTO & JOHNNY Santo (steel guitar) & brother Johnny (rhythm guitar) Farina from Brooklyn	
1/18/60	20	24	1. Santo & Johnny .... [I] "Sleep Walk"(1)	Canadn-Am. 1001
9/26/60	11	36	2. Encore .... [I]	Canadn-Am. 1002
6/26/61	80	13	3. Hawaii .... [I]	Canadn-Am. 1004
			FATHER GUIDO SARDUCCI real name: Don Novello - featured on "Saturday Night Live"	
5/10/80	179	2	1. Live at St. Douglas Convent .... [C]	Warner 3440
			ESTHER SATTERFIELD	
7/24/76	180	4	1. The Need To Be .... produced, arranged and orchestrated by Chuck Mangione	A&M 3411
			SATURDAY NIGHT BAND a Jesse Boyce & Moses Dillard disco production	
5/27/78	125	17	1. Come On Dance, Dance	Prelude 12155
			MERL SAUNDERS session keyboardist	
6/02/73	197	5	1. Fire Up .... [I] featuring Jerry Garcia & Tom Fogerty (guitars)	Fantasy 9421
			SAVAGE GRACE	
6/06/70	182	8	1. Savage Grace	Reprise 6399
			TELLY SAVALAS Lt. Theo Kojak of the TV series "Kojak"	
1/04/75	117	8	1. Telly .... Telly both narrates and sings	MCA 436
			SAVOY BROWN British blues-rock band led by guitarist Kim Simmonds	
4/12/69	182	2	1. Blue Matter .... side 2: recorded live	Parrot 71027
9/13/69	71	14	2. A Step Further .... side 2: a live Boogie Medley	Parrot 71029
4/25/70	121	18	3. Raw Sienna	Parrot 71036
10/17/70	39	19	4. Looking In	Parrot 71042
9/18/71	75	17	5. Street Corner Talking	Parrot 71047
3/18/72	34	21	6. Hellbound Train	Parrot 71052
11/04/72	151	10	7. Lion's Share	Parrot 71057
6/30/73	84	14	8. Jack The Toad	Parrot 71059
4/20/74	101	8	9. Boogie Brothers	London 638
11/22/75	153	7	10. Wire Fire	London 659
7/25/81	185	4	11. Rock 'n' Roll Warriors	Town House 7002
			SAWYER BROWN 5-member country band - Mark Miller, lead singer	
2/23/85	140	7+	1. Sawyer Brown	Capitol 12391
			SAXON British heavy-metal rock quintet - Biff Byford, lead vocals	
6/18/83	155	10	1. Power & The Glory	Carrere 38719
4/14/84	174	5	2. Crusader	Carrere 39284
			LEO SAYER English singer/songwriter	
2/08/75	16	22	1. Just A Boy .... "Long Tall Glasses (I Can Dance)"(9)	Warner 2836
10/11/75	125	7	2. Another Year	Warner 2885
11/27/76	10	51	▲ 3. Endless Flight .... "You Make Me Feel Like Dancing"(1)/"When I Need You"(1)	Warner 2962
10/22/77	37	15	4. Thunder In My Heart	Warner 3089
8/19/78	101	14	5. Leo Sayer	Warner 3200
10/18/80	36	23	6. Living In A Fantasy .... "More Than I Can Say"(2)	Warner 3483

DATE CHARTED	PEAK POS	WKS CHRT'D	ARTIST — Album Title	LABEL & NUMBER
			BOZ SCAGGS singer/songwriter from Ohio - original member of the Steve Miller Band	
4/17/71	124	9	1. Moments	Columbia 30454
12/11/71	198	2	2. Boz Scaggs & Band	Columbia 30796
9/23/72	138	9	3. My Time	Columbia 31384
3/23/74	81	20	4. Slow Dancer	Columbia 32760
7/13/74	171	5	5. Boz Scaggs .... [E] reissue of his first album - featuring guitarist Duane Allman	Atlantic 8239
3/20/76	2(5)	115	▲ 6. **Silk Degrees** .... "Lowdown"(3)/"Lido Shuffle"	Columbia 33920
12/10/77	11	23	▲ 7. Down Two Then Left	Columbia 34729
4/19/80	8	33	▲ 8. **Middle Man**	Columbia 36106
11/29/80	24	26	● 9. Hits! .... [G]	Columbia 36841
			SCANDAL featuring Patty Smyth New York-based rock band	
1/29/83	39	32	1. Scandal .... [M]	Columbia 38194
8/04/84	17	36+	● 2. Warrior .... "The Warrior"(7)	Columbia 39173
			JOEY SCARBURY	
8/22/81	104	9	1. America's Greatest Hero .... "Theme from Greatest American Hero (Believe It Or Not)"(2)	Elektra 537
			KERMIT SCHAFER collection of 'bloopers' by radio & TV producer Schafer - died on 3/8/79	
1/27/58	17	1	1. Pardon My Blooper! Volume 6 .... [C] narrator: George de Holczer	Jubilee 6
			MICHAEL SCHENKER Group German - former lead guitarist of UFO	
9/20/80	100	14	1. The Michael Schenker Group	Chrysalis 1302
10/24/81	81	8	2. MSG	Chrysalis 1336
4/09/83	151	7	3. Assault Attack	Chrysalis 1393
			LALO SCHIFRIN Argentinian pianist/conductor/composer	
12/22/62	35	3	1. Bossa Nova - New Brazilian Jazz .... [I]	Audio Fidel. 1981
12/30/67	47	31	2. music from Mission: Impossible .... [I]	Dot 25831
			PETER SCHILLING German singer/songwriter	
10/08/83	61	23	1. Error In The System .... "Major Tom (Coming Home)"	Elektra 60265
			TIMOTHY B. SCHMIT member of Poco and the Eagles	
11/10/84	160	5	1. Playin' It Cool	Asylum 60359
			JOHN SCHNEIDER Bo Duke of TV's "The Dukes Of Hazzard"	
6/27/81	37	22	1. Now Or Never	Scotti Br. 37400
12/05/81	155	7	2. White Christmas .... [X]	Scotti Br. 37617
11/17/84	111	12	3. Too Good To Stop Now	MCA 5495
			NEAL SCHON & JAN HAMMER Neal (lead guitarist of Journey); Jan (keyboards/drums) - also see Sammy Hagar	
10/17/81	115	8	1. Untold Passion	Columbia 37600
2/05/83	122	12	2. Here To Stay	Columbia 38428
			DICK SCHORY'S Percussion Pops Orchestra	
6/29/59	11	26	1. Music For Bang, Baa room and Harp .... [I]	RCA 1866
4/20/63	13	13	2. Supercussion .... [I]	RCA 2613

DATE CHARTED	PEAK POS	WKS CHRT'D	ARTIST — Album Title	LABEL & NUMBER
			EDDIE SCHWARTZ Canadian singer/songwriter	
2/06/82	195	6	1. No Refuge	Atco 141
			SCORPIONS German heavy-metal rock quintet led by Rudolf Schenker (guitar - Michael's brother), & Klaus Meine (vocals)	
7/28/79	55	23	1. Lovedrive .... Michael Schenker. lead guitar on 3 tracks	Mercury 3795
11/17/79	180	4	2. Best Of Scorpions .... [E-K]	RCA 3516
5/17/80	52	21	● 3. Animal Magnetism	Mercury 3825
3/27/82	10	74	▲ 4. **Blackout**	Mercury 4039
3/17/84	6	53	▲ 5. **Love At First Sting** .... "Rock You Like A Hurricane"	Mercury 814981
8/04/84	175	4	6. Best of Scorpions, Vol. 2 .... [E-K]	RCA 5085
			CHRISTOPHER SCOTT	
10/04/69	175	3	1. Switched-On Bacharach .... [I] Burt Bacharach songs performed on a Moog Synthesizer	Decca 75141
			MARILYN SCOTT	
4/14/79	189	4	1. Dreams Of Tomorrow	Atco 109
			PEGGY SCOTT & JO JO BENSON	
3/01/69	196	5	1. Soulshake .... "Lover's Holiday"/"Pickin' Wild Mountain Berries"	SSS Int'l. 1
			TOM SCOTT pop-jazz saxophonist	
4/27/74	141	16	1. Tom Scott & The L.A. Express .... [I] Express: backing band (also on album #2)	Ode 77021
3/15/75	18	27	2. Tom Cat .... [I]	Ode 77029
12/20/75	42	25	3. New York Connection .... [I]	Ode 77033
9/10/77	87	14	4. Blow It Out .... [I]	Ode 34966
11/18/78	123	13	5. Intimate Strangers .... [I]	Columbia 35557
12/15/79	162	6	6. Street Beat .... [I]	Columbia 36137
7/11/81	123	11	7. Apple Juice .... [I-L]	Columbia 37419
9/25/82	164	7	8. Desire .... [I]	Musician 60162
			GIL SCOTT-HERON socio-political poet/singer	
12/20/80	159	6	1. Real Eyes	Arista 9540
9/26/81	106	27	2. Reflections	Arista 9566
10/02/82	123	9	3. Moving Target	Arista 9606
			GIL SCOTT-HERON & BRIAN JACKSON keyboard duo: Gil is the lyricist; Brian composes the music	
2/01/75	30	17	1. The First Minute Of A New Day .... featuring backup group: The Midnight Band	Arista 4030
11/08/75	103	5	2. From South Africa To South Carolina	Arista 4044
11/13/76	168	5	3. It's Your World .... [L]	Arista 5001 [2]
10/22/77	130	5	4. Bridges	Arista 4147
9/09/78	61	21	5. Secrets	Arista 4189
3/08/80	82	12	6. 1980	Arista 9514
			EARL SCRUGGS Revue legendary bluegrass banjo stylist - also see Flatt & Scruggs	
9/22/73	169	5	1. The Earl Scruggs Revue .... with sons Randy, Gary & Steve	Columbia 32426
6/21/75	104	10	2. Anniversary Special, Volume One .... with a host of pop and country guest artists	Columbia 33416
4/17/76	161	4	3. The Earl Scruggs Revue, Volume II	Columbia 34090

SEA LEVEL
jazzy blues-rock band formed by 3 members of the Allman Brothers Band

3/05/77	43	15	1. Sea Level	Capricorn 0178
2/04/78	31	16	2. Cats On The Coast	Capricorn 0198
10/28/78	137	16	3. On The Edge	Capricorn 0212
8/23/80	152	6	4. Ball Room	Arista 9531

SEATRAIN
fusion rock band formed by 2 members of the Blues Project

5/17/69	168	4	1. Sea Train	A&M 4171
1/30/71	48	23	2. Seatrain	Capitol 659
10/09/71	91	9	3. The Marblehead Messenger	Capitol 829
			above 2 albums produced by George Martin	

JOHNNY SEA

8/06/66	147	2	1. Day For Decision	Warner 1659
			patriotic songs	

SEAWIND
jazz/R&B sextet formed in Hawaii - Pauline Wilson, lead singer

5/07/77	188	2	1. Seawind	CTI 5002
1/21/78	122	7	2. Window Of A Child	CTI 5007
3/24/79	143	14	3. Light The Light	Horizon 734
10/25/80	83	11	4. Seawind	A&M 4824

SEALS & CROFTS
Jim Seals & Dash Crofts - both from Texas

10/31/70	122	10	1. Down Home	TA 5004
12/04/71	133	20	2. Year of Sunday	Warner 2568
9/02/72	7	109	● 3. **Summer Breeze**	Warner 2629
			"Summer Breeze"(6)	
4/21/73	4	77	● 4. **Diamond Girl**	Warner 2699
			"Diamond Girl"(6)	
3/02/74	14	34	● 5. Unborn Child	Warner 2761
8/10/74	86	12	6. Seals & Crofts I And II [E-R]	Warner 2809 [2]
			reissue of first two albums on TA Records: "Seals & Crofts" & "Down Home"	
4/05/75	30	23	● 7. I'll Play For You	Warner 2848
11/15/75	11	54	● 8. Greatest Hits [G]	Warner 2886
5/01/76	37	29	● 9. Get Closer	Warner 2907
			"Get Closer"(6)	
12/11/76	73	10	10. Sudan Village	Warner 2976
10/08/77	118	7	11. One On One [S]	Warner 3076
5/13/78	78	13	12. Takin' It Easy	Warner 3163

SEARCHERS
rock quartet from Liverpool, England

4/11/64	22	21	1. Meet The Searchers/Needles & Pins	Kapp 3363
6/20/64	120	8	2. Hear! Hear! [E-L]	Mercury 60914
			recorded at the Star Club in Hamburg, Germany "Love Potion Number Nine"(3)	
8/29/64	97	14	3. This Is Us	Kapp 3409
3/20/65	112	7	4. The New Searchers LP	Kapp 3412
10/23/65	149	2	5. The Searchers No. 4	Kapp 3449
3/15/80	191	2	6. The Searchers	Sire 6082

JOHN SEBASTIAN
lead singer of the Lovin' Spoonful

3/28/70	20	31	1. John B. Sebastian	MGM 4654
			album also released on Reprise 6379	
10/10/70	129	3	2. John Sebastian Live [L]	MGM 4720
4/24/71	75	13	3. cheapo-cheapo productions presents Real Live John Sebastian [L]	Reprise 2036

DATE CHARTED	PEAK POS	WKS CHRT'D	ARTIST — Album Title	LABEL & NUMBER
9/18/71	**93**	9	4. The Four Of Us	Reprise 2041
5/15/76	**79**	10	5. Welcome Back .... "Welcome Back"(1)	Reprise 2249
			NEIL SEDAKA born on 3/13/39 in Brooklyn, New York	
1/05/63	**55**	9	1. Neil Sedaka Sings His Greatest Hits .... [G] "Oh! Carol"(9)/"Stairway To Heaven"(9)/"Calendar Girl"(4)/ "Happy Birthday, Sweet Sixteen"(6)/ "Breaking Up Is Hard To Do"(1)/"Next Door To An Angel"(5)	RCA 2627
12/07/74	**23**	62	● 2. Sedaka's Back .... compilation of cuts from 3 albums made in Britain "Laughter In The Rain"(1)	Rocket 463
3/01/75	**161**	4	3. Neil Sedaka Sings His Greatest Hits .... [R-G] reissue of album #1	RCA 0928
10/11/75	**16**	32	● 4. The Hungry Years .... "Bad Blood"(1)/"Breaking Up Is Hard To Do"(8)	Rocket 2157
5/01/76	**26**	22	5. Steppin' Out	Rocket 2195
9/18/76	**159**	4	6. Solitaire .... [E] recorded in 1972 - formerly on Kirshner Records 117	RCA 1790
5/28/77	**59**	7	7. A Song	Elektra 102
10/22/77	**143**	5	8. Neil Sedaka's Greatest Hits .... [G]	Rocket 2297
5/17/80	**135**	13	9. In The Pocket	Elektra 259
			SEEDS Los Angeles psychedelic rock quartet - Sky Saxon, lead singer	
1/07/67	**132**	7	1. The Seeds .... "Pushin' Too Hard"	GNP Cres. 2023
8/12/67	**87**	8	2. Future	GNP Cres. 2038
			PETE SEEGER legendary folk singer - member of the Weavers	
12/14/63	**42**	36	1. We Shall Overcome .... [L] recorded at Carnegie Hall on 6/8/63	Columbia 8901
5/17/75	**181**	4	2. Together In Concert .... [L] PETE SEEGER & ARLO GUTHRIE	Reprise 2214 [2]
			SEEKERS pop/folk Australian-born quartet: Judith Durham, lead singer - also see New Seekers	
6/05/65	**145**	3	1. The Seekers	Marvel 2060
6/12/65	**62**	16	2. The New Seekers	Capitol 2319
9/25/65	**123**	6	3. A World Of Our Own	Capitol 2369
2/25/67	**10**	28	4. **Georgy Girl** .... "Georgy Girl"(2)	Capitol 2431
8/19/67	**97**	10	5. The Best Of The Seekers .... [G] "I'll Never Find Another You"(4)	Capitol 2746
			GEORGE SEGAL movie actor	
9/02/67	**199**	2	1. The Yama Yama Man .... George sings and plays the banjo	Philips 242
			BOB SEGER born on 5/6/45 in Ann Arbor, Michigan	
			BOB SEGER SYSTEM:	
2/08/69	**62**	10	1. Ramblin' Gamblin' Man	Capitol 172
10/31/70	**171**	4	2. Mongrel	Capitol 499
			BOB SEGER:	
7/22/72	**180**	11	3. Smokin' O.P.'s	Palladium 1006
3/03/73	**188**	6	4. Back In '72	Palladium 2126
4/12/75	**131**	18	5. Beautiful Loser	Capitol 11378
			BOB SEGER & THE SILVER BULLET BAND:	
5/01/76	**34**	140	▲ 6. 'Live' Bullet .... [L] recorded at Cobo Hall, Detroit, Michigan	Capitol 11523 [2]

DATE CHARTED	PEAK POS	WKS CHRT'D	ARTIST — Album Title	LABEL & NUMBER
11/13/76	**8**	88	▲ 7. **Night Moves** .... "Night Moves"(4)	Capitol 11557
5/27/78	**4**	110	▲ 8. **Stranger in Town** .... "Still The Same"(4)/"Old Time Rock & Roll"	Capitol 11698
3/15/80	**1(6)**	110	▲ 9. **Against The Wind** .... "Fire Lake"(6)/"Against The Wind"(5)	Capitol 12041
9/26/81	**3**	51	▲ 10. **Nine Tonight** .... [L] "Tryin' To Live My Life Without You"(5)	Capitol 12182 [2]
1/15/83	**5**	39	▲ 11. **The Distance** .... "Shame On The Moon"(2)	Capitol 12254

SELECTER
Pauline Black, lead singer of British ska/rock group

5/03/80	**175**	4	1. Too Much Pressure	Chrysalis 1274

MICHAEL SEMBELLO
session guitarist/producer/composer/arranger/vocalist

10/08/83	**80**	10	1. Bossa Nova Hotel .... "Maniac"(1)	Warner 23920

SERENDIPITY SINGERS
pop/folk group organized at the University of Colorado

3/07/64	**11**	29	1. The Serendipity Singers .... "Don't Let The Rain Come Down (Crooked Little Man)"(6)	Philips 115
6/27/64	**68**	15	2. The Many Sides Of The Serendipity Singers	Philips 134
1/16/65	**149**	2	3. Take Your Shoes Off with the Serendipity Singers	Philips 151

SESAME STREET - see CHILDRENS section

707
Detroit-bred rock group

2/07/81	**159**	6	1. The Second Album	Casablanca 7248
7/03/82	**129**	9	2. Mega Force	Boardwalk 33253

DOC SEVERINSEN
trumpet virtuoso - leader of the "Tonight Show" orchestra

8/27/66	**147**	2	1. Fever! .... [I]	Command 893
11/26/66	**133**	6	2. Command Performances .... [I]	Command 904
10/16/71	**185**	2	3. Brass Roots	RCA 4522
4/29/72	**74**	19	4. Brass On Ivory .... [I] HENRY MANCINI & DOC SEVERINSEN	RCA 4629
6/09/73	**185**	3	5. Brass, Ivory & Strings .... [I] HENRY MANCINI & DOC SEVERINSEN	RCA 0098
4/17/76	**189**	4	6. Night Journey .... [I]	Epic 34078

SEX PISTOLS
notorious British punk-rock quartet led by Johnny Rotten & Sid Vicious (died on 2/2/79)

12/10/77	**106**	12	1. Never Mind The Bollocks, Here's The Sex Pistols	Warner 3147

PHIL SEYMOUR
vocalist/drummer with the Dwight Twilley Band

2/21/81	**64**	16	1. Phil Seymour	Boardwalk 36996

SHA NA NA
'50's rock & roll specialists led by John "Bowzer" Baumann

12/13/69	**183**	7	1. Rock & Roll Is Here To Stay!	Kama Sutra 2010
8/07/71	**122**	9	2. Sha Na Na .... [L] side 1: live; side 2: studio	Kama Sutra 2034
7/01/72	**156**	14	3. The Night Is Still Young	Kama Sutra 2050
4/21/73	**38**	24	● 4. The Golden Age Of Rock 'N' Roll .... [L]	Kama Sutr. 2073[2]
12/01/73	**140**	11	5. From The Streets Of New York .... [L]	Kama Sutra 2075
6/01/74	**165**	6	6. Hot Sox	Kama Sutra 2600
8/09/75	**162**	4	7. Sha Na Now	Kama Sutra 2605

DATE CHARTED	PEAK POS	WKS CHRT'D	ARTIST — Album Title	LABEL & NUMBER
			SHADOWFAX jazz fusion sextet	
11/19/83	145	19	1. Shadowdance .... [I]	Windham Hill 1029
11/17/84	126	20	2. The Dreams Of Children .... [I]	Windham Hill 1038
			SHADOWS OF KNIGHT Chicago-area "garage band" - Jim Sohns, lead singer	
5/14/66	46	18	1. Gloria .... "Gloria"(10)	Dunwich 666
			SHAKTI - see JOHN McLAUGHLIN	
			SHALAMAR soul/dance trio: Howard Hewett, lead singer	
5/21/77	48	14	1. Uptown Festival	Soul Train 2289
11/04/78	171	4	2. Disco Gardens	Solar 2895
11/10/79	23	36	● 3. Big Fun .... "The Second Time Around"(8)	Solar 3479
1/10/81	40	36	● 4. Three For Love	Solar 3577
10/24/81	115	15	5. Go For It	Solar 3984
2/20/82	35	25	● 6. Friends	Solar 28
8/06/83	38	23	7. The Look .... "Dead Giveaway"	Solar 60239
12/08/84	90	18+	8. Heart Break	Solar 60385
			SHANGRI-LAS Queens, New York "girl group" - Mary Weiss, lead singer	
3/13/65	109	6	1. Leader Of The Pack .... side 2 has live sounds dubbed in "Remember (Walkin' In The Sand)"(5)/"Leader Of The Pack"(1)	Red Bird 101
			BUD SHANK jazz-oriented saxophonist	
2/12/66	56	21	1. Michelle .... [I] with Chet Baker (flugelhorn)	World Pac. 21840
			RAVI SHANKAR classical sitarist from India - also see Soundtrack "Gandhi"	
7/15/67	161	7	1. West Meets East .... [I] YEHUDI MENUHIN (violin) & RAVI SHANKAR	Angel 36418
7/29/67	148	7	2. Ravi Shankar in New York .... [I]	World Pac. 21441
11/18/67	43	19	3. Ravi Shankar At The Monterey International Pop Festival .... [I-L]	World Pac. 21442
8/03/68	140	4	4. Ravi Shankar in San Francisco .... [I-L]	World Pac. 21449
1/11/75	176	3	5. Shankar Family & Friends .... George Harrison producer/guitarist	Dark Horse 22002
			SHANNON New Yorker Shannon Greene	
2/11/84	32	37	● 1. Let The Music Play .... "Let The Music Play"(8)	Mirage 90134
			DEL SHANNON born Charles Westover on 12/30/39 in Coopersville, Michigan	
6/22/63	12	26	1. Little Town Flirt .... "Runaway"(1)/"Hats Off To Larry"(5)	Big Top 1308
12/12/81	123	14	2. Drop Down And Get Me .... produced by Tom Petty	Elektra 568
			SHARKS British rock quartet formed by Andy Fraser (Free) & guitarist Chris Spedding	
8/25/73	189	4	1. First Water	MCA 351
			DEE DEE SHARP born Dione LaRue on 9/9/45 in Philadelphia	
6/23/62	44	17	1. It's Mashed Potato Time .... "Mashed Potato Time"(2)/"Gravy (For My Mashed Potatoes)"(9)	Cameo 1018
11/17/62	117	4	2. Down To Earth .... CHUBBY CHECKER/DEE DEE SHARP	Cameo 1029

DATE CHARTED	PEAK POS	WKS CHRT'D	ARTIST — Album Title	LABEL & NUMBER
			BOB SHARPLES	
10/09/61	11	25	1. Pass In Review .... [I] featuring patriotic songs	London P. 4 44001
			MARLENA SHAW	
7/05/75	159	5	1. Who Is This Bitch, Anyway?	Blue Note 397
4/02/77	62	14	2. Sweet Beginnings	Columbia 34458
4/08/78	171	4	3. Acting Up	Columbia 35073
			ROBERT SHAW Chorale Shaw organized his singing group in 1948	
12/23/57	5	4	● 1. **Christmas Hymns And Carols** .... [X]	RCA 1711
12/22/58	13	3	2. Christmas Hymns And Carols .... [X-R] made top 10 on Billboard's special Christmas charts (1963)	RCA 1711
5/25/59	21	1	3. Deep River and Other Spirituals	RCA 2247
4/27/63	27	10	4. This Is My Country .... with the RCA Victor Symphony Orchestra	RCA 2662
			ROLAND SHAW Orchestra English	
2/27/65	38	25	1. Themes From The James Bond Thrillers .. [I]	London 412
2/05/66	119	5	2. More Themes From The James Bond Thrillers .... [I]	London 445
			SANDIE SHAW 18-year-old songstress from England	
6/12/65	100	4	1. Sandie Shaw	Reprise 6166
			TOMMY SHAW lead guitarist of Styx	
10/20/84	50	25	1. Girls With Guns	A&M 5020
			GEORGE SHEARING Quintet English piano stylist - born blind - came to U.S. in 1947	
10/06/56	20	1	1. Velvet Carpet .... [I]	Capitol 720
10/07/57	13	3	2. Black Satin .... [I]	Capitol 858
8/25/58	17	2	3. Burnished Brass .... [I]	Capitol 1038
7/25/60	11	23	4. White Satin	Capitol 1334
10/30/61	82	14	5. Satin Affair	Capitol 1628
5/05/62	27	16	6. Nat King Cole Sings/George Shearing Plays	Capitol 1675
			SHEILA E. Sheila Escovedo - daughter of Pete Escovedo (Santana/Azteca)	
7/07/84	28	40+	● 1. Sheila E. in The Glamorous Life .... "The Glamorous Life"(7)	Warner 25107
			PETE SHELLEY English - lead singer of the Buzzcocks	
6/26/82	121	10	1. Homosapien	Arista 6602
7/23/83	151	5	2. XL1	Arista 8017
			T.G. SHEPPARD born Bill Browder in Humbolt, Tennessee - T.G.: The Good	
4/25/81	119	12	1. I Love 'Em All	Warner 3528
1/30/82	152	13	2. Finally!	Warner 3600
6/11/83	189	3	3. T.G. Sheppard's Greatest Hits .... [G]	Warner 23841
			SHERBS Australian quintet originally known as Sherbet	
2/28/81	100	16	1. The Skill	Atco 137
			TONY SHERIDAN - see BEATLES	

DATE CHARTED	PEAK POS	WKS CHRT'D	ARTIST — Album Title	LABEL & NUMBER
			ALLAN SHERMAN comedy writer-producer of TV's "I've Got A Secret" - died on 11/21/73 (48)	
11/03/62	1(2)	51	● 1. **My Son, The Folk Singer** .... [C]	Warner 1475
1/19/63	1(1)	47	2. **My Son, The Celebrity** .... [C]	Warner 1487
8/17/63	1(8)	32	3. **My Son, The Nut** .... [C] "Hello Mudduh, Hello Fudduh!"(2)	Warner 1501
4/11/64	25	19	4. Allan In Wonderland .... [C]	Warner 1539
11/21/64	53	14	5. Peter And The Commissar .... [C] ALLAN SHERMAN/BOSTON POPS/ARTHUR FIEDLER	RCA 2773
11/28/64	32	17	6. For Swingin' Livers Only! .... [C]	Warner 1569
12/18/65	88	11	7. My Name Is Allan .... [C]	Warner 1604
			BOBBY SHERMAN regular on TV's "Shindig" - Jeremy Bolt on TV's "Here Come The Brides"	
11/08/69	11	35	● 1. Bobby Sherman .... "Little Woman"(3)	Metromedia 1014
4/11/70	10	48	● 2. **Here Comes Bobby** .... "La La La (If I Had You)"(9)/"Easy Come, Easy Go"(9)	Metromedia 1028
10/24/70	20	26	● 3. With Love, Bobby .... "Julie, Do Ya Love Me"(5)	Metromedia 1032
4/24/71	48	14	4. Portrait Of Bobby	Metromedia 1040
10/09/71	71	8	5. Getting Together	Metromedia 1045
3/25/72	83	9	6. Bobby Sherman's Greatest Hits .... [G]	Metromedia 1048
			SHIRELLES female quartet from Passaic, New Jersey - Shirley Alston, lead singer - Micki Harris died on 6/10/82 (42)	
5/05/62	59	13	1. Baby It's You .... "Baby It's You"(8)/"Soldier Boy"(1)	Scepter 504
1/26/63	19	49	2. The Shirelles Greatest Hits .... [G] "Will You Love Me Tomorrow"(1)/ "Dedicated To The One I Love"(3)/"Mama Said"(4)	Scepter 507
6/29/63	68	9	3. Foolish Little Girl .... "Foolish Little Girl"(4)	Scepter 511
			SHIRLEY and COMPANY Shirley Goodman of Shirley & Lee	
8/02/75	169	3	1. Shame Shame Shame	Vibration 128
			DONALD SHIRLEY pianist - born in Kingston, Jamaica on 1/27/27	
4/02/55	14	2	1. Tonal Expressions .... [I]	Cadence 1001
			SHOCKING BLUE Dutch quartet - Mariska Veres, lead singer	
2/14/70	31	17	1. The Shocking Blue .... "Venus"(1)	Colossus 1000
			SHOES rock quartet from Zion, Illinois	
10/13/79	50	12	1. Present Tense	Elektra 244
2/07/81	140	7	2. Tongue Twister	Elektra 303
			SHOOTING STAR Kansas City-based rock quintet - Van McLain & Gary West, leaders	
3/15/80	147	14	1. Shooting Star	Virgin 13133
9/19/81	92	30	2. Hang On For Your Life	Epic 37407
8/07/82	82	9	3. III Wishes	Epic 38020
7/30/83	162	6	4. Burning	Epic 38683
			BOBBY SHORT pianist/vocalist	
3/04/72	169	8	1. Bobby Short Loves Cole Porter	Atlantic 606 [2]

DATE CHARTED	PEAK POS	WKS CHRT'D	ARTIST — Album Title	LABEL & NUMBER
			WAYNE SHORTER	
			jazz saxophonist	
7/12/75	183	3	1. Native Dancer	Columbia 33418
			featuring Milton Nascimento, Herbie Hancock & Airto Moreira	
			SHOTGUN	
4/29/78	172	5	1. Good, Bad & Funky	ABC 1060
5/05/79	163	4	2. Shotgun III	MCA 1118
			SHRIEKBACK	
			British: Dave Allen (Gang Of Four), Barry Andrews (XTC) and Carl Marsh	
6/25/83	188	3	1. Care	Warner 23874
			MICHAEL SHRIEVE -	
			see SAMMY HAGAR/STOMU YAMASHTA	
			SIDE EFFECT	
			R&B/funk quartet	
3/19/77	115	13	1. What You Need	Fantasy 9513
1/07/78	86	15	2. Goin' Bananas	Fantasy 9537
1/20/79	135	8	3. Rainbow Visions	Fantasy 9569
			SIEGEL-SCHWALL BAND -	
			see SAN FRANCISCO SYMPHONY	
			BUNNY SIGLER	
2/25/78	77	13	1. Let Me Party With You	Gold Mind 7502
4/07/79	119	9	2. I've Always Wanted To Sing...Not Just Write Songs	Gold Mind 9503
			backing band on above albums: Instant Funk	
			SILK	
11/08/69	191	2	1. Smooth As Raw Silk	ABC 694
			BEVERLY SILLS	
			soprano opera star	
1/03/76	113	6	1. Music of Victor Herbert	Angel 37160
			with Andre Kostelanetz conducting the London Symphony Orchestra	
			SILVER	
			country-rock quintet led by John Batdorf (Batdorf & Rodney)	
9/25/76	142	6	1. Silver	Arista 4076
			SILVER APPLES	
			electronic rock duo: Dan Taylor & Simeon	
8/03/68	193	3	1. Silver Apples	Kapp 3562
			SILVER CONDOR	
			rock quintet led by Joe Cerisano (vocals) & Earl Slick (guitar)	
7/04/81	141	12	1. Silver Condor	Columbia 37163
			SILVER CONVENTION	
			female disco trio from Munich, Germany	
9/13/75	10	25	● 1. **Save Me**	Midland Int. 1129
			"Fly, Robin, Fly"(1)	
4/10/76	13	24	2. Silver Convention	Midland Int. 1369
			"Get Up And Boogie (That's Right)"(2)	
11/13/76	65	12	3. Madhouse	Midland Int. 1824
7/16/77	73	10	4. Golden Girls	Midsong Int. 2296
			HORACE SILVER Quintet	
			jazz pianist	
6/12/65	95	10	1. Song For My Father (Cantiga Para Meu Pai) .... [I]	Blue Note 84185
2/26/66	130	2	2. The Cape Verdean Blues .... [I]	Blue Note 84220
			with J.J. Johnson (trombone) on side 2	

DATE CHARTED	PEAK POS	WKS CHRT'D	ARTIST — Album Title	LABEL & NUMBER
			SHEL SILVERSTEIN satirical/novelty songwriter ("A Boy Named Sue")	
1/20/73	**155**	8	1. Freakin' At The Freakers Ball .... [N] backing band: Dr. Hook & The Medicine Show	Columbia 31119
			HARRY SIMEONE Chorale	
1/06/62	**119**	2	● 1. Sing We Now Of Christmas .... [X] "The Little Drummer Boy"	20th Fox 3002
12/22/62	**44**	2	2. Sing We Now Of Christmas .... [X-R] album later repackaged as "The Little Drummer Boy" - made top 10 on Billboard's special Xmas charts (1963-69)	20th Fox 3002
			GENE SIMMONS bass guitarist of Kiss	
10/14/78	**22**	22	▲ 1. Gene Simmons	Casablanca 7120
			GENE SIMMONS	
11/14/64	**132**	5	1. jumpin' Gene Simmons .... "Haunted House"	Hi 32018
			PATRICK SIMMONS original member of the Doobie Brothers	
5/07/83	**52**	11	1. Arcade	Elektra 60225
			RICHARD SIMMONS - see AEROBICS section	
			SIMON & GARFUNKEL Paul Simon & Art Garfunkel - recorded in high school as Tom & Jerry	
1/22/66	**30**	31	● 1. Wednesday Morning, 3 AM .... contains original unmixed version of "The Sounds Of Silence"	Columbia 9049
2/19/66	**21**	143	● 2. Sounds of Silence .... "The Sounds Of Silence"(1)/"I Am A Rock"(3)	Columbia 9269
11/12/66	**4**	145	● 3. **Parsley, Sage, Rosemary and Thyme** .... "Homeward Bound"(5)/"Scarborough Fair/Canticle"	Columbia 9363
3/16/68	**1(9)**	69	● 4. **The Graduate** .... [S] includes 4 previously released Simon & Grafunkel songs - the two "Mrs. Robinson" cuts are not the hit versions	Columbia 3180
4/27/68	**1(7)**	66	● 5. **Bookends** "Mrs. Robinson"(1) side 2: singles hits previously unavailable on an album	Columbia 9529
2/14/70	**1(10)**	85	● 6. **Bridge Over Troubled Water** .... "The Boxer"(7)/"Bridge Over Troubled Water"(1)/ "Cecilia"(4)	Columbia 9914
7/01/72	**5**	126	● 7. **Simon And Garfunkel's Greatest Hits** ... [G]	Columbia 31350
3/13/82	**6**	34	● 8. **The Concert In Central Park** .... [L] recorded in New York City's Central Park on 9/19/81	Warner 3654 [2]
			CARLY SIMON born on 6/25/45 in New York City - recorded with sister Lucy as the Simon Sisters	
4/24/71	**30**	25	1. Carly Simon .... "That's The Way I've Always Heard It Should Be"(10)	Elektra 74082
11/27/71	**30**	31	● 2. Anticipation	Elektra 75016
12/09/72	**1(5)**	71	● 3. **No Secrets** .... "You're So Vain"(1)	Elektra 75049
2/02/74	**3**	35	● 4. **Hotcakes** .... "Mockingbird"(5-with James Taylor)	Elektra 1002
5/03/75	**10**	17	5. **Playing Possum**	Elektra 1033
12/06/75	**17**	19	● 6. The Best Of Carly Simon .... [G]	Elektra 1048
6/26/76	**29**	13	7. Another Passenger	Elektra 1064
4/22/78	**10**	29	▲ 8. **Boys In The Trees** .... "You Belong To Me"(6)	Elektra 128
6/30/79	**45**	13	9. Spy	Elektra 506
7/12/80	**36**	32	10. Come Upstairs .... "Jesse"	Warner 3443
10/17/81	**50**	24	11. Torch .... featuring jazz and blues songs of the '30s and '40s	Warner 3592
10/08/83	**69**	17	12. Hello Big Man	Warner 23886

DATE CHARTED	PEAK POS	WKS CHRT'D	ARTIST — Album Title	LABEL & NUMBER
			JOE SIMON soul singer - born on 9/2/43 in Simmesport, Louisiana	
6/21/69	**81**	17	1. The Chokin' Kind	Sound Stage 15006
11/29/69	**192**	2	2. Joe Simon...better than ever	Sound Stage 15008
4/03/71	**153**	12	3. The Sounds Of Simon	Spring 4701
3/25/72	**71**	12	4. Drowning In The Sea Of Love	Spring 5702
12/30/72	**147**	8	5. The Best Of Joe Simon .... [G]	Sound Stage 15009
2/17/73	**97**	12	6. The Power Of Joe Simon	Spring 5704
7/19/75	**129**	12	7. Get Down .... "Get Down, Get Down (Get On The Floor)"(8)	Spring 6706
			PAUL SIMON born on 10/13/42 in Newark, New Jersey - also see Simon & Garfunkel	
2/12/72	**4**	36	● 1. **Paul Simon** .... "Mother And Child Reunion"(4)	Columbia 30750
5/26/73	**2(2)**	48	● 2. **There Goes Rhymin' Simon** .... "Kodachrome"(2)/"Loves Me Like A Rock"(2)	Columbia 32280
3/23/74	**33**	17	● 3. Paul Simon In Concert/Live Rhymin' .... [L]	Columbia 32855
10/25/75	**1(1)**	40	● 4. **Still Crazy After All These Years** .... "My Little Town"(9 - Simon & Garfunkel)/ "50 Ways To Leave Your Lover"(1)	Columbia 33540
12/03/77	**18**	23	▲ 5. Greetest Hits, Etc. .... [G] "Slip Slidin' Away"(5)	Columbia 35032
9/06/80	**12**	26	● 6. One-Trick Pony .... [S] Paul starred in the film "Late In The Evening"(6)	Warner 3472
11/19/83	**35**	18	7. Hearts And Bones	Warner 23942
			NINA SIMONE born Eunice Waymon on 2/21/33 in Tryon, North Carolina	
3/06/61	**23**	1	1. Nina At Newport .... [L]	Colpix 412
9/19/64	**102**	11	2. Nina Simone In Concert .... [L]	Philips 135
6/26/65	**99**	8	3. I Put A Spell On You	Philips 172
10/16/65	**139**	7	4. Pastel Blues	Philips 187
11/05/66	**110**	9	5. Wild Is The Wind	Philips 207
11/25/67	**158**	4	6. Silk & Soul	RCA 3837
4/19/69	**187**	3	7. The Best Of Nina Simone .... [K]	Philips 298
3/14/70	**149**	12	8. Black Gold .... [L]	RCA 4248
7/25/70	**189**	3	9. The Best Of Nina Simone .... [K]	RCA 4374
8/21/71	**190**	4	10. Here Comes The Sun	RCA 4536
			SIMPLE MINDS British sextet - Jim Kerr, lead singer	
2/19/83	**69**	19	1. New Gold Dream (81-82-83-84)	A&M 4928
2/18/84	**64**	24	2. Sparkle In The Rain	A&M 4981
			VALERIE SIMPSON also see Ashford & Simpson	
7/31/71	**159**	6	1. Valerie Simpson Exposed	Tamla 311
8/26/72	**162**	6	2. Valerie Simpson	Tamla 317
			FRANK SINATRA one of the world's greatest popular song stylists - born Francis Albert Sinatra on 12/12/15 in Hoboken, New Jersey	
5/28/55	**2(18)**	42	1. **in the Wee Small Hours**	Capitol 581
3/31/56	**2(1)**	66	● 2. **songs for Swingin' Lovers!** .... "I've Got You Under My Skin"	Capitol 653
12/22/56	**8**	25	● 3. **This is Sinatra!** .... [G] "Young At Heart"(2-'54)/"Three Coins In The Fountain"(7-'54)/ "Learnin' The Blues"(1)/"Love And Marriage"(5)/ "(Love Is) The Tender Trap"(7)	Capitol 768
3/02/57	**5**	14	4. **Close To You** .... featuring The Hollywood String Quartet	Capitol 789
5/27/57	**2(1)**	42	5. **a Swingin' Affair!**	Capitol 803

DATE CHARTED	PEAK POS	WKS CHRT'D		ARTIST — Album Title	LABEL & NUMBER
9/23/57	3	29		6. **Where are you?**	Capitol 855
11/11/57	2(1)	27		7. **Pal Joey** .... [S]	Capitol 912
				Frank plays Joey Evans and sings on 6 of the tracks "The Lady Is A Tramp"	
12/30/57	18	2	●	8. a Jolly Christmas from Frank Sinatra ...... [X]	Capitol 894
2/03/58	1(5)	71		9. **Come fly with me**	Capitol 920
4/28/58	8	7		10. **This Is Sinatra, Volume Two** .... [G]	Capitol 982
				"Hey! Jealous Lover"(3)	
6/02/58	12	1		11. The Frank Sinatra Story .... [K]	Columbia 6 [2]
				"All Or Nothing At All"/"You'll Never Know"/"Nancy"	
9/29/58	1(5)	120	●	12. **Frank Sinatra sings for Only The Lonely**	Capitol 1053
2/09/59	2(8)	140	●	13. **Come Dance With Me!**	Capitol 1069
6/01/59	8	15		14. **Look to Your Heart** .... [K]	Capitol 1164
8/24/59	2(2)	73		15. **No One Cares**	Capitol 1221
8/22/60	1(9)	86	●	16. **Nice 'n' Easy**	Capitol 1417
2/13/61	3	36		17. **Sinatra's Swingin' Session!!!**	Capitol 1491
4/10/61	4	60		18. **All The Way** .... [G]	Capitol 1538
				"All The Way"(2)/"Witchcraft"(6)/"High Hopes"	
5/01/61	4	35		19. **Ring-A-Ding Ding!**	Reprise 1001
				the first album for Sinatra's own record company	
8/14/61	6	22		20. **Sinatra Swings**	Reprise 1002
				"That Old Black Magic"	
8/14/61	8	39		21. **Come Swing With Me!**	Capitol 1594
11/06/61	3	42		22. **I Remember Tommy...**	Reprise 1003
				songs popularized by Tommy Dorsey	
3/17/62	8	31		23. **Sinatra & Strings**	Reprise 1004
				"Night And Day"/"Misty"/"Stardust"	
4/21/62	19	29		24. Point Of No Return	Capitol 1676
8/18/62	15	18		25. Sinatra Sings...of love and things .... [K]	Capitol 1729
9/01/62	18	16		26. Sinatra and Swingin' Brass	Reprise 1005
				"I Get A Kick Out Of You"	
11/10/62	25	17		27. All Alone	Reprise 1007
12/22/62	120	2		28. a Jolly Christmas from Frank Sinatra .... [X-R]	Capitol 894
				album later repackaged as "The Sinatra Christmas Album" - made top 10 on Billboard's special Christmas charts (1984)	
2/02/63	5	42		29. **Sinatra-Basie**	Reprise 1008
				FRANK SINATRA/COUNT BASIE	
6/22/63	6	35		30. **The Concert Sinatra**	Reprise 1009
9/28/63	129	4		31. Tell Her You Love Her .... [K]	Capitol 1919
10/05/63	8	43	●	32. **Sinatra's Sinatra**	Reprise 1010
				newly recorded Sinatra favorites	
4/11/64	10	24		33. **Days Of Wine And Roses, Moon River, and other academy award winners**	Reprise 1011
5/30/64	116	7		34. America, I Hear You Singing	Reprise 2020
				FRANK SINATRA/BING CROSBY/FRED WARING	
8/22/64	13	31		35. It Might As Well Be Swing	Reprise 1012
				FRANK SINATRA/COUNT BASIE	
12/19/64	19	28		36. Softly, As I Leave You	Reprise 1013
7/03/65	9	44		37. **Sinatra '65**	Reprise 6167
8/21/65	5	69	●	38. **September Of My Years**	Reprise 1014
				"It Was A Very Good Year"	
12/25/65	9	32	●	39. **A Man And His Music** .... [K]	Reprise 1016 [2]
				an anthology of Sinatra's career, narrated and sung by him	
12/25/65	30	16		40. My Kind Of Broadway	Reprise 1015
4/23/66	34	14		41. Moonlight Sinatra	Reprise 1018
6/18/66	1(1)	73	●	42. **Strangers In The Night**	Reprise 1017
				"Strangers In The Night"(1)	
8/20/66	9	44	●	43. **Sinatra At The Sands** .... [L]	Reprise 1019 [2]
				with Count Basie & The Orchestra	
12/31/66	6	61	●	44. **That's Life**	Reprise 1020
				"That's Life"(4)	

DATE CHARTED	PEAK POS	WKS CHRT'D	ARTIST — Album Title	LABEL & NUMBER
4/15/67	19	28	45. Francis Albert Sinatra & Antonio Carlos Jobim .... Jobim: Brazilian songwriter/guitarist/vocalist	Reprise 1021
7/29/67	195	2	46. The Movie Songs .... [K] Frank's greatest movie song hits ('54-'60)	Capitol 2700
9/16/67	24	23	47. Frank Sinatra .... "Somethin' Stupid"(1-with Nancy Sinatra)	Reprise 1022
2/24/68	78	13	48. Francis A. & Edward K. .... FRANK SINATRA & DUKE ELLINGTON	Reprise 1024
9/07/68	55	25	● 49. Frank Sinatra's Greatest Hits! .... [G]	Reprise 1025
12/28/68	18	28	● 50. Cycles	Reprise 1027
5/10/69	11	19	● 51. My Way	Reprise 1029
8/23/69	186	3	52. Close-Up .... [R] reissue of albums #3 & #10 above	Capitol 254 [2]
9/06/69	30	16	53. A Man Alone & Other Songs of Rod McKuen	Reprise 1030
4/11/70	101	10	54. Watertown	Reprise 1031
4/24/71	73	15	55. Sinatra & Company .... with Antonio Carlos Jobim on side one	Reprise 1033
6/10/72	88	17	56. Frank Sinatra's Greatest Hits, Vol. 2 .... [G]	Reprise 1034
10/27/73	13	22	● 57. Ol' Blue Eyes Is Back	Reprise 2155
8/03/74	48	12	58. Some Nice Things I've Missed	Reprise 2195
12/07/74	37	12	59. Sinatra - The Main Event Live .... [L] recorded at New York's Madison Square Garden - with Woody Herman & The Young Thundering Herd	Reprise 2207
1/04/75	170	3	60. Round #1 .... [K]	Capitol 11357 [2]
4/12/80	17	24	● 61. Trilogy: Past, Present, Future .... "Theme From New York, New York"	Reprise 2300 [3]
12/05/81	52	13	62. She Shot Me Down	Reprise 2305
8/25/84	58	13	63. L.A. Is My Lady .... with Quincy Jones & Orchestra	Qwest 25145

NANCY SINATRA
daughter of Frank Sinatra

DATE CHARTED	PEAK POS	WKS CHRT'D	ARTIST — Album Title	LABEL & NUMBER
3/12/66	5	42	● 1. **Boots** .... "These Boots Are Made For Walkin'"(1)	Reprise 6202
6/04/66	41	15	2. How Does That Grab You? .... "How Does That Grab You, Darlin'?"(7)	Reprise 6207
9/03/66	122	7	3. Nancy in London	Reprise 6221
2/18/67	18	24	4. Sugar .... "Sugar Town"(5)	Reprise 6239
9/02/67	43	26	5. Country, My Way	Reprise 6251
1/13/68	37	32	6. Movin' With Nancy .... [TV] guests: Frank Sinatra, Dean Martin & Lee Hazlewood	Reprise 6277
4/13/68	13	44	● 7. Nancy & Lee .... NANCY SINATRA & LEE HAZLEWOOD	Reprise 6273
5/03/69	91	8	8. Nancy	Reprise 6333
10/03/70	99	7	9. Nancy's Greatest Hits .... [G] "Somethin' Stupid"(1-with Frank Sinatra)	Reprise 6409

PETE SINFIELD
English - lyrical partner of Robert Fripp in King Crimson

DATE CHARTED	PEAK POS	WKS CHRT'D	ARTIST — Album Title	LABEL & NUMBER
10/06/73	190	5	1. Still	Manticore 66667

SINGING NUN
Jeanine Deckers, from the Fichermont, Belgium nuns convent (died 3/31/85-52) - also see "The Singing Nun" soundtrack by Debbie Reynolds

DATE CHARTED	PEAK POS	WKS CHRT'D	ARTIST — Album Title	LABEL & NUMBER
11/09/63	1(10)	39	● 1. **The Singing Nun** .... [F]	Philips 203
4/11/64	90	14	2. Her Joy, Her Songs .... [F]	Philips 209

SIOUXSIE & THE BANSHEES
British group

DATE CHARTED	PEAK POS	WKS CHRT'D	ARTIST — Album Title	LABEL & NUMBER
7/07/84	157	7	1. Hyaena	Geffen 24030

DATE CHARTED	PEAK POS	WKS CHRT'D	ARTIST — Album Title	LABEL & NUMBER
			SIR DOUGLAS QUINTET 'Tex-Mex' rock band led by Doug Sahm from San Antonio - also see Doug Sahm Band	
4/19/69	**81**	11	1. Mendocino	Smash 67115
2/14/81	**184**	4	2. Border Wave	Takoma 7088
			SIR LORD BALTIMORE rock trio - John Garner, lead singer	
2/06/71	**198**	2	1. Kingdom Come	Mercury 61328
			SISTER SLEDGE Kathy, Debbie, Kim and Joni Sledge	
2/24/79	**3**	33	▲ 1. **We Are Family** "He's The Greatest Dancer"(9)/"We Are Family"(2)	Cotillion 5209
3/08/80	**31**	15	2. Love Somebody Today	Cotillion 16012
2/28/81	**42**	29	3. All American Girls	Cotillion 16027
2/13/82	**69**	14	4. The Sisters	Cotillion 5231
6/04/83	**169**	8	5. Bet Cha Say That To All The Girls	Cotillion 90069
			RICKY SKAGGS country/bluegrass singer	
6/12/82	**77**	30	● 1. Waitin' For The Sun To Shine	Epic 37193
10/16/82	**61**	12	● 2. Highways & Heartaches	Epic 37996
11/10/84	**180**	5	3. Country Boy	Epic 39410
3/09/85	**181**	4	4. Favorite Country Songs [K]	Epic 39409
			SKY rock trio led by Doug Fieger (Knack)	
12/19/70	**160**	6	1. Sky	RCA 4457
			SKY classical/rock group led by classical guitarist John Williams	
11/01/80	**125**	15	1. Sky [I]	Arista 8302 [2]
5/02/81	**181**	3	2. Sky 3 [I]	Arista 4288
			SKYLARK Canadian quartet - Donny Gerrard & Ms. B.J. Cook, lead singers	
4/07/73	**102**	16	1. Skylark "Wildflower"(9)	Capitol 11048
			SKYY New York City-based 8-piece dance/funk band	
5/19/79	**117**	9	1. Skyy	Salsoul 8517
3/15/80	**61**	23	2. Skyway	Salsoul 8532
12/06/80	**85**	20	3. Skyyport	Salsoul 8537
11/21/81	**18**	33	● 4. Skyy Line	Salsoul 8548
11/20/82	**81**	13	5. Skyyjammer	Salsoul 8555
8/06/83	**183**	3	6. Skyylight	Salsoul 8562
			SLADE English hard-rock quartet, Noddy Holder, lead singer	
10/07/72	**158**	11	1. Slade Alive! [L]	Polydor 5508
2/17/73	**69**	26	2. Slayed?	Polydor 5524
10/20/73	**129**	7	3. Sladest [K] "Cum On Feel The Noize"	Reprise 2173
3/09/74	**168**	5	4. Stomp Your Hands, Clap Your Feet	Warner 2770
7/05/75	**93**	14	5. Slade In Flame [S] Slade starred in the film "Flame"	Warner 2865
5/05/84	**33**	23	6. Keep Your Hands Off My Power Supply "Run Runaway"	CBS Assoc. 39336
			FELIX SLATKIN conductor of a studio orchestra - died on 2/9/63 (47)	
4/06/63	**20**	12	1. Our Winter Love [I]	Liberty 7287

DATE CHARTED	PEAK POS	WKS CHRT'D	ARTIST — Album Title	LABEL & NUMBER
			SLAVE Dayton, Ohio 8-man funk band	
4/09/77	**22**	28	● 1. Slave	Cotillion 9914
12/17/77	**67**	15	2. The Hardness Of The World	Cotillion 5201
8/19/78	**78**	10	3. The Concept	Cotillion 5206
12/08/79	**92**	15	4. Just a Touch of Love	Cotillion 5217
11/01/80	**53**	34	● 5. Stone Jam	Cotillion 5224
10/10/81	**46**	23	6. Show Time	Cotillion 5227
1/15/83	**177**	6	7. Visions Of The Lite	Cotillion 90024
10/22/83	**168**	5	8. Bad Enuff	Cotillion 90118
			PERCY SLEDGE soul singer from Leighton, Alabama	
6/04/66	**37**	21	1. When A Man Loves A Woman .... "When A Man Loves A Woman"(1)	Atlantic 8125
11/26/66	**136**	3	2. Warm & Tender Soul	Atlantic 8132
8/05/67	**178**	3	3. The Percy Sledge Way	Atlantic 8146
5/25/68	**148**	6	4. Take Time To Know Her	Atlantic 8180
3/01/69	**133**	11	5. The Best Of Percy Sledge .... [G]	Atlantic 8210
			GRACE SLICK Jefferson Airplane/Starship lead singer - also see Paul Kantner	
5/04/68	**166**	4	1. Conspicuous Only In Its Absence .... [E-L] THE GREAT SOCIETY with GRACE SLICK recorded in 1965 - features early versions of 'Somebody To Love' & 'White Rabbit'	Columbia 9624
2/09/74	**127**	7	2. Manhole .... with David Crosby and members of Jefferson Starship	Grunt 0347
4/05/80	**32**	16	3. Dreams	RCA 3544
2/14/81	**48**	14	4. Welcome To The Wrecking Ball!	RCA 3851
			SLY & THE FAMILY STONE San Francisco funk/rock band featuring Sly Stone (Sylvester Stewart), brother Freddie Stone, sister Rose Stone and Larry Graham (1-5)	
5/04/68	**142**	7	1. Dance To The Music .... "Dance To The Music"(8)	Epic 26371
12/07/68	**195**	5	2. Life	Epic 26397
4/26/69	**13**	102	● 3. Stand! .... "Everyday People"(1)	Epic 26456
11/07/70	**2(1)**	79	● 4. **Greatest Hits** .... [G] "Hot Fun In The Summertime"(2)/ "Thank You (Falettinme Be Mice Elf Agin)"(1)	Epic 30325
11/13/71	**1(2)**	31	● 5. **There's A Riot Goin' On** .... "Family Affair"(1)	Epic 30986
6/30/73	**7**	33	● 6. **Fresh**	Epic 32134
7/27/74	**15**	15	● 7. Small Talk	Epic 32930
11/08/75	**45**	10	8. High On You .... shown only as Sly Stone	Epic 33835
11/10/79	**152**	3	9. Back On The Right Track	Warner 3303
			SMALL FACES British: Steve Marriott (guitar), Ronnie Lane (bass), Ian McLagan (organ), Kenny Jones (drums) - also see Faces	
3/16/68	**178**	3	1. There Are But Four Small Faces .... "Itchycoo Park"	Immediate 52002
9/21/68	**159**	9	2. Ogdens' Nut Gone Flake	Immediate 52008
8/05/72	**176**	10	3. Early Faces .... [E]	Pride 0001
3/17/73	**189**	6	4. Ogdens' Nut Gone Flake .... [R]	Abkco 4225
			MILLIE SMALL 16-year-old from Jamaica	
8/08/64	**132**	5	1. My Boy Lollipop .... "My Boy Lollipop"(2)	Smash 67055

DATE CHARTED	PEAK POS	WKS CHRT'D	ARTIST — Album Title	LABEL & NUMBER
			SMITH Gayle McCormick, lead singer	
8/23/69	**17**	28	1. a group called Smith .... "Baby It's You"(5)	Dunhill 50056
7/04/70	**74**	12	2. Minus-Plus	Dunhill 50081
			CAL SMITH member of Ernest Tubb's Texas Troubadours	
9/06/69	**170**	2	1. Cal Smith Sings	Kapp 3608
4/14/73	**191**	3	2. I've Found Someone Of My Own	Decca 75369
			CONNIE SMITH	
5/22/65	**105**	5	1. Connie Smith .... "Once A Day"	RCA 3341
			FRANKIE SMITH	
8/08/81	**54**	10	1. Children Of Tomorrow .... "Double Dutch Bus"	WMOT 37391
			HURRICANE SMITH English producer (Pink Floyd) and engineer (Beatles) - real name: Norman Smith	
1/06/73	**53**	18	1. Hurricane Smith .... "Oh, Babe, What Would You Say?"(3)	Capitol 1139
			JERRY SMITH & His Pianos also see Magic Organ	
7/26/69	**200**	2	1. Truck Stop .... [I]	ABC 692
			JIMMY SMITH jazz organist from Philadelphia - born on 12/8/25	
2/17/62	**28**	51	1. Midnight Special .... [I] with Stanley Turrentine (sax) & Kenny Burrell (guitar)	Blue Note 84078
6/02/62	**10**	34	2. Bashin' .... [I] "Walk On The Wild Side"	Verve 8474
3/09/63	**14**	22	3. Back At The Chicken Shack .... [I] with Stanley Turrentine & Kenny Burrell	Blue Note 84117
5/18/63	**11**	30	4. Hobo Flats .... [I]	Verve 8544
11/09/63	**25**	33	5. Any Number Can Win .... [I]	Verve 8552
11/09/63	**64**	8	6. Rockin' The Boat .... [E-I] with Lou Donaldson (alto sax)	Blue Note 84141
11/30/63	**108**	4	7. Blue Bash! .... [I] KENNY BURRELL/JIMMY SMITH	Verve 8553
4/18/64	**16**	31	8. Who's Afraid Of Virginia Woolf? .... [I]	Verve 8583
8/01/64	**86**	20	9. Prayer Meetin' .... [E-I] with Stanley Turrentine (tenor sax)	Blue Note 84164
9/19/64	**12**	32	10. The Cat .... [I]	Verve 8587
5/08/65	**35**	24	11. Monster .... [I]	Verve 8618
9/18/65	**15**	31	12. Organ Grinder Swing .... [I] featuring Kenny Burrell (guitar) & Grady Tate (drums)	Verve 8628
3/12/66	**28**	27	13. Get My Mojo Workin' .... [I]	Verve 8641
9/10/66	**77**	14	14. Hoochie Cooche Man .... [I]	Verve 8667
11/12/66	**121**	9	15. "Bucket"! .... [E-I]	Blue Note 84235
5/20/67	**129**	23	16. Jimmy & Wes The Dynamic Duo .... [I] JIMMY SMITH & WES MONTGOMERY	Verve 8678
10/07/67	**60**	20	17. Respect .... [I]	Verve 8705
12/09/67	**185**	4	18. The Best Of Jimmy Smith .... [G-I]	Verve 8721
6/08/68	**128**	4	19. Jimmy Smith's Greatest Hits! .... [G-I]	Blue Note 89901 [2]
10/26/68	**169**	10	20. Livin' It Up! .... [I]	Verve 8750
7/26/69	**144**	3	21. The Boss .... [I] featuring George Benson (guitar)	Verve 8770
5/23/70	**197**	3	22. Groove Drops .... [I]	Verve 8794
			KATE SMITH popular singer of radio and television - born on 5/1/07	
12/21/63	**83**	18	1. Kate Smith at Carnegie Hall .... [L]	RCA 2819
10/31/64	**145**	2	2. The Sweetest Sounds	RCA 2921

DATE CHARTED	PEAK POS	WKS CHRT'D	ARTIST — Album Title	LABEL & NUMBER
1/15/66	**36**	24	3. How Great Thou Art	RCA 3445
6/25/66	**130**	3	4. The Kate Smith Anniversary Album	RCA 3535
			medleys of songs she introduced on radio	
12/03/66	**148**	2	5. Kate Smith Today	RCA 3670

KATHY SMITH - see AEROBICS section

KEELY SMITH
born on 3/9/32 in Norfolk, Virgina - also see Louis Prima

10/20/58	**14**	8	1. Politely!	Capitol 1073
5/25/59	**23**	9	2. Swingin' Pretty	Capitol 1145
1/04/60	**40**	1	3. Be My Love	Dot 3241

LONNIE SMITH
soul/jazz organist

5/16/70	**186**	2	1. Move Your Hand .... [I-L]	Blue Note 84326

LONNIE LISTON SMITH
jazz/funk keyboardist

LONNIE LISTON SMITH & THE COSMIC ECHOES:

5/24/75	**85**	13	1. Expansions	Flying Dtch. 0934
10/18/75·	**74**	15	2. Visions Of A New World	Flying Dtch. 1196
4/10/76	**75**	14	3. Reflections Of A Golden Dream	Flying Dtch. 1460
12/11/76	**73**	20	4. Renaissance	RCA 1822

LONNIE LISTON SMITH:

7/30/77	**58**	11	5. Live! .... [I-L]	RCA 2433
4/22/78	**120**	13	6. Loveland	Columbia 35332
2/17/79	**123**	8	7. Exotic Mysteries	Columbia 35654
7/30/83	**193**	2	8. Dreams Of Tomorrow	Doctor Jazz 38447
			Donald Smith (Lonnie's brother), lead vocalist on above albums	

O.C. SMITH
Ocie Lee Smith - replaced Joe Williams as lead singer with Count Basie

6/15/68	**19**	42	1. Hickory Holler Revisited	Columbia 9680
			"Little Green Apples"(2)	
3/01/69	**50**	15	2. For Once In My Life	Columbia 9756
10/18/69	**58**	16	3. O.C. Smith At Home	Columbia 9908
9/19/70	**177**	5	4. O.C. Smith's Greatest Hits .... [G]	Columbia 30227
7/31/71	**159**	7	5. Help Me Make It Through The Night	Columbia 30664

PATTI SMITH Group
punk-rocker from Chicago

12/13/75	**47**	17	1. Horses	Arista 4066
11/27/76	**122**	8	2. Radio Ethiopia	Arista 4097
4/08/78	**20**	23	3. Easter	Arista 4171
			"Because The Night"	
5/19/79	**18**	19	4. Wave	Arista 4221
			produced by Todd Rundgren	

REX SMITH
starred in several Broadway musicals

4/28/79	**19**	19	● 1. Sooner Or Later	Columbia 35813
			"You Take My Breath Away"(10)	
1/12/80	**165**	3	2. Forever, Rex Smith	Columbia 36275
8/22/81	**167**	4	3. Everlasting Love	Columbia 37494

SAMMI SMITH

2/13/71	**33**	21	1. Help Me Make It Through The Night	Mega 1000
			"Help Me Make It Through The Night"(8)	
8/21/71	**191**	2	2. Lonesome	Mega 1007

SMITHS
English quartet - Stephen Morrissey, lead singer

5/05/84	**150**	11	1. The Smiths	Sire 25065
3/02/85	**130+**	6+	2. Meat Is Murder	Sire 25269

DATE CHARTED	PEAK POS	WKS CHRT'D	ARTIST — Album Title	LABEL & NUMBER
			SMOKESTACK LIGHTNIN' white blues quartet - Ronnie Darling, lead singer	
4/12/69	**200**	2	1. Off The Wall	Bell 6026
			SMOKIE Chris Norman, lead singer of pop/rock quartet	
1/22/77	**173**	6	1. Midnight Cafe	RSO 3005
			SMOTHERS BROTHERS comedians Tom & Dick Smothers - hosts of their own TV comedy variety series, 1967-70	
10/20/62	**26**	66	● 1. The Two Sides Of The Smothers Brothers .... [C] side 1: comedy; side 2: serious singing	Mercury 20675
4/06/63	**27**	63	● 2. (Think Ethnic!) .... [C]	Mercury 20777
7/13/63	**45**	50	● 3. The Songs And Comedy of The Smothers Brothers! .... [C] their first album	Mercury 20611
12/14/63	**13**	33	4. Curb Your Tongue, Knave! .... [C]	Mercury 20862
5/23/64	**23**	28	5. It Must Have Been Something I Said! .... [C]	Mercury 20904
12/19/64	**58**	20	6. Tour De Farce American History And Other Unrelated Subjects .... [C]	Mercury 20948
6/05/65	**57**	10	7. Aesop's Fables The Smothers Brothers Way .... [C]	Mercury 20989
10/16/65	**39**	28	8. Mom Always Liked You Best! .... [C]	Mercury 21051
8/13/66	**119**	6	9. Golden Hits Of The Smothers Brothers, Vol. 2 .... [C] new versions of their classics (there is no volume 1)	Mercury 21089
11/16/68	**164**	4	10. Smothers Comedy Brothers Hour .... [C]	Mercury 61193
			SNAIL	
7/08/78	**135**	12	1. Snail	Cream 1009
11/10/79	**186**	2	2. Flow	Cream 1012
			SNEAKER Los Angeles-based sextet	
12/12/81	**149**	17	1. Sneaker	Handshake 37631
			SNIFF 'n' the TEARS British - Paul Roberts, lead singer	
7/28/79	**35**	17	1. Fickle Heart .... "Driver's Seat"	Atlantic 19242
9/19/81	**192**	2	2. Love Action	MCA 5242
			PHOEBE SNOW born Phoebe Laub on 7/17/52 in New York City	
9/07/74	**4**	58	● 1. **Phoebe Snow** .... "Poetry Man"(5)	Shelter 2109
2/14/76	**13**	22	● 2. Second Childhood	Columbia 33952
11/06/76	**29**	21	3. It Looks Like Snow	Columbia 34387
10/22/77	**73**	15	4. Never Letting Go	Columbia 34875
10/28/78	**100**	7	5. Against The Grain	Columbia 35456
4/04/81	**51**	18	6. Rock Away	Mirage 19297
			TERRY SNYDER & THE ALL-STARS - see ENOCH LIGHT Terry died on 3/15/63 (47)	
			GINO SOCCIO techno-disco artist from Montreal, Canada	
4/21/79	**79**	13	1. Outline	RFC 3309
5/23/81	**96**	14	2. Closer	Atlantic 16042

DATE CHARTED	PEAK POS	WKS CHRT'D	ARTIST — Album Title	LABEL & NUMBER
			SOFT CELL British electro-rock duo: Marc Almond & David Ball	
1/30/82	22	41	1. Non-Stop Erotic Cabaret .... "Tainted Love"(8)	Sire 3647
8/14/82	57	14	2. Non-Stop Ecstatic Dancing .... [M]	Sire 23694
2/26/83	84	8	3. The Art of Falling Apart .... includes a bonus mini LP	Sire 23769 [2]
			SOFT MACHINE British experimental rock trio	
12/21/68	160	9	1. The Soft Machine	Probe 4500
			JOANIE SOMMERS first heard as the vocalist for "Pepsi-Cola" jingles	
9/22/62	103	3	1. Johnny Get Angry .... "Johnny Get Angry"(7)	Warner 1470
			SONNY & CHER Salvatore Bono & Cherilyn LaPier (married 1964-1974) - hosts of their own TV comedy/musical variety series (1971-1977)	
8/21/65	2(8)	44	● 1. **Look At Us** .... "I Got You Babe"(1)	Atco 177
10/23/65	69	16	2. Baby Don't Go .... [E] Sonny & Cher (5 cuts), Lettermen (3), Bill Medley (3) "Baby Don't Go"(8)	Reprise 6177
4/16/66	34	20	3. The Wondrous World Of Sonny & Cher	Atco 183
3/25/67	45	29	4. In Case You're In Love .... "The Beat Goes On"(6)	Atco 203
5/27/67	73	18	5. Good Times .... [S] Sonny & Cher star as themselves in the film	Atco 214
8/12/67	23	64	6. The Best of Sonny & Cher .... [G]	Atco 219
10/02/71	35	40	● 7. Sonny & Cher Live .... [L]	Kapp 3654
2/26/72	14	29	● 8. All I Ever Need Is You .... "All I Ever Need Is You"(7)/"A Cowboys Work Is Never Done"(8)	Kapp 3660
9/09/72	122	12	9. The Two Of Us .... [R] reissue of albums 1 & 4 above	Atco 804 [2]
6/30/73	132	6	10. Mama Was A Rock And Roll Singer Papa Used To Write All Her Songs	MCA 2101
12/22/73	175	7	11. Sonny & Cher Live In Las Vegas, Vol. 2 .... [L]	MCA 8004 [2]
9/28/74	146	6	12. Greatest Hits .... [G]	MCA 2117
			SONS OF CHAMPLIN San Francisco 7-man rock band led by Bill Champlin	
6/14/69	137	9	1. Loosen Up Naturally	Capitol 200 [2]
11/08/69	171	6	2. The Sons	Capitol 332
6/09/73	186	5	3. Welcome To The Dance	Columbia 32341
6/05/76	117	10	4. A Circle Filled With Love	Ariola Am. 50007
5/28/77	188	4	5. Loving Is Why	Ariola Am. 50017
			SOPWITH CAMEL San Francisco quintet	
10/28/67	191	2	1. Sopwith Camel	Kama Sutra 8060
			S.O.S. BAND Atlanta funk/R&B band - Mary Davis, lead singer	
6/28/80	12	20	● 1. S.O.S .... "Take Your Time (Do It Right)"(3)	Tabu 36332
8/22/81	117	6	2. Too	Tabu 37449
12/25/82	172	8	3. S.O.S. III	Tabu 38352
8/27/83	47	29	● 4. On The Rise	Tabu 38697
9/01/84	60	27	5. Just The Way You Like It	Tabu 39332
			SOUL CHILDREN	
9/06/69	154	6	1. Soul Children	Stax 2018
4/29/72	159	6	2. Genesis	Stax 3003

DATE CHARTED	PEAK POS	WKS CHRT'D	ARTIST — Album Title	LABEL & NUMBER
			SOUL SURVIVORS white-soul band from New York City and Philadelphia	
11/18/67	**123**	13	1. When The Whistle Blows Anything Goes .... "Expressway To Your Heart"(4)	Crimson 502
			DAVID SOUL Ken Hutchinson of TV's "Starsky & Hutch"	
1/22/77	**40**	22	1. David Soul .... "Don't Give Up On Us"(1)	Private S. 2019
9/10/77	**86**	7	2. Playing To An Audience Of One	Private S. 7001
			SOULFUL STRINGS Chicago studio group - Richard Evans, conductor	
8/26/67	**166**	15	1. Paint It Black .... [I]	Cadet 776
11/11/67	**59**	34	2. Groovin' With The Soulful Strings .... [I]	Cadet 796
8/03/68	**189**	4	3. Another Exposure .... [I]	Cadet 805
5/03/69	**125**	6	4. In Concert/Back By Demand .... [I-L]	Cadet 820
11/29/69	**183**	4	5. Spring Fever .... [I]	Cadet 834
			SOUNDS OF SUNSHINE	
8/14/71	**187**	8	1. Love Means You Never Have To Say You're Sorry	Ranwood 8089
			SOUNDS ORCHESTRAL English - Johnny Pearson on piano	
5/29/65	**11**	28	1. Cast Your Fate To The Wind .... [I] "Cast Your Fate To The Wind"(10)	Parkway 7046
			JOE SOUTH singer/songwriter from Atlanta, Georgia	
2/08/69	**117**	14	1. Introspect .... "Games People Play"	Capitol 108
1/17/70	**60**	23	2. Don't It Make You Want To Go Home? .... "Walk A Mile In My Shoes"	Capitol 392
9/12/70	**125**	11	3. Joe South's Greatest Hits .... [G]	Capitol 450
			SOUTHER, HILLMAN, FURAY Band J.D. Souther, Chris Hillman, Richie Furay	
7/20/74	**11**	22	● 1. The Souther, Hillman, Furay Band	Asylum 1006
6/21/75	**39**	11	2. Trouble In Paradise	Asylum 1036
			J.D. SOUTHER John David Souther	
5/08/76	**85**	11	1. Black Rose	Asylum 1059
9/22/79	**41**	22	2. You're Only Lonely .... "You're Only Lonely"(7)	Columbia 36093
			SOUTHERN COMFORT - **see MATTHEWS' SOUTHERN COMFORT**	
			SOUTHSIDE JOHNNY & THE ASBURY JUKES Johnny Lyon, leader of rock band formed in Asbury Park, New Jersey	
7/10/76	**125**	9	1. I Don't Want To Go Home	Epic 34180
5/07/77	**85**	9	2. This Time It's For Real .... with guests: The Coasters, The Drifters, The Five Satins	Epic 34668
11/04/78	**112**	20	3. Hearts Of Stone .... above 3 albums produced by Miami Steve Van Zandt	Epic 35488
8/18/79	**48**	14	4. The Jukes	Mercury 3793
6/14/80	**67**	15	5. Love Is A Sacrifice	Mercury 3836
5/09/81	**80**	12	6. Live - Reach Up And Touch The Sky .... [L]	Mercury 8602 [2]
10/01/83	**154**	6	7. Trash It Up!	Mirage 90113
9/08/84	**164**	8	8. In The Heat	Mirage 90186
			RED SOVINE full name: Woodrow Wilson Sovine - died on 4/4/80 (61)	
9/11/76	**119**	6	1. Teddy Bear	Starday 968

DATE CHARTED	PEAK POS	WKS CHRT'D	ARTIST — Album Title	LABEL & NUMBER
			SPANDAU BALLET English quintet - Tony Hadley, lead singer	
5/14/83	**19**	37	1. True .... "True"(4)	Chrysalis 41403
8/18/84	**50**	16	2. Parade	Chrysalis 41473
			SPANKY & OUR GANG Elaine "Spanky" McFarlane, lead singer	
9/09/67	**77**	15	1. Spanky And Our Gang .... "Sunday Will Never Be The Same"(9)	Mercury 61124
4/27/68	**56**	25	2. Like To Get To Know You	Mercury 61161
2/15/69	**101**	7	3. Anything You Choose/Without Rhyme Or Reason	Mercury 61183
11/01/69	**91**	17	4. Spanky's Greatest Hit(s) .... [G]	Mercury 61227
			SPARKS brothers Ron & Russell Mael	
8/24/74	**101**	14	1. Kimono My House	Island 9272
2/08/75	**63**	13	2. Propaganda	Island 9312
11/29/75	**169**	6	3. Indiscreet	Island 9345
8/15/81	**182**	2	4. Whomp That Sucker	RCA 4091
5/22/82	**173**	6	5. Angst In My Pants	Atlantic 19347
4/30/83	**88**	17	6. Sparks In Outer Space	Atlantic 80055
			SPECIALS 7-man 'ska' band from Coventry, England	
1/26/80	**84**	21	1. The Specials	Chrysalis 1265
11/08/80	**98**	5	2. More Specials	Chrysalis 1303
			JIMMIE SPHEERIS	
9/20/75	**135**	6	1. The Dragon Is Dancing	Epic 33565
			SPIDER Amanda Blue, lead singer of New York-based quintet	
5/17/80	**130**	10	1. Spider	Dreamland 5000
7/11/81	**185**	2	2. Between The Lines	Dreamland 5007
			SPIDERS FROM MARS David Bowie's backup band	
4/03/76	**197**	2	1. Spiders From Mars	Pye 12125
			SPINAL TAP - see SOUNDTRACK "This Is Spinal Tap"	
			SPINNERS R&B quintet founded by Harvey Fuqua in Detroit in 1957 - Philippe Wynne, lead singer ('72-'77) died 7/14/84 (43)	
11/14/70	**199**	2	1. 2nd Time Around	V.I.P. 405
4/21/73	**14**	28	● 2. Spinners .... "I'll Be Around"(3)/"Could It Be I'm Falling In Love"(4)	Atlantic 7256
5/12/73	**124**	10	3. The Best of The Spinners .... [E]	Motown 769
3/16/74	**16**	35	● 4. Mighty Love	Atlantic 7296
12/14/74	**9**	26	● 5. **New And Improved** .... "Then Came You"(1-with Dionne Warwick)	Atlantic 18118
8/09/75	**8**	26	● 6. **Pick Of The Litter** .... "They Just Can't Stop It the (Games People Play)"(5)	Atlantic 18141
12/13/75	**20**	21	7. Spinners Live! .... [L]	Atlantic 910 [2]
7/31/76	**25**	30	● 8. Happiness Is Being With The Detroit Spinners .... "The Rubberband Man"(2)	Atlantic 18181
4/02/77	**26**	13	9. Yesterday, Today & Tomorrow	Atlantic 19100
12/24/77	**57**	13	10. Spinners/8	Atlantic 19146
5/20/78	**115**	9	11. The Best of Spinners .... [G]	Atlantic 19179
5/26/79	**165**	4	12. From Here To Eternally	Atlantic 19219

DATE CHARTED	PEAK POS	WKS CHRT'D	ARTIST — Album Title	LABEL & NUMBER
1/19/80	32	20	13. Dancin' And Lovin' .... "Working My Way Back To You/Forgive Me, Girl"(2)	Atlantic 19256
6/21/80	53	13	14. Love Trippin' .... "Cupid/I've Loved You For A Long Time"(4)	Atlantic 19270
4/04/81	128	6	15. Labor Of Love	Atlantic 16032
1/16/82	196	4	16. Can't Shake This Feelin'	Atlantic 19318
1/08/83	167	6	17. Grand Slam	Atlantic 80020
			SPIRAL STARECASE pop/rock quintet from Sacramento, California - Pat Upton, lead singer	
6/14/69	79	16	1. More Today Than Yesterday	Columbia 9852
			SPIRIT Los Angeles rock fusion group - Jay Ferguson, lead singer (1-8)	
4/20/68	31	32	1. Spirit	Ode 44004
1/18/69	22	21	2. The Family That Plays Together	Ode 44014
8/23/69	55	15	3. Clear Spirit	Ode 44016
12/26/70	63	14	● 4. Twelve Dreams Of Dr. Sardonicus	Epic 30267
3/18/72	63	14	5. Feedback	Epic 31175
7/22/72	189	7	6. The Family That Plays Together .... [R]	Epic 31461
7/21/73	120	12	7. The Best Of Spirit .... [G]	Epic 32271
8/25/73	191	4	8. Spirit .... [R] reissue of albums 1 & 3 above	Epic 31457 [2]
6/07/75	147	9	9. Spirit Of '76	Mercury 804 [2]
7/31/76	179	4	10. Farther Along	Mercury 1094
			SPLINTER English duo: Bill Elliott & Bob Purvis - produced by George Harrison	
10/26/74	81	14	1. The Place I Love	Dark Horse 22001
			SPLIT ENZ sextet from New Zealand, led by brothers Tim & Neil Finn	
8/30/80	40	25	1. True Colours .... record pressed in laser-etched vinyl	A&M 4822
5/23/81	45	19	2. Waiata	A&M 4848
5/08/82	58	20	3. Time And Tide	A&M 4894
7/21/84	137	10	4. Conflicting Emotions	A&M 4963
			SPOOKY TOOTH British hard-rock group led by Gary Wright & Mike Harrison	
8/16/69	44	18	1. Spooky Two	A&M 4194
3/21/70	92	14	2. Ceremony .... with special electronic overdubs by Pierre Henry	A&M 4225
8/15/70	84	13	3. The Last Puff	A&M 4266
6/05/71	152	7	4. Tobacco Road .... [E-R] reissue of their 1st album entitled "It's All About..."	A&M 4300
5/19/73	84	14	5. You Broke My Heart So I Busted Your Jaw ...	A&M 4385
11/10/73	99	10	6. Witness	Island 9337
9/21/74	130	8	7. The Mirror .... above 3 albums with Mick Jones (Foreigner), lead guitarist	Island 9292
4/24/76	172	4	8. That Was Only Yesterday .... [K] GARY WRIGHT/SPOOKY TOOTH (includes cuts from above A&M albums, plus cuts from solo albums by Wright)	A&M 3528 [2]
			SPORTS Stephen Cummings, lead singer of Australian sextet	
11/24/79	194	2	1. Don't Throw Stones	Arista 4249
			DUSTY SPRINGFIELD born Mary O'Brien on 4/16/39 in London, England	
6/27/64	62	13	1. Stay Awhile/I Only Want To Be With You .... "Wishin' And Hopin'"(6)	Philips 133
12/05/64	136	3	2. Dusty	Philips 156

DATE CHARTED	PEAK POS	WKS CHRT'D		ARTIST — Album Title	LABEL & NUMBER
7/16/66	77	10		3. You Don't Have To Say You Love Me .... "You Don't Have To Say You Love Me"(4)	Philips 210
12/24/66	137	3		4. Dusty Springfield's Golden Hits .... [G]	Philips 220
12/23/67	135	7		5. The Look of Love	Philips 256
3/15/69	99	14		6. Dusty In Memphis .... "Son-Of-A Preacher Man"(10)	Atlantic 8214
2/28/70	107	13		7. A Brand New Me	Atlantic 8249

RICK SPRINGFIELD
Australian - played Noah Drake on TV's "General Hospital"

DATE CHARTED	PEAK POS	WKS CHRT'D		ARTIST — Album Title	LABEL & NUMBER
8/12/72	35	17		1. Beginnings .... "Speak To The Sky"	Capitol 11047
3/14/81	7	73	▲	2. **Working Class Dog** .... "Jessie's Girl"(1)/"I've Done Everything For You"(8)	RCA 3697
3/27/82	2(3)	35	▲	3. **Success Hasn't Spoiled Me Yet** .... "Don't Talk To Strangers"(2)	RCA 4125
12/18/82	159	8		4. Wait For Night .... [E-R] originally released in 1976 on Chelsea Records	RCA 4235
4/30/83	12	57	▲	5. Living in Oz .... "Affair Of The Heart"(9)	RCA 4660
4/07/84	16	36	▲	6. Hard To Hold .... [S] Rick starred in the film "Love Somebody"(5)	RCA 4935
12/08/84	78	13		7. Beautiful Feelings .... [E] vocals recorded in '78 and all new music tracks added in '84	Mercury 824107

SPRINGFIELDS
English folk trio featuring Dusty & brother Tom Springfield

DATE CHARTED	PEAK POS	WKS CHRT'D	ARTIST — Album Title	LABEL & NUMBER
10/27/62	91	4	1. Silver Threads & Golden Needles	Philips 052

BRUCE SPRINGSTEEN
born on 9/23/49 in Freehold, New Jersey

DATE CHARTED	PEAK POS	WKS CHRT'D		ARTIST — Album Title	LABEL & NUMBER
7/26/75	60	36	●	1. Greetings From Asbury Park, N.J.	Columbia 31903
7/26/75	59	34	●	2. The Wild, The Innocent & The E Street Shuffle .... above 2 albums originally released in 1973	Columbia 32432
9/13/75	3	60+	●	3. **Born To Run**	Columbia 33795
6/17/78	5	83	▲	4. **Darkness on the Edge of Town**	Columbia 35318
11/01/80	1(4)	75	▲	5. **The River** .... "Hungry Heart"(5)	Columbia 36854 [2]
10/09/82	3	29	●	6. **Nebraska** .... recorded on a 4-track cassette recorder at home	Columbia 38358
6/23/84	1(7)	42+	▲	7. **Born In The U.S.A.** .... "Dancing In The Dark"(2)/"Cover Me"(7)/ "Born In The U.S.A."(9)/"I'm On Fire"	Columbia 38653

SPYRO GYRA
Buffalo-based jazz/pop band led by sax man Jay Beckenstein

DATE CHARTED	PEAK POS	WKS CHRT'D		ARTIST — Album Title	LABEL & NUMBER
5/20/78	99	12		1. Spyro Gyra .... [I]	Amherst 1014
4/07/79	27	41	●	2. Morning Dance .... [I]	Infinity 9004
3/22/80	19	29		3. Catching The Sun .... [I]	MCA 5108
11/01/80	49	30		4. Carnaval .... [I]	MCA 5149
8/29/81	41	27		5. Freetime .... [I]	MCA 5238
10/23/82	46	24		6. Incognito .... [I]	MCA 5368
8/13/83	66	16		7. City Kids .... [I]	MCA 5431
7/14/84	59	19		8. Access All Areas .... [I-L]	MCA 6893 [2]

SPYS
members Al Greenwood & Ed Gagliardi were formerly with Foreigner

DATE CHARTED	PEAK POS	WKS CHRT'D	ARTIST — Album Title	LABEL & NUMBER
8/14/82	138	10	1. Spys	EMI America 17073

SQUEEZE
English new wave quintet led by Chris Difford & Glenn Tilbrook

DATE CHARTED	PEAK POS	WKS CHRT'D	ARTIST — Album Title	LABEL & NUMBER
4/26/80	71	24	1. Argybargy	A&M 4802
5/30/81	44	25	2. East Side Story.. .... Elvis Costello, co-producer "Tempted"	A&M 4854

DATE CHARTED	PEAK POS	WKS CHRT'D	ARTIST — Album Title	LABEL & NUMBER
5/29/82	**32**	30	3. Sweets From A Stranger	A&M 4899
1/08/83	**47**	21	4. Singles-45's and under .... [K]	A&M 4922
			BILLY SQUIER	
			Boston-bred heavy-metal rock guitarist	
6/07/80	**169**	12	1. The Tale Of The Tape	Capitol 12062
5/02/81	**5**	111	▲ 2. **Don't Say No**	Capitol 12146
			"The Stroke"	
8/07/82	**5**	50	▲ 3. **Emotions in Motion**	Capitol 12217
8/04/84	**11**	29	▲ 4. Signs of Life	Capitol 12361
			CHRIS SQUIRE	
			English - bass player of Yes	
1/24/76	**69**	12	1. Fish Out Of Water	Atlantic 18159
			with guests Bill Bruford (drums) & Patrick Moraz (keyboards)	
			SRC	
			Detroit psychedelic rock sextet	
9/28/68	**147**	4	1. SRC	Capitol 2991
6/14/69	**134**	9	2. Milestones	Capitol 134
			STACKRIDGE	
			English septet produced by George Martin	
12/28/74	**191**	9	1. Pinafore Days	Sire 7503
			JIM STAFFORD	
			host of a summer variety TV show in 1975	
3/16/74	**55**	33	1. Jim Stafford .... [N]	MGM 4947
			"Spiders & Snakes"(3)/"Wildwood Weed"(7)	
			JO STAFFORD	
			member of Tommy Dorsey's vocal group, the Pied Pipers	
12/29/56	**13**	8	1. Ski Trails	Columbia 910
			with husband Paul Weston, conductor; and the Norman Luboff Choir	
			TERRY STAFFORD	
			from Amarillo, Texas	
5/16/64	**81**	11	1. Suspicion!	Crusader 1001
			"Suspicion"(3)	
			STAIRSTEPS - see FIVE STAIRSTEPS	
			STALLION	
3/26/77	**191**	9	1. Stallion	Casablanca 7040
			STAMPEDERS	
			Canadian country-rock trio	
10/23/71	**172**	6	1. Sweet City Woman	Bell 6068
			"Sweet City Woman"(8)	
			JOE STAMPLEY - see MOE BANDY	
			STANDELLS	
			Los Angeles-area punk rock quintet - Dick Todd, lead singer	
7/02/66	**52**	16	1. Dirty Water	Tower 5027
			STANKY BROWN GROUP	
			New York City-area rock group	
5/15/76	**192**	3	1. Our Pleasure To Serve You	Sire 7516
3/05/77	**195**	2	2. If The Lights Don't Get You The Helots Will	Sire 7529
4/29/78	**192**	5	3. Stanky Brown	Sire 6053
			MICHAEL STANLEY Band	
			rock group from Cleveland, Ohio led by Michael Stanley	
9/13/75	**184**	3	1. You break it...You bought it!	Epic 33492
7/08/78	**99**	18	2. Cabin Fever	Arista 4182
8/04/79	**148**	5	3. Greatest Hints	Arista 4236
9/27/80	**86**	32	4. Heartland	EMI America 17040

DATE CHARTED	PEAK POS	WKS CHRT'D	ARTIST — Album Title	LABEL & NUMBER
8/01/81	79	15	5. North Coast	EMI America 17056
9/04/82	136	6	6. MSB	EMI America 17071
9/24/83	64	17	7. You Can't Fight Fashion	EMI America 17100

PAUL STANLEY
Kiss' rhythm guitarist

10/14/78	40	18	▲ 1. Paul Stanley	Casablanca 7123

STAPLE SINGERS
Roebuck 'Pop' Staples and daughters Mavis, Cleo & Yvonne

3/20/71	117	11	1. The Staple Swingers	Stax 2034
2/26/72	19	37	2. Bealtitude: Respect Yourself .... "I'll Take You There"(1)	Stax 3002
8/25/73	102	21	3. Be What You Are .... "If You're Ready (Come Go With Me)"(9)	Stax 3015
9/14/74	125	9	4. City In The Sky	Stax 5515
11/01/75	20	18	5. Let's Do It Again .... [S] "Let's Do It Again"(1)	Curtom 5005
			STAPLES:	
9/25/76	155	5	6. Pass It On	Warner 2945

MAVIS STAPLES
lead singer of the Staple Singers

9/12/70	188	4	1. Only For The Lonely	Volt 6010

POP STAPLES - see ALBERT KING

STARBUCK
Atlanta septet - Bruce Blackman, lead singer

7/24/76	78	14	1. Moonlight Feels Right .... "Moonlight Feels Right"(3)	Private S. 2013
6/11/77	182	2	2. Rock 'n Roll Rocket	Private S. 2027

STARCASTLE
6-man progressive rock group - Terry Luttrell, lead singer

3/13/76	95	15	1. Starcastle	Epic 33914
2/05/77	101	11	2. Fountains Of Light	Epic 34375
11/19/77	156	3	3. Citadel	Epic 34935

STARGARD
disco-funk female trio

3/04/78	26	13	1. Stargard	MCA 2321
7/04/81	186	2	2. Back 2 Back	Warner 3456

STARLAND VOCAL BAND
quartet led by Bill Danoff and his wife Taffy

5/29/76	20	25	1. Starland Vocal Band .... "Afternoon Delight"(1)	Windsong 1351
6/11/77	104	13	2. Rear View Mirror	Windsong 2239

STARPOINT

5/09/81	138	8	1. Keep On It	Choc. City 2018

EDWIN STARR
born Charles Hatcher on 1/21/42 in Nashville

5/17/69	73	13	1. 25 Miles .... "Twenty-Five Miles"(6)	Gordy 940
9/05/70	52	13	2. War & Peace .... "War"(1)	Gordy 948
7/31/71	178	7	3. Involved	Gordy 956
1/20/79	80	14	4. Clean	20th Century 559
7/28/79	115	8	5. Happy Radio	20th Century 591

RINGO STARR
born Richard Starkey on 7/7/40 in Liverpool, England - he replaced Pete Best as the Beatles' drummer, August, 1962

5/16/70	22	14	1. Sentimental Journey	Apple 3365
10/17/70	65	15	2. Beaucoups of Blues	Apple 3368

DATE CHARTED	PEAK POS	WKS CHRT'D	ARTIST — Album Title	LABEL & NUMBER
11/17/73	2(2)	37	● 3. **Ringo** .... featuring backing by the other 3 Beatles "Photograph"(1)/"You're Sixteen"(1)/"Oh My My"(5)	Apple 3413
11/30/74	8	25	● 4. **Goodnight Vienna** .... guests: John Lennon and Elton John "Only You"(6)/"No No Song"(3)	Apple 3417
12/06/75	30	11	5. Blast From Your Past .... [G] "It Don't Come Easy"(4)/"Back Off Boogaloo"(9)	Apple 3422
10/16/76	28	9	6. Ringo's Rotogravure .... guests: McCartney & Lennon, Eric Clapton, Peter Frampton	Atlantic 18193
10/15/77	162	6	7. Ringo the 4th	Atlantic 19108
5/20/78	129	6	8. Bad Boy	Portrait 35378
11/14/81	98	12	9. Stop And Smell The Roses .... guests: Paul McCartney & George Harrison	Boardwalk 33246
			STARS ON session musicians from Holland, performing hit song medleys	
5/09/81	9	24	● 1. **Stars On Long Play** .... side 1: Beatles' medley	Radio 16044
10/31/81	120	6	2. Stars On Long Play II	Radio 19314
5/08/82	163	6	3. Stars On Long Play III .... side 1: Rolling Stones medley; side 2: Stevie Wonder medley	Radio 19349
			STARZ New York-based rock quintet - Michael Lee Smith, lead singer	
9/11/76	123	13	1. Starz	Capitol 11539
4/16/77	89	8	2. Violation .... "Cherry Baby"	Capitol 11617
2/11/78	105	9	3. Attention Shoppers!	Capitol 11730
			STATLER BROTHERS Harold & Don Reid (brothers), Lew DeWitt, Phil Balsley	
2/26/66	125	3	1. Flowers On The Wall .... "Flowers On The Wall"(4)	Columbia 9249
1/30/71	126	11	2. Bed Of Rose's	Mercury 61317
10/16/71	181	2	3. Pictures Of Moments To Remember	Mercury 61349
9/13/75	121	20	● 4. The Best of The Statler Bros. .... [G]	Mercury 1037
6/10/78	155	9	● 5. Entertainers...On And Off The Record	Mercury 5007
12/16/78	183	4	● 6. The Statler Brothers Christmas Card ...... [X]	Mercury 5012
7/14/79	183	2	● 7. The Originals	Mercury 5016
2/02/80	153	11	● 8. The Best Of The Statler Bros. Ride's Again, Volume II .... [G]	Mercury 5024
9/06/80	169	5	9. 10th Anniversary .... title refers to their tenure with Mercury Records	Mercury 5027
7/11/81	103	9	10. Years Ago	Mercury 6002
6/25/83	193	5	11. Today	Mercury 812184
5/26/84	177	4	12. Atlanta Blue	Mercury 818652
			CANDI STATON formerly married to Clarence Carter	
2/27/71	188	2	1. Stand By Your Man	Fame 4202
6/26/76	129	14	2. Young Hearts Run Free	Warner 2948
7/28/79	129	6	3. Chance	Warner 3333
			DAKOTA STATON jazz stylist born in Pittsburgh on 6/3/31	
2/24/58	4	52	1. **The Late, Late Show**	Capitol 876
10/27/58	22	1	2. Dynamic!	Capitol 1054
6/01/59	23	9	3. Crazy He Calls Me	Capitol 1170
11/16/59	47	3	4. Time To Swing	Capitol 1241
			STATUS QUO English rock quartet	
4/17/76	148	7	1. Status Quo	Capitol 11509

DATE CHARTED	PEAK POS	WKS CHRT'D	ARTIST — Album Title	LABEL & NUMBER
			STEALERS WHEEL English group featuring Gerry Rafferty & Joe Egan	
2/24/73	50	22	1. Stealers Wheel .... "Stuck In The Middle With You"(6)	A&M 4377
4/13/74	181	3	2. Ferguslie Park	A&M 4419
			STEAM New York City session musicians	
1/10/70	84	13	1. Steam .... "Na Na Hey Hey Kiss Him Goodbye"(1)	Mercury 61254
			STEEL BREEZE Ric Jacobs, lead singer of 6-man pop band from California	
9/18/82	50	28	1. Steel Breeze .... "You Don't Want Me Anymore"	RCA 4424
			STEEL PULSE reggae quintet from Birmingham, England	
7/17/82	120	13	1. True Democracy	Elektra 60113
3/31/84	154	12	2. Earth Crisis	Elektra 60315
			STEELEYE SPAN English traditional folk group - Maddy Prior, lead singer	
12/06/75	143	6	1. All Around My Hat	Chrysalis 1091
3/25/78	191	3	2. Storm Force Ten	Chrysalis 1151
			STEELY DAN sophisticated pop/jazz group, reduced to a duo (Donald Fagen & Walter Becker) beginning with album #4	
12/02/72	17	59	● 1. Can't Buy A Thrill .... "Do It Again"(6)/"Reeling In The Years"	ABC 758
7/21/73	35	34	● 2. Countdown To Ecstasy	ABC 779
3/30/74	8	36	● 3. **Pretzel Logic** .... "Rikki Don't Lose That Number"(4)	ABC 808
4/12/75	13	26	● 4. Katy Lied	ABC 846
5/22/76	15	29	● 5. The Royal Scam	ABC 931
10/15/77	3	60	▲ 6. **Aja** .... "Peg"/"Deacon Blues"	ABC 1006
11/18/78	30	22	▲ 7. Greatest Hits .... [G]	ABC 1107 [2]
12/06/80	9	36	▲ 8. **Gaucho** .... "Hey Nineteen"(10)	MCA 6102
7/03/82	115	9	9. Steely Dan gold .... [G]	MCA 5324
			DAVID STEINBERG television and film comedian/producer	
1/23/71	182	6	1. Disguised As A Nomal Person .... [C]	Elektra 74065
			JIM STEINMAN writer & producer for Meat Loaf	
5/16/81	63	17	1. Bad For Good	Cleve. I. 36531
			VAN STEPHENSON singer/songwriter from Nashville	
6/02/84	54	20	1. Righteous Anger	MCA 5482
			STEPPENWOLF hard-rock quintet led by John Kay	
3/09/68	6	87	● 1. **Steppenwolf** .... "Born To Be Wild"(2)	Dunhill 50029
10/05/68	3	52	● 2. **The Second** .... "Magic Carpet Ride"(3)	Dunhill 50037
3/15/69	7	29	3. **At Your Birthday Party** .... "Rock Me"(10)	Dunhill 50053
7/05/69	29	19	4. Early Steppenwolf .... [E-L] recorded in 1967 when band was known as Sparrow - side 2 is a 21-1/2 minute version of "The Pusher"	Dunhill 50060
11/15/69	17	46	● 5. Monster	Dunhill 50066
4/18/70	7	53	● 6. **Steppenwolf 'Live'** .... [L]	Dunhill 50075 [2]

DATE CHARTED	PEAK POS	WKS CHRT'D	ARTIST — Album Title	LABEL & NUMBER
11/21/70	19	17	● 7. Steppenwolf 7	Dunhill 50090
3/06/71	24	36	● 8. Steppenwolf Gold/Their Great Hits .... [G]	Dunhill 50099
10/02/71	54	11	9. For Ladies Only	Dunhill 50110
6/17/72	62	13	10. Rest In Peace .... [K]	Dunhill 50124
2/24/73	152	9	11. 16 Greatest Hits .... [G]	Dunhill 50135
9/21/74	47	12	12. Slow Flux	Mums 33093
9/20/75	155	4	13. Hour Of The Wolf	Epic 33583

STEVE & EYDIE - see STEVE LAWRENCE & EYDIE GORME

APRIL STEVENS - see NINO TEMPO

CAT STEVENS
English - born Stephen Georgiou on 7/21/48 - currently a Muslim (Yusuf Islam) living in London

DATE CHARTED	PEAK POS	WKS CHRT'D	ARTIST — Album Title	LABEL & NUMBER
2/06/71	8	79	● 1. **Tea for the Tillerman** .... "Wild World"	A&M 4280
3/20/71	164	16	● 2. Mona Bone Jakon .... Cat's 1st A&M album	A&M 4260
4/03/71	173	12	3. Matthew & Son/New Masters .... [E-R] two record set of Cat's first two albums (1967-68)	Deram 18005-10 [2]
10/09/71	2(1)	67	● 4. **Teaser And The Firecat** .... "Peace Train"(7)/"Morning Has Broken"(6)	A&M 4313
1/08/72	94	10	5. Very Young And Early Songs .... [E-K]	Deram 18061
10/14/72	1(3)	48	● 6. **Catch Bull At Four**	A&M 4365
7/28/73	3	43	● 7. **Foreigner**	A&M 4391
4/13/74	2(3)	36	● 8. **Buddha And The Chocolate Box** .... "Oh Very Young"(10)	A&M 3623
7/12/75	6	45	● 9. **Greatest Hits** .... [G] "Another Saturday Night"(6)	A&M 4519
12/13/75	13	19	● 10. Numbers	A&M 4555
5/21/77	7	23	● 11. **Izitso**	A&M 4702
12/23/78	33	15	12. Back To Earth	A&M 4735
12/15/84	165	8	13. Footsteps In The Dark .... [K] selections from his 9 A&M studio LPs + 3 more songs	A&M 3736

RAY STEVENS
born on 1/24/41 in Clarkdale. Georgia

DATE CHARTED	PEAK POS	WKS CHRT'D	ARTIST — Album Title	LABEL & NUMBER
9/15/62	135	2	1. 1,837 seconds of Humor .... [N] "Ahab The Arab"(5)	Mercury 60732
6/21/69	57	13	2. Gitarzan .... [N] "Gitarzan"(8)	Monument 18115
6/13/70	35	19	3. Everything Is Beautiful .... "Everything Is Beautiful"(1)	Barnaby 35005
12/12/70	141	8	4. Ray Stevens...Unreal!!!	Barnaby 30092
9/04/71	95	8	5. Ray Stevens' Greatest Hits .... [G]	Barnaby 30770
2/05/72	175	9	6. Turn Your Radio On .... inspirational songs	Barnaby 30809
6/15/74	159	11	7. Boogity Boogity .... [N] "The Streak"(1)	Barnaby 6003
6/28/75	106	14	8. Misty	Barnaby 6012
12/27/75	173	4	9. The Very Best of Ray Stevens .... [G]	Barnaby 6018
3/15/80	132	8	10. Shriner's Convention .... [N]	RCA 3574
1/19/85	118	12 +	11. He Thinks He's Ray Stevens .... [N]	MCA 5517

B.W. STEVENSON
Austin. Texas native

DATE CHARTED	PEAK POS	WKS CHRT'D	ARTIST — Album Title	LABEL & NUMBER
9/15/73	45	14	1. My Maria .... "My Maria"(9)	RCA 0088

AL STEWART
born on 9/5/45 in Glasgow. Scotland

DATE CHARTED	PEAK POS	WKS CHRT'D	ARTIST — Album Title	LABEL & NUMBER
6/01/74	133	14	1. Past, Present And Future	Janus 3063
3/01/75	30	23	2. Modern Times	Janus 7012

DATE CHARTED	PEAK POS	WKS CHRT'D	ARTIST — Album Title	LABEL & NUMBER
10/09/76	5	48	▲ 3. **Year Of The Cat** .... "Year Of The Cat"(8)	Janus 7022
10/07/78	10	31	▲ 4. **Time Passages** .... "Time Passages"(7)	Arista 4190
9/13/80	37	13	5. 24 Carrots	Arista 9520
11/14/81	110	11	6. Live/Indian Summer .... [L] 3 of 4 sides are live	Arista 8607 [2]
			AMII STEWART cabaret star from Washington, D.C.	
3/17/79	19	23	● 1. Knock On Wood .... "Knock On Wood"(1)	Ariola 50054
			BILLY STEWART killed in an auto crash on 1/17/70 (32)	
7/03/65	97	10	1. I Do Love You	Chess 1496
5/07/66	138	6	2. Unbelievable .... "Summertime"(10)	Chess 1499
			GARY STEWART	
8/16/80	165	3	1. Cactus And A Rose	RCA 3627
			JERMAINE STEWART	
3/02/85	92+	6+	1. The Word Is Out	Arista 8261
			JOHN STEWART member of the Kingston Trio 1961-1967	
6/21/69	193	3	1. California Bloodlines	Capitol 203
1/15/72	195	2	2. The Lonesome Picker Rides Again	Warner 1948
7/06/74	195	2	3. The Phoenix Concerts-Live .... [L]	RCA 0265 [2]
5/17/75	150	6	4. Wingless Angels	RCA 0816
11/26/77	126	8	5. Fire In The Wind	RSO 3027
5/19/79	10	28	6. **Bombs Away Dream Babies** .... "Gold"(5-with Stevie Nicks)	RSO 3051
4/12/80	85	10	7. Dream Babies Go Hollywood	RSO 3074
			ROD STEWART born on 1/10/45 in London, England - also see Jeff Beck, Faces, and Python Lee Jackson	
12/13/69	139	27	1. The Rod Stewart Album	Mercury 61237
6/20/70	27	53	2. Gasoline Alley	Mercury 61264
6/19/71	1(4)	52	● 3. **Every Picture Tells A Story** .... "Maggie May"(1)	Mercury 609
8/12/72	2(3)	36	● 4. **Never A Dull Moment**	Mercury 646
7/07/73	31	25	● 5. Sing It Again Rod .... [G]	Mercury 680
1/05/74	63	11	6. Rod Stewart/Faces Live - Coast To Coast Overture and Beginners .... [L]	Mercury 697
10/26/74	13	14	7. Smiler	Mercury 1017
9/06/75	9	29	● 8. **Atlantic Crossing**	Warner 2875
5/15/76	90	26	● 9. The Best Of Rod Stewart .... [G] all Mercury albums feature members of the Faces	Mercury 7507 [2]
7/17/76	2(5)	57	▲ 10. **A Night On The Town** .... "Tonight's The Night (Gonna Be Alright)"(1)	Warner 2938
11/26/77	2(6)	47	▲ 11. **Foot Loose & Fancy Free** .... "You're In My Heart (The Final Acclaim)"(4)	Warner 3092
12/23/78	1(3)	37	▲ 12. **Blondes Have More Fun** .... "Da Ya Think I'm Sexy?"(1)	Warner 3261
11/24/79	22	19	▲ 13. Rod Stewart Greatest Hits .... [G]	Warner 3373
12/06/80	12	21	▲ 14. Foolish Behaviour .... "Passion"(5)	Warner 3485
11/21/81	11	31	▲ 15. Tonight I'm Yours .... "Young Turks"(5)	Warner 3602
11/20/82	46	13	16. Absolutely Live .... [L]	Warner 23743 [2]

DATE CHARTED	PEAK POS	WKS CHRT'D	ARTIST — Album Title	LABEL & NUMBER
6/25/83	30	22	17. Body Wishes	Warner 23877
6/30/84	18	35	18. Camouflage	Warner 25095
			"Infatuation"(6)/"Some Guys Have All The Luck"(10)	
			SANDY STEWART	
			Sandy was a regular on the Eddie Fisher and Perry Como TV shows	
4/06/63	138	2	1. My Coloring Book	Colpix 441
			WYNN STEWART	
7/22/67	158	8	1. It's Such A Pretty World Today	Capitol 2737
			STILLER & MEARA - see SHELLEY BERMAN	
			STEPHEN STILLS	
			member of Buffalo Springfield - also see Crosby, Stills & Nash	
8/31/68	12	37	● 1. Super Session	Columbia 9701
			MIKE BLOOMFIELD/AL KOOPER/STEVE STILLS	
11/28/70	3	39	● 2. **Stephen Stills**	Atlantic 7202
			guests: Jimi Hendrix, Eric Clapton, David Crosby, Graham Nash "Love The One You're With"	
7/17/71	8	20	● 3. **Stephen Stills 2**	Atlantic 7206
4/29/72	4	30	● 4. **Manassas**	Atlantic 903 [2]
5/12/73	26	18	5. Down The Road	Atlantic 7250
			above 2 albums feature Stills' band, Manassas	
7/05/75	19	17	6. Stills	Columbia 33575
12/27/75	42	11	7. Stephen Stills Live .... [L]	Atlantic 18156
5/15/76	31	15	8. Illegal Stills	Columbia 34148
10/09/76	26	18	● 9. Long May You Run	Reprise 2253
			STILLS-YOUNG BAND (Neil Young)	
1/08/77	127	5	10. Still Stills-The Best Of Stephen Stills .... [G]	Atlantic 18201
11/11/78	83	4	11. Thoroughfare Gap	Columbia 35380
9/01/84	75	12	12. Right By You	Atlantic 80177
			SONNY STITT	
			jazz saxophonist - died on 7/22/82 (58)	
4/08/67	172	2	1. What's New!!! .... [I]	Roulette 25343
			STONE CITY BAND - see RICK JAMES	
			STONE FURY	
			heavy-metal quartet - Lenny Wolf, lead singer	
11/24/84	144	12	1. Burns Like A Star	MCA 5522
			STONE PONEYS - see LINDA RONSTADT	
			KIRBY STONE Four	
			Kirby Stone, Eddie Hall, Larry Foster, Mike Gardner	
8/25/58	13	9	1. Baubles, Bangles And Beads	Columbia 1211
			SLY STONE - see SLY & THE FAMILY STONE	
			STOOGES - see IGGY POP	
			PAUL STOOKEY	
			Paul of Peter, Paul & Mary	
8/21/71	42	15	1. Paul and	Warner 1912
			"Wedding Song (There Is Love)"	
			STORIES	
			New York rock quartet led by Michael Brown (keyboards) & Ian Lloyd (vocals)	
7/01/72	182	9	1. Stories	Kama Sutra 2051
7/28/73	29	19	2. About Us	Kama Sutra 2068
			"Brother Louie"(1)	

DATE CHARTED	PEAK POS	WKS CHRT'D	ARTIST — Album Title	LABEL & NUMBER
			GEORGE STRAIT country singer from San Marcos, Texas	
3/03/84	**163**	7	● 1. Right Or Wrong	MCA 5450
11/10/84	**139**	16	2. Does Fort Worth Ever Cross Your Mind	MCA 5518
			BILLY STRANGE session guitarist	
10/24/64	**135**	5	1. The James Bond Theme .... [I]	Crescendo 2004
7/03/65	**146**	3	2. English Hits Of '65 .... [I]	Crescendo 2009
			STRANGELOVES producers Bob Feldman, Jerry Goldstein, Richard Gottehrer	
11/13/65	**141**	2	1. I Want Candy	Bang 211
			STRAWBERRY ALARM CLOCK west coast psychedelic rock sextet	
11/04/67	**11**	24	1. Incense And Peppermints .... "Incense And Peppermints"(1)	Uni 73014
			STRAWBS British progressive rock band led by David Cousins	
7/15/72	**191**	5	1. Grave New World	A&M 4344
4/28/73	**121**	9	2. Bursting At The Seams	A&M 4383
3/02/74	**94**	17	3. Hero and Heroine	A&M 3607
3/08/75	**47**	13	4. Ghosts	A&M 4506
10/11/75	**147**	6	5. Nomadness	A&M 4544
10/30/76	**144**	5	6. Deep Cuts	Oyster 1603
8/06/77	**175**	4	7. Burning For You	Oyster 1604
			STRAY CATS rockabilly trio from Long Island, New York led by Brian Setzer	
7/03/82	**2(15)**	74	▲ 1. **Built For Speed** .... "Rock This Town"(9)/"Stray Cat Strut"(3)	EMI America 17070
9/10/83	**14**	29	● 2. Rant n' Rave with the Stray Cats .... "(She's) Sexy + 17"(5)	EMI America 17102
			JANEY STREET New York native	
11/03/84	**145**	6	1. Heroes, Angels & Friends	Arista 8219
			STREETS American quartet led by Steve Walsh (Kansas)	
12/03/83	**166**	11	1. 1st	Atlantic 80117
			BARBRA STREISAND born on 4/24/42 in Brooklyn, New York - leading stage and screen actress since 1962	
4/13/63	**8**	101	● 1. **The Barbra Streisand Album** .... "Happy Days Are Here Again"	Columbia 8807
9/14/63	**2(3)**	74	● 2. **The Second Barbara Streisand Album**	Columbia 8854
2/29/64	**5**	74	● 3. **The Third Album**	Columbia 8954
5/02/64	**2(3)**	51	● 4. **Funny Girl** .... [OC] based on the early life of Fanny Brice	Capitol 2059
10/03/64	**1(5)**	84	● 5. **People** .... "People"(5)	Columbia 9015
5/22/65	**2(3)**	68	● 6. **My Name Is Barbra**	Columbia 9136
11/06/65	**2(3)**	48	● 7. **My Name Is Barbra, Two...**	Columbia 9209
4/09/66	**3**	36	● 8. **Color Me Barbra**	Columbia 9278
11/19/66	**5**	29	9. **Je m'appelle Barbra**	Columbia 9347
11/11/67	**12**	23	10. Simply Streisand	Columbia 9482
9/28/68	**12**	108	● 11. Funny Girl .... [S] screen version of the above Broadway musical	Columbia 3220
10/12/68	**30**	20	12. A Happening In Central Park .... [L]	Columbia 9710
9/06/69	**31**	40	13. What About Today?	Columbia 9816
11/15/69	**49**	33	14. Hello, Dolly! .... [S]	20th Century 5103
2/28/70	**32**	30	● 15. Barbra Streisand's Greatest Hits .... [G]	Columbia 9968

DATE CHARTED	PEAK POS	WKS CHRT'D	ARTIST — Album Title	LABEL & NUMBER
7/25/70	108	24	16. On A Clear Day You Can See Forever .... [S]	Columbia 30086
2/06/71	186	6	17. The Owl and the Pussycat .... [S-T] comedy dialogue highlights (Streisand/George Segal) from the film - background music by Blood, Sweat & Tears	Columbia 30401
2/20/71	10	29	● 18. **Stoney End** .... "Stoney End"(6)	Columbia 30378
9/18/71	11	26	● 19. Barbra Joan Streisand	Columbia 30792
11/18/72	19	27	● 20. Live Concert At The Forum .... [L]	Columbia 31760
11/24/73	64	16	21. Barbra Streisand...and other musical instruments .... featuring a host of musicians & instruments from many countries	Columbia 32655
2/16/74	1(2)	31	● 22. **The Way We Were** .... not the soundtrack album (see Soundtracks) "The Way We Were"(1)	Columbia 32801
11/16/74	13	24	● 23. ButterFly	Columbia 33095
3/29/75	6	25	● 24. **Funny Lady** .... [S] film is the sequel to "Funny Girl"	Arista 9004
11/01/75	12	20	● 25. Lazy Afternoon	Columbia 33815
3/06/76	46	14	26. Classical Barbra .... [F] with the Columbia Symphony Orchestra	Columbia 33452
12/11/76	1(6)	51	▲ 27. **A Star Is Born** .... [S-L] Kris Kristofferson sings on 5 of the 12 tracks (all but 4 tracks are live) - third version of the 1937 film classic "Evergreen"(1)	Columbia 34403
7/02/77	3	25	▲ 28. **Streisand Superman** .... "My Heart Belongs To Me"(4)	Columbia 34830
6/17/78	12	27	▲ 29. Songbird	Columbia 35375
12/02/78	1(3)	46	▲ 30. **Barbra Streisand's Greatest Hits,** **Volume 2** .... [G] "You Don't Bring Me Flowers"(1-with Neil Diamond)	Columbia 35679
7/07/79	20	18	● 31. The Main Event .... [S] 3 versions of title song - others by various artists "The Main Event/Fight"(3)	Columbia 36115
11/03/79	7	26	▲ 32. **Wet** .... "No More Tears (Enough Is Enough)"(1-with Donna Summer)	Columbia 36258
10/11/80	1(3)	49	▲ 33. **Guilty** .... "Woman In Love"(1)/"Guilty"(3-with Barry Gibb)/ "What Kind Of Fool"(10-with Barry Gibb)	Columbia 36750
12/12/81	10	100	▲ 34. **Memories** .... [K]	Columbia 37678
12/19/81	108	5	● 35. A Christmas Album .... [X-R] originally charted 12/2/67 (Pos. 1-5 wks.) on Billboard's special Christmas charts (also on 1968, 70-71, 83-84)	Columbia 9557
11/26/83	9	26	▲ 36. **Yentl** .... [S] Barbra is the first woman to produce, direct, write & perform a film's title role	Columbia 39152
10/27/84	19	24+	▲ 37. Emotion	Columbia 39480

STRIKERS
7-man New York City funk band

8/29/81	174	3	1. The Strikers	Prelude 14100

JUD STRUNK
killed in a plane crash on 10/15/81 (45)

5/05/73	138	9	1. Daisy A Day	MGM 4898

STUFF
New York's top session musicians

11/27/76	163	3	1. Stuff .... [I]	Warner 2968
7/30/77	61	13	2. More Stuff .... [I]	Warner 3061

STYLE COUNCIL
English duo: Paul Weller (The Jam) & Mick Talbot

10/22/83	172	5	1. Introducing The Style Council .... [M]	Polydor 815277
4/07/84	56	22	2. My Ever Changing Moods	Geffen 4029

DATE CHARTED	PEAK POS	WKS CHRT'D	ARTIST — Album Title	LABEL & NUMBER
			STYLISTICS	
			Philadelphia soul quintet - Russell Thompkins, Jr., lead singer	
12/18/71	23	38	● 1. The Stylistics	Avco 33023
			"You Are Everything"(9)/"Betcha By Golly, Wow"(3)	
11/11/72	32	38	● 2. Round 2: The Stylistics	Avco 11006
			"I'm Stone In Love With You"(10)/"Break Up To Make Up"(5)	
11/24/73	66	44	3. Rockin' Roll Baby	Avco 11010
			"You Make Me Feel Brand New"(2)	
5/25/74	14	31	● 4. Let's Put It All Together	Avco 69001
11/02/74	43	16	5. Heavy	Avco 69004
2/22/75	41	30	6. The Best of The Stylistics .... [G]	Avco 69005
6/14/75	72	13	7. Thank You Baby	Avco 69008
11/08/75	99	11	8. You Are Beautiful	Avco 69010
6/19/76	117	6	9. Fabulous	H&L 69013
11/08/80	127	12	10. Hurry Up This Way Again	TSOP 36470
			STYX	
			Chicago-based rock quintet: Dennis DeYoung (vocals/keyboards), Tommy Shaw (lead guitar), James Young (guitar), and John (drums) & brother Chuck Panozzo (bass)	
2/09/74	192	2	1. The Serpent Is Rising	Wooden N. 0287
11/09/74	154	12	2. Man Of Miracles	Wooden N. 0638
1/25/75	20	19	● 3. Styx II	Wooden N. 1012
			originally released in 1973 (Styx I did not chart) "Lady"(6)	
12/20/75	58	50	● 4. Equinox	A&M 4559
10/30/76	66	18	● 5. Crystal Ball	A&M 4604
			Tommy Shaw's first album with group (replaces John Curulewski)	
7/30/77	6	127	▲ 6. **The Grand Illusion**	A&M 4637
			"Come Sail Away"(8)	
9/30/78	6	92	▲ 7. **Pieces of Eight**	A&M 4724
10/13/79	2(1)	60	▲ 8. **Cornerstone**	A&M 3711
			"Babe"(1)	
1/31/81	1(3)	61	▲ 9. **Paradise Theater**	A&M 3719
			"The Best Of Times"(3)/"Too Much Time On My Hands"(9)	
3/19/83	3	34	▲ 10. **Kilroy Was Here**	A&M 3734
			"Mr. Roboto"(3)/"Don't Let It End"(6)	
4/21/84	31	15	11. Caught In The Act - Live .... [L]	A&M 6514 [2]
			SUGARHILL GANG	
			New York City rap/funk trio	
1/30/82	50	18	1. 8th Wonder	SugarHill 249
			SUGARLOAF	
			rock quartet from Denver, Colorado - Jerry Corbetta, lead singer	
8/15/70	24	29	1. Sugarloaf	Liberty 7640
			"Green-Eyed Lady"(3)	
2/13/71	111	9	2. Spaceship Earth	Liberty 11010
4/12/75	152	6	3. Don't Call Us-We'll Call You	Claridge 1000
			"Don't Call Us, We'll Call You"(9)	
			KASIM SULTON	
			bass player of Todd Rundgren's Utopia	
2/27/82	197	2	1. Kasim	EMI America 17063
			DONNA SUMMER	
			born LaDonna Gaines on 12/31/48 in Boston, Massachusetts	
11/01/75	11	30	● 1. Love To Love You Baby	Oasis 5003
			"Love To Love You Baby"(2)	
3/27/76	21	27	● 2. A Love Trilogy	Oasis 5004
11/06/76	29	26	● 3. Four Seasons Of Love	Casablanca 7038
6/04/77	18	40	● 4. I Remember Yesterday	Casablanca 7056
			"I Feel Love"(6)	
11/26/77	26	57	● 5. Once Upon A Time...	Casablanca 7078 [2]

DATE CHARTED	PEAK POS	WKS CHRT'D	ARTIST — Album Title	LABEL & NUMBER
9/16/78	1(1)	75	▲ 6. **Live And More** .... [L] one of four sides is a studio recording "MacArthur Park"(1)/"Heaven Knows"(4)	Casablanca 7119 [2]
5/12/79	1(6)	49	▲ 7. **Bad Girls** .... "Hot Stuff"(1)/"Bad Girls"(1)/"Dim All The Lights"(2)	Casablanca 7150 [2]
11/03/79	1(1)	39	▲ 8. **On The Radio-Greatest Hits-Volumes I &** **II** .... [G] "Last Dance"(3)/"No More Tears (Enough Is Enough)"(1-with Barbra Streisand)/"On The Radio"(5)	Casablanca 7191 [2]
10/11/80	50	15	9. Walk Away - Collector's Edition (The Best Of 1977-1980) .... [G]	Casablanca 7244
11/08/80	13	18	● 10. The Wanderer .... "The Wanderer"(3)	Geffen 2000
8/14/82	20	37	● 11. Donna Summer .... "Love Is In Control (Finger On The Trigger)"(10)	Geffen 2005
7/16/83	9	32	● 12. **She Works Hard For The Money** .... "She Works Hard For The Money"(3)	Mercury 812265
9/22/84	40	17	13. Cats Without Claws	Geffen 24040
			ANDY SUMMERS/ROBERT FRIPP Andy is lead guitarist of Police; Robert is leader of King Crimson	
11/06/82	60	11	1. I Advance Masked .... [I]	A&M 4913
10/20/84	155	5	2. Bewitched .... [I]	A&M 5011
			BILL SUMMERS & SUMMERS HEAT percussionist - formerly with Herbie Hancock's Head Hunters	
4/04/81	129	15	1. Call It What You Want	MCA 5176
12/12/81	92	16	2. Jam The Box!	MCA 5266
			SUN Dayton, Ohio soul-funk band	
5/06/78	69	22	● 1. Sunburn	Capitol 11723
7/21/79	85	10	2. Destination: Sun	Capitol 11941
			SUNGLOWS 10-man Latin polka band from Texas	
8/14/65	148	2	1. the original Peanuts .... [I]	Sunglow 103
			SUNNY & THE SUNLINERS San Antonio, Texas band led by Sunny Ozuna	
11/02/63	142	2	1. Talk To Me	Tear Drop 2000
			SUNSHINE BAND - see KC	
			SUNSHINE COMPANY Mary Nance, lead singer of Southern California quintet	
10/21/67	126	10	1. Happy Is The Sunshine Company	Imperial 12359
			SUPERSAX jazz band that plays Charlie Parker choruses in harmony	
7/14/73	169	7	1. Supersax plays Bird .... [I]	Capitol 11177
4/06/74	182	3	2. Supersax plays Bird, Volume 2/Salt Peanuts .... [I]	Capitol 11271
			SUPERTRAMP British rock quintet: Rick Davies (vocals/keyboards), Roger Hodgson (guitar), John Helliwell (sax), Dougie Thomson (bass), & Bob Benberg (drums)	
12/07/74	38	76	● 1. Crime Of The Century .... "Bloody Well Right"/"Dreamer"	A&M 3647
12/13/75	44	28	2. Crisis? What Crisis?	A&M 4560
4/23/77	16	49	● 3. Even In The Quietest Moments... .... "Give A Little Bit"	A&M 4634
3/04/78	158	5	4. Supertramp .... [E] their first album - recorded in 1970	A&M 4665
3/31/79	1(6)	88	▲ 5. **Breakfast In America** .... "The Logical Song"(6)/"Take The Long Way Home"(10)	A&M 3708

DATE CHARTED	PEAK POS	WKS CHRT'D	ARTIST — Album Title	LABEL & NUMBER
10/11/80	8	26	● 6. **Paris** .... [L] recorded at the Paris Pavilion on 11/29/79	A&M 6702 [2]
11/13/82	5	28	● 7. **...famous last words...** .... "It's Raining Again"	A&M 3732

SUPREMES
Diana Ross, lead singer; Mary Wilson & Florence Ballard
(Flo died on 2/21/76-32) - Cindy Birdsong replaced Flo in 1967:
Jean Terrell replaced Diana in 1970

DATE CHARTED	PEAK POS	WKS CHRT'D	ARTIST — Album Title	LABEL & NUMBER
9/19/64	2(4)	89	1. **Where Did Our Love Go** .... "Where Did Our Love Go"(1)/"Baby Love"(1)/ "Come See About Me"(1)	Motown 621
11/28/64	21	21	2. A Bit Of Liverpool	Motown 623
3/20/65	79	8	3. The Supremes sing Country Western & Pop	Motown 625
5/08/65	75	19	4. We Remember Sam Cooke	Motown 629
8/21/65	6	37	5. **More Hits By The Supremes** .... "Stop! In The Name Of Love"(1)/"Back In My Arms Again"(1)	Motown 627
11/13/65	11	54	6. The Supremes at the Copa .... [L]	Motown 636
3/19/66	8	55	7. **I Hear A Symphony** .... "I Hear A Symphony"(1)/"My World Is Empty Without You"(5)	Motown 643
9/24/66	1(2)	60	8. **The Supremes A' Go-Go** .... "Love Is Like An Itching In My Heart"(9)/ "You Can't Hurry Love"(1)	Motown 649
2/18/67	6	29	9. **The Supremes sing** **Holland-Dozier-Holland** .... Brian Holland, Lamont Dozier, Eddie Holland "You Keep Me Hangin' On"(1)/ "Love Is Here And Now You're Gone"(1)	Motown 650
6/17/67	20	19	10. The Supremes Sing Rodgers & Hart .... songwriting team: Richard Rodgers & Lorenz Hart	Motown 659
			DIANA ROSS & THE SUPREMES:	
9/30/67	1(5)	89	11. **Diana Ross and the Supremes Greatest** **Hits** .... [G] "The Happening"(1)	Motown 663 [2]
4/27/68	18	29	12. Reflections .... "Reflections"(2)/"In And Out Of Love"(9)	Motown 665
10/05/68	57	18	13. Live at London's Talk Of The Town .... [L]	Motown 676
10/05/68	150	12	14. Funny Girl .... version of the Styne/Merrill musical	Motown 672
11/30/68	2(1)	32	15. **Diana Ross & the Supremes Join the** **Temptations** .... "I'm Gonna Make You Love Me"(2)	Motown 679
12/14/68	14	21	16. Love Child .... "Love Child"(1)	Motown 670
12/28/68	1(1)	34	17. TCB .... [TV] DIANA ROSS & THE SUPREMES with THE TEMPTATIONS	Motown 682
6/21/69	24	18	18. Let The Sunshine In .... "I'm Livin' In Shame"(10)	Motown 689
10/25/69	28	18	19. Together .... DIANA ROSS & THE SUPREMES with THE TEMPTATIONS	Motown 692
11/29/69	33	20	20. Cream Of The Crop .... "Someday We'll Be Together"(1)	Motown 694
12/06/69	38	12	21. On Broadway .... [TV] DIANA ROSS & THE SUPREMES with THE TEMPTATIONS	Motown 699
1/10/70	31	25	22. Diana Ross & the Supremes Greatest Hits, Volume 3 .... [G]	Motown 702
5/16/70	46	18	23. Farewell .... [L] Diana's last performance with The Supremes - recorded at the Frontier Hotel, Las Vegas (1/14/70)	Motown 708 [2]
			THE SUPREMES:	
6/06/70	25	19	24. Right On .... "Up The Ladder To The Roof"(10)	Motown 705
10/17/70	113	16	25. The Magnificent 7 .... SUPREMES & FOUR TOPS	Motown 717
10/24/70	68	17	26. New Ways But Love Stays .... "Stoned Love"(7)	Motown 720

DATE CHARTED	PEAK POS	WKS CHRT'D	ARTIST — Album Title	LABEL & NUMBER
6/26/71	**85**	10	27. Touch	Motown 737
6/26/71	**154**	6	28. The Return Of The Magnificent Seven .... SUPREMES & FOUR TOPS	Motown 736
1/08/72	**160**	6	29. Dynamite .... SUPREMES & FOUR TOPS	Motown 745
5/27/72	**54**	15	30. Floy Joy	Motown 751
11/25/72	**129**	13	31. The Supremes	Motown 756
6/29/74	**66**	15	32. Anthology (1962-1969) .... [G]	Motown 794 [3]
6/28/75	**152**	8	33. The Supremes	Motown 828
5/22/76	**42**	15	34. High Energy	Motown 863

SURFARIS
surf band from Glendora, California

8/10/63	**15**	51	1. Wipe Out .... [I] "Wipe Out"(2)	Dot 25535
11/30/63	**94**	11	2. The Surfaris play Wipe Out and others .... [I] "Wipe Out" is not the hit version	Decca 74470
3/07/64	**120**	5	3. Hit City 64	Decca 74487

SURVIVOR
midwest rock quintet led by Dave Bickler & Jim Peterik

3/29/80	**169**	7	1. Survivor	Scotti Br. 7107
10/24/81	**82**	25	2. Premonition	Scotti Br. 37549
6/26/82	**2(4)**	41	▲ 3. **Eye Of The Tiger** .... "Eye Of The Tiger"(1)	Scotti Br. 38062
10/22/83	**82**	9	4. Caught In The Game	Scotti Br. 38791
9/29/84	**30+**	28+	● 5. Vital Signs .... "High On You"(8)	Scotti Br. 39578

SUSAN
New York rock quartet

5/05/79	**169**	5	1. Falling In Love Again	RCA 3372

SUTHERLAND BROTHERS & QUIVER
English: Iain & Gavin Sutherland with group Quiver

8/18/73	**77**	17	1. Lifeboat	Island 9326
5/11/74	**193**	3	2. Dream Kid	Island 9341
5/08/76	**195**	2	3. Reach For The Sky	Columbia 33982

BILLY SWAN

12/07/74	**21**	16	1. I Can Help .... "I Can Help"(1)	Monument 33279

BRAD SWANSON & his Whispering Organ Sound

10/18/69	**185**	2	1. Quentin's Theme .... [I]	Thunderbird 9004

SWEAT BAND
P-funk trio who played in "Bootsy's Rubber Band"

12/13/80	**150**	8	1. Sweat Band	Uncle Jam 36857

SWEET
English rock band - Brian Connolly. lead singer

7/28/73	**191**	4	1. The Sweet .... "Little Willy"(3)	Bell 1125
7/26/75	**25**	44	● 2. Desolation Boulevard .... "Ballroom Blitz"(5)/"Fox On The Run"(5)	Capitol 11395
3/06/76	**27**	13	3. Give Us A Wink	Capitol 11496
5/14/77	**151**	4	4. Off The Record	Capitol 11636
2/18/78	**52**	28	5. Level Headed .... "Love Is Like Oxygen"(8)	Capitol 11744
5/12/79	**151**	5	6. Cut Above The Rest	Capitol 11929

SWEET INSPIRATIONS
studio vocal group led by Cissy Houston

4/06/68	**90**	6	1. The Sweet Inspirations	Atlantic 8155

DATE CHARTED	PEAK POS	WKS CHRT'D	ARTIST — Album Title	LABEL & NUMBER
			SWEET SENSATION 8-man British soul band - Marcel King, lead singer	
5/03/75	163	7	1. Sad Sweet Dreamer	Pye 12110
			SWEET THUNDER soul quartet - Charles Buie, leader	
7/15/78	125	11	1. Sweet Thunder	Fntsy./WMOT 9547
			SWEETWATER	
9/13/69	200	2	1. Sweetwater	Reprise 6313
			RACHEL SWEET teenage rock singer from Akron, Ohio	
8/04/79	97	9	1. Fool Around	Stiff 36101
3/22/80	123	11	2. Protect The Innocent	Stiff 36337
9/05/81	124	7	3. ...And Then He Kissed Me	ARC 37077
			SWINGING BLUE JEANS rock quartet from Liverpool, England	
5/30/64	90	9	1. Hippy Hippy Shake	Imperial 12261
			SWINGIN' MEDALLIONS 8-man rock band from South Carolina	
7/30/66	88	12	1. Double Shot (Of My Baby's Love)	Smash 67083
			SWINGLE SINGERS Ward Swingle (American) & his wordless French singers	
10/26/63	15	74	1. Bach's Greatest Hits ... [I]	Philips 097
5/30/64	65	17	2. Going Baroque ... [I]	Philips 126
2/20/65	140	6	3. Anyone for Mozart?	Philips 149
			SWITCH 6-member soul/funk band from Detroit, discovered by Jermaine Jackson	
9/02/78	37	33	1. Switch	Gordy 980
6/02/79	37	36	2. Switch II	Gordy 988
4/12/80	57	14	3. Reaching For Tomorrow	Gordy 993
11/15/80	85	17	4. This Is My Dream	Gordy 999
11/21/81	174	4	5. Switch V	Gordy 1007
			KEITH SYKES rockabilly singer from Memphis	
11/22/80	147	11	1. I'm Not Strange I'm Just Like You	Backstreet 3265
			SYLVAIN SYLVAIN ex-New York Dolls guitarist	
2/16/80	123	8	1. Sylvain Sylvain	RCA 3475
			SYLVERS Memphis family of 9 brothers and sisters	
3/03/73	180	7	1. The Sylvers	Pride 0007
8/04/73	164	5	2. The Sylvers II	Pride 0026
2/14/76	58	25	3. Showcase "Boogie Fever"(1)	Capitol 11465
11/20/76	80	18	4. Something Special "Hot Line"(5)	Capitol 11580
11/26/77	134	13	5. New Horizons	Capitol 11705
9/16/78	132	8	6. Forever Yours	Casablanca 7103
			FOSTER SYLVERS member of the Sylvers (age 11 in '73)	
7/21/73	159	7	1. Foster Sylvers	Pride 0027
			SYLVESTER San Francisco disco star Sylvester James	
8/05/78	28	42	● 1. Step II	Fantasy 9556
4/28/79	63	15	2. Stars	Fantasy 9579

DATE CHARTED	PEAK POS	WKS CHRT'D	ARTIST — Album Title	LABEL & NUMBER
11/24/79	123	12	3. Living Proof .... [L] side 4: studio	Fantasy 79010 [2]
9/27/80	147	8	4. Sell My Soul	Honey 9601
7/11/81	156	4	5. Too Hot To Sleep	Honey 9607
3/19/83	168	5	6. All I Need	Megatone 1005

SYLVIA
country singer Sylvia Kirby Allen from Kokomo, Indiana

DATE CHARTED	PEAK POS	WKS CHRT'D	ARTIST — Album Title	LABEL & NUMBER
5/09/81	139	11	1. Drifter	RCA 3986
8/07/82	56	33	● 2. Just Sylvia	RCA 4312
6/18/83	77	11	3. Snapshot	RCA 4672
4/28/84	178	4	4. Surprise	RCA 4960

SYLVIA
Sylvia Robinson of Mickey & Sylvia

DATE CHARTED	PEAK POS	WKS CHRT'D	ARTIST — Album Title	LABEL & NUMBER
6/02/73	70	12	1. Pillow Talk .... "Pillow Talk"(3)	Vibration 126

SYNDICATE OF SOUND
rock quintet from San Jose, California

DATE CHARTED	PEAK POS	WKS CHRT'D	ARTIST — Album Title	LABEL & NUMBER
8/27/66	148	2	1. Little Girl .... "Little Girl"(8)	Bell 6001

SYNERGY
electronic equipment performed & programmed by Larry Fast

DATE CHARTED	PEAK POS	WKS CHRT'D	ARTIST — Album Title	LABEL & NUMBER
6/21/75	66	18	1. Electronic Realizations for Rock Orchestra .... [I]	Passport 98009
6/26/76	144	11	2. Sequencer .... [I]	Passport 98014
9/16/78	146	6	3. Cords .... [I]	Passport 6000

SYREETA
Syreeta Wright - formerly married to Stevie Wonder

DATE CHARTED	PEAK POS	WKS CHRT'D	ARTIST — Album Title	LABEL & NUMBER
8/12/72	185	8	1. Syreeta	MoWest 113
7/20/74	116	17	2. Stevie Wonder presents Syreeta .... above 2 albums produced by Stevie Wonder	Motown 808
5/17/80	73	15	3. Syreeta	Tamla 372
8/08/81	127	9	4. Billy Preston & Syreeta	Motown 958
1/30/82	189	3	5. Set My Love In Motion	Tamla 376

SYSTEM
New York City-based techno-funk duo: Mic Murphy & David Frank

DATE CHARTED	PEAK POS	WKS CHRT'D	ARTIST — Album Title	LABEL & NUMBER
3/12/83	94	23	1. Sweat	Mirage 90062
3/31/84	182	5	2. X-Periment	Mirage 90146

GABOR SZABO
Hungarian-born jazz guitarist - died on 2/26/82

DATE CHARTED	PEAK POS	WKS CHRT'D	ARTIST — Album Title	LABEL & NUMBER
1/28/67	140	4	1. Spellbinder .... [I]	Impulse! 9123
1/13/68	194	2	2. The Sorcerer .... [I-L]	Impulse! 9146
6/15/68	157	3	3. Bacchanal .... [I]	Skye 3
8/16/69	143	7	4. Gabor Szabo 1969 .... [I]	Skye 9
5/16/70	162	10	5. Lena & Gabor .... LENA HORNE & GABOR SZABO	Skye 15

TACO
Taco Ockerse - Indonesian/Dutch

DATE CHARTED	PEAK POS	WKS CHRT'D	ARTIST — Album Title	LABEL & NUMBER
7/23/83	23	24	1. After Eight .... "Puttin' On The Ritz"(4)	RCA 4818

TALK TALK
rock quartet from Britain - Mark Hollis, lead singer

DATE CHARTED	PEAK POS	WKS CHRT'D	ARTIST — Album Title	LABEL & NUMBER
9/18/82	132	16	1. The Party's Over	EMI America 17083
4/07/84	42	22	2. It's My Life	EMI America 17113

DATE CHARTED	PEAK POS	WKS CHRT'D	ARTIST — Album Title	LABEL & NUMBER
			TALKING HEADS New York City new-wave quartet led by David Byrne - also see Tom Tom Club	
10/08/77	**97**	29	1. Talking Heads: 77	Sire 6036
8/12/78	**29**	42	● 2. More Songs About Buildings And Food .... "Take Me To The River"	Sire 6058
9/01/79	**21**	30	3. Fear Of Music	Sire 6076
11/01/80	**19**	27	4. Remain In Light .... above 3 albums produced by Brian Eno	Sire 6095
4/17/82	**31**	14	5. The Name Of This Band Is Talking Heads .... [L]	Sire 3590 [2]
6/25/83	**15**	51	● 6. Speaking In Tongues .... "Burning Down The House"(9)	Sire 23883
9/22/84	**41**	29+	● 7. Stop Making Sense .... [S-L] film is a live concert at The Pantages Theatre in Hollywood (December, 1983)	Sire 25121
			TANGERINE DREAM German synthesists: Edgar Froese, Chris Franks, Peter Baumann	
7/06/74	**196**	2	1. Phaedra .... [I]	Virgin 13108
4/02/77	**158**	7	2. Stratosfear .... [I]	Virgin 34427
7/23/77	**153**	6	3. Sorcerer .... [S-I]	MCA 2277
12/03/77	**178**	2	4. Encore .... [I-L]	Virgin 35014 [2]
5/09/81	**115**	10	5. Thief .... [S-I] Johannes Schmoelling replaces Peter Baumann	Elektra 521
11/21/81	**195**	2	6. Exit .... [I]	Elektra 557
			MARC TANNER Band	
3/03/79	**140**	8	1. No Escape	Elektra 168
			TANTRUM	
1/19/80	**199**	3	1. Rather Be Rockin'	Ovation 1747
			TARNEY/SPENCER Band Australian duo: Alan Tarney/Trevor Spencer	
7/29/78	**174**	4	1. Three's A Crowd	A&M 4692
5/12/79	**181**	4	2. Run For Your Life	A&M 4757
			TASTE Irish rock trio led by Rory Gallagher	
8/16/69	**133**	9	1. Taste	Atco 296
			TASTE OF HONEY Janice Marie Johnson & Hazel Payne	
6/17/78	**6**	27	▲ 1. **A Taste of Honey** .... "Boogie Oogie Oogie"(1)	Capitol 11754
7/14/79	**59**	13	2. Another Taste	Capitol 11951
8/02/80	**36**	32	3. Twice As Sweet .... "Sukiyaki"(3)	Capitol 12089
4/24/82	**73**	12	4. Ladies Of The Eighties	Capitol 12173
			TAVARES five Tavares brothers from New Bedford, Massachusetts	
2/09/74	**160**	8	1. Check It Out	Capitol 11258
9/21/74	**121**	23	2. Hard Core Poetry	Capitol 11316
8/09/75	**26**	17	3. In The City .... "It Only Takes A Minute"(10)	Capitol 11396
6/12/76	**24**	31	4. Sky High! .... "Heaven Must Be Missing An Angel"	Capitol 11533
4/30/77	**59**	22	5. Love Storm	Capitol 11628
10/15/77	**72**	10	6. The Best Of Tavares .... [G]	Capitol 11701
5/13/78	**115**	8	7. Future Bound	Capitol 11719
2/03/79	**92**	11	8. Madam Butterfly	Capitol 11874
3/08/80	**75**	7	9. Supercharged	Capitol 12026
12/11/82	**137**	11	10. New Directions	RCA 4357

DATE CHARTED	PEAK POS	WKS CHRT'D	ARTIST — Album Title	LABEL & NUMBER
			TAXXI British rock trio	
12/25/82	**161**	11	1. States Of Emergency	Fantasy 9617
			ALEX TAYLOR James Taylor's older brother	
3/20/71	**190**	2	1. With Friends And Neighbors	Capricorn 860
			JAMES TAYLOR born on 3/12/48 in Boston - married to Carly Simon ('72-'82)	
3/14/70	**3**	102	● 1. **Sweet Baby James** .... "Fire And Rain"(3)	Warner 1843
10/03/70	**62**	28	2. James Taylor .... [E] recorded in 1968 in London	Apple 3352
2/06/71	**74**	8	3. James Taylor and the original Flying Machine-1967 .... [E] Flying Machine: New York group formed by Danny Kortchmar	Euphoria 2
5/08/71	**2(4)**	45	● 4. **Mud Slide Slim And The Blue Horizon** .... "You've Got A Friend"(1)	Warner 2561
11/25/72	**4**	25	● 5. **One Man Dog**	Warner 2660
7/13/74	**13**	18	6. Walking Man	Warner 2794
5/31/75	**6**	27	● 7. **Gorilla** .... "How Sweet It Is (To Be Loved By You)"(5)	Warner 2866
7/04/76	**16**	24	● 8. In The Pocket	Warner 2912
12/04/76	**23**	41	▲ 9. Greatest Hits .... [G]	Warner 2979
7/09/77	**4**	39	▲ 10. **JT** .... "Handy Man"(4)	Columbia 34811
5/12/79	**10**	23	● 11. **Flag**	Columbia 36058
3/21/81	**10**	23	● 12. **Dad Loves His Work** .... "Her Town Too"(with J.D. Souther)	Columbia 37009
			JOHNNIE TAYLOR replaced Sam Cooke as lead singer of the Soul Stirrers gospel group	
1/25/69	**42**	18	1. Who's Making Love... .... "Who's Making Love"(5)	Stax 2005
4/26/69	**126**	9	2. Raw Blues	Stax 2008
7/05/69	**109**	6	3. The Johnnie Taylor Philosophy Continues ...	Stax 2023
12/19/70	**141**	5	4. Johnnie Taylor's Greatest Hits .... [G]	Stax 2032
4/17/71	**116**	11	5. One Step Beyond	Stax 2030
7/14/73	**54**	20	6. Taylored in Silk	Stax 3014
6/08/74	**182**	8	7. Super Taylor	Stax 5509
3/13/76	**5**	28	● 8. **Eargasm** .... "Disco Lady"(1)	Columbia 33951
3/19/77	**51**	11	9. Rated Extraordinaire	Columbia 34401
5/06/78	**164**	6	10. Ever Ready	Columbia 35340
			KATE TAYLOR James Taylor's sister	
3/27/71	**88**	8	1. Sister Kate	Cotillion 9045
			LITTLE JOHNNY TAYLOR real name: Johnny Young	
11/09/63	**140**	2	1. Little Johnny Taylor	Galaxy 203
			LIVINGSTON TAYLOR James Taylor's younger brother	
7/25/70	**82**	20	1. Livingston Taylor	Atco 334
12/18/71	**147**	10	2. Liv	Capricorn 863
11/03/73	**189**	5	3. Over The Rainbow	Capricorn 0114
			MICK TAYLOR guitarist with the Rolling Stones (1969-74)	
7/21/79	**119**	5	1. Mick Taylor	Columbia 35076

DATE CHARTED	PEAK POS	WKS CHRT'D	ARTIST — Album Title	LABEL & NUMBER
			R. DEAN TAYLOR Canadian	
2/20/71	**198**	1	1. I Think, Therefore I Am .... "Indiana Wants Me"(5)	Rare Earth 522
			ROGER TAYLOR Queen's drummer	
5/09/81	**121**	10	1. Fun In Space	Elektra 522
			T-BONES a Joe Saraceno studio production	
2/12/66	**75**	12	1. No Matter What Shape (Your Stomach's In) .... [I] "No Matter What Shape (Your Stomach's In)"(3)	Liberty 7439
			T-CONNECTION dance/disco group formed in the Bahamas	
5/14/77	**109**	11	1. Magic	Dash 30004
1/21/78	**139**	11	2. On Fire	Dash 30008
1/27/79	**51**	19	3. T-Connection	Dash 30009
11/24/79	**188**	3	4. Totally Connected	Dash 30014
3/21/81	**138**	8	5. Everything Is Cool	Capitol 12128
3/20/82	**123**	10	6. Pure & Natural	Capitol 12191
			TEARDROP EXPLODES English new wave group - Julian Cope, lead singer	
2/28/81	**156**	6	1. Kilimanjaro	Mercury 4016
2/06/82	**176**	4	2. Wilder	Mercury 4035
			TEARS FOR FEARS British duo: Roland Orzabal & Curt Smith	
5/07/83	**73**	27	1. The Hurting	Mercury 811039
3/30/85	**60+**	2+	2. Songs From The Big Chair	Mercury 824300
			TEE SET Dutch quintet	
5/16/70	**158**	6	1. Ma Belle Amie .... "Ma Belle Amie"(5)	Colossus 1001
			TEENAGERS featuring Frankie Lymon Frankie died on 2/28/68 (25)	
1/19/57	**19**	1	1. The Teenagers featuring Frankie Lymon .... "Why Do Fools Fall In Love"(6)	Gee 701
			NINO TEMPO & APRIL STEVENS brother and sister	
11/23/63	**48**	14	1. Deep Purple .... "Deep Purple"(1)	Atco 156
			TEMPTATIONS original group: David Ruffin, Eddie Kendricks, Otis Williams, Melvin Franklin, Paul Williams (died 8/17/73-34)	
5/09/64	**95**	11	1. Meet The Temptations .... "The Way You Do The Things You Do"	Gordy 911
4/03/65	**35**	26	2. The Temptations Sing Smokey .... tribute to songwriter/producer Smokey Robinson "My Girl"(1)	Gordy 912
11/27/65	**11**	37	3. Temptin' Temptations	Gordy 914
7/09/66	**12**	35	4. Gettin' Ready	Gordy 918
12/17/66	**5**	120	5. **The Temptations Greatest Hits** .... [G] "Beauty Is Only Skin Deep"(3)	Gordy 919
4/01/67	**10**	51	6. **Temptations Live!** .... [L]	Gordy 921
8/12/67	**7**	36	7. **With A Lot O' Soul** .... "(I Know) I'm Losing You"(8)/"All I Need"(8)/ "You're My Everything"(6)	Gordy 922
12/23/67	**13**	44	8. The Temptations in a Mellow Mood	Gordy 924
5/25/68	**13**	41	9. Wish It Would Rain .... "I Wish It Would Rain"(4)	Gordy 927

DATE CHARTED	PEAK POS	WKS CHRT'D	ARTIST — Album Title	LABEL & NUMBER
11/30/68	2(1)	32	10. **Diana Ross & the Supremes Join the Temptations** .... "I'm Gonna Make You Love Me"(2)	Motown 679
12/28/68	1(1)	34	11. **TCB** .... [TV] DIANA ROSS & THE SUPREMES with THE TEMPTATIONS	Motown 682
1/04/69	15	24	12. Live At The Copa .... [L] Dennis Edwards replaces David Ruffin	Gordy 938
3/15/69	4	40	13. **Cloud Nine** .... "Cloud Nine"(6)/"Run Away Child, Running Wild"(6)	Gordy 939
8/09/69	24	16	14. The Temptations Show .... [TV] with guests Kaye Stevens & George Kirby	Gordy 933
10/11/69	5	41	15. **Puzzle People** .... "I Can't Get Next To You"(1)	Gordy 949
10/25/69	28	18	16. Together .... DIANA ROSS & THE SUPREMES with THE TEMPTATIONS	Motown 692
12/06/69	38	12	17. On Broadway .... [TV] DIANA ROSS & THE SUPREMES with THE TEMPTATIONS	Motown 699
4/04/70	9	30	18. **Psychedelic Shack** .... "Psychedelic Shack"(7)	Gordy 947
8/22/70	21	18	19. Live at London's Talk of The Town .... [L]	Gordy 953
9/26/70	15	70	20. Temptations Greatest Hits II .... [G] "Ball Of Confusion (That's What The World Is Today)"(3)	Gordy 954
5/08/71	16	35	21. Sky's The Limit .... "Just My Imagination (Running Away With Me)"(1)	Gordy 957
1/29/72	24	22	22. Solid Rock .... Damon Harris replaces Eddie Kendricks	Gordy 961
8/19/72	2(2)	44	23. **All Directions** .... "Papa Was A Rollin' Stone"(1)	Gordy 962
3/10/73	7	28	24. **Masterpiece** .... "Masterpiece"(7)	Gordy 965
9/15/73	65	26	25. Anthology .... [G]	Motown 782 [3]
12/29/73	19	22	26. 1990	Gordy 966
2/08/75	13	36	27. A Song For You	Gordy 969
11/29/75	40	20	28. House Party	Gordy 973
4/03/76	29	20	29. Wings Of Love	Gordy 971
9/11/76	53	14	30. The Temptations Do The Temptations	Gordy 975
12/10/77	113	13	31. Hear To Tempt You	Atlantic 19143
5/17/80	45	14	32. Power	Gordy 994
8/29/81	119	9	33. The Temptations	Gordy 1006
5/01/82	37	18	34. Reunion .... Ruffin & Kendricks return for this album	Gordy 6008
3/19/83	159	9	35. Surface Thrills	Gordy 6032
4/21/84	152	9	36. Back To Basics	Gordy 6085
11/17/84	55	21+	37. Truly For You	Gordy 6119
			10cc English art-rock group which evolved from Hotlegs	
8/10/74	81	14	1. Sheet Music	UK 53107
4/19/75	15	25	2. The Original Soundtrack .... "I'm Not In Love"(2)	Mercury 1029
9/13/75	161	5	3. 100cc .... [K]	UK 53110
2/14/76	47	13	4. How Dare You! .... Kevin Godley & Lol Creme's last album as members	Mercury 1061
5/14/77	31	20	5. Deceptive Bends .... "The Things We Do For Love"(5)	Mercury 3702
12/24/77	146	6	6. Live And Let Live .... [L]	Mercury 8600 [2]
10/14/78	69	17	7. Bloody Tourists	Polydor 6161
12/22/79	188	4	8. Greatest Hits 1972-1978 .... [G]	Polydor 6244
5/17/80	180	2	9. Look Hear?	Warner 3442

DATE CHARTED	PEAK POS	WKS CHRT'D	ARTIST — Album Title	LABEL & NUMBER
			TEN WHEEL DRIVE with GENYA RAVAN jazz-rock band led by vocalist Genya Ravan	
1/10/70	**151**	16	1. Construction #1	Polydor 4008
8/01/70	**161**	8	2. Brief Replies	Polydor 4024
6/19/71	**190**	5	3. Peculiar Friends	Polydor 4062
			TEN YEARS AFTER British blues-rock group led by guitarist/vocalist Alvin Lee	
8/10/68	**115**	14	1. Undead .... [L]	Deram 18016
2/22/69	**61**	18	2. Stonedhenge	Deram 18021
8/30/69	**20**	23	3. Ssssh	Deram 18029
4/18/70	**14**	30	4. Cricklewood Green	Deram 18038
12/12/70	**21**	16	5. Watt	Deram 18050
8/28/71	**17**	26	● 6. A Space In Time .... "I'd Love To Change The World"	Columbia 30801
4/08/72	**55**	18	7. Alvin Lee & Company .... [K]	Deram 18064
10/14/72	**43**	25	8. Rock & Roll Music To The World	Columbia 31779
6/23/73	**39**	21	9. Recorded Live .... [L]	Columbia 32290 [2]
5/18/74	**81**	14	10. Positive Vibrations	Columbia 32851
7/19/75	**174**	5	11. Goin' Home! Their Greatest Hits .... [K] includes "I'm Going Home" (recorded live at Woodstock)	Deram 18072
			TONI TENNILLE half of Captain & Tennille duo	
6/09/84	**142**	11	1. More Than You Know .... features standards from the '30s and '40s	Mirage 90162
			TAMMI TERRELL - see MARVIN GAYE	
			SONNY TERRY & BROWNIE McGHEE blues duo	
4/07/73	**185**	5	1. Sonny & Brownie	A&M 4379
			JOE TEX born Joseph Arrington in Rogers, Texas - died on 8/13/82 (49)	
2/06/65	**124**	7	1. Hold What You've Got .... "Hold What You've Got"(5)	Atlantic 8106
11/27/65	**142**	7	2. The New Boss	Atlantic 8115
5/07/66	**108**	8	3. The Love You Save	Atlantic 8124
9/02/67	**168**	4	4. The Best Of Joe Tex .... [G]	Atlantic 8144
2/24/68	**84**	17	5. Live and Lively .... [L] "Skinny Legs And All"(10)	Atlantic 8156
7/27/68	**154**	7	6. Soul Country	Atlantic 8187
7/19/69	**190**	5	7. Buying A Book	Atlantic 8231
4/22/72	**17**	21	8. I Gotcha .... "I Gotcha"(2)	Dial 6002
5/07/77	**108**	9	9. Bumps & Bruises	Epic 34666
			TEXTONES quintet led by singer/guitarist Carla Olson	
11/24/84	**176**	8	1. Midnight Mission	Gold Mt. 86010
			THEE PROPHETS pop/rock quartet from Milwaukee	
6/28/69	**163**	3	1. Playgirl	Kapp 3596
			THEM Irish rock quintet led by Van Morrison	
7/24/65	**54**	23	1. Them .... "Gloria"/"Here Comes The Night"	Parrot 71005
4/16/66	**138**	6	2. Them Again	Parrot 71008
7/22/72	**154**	11	3. Them Featuring Van Morrison .... [R] reissue (condensed) of their first 2 albums	Parrot 71053 [2]

DATE CHARTED	PEAK POS	WKS CHRT'D	ARTIST — Album Title	LABEL & NUMBER
			THEO VANESS French disco act	
6/16/79	**145**	6	1. Bad Bad Boy	Prelude 12165
			MIKE THEODORE Orchestra a studio disco production	
10/01/77	**178**	2	1. Cosmic Wind	Westbound 305
			THIN LIZZY Irish rock quartet led by Phil Lynott	
4/17/76	**18**	28	● 1. Jailbreak "The Boys Are Back In Town"	Mercury 1081
11/13/76	**52**	11	2. Johnny The Fox	Mercury 1119
9/24/77	**39**	11	3. Bad Reputation	Mercury 1186
7/22/78	**84**	12	4. Live And Dangerous [L]	Warner 3213 [2]
6/02/79	**81**	12	5. Black Rose/A Rock Legend	Warner 3338
11/29/80	**120**	10	6. Chinatown	Warner 3496
2/20/82	**157**	11	7. Renegade	Warner 3622
5/28/83	**159**	5	8. Thunder And Lightning	Warner 23831
1/28/84	**185**	3	9. 'Life'-Live [L]	Warner 23986 [2]
			THIRD POWER	
7/04/70	**194**	2	1. Believe	Vanguard 6554
			THIRD WORLD reggae fusion band from Jamaica	
11/25/78	**55**	24	1. Journey To Addis	Island 9554
7/21/79	**157**	5	2. The Story's Been Told	Island 9569
8/30/80	**186**	2	3. Third World, Prisoner in The Street [S-L]	Island 9616
7/25/81	**186**	3	4. Rock The World	Columbia 37402
3/20/82	**63**	27	5. You've Got The Power Stevie Wonder produced & performed on 2 tracks	Columbia 37744
10/01/83	**137**	7	6. All The Way Strong	Columbia 38687
			38 SPECIAL Donnie Van Zant, leader - younger brother of Lynyrd Skynyrd's Ronnie Van Zant	
5/28/77	**148**	5	1. 38 Special	A&M 4638
1/05/80	**57**	19	2. Rockin' Into The Night	A&M 4782
2/21/81	**18**	57	▲ 3. Wild-Eyed Southern Boys	A&M 4835
5/29/82	**10**	42	▲ 4. Special Forces "Caught Up In You"(10)	A&M 4888
12/03/83	**22**	39	▲ 5. Tour De Force	A&M 4971
			B.J. THOMAS born Billy Joe Thomas on 8/7/42 in Hugo, Oklahoma	
1/18/69	**133**	12	1. On My Way "Hooked On A Feeling"(5)	Scepter 570
11/08/69	**90**	28	2. Greatest Hits, Volume 1 [G] "I'm So Lonesome I Could Cry"(8)	Scepter 578
1/03/70	**12**	41	● 3. Raindrops Keep Fallin' On My Head "Raindrops Keep Fallin' On My Head"(1)	Scepter 580
5/02/70	**72**	20	4. Everybody's Out Of Town "I Just Can't Help Believing"(9)	Scepter 582
12/12/70	**67**	24	5. Most Of All	Scepter 586
11/20/71	**92**	13	6. Greatest Hits, Volume Two [G]	Scepter 597
5/20/72	**145**	9	7. Billy Joe Thomas	Scepter 5101
3/29/75	**59**	14	8. Reunion "(Hey Won't You Play) Another Somebody Done Somebody Wrong Song"(1)	ABC 858
8/27/77	**114**	12	9. B.J. Thomas	MCA 2286
5/21/83	**193**	3	10. New Looks	Cleve. I. 38561

DATE CHARTED	PEAK POS	WKS CHRT'D	ARTIST — Album Title	LABEL & NUMBER
			CARLA THOMAS daughter of Rufus Thomas	
3/05/66	**134**	10	1. Comfort Me	Stax 706
10/15/66	**130**	5	2. Carla	Stax 709
4/22/67	**36**	31	3. King & Queen .... OTIS REDDING & CARLA THOMAS	Stax 716
7/01/67	**133**	6	4. The Queen Alone	Stax 718
7/05/69	**151**	5	5. Memphis Queen	Stax 2019
7/19/69	**190**	4	6. The Best Of Carla Thomas .... [G] "Gee Whiz (Look At His Eyes)"(10-'61)	Atlantic 8232
			IRMA THOMAS R&B vocalist from Panchatla, Louisiana	
6/27/64	**104**	8	1. Wish Someone Would Care	Imperial 12266
			LILLO THOMAS	
10/06/84	**186**	3	1. All Of You	Capitol 12346
			MARLO THOMAS - see CHILDRENS section	
			RAY THOMAS English - member of the Moody Blues (flute/harmonica)	
8/09/75	**68**	11	1. From Mighty Oaks	Threshold 16
8/14/76	**147**	5	2. Hopes Wishes & Dreams	Threshold 17
			RUFUS THOMAS R&B singer, dance creator, disc jockey	
12/28/63	**138**	3	1. Walking The Dog .... "Walking The Dog"(10)	Stax 704
4/03/71	**147**	5	2. Rufus Thomas Live/Doing The Push & Pull At P.J.'s .... [L]	Stax 2039
			TIMMY THOMAS native of Evansville, Indiana	
1/20/73	**53**	15	1. Why Can't We Live Together .... "Why Can't We Live Together"(3)	Glades 6501
			THOMPSON TWINS Tom Bailey (English), Alannah Currie (New Zealand), Joe Leeway (South Africa)	
6/26/82	**148**	8	1. In The Name Of Love	Arista 6601
2/26/83	**34**	25	2. Side Kicks .... "Lies"	Arista 6607
3/17/84	**10**	53	▲ 3. **Into The Gap** .... "Hold Me Now"(3)	Arista 8200
			ROBBIN THOMPSON Band played in Bruce Springsteen's early Steel Mill band	
10/25/80	**168**	11	1. (two "b's" please)	Ovation 1759
			RICHARD THOMPSON English - founding member of Fairport Convention	
7/30/83	**186**	5	1. Hand Of Kindness	Hannibal 1313
3/09/85	**104+**	5+	2. Across A Crowded Room	Polydor 825421
			SUE THOMPSON born Eva Sue McKee on 7/19/26 in Nevada, Missouri	
3/20/65	**134**	3	1. Paper Tiger	Hickory 121
			ALI THOMSON Scottish - younger brother of Supertramp's Dougie Thomson	
7/05/80	**99**	15	1. Take A Little Rhythm	A&M 4803
			BIG MAMA THORNTON Willie Mae's 1953 version of "Hound Dog" hit #1 on the R&B charts - died on 7/25/84 (57)	
8/30/69	**198**	2	1. Stronger Than Dirt	Mercury 61225

DATE CHARTED	PEAK POS	WKS CHRT'D	ARTIST — Album Title	LABEL & NUMBER
			GEORGE THOROGOOD & The Destroyers Delaware rock & blues quartet	
12/09/78	**33**	47	● 1. Move It On Over	Rounder 3024
9/01/79	**78**	10	2. Better Than The Rest .... [E] recorded in 1974	MCA 3091
11/08/80	**68**	12	3. More George Thorogood and the Destroyers	Rounder 3045
8/28/82	**43**	21	4. Bad To The Bone	EMI America 17076
3/02/85	**40+**	6+	5. Maverick	EMI America 17145
			BILLY THORPE Australian	
5/05/79	**39**	23	1. Children Of The Sun .... originally released on Capricorn 0221	Polydor 6228
11/08/80	**151**	5	2. 21st Century Man	Elektra 294
			THP ORCHESTRA Canadian disco production	
2/04/78	**65**	19	1. Two Hot For Love!	Butterfly 005
			THREE DEGREES Fayette Pinkney, Sheila Ferguson & Valerie Holiday	
8/08/70	**139**	7	1. "Maybe"	Roulette 42050
12/14/74	**28**	15	2. The Three Degrees .... "When Will I See You Again"(2)	Phil. Int. 32406
6/21/75	**99**	8	3. International	Phil. Int. 33162
1/17/76	**199**	1	4. The Three Degrees Live .... [L]	Phil. Int. 33840
12/23/78	**169**	8	5. New Dimensions	Ariola 50044
			THREE DOG NIGHT Danny Hutton, Chuck Negron & Cory Wells	
1/25/69	**11**	62	● 1. Three Dog Night .... "One"(5)	Dunhill 50048
7/12/69	**16**	74	● 2. Suitable for Framing .... "Easy To Be Hard"(4)/"Eli's Coming"(10)	Dunhill 50058
11/29/69	**6**	72	● 3. **Captured Live At The Forum** .... [L]	Dunhill 50068
5/02/70	**8**	48	● 4. It Ain't Easy .... "Mama Told Me (Not To Come)"(1)	Dunhill 50078
12/12/70	**14**	64	● 5. Naturally .... "Joy To The World"(1)/"Liar"(7)	Dunhill 50088
2/27/71	**5**	61	● 6. **Golden Bisquits** .... [G]	Dunhill 50098
10/23/71	**8**	34	● 7. Harmony .... "An Old Fashioned Love Song"(4)/"Never Been To Spain"(5)	Dunhill 50108
7/29/72	**6**	40	● 8. **Seven Separate Fools** .... "Black & White"(1)	Dunhill 50118
3/17/73	**18**	27	● 9. Around The World With Three Dog Night .... [L]	Dunhill 50138 [2]
10/20/73	**26**	17	● 10. Cyan .... "Shambala"(3)	Dunhill 50158
4/06/74	**20**	22	● 11. Hard Labor .... "The Show Must Go On"(4)	Dunhill 50168
12/21/74	**15**	17	● 12. Joy To The World-Their Greatest Hits .... [G]	Dunhill 50178
6/21/75	**70**	12	13. Coming Down Your Way	ABC 888
4/24/76	**123**	6	14. American Pastime	ABC 928
			THREE SUNS instrumental (organ/accordion/guitar) trio	
5/28/55	**13**	5	1. Soft and Sweet .... [I]	RCA 1041
8/18/56	**19**	1	2. High Fi and Wide .... [I]	RCA 1249
1/26/57	**16**	6	3. Midnight For Two .... [I]	RCA 1333
			THRILLS New York-based rock quartet	
6/27/81	**199**	4	1. First Thrills	G&P 1002

DATE CHARTED	PEAK POS	WKS CHRT'D	ARTIST — Album Title	LABEL & NUMBER
			THUNDERCLAP NEWMAN British trio: Andy Newman, Speedy Keen, Jimmy McCulloch	
10/10/70	161	10	1. Hollywood Dream .... produced by Pete Townshend "Something In The Air"	Track 8264
			TIERRA Los Angeles septet - 3 members were formerly with El Chicano	
12/27/80	38	21	1. City Nights	Boardwalk 36995
			JOHNNY TILLOTSON born on 4/20/39 in Jacksonville, Florida	
4/14/62	120	5	1. Johnny Tillotson's Best .... [G] "Poetry In Motion"(2)/"Without You"(7)	Cadence 3052
7/21/62	8	31	2. **It Keeps Right On A-Hurtin'** .... "It Keeps Right On A-Hurtin"(3)	Cadence 3058
2/22/64	48	14	3. Talk Back Trembling Lips .... "Talk Back Trembling Lips"(7)	MGM 4188
2/06/65	148	3	4. She Understands Me	MGM 4270
			TIME sextet from Minneapolis - Morris Day, lead vocals	
9/12/81	50	32	● 1. The Time	Warner 3598
9/25/82	26	33	● 2. What Time Is It?	Warner 23701
7/28/84	24	37 +	▲ 3. Ice Cream Castle	Warner 25109
			TIN TIN Australian duo: Steve Kipner & Steve Groves	
6/05/71	197	1	1. Tin Tin	Atco 350
			TINY TIM born Herbert Khaury on 4/12/25 in New York City	
5/04/68	7	32	1. **God Bless Tiny Tim** .... [N] "Tip-Toe Thru' The Tulips With Me"	Reprise 6292
			CAL TJADER Latin jazz vibraphonist - died on 5/5/82 (56)	
9/28/63	79	14	1. Several Shades Of Jade .... [I]	Verve 8507
4/17/65	52	22	2. Soul Sauce .... [I]	Verve 8614
			TKO	
4/14/79	181	2	1. Let It Roll	Infinity 9005
			TOBY BEAU	
10/14/78	40	23	1. Toby Beau .... "My Angel Baby"	RCA 2771
			TOKENS Brooklyn quartet - former backup group for Neil Sedaka	
1/27/62	54	16	1. The Lion Sleeps Tonight .... "The Lion Sleeps Tonight"(1)	RCA 2514
5/21/66	148	2	2. I Hear Trumpets Blow	B.T. Puppy 1000
7/22/67	134	6	3. Back To Back .... TOKENS (side 1)/HAPPENINGS (side 2)	B.T. Puppy 1002
			TOM TOM CLUB group formed by Chris Frantz & Tina Weymouth of Talking Heads	
10/24/81	23	33	● 1. Tom Tom Club	Sire 3628
8/20/83	73	13	2. Close To The Bone	Sire 23916
			TOMITA Isao Tomita - Japanese electronic classical musician	
8/31/74	57	25	1. Snowflakes Are Dancing .... [I] electronic performances of music by Debussy	RCA 0488
5/24/75	49	12	2. Moussorgsky: Pictures At An Exhibition .... [I]	RCA 0838
2/14/76	71	12	3. Firebird .... [I] interpretations of music by Stravinsky, Debussy, & Moussorgsky	RCA 11312

DATE CHARTED	PEAK POS	WKS CHRT'D	ARTIST — Album Title	LABEL & NUMBER
1/08/77	67	13	4. Holst: The Planets .... [I]	RCA 1919
2/18/78	115	10	5. Kosmos .... [I]	RCA 2616
3/03/79	152	6	6. The Bermuda Triangle .... [I]	RCA 2885
2/09/80	174	5	7. Ravel: Bolero .... [I]	RCA 3412
			LILY TOMLIN member of TV's "Laugh-In" series ('70-'73)	
3/27/71	15	25	1. This is a Recording .... [C]	Polydor 4055
3/25/72	41	22	2. And That's The Truth .... [C]	Polydor 5023
11/12/77	120	6	3. On Stage .... [C]	Arista 4142
			TOMMY TUTONE San Francisco rock band led by Tommy Heath	
5/24/80	68	13	1. Tommy Tutone	Columbia 36372
2/06/82	20	30	2. Tommy Tutone-2 .... "867-5309/Jenny"(4)	Columbia 37401
10/29/83	179	3	3. National Emotion	Columbia 38425
			GARY TOMS Empire	
9/27/75	178	3	1. 7-6-5-4-3-2-1 Blow Your Whistle	PIP 6814
			OSCAR TONEY, JR.	
7/29/67	192	5	1. For Your Precious Love	Bell 6006
			TOOTS & THE MAYTALS Jamaican band led by Frederick "Toots" Hibbert	
11/01/75	164	13	1. Funky Kingston	Island 9330
7/17/76	157	5	2. Reggae Got Soul	Mango 9374
			TORNADOES English quintet	
1/05/63	45	17	1. The Original Telstar .... [I] "Telstar"(1)	London 3279
			TORONTO Holly Woods, lead singer of rock group from Canada	
8/30/80	185	4	1. Lookin' For Trouble	A&M 4821
9/04/82	162	10	2. Get It On Credit	Network 60153
			RICHARD TORRANCE & EUREKA	
3/08/75	107	17	1. Belle Of The Ball	Shelter 2134
			PETER TOSH born Winston MacIntosh in Jamaica - former member of Bob Marley's Wailers	
7/31/76	199	2	1. Legalize It	Columbia 34253
12/09/78	104	20	2. Bush Doctor	Rolling S. 39109
8/04/79	123	10	3. Mystic Man	Rolling S. 39111
7/18/81	91	13	4. Wanted Dread & Alive	EMI America 17055
6/18/83	59	17	5. Mama Africa	EMI America 17095
9/22/84	152	8	6. Captured Live .... [L]	EMI America 17126
			TOTO Los Angeles-based studio musicians	
10/21/78	9	48	▲ 1. **Toto** .... "Hold The Line"(5)	Columbia 35317
11/17/79	37	29	● 2. Hydra	Columbia 36229
2/07/81	41	10	3. Turn Back	Columbia 36813
4/24/82	4	82	▲ 4. **Toto IV** .... "Rosanna"(2)/"Africa"(1)/"I Won't Hold You Back"(10)	Columbia 37728
11/24/84	42	20+	● 5. Isolation	Columbia 38962
12/22/84	168	8	6. Dune .... [S-I] featuring The Vienna Symphony Orchestra	Polydor 823770

DATE CHARTED	PEAK POS	WKS CHRT'D	ARTIST — Album Title	LABEL & NUMBER
			TOWER OF POWER brass oriented Oakland-area R&B/funk band	
4/10/71	106	12	1. East Bay Grease	San Francisco 204
6/17/72	85	20	2. Bump City	Warner 2616
6/02/73	15	31	3. Tower Of Power	Warner 2681
3/09/74	26	35	4. Back to Oakland	Warner 2749
1/25/75	22	16	5. Urban Renewal .... Lenny Williams, lead singer on above 3 albums	Warner 2834
10/11/75	67	11	6. In The Slot	Warner 2880
5/22/76	99	8	7. Live And In Living Color .... [L]	Warner 2924
9/11/76	42	17	8. Ain't Nothin' Stoppin' Us Now	Columbia 34302
4/22/78	89	8	9. We Came To Play!	Columbia 34906
8/11/79	106	12	10. Back On The Streets	Columbia 35784
			PETE TOWNSHEND English - lead guitarist/songwriter of The Who	
11/18/72	69	17	1. Who Came First	Track 79189
10/15/77	45	12	2. Rough Mix .... PETE TOWNSHEND/RONNIE LANE (Small Faces) with guests Eric Clapton & John Entwistle	MCA 2295
5/17/80	5	30	● 3. **Empty Glass** .... "Let My Love Open The Door"(9)	Atco 100
7/10/82	26	26	4. All The Best Cowboys Have Chinese Eyes	Atco 149
3/26/83	35	13	5. Scoop .... [K] primarily a collection of Townshend's demo recordings	Atco 90063 [2]
			SIMON TOWNSHEND Pete Townshend's younger brother by 18 years	
12/03/83	169	7	1. Sweet Sound .... produced by Pete Townshend	21 Records 815708
			TOYS New York trio: Barbara Harris, Barbara Parritt, June Monteiro	
2/05/66	92	8	1. The Toys sing "A Lover's Concerto" and "Attack!" .... "A Lover's Concerto"(2)	DynoVoice 9002
			TRAFFIC British - original group: Steve Winwood, Dave Mason, Jim Capaldi and Chris Wood (died 7/12/83-39)	
4/27/68	88	22	1. Mr. Fantasy	United Art. 6651
11/30/68	17	26	2. Traffic	United Art. 6676
5/17/69	19	22	3. Last Exit	United Art. 6702
1/03/70	48	14	4. Best Of Traffic .... [G]	United Art. 5500
7/11/70	5	38	● 5. **John Barleycorn Must Die**	United Art. 5504
10/02/71	26	19	6. Welcome To The Canteen .... [L]	United Art. 5550
12/11/71	7	30	● 7. **The Low Spark Of High Heeled Boys**	Island 9306
2/03/73	6	29	● 8. **Shoot Out At The Fantasy Factory**	Island 9323
11/03/73	29	24	9. Traffic-On The Road .... [L]	Island 9336 [2]
9/28/74	9	27	● 10. **When The Eagle Flies**	Asylum 1020
5/03/75	155	3	11. Heavy Traffic .... [G]	United Art. 421
9/27/75	193	4	12. More Heavy Traffic .... [G]	United Art. 526
			TRAMMPS originally session musicians and singers from Philadelphia	
7/05/75	159	4	1. Trammps	Gld. Fleece 33163
5/15/76	50	24	2. Where The Happy People Go	Atlantic 18172
1/22/77	46	49	● 3. Disco Inferno	Atlantic 18211
12/17/77	85	13	4. The Trammps III	Atlantic 19148
9/09/78	139	6	5. The Best Of The Trammps .... [G]	Atlantic 19194
5/26/79	184	2	6. The Whole World's Dancing	Atlantic 19210

DATE CHARTED	PEAK POS	WKS CHRT'D	ARTIST — Album Title	LABEL & NUMBER
			TRAPEZE British rock group	
11/02/74	172	6	1. The Final Swing .... [E-K] featuring Glenn Hughes (Deep Purple)	Threshold 11
1/04/75	146	6	2. Hot Wire	Warner 2828
			TRASHMEN Minneapolis/St. Paul surf quartet	
2/15/64	48	15	1. Surfin' Bird .... "Surfin' Bird"(4)	Garrett 200
			MARY TRAVERS Mary of Peter, Paul & Mary	
4/17/71	71	29	1. Mary	Warner 1907
4/29/72	157	5	2. Morning Glory	Warner 2609
2/24/73	169	6	3. All My Choices	Warner 2677
7/20/74	200	1	4. Circles	Warner 2795
3/11/78	186	5	5. It's In Everyone Of Us	Chrysalis 1168
			PAT TRAVERS Band Canadian blues-rock guitarist/vocalist	
12/17/77	70	22	1. Putting It Straight	Polydor 6121
10/21/78	99	16	2. Heat In The Street	Polydor 6170
7/21/79	29	22	3. Pat Travers Band Live! Go For What You Know .... [L] "Boom Boom (Out Go The Lights)"	Polydor 6202
4/05/80	20	25	4. Crash And Burn	Polydor 6262
3/28/81	37	15	5. Radio Active	Polydor 6313
11/06/82	74	13	6. Pat Travers' Black Pearl .... Black Pearl is Pat's backing band	Polydor 6361
5/05/84	108	8	7. Hot Shot	Polydor 821064
			JOHN TRAVOLTA starred in "Saturday Night Fever," "Grease" and "Urban Cowboy"	
5/22/76	39	22	1. John Travolta .... "Let Her In"(10)	Midland Int. 1563
3/12/77	66	9	2. Can't Let You Go	Midland Int. 2211
12/23/78	161	7	3. Travolta Fever .... [R] reissue of his first 2 albums above	Midsong Int. 001 [2]
			TREMELOES British quartet	
6/24/67	119	8	1. Here Comes My Baby	Epic 26310
			T. REX British group led by Marc Bolan - died on 9/16/77 (28)	
5/01/71	188	5	1. T-Rex	Reprise 6440
11/06/71	32	34	2. Electric Warrior .... "Bang A Gong (Get It On)"(10)	Reprise 6466
8/26/72	17	24	3. The Slider	Reprise 2095
10/07/72	133	12	4. Tyrannosaurus Rex (A Beginning) .... [E-R] reissue of two 1968 albums: "My People Were Fair And Had Sky In Their Hair..." & "Prophets, Seers & Sages"	A&M 3514 [2]
4/28/73	102	10	5. Tanx	Reprise 2132
			TRIUMPH Gil Moore, Rik Emmett, & Mike Levine - from Toronto, Canada	
5/05/79	48	28	1. Just A Game	RCA 3224
5/19/79	185	2	2. Rock & Roll Machine .... their first album	RCA 2982
3/29/80	32	18	3. Progessions Of Power	RCA 3524
9/19/81	23	57+ ●	4. Allied Forces	RCA 3902
1/29/83	26	27 ●	5. Never Surrender	RCA 4382
12/08/84	35	18+	6. Thunder Seven	MCA 5537

DATE CHARTED	PEAK POS	WKS CHRT'D	ARTIST — Album Title	LABEL & NUMBER
			TRIUMVIRAT German synthesized rock trio	
8/10/74	**55**	17	1. Illusions On A Double Dimple	Harvest 11311
6/07/75	**27**	17	2. Spartacus	Capitol 11392
8/07/76	**85**	8	3. Old Loves Die Hard	Capitol 11551
			TROGGS British foursome - Reg Presley, lead singer	
9/03/66	**52**	16	1. Wild Thing .... "Wild Thing"(1)	Fontana 67556
5/18/68	**109**	9	2. **Love Is All Around** .... "Love Is All Around"(7)	Fontana 67576
			TROOPER Canadian rock quintet	
8/26/78	**182**	4	1. Thick As Thieves	MCA 2377
			TROPEA eclectic guitarist, John Tropea	
3/20/76	**138**	7	1. Tropea .... [I]	Marlin 2200
5/14/77	**149**	7	2. Short Trip To Space .... [I]	Marlin 2204
			TROUBADOURS DU ROI BAUDOUIN choir and percussionists consisting of 45 boys and 15 teachers from the Kamina School in the Congo	
8/02/69	**184**	5	1. Missa Luba .... [F]	Philips 606
			TROUBLE FUNK	
5/08/82	**121**	14	1. Drop The Bomb	SugarHill 266
			ROBIN TROWER English rock guitarist - member of Procol Harum - James Dewar, vocalist (except 9 & 10)	
5/12/73	**106**	24	1. Twice Removed From Yesterday	Chrysalis 1039
4/20/74	**7**	31	● 2. **Bridge Of Sighs**	Chrysalis 1057
3/01/75	**5**	17	● 3. **For Earth Below**	Chrysalis 1073
3/27/76	**10**	20	4. **Robin Trower Live!** .... [L]	Chrysalis 1089
10/09/76	**24**	19	● 5. Long Misty Days	Chrysalis 1107
10/01/77	**25**	19	● 6. In City Dreams	Chrysalis 1148
8/26/78	**37**	17	7. Caravan To Midnight	Chrysalis 1189
3/01/80	**34**	15	8. Victims Of The Fury	Chrysalis 1215
3/21/81	**37**	16	9. B.L.T. .... B.L.T.: Jack Bruce, Bill Lordan, Robin Trower	Chrysalis 1324
1/30/82	**109**	6	10. Truce .... JACK BRUCE/ROBIN TROWER	Chrysalis 1352
10/01/83	**191**	2	11. Back It Up	Chrysalis 41420
			ANDREA TRUE Connection disco singer/actress from Nashville	
6/19/76	**47**	17	1. More, More, More .... "More, More, More"(4)	Buddah 5670
			GIL TRYTHALL	
2/07/70	**157**	6	1. Switched On Nashville/Country Moog .... [I] synthesized country hits	Athena 6003
			TUBES San Francisco theatre rock troupe - Fee Waybill, lead singer	
8/02/75	**113**	18	1. The Tubes	A&M 4534
5/15/76	**46**	15	2. Young And Rich	A&M 4580
5/28/77	**122**	6	3. Now	A&M 4632
3/11/78	**82**	8	4. What Do You Want From Live .... [L]	A&M 6003 [2]
3/31/79	**46**	18	5. Remote Control	A&M 4751
5/30/81	**36**	27	6. The Completion Backward Principle	Capitol 12151

DATE CHARTED	PEAK POS	WKS CHRT'D	ARTIST — Album Title	LABEL & NUMBER
8/29/81	148	6	7. T.R.A.S.H. (Tubes Rarities And Smash Hits) .... [K]	A&M 4870
4/02/83	18	34	8. Outside Inside	Capitol 12260
			"She's A Beauty"(10)	
3/23/85	89+	3+	9. Love Bomb	Capitol 12381

LOUISE TUCKER
English classical-styled vocalist

8/06/83	127	10	1. Midnight Blue	Arista 8088
			with Charlie Skarbek (vocals/guitars/synthesizers)	

TANYA TUCKER
born on 10/10/58 in Seminole, Texas

3/30/74	159	6	1. Would You Lay With me (In A Field Of Stone)	Columbia 32744
5/17/75	113	7	● 2. Tanya Tucker	MCA 2141
12/02/78	54	22	● 3. TNT	MCA 3066
12/01/79	121	8	4. Tear Me Apart	MCA 5106
8/01/81	180	3	5. Should I Do It	MCA 5228

TUFF DARTS
New York new-wave rock quintet

3/18/78	156	6	1. Tuff Darts!	Sire 6048

IKE & TINA TURNER
R&B/rock duo (married '58-'76) - Ike was an A&R man/ producer/session guitarist in the Fifties

2/06/65	126	6	1. Live! The Ike & Tina Turner Show .... [L]	Warner 1579
4/19/69	91	12	2. Outta Season	Blue Thumb 5
7/19/69	142	9	3. In Person .... [L]	Minit 24018
9/27/69	102	5	4. River Deep-Mountain High	A&M 4178
			Phil Spector, producer - recorded in 1966	
11/22/69	176	3	5. The Hunter	Blue Thumb 11
5/16/70	130	19	6. Come Together	Liberty 7637
12/05/70	25	38	7. Workin' Together	Liberty 7650
			"Proud Mary"(4)	
7/10/71	25	22	● 8. Live At Carnegie Hall/What You Hear Is What You Get .... [L]	United Art. 9953 [2]
11/20/71	108	10	9. 'Nuff Said	United Art. 5530
7/22/72	160	9	10. Feel Good	United Art. 5598
12/22/73	163	6	11. Nutbush City Limits	United Art. 180

SPYDER TURNER
born Dwight Turner in Beckley, West Virginia

3/25/67	158	3	1. Stand By Me	MGM 4450

TINA TURNER
born Annie Mae Bullock on 11/26/38 in Nutbush, Tennessee

9/20/75	155	5	1. Acid Queen	United Art. 495
			Tina played the Acid Queen in the film "Tommy"	
6/16/84	3	43+	▲ 2. Private Dancer	Capitol 12330
			"What's Love Got To Do With It"(1)/"Better Be Good To Me"(5)/ "Private Dancer"(7)	

STANLEY TURRENTINE
jazz tenor saxophonist - also see Jimmy Smith

1/07/67	149	2	1. Rough 'N Tumble .... [I]	Blue Note 84240
11/02/68	193	3	2. The Look Of Love .... [I]	Blue Note 84286
3/20/71	182	3	3. Sugar .... [I]	CTI 6005
10/19/74	69	21	4. Pieces Of Dreams .... [I]	Fantasy 9465
11/16/74	185	7	5. The Baddest Turrentine .... [K-I]	CTI 6048
3/08/75	110	13	6. The Sugar Man .... [K-I]	CTI 6052
5/10/75	65	14	7. In The Pocket	Fantasy 9478
11/01/75	76	16	8. Have You Ever Seen The Rain .... [I]	Fantasy 9493

DATE CHARTED	PEAK POS	WKS CHRT'D	ARTIST — Album Title	LABEL & NUMBER
6/12/76	**100**	14	9. Everybody Come On Out .... [I]	Fantasy 9508
11/27/76	**96**	14	10. The Man With The Sad Face .... [I]	Fantasy 9519
9/10/77	**84**	9	11. Nightwings .... [I]	Fantasy 9534
3/18/78	**63**	12	12. West Side Highway .... [I]	Fantasy 9548
9/16/78	**106**	13	13. What About You! .... [I]	Fantasy 9563
10/10/81	**162**	3	14. Tender Togetherness	Elektra 534

TURTLES
Los Angeles-based pop group featuring Mark Volman & Howard Kaylan (Flo & Eddie)

DATE CHARTED	PEAK POS	WKS CHRT'D	ARTIST — Album Title	LABEL & NUMBER
10/23/65	**98**	19	1. It Ain't Me Babe .... "It Ain't Me Babe"(8)	White Whale 7111
4/29/67	**25**	22	2. Happy Together .... "Happy Together"(1)/"She'd Rather Be With Me"(3)	White Whale 7114
11/18/67	**7**	39	● 3. **The Turtles! Golden Hits** .... [G]	White Whale 7115
11/16/68	**128**	12	4. The Turtles Present The Battle of the Bands .... "Elenore"(6)/"You Showed Me"(6)	White Whale 7118
11/01/69	**117**	9	5. Turtle Soup	White Whale 7124
4/11/70	**146**	9	6. The Turtles! More Golden Hits .... [G]	White Whale 7127
12/21/74	**194**	7	7. The Turtles' Greatest Hits/Happy Together Again .... [G]	Sire 3703 [2]

TUXEDO JUNCTION

DATE CHARTED	PEAK POS	WKS CHRT'D	ARTIST — Album Title	LABEL & NUMBER
2/18/78	**56**	32	1. Tuxedo Junction .... disco versions of '40s songs	Butterfly 007

TWENNYNINE with LENNY WHITE
R&B/funk band led by Lenny (former drummer of Return To Forever)

DATE CHARTED	PEAK POS	WKS CHRT'D	ARTIST — Album Title	LABEL & NUMBER
12/08/79	**54**	16	1. Best of Friends	Elektra 223
11/01/80	**106**	8	2. Twennynine with Lenny White	Elektra 304
12/05/81	**162**	5	3. Just Like Dreamin'	Elektra 551

20/20
pop/rock quartet originally from Tulsa, Oklahoma

DATE CHARTED	PEAK POS	WKS CHRT'D	ARTIST — Album Title	LABEL & NUMBER
11/03/79	**138**	13	1. 20/20	Portrait 36205
6/20/81	**127**	12	2. Look Out!	Portrait 37050

DWIGHT TWILLEY
first 2 albums shown as Dwight Twilley Band - with fellow Tulsa, Oklahoma native Phil Seymour

DATE CHARTED	PEAK POS	WKS CHRT'D	ARTIST — Album Title	LABEL & NUMBER
7/31/76	**138**	14	1. Sincerely .... "I'm On Fire"	Shelter 52001
10/08/77	**70**	13	2. Twilley Don't Mind	Arista 4140
3/24/79	**113**	9	3. Twilley	Arista 4214
3/13/82	**109**	11	4. Scuba Divers	EMI America 17064
2/18/84	**39**	21	5. Jungle .... "Girls"	EMI America 17107

TWISTED SISTER
Long Island, N.Y. heavy-metal quintet - Dee Snider, lead singer

DATE CHARTED	PEAK POS	WKS CHRT'D	ARTIST — Album Title	LABEL & NUMBER
8/27/83	**130**	14	1. You Can't Stop Rock 'N' Roll	Atlantic 80074
7/07/84	**15**	40 + ▲	2. Stay Hungry .... "We're Not Gonna Take It"	Atlantic 80156

CONWAY TWITTY
born Harold Jenkins on 9/1/33 in Friars Point, Mississippi - Conway had 36 consecutive Top 5 hits on the Country Singles charts ('68-'77)

DATE CHARTED	PEAK POS	WKS CHRT'D	ARTIST — Album Title	LABEL & NUMBER
8/16/69	**161**	3	1. I Love You More Today	Decca 75131
7/04/70	**65**	26	● 2. Hello Darlin'	Decca 75209
1/23/71	**140**	7	3. Fifteen Years Ago	Decca 75248
3/13/71	**78**	14	4. We Only Make Believe .... LORETTA LYNN & CONWAY TWITTY	Decca 75251
5/22/71	**91**	9	5. How Much More Can She Stand	Decca 75276

DATE CHARTED	PEAK POS	WKS CHRT'D	ARTIST — Album Title	LABEL & NUMBER
9/18/71	142	8	6. I Wonder What She'll Think About Me Leaving	Decca 75292
3/04/72	106	13	● 7. Lead Me On	Decca 75326
			CONWAY TWITTY & LORETTA LYNN	
4/08/72	130	9	8. I Can't See Me Without You	Decca 75335
8/25/73	153	9	9. Louisiana Woman-Mississippi Man	MCA 335
			CONWAY TWITTY-LORETTA LYNN	
9/15/73	134	9	● 10. You've Never Been This Far Before/Baby's Gone	MCA 359
2/13/82	144	15	11. Southern Comfort	Elektra 60005

TWO TONS O' FUN
Martha Wash & Izora Armstead (changed name to: Weather Girls)

5/17/80	91	11	1. Two Tons O' Fun	Honey 9584

TYCOON

3/31/79	41	17	1. Tycoon	Arista 4215

BONNIE TYLER
British songstress

6/03/78	16	17	● 1. It's A Heartache	RCA 2821
			"It's A Heartache"(3)	
2/17/79	145	5	2. Diamond Cut	RCA 3072
8/06/83	4	32	▲ 3. **Faster Than The Speed Of Night**	Columbia 38710
			"Total Eclipse Of The Heart"(1)	

TYMES
sweet soul quintet from Philadelphia

8/03/63	15	20	1. So Much In Love	Parkway 7032
			"So Much In Love"(1)/"Wonderful! Wonderful!"(7)	
12/21/63	117	10	2. The Sound Of The Wonderful Tymes	Parkway 7038
3/07/64	122	4	3. Somewhere	Parkway 7039

McCOY TYNER
jazz pianist

6/14/75	161	5	1. Atlantis .... [I-L]	Milestone 55002 [2]
1/03/76	198	2	2. Trident .... [I]	Milestone 9063
			with Ron Carter (bass) & Elvin Jones (drums)	
6/12/76	128	11	3. Fly With The Wind .... [I]	Milestone 9067
			with Hubert Laws (flute), Billy Cobham (drums) & Ron Carter	
1/22/77	187	3	4. Focal Point .... [I]	Milestone 9072
7/09/77	167	5	5. Supertrios .... [I]	Milestone 55003 [2]
			record 1 with Ron Carter & Tony Williams (drums); record 2 with Eddie Gomez (bass) & Jack DeJohnette (drums)	
1/28/78	171	8	6. Inner Voices .... [I]	Milestone 9079
			with Earl Klugh (guitar)	
10/14/78	170	3	7. The Greeting .... [I-L]	Milestone 9085
5/26/79	66	11	8. Together .... [I]	Milestone 9087
			with Freddie Hubbard (trumpet), Stanley Clarke (bass), & Hubert Laws	

TYZIK
Jeff Tyzik - jazz trumpeter/flugelhornist

9/08/84	172	6	1. Jammin' In Manhattan	Polydor 821605

UB40
British reggae octet - UB40=British unemployment benefit form

11/26/83	39	38	1. Labour of Love	A&M 4980
11/10/84	60	22 +	2. Geffery Morgan...	A&M 5033

UBIQUITY
Roy Ayers' backing group

4/08/78	146	4	1. Starbooty	Elektra 120

DATE CHARTED	PEAK POS	WKS CHRT'D	ARTIST — Album Title	LABEL & NUMBER
			UFO British hard-rock group led by Phil Mogg (vocals) & Michael Schenker (guitar 1-5)	
8/09/75	**71**	13	1. Force It	Chrysalis 1074
6/19/76	**169**	4	2. No Heavy Petting	Chrysalis 1103
6/11/77	**23**	24	3. Lights Out	Chrysalis 1127
7/29/78	**41**	18	4. Obsession	Chrysalis 1182
2/03/79	**42**	15	5. Strangers In The Night .... [L]	Chrysalis 1209 [2]
1/19/80	**51**	13	6. No Place to Run	Chrysalis 1239
1/31/81	**77**	11	7. The Wild The Willing And The Innocent	Chrysalis 1307
2/20/82	**82**	14	8. Mechanix	Chrysalis 1360
4/30/83	**153**	5	9. Making Contact	Chrysalis 41402
			U.K. British: John Wetton, Eddie Jobson & Terry Bozzio	
5/20/78	**65**	15	1. U.K. .... Bill Bruford & Allan Holdsworth were members on this album	Polydor 6146
3/24/79	**45**	11	2. Danger Money	Polydor 6194
10/20/79	**109**	6	3. Night After Night .... [L]	Polydor 6234
			TRACEY ULLMAN British singer/actress	
3/24/84	**34**	20	1. You Broke My Heart In 17 Places .... "They Don't Know"(8)	MCA 5471
			ULTIMATE studio disco production from Philadelphia	
3/03/79	**157**	11	1. Ultimate	Casablanca 7128
			ULTIMATE SPINACH psychedelic rock quintet from Boston	
2/24/68	**34**	24	1. Ultimate Spinach	MGM 4518
11/09/68	**198**	2	2. Behold & See	MGM 4570
			ULTRAVOX British electronic rock quartet led by Midge Ure	
9/13/80	**164**	9	1. Vienna	Chrysalis 1296
10/24/81	**144**	6	2. Rage In Eden	Chrysalis 1338
3/12/83	**61**	17	3. Quartet .... "Reap The Wild Wind"	Chrysalis 1394
5/19/84	**115**	9	4. Lament	Chrysalis 41459
			UNDERGROUND SUNSHINE rock quartet - 2 members from Wisconsin; 2 from Germany	
11/08/69	**161**	3	1. Let There Be Light .... "Birthday"	Intrepid 74003
			UNDERTONES Irish punk rock quintet led by Feargal Sharkey	
1/26/80	**154**	7	1. The Undertones	Sire 6081
			UNDISPUTED TRUTH soul group founded and produced by Norman Whitfield	
7/24/71	**43**	18	1. The Undisputed Truth .... "Smiling Faces Sometimes"(3)	Gordy 955
2/05/72	**114**	12	2. Face To Face With The Truth	Gordy 959
8/18/73	**191**	2	3. Law Of The Land	Gordy 963
6/21/75	**186**	2	4. Cosmic Truth	Gordy 970
11/22/75	**173**	4	5. Higher Than High	Gordy 972
1/29/77	**66**	17	6. Method To The Madness	Whitfield 2967
			UNICORN country-rock quartet produced by David Gilmour	
10/26/74	**129**	5	1. Blue Pine Trees	Capitol 11334
			UNION GAP - see GARY PUCKETT	

DATE CHARTED	PEAK POS	WKS CHRT'D	ARTIST — Album Title	LABEL & NUMBER
			UNITED STATES AIR FORCE BAND	
6/29/63	102	6	1. The United States Air Force Band .... with The Singing Sergeants on 4 tracks	RCA 2686
			UNITED STATES MARINE BAND	
6/15/63	22	9	1. The United States Marine Band .... [I]	RCA 2687
			UNITED STATES NAVY BAND	
6/15/63	38	7	1. The United States Navy Band .... with The Sea Chanters on 2 tracks	RCA 2688
			UNITED STATES OF AMERICA electronic rock quintet - Dorothy Moskowitz, lead singer	
5/04/68	181	9	1. The United States Of America	Columbia 9614
			UNLIMITED TOUCH	
6/20/81	142	7	1. Unlimited Touch	Prelude 12184
			UP WITH PEOPLE a "sing-out" musical production featuring various young singing talent	
7/23/66	61	14	1. Up With People!	Pace 1101
			URIAH HEEP British heavy-metal rock quintet led by David Byron (lead singer 1-11) & Mick Box (lead guitar)	
10/03/70	186	4	1. Uriah Heep	Mercury 61294
1/30/71	103	9	2. Salisbury	Mercury 61319
9/25/71	93	20	3. Look At Yourself	Mercury 614
6/17/72	23	38	● 4. Demons And Wizards .... "Easy Livin"	Mercury 630
12/02/72	31	22	● 5. The Magician's Birthday	Mercury 652
5/05/73	37	30	● 6. Uriah Heep Live .... [L]	Mercury 7503 [2]
10/06/73	33	23	● 7. Sweet Freedom	Warner 2724
7/06/74	38	15	8. Wonderworld	Warner 2800
8/02/75	85	10	9. Return To Fantasy	Warner 2869
3/20/76	145	6	10. The Best Of Uriah Heep .... [G]	Mercury 1070
6/26/76	161	3	11. High And Mighty	Warner 2949
4/30/77	166	3	12. Firefly	Warner 3013
11/04/78	186	5	13. Fallen Angel	Chrysalis 1204
8/07/82	56	16	14. Abominog	Mercury 4057
6/04/83	159	10	15. Head First	Mercury 812313
			USA-EUROPEAN CONNECTION a Boris Midney disco production	
4/08/78	66	19	1. Come Into My Heart	Marlin 2212
			UTOPIA Todd Rundgren, leader	
11/09/74	34	15	1. Todd Rundgren's Utopia	Bearsville 6954
11/15/75	66	9	2. Todd Rundgren's Utopia/Another Live ...... [L]	Bearsville 6961
2/26/77	79	7	3. RA	Bearsville 6965
9/24/77	73	8	4. Oops! Wrong Planet	Bearsville 6970
1/26/80	32	21	5. Adventures In Utopia .... "Set Me Free"	Bearsville 6991
10/25/80	65	9	6. Deface The Music .... a Beatles parody	Bearsville 3487
3/20/82	102	10	7. Swing To The Right	Bearsville 3666
10/16/82	84	19	8. Utopia .... album 2 is a bonus 5 track LP	Network 60183 [2]
2/11/84	74	12	9. Oblivion	Passport 6029
3/16/85	161+	4+	10. POV	Passport 6044

DATE CHARTED	PEAK POS	WKS CHRT'D	ARTIST — Album Title	LABEL & NUMBER
			U2 rock band from Dublin, Ireland: Paul "Bono" Hewson (vocals), Dave "the Edge" Evans (guitar), Adam Clayton (bass), Larry Mullen Jr. (drums)	
3/14/81	63	25	1. Boy	Island 9646
11/07/81	104	16	2. October	Island 9680
3/19/83	12	92+ ▲	3. War .... "New Year's Day"/"Sunday Bloody Sunday"	Island 90067
12/10/83	28	70+ ●	4. Under A Blood Red Sky .... [M-L]	Island 90127
10/20/84	12	25+ ▲	5. The Unforgettable Fire	Island 90231
			JERRY VALE born Genaro Vitaliano on 7/8/32 in the Bronx, New York	
8/25/62	60	48	1. I Have But One Heart	Columbia 8597
2/23/63	34	25	2. Arrivederci, Roma	Columbia 8755
9/07/63	22	35	3. The Language Of Love	Columbia 8843
2/22/64	28	18	4. Till The End Of Time	Columbia 8916
8/29/64	26	22	5. Be My Love	Columbia 8981
1/30/65	55	18	6. Standing Ovation! .... [L] recorded at Carnegie Hall on 5/30/64	Columbia 9073
3/06/65	30	23	7. Have You Looked Into Your Heart	Columbia 9113
10/16/65	42	17	8. There Goes My Heart	Columbia 9187
2/12/66	38	17	9. It's Magic	Columbia 9244
7/02/66	111	4	10. Great Moments On Broadway	Columbia 9289
3/18/67	117	23	11. The Impossible Dream	Columbia 9383
9/16/67	128	6	12. Time Alone Will Tell	Columbia 9484
3/16/68	163	7	13. You Don't Have To Say You Love Me	Columbia 9574
8/10/68	135	20	14. This Guy's In Love With You	Columbia 9694
2/15/69	90	12	15. Till	Columbia 9757
7/05/69	180	4	16. Where's The Playground Susie?	Columbia 9838
11/01/69	193	2	17. With Love, Jerry Vale .... [K]	Columbia 16 [2]
2/14/70	196	2	18. Jerry Vale Sings 16 Greatest Hits Of The 60's	Columbia 9982
6/27/70	189	4	19. Let It Be	Columbia 1021
2/12/72	200	2	20. Jerry Vale Sings The Great Hits Of Nat King Cole	Columbia 31147
			RITCHIE VALENS real name: Richard Valenzuela - died in a plane crash with Buddy Holly & the Big Bopper on 2/3/59 (17)	
4/06/59	23	6	1. Ritchie Valens .... "Donna"(2)/"La Bamba"	Del-Fi 1201
			DAVE VALENTIN jazz/Latin flutist from the South Bronx, New York	
10/25/80	194	2	1. Land Of The Third Eye .... [I]	GRP 5009
8/08/81	184	4	2. Pied Piper .... [I]	GRP 5505
			VALJEAN pianist Valjean Johns from Shattuck, Oklahoma	
7/28/62	113	5	1. The Theme From Ben Casey .... [I]	Carlton 143
			FRANKIE VALLI born Frank Castelluccio on 5/3/37 - also see the Four Seasons	
7/22/67	34	23	1. Frankie Valli-Solo .... "Can't Take My Eyes Off You"(2)	Philips 247
8/10/68	176	5	2. Timeless	Philips 274
3/29/75	51	28	3. Closeup .... "My Eyes Adored You"(1)/"Swearin' To God"(6)	Private S. 2000
12/13/75	107	8	4. Our Day Will Come	Private S. 2006

DATE CHARTED	PEAK POS	WKS CHRT'D	ARTIST — Album Title	LABEL & NUMBER
12/20/75	132	8	5. Frankie Valli Gold .... [G]	Private S. 2001
8/26/78	160	7	6. Frankie Valli...Is The Word .... "Grease"(1)	Warner 3233
			VAN HALEN heavy-metal rock band formed in Pasadena, California: David Lee Roth (vocals), Edward (guitar) & Alex Van Halen (drums), and Michael Anthony (bass)	
3/11/78	19	169	▲ 1. **Van Halen** .... "You Really Got Me"	Warner 3075
4/14/79	6	47	▲ 2. **Van Halen II** .... "Dance The Night Away"	Warner 3312
4/19/80	6	31	▲ 3. **Women and Children First**	Warner 3415
5/30/81	5	23	▲ 4. **Fair Warning**	Warner 3540
5/08/82	3	65	▲ 5. **Diver Down** .... "(Oh) Pretty Woman"	Warner 3677
1/28/84	2(5)	63+	▲ 6. **1984 (MCMLXXXIV)** .... "Jump(1)/"I'll Wait"/"Panama"	Warner 23985
			JOHNNY VAN ZANT Band brother of Ronnie (Lynyrd Skynyrd) & Donnie Van Zant (38 Special)	
9/06/80	48	15	1. No More Dirty Deals	Polydor 6289
6/13/81	119	10	2. Round Two	Polydor 6322
9/18/82	159	6	3. The Last Of The Wild Ones	Polydor 6355
			VANDENBERG Dutch hard-rock quartet led by Adrian Vandenberg & Bert Heerink	
1/08/83	65	18	1. Vandenberg	Atco 90005
1/28/84	169	7	2. Heading For A Storm	Atco 90121
			LUTHER VANDROSS soul singer/producer/songwriter from New York	
9/19/81	19	36	● 1. Never Too Much	Epic 37451
10/16/82	20	36	▲ 2. Forever, For Always, For Love	Epic 38235
12/24/83	32	41	▲ 3. Busy Body	Epic 39196
			VANGELIS Greek keyboardist - real name: Evangelos Papathanassiou - also see Jon & Vangelis	
10/17/81	1(4)	57	▲ 1. **Chariots Of Fire** .... [S-I] film is based on the true story of 2 members of Britain's 1924 Olympic team "Chariots Of Fire-Titles"(1)	Polydor 6335
			VANILLA FUDGE New York psychedelic rock quartet - Mark Stein, lead singer	
9/16/67	6	80	● 1. **Vanilla Fudge** .... "You Keep Me Hangin' On"(6)	Atco 224
3/02/68	17	33	2. The Beat Goes On	Atco 237
7/13/68	20	33	3. Renaissance	Atco 244
3/01/69	16	27	4. Near the Beginning .... [L] side 2 recorded live	Atco 278
10/25/69	34	13	5. Rock & Roll	Atco 303
			VANITY real name: Denise Matthews (former leader of Vanity 6)	
9/22/84	62	23	1. Wild Animal	Motown 6102
			VANITY 6 female dance-funk trio led by Vanity - also see Apollonia 6	
10/02/82	45	31	1. Vanity 6	Warner 23716
			GINO VANNELLI Canadian singer/songwriter	
9/28/74	60	30	1. Powerful People	A&M 3630
7/19/75	66	23	2. Storm at Sunup	A&M 4533
8/14/76	32	22	3. The Gist of The Gemini	A&M 4596

DATE CHARTED	PEAK POS	WKS CHRT'D	ARTIST — Album Title	LABEL & NUMBER
11/19/77	**33**	16	4. A Pauper In Paradise .... side 2 with the Royal Philharmonic Orchestra	A&M 4664
9/30/78	**13**	35	▲ 5. Brother To Brother .... "I Just Wanna Stop"(4)	A&M 4722
4/11/81	**15**	26	6. Nightwalker .... "Living Inside Myself"(6)	Arista 9539
9/19/81	**172**	2	7. The Best Of Gino Vannelli .... [G]	A&M 3729
			RANDY VANWARMER	
6/02/79	**81**	10	1. Warmer .... "Just When I Needed You Most"(4)	Bearsville 6988
			VAPORS British pub-rock quartet - David Fenton, lead singer	
8/16/80	**62**	28	1. New Clear Days	United Art. 1049
4/04/81	**109**	9	2. Magnets	Liberty 1090
			SARAH VAUGHAN jazz-styled singer from Newark, New Jersey	
11/24/56	**20**	2	1. Linger Awhile	Columbia 914
12/01/56	**21**	1	2. Sassy	EmArcy 36089
4/13/57	**14**	10	3. Great Songs From Hit Shows	Mercury 100 [2]
8/19/57	**14**	9	4. Sarah Vaughan sings George Gershwin	Mercury 101 [2]
7/01/72	**173**	12	5. Sarah Vaughan/Michel Legrand .... Legrand: composer/conductor/arranger	Mainstream 361
			STEVIE RAY VAUGHAN & Double Trouble lead guitarist on David Bowie's "Let's Dance" album	
7/23/83	**38**	33	1. Texas Flood	Epic 38734
6/23/84	**31**	38	2. Couldn't Stand The Weather	Epic 39304
			BILLY VAUGHN & His Orchestra Dot Records musical director - arranger/conductor for Pat Boone and other Dot artists	
4/21/58	**5**	68	● 1. **Sail Along Silv'ry Moon** .... [I] "Sail Along Silvery Moon"(5)/"Raunchy"(10)	Dot 3100
10/13/58	**15**	45	2. Billy Vaughn Plays The Million Sellers .... [I]	Dot 3119
5/04/59	**20**	3	3. Billy Vaughn Plays .... [I]	Dot 3156
5/25/59	**7**	108	● 4. **Blue Hawaii** .... [I]	Dot 3165
1/18/60	**36**	1	5. Golden Saxophones .... [I]	Dot 3205
3/21/60	**1(2)**	62	● 6. **Theme from A Summer Place** .... [I]	Dot 3276
8/15/60	**5**	21	7. **Look For A Star** .... [I]	Dot 3322
12/19/60	**5**	23	8. **Theme from The Sundowners** .... [I]	Dot 3349
4/24/61	**11**	43	9. Orange Blossom Special and Wheels ...... [I]	Dot 3366
10/09/61	**17**	25	10. Golden Waltzes .... [I]	Dot 3280
12/04/61	**20**	18	11. Berlin Melody .... [I]	Dot 3396
3/24/62	**18**	12	12. Greatest String Band Hits	Dot 3409
6/02/62	**14**	16	13. Chapel By The Sea .... [I]	Dot 3424
9/15/62	**10**	27	14. **A Swingin' Safari** .... [I]	Dot 3458
12/29/62	**145**	1	15. Christmas Carols .... [X-I] originally released in 1958	Dot 3148
2/16/63	**17**	32	16. 1962's Greatest Hits .... [I]	Dot 25497
6/15/63	**15**	16	17. Sukiyaki and 11 Hawaiian Hits .... [I]	Dot 25523
11/09/63	**94**	8	18. Number 1 Hits, Vol. #1 .... [I]	Dot 25540
2/01/64	**51**	17	19. Blue Velvet & 1963's Great Hits .... [I]	Dot 25559
6/20/64	**144**	4	20. Forever .... [I]	Dot 25578
8/29/64	**141**	3	21. Another Hit Album! .... [I]	Dot 25593
1/02/65	**18**	29	22. Pearly Shells .... [I]	Dot 25605
4/24/65	**45**	15	23. Mexican Pearls .... [I]	Dot 25628
10/09/65	**31**	29	24. Moon Over Naples .... [I]	Dot 25654
2/12/66	**56**	14	25. Michelle .... [I]	Dot 25679

DATE CHARTED	PEAK POS	WKS CHRT'D	ARTIST — Album Title	LABEL & NUMBER
7/23/66	149	2	26. Great Country Hits .... [I]	Dot 25698
10/22/66	44	35	27. Alfie .... [I]	Dot 25751
3/18/67	114	20	28. Sweet Maria	Dot 25782
5/13/67	130	7	29. That's Life & Pineapple Market .... [I]	Dot 25788
7/29/67	147	2	30. Josephine .... [E-I]	Dot 25796
8/12/67	161	5	31. I Love You	Dot 25813
			shown as The Billy Vaughn Singers (also on #28 above)	
9/23/67	159	8	32. Golden Hits/The Best Of Billy Vaughn .... [G-I]	Dot 25811
			"Melody Of Love"(2-'55)/"The Shifting Whispering Sands" (5-'55)	
10/28/67	200	2	33. Ode To Billy Joe .... [I]	Dot 25828
9/28/68	198	3	34. A Current Set Of Standards .... [I]	Dot 25882
5/17/69	95	16	35. The Windmills Of Your Mind .... [I]	Dot 25937
3/14/70	188	2	36. Winter World Of Love .... [I]	Dot 25975

BOBBY VEE
born Robert Velline on 4/30/43 in Fargo, North Dakota

DATE CHARTED	PEAK POS	WKS CHRT'D	ARTIST — Album Title	LABEL & NUMBER
3/20/61	18	15	1. Bobby Vee	Liberty 7181
			"Devil Or Angel"(6)/"Rubber Ball"(6)	
10/30/61	85	8	2. Bobby Vee sings Hits Of The Rockin' '50's	Liberty 7205
2/03/62	91	14	3. Take Good Care Of My Baby	Liberty 7211
			"Take Good Care Of My Baby"(1)/"Run To Him"(2)	
7/21/62	42	23	4. Bobby Vee Meets The Crickets	Liberty 7228
7/21/62	121	6	5. A Bobby Vee Recording Session	Liberty 7232
11/03/62	24	44	6. Bobby Vee's Golden Greats .... [G]	Liberty 7245
12/15/62	136	3	7. Merry Christmas From Bobby Vee .... [X]	Liberty 7267
4/13/63	102	5	8. The Night Has A Thousand Eyes	Liberty 7285
			"The Night Has A Thousand Eyes"(3)	
6/01/63	91	8	9. Bobby Vee Meets The Ventures	Liberty 7289
6/27/64	146	2	10. Bobby Vee sings The New Sound From England!	Liberty 7352
10/07/67	66	12	11. Come Back When You Grow Up	Liberty 7534
			"Come Back When You Grow Up"(3)	
4/27/68	187	7	12. Just Today	Liberty 7554

TATA VEGA
DATE CHARTED	PEAK POS	WKS CHRT'D	ARTIST — Album Title	LABEL & NUMBER
4/21/79	170	8	1. Try My Love	Tamla 360

MARTHA VELEZ
DATE CHARTED	PEAK POS	WKS CHRT'D	ARTIST — Album Title	LABEL & NUMBER
5/15/76	153	17	1. Escape From Babylon	Sire 7515
			produced by Bob Marley	

VELVET UNDERGROUND
New York seminal rock quartet featuring Lou Reed & John Cale

DATE CHARTED	PEAK POS	WKS CHRT'D	ARTIST — Album Title	LABEL & NUMBER
5/13/67	171	13	1. The Velvet Underground & Nico	Verve 5008
			Nico: German female singer - produced by Andy Warhol	
3/16/68	199	2	2. White Light/White Heat	Verve 5046
3/09/85	87+	5+	3. VU .... [E]	Verve 823721
			collection of previously unreleased material from 1968-69	

VENTURES
instrumental quartet from Tacoma, Washington featuring guitarists Bob Bogle (bass), Don Wilson (rhythm) and Nokie Edwards (lead)

DATE CHARTED	PEAK POS	WKS CHRT'D	ARTIST — Album Title	LABEL & NUMBER
12/05/60	11	37	1. Walk Don't Run .... [I]	Dolton 8003
			"Walk-Don't Run"(2)	
6/26/61	39	14	2. Another Smash!!! .... [I]	Dolton 8006
9/18/61	105	14	3. The Ventures .... [I]	Dolton 8004
10/02/61	94	17	4. The Colorful Ventures .... [I]	Dolton 8008
1/20/62	24	29	5. Twist With The Ventures .... [I]	Dolton 8010
5/19/62	41	11	6. The Ventures' Twist Party, Vol. 2 .... [I]	Dolton 8014
8/11/62	45	12	7. Mashed Potatoes And Gravy .... [I]	Dolton 8016

DATE CHARTED	PEAK POS	WKS CHRT'D	ARTIST — Album Title	LABEL & NUMBER
11/24/62	93	8	8. Going To The Ventures Dance Party! .... [I]	Dolton 8017
1/05/63	8	40	● 9. **The Ventures play Telstar, The Lonely Bull** .... [I]	Dolton 8019
5/04/63	30	28	10. "Surfing" .... [I]	Dolton 8022
6/01/63	91	8	11. Bobby Vee Meets The Ventures	Liberty 7289
6/08/63	101	14	12. The Ventures Play The Country Classics .... [I]	Dolton 8023
8/31/63	30	33	13. Let's Go! .... [I]	Dolton 8024
1/25/64	27	18	14. (The) Ventures In Space .... [I]	Dolton 8027
7/18/64	32	19	15. The Fabulous Ventures .... [I]	Dolton 8029
10/10/64	17	24	16. Walk, Don't Run, Vol. 2 .... [I] "Walk-Don't Run '64"(8)	Dolton 8031
2/13/65	31	24	17. The Ventures Knock Me Out! .... [I]	Dolton 8033
6/19/65	27	30	18. The Ventures On Stage .... [I-L]	Dolton 8035
8/07/65	96	13	19. Play Guitar with the Ventures .... how to play lead, bass and rhythm guitar	Dolton 16501
9/25/65	16	35	20. The Ventures a go-go .... [I]	Dolton 8037
2/12/66	33	22	21. Where The Action Is .... [I]	Dolton 8040
3/05/66	42	21	22. The Ventures/Batman Theme .... [I]	Dolton 8042
6/11/66	39	25	23. Go With The Ventures! .... [I]	Dolton 8045
9/17/66	33	26	24. Wild Things! .... [I]	Dolton 8047
2/18/67	57	26	25. Guitar Freakout .... [I]	Dolton 8050
6/03/67	69	15	26. Super Psychedelics .... [I]	Liberty 8052
9/02/67	50	44	● 27. Golden Greats By The Ventures .... [I]	Liberty 8053
12/23/67	55	21	28. $1,000,000.00 Weekend .... [I]	Liberty 8054
5/25/68	169	6	29. Flights Of Fantasy .... [I]	Liberty 8055
8/24/68	128	9	30. The Horse .... [I] Jerry McGee replaces Nokie Edwards (lead guitar)	Liberty 8057
1/18/69	157	14	31. Underground Fire .... [I]	Liberty 8059
5/10/69	11	24	● 32. Hawaii Five-O .... [I] "Hawaii Five-O"(4)	Liberty 8061
12/13/69	81	12	33. Swamp Rock .... [I]	Liberty 8062
3/14/70	154	5	34. More Golden Greats .... [I]	Liberty 8060
10/10/70	91	21	35. The Ventures 10th Anniversary Album ..... [I]	Liberty 35000 [2]
1/15/72	195	3	36. Theme From Shaft .... [I]	United Art. 5547
3/18/72	146	3	37. Joy/The Ventures play the classics .... [I]	United Art. 5575

BILLY VERA - see BILLY & THE BEATERS

TOM VERLAINE
lead singer of Television

10/10/81	177	3	1. Dreamtime	Warner 3539

VILLAGE PEOPLE
New York campy disco act

10/01/77	54	86	● 1. Village People	Casablanca 7064
3/25/78	24	69	▲ 2. Macho Man	Casablanca 7096
10/21/78	3	45	▲ 3. **Cruisin'** .... "Y.M.C.A."(2)	Casablanca 7118
4/14/79	8	21	▲ 4. **Go West** .... "In The Navy"(3)	Casablanca 7144
10/20/79	32	20	● 5. Live and Sleazy .... [L] record 1: live; record 2: studio	Casablanca 7183 [2]
6/21/80	47	12	6. Can't Stop The Music .... [S] the group appears as themselves in the film	Casablanca 7220
8/01/81	138	4	7. Renaissance	RCA 4105

VILLAGE STOMPERS
Greenwich Village, New York dixieland band

11/02/63	5	30	1. **Washington Square** .... [I] "Washington Square"(2)	Epic 26078
4/25/64	139	3	2. More Sounds of Washington Square .... [I]	Epic 26090

DATE CHARTED	PEAK POS	WKS CHRT'D	ARTIST — Album Title	LABEL & NUMBER
			GENE VINCENT & His Blue Caps born Eugene Vincent Craddock on 2/11/35 - died on 10/12/71 (36)	
9/29/56	16	2	1. Bluejean Bop!	Capitol 764
			BOBBY VINTON born Stanley Robert Vinton on 4/16/41 in Canonsburg, Penn.	
8/04/62	5	27	1. **Roses Are Red** .... "Roses Are Red (My Love)"(1)/"Mr. Lonely"(1-'64)	Epic 26020
1/05/63	137	2	2. Bobby Vinton sings the Big Ones	Epic 26035
8/10/63	10	33	3. **Blue Velvet** .... "Blue On Blue"(3)/"Blue Velvet"(1)	Epic 26068
2/01/64	8	28	4. **There! I've Said It Again** .... "There! I've Said It Again"(1)/ "My Heart Belongs To Only You"(9)	Epic 26081
7/25/64	31	12	5. Tell Me Why	Epic 26113
10/03/64	12	38	● 6. Bobby Vinton's Greatest Hits .... [G]	Epic 26098
1/16/65	18	13	7. Mr. Lonely .... album 1 above also contains the hit version of the title song	Epic 26136
7/03/65	116	5	8. Bobby Vinton Sings for Lonely Nights	Epic 26154
2/12/66	110	5	9. Satin Pillows and Careless	Epic 26182
12/16/67	41	33	10. Please Love Me Forever .... "Please Love Me Forever"(6)	Epic 26341
6/15/68	164	8	11. Take Good Care Of My Baby	Epic 26382
1/04/69	21	24	12. I Love How You Love Me .... "I Love How You Love Me"(9)	Epic 26437
6/14/69	69	12	13. Vinton	Epic 26471
1/17/70	138	8	14. Bobby Vinton's Greatest Hits Of Love .... [K]	Epic 26517
4/11/70	90	6	15. My Elusive Dreams	Epic 26540
4/08/72	72	15	16. Ev'ry Day Of My Life	Epic 31286
7/29/72	77	14	17. Sealed With A Kiss	Epic 31642
11/25/72	119	16	18. Bobby Vinton's All-Time Greatest Hits .... [G]	Epic 31487 [2]
11/30/74	16	22	● 19. Melodies Of Love .... "My Melody Of Love"(3)	ABC 851
12/07/74	109	5	20. With Love .... [K]	Epic 32921
6/28/75	154	5	21. Bobby Vinton Sings The Golden Decade Of Love .... [K] songs from the fifties	Epic 33468 [2]
7/19/75	108	5	22. Heart Of Hearts	ABC 891
12/27/75	161	7	23. The Bobby Vinton Show .... Bobby hosted a TV variety show in 1975	ABC 924
6/11/77	183	2	24. The Name Is Love	ABC 981
			VISAGE British dance/rock sextet - Steve Strange, lead singer	
8/08/81	178	4	1. Visage .... [M]	Polydor 501
			VISCOUNTS New Jersey instrumental quintet led by brothers Bobby & Joe Spievak	
1/29/66	144	2	1. Harlem Nocturne .... [I]	Amy 8008
			JOE VITALE percussionist/keyboardist for both Joe Walsh and the Eagles	
7/04/81	181	3	1. Plantation Harbor	Asylum 529
			VOGUES quartet from Turtle Creek, Pennsylvania	
2/12/66	137	7	1. Five O'Clock World .... "Five O'Clock World"(4)	Co & Ce 1230
9/07/68	29	30	2. Turn Around, Look At Me .... "Turn Around, Look At Me"(7)/"My Special Angel"(7)	Reprise 6314
2/15/69	30	23	3. Till	Reprise 6326

DATE CHARTED	PEAK POS	WKS CHRT'D	ARTIST — Album Title	LABEL & NUMBER
9/27/69	115	9	4. Memories	Reprise 6347
1/10/70	148	9	5. The Vogues' Greatest Hits .... [G] "You're The One"(4-'65)	Reprise 6371
			VOICES OF EAST HARLEM gospel-styled black vocal group	
10/10/70	191	3	1. Right On Be Free	Elektra 74080
			ANDREAS VOLLENWEIDER electro-acoustic harpist from Zurich, Switzerland	
12/01/84	121	18	1. ...Behind The Gardens-Behind The Wall-Under The Tree... .... [I]	CBS 37793
12/15/84	149	15	2. Caverna Magica (...Under The Tree-In The Cave...) .... [I]	CBS 37827
3/02/85	86	6+	3. White Winds .... [I]	FM/CBS 39963
			ROGER VOUDOURIS Sacramento, California vocalist/guitarist	
7/07/79	171	3	1. Radio Dream	Warner 3290
			VOYAGE European disco group	
4/08/78	40	21	1. Voyage	Marlin 2213
12/16/78	47	27	2. Fly Away	Marlin 2225
			V.S.O.P. Herbie Hancock (piano), Freddie Hubbard (trumpet), Wayne Shorter (sax), Ron Carter (bass), Tony Williams (drums)	
11/12/77	123	5	1. The Quintet ....[I-L]	Columbia 34976 [2]
			JACK WAGNER Frisco Jones of TV's "General Hospital"	
9/22/84	44	29	1. All I Need .... [M] "All I Need"(2)	Qwest 25089
			PORTER WAGONER born on 8/12/30 in West Plains, Missouri - host of his own TV variety series beginning in 1960	
7/01/67	199	1	1. The Cold Hard Facts Of Life	RCA 3797
3/15/69	161	8	2. The Carroll County Accident	RCA 4116
3/22/69	184	4	3. Just The Two Of Us .... PORTER WAGONER & DOLLY PARTON	RCA 4039
8/16/69	162	5	4. Always, Always .... PORTER WAGONER & DOLLY PARTON	RCA 4186
4/04/70	137	7	5. Porter Wayne And Dolly Rebecca .... PORTER WAGONER & DOLLY PARTON	RCA 4305
5/16/70	190	2	6. You Got-ta Have A License	RCA 4286
10/10/70	191	2	7. Once More .... PORTER WAGONER & DOLLY PARTON	RCA 4388
3/13/71	142	3	8. Two Of A Kind .... PORTER WAGONER & DOLLY PARTON	RCA 4490
			WAIKIKIS Belgian instrumental group	
1/16/65	93	9	1. Hawaii Tattoo .... [I]	Kapp 3366
			WAILERS teenage quintet (in 1959) from Tacoma, Washington	
6/27/64	127	6	1. Tall Cool One .... title song originally released in 1959	Imperial 12262
			LOUDON WAINWRIGHT III satirical folksinger/songwriter	
3/03/73	102	13	1. Album III .... "Dead Skunk"	Columbia 31462
3/15/75	156	5	2. Unrequited	Columbia 33369
6/19/76	188	4	3. T Shirt	Arista 4063

DATE CHARTED	PEAK POS	WKS CHRT'D	ARTIST — Album Title	LABEL & NUMBER
			JOHN WAITE	
			British - lead singer of the Babys	
7/17/82	68	21+	1. Ignition	Chrysalis 1376
7/14/84	10	39+ ●	2. **No Brakes**	EMI America 17124
			"Missing You"(1)	
			WAITRESSES	
			Akron, Ohio-based sextet - Patty Donahue, lead singer	
2/06/82	41	24	1. Wasn't Tomorrow Wonderful?	Polydor 6346
12/18/82	128	10	2. I Could Rule The World If I Could Only	
			Get The Parts .... [M]	Polydor 507
6/04/83	155	5	3. Bruiseology	Polydor 810980
			TOM WAITS	
			gravelly voiced monologue song stylist	
11/29/75	164	6	1. Nighthawks At The Diner .... [L]	Asylum 2008 [2]
11/06/76	89	5	2. Small Change	Asylum 1078
10/22/77	113	8	3. Foreign Affairs	Asylum 1117
11/18/78	181	4	4. Blue Valentine	Asylum 162
10/04/80	96	10	5. Heartattack And Vine	Asylum 295
10/29/83	167	7	6. Swordfishtrombones	Island 90095
			RICK WAKEMAN	
			English - former keyboardist of the Strawbs and Yes	
3/24/73	30	45 ●	1. The Six Wives of Henry VIII .... [I]	A&M 4361
6/15/74	3	27 ●	2. **Journey To The Centre Of The Earth** .... [L]	A&M 3621
			with the London Symphony Orchestra	
4/19/75	21	5	3. The Myths and Legends of King Arthur	
			and the Knights of the Round Table	A&M 4515
			with the English Chamber Choir and orchestra	
5/15/76	67	8	4. No Earthly Connection	A&M 4583
			with the English Rock Ensemble	
2/26/77	126	7	5. White Rock .... [S-I]	A&M 4614
			film based on the Innsbruck Winter Games	
12/17/77	128	8	6. Rick Wakeman's Criminal Record .... [I]	A&M 4660
			with fellow Yes-men Chris Squire & Alan White	
7/21/79	170	5	7. Rhapsodies .... [I]	A&M 6501 [2]
			NARADA MICHAEL WALDEN	
			formerly with John McLaughlin's Mahavishnu Orchestra (drums)	
3/10/79	103	16	1. Awakening	Atlantic 19222
1/05/80	74	19	2. The Dance Of Life	Atlantic 19259
10/18/80	103	8	3. Victory	Atlantic 19279
6/05/82	135	6	4. Confidence	Atlantic 19351
			DAVID T. WALKER	
			studio session guitarist	
2/09/74	187	8	1. Press On .... [I]	Ode 77020
9/04/76	166	5	2. On Love	Ode 77035
			JERRY JEFF WALKER	
			'outlaw' country-rock singer/songwriter	
12/15/73	160	11 ●	1. Viva Terlingua!	MCA 382
1/11/75	141	8	2. Walker's Collectibles	MCA 450
10/04/75	119	7	3. Ridin' High	MCA 2156
7/04/76	109	10	4. It's A Good Night For Singin'	MCA 2202
5/28/77	60	21	5. A Man Must Carry On	MCA 6003 [2]
			side 4: live recordings	
7/01/78	111	9	6. Contrary To Ordinary	MCA 3041
7/19/80	185	3	7. The Best Of Jerry Jeff Walker .... [G]	MCA 5128
6/20/81	188	3	8. Reunion	SouthCoast 5199

DATE CHARTED	PEAK POS	WKS CHRT'D	ARTIST — Album Title	LABEL & NUMBER
			JIMMIE WALKER J.J. Evans of the TV show "Good Times"	
5/31/75	130	12	1. Dyn-O-Mite .... [C]	Buddah 5635
			JR. WALKER & THE ALL STARS Jr. (born Autry DeWalt, Jr.) began as a session tenor sax player	
7/10/65	108	35	1. Shotgun .... "Shotgun"(4)	Soul 701
4/09/66	130	7	2. Soul Session .... [I]	Soul 702
9/03/66	64	13	3. Road Runner	Soul 703
10/07/67	119	11	4. "Live!" .... [L]	Soul 705
2/08/69	172	4	5. Home Cookin' .... "What Does It Take (To Win Your Love)"(4)	Soul 710
6/28/69	43	18	6. Greatest Hits .... [G]	Soul 718
1/17/70	92	22	7. What Does It Take To Win Your Love	Soul 721
10/03/70	110	5	8. A Gasssss	Soul 726
7/24/71	91	14	9. Rainbow Funk	Soul 732
1/08/72	142	16	10. Moody Jr.	Soul 733
			WALL OF VOODOO electronic-rock group from L.A. - Stanard Ridgway, lead singer	
10/17/81	177	2	1. Dark Continent	I.R.S. 70022
1/15/83	45	23	2. Call Of The West	I.R.S. 70026
			JERRY WALLACE born on 12/15/38 in Kansas City, Missouri	
11/07/64	96	7	1. In The Misty Moonlight	Challenge 619
3/03/73	179	8	2. Do You Know What It's Like To Be Lonesome?	MCA 301
			JOE WALSH rock guitarist - member of the James Gang and the Eagles	
10/21/72	79	29	1. Barnstorm .... LP title is also the name of Walsh's band	Dunhill 50130
6/23/73	6	54	● 2. **The Smoker You Drink, The Player You Get** .... "Rocky Mountain Way"	Dunhill 50140
1/04/75	11	22	● 3. So What	Dunhill 50171
4/10/76	20	18	4. You Can't Argue With A Sick Mind .... [L]	ABC 932
6/10/78	8	27	▲ 5. **But Seriously, Folks...** .... "Life's Been Good"	Asylum 141
10/28/78	71	7	6. The Best Of Joe Walsh .... [G] includes "Funk #49" & "Walk Away" by the James Gang	ABC 1083
5/23/81	20	18	7. There Goes The Neighborhood	Asylum 523
7/09/83	48	14	8. You Bought It-You Name It	Warner 23884
			STEVE WALSH lead singer/keyboardist of Kansas	
2/16/80	124	6	1. Schemer-Dreamer	Kirshner 36320
			WALTER WANDERLEY Brazilian Bossa Nova organist	
9/03/66	22	41	1. Rain Forest .... [I] "Summer Samba"	Verve 8658
			WANG CHUNG British rock trio - formerly Huang Chung	
2/25/84	30	37	1. Points On The Curve .... "Dance Hall Days"	Geffen 4004
			DEXTER WANSEL R&B keyboardist/synthesizer player and producer/arranger	
4/30/77	168	3	1. What The World Is Coming To	Phil. Int. 34487
4/01/78	139	6	2. Voyager	Phil. Int. 34985

DATE CHARTED	PEAK POS	WKS CHRT'D	ARTIST — Album Title	LABEL & NUMBER
			WAR Latin jazz/funk band from Long Beach, California	
			ERIC BURDON & WAR:	
5/16/70	18	27	1. Eric Burdon Declares "War" .... "Spill The Wine"(3)	MGM 4663
12/26/70	82	9	2. The Black-Man's Burdon	MGM 4710 [2]
			WAR:	
4/24/71	190	6	3. War	United Art. 5508
11/20/71	16	49	● 4. All Day Music	United Art. 5546
11/18/72	1(2)	68	● 5. **The World Is A Ghetto** .... "The World Is A Ghetto"(7)/"The Cisco Kid"(2)	United Art. 5652
9/01/73	6	36	● 6. **Deliver The Word** .... "Gypsy Man"(8)	United Art. 128
3/23/74	13	35	● 7. War Live! .... [L]	United Art. 193 [2]
7/05/75	8	31	● 8. **Why Can't We Be Friends?** .... "Why Can't We Be Friends?"(6)/"Low Rider"(7)	United Art. 441
9/04/76	6	21	▲ 9. **Greatest Hits** .... [G] "Summer"(7)	United Art. 648
12/25/76	140	5	10. Love Is All Around .... [E] WAR featuring ERIC BURDON recorded 1969-70	ABC 988
7/23/77	23	14	● 11. Platinum Jazz .... [K]	Blue Note 690 [2]
12/03/77	15	23	● 12. Galaxy	MCA 3030
8/19/78	69	6	13. Youngblood .... [S]	United Art. 904
4/14/79	41	16	● 14. The Music Band	MCA 3085
12/08/79	111	13	15. The Music Band 2	MCA 3193
3/20/82	48	27	16. Outlaw	RCA 4208
7/23/83	164	4	17. Life (Is So Strange)	RCA 4598
			ANITA WARD	
5/26/79	8	19	1. **Songs Of Love** .... "Ring My Bell"(1)	Juana 200,004
			FRED WARING & The PENNSYLVANIANS glee club/bandleader since early 20's - died on 7/29/84 (84)	
9/09/57	25	1	1. Fred Waring And The Pennsylvanians In Hi-Fi	Capitol 845
12/23/57	6	3	2. **Now Is The Caroling Season** .... [X]	Capitol 896
12/22/58	19	3	3. Now Is The Caroling Season .... [X-R]	Capitol 896
5/30/64	116	7	4. America, I Hear You Singing .... FRANK SINATRA/BING CROSBY/FRED WARING	Reprise 2020
			JENNIFER WARNES lead actress in the Los Angeles production of "Hair"	
2/26/77	43	18	1. Jennifer Warnes .... "Right Time Of The Night"(6)	Arista 4062
6/09/79	94	23	2. Shot Through The Heart	Arista 4217
			RUSTY WARREN singer/story teller of adult comedy	
11/07/60	8	181	1. **Knockers Up!** .... [C]	Jubilee 2029
5/08/61	55	40	2. Songs For Sinners .... [C] Rusty's first album release	Jubilee 2024
5/22/61	21	51	3. Sin-Sational .... [C]	Jubilee 2034
12/18/61	31	50	4. Rusty Warren Bounces Back .... [C]	Jubilee 2039
11/03/62	22	32	5. Rusty Warren In Orbit .... [C]	Jubilee 2044
10/19/63	52	18	6. Banned In Boston? .... [C]	Jubilee 2049
1/01/66	124	7	7. More Knockers Up! .... [C]	Jubilee 2059

DATE CHARTED	PEAK POS	WKS CHRT'D	ARTIST — Album Title	LABEL & NUMBER
			DIONNE WARWICK born on 12/12/41 in East Orange, New Jersey - also see Soundtracks "Love Machine" and "The Woman In Red" (Stevie Wonder)	
9/12/64	68	20	1. Make Way For Dionne Warwick .... "Walk On By"(6)	Scepter 523
3/06/65	107	9	2. The Sensitive Sound of Dionne Warwick	Scepter 528
1/01/66	45	29	3. Here I Am	Scepter 531
4/16/66	76	11	4. Dionne Warwick in Paris .... [L]	Scepter 534
1/07/67	18	66	● 5. Here Where There is Love .... "Alfie"	Scepter 555
5/13/67	169	9	6. On Stage and in The Movies	Scepter 559
9/16/67	22	31	7. The Windows of The World .... "I Say A Little Prayer"(4)	Scepter 563
11/18/67	10	69	8. **Dionne Warwick's Golden Hits,** **Part One** .... [G] "Anyone Who Had A Heart"(8-'64)	Scepter 565
3/09/68	6	48	● 9. **Valley of the Dolls** .... "(Theme From) Valley Of The Dolls"(2)/ "Do You Know The Way To San Jose"(10)	Scepter 568
12/14/68	18	39	10. Promises, Promises .... "This Girl's In Love With You"(7)	Scepter 571
4/05/69	11	28	11. Soulful	Scepter 573
8/16/69	31	24	● 12. Dionne Warwick's Greatest Motion Picture Hits .... [K]	Scepter 575
11/01/69	28	28	13. Dionne Warwick's Golden Hits, Part 2...... [G] "Message To Michael"(8-'66)	Scepter 577
5/02/70	23	39	14. I'll Never Fall In Love Again .... "I'll Never Fall In Love Again"(6)	Scepter 581
12/12/70	37	24	15. Very Dionne	Scepter 587
10/30/71	48	17	● 16. The Dionne Warwicke Story .... [L]	Scepter 596 [2]
1/29/72	54	14	17. Dionne	Warner 2585
4/08/72	169	5	18. From Within .... [K]	Scepter 598 [2]
2/03/73	178	8	19. Just Being Myself	Warner 2658
3/08/75	167	6	20. Then Came You .... "Then Came You"(1-with Spinners)	Warner 2846
12/06/75	137	15	21. Track of the Cat	Warner 2893
2/19/77	49	13	22. A Man And A Woman .... [L] ISAAC HAYES & DIONNE WARWICK	HBS 996 [2]
7/02/77	188	7	23. Only Love Can Break A Heart .... [K]	Musicor 2501
6/09/79	12	54	▲ 24. Dionne .... album produced by Barry Manilow "I'll Never Love This Way Again"(5)	Arista 4230
8/09/80	23	25	25. No Night So Long	Arista 9526
6/13/81	72	14	26. Hot! Live and Otherwise .... [L] 3 of 4 sides are live recordings	Arista 8605 [2]
5/22/82	83	12	27. Friends In Love	Arista 9585
10/30/82	25	28	28. Heartbreaker .... album produced by Barry Gibb "Heartbreaker"(10)	Arista 9609
10/29/83	57	17	29. How Many Times Can We Say Goodbye .... album produced by Luther Vandross	Arista 8104
3/02/85	106+	6+	30. Finder Of Lost Loves	Arista 8262
			WAS (NOT WAS) Detroit duo: Don Fagenson & David Weiss	
10/15/83	134	9	1. Born To Laugh At Tornadoes	Geffen 4016
			DINAH WASHINGTON real name: Ruth Jones - renown as "Queen Of The Blues" - died on 12/14/63 (39)	
2/01/60	34	10	1. What a diffrence a day makes! .... "What A Diffrence A Day Makes"(8)	Mercury 20479
1/23/61	10	13	2. **Unforgettable**	Mercury 20572

DATE CHARTED	PEAK POS	WKS CHRT'D	ARTIST — Album Title	LABEL & NUMBER
12/18/61	56	15	3. September In The Rain	Mercury 20638
6/23/62	33	25	4. Dinah '62	Roulette 25170
10/20/62	78	9	5. Drinking Again	Roulette 25183
11/17/62	131	4	6. I Wanna Be Loved .... with the Quincy Jones Orchestra	Mercury 20729
2/23/63	61	12	7. Back To The Blues	Roulette 25189
4/04/64	130	6	8. A Stranger On Earth	Roulette 25253

GROVER WASHINGTON, JR.
jazz/R&B saxophonist from Buffalo, New York

1/01/72	62	25	1. Inner City Blues .... [I]	Kudu 03
9/09/72	111	17	2. All The King's Horses .... [I]	Kudu 07
7/14/73	100	14	3. Soul Box .... [I]	Kudu 1213 [2]
3/08/75	10	34	4. **Mister Magic** .... [I]	Kudu 20
11/15/75	10	30	5. **Feels So Good** .... [I]	Kudu 24
1/15/77	31	16	6. A Secret Place .... [I]	Kudu 32
1/07/78	11	32	7. Live At The Bijou .... [I-L]	Kudu 3637 [2]
10/21/78	35	23	8. Reed Seed .... [I] backed by the jazz ensemble, Locksmith	Motown 910
4/28/79	24	19	9. Paradise .... [I]	Elektra 182
3/08/80	24	22	10. Skylarkin' .... [I]	Motown 933
9/13/80	96	10	11. Baddest .... [I-K]	Motown 940 [2]
11/15/80	5	52	▲ 12. **Winelight** .... [I] "Just The Two Of Us"(2-with Bill Withers)	Elektra 305
10/24/81	149	7	13. Anthology .... [I-K]	Motown 961 [2]
12/12/81	28	27	14. Come Morning .... [I]	Elektra 562
12/11/82	50	25	15. The Best Is Yet To Come	Elektra 60215
11/10/84	79	22+	16. Inside Moves	Elektra 60318

W.A.S.P.
Los Angeles-based heavy-metal quartet led by Blackie Lawless

10/06/84	74	27+	1. W.A.S.P.	Capitol 12343

MUDDY WATERS
legendary bluesman from Chicago (real name: McKinley Morganfield) - died on 4/30/83 (68)

11/09/68	127	8	1. Electric Mud	Cadet Concept 314
9/27/69	70	10	2. Fathers And Sons .... [L] with Otis Spann, Michael Bloomfield, Paul Butterfield - side 2 recorded live	Chess 127 [2]
2/19/77	143	7	3. Hard Again	Blue Sky 34449
2/25/78	157	6	4. I'm Ready	Blue Sky 34928
5/16/81	192	2	5. King Bee .... above 3 albums produced by rock guitarist Johnny Winter	Blue Sky 37064

ROGER WATERS
Pink Floyd's bassist

5/19/84	31	18	1. The Pros And Cons Of Hitch Hiking	Columbia 39290

DOC WATSON
banjo/guitar player of traditional folk and country music

8/30/75	193	3	1. Memories .... with son Merle Watson on guitar	United Art. 423 [2]

JOHNNY "Guitar" WATSON
R&B/funk guitarist and keyboardist from Houston, Texas

8/07/76	52	22	● 1. Ain't That A Bitch	DJM 3
4/16/77	20	27	● 2. A Real Mother For Ya	DJM 7
12/24/77	84	14	3. Funk Beyond The Call Of Duty	DJM 714
10/28/78	157	7	4. Giant	DJM 19

DATE CHARTED	PEAK POS	WKS CHRT'D	ARTIST — Album Title	LABEL & NUMBER
7/05/80	115	14	5. Love Jones	DJM 31
6/27/81	177	3	6. Johnny "Guitar" Watson And The Family Clone	DJM 501
			all instruments played by Johnny	

WATSONIAN INSTITUTE
The Johnny "Guitar" Watson band

4/15/78	154	4	1. Master Funk	DJM 13

WATTS 103rd STREET RHYTHM BAND
soul/funk band led by Charles Wright

4/19/69	140	5	1. Together .... "Do Your Thing"	Warner 1761
10/18/69	145	4	2. In The Jungle, Babe	Warner 1801

CHARLES WRIGHT & THE WATTS 103RD STREET BAND:

8/08/70	182	10	3. Express Yourself	Warner 1864
5/15/71	147	11	4. You're So Beautiful	Warner 1904

ERNIE WATTS
saxophonist with the NBC "Tonight Show" orchestra - accompanied the Rolling Stones on their 1981 tour

2/20/82	161	12	1. Chariots of Fire .... [I]	Qwest 3637

FEE WAYBILL
lead singer of the Tubes

11/10/84	146	6	1. Read My Lips	Capitol 12369

WAYLON & WILLIE -
see WAYLON JENNINGS/WILLIE NELSON

JOHN WAYNE
America's favorite actor - died on 6/11/79 (72)

3/03/73	66	16	1. America, Why I Love Her .... [T]	RCA 4828
			a narrative tribute (with orchestra & chorus) to America	

WE FIVE
quintet led by John Stewart's brother, Mike Stewart

10/16/65	32	30	1. You Were On My Mind .... "You Were On My Mind"(3)	A&M 4111
1/27/68	172	6	2. Make Someone Happy	A&M 4138

WEATHER REPORT
jazz/fusion quintet led by Josef Zawinul (keyboards) and Wayne Shorter (sax)

7/24/71	191	4	1. Weather Report .... [I]	Columbia 30661
7/15/72	147	6	2. I Sing The Body Electric .... [I-L] side 2 recorded live at Tokyo, Japan	Columbia 31352
5/26/73	85	17	3. Sweetnighter .... [I]	Columbia 32210
6/22/74	46	23	4. Mysterious Traveller .... [I]	Columbia 32494
6/07/75	31	14	5. Tale Spinnin' .... [I]	Columbia 33417
4/17/76	42	12	6. Black Market .... [I]	Columbia 34099
4/02/77	30	22	● 7. Heavy Weather .... [I]	Columbia 34418
10/28/78	52	14	8. Mr. Gone .... [I]	ARC 35358
10/06/79	47	11	9. 8:30 .... [I-L] 3 of 4 sides are live concert recordings	ARC 36030 [2]
12/13/80	57	14	10. Night Passage .... [I]	ARC 36793
2/20/82	68	11	11. Weather Report .... [I]	ARC 37616
3/19/83	96	10	12. Procession .... [I]	Columbia 38427
3/24/84	136	8	13. Domino Theory .... [I]	Columbia 39147

JIM WEATHERLY
pop/country songwriter and singer

9/28/74	94	14	1. The Songs of Jim Weatherly .... "The Need To Be"	Buddah 5608

DATE CHARTED	PEAK POS	WKS CHRT'D	ARTIST — Album Title	LABEL & NUMBER
			DENNIS WEAVER starred in TV's "McCloud," "Gentle Ben," and "Gunsmoke"	
5/13/72	191	2	1. Dennis Weaver	Im'press 1614
			WEAVERS folk quartet: Pete Seeger (replaced by Erik Darling on album 1), Lee Hays (died 8/26/81), Fred Hellerman & Ronnie Gilbert	
1/23/61	126	13	1. The Weavers at Carnegie Hall, Vol. 2 .... [L] recorded on 4/1/60	Vanguard 9075
3/13/61	24	7	2. The Weavers at Carnegie Hall .... [E-L] recorded on Christmas Eve, 1955	Vanguard 9010
			JACK WEBB Jack narrates the introduction to songs played by a 7-man jazz combo led by Matty Matlock (clarinet) - also see Ray Heindorf	
9/03/55	2(2)	14	1. **Pete Kelly's Blues** .... [T-I] played by the same band which did the scoring for the film	RCA 1126
			BOB WEIR member of the Grateful Dead - also see Kingfish, and Bobby & The Midnites	
6/17/72	68	15	1. Ace	Warner 2627
2/11/78	69	16	2. Heaven Help The Fool	Arista 4155
			TIM WEISBERG light jazz fusion flautist	
12/29/73	160	4	1. Dreamspeaker .... [I-L] side 1: live; side 2: studio	A&M 3045
11/23/74	100	13	2. Tim Weisberg 4 .... [I]	A&M 3658
10/11/75	105	7	3. Listen To The City .... [I]	A&M 4545
10/02/76	148	7	4. Live At Last! .... [I-L]	A&M 4600
8/20/77	108	12	5. The Tim Weisberg Band .... [I]	United Art. 773
5/06/78	159	6	6. Rotations .... [I]	United Art. 857
9/16/78	8	35	7. **Twin Sons Of Different Mothers** .... DAN FOGELBERG & TIM WEISBERG	Full Moon 35339
4/14/79	114	11	8. Night-Rider! .... [I]	MCA 3084
6/09/79	169	4	9. Smile!/The Best Of Tim Weisberg .... [I-G]	A&M 4749
8/02/80	171	7	10. Party of One .... [I]	MCA 5125
			ERIC WEISSBERG bluegrass musician	
1/27/73	1(3)	25	● 1. **Dueling Banjos** .... [I] except for the title song, all tunes performed by Weissberg & Marshall Brickman (previously released on LP "New Dimensions in Banjo & Bluegrass") "Dueling Banjos"(2-by Weissberg & Steve Mandell)	Warner 2683
10/20/73	196	2	2. Rural Free Delivery .... ERIC WEISSBERG & DELIVERANCE	Warner 2720
			BOB WELCH guitarist with Fleetwood Mac ('71-74) - also see Paris	
10/08/77	12	46	▲ 1. French Kiss .... "Sentimental Lady"(8)	Capitol 11663
3/10/79	20	17	● 2. Three Hearts	Capitol 11907
12/01/79	105	8	3. The Other One	Capitol 12017
10/11/80	162	5	4. Man Overboard	Capitol 12107
			LENNY WELCH born on 5/15/38 in Asbury Park, New Jersey	
2/01/64	73	10	1. Since I Fell For You .... "Since I Fell For You"(4)	Cadence 3068
1/01/66	147	2	2. Since I Fell For You .... [R]	Columbia 9230
			LAWRENCE WELK leader of polka and dance bands since mid 1920's - began his TV show in 1955	
1/28/56	5	15	1. **Lawrence Welk and His Sparkling Strings** .... [I]	Coral 57011
3/31/56	13	2	2. TV Favorites	Coral 57025

DATE CHARTED	PEAK POS	WKS CHRT'D	ARTIST — Album Title	LABEL & NUMBER
3/31/56	18	2	3. Shamrocks and Champagne	Coral 57036
5/12/56	6	17	4. **Bubbles In The Wine**	Coral 57038
			title song is Lawrence's theme song	
8/18/56	10	30	5. **Say It With Music** .... [I!	Coral 57041
			medleys of 36 dance favorites	
8/25/56	17	4	6. Champagne Pops Parade	Coral 57078
10/20/56	18	1	7. Moments To Remember .... [I]	Coral 57068
12/22/56	8	3	8. **Merry Christmas** .... [X]	Coral 57093
3/16/57	20	1	9. Pick-a-Polka! .... [I]	Coral 57067
5/20/57	17	5	10. Waltz with Lawrence Welk .... [I]	Coral 57119
			medleys of 24 favorite waltzes	
10/21/57	19	2	11. Lawrence Welk plays Dixieland .... [I]	Coral 57146
			featuring Pete Fountain on clarinet	
12/23/57	18	3	12. Jingle Bells .... [X]	Coral 57186
12/19/60	4	29	13. **Last Date** .... [I]	Dot 3350
1/30/61	1(11)	64	● 14. **Calcutta!** .... [I]	Dot 3359
			"Calcutta"(1)	
8/07/61	2(1)	49	15. **Yellow Bird** .... [I]	Dot 3389
			above 2 albums feature Frank Scott on harpsichord	
1/06/62	4	48	16. **Moon River** .... [I]	Dot 3412
1/06/62	100	3	17. Silent Night and 13 other best loved Christmas songs ....[X-I]	Dot 3397
5/26/62	6	20	18. **Young World** .... [I]	Dot 3428
9/15/62	9	15	19. **Baby Elephant Walk and Theme From The Brothers Grimm** .... [I]	Dot 8457
12/29/62	140	1	20. Silent Night and 13 other best loved Christmas songs .... [X-R]	Dot 3397
3/09/63	34	25	21. Waltz Time .... [I]	Dot 25499
4/06/63	20	28	22. 1963's Early Hits .... [I]	Dot 25510
8/10/63	33	28	23. Scarlett O'Hara .... [I]	Dot 25528
12/07/63	29	26	24. Wonderful! Wonderful! .... [I]	Dot 25552
4/11/64	37	19	25. Early Hits Of 1964 .... [I]	Dot 25572
4/25/64	127	5	26. A tribute to the All-Time Greats .... [I]	Dot 25544
8/08/64	73	16	27. the Lawrence Welk Television Show 10th Anniversary	Dot 25591
1/09/65	115	6	28. The Golden Millions .... [I]	Dot 25611
			12 songs made famous by female singers	
4/03/65	108	12	29. My First Of 1965 .... [I]	Dot 25616
4/17/65	57	12	30. Apples & Bananas .... [I]	Dot 25629
1/29/66	93	6	31. Today's Great Hits .... [I]	Dot 25663
3/26/66	106	5	32. Champagne On Broadway .... [I]	Dot 25688
12/03/66	12	41	● 33. Winchester Cathedral .... [I]	Dot 25774
4/15/67	72	18	34. Lawrence Welk's "Hits Of Our Time" .... [I]	Dot 25790
10/14/67	130	12	35. Golden Hits/The Best Of Lawrence Welk .... [I-G]	Dot 25812
4/06/68	130	12	36. Love Is Blue .... [I]	Ranwood 8003
2/08/69	173	8	37. Memories .... [I]	Ranwood 8044
4/19/69	55	20	38. Galveston .... [I]	Ranwood 8049
9/13/69	176	4	39. Lawrence Welk plays I Love You Truly and other songs of love .... [I]	Ranwood 8053
11/15/69	145	7	40. Jean .... [I]	Ranwood 8060
12/12/70	133	17	41. Candida	Ranwood 8083
12/23/72	149	10	42. Reminiscing .... [I-K]	Ranwood 5001 [2]
			FREDDY WELLER guitarist with Paul Revere & The Raiders	
8/16/69	144	7	1. Games People Play/These Are Not My People	Columbia 9904

400

DATE CHARTED	PEAK POS	WKS CHRT'D	ARTIST — Album Title	LABEL & NUMBER
			ORSON WELLES legendary American actor	
8/22/70	66	16	1. The Begatting of The President .... [C] tongue-in-cheek history of contemporary America (biblical style)	Mediarts 41-2
			MARY WELLS born on 5/13/43 in Detroit, Michigan	
3/16/63	49	8	1. Two Lovers and other great hits	Motown 607
5/16/64	42	16	2. Together .... MARVIN GAYE & MARY WELLS	Motown 613
5/30/64	18	37	3. Greatest Hits .... [G] "The One Who Really Loves You"(8)/ "You Beat Me To The Punch"(9)/"My Guy"(1)	Motown 616
7/25/64	111	12	4. Mary Wells Sings My Guy	Motown 617
5/01/65	145	4	5. Mary Wells	20th Century 3171
			DAVID WERNER	
9/01/79	65	11	1. David Werner	Epic 36126
			FRED WESLEY & THE HORNY HORNS funk band led by former members of James Brown's J.B.'s: Fred Wesley (trombone), Maceo Parker (sax) - also see J.B.'s	
4/30/77	181	5	1. A Blow For Me, A Toot To You	Atlantic 18214
			WEST, BRUCE & LAING power-rock trio: Leslie West (guitar/vocals-Mountain), Jack Bruce (bass-Cream) & Corky Laing (drums-Mountain)	
11/04/72	26	20	1. Why Dontcha	Windfall 31929
7/28/73	87	10	2. Whatever Turns You On	Windfall 32216
5/11/74	165	6	3. Live 'N' Kickin' .... [L]	Windfall 33899
			DOTTIE WEST country singer from Tennessee - also see Kenny Rogers	
4/11/81	126	15	1. Wild West	Liberty 1062
			LESLIE WEST lead guitarist and vocalist of Mountain	
9/06/69	72	14	1. Leslie West - Mountain .... West formed the group Mountain named after this title	Windfall 4500
4/19/75	168	6	2. The Great Fatsby .... with guest guitarist, Mick Jagger	Phantom 0954
			MAE WEST leading sex symbol of the thirties - died on 11/22/80 (87)	
7/23/66	116	5	1. Way Out West .... Mae sings rock 'n' roll, backed by the group Somebody's Chyldren	Tower 5028
			PAUL WESTON top arranger and conductor of mood music since 1934 - married to Jo Stafford	
10/29/55	15	1	1. Mood For 12 .... [I]	Columbia 693
9/01/56	12	5	2. Solo Mood .... [I] both albums feature same group of 12 big band soloists	Columbia 879
			WET WILLIE Southern rock band led by brothers Jimmy & Jack Hall	
5/12/73	189	4	1. Drippin' Wet!/Live .... [L]	Capricorn 0113
6/01/74	41	24	2. Keep On Smilin' .... "Keep On Smilin'"(10)	Capricorn 0128
3/08/75	114	7	3. Dixie Rock	Capricorn 0149
4/03/76	133	7	4. The Wetter The Better	Capricorn 0166
6/04/77	191	2	5. Left Coast Live .... [L]	Capricorn 0182
1/21/78	118	8	6. Manorisms	Epic 34983
3/18/78	158	6	7. Greatest Hits .... [G]	Capricorn 0200
6/09/79	172	11	8. Which One's Willie?	Epic 35794

DATE CHARTED	PEAK POS	WKS CHRT'D	ARTIST — Album Title	LABEL & NUMBER
			WHAM! English duo: George Michael & Andrew Ridgely	
8/20/83	83	17+	1. Fantastic	Columbia 38911
11/10/84	1(3)	22+ ▲	2. **Make It Big** .... "Wake Me Up Before You Go-Go"(1)/"Careless Whisper"(1)	Columbia 39595
			BILLY EDD WHEELER wrote "The Reverend Mr. Black" (Kingston Trio)	
2/13/65	132	3	1. Memories Of America/Ode To The Little Brown Shack Out Back	Kapp 3425
			WHISPERS soul quintet led by twin brothers Wallace & Walter Scott	
5/13/72	186	2	1. The Whispers' Love Story	Janus 3041
8/28/76	189	6	2. One For The Money	Soul Train 1450
7/16/77	65	10	3. Open Up Your Love	Soul Train 2270
5/27/78	77	28	4. Headlights	Solar 2774
4/14/79	146	9	5. Whisper In Your Ear	Solar 3105
1/05/80	6	35 ▲	6. **The Whispers** .... "And The Beat Goes On"	Solar 3521
1/17/81	23	27 ●	7. Imagination	Solar 3578
10/03/81	100	9	8. This Kind Of Lovin'	Solar 3976
1/23/82	35	25 ●	9. Love Is Where You Find It	Solar 27
3/13/82	180	5	10. The Best Of The Whispers .... [G]	Solar 4242
4/02/83	37	29	11. Love For Love	Solar 60216
12/01/84	88	19+	12. So Good	Solar 60356
			IAN WHITCOMB English	
7/10/65	125	13	1. You Turn Me On! .... "You Turn Me On"(8)	Tower 5004
			WHITE PLAINS English production by Roger Greenaway & Roger Cook	
8/22/70	166	4	1. My Baby Loves Lovin'	Deram 18045
			WHITESNAKE British heavy-metal sextet led by former Deep Purple members David Coverdale (vocals) & Jon Lord (keyboards)	
8/16/80	90	16	1. Ready An' Willing	Mirage 19276
12/27/80	146	12	2. Live....In The Heart Of The City .... [L]	Mirage 19292
5/30/81	151	6	3. Come An' Get It	Mirage 16043
5/19/84	40	42	4. Slide It In	Geffen 4018
			WHITE WOLF heavy-metal quintet from Western Canada - Don Wilk, lead singer	
2/16/85	162	6	1. Standing Alone	RCA 8042
			BARRY WHITE producer of Love Unlimited (his female backing trio) and Love Unlimited Orchestra (his studio orchestra)	
4/21/73	16	63 ●	1. I've Got So Much To Give .... "I'm Gonna Love You Just A Little More Baby"(3)	20th Century 407
11/17/73	20	37 ●	2. Stone Gon' .... "Never, Never Gonna Give Ya Up"(7)	20th Century 423
9/07/74	1(1)	38 ●	3. **Can't Get Enough** .... "Can't Get Enough Of Your Love, Babe"(1)/ "You're The First, The Last, My Everything"(2)	20th Century 444
4/12/75	17	17 ●	4. Just Another Way To Say I Love You .... "What Am I Gonna Do With You"(8)	20th Century 466
11/15/75	23	25 ●	5. Barry White's Greatest Hits .... [G]	20th Century 493
2/14/76	42	15	6. Let The Music Play	20th Century 502
11/27/76	125	9	7. Is This Whatcha Wont?	20th Century 516
9/17/77	8	33 ▲	8. **Barry White Sings For Someone You Love** "It's Ecstasy When You Lay Down Next To Me"(4)	20th Century 543
10/28/78	36	28 ▲	9. Barry White The Man	20th Century 571

DATE CHARTED	PEAK POS	WKS CHRT'D	ARTIST — Album Title	LABEL & NUMBER
4/28/79	67	9	● 10. The Message Is Love	Un. Gold 35763
8/18/79	132	6	11. I Love To Sing The Songs I Sing	20th Century 590
7/26/80	85	11	12. Barry White's Sheet Music	Un. Gold 36208
10/02/82	148	6	13. Change	Un. Gold 38048

LENNY WHITE
percussionist with Return To Forever - also see Twennynine

DATE CHARTED	PEAK POS	WKS CHRT'D	ARTIST — Album Title	LABEL & NUMBER
1/31/76	177	3	1. Venusian Summer ... [I]	Nemperor 435

TONY JOE WHITE
"swamp rock" singer from the Louisiana Bayous

7/26/69	51	16	1. Black And White	Monument 18114
			"Polk Salad Annie"(8)	
11/22/69	183	3	2. ...Continued	Monument 18133
3/06/71	167	4	3. Tony Joe White	Warner 1900

PAUL WHITEMAN
the #1 orchestra leader of the 1920s - died on 12/29/67 (77)

1/19/57	20	1	1. Paul Whiteman/50th Anniversary	Grand Awrd. 901[2]
			reunion with many of the great alumni of the Whiteman Orchestra: Tommy & Jimmy Dorsey, Bing Crosby, Hoagy Carmichael, Jack Teagarden & others	

MARGARET WHITING
one of the most popular female vocalists of the forties

2/18/67	109	8	1. The Wheel Of Hurt	London 497

BOBBY WHITLOCK
member of Delaney & Bonnie and Derek & the Dominoes

4/01/72	140	10	1. Bobby Whitlock	Dunhill 50121
11/04/72	190	3	2. Raw Velvet	Dunhill 50131

SLIM WHITMAN
born Ottis Whitman on 1/24/24

10/25/80	175	3	1. Songs I Love To Sing	Cleve. I. 36768
12/13/80	184	4	2. Christmas with Slim Whitman ... [X]	Cleve. I. 36847

ROGER WHITTAKER
English MOR singer - born in Nairobi, Africa

5/03/75	31	24	● 1. "The Last Farewell" and other hits	RCA 0855
5/05/79	115	5	2. When I Need You	RCA 3355
12/08/79	157	10	3. Mirrors Of My Mind	RCA 3501
2/09/80	154	12	4. Voyager	RCA 3518
11/29/80	175	2	5. With Love	RCA 3778
6/13/81	177	3	6. Live In Concert ... [L]	RCA 4057 [2]

WHO
English: Roger Daltrey (vocals), Pete Townshend (guitar/songwriter), John Entwistle (bass), Keith Moon (drums - died 9/7/78-32) - replaced by Kenny Jones

5/20/67	67	21	1. Happy Jack	Decca 74892
			album released in England entitled "A Quick One"	
1/06/68	48	23	2. The Who Sell Out	Decca 74950
			"I Can See For Miles"(9)	
10/26/68	39	10	3. Magic Bus-The Who On Tour ... [K]	Decca 75064
6/07/69	4	126	● 4. Tommy	Decca 7205 [2]
			also see Various-Rock Operas and Soundtrack versions "Pinball Wizard"	
5/30/70	4	44	● 5. Live At Leeds ... [L]	Decca 79175
8/14/71	4	41	● 6. Who's next	Decca 79182
			"Won't Get Fooled Again"	
11/20/71	11	21	● 7. Meaty Beaty Big And Bouncy ... [G]	Decca 79184
11/10/73	2(1)	40	● 8. Quadrophenia	MCA 10004
			Townshend's second rock opera (also see film version below)	
10/26/74	15	15	● 9. Odds & Sods ... [K]	Track 2126
			previously unreleased recordings from 1964-72	

DATE CHARTED	PEAK POS	WKS CHRT'D	ARTIST — Album Title	LABEL & NUMBER
12/21/74	185	4	10. A Quick One (Happy Jack)/Sell Out .... [R] reissue of albums 1 & 2 above	Track 4067 [2]
10/25/75	8	25	● 11. **The Who By Numbers** .... "Squeeze Box"	MCA 2161
9/09/78	2(2)	30	▲ 12. **Who Are You**	MCA 3050
6/30/79	8	25	▲ 13. **The Kids Are Alright** .... [S-L] film features interviews & performances from the groups past 15 years	MCA 11005 [2]
10/13/79	46	16	14. Quadrophenia .... [S] also see original version above side 4: oldies by The Ronettes, The Crystals and others	Polydor 6235 [2]
4/04/81	4	20	▲ 15. **Face Dances** .... "You Better You Bet"	Warner 3516
10/17/81	52	19	16. Hooligans .... [K] recordings from 1965-1978	MCA 12001 [2]
9/25/82	8	32	● 17. **It's Hard**	Warner 23731
5/21/83	94	13	18. Who's Greatest Hits .... [G]	MCA 5408
12/01/84	81	14	19. Who's Last .... [L]	MCA 8018 [2]

WHODINI
Brooklyn-based rap duo: Jalil Hutchins & John Fletcher

11/24/84	35	20 +	● 1. Escape	Jive 8251

WICHITA TRAIN WHISTLE
Mike Nesmith (Monkees) producer

8/03/68	144	7	1. Mike Nesmith Presents/The Wichita Train Whistle Sings .... [I]	Dot 25861

WIDOWMAKER
hard rock quintet - John Butler, lead singer

6/11/77	150	9	1. Too Late To Cry	United Art. 723

RUSTY WIER
country/rock singer from Austin, Texas

7/19/75	103	14	1. Don't It Make You Wanna Dance?	20th Century 469
1/17/76	131	9	2. Rusty Wier	20th Century 495

WILBURN BROTHERS
country duo: Teddy & Doyle Wilburn

3/28/70	143	2	1. Little Johnny From Down The Street	Decca 75173

WILD CHERRY
Cleveland, Ohio electrified funk band - Bob Parissi, lead singer

7/24/76	5	29	▲ 1. **Wild Cherry** .... "Play That Funky Music"(1)	Sweet City 34195
4/02/77	51	9	2. Electrified Funk	Sweet City 34462
2/18/78	84	9	3. I Love My Music	Sweet City 35011

WILD MAN STEVE
disc jockey Steve Gallon

11/01/69	185	6	1. My Man! Wild Man! .... [C]	Raw 7000
6/06/70	179	2	2. Wild! Wild! Wild! Wild! .... [C]	Raw 7001

WILD ONES
New York City party band

11/20/65	149	2	1. The Arthur Sound .... [L]	United Art. 3450

WILD TURKEY
British rock quintet led by ex-Jethro Tull bassist Glen Cornick

5/06/72	193	3	1. Battle Hymn	Reprise 2070

EUGENE WILDE
real name: Ron Broomfield of the Miami-based family group Life

1/26/85	97	11 +	1. Eugene Wilde	Philly W. 90239

DATE CHARTED	PEAK POS	WKS CHRT'D	ARTIST — Album Title	LABEL & NUMBER
			KIM WILDE English - daughter of Marty Wilde ("Bad Boy")	
6/05/82	86	22	1. Kim Wilde .... "Kids In America"	EMI Amer. 17065
2/09/85	84	9+	2. Teases & Dares	MCA 5550
			MATTHEW WILDER New York City native	
1/07/84	49	16	1. I Don't Speak The Language .... "Break My Stride"(5)	Private I 39112
			ANDY WILLIAMS born on 12/3/30 in Wall Lake, Iowa - host of his own NBC-TV musical/variety series (1962-1971)	
1/25/60	38	4	1. Lonely Street .... "Lonely Street"(5)	Cadence 3030
3/03/62	19	36	2. "Danny Boy" and other songs I love to sing	Columbia 8551
4/07/62	59	44	3. Andy Williams' Best .... [G] "Canadian Sunset"(7)/"Butterfly"(1)/ "I Like Your Kind Of Love"(8)/"Are You Sincere"(3)/ "The Village Of St. Bernadette"(7)	Cadence 3054
5/12/62	3	176	● 4. **Moon River & Other Great Movie Themes**	Columbia 8609
10/20/62	16	44	5. Warm And Willing	Columbia 8679
1/12/63	54	43	6. Million Seller Songs .... [K]	Cadence 3061
4/20/63	1(16)	107	● 7. **Days of Wine and Roses** .... "Can't Get Used To Losing You"(2)	Columbia 8815
1/25/64	9	24	● 8. **The Wonderful World Of Andy Williams** ...... with members of Andy's family	Columbia 8937
5/09/64	5	63	● 9. **The Academy Award Winning "Call Me Irresponsible"**	Columbia 8971
9/26/64	5	33	● 10. **The Great Songs From "My Fair Lady" and other Broadway hits**	Columbia 9005
4/10/65	4	65	● 11. **Dear Heart**	Columbia 9138
5/22/65	61	18	12. Hawaiian Wedding Song .... [R] reissue of Cadence LP "To You Sweetheart, Aloha"	Columbia 9123
7/03/65	112	6	13. Canadian Sunset .... [R] reissue of Cadence album #3 above	Columbia 9124
2/05/66	23	23	14. Andy Williams' Newest Hits .... [K]	Columbia 9183
5/14/66	6	54	● 15. **The Shadow of Your Smile**	Columbia 9299
1/21/67	21	22	16. In The Arms Of Love	Columbia 9333
5/13/67	5	79	● 17. **Born Free**	Columbia 9480
11/18/67	8	36	● 18. **Love, Andy**	Columbia 9566
6/08/68	9	40	● 19. **Honey**	Columbia 9662
2/01/69	139	7	20. The Andy Williams Sound of Music .... [K]	Columbia 5 [2]
5/17/69	9	23	● 21. **Happy Heart**	Columbia 9844
11/08/69	27	21	● 22. Get Together With Andy Williams .... with The Osmonds on 3 tracks	Columbia 9922
3/07/70	42	20	● 23. Andy Williams' Greatest Hits .... [G]	Columbia 9979
6/13/70	43	19	24. Raindrops Keep Fallin' On My Head	Columbia 9896
11/14/70	81	17	25. The Andy Williams Show .... [L]	Columbia 30105
2/20/71	3	33	● 26. **Love Story** .... "(Where Do I Begin) Love Story"(9)	Columbia 30497
8/28/71	54	12	27. You've Got A Friend	Columbia 30797
1/08/72	123	5	28. The Impossible Dream .... [K]	Columbia 31064 [2]
4/08/72	29	26	● 29. Love Theme From "The Godfather"	Columbia 31303
9/30/72	86	18	30. Alone Again (Naturally)	Columbia 31625
7/07/73	174	5	31. Andy Williams' Greatest Hits, Vol. 2 .... [G]	Columbia 32384
11/17/73	185	6	32. Solitaire	Columbia 32383
12/28/74	150	4	33. You Lay So Easy On My Mind	Columbia 33234

DATE CHARTED	PEAK POS	WKS CHRT'D	ARTIST — Album Title	LABEL & NUMBER
			DANNY WILLIAMS native of Port Elizabeth, South Africa	
6/13/64	122	5	1. "White On White"(9)	United Art. 3359
			DENIECE WILLIAMS member of Stevie Wonder's back-up group, Wonderlove (1971-76)	
10/30/76	33	36	● 1. This is Niecy	Columbia 34242
11/19/77	66	20	2. Song Bird	Columbia 34911
			JOHNNY MATHIS & DENIECE WILLIAMS	
7/29/78	19	16	● 3. That's What Friends Are For	Columbia 35435
8/18/79	96	8	4. When Love Comes Calling	ARC 35568
4/04/81	74	32	5. My Melody	ARC 37048
4/17/82	20	22	6. Niecy	ARC 37952
			"It's Gonna Take A Miracle"(10)	
6/04/83	54	19	7. I'm So Proud	Columbia 38622
6/09/84	26	19	8. Let's Hear It For The Boy	Columbia 39366
			"Let's Hear It For The Boy"(1)	
			DON WILLIAMS leader of the Pozo-Seco Singers	
1/27/79	161	7	1. Expressions	ABC 1069
10/04/80	57	31	● 2. I Believe In You	MCA 5133
7/25/81	109	11	3. Especially For You	MCA 5210
5/01/82	166	8	4. Listen To The Radio	MCA 5306
			HANK WILLIAMS, JR. son of country music's first superstar, Hank Williams	
1/02/65	16	37	● 1. Your Cheatin' Heart .... [S] film is Hank Williams' life story (Hank is played by George Hamilton - songs sung by Hank, Jr.)	MGM 4260
8/07/65	139	3	2. Father & Son .... HANK WILLIAMS, SR. & HANK WILLIAMS, JR. Hank, Jr.'s vocals are dubbed in to create a duet effect	MGM 4276
11/02/68	189	3	3. A Time To Sing .... [S] Hank plays a young country singer (Grady Dodd) in the film	MGM 4540
6/21/69	164	4	4. Songs My Father Left Me .... Hank, Jr. adds melodies to unfinished songs (lyrics) written by his father	MGM 4621
10/18/69	187	2	5. Live At Cobo Hall, Detroit .... [L]	MGM 4644
6/21/80	154	17	6. Habits Old and New	Elektra 278
2/21/81	82	15	7. Rowdy	Elektra 330
9/05/81	76	23	● 8. The Pressure Is On	Elektra 535
5/08/82	123	20	9. High Notes	Elektra 60100
11/13/82	107	70	▲ 10. Hank Williams, Jr.'s Greatest Hits .... [G]	Elektra 60193
4/23/83	64	16	11. Strong Stuff	Elektra 60223
11/19/83	116	13	● 12. Man Of Steel	Warner 23924
6/09/84	100	19	● 13. Major Moves	Warner 25088
			JOHN WILLIAMS - see BOSTON POPS ORCHESTRA	
			LENNY WILLIAMS former lead singer of Tower Of Power	
8/06/77	99	26	1. Choosing You	ABC 1023
7/22/78	87	25	● 2. Spark of Love	ABC 1073
7/07/79	108	9	3. Love Current	MCA 3155
11/15/80	185	2	4. Let's Do It Today	MCA 5147
			MASON WILLIAMS one of the writers for the Smothers Brothers TV show	
6/29/68	14	34	1. The Mason Williams Phonograph Record ...... "Classical Gas"(2)	Warner 1729
12/28/68	164	8	2. The Mason Williams Ear Show	Warner 1766
5/10/69	44	17	3. Music By Mason Williams	Warner 1788

DATE CHARTED	PEAK POS	WKS CHRT'D	ARTIST — Album Title	LABEL & NUMBER
			PAUL WILLIAMS composer of numerous pop hits - also see Soundtrack "Phantom Of The Paradise"	
12/25/71	141	21	1. Just An Old Fashioned Love Song	A&M 4327
12/02/72	159	14	2. Life Goes On	A&M 4367
3/02/74	165	10	3. Here Comes Inspiration	A&M 3606
11/23/74	95	6	4. A Little Bit Of Love	A&M 3655
12/13/75	146	6	5. Ordinary Fool	A&M 4550
8/06/77	155	8	6. Classics ... [K]	A&M 4701
			ROBIN WILLIAMS Mork of TV series "Mork & Mindy"	
7/21/79	10	22	● 1. **Reality...What A Concept** ... [C]	Casablanca 7162
4/02/83	119	9	2. Throbbing Python Of Love ... [C]	Casablanca 811150
			ROGER WILLIAMS America's best selling popular pianist	
3/31/56	19	2	1. Roger Williams ... [I] "Autumn Leaves"(1)	Kapp 1012
8/25/56	19	3	2. Daydreams ... [I]	Kapp 1031
10/27/56	16	2	3. Roger Williams plays the wonderful Music of the Masters ... [I] classical melodies	Kapp 1040
3/23/57	6	67	● 4. **Songs Of The Fabulous Fifties** ... [I]	Kapp 5000 [2]
10/07/57	20	5	5. Almost Paradise ... [I]	Kapp 1063
11/04/57	19	2	6. Songs Of The Fabulous Forties ... [I]	Kapp 5003 [2]
3/31/58	4	94	● 7. **Till** ... [I]	Kapp 1081
2/23/59	10	58	8. **Near You** ... [I] "Near You"(10)	Kapp 1112
6/15/59	11	24	● 9. More Songs Of The Fabulous Fifties ... [I]	Kapp 1130
10/26/59	8	34	10. **With These Hands** ... [I]	Kapp 1147
12/28/59	12	2	11. Christmas Time ... [X-I]	Kapp 1164
4/04/60	25	10	12. Always ... [I]	Kapp 1172
12/19/60	5	39	13. **Temptation** ... [I]	Kapp 1217
9/11/61	49	15	14. Yellow Bird ... [I]	Kapp 1244
10/02/61	35	11	15. Songs Of The Soaring '60s ... [I]	Kapp 1251
12/25/61	105	3	16. Christmas Time ... [X-R]	Kapp 1164
2/03/62	44	23	● 17. Greatest Hits ... [G-I]	Kapp 3260
3/17/62	9	46	18. **Maria** ... [I]	Kapp 3266
9/15/62	27	30	19. Mr. Piano ... [I]	Kapp 3290
4/20/63	122	13	20. Country Style ... [I]	Kapp 3305
10/12/63	59	12	21. For You ... [I]	Kapp 3336
2/08/64	27	19	22. The Solid Gold Steinway ... [I]	Kapp 3354
4/04/64	108	8	23. 10th Anniversary/Limited Edition ... [R] reissue of albums #9 & 12 above, plus "Roger Williams plays Gershwin"	Kapp 1 [3]
9/05/64	126	9	24. Academy Award Winners ... [I]	Kapp 3406
4/10/65	118	6	25. Roger Williams plays The Hits ... [I]	Kapp 3414
10/09/65	63	18	26. Summer Wind ... [I]	Kapp 3434
12/25/65	130	7	27. Autumn Leaves-1965 ... [I]	Kapp 3452
3/26/66	24	67	28. I'll Remember You ... [I]	Kapp 3470
12/10/66	7	69	● 29. **Born Free** ... [I] "Born Free"(7)	Kapp 3501
5/13/67	51	27	30. Roger! ... [I]	Kapp 3512
9/09/67	87	29	31. Roger Williams/Golden Hits ... [G-I]	Kapp 3530
3/02/68	164	5	32. More Than A Miracle ... [I]	Kapp 3550
1/25/69	131	10	33. Only For Lovers ... [I]	Kapp 3565
5/31/69	60	11	34. Happy Heart ... [I]	Kapp 3595
8/09/69	147	10	35. Love Theme From "Romeo & Juliet" ... [I]	Kapp 3610

DATE CHARTED	PEAK POS	WKS CHRT'D	ARTIST — Album Title	LABEL & NUMBER
3/06/71	**112**	13	36. Love Story .... [I]	Kapp 3645
9/18/71	**187**	3	37. Summer of '42 .... [I]	Kapp 3650
4/08/72	**187**	8	38. Love Theme from "The Godfather" .... [I]	Kapp 3665
			TONY WILLIAMS jazz-fusion drummer - also see V.S.O.P.	
5/12/79	**113**	7	1. The Joy Of Flying .... with guests George Benson, Herbie Hancock & Jan Hammer	Columbia 35705
			WILMER & THE DUKES R&B/rock quintet led by Wilmer Alexander, Jr.	
8/16/69	**173**	3	1. Wilmer & The Dukes	Aphrodisiac 6001
			AL WILSON member of the Jewels and the Rollers	
12/22/73	**70**	17	1. Show And Tell .... "Show And Tell"(1)	Rocky Road 3601
10/19/74	**171**	7	2. La La Peace Song	Rocky Road 3700
7/10/76	**185**	2	3. I've Got A Feeling	Playboy 410
			CARL WILSON member of the Beach Boys	
5/02/81	**185**	2	1. Carl Wilson	Caribou 37010
			DENNIS WILSON member of the Beach Boys - died on 12/28/83 (39)	
9/10/77	**96**	8	1. Pacific Ocean Blue	Caribou 34353
			FLIP WILSON host of his own TV variety show (1970-74)	
8/26/67	**34**	63	1. Cowboys & Colored People .... [C]	Atlantic 8149
6/01/68	**147**	7	2. You Devil You .... [C]	Atlantic 8179
2/28/70	**17**	54	● 3. "The Devil made me buy this dress" .... [C]	Little David 1000
1/02/71	**45**	15	4. "Flip" - The Flip Wilson Show .... [C]	Little David 2000
5/13/72	**63**	15	5. Geraldine/Don't Fight The Feeling .... [C] above 2 albums feature actual skits and guests from his TV show	Little David 1001
			HANK WILSON - see LEON RUSSELL	
			J. FRANK WILSON & The Cavaliers band formed in San Angelo, Texas	
11/14/64	**54**	14	1. Last Kiss .... "Last Kiss"(2)	Josie 4006
			JACKIE WILSON replaced Clyde McPhatter in Billy Ward & The Dominoes (1953-56) - died on 1/21/84 (49)	
11/24/62	**137**	2	1. Jackie Wilson At The Copa .... [L]	Brunswick 754108
4/27/63	**36**	21	2. Baby Workout .... "Baby Workout"(5)	Brunswick 754110
1/14/67	**108**	7	3. Whispers	Brunswick 754122
11/25/67	**163**	4	4. Higher And Higher .... "(Your Love Keeps Lifting Me) Higher And Higher"(6)	Brunswick 754130
6/01/68	**195**	3	5. Manufacturers of Soul .... JACKIE WILSON/COUNT BASIE	Brunswick 754134
			NANCY WILSON jazz stylist from Columbus, Ohio	
5/05/62	**30**	21	1. Nancy Wilson/Cannonball Adderley	Capitol 1657
9/15/62	**49**	18	2. Hello Young Lovers	Capitol 1767
4/06/63	**18**	46	3. Broadway-My Way	Capitol 1828
8/17/63	**11**	58	4. Hollywood-My Way	Capitol 1934
1/25/64	**4**	42	5. **Yesterday's Love Songs/Today's Blues**	Capitol 2012
5/30/64	**10**	30	6. **Today, Tomorrow, Forever**	Capitol 2082
9/05/64	**4**	31	7. **How Glad I Am**	Capitol 2155
2/06/65	**24**	29	8. The Nancy Wilson Show! .... [L] recorded at the Cocoanut Grove in Los Angeles	Capitol 2136
6/05/65	**7**	21	9. **Today-My Way**	Capitol 2321

DATE CHARTED	PEAK POS	WKS CHRT'D	ARTIST — Album Title	LABEL & NUMBER
8/28/65	**17**	24	10. Gentle Is My Love	Capitol 2351
2/05/66	**44**	18	11. From Broadway With Love	Capitol 2433
5/28/66	**15**	33	12. A Touch Of Today	Capitol 2495
8/27/66	**35**	23	13. Tender Loving Care	Capitol 2555
1/28/67	**35**	21	14. Nancy-Naturally	Capitol 2634
6/03/67	**40**	15	15. Just For Now	Capitol 2712
9/02/67	**46**	19	16. Lush Life	Capitol 2757
2/03/68	**115**	17	17. Welcome To My Love	Capitol 2844
6/01/68	**51**	24	18. Easy	Capitol 2909
8/31/68	**145**	14	19. The Best Of Nancy Wilson .... [G]	Capitol 2947
10/12/68	**122**	7	20. The Sound Of Nancy Wilson	Capitol 2970
2/08/69	**117**	14	21. Nancy	Capitol 148
7/05/69	**122**	15	22. Son of a Preacher Man	Capitol 234
8/23/69	**193**	2	23. Close-Up .... [R] reissue of albums #3 & 4 above	Capitol 256 [2]
11/08/69	**92**	18	24. Hurt So Bad	Capitol 353
3/28/70	**155**	5	25. Can't Take My Eyes Off You	Capitol 429
11/28/70	**54**	21	26. Now I'm A Woman	Capitol 541
6/12/71	**185**	3	27. The Right To Love .... [R] reissue (new title) of album #16 above	Capitol 763
7/17/71	**185**	5	28. But Beautiful	Capitol 798
12/25/71	**151**	6	29. Kaleidoscope	Capitol 852
9/28/74	**97**	18	30. All In Love Is Fair	Capitol 11317
7/26/75	**119**	10	31. Come Get To This	Capitol 11386
5/01/76	**126**	13	32. This Mother's Daughter	Capitol 11518
7/30/77	**198**	1	33. I've Never Been To Me	Capitol 11659
9/08/84	**144**	9	34. The Two Of Us .... RAMSEY LEWIS & NANCY WILSON	Columbia 39326

JESSE WINCHESTER
Canadian citizen, originally from Shreveport, Louisiana

12/30/72	**193**	5	1. Third Down, 110 To Go	Bearsville 2102
5/28/77	**115**	16	2. Nothing But A Breeze .... supporting vocals: Emmylou Harris, Anne Murray & Nicolette Larson	Bearsville 6968
8/26/78	**156**	7	3. A Touch On The Rainy Side	Bearsville 6984
6/27/81	**188**	2	4. Talk Memphis	Bearsville 6989

WIND IN THE WILLOWS
Deborah Harry (Blondie) was a member

8/17/68	**195**	3	1. The Wind In The Willows	Capitol 2956

KAI WINDING
Danish - trombonist with Stan Kenton - died on 5/6/83 (60)

8/10/63	**67**	24	1. More!!! .... [I] album originally titled "Soul Surfin'" - featuring Kenny Burrell (guitar) "More"(8)	Verve 8551

WING & A PRAYER FIFE & DRUM CORPS.
New York studio disco production

2/14/76	**47**	16	1. Babyface	Wing & Prayer 3025

PETE WINGFIELD
English

12/06/75	**165**	5	1. Breakfast Special .... "Eighteen With A Bullet"	Island 9333

WINGS - see PAUL McCARTNEY

DATE CHARTED	PEAK POS	WKS CHRT'D	ARTIST — Album Title	LABEL & NUMBER
			GEORGE WINSTON contemporary piano soloist	
3/12/83	**54**	87 +	● 1. December .... [X-I]	Windham Hill 1025
5/12/84	**127**	11 +	2. Winter Into Spring .... [I] recorded March, 1982	Windham Hill 1019
6/02/84	**142**	13	3. Autumn .... [I] recorded June, 1980	Windham Hill 1012
			WINSTONS soul sextet from Washington, D.C.	
8/02/69	**78**	12	1. Color Him Father .... "Color Him Father"(7)	Metromedia 1010
			EDGAR WINTER born in Beaumont, Texas on 12/28/46 - younger brother of Johnny Winter - group features Rick Derringer, Ronnie Montrose & Dan Hartman	
6/27/70	**196**	2	1. Entrance	Epic 26503
			EDGAR WINTER'S WHITE TRASH:	
5/01/71	**111**	19	2. Edgar Winter's White Trash .... introducing Jerry laCroix (lead singer)	Epic 30512
3/25/72	**23**	25	● 3. Roadwork .... [L]	Epic 31249 [2]
			EDGAR WINTER GROUP:	
12/09/72	**3**	80	● 4. **They Only Come Out At Night** .... album introduces Ronnie Montrose & Dan Hartman in group "Frankenstein"(1)/"Free Ride"	Epic 31584
5/25/74	**13**	23	● 5. Shock Treatment .... Rick Derringer replaces Montrose as lead guitarist (Rick also appears on previous 3 albums)	Epic 32461
6/21/75	**69**	10	6. Jasmine Nightdreams .... solo album by Edgar	Blue Sky 33483
10/18/75	**124**	8	7. The Edgar Winter Group with Rick Derringer	Blue Sky 33798
6/19/76	**89**	9	8. Together .... [L] JOHNNY & EDGAR WINTER Johnny also appears on albums 1 & 3	Blue Sky 34033
			JOHNNY WINTER born in Leland, Mississippi on 2/23/44	
4/12/69	**49**	20	1. The Progressive Blues Experiment	Imperial 12431
5/10/69	**24**	23	2. Johnny Winter	Columbia 9826
9/27/69	**111**	6	3. The Johnny Winter Story .... [E]	GRT 10010
12/06/69	**55**	17	4. Second Winter	Columbia 9947 [2]
9/26/70	**154**	4	5. Johnny Winter And .... with Rick Derringer and the McCoys as backup band	Columbia 30221
3/13/71	**40**	27	● 6. Live/Johnny Winter And .... [L]	Columbia 30475
4/07/73	**22**	24	7. Still Alive And Well	Columbia 32188
2/23/74	**42**	16	8. Saints & Sinners	Columbia 32715
12/07/74	**78**	12	9. John Dawson Winter III	Blue Sky 33292
3/06/76	**93**	12	10. Captured Live! .... [L]	Blue Sky 33944
6/19/76	**89**	9	11. Together .... [L] JOHNNY & EDGAR WINTER Edgar also appears on albums 2,4,13	Blue Sky 34033
7/23/77	**146**	8	12. Nothin' But The Blues .... with Muddy Waters and his band	Blue Sky 34813
8/26/78	**141**	4	13. White, Hot & Blue	Blue Sky 35475
8/04/84	**183**	4	14. Guitar Slinger	Alligator 4735
			PAUL WINTER Sextet jazz group of students from universities in the Chicago area	
12/29/62	**109**	4	1. Jazz Meets The Bossa Nova .... [I]	Columbia 8725

DATE CHARTED	PEAK POS	WKS CHRT'D	ARTIST — Album Title	LABEL & NUMBER
			JONATHAN WINTERS comedian - master of improvisation	
2/01/60	18	54	1. The Wonderful World Of Jonathan Winters .... [C]	Verve 15009
9/19/60	25	11	2. Down To Earth .... [C]	Verve 15011
5/29/61	19	42	3. Here's Jonathan .... [C]	Verve 15025
9/01/62	127	3	4. Another Day, Another World .... [C]	Verve 15032
3/21/64	145	2	5. Jonathan Winters' Mad, Mad, Mad, Mad World .... [K-C]	Verve 15041
12/19/64	148	2	6. Whistle Stopping with Jonathan Winters .... [C]	Verve 15037
			ROBERT WINTERS & FALL polio victim confined to a wheelchair since age 5	
5/09/81	71	8	1. Magic Man	Buddah 5732
			STEVE WINWOOD lead singer of Spencer Davis Group, Blind Faith and Traffic - also see Stomu Yamashta	
5/29/71	93	8	1. Winwood .... [K] compiled from albums recorded with above named groups	United Art. 9950 [2]
7/16/77	22	17	2. Steve Winwood	Island 9494
1/17/81	3	43	● 3. **Arc Of A Diver** .... "While You See A Chance"(7)	Island 9576
8/21/82	28	25	4. Talking Back To The Night	**Island 9777**
			WIRE TRAIN rock quartet led by Kevin Hunter & Kurt Herr	
2/18/84	150	9	1. In A Chamber	Columbia 38998
			WISHBONE ASH British progressive rock quartet featuring the dual lead guitars of Andy Powell & Ted Turner	
9/11/71	174	7	1. Pilgrimage	Decca 75295
6/24/72	169	13	2. Argus	Decca 75437
4/28/73	44	15	3. Wishbone Four	MCA 327
12/01/73	82	18	4. Live Dates .... [L]	MCA 8006 [2]
11/30/74	88	13	5. There's The Rub .... Laurie Wisefield replaces Ted Turner	MCA 464
3/27/76	136	9	6. Locked In	Atlantic 18164
12/18/76	154	9	7. New England	Atlantic 18200
11/05/77	166	4	8. Front Page News	MCA 2311
3/29/80	179	2	9. Just Testing	MCA 3221
1/23/82	192	4	10. Hot Ash .... [K-L]	MCA 5283
			WITCH QUEEN studio disco production	
4/28/79	158	6	1. Witch Queen	Roadshow 3312
			BILL WITHERS born in Slab Fork, West Virginia on 7/4/38	
6/26/71	39	33	1. Just As I Am .... "Ain't No Sunshine"(3)	Sussex 7006
5/20/72	4	43	● 2. **Still Bill** .... "Lean On Me"(1)/"Use Me"(2)	Sussex 7014
4/21/73	63	21	3. Bill Withers Live At Carnegie Hall .... [L]	Sussex 7025 [2]
4/06/74	67	21	4. + 'Justments	Sussex 8032
5/17/75	182	2	5. The Best Of Bill Withers .... [G]	Sussex 8037
11/08/75	81	15	6. Making Music	Columbia 33704
11/06/76	169	4	7. Naked & Warm	Columbia 34327
10/29/77	39	26	● 8. Menagerie	Columbia 34903
3/17/79	134	9	9. 'Bout Love	Columbia 35596
5/16/81	183	3	10. Bill Withers' Greatest Hits .... [G] "Just The Two Of Us"(2-with Grover Washington, Jr.)	Columbia 37199

DATE CHARTED	PEAK POS	WKS CHRT'D	ARTIST — Album Title	LABEL & NUMBER
			JIMMY WITHERSPOON legendary blues singer	
3/08/75	**176**	2	1. Love Is A Five Letter Word	Capitol 11360
			PETER WOLF former lead singer of J. Geils Band	
8/11/84	**24**	26	1. Lights Out	EMI America 17121
			BOBBY WOMACK top session guitarist - Bobby and his four brothers formed the Valentinos	
12/28/68	**174**	2	1. Fly Me To The Moon	Minit 24014
4/17/71	**188**	5	2. The Womack "Live" .... [L]	Liberty 7645
12/04/71	**83**	17	3. Communication	United Art. 5539
6/24/72	**43**	48	4. Understanding	United Art. 5577
1/13/73	**50**	20	5. Across 110th Street .... [S]	United Art. 5225
7/07/73	**37**	21	6. Facts Of Life	United Art. 043
2/09/74	**85**	19	7. Lookin' For A Love Again .... "Lookin' For A Love"(10)	United Art. 199
12/14/74	**142**	7	8. Bobby Womack's Greatest Hits .... [G]	United Art. 346
5/24/75	**126**	4	9. I Don't Know What The World Is Coming To	United Art. 353
1/17/76	**147**	11	10. Safety Zone	United Art. 544
12/26/81	**29**	23	11. The Poet	Beverly G. 10000
4/07/84	**60**	14	12. The Poet II .... with guest vocalist Patti LaBelle	Beverly G. 10003
			WOMENFOLK female folk quintet	
5/02/64	**118**	6	1. The Womenfolk	RCA 2832
			STEVIE WONDER born Steveland Morris on 5/13/50 in Saginaw, Michigan	
7/13/63	**1(1)**	20	1. **Little Stevie Wonder/The 12 Year Old Genius** .... [L] "Fingertips"(1)	Tamla 240
6/18/66	**33**	25	2. Up-Tight Everything's Alright .... "Uptight (Everything's Alright)"(3)/"Blowin' In The Wind"(9)	Tamla 268
1/28/67	**92**	7	3. Down To Earth .... "A Place In The Sun"(9)	Tamla 272
9/30/67	**45**	13	4. I Was Made To Love Her .... "I Was Made To Love Her"(2)	Tamla 279
4/27/68	**37**	29	5. Greatest Hits .... [G]	Tamla 282
1/11/69	**50**	18	6. For Once In My Life .... "Shoo-Be-Doo-Be-Doo-Da-Day"(9)/"For Once In My Life"(2)	Tamla 291
10/11/69	**34**	20	7. My Cherie Amour .... "My Cherie Amour"(4)/"Yester-Me, Yester-You, Yesterday"(7)	Tamla 296
4/11/70	**81**	15	8. Stevie Wonder Live .... [L]	Tamla 298
8/29/70	**25**	16	9. Signed Sealed & Delivered .... "Signed, Sealed, Delivered I'm Yours"(3)/ "Heaven Help Us All"(9)	Tamla 304
5/08/71	**62**	27	10. Where I'm Coming From .... "If You Really Love Me"(8)	Tamla 308
11/20/71	**69**	12	11. Stevie Wonder's Greatest Hits, Vol. 2 .... [G]	Tamla 313
3/25/72	**21**	35	12. Music Of My Mind	Tamla 314
11/18/72	**3**	109	13. **Talking Book** .... "Superstition"(1)/"You Are The Sunshine Of My Life"(1)	Tamla 319
8/18/73	**4**	89	14. **Innervisions** .... "Higher Ground"(4)/"Living For The City"(8)	Tamla 326
8/10/74	**1(2)**	65	15. **Fulfillingness' First Finale** .... "You Haven't Done Nothin"(1)/"Boogie On Reggae Woman"(3)	Tamla 332
10/16/76	**1(14)**	80	16. **Songs In The Key Of Life** .... double LP also includes a bonus 4 song 7" E.P. "I Wish"(1)/"Sir Duke"(1)	Tamla 340 [2]

DATE CHARTED	PEAK POS	WKS CHRT'D	ARTIST — Album Title	LABEL & NUMBER
12/24/77	**34**	13	17. Looking Back .... [K] compilation of recordings from 1962-1971	Motown 804 [3]
11/24/79	**4**	22	18. **Journey Through The Secret Life of Plants** .... "Send One Your Love"(4)	Tamla 371 [2]
11/15/80	**3**	40	▲ 19. **Hotter Than July** .... "Master Blaster (Jammin')"(5)	Tamla 373
5/29/82	**4**	28	● 20. **Stevie Wonder's Original Musiquarium I** .... [G] compilation of hits from 1972-1982 "That Girl"(4)	Tamla 6002 [2]
9/22/84	**4**	29+	▲ 21. **The Woman in Red** .... [S] "I Just Called To Say I Love You"(1) featuring Dionne Warwick on 3 songs	Motown 6108

BRENTON WOOD

7/22/67	**184**	2	1. Oogum Boogum .... "Gimme Little Sign"(9)	Double Shot 5002

RON WOOD
original guitarist of Faces - currently with the Rolling Stones

7/19/75	**118**	6	1. Now Look	Warner 2872
5/12/79	**45**	13	2. Gimme Some Neck	Columbia 35702
9/19/81	**164**	5	3. 1234	Columbia 37473

ROY WOOD
English - leader of the Move - founded Electric Light Orchestra

11/03/73	**173**	6	1. Boulders	United Art. 168

WOODY WOODBURY
adult comedy storyteller

3/07/60	**10**	78	1. **Woody Woodbury Looks at love and life** .... [C]	Stereoddities 1
6/13/60	**16**	59	2. Woody Woodbury's Laughing Room .... [C]	Stereoddities 2
1/20/62	**46**	21	3. Woody Woodbury's Saloonatics .... [C]	Stereoddities 4

STEVIE WOODS

12/05/81	**153**	25	1. Take Me To Your Heaven	Cotillion 5229

BRUCE WOOLLEY & The Camera Club
British

3/08/80	**184**	2	1. Bruce Woolley & The Camera Club	Columbia 36301

WRABIT
Canadian rock sextet - Lou Nadeau, lead singer

2/06/82	**157**	8	1. Wrabit	MCA 5268

LINK WRAY
rock guitarist - American Indian from North Carolina -
also see Robert Gordon

7/24/71	**186**	4	1. Link Wray .... recorded at his 3-track shack in Maryland	Polydor 4064

BERNARD WRIGHT
16 year-old R&B/funk keyboardist

3/14/81	**116**	14	1. 'Nard	GRP 5011

BETTY WRIGHT
background singer with KC. and Peter Brown

2/26/72	**123**	6	1. I Love The Way You Love .... "Clean Up Woman"(6)	Alston 388
6/17/78	**26**	36	2. Betty Wright Live .... [L]	Alston 4408
6/02/79	**138**	6	3. Betty Travelin' In The Wright Circle	Alston 4410

DATE CHARTED	PEAK POS	WKS CHRT'D	ARTIST — Album Title	LABEL & NUMBER
			GARY WRIGHT keyboardist/vocalist with Spooky Tooth	
8/23/75	**7**	75	● 1. **The Dream Weaver** .... "Dream Weaver"(2)/"Love Is Alive"(2)	Warner 2868
4/24/76	**172**	4	2. That Was Only Yesterday .... [E-K] GARY WRIGHT/SPOOKY TOOTH includes cuts from his work with Spooky Tooth and his early solo albums	A&M 3528 [2]
1/22/77	**23**	15	3. The Light of Smiles	Warner 2951
12/10/77	**117**	9	4. Touch And Gone	Warner 3137
3/17/79	**147**	5	5. Headin' Home	Warner 3244
6/27/81	**79**	19	6. The Right Place	Warner 3511
			BILL WYMAN bass guitarist of the Rolling Stones	
6/15/74	**99**	11	1. Monkey Grip	Rolling S. 59102
3/27/76	**166**	5	2. Stone Alone	Rolling S. 79103
			TAMMY WYNETTE born Wynette Pugh on 5/5/42 near Tupelo, Mississippi	
9/07/68	**147**	15	1. D-I-V-O-R-C-E	Epic 26392
2/08/69	**43**	21	2. Stand By Your Man	Epic 26451
5/17/69	**189**	3	3. Inspiration	Epic 26423
9/06/69	**37**	61	● 4. Tammy's Greatest Hits .... [G]	Epic 26486
2/21/70	**83**	11	5. The Ways To Love A Man	Epic 26519
5/16/70	**85**	17	6. Tammy's Touch	Epic 26549
8/15/70	**145**	2	7. The World Of Tammy Wynette .... [K]	Epic 503 [2]
10/31/70	**119**	14	8. The First Lady	Epic 30213
5/22/71	**115**	10	9. We Sure Can Love Each Other	Epic 30658
9/18/71	**118**	8	10. Tammy's Greatest Hits, Volume II .... [G]	Epic 30733
11/13/71	**169**	6	11. We Go Together .... TAMMY WYNETTE & GEORGE JONES married 1968-1975	Epic 30802
4/08/72	**133**	9	12. Bedtime Story	Epic 31285
			X Los Angeles punk-rock band - Exene Cervenka & John Doe, lead singers	
6/06/81	**165**	5	1. Wild Gift	Slash 107
7/17/82	**76**	15	2. Under The Big Black Sun	Elektra 60150
10/08/83	**86**	23	3. More Fun In The New World	Elektra 60283
			XAVIER 8-member group - lead vocals by Xavier Smith & Ayanna Little	
4/24/82	**129**	7	1. Point Of Pleasure	Liberty 51116
			XTC British new-wave rock band	
1/26/80	**176**	8	1. Drums And Wires	Virgin 13134
11/22/80	**41**	24	2. Black Sea	Virgin 13147
3/20/82	**48**	20	3. English Settlement	Epic 37943
2/25/84	**145**	5	4. Mummer	Geffen 4027
11/10/84	**178**	5	5. The Big Express	Geffen 24054
			Y&T Dave Meniketti, lead singer/lead guitarist of San Francisco heavy-metal rock quartet	
9/10/83	**103**	12	1. Mean Streak	A&M 4960
8/18/84	**46**	17	2. In Rock We Trust	A&M 5007

DATE CHARTED	PEAK POS	WKS CHRT'D	ARTIST — Album Title	LABEL & NUMBER
			YACHTS British rock quartet	
10/20/79	179	3	1. S.O.S.	Polydor 6220
			STOMU YAMASHTA Japanese eclectic composer/percussionist	
8/21/76	60	12	1. Go	Island 9387
			STOMU YAMASHTA/STEVE WINWOOD/MICHAEL SHRIEVE	
10/15/77	156	6	2. Go Too	Arista 4138
			both albums feature the guitar work of Al DiMeola	
			"WEIRD AL" YANKOVIC comical accordionist, specializing in parodies	
5/21/83	139	8	1. "Weird Al" Yankovic .... [N]	Rock 'n' R. 38679
3/17/84	17	23	● 2. "Weird Al" Yankovic In 3-D .... [N] "Eat It"	Rock 'n' R. 39221
			YARBROUGH & PEOPLES Cavin Yarbrough & Alisa Peoples	
12/27/80	16	24	● 1. The Two Of Us	Mercury 3834
4/14/84	90	16	2. Be A Winner	Total Exp. 5700
			GLENN YARBROUGH lead singer of the Limeliters (1959-63)	
9/19/64	142	4	1. One More Round	RCA 2905
5/08/65	112	8	2. Come Share My Life	RCA 3301
6/12/65	35	24	3. Baby The Rain Must Fall	RCA 3422
11/06/65	75	12	4. It's Gonna Be Fine	RCA 3472
6/25/66	61	24	5. The Lonely Things	RCA 3539
11/05/66	85	9	6. Live At The hungry i .... [L]	RCA 3661
5/27/67	159	14	7. For Emily, Whenever I May Find Her	RCA 3801
9/16/67	141	18	8. Honey & Wine	RCA 3860
11/09/68	188	2	9. Each Of Us Alone (the words and music of Rod McKuen)	Warner 1736
5/10/69	189	4	10. Glenn Yarbrough Sings The Rod McKuen Songbook .... [K] all songs on albums 5,9 & 10 composed by Rod McKuen	RCA 6018 [2]
			YARDBIRDS legendary British rock band featuring Eric Clapton & Jeff Beck; evolved into Led Zeppelin - Keith Relf (original lead singer) died on 5/14/76 (33)	
7/31/65	96	11	1. For Your Love .... "For Your Love"(6)	Epic 26167
12/18/65	53	33	2. Having a Rave Up with The Yardbirds .... side 2: live tracks from first British album "Five Live Yardbirds" "Heart Full Of Soul"(9)/"I'm A Man"	Epic 26177
8/27/66	52	16	3. Over Under Sideways Down	Epic 26210
4/29/67	28	37	4. The Yardbirds' Greatest Hits .... [G] "Shapes Of Things"	Epic 26246
8/12/67	80	8	5. Little Games	Epic 26313
10/03/70	155	6	6. The Yardbirds/Featuring Performances By Jeff Beck, Eric Clapton, Jimmy Page .... [K]	Epic 30135 [2]
			PETER YARROW Peter of Peter, Paul & Mary	
3/04/72	163	8	1. Peter	Warner 2599
			YAZ British duo: Vince Clarke & Alison Moyet - formerly Yazoo	
10/02/82	92	32	1. Upstairs At Eric's	Sire 23737
8/13/83	69	13	2. You And Me Both	Sire 23903

DATE CHARTED	PEAK POS	WKS CHRT'D	ARTIST — Album Title	LABEL & NUMBER
			YELLO Swiss computer/synthesizer trio	
7/16/83	184	4	1. You Gotta Say Yes To Another Excess	Elektra 60271
			YELLOWJACKETS Los Angeles-based pop/jazz trio	
5/28/83	145	10	1. Mirage A Trois .... [I]	Warner 23813
			YELLOW MAGIC ORCHESTRA Japanese electronic trio	
1/26/80	81	21	1. Yellow Magic Orchestra .... [I]	Horizon 736
9/20/80	177	2	2. X Multiplies	A&M 4813
			YES British progressive rock band - original lineup: Jon Anderson (vocals), Steve Howe (guitars), Chris Squire (bass), Bill Bruford (drums), Tony Kaye (keyboards)	
5/08/71	40	50	● 1. The Yes Album	Atlantic 8243
1/22/72	4	46	● 2. **Fragile** .... Rick Wakeman replaces Tony Kaye on keyboards "Roundabout"	Atlantic 7211
10/07/72	3	32	● 3. **Close To The Edge**	Atlantic 7244
5/26/73	12	32	● 4. Yessongs .... [L] Alan White replaces Bill Bruford on drums	Atlantic 100 [3]
2/02/74	6	27	● 5. **Tales From Topographic Oceans**	Atlantic 908
12/28/74	5	16	● 6. **Relayer** .... Patrick Moraz replaces Rick Wakeman on keyboards	Atlantic 18122
3/22/75	17	12	7. Yesterdays .... [K] featuring cuts from their first 2 albums (uncharted) "Yes" and "Time and a Word"	Atlantic 19134
7/30/77	8	21	● 8. **Going For The One** .... Rick Wakeman returns as a replacement for Patrick Moraz	Atlantic 19106
10/14/78	10	14	▲ 9. **Tormato**	Atlantic 19202
9/13/80	18	19	10. Drama .... Geoff Downes & Trevor Horn replace Wakeman & Anderson	Atlantic 16019
12/20/80	43	12	11. Yesshows .... [L] concert recordings from 1976-1978	Atlantic 510 [2]
1/09/82	142	5	12. Classic Yes .... [K]	Atlantic 19320
12/03/83	5	53	▲ 13. **90125** .... re-formed group: Jon Anderson, Trevor Rabin (guitars), Chris Squire, Alan White and Tony Kaye "Owner Of A Lonely Heart"(1)	Atco 90125
			YIPES! Milwaukee rock quintet - Pat McCurdy, lead singer	
10/06/79	177	4	1. Yipes!	Millennium 7745
			DENNIS YOST - see CLASSICS IV	
			YOUNG AMERICANS 36-member chorus	
4/19/69	178	3	1. Time For Livin'	ABC 659
			YOUNGBLOODS folk-rock group led by Jesse Colin Young	
3/25/67	131	8	1. The Youngbloods .... "Get Together"(5-'69)	RCA 3724
5/10/69	118	29	2. Elephant Mountain	RCA 4150
9/05/70	144	10	3. The Best Of The Youngbloods .... [G]	RCA 4399
10/31/70	80	13	4. Rock Festival .... [L]	Raccoon 1878
7/24/71	157	8	5. Ride The Wind .... [L]	Raccoon 2563
8/07/71	186	3	6. Sunlight .... [K]	RCA 4561
12/04/71	160	5	7. Good And Dusty	Raccoon 2566
12/09/72	185	10	8. High On A Ridge Top	Raccoon 2653

DATE CHARTED	PEAK POS	WKS CHRT'D	ARTIST — Album Title	LABEL & NUMBER
			YOUNG-HOLT UNLIMITED Eldee Young & Isaac "Red" Holt - 2/3 of the Ramsey Lewis Trio	
1/14/67	**132**	6	1. Wack Wack .... [I] shown as Young-Holt Trio	Brunswick 754121
1/04/69	**9**	30	2. **Soulful Strut** .... [I] "Soulful Strut"(3)	Brunswick 754144
8/16/69	**185**	6	3. Just A Melody .... [I]	Brunswick 754150
			BARRY YOUNG	
1/01/66	**67**	12	1. One Has My Name	Dot 25672
			JESSE COLIN YOUNG real name: Perry Miller - leader of the Youngbloods	
3/25/72	**157**	6	1. Together	Raccoon 2588
10/06/73	**51**	44	2. Song For Juli	Warner 2734
2/09/74	**172**	6	3. The Soul Of A City Boy .... [E-R] reissue of Jesse's first album (released in 1964)	Capitol 11267
4/20/74	**37**	29	4. Light Shine	Warner 2790
3/22/75	**26**	14	5. Songbird	Warner 2845
3/27/76	**34**	15	6. On The Road .... [L]	Warner 2913
4/02/77	**64**	9	7. Love on the Wing	Warner 3033
12/09/78	**165**	2	8. American Dreams	Elektra 157
			JOHN PAUL YOUNG Australian	
11/11/78	**119**	18	1. Love Is In The Air .... "Love Is In The Air"(7)	Scotti Br. 7101
			NEIL YOUNG Canadian-born - member of Buffalo Springfield and Crosby, Stills, Nash & Young - featuring backup band, Crazy Horse	
6/21/69	**34**	98	● 1. Everybody Knows This Is Nowhere .... "Cinnamon Girl"/"Down By The River"	Reprise 6349
9/19/70	**8**	66	● 2. **After The Gold Rush**	Reprise 6383
3/04/72	**1(2)**	41	● 3. **Harvest** .... "Heart Of Gold"(1)	Reprise 2032
11/25/72	**45**	21	4. Journey Through The Past .... [S] side 1: new versions of Buffalo Springfield and CSN&Y hits	Warner 6480 [2]
10/27/73	**22**	18	● 5. Time Fades Away .... [L] guests: David Crosby & Graham Nash	Reprise 2151
8/03/74	**16**	18	● 6. On The Beach	Reprise 2180
7/12/75	**25**	12	7. Tonight's The Night	Reprise 2221
11/29/75	**25**	21	8. Zuma	Reprise 2242
10/09/76	**26**	18	● 9. Long May You Run .... STILLS-YOUNG BAND (Stephen Stills)	Reprise 2253
7/02/77	**21**	15	● 10. American Stars 'N Bars .... guests: Linda Ronstadt & Emmylou Harris	Reprise 2261
11/26/77	**43**	18	● 11. Decade .... [K]	Reprise 2257 [3]
10/21/78	**7**	30	● 12. **Comes A Time**	Reprise 2266
7/21/79	**8**	39	▲ 13. **Rust Never Sleeps**	Reprise 2295
12/08/79	**15**	24	● 14. Live Rust .... [L]	Reprise 2296 [2]
11/22/80	**30**	16	15. Hawks & Doves	Reprise 2297
11/21/81	**27**	17	16. Re-ac-tor	Reprise 2304
1/22/83	**19**	17	17. Trans	Geffen 2018
8/20/83	**46**	15	18. Everybody's Rockin' .... NEIL & the SHOCKING PINKS	Geffen 4013
			PAUL YOUNG English	
4/14/84	**79**	20	1. No Parlez	Columbia 38976

DATE CHARTED	PEAK POS	WKS CHRT'D	ARTIST — Album Title	LABEL & NUMBER
			LONNIE YOUNGBLOOD - see JIMI HENDRIX	
			TIMI YURO	
			born Rosemarie Yuro on 8/4/41 in Chicago	
9/18/61	**51**	13	1. Timi Yuro	Liberty 3208
			"Hurt"(4)	
			YUTAKA	
			Yutaka Yokokura - Japanese jazz/fusion keyboardist	
7/11/81	**174**	4	1. Love Light .... [I]	Alfa 10004
			JOHN ZACHERLE	
11/10/62	**44**	10	1. Monster Mash .... [N]	Parkway 7018
			"Dinner With Drac"(6-'58)	
			ZAGER & EVANS	
			Denny Zager & Rick Evans	
8/02/69	**30**	13	1. 2525 (Exordium & Terminus)	RCA 4214
			"In The Year 2525"(1)	
			MICHAEL ZAGER Band	
			keyboardist with Ten Wheel Drive	
4/22/78	**120**	13	1. Let's All Chant	Private S. 7013
			ZAPP	
			Dayton, Ohio funk group fronted by Roger & Zapp Troutman - also see Roger	
9/27/80	**19**	19	● 1. Zapp	Warner 3463
			with Bootsy Collins (guitars)	
8/14/82	**25**	19	● 2. Zapp II	Warner 23583
9/03/83	**39**	22	3. Zapp III	Warner 23875
			FRANK ZAPPA	
			born on 12/21/40 in Baltimore, Maryland - rock music's leading satirist - formed The Mothers Of Invention in 1966	
			MOTHERS OF INVENTION:	
2/11/67	**130**	23	1. Freak Out!	Verve 5005 [2]
			original members: Frank Zappa, Ray Collins, Elliot Ingber, Roy Estrada, Jim Black	
7/08/67	**41**	22	2. Absolutely Free	Verve 5013
3/16/68	**30**	19	3. We're Only In It For The Money	Verve 5045
			album art work is a parody of the Beatles' "Sgt. Pepper" LP	
6/08/68	**159**	5	4. Lumpy Gravy .... [I]	Verve 8741
			Frank Zappa conducts the Abnuceals Emuukha Electric Symphony Orchestra (50-man session band) - Zappa's first solo album	
12/21/68	**110**	12	5. Cruising with Ruben & The Jets	Verve 5055
			a parody of '50s R&B/rock music	
4/05/69	**151**	9	6. Mothermania/The Best Of The Mothers . [K]	Verve 5068
			selections from the first 3 albums above	
5/03/69	**43**	11	7. Uncle Meat	Bizarre 2024 [2]
			basically instrumentals for an unfinished movie	
11/29/69	**173**	6	8. Hot Rats .... [I]	Bizarre 6356
			FRANK ZAPPA (with guests Captain Beefheart and Jean-Luc Ponty)	
3/14/70	**94**	8	9. Burnt Weeny Sandwich .... [I]	Bizarre 6370
9/26/70	**189**	3	10. Weasels Ripped My Flesh .... [L]	Bizarre 2028
			live tracks and studio recordings from 1967-69	
11/21/70	**119**	14	11. Chunga's Revenge	Bizarre 2030
			FRANK ZAPPA	
8/21/71	**38**	15	12. The Mothers/Fillmore East-June 1971 ..... [L]	Bizarre 2042
10/30/71	**59**	13	13. Frank Zappa's 200 Motels .... [S]	United Art. 9956 [2]
			with the Royal Philharmonic Orchestra film follows the exploits of the Mothers of Invention	
4/22/72	**85**	9	14. Just Another Band From L.A. .... [L]	Bizarre 2075
			recorded live at UCLA, Los Angeles on 8/7/71	

DATE CHARTED	PEAK POS	WKS CHRT'D	ARTIST — Album Title	LABEL & NUMBER
9/09/72	152	7	15. Waka/Jawaka - Hot Rats .... [I] FRANK ZAPPA	Reprise 2094
10/06/73	32	50	● 16. Over-nite Sensation	DiscReet 2149
4/20/74	10	43	● 17. **Apostrophe (')**	DiscReet 2175
			FRANK ZAPPA "Don't Eat The Yellow Snow"	
10/05/74	27	18	18. Roxy & Elsewhere .... [L]	DiscReet 2202 [2]
7/19/75	26	12	19. One Size Fits All	DiscReet 2216
11/01/75	66	8	20. Bongo Fury .... [L] FRANK ZAPPA/CAPTAIN BEEFHEART/THE MOTHERS	DiscReet 2234
			FRANK ZAPPA:	
11/27/76	61	13	21. Zoot Allures	Warner 2970
4/15/78	57	8	22. Zappa in New York .... [L]	DiscReet 2290 [2]
10/21/78	147	6	23. Studio Tan .... [I]	DiscReet 2291
2/17/79	175	4	24. Sleep Dirt .... [I]	DiscReet 2292
3/24/79	21	23	25. Sheik Yerbouti .... [2] "Dancin' Fool"	Zappa 1501 [2]
6/02/79	168	4	26. Orchestral Favorites .... [I]	DiscReet 2294
9/22/79	27	25	27. Joe's Garage, Act I	Zappa 1603
12/15/79	53	12	28. Joe's Garage, Acts II & III	Zappa 1502 [2]
5/30/81	66	11	29. Tinsel Town Rebellion .... [L]	Barking P. 37336 [2]
10/03/81	93	7	30. You Are What You Is	Barking P. 37537 [2]
6/12/82	23	22	31. Ship arriving too late to save a drowning witch	Barking P. 38066
			"Valley Girl"	
4/16/83	153	5	32. The Man From Utopia	Barking P. 38403

ZEBRA
rock trio founded in New Orleans

DATE CHARTED	PEAK POS	WKS CHRT'D	ARTIST — Album Title	LABEL & NUMBER
5/14/83	29	28	1. Zebra	Atlantic 80054
9/22/84	84	11	2. No Tellin' Lies	Atlantic 80159

SI ZENTER & His Orchestra
played first trombone for Jimmy Dorsey, Harry James and Les Brown

DATE CHARTED	PEAK POS	WKS CHRT'D	ARTIST — Album Title	LABEL & NUMBER
12/18/61	65	8	1. Big Band Plays The Big Hits .... [I]	Liberty 7197
3/17/62	107	12	2. Up A Lazy River (Big Band Plays The Big Hits: Vol. 2) .... [I]	Liberty 7216
9/01/62	108	6	3. The Stripper and Other Big Band Hits ...... [I]	Liberty 7247
2/09/63	139	5	4. Desafinado .... [I]	Liberty 7273

ZEPHYR
rock quintet led by Candy Givens (vocals) & Tommy Bolin (guitar)

DATE CHARTED	PEAK POS	WKS CHRT'D	ARTIST — Album Title	LABEL & NUMBER
12/20/69	48	26	1. Zephyr	Probe 4510

WARREN ZEVON
Canadian-born singer/songwriter

DATE CHARTED	PEAK POS	WKS CHRT'D	ARTIST — Album Title	LABEL & NUMBER
8/28/76	189	2	1. Warren Zevon	Asylum 1060

2/25/78	8	28	● 2. **Excitable Boy** ....
			       above 2 albums produced by Jackson Browne
			       "Werewolves Of London"
				Asylum 118

3/08/80	20	16	3. Bad Luck Streak In Dancing School	Asylum 509
1/17/81	80	10	4. Stand In The Fire .... [L]	Asylum 519
8/14/82	93	13	5. The Envoy	Asylum 60159

ZOMBIES
British rock quintet featuring Rod Argent (keyboards) &
Colin Blunstone (vocals)

DATE CHARTED	PEAK POS	WKS CHRT'D	ARTIST — Album Title	LABEL & NUMBER
2/27/65	39	17	1. The Zombies	Parrot 71001
			"She's Not There"(2)/"Tell Her No"(6)	
3/15/69	95	13	2. Odessey & Oracle	Date 4013
			"Time Of The Season"(3)	

DATE CHARTED	PEAK POS	WKS CHRT'D		ARTIST — Album Title	LABEL & NUMBER
				ZZ TOP rock trio from El Paso, Texas: Billy Gibbons (guitar). Dusty Hill (bass) and Frank Beard (drums)	
5/06/72	**104**	10		1. Rio Grande Mud	London 612
8/04/73	**8**	81	●	2. **Tres Hombres**	London 631
5/17/75	**10**	47	●	3. **Fandango!** .... [L] side 1: live; side 2: studio	London 656
1/22/77	**17**	24	●	4. Tejas	London 680
12/17/77	**94**	19	●	5. The Best Of ZZ Top .... [G]	London 706
11/24/79	**24**	43	▲	6. Deguello	Warner 3361
8/08/81	**17**	22	●	7. El Loco	Warner 3593
4/23/83	**9**	103+	▲	8. **Eliminator** .... "Legs"(8)	Warner 23774

ALBUMS
BY
CATEGORY

This section lists, by category, those albums which are not already listed in the artist section. The albums are listed either alphabetically by title or alphabetically by artist. Some of these categories also include cross references to the main artist section. The headings and symbols are the same as those used in the artist section unless otherwise indicated.

The Categories:

SOUNDTRACKS

ORIGINAL CASTS

TELEVISION SHOWS

VARIOUS ARTISTS:

Label Compilations

Radio/TV Celebrity Compilations

Concerts/Festivals

Rock Operas/Concept Albums

Jazz

Dance/Disco

AEROBICS

CHILDRENS

CHRISTMAS

CLASSICAL

COMEDY

MISCELLANEOUS

RELIGIOUS

TRIBUTES

DATE CHARTED	PEAK POS	WKS CHRT'D	ALBUM TITLE	LABEL & NUMBER

SOUNDTRACKS

The film stars are listed directly below the title.
Also shown are the Composer (cp)/Conductor (cd)/Lyricist (ly)/
Musicwriter (mu)/Performer (pf)/Songwriter [music & lyrics] (sw)
The following symbols are also used in this section:
[I] Instrumental/[M] Musical/[O] Oldies/[R] Reissue/
[V] Various Artists

Across 110th Street - see Bobby Womack
Anthony Quinn/Yaphet Kotto/Anthony Franciosa

Advance To The Rear - see New Christy
Minstrels
Glenn Ford/Stella Stevens/Melvyn Douglas

3/31/84	12	22	● 1. Against All Odds .... [V] Rachel Ward/Jeff Bridges/James Woods side 2: instrumentals - cp/pf: Larry Carlton/Michel Colombier "Against All Odds (Take A Look At Me Now)"(1-Phil Collins)	Atlantic 80152
4/18/70	104	19	2. Airport .... [I] Burt Lancaster/Dean Martin - cp/cd: Alfred Newman	Decca 79173
12/05/60	7	47	3. **Alamo, The** .... [I+V] John Wayne/Richard Widmark/Laurence Harvey cp/cd: Dimitri Tiomkin	Columbia 8358
			Alice's Restaurant - see Arlo Guthrie	
7/07/79	113	8	4. Alien .... [I] Tom Skerritt/Sigourney Weaver - cp: Jerry Goldsmith; cd: Lionel Newman; pf: National Philharmonic Orchestra	20th Century 593
3/22/80	36	23	5. All That Jazz .... [M] Roy Scheider/Jessica Lange - cd: Ralph Burns	Casablanca 7198
12/03/83	165	7	6. All The Right Moves .... [V] Tom Cruise/Lea Thompson/Craig T. Nelson	Casablanca 814449
11/27/76	48	9	7. All This And World War II .... [V] features 28 Lennon & McCartney songs (performed by various artists) and a book of the lyrics	20th Cent. 522[2]
			Amadeus - see Neville Marriner Tom Hulce/F. Murray Abraham	
3/01/80	7	25	● 8. **American Gigolo** .... [I+V] Richard Gere/Lauren Hutton side 2: instrumentals - cp/pf: Giorgio Moroder "Call Me"(1-Blondie)	Polydor 6259
9/01/73	10	60	● 9. **American Graffiti** .... [V-O] director George Lucas' 1st major film - stars Ronny Howard & newcomers Richard Dreyfuss, Cindy Williams & Harrison Ford - also see "More American Graffiti"	MCA 8001 [2]
4/08/78	31	11	10. American Hot Wax .... [V-O] based on the life of disc jockey Alan Freed - record 1: live: record 2: original '50s recordings	A&M 6500 [2]
9/02/78	71	18	11. Animal House .... [V-O] John Belushi/Tim Matheson - National Lampoon's 1st film	MCA 3046
5/29/82	35	31	▲ 12. Annie .... [M] Aileen Quinn (Annie)/Carol Burnett/Albert Finney mu: Charles Strouse/ly: Martin Charnin; cd: Ralph Burns - also see Original Cast ('77)	Columbia 38000
			Annie Get Your Gun - see "Those Glorious MGM Musicals"	
1/17/81	141	9	13. Any Which Way You Can .... [V] Clint Eastwood/Sondra Locke featuring songs by various country artists	Warner 3499
1/09/61	18	15	14. Apartment, The .... [I] Jack Lemmon/Shirley MacLaine/Fred MacMurray cp: Adolph Deutsch; cd: Mitchell Powell	United Art. 3105
			April Love - see Pat Boone Pat Boone/Shirley Jones	
			Arabesque - see Henry Mancini Gregory Peck/Sophia Loren	
1/23/71	137	10	15. Aristocats, The .... special story book album from the Walt Disney original cast - narration by Sterling Holloway/songs by Phil Harris	Disneyland 3995

SOUNDTRACKS

DATE CHARTED	PEAK POS	WKS CHRT'D	ALBUM TITLE	LABEL & NUMBER
4/13/57	1(10)	88	16. **Around The World In 80 Days** .... [I] David Niven/Cantinflas/Robert Newton/Shirley MacLaine cp/cd: Victor Young - also see New World Theatre Orchestra	Decca 79046
9/05/81	32	22	17. Arthur (The Album) .... [I+V] Dudley Moore/Liza Minnelli/John Gielgud side 2: instrumentals - cp: Burt Bacharach "Arthur's Theme" (1-Christopher Cross)	Warner 3582
1/20/62	57	18	18. Babes In Toyland .... [M] Tommy Sands/Annette/Ray Bolger/Ed Wynn adaptation of Victor Herbert's operetta by George Bruns & Mel Leven	Buena Vista 4022
12/07/68	183	5	19. Barbarella .... Jane Fonda - ly: Bob Crewe; mu: Charles Fox	DynoVoice 31908
2/14/76	132	15	20. Barry Lyndon .... [I] Ryan O'Neal/Marisa Berenson - classical & traditional music adapted & conducted by Leonard Rosenman	Warner 2903
			Beach Party - see Annette Annette/Frankie Avalon/Robert Cummings	
6/02/84	14	21	● 21. Beat Street, Volume 1 .... [V] Rae Dawn Chong/Guy Davis	Atlantic 80154
9/29/84	137	9	22. Beat Street, Volume 2 .... [V] 2nd album of music from "Beat Street"	Atlantic 80158
5/09/64	147	3	23. Becket .... [I] Richard Burton/Peter O'Toole cp: Laurence Rosenthal; cd: Muir Mathieson	Decca 79117
4/25/60	6	98	24. **Ben-Hur** .... [I] Charlton Heston - cp: Miklos Rozsa; cd: Carlo Savina includes a full-color book about the movie	MGM 1
			Benny Goodman Story - see Benny Goodman	
8/07/82	63	15	25. Best Little Whorehouse In Texas .... [M] Burt Reynolds/Dolly Parton - sw: Carol Hall/Dolly Parton	MCA 6112
1/12/85	4+	13+	● 26. **Beverly Hills Cop** .... [V] Eddie Murphy "Neutron Dance"(6-Pointer Sisters)/"The Heat Is On"(2-Glenn Frey)	MCA 5547
11/12/66	102	13	27. Bible, The .... [I] featuring many top stars - cp: Toshiro Mayuzumi; cd: Franco Ferrara	20th Century 4184
			Bible, The - see Art Linkletter George C. Scott/Ava Gardner/John Huston/Richard Harris	
10/22/83	17	77+ ▲	28. Big Chill .... [V-O] William Hurt/Glenn Close/Jobeth Williams/Jeff Goldblum	Motown 6062
4/28/84	85	43+	29. Big Chill (More Songs From The Original Soundtrack) .... [V-O] includes 4 Motown songs not in the film	Motown 6094
			Bill Cosby "Himself" - see Bill Cosby	
10/09/71	135	7	30. Billy Jack .... [I+V] Tom Laughlin/Delores Taylor - cp/cd: Mundell Lowe "One Tin Soldier"(Coven) - also see "Trial of Billy Jack"	Warner 1926
1/05/74	167	5	31. Billy Jack .... [R]	Warner 1001
1/05/63	33	22	32. Billy Rose's Jumbo .... [M] Doris Day/Stephen Boyd/Jimmy Durante/Martha Raye mu: Richard Rodgers; ly: Lorenz Hart; cd: George Stoll	Columbia 2260
			Black Caesar - see James Brown Fred Williamson/Art Lund/Julius Harris	
11/27/71	176	10	33. Bless The Beasts & Children .... [I+V] stars 6 teenage boys - sw: Barry DeVorzon/Perry Botkin, Jr.	A&M 4322
			Blow-Up - see Herbie Hancock Vanessa Redgrave/David Hemmings/Sarah Miles	
			Blue Hawaii - see Elvis Presley Elvis (Chad Gates)/Joan Blackman/Angela Lansbury	
			Blues Brothers - see Blues Brothers John Belushi/Dan Aykroyd	

DATE CHARTED	PEAK POS	WKS CHRT'D	ALBUM TITLE	LABEL & NUMBER
4/06/68	12	21	34. Bonnie And Clyde .... [I] Warren Beatty/Faye Dunaway - cp: Charles Strouse includes excerpts of the original dialogue - also see Flatt & Scruggs	Warner 1742
7/30/66	42	48	35. Born Free .... [I] Virginia McKenna/Bill Travers - cp/cd: John Barry Breakfast At Tiffany's - see Henry Mancini Audrey Hepburn/George Peppard	MGM 4368
3/09/85	36+	5+	36. Breakfast Club, The .... [V] Molly Ringwald/Anthony Michael Hall/Emilio Estevez/ Paul Gleason/Judd Nelson	A&M 5045
6/02/84	8	23	▲ 37. **Breakin'** .... [V] Lucinda Dickey/Adolfo Quinones/Michael Chambers "Breakin'...There's No Stopping Us"(9-Ollie & Jerry)	Polydor 821919
1/12/85	52	13	38. Breakin' 2 Electric Boogaloo .... [V] Lucinda Dickey/Adolfo Quinones/Michael Chambers	Polydor 823696
7/05/80	123	6	39. Bronco Billy .... [V] Clint Eastwood/Sondra Locke featuring songs by Merle Haggard & Ronnie Milsap	Elektra 512
7/22/78	86	13	40. Buddy Holly Story .... vocals by Gary Busey (portrays Buddy) Bustin' Loose - see Roberta Flack Richard Pryor/Cicely Tyson	Epic 35412
11/29/69	16	74	● 41. Butch Cassidy And The Sundance Kid ... [I+V] Paul Newman/Robert Redford - cp/cd: Burt Bacharach "Raindrops Keep Fallin' On My Head"(1-B.J. Thomas)	A&M 4227
4/27/63	2(2)	55	42. **Bye Bye Birdie** .... [M] Ann-Margret/Jesse Pearson/Janet Leigh/Dick Van Dyke mu: Charles Strouse; ly: Lee Adams; cd: Johnny Green - also see Original Cast ('60)	RCA 1081
3/18/72	25	72	● 43. Cabaret .... [M] Liza Minnelli/Michael York/Joel Grey mu: John Kander; ly: Fred Ebb - also see Original Cast ('67)	ABC 752
8/23/80	78	12	44. Caddyshack .... [V] Chevy Chase/Bill Murray/Rodney Dangerfield/Ted Knight side 1: Kenny Loggins; side 2: various artists "I'm Alright"(7-Kenny Loggins)	Columbia 36737
11/11/67	11	87	● 45. Camelot .... [M] Richard Harris/Vanessa Redgrave - mu: Frederick Loewe; ly: Alan Jay Lerner; cd: Alfred Newman - also see Original Cast ('61)/Living Strings/Percy Faith	Warner 1712
5/02/60	3	68	46. **Can-Can** .... [M] Frank Sinatra/Shirley MacLaine/Maurice Chevalier/Louis Jourdan sw: Cole Porter; cd: Nelson Riddle Can't Stop The Music - see Village People Village People/Valerie Perrine/Bruce Jenner	Capitol 1301
2/01/69	49	16	47. Candy .... [I+V] Ewa Aulin (Candy) - cp/cd: Dave Grusin featuring songs performed by the Byrds and Steppenwolf Car Wash - see Rose Royce George Carlin/Richard Pryor/Ivan Dixon	ABC 9
2/08/64	100	9	48. Cardinal, The .... [I] Tom Tryon/John Huston/Carol Lynley - cp/cd: Jerome Moross	RCA 1084
2/25/56	2(1)	59	● 49. **Carousel** .... [M] Gordon MacRae/Shirley Jones - mu: Richard Rodgers; ly: Oscar Hammerstein II; cd: Alfred Newman - also see Original Cast (special version '62)	Capitol 694
9/05/64	141	3	50. Carpetbaggers, The .... [I] George Peppard/Alan Ladd - cp/cd: Elmer Bernstein Carry It On - see Joan Baez	Ava 45
5/13/67	22	21	51. Casino Royale .... [I] Peter Sellers/David Niven - cp/cd: Burt Bacharach Cat Ballou - see Nat King Cole Jane Fonda/Lee Marvin/Michael Callan	Colgems 5005
4/17/82	47	14	52. Cat People .... [I] Nastassia Kinski/Malcolm McDowell - cp: Giorgio Moroder Charade - see Henry Mancini Cary Grant/Audrey Hepburn	Backstreet 6107

DATE CHARTED	PEAK POS	WKS CHRT'D	ALBUM TITLE	LABEL & NUMBER
			Chariots Of Fire - see Vangelis Ian Charleson/Ben Cross	
			Children Of Sanchez - see Chuck Mangione Anthony Quinn/Dolores Del Rio/Katy Jurado	
11/09/68	**58**	28	53. Chitty Chitty Bang Bang .... [M] Dick Van Dyke/Sally Ann Howes/Lionel Jeffries sw: Richard M. Sherman/Robert B. Sherman	United Art. 5188
			Christiane F. - see David Bowie Natja Brunkhorst/Thomas Haustein	
1/21/84	**177**	5	54. Christine .... [V-O] Keith Gordon/John Stockwell	Motown 6086
			Christmas Carol - see "Scrooge"	
			Clambake - see Elvis Presley Elvis (Scott Heywood)/Shelley Fabares/Will Hutchins	
			Claudine - see Gladys Knight & The Pips James Earl Jones/Diahann Carroll	
6/22/63	**2(3)**	27	55. **Cleopatra** .... [I] Elizabeth Taylor/Richard Burton/Rex Harrison cp/cd: Alex North	20th Century 5008
8/18/73	**109**	10	56. Cleopatra Jones .... [I-V] Tamara Dobson/Bernie Casey - cp/cd: J.J. Johnson	Warner 2719
2/05/72	**34**	31	57. Clockwork Orange .... [I] Malcolm McDowell/Patrick Magee - features classical pieces & the electronic synthesizer compositions of Walter Carlos - also see Walter Carlos	Warner 2573
1/07/78	**17**	16	● 58. Close Encounters Of The Third Kind .... [I] Richard Dreyfuss/Teri Garr - cp/cd: John Williams - also see Zubin Mehta	Arista 9500
3/29/80	**40**	20	● 59. Coal Miner's Daughter .... [I] based on Loretta Lynn's life - Sissy Spacek plays Loretta & performs the vocals	MCA 5107
9/23/72	**198**	2	60. Come Back Charleston Blue .... Godfrey Cambridge/Raymond St. Jacques - cp/cd: Donny Hathaway	Atco 7010
6/12/82	**162**	5	61. Conan The Barbarian .... [I] Arnold Schwarzenegger - cp/cd: Basil Poledouris	MCA 6108
			Cornbread, Earl and Me - see Blackbyrds Moses Gunn/Bernie Casey/Keith Wilkes	
1/19/85	**93**	10	62. Cotton Club .... Richard Gere/Gregory Hines - story based on a Harlem night- club, featuring jazz standards from 1927-36 - cd: Bob Wilder	Geffen 24062
12/01/84	**120**	15	63. Country .... [I + V] Jessica Lange/Sam Shepard - cp/cd: Charles Gross; pf: George Winston/Darol Anger/Mark Isham/Mike Marshall	Windham Hill 1039
12/01/58	**21**	1	64. Damn Yankees .... [M] Tab Hunter/Gwen Verdon - sw: Richard Adler/Jerry Ross - also see Original Cast ('55)	RCA 1047
8/01/70	**113**	7	65. Darling Lili .... Julie Andrews/Rock Hudson songs peformed by Julie Andrews & Henry Mancini	RCA 1000
2/11/84	**181**	4	66. D.C. Cab .... [V] Mr. T/Gary Busey/Anne DeSalvo/Max Gail	MCA 6128
			Death Wish II - see Jimmy Page Charles Bronson/Jill Ireland/Vincent Gardenia	
1/22/55	**4**	15	67. **Deep In My Heart** .... [M] features many stars - based on the life and the melodies of Sigmund Romberg - cd: Adolph Deutsch	MGM 3153
7/02/77	**70**	10	68. Deep, The .... [I + V] Nick Nolte/Jacqueline Bisset/Robert Shaw - cp/cd: John Barry	Casablanca 7060
			Deliverance - see Eric Weissberg Burt Reynolds/Jon Voight/Ned Beatty/Ronny Cox	
			Devil's Angels - see Davie Allan John Cassavetes/Beverly Adams	
1/08/72	**74**	12	69. Diamonds Are Forever .... [I] Sean Connery/Jill St. John - cp/cd: John Barry	United Art. 5220
			Divine Madness - see Bette Midler	
10/14/67	**55**	44	● 70. Doctor Dolittle .... [M] Rex Harrison/Samantha Eggar/Anthony Newley sw: Leslie Bricusse; cd: Lionel Newman	20th Century 5101

DATE CHARTED	PEAK POS	WKS CHRT'D	ALBUM TITLE	LABEL & NUMBER
7/27/63	82	10	71. Dr. No .... Sean Connery/Ursula Andress - cp: Monty Norman	United Art. 5108
3/19/66	1(1)	157	● 72. **Doctor Zhivago** .... [I] Omar Sharif/Julie Christie - cp/cd: Maurice Jarre	MGM 6
2/19/72	173	5	73. Dollar ($) .... [I + V] Warren Beatty/Goldie Hawn - cp/cd: Quincy Jones	Reprise 2051
			Don't Knock The Twist - see Chuck Berry	
			Double Trouble - see Elvis Presley Elvis (Guy Lambert)/Annette Day/John Williams	
			Dune - see Toto Kyle MacLachlan/Kenneth McMillan/Sting	
			Easter Parade - see "Those Glorious MGM Musicals"	
9/06/69	6	72	● 74. **Easy Rider** .... [V] Peter Fonda/Dennis Hopper/Jack Nicholson featuring songs by Jimi Hendrix, Steppenwolf & The Byrds	Dunhill 50063
			Eddie & The Cruisers - see John Cafferty Michael Pare/Tom Berenger	
			Eddy Duchin Story - see Carmen Cavallaro Tyrone Power/Kim Novak	
8/04/62	35	13	75. El Cid .... [I] Charlton Heston/Sophia Loren - cp/cd: Miklos Rozsa	MGM 3977
10/20/73	194	2	76. Electra Glide In Blue .... [I + V] Robert Blake/Billy (Green) Bush - cp: James William Guercio includes a booklet of pictures & 2 posters	United Art. 062
9/01/84	94	9	77. Electric Dreams .... [V] Lenny Von Dohlen/Virginia Madsen includes 2 songs by Culture Club	Virgin 39600
			Electric Horseman - see Willie Nelson Robert Redford/Jane Fonda/Willie Nelson	
			Elvis - That's The Way It Is - see Elvis Presley	
5/17/80	4	28	● 78. **Empire Strikes Back** .... [I] Mark Hamill/Harrison Ford/Carrie Fisher cp/cd: John Williams; pf: London Symphony Orchestra also see Various-Jazz section "Empire Jazz"/Meco	RSO 4201 [2]
9/06/80	178	4	79. Empire Strikes Back/The Adventures Of Luke Skywalker .... storyline excerpts from the film (narrator: Malachi Throne)	RSO 3081
8/01/81	9	20	● 80. **Endless Love** .... [I + V] Brooke Shields/Martin Hewitt "Endless Love"(1-Diana Ross & Lionel Richie)	Mercury 2001
			Endless Summer - see Sandals	
7/03/82	37	31	● 81. E.T. - The Extra-Terrestrial .... [I] Henry Thomas/Peter Coyote/Dee Wallace - cp/cd: John Williams	MCA 6109
1/20/79	78	15	82. Every Which Way But Loose .... [V] Clint Eastwood/Sondra Locke featuring songs by Eddie Rabbitt, Charlie Rich & Mel Tillis	Elektra 503
1/16/61	1(14)	89	● 83. **Exodus** .... [I] Paul Newman/Eva Marie Saint - cp/cd: Ernest Gold - also see Hollywood Studio Orchestra	RCA 1058
			Exorcist - see Mike Oldfield	
			Experiment In Terror - see Henry Mancini Glenn Ford/Lee Remick/Stefanie Powers	
8/12/78	124	9	84. Eyes Of Laura Mars .... [I + V] Faye Dunaway/Tommy Lee Jones	Columbia 35487
			Falcon And The Snowman - see Pat Metheny Timothy Hutton/Sean Penn	
6/13/64	147	2	85. Fall Of The Roman Empire .... [I] Sophia Loren/Stephen Boyd - cp/cd: Dimitri Tiomkin	Columbia 2460
6/07/80	7	82	▲ 86. **Fame** .... [M] inspired by the students of New York's High School of The Performing Arts "Fame"(4-Irene Cara)	RSO 3080

SOUNDTRACKS

DATE CHARTED	PEAK POS	WKS CHRT'D	ALBUM TITLE	LABEL & NUMBER
9/25/61	**88**	13	87. Fanny .... [I] Leslie Caron/Maurice Chevalier/Charles Boyer cp: Harold Rome; cd: Morris Stoloff - also see Original Cast ('55)	Warner 1416
8/28/82	**54**	20	88. Fast Times At Ridgemont High .... [V] Sean Penn/Phoebe Cates featuring songs by 20 top rock artists	Full Moon 60158 [2]
			Ferry Cross The Mersey - see Gerry & The Pacemakers	
10/30/71	**30**	90	● 89. Fiddler on the Roof .... [M] Topol - mu: Jerry Bock; ly: Sheldon Harnick; cd: John Williams - also see Ferrante & Teicher/Herschel Bernardi/ Original Cast ('64)	Untd. Art. 10900[2]
10/05/68	**90**	26	90. Finian's Rainbow .... [M] Fred Astaire/Petula Clark/Tommy Steele ly: E.Y. Harburg; mu: Burton Lane; cd: Ray Heindorf	Warner 2550
6/24/67	**107**	28	91. Fistful Of Dollars .... [I] Clint Eastwood/Marianne Koch - cp/cd: Ennio Morricone - also see Hugo Montenegro	RCA 1135
10/12/59	**22**	10	92. Five Pennies .... [M] Danny Kaye/Louis Armstrong based on the life of bandleader Loring "Red" Nichols	Dot 29500
			Flame - see Slade	
			Flash Gordon - see Queen Sam Jones/Melody Anderson/Max Von Sydow	
2/16/85	**130**	8	93. Flamingo Kid .... [V-O] Matt Dillon/Richard Crenna/Hector Elizondo/Jessica Walter	Motown 6131
4/30/83	**1(2)**	78	▲ 94. **Flashdance** .... [V] Jennifer Beals/Michael Nouri "Flashdance...What A Feeling"(1-Irene Cara)/ "Maniac"(1-Michael Sembello)	Casablanca 811492
12/25/61	**15**	35	95. Flower Drum Song .... [M] Nancy Kwan/James Shigeta/Miyoshi Umeki mu: Richard Rodgers; ly: Oscar Hammerstein II; cd: Alfred Newman - also see Original Cast ('59)	Decca 79098
5/06/78	**5**	24	▲ 96. FM .... [V] Michael Brandon/Eileen Brennan/Alex Karras/Martin Mull featuring songs by 17 top rock artists	MCA 12000 [2]
			Follow The Boys - see Connie Francis Connie Francis/Paula Prentiss/Russ Tamblyn/Richard Long	
2/18/84	**1(10)**	55	▲ 97. **Footloose** .... [V] Kevin Bacon/Lori Singer - "Footloose"(1-Kenny Loggins)/ "Let's Here It For The Boy"(1-Deniece Williams)/ "Almost Paradise"(7-Mike Reno & Ann Wilson)	Columbia 39242
			For A Few Dollars More - see Leroy Holmes/Hugo Montenegro Clint Eastwood/Lee Van Cleef/Gian Maria Volonte	
9/14/68	**192**	2	98. For Love of Ivy .... [I + V] Sidney Poitier/Abbey Lincoln (Ivy) - cp/cd: Quincy Jones	ABC 7
			For The First Time - see Mario Lanza Mario Lanza/Zsa Zsa Gabor	
7/25/81	**84**	19	99. For Your Eyes Only .... [I] Roger Moore/Carole Bouquet/Topol - cp/cd: Bill Conti "For Your Eyes Only"(4-Sheena Easton)	Liberty 1109
9/02/78	**102**	7	100. Foul Play .... [I + V] Goldie Hawn/Chevy Chase - cp/cd: Charles Fox "Copacabana" (8-Barry Manilow)	Arista 9501
			Foxy Brown - see Willie Hutch Pam Grier/Peter Brown/Terry Carter	
			Frankie And Johnny - see Elvis Presley Elvis (Johnny)/Donna Douglas (Frankie)/Nancy Kovack	
			Friends - see Elton John Sean Bury/Anicee Alvina	
5/02/64	**27**	34	101. From Russia with Love .... [I] Sean Connery/Daniela Bianchi - cp/cd: John Barry	United Art. 5114
			Fun In Acapulco - see Elvis Presley Elvis (Mike Windgren)/Ursula Andress/Elsa Cardenas	

DATE CHARTED	PEAK POS	WKS CHRT'D	ALBUM TITLE	LABEL & NUMBER
			Funny Girl - see Barbra Streisand (both Soundtrack & Original Cast)/Supremes Barbra Streisand/Omar Sharif	
			Funny Lady - see Barbra Streisand Barbra Streisand/James Caan/Omar Sharif	
4/30/83	168	3	102. Gandhi .... [I] Ben Kingsley - cp: Ravi Shankar/George Fenton; cd: George Fenton - features Ravi Shankar on the sitar	RCA 4557
7/07/84	6	34	103. **Ghostbusters** .... [V] Bill Murray/Dan Aykroyd/Sigourney Weaver "Ghostbusters"(1-Ray Parker Jr.)	Arista 8246
			G.I. Blues - see Elvis Presley Elvis (Tulsa McCauley)/Juliet Prowse/James Douglas	
12/29/56	16	7	104. Giant .... [I] Elizabeth Taylor/Rock Hudson/James Dean cp/cd: Dimitri Tiomkin	Capitol 773
6/23/58	1(10)	172	● 105. **Gigi** .... [M] Leslie Caron/Maurice Chevalier/Louis Jordan ly: Alan Jay Lerner/mu: Frederick Loewe; cd: Andre Previn	MGM 3641
			Girl Happy - see Elvis Presley Elvis (Rusty Wells)/Shelley Fabares/Gary Crosby	
			Girls! Girls! Girls! - see Elvis Presley Elvis (Ross Carpenter)/Stella Stevens/Laurel Goodwin	
			Give My Regards To Broad Street - see Paul McCartney Paul McCartney/Bryan Brown/Ringo Starr	
4/08/72	21	35	106. Godfather, The .... [I] Marlon Brando/Al Pacino/James Caan/Robert Duvall cp: Nino Rota; cd: Carlo Savina	Paramount 1003
3/08/75	184	2	107. Godfather, Part II .... [I] Al Pacino/Robert DeNiro/Robert Duvall cp: Nino Rota/Carmine Coppola; cd: Carmine Coppola	ABC 856
4/14/73	50	51	108. Godspell .... [M] rock musical based on the gospel according to St. Matthew music and lyrics by Stephen Schwartz - also see Original Cast ('71)	Bell 1118
			Goin' Coconuts - see Donny & Marie Osmond	
12/12/64	1(3)	70	109. **Goldfinger** .... [I] Sean Connery/Gert Frobe (Goldfinger) - cp/cd: John Barry "Goldfinger"(8-Shirley Bassey)	United Art. 5117
7/03/61	64	13	110. Gone With The Wind .... [I] Clark Gable/Vivien Leigh/Leslie Howard/Olivia de Havilland cp/cd: Max Steiner (new recording of film sound track)	RCA Camden 625
10/14/67	24	36	111. Gone With The Wind .... [I] first album taken directly from the film sound track (premiered in 1939) - cp/cd: Max Steiner - also see Muir Mathieson	MGM 10
2/10/68	4	52	● 112. **Good, The Bad and The Ugly** ...... [I] Clint Eastwood/Lee Van Cleef - cp/cd: Ennio Morricone - also see Hugo Montenegro	United Art. 5172
			Good Times - see Sonny & Cher	
			Goodbye, Columbus - see Association Richard Benjamin/Jack Klugman/Ali MacGraw	
12/06/69	164	5	113. Goodbye, Mr. Chips .... [M] Peter O'Toole/Petula Clark/Sir Michael Redgrave sw: Leslie Bricusse; cd: John Williams	MGM 19
			Graduate, The - see Simon & Garfunkel Dustin Hoffman/Anne Bancroft/Katharine Ross	
3/18/67	76	28	114. Grand Prix .... [I] James Garner/Eva Marie Saint - cp/cd: Maurice Jarre	MGM 8
5/20/78	1(12)	77	▲ 115. **Grease** .... [M] Olivia Newton-John/John Travolta "You're The One That I Want"(1)/"Summer Nights"(5)/ "Hopelessly Devoted To You"(3-Olivia solo)/ "Grease"(1-Frankie Valli)	RSO 4002 [2]
6/19/82	71	13	116. Grease 2 .... [M] Maxwell Caulfield/Michelle Pfeiffer	RSO 3803

SOUNDTRACKS

DATE CHARTED	PEAK POS	WKS CHRT'D	ALBUM TITLE	LABEL & NUMBER
9/21/63	**50**	21	● 117. Great Escape .... [I] Steve McQueen/James Garner - cp/cd: Elmer Bernstein	United Art. 5107
4/20/74	**85**	16	118. Great Gatsby .... [I–V] Robert Redford/Mia Farrow includes 18 songs from the '20s - cp: Nelson Riddle	Paramount 3001 [2]
			Great Muppet Caper - see Muppets (Childrens section)	
			Great Race - see Henry Mancini Tony Curtis/Jack Lemmon/Natalie Wood	
6/25/77	**166**	8	119. Greatest, The .... [I+V] based on the life story of Muhammad Ali - Muhammad Ali/Ernest Borgnine - cp: Michael Masser	Arista 7000
4/17/65	**82**	13	120. Greatest Story Ever Told .... features many top stars - cp/cd: Alfred Newman	United Art. 5120
7/07/84	**143**	7	121. Gremlins .... [I+V] Zach Galligan/Phoebe Cates	Geffen 24044
4/27/68	**177**	3	122. Guess Who's Coming To Dinner .... [I] Spencer Tracy/Katharine Hepburn/Sidney Poitier cp/cd: Frank DeVol	Colgems 108
9/25/61	**48**	14	123. Guns Of Navarone .... [I] Gregory Peck/David Niven/Anthony Quinn cp/cd: Dimitri Tiomkin	Columbia 8455
12/15/62	**10**	32	124. **Gypsy** .... [M] Rosalind Russell/Natalie Wood/Karl Malden - mu: Jule Styne; ly: Stephen Sondheim - also see Original Cast ('59)	Warner 1480
4/07/79	**65**	16	● 125. Hair .... [M] John Savage/Treat Williams/Beverly D'Angelo mu/cd: Galt MacDermot; ly: Gerome Ragni & James Rado also see Original Cast ('68)/Various-"Disco Spectacular"	RCA 3274 [2]
8/17/68	**193**	4	126. Hang 'Em High .... [I] Clint Eastwood/Inger Stevens - cp/cd: Dominic Frontiere	United Art. 5179
3/23/68	**166**	9	127. Happiest Millionaire .... [M] Fred MacMurray/Tommy Steele/Greer Garson sw: Richard M. Sherman/Robert B. Sherman; cd: Jack Elliott	Buena Vista 5001
			Hard Day's Night - see Beatles	
			Hard To Hold - see Rick Springfield	
			Harder They Come - see Jimmy Cliff	
			Harum Scarum - see Elvis Presley Elvis (Johnny Tyronne)/Mary Ann Mobley/Fran Jeffries	
			Hatari! - see Henry Mancini John Wayne/Red Buttons/Hardy Kruger	
			Having A Wild Weekend - see Dave Clark Five	
11/19/66	**85**	16	128. Hawaii .... [I] Julie Andrews/Richard Harris - cp/cd: Elmer Bernstein	United Art. 5143
			Head - see Monkees Monkees/Annette Funicello/Victor Mature	
8/08/81	**12**	28	● 129. Heavy Metal .... [V] animated film - featuring songs by 13 rock artists	Asylum 90004 [2]
2/03/58	**25**	1	130. Helen Morgan Story .... Ann Blyth (portrays Helen)/Paul Newman vocals performed by Gogi Grant; cd: Ray Heindorf	RCA 1030
			Hello, Dolly! - see Barbra Streisand Barbra Streisand/Walter Matthau/Michael Crawford - also see Original Cast ('64)	
9/30/67	**165**	2	131. Hells Angels On Wheels .... [I] Adam Roarke/Jack Nicholson - cp/cd: Stu Phillips	Smash 67094
10/11/69	**184**	3	132. Hell's Angels '69 .... Tom Stern/Conny Van Dyke/Jeremy Slate - cp/cd: Tony Bruno above 2 films feature actual members of the Hells Angels	Capitol 303
			Help! - see Beatles	
			Hey Boy! Hey Girl! - see Louis Prima & Keely Smith	
			Hey, Let's Twist! - see Joey Dee	

DATE CHARTED	PEAK POS	WKS CHRT'D	ALBUM TITLE	LABEL & NUMBER
8/25/56	5	28	133. **High Society** .... [M] adapted from the play "Philadelphia Story" Bing Crosby/Grace Kelly/Frank Sinatra - sw: Cole Porter "True Love"(3-Bing Crosby & Grace Kelly)	Capitol 750
			Hold On! - see Herman's Hermits Peter Noone/Shelley Fabares/Sue Ane Langdon	
			Honeysuckle Rose - see Willie Nelson Willie Nelson/Dyan Cannon/Amy Irving/Slim Pickens	
4/20/63	4	84	● 134. **How The West Was Won** .... features many top stars - cd: Alfred Newman	MGM 5
			How To Beat The High Cost Of Loving - see Hubert Laws & Earl Klugh Susan Saint James/Jane Curtin/Jessica Lange	
4/22/67	146	4	135. **How To Succeed In Business Without** **Really Trying** .... [M] Robert Morse/Michele Lee/Rudy Vallee - sw: Frank Loesser; cd: Nelson Riddle - also see Original Cast ('61)	United Art. 5151
4/22/67	153	2	136. **Hurry Sundown** .... [I] Michael Caine/Jane Fonda - cp/cd: Hugo Montenegro	RCA 1133
			I Could Go On Singing - see Judy Garland Judy Garland/Dirk Bogarde/Jack Klugman	
			I Walk The Line - see Johnny Cash Gregory Peck/Tuesday Weld/Estelle Parsons	
			I Want To Live! - see Gerry Mulligan Susan Hayward	
4/14/79	174	5	137. **Ice Castles** .... [I] Robby Benson/Lynn-Holly Johnson - cp/cd: Marvin Hamlisch	Arista 9502
12/20/80	130	9	138. **Idolmaker, The** .... [V] Ray Sharkey/Tovah Feldshuh/Peter Gallagher - sw: Jeff Barry	A&M 4840
9/30/67	153	11	139. **In The Heat Of The Night** .... [I+V] Sidney Poitier/Rod Steiger - cp/cd: Quincy Jones	United Art. 5160
6/16/84	42	11	140. **Indiana Jones and the Temple Of Doom**.... [I] Harrison Ford/Kate Capshaw/Ke Huy Quan - cp/cd: John Williams	Polydor 821592
10/19/68	136	5	141. **Interlude** .... [I] Oskar Werner/Barbara Ferris - mixture of traditional classical works and new compositions by Georges Delerue	Colgems 5007
11/13/65	133	2	142. **Ipcress File** .... [I] Michael Caine/Nigel Green/Sue Lloyd - cp/cd: John Barry	Decca 79124
9/14/63	69	11	143. **Irma La Douce** .... [I] Jack Lemmon/Shirley MacLaine - cp/cd: Andre Previn also see Original Cast ('60)	United Art. 5109
			It Happened At The World's Fair - see Elvis Presley Elvis (Mike Edwards)/Joan O'Brien/Gary Lockwood	
12/21/63	101	11	144. **It's A Mad, Mad, Mad, Mad World** .... [I] star-studded comedy - cp/cd: Ernest Gold	United Art. 5110
11/22/80	137	11	145. **It's My Turn** .... [I+V] Jill Clayburgh/Michael Douglas - cp/cd: Patrick Williams "It's My Turn"(9-Diana Ross)	Motown 947
			Jack Johnson - see Miles Davis **James Bond** - see: Casino Royale On Her Majesty's Secret Service Dr. No Spy Who Loved Me For Your Eyes Only Thunderball From Russia With Love You Only Live Twice Goldfinger also: Roland Shaw/Billy Strange/ Live And Let Die Soundtrack Compilations: Moonraker Music To Read James Bond By Octopussy **Janis** - see Janis Joplin	
7/26/75	30	17	146. **Jaws** .... [I] Roy Scheider/Richard Dreyfuss/Robert Shaw cp/cd: John Williams	MCA 2087
			Jazz Singer - see Neil Diamond Neil Diamond/Laurence Olivier/Lucie Arnaz	

SOUNDTRACKS

DATE CHARTED	PEAK POS	WKS CHRT'D	ALBUM TITLE	LABEL & NUMBER
6/30/73	21	39	● 147. Jesus Christ Superstar .... [M] Ted Neely/Yvonne Elliman/Carl Anderson/Barry Dennen mu: Andrew Lloyd Webber: ly: Tim Rice also see Various ('70)/Original Cast ('72)/Percy Faith	MCA 11000 [2]
			Jimi Hendrix - see Jimi Hendrix	
			Jonathan Livingston Seagull - see Neil Diamond James Franciscus/Juliet Mills - also see Richard Harris	
			Journey Through The Past - see Neil Young	
2/03/68	19	34	148. Jungle Book .... Disney cartoon based on Rudyard Kipling's "Mowgli" stories sw: Richard M. Sherman/Robert B. Sherman	Disneyland 3948
7/21/84	114	12	149. Karate Kid .... [V] Ralph Macchio/Noriyuki "Pat" Morita/Elisabeth Shue	Casablanca 822213
			Kids Are Alright - see Who	
7/21/56	1(1)	274	● 150. **King And I** .... [M] Yul Brynner/Deborah Kerr - mu: Richard Rodgers: ly: Oscar Hammerstein II; cd: Alfred Newman	Capitol 740
			King Creole - see Elvis Presley Elvis (Danny Fisher)/Carolyn Jones/Walter Matthau	
1/08/77	123	8	151. King Kong .... [I] Jeff Bridges/Jessica Lange - cp/cd: John Barry	Reprise 2260
4/16/83	162	6	152. King of Comedy .... [V] Robert DeNiro/Jerry Lewis/Tony Randall "Back On The Chain Gang"(5-Pretenders)	Warner 23765
11/06/61	10	39	153. **King of Kings** .... [I] Jeffrey Hunter (Jesus Christ) - cp/cd: Miklos Rozsa includes a full-color book about the movie	MGM 2
			Kissin' Cousins - see Elvis Presley Elvis (Josh Morgan)/Jodie Tatum)/Arthur O'Connell	
3/02/85	107+	2+	154. Last Dragon, The .... [V] Taimak/Julius J. Carry III/Chris Murney/Leo O'Brien/Vanity "Rhythm Of The Night"(DeBarge)	Motown 6128
			Lady Sings The Blues - see Diana Ross Diana Ross/Billy Dee Williams/Richard Pryor	
			Last Tango in Paris - see Gato Barbieri Marlon Brando/Maria Schneider	
			Last Waltz - see Band	
3/02/63	2(2)	86	155. **Lawrence Of Arabia** .... [I] Peter O'Toole/Alec Guinness/Anthony Quinn cp/cd: Maurice Jarre: pf: London Philharmonic Orchestra	Colpix 514
1/18/75	180	3	156. Lenny .... Dustin Hoffman (portrays Lenny Bruce) featuring monologues from the film	United Art. 359
			Let It Be - see Beatles	
			Let The Good Times Roll - see Various- Radio/TV Celebrity: Richard Nader	
			Let's Do It Again - see Staple Singers Sidney Poitier/Bill Cosby/Jimmie Walker/John Amos	
			Life Of Brian - see Monty Python	
5/30/64	110	6	157. Lilies Of The Field .... [I] Sidney Poitier - cp-cd: Jerry Goldsmith	Epic 26094
5/03/69	182	7	158. Lion in Winter .... [I] Peter O'Toole/Katharine Hepburn - cp/cd: John Barry	Columbia 3250
11/08/75	145	6	159. Lisztomania .... [M] Roger Daltrey/Rick Wakeman/Ringo Starr based on the life & compositions of Franz Liszt	A&M 4546
7/28/73	17	15	160. Live And Let Die .... [I] Roger Moore/Jane Seymour - cp/cd: George Martin "Live And Let Die"(2-Paul McCartney & Wings)	United Art. 100
1/27/68	188	7	161. Live For Life .... [I] Yves Montand/Candice Bergen - cp/cd: Francis Lai	United Art. 5165
9/22/62	63	6	162. Lolita .... [I] Peter Sellers/Sue Lyon (Lolita) cp/cd: Nelson Riddle	MGM 4050

DATE CHARTED	PEAK POS	WKS CHRT'D	ALBUM TITLE	LABEL & NUMBER
			Looking For Love - see Connie Francis Connie Francis/Jim Hutton/Susan Oliver	
11/26/77	134	8	163. Looking For Mr. Goodbar .... [V] Diane Keaton/Richard Gere/Tuesday Weld featuring top R&B hits of the '70s	Columbia 35029
3/27/65	123	5	164. Lord Jim .... [I] Peter O'Toole/James Mason/Curt Jurgens/Eli Wallach cp: Bronislau Kaper; cd: Muir Mathieson	Colpix 521
12/09/78	39	12	165. Lord Of The Rings .... [I] animated film based on the novels of J.R.R. Tolkien cp/cd: Leonard Rosenman - also see Bo Hansson	Fantasy 1 [2]
2/03/73	58	21	166. Lost Horizon .... [M] Peter Finch/Liv Ullmann/Charles Boyer/John Gielgud mu/cd: Burt Bacharach; ly: Hal David	Bell 1300
8/28/71	172	7	167. Love Machine .... Dyan Cannon/John Phillip Law - cp/cd: Artie Butler includes several songs performed by Dionne Warwick	Scepter 595
			Love Me Or Leave Me - see Doris Day Doris Day/James Cagney/Cameron Mitchell	
			Love Me Tender - see Elvis Presley Elvis (Clint)/Richard Egan/Debra Paget	
1/02/71	2(6)	39	● 168. Love Story .... [I] Ali MacGraw/Ryan O'Neal - cp/cd: Francis Lai	Paramount 6002
			Loving You - see Elvis Presley Elvis (Deke Rivers)/Lizabeth Scott/Dolores Hart	
			Mack - see Willie Hutch Max Julien/Richard Pryor/Don Gordon	
			Mackintosh & T.J. - see Waylon Jennings Roy Rogers/Clay O'Brien/Joan Hackett	
			Mad Dogs & Englishmen - see Joe Cocker	
3/21/70	106	12	169. Magic Christian .... Peter Sellers/Ringo Starr - cp/cd: Ken Thorne includes 3 songs performed by Badfinger - also see Badfinger	Cmmnwealth 6004
			Magical Mystery Tour - see Beatles	
			Mahogany - see Diana Ross Diana Ross/Billy Dee Williams/Anthony Perkins	
			Main Event - see Barbra Streisand Barbra Streisand/Ryan O'Neal	
4/13/74	196	3	170. Mame .... [M] Lucille Ball/Beatrice Arthur - sw: Jerry Herman also see Original Cast ('66)	Warner 2773
11/19/66	10	93	● 171. Man And A Woman .... [F] Jean-Louis Trintignant/Anouk Aimee - cp: Francis Lai grand prize winner of the 1966 Cannes Film Festival	United Art. 5147
12/09/72	76	17	172. Man Of La Mancha .... [M] Peter O'Toole/Sophia Loren - mu: Mitch Leigh; ly: Joe Darion; cd: Laurence Rosenthal - also see Original Cast ('66)	United Art. 9906
3/24/56	2(4)	17	173. Man With The Golden Arm .... [I] Frank Sinatra/Eleanor Parker/Kim Novak cp/cd: Elmer Bernstein jazz sequences played by Shorty Rogers & His Giants	Decca 78257
7/28/79	94	11	174. Manhattan .... [I] Woody Allen/Diane Keaton/Meryl Streep/Mariel Hemingway cp: George Gershwin; cd: Zubin Mehta & The N.Y. Philharmonic	Columbia 36020
10/03/64	1(14)	114	● 175. Mary Poppins .... [M] Julie Andrews/Dick Van Dyke/David Tomlinson/Glynis Johns sw: Richard M. Sherman/Robert B. Sherman; cd: Irwin Kostal	Buena Vista 4026
8/04/73	141	8	176. Mary Poppins .... [R] reissue of the Walt Disney Classic	Buena Vista 5005
7/11/70	120	16	177. M*A*S*H Elliott Gould/Donald Southerland - cp: Johnny Mandel includes dialogue excerpts from the film	Columbia 3520
			McVicar - see Roger Daltrey	
8/18/79	170	5	178. Meatballs .... [V] Bill Murray/Chris Makepeace - mu: Elmer Bernstein "Makin' It"(5-David Naughton)	RSO 3056

SOUNDTRACKS

DATE CHARTED	PEAK POS	WKS CHRT'D	ALBUM TITLE	LABEL & NUMBER
8/25/84	110	13	179. Metropolis .... [V] Gustav Frohlich/Brigitte Helm - 1926 film restored and presented with a contemporary score - cp: Giorgio Moroder	Columbia 39526
8/09/69	19	57	● 180. Midnight Cowboy .... [I+V] Dustin Hoffman/Jon Voight "Everybody's Talkin'"(6-Nilsson)	United Art. 5198
11/25/78	59	26	181. Midnight Express .... [I] Brad Davis/John Hurt/Randy Quaid - cp/cd: Giorgio Moroder	Casablanca 7114
			Mike's Murder - see Joe Jackson Debra Winger/Mark Keyloun/Darrell Larson	
7/20/63	15	74	182. Mondo Cane .... [I] documentary depicting various cultures around the world - cp: Riz Ortolani & Nino Oliviero	United Art. 5105
			Monterey Pop - see Otis Redding/ Jimi Hendrix	
			Monty Python & The Holy Grail - see Monty Python	
8/18/79	159	4	183. Moonraker .... [I] Roger Moore/Lois Chiles - cp/cd: John Barry	United Art. 971
			More - see Pink Floyd Mimsi Farmer/Klaus Grunberg	
8/11/79	84	12	184. More American Graffiti .... [V-O] Ron Howard/Cindy Williams/Charles Martin Smith/Paul Le Mat also see VARIOUS-Radio/TV Celebrity: Wolfman Jack	MCA 11006 [2]
			Mrs. Brown, You've Got A Lovely Daughter - see Herman's Hermits Peter Noone/Stanley Holloway	
			Muppet Movie - see Muppets (Childrens section)	
8/11/62	2(6)	56	● 185. **Music Man** .... [M] Robert Preston/Shirley Jones - cp: Meredith Willson; cd: Ray Heindorf - also see Original Cast ('58)	Warner 1459
1/05/63	14	20	186. Mutiny On The Bounty .... [I] Marlon Brando/Trevor Howard cp: Bronislau Kaper; cd: Robert Armbruster includes a full-color souvenir book	MGM 4
10/10/64	4	111	● 187. **My Fair Lady** .... [M] Audrey Hepburn/Rex Harrison/Stanley Holloway mu: Frederick Loewe; ly: Alan Jay Lerner; cd: Andre Previn also see Nat King Cole/Percy Faith/Ferrante & Teicher/ Sammy Kaye/Andre Previn/Andy Williams/Original Cast ('56)	Columbia 2600
7/19/75	80	13	188. Nashville .... [V] Henry Gibson/Lily Tomlin/Ronee Blakley/Shelley Duvall	ABC 893
1/30/61	2(5)	74	189. **Never On Sunday** .... [I] Melina Mercouri/Jules Dassin - cp/cd: Manos Hadjidakis also see Original Cast "Ilya Darling"	United Art. 5070
7/16/77	50	14	190. New York, New York .... [M] Liza Minnelli/Robert DeNiro sw: John Kander/Fred Ebb; cd: Ralph Burns	United Art. 750 [2]
8/22/81	189	5	191. Night The Lights Went Out in Georgia ..... [V] Kristy McNichol/Dennis Quaid/Mark Hamill	Mirage 16051
			Nighthawks - see Keith Emerson Sylvester Stallone/Rutger Hauer/Billy Dee Williams	
12/27/80	77	15	192. 9 To 5 .... Jane Fonda/Lily Tomlin/Dolly Parton - cp/cd: Charles Fox "9 To 5"(1-Dolly Parton)	20th Century 627
			1984 - see Eurythmics John Hurt/Richard Burton	
			Norwood - see Glen Campbell Glen Campbell/Kim Darby/Joe Namath/Carol Lynley	
			O Lucky Man! - see Alan Price Malcolm McDowell	
7/16/83	137	5	193. Octopussy .... [I] Roger Moore/Maud Adams - cp/cd: John Barry	A&M 4967
7/27/68	190	2	194. Odd Couple .... [I] Jack Lemmon/Walter Matthau - cp/cd: Neal Hefti includes excerpts of comedy from the film	Dot 25862

DATE CHARTED	PEAK POS	WKS CHRT'D	ALBUM TITLE	LABEL & NUMBER
10/30/82	**38**	23	195. Officer And A Gentleman .... [V] Richard Gere/Debra Winger/David Keith/Louis Gossett, Jr. "Up Where We Belong"(1-Joe Cocker & Jennifer Warnes) includes songs by ZZ Top, Pat Benatar and Dire Straits	Island 90017
9/17/55	**1(4)**	305	● 196. **Oklahoma!** .... [M] Gordon MacRae/Shirley Jones - mu: Richard Rodgers: ly: Oscar Hammerstein II; cd: Jay Blackton	Capitol 595
12/28/68	**20**	91	● 197. Oliver! .... [M] Mark Lester (Oliver)/Ron Moody/Jack Wild/Oliver Reed sw: Lionel Bart; cd: John Green also see Original Cast ('62)/Mantovani	Colgems 5501
			On A Clear Day You Can See Forever - see Barbra Streisand Barbra Streisand/Yves Montand - also see Original Cast ('65)	
2/27/82	**147**	11	198. On Golden Pond .... [I] Henry Fonda/Katharine Hepburn - cp/cd: Dave Grusin includes dialogue excerpts from the film	MCA 6106
2/07/70	**103**	13	199. On Her Majesty's Secret Service .... [I+V] George Lazenby/Diana Rigg/Telly Savalas - cp/cd: John Barry	United Art. 5204
4/17/76	**158**	7	200. One Flew Over The Cuckoo's Nest .... [I] Jack Nicholson/Louise Fletcher - cp: Jack Nitzsche	Fantasy 9500
			One On One - see Seals & Crofts Robby Benson/Annette O'Toole/G.D. Spradlin	
			One-Trick Pony - see Paul Simon	
3/19/66	**118**	5	201. Our Man Flint .... [I] James Coburn/Lee J. Cobb/Gila Golan - cp/cd: Jerry Goldsmith	20th Century 4179
			Owl and the Pussycat - see Barbra Streisand Barbra Streisand/George Segal	
10/25/69	**28**	56	● 202. Paint Your Wagon .... [M] Lee Marvin/Clint Eastwood/Jean Seberg mu: Frederick Loewe; ly: Alan Jay Lerner	Paramount 1001
9/23/57	**9**	14	203. **Pajama Game** .... [M] Doris Day/John Raitt - sw: Richard Adler/Jerry Ross; cd: Ray Heindorf	Columbia 5210
			Pal Joey - see Frank Sinatra Frank Sinatra/Rita Hayworth/Kim Novak	
8/04/73	**154**	12	204. Paper Moon .... [V-O] Ryan O'Neal/Tatum O'Neal featuring original recordings from the early thirties by Bing Crosby, Paul Whiteman, Tommy Dorsey and others	Paramount 1012
			Paradise, Hawaiian Style - see Elvis Presley Elvis (Rick Richards)/Suzanne Leigh/James Shigeta	
10/23/61	**92**	8	205. Parent Trap! .... [V+I] Hayley Mills/Brian Keith/Maureen O'Hara - cd: Tutti Camarata "Let's Get Together"(8-Hayley Mills) side 2: Camarata conducts Themes From Great Motion Pictures	Buena Vista 3309
9/25/61	**45**	12	206. Parrish .... [I] Troy Donahue/Claudette Colbert - cp/cd: Max Steiner side 2: "Popular Piano Concertos" by George Greeley	Warner 1413
2/05/83	**169**	6	207. Party Party .... [V] featuring recordings by Sting, Elvis Costello & 9 others	A&M 3212
			Pat Garrett & Billy The Kid - see Bob Dylan James Coburn/Kris Kristofferson/Jason Robards	
5/22/71	**117**	8	208. Patton .... [I] George C. Scott/Karl Malden - cp/cd: Jerry Goldsmith includes Scott's rendition of Patton's address to his troops	20th Century 4208
1/23/82	**188**	2	209. Pennies From Heaven .... [M-O] Steve Martin/Bernadette Peters - featuring songs from the thirties by the original artists	Warner 3639 [2]

			Pete Kelly's Blues - see Peggy Lee &
			    Ella Fitzgerald/Ray Heindorf &
			    Matty Matlock/Jack Webb
			Jack Webb/Janet Leigh/Peggy Lee/Lee Marvin	

SOUNDTRACKS

DATE CHARTED	PEAK POS	WKS CHRT'D	ALBUM TITLE	LABEL & NUMBER
12/24/77	**131**	10	210. Pete's Dragon .... [M] Helen Reddy/Jim Dale/Mickey Rooney/Red Buttons sw: Al Kasha/Joel Hirschhorn; cd: Irwin Kostal	Capitol 11704
2/23/63	**88**	7	211. Phaedra .... [I] Melina Mercouri/Anthony Perkins - cp/cd: Mikis Theodorakis	United Art. 5102
3/01/75	**194**	1	212. Phantom Of The Paradise .... [M] Paul Williams/William Finley/Jessica Harper sw: Paul Williams	A&M 3653
5/05/56	**6**	18	213. **Picnic** .... [I] William Holden/Kim Novak/Rosalind Russell cp: George Duning; cd: Morris Stoloff "Moonglow and Theme From Picnic"(1-Morris Stoloff)	Decca 78320
			Pink Panther - see Henry Mancini Peter Sellers/David Niven/Robert Wagner/Capucine	
			Pipe Dreams - see Gladys Knight Gladys Knight/Barry Hankerson	
8/28/82	**166**	6	214. Pirate Movie .... [M] Kristy McNichol/Christopher Atkins based on Gilbert & Sullivan's "Pirates Of Penzance"	Polydor 9503 [2]
7/27/68	**195**	3	215. Planet Of The Apes .... [I] Charlton Heston/Roddy McDowall - cp/cd: Jerry Goldsmith	Project 3 5023
7/17/82	**168**	5	216. Poltergeist .... [I] Jobeth Williams/Craig T. Nelson - cp/cd: Jerry Goldsmith	MGM 5408
12/27/80	**115**	10	217. Popeye .... [M] Robin Williams/Shelley Duvall - sw: Harry Nilsson	Boardwalk 36880
7/13/59	**8**	92	● 218. **Porgy and Bess** .... [M] Sidney Poitier/Dorothy Dandridge - mu: George Gershwin; ly: DuBose Heyward/Ira Gershwin; cd: Andre Previn also see Harry Belafonte/Ray Charles/Percy Faith/ Leontyne Price	Columbia 2016
			Purple Rain - see Prince Prince/Apollonia Kotero/Morris Day	
			Quadrophenia - see Who Phil Daniels/Leslie Ash/Sting	
4/17/82	**154**	6	219. Quest For Fire .... [I] Everett McGill/Rae Dawn Chong - cp: Philippe Sarde	RCA 4274
1/23/82	**134**	9	220. Ragtime .... [I] James Cagney/Howard Rollins - cp/cd: Randy Newman	Elektra 565
7/04/81	**62**	13	221. Raiders Of The Lost Ark .... [I] Harrison Ford/Karen Allen cp/cd: John Williams; pf: London Symphony Orchestra	Columbia 37373
			Rainbow Bridge - see Jimi Hendrix	
6/11/83	**20**	17	222. Return Of The Jedi .... [I] Mark Hamill/Harrison Ford/Carrie Fisher/Billy Dee Williams cp/cd: John Williams; pf: London Symphony Orchestra	RSO 811767
			Rhinestone - see Dolly Parton Sylvester Stallone/Dolly Parton	
			Richard Pryor Live On The Sunset Strip - see Richard Pryor	
			Richard Pryor: Here And Now - see Richard Pryor	
			Ride The Wild Surf - see Jan & Dean Tab Hunter/Fabian/Barbara Eden	
			Right On! - see Last Poets David Nelson/Felipe Luciano/Gylan Kain	
6/21/80	**125**	8	223. Roadie .... [V] Meat Loaf/Art Carney/Kaki Hunter featuring recordings by 16 rock and country artists	Warner 3441 [2]
7/18/64	**56**	14	224. Robin And The 7 Hoods .... [M] Frank Sinatra/Dean Martin/Bing Crosby/Sammy Davis, Jr. sw: Sammy Cahn/James Van Heusen; cd: Nelson Riddle	Reprise 2021
6/02/79	**118**	6	225. Rock 'N' Roll High School .... [V] P.J. Soles/Vincent Van Patten/Dey Young/Ramones featuring recordings by 11 rock acts	Sire 6070
3/09/57	**16**	9	226. Rock, Pretty Baby .... Sal Mineo/John Saxon/Luana Patten cp: Henry Mancini; pf: Jimmy Daley & The Ding-A-Lings	Decca 8429

DATE CHARTED	PEAK POS	WKS CHRT'D	ALBUM TITLE	LABEL & NUMBER
3/05/77	4	34	▲ 227. **Rocky** .... Sylvester Stallone/Talia Shire - cp/cd: Bill Conti "Gonna Fly Now"(1-Bill Conti)	United Art. 693
8/25/79	147	5	228. Rocky II .... [I] Sylvester Stallone/Talia Shire - cp/cd: Bill Conti	United Art. 972
7/10/82	15	19	● 229. Rocky III .... Sylvester Stallone/Talia Shire/Mr. T - cp/cd: Bill Conti "Eye Of The Tiger"(1-Survivor)	Liberty 51130
4/15/78	49	58	● 230. Rocky Horror Picture Show.................. [M] Tim Curry/Susan Sarandon/Barry Bostwick - sw: Richard O'Brien	Ode 21653
8/23/75	156	6	231. Rollerball .... [I] James Caan/John Houseman/Maud Adams cd: Andre Previn; pf: London Symphony Orchestra	United Art. 470
6/16/62	5	28	232. **Rome Adventure** .... [I] Troy Donahue/Suzanne Pleshette/Angie Dickinson cp: Max Steiner - side 2: "Neapolitan Favorites" by The Cafe Milano Orch. "Al Di La"(6-Emilio Pericoli)	Warner 1458
2/08/69	2(2)	74	● 233. **Romeo & Juliet** .... Leonard Whiting/Olivia Hussey - cp/cd: Nino Rota includes dialogue highlights	Capitol 2993
			Rose, The - see Bette Midler Bette Midler/Alan Bates/Frederic Forrest	
			Roustabout - see Elvis Presley Elvis (Charlie Rogers)/Barbara Stanwyck/Joan Freeman	
10/31/70	148	6	234. R.P.M. .... [I+V] Anthony Quinn/Ann-Margret/Gary Lockwood sw: Barry DeVorzon & Perry Botkin, Jr.	Bell 1203
			Rumble Fish - see Stewart Copland Matt Dillon/Mickey Rourke/Diane Lane	
12/19/70	199	4	235. Ryan's Daughter .... [I] Robert Mitchum/Sarah Miles - cp/cd: Maurice Jarre	MGM 27
			St. Louis Blues - see Nat King Cole	
10/23/65	89	15	236. Sandpiper, The .... [I] Elizabeth Taylor/Richard Burton/Eva Marie Saint cp: Johnny Mandel; cd: Robert Armbruster	Mercury 61032
11/26/77	1(24)	120	▲ 237. **Saturday Night Fever** .... [V] John Travolta - biggest selling soundtrack album of all-time "If I Can't Have You"(1-Yvonne Elliman) - also see Bee Gees	RSO 4001 [2]
12/26/70	95	8	238. Scrooge .... [M-X] a version of Charles Dicken's "A Christmas Carol" Albert Finney (Scrooge)/Alec Guinness/Edith Evans sw: Leslie Bricusse; cd: Ian Fraser	Columbia 30258
			Serenade - see Mario Lanza Mario Lanza/Joan Fontaine	
			Seven Hills Of Rome - see Mario Lanza Mario Lanza/Renato Roscel/Marisa Allasio	
10/17/64	148	3	239. 7th Dawn .... [I] William Holden/Susannah York - cp/cd: Riz Ortolani	United Art. 5115
12/30/72	163	11	240. 1776 .... [M] William Daniels/Howard Da Silva - sw: Sherman Edwards also see Original Cast ('69)	Columbia 31741
8/12/78	5	28	▲ 241. **Sgt. Pepper's Lonely Hearts Club Band** .... [M] Peter Frampton/Bee Gees - sw: John Lennon/Paul McCartney film inspired by the Beatles "Sgt. Pepper's" album "Got To Get You Into My Life"(9-Earth, Wind & Fire)	RSO 4100 [2]
			Shaft - see Isaac Hayes Richard Roundtree/Moses Gunn/Gwenn Mitchell	
7/21/73	147	9	242. Shaft in Africa .... [I] Richard Roundtree/Vonetta McGee - cp/cd: Johnny Pate	ABC 793
8/26/72	100	16	243. Shaft's Big Score! .... Richard Roundtree - cp: Gordon Parks; cd: Dick Hazard	MGM 36
1/23/82	171	8	244. Sharky's Machine .... [V] Burt Reynolds/Rachel Ward/Bernie Casey/Brian Keith featuring songs by Sarah Vaughan, Peggy Lee & other jazz greats	Warner 3653

SOUNDTRACKS

DATE CHARTED	PEAK POS	WKS CHRT'D	ALBUM TITLE	LABEL & NUMBER
10/09/65	147	2	245. Shenandoah .... [I] James Stewart - cp: Frank Skinner; cd: Joseph Gershenson	Decca 79125
			Show Boat - see "Those Glorious MGM Musicals"	
			Silencers - see Dean Martin Dean Martin/Stella Stevens/Daliah Lavi	
			Sing Boy Sing - see Tommy Sands Tommy Sands/Lili Gentle/Edmond O'Brien	
			Singin' In The Rain - see "Those Glorious MGM Musicals"	
			Singing Nun - see Debbie Reynolds Debbie Reynolds/Ricardo Montalban/Greer Garson	
			Slaughter's Big Rip-Off - see James Brown Jim Brown (football player)/Brock Peters/Ed McMahon	
9/06/80	103	11	246. Smokey And The Bandit 2 .... [V] Burt Reynolds/Sally Field/Jackie Gleason/Jerry Reed featuring songs by 8 top country stars	MCA 6101
12/06/80	187	2	247. Somewhere in Time .... [I] Christopher Reeve/Jane Seymour - cp/cd: John Barry	MCA 5154
			Son Of Dracula - see Nilsson	
1/23/71	95	8	248. Song of Norway .... [M] Florence Henderson/Toralv Maurstad - based on the life & music of Norwegian classical composer Edvard Grieg	ABC 14
			Song Remains The Same - see Led Zeppelin	
			SongWriter - see Willie Nelson & Kris Kristofferson	
			Sorcerer - see Tangerine Dream Roy Scheider/Bruno Cremer/Francisco Rabal	
			Soul To Soul - see Various-Concerts	
3/20/65	1(2)	233	● 249. **Sound Of Music, The** .... [M] Julie Andrews/Christopher Plummer - story of Maria Trapp's family - mu: Richard Rodgers; ly: Oscar Hammerstein II; cd: Irwin Kostal - also see Original Cast ('59)	RCA 2005
6/12/82	168	12	250. Soup For One .... [V] Saul Rubinek/Marcia Strassman/Gerrit Graham sw/cd: Bernard Edwards & Nile Rodgers	Mirage 19353
3/31/58	1(31)	262	● 251. **South Pacific** .... [M] Rossano Brazzi/Mitzi Gaynor/John Kerr - mu: Richard Rodgers; ly: Oscar Hammerstein II; cd: Alfred Newman	RCA 1032
			Sparkle - see Aretha Franklin Irene Cara/Philip Thomas/Lonette McKee	
			Speedway - see Elvis Presley Elvis (Steve Grayson)/Nancy Sinatra/Bill Bixby	
			Spinout - see Elvis Presley Elvis (Mike McCoy)/Shelley Fabares/Diane McBain	
8/27/77	40	16	252. Spy Who Loved Me .... [I] Roger Moore/Barbara Bach - cp/cd: Marvin Hamlisch "Nobody Does It Better"(2-Carly Simon)	United Art. 774
10/26/68	98	20	253. Star! .... [M] Julie Andrews/Richard Crenna/Michael Craig based on the life of English stage star, Gertrude Lawrence	20th Century 5102
			Star Is Born - see Barbra Streisand Barbra Steisand/Kris Kristofferson	
1/05/80	50	11	● 254. Star Trek - The Motion Picture .... [I] William Shatner/Leonard Nimoy/DeForest Kelley cp/cd: Jerry Goldsmith	Columbia 36334
7/17/82	61	9	255. Star Trek II - The Wrath Of Khan................ [I] William Shatner/Leonard Nimoy/DeForest Kelley cp/cd: James Horner	Atlantic 19363
6/23/84	82	8	256. Star Trek III - The Search For Spock .... [I] William Shatner/DeForest Kelley - cp/cd: James Horner includes bonus 12" single "The Search For Spock"	Capitol 12360
6/18/77	2(3)	53	▲ 257. **Star Wars** .... [I] Mark Hamill/Harrison Ford/Carrie Fisher/Alec Guinness cp/cd: John Williams; pf: London Symphony Orchestra "Star Wars (Main Title)"(1) - also see Meco/Zubin Mehta	20th Centry. 541[2]

DATE CHARTED	PEAK POS	WKS CHRT'D	ALBUM TITLE	LABEL & NUMBER
12/17/77	36	10	● 258. Star Wars, The Story Of .... storyline excerpts from the film - narrator: Roscoe Browne	20th Century 550
5/12/62	12	19	259. State Fair .... [M] Pat Boone/Ann-Margret/Bobby Darin - mu: Richard Rodgers; ly: Oscar Hammerstein II; cd: Alfred Newman	Dot 29011
7/16/83	6	27	▲ 260. **Staying Alive** .... [V] John Travolta - side 1: Bee Gees; side 2: Various Artists "Far From Over"(10-Frank Stallone)	RSO 813269
6/06/70	200	2	261. Sterile Cuckoo .... Liza Minnelli/Wendell Burton - cp/cd: Fred Karlin featuring "Come Saturday Morning" by The Sandpipers	Paramount 5009
1/26/74	1(5)	41	● 262. **Sting, The** .... [I] Paul Newman/Robert Redford/Robert Shaw - cp: Scott Joplin; cd/pianist: Marvin Hamlisch "The Entertainer"(3-Marvin Hamlisch)	MCA 390
			Stop Making Sense - see Talking Heads	
9/12/70	91	9	263. Strawberry Statement .... [V] Bruce Davison/Kim Darby/James Coco featuring songs by Crosby, Stills, Nash & Young	MGM 14 [2]
6/16/84	32	21	264. Streets Of Fire .... [V] Michael Pare/Diane Lane/Rick Moranis/Amy Madigan "I Can Dream About You"(6-Dan Hartman)	MCA 5492
8/28/82	152	7	265. Summer Lovers .... [V] Peter Gallagher/Daryl Hannah/Valerie Quennessen - featuring songs by Elton John, Tina Turner, Chicago, plus 6 others "Hard To Say I'm Sorry"(1-Chicago)	Warner 23695
9/11/71	52	34	266. Summer Of '42 .... [I] Jennifer O'Neill/Gary Grimes - cp/cd: Michel Legrand	Warner 1925
			Sunday In New York - see Peter Nero Cliff Robertson/Rod Taylor/Jane Fonda/Robert Culp	
			Superfly - see Curtis Mayfield Ron O'Neal/Carl Lee/Julius Harris	
			Super Fly T.N.T. - see Osibisa Ron O'Neal/Roscoe Lee Browne/Sheila Frazier	
1/13/79	44	13	267. Superman - The Movie .... [I] Christopher Reeve/Margot Kidder/Marlon Brando/Gene Hackman cp/cd: John Williams; pf: London Symphony Orchestra	Warner 3257 [2]
7/04/81	133	9	268. Superman II .... [I] Christopher Reeve/Margot Kidder/Gene Hackman cp/cd: Ken Thorne (from John Williams' original material)	Warner 3505
7/02/83	163	3	269. Superman III .... [I+V] Christopher Reeve/Richard Pryor/Annette O'Toole cp: John Williams/Ken Thorne/Giorgio Moroder	Warner 23879
3/08/69	72	22	270. Sweet Charity .... [M] Shirley MacLaine/Sammy Davis, Jr. - mu: Cy Coleman; ly: Dorothy Fields - also see Original Cast ('66)	Decca 71502
7/03/71	139	19	271. Sweet Sweetback's Baadasssss Song .... cp & star: Melvin Van Peebles	Stax 3001
10/27/84	34	16	● 272. Teachers .... [V] Nick Nolte/Jobeth Williams/Judd Hirsch/Ralph Macchio features songs by 38 Special, Joe Cocker and 8 others	Capitol 12371
1/05/80	80	9	273. "10" .... Bo Derek/Dudley Moore/Julie Andrews - cp/cd: Henry Mancini	Warner 3399
4/21/84	111	10	274. Terms of Endearment .... [I+V] Shirley MacLaine/Debra Winger - cp: Michael Gore	Capitol 12329
5/13/78	10	27	▲ 275. **Thank God It's Friday** .... [V] Jeff Goldblum/Valerie Landsburg - includes bonus 12" single "Last Dance"(3-Donna Summer)	Casablanca 7099 [2]
6/22/74	128	14	276. That's Entertainment .... [M] musical highlights from MGM's greatest musicals (1929-1958)	MCA 11002 [2]
			That's The Way Of The World - see **Earth, Wind & Fire**	
1/22/55	6	7	277. **There's No Business Like Show Business** .... [M] Ethel Merman/Donald O'Connor/Dan Dailey - sw: Irving Berlin	Decca 8091
			Thief - see Tangerine Dream James Caan/Tuesday Weld/Willie Nelson	

SOUNDTRACKS

DATE CHARTED	PEAK POS	WKS CHRT'D	ALBUM TITLE	LABEL & NUMBER
12/22/84	179	4	278. Thief Of Hearts .... [V] Steven Bauer/Barbara Williams/John Getz	Casablanca 822942
			Third World, Prisoner In The Street - see Third World	
			This Is Elvis - see Elvis Presley	
4/28/84	121	10	279. This Is Spinal Tap .... Christopher Guest/Michael McKean - parody of a rock group	Polydor 817846
8/31/68	182	6	280. Thomas Crown Affair .... [I] Steve McQueen/Faye Dunaway - cp/cd: Michel Legrand "The Windmills Of Your Mind" sung by Noel Harrison	United Art. 5182
4/15/67	16	48	● 281. Thoroughly Modern Millie .... [M] Julie Andrews/Mary Tyler Moore/Carol Channing cd: Andre Previn	Decca 71500
9/15/73	184	6	282. Those Glorious MGM Musicals: Show Boat/Annie Get Your Gun . [M-R] reissue of "Show Boat"(1-'51) & "Annie Get Your Gun"(3-'50)	MGM 42 [2]
9/15/73	185	7	283. Those Glorious MGM Musicals: Singin' In The Rain/Easter Parade .... [M-R] reissue of "Singin' In The Rain"(2-'52) & "Easter Parade"('48)	MGM 40 [2]
			Three Tough Guys - see Isaac Hayes Isaac Hayes/Fred Williamson/Lino Ventura	
12/11/65	10	28	284. Thunderball .... [I] Sean Connery/Claudine Auger - cp/cd: John Barry	United Art. 5132
			Time To Sing - see Hank Williams, Jr. Hank Williams, Jr./Shelley Fabares/Ed Begley	
9/27/80	37	17	285. Times Square .... [V] Tim Curry/Trini Alvarado/Robin Johnson featuring recordings by 20 rock artists	RSO 4203 [2]
9/23/67	16	22	286. To Sir, With Love .... [I + V] Sidney Poitier/Judy Geeson "To Sir With Love"(1-Lulu)	Fontana 67569
			Together Brothers - see Love Unlimited Orchestra Anthony Wilson/Kim Dorsey/Owen Pace	
3/21/64	38	20	287. Tom Jones .... [I] Albert Finney/Susannah York - cp/cd: John Addison	United Art. 5113
3/29/75	2(1)	35	● 288. Tommy .... [M] rock opera featuring Roger Daltrey, Ann-Margret, Oliver Reed, Elton John - all but 4 songs written by Pete Townshend also see The Who/Various "Rock Operas"	Polydor 9502 [2]
2/26/83	144	12	289. Tootsie .... Dustin Hoffman/Jessica Lange - mu: Dave Grusin; lyrics: Alan & Marilyn Bergman; vocals: Stephen Bishop	Warner 23781
1/09/65	150	2	290. Topkapi .... [I] Melina Mercouri/Peter Ustinov - cp: Manos Hadjidakis	United Art. 5118
2/01/75	158	3	291. Towering Inferno .... [I] Paul Newman/Steve McQueen/William Holden cp/cd: John Williams	Warner 2840
12/21/74	130	8	292. Trial of Billy Jack .... Tom Laughlin/Delores Taylor - cp/cd: Elmer Bernstein	ABC 853
7/31/82	135	5	293. Tron .... [I] Jeff Bridges/Bruce Boxleitner - cp: Wendy Carlos; cd: Douglas Gamley; pf: London Philharmonic Orchestra	CBS 37782
			Trouble Man - see Marvin Gaye Robert Hooks/Paul Winfield/Ralph Waite/Paula Kelly	
			Truck Turner - see Isaac Hayes Isaac Hayes/Yaphet Kotto	
8/02/69	77	12	294. True Grit .... [I] John Wayne/Glen Campbell/Kim Darby - cp/cd: Elmer Bernstein	Capitol 263
			Two For The Road - see Henry Mancini Audrey Hepburn/Albert Finney	
12/03/83	26	17	▲ 295. Two Of A Kind .... [V] John Travolta/Olivia Newton-John "Twist Of Fate"(5-Olivia Newton-John)	MCA 6127
			200 Motels - see Frank Zappa Frank Zappa/Ringo Starr/Theodore Bikel	

DATE CHARTED	PEAK POS	WKS CHRT'D	ALBUM TITLE	LABEL & NUMBER
7/13/68	24	120	● 296. 2001: A Space Odyssey .... [I] Gary Lockwood/Keir Dullea features classical music by various orchestras	MGM 13
10/10/70	147	7	297. 2001: A Space Odyssey (volume two) .... [I] only a few tracks are from the original soundtrack	MGM 4722
2/02/85	173	5	298. 2010 .... [I] Roy Scheider/John Lithgow - cp: David Shire	A&M 5038
7/18/64	11	33	299. Unsinkable Molly Brown .... [M] Debbie Reynolds/Harve Presnell - sw: Meredith Willson; cd: Robert Armbruster - also see Original Cast ('60)	MGM 4232
			Up In Smoke - see Cheech & Chong	
5/12/84	185	3	300. Up The Creek .... [V] Tim Matheson/Jennifer Runyon/Dan Monahan/Stephen Furst featuring recordings by 9 pop/rock artists	Pasha 39333
			Uptight - see Booker T. & The MG's Raymond St. Jacques/Ruby Dee/Frank Silvera	
5/17/80	3	47	▲ 301. Urban Cowboy .... [V] John Travolta/Debra Winger "Lookin' For Love"(5-Johnny Lee)	Asylum 90002 [2]
1/10/81	134	6	302. Urban Cowboy II .... [V] more music from the original soundtrack above 2 albums feature recordings by 16 country/pop artists	Full Moon 36921
			Valley - see Pink Floyd Bulle Ogier/Jean-Pierre Kalfon/the Mapuga Tribe	
2/03/68	11	27	303. Valley Of The Dolls .... Barbara Parkins/Patty Duke/Sharon Tate/Susan Hayward sw: Dory & Andre Previn; cd: Johnny Williams	20th Century 4196
6/05/82	174	4	304. Victor/Victoria .... [M] Julie Andrews/James Garner/Robert Preston mu/cd: Henry Mancini; ly: Leslie Bricusse	MGM 5407
1/04/64	145	3	305. Victors, The .... [I] George Peppard/George Hamilton/Eli Wallach cp/cd: Sol Kaplan	Colpix 516
3/02/85	16+	6+	306. Vision Quest .... [V] Matthew Modine/Linda Fiorentino/Michael Schoeffling "Only The Young"(9-Journey)/"Crazy For You"(Madonna)	Geffen 24063
6/30/62	33	18	307. Walk On The Wild Side .... [I] Laurence Harvey/Jane Fonda - cp/cd: Elmer Bernstein	Ava 4
8/17/68	189	3	308. War and Peace .... [I] Ludmilla Savelyeva/Vyacheslav Tikhonov/Sergei Bondarchuk cp: Vyacheslav Ovchinnikov - a Russian film production	Melodiya 2918
5/05/79	125	8	309. Warriors, The .... [V] Michael Beck/Thomas Waites/James Remar	A&M 4761
			Wattstax - see Various-Concerts	
2/16/74	20	15	● 310. Way We Were .... [I] Barbra Streisand/Robert Redford - cp: Marvin Hamlisch	Columbia 32830
10/23/61	1(54)	198	● 311. West Side Story .... [M] Natalie Wood/Richard Beymer/Rita Moreno/George Chakiris mu: Leonard Bernstein; ly: Stephen Sondheim; cd: Johnny Green also see Ferrante & Teicher/Stan Kenton/Original Cast ('58)	Columbia 2070
			What Did You Do In The War, Daddy? - see Henry Mancini James Coburn/Dick Shawn/Aldo Ray/Carroll O'Connor	
8/07/65	14	22	312. What's New Pussycat? .... [I+V] Peter Sellers/Peter O'Toole - mu: Burt Bacharach ly: Hal David - "What's New Pussycat?"(3-Tom Jones)	United Art. 5117
			What's Up, Tiger Lily? - see Lovin' Spoonful Woody Allen	
			When The Boys Meet The Girls - see Connie Francis Connie Francis/Harve Presnell/Herman's Hermits	
			White Rock - see Rick Wakeman	
9/03/66	119	5	313. Who's Afraid Of Virginia Woolf? .... [I] Elizabeth Taylor/Richard Burton - cp/cd: Alex North	Warner 1656

DATE CHARTED	PEAK POS	WKS CHRT'D	ALBUM TITLE	LABEL & NUMBER
			Wild Angels - see Davie Allan Peter Fonda/Nancy Sinatra - cp/cd: Mike Curb	
10/18/69	**192**	2	314. Wild Bunch .... [I] William Holden/Ernest Borgnine - cp/cd: Jerry Fielding	Warner 1814
7/06/68	**12**	32	315. Wild In The Streets .... Christopher Jones/Diana Varsi/Shelley Winters sw: Barry Mann/Cynthia Weil; cd: Mike Curb	Tower 5099
10/21/78	**40**	17	● 316. Wiz, The .... [M] a soul musical version of "The Wizard Of Oz" Diana Ross/Michael Jackson - sw: Charlie Smalls; cd: Quincy Jones - also see Original Cast ('75)	MCA 14000 [2]
			Woman In Red - see Stevie Wonder Gene Wilder/Charles Grodin/Judith Ivey/Gilda Radner	
			Wonderwall - see George Harrison	
			Woodstock - see Various-Concerts	
			Xanadu - see Olivia Newton-John/ELO Olivia Newton-John/Gene Kelly	
8/07/65	**82**	10	317. Yellow Rolls-Royce .... Ingrid Bergman/Rex Harrison/Shirley MacLaine/Omar Shariff cp/cd: Riz Ortolani	MGM 4292
			Yellow Submarine - see Beatles	
			Yentl - see Barbra Streisand Barbra Streisand/Mandy Patinkin/Amy Irving	
			Yes, Giorgio - see Luciano Pavarotti Luciano Pavarotti/Kathryn Harrold/Eddie Albert	
10/29/77	**17**	15	● 318. You Light Up My Life .... Didi Conn/Joe Silver - cp/cd: Joseph Brooks	Arista 4159
7/15/67	**27**	26	319. You Only Live Twice .... [I] Sean Connery - cp/cd: John Barry	United Art. 5155
			You're A Big Boy Now - see Lovin' Spoonful Peter Kastner/Rip Torn/Geraldine Page/Julie Harris	
			Young At Heart - see Doris Day	
3/22/75	**128**	8	320. Young Frankenstein .... Gene Wilder/Peter Boyle - album of storyline excerpts	ABC 870
			Youngblood - see War Lawrence-Hilton Jacobs/Bryan O'Dell/Ren Woods	
			Your Cheatin' Heart - Hank Williams, Jr. George Hamilton/Susan Oliver/Red Buttons/Arthur O'Connell	
4/11/70	**128**	8	321. Z .... Yves Montand/Irene Papas cp: Mikis Theodorakis; cd: Bernard Gerard	Columbia 3370
			Ziggy Stardust - The Motion Picture - see David Bowie	
5/01/65	**26**	79	322. Zorba The Greek .... [I] Anthony Quinn/Irene Papas - cp/cd: Mikis Theodorakis also see Original Cast "Zorba"('69-an adaptation)	20th Century 4167

SOUNDTRACK COMPILATIONS

DATE CHARTED	PEAK POS	WKS CHRT'D	ALBUM TITLE	LABEL & NUMBER
2/08/69	**198**	2	1. Best Of The Soundtracks .... from 5 American International motion pictures	Tower 5148
1/23/61	**2(3)**	81	2. **Great Motion Picture Themes** .... [I] "Exodus" Ferrante & Teicher/"Never On Sunday" Don Costa	United Art. 3122
9/25/61	**129**	5	3. Great Motion Picture Themes (More Original Sound Tracks And Hit Music) .... [I] "Gone With The Wind" Ferrante & Teicher/"Bonanza" Al Caiola	United Art. 3158
3/13/65	**72**	27	4. Music To Read James Bond By .... Ferrante & Teicher, Al Caiola and others perform Bond themes	United Art. 6415
5/19/62	**31**	16	5. Original Motion Picture Hit Themes .... "Town Without Pity" Gene Pitney/"Tonight" Ferrante & Teicher	United Art. 3197

DATE CHARTED	PEAK POS	WKS CHRT'D	ALBUM TITLE	LABEL & NUMBER
			ORIGINAL CASTS The original cast stars are listed directly below the title. Also shown are the Lyricist (ly)/Musicwriter (mu)/Songwriter (sw)	
9/23/78	**161**	5	1. Ain't Misbehavin' .... Ken Page/Nell Carter/Andre De Shields - based on the life and compositions of Fats Waller	RCA 2965 [2]
4/21/62	**21**	16	2. All American .... Ray Bolger/Eileen Herlie/Ron Husmann mu: Charles Strouse: ly: Lee Adams	Columbia 2160
6/18/77	**81**	39	▲ 3. Annie .... Andrea McArdle/Reid Shelton - mu: Charles Strouse; ly: Martin Charnin - also see Soundtrack ('82)	Columbia 34712
12/30/57	**12**	5	4. Annie Get Your Gun .... Mary Martin/John Raitt - sw: Irving Berlin - San Francisco/ Los Angeles production selected by NBC for a TV spectacular (introduced on Broadway in 1946 - starring Ethel Merman)	Capitol 913
8/06/66	**113**	7	5. Annie Get Your Gun .... Ethel Merman/Bruce Yarnell - sw: Irving Berlin new production from the Music Theater of Lincoln Center	RCA 1124
5/23/70	**168**	7	6. Applause .... Lauren Bacall - mu: Charles Strouse; ly: Lee Adams based on the film "All About Eve"	ABC 11
12/17/66	**113**	9	7. Apple Tree, The .... Barbara Harris/Larry Blyden/Alan Alda mu: Jerry Bock; ly: Sheldon Harnick	Columbia 3020
2/20/65	**143**	2	8. Bajour .... Chita Rivera/Nancy Dussault/Herschel Bernardi sw: Walter Marks	Columbia 2700
5/08/65	**138**	4	9. Baker Street (A Musical Adventure Of Sherlock Holmes) .... Fritz Weaver/Inga Swenson - sw: Marian Grudeff/Raymond Jessel adapted from the stories by Sir Arthur Conan Doyle	MGM 7000
2/09/57	**20**	1	10. Bells are Ringing .... Judy Holliday/Sydney Chaplin - mu: Jule Styne; ly: Betty Comden/Adolph Green	Columbia 5170
12/26/64	**132**	8	11. Ben Franklin In Paris .... Robert Preston/Ulla Sallert - mu: Mark Sandrich, Jr.; ly: Sidney Michaels	Capitol 2191
12/15/62	**73**	20	12. Beyond The Fringe .... all-male cast of 4: Dudley Moore/Alan Bennett/Peter Cook/ Jonathan Miller - primarily consists of comedy excerpts	Capitol 1792
6/14/69	**195**	3	13. Boys in the Band .... Kenneth Nelson/Peter White - LP is all dialogue from the play	A&M 6001 [2]
7/18/60	**12**	61	14. Bye Bye Birdie .... Chita Rivera/Dick Van Dyke/Kay Medford/Dick Gautier (Conrad Birdie) - mu: Charles Strouse: ly: Lee Adams - also see Soundtrack ('63)	Columbia 5510
1/07/67	**37**	39	15. Cabaret .... Jill Haworth/Jack Gilford/Bert Convy/Lotte Lenya mu: John Kander; ly: Fred Ebb - also see Soundtrack ('72)	Columbia 3040
1/23/61	**1(6)**	265	● 16. Camelot .... Richard Burton/Julie Andrews/Robert Goulet mu: Frederick Loewe; ly: Alan Jay Lerner also see Percy Faith/Soundtrack ('67)	Columbia 2031
4/19/69	**171**	4	17. Canterbury Tales .... George Rose/Hermione Baddeley/Martyn Green mu: Richard Hill/John Hawkins; ly: Nevill Coghill	Capitol 229
5/29/61	**1(1)**	67	18. Carnival .... Anna Maria Alberghetti/James Mitchell - sw: Bob Merrill	MGM 3946
11/10/62	**12**	19	19. Carousel .... version of the Rodgers & Hammerstein musical - produced by Enoch Light and featuring vocalists Alfred Drake & Roberta Peters - also see Soundtrack ('56)	Command 843
			Catherine Wheel - see David Byrne	

ORIGINAL CASTS

DATE CHARTED	PEAK POS	WKS CHRT'D		ALBUM TITLE	LABEL & NUMBER
11/06/82	**86**	22		20. Cats .... original London Cast - Wayne Sleep/Paul Nicholas/Elaine Paige sw: Andrew Lloyd Webber - based on 'Old Possum's Book of Practical Cats' by T.S. Eliot - featuring the song "Memory"	Geffen 2017 [2]
2/26/83	**113**	41+		21. Cats .... entire Broadway cast - Ken Page/Betty Buckley/Timothy Scott	Geffen 2031 [2]
2/26/83	**131**	14		22. Cats .... selections from the original Broadway Cast	Geffen 2026
8/23/75	**73**	10		23. Chicago .... Gwen Verdon/Chita Rivera/Jerry Orbach mu: John Kander; ly: Fred Ebb	Arista 9005
8/16/75	**98**	49	●	24. Chorus Line, A .... Pamela Blair/Wayne Cilento/Priscilla Lopez/Donna McKechnie mu: Marvin Hamlisch; ly: Edward Kleban	Columbia 33581
4/29/57	**15**	1		25. Cinderella - mu: Richard Rodgers; ly: Oscar Hammerstein Julie Andrews a special CBS-TV production (3/31/57)	Columbia 5190
6/20/70	**178**	2		26. Company .... Dean Jones/Barbara Barrie - sw: Stephen Sondheim	Columbia 3550
8/02/69	**195**	2		27. Dames At Sea .... Bernadette Peters/David Christmas/Tamara Long/Sally Stark mu: Jim Wise; ly: George Haimsohn/Robin Miller	Columbia 3330
6/11/55	**6**	13		28. **Damn Yankees** .... Gwen Verdon/Stephen Douglass/Ray Walston sw: Richard Adler/Jerry Ross - also see Soundtrack ('58)	RCA 1021
4/05/69	**128**	8		29. Dear World .... Angela Lansbury/Milo O'Shea - sw: Jerry Herman	Columbia 3260
8/24/59	**44**	2		30. Destry Rides Again .... Andy Griffith/Dolores Gray/Scott Brady - sw: Harold Rome	Decca 79075
5/22/65	**81**	9		31. Do I Hear A Waltz? .... Elizabeth Allen/Sergio Franchi/Carol Bruce mu: Richard Rodgers; ly: Stephen Sondheim	Columbia 2770
3/20/61	**12**	23		32. Do Re Mi .... Phil Silvers/Nancy Walker - mu: Jule Styne; ly: Betty Comden/Adolph Green	RCA 2002
7/31/61	**58**	9		33. Donnybrook! .... Eddie Foy/Art Lund/Joan Fagan - sw: Johnny Burke based on the movie "The Quiet Man" by Maurice Walsh	Kapp 8500
5/22/82	**11**	29		34. Dreamgirls .... Jennifer Holliday/Loretta Devine/Cleavant Derricks mu: Henry Krieger; ly: Tom Eyen	Geffen 2007
				Evening With Mike Nichols And Elaine May - see Mike Nichols & Elaine May	
8/23/80	**105**	19	●	35. Evita .... Patti LuPone/Mandy Patinkin/Bob Gunton mu: Andrew Lloyd Webber; ly: Tim Rice (based on the life of Argentinian Eva Peron) - also see the artist 'Festival'	MCA 11007 [2]
7/25/64	**96**	8		36. Fade Out-Fade In .... Carol Burnett/Jack Cassidy/Lou Jacobi mu: Jule Styne; ly: Betty Comden/Adolph Green	ABC-Para. 3
1/22/55	**7**	1		37. **Fanny** .... Ezio Pinza/Walter Slezak/Florence Henderson - sw: Harold Rome - also see Soundtrack ('61)	RCA 1015
8/03/63	**117**	6		38. Fantasticks .... Kenneth Nelson/Jerry Orbach/Rita Gardner mu: Harvey Schmidt; ly: Tom Jones	MGM 3872
10/31/64	**7**	206	●	39. **Fiddler On The Roof** .... Zero Mostel/Maria Karnilova/Beatrice Arthur mu: Jerry Bock; ly: Sheldon Harnick also see Soundtrack ('71)/Herschel Bernardi	RCA 1093
1/11/60	**7**	88		40. **Fiorello!** .... Tom Bosley/Patricia Wilson/Ellen Hanley/Howard Da Silva mu: Jerry Bock; ly: Sheldon Harnick	Capitol 1321
7/03/65	**111**	8		41. Flora, The Red Menace .... Liza Minnelli/Bob Dishy - mu: John Kander; ly: Fred Ebb	RCA 1111

DATE CHARTED	PEAK POS	WKS CHRT'D	ALBUM TITLE	LABEL & NUMBER
1/12/59	1(3)	151	● 42. **Flower Drum Song** .... Miyoshi Umeki/Larry Blyden/Pat Suzuki - mu: Richard Rodgers; ly: Oscar Hammerstein II - also see Sountrack ('61)	Columbia 2009
6/05/71	172	3	43. Follies .... Alexis Smith/Gene Nelson/Yvonne De Carlo/Dorothy Collins sw: Stephen Sondheim	Capitol 761
1/17/81	120	11	44. 42nd Street .... Tammy Grimes/Jerry Orbach - mu: Harry Warren; ly: Al Dubin	RCA 3891
			Funny Girl - see Barbra Streisand (both Original Cast and Soundtrack) Barbra Streisand/Sydney Chaplin - mu: Jule Styne; ly: Bob Merrill	
7/07/62	60	14	45. Funny Thing Happened On The Way To The Forum, A .... Zero Mostel/Jack Gilford/David Burns - sw: Stephen Sondheim	Capitol 1717
2/24/62	81	9	46. Gay Life, The .... Walter Chiari/Barbara Cook/Jules Munshin sw: Howard Dietz/Arthur Schwartz	Capitol 1560
5/25/68	161	6	47. George M! .... Joel Grey/Betty Ann Grove - based on the life and compositions of George Michael Cohan	Columbia 3200
1/25/64	33	14	48. Girl Who Came To Supper .... Jose Ferrer/Florence Henderson - sw: Noel Coward	Columbia 2420
8/07/71	34	79	● 49. Godspell .... Stephen Nathan/David Haskell - sw: Stephen Schwartz based upon the gospel according to St. Matthew also see Soundtrack ('73)	Bell 1102
12/19/64	36	16	50. Golden Boy .... Sammy Davis, Jr./Billy Daniels - mu: Charles Strouse; ly: Lee Adams	Capitol 2124
1/01/66	118	4	51. Great Waltz, The .... Giorgio Tozzi/Jean Fenn - musical based on the lives and compositions of Johann Strauss, Sr. & Jr.	Capitol 2426
7/20/59	13	116	52. Gypsy .... Ethel Merman/Jack Klugman/Sandra Church - mu: Jule Styne; ly: Stephen Sondheim - based on memoirs of Gypsy Rose Lee also see Soundtrack ('62)	Columbia 2017
8/03/68	1(13)	151	● 53. **Hair** .... Gerome Ragni/James Rado/Lynn Kellogg - mu: Galt MacDermot; ly: Gerome Ragni/James Rado - also see Soundtrack ('79)/ Various-Concept "DisinHAIRited"	RCA 1150
5/10/69	186	4	54. Hair .... original London cast - Paul Nicholas/Oliver Tobias	Atco 7002
6/12/65	103	14	55. Half A Sixpence .... Tommy Steele/Polly James - sw: David Heneker	RCA 1110
8/15/64	128	13	56. Hamlet .... Richard Burton/Hume Cronyn/Alfred Drake/Eileen Herlie a 4-album set of dialogue from Shakespeare's play	Columbia 702 [4]
7/03/61	84	6	57. Happiest Girl In The World .... Cyril Ritchard/Janice Rule - mu: Jacques Offenbach; ly: E.Y. Harburg	Columbia 2050
2/22/64	1(1)	90	● 58. **Hello, Dolly!** .... Carol Channing/David Burns/Eileen Brennan - sw: Jerry Herman also see Barbra Streisand (Soundtrack '69)	RCA 1087
11/16/63	38	17	59. Here's Love .... Janis Paige/Craig Stevens - sw: Meredith Willson based on "Miracle On 34th Street"	Columbia 2400
5/16/64	76	20	60. High Spirits .... Beatrice Lillie/Tammy Grimes/Edward Woodward sw: Hugh Martin/Timothy Gray - based on Noel Coward's "Blithe Spirit"	ABC-Para. 1
11/27/61	19	47	61. How To Succeed In Business Without Really Trying .... Robert Morse/Rudy Vallee - sw: Frank Loesser also see Soundtrack ('67)	RCA 1066

DATE CHARTED	PEAK POS	WKS CHRT'D	ALBUM TITLE	LABEL & NUMBER
7/21/62	125	5	62. I Can Get It For You Wholesale .... Lillian Roth/Jack Kruschen/Elliott Gould - sw: Harold Rome cast includes Barbra Streisand in her first Broadway show	Columbia 2180
1/14/67	84	16	63. I Do! I Do! .... Mary Martin/Robert Preston - mu: Harvey Schmidt; ly: Tom Jones	RCA 1128
1/30/65	126	8	64. I Had A Ball .... Buddy Hackett/Richard Kiley - sw: Jack Lawrence/Stan Freeman	Mercury 6210
6/17/67	177	8	65. Illya Darling .... Melina Mercouri/Orson Bean - mu: Manos Hadjidakis; ly: Joe Darion - based on the film "Never On Sunday"	United Art. 9901
12/05/60	9	33	66. **Irma La Douce** .... Elizabeth Seal/Keith Michell/Clive Revill mu: Marguerite Monnot; original lyrics: Alexandre Breffort also see Soundtrack ('63)	Columbia 2029
1/04/64	87	5	67. Jennie .... Mary Martin/George Wallace/Robin Bailey mu: Arthur Schwartz; ly: Howard Dietz	RCA 1083
1/08/72	31	10	68. Jesus Christ Superstar .... Ben Vereen/Jeff Fenbolt/Yvonne Elliman/Bob Bingham mu: Andrew Lloyd Webber; ly: Tim Rice also see Various ('70)/Soundtrack ('73)/Percy Faith	Decca 1503
3/14/70	187	4	69. Joy .... Oscar Brown Jr./Jean Pace/Sivuca - sw: various	RCA 1166
12/25/61	80	12	70. Kean .... Alfred Drake/Lee Venora - sw: Robert Wright/George Forrest Kismet - see Mantovani	Columbia 2120
3/24/62	139	3	71. Kwamina .... Sally Ann Howes/Terry Carter - sw: Richard Adler	Capitol 1645
9/24/83	52	15	72. La Cage Aux Folles .... George Hearn/Gene Barry - sw: Jerry Herman	RCA 4824
12/29/56	19	3	73. Li'l Abner .... Edith Adams/Peter Palmer/Howard St. John/Stubby Kaye mu: Gene de Paul; ly: Johnny Mercer	Columbia 5150
1/19/63	44	10	74. Little Me .... Sid Caesar/Virginia Martin/Nancy Andrews mu: Cy Coleman; ly: Carolyn Leigh	RCA 1078
5/05/73	94	12	75. Little Night Music, A .... Glynis Johns/Len Cariou/Hermione Gingold - sw: Stephen Sondheim - based on the film "Smiles Of A Summer Night"	Columbia 32265
1/11/69	185	2	76. Maggie Flynn .... Shirley Jones/Jack Cassidy - sw: Hugo Peretti/ Luigi Creatore/George David Weiss	RCA 2009
7/02/66	23	66	● 77. Mame .... Angela Lansbury/Beatrice Arthur - sw: Jerry Herman based on the movie "Auntie Mame" - also see Soundtrack ('74)	Columbia 3000
1/22/66	31	167	● 78. Man of La Mancha .... Richard Kiley/Irving Jacobson/Joan Diener - mu: Mitch Leigh; ly: Joe Darion - an adaptation of "Don Quixote" - featuring the song "The Impossible Dream" - also see Soundtrack ('72)	Kapp 4505
10/17/64	137	4	79. Merry Widow, The .... Patrice Munsel/Bob Wright - sw: Franz Lehar	RCA 1094
11/18/61	10	41	80. **Milk and Honey** .... Robert Weede/Mimi Benzell/Molly Picon - sw: Jerry Herman	RCA 1065
12/01/62	14	24	81. Mr. President .... Robert Ryan/Nanette Fabray - sw: Irving Berlin also see Perry Como	Columbia 2270
8/04/56	11	4	82. Most Happy Fella, The .... Robert Weede/Jo Sullivan - sw: Frank Loesser	Columbia 2330

DATE CHARTED	PEAK POS	WKS CHRT'D	ALBUM TITLE	LABEL & NUMBER
2/24/58	1(12)	245	● 83. **Music Man, The** .... Robert Preston/Barbara Cook - sw: Meredith Willson also see Soundtrack ('62)	Capitol 990
4/28/56	1(15)	480	● 84. **My Fair Lady** .... Rex Harrison/Julie Andrews - mu: Frederick Loewe; ly: Alan Jay Lerner - adapted from Bernard Shaw's "Pygmalion" - also see Soundtrack ('64)	Columbia 5090
8/05/57	17	3	85. New Girl in Town .... Gwen Verdon/Thelma Ritter/George Wallace - sw: Bob Merrill	RCA 1027
3/13/71	61	19	86. No, No, Nanette .... Ruby Keeler/Jack Gilford/Bobby Van/Helen Gallagher mu: Vincent Youmans; ly: Irving Caesar/Otto Harbach	Columbia 30563
4/21/62	5	62	87. **No Strings** .... Richard Kiley/Diahann Carroll - sw: Richard Rodgers	Capitol 1695
11/03/62	4	99	● 88. **Oliver!** .... Clive Revill/Georgia Brown/Bruce Prochnik (Oliver) sw: Lionel Bart - also see Soundtrack ('68)/Mantovani	RCA 2004
12/11/65	59	32	89. On A Clear Day You Can See Forever .... Barbara Harris/John Cullum/Tito Vandis mu: Burton Lane; ly: Alan Jay Lerner also see Barbra Streisand (Soundtrack '70)	RCA 2006
1/04/64	37	15	90. 110 In The Shade .... Robert Horton/Inga Swenson/Stephen Douglass mu: Harvey Schmidt; ly: Tom Jones	RCA 1085
			Over Here! - see Andrews Sisters sw: Richard M. Sherman/Robert B. Sherman	
4/02/55	4	7	91. **Peter Pan** .... Mary Martin/Cyril Ritchard - mu: Mark Charlap/Jule Styne; ly: Carolyn Leigh/Betty Comden/Adolph Green	RCA 1019
1/13/73	129	10	92. Pippin .... Ben Vereen/Jill Clayburgh - sw: Stephen Schwartz	Motown 760
6/06/81	178	3	93. Pirates of Penzance .... Kevin Kline/Estelle Parsons/Linda Ronstadt/Rex Smith ly: W.S. Gilbert; mu: Sir Arthur Sullivan also see Soundtrack "Pirate Movie"	Elektra 601 [2]
1/25/69	95	12	94. Promises, Promises .... Jerry Orbach/Jill O'Hara/Edward Winter - mu: Burt Bacharach; ly: Hal David - based on the screenplay "The Apartment"	United Art. 9902
6/13/70	138	5	95. Purlie .... Cleavon Little/Melba Moore - mu: Gary Geld; ly: Peter Udell	Ampex 40101
5/25/59	47	1	96. Redhead .... Gwen Verdon/Richard Kiley - mu: Albert Hague; ly: Dorothy Fields	RCA 1048
4/10/65	54	34	97. Roar Of The Greasepaint - The Smell Of The Crowd .... Anthony Newley/Cyril Ritchard - sw: Anthony Newley/ Leslie Bricusse	RCA 1109
11/27/61	36	22	98. Sail Away .... Elaine Stritch/James Hurst - sw: Noel Coward	Capitol 1643
5/17/69	174	6	99. 1776 .... William Daniels/Paul Hecht/Roy Poole - sw: Sherman Edwards also see Soundtrack ('72)	Columbia 3310
6/22/63	15	17	100. She Loves Me .... Barbara Cook/Daniel Massey/Barbara Baxley/Jack Cassidy mu: Jerry Bock; ly: Sheldon Harnick	MGM 4118 [2]
9/15/62	95	6	101. Show Boat .... version of the Jerome Kern & Oscar Hammerstein II musical, featuring John Raitt, Barbara Cook and William Warfield	Columbia 2220
4/16/55	9	5	102. **Silk Stockings** .... Hildegarde Neff/Don Ameche/Gretchen Wyler - sw: Cole Porter	RCA 1016
1/08/66	128	8	103. Skyscraper .... Julie Harris/Peter Marshall/Charles Nelson Reilly mu: James Van Heusen - ly: Sammy Cahn	Capitol 2422

ORIGINAL CASTS

DATE CHARTED	PEAK POS	WKS CHRT'D	ALBUM TITLE	LABEL & NUMBER
12/21/59	1(16)	227	● 104. **Sound Of Music, The** .... Mary Martin/Theodore Bikel - mu: Richard Rodgers; ly: Oscar Hammerstein II - also see Soundtrack ('65)	Columbia 2020
11/24/62	3	76	105. **Stop The World - I Want To Get Off** .... Anthony Newley/Anna Quayle - sw: Leslie Bricusse/ Anthony Newley - also see Mantovani	London 88001
4/07/62	81	11	106. Subways Are For Sleeping .... Sydney Chaplin/Carol Lawrence/Orson Bean mu: Jule Styne; ly: Betty Comden/Adolph Green	Columbia 2130
8/25/84	149	11	107. Sunday in the Park with George .... Mandy Patinkin/Bernadette Peters - sw: Stephen Sondheim	RCA 5042 [2]
6/09/79	78	11	108. Sweeny Todd - The Demon Barber of Fleet Street .... Angela Lansbury/Len Cariou - sw: Stephen Sondheim	RCA 3379 [2]
3/12/66	92	16	109. Sweet Charity .... Gwen Verdon/John McMartin - mu: Cy Coleman; ly: Dorothy Fields - also see Soundtrack ('69)	Columbia 2900
1/16/61	15	34	110. Tenderloin .... Maurice Evans/Ron Husmann/Wayne Miller/Eileen Rodgers mu: Jerry Bock; ly: Sheldon Harnick	Capitol 1492
3/24/79	167	6	111. They're Playing Our Song .... Robert Klein/Lucie Arnaz - mu: Marvin Hamlisch; ly: Carole Bayer Sager	Casablanca 7141
8/06/66	145	2	112. Time For Singing, A .... Ivor Emmanuel/Tessie O'Shea/Shani Wallis mu: John Morris; ly: Gerald Freedman/John Morris based on the novel "How Green Was My Valley"	Warner 1639
7/27/63	64	11	113. Tovarich .... Vivian Leigh/Jean-Pierre Aumont/Alexander Scourby mu: Lee Pockriss; ly: Anne Croswell	Capitol 1940
5/08/76	200	2	114. Treemonisha .... Carmen Balthrop/Betty Allen/Curtis Rayam - sw: Scott Joplin; cd: Gunther Schuller; pf: Houston Grand Opera	DG 2707 [2]
12/26/60	6	48	115. **Unsinkable Molly Brown** .... Tammy Grimes/Harve Presnell - sw: Meredith Willson also see Soundtrack ('64)	Capitol 1509
3/17/58	5	191	● 116. **West Side Story** .... Carol Lawrence/Larry Kert/Chita Rivera/Art Smith mu: Leonard Bernstein; ly: Stephen Sondheim also see Soundtrack ('61)	Columbia 5230
4/04/64	28	14	117. What Makes Sammy Run? .... Steve Lawrence/Sally Ann Howes/Robert Alda - sw: Ervin Drake	Columbia 2440
1/30/61	6	40	118. **Wildcat** .... Lucille Ball/Keith Andes - mu: Cy Coleman; ly: Carolyn Leigh	RCA 1060
5/03/75	43	16	119. Wiz, The .... Stephanie Mills/Tiger Haynes/Ted Ross/Hinton Battle sw: Charlie Smalls - also see Soundtrack ('78)	Atlantic 18137
6/27/81	196	2	120. Woman Of The Year .... Lauren Bacall/Harry Guardino - mu: John Kander; ly: Fred Ebb	Arista 8303
7/01/67	165	5	121. You're A Good Man, Charlie Brown .... Gary Burghoff/Bob Balaban/Bill Hinnant/Reva Rose sw: Clark Gesner - based on the comic strip "Peanuts"	MGM 9
1/25/69	177	7	122. Zorba .... Herschel Bernardi/Maria Karnilova - mu: John Kander; ly: Fred Ebb - also see Soundtrack "Zorba The Greek" ('65)	Capitol 118

DATE CHARTED	PEAK POS	WKS CHRT'D	ALBUM TITLE	LABEL & NUMBER

TELEVISION SHOWS

The stars of the show are listed directly below the title.

DATE CHARTED	PEAK POS	WKS CHRT'D	ALBUM TITLE	LABEL & NUMBER
11/20/71	8	22	● 1. **All In The Family** .... [C] Carroll O'Connor/Jean Stapleton/Rob Reiner/Sally Struthers comedy excerpts from the show	Atlantic 7210
12/30/72	129	8	2. All In The Family - 2nd Album .... [C] more comedy excerpts from the show	Atlantic 7232
4/23/66	112	8	3. Batman .... [I-T] Adam West/Burt Ward - cd: Nelson Riddle - music and dialogue excerpts from the show - also see Neal Hefti/Marketts	20th Century 4180
10/21/78	144	6	4. Battlestar Galactica .... [I] Lorne Greene/Richard Hatch/Dirk Benedict cp/cd: Stu Phillips; pf: Los Angeles Philharmonic Orchestra	MCA 3051
			Ben Casey - see Valjean	
11/24/62	66	9	5. Bonanza .... Lorne Greene/Michael Landon/Dan Blocker/Pernell Roberts songs performed by each of the stars	RCA 2583
5/13/72	108	19	6. Brady Bunch (Meet The) .... featuring songs by the 6 kids of the 1969-74 series	Paramount 6032
5/09/81	136	13	7. Cosmos (The Music Of) .... [I] selections from PBS television series hosted by Carl Sagan - featuring classical works plus selections by Vangelis	RCA 4003
			Dallas - see Floyd Cramer	
8/02/69	18	19	8. Dark Shadows .... [I] Jonathan Frid/David Selby - cp/cd: Robert Cobert	Philips 314
4/17/82	93	14	9. Dukes Of Hazzard .... John Schneider/Tom Wopat/Sorrell Booke/James Best narration & vocals by members of the cast	Scotti Br. 37712
			Fame - see Kids From Fame Flying Nun - see Sally Field	
5/23/70	196	4	10. Hee Haw (The Stars Of) .... Buck Owens/Roy Clark/The Hagers/Buddy Alan/Susan Raye	Capitol 437
10/19/68	105	17	11. Laugh-In .... [C] Dan Rowan/Dick Martin/Arte Johnson/Judy Carne & cast	Epic 15118
4/05/69	88	10	12. Laugh-in '69 .... [C] above 2 albums feature comedy/musical highlights by the cast	Reprise 6335
			Man From U.N.C.L.E. - see Hugo Montenegro Mickey Mouse Club - see Childrens section	
7/23/66	120	15	13. Mickie Finn's - America's No.1 Speakeasy .... [L] San Diego night club specializing in "Gay '90s" music - featuring pianist Fred Finn and his wife Mickie (banjo)	Dunhill 50009
			Mission: Impossible - see Lalo Schifrin Mr. Lucky - see Henry Mancini MTV - see Various-Radio/TV Celebrity Muppet Show - see Childrens section	
5/09/60	30	2	14. One Step Beyond (Music From) .... [I] from the "Alcoa Presents" TV series - Harry Lubin conducts the Berliner Symphoniker orchestra	Decca 8970
			Peter Gunn - see Henry Mancini	
			Roaring Twenties - see Dorothy Provine Roots - see Quincy Jones	

TELEVISION SHOWS

DATE CHARTED	PEAK POS	WKS CHRT'D	ALBUM TITLE	LABEL & NUMBER
			Sanford & Son - see Redd Foxx	
12/25/76	**38**	13	15. Saturday Night Live! .... [C] John Belushi/Dan Aykroyd/Chevy Chase/Jane Curtin & cast	Arista 4107
			Sesame Street - see Childrens section	
4/20/59	**3**	28	16. **77 Sunset Strip** .... [I] Efrem Zimbalist, Jr./Roger Smith/Ed "Kookie" Byrnes musical director: Warren Barker	Warner 1289
10/04/80	**115**	6	17. Shogun .... [I] TV film starring Richard Chamberlain - cp/cd: Maurice Jarre	RSO 3088
12/01/73	**34**	23	18. Sunshine .... TV film starring Christina Raines and Cliff DeYoung music composed by John Denver; vocals by Cliff DeYoung	MCA 387
			Taxi - see Bob James	
12/21/74	**30**	11	● 19. Tonight Show/Here's Johnny .... [C] actual musical and comedy excerpts from the TV show hosted by Johnny Carson since 10/1/62	Casablanca 1296 [2]
11/10/58	**2(4)**	89	20. **Victory At Sea, Vol 2** .... [I]	RCA 2226
9/11/61	**7**	32	21. **Victory At Sea, Vol. 3** .... [I] above 2 albums are orchestral suites from the NBC-TV series which featured actual film of World War II naval battles cp: Richard Rodgers; cd: Robert Russell Bennett	RCA 2523
			Waltons - see Christmas section	

TELEVISION SPECIALS:

Aloha From Hawaii via Satellite -
see Elvis Presley

Cinderella - see Original Casts

Diana! - see Diana Ross

Elvis - see Elvis Presley

Elvis in Concert - see Elvis Presley

Goin' Back To Indiana - see Jackson 5

Liza With A "Z" - see Liza Minnelli

Movin' With Nancy - see Nancy Sinatra

On Broadway - see Supremes & Temptations

Point!, The - see Nilsson

Really Rosie - see Carole King

TCB - see Supremes/Temptations

Temptations Show - see Temptations

DATE CHARTED	PEAK POS	WKS CHRT'D	LABEL — Album Title	LABEL & NUMBER

VARIOUS ARTISTS - Label Compilations
a sampling of artists and/or songs are listed beneath each album title

A&M

2/17/68	194	4	1. Family Portrait .... Herb Alpert & The Tijuana Brass/Sergio Mendes & Brasil '66	A&M 19002

ATCO

3/01/69	178	5	2. The Super Groups .... Cream/Iron Butterfly/Rascals/Buffalo Springfield/Bee Gees	Atco 279

ATLANTIC

4/06/68	187	3	3. History of Rhythm & Blues, volume 1/ The Roots 1947-52 .... Ravens/Orioles/Clovers/Cardinals/Ruth Brown/Joe Turner	Atlantic 8161
3/30/68	173	5	4. History of Rhythm & Blues, volume 2/ The Golden Years 1953-55 .... Ruth Brown/Joe Turner/Drifters/Lavern Baker/Chords	Atlantic 8162
4/06/68	189	3	5. History of Rhythm & Blues, volume 3/ Rock & Roll 1956-57 .... Clyde McPhatter/Coasters/Ivory Joe Hunter/Chuck Willis	Atlantic 8163
4/06/68	180	4	6. History of Rhythm & Blues, volume 4/ The Big Beat 1958-60 .... Ray Charles/Ben E. King/Drifters/Coasters/Bobby Darin	Atlantic 8164
11/24/56	20	2	7. Rock & Roll Forever .... 14 selections by Atlantic's top R&B artists	Atlantic 1239
3/19/66	107	19	8. Solid Gold Soul .... Otis Redding/Joe Tex/Wilson Pickett/Solomon Burke/Ben E. King	Atlantic 8116
8/05/67	12	60	9. The Super Hits .... "Respect" Aretha Franklin/"Good Lovin'" Young Rascals	Atlantic 501
7/20/68	76	33	10. The Super Hits, Vol. 2 .... "Groovin'" Rascals/"Soul Man" Sam & Dave	Atlantic 8188
11/23/68	68	19	11. The Super Hits, Vol. 3 .... "Tighten Up" Archie Bell/"Sunshine Of Your Love" Cream	Atlantic 8203
7/19/69	164	10	12. The Super Hits, Vol. 4 .... "Fire" Arthur Brown/"People Got To Be Free" Rascals	Atlantic 8224
3/16/68	146	22	13. This Is Soul .... "Sweet Soul Music" Arthur Conley/"On Broadway" Drifters	Atlantic 8170

BUDDAH

3/22/69	105	9	14. Bubble Gum Music Is The Naked Truth .... 1910 Fruitgum Co./Ohio Express/Lemon Pipers	Buddah 5032

CAPITOL

3/07/70	200	1	15. New Spirit Of Capitol .... sampling of current releases by 13 Capitol rock artists	Capitol 6
6/29/68	130	9	16. Super Oldies/Vol. 3 .... "Ode To Billie Jo" Bobbie Gentry/"Nobody But Me" Human Beinz	Capitol 2910 [2]
7/12/69	196	2	17. Super Oldies/Vol. 5 .... "Galveston" Glen Campbell/"Ramblin' Rose" Nat King Cole	Capitol 216 [2]
6/01/59	5	3	18. **What's New? on Capitol Stereo, vol. 1** .... preview of 12 new Capitol stereo albums	Capitol SN-1
7/10/65	107	7	19. World Of Country Music .... 24 hits by 24 Capitol Records' country artists	Capitol 5 [2]

CAPRICORN

7/30/77	142	11	20. South's Greatest Hits .... Allman Bros./Lynyrd Skynyrd/Charlie Daniels/Marshall Tucker	Capricorn 0187

VARIOUS ARTISTS

DATE CHARTED	PEAK POS	WKS CHRT'D	LABEL — Album Title	LABEL & NUMBER
			CBS	
6/27/81	51	9	21. Exposed/A Cheap Peek At Today's Provocative New Rock .... featuring 11 emerging rock artists on the CBS Label family	CBS 37124 [2]
12/05/81	124	5	22. Exposed II .... featuring 11 more up and coming rock artists on CBS	CBS 37601 [2]
			COLUMBIA	
3/13/71	85	7	23. Different Strokes .... 19 rock songs by 19 Columbia/Epic artists	Columbia 12
8/09/69	151	2	24. Heavy Hits! .... Byrds/Blood, Sweat & Tears/Moby Grape/Laura Nyro/Taj Mahal	Columbia 9840
2/28/70	128	3	25. Heavy Sounds .... Chicago/Big Brother & The Holding Co./It's A Beautiful Day	Columbia 9952
3/18/72	165	6	26. Music People, The .... selections from 40 rock artists on the CBS Labels	Columbia 31280 [3]
7/05/69	182	7	27. Rock's Greatest Hits .... "Red Rubber Ball" Cyrkle/"Turn! Turn! Turn!" Byrds	Columbia 11 [2]
7/20/63	72	12	28. Songs For A Summer Night .... 24 songs by 24 popular artists on the Columbia label	Columbia 2 [2]
6/05/61	1(9)	40	29. **Stars For A Summer Night** .... 25 perfomances by 22 pop and classical artists	Columbia 1 [2]
11/14/70	197	2	30. Super Rock .... 20 selections from Columbia's rock album roster	Columbia 30121 [2]
			DOT	
10/14/67	177	4	31. Golden Instrumentals .... [I] "Tequila" Champs/"Sleepwalk" Santo & Johnny	Dot 25820
			DUNHILL	
8/08/70	197	2	32. Big Hits Now .... 1969-70 hits by 8 ABC/Dunhill artists	Dunhill 50085
12/13/69	166	5	33. Original Hits Of Right Now .... Three Dog Night/Steppenwolf/Grassroots/Smith/Mama Cass	Dunhill 50070
7/26/69	144	7	34. Treasury of Great Contemporary Hits .... "Monday, Monday" Mamas & Papas/"Born To Be Wild" Steppenwolf	Dunhill 50057
			END	
3/20/61	19	23	35. 12 + 3 = 15 Hits .... Flamingos/Chantels/Little Anthony & The Imperials/Dubs	End 310
			FONTANA	
9/09/67	197	1	36. England's Greatest Hits .... Troggs/Wayne Fontana & The Mindbenders/Dusty Springfield	Fontana 67570
			HI	
9/27/69	189	2	37. The Greatest Hits From Memphis .... "Smokie" Bill Black's Combo/"Haunted House" Gene Simmons	Hi 32049
			IMMEDIATE	
12/28/68	200	2	38. An Anthology Of British Blues, Vol. 2 .... John Mayall & The Bluesbreakers/Eric Clapton & Jimmy Page	Immediate 52014
			LAURIE	
1/18/64	80	8	39. Pick Hits of the Radio Good Guys .... "He's So Fine" Chiffons/"The Wanderer" Dion	Laurie 2021 [2]
			LIBERTY	
9/27/69	196	2	40. Underground Gold .... Canned Heat/Traffic/Spencer Davis Group/Johnny Winter	Liberty 7625

DATE CHARTED	PEAK POS	WKS CHRT'D	LABEL — Album Title	LABEL & NUMBER
			MGM	
6/13/70	175	4	41. The Core of Rock .... Janis Ian/Richie Havens/Blues Project/Tim Hardin	MGM 4669
			MOTOWN	
7/09/83	114	9	42. Motown Story: The First Twenty-Five Years .... narrated by Lionel Richie and Smokey Robinson, with comments, interviews and music by Motown's major artists	Motown 6048 [5]
2/22/69	159	4	43. Motown Winners' Circle/No. 1 Hits, Vol. 1 .... "Shop Around"/"Fingertips"/"Where Did Our Love Go"/"Playboy"	Gordy 835
2/22/69	135	5	44. Motown Winners' Circle/No. 1 Hits, Vol. 2 .... "My Guy"/"My Girl"/"Do You Love Me"/"Uptight"	Gordy 936
4/11/64	84	11	45. 16 Original Big Hits .... "Please Mr. Postman" Marvelettes/"Money" Barrett Strong	Motown 614
1/15/66	108	5	46. 16 Original Big Hits, Volume 4 .... "Baby Love" Supremes/"My Guy" Mary Wells	Motown 633
11/05/66	57	19	47. 16 Original Big Hits, Volume 5 .... "My Girl" Temptations/"I Can't Help Myself" Four Tops	Motown 651
2/25/67	95	25	48. 16 Original Big Hits, Volume 6 .... "Going To A Go-Go" Miracles/"Ain't That Peculiar" Marvin Gaye	Motown 655
10/14/67	81	18	49. 16 Original Big Hits, Volume 7 .... "How Sweet It Is" Jr. Walker/"I Hear A Symphony" Supremes	Motown 661
12/30/67	163	7	50. 16 Original Big Hits, Volume 8 .... "Jimmy Mack" Martha & The Vandellas/"Travlin' Man" Stevie Wonder	Motown 666
11/16/68	173	9	51. 16 Original Big Hits, Volume 9 .... "All I Need" Temptations/"Bernadette" Four Tops	Motown 668
4/12/80	150	6	52. 20/20 - Twenty No. 1 Hits From Twenty Years At Motown .... 20 #1 Pop/Black Motown hits from 1969-1979	Motown 937 [2]
6/04/83	42	28	53. 25 #1 Hits From 25 Years .... all but 1 song hit #1 on the "Hot 100" ('61-'81)	Motown 5308 [2]
6/11/83	107	9	54. 25 Years of Grammy Greats .... features 10 Motown hits nominated for Grammys	Motown 5309
			ORIGINAL SOUND	
9/21/59	12	183	55. Oldies But Goodies .... "Earth Angel" Penguins/"In The Still Of The Night" 5 Satins	Original Snd. 5001
8/14/61	12	54	56. Oldies But Goodies, Vol. 3 .... "Come Go With Me" Dell-Vikings/"Sea Cruise" Frankie Ford	Original Snd. 5004
6/16/62	15	39	57. Oldies But Goodies, Vol. 4 .... "Silhouettes" Rays/"Blue Suede Shoes" Carl Perkins	Original Snd. 5005
6/01/63	16	31	58. Oldies But Goodies, Vol. 5 .... "Alley-Oop" Hollywood Argyles/"Little Star" Elegants	Original Snd. 5007
1/25/64	31	11	59. Oldies But Goodies, Vol. 6 .... "Raindrops" Dee Clark/"Quarter To Three" Gary U.S. Bonds	Original Snd. 5011
1/09/65	121	9	60. Oldies But Goodies, Vol. 7 .... "Handy Man" Jimmy Jones/"Donna" Ritchie Valens above 6 albums are R&B/rock oldies collections by the labels' owner, Art Laboe	Original Snd. 5012
			PARKWAY	
11/24/62	110	7	61. All The Hits By All The Stars .... 9 of 12 cuts were Top 10 hits by Cameo/Parkway artists	Parkway 7013
			PARROT	
5/13/67	87	18	62. Greatest Hits From England .... "Go Now" Moody Blues/"She's Not There" Zombies/"Gloria" Them	Parrot 71010

VARIOUS ARTISTS

DATE CHARTED	PEAK POS	WKS CHRT'D	LABEL — Album Title	LABEL & NUMBER
			PHILADELPHIA INTERNATIONAL	
8/06/77	**121**	9	63. Let's Clean Up The Ghetto .... featuring the artists of Philadelphia International Records	Phil. Int. 34659
			RCA	
10/15/55	**9**	8	64. **Pop Shopper** .... 12 selections from RCA Victor's album releases	RCA 12-13
11/30/59	**2(7)**	78	● 65. **60 Years Of Music America Loves Best** .... performances by RCA Victor artists, from Caruso to Belafonte	RCA 6074 [2]
10/31/60	**6**	59	66. **60 Years Of Music America Loves Best, Volume II** .... 30 performances by RCA artists, from Sousa to Eddie Fisher	RCA 6088 [2]
9/04/61	**5**	40	67. **60 Years Of Music America Loves Best, Volume III (Popular)** .... "Frenesi" Artie Shaw/"Night And Day" Frank Sinatra	RCA 1509
			ROULETTE	
7/27/63	**97**	6	68. Golden Goodies, Vol. 1 .... Heartbeats/Harptones/Angels/Frankie Lymon/Devotions	Roulette 25207
7/20/63	**89**	5	69. Golden Goodies, Vol. 2 .... "Gee" Crows/"Why Do Fools Fall In Love" Frankie Lymon	Roulette 25210
8/03/63	**112**	4	70. Golden Goodies, Vol. 3 .... "Speedoo" Cadillacs/"16 Candles" Crests/"Maybe" Chantels	Roulette 25218
7/27/63	**124**	4	71. Golden Goodies, Vol. 5 .... "Book Of Love" Monotones/"So Fine" Fiestas/"Zoom" Cadillacs	Roulette 25215
8/03/63	**86**	3	72. Golden Goodies, Vol. 6 .... "Most Of All" Moonglows/"When You Dance" Turbans above 5 albums are part of a 19 volume oldies series	Roulette 25216
3/20/65	**44**	18	73. 20 Original Winners Of 1964 .... "My Boy Lollipop" Millie Small/"California Sun" Rivieras	Roulette 25293
			SIRE	
4/28/73	**160**	8	74. History Of British Blues, Volume One .... John Mayall/Fleetwood Mac/Yardbirds and others ('62-'70)	Sire 3701 [2]
6/01/74	**198**	2	75. History Of British Rock .... Kinks/Searchers/Rod Stewart/Dave Clark 5 plus 24 more	Sire 3702 [2]
12/21/74	**141**	11	76. History Of British Rock, Vol. 2 .... Beatles/Donovan/Hollies/Cream/Who plus 28 more artists	Sire 3705 [2]
11/22/75	**145**	10	77. History Of British Rock, Volume 3 .... Animals/Zombies/Badfinger/Elton John plus 24 more artists	Sire 3712 [2]
			STAX	
4/05/69	**172**	3	78. Soul Explosion .... 28 songs by 12 artists from Stax Records	Stax 2007 [2]

DATE CHARTED	PEAK POS	WKS CHRT'D	ALBUM TITLE	LABEL & NUMBER

VARIOUS ARTISTS - Radio/TV Celebrity Compilations
collections of hits gathered together by famous radio and TV names

ALAN FREED

2/17/62	**99**	7	1. Alan Freed's Memory Lane .... 14 original fifties R&B hits (narrated by Alan) also see Soundtrack "American Hot Wax"	End 314

DICK CLARK

7/14/73	**27**	18	● 2. Dick Clark/20 Years Of Rock 'N Roll .... original hits from 1953-1972	Buddah 5133 [2]

DR. DEMENTO

11/29/75	**198**	2	3. Dr. Demento's Delights .... [N] includes "They're Coming To Take Me Away, Ha-Haaa!" & "Hello Mudduh, Hello Fadduh!"	Warner 2855

MTV

3/02/85	**91**	6+	4. MTV's Rock 'N Roll To Go .... all proceeds from album are donated to cancer research "Drive" Cars/"She Bop" Cyndi Lauper/"Lucky Star" Madonna/ "King Of Pain" Police/"Hold Me Now" Thompson Twins	Elektra 60399

MURRAY THE K

10/09/61	**63**	29	5. Murray the "K's" Sing Along with the Original Golden Gassers .... "Party Doll" Buddy Knox/"Honeycomb" Jimmie Rodgers Murray The K: disc jockey Murray Kaufman	Roulette 25159
12/25/61	**26**	15	6. Murray the K's Blasts From The Past .... "Sweet Little 16" Chuck Berry/"Bo Diddley" Bo Diddley	Chess 1461
8/04/62	**124**	13	7. Murray the K's Gassers For Submarine Race Watchers .... "Tears On My Pillow" Little Anthony/"Maybe" Chantels	Chess 1470
7/20/63	**69**	10	8. Murray the K's 1962 Boss Golden Gassers ... "Duke Of Earl" Gene Chandler/"Rama Lama Ding Dong" Edsels	Scepter 510
11/30/63	**148**	2	9. Murray The K - Live From The Brooklyn Fox .... [L] Jan & Dean/Gene Pitney/Miracles/Shirelles/Ronettes	KFM 1001

RICHARD NADER

7/28/73	**117**	9	10. Let The Good Times Roll .... [S-L] Richard Nader's Rock & Roll Revival show featuring Little Richard, Fats Domino, Chubby Checker and Bo Diddley	Bell 9002 [2]

WOLFMAN JACK

4/05/75	**84**	10	11. More American Graffiti .... collection of oldies inspired by, but not included in the film "American Graffiti" - introductions by Wolfman Jack	MCA 8007 [2]

DATE CHARTED	PEAK POS	WKS CHRT'D	ALBUM TITLE	LABEL & NUMBER
			## VARIOUS ARTISTS - Concerts/Festivals	
2/22/64	43	17	1. Apollo Saturday Night .... 11/16/63 concert - Otis Redding/Ben E. King/The Coasters	Atco 159
4/08/72	191	4	2. Big Sur Festival/One Hand Clapping .... 8th annual folk festival featuring Joan Baez and 5 others	Columbia 31138
7/22/78	84	10	3. California Jam 2 .... 3/18/78 concert in Ontario, California - Aerosmith/Heart/ Ted Nugent/Santana and 4 others	Columbia 35389 [2]
			Concert For Bangla Desh - see George Harrison	
4/18/81	36	12	4. Concerts For The People Of Kampuchea .... December, 1979 four day benefit concert in London, England The Who/Paul McCartney/Pretenders/Rockestra and 6 others	Atlantic 7005 [2]
9/18/71	47	9	5. First Great Rock Festivals Of The Seventies: Isle Of Wight/Atlanta Pop Festival .... Jimi Hendrix/Allman Brothers/Johnny Winter and 11 others	Columbia 30805[3]
7/15/72	40	16	6. Fillmore: The Last Days .... Bill Graham's Fillmore-San Francisco rock shows ran from 11/6/65-7/4/71 - album includes a booklet & 7" interview record	Fillmore 31390 [3]
			Last Waltz - see Band	
10/25/69	200	2	7. Live At Bill Graham's Fillmore West .... Mike Bloomfield/Taj Mahal/Nick Gravenites	Columbia 9893
			Live At Yankee Stadium - see Isley Brothers	
10/07/72	186	7	8. Mar y Sol .... Rock festival held in Puerto Rico for 4 days in April, 1972 Allman Bros./John McLaughlin/Emerson, Lake & Palmer/Dr. John	Atco 705 [2]
			Monterey International Pop Festival - see Otis Redding/Jimi Hendrix	
			Montreux Jazz Festival - see Various-Jazz "Casino Lights"	
6/08/63	47	14	9. Motor-Town Review, Vol. 1 .... recorded at New York's Apollo Theatre	Motown 609
5/30/64	102	5	10. Motortown Review, Vol. 2 .... recorded at Detroit's Fox Theatre	Motown 615
12/18/65	111	7	11. Motortown Review In Paris .... recorded at Olympia Music Hall in Paris, France	Tamla 264
8/23/69	177	5	12. Motortown Review Live .... above 4 albums feature Motown's top recording artists	Motown 688
4/11/70	105	4	13. Motown at the Hollywood Palace .... Supremes/Jackson 5/Stevie Wonder/Gladys Knight & The Pips	Motown 703
8/18/79	171	4	14. Music for UNICEF Concert/A Gift Of Song .... benefit concert on 1/9/79 at the United Nations Abba/Bee Gees/Rod Stewart/Donna Summer/John Denver	Polydor 6214
12/22/79	19	18	● 15. No Nukes/The MUSE Concerts For A Non-Nuclear Future .... benefit concerts at New York's Madison Square Garden Jackson Browne/Bruce Springsteen/Tom Petty/Doobie Bros.	Asylum 801 [3]
11/07/64	95	8	16. Saturday Night At The Uptown .... concert featuring the Drifters, Wilson Pickett, Patti LaBelle and others at the Uptown Theatre in Philadelphia	Atlantic 8101
5/23/81	106	12	17. Secret Policeman's Ball/The Music .... Pete Townshend/Tom Robinson/Neil Innes/John Williams	Island 9630
3/20/82	29	16	18. Secret Policeman's Other Ball/ The Music .... Sting/Jeff Beck & Eric Clapton/Phil Collins/Donovan above 2 albums are benefit concerts recorded in London	Island 9698
9/25/71	112	10	19. Soul To Soul .... [S] concert film featuring Roberta Flack/Wilson Pickett/ Eddie Harris & Les McCann/Ike & Tina Turner/Staple Singers	Atlantic 7207

VARIOUS ARTISTS

DATE CHARTED	PEAK POS	WKS CHRT'D	ALBUM TITLE	LABEL & NUMBER
9/02/67	**145**	4	20. Stax/Volt Revue - Live In London .... Booker T. & The MG's/Sam & Dave/Otis Redding and 3 others	Stax 721
			Tarantella - see Chuck Mangione	
9/26/81	**173**	3	21. Urgh! A Music War .... previously unreleased live performances by Police/Go-Go's/ Devo/Joan Jett & The Blackhearts and 24 other rock acts	A&M 6019 [2]
7/24/76	**153**	6	22. Volunteer Jam .... side 1: Charlie Daniels Band: side 2: Marshall Tucker Band, Dicky Betts and others	Capricorn 0172
7/19/80	**104**	9	23. Volunteer Jam VI .... guests: Ted Nugent/Wet Willie/Crystal Gayle & others	Epic 36438 [2]
7/25/81	**149**	4	24. Volunteer Jam VII .... above 3 albums are concerts hosted by the Charlie Daniels Band which were held in Tennessee	Epic 37178
2/17/73	**28**	17	● 25. Wattstax: The Living Word .... [S] Isaac Hayes/Staple Singers/Rufus & Carla Thomas/Eddie Floyd	Stax 3010 [2]
9/15/73	**157**	5	26. Wattstax 2: The Living Word .... [S] above 2 albums are from the Soundtrack of the filmed concert in memory of the 7th anniversary of the Watts' riots	Stax 3018 [2]
6/06/70	**1(4)**	68	● 27. **Woodstock** .... [S] film of historic rock festival near Woodstock, New York on August 15-17, 1969 - Jimi Hendrix/Crosby. Stills, Nash & Young/Santana/The Who/Ten Years After/Joe Cocker/Sha-Na-Na	Cotillion 500 [3]
4/10/71	**7**	17	● 28. **Woodstock Two** .... [S] more songs from the festival - Jefferson Airplane/Joan Baez/ Melanie/Mountain/Canned Heat/Butterfield Blues Band	Cotillion 400 [2]

DATE CHARTED	PEAK POS	WKS CHRT'D	ALBUM TITLE	LABEL & NUMBER
			VARIOUS ARTISTS - Rock Operas/ Concept Albums	
3/16/85	105+	4+	1. Chess .... a new musical written by Tim Rice and Abba's Benny Anderson & Bjorn Ulvaeus - features vocalists Murray Head, Elaine Paige & Barbara Dickson, and the London Symphony Orchestra	Chess 5340 [2]
2/14/70	95	13	2. DisinHAIRited .... songs written for, but not included in the musical "Hair"	RCA 1163
10/13/84	75	10	3. Every Man Has A Woman .... all songs written by Yoko Ono - featuring John Lennon, Sean Ono Lennon, Harry Nilsson, Elvis Costello, Eddie Money, Rosanne Cash, Roberta Flack and others	Casablanca 823490
			Godspell - see Soundtrack and Original Cast versions	
			Hair - see Soundtrack and Original Cast versions	
11/21/70	1(3)	101	● 4. **Jesus Christ Superstar** .... a rock opera featuring Ian Gillan (Jesus), Murray Head and Yvonne Elliman - mu: Andrew Lloyd Webber: ly: Tim Rice also see Soundtrack and Original Cast versions	Decca 7206 [2]
4/03/71	84	12	5. Joseph and the Amazing Technicolor Dreamcoat .... Andrew Lloyd Webber & Tim Rice's first rock opera	Scepter 588
1/15/83	109	14	6. Kris, Willie, Dolly & Brenda...the winning hand .... KRIS KRISTOFFERSON, WILLIE NELSON, DOLLY PARTON & BRENDA LEE - a Fred Foster production	Monmnt.38389[2]
12/06/80	154	13	7. Legend Of Jesse James .... a biographical album written and composed by Paul Kennerley - featuring Levon Helm (Jesse), Johnny Cash, Emmylou Harris, Charlie Daniels and Albert Lee	A&M 3718
2/07/76	10	51	▲ 8. **The Outlaws** .... WAYLON JENNINGS, WILLIE NELSON, JESSI COLTER, TOMPALL GLASER	RCA 1321
12/27/75	192	3	9. Threads of Glory - 200 years of America in words & music .... 6 volume boxed set tracing America's history using music, sound effects & many famous guest narrators (Ronald Reagan/ Henry Fonda/Burt Lancaster/Walter Pidgeon and 23 more)	Ln. Ph. 4 14000 [6]
12/09/72	5	38	● 10. **Tommy** .... featuring the London Symphony Orchestra and English Chamber Choir with guests Pete Townshend, Roger Daltrey, Rod Stewart, Ringo Starr and others - also see The Who/Soundtrack versions	Ode 99001 [2]
12/18/71	185	7	11. Truth Of Truths - A Contemporary Rock Opera .... based on the Old and New Testaments - featuring Jim Backus (God) and Donnie Brooks (Jesus) - concept by Ray Ruff	Oak 1001 [2]
8/12/78	98	25	12. War Of The Worlds .... musical version by Jeff Wayne of H.G. Wells' classic story - narration by Richard Burton: songs performed by Justin Hayward, David Essex and others	Columbia 35290 [2]
7/22/78	181	4	13. White Mansions .... a portrayal of life in the Confederate States of America 1861-1865 - written by Paul Kennerley, with songs performed by Waylon Jennings, Jessi Colter and others	A&M 6004

DATE CHARTED	PEAK POS	WKS CHRT'D	ALBUM TITLE	LABEL & NUMBER
			VARIOUS ARTISTS - Jazz	
8/05/78	**151**	6	1. Alivemutherforya .... [I-L] quintet of jazz/fusion musicians from the CBS Records family	Columbia 35349
11/13/82	**63**	19	2. Casino Lights .... [L] recorded live at the Montreux Jazz Festival in Switzerland	Warner 23718
2/06/82	**105**	11	3. Echoes Of An Era .... contemporary jazz artists (Chaka Khan/Freddie Hubbard/ Chick Corea & others) performing classic songs	Elektra 60021
8/02/80	**168**	5	4. Empire Jazz .... [I] adaptation by 10 jazz musicians of "The Empire Strikes Back"	**RSO** 3085
7/09/55	**5**	11	5. I Like Jazz! .... [K] a sampling of the development of jazz (ragtime, swing, etc.)	Columbia 1
1/27/79	**122**	8	6. Milestone Jazzstars In Concert .... [I-L] McCoy Tyner/Ron Carter/Sonny Rollins/Al Foster	Milestone 55006 [2]
10/20/84	**108**	25	7. Windham Hill Records Sampler '84 .... [I] George Winston/Michael Hedges/Alex de Grassi and 6 others	Windham Hill 1035
			VARIOUS ARTISTS - Dance/Disco	
6/27/64	**102**	6	1. dance Discotheque .... Peter Duchin/Tommy Dorsey, and the Discotheque Orchestra	Decca 74556
12/24/77	**115**	11	2. Disco Boogie .... 10 Salsoul artists perform their disco hits	Salsoul 0101 [2]
7/26/75	**153**	5	3. Disco Gold .... an early album of new disco-mixed songs	Scepter 5120
7/15/78	**115**	12	4. Disco Party .... disco hits by 12 artists from the T.K. Record family	Marlin 2207/8 [2]
4/28/79	**159**	5	5. Disco Spectacular Inspired by the Film "Hair" .... Evelyn King, Vicki Sue Robinson and 3 other disco groups	RCA 3356
9/08/84	**147**	9	6. Electric Breakdance .... Newcleus/Grandmaster Flash & Melle Mel/Twilight 22	Dominion 2320
4/10/76	**177**	2	7. Hustle Hits! .... original long disco versions by Kool & The Gang and 5 others	De-Lite 2019
7/28/79	**21**	25	● 8. Night At Studio 54 .... specially sequenced disco favorites at the New York club	Casablanca 7161 [2]
9/06/80	**69**	7	9. Winners .... 15 specially sequenced disco tracks for dancing	I&M 017

DATE CHARTED	PEAK POS	WKS CHRT'D	ARTIST — Album Title	LABEL & NUMBER
			AEROBICS albums for aerobic exercising - with music, narration, instructions and illustrations	
			BARBARA ANN AUER	
6/20/81	**145**	15	1. Aerobic Dancing .... written by Barbara; narration by Alan de Mause - music by the Salsoul Orchestra and others	Gateway 7610
			CARLA CAPUANO	
3/13/82	**152**	8	2. Aerobic Dance Hits, volume one .... music by Kool & The Gang and others	Casablanca 7263
			JULIE CONWAY	
1/09/61	**73**	17	3. Good Housekeeping's Plan For Reducing Off-The-Record .... music: The Bob Prince Quartet - the 1st "aerobics" album	Harmony 7143
			JANE FONDA	
5/29/82	**15**	120	▲ 4. Jane Fonda's Workout Record .... music: Jacksons/REO Speedwagon/Brothers Johnson/Boz Scaggs	Columbia 38054 [2]
5/21/83	**117**	7	5. Jane Fonda's Workout Record For Pregnancy, Birth And Recovery .... music by a special studio group	Columbia 38675 [2]
8/18/84	**135**	10	6. Jane Fonda's Workout Record - New And Improved .... music: Michael Jackson/REO Speedwagon/Sylvester/Quincy Jones	Columbia 39287 [2]
			LINDA FRATIANNE	
2/20/82	**174**	7	7. Dance & Exercise With The Hits .... music performed by The Beachwood All-Stars (studio group)	Columbia 37653
			JOANIE GREGGAINS	
6/18/83	**177**	4	8. Aerobic Shape-Up II .... music by studio musicians	Parade 106
			CAROL HENSEL	
3/21/81	**56**	55	9. Carol Hensel's Exercise & Dance Program ..... originally titled "Dancersize" on Vintage 7701	Vintage 7713
12/19/81	**70**	28	10. Carol Hensel's Exercise & Dance Program, Volume 2	Vintage 7733
1/22/83	**104**	12	11. Carol Hensel's Exercise & Dance Program, Volume 3 .... above 3 albums feature music by studio musicians	Vintage 30004
			JUDI SHEPPARD MISSETT	
12/05/81	**117**	20	● 12. Jazzercise .... music by studio musicians	MCA 5272
			DEBBIE REYNOLDS	
5/26/84	**182**	3	13. Do It Debbie's Way .... music by a "switched on swing" big band	K-Tel 9190
			RICHARD SIMMONS	
6/05/82	**44**	40	▲ 14. Reach .... songs sung by Simmons, backed by studio musicians	Elektra 60122
			KATHY SMITH	
3/13/82	**144**	13	15. Kathy Smith's Aerobic Fitness .... music by studio musicians	MuscleTone 72151

DATE CHARTED	PEAK POS	WKS CHRT'D		ALBUM TITLE	LABEL & NUMBER
				CHILDRENS children oriented albums	
				MICKEY MOUSE	
5/03/75	**51**	13		1. Mickey Mouse Club .... [TV] Jimmie Dodd/Annette/Spin & Marty/Mouseketeers	Disneyland 1362
4/12/80	**35**	27	▲	2. Mickey Mouse Disco .... disco songs performed by session musicians	Disneyland 2504
				SESAME STREET/MUPPETS	
7/25/70	**23**	54	●	3. Sesame Street Book & Record .... [TV] Loretta Long/Bob McGrath/Jim Henson's Muppets & cast	Columbia 1069
12/11/71	**78**	10		4. Sesame Street 2 .... [TV] above 2 albums feature songs performed by original TV cast	Warner 2569
9/09/78	**75**	10	●	5. Sesame Street Fever .... parody of "Saturday Night Fever" - with guest, Robin Gibb	Sesame St. 79005
8/15/70	**126**	11		6. Bob McGrath from Sesame Street .... "Sesame Street" co-star talks and sings with a children's chorus	Affinity 1001
8/01/70	**86**	13		7. Susan sings songs from Sesame Street .... Susan (Loretta Long) sings with a children's chorus	Scepter 584
12/25/71	**189**	4		8. The Muppet Alphabet Album .... Muppets: puppeteers created by Jim Henson for TV's "Sesame Street" - includes blackboard, chalk and a set of letters	Columbia 25503
7/21/79	**32**	34	●	9. The Muppet Movie .... [S] "Rainbow Connection" - Kermit	Atlantic 16001
7/11/81	**66**	11		10. The Great Muppet Caper .... [S]	Atlantic 16047
1/21/78	**153**	5		11. The Muppet Show .... [TV] featuring Frank Oz performing as Fozzie Bear & Miss Piggy	Arista 4152
11/10/79	**26**	12	▲	12. A Christmas Together .... [X] JOHN DENVER & THE MUPPETS	RCA 3451
				VARIOUS ARTISTS	
1/10/81	**156**	5		13. In Harmony - A Sesame Street Record .... Doobie Brothers/Carly Simon/James Taylor and 12 others	Sesame St. 3481
11/21/81	**129**	10		14. In Harmony 2 .... Billy Joel/Bruce Springsteen/Kenny Loggins and 9 others above 2 albums are family-oriented, featuring superstars	Columbia 37641
1/06/73	**68**	58	●	15. Free To Be...You And Me .... songs and stories for children, starring Marlo Thomas with guests Diana Ross, Alan Alda, Harry Belafonte, Mel Brooks, Carol Channing, Tom Smothers, Dick Cavett and others	Bell 1110

Also see the following names for more Children oriented albums:

Archies
Chipmunks
Tom Glazer
Hardy Boys
Carole King
Limeliters
Art Linkletter
Lou Monte
Cyril Ritchard
Royal Guardsmen
Soupy Sales

Soundtracks:
Annie (also Original Cast &
  Christmas albums)
Aristocats
Jungle Book
Lord of The Rings
Mary Poppins
Popeye
Scrooge

DATE CHARTED	PEAK POS	WKS CHRT'D	ARTIST — Album Title	LABEL & NUMBER
			CHRISTMAS The following various artist/specialty Christmas albums made Billboard's regular Top LPs charts:	
11/20/82	**96**	9	1. Annie's Christmas .... children's story with music, narration and dialogue - Annie: Robin Ignico; narrator: William Woodson	Columbia 38361
12/25/82	**172**	4	2. Country Christmas, A .... Charley Pride/Alabama/Willie Nelson/Jim Ed Brown + 6 others	RCA 4396
12/30/57	**19**	3	3. Merry Christmas .... [EP] 7″ E.P. (originally released as a 10″ LP in 1952) Ames Brothers/Don Cornell/Johnny Desmond/Eileen Barton	Coral 82003
12/21/74	**125**	2	4. The Walton's Christmas Album .... album cover pictures TV's "The Waltons" - songs performed by The Holiday Singers - narration by Earl Hamner (creator of The Waltons)	Columbia 33193
			For the years 1963 thru 1973, Billboard did not chart Christmas albums on their regular Top LPs charts. Instead, they issued special Christmas charts for 3-4 weeks during each Christmas season. These special charts were discontinued from 1974 thru 1982 when Billboard again charted Christmas albums on their regular album charts. For the years 1983 and 1984, Billboard again issued special Christmas charts; however, they also listed the best selling Christmas albums on their regular Top LPs charts. The following list includes only those albums which made the TOP 10 of Billboard's special CHRISTMAS ALBUMS chart, and never made Billboard's regular Top LPs charts. The number in brackets after title indicates total years (Christmas seasons) album made Billboard's Christmas charts.	
			HERB ALPERT & THE TIJUANA BRASS	
12/07/68	**1(2)**	8	● 1. Herb Alpert & The Tijuana Brass Christmas Album [2 yrs.] .... [I]	A&M 4166
			JULIE ANDREWS	
12/02/67	**9**	1	2. A Christmas Treasure .... with the orchestra, harpsichord & arrangements of Andre Previn	RCA 3829
			JOAN BAEZ	
12/03/66	**6**	5	3. Noel [2 yrs.]	Vanguard 79230
			BEACH BOYS	
12/05/64	**6**	3	● 4. The Beach Boys' Christmas Album [2 yrs.] .. "Little Saint Nick"/"The Man With All The Toys"	Capitol 2164
			TONY BENNETT	
12/14/68	**10**	1	5. Snowfall/The Tony Bennett Christmas Album	Columbia 9739
			BOSTON POPS ORCHESTRA/ARTHUR FIEDLER	
12/19/70	**9**	1	6. A Christmas Festival .... [I]	Polydor 5004
			BRADY BUNCH	
12/25/71	**6**	1	7. Merry Christmas from the Brady Bunch	Paramount 5026
			JAMES BROWN	
12/13/69	**10**	1	8. A Soulful Christmas	King 1040
			GLEN CAMPBELL	
12/07/68	**1(2)**	6	● 9. That Christmas Feeling [2 yrs.]	Capitol 2978

CHRISTMAS

DATE CHARTED	PEAK POS	WKS CHRT'D	ARTIST — Album Title	LABEL & NUMBER
			RAMSEY LEWIS TRIO	
12/19/64	8	2	27. More Sounds of Christmas .... [I]	Argo 745
			BARBARA MANDRELL	
12/15/84	8	2	28. Christmas At Our Home	MCA 5519
			MANTOVANI & His Orchestra	
12/14/63	7	3	29. Christmas Greetings From Mantovani [2 yrs.] .... [I]	London 338
			DEAN MARTIN	
12/03/66	1(1)	14	● 30. The Dean Martin Christmas Album [4 yrs.] .	Reprise 6222
			AL MARTINO	
12/12/64	8	2	31. A Merry Christmas	Capitol 2165
			JOHNNY MATHIS	
11/30/63	2(2)	7	32. Sounds Of Christmas [2 yrs.]	Mercury 60837
12/06/69	1(1)	15	● 33. Give Me Your Love For Christmas [4 yrs.]	Columbia 9923
			MORMON TABERNACLE CHOIR	
12/11/65	8	1	● 34. The Joy of Christmas .... with Leonard Bernstein conducting the New York Philharmonic	Columbia 6499
12/20/69	3	4	35. Handel: Messiah [3 yrs.] .... with Eugene Ormandy conducting The Philadelphia Orchestra featured vocalists: Eileen Farrell (soprano) & William Warfield (baritone)	Columbia 607 [2]
			JIM NABORS	
12/09/67	1(1)	17	● 36. Jim Nabors' Christmas Album [6 yrs.]	Columbia 9531
			NEW CHRISTY MINSTRELS	
12/28/63	5	1	37. Merry Christmas!	Columbia 8896
			WAYNE NEWTON	
12/03/66	10	3	38. Songs For A Merry Christmas	Capitol 2588
			PARTRIDGE FAMILY	
12/04/71	1(4)	6	● 39. A Partridge Family Christmas Card [2 yrs.]	Bell 6066
			LUCIANO PAVAROTTI	
12/17/83	6	4	● 40. O Holy Night [2 yrs.] .... with Kurt Adler conducting the National Philharmonic (recorded 1976)	London 26473
			ELVIS PRESLEY	
12/05/70	2(3)	5	41. Elvis' Christmas Album [2 yrs.] .... 8 of 10 songs are from his 1957 Christmas album "If Every Day Was Like Christmas"/"Mama Liked The Roses"	RCA Camden 2428
12/04/71	1(3)	12	▲ 42. Elvis sings The Wonderful World of Christmas [3 yrs.] .... an all new Christmas LP (recorded May, 1971)	RCA LSP-4579
			CHARLEY PRIDE	
12/12/70	5	6	43. Christmas in My Home Town [3 yrs.]	RCA 4406

CHRISTMAS

DATE CHARTED	PEAK POS	WKS CHRT'D	ARTIST — Album Title	LABEL & NUMBER
			LOU RAWLS	
12/02/67	**2(1)**	5	44. Merry Christmas Ho! Ho! Ho!	Capitol 2790
			PAUL REVERE & THE RAIDERS	
12/09/67	**10**	1	45. A Christmas Present . . . And Past	Columbia 9555
			ROBERT SHAW CHORALE & ORCHESTRA	
12/07/68	**8**	2	46. Handel: Messiah .... "Messiah" was composed by George Frideric Handel from 8/22 to 9/14, 1741	RCA 6175
			BOBBY SHERMAN	
12/12/70	**2(1)**	3	47. Bobby Sherman Christmas Album	Metromedia 1038
			HARRY SIMEONE CHORALE	
12/03/66	**5**	4	48. O Bambino/The Little Drummer Boy [3 yrs.]. Includes Simeone's new recording of "The Little Drummer Boy"	Kapp 3450
			SINATRA FAMILY	
12/13/69	**3**	2	49. The Sinatra Family Wish You A Merry Christmas .... Frank and daughters Nancy & Tina, and son Frank Jr.	Reprise 1026
			JIMMY SMITH	
12/05/64	**8**	1	50. Christmas '64 .... [I]	Verve 8604
			SUPREMES	
12/11/65	**6**	3	51. Merry Christmas	Motown 638
			TEMPTATIONS	
12/19/70	**4**	5	52. The Temptations' Christmas Card [3 yrs.]	Gordy 951
12/17/83	**6**	2	53. Give Love At Christmas	Gordy 998
			VENTURES	
12/18/65	**9**	2	54. The Ventures' Christmas Album .... [I]	Dolton 8038
			ANDY WILLIAMS	
11/30/63	**1(9)**	26	● 55. The Andy Williams Christmas Album [8 yrs.]	Columbia 8887
12/18/65	**1(3)**	12	● 56. Merry Christmas [4 yrs.]	Columbia 9220
			VARIOUS ARTISTS	
12/09/72	**7**	3	57. Christmas Album, The [2 yrs.] .... features songs by Barbra Streisand, Mahalia Jackson, Johnny Mathis, Frank Sinatra, Tony Bennett, Johnny Cash & 14 others	Columbia 30763 [2]
12/01/73	**7**	1	58. Christmas Greetings from Nashville .... features Eddy Arnold, Chet Atkins, Jim Reeves & 7 others	RCA 0262
12/08/73	**1(1)**	3	59. Motown Christmas, A .... Temptations/Stevie Wonder/Jackson Five/Miracles/Supremes	Motown 795 [2]
12/05/70	**7**	1	60. Peace On Earth .... Beach Boys/Glen Campbell/Nat King Cole/Lettermen + 13 others	Capitol 585 [2]

DATE CHARTED	PEAK POS	WKS CHRT'D	ARTIST — Album Title	LABEL & NUMBER
12/23/72	6	3	61. Phil Spector's Christmas Album [2 yrs.] .... Crystals/Ronettes/Darlene Love/Bob B. Soxx & Blue Jeans - reissue of "A Christmas Gift For You" (Philles/1963)	Apple 3400
12/06/69	8	2	62. Soul Christmas [2 yrs.] .... Otis Redding/Clarence Carter/Joe Tex plus 5 others	Atco 269

Refer to the following names in the Artist Section for the
Christmas albums that made the regular Top LPs charts:

Ames Brothers	Ramsey Lewis	Kenny Rogers (2)
Harry Belafonte	Norman Luboff Choir	Royal Guardsmen
Pat Boone	Mannheim Steamroller	Salsoul Orchestra (2)
Carpenters (2)	Mantovani	John Schneider
Chipmunks (2)	Johnny Mathis	Robert Shaw Chorale
Perry Como (2)	Meco	Harry Simeone Chorale
Ray Conniff (2)	George Melachrino	Frank Sinatra
Bing Crosby (3)	Mitch Miller (2)	Statler Brothers
John Denver (2)	Montana Orchestra	Barbra Streisand
Frank DeVol	Mormon Tabernacle Choir	Billy Vaughn
Tennessee Ernie Ford	Anne Murray	Bobby Vee
Jackie Gleason	Willie Nelson	Fred Waring
Emmylou Harris	Oak Ridge Boys	Lawrence Welk (3)
Engelbert Humperdinck	Osmonds	Slim Whitman
Mahalia Jackson	Philadelphia Orchestra	Roger Williams
Kingston Trio	Elvis Presley	George Winston
Mario Lanza	Leontyne Price	Soundtrack - Scrooge
Lennon Sisters	Robert Rheims (2)	

DATE CHARTED	PEAK POS	WKS CHRT'D	ALBUM TITLE	LABEL & NUMBER
			CLASSICAL various artist compilations	
4/25/64	**70**	15	1. Great Voices Of The Century .... 12 classical greats including Enrico Caruso & John McCormack	Angel 4
7/15/72	**176**	7	2. Metropolitan Opera Gala honoring Sir Rudolf Bing .... [L] Bing: general manager of the Opera from 1950-1972 featuring opera stars Leontyne Price, Placido Domingo, Robert Merrill, Martina Arroyo and 6 others	DG 2530 260
10/08/66	**49**	21	3. Opening Nights at the Met .... historic recordings by opera stars who performed at New York's old Metropolitan Opera House from 1883-1965	RCA 6171 [3]
9/04/61	**6**	18	4. **60 Years Of Music America Loves Best, Volume III (Red Seal)** .... Caruso/Fiedler/Toscanini plus 9 more classical greats	RCA 2574
5/11/63	**39**	8	5. Sound of Genius .... 19 favorites by 18 of Columbia's greatest classical artists	Columbia SGS 1 [2]
6/16/62	**24**	14	6. Summer Festival .... 19 favorites by 20 of RCA's greatest classical artists	RCA 6097 [2]

Refer to the following names in the Artist Section for more classical albums:

Geza Anda	Reverberi
Leonard Bernstein (2)	Sviatoslav Richter
Jussi Bjoerling	Waldo de Los Rios
Boston Pops/Arthur Fiedler (18)	Royal Philharmonic Orchestra (3)
Boston Pops/John Williams	Arthur Rubinstein (2)
Boston Symphony Orchestra (3)	San Francisco Symphony Orchestra
Benjamin Britten	Beverly Sills
Maria Callas	Swingle Singers
Walter Carlos (4)	Tomita (7)
Cleveland Orchestra	
Van Cliburn (5)	SOUNDTRACKS:
Placido Domingo (3)	Barry Lyndon
Antal Dorati (2)	Clockwork Orange
Carmen Dragon	Interlude
Virgil Fox	Manhattan
James Galway	Rollerball
Philip Glass	Song of Norway
Morton Gould (2)	2001: A Space Odyssey (2)
George Greeley	War & Peace
Vladimir Horowitz (5)	
Mario Lanza (7)	ORIGINAL CAST:
Neville Marriner	The Merry Widow
Zubin Mehta (2)	Treemonisha
Mormon Tabernacle Choir (4)	
Leonard Pennario	TELEVISION SHOWS:
Philadelphia Orchestra (3)	Cosmos
Leontyne Price (5)	Victory At Sea (2)

DATE CHARTED	PEAK POS	WKS CHRT'D	ALBUM TITLE	LABEL & NUMBER
			COMEDY comedy concept productions	
12/29/62	**47**	12	1. At Home With That Other Family .... parody of Russia's Krushchevs - George Segal, Joan Rivers	Roulette 25203
1/11/69	**190**	6	2. Beware Of Greeks Bearing Gifts .... starring Susan Anspach & Joe Silver + 7 others	Musicor 3173
6/05/71	**148**	9	3. Child's Garden Of Grass (A Pre-Legalization Comedy) .... narrated by Michael Gwynne & Carl Esser	Elektra 75012
1/16/71	**185**	3	4. Earle Doud Presents Spiro T. Agnew Is A Riot! .... featuring Stanley Myron Handelman with Rich Little, Vincent Price and Pat McCormick	Cadet Concept 1
7/22/72	**178**	6	5. Everything You Always Wanted To Know About The Godfather - But Don't Ask .... starring Chuck McCann (The Godfather) & Steve Landesberg	Columbia 31608
7/11/64	**96**	14	6. First Nine Months are the hardest! .... starring Len Weinrib & Joyce Jameson - director: Carl Reiner	Capitol 2034
10/19/63	**87**	10	7. Fool Britannia .... Peter Sellers/Joan Collins/Anthony Newley	Acappella 1
12/18/65	**93**	9	8. James Blonde, Secret Agent 006.95, "The Man From T.A.N.T.E." .... starring Marty Brill & Larry Foster	Colpix 495
11/06/71	**183**	7	9. Jewish American Princess .... starring Judy Graubart, Frank Gallop, Lou Jacobi + 6 others	Bell 6063
1/20/68	**176**	5	10. Lyndon Johnson's Lonely Hearts Club Band .... featuring the actual recorded voices of political leaders	Atco 230
12/17/66	**72**	10	11. New First Family, 1968 .... starring David Frye & John Byner + 4 others	Verve 15054
12/29/62	**27**	13	12. Other Family, The .... starring Larry Foster, Marty Brill and Toby Deane	Laurie 5000
9/10/66	**40**	14	13. Our Wedding Album or The Great Society Affair .... spoof of President Johnson's family - with Kenny Solms, Gail Parent, Fannie Flagg, Robert Klein & Jo Ann Worley	Jamie 3028
1/12/63	**35**	13	14. President Strikes Back! .... an answer album to Vaughn Meader's "The First Family" starring Marc London and Sylvia Miles	Kapp 1322
6/23/73	**62**	18	15. Watergate Comedy Hour .... with Frank Welker (Nixon), Fannie Flagg and 5 others	Hidden 11202
11/27/65	**3**	25	● 16. **Welcome to the LBJ Ranch!** .... featuring the actual recorded voices of political leaders	Capitol 2423
4/02/66	**22**	18	17. When You're In Love The Whole World Is Jewish .... starring Betty Walker, Lou Jacobi, Frank Gallop and 4 others	Kapp 4506
10/14/67	**165**	5	18. Yiddish Are Coming! The Yiddish Are Coming! .... starring Lou Jacobi, Betty Walker, Frank Gallop and 7 others	Verve 15058
9/18/65	**9**	34	19. **You Don't Have To Be Jewish** .... starring Betty Walker, Lou Jacobi, Frank Gallop and 5 others	Kapp 4503

Refer to the following names in the Artist Section
for more comedy albums:

Dayton Allen
Steve Allen
Woody Allen
Don Ameche & Frances Langford (2)
Gertrude Berg
Edgar Bergen & Charlie McCarthy -
   see W.C. Fields
Shelley Berman (5)
Lenny Bruce (2)
Victor Buono
Godfrey Cambridge (2)
George Carlin (9)
Cheech & Chong (7)
Cassius Clay
Myron Cohen
Pat Cooper
Bill Cosby (18)
Bill Dana (7)
Rodney Dangerfield (2)
W.C. Fields (2)
Firesign Theatre (8)
Fannie Flagg
Redd Foxx (3)
Stan Freberg
David Frye (4)
Dave Gardner (6)

Dick Gregory (2)
Wes Harrison
Bob Hope
Hudson & Landry (3)
Jerry Jordan
Robert Klein
Tom Lehrer (2)
Rich Little
Moms Mabley (13)
Charlie Manna
Pigmeat Markham
Steve Martin (4)
Groucho Marx/Marx Bros. (2)
Jackie Mason
Bob & Doug McKenzie
Vaughn Meader (2)
Monty Python (6)
Martin Mull (2)
Eddie Murphy (2)
National Lampoon (3)
Bob Newhart (6)
Mike Nichols & Elaine May (3)
Pat Paulsen
Richard Pryor (10)
Gilda Radner
Carl Reiner & Mel Brooks

Don Rickles (2)
Joan Rivers
Mort Sahl (2)
Father Guido Sarducci
Kermit Schafer
Allan Sherman (7)
Smothers Brothers (10)
David Steinberg
Lily Tomlin (3)
Jimmie Walker
Rusty Warren (7)
Orson Welles
Wild Man Steve (2)
Robin Williams (2)
Flip Wilson (5)
Jonathan Winters (6)
Woody Woodbury (3)

TELEVISION SECTiON:
All In The Family (2)
Laugh-In (2)
Saturday Night Live
Tonight Show/
   Johnny Carson

DATE CHARTED	PEAK POS	WKS CHRT'D	ALBUM TITLE	LABEL & NUMBER

MISCELLANEOUS

The following albums, because of their unusual content, are listed in this section and are categorized with special headings.

BASEBALL

11/22/69	197	1	1. The Amazing Mets .... featuring the singing voices of the New York Mets - 1969 World Series Champs (note label number)	Buddah 1969

CARS

12/14/63	27	18	2. Big Sounds Of The Drags! .... actual sounds of drag racing at a quarter-mile track	Capitol 2001
2/15/64	138	3	3. Hot Rod Hootenanny .... [N] novelty hot rod songs featuring The Weirdos and the voice of Mr. Gasser (Ed "Big Daddy" Roth)	Capitol 2010
12/14/63	62	15	4. Hot Rod Rally .... car songs by The Super Stocks/Hot Rod Rog/Shutdown Douglas	Capitol 1997
7/13/63	7	46	5. Shut Down .... "Shut Down" Beach Boys/"Black Denim Trousers" Cheers, plus 10 other car oriented songs	Capitol 1918

HOOTENANNY

7/20/63	99	6	6. At The Hootenanny .... [L] Chad Mitchell Trio/Terry Gilkyson/David Hill and 4 others	Kapp 3330
8/31/63	128	4	7. The Original Hootenanny .... Limeliters/Judy Collins/Bud & Travis and 9 more folk artists	Crestview 806

MINSTREL SHOW

5/26/56	9	9	8. Gentlemen, Be Seated .... recreation of a complete minstrel show (conducted by Allen Roth) - also see Eric Rogers "Vaudeville"	Epic 3238

OLYMPICS

7/14/84	92	13	9. Official Music Of The XXIIIrd Olympiad Los Angeles 1984 .... performances by 12 contemporary pop/rock/jazz artists	Columbia 39322 [2]

PARODY

12/05/64	129	3	10. Dracula's Greatest Hits .... [N] parodies of popular songs by Dracula (Gene Moss) "I Want To Bite Your Hand"	RCA 2977
7/28/62	108	14	11. Mad "Twists" Rock 'n' Roll .... [N] a parody of pop music - "She Got A Nose Job"	Big Top 1305

RADIO

3/01/69	31	17	12. Themes Like Old Times .... 180 of the most famous original radio themes	Viva 36018 [2]

SEX

1/19/63	59	19	13. How To Strip For Your Husband .... [I] instrumentals by Sonny Lester, with booklet "How To Strip For Your Husband" by strip-teaser Ann Corio	Roulette 25186
10/16/71	181	4	14. Way to become The Sensuous Woman by "J" .... based on the best-selling book - spoken word by Connie Z.; background music by Tony Camillo	Atlantic 7209

SOUNDS

3/27/71	176	8	15. Songs of the Humpback Whale .... actual recorded sounds of Whales near Bermuda	Capitol 620

MISCELLANEOUS

DATE CHARTED	PEAK POS	WKS CHRT'D	ALBUM TITLE	LABEL & NUMBER
			SPACE	
9/06/69	**185**	5	16. Apollo 11: Flight To The Moon .... actual voice transmissions of America's space missions - narrated by astronaut Walter M. Schirra, Jr.	Bell 1100
			ZODIAC	
2/28/70	**180**	3	17. The Astromusical House Of... .... [I] series of 12 albums, each named after a zodiac sign - music selected is supposed to reflect the character of the sign	Astro 1001/1012
12/06/69	**147**	15	18. Signs Of The Zodiac .... series of 12 albums about the signs of the zodiac - script: Jacques Wilson; electronic music: Mort Garson	A&M 4211/22
7/15/67	**118**	9	19. The Zodiac: Cosmic Sounds .... script (Jacques Wilson) and music (Mort Garson) about the 12 signs of the zodiac	Elektra 74009

RELIGIOUS

Refer to the Artist Section for complete chart data on the following religious oriented albums:

Harry Belafonte - My Lord What A Mornin'

Brook Benton - If You Believe

Leonard Bernstein - Mass

Pat Boone - A Closer Walk With Thee/Hymns We Love

Boston Symphony Orchestra - Mozart: Requiem Mass

Glen Campbell - Oh Happy Day

Johnny Cash - The Holy Land

Perry Como - When You Come To The End Of The Day

Electric Prunes - Mass In F Minor

Ella Fitzgerald - Brighten The Corner

Tennessee Ernie Ford - 7 albums

Connie Francis - In The Summer Of His Years

Aretha Franklin - Amazing Grace

Nikki Giovanni - Truth Is On Its Way

Edwin Hawkins - 3 albums

David Houston - David

Jerry Jordan - Phone Call From God

Mario Lanza - I'll Walk With God

Limeliters - Makin' A Joyful Noise

Art Linkletter - For Children Of The World, Art Linkletter narrates "The Bible...In The Beginning"

Mantovani - Songs Of Praise

Johnny Mathis - Good Night Dear Lord

Mormon Tabernacle Choir - The Lord's Prayer (Vols. 1 & 2)

Jim Nabors - The Lord's Prayer/How Great Thou Art

Willie Nelson - The Troublemaker

Buck Owens - Your Mother's Prayer

Pope John XXIII - Pope John XXIII

Pope John Paul II - Pope John Paul II Sings At The Festival Of Sacrosong

Elvis Presley - Peace In The Valley/His Hand in Mine/ How Great Thou Art/You'll Never Walk Alone/He Touched Me/ He Walks Beside Me

Charley Pride - Did You Think To Pray

Boots Randolph - Sunday Sax

Charlie Rich - Silver Linings

Robert Shaw - Deep River and Other Spirituals

Singing Nun - The Singing Nun/Her Joy, Her Songs

Kate Smith - How Great Thou Art

Ray Stevens - Turn Your Radio On

Tammy Wynette - Inspiration

Various-Rock Operas/Concept - Truth Of Truths

TRIBUTES

The indented artists perform music originally written and/or performed by the artist shown in capital letters.

PAUL ANKA - Annette
JOHANN SEBASTIAN BACH - Swingle Singers
BURT BACHARACH/HAL DAVID:
  Ed Ames
  Anita Kerr
  Johnny Mathis
  Christopher Scott
  Renaissance.
BEATLES:
  Chet Atkins
  George Benson (Abbey Road)
  Booker T. & The MG's (Abbey Road)
  Brothers Four
  Chipmunks
  Percy Faith
  Hollyridge Strings (2)
  George Martin
  Joshua Rifkin
  Soundtrack "All This & World War II"
BEACH BOYS - Hollyridge Strings
IRVING BERLIN:
  Enoch Light
  Guy Lombardo
  Mantovani
CHUCK BERRY - Bill Black
CARUSO - Mario Lanza
RAY CHARLES - Bobby Darin
NAT KING COLE:
  Jerry Vale
  Hollyridge Strings
SAM COOKE - Supremes
CREAM - Rubber Band
TOMMY DORSEY - Frank Sinatra
BOB DYLAN - Joan Baez
DUKE ELLINGTON - Andre Previn
STEPHEN FOSTER - Mantovani
RUDOLF FRIML - Mantovani
LEFTY FRIZZELL - Willie Nelson
GERSHWINS:
  Ella Fitzgerald
  Sarah Vaughan
W.C. HANDY:
  101 Strings
  Nat King Cole

JIMI HENDRIX - Rubber Band
VICTOR HERBERT:
  Beverly Sills
  Andre Kostelanetz
HOLLAND-DOZIER-HOLLAND - Supremes
BERT KAEMPFERT:
  Al Hirt
  Johnny Mathis
KRIS KRISTOFFERSON - Willie Nelson
MAMAS & THE PAPAS - Classics IV
ROD McKUEN:
  Frank Sinatra
  Glenn Yarbrough
GLENN MILLER - Boston Pops Orchestra
CHARLIE MINGUS - Joni Mitchell
MONKEES - Golden Gate Strings
HELEN MORGAN - Polly Bergen
WOLFGANG AMADEUS MOZART:
  Swingle Singers
  Neville Marriner
CHARLIE PARKER - Supersax (2)
COLE PORTER:
  Ella Fitzgerald
  Bobby Short
ELVIS PRESLEY:
  Merle Haggard
  Hollyridge Strings
JIM REEVES - Ronnie Milsap
SMOKEY ROBINSON - Temptations
JIMMIE RODGERS - Merle Haggard
RICHARD RODGERS & LORENZ HART:
  Ella Fitzgerald
  Supremes
PAUL SIMON - Boston Pops Orchestra
STARS of the LONDON PALLADIUM - Sammy Davis, Jr.
RICHARD STRAUSS - Mantovani
FATS WALLER - Louis Armstrong
DIONNE WARWICK - Dells
JIMMY WEBB - Glen Campbell
HANK WILLIAMS:
  Floyd Cramer
  Charlie Rich
BOB WILLS - Merle Haggard

TOP ARTIST
and
ALBUM
ACHIEVEMENTS

THE TOP 200 ARTISTS — 1955-1985

RANK	POINTS	RANK	POINTS
1. Elvis Presley	20,050	51. Dean Martin	4630
2. Frank Sinatra	17,025	52. Linda Ronstadt	4578
3. Johnny Mathis	12,886	53. Neil Young	4536
4. Beatles	11,544	54. Frank Zappa/Mothers Of Invention	4511
5. Rolling Stones	11,516	55. Kinks	4501
6. Barbra Streisand	10,956	56. Isley Brothers	4487
7. Mantovani	9821	57. Earth, Wind & Fire	4368
8. Ray Conniff	9612	58. Santana	4335
9. Temptations	9123	59. Four Seasons	4331
10. Beach Boys	8363	60. Grand Funk Railroad	4288
11. Lawrence Welk	8361	61. Perry Como	4265
12. Bob Dylan	7986	62. Bill Cosby	4257
13. Andy Williams	7884	63. Olivia Newton-John	4250
14. Elton John	7631	64. Isaac Hayes	4232
15. Supremes	7464	65. Barry Manilow	4167
16. Kingston Trio	7438	66. Led Zeppelin	4106
17. Neil Diamond	7326	67. Johnny Cash	4052
18. Roger Williams	7298	68. Doors	4052
19. Henry Mancini	7294	69. Eric Clapton	4022
20. Ray Charles	7285	70. Four Tops	4014
21. James Brown	7128	71. Gladys Knight & The Pips	3994
22. Aretha Franklin	7010	72. Grateful Dead	3973
23. Billy Vaughn	6789	73. Kiss	3956
24. Mitch Miller	6635	74. Pink Floyd	3956
25. Herb Alpert & The Tijuana Brass	6603	75. Miracles	3924
26. Ventures	6399	76. Moody Blues	3888
27. Nat King Cole	5901	77. Three Dog Night	3884
28. Diana Ross	5823	78. Peter, Paul & Mary	3862
29. Bee Gees	5800	79. Al Martino	3819
30. Stevie Wonder	5752	80. Percy Faith	3817
31. Chicago	5729	81. Carole King	3788
32. Harry Belafonte	5712	82. Bobby Vinton	3775
33. Nancy Wilson	5570	83. Ferrante & Teicher	3769
34. Jefferson Airplane/Starship	5529	84. Al Hirt	3758
35. Lettermen	5420	85. Chubby Checker	3739
36. Willie Nelson	5417	86. Pat Boone	3719
37. David Bowie	5405	87. Daryl Hall & John Oates	3716
38. Dionne Warwick	5373	88. Tom Jones	3715
39. Paul McCartney/Wings	5334	89. Donna Summer	3703
40. John Denver	5312	90. John Lennon/Plastic Ono Band	3692
41. Jethro Tull	5137	91. Jimmy Smith	3687
42. Joan Baez	5000	92. Commodores	3686
43. Marvin Gaye	4964	93. Connie Francis	3679
44. Who	4911	94. Dave Brubeck Quartet	3677
45. Glen Campbell	4775	95. Ramsey Lewis	3674
46. Rod Stewart	4766	96. Doobie Brothers	3650
47. Kenny Rogers	4763	97. Yes	3624
48. Jacksons	4750	98. Steve Miller Band	3590
49. Enoch Light	4710	99. War	3573
50. Jimi Hendrix	4676	100. Anne Murray	3571

THE TOP 200 ARTISTS — 1955-1985 Cont'd.

RANK	POINTS	RANK	POINTS
101. Queen	3563	151. Emerson, Lake & Palmer	2779
102. James Taylor	3533	152. Spinners	2774
103. Tony Bennett	3525	153. Paul Revere & The Raiders	2747·
104. Lou Rawls	3519	154. Leon Russell	2745
105. Jackie Gleason	3516	155. Peggy Lee	2744
106. Fleetwood Mac	3443	156. Otis Redding	2741
107. Electric Light Orchestra	3362	157. Stephen Stills	2737
108. Engelbert Humperdinck	3360	158. Trini Lopez	2729
109. Donovan	3348	159. Crusaders	2728
110. Grover Washington, Jr.	3316	160. B.B. King	2719
111. Creedence Clearwater Revival	3295	161. Bob James	2708
112. Cat Stevens	3276	162. Gordon Lightfoot	2699
113. Roberta Flack	3273	163. Van Morrison	2683
114. Joni Mitchell	3237	164. Bob Seger	2677
115. Alice Cooper	3164	165. Barry White	2671
116. George Benson	3148	166. Genesis	2664
117. America	3146	167. Journey	2663
118. Deep Purple	3129	168. Traffic	2663
119. 5th Dimension	3126	169. Animals	2645
120. Ricky Nelson	3114	170. Crosby, Stills & Nash	2576
121. Simon & Garfunkel	3114	171. Eddy Arnold	2571
122. O'Jays	3098	172. Bobby Darin	2566
123. Waylon Jennings	3092	173. Quincy Jones	2549
124. Judy Collins	3091	174. Chuck Mangione	2546
125. Eagles	3089	175. Paul Anka	2510
126. Bert Kaempfert	3074	176. Seals & Crofts	2502
127. Carly Simon	3068	177. John Gary	2491
128. Carpenters	3067	178. The Band	2485
129. George Harrison	3053	179. Jerry Vale	2482
130. Brenda Lee	3042	180. Helen Reddy	2469
131. Robert Goulet	3040	181. Smokey Robinson	2466
132. Al Green	3037	182. Marshall Tucker Band	2464
133. Steppenwolf	3024	183. Herbie Hancock	2434
134. Black Sabbath	3008	184. Rufus	2427
135. Johnny Rivers	2994	185. Guess Who	2424
136. J. Geils Band	2986	186. Herman's Hermits	2410
137. Billy Joel	2971	187. Lynyrd Skynyrd	2406
138. Kool & The Gang	2968	188. Steely Dan	2400
139. Righteous Brothers	2964	189. Aerosmith	2394
140. Peter Nero	2959	190. Cream	2393
141. Ohio Players	2942	191. Jack Jones	2392
142. Allman Brothers Band	2935	192. Mamas & The Papas	2390
143. Byrds	2922	193. Boston Pops Orchestra/Arthur Fiedler	2387
144. Styx	2860	194. Cher	2382
145. Monkees	2859	195. Herbie Mann	2358
146. Rush	2841	196. Dolly Parton	2351
147. Sergio Mendes & Brasil '66	2840	197. Kansas	2350
148. Poco	2809	198. Dan Fogelberg	2341
149. Dave Clark Five	2802	199. Bruce Springsteen	2340
150. Tennessee Ernie Ford	2780	200. Ted Nugent	2339

Artist's points are calculated using the following formula:

1. Each artist's charted albums are given points based on their highest charted position (#1=200 points; #2=199 points, etc.).
2. Bonus points are added to each album based on its highest charted position (#1=150 points; #2-5=125 points; #6-10=100; #11-20=50; #21-40=25; #41-100=10).
3. Total weeks charted are added in.
4. Total weeks an artist held the #1 position are also added in.

Christmas albums are given full point value for their first chart appearance. Their seasonal re-entry on the charts are only counted for total weeks charted with no points awarded for highest position.

When two artists combine for a hit album (Ex: Supremes/Temptations; Kenny Rogers/Dolly Parton) the full point value is given to each artist.

Artists such as 'Simon and Garfunkel,' 'Sonny & Cher', 'Marvin Gaye & Tammi Terrell' and 'Loggins & Messina' are considered regular recording teams and their points are not shared by either of the artists individually.

THE TOP 200 ARTISTS — (A-Z)

Artist	Points	Artist	Points	Artist	Points
Aerosmith	189	Crusaders	159	Engelbert Humperdinck	108
Allman Brothers Band	142	Bobby Darin	172	Isley Brothers	56
Herb Alpert & The Tijuana Brass	25	Deep Purple	118	Jacksons	48
America	117	John Denver	40	Bob James	161
Animals	169	Neil Diamond	17	Jefferson Airplane/Starship	34
Paul Anka	175	Donovan	109	Waylon Jennings	123
Eddy Arnold	171	Doobie Brothers	96	Jethro Tull	41
Joan Baez	42	Doors	68	Billy Joel	137
The Band	178	Bob Dylan	12	Elton John	14
Beach Boys	10	Eagles	125	Jack Jones	191
Beatles	4	Earth, Wind & Fire	57	Quincy Jones	173
Bee Gees	29	Electric Light Orchestra	107	Tom Jones	88
Harry Belafonte	32	Emerson, Lake & Palmer	151	Journey	167
Tony Bennett	103	Percy Faith	80	Bert Kaempfert	126
George Benson	116	Ferrante & Teicher	83	Kansas	197
Black Sabbath	134	5th Dimension	119	B.B. King	160
Pat Boone	86	Roberta Flack	113	Carole King	81
Boston Pops Orchestra	193	Fleetwood Mac	106	Kingston Trio	16
David Bowie	37	Dan Fogelberg	198	Kinks	55
James Brown	21	Tennessee Ernie Ford	150	Kiss	73
Dave Brubeck Quartet	94	Four Seasons	59	Gladys Knight & The Pips	71
Byrds	143	Four Tops	70	Kool & The Gang	138
Glen Campbell	45	Connie Francis	93	Led Zeppelin	66
Carpenters	128	Aretha Franklin	22	Brenda Lee	130
Johnny Cash	67	John Gary	177	Peggy Lee	155
Ray Charles	20	Marvin Gaye	43	John Lennon/	
Chubby Checker	85	J. Geils Band	136	Plastic Ono Band	90
Cher	194	Genesis	166	Lettermen	35
Chicago	31	Jackie Gleason	105	Ramsey Lewis	95
Eric Clapton	69	Robert Goulet	131	Enoch Light	49
Dave Clark Five	149	Grand Funk Railroad	60	Gordon Lightfoot	162
Nat King Cole	27	Grateful Dead	72	Trini Lopez	158
Judy Collins	124	Al Green	132	Lynyrd Skynyrd	187
Commodores	92	Guess Who	185	Mamas & The Papas	192
Perry Como	61	Daryl Hall & John Oates	87	Henry Mancini	19
Ray Conniff	8	Herbie Hancock	183	Chuck Mangione	174
Alice Cooper	115	George Harrison	129	Barry Manilow	65
Bill Cosby	62	Isaac Hayes	64	Herbie Mann	195
Cream	190	Jimi Hendrix	50	Mantovani	7
Creedence Clearwater Revival	111	Herman's Hermits	186	Marshall Tucker Band	182
Crosby, Stills & Nash	179	Al Hirt	84	Dean Martin	51

THE TOP 20 ARTISTS BY DECADE

Fifties ('55-'59)

1. Frank Sinatra 5323
2. Johnny Mathis 4159
3. Mantovani 3939
4. Elvis Presley 3731
5. Harry Belafonte 3159
6. Lawrence Welk 3153
7. Roger Williams 3135
8. Mitch Miller 3075
9. Pat Boone 2941
10. Jackie Gleason 2920
11. Ray Conniff 2323
12. Nat King Cole 2290
13. Perry Como 2186
14. Tennessee Ernie Ford 2058
15. Kingston Trio 2015
16. Four Freshmen 1560
17. Dave Brubeck Quartet 1373
18. Billy Vaughn 1306
19. Mario Lanza 1293
20. Lester Lanin 1253

Sixties ('60-'69)

1. Frank Sinatra 10,033
2. Elvis Presley 8561
3. Beatles 8002
4. Ray Conniff 6632
5. Ray Charles 6368
6. Andy Williams 6278
7. Ventures 6139
8. Johnny Mathis 6012
9. Mantovani 5759
10. Supremes 5683
11. Billy Vaughn 5468
12. Kingston Trio 5423
13. Henry Mancini 5410
14. Beach Boys 5118
15. Lawrence Welk 5111
16. Rolling Stones 5081
17. Temptations 4928
18. Nancy Wilson 4863
19. Lettermen 4802
20. Barbra Streisand 4729

Seventies ('70-'79)

1. Elvis Presley 6736
2. Elton John 6361
3. Neil Diamond 4766
4. Barbra Streisand 4762
5. Rolling Stones 4537
6. Chicago 4443
7. John Denver 4443
8. Bob Dylan 4360
9. Jethro Tull 4096
10. Paul McCartney/Wings 4081
11. Grand Funk Railroad 3977
12. David Bowie 3933
13. Diana Ross 3927
14. Jackson 5 3823
15. Bee Gees 3707
16. Isaac Hayes 3691
17. Carole King 3511
18. Rod Stewart 3482
19. Temptations 3431
20. Neil Young 3389

Eighties ('80-'85)

1. Willie Nelson 3035
2. Kenny Rogers 2991
3. Rolling Stones 1898
4. Diana Ross 1896
5. Neil Diamond 1794
6. Daryl Hall & John Oates 1790
7. Alabama 1740
8. Pat Benatar 1719
9. Rush 1703
10. Journey 1674
11. AC/DC 1657
12. Duran Duran 1628
13. Billy Joel 1537
14. Elvis Costello 1512
15. Rick Springfield 1489
16. David Bowie 1472
17. Barbra Streisand 1465
18. Linda Ronstadt 1462
19. Van Halen 1445
20. Police 1359

TOP ARTIST ACHIEVEMENTS

MOST CHARTED ALBUMS

1. ELVIS PRESLEY 90
2. FRANK SINATRA 62
3. JOHNNY MATHIS 60
4. RAY CONNIFF 49
5. JAMES BROWN 47
6. MANTOVANI 45
7. LAWRENCE WELK 41
8. HENRY MANCINI 38
9. BARBRA STREISAND 37
10. TEMPTATIONS 37
11. BEACH BOYS 37
12. ROGER WILLIAMS 37
13. RAY CHARLES 37
14. VENTURES 37
15. BILLY VAUGHN 36
16. BEATLES 35
17. SUPREMES 34
18. NANCY WILSON 34
19. ANDY WILLIAMS 33
20. ARETHA FRANKLIN 33

MOST #1 ALBUMS

1. BEATLES 15
2. ELVIS PRESLEY 9
3. ROLLING STONES 9
4. ELTON JOHN 7
5. PAUL McCARTNEY/WINGS 7
6. LED ZEPPELIN 6
7. BARBRA STREISAND 5
8. KINGSTON TRIO 5
9. HERB ALPERT & THE TIJUANA BRASS 5
10. CHICAGO 5
11. FRANK SINATRA 4
12. EAGLES 4
13. MONKEES 4
14. BOB DYLAN 3
15. SUPREMES 3
16. MITCH MILLER 3
17. BEE GEES 3
18. STEVIE WONDER 3
19. JOHN DENVER 3
20. LINDA RONSTADT 3

TOP ARTIST ACHIEVEMENTS

MOST WEEKS HELD #1 POSITION

1. BEATLES 119
2. ELVIS PRESLEY 64
3. KINGSTON TRIO 46
4. ELTON JOHN 39
5. ROLLING STONES 38
6. HARRY BELAFONTE 37
7. FLEETWOOD MAC 37
8. MONKEES 37
9. MICHAEL JACKSON 37
10. BEE GEES 31
11. LED ZEPPELIN 28
12. EAGLES 27
13. HERB ALPERT & THE TIJUANA BRASS 26
14. SIMON & GARFUNKEL 26
15. PRINCE 24
16. HENRY MANCINI 22
17. CHICAGO 22
18. PAUL McCARTNEY/WINGS 22
19. FRANK SINATRA 20
20. ENOCH LIGHT 20

MOST TOP 10 ALBUMS

1. FRANK SINATRA 31
2. ROLLING STONES 29
3. ELVIS PRESLEY 25
4. BEATLES 23
5. BARBRA STREISAND 19
6. JOHNNY MATHIS 16
7. BOB DYLAN 14
8. KINGSTON TRIO 14
9. MITCH MILLER 14
10. BEACH BOYS 13
11. ELTON JOHN 13
12. RAY CONNIFF 12
13. ANDY WILLIAMS 12
14. NEIL DIAMOND 12
15. CHICAGO 12
16. PAUL McCARTNEY/WINGS 12
17. MANTOVANI 11
18. TEMPTATIONS 10
19. LAWRENCE WELK 10
20. LED ZEPPELIN 10

TOP ARTIST ACHIEVEMENTS

MOST TOP 40 ALBUMS

1. ELVIS PRESLEY 49
2. FRANK SINATRA 49
3. ROLLING STONES 31
4. BARBRA STREISAND 31
5. TEMPTATIONS 28
6. JOHNNY MATHIS 27
7. BEATLES 27
8. MANTOVANI 26
9. RAY CONNIFF 26
10. BOB DYLAN 25
11. LAWRENCE WELK 24
12. ELTON JOHN 23
13. BEACH BOYS 20
14. NEIL DIAMOND 20
15. ANDY WILLIAMS 19
16. SUPREMES 19
17. KINGSTON TRIO 19
18. ROGER WILLIAMS 19
19. ARETHA FRANKLIN 19
20. BILLY VAUGHN 18

Ties are broken according to rank in the 'Top 200 Artists 1955-1985' section.

Christmas albums are accounted for in the above 5 categories for their first chart appearance only. Their seasonal re-entry is not added to the totals.

THE TOP 100 ALBUMS — 1955 - 1985

Following is a listing, in rank order, of the Top #1 Albums from 1955 through March, 1985. The ranking is based on total weeks at #1 - ties are broken by total weeks charted.

Columnar headings show the following data:

PK YR : Year album reached its peak position
WKS CHR : Total weeks charted
WKS @ #1 : Total weeks album held the #1 position

PK YR	WKS CHR	WKS @ #1	RANK	TITLE	Artist
62	198	54	1.	WEST SIDE STORY	Soundtrack
83	120	37	2.	THRILLER	Michael Jackson
58	262	31	3.	SOUTH PACIFIC	Soundtrack
77	134	31	4.	RUMOURS	Fleetwood Mac
56	99	31	5.	CALYPSO	Harry Belafonte
78	120	24	6.	SATURDAY NIGHT FEVER	Bee Gees/Soundtrack
84	39	24	7.	PURPLE RAIN	Prince/Soundtrack
61	79	20	8.	BLUE HAWAII	Elvis Presley/ Soundtrack
67	70	18	9.	MORE OF THE MONKEES	Monkees
83	75	17	10.	SYNCHRONICITY	Police
55	37	17	11.	LOVE ME OR LEAVE ME	Doris Day/Soundtrack
60	277	16	12.	THE SOUND OF MUSIC	Original Cast
63	107	16	13.	DAYS OF WINE AND ROSES	Andy Williams
56	480	15	14.	MY FAIR LADY	Original Cast
71	302	15	15.	TAPESTRY	Carole King
67	168	15	16.	SGT. PEPPER'S LONELY HEARTS CLUB BAND	Beatles
59	118	15	17.	THE KINGSTON TRIO AT LARGE	Kingston Trio
80	115	15	18.	THE WALL	Pink Floyd
81	101	15	19.	HI INFIDELITY	REO Speedwagon
82	90	15	20.	BUSINESS AS USUAL	Men At Work
65	114	14	21.	MARY POPPINS	Soundtrack
60	108	14	22.	THE BUTTON-DOWN MIND OF BOB NEWHART	Bob Newhart
62	101	14	23.	MODERN SOUNDS IN COUNTRY AND WESTERN MUSIC	Ray Charles
61	89	14	24.	EXODUS	Soundtrack
76	80	14	25.	SONGS IN THE KEY OF LIFE	Stevie Wonder
64	51	14	26.	A HARD DAY'S NIGHT	Beatles/Soundtrack
69	151	13	27.	HAIR	Original Cast
60	124	13	28.	PERSUASIVE PERCUSSION	Enoch Light/ Terry Snyder
61	97	13	29.	JUDY AT CARNEGIE HALL	Judy Garland
66	78	13	30.	THE MONKEES	Monkees
58	245	12	31.	THE MUSIC MAN	Original Cast
62	96	12	32.	BREAKFAST AT TIFFANY'S	Henry Mancini/ Soundtrack
78	77	12	33.	GREASE	Soundtrack
60	73	12	34.	SOLD OUT	Kingston Trio
62	49	12	35.	THE FIRST FAMILY	Vaughn Meader
69	116	11	36.	ABBEY ROAD	Beatles
64	71	11	37.	MEET THE BEATLES!	Beatles
61	64	11	38.	CALCUTTA!	Lawrence Welk
58	172	10	39.	GIGI	Soundtrack
59	117	10	40.	THE MUSIC FROM PETER GUNN	Henry Mancini

PK YR	WKS CHR	WKS @ #1	RANK	TITLE	Artist
60	111	10	41.	G.I. BLUES	Elvis Presley/ Soundtrack
74	104	10	42.	ELTON JOHN - GREATEST HITS	Elton John
76	97	10	43.	FRAMPTON COMES ALIVE!	Peter Frampton
57	88	10	44.	AROUND THE WORLD IN 80 DAYS	Soundtrack
70	85	10	45.	BRIDGE OVER TROUBLED WATER	Simon & Garfunkel
81	81	10	46.	4	Foreigner
60	60	10	47.	STRING ALONG	Kingston Trio
84	55	10	48.	FOOTLOOSE	Soundtrack
56	49	10	49.	ELVIS PRESLEY	Elvis Presley
63	39	10	50.	THE SINGING NUN	Singing Nun
57	29	10	51.	LOVING YOU	Elvis Presley/ Soundtrack
68	144	9	52.	THE BEATLES [WHITE ALBUM]	Beatles
66	129	9	53.	WHAT NOW MY LOVE	Herb Alpert & The Tijuana Brass
82	93	9	54.	AMERICAN FOOL	John Cougar
60	86	9	55.	NICE 'N' EASY	Frank Sinatra
65	71	9	56.	BEATLES '65	Beatles
70	69	9	57.	COSMO'S FACTORY	Creedence Clearwater Revival
68	69	9	58.	THE GRADUATE	Simon & Garfunkel/ Soundtrack
82	61	9	59.	ASIA	Asia
81	58	9	60.	TATTOO YOU	Rolling Stones
79	57	9	61.	THE LONG RUN	Eagles
72	51	9	62.	CHICAGO V	Chicago
65	44	9	63.	HELP!	Beatles/Soundtrack
71	42	9	64.	PEARL	Janis Joplin
61	40	9	65.	STARS FOR A SUMMER NIGHT	Various Artists
58	204	8	66.	SING ALONG WITH MITCH	Mitch Miller & The Gang
65	185	8	67.	WHIPPED CREAM & OTHER DELIGHTS	Herb Alpert & The Tijuana Brass
59	126	8	68.	HERE WE GO AGAIN!	Kingston Trio
77	107	8	69.	HOTEL CALIFORNIA	Eagles
57	93	8	70.	LOVE IS THE THING	Nat King Cole
73	91	8	71.	GOODBYE YELLOW BRICK ROAD	Elton John
68	87	8	72.	MAGICAL MYSTERY TOUR	Beatles/Soundtrack
78	76	8	73.	52ND STREET	Billy Joel
80	74	8	74.	DOUBLE FANTASY	John Lennon/ Yoko Ono
68	66	8	75.	CHEAP THRILLS	Big Brother & The Holding Company
63	32	8	76.	MY SON, THE NUT	Allan Sherman
62	185	7	77.	PETER, PAUL & MARY	Peter, Paul & Mary
58	125	7	78.	TCHAIKOVSKY: PIANO CONCERTO NO. 1	Van Cliburn
69	109	7	79.	BLOOD, SWEAT & TEARS	Blood, Sweat & Tears
69	98	7	80.	LED ZEPPELIN II	Led Zeppelin
68	66	7	81.	BOOKENDS	Simon & Garfunkel
61	57	7	82.	STEREO 35/MM	Enoch Light
76	51	7	83.	WINGS AT THE SPEED OF SOUND	Paul McCartney/ Wings
80	51	7	84.	EMOTIONAL RESCUE	Rolling Stones
72	48	7	85.	AMERICAN PIE	Don McLean
75	43	7	86.	CAPTAIN FANTASTIC AND THE BROWN DIRT COWBOY	Elton John

PK YR	WKS CHR	WKS @ #1	RANK	TITLE	Artist
84	42	7	87.	BORN IN THE U.S.A	Bruce Springsteen
79	41	7	88.	IN THROUGH THE OUT DOOR	Led Zeppelin
71	38	7	89.	ALL THINGS MUST PASS	George Harrison
61	265	6	90.	CAMELOT	Original Cast
66	164	6	91.	GOING PLACES	Herb Alpert & The Tijuana Brass
80	110	6	92.	AGAINST THE WIND	Bob Seger & The Silver Bullet Band
70	88	6	93.	ABRAXAS	Santana
79	88	6	94.	BREAKFAST IN AMERICA	Supertramp
66	77	6	95.	REVOLVER	Beatles
64	74	6	96.	HELLO, DOLLY!	Louis Armstrong
80	73	6	97.	GLASS HOUSES	Billy Joel
82	72	6	98.	BEAUTY AND THE BEAT	Go-Go's
56	64	6	99.	BELAFONTE	Harry Belafonte
66	59	6	100.	RUBBER SOUL	Beatles

TOP 100 ALBUMS
(A-Z by Artist)

THE TOP ALBUMS BY DECADE

THE TOP #1 ALBUMS
1955-1959

PK YR	WKS CHR	WKS @ #1	RANK	TITLE	Artist
58	262	31	1.	SOUTH PACIFIC	Soundtrack
56	99	31	2.	CALYPSO	Harry Belafonte
55	37	17	3.	LOVE ME OR LEAVE ME	Doris Day/Soundtrack
56	480	15	4.	MY FAIR LADY	Original Cast
59	118	15	5.	THE KINGSTON TRIO AT LARGE	Kingston Trio
58	245	12	6.	THE MUSIC MAN	Original Cast
58	172	10	7.	GIGI	Soundtrack
59	117	10	8.	THE MUSIC FROM PETER GUNN	Henry Mancini
57	88	10	9.	AROUND THE WORLD IN 80 DAYS	Soundtrack
56	49	10	10.	ELVIS PRESLEY	Elvis Presley
57	29	10	11.	LOVING YOU	Elvis Presley/ Soundtrack
58	204	8	12.	SING ALONG WITH MITCH	Mitch Miller & The Gang
59	126	8	13.	HERE WE GO AGAIN!	Kingston Trio
57	93	8	14.	LOVE IS THE THING	Nat King Cole
58	125	7	15.	TCHAIKOVSKY: PIANO CONCERTO NO. 1	Van Cliburn
56	64	6	16.	BELAFONTE	Harry Belafonte
55	27	6	17.	STARRING SAMMY DAVIS, JR.	Sammy Davis, Jr.
59	295	5	18.	HEAVENLY	Johnny Mathis
58	120	5	19.	FRANK SINATRA SINGS FOR ONLY THE LONELY	Frank Sinatra
58	71	5	20.	COME FLY WITH ME	Frank Sinatra
59	63	5	21.	EXOTICA	Martin Denny
56	32	5	22.	ELVIS	Elvis Presley
56	305	4	23.	OKLAHOMA!	Soundtrack
57	7	4	24.	ELVIS' CHRISTMAS ALBUM	Elvis Presley
58	490	3	25.	JOHNNY'S GREATEST HITS	Johnny Mathis
59	151	3	26.	FLOWER DRUM SONG	Original Cast
58	33	2	27.	RICKY	Ricky Nelson
55	24	2	28.	LONESOME ECHO	Jackie Gleason
55	21	2	29.	CRAZY OTTO	Crazy Otto
58	5	2	30.	CHRISTMAS SING-ALONG WITH MITCH	Mitch Miller & The Gang
56	274	1	31.	THE KING AND I	Soundtrack
59	231	1	32.	FILM ENCORES	Mantovani
58	195	1	33.	THE KINGSTON TRIO	Kingston Trio
56	99	1	34.	THE EDDY DUCHIN STORY	Carmen Cavallaro/ Soundtrack
58	7	1	35.	MERRY CHRISTMAS	Bing Crosby

THE TOP #1 ALBUMS
1960-1969

PK YR	WKS CHR	WKS @ #1	RANK	TITLE	Artist
62	198	54	1.	WEST SIDE STORY	Soundtrack
61	79	20	2.	BLUE HAWAII	Elvis Presley/ Soundtrack
67	70	18	3.	MORE OF THE MONKEES	Monkees
60	277	16	4.	THE SOUND OF MUSIC	Original Cast
63	107	16	5.	DAYS OF WINE AND ROSES	Andy Williams
67	168	15	6.	SGT. PEPPER'S LONELY HEARTS CLUB BAND	Beatles
65	114	14	7.	MARY POPPINS	Soundtrack
60	108	14	8.	THE BUTTON-DOWN MIND OF BOB NEWHART	Bob Newhart
62	101	14	9.	MODERN SOUNDS IN COUNTRY AND WESTERN MUSIC	Ray Charles
61	89	14	10.	EXODUS	Soundtrack
64	51	14	11.	A HARD DAY'S NIGHT	Beatles/Soundtrack
69	151	13	12.	HAIR	Original Cast
60	124	13	13.	PERSUASIVE PERCUSSION	Enoch Light/ Terry Snyder
61	97	13	14.	JUDY AT CARNEGIE HALL	Judy Garland
66	78	13	15.	THE MONKEES	Monkees
62	96	12	16.	BREAKFAST AT TIFFANY'S	Henry Mancini/ Soundtrack
60	73	12	17.	SOLD OUT	Kingston Trio
62	49	12	18.	THE FIRST FAMILY	Vaughn Meader
69	116	11	19.	ABBEY ROAD	Beatles
64	71	11	20.	MEET THE BEATLES!	Beatles
61	64	11	21.	CALCUTTA!	Lawrence Welk
60	111	10	22.	G.I. BLUES	Elvis Presley/ Soundtrack
60	60	10	23.	STRING ALONG	Kingston Trio
63	39	10	24.	THE SINGING NUN	Singing Nun
68	144	9	25.	THE BEATLES [White Album]	Beatles
66	129	9	26.	WHAT NOW MY LOVE	Herb Alpert & The Tijuana Brass
60	86	9	27.	NICE 'N' EASY	Frank Sinatra
65	71	9	28.	BEATLES '65	Beatles
68	69	9	29.	THE GRADUATE	Simon & Garfunkel/ Soundtrack
65	44	9	30.	HELP!	Beatles/Soundtrack
61	40	9	31.	STARS FOR A SUMMER NIGHT	Various Artists
65	185	8	32.	WHIPPED CREAM & OTHER DELIGHTS	Herb Alpert & The Tijuana Brass
68	87	8	33.	MAGICAL MYSTERY TOUR	Beatles/Soundtrack
68	66	8	34.	CHEAP THRILLS	Big Brother & The Holding Company
63	32	8	35.	MY SON, THE NUT	Allan Sherman
62	185	7	36.	PETER, PAUL & MARY	Peter, Paul & Mary
69	109	7	37.	BLOOD, SWEAT & TEARS	Blood, Sweat & Tears
69	98	7	38.	LED ZEPPELIN II	Led Zeppelin
68	66	7	39.	BOOKENDS	Simon & Garfunkel
61	57	7	40.	STEREO 35/MM	Enoch Light

THE TOP #1 ALBUMS
1970-1979

PK YR	WKS CHR	WKS @ #1	RANK	TITLE	Artist
77	134	31	1.	RUMOURS	Fleetwood Mac
78	120	24	2.	SATURDAY NIGHT FEVER	Bee Gees/Soundtrack
71	302	15	3.	TAPESTRY	Carole King
76	80	14	4.	SONGS IN THE KEY OF LIFE	Stevie Wonder
78	77	12	5.	GREASE	Soundtrack
74	104	10	6.	ELTON JOHN - GREATEST HITS	Elton John
76	97	10	7.	FRAMPTON COMES ALIVE!	Peter Frampton
70	85	10	8.	BRIDGE OVER TROUBLED WATER	Simon & Garfunkel
70	69	9	9.	COSMO'S FACTORY	Creedence Clearwater Revival
79	57	9	10.	THE LONG RUN	Eagles
72	51	9	11.	CHICAGO V	Chicago
71	42	9	12.	PEARL	Janis Joplin
77	107	8	13.	HOTEL CALIFORNIA	Eagles
73	91	8	14.	GOODBYE YELLOW BRICK ROAD	Elton John
78	76	8	15.	52ND STREET	Billy Joel
76	51	7	16.	WINGS AT THE SPEED OF SOUND	Paul McCartney/ Wings
72	48	7	17.	AMERICAN PIE	Don McLean
75	43	7	18.	CAPTAIN FANTASTIC AND THE BROWN DIRT COWBOY	Elton John
79	41	7	19.	IN THROUGH THE OUT DOOR	Led Zeppelin
71	38	7	20.	ALL THINGS MUST PASS	George Harrison
70	88	6	21.	ABRAXAS	Santana
79	88	6	22.	BREAKFAST IN AMERICA	Supertramp
79	55	6	23.	SPIRITS HAVING FLOWN	Bee Gees
77	51	6	24.	A STAR IS BORN	Barbra Streisand
79	49	6	25.	BAD GIRLS	Donna Summer
75	41	6	26.	PHYSICAL GRAFFITI	Led Zeppelin
76	133	5	27.	EAGLES/THEIR GREATEST HITS 1971-1975	Eagles
74	93	5	28.	YOU DON'T MESS AROUND WITH JIM	Jim Croce
79	87	5	29.	MINUTE BY MINUTE	Doobie Brothers
73	73	5	30.	CHICAGO VI	Chicago
75	72	5	31.	CHICAGO IX - Chicago's Greatest Hits	Chicago
73	71	5	32.	NO SECRETS	Carly Simon
72	61	5	33.	HONKY CHATEAU	Elton John
73	56	5	34.	BROTHERS AND SISTERS	Allman Brothers Band
75	56	5	35.	ONE OF THESE NIGHTS	Eagles
72	54	5	36.	FIRST TAKE	Roberta Flack
77	47	5	37.	SIMPLE DREAMS	Linda Ronstadt
72	44	5	38.	SEVENTH SOJOURN	Moody Blues
74	41	5	39.	THE STING	Soundtrack
72	40	5	40.	AMERICA	America

THE TOP #1 ALBUMS
1980-1985

PK YR	WKS CHR	WKS @ #1	RANK	TITLE	Artist
83	120	37	1.	THRILLER	Michael Jackson
84	39	24	2.	PURPLE RAIN	Prince/Soundtrack
83	75	17	3.	SYNCHRONICITY	Police
80	115	15	4.	THE WALL	Pink Floyd
81	101	15	5.	HI INFIDELITY	REO Speedwagon
82	90	15	6.	BUSINESS AS USUAL	Men At Work
81	81	10	7.	4	Foreigner
84	55	10	8.	FOOTLOOSE	Soundtrack
82	93	9	9.	AMERICAN FOOL	John Cougar
82	61	9	10.	ASIA	Asia
81	58	9	11.	TATTOO YOU	Rolling Stones
80	74	8	12.	DOUBLE FANTASY	John Lennon/ Yoko Ono
80	51	7	13.	EMOTIONAL RESCUE	Rolling Stones
84	42	7	14.	BORN IN THE U.S.A	Bruce Springsteen
80	110	6	15.	AGAINST THE WIND	Bob Seger & The Silver Bullet Band
80	73	6	16.	GLASS HOUSES	Billy Joel
82	72	6	17.	BEAUTY AND THE BEAT	Go-Go's
85	11	6	18.	NO JACKET REQUIRED	Phil Collins
82	45	5	19.	MIRAGE	Fleetwood Mac
80	43	5	20.	THE GAME	Queen
80	75	4	21.	THE RIVER	Bruce Springsteen
82	70	4	22.	FREEZE-FRAME	J. Geils Band
82	57	4	23.	CHARIOTS OF FIRE	Vangelis/Soundtrack
81	52	4	24.	MISTAKEN IDENTITY	Kim Carnes
83	74	3	25.	CAN'T SLOW DOWN	Lionel Richie
81	61	3	26.	PARADISE THEATER	Styx
80	49	3	27.	GUILTY	Barbra Streisand
81	39	3	28.	LONG DISTANCE VOYAGER	Moody Blues
81	30	3	29.	FOR THOSE ABOUT TO ROCK WE SALUTE YOU	AC/DC
82	29	3	30.	TUG OF WAR	Paul McCartney
85	22	3	31.	MAKE IT BIG	Wham!
85	19	3	32.	LIKE A VIRGIN	Madonna
85	5	3	33.	WE ARE THE WORLD	USA for Africa
80	181	2	34.	KENNY ROGER'S GREATEST HITS	Kenny Rogers
83	78	2	35.	FLASHDANCE	Soundtrack
81	146	1	36.	ESCAPE	Journey
81	141	1	37.	BELLA DONNA	Stevie Nicks
83	81	1	38.	METAL HEALTH	Quiet Riot
84	79	1	39.	SPORTS	Huey Lewis & The News
81	54	1	40.	PRECIOUS TIME	Pat Benatar

ALBUMS OF LONGEVITY
Albums charted 100 weeks or more

PK YR	PK POS	WKS CHR	RANK	TITLE	Artist
73	1	566+	1.	THE DARK SIDE OF THE MOON	Pink Floyd
58	1	490	2.	JOHNNY'S GREATEST HITS	Johnny Mathis
56	1	480	3.	MY FAIR LADY	Original Cast
56	1	305	4.	OKLAHOMA!	Soundtrack
71	1	302	5.	TAPESTRY	Carole King
59	1	295	6.	HEAVENLY	Johnny Mathis
60	1	277	7.	THE SOUND OF MUSIC	Original Cast
57	2	277	8.	HYMNS	Tennessee Ernie Ford
56	1	274	9.	THE KING AND I	Soundtrack
61	1	265	10.	CAMELOT	Original Cast
58	1	262	11.	SOUTH PACIFIC	Soundtrack
58	1	245	12.	THE MUSIC MAN	Original Cast
71	2	234	13.	LED ZEPPELIN IV	Led Zeppelin
65	1	233	14.	THE SOUND OF MUSIC	Soundtrack
72	4	233	15.	HOT ROCKS 1964-1971	Rolling Stones
59	1	231	16.	FILM ENCORES	Mantovani
65	7	206	17.	FIDDLER ON THE ROOF	Original Cast
58	1	204	18.	SING ALONG WITH MITCH	Mitch Miller & The Gang
62	1	198	19.	WEST SIDE STORY	Soundtrack
58	1	195	20.	THE KINGSTON TRIO	Kingston Trio
62	5	191	21.	WEST SIDE STORY	Original Cast
65	1	185	22.	WHIPPED CREAM & OTHER DELIGHTS	Herb Alpert & The Tijuana Brass
62	1	185	23.	PETER, PAUL & MARY	Peter, Paul & Mary
60	12	183	24.	OLDIES BUT GOODIES	Various Artists
80	1	181	25.	KENNY ROGERS' GREATEST HITS	Kenny Rogers
61	8	181	26.	KNOCKERS UP!	Rusty Warren
59	11	181	27.	THE BUDDY HOLLY STORY	Buddy Holly
59	2	178	28.	FROM THE HUNGRY I	Kingston Trio
63	3	176	29.	MOON RIVER & OTHER GREAT MOVIE THEMES	Andy Williams
74	1	175	30.	JOHN DENVER'S GREATEST HITS	John Denver
60	6	174	31.	ENCORE OF GOLDEN HITS	Platters
58	1	172	32.	GIGI	Soundtrack
59	4	171	33.	MORE SING ALONG WITH MITCH	Mitch Miller & The Gang
69	17	171	34.	CHICAGO TRANSIT AUTHORITY	Chicago
73	1	169	35.	THE BEATLES/1967-1970	Beatles
80	3	169	36.	OFF THE WALL	Michael Jackson
78	19	169	37.	VAN HALEN	Van Halen
67	1	168	38.	SGT. PEPPER'S LONELY HEARTS CLUB BAND	Beatles
60	3	168	39.	BELAFONTE AT CARNEGIE HALL	Harry Belafonte
67	31	167	40.	MAN OF LA MANCHA	Original Cast
66	1	164	41.	GOING PLACES	Herb Alpert & The Tijuana Brass
61	2	164	42.	TIME OUT FEATURING "TAKE FIVE"	Dave Brubeck Quartet

PK YR	PK POS	WKS CHR	RANK	TITLE	Artist
73	3	164	43.	THE BEATLES/1962-1966	Beatles
65	6	163	44.	SOUTH OF THE BORDER	Herb Alpert & The Tijuana Brass
62	3	162	45.	RAMBLIN' ROSE	Nat King Cole
81	16	161	46.	FEELS SO RIGHT	Alabama
66	1	157	47.	DOCTOR ZHIVAGO	Soundtrack
63	24	157	48.	THE LONELY BULL	Herb Alpert & The Tijuana Brass
74	1	155	49.	ENDLESS SUMMER	Beach Boys
81	5	153	50.	ZENYATTA MONDATTA	Police
66	19	152	51.	WHY IS THERE AIR?	Bill Cosby
69	1	151	52.	HAIR	Original Cast
59	1	151	53.	FLOWER DRUM SONG	Original Cast
62	5	149	54.	I LEFT MY HEART IN SAN FRANCISCO	Tony Bennett
76	1	148	55.	FLEETWOOD MAC	Fleetwood Mac
81	1	146	56.	ESCAPE	Journey
66	4	145	57.	PARSLEY, SAGE, ROSEMARY AND THYME	Simon & Garfunkel
68	1	144	58.	THE BEATLES [WHITE ALBUM]	Beatles
68	21	143	59.	SOUNDS OF SILENCE	Simon & Garfunkel
68	52	143	60.	THE SEA	San Sebastian Strings
81	1	141	61.	BELLA DONNA	Stevie Nicks
59	2	140	62.	COME DANCE WITH ME!	Frank Sinatra
60	4	140	63.	PAUL ANKA SINGS HIS BIG 15	Paul Anka
69	4	140	64.	IN-A-GADDA-DA-VIDA	Iron Butterfly
62	14	140	65.	ROY ORBISON'S GREATEST HITS	Roy Orbison
62	15	140	66.	JOAN BAEZ	Joan Baez
65	.32	140	67.	I STARTED OUT AS A CHILD	Bill Cosby
76	34	140	68.	'LIVE' BULLET	Bob Seger & The Silver Bullet Band
79	18	139	69.	THE CARS	Cars
78	2	137	70.	THE STRANGER	Billy Joel
69	20	136	71.	ON THE THRESHOLD OF A DREAM	Moody Blues
77	1	134	72.	RUMOURS	Fleetwood Mac
59	2	134	73.	INSIDE SHELLEY BERMAN	Shelley Berman
70	4	134	74.	CHICAGO II	Chicago
76	1	133	75.	EAGLES/THEIR GREATEST HITS 1971-1975	Eagles
59	4	131	76.	STILL MORE! SING ALONG WITH MITCH	Mitch Miller & The Gang
64	20	131	77.	THE KINGSMEN IN PERSON	Kingsmen
66	1	129	78.	WHAT NOW MY LOVE	Herb Alpert & The Tijuana Brass
82	3	129+	79.	LIONEL RICHIE	Lionel Richie
83	6	129	80.	RIO	Duran Duran
75	11	128	81.	TOYS IN THE ATTIC	Aerosmith
66	21	128	82.	BILL COSBY IS A VERY FUNNY FELLOW, RIGHT!	Bill Cosby
78	6	127	83.	THE GRAND ILLUSION	Styx
59	1	126	84.	HERE WE GO AGAIN!	Kingston Trio
70	4	126	85.	TOMMY	Who

PK YR	PK POS	WKS CHR	RANK	TITLE	Artist
72	5	126	86.	SIMON AND GARFUNKEL'S GREATEST HITS	Simon & Garfunkel
66	7	126	87.	SERGIO MENDES & BRASIL '66	Sergio Mendes & Brasil '66
58	1	125	88.	TCHAIKOVSKY: PIANO CONCERTO NO. 1	Van Cliburn
83	9	125+	89.	PRINCE **1999**	Prince
62	13	125	90.	JOAN BAEZ, VOL. 2	Joan Baez
60	1	124	91.	PERSUASIVE PERCUSSION	Enoch Light/ Terry Snyder
78	21	123	92.	INFINITY	Journey
82	7	122	93.	GET LUCKY	Loverboy
80	12	122	94.	IN THE HEAT OF THE NIGHT	Pat Benatar
68	13	122	95.	JOHNNY CASH AT FOLSOM PRISON	Johnny Cash
67	2	121	96.	THE DOORS	Doors
83	1	120+	97.	THRILLER	Michael Jackson
78	1	120	98.	SATURDAY NIGHT FEVER	Bee Gees/Soundtrack
58	1	120	99.	FRANK SINATRA SINGS FOR ONLY THE LONELY	Frank Sinatra
67	5	120	100.	THE TEMPTATIONS GREATEST HITS	Temptations
83	15	120	101.	JANE FONDA'S WORKOUT RECORD	Jane Fonda
68	24	120	102.	2001: A SPACE ODYSSEY	Soundtrack
73	2	119	103.	THE BEST OF BREAD	Bread
72	21	119	104.	TOULOUSE STREET	Doobie Brothers
59	1	118	105.	THE KINGSTON TRIO AT LARGE	Kingston Trio
72	7	118	106.	MACHINE HEAD	Deep Purple
67	7	118	107.	RELEASE ME	Engelbert Humperdinck
59	1	117	108.	THE MUSIC FROM PETER GUNN	Henry Mancini
78	30	117	109.	STARDUST	Willie Nelson
69	1	116	110.	ABBEY ROAD	Beatles
74	1	116	111.	BAND ON THE RUN	Paul McCartney/ Wings
80	6	116	112.	CHRISTOPHER CROSS	Christopher Cross
60	13	116	113.	GYPSY	Original Cast
80	1	115	114.	THE WALL	Pink Floyd
76	2	115	115.	SILK DEGREES	Boz Scaggs
80	3	115	116.	THE JAZZ SINGER	Neil Diamond/ Soundtrack
79	28	115	117.	GREATEST HITS	Waylon Jennings
65	1	114	118.	MARY POPPINS	Soundtrack
58	2	114	119.	WARM	Johnny Mathis
62	10	114	120.	JOAN BAEZ IN CONCERT	Joan Baez
82	14	114	121.	MOUNTAIN MUSIC	Alabama
77	4	113	122.	FOREIGNER	Foreigner
66	6	113	123.	THE BEST OF THE ANIMALS	Animals
72	70	113	124.	SITTIN' IN	Loggins & Messina
78	12	112	125.	THE GAMBLER	Kenny Rogers
60	1	111	126.	G.I. BLUES	Elvis Presley/ Soundtrack
72	2	111	127	BIG BAMBU	Cheech & Chong
64	4	111	128.	MY FAIR LADY	Soundtrack

PK YR	PK POS	WKS CHR	RANK	TITLE	Artist
81	5	111	129.	DON'T SAY NO	Billy Squier
80	1	110	130.	AGAINST THE WIND	Bob Seger & The Silver Bullet Band
78	4	110	131.	STRANGER IN TOWN	Bob Seger & The Silver Bullet Band
75	9	110	132.	ALIVE!	Kiss
69	1	109	133.	BLOOD, SWEAT & TEARS	Blood, Sweat & Tears
81	2	109	134.	GHOST IN THE MACHINE	Police
72	3	109	135.	TALKING BOOK	Stevie Wonder
72	7	109	136.	SUMMER BREEZE	Seals & Crofts
60	1	108	137.	THE BUTTON-DOWN MIND OF BOB NEWHART	Bob Newhart
69	4	108	138.	SANTANA	Santana
60	7	108	139.	BLUE HAWAII	Billy Vaughn
68	12	108	140.	FUNNY GIRL	Barbra Streisand/ Soundtrack
63	1	107	141.	DAYS OF WINE AND ROSES	Andy Williams
77	1	107	142.	HOTEL CALIFORNIA	Eagles
58	3	107	143.	BUT NOT FOR ME/AHMAD JAMAL AT THE PERSHING	Ahmad Jamal
60	5	107	144.	SENTIMENTAL SING ALONG WITH MITCH	Mitch Miller & The Gang
69	6	107	145.	CROSBY, STILLS & NASH	Crosby, Stills & Nash
67	5	106	146.	ARE YOU EXPERIENCED?	Jimi Hendrix Experience
66	7	106	147.	WONDERFULNESS	Bill Cosby
66	1	105	148.	IF YOU CAN BELIEVE YOUR EYES AND EARS	Mamas & The Papas
65	5	105	149.	THE BEST OF HERMAN'S HERMITS	Herman's Hermits
58	5	105	150.	GEMS FOREVER	Mantovani
62	7	105	151.	THE BEST OF THE KINGSTON TRIO	Kingston Trio
73	8	105	152.	BEHIND CLOSED DOORS	Charlie Rich
81	13	105	153.	LOVERBOY	Loverboy
74	1	104	154.	ELTON JOHN - GREATEST HITS	Elton John
75	2	104	155.	LOVE WILL KEEP US TOGETHER	Captain & Tennille
64	3	104	156.	HONEY IN THE HORN	Al Hirt
81	21	104	157.	BLIZZARD OF OZZ	Ozzy Osbourne
83	45	104	158.	BILLY IDOL	Billy Idol
78	6	103	159.	PARALLEL LINES	Blondie
83	9	103+	160.	ELIMINATOR	ZZ Top
81	9	103	161.	BREAKIN' AWAY	Al Jarreau
80	22	103	162.	LOST IN LOVE	Air Supply
78	33	103	163.	TEN YEARS OF GOLD	Kenny Rogers
63	2	102	164.	TRINI LOPEZ AT PJ'S	Trini Lopez
68	3	102	165.	DAYS OF FUTURE PASSED	Moody Blues
70	3	102	166.	SWEET BABY JAMES	James Taylor
73	7	102	167.	THE CAPTAIN AND ME	Doobie Brothers
69	13	102	168.	STAND!	Sly & The Family Stone
81	1	101	169.	HI INFIDELITY	REO Speedwagon

PK YR	PK POS	WKS CHR	RANK	TITLE	Artist
62	1	101	170.	MODERN SOUNDS IN COUNTRY AND WESTERN MUSIC	Ray Charles
71	1	101	171.	JESUS CHRIST SUPERSTAR	Various Artists
76	3	101	172.	BOSTON	Boston
63	8	101	173.	THE BARBRA STREISAND ALBUM	Barbra Streisand
76	7	100	174.	DREAMBOAT ANNIE	Heart
59	7	100	175.	PARTY SING ALONG WITH MITCH	Mitch Miller & The Gang
81	10	100	176.	MEMORIES	Barbra Streisand
60	17	100	177.	CONNIE'S GREATEST HITS	Connie Francis
80	17	100	178.	VOICES	Daryl Hall & John Oates
79	25	100	179.	REGGATTA DE BLANC	Police

PK YR : Year album reached its peak position
PK POS : Highest charted position album attained
WKS CHR : Total weeks charted
+ : Album still charted as of the March 30, 1985 issue.

ALBUMS OF LONGEVITY (A-Z by Artist)

Aerosmith 81
Air Supply 162
Alabama 46,121
Herb Alpert/Tijuana Brass
.... 22,41,44,48,78
Animals 123
Paul Anka 63
Joan Baez 66,90,120
Beach Boys 49
Beatles 35,38,43,58,110
Bee Gees 98
Harry Belafonte 39
Pat Benatar 94
Tony Bennett 54
Shelley Berman 73
Blondie 159
Blood, Sweat, & Tears 133
Boston 172
Bread 103
Dave Brubeck Quartet 42
Captain & Tennille 155
Cars 69
Johnny Cash 95
Ray Charles 170
Cheech & Chong 127
Chicago 34,74
Van Cliburn 88
Nat King Cole 45
Bill Cosby 51,67,82,147
Crosby, Stills & Nash 145
Christopher Cross 112
Deep Purple 106
John Denver 30
Neil Diamond 116
Doobie Brothers 104,167
Doors 96
Duran Duran 80
Eagles 75,142
Fleetwood Mac 55,72
Jane Fonda 101
Tennessee Ernie Ford 8
Foreigner 122
Connie Francis 177
Daryl Hall & John Oats 178
Heart 174
Jimi Hendrix 146
Herman's Hermits 149

Al Hirt 156
Buddy Holly 27
Engelbert Humperdinck 107
Billy Idol 158
Iron Butterfly 64
Michael Jackson 36,97
Ahmad Jamal 143
Al Jarreau 161
Waylon Jennings 117
Billy Joel 70
Elton John 154
Journey 56,92
Carole King 5
Kingsmen 77
Kingston Trio .. 20,28,84,105,151
Kiss 132
Led Zeppelin 13
Enoch Light 91
Loggins & Messina 124
Trini Lopez 164
Loverboy 93,153
Mamas & The Papas 148
Henry Mancini 108
Mantovani 16,150
Johnny Mathis 2,6,119
Paul McCartney 111
Sergio Mendes & Brasil '66 87
Mitch Miller 18,33,76,144,175
Moody Blues 71,165
Willie Nelson 109
Bob Newhart 137
Stevie Nicks 61
Roy Orbison 65
Ozzy Osbourne 157
Peter, Paul & Mary 23
Pink Floyd 1,114
Platters 31
Police 50,134,179
Elvis Presley 126
Prince 89
Reo Speedwagon 169
Charlie Rich 152
Lionel Richie 79
Kenny Rogers 25,125,163
Rolling Stones 15
San Sebastian Strings 60
Santana 138

Boz Scaggs 115
Seals & Crofts 136
Bob Seger 68,130,131
Simon & Garfunkel 57,59,86
Frank Sinatra 62,99
Sly & The Family Stone 168
Billy Squier 129
Barbra Streisand 140,173,176
Styx 83
James Taylor 166
Temptations 100
Van Halen 37
Billy Vaughn 139
Rusty Warren 26
Who 85
Andy Williams 29,141
Stevie Wonder 135
ZZ Top 160

SOUNDTRACKS:
Doctor Zhivago 47
Gigi 32
King And I 9
Mary Poppins 118
My Fair Lady 128
Oklahoma! 4
Saturday Night Fever 98
Sound Of Music 14
South Pacific 11
2001: A Space Odyssey 102
West Side Story 19

ORIGINAL CASTS:
Camelot 10
Fiddler On The Roof 17
Flower Drum Song 53
Gypsy 113
Hair 52
Man Of La Mancha 40
Music Man 12
My Fair Lady 3
Sound Of Music 7
West Side Story 21

VARIOUS ARTISTS:
Jesus Christ Superstar 171
Oldies But Goodies 24

#1 ALBUMS
LISTED
CHRONOLOGICALLY

#1 ALBUMS LISTED CHRONOLOGICALLY

For the years 1958 through 1963, when separate stereo and mono charts were published each week, there are special columns on the right side of the page to show the weeks each album held the #1 spot on each of these pop charts. If an album peaked at #1 on both the mono and stereo charts in the same week, it is counted as only 1 week at #1. Therefore the grand total of an albums weeks at #1 on all charts may equal more than the total shown on the left side of the page.

The date shown is the earliest date that an album hit #1 on any of the three pop charts. Some dates are duplicated because different albums peaked at #1 on the same date on different charts.

DATE	: Date album first hit the #1 position.
WKS	: Total weeks album held the #1 position.
*	: Album appeared non-consecutively at the #1 position.

CHARTS COLUMN:

1 CH	: One chart published
ST	: Stereo chart
MO	: Mono chart

The #1 album of each year is shown in bold type and is based on total weeks at the #1 spot - ties are broken by total weeks charted. The album qualifies for the award only in the year that it first peaked at #1.

292 albums have hit the #1 position on Billboard's pop charts from 1955 through March, 1985.

1955

Two albums from 1954 continued into 1955 at the #1 spot: "The Student Prince" Mario Lanza (18 wks.) and "Music, Martinis And Memories" Jackie Gleason (2 wks.). For all of 1955 and up to 3/24/56, the LP chart was published mainly on a bi-weekly basis. The chart was considered 'frozen' for a non-published week and, therefore, each position on the published chart was counted twice. In addition to these bi-weekly 'frozen' charts, there were 5 other weeks of unpublished charts which did not count toward weeks at the #1 spot.

	DATE	WKS	ALBUM TITLE	ARTIST
1.	5/28	2	CRAZY OTTO	Crazy Otto
2.	6/11	6	STARRING SAMMY DAVIS JR.	Sammy Davis, Jr.
3.	7/23	2	LONESOME ECHO	Jackie Gleason
4.	8/06	17	LOVE ME OR LEAVE ME	Doris Day/Soundtrack

1956

Beginning with 3/24/56, Billboard published the LP chart on a weekly basis. From the 1st of the year to that date, there were 2 published charts, 2 frozen charts and 7 weeks of unpublished charts.

	DATE	WKS	ALBUM TITLE	ARTIST
1.	1/28	4	OKLAHOMA!	Soundtrack
2.	3/24	6	BELAFONTE	Harry Belafonte
3.	5/05	10	ELVIS PRESLEY	Elvis Presley
4.	7/14	15*	MY FAIR LADY peaked at #1 in 4 consecutive years: '56 (8 wks.), '57 (1 wk.), '58 (3 wks.) & '59 (3 wks.-Stereo chart)	Original Cast
5.	9/08	31*	**CALYPSO**	Harry Belafonte
6.	10/06	1	THE KING AND I	Soundtrack
7.	10/13	1	THE EDDY DUCHIN STORY	Carmen Cavallaro/Soundtrack
8.	12/08	5	ELVIS	Elvis Presley

1957

	DATE	WKS	ALBUM TITLE	ARTIST
1.	5/27	8	LOVE IS THE THING	Nat King Cole
2.	7/22	10*	AROUND THE WORLD IN 80 DAYS	Soundtrack
3.	7/29	10	LOVING YOU	Elvis Presley/Soundtrack
4.	12/16	4*	ELVIS' CHRISTMAS ALBUM	Elvis Presley
5.	12/30	1	MERRY CHRISTMAS	Bing Crosby

1958

Multiple Charts

	DATE	WKS	ALBUM TITLE	ARTIST	1 CH	ST	MO
1.	1/20	2	RICKY	Ricky Nelson	2	—	—
2.	2/10	5	COME FLY WITH ME	Frank Sinatra	5	—	—
3.	3/17	12*	THE MUSIC MAN	Original Cast	12	—	—
4.	5/19	31*	SOUTH PACIFIC 3 wks. #1 in '58; 28 wks. #1 on Stereo charts beginning 5/25/59	Soundtrack	3	28	—
5.	6/09	3*	JOHNNY'S GREATEST HITS	Johnny Mathis	3	—	—
6.	7/21	10*	GIGI 3 wks. #1 in '58; 3 wks. #1 on solo chart in '59, and 4 wks. #1 on Mono charts beginning 5/25/59	Soundtrack	6	—	4
7.	8/11	7*	TCHAIKOVSKY: PIANO CONCERTO NO. 1	Van Cliburn	7	—	—
8.	10/06	8*	SING ALONG WITH MITCH	Mitch Miller	8	—	—
9.	10/13	5	FRANK SINATRA SINGS FOR ONLY THE LONELY	Frank Sinatra	5	—	—
10.	11/24	1	THE KINGSTON TRIO	Kingston Trio	1	—	—
11.	12/29	2	CHRISTMAS SING-ALONG WITH MITCH	Mitch Miller	2	—	—

1959

Multiple Charts

	DATE	WKS	ALBUM TITLE	ARTIST	1 CH	ST	MO
1.	2/02	3	FLOWER DRUM SONG	Original Cast	3	—	—
2.	2/23	10	THE MUSIC FROM PETER GUNN	Henry Mancini	10	—	—
			5/25/59: **separate Stereo and Mono charts begin**				
3.	6/22	5	EXOTICA	Martin Denny	—	—	5
4.	7/13	1	FILM ENCORES	Mantovani	—	1	—
5.	7/27	15	THE KINGSTON TRIO AT LARGE	Kingston Trio	—	—	15
6.	11/09	5	HEAVENLY	Johnny Mathis	—	—	5
7.	12/14	8	HERE WE GO AGAIN!	Kingston Trio	—	2	8

1960

	DATE	WKS	ALBUM TITLE	ARTIST	1 CH	ST	MO
1.	1/11	1	THE LORD'S PRAYER	Mormon Tabernacle Choir	—	1	—
2.	1/25	16	**THE SOUND OF MUSIC**	Original Cast	—	15	12
3.	4/25	13*	PERSUASIVE PERCUSSION	Enoch Light/ Terry Snyder	—	13	—
4.	5/02	2*	THEME FROM A SUMMER PLACE	Billy Vaughn	—	—	2
5.	5/09	12*	SOLD OUT	Kingston Trio	—	3	10
6.	7/25	14*	THE BUTTON-DOWN MIND OF BOB NEWHART	Bob Newhart	—	—	14
7.	8/29	10*	STRING ALONG	Kingston Trio	—	10	5
8.	10/24	9*	NICE 'N' EASY	Frank Sinatra	—	9	1
9.	12/05	10*	G.I. BLUES	Elvis Presley/ Soundtrack	—	2	8

1961

	DATE	WKS	ALBUM TITLE	ARTIST	1 CH	ST	MO
1.	1/09	1	THE BUTTON-DOWN MIND STRIKES BACK!	Bob Newhart	—	—	1
2.	1/16	5*	WONDERLAND BY NIGHT	Bert Kaempfert	—	—	5
3.	1/23	14*	EXODUS	Soundtrack	—	14	3
4.	3/13	11*	CALCUTTA!	Lawrence Welk	—	11	8
5.	6/05	6	CAMELOT	Original Cast	—	—	6
6.	7/17	9	STARS FOR A SUMMER NIGHT	Various Artists	—	9	4
7.	7/17	1	CARNIVAL	Original Cast	—	—	1
8.	8/21	3	SOMETHING FOR EVERYBODY	Elvis Presley	—	—	3
9.	9/11	13	JUDY AT CARNEGIE HALL	Judy Garland	—	9	13
10.	11/18	7	STEREO 35/MM	Enoch Light	—	7	—
11.	12/11	20	**BLUE HAWAII**	Elvis Presley/ Soundtrack	—	4	20

1962

	DATE	WKS	ALBUM TITLE	ARTIST	1 CH	ST	MO
1.	1/13	1	HOLIDAY SING ALONG WITH MITCH	Mitch Miller	—	1	—
2.	2/10	12*	BREAKFAST AT TIFFANY'S	Henry Mancini/ Soundtrack	—	12	—
3.	5/05	54*	**WEST SIDE STORY** most weeks at #1 for the '55-'85 era	Soundtrack	—	53	12
4.	6/23	14	MODERN SOUNDS IN COUNTRY AND WESTERN MUSIC	Ray Charles	—	1	14
5.	10/20	7*	PETER, PAUL & MARY returned to the #1 spot for 1 week on 10/26/63	Peter, Paul & Mary	1	—	6
6.	12/01	2	MY SON, THE FOLK SINGER	Allan Sherman	—	—	2
7.	12/15	12	THE FIRST FAMILY	Vaughn Meader	—	—	12

1963

	DATE	WKS	ALBUM TITLE	ARTIST	1 CH	ST	MO
1.	3/09	1	MY SON, THE CELEBRITY	Allan Sherman	—	—	1
2.	3/09	1	JAZZ SAMBA	Stan Getz/Charlie Byrd	—	1	—
3.	3/16	5	SONGS I SING ON THE JACKIE GLEASON SHOW	Frank Fontaine	—	—	5
4.	5/04	16	**DAYS OF WINE AND ROSES**	Andy Williams	1	11	15
			8/17/63: Stereo & Mono charts combined into one single chart				
5.	8/24	1	LITTLE STEVIE WONDER/THE 12 YEAR OLD GENIUS	Stevie Wonder	1	—	—
6.	8/31	8	MY SON, THE NUT	Allan Sherman	8	—	—
7.	11/02	5	IN THE WIND	Peter, Paul & Mary	5	—	—
8.	12/07	10	THE SINGING NUN	The Singing Nun	10	—	—

1964

	DATE	WKS	ALBUM TITLE	ARTIST
1.	2/15	11	MEET THE BEATLES!	Beatles
2.	5/02	5	THE BEATLES' SECOND ALBUM	Beatles
3.	6/06	1	HELLO, DOLLY!	Original Cast
4.	6/13	6	HELLO, DOLLY!	Louis Armstrong
5.	7/25	14	**A HARD DAY'S NIGHT**	Beatles/Soundtrack
6.	10/31	5	PEOPLE	Barbra Streisand
7.	12/05	4	BEACH BOYS CONCERT	Beach Boys

1965

	DATE	WKS	ALBUM TITLE	ARTIST
1.	1/02	1	ROUSTABOUT	Elvis Presley/Soundtrack
2.	1/09	9	BEATLES '65	Beatles
3.	3/13	14*	**MARY POPPINS**	Soundtrack
4.	3/20	3	GOLDFINGER	Soundtrack
5.	7/10	6	BEATLES VI	Beatles
6.	8/21	3	OUT OF OUR HEADS	Rolling Stones
7.	9/11	9	HELP!	Beatles/Soundtrack
8.	11/13	2	THE SOUND OF MUSIC	Soundtrack
9.	11/27	8*	WHIPPED CREAM & OTHER DELIGHTS	Herb Alpert & The Tijuana Brass

1966

	DATE	WKS	ALBUM TITLE	ARTIST
1.	1/08	6	RUBBER SOUL	Beatles
2.	3/05	6*	GOING PLACES	Herb Alpert & The Tijuana Brass
3.	3/12	5	BALLADS OF THE GREEN BERETS	SSgt Barry Sadler
4.	5/21	1	IF YOU CAN BELIEVE YOUR EYES AND EARS	Mamas & The Papas
5.	5/28	9*	WHAT NOW MY LOVE	Herb Alpert & The Tijuana Brass
6.	7/23	1	STRANGERS IN THE NIGHT	Frank Sinatra
7.	7/30	5	"YESTERDAY" ... AND TODAY	Beatles
8.	9/10	6	REVOLVER	Beatles
9.	10/22	2	THE SUPREMES A' GO-GO	Supremes
10.	11/05	1	DOCTOR ZHIVAGO	Soundtrack
11.	11/12	13	**THE MONKEES**	Monkees

1967

	DATE	WKS	ALBUM TITLE	ARTIST
1.	2/11	18	MORE OF THE MONKEES	Monkees
2.	6/17	1	SOUNDS LIKE	Herb Alpert & The Tijuana Brass
3.	6/24	1	HEADQUARTERS	Monkees
4.	7/01	15	SGT. PEPPER'S LONELY HEARTS CLUB BAND	Beatles
5.	10/14	2	ODE TO BILLIE JOE	Bobbie Gentry
6.	10/28	5	DIANA ROSS AND THE SUPREMES GREATEST HITS	Supremes
7.	12/02	5	PISCES, AQUARIUS, CAPRICORN & JONES LTD.	Monkees

1968

	DATE	WKS	ALBUM TITLE	ARTIST
1.	1/06	8	MAGICAL MYSTERY TOUR	Beatles
2.	3/02	5	BLOOMING HITS	Paul Mauriat
3.	4/06	9*	THE GRADUATE	Simon & Garfunkel/Soundtrack
4.	5/25	7*	BOOKENDS	Simon & Garfunkel
5.	7/27	2	THE BEAT OF THE BRASS	Herb Alpert & The Tijuana Brass
6.	8/10	4	WHEELS OF FIRE	Cream
7.	9/07	4*	WAITING FOR THE SUN	Doors
8.	9/28	1	TIME PEACE/THE RASCALS' GREATEST HITS	Rascals
9.	10/12	8*	CHEAP THRILLS	Big Brother & The Holding Company
10.	11/16	2	ELECTRIC LADYLAND	Jimi Hendrix Experience
11.	12/21	5*	WICHITA LINEMAN	Glen Campbell
12.	12/28	9*	THE BEATLES [WHITE ALBUM]	Beatles

1969

	DATE	WKS	ALBUM TITLE	ARTIST
1.	2/08	1	TCB	Supremes & Temptations
2.	3/29	7*	BLOOD, SWEAT & TEARS	Blood, Sweat & Tears
3.	4/26	13	HAIR	Original Cast
4.	8/23	4	JOHNNY CASH AT SAN QUENTIN	Johnny Cash
5.	9/20	2	BLIND FAITH	Blind Faith
6.	10/04	4	GREEN RIVER	Creedence Clearwater Revival
7.	11/01	11*	ABBEY ROAD	Beatles
8.	12/27	7*	LED ZEPPELIN II	Led Zeppelin

1970

	DATE	WKS	ALBUM TITLE	ARTIST
1.	3/07	10	BRIDGE OVER TROUBLED WATER	Simon & Garfunkel
2.	5/16	1	DEJA VU	Crosby, Stills, Nash & Young
3.	5/23	3	McCARTNEY	Paul McCartney
4.	6/13	4	LET IT BE	Beatles/Soundtrack
5.	7/11	4	WOODSTOCK	Various Artists/Soundtrack
6.	8/08	2	BLOOD, SWEAT & TEARS 3	Blood, Sweat & Tears
7.	8/22	9	COSMO'S FACTORY	Creedence Clearwater Revival
8.	10/24	6*	ABRAXAS	Santana
9.	10/31	4	LED ZEPPELIN III	Led Zeppelin

1971

	DATE	WKS	ALBUM TITLE	ARTIST
1.	1/02	7	ALL THINGS MUST PASS	George Harrison
2.	2/20	3*	JESUS CHRIST SUPERSTAR	Various Artists
3.	2/27	9	PEARL	Janis Joplin
4.	5/15	1	4 WAY STREET	Crosby, Stills, Nash & Young
5.	5/22	4	STICKY FINGERS	Rolling Stones
6.	6/19	15	TAPESTRY	Carole King
7.	10/02	4	EVERY PICTURE TELLS A STORY	Rod Stewart
8.	10/30	1	IMAGINE	John Lennon
9.	11/06	1	SHAFT	Isaac Hayes/Soundtrack
10.	11/13	5	SANTANA III	Santana
11.	12/18	2	THERE'S A RIOT GOIN' ON	Sly & The Family Stone

1972

	DATE	WKS	ALBUM TITLE	ARTIST
1.	1/01	3	MUSIC	Carole King
2.	1/22	7	AMERICAN PIE	Don McLean
3.	3/11	2	HARVEST	Neil Young
4.	3/25	5	AMERICA	America
5.	4/29	5	FIRST TAKE	Roberta Flack
6.	6/03	2	THICK AS A BRICK	Jethro Tull
7.	6/17	4	EXILE ON MAIN ST.	Rolling Stones
8.	7/15	5	HONKY CHATEAU	Elton John
9.	8/19	9	CHICAGO V	Chicago
10.	10/21	4	SUPERFLY	Curtis Mayfield/Soundtrack
11.	11/18	3	CATCH BULL AT FOUR	Cat Stevens
12.	12/09	5	SEVENTH SOJOURN	Moody Blues

1973

	DATE	WKS	ALBUM TITLE	ARTIST
1.	1/13	5	NO SECRETS	Carly Simon
2.	2/17	2	THE WORLD IS A GHETTO	War
3.	3/03	2	DON'T SHOOT ME I'M ONLY THE PIANO PLAYER	Elton John
4.	3/17	3	DUELING BANJOS	Eric Weissberg
5.	4/07	2	LADY SINGS THE BLUES	Diana Ross/Soundtrack
6.	4/21	1	BILLION DOLLAR BABIES	Alice Cooper
7.	4/28	1	THE DARK SIDE OF THE MOON	Pink Floyd
8.	5/05	1	ALOHA FROM HAWAII VIA SATELLITE	Elvis Presley
9.	5/12	2	HOUSES OF THE HOLY	Led Zeppelin
10.	5/26	1	THE BEATLES/1967-1970	Beatles
11.	6/02	3	RED ROSE SPEEDWAY	Paul McCartney & Wings
12.	6/23	5	LIVING IN THE MATERIAL WORLD	George Harrison
13.	7/28	5*	CHICAGO VI	Chicago
14.	8/18	1	A PASSION PLAY	Jethro Tull
15.	9/08	5	BROTHERS AND SISTERS	Allman Brothers Band
16.	10/13	4	GOATS HEAD SOUP	Rolling Stones
17.	11/10	8	GOODBYE YELLOW BRICK ROAD	Elton John

1974

	DATE	WKS	ALBUM TITLE	ARTIST
1.	1/05	1	THE SINGLES 1969-1973	Carpenters
2.	1/12	5	YOU DON'T MESS AROUND WITH JIM	Jim Croce
3.	2/16	4	PLANET WAVES	Bob Dylan
4.	3/16	2	THE WAY WE WERE	Barbra Streisand
5.	3/30	3*	JOHN DENVER'S GREATEST HITS	John Denver
6.	4/13	4*	BAND ON THE RUN	Paul McCartney & Wings
7.	4/27	1	CHICAGO VII	Chicago
8.	5/04	5	THE STING	Soundtrack (Marvin Hamlisch)
9.	6/22	2	SUNDOWN	Gordon Lightfoot
10.	7/13	4	CARIBOU	Elton John
11.	8/10	1	BACK HOME AGAIN	John Denver
12.	8/17	4	461 OCEAN BOULEVARD	Eric Clapton
13.	9/14	2	FULFILLINGNESS' FIRST FINALE	Stevie Wonder
14.	9/28	1	BAD COMPANY	Bad Company
15.	10/05	1	ENDLESS SUMMER	Beach Boys
16.	10/12	1	IF YOU LOVE ME, LET ME KNOW	Olivia Newton-John
17.	10/19	1	NOT FRAGILE	Bachman-Turner Overdrive
18.	10/26	1	CAN'T GET ENOUGH	Barry White
19.	11/02	1	SO FAR	Crosby, Stills, Nash & Young
20.	11/09	1	WRAP AROUND JOY	Carole King
21.	11/16	1	WALLS AND BRIDGES	John Lennon
22.	11/23	1	IT'S ONLY ROCK 'N ROLL	Rolling Stones
23.	11/30	10	**ELTON JOHN - GREATEST HITS**	Elton John

1975

	DATE	WKS	ALBUM TITLE	ARTIST
1.	2/08	1	FIRE	Ohio Players
2.	2/15	1	HEART LIKE A WHEEL	Linda Ronstadt
3.	2/22	1	AWB	Average White Band
4.	3/01	2	BLOOD ON THE TRACKS	Bob Dylan
5.	3/15	1	HAVE YOU NEVER BEEN MELLOW	Olivia Newton-John
6.	3/22	6	PHYSICAL GRAFFITI	Led Zeppelin
7.	5/03	2	CHICAGO VIII	Chicago
8.	5/17	3	THAT'S THE WAY OF THE WORLD	Earth, Wind & Fire/Soundtrack
9.	6/07	7*	**CAPTAIN FANTASTIC AND THE BROWN DIRT COWBOY** album debuted at #1	Elton John
10.	7/19	1	VENUS AND MARS	Paul McCartney/Wings
11.	7/26	5	ONE OF THESE NIGHTS	Eagles
12.	9/06	4*	RED OCTOPUS	Jefferson Starship
13.	9/13	1	THE HEAT IS ON	Isley Brothers
14.	9/20	1	BETWEEN THE LINES	Janis Ian
15.	10/04	2	WISH YOU WERE HERE	Pink Floyd
16.	10/18	2	WINDSONG	John Denver
17.	11/08	3	ROCK OF THE WESTIES album debuted at #1	Elton John
18.	12/06	1	STILL CRAZY AFTER ALL THESE YEARS	Paul Simon
19.	12/13	5	CHICAGO IX - CHICAGO'S GREATEST HITS	Chicago

1976

	DATE	WKS	ALBUM TITLE	ARTIST
1.	1/17	3	GRATITUDE	Earth, Wind & Fire
2.	2/07	5	DESIRE	Bob Dylan
3.	3/13	5*	EAGLES/THEIR GREATEST HITS 1971-1975	Eagles
4.	4/10	10*	FRAMPTON COMES ALIVE!	Peter Frampton
5.	4/24	7*	WINGS AT THE SPEED OF SOUND	Paul McCartney/Wings
6.	5/01	2	PRESENCE	Led Zeppelin
7.	5/15	4*	BLACK AND BLUE	Rolling Stones
8.	7/31	2	BREEZIN'	George Benson
9.	9/04	1	FLEETWOOD MAC	Fleetwood Mac
10.	10/16	14*	SONGS IN THE KEY OF LIFE album debuted at #1	Stevie Wonder

1977

	DATE	WKS	ALBUM TITLE	ARTIST
1.	1/15	8*	HOTEL CALIFORNIA	Eagles
2.	1/22	1	WINGS OVER AMERICA	Paul McCartney/Wings
3.	2/12	6	A STAR IS BORN	Barbra Streisand/Soundtrack
4.	4/02	31*	RUMOURS	Fleetwood Mac
5.	7/16	1	BARRY MANILOW/LIVE	Barry Manilow
6.	12/03	5	SIMPLE DREAMS	Linda Ronstadt

1978

	DATE	WKS	ALBUM TITLE	ARTIST
1.	1/21	24	SATURDAY NIGHT FEVER	Bee Gees/Soundtrack
2.	7/08	1	CITY TO CITY	Gerry Rafferty
3.	7/15	2	SOME GIRLS	Rolling Stones
4.	7/29	12*	GREASE	Soundtrack
5.	9/16	2*	DON'T LOOK BACK	Boston
6.	11/04	1	LIVING IN THE USA	Linda Ronstadt
7.	11/11	1	LIVE AND MORE	Donna Summer
8.	11/18	8*	52ND STREET	Billy Joel

1979

	DATE	WKS	ALBUM TITLE	ARTIST
1.	1/06	3	BARBRA STREISAND'S GREATEST HITS, VOLUME 2	Barbra Streisand
2.	2/03	1	BRIEFCASE FULL OF BLUES	Blues Brothers
3.	2/10	3	BLONDES HAVE MORE FUN	Rod Stewart
4.	3/03	6*	SPIRITS HAVING FLOWN	Bee Gees
5.	4/07	5*	MINUTE BY MINUTE	Doobie Brothers
6.	5/19	6*	BREAKFAST IN AMERICA	Supertramp
7.	6/16	6*	BAD GIRLS	Donna Summer
8.	8/11	5	GET THE KNACK	Knack
9.	9/15	7	IN THROUGH THE OUT DOOR	Led Zeppelin
10.	11/03	9	THE LONG RUN	Eagles

1980

	DATE	WKS	ALBUM TITLE	ARTIST
1.	1/05	1	ON THE RADIO-GREATEST HITS- VOLUMES I & II	Donna Summer
2.	1/12	1	BEE GEES GREATEST	Bee Gees
3.	1/19	15	THE WALL	Pink Floyd
4.	5/03	6	AGAINST THE WIND	Bob Seger & The Silver Bullet Band
5.	6/14	6	GLASS HOUSES	Billy Joel
6.	7/26	7	EMOTIONAL RESCUE	Rolling Stones
7.	9/13	1	HOLD OUT	Jackson Browne
8.	9/20	5	THE GAME	Queen
9.	10/25	3*	GUILTY	Barbra Streisand
10.	11/08	4	THE RIVER	Bruce Springsteen
11.	12/13	2	KENNY ROGERS' GREATEST HITS	Kenny Rogers
12.	12/27	8	DOUBLE FANTASY	John Lennon/Yoko Ono

1981

	DATE	WKS	ALBUM TITLE	ARTIST
1.	2/21	15*	HI INFIDELITY	REO Speedwagon
2.	4/04	3*	PARADISE THEATER	Styx
3.	6/27	4	MISTAKEN IDENTITY	Kim Carnes
4.	7/25	3	LONG DISTANCE VOYAGER	Moody Blues
5.	8/15	1	PRECIOUS TIME	Pat Benatar
6.	8/22	10*	4	Foreigner
7.	9/05	1	BELLA DONNA	Stevie Nicks
8.	9/12	1	ESCAPE	Journey
9.	9/19	9	TATTOO YOU	Rolling Stones
10.	12/26	3	FOR THOSE ABOUT TO ROCK WE SALUTE YOU	AC/DC

1982

	DATE	WKS	ALBUM TITLE	ARTIST
1.	2/06	4	FREEZE-FRAME	J. Geils Band
2.	3/06	6	BEAUTY AND THE BEAT	Go-Go's
3.	4/17	4	CHARIOTS OF FIRE	Vangelis/Soundtrack
4.	5/15	9*	ASIA	Asia
5.	5/29	3	TUG OF WAR	Paul McCartney
6.	8/07	5	MIRAGE	Fleetwood Mac
7.	9/11	9	AMERICAN FOOL	John Cougar
8.	11/13	15	BUSINESS AS USUAL	Men At Work

1983

	DATE	WKS	ALBUM TITLE	ARTIST
1.	2/26	37*	THRILLER	Michael Jackson
2.	6/25	2	FLASHDANCE	Soundtrack
3.	7/23	17*	SYNCHRONICITY	Police
4.	1/26	1	METAL HEALTH	Quiet Riot
5.	12/03	3	CAN'T SLOW DOWN	Lionel Richie

1984

	DATE	WKS	ALBUM TITLE	ARTIST
1.	4/21	10	FOOTLOOSE	Soundtrack
2.	6/30	1	SPORTS	Huey Lewis & The News
3.	7/07	7*	BORN IN THE U.S.A.	Bruce Springsteen
4.	8/04	24	PURPLE RAIN	Prince & The Revolution/Soundtrack

1985

	DATE	WKS	ALBUM TITLE	ARTIST
1.	2/09	3	LIKE A VIRGIN	Madonna
2.	3/02	3	MAKE IT BIG	Wham!
3.	3/23	1	CENTERFIELD	John Fogerty
4.	3/30	6*	NO JACKET REQUIRED	Phil Collins
5.	4/27	3	WE ARE THE WORLD	USA for Africa

Joel Whitburn's

TOP
POP
COLLECTION

Joel Whitburn's
TOP POP
1955 -1982

The definitive listing of every 45 rpm record to ever hit the "Hot 100", arranged by artist, in the same basic format as the "Top Pop Albums 1955 -1985" book.
692 Pages. Hardcover $40.00   Softcover $30.00

Joel Whitburn's
POP ANNUAL
1955 -1982

The only book that breaks down the "Hot 100" year by year. Lists in rank order, for each year, all singles to appear on the "Hot 100". 679 Pages.   Softcover $30.00

Billboard's
TOP 1000
1955 -1984
by Joel Whitburn

The all-time one thousand hottest singles of rock's entire 30-year span, ranked side by side, hit by hit.
80 Pages.   Softcover $15.00

Joel Whitburn's
BUBBLING UNDER THE HOT 100
1959 -1981

Lists over 4,000 hits that never made the "Hot 100". The only reference book of its kind.
235 Pages.   Softcover $30.00.

OTHER POP HITS!

Joel Whitburn's
MUSIC YEARBOOK
1984

The complete story of 1984's charted music in one concise volume. Covers 14 major Billboard charts. Updates all previous Record Research books, plus complete data on 6 additional charts. 272 Pages. Softcover $25.00 (Music Yearbook 1983 also available for $25.00)

UP AND COMING!

Top Pop 1900 -1955
Top Black 1942 -1985
Top Country 1944 -1985

For more information on the complete Record Research line of books, write for a free catalog. When ordering the above books, please include check or money order for full amount plus $3.00 for postage and handling. Overseas orders add $3.00 per book. All Canadian orders must be paid in U.S. dollars.

P.O. BOX 200
Menomonee Falls, Wisconsin 53051